JANE'S
FIGHTING SHIPS
1939

JANE'S
FIGHTING SHIPS
1939

A Reprint of the 1939 Edition of Fighting Ships
Founded by
FRED T. JANE

Edited by
FRANCIS E. McMURTRIE

ARCO PUBLISHING, INC.
219 Park Avenue South, New York, N.Y. 10003

Second U.S. Edition, First Printing, 1980

Library of Congress Catalog Card Number 69-14519
ISBN 0-668-02431-3

First published by Sampson Low Marston in 1939
This edition first published by Arco Publishing, Inc. in 1969
Copyright 1939 Sampson Low Marston & Company Limited

Printed in the United States of America

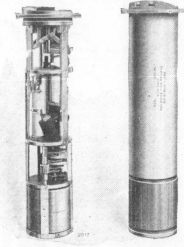

ADVERTISERS IN 1939 EDITION

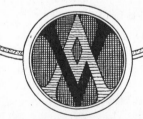

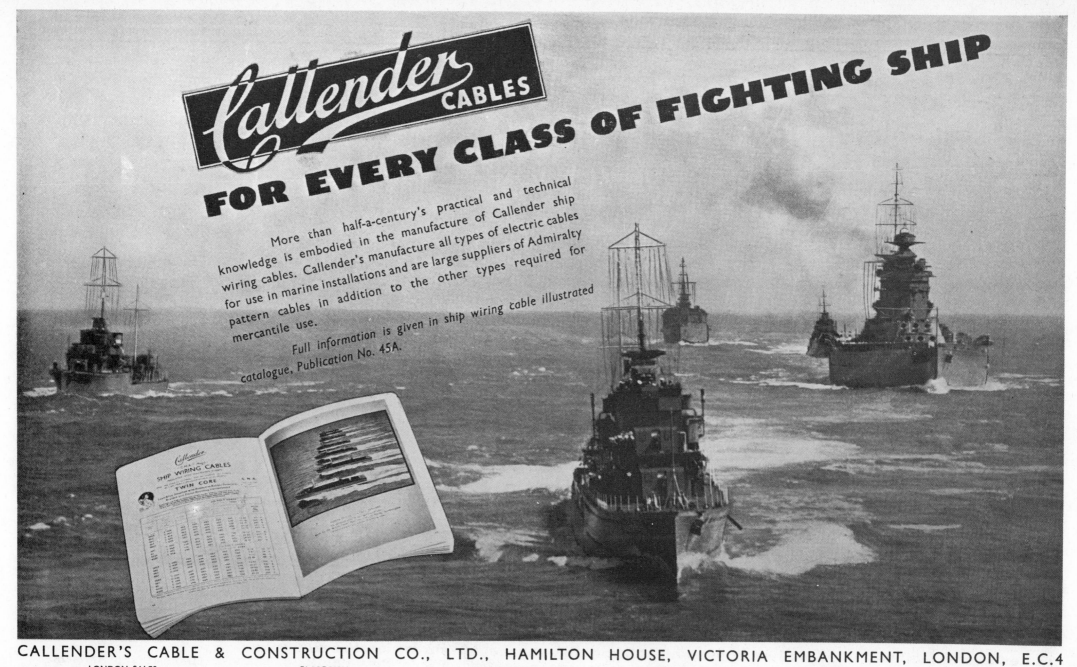

CLASSIFIED LIST OF ADVERTISERS.

Leading the World

POWER BOATS
Tradition · Enterprise · Craftsmanship

Creating and maintaining a standard of superiority unapproached elsewhere *POWER BOATS* led and are leading all practical progressive developments of High Speed Naval Architecture.

The name is a guarantee of perfection of design and a mark typifying excellence of workmanship and quality of material.

In the Royal Navy there are more fast Motor Boats of this manufacture, both for Offense and Service duties than all other makes together; and they have been, and are being, supplied in greater numbers throughout the World than any other British type of similar characteristics.

THE BRITISH POWER BOAT COMPANY, LTD

HYTHE   SOUTHAMPTON   ENGLAND

Owners and operators of the World's largest factory devoted to the manufacture of High Speed Motor Craft

Contractors to The Admiralty, The War Office, The Air Ministry, Dominion Colonial and Foreign Governments

Telephone : Hythe, Southampton 201 (10 lines)
Telegrams :   *POWER* Hythe, Southampton

THE NEW *POWER* 70 MOTOR TORPEDO BOAT

Armament : Two 21″ or Four 18″ Torpedoes ; Two or three power-worked Gun Turrets mounting Machine Guns ; Smoke-Screen Apparatus; Depth Charges.   Machinery: Three 1,000 h.p. Rolls-Royce — *POWER* — Merlin Marine Units. Maximum Speed: In excess of 44 Knots. Maximum Endurance: 2,130 sea miles on main engines. The smallest target silhouette and greatest acceleration for attack of any Motor Torpedo Boat afloat

DELETED BY THE CENSOR

CLASSIFIED LIST OF ADVERTISERS—*continued.*

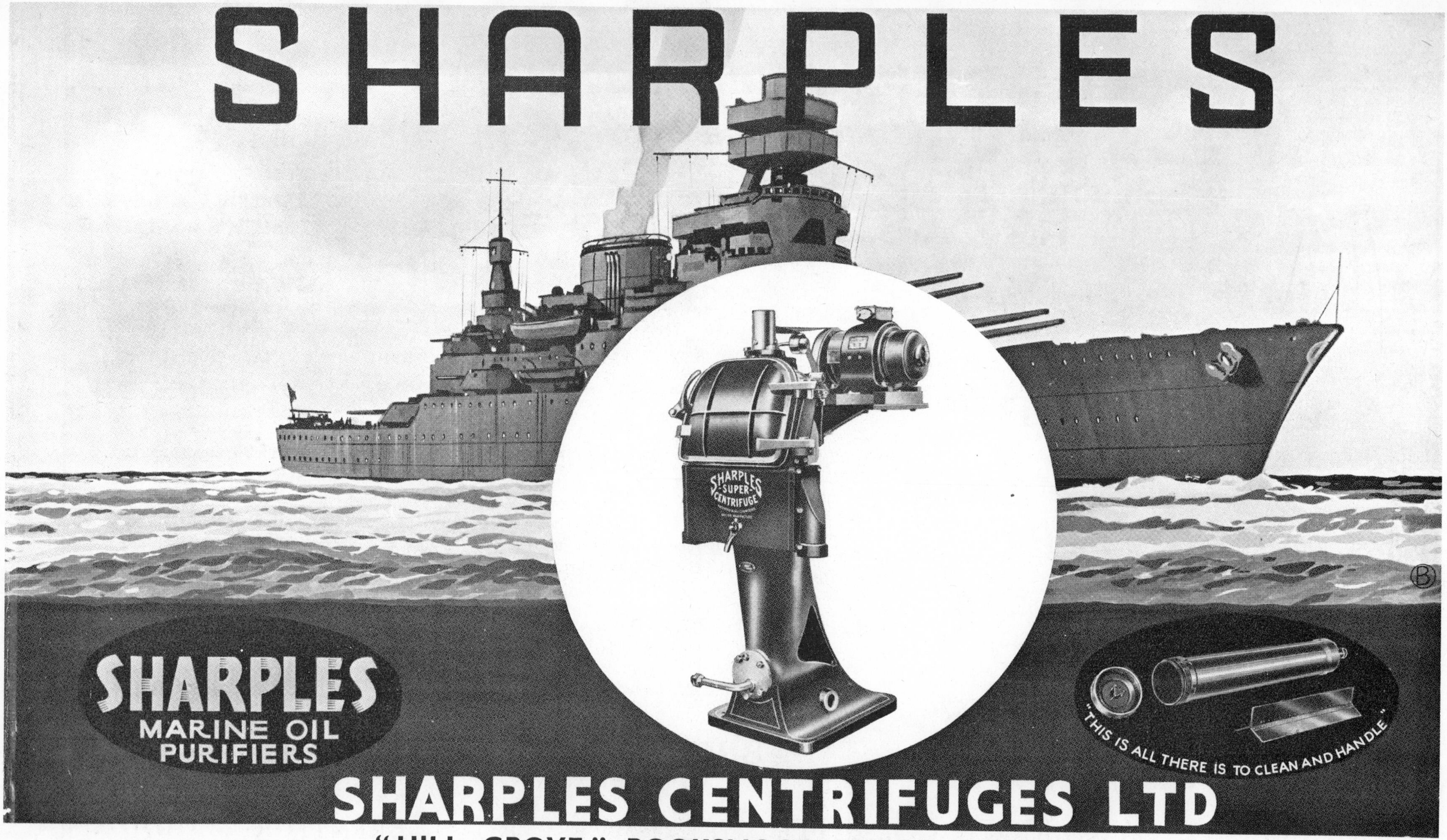

"HILL GROVE," ROOKSMOOR, WOODCHESTER,
Near STROUD, GLOS.
Telephone No.: AMBERLEY 151.

Walker's
"Trident" and "Excelsior"
Electric Ship-Logs
(Naval Pattern)

"Trident" Electric Register.

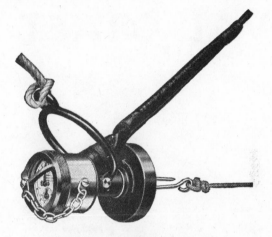

"Excelsior" Electric Register
(Sling pattern).

With these two types of instrument we offer an accurate means of obtaining "distance run" in every class of surface ship, from the Motor Torpedo Boat to the largest Battleship. Walker's Logs are accurate, reliable and moderate in price. Simple and robust in design, they are easily serviced, and have proved after years of regular use to be dependable under the most severe conditions at sea. The "Excelsior" Electric Log is of new design, and highly recommended for very high speed craft. It has been proved accurate up to 40 knots.

Write for illustrated booklets.

AS SUPPLIED TO THE BRITISH NAVY

Chart House Receiver.

Conning House Repeater
(Instrument Panel Type).

Thos. Walker & Son, Ltd..
58, Oxford Street. Birmingham, Eng.
T.W

Examples of
THORNYCROFT
NAVAL CRAFT

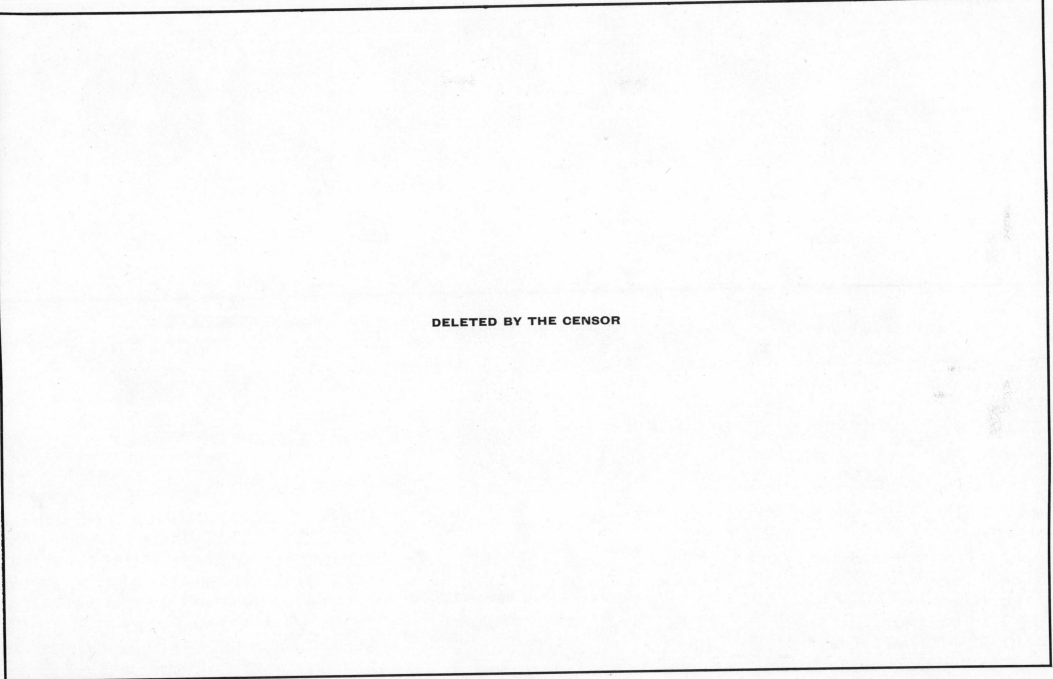

DELETED BY THE CENSOR

DELETED BY THE CENSOR

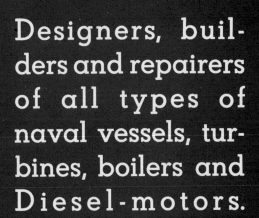

Record Speed 45 Knots

Flotilla Leader "TASHKENT" Russian Navy

3000 Tons

ODERO TERNI ORLANDO

DESIGNERS AND BUILDERS:	BUILT AND BUILDING:	
WARSHIPS OF ALL TYPES & SUBMARINES	WARSHIPS . . .	412.790 Tons disp.
MERCHANT SHIPS OF ALL SIZES	SUBMARINES . .	47.226 " "
GUNS OF ALL CALIBRES - AMMUNITIONS	MERCHANT SHIPS .	660.346 Reg. T.
MARINE ENGINES - BOILERS	MARINE ENGINES .	3.800.000 H.P.
PARSONS TURBINES - DIESEL ENGINES	ARTILLERY . . .	over 9000 guns
AUXILIARY MACHINERY		
SHIP REPAIRS AND RECONDITIONING		

III
IMPIANTO BINATO

You will be interested in Brochure No. 471, on Firth-Brown Forgings. May we send you a copy?

COMPLETE SET OF HOLLOW FORGED SEAMLESS BOILER DRUMS

FORGINGS FOR TWO THRUST SHAFTS

GROUP OF FORGED STEEL TURBINE WHEELS

THE
FORGINGS
FOR THE
QUEEN ELIZABETH
WERE MADE
BY

THOS. FIRTH & JOHN BROWN LIMITED.
ATLAS & NORFOLK WORKS, SHEFFIELD.
LONDON OFFICE: 8, THE SANCTUARY WESTMINSTER, S.W.I.

30 adv.

31 adv.

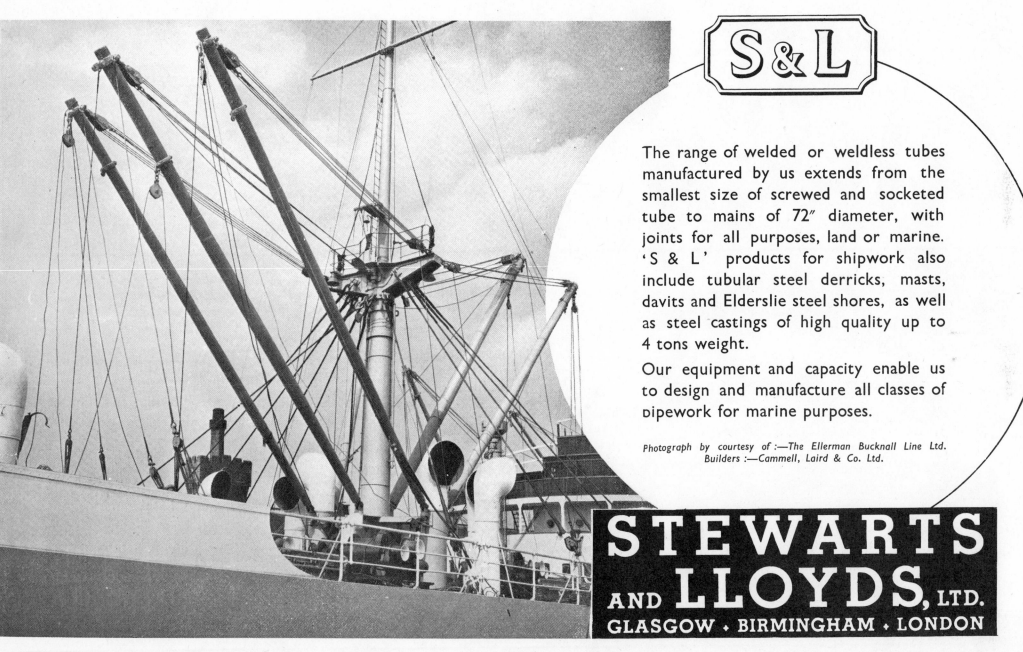

33 adv.

FOR MAXIMUM POWER TRANSMISSION

HENDRYS'

LAMINATED BELTING

(Regd. Trade Mark)

Made up to 1″ thick from solid leather in a single ply and in any width up to 48″, every Hendry belt is endless there being no metal or cemented joints to cause vibration. And, being made from leather, a Hendry belt gives a smooth elastic drive and lasts longer because it does not disintegrate. Ideal over small pulleys and for heavy-duty main drives, Hendry belting will give you efficient power transmission.

Sole Manufacturers :

James Hendry Ltd., Bridgeton, Glasgow

BRANCHES :
LONDON, BIRMINGHAM, MANCHESTER & JOHANNESBURG

CONTRACTORS TO THE ADMIRALTY

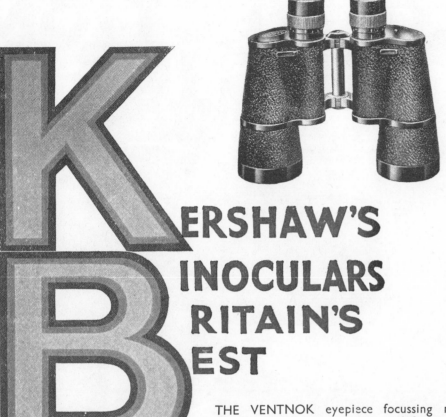

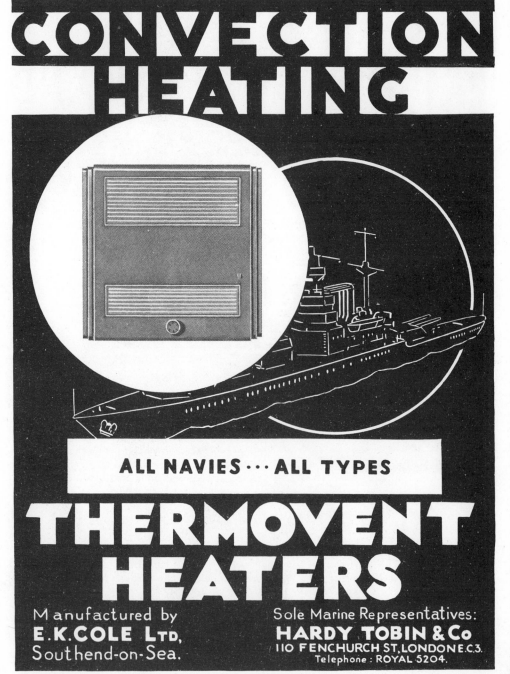

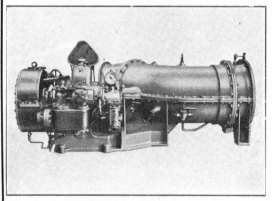

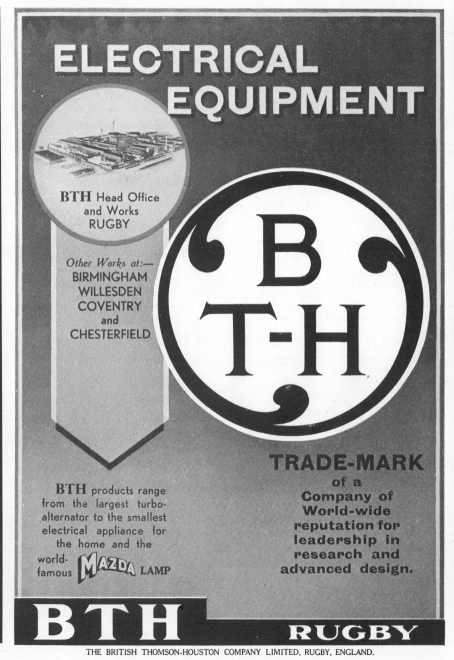

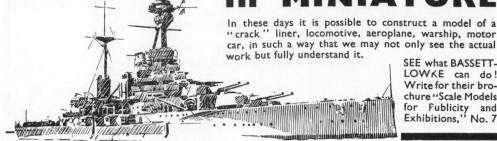
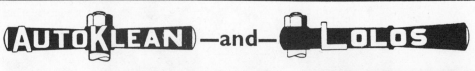
44 adv.

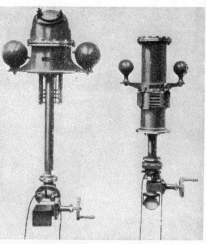

BOOKS
about ships

YACHTS, YACHTING AND SAILING.
Edited by Paymr. Lieut.-Commdr. E. C. Talbot-Booth, R.N.R. 5th Edition. *With over* 1,500 *illustrations,* 7s. 6d. net. This "DUMPY" BOOK contains a wealth of interesting information that all yachtsmen and amateur seamen will appreciate. The illustrations include a colour section of nearly 1,200 yacht club flags.

SHIPS OF THE NORTH ATLANTIC.
Edited by A. G. Horton White. With hundreds of illustrations, 7s. 6d. net. A complete account of the Blue Riband route, its history and the liners of the present time. This is a "DUMPY" BOOK and contains scale plans of all the leading ships.

SHIPS OF THE WORLD'S BATTLEFLEETS.
By Paymr. Lieut.-Commdr. E. C. Talbot-Booth, R.N.R. 2nd Edition. *Fully illustrated,* 3s. 6d. net. Excellent illustrations and details and histories of the capital ships and large cruisers of the principal navies make this a very useful pocket book.

WATERLINE SHIP MODELS.
By Paymr. Lieut.-Commdr. E. C. Talbot-Booth, R.N.R., 3s. 6d. net. The ideal book for the model enthusiast, giving model plans and half-tone illustrations of nearly 40 well-known ships.

MERCHANT SHIPS, 1940
Edited by Paymr. Lieut.-Commdr. E. C. TALBOT-BOOTH, R.N.R. Nearly 2,500 *illustrations in colour and black and white.* £2 12s. 6d. net.
The most complete illustrated volume published dealing with the world's merchant vessels. *Merchant Ships* contains scale drawings and details of 7,000 British and foreign-owned ships, also a full list of shipping companies, and fleets, cross-indexed for reference, and illustrations of nearly 800 funnel colourings. *Merchant Ships* is recognised as the foremost work used in identifying merchant vessels.

SHIPS OF THE ROYAL NAVY.
Edited by Francis E. McMurtrie (Editor of "JANE'S Fighting Ships") New and Revised Edition. With over 120 *illustrations,* 3s. 6d. net.
A leading Service paper has described this small volume as "The Ideal Non-Technical Handbook." Each type of ship in the Royal Navy is photographically illustrated and the various classes are described in chronological order, so that the development of each type can be readily understood and appreciated.

SHIPS AND THE SEA.
5th Edition. Edited by Paymr. Lieut.-Commdr. E. C. TALBOT-BOOTH, R.N.R. With over 1,000 *illustrations,* 7s. 6d. net.
One of the finest little ship books ever published, this "DUMPY" BOOK contains an extraordinary amount of information on every conceivable phase of shipping and seamanship.

★　　　★　　　★

THE "DUMPY BOOKS" are a remarkable series of compact pocket books (5¼ ins. × 4¼ ins.) noted for the immense quantity of matter and illustrations they contain. May we send you a prospectus of this series and numerous other books? Send us a post-card asking for our Prospectus of Naval and Aircraft Books.

THE WORLD'S WARSHIPS.
By Francis E. McMurtrie (Editor of "Jane's Fighting Ships") Fully illustrated, 3s. 6d. net. As a concise guide to the World's War Fleets at a moderate price this little book is unequalled. It gives essential information in tabular form, interspersed with illustrations.

ALL THE WORLD'S FIGHTING FLEETS.
Edited by Paymr. Lieut.-Commdr. E. C. Talbot-Booth, R.N.R. 2nd Edition. *Nearly* 300 *illustrations,* 7s. 6d. net. Another compact "DUMPY" BOOK which will be valuable to everyone interested in Naval Matters and the Navies of the World.

THE NAVAL CALENDAR.
Edited by Paymr. Lieut.-Commdr. E. C. Talbot-Booth, R.N.R. With over 100 *illustrations,* 3s. 6d. net. A small pocket book containing the leading particulars of the world's fighting ships.

OUR NAVY FOR 1,000 YEARS.
By Rear-Admiral Sir S. Eardley-Wilmot. Profusely illustrated, 3s. 6d. net. The author tells the story of the British Navy as an epic of courage and adventure.

Get these books from your bookshop, they are published by Sampson Low, 100 Southwark Street, London

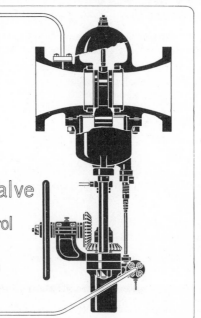

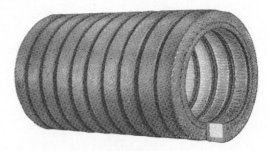

THO^S W. WARD LIMITED

T<small>HE</small> **INTERNATIONAL PAINT & COMPOSITIONS** C<small>O</small>. L<small>TD</small>.

Suppliers of Ships' Compositions to the British Admiralty for nearly half a century

---

Manufacturers of such world-renowned specialities as:

"INTERNATIONAL" PROTECTIVE AND ANTI-FOULING COMPOSITIONS
which are used on three times the number of vessels painted with any other brand

"SUNLIGHT" ENAMEL   Unrivalled for gloss and durability

NON-SLIP DECK PAINT   Ready mixed for use on steel decks

"TANCTECTOL"   Tank interior protective—withstands permanent immersion in
petroleum products

"PINTOFF"   The most efficient paint remover known; has no injurious effect on
subsequent paint coatings

ALSO ALL READY MIXED AND PASTE PAINTS

The " INTERNATIONAL " Organisation is the World's largest supplier of compositions to shipping
Suppliers to the principal Navies of the World including :

GREAT BRITAIN	FRANCE	FINLAND	NORWAY	BRAZIL	ARGENTINE
AUSTRALIA	GERMANY	GREECE	SWEDEN	CHILE	RUSSIA
CANADA	SPAIN	NETHERLANDS	TURKEY	PERU	

Main Factory: FELLING-ON-TYNE, ENGLAND

Head Office:

Telegraphic Address:
" Corrofoul, Sowest, London"

Telephone:
VICTORIA 3161 (7 Lines)

Grosvenor Gardens House, Grosvenor Gardens, LONDON, S.W.1

AN EXAMPLE OF RECONSTRUCTION.

H.M.S. Renown before reconstruction.

1933, *Stephen Cribb.*

H.M.S. Renown after reconstruction.

1939, *courtesy " Hampshire Telegraph and Post," Portsmouth.*

[*Frontispiece*

JANE'S FIGHTING SHIPS

1939

(ISSUED NOVEMBER, 1939)

FOUNDED IN **1897** BY FRED T. JANE

FORTY-THIRD YEAR OF ISSUE

EDITOR :
FRANCIS E. McMURTRIE, A.I.N.A.

SAMPSON LOW, MARSTON & CO., LTD. LONDON MCMXXXIX

CONTENTS.

FOREWORD

THOUGH "Fighting Ships" this year has made its appearance several weeks earlier than usual, it will be found that the amount of fresh material contained in the present volume is well above the normal. Not only are there particulars and pictures of more new ships than for twenty years past, but many older ones have undergone alteration in appearance or armament. An outstanding example of this appears in the frontispiece, H.M.S. *Renown*. Incidentally, it may be of interest to mention that this was the third subject to be selected for the frontispiece, two others having to be discarded for reasons connected with the War.

It has been no easy feat to adjust the make-up of a volume so full of fresh matter without adding any appreciable number of pages to the total; but by careful rearrangement and the discarding of sundry non-essential features, this has been accomplished. One change which has helped has been the elimination of the separate pages hitherto devoted to summaries of the fleets of the principal Powers, and the substitution in the introductory section of a table which shows at a glance how their navies compare so far as the more important categories are concerned. It is felt that at the present time the reference value of such a compact table should be considerable.

In the 1940 issue it is probable that the changes will be quite as many. Quite apart from the rapid development of the many large shipbuilding programmes in hand, with a first-class war in progress —even should it not spread—casualties are bound to occur. Those officially reported before going to press have been indicated by special notes in the text in preference to last-minute excisions.

Every effort will be made to bring out the 1940 edition at the earliest date feasible, since the reference value in war time of an up-to-date copy of "Fighting Ships" was abundantly proved in 1914–18, and needs no further stressing.

Capital ships under construction or on order in various countries now number 34. Of this number, ten (including the four British units of the *Lion* class) are believed to be designed for displacements of between 40,000 and 45,000 tons.

The British Navy Estimates for 1939, with supplementary votes up to the outbreak of war, comprise the largest number of vessels authorised for construction in any single year since 1918. Though only seven ships of considerable size and importance are included, the provision of 16 destroyers, 22 escort vessels, 20 minesweepers, 107 trawlers and 56 patrol vessels of the whaler type have served to expand the programme well beyond the usual limits. Two novel items are a Royal yacht and a hospital ship, though it is fairly certain that the former will not now be begun until peace returns.

Though for obvious reasons it has not been possible to give such complete data as in normal times of new British warships, all fresh information already published up to September 2 has been incorporated in this issue. It includes photographs of the reconstructed *Renown*, to one of which reference is made above; of the aircraft carrier *Furious*, as refitted, with an island superstructure; of the new 10,000-ton cruiser *Belfast*, and ex-cruiser *Cairo*, now an anti-aircraft ship; of two of the destroyers of the *Javelin* class; and of the latest design of motor torpedo boat and other craft of less note. H.M.A.S. *Adelaide* is shown as rebuilt, with three funnels instead of the original four, which the majority will doubtless consider an improvement from the artistic standpoint.

In other sections of the book the high standard of "Fighting Ships" will be found to have been well maintained. Several new photographs will be found in the Argentine, Brazilian and Chilean sections. No one who has read that classic of future war yarns, "The Captain of the *Mary Rose*," written by the late Sir William Laird Clowes and illustrated by Fred. T. Jane, the founder of "Fighting Ships," can fail to notice with regret the disappearance from the Chilean Navy this year of the *Capitan Prat*, the highly original design of which was the basis of the story in question.

Sketches showing the main features of the new Danish and Norwegian torpedo craft have been obtained. In each case these are the largest vessels of this category ever laid down by those countries. In the case of the Royal Swedish Navy, two small capital ships of the coast defence type have been ordered, the first construction of this kind on which Sweden has embarked since the *Drottning Victoria* and *Gustaf V* were authorised in 1914. The Swedish section has undergone a particularly thorough revision this year.

An exceptionally heavy programme of new construction has been initiated in France. With two supplementary votes, the total number of ships provided for under the 1938–39 Estimates exceeds 100, a record for recent times. Though some improvement in the rate of shipbuilding has been secured, it still lags behind that of Germany and Italy. Though the 35,000-ton battleship *Clemenceau* was laid down in January last, a start is not expected to be made with her sister ship, the *Gascogne*, before the end of this year. On the other hand, somewhat better progress appears to have been made with some of the new torpedo craft, half-a-dozen of the destroyers of *Le Hardi* class having now entered the water, while the name-ship herself is said to be due for completion this year. But submarine construction seems to be proceeding at a slower pace, the only launch reported this year being that of the *Aurore* last July. As she belongs to the 1936 programme, this can scarcely be considered satisfactory, though change in design is believed to have been mainly responsible for the delay. At least two of the new minesweepers of the *Elan* class have been commissioned and eleven more have been launched. The river gunboat *Jouffroy d'Abbans*, projected several years back for duty on the China Station, is not to be built, the funds allotted for her construction being devoted instead to the provision of a sailing vessel for service in the Pacific.

Germany has launched her first two 35,000-ton battleships, the *Bismarck* and *Tirpitz*, while two more are building. The first of the two aircraft carriers of 19,250 tons, the *Graf Zeppelin*, was set afloat towards the end of last year, but there is no news of the sister ship having followed her. All five of the 10,000-ton cruisers of the *Admiral Hipper* class have been launched, and the first pair are in service. Six destroyers of the *Roeder* class and all 16 of the *Maass* class have also been completed, but slower progress seems to have been made with the numerous 600-ton torpedo boats under construction. Though the first dozen of these were reported to have been laid down as far back as 1936, none had been photographed at sea up to the time of going to press. Such unexpected delay suggests that there must have been some radical change in the design of the vessels, especially as all the 12 minesweepers laid down in 1936, which are of the same displacement, have passed into service.

Additions continue to be made to the long list of depot ships and tenders which the German Navy possesses. Some of these are new ships, but the majority have been purchased or converted from other duties. It may be assumed that most of the former Czechoslovakian and some of the Polish river craft have now been incorporated in the German flotillas.

In this year's "Fighting Ships" there will be found up-to-date photographs of practically every important type in the German Navy. To provide these, a very large number of prints had to be purchased or otherwise obtained, some of them on the eve of hostilities.

The Royal Hellenic Navy has added two British-built destroyers, four trawlers (fitted as minelayers) and an oiler to its effective strength since last year. Roumania is building two minelayers—one of which has been launched—and two submarines in her own naval dockyard at Galatz. Yugoslavia has had a patrol vessel built in Italy and has ordered two submarines in Germany, though when, if ever, she will obtain delivery of the latter is decidedly doubtful. A big new destroyer, to be an improved edition of the *Dubrovnik*, is under construction at Split, the engines and boilers being supplied by Messrs. Yarrow.

Neither of the first pair of Italy's four 35,000-ton battleships has yet been completed, and only one of the twelve high speed cruisers of the *Regolo* class appears to have been laid down. No official details of the two cruisers of the *Ciano* class have yet been published, but those given in the present volume are believed to be reliable. On the other hand, the construction of submarines continues briskly, and it is probable that by now additional units have been put in hand.

Notwithstanding the difficulty of obtaining information of any kind concerning the Japanese fleet, "Fighting Ships" has succeeded in securing 15 fresh photographs in this section. There is still, unfortunately, a considerable dearth of details of new construction, though no pains have been spared to tap all possible sources of news. Apart from capital ships and cruisers, it is plain from the data collected that a steady flow of construction in destroyers, submarines and lighter vessels is proceeding.

In the Netherlands there is great activity in warship building. This will before long be supplemented by the ordering of three small capital ships of high speed, if the recommendations of the technical committee appointed to report on the subject are followed. New ships illustrated for the first time include the gunnery training ship *Van Kinsbergen*, submarine *O19* and the minelayer *Willem van der Zaan*. Several additional photographs of vessels of the East Indies Gouvernementsmarine have been provided.

Fortunately the Polish Navy section had been brought right up to date before the war began, a good picture of the new submarine *Orzel* being amongst the illustrations added.

The Russian Navy continues to be a difficult problem, very little reliable information being obtainable, but everything goes to suggest that shipbuilding still proceeds at a very slow rate. Efforts to widen the scope of construction continue, and a destroyer is understood to have been completed in the new shipyard at Vladivostok.

Spain is engaged in reorganising her naval material, following the close of the Civil War. No official revision having been received in time for this year's issue, the information in this section is less complete than had been hoped, but there are several new illustrations.

Of the Royal Thai Navy (formerly known as Siamese) there is little fresh news beyond the disappearance of certain obsolete vessels replaced by new construction. Nor is there any outstanding novelty in the Turkish section, though particulars of the new ships ordered in England are given.

Far otherwise is it with the United States Navy, in which expansion is still the order of the day. Eight new battleships are now on order, though only three had been definitely laid down when this section was printed. A fine selection of photos will be found of the cruiser *Wichita*, which, now that she is completed, proves to be of a new type, combining features of both the *Minneapolis* and *Brooklyn* classes. Two other novel designs are those of the *Atlanta* and *Cleveland* types, though full official details of both have still to be released. Steady progress is being made with destroyer and submarine programmes, and many new auxiliaries are building.

A new subsidiary Navy has made its appearance in the Philippines, with material provided by that ubiquitous firm, Messrs. John I. Thornycroft & Co. Ltd.

New sail training vessels illustrated for the first time this year are the Belgian *Mercator*, Roumanian *Mircea* and Uruguayan *Aspirante*.

Our best thanks are due to the various Admiralties, Ministries of Marine, Ministries of Defence, Navy Departments and Naval Staffs who have assisted officially by revising sundry sections of the book, as well as to their Naval Attachés and representatives in London. These latter include Vice-Admiral Juan T. Gerken and Commander G. H. Trudgett, of the Chilean Navy; Rear-Admiral Bruno Brivonesi, Royal Italian Navy; Captain C. Denis de Rivoyre, French Navy ; Captain Alan G. Kirk, Commander W. K. Harrill and Commander Gordon W. Nelson (C.C.), of the United States Navy; Captain T. Kondo, I.J.N.; Captain G. E. F. Boldt-Christmas, Royal Swedish Navy; Captain José S. Zuloaga, Argentine Navy; Captain S. Matessis, Royal Hellenic Navy; Captain G. St. Dumitrescu, C.V.O., Royal Roumanian Navy; Engineer Captain Natal Arnaud, Brazilian Navy; Commander Holger Gröndahl, Finnish Navy; Commander T. Stoklasa, Polish Navy; Lieut.-Commander A. de Booy, Royal Nether-

land Navy; Lieut.-Commander S. Cakir, Turkish Navy; Paymaster Lieut.-Commander P. Perry, Royal Australian Navy; and the Secretary to the High Commissioner for Canada.

A record number of correspondents in all parts of the world have forwarded information and photographs this year, proof of the steadily increasing number of subscribers to "Fighting Ships." Particularly useful has been the aid rendered by Commander P. Vincent-Bréchignac, Editor of "Flottes de Combat"; Captain G. V. Stewart, U.S.N., Secretary-Treasurer of the United States Naval Institute; Kapitänleutnant Alexander Bredt, Editor of "Taschenbuch der Kriegsflotten"; Redaktör K.-E. Westerlund, of "Sveriges Flotta"; and Mr. K. A. Knowles, Editor of "Our Navy."

Private individuals who have helped materially this year include Dott. Ing. L. Accorsi; Capitaine de Frégate M. Adam; Lieutenant L. F. Bouman; Mr. William H. Davis; Mr. George Dott; Mr. F. W. Endert; Mr. William A. Fuller; Mr. R. H. Gibson; Dr. Erich Gröner; Mr. Eric H. Hanson; Mr. D. Gibson Harris; Midshipman T. B. Healey, R.N.R.; Mr. F. H. James; Registrator Ossi Janson; Mr. Jay Launer; M. Maurice Lebigre; M. Henri Le Masson; Lieut.-Commander A. J. McHattie, R.N.R.; Primeiro Tenente Aluino Martins da Silva; Dr. Ing. W. V. Mendl, M.I.N.A.; Mr. R. Perkins; Mr. C. W. E. Richardson; Mr. Douglas Robinson; Mr. Stephen C. Rowan, Junior; Mr. George Rutkowski, Junior; Ir. R. F. Scheltema de Heere; Orlogskaptajn R. Steen Steensen; Mr. Paul J. Tasso; Mr. Matthew Thomlinson; Mr. L. F. Williams; and Mr. David Woodward. There are many others besides who prefer that their names should not be mentioned.

Those to whom in the past the name of Capitan de Corbeta Mateo Mille y Garcia will have become familiar through his many photographic contributions to "Fighting Ships" will learn with regret that authentic news of his death has been received this year. According to information furnished through the courtesy of the Duke of Alba, he was imprisoned by the Republicans in Madrid at the beginning of the Civil War and later disappeared. He is believed to have been murdered after being taken out of prison under the pretext of being transferred to a safer place.

For the extent and variety of the illustrations in this year's "Fighting Ships" thanks are largely due to Lieut.-Commander T. Davys Manning, V.D., R.N.V.R., who before proceeding on service was able to provide the bulk of the photographic contents, besides contributing the historical particulars of British warship names. Special mention must also be made of the name of Mr. Maurice Prendergast whose former editorial experience has so often been placed at the disposal of "Fighting Ships."

Various shipbuilding firms in this country and elsewhere have also been very helpful in furnishing photographs and information.

The Editor does not wish to enlarge on his own share in the work accomplished during the past nine months, since those who peruse the pages that follow should be able to form their own conclusions as to its quality.

Errors and omissions it is impossible altogether to avoid, but those who may notice either should write to the Editor, care of the Publishers, at the address given on the title page. It should also be noted that Press illustrations of warships, though seldom suitable for reproduction, are often of considerable value for reference.

THE PUBLISHERS.

NAVAL STRENGTH OF LEADING POWERS, SEPTEMBER, 1939

(Completed Ships Only)

	CAPITAL SHIPS	AIRCRAFT CARRIERS	HEAVY CRUISERS	OTHER CRUISERS	ANTI-AIRCRAFT SHIPS	DESTROYERS	SUBMARINES	T.B.	M.T.B.
BRITISH	15[1]	6[2]	15	43[1]	6[1]	179	57	—	26
U.S.A.	15	5	18	17	—	215	87	—	—
JAPANESE	9	5	12	27	—	112	59	12	—
FRENCH	7	1	7	12	—	59	78	12	1
ITALIAN	4[1]	—	7	14	—	61	104	70	72
GERMAN	5	—	2	6	—	22	65	12	30
RUSSIAN	3	1	—	5	—	30[3]	150[3]	19	100[3]

[1] Including 2 under reconstruction.　　　[2] Including H.M.S. *Argus*, but not H.M.S. *Courageous*.　　　[3] Approximate estimate.

NOTES ON NAVAL TREATIES

SPECIAL NOTE:—On September 6th, 1939, the British Government gave notice of suspension of all its obligations under the Three-Power Treaty and the Agreements with Russia and Poland.

A. By the Three-Power Treaty of the 25th March, 1936, the British, United States, and French Governments agreed, for the period 1937 to 1942 inclusive, to exchange information about new construction and not to construct or acquire any new ships save those falling within certain qualitative limitations.

The following classifications and age limits were agreed upon:

1. *Capital Ships:* Surface vessels of war, other than aircraft carriers, mounting guns of calibre exceeding 8 inches; divided into two sub-categories (a) those exceeding 10,000 tons and (b) those not exceeding 8,000 tons; age limit, 26 years.

2. *Aircraft Carriers:* Surface vessels of war, designed or adapted primarily to carry and operate aircraft at sea; divided into two sub-categories (a) those fitted with a flight deck, and (b) those not so fitted; age limit, 20 years.

3. *Light Surface Vessels:* Surface vessels of war, other than aircraft carriers, minor war vessels or auxiliary vessels, displacing from 100 to 10,000 tons and mounting guns not exceeding 8 inches calibre; divided into three sub-categories (a) those carrying a gun exceeding 6.1 inches calibre (b) those not carrying such a gun and displacing more than 3,000 tons, and (c) those not carrying such a gun and not displacing more than 3,000 tons; age limits, for sub-categories (a) and (b), 20 years (but, if laid down before 1920, 16 years); for sub-category (c), 16 years.

4. *Submarines:* Age limit, 13 years.

5. *Minor War Vessels:* Surface vessels of war, other than auxiliary vessels, displacing from 100 to 2,000 tons, not carrying a gun exceeding 6.1 inches calibre, or designed to launch torpedoes, or for a speed of more than 20 knots.

6. *Auxiliary Vessels:* Naval surface vessels, displacing more than 100 tons, not specifically built or normally employed as fighting ships, not carrying a gun exceeding 6.1 inches calibre or more than four guns exceeding 3 inches calibre or designed to launch torpedoes or carrying armour or more than two catapults or designed for more than 28 knots.

7. *Small Craft:* Naval surface vessels not exceeding 100 tons displacement.

For the period of the Treaty, the following qualitative limitations were agreed upon:

1. No capital ships are to be built or acquired which displace more than 35,000 tons[1] or less than 17,500 tons or carry a gun exceeding 16 inches calibre or a main armament of guns of less than 10 inches calibre.

2. No aircraft carrier to be built or acquired which displaces more than 23,000 tons or carries a gun exceeding 6.1 inches calibre or more than ten guns exceeding 5.25 inches calibre.

3. No light surface vessel of sub-category (a) and no light surface vessel of sub-category (b) which displaces more than 8,000 tons to be built or acquired

(subject to an "escalator" clause raising the limit to 10,000 tons and guns of 8 inches calibre).

4. No submarines to be built or acquired which displace more than 2,000 tons or carry a gun exceeding 5.1 inches calibre.

B. By the Treaty with Great Britain, dated the 17th July, 1937, Russia adopted the same provisions as to exchange of information, definitions, age limits, and qualitative limitations, subject to the following reservations.

1. Russia has the right to build or acquire seven light surface vessels of sub-category (a), having a displacement not exceeding 8,000 tons and a main armament of 7.1 inch guns.

2. Russian vessels stationed in the Far East are not subject to the above qualitative limitations, and the provisions for exchange of information do not apply to Russian vessels constructed in the Far East unless and until they are transferred to other stations.

C. On the 2nd December, 1938, Italy formally acceded to the Three-Power Treaty.

D. By the Treaty with Great Britain dated the 27th April, 1938, Poland agreed to adopt the same provisions as to exchange of information, definitions, age limits and qualitative limitations.

E. By the Treaty with Great Britain dated the 21st December, 1938, Denmark, Finland, Norway and Sweden agreed to adopt the same provisions as to exchange of information, definitions, age limits and qualitative limitations, subject to the following reservation:—

Each of these four powers has the right to build or acquire three capital ships of sub-category (b), having a main armament of guns of between 8 inches and 10 inches calibre.

F. The Anglo-German position: From the 17th July, 1937 until the 27th April, 1939, Germany was bound by an Agreement with Great Britain to exchange information in the manner provided by the Three-Power Treaty and to recognize its definitions, age limits and qualitative limitations. In repudiating that Agreement on the latter date, Germany expressed her desire that "the qualitative provisions of the Anglo-German Agreement" should remain unaffected. It is not clear from this whether Germany still regards herself as bound to restrict her light surface vessels of sub-category (a) to the five allowed her under the Agreement or only by the definition clause in the Three-Power Treaty which limits light surface vessels to 10,000 tons and 8 inch guns.

---

[1] By a Protocol dated the 30th June, 1938, Great Britain, the United States and France agreed to increase the qualitative limitation for capital ships of sub-category (a) from 35,000 to 45,000 tons. Russia, Italy and Poland have since acceded to this Protocol and Germany did so before her repudiation of the Anglo-German Naval Agreement.

CHANGES IN THIS EDITION

Ships Added

British:

INDEFATIGABLE
WELSHMAN
MILNE
MARKSMAN
MARNE
MARTIN
MATCHLESS
METEOR
MUSKETEER
MYRMIDON
NAPIER
NESTOR
NERISSA
NIZAM
NOBLE
NONPAREIL
NORMAN
NORSEMAN
ERNE
IBIS
ATHERSTONE
BERKELEY
CATTISTOCK
CLEVELAND
COTSWOLD
COTTESMORE
EGLINTON
EXMOOR
FERNIE
GARTH
HAMBLEDON
HOLDERNESS
MENDIP
MEYNELL
PYTCHLEY
QUANTOCK
QUORN
SOUTHDOWN
TYNEDALE
WHADDON
BANGOR
BLACKPOOL
BRIDLINGTON
BRIDPORT
BLYTH
PETERHEAD
POLRUAN
RYE
ROTHESAY
TENBY
BARNEHURST
BARNSTONE
ACACIA
ALMOND
ASH
BAY
BIRCH
BLACKTHORN
CHESTNUT
DEODAR
ELM
FIR
HAZEL
HICKORY
JUNIPER
MANGROVE
OLIVE
PINE
ROWAN
WALNUT
WISTARIA

Ships Deleted (Lost, condemned, sold or otherwise non-effective)

British:

STRATHCOE
(ex-*Vernon*)

Ships Added

British—contd.

WHITETHORN
AMBER
BERYL
CORAL
JADE
MOONSTONE
GUAVA
ALDER
BEECH
BERBERIS
HORNBEAM
LARCH
MAPLE
MYRTLE
OAK
TAMARISK
REDWOOD
JENNET
PUNNET
RENNET
QUANNET
BRINE
KILMUN
(Also 67 Trawlers to be renamed)

R. Aus. Navy:
PERTH
(From R.N.)

R. Canadian Navy:
SKIDEGATE

S. African Navy:
CRASSULA
KOMMETJE

Straits Settlements:
PANJI

Kenya:
NDOVU
ALHATHARI

Argentine:
KING

Ships Deleted (Lost, condemned, sold or otherwise non-effective)

R. Canadian Navy:
FESTUBERT
YPRES

Canadian Govt. Vessels:
LILLOOET
ALACHASSE
ULNA
PREVENTOR

Argentine:
KING (old)
MURATURE (old)

Albanian:
(All vessels)

Ships Added

Belgian:
MERCATOR

Brazilian:
AMAPÁ
IGUAPE
ITAJAHY
ITACURUSSÁ

Chilean:
HUEMUL
LEUCOTON

Colombian:
MARISCAL SUCRE

Cuba:
COLUMBIA

Dominican:
PRESIDENTE TRUJILLO
RAMSIS

Egyptian:
DARFEEL
RAQIB

French:
AVENTURIER
OPINIATRE
INTREPIDE
TÉMÉRAIRE
DESAIX
HOCHE
MARCEAU
KLÉBER
L'ALSACIEN
LE BRETON
LE SAVOYARD
LE CORSE
LE TUNISIEN
LE NORMAND
LE PARISIEN
LE PROVENCAL
LE NICOIS
LE SAINTONGEAIS

Ships Deleted (Lost, condemned, sold or otherwise non-effective)

Brazilian:
ALAGOAS

Chilean:
CAPITAN PRAT

Czechoslovakian:
(All vessels)

Egyptian:
ABDEL MONAYM

Finnish:
VMV 3
VMV 4

French:
AVENTURIER (old)
VTB 9
PHÉNIX
NYMPHE
ALTAIR
DUCOUÉDIC
JOUFFROY D'ABBANS

Ships Added

French—contd.

VTB 15—40
PHÉNIX (new)
AGATHE
CORAIL
ESCARBOUCLE
ANTIGONE
ARTEMIS
GORGONE
HERMIONE
ANDROMAQUE
ARMIDE
ANDROMÈDE
ASTRÉE
CLORINDE
CORNÉLIE
LA FURIEUSE
LA JOYEUSE
LA TROMPEUSE
CH 17—21
CH 47
CH 48
BENGALI
CORMORAN
GOELAND
IBIS
MOUETTE
PELICAN
LAPÉROUSE (new)
IMPASSIBLE
SAONE
SEINE
LIAMONE
MEDJERDA
CHARENTE
MAYENNE
BAISE
ACTIF
LA GRANDIÈRE

Greek:
ALIAKMON
NESTOS
STRYMON
AXIOS
ARGO
T 3
T 4

Italian:
AMMIRAGLIO COSTANZO CIANO
SAINT BON
CAGNI
MILLO
CARACCIOLO
MALASPINA
GENERALE LIUZZI
TARANTINI
METAURO
SILE
SEBETO
RAPALLO
TAORMINA
NEREO
SALVORE
PORTO QUIETO

Ships Deleted (Lost, condemned, sold or otherwise non-effective)

Italian:
QUARTO
PREMUDA
ARDIMENTOSO
C. ROSSAROL
CORTELLAZZO
MONFALCONE
I. NIEVO
INSIDIOSO
A. VITTURI
A. BAFILE
T. FARINATI
C. DEL GRECO
M.A.S. 418
M.A.S. 96
M.A.S. 188
M.A.S. 212
FAA DI BRUNO (old)

CHANGES IN THIS EDITION—*continued.*

Ships Added	Ships Deleted (Lost, condemned, sold or otherwise non-effective)	Ships Added	Ships Deleted (Lost, condemned, sold or otherwise non-effective)	Ships Added	Ships Deleted (Lost, condemned, sold or otherwise non-effective)	Ships Added	Ships Deleted (Lost, condemned, sold or otherwise non-effective)
Italian—contd. PORTO SDOBBA PORTO FOSSONE PORTO VENERE PORTO BUSO PORTO RECANATI PORTO SALVO PORTO PISANO	***Italian—contd.*** MONTE GRAPPA MONTELLO MONTE CENGIO MONTE NOVEGNO TEVERE	***Roumanian:*** AMIRAL MURGESCU TAIFUN	***Roumanian:*** MAIOR SONTU GHEORGHE MAIOR ENE CONSTANTIN MAIOR GRIGORE IOAN CAPITAN NICOLAE LASCAR BOGDAN	***Turkish:*** DEMIRHISAR SULTANHISAR GAYRET MUAVENET BURAK REIS MURAT REIS ORUÇ REIS ULUÇ ALI REIS SIVRIHISAR YÜZBAŞI HAKKI ATAK		***Venezuelan:*** CARIBE	***Venezuelan:*** 21 DE JULIO
Japanese: KATORI OYASIO HATUKAZE NATUSIO HAYASIO YUKIKAZE ISOKAZE I 17—I 24 SUBMARINE CHASER 7 MINESWEEPERS 11, 12 SOKUTEN *ex*-YUNG CHI FUSIMI	***Japanese:*** RO. 54, 55	***Russian:*** MOSKVA KHARKOV KIEV PEREKOP STALINSK VOLOCHEVKA CHEKA KAPSIUL PARAVAN VEKHA PODSEKATEL STRELA	***Russian:*** KAPSIUL (old)	***U.S.A.:*** IOWA NEW JERSEY CLEVELAND COLUMBIA WOOLSEY LUDLOW WILKES NICHOLSON SWANSON INGRAHAM EDISON ERICSSON P.T. 1—6 GAR GRAMPUS GRAYLING GRAYBACK GRENADIER GUDGEON CASCO MACKINAC SEMMES VULCAN SANTA RITA SANTA INEZ ARUNDEL MAHONING NAUGATUCK RARITAN AGASSIZ BONHAM BOUTWELL CARTIGAN NEMAHA AMERICAN SEAMAN JOSEPH CONRAD	***U.S.A.:*** MONOCACY GOLDEN GATE GUARD MACKINAC (old) TIOGA PETREL	***Yugoslav:*** BJELI ORAO PERUN MOCNI LOVCEN	***Yugoslav:*** MOCNI (old)
Netherlands: DE ZEVEN PROVINCIEN KIJKDUIN HEEMSKERCK ISAÄC SWEERS MOK I, MOK II D 1 CHERIBON POOLSTER	***Netherlands:*** WILLEM VAN EWIJK	***Spanish:*** OVIEDO TOLEDO BADAJOZ C. PEREZ T. AGUILAR XAUEN (salved)	***Spanish:*** CHURRUCA				
Norwegian: ODIN TOR BALDER DJERV DRISTIG OTRA RAUMA		***Swedish:*** U 1 U 2 T 1—4 Nos. 71—76 Nos. 10—12 Nos. 14, 15, 41, 45 Nos. 5—9 Nos. 1, 3		***Philippines:*** Q 1—5			
Polish: KAPER KRAKUS SOKOL NUREK	***Polish:*** KUJAWIAK ***Portuguese:*** AVE LIMPOPO	***Thai:*** No. 9	***Thai:*** SUA KHAMRONSIN-DHU SUA TAYARNCHOL Nos. 1—4 MONGKUT RAJAKUMARN BALI SUGRIB SRIYA MONTHON	***Uruguayan:*** HURACÁN ZAPICÁN ASPIRANTE			

ABBREVIATIONS: (A) signifies Argentine, (Br) Brazilian, (Chil) Chilian, (C) Chinese, (Cu) Cuban, (Da) Danish, (F) French, (G) German, (Gr) Grecian, (I) Italian, (J) Japanese, (N) Netherlands, (Nor) Norwegian, (P) Peruvian, (Po) Polish, (Port) Portuguese, (Ro) Roumanian, (Rus) Russian, (Sp) Spanish, (Sw) Swedish, (T) Turkish, (U.S.) United States.   No descriptive term implies British Empire.

BRITISH ROYAL NAVY.

Uniforms.

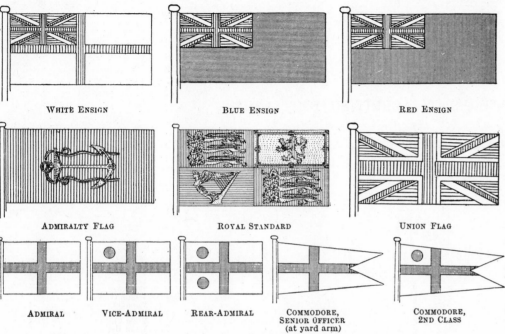

WHITE ENSIGN   BLUE ENSIGN   RED ENSIGN

ADMIRALTY FLAG   ROYAL STANDARD   UNION FLAG

ADMIRAL   VICE-ADMIRAL   REAR-ADMIRAL   COMMODORE, SENIOR OFFICER (at yard arm)   COMMODORE, 2ND CLASS

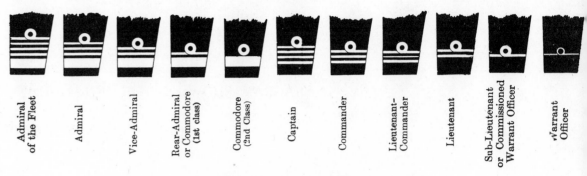

Admiral of the Fleet — Admiral — Vice-Admiral — Rear-Admiral or Commodore (1st class) — Commodore (2nd Class) — Captain — Commander — Lieutenant-Commander — Lieutenant — Sub-Lieutenant or Commissioned Warrant Officer — Warrant Officer

Colour of Ships.

Warships in Home waters, dark grey; in Mediterranean, China, East Indies, America and West Indies, light grey, except submarines, very dark grey in Home waters, dark blue in Mediterranean and dark olive-green on China Station. Escort Vessels in East Indies and Red Sea, white with light grey upperworks (and in some cases, yellow funnels). Escort Vessels on America and West Indies, New Zealand and Africa Stations, grey all over. Surveying Vessels have white hulls with yellow funnels. All Destroyers (but no Leaders) have their Pendant Numbers on bows and across sterns. Submarines have their Class Letter and Numbers painted on sides of Conning Tower, and in case of those with names on China Station, distinctive letters.

Programme.

Recent Construction.

1935. 3 Cruisers, 1 Flotilla Leader, 15 Destroyers, 3 Submarines, 1 Submarine Depot Ship, 1 Escort Vessel, 3 Minesweepers, 2 Patrol Vessels, 1 Surveying Vessel, 20 Trawlers, 1 Mining Tender, 6 Torpedo Boats, 2 Boom Defence Vessels.

1936. 2 Battleships, 2 Aircraft Carriers, 7 Cruisers, 1 Flotilla Leader, 16 Destroyers, 2 Escort Vessels, 3 Minesweepers, 1 Patrol Vessel, 8 Submarines, 1 Gunboat, 2 Surveying Vessels, 2 Trawlers, 1 Minelayer, 7 Torpedo Boats, etc., 2 Fleet Tugs, 5 Boom Defence Vessels, 1 Cable Vessel, 2 Motor Minesweepers.

1937. 3 Battleships, 2 Aircraft Carriers, 7 Cruisers, 16 Destroyers, 7 Submarines, 2 Depot Ships, 3 Escort Vessels, 4 Minesweepers, 3 Patrol Vessels, 1 Surveying Vessel, 2 Gunboats, 10 Torpedo Boats, 6 Boom Working Vessels, 10 Boom Defence Vessels, 2 Minelayers, 1 Fleet Tug.

1938. 2 Battleships, 1 Aircraft Carrier, 7 Cruisers, 3 Submarines, 2 Depot Ships, 1 Fleet Air Arm Repair Ship, 3 Minelayers, 2 Gunboats, 7 Torpedo Boats, 5 Boom Working Vessels, 1 Fleet Tug.

1939. 2 Battleships, 1 Aircraft Carrier, 4 Cruisers, 16 Destroyers, 4 Submarines, 22 Escort Vessels, 20 Minesweepers, 1 Minelayer, 1 Depot Ship, 1 Gunboat, 6 Torpedo Boats, 8 Boom Defence Vessels, 1 Royal Yacht, 1 Hospital Ship, 107 Trawlers, 56 Patrol Vessels, 1 Cable Vessel, 1 Fleet Tug.

Relative Ranks, Non-Executive Branches.

Engineer Officers have same as above, with purple between stripes.

Medical	,,	,,	,,	,, scarlet	,,	,,
Dental	,,	,,	,,	,, orange	,,	,,
Accountant	,,	,,	,,	,, white	,,	,,
Instructor	,,	,,	,,	,, light blue	,,	,,
Shipwright	,,	,,	,,	,, silver grey	,,	,,
Wardmaster	,,	,,	,,	,, maroon	,,	,,
Electrical	,,	,,	,,	,, dark green	,,	,,
Ordnance	,,	,,	,,	,, dark blue	,,	,,

Navy Estimates and Personnel.

(1936) £81,289,000.   (1937) £105,065,000.   (1938) £131,512,519.   (1939) £149,399,000.
Personnel: 101,154.   Personnel: 112,000.   Personnel: 121,000.   Personnel: 133,000.

Minister for Co-ordination of Defence: Admiral of the Fleet Lord Chatfield, G.C.B., O.M., K.C.M.G., C.V.O., D.C.L.

Board of Admiralty.

First Lord: The Right Hon. Winston Churchill, C.H., M.P.
First Sea Lord and Chief of Naval Staff: Admiral of the Fleet Sir Dudley Pound, G.C.B., G.C.V.O.
Second Sea Lord and Chief of Naval Personnel: Admiral Sir Charles Little, K.C.B
Third Sea Lord and Controller: Rear-Admiral B. A. Fraser, C.B.
Fourth Sea Lord and Chief of Supplies and Transport: Rear-Admiral G. S. Arbuthnot, C.B., D.S.O.
Fifth Sea Lord and Chief of Naval Air Services: Vice-Admiral the Hon. Sir Alexander Ramsay, K.C.B., K.C.V.O., D.S.O.
Deputy Chief of the Naval Staff: Rear-Admiral Tom Phillips, C.B.
Civil Lord: Captain A. U. M. Hudson, M.P.
Parliamentary and Financial Secretary: Geoffrey Shakespeare, Esq., M.P.
Permanent Secretary: Sir Archibald Carter, K.C.B., K.C.I.E.

Committee of Imperial Defence.

Chairman: The Prime Minister.
Deputy Chairman: The Minister for Co-ordination of Defence.
Members: H. M. Secretaries of State for War, Air, Foreign Affairs, Dominions, Colonies, India; The First Lord of the Admiralty; The First Sea Lord and Chief of Naval Staff; Chief of the Imperial General Staff; Chief of the Air Staff. Also representatives of H.M. Treasury and other Government Departments.

Director of Naval Construction.

Sir Stanley V. Goodall, K.C.B., O.B.E.

Mercantile Marine.

(From "Lloyd's Register," 1939.)
Total for whole of British Empire, 9,488 vessels of 21,215,261 gross tonnage.

1

A

DIAGRAM SHOWING THE OUTSTANDING FEATURES OF A BRITISH BATTLESHIP.

(H.M.S. BARHAM, OF QUEEN ELIZABETH TYPE.)

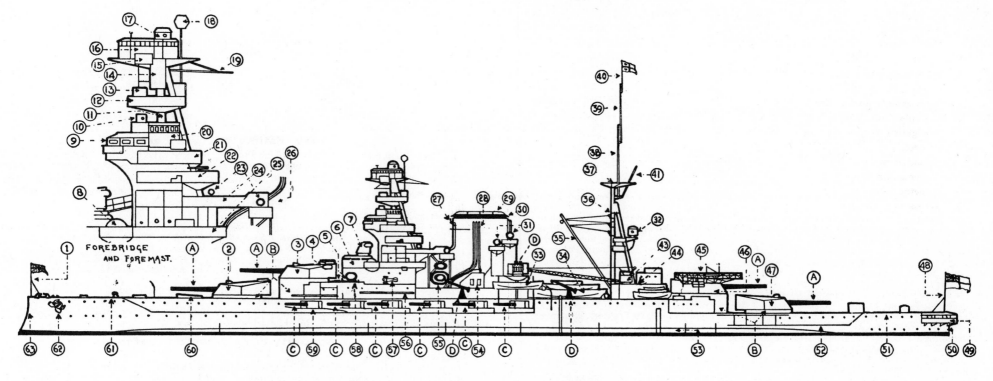

FOREBRIDGE AND FOREMAST.

(FOR KEY TO VARIOUS NUMBERED POINTS, SEE OPPOSITE.)

KEY TO DIAGRAM OPPOSITE.

A, A, A, A. Primary armament.
B, B. Barbettes.
C, C, C, C, C, C. Secondary armament of 6-inch guns.
D, D, D. High angle (anti-aircraft) guns.

1.	Jackstaff.	32.	Tower.
2.	" A " turret.	33.	Boat in davits.
3.	" B " turret.	34.	Boom boats.
4.	Rangefinder (R.F.).	35.	Main derrick (for boats, etc.).
5.	Saluting guns.	36.	Tripod mainmast.
6.	Conning tower (C.T.).	37.	Maintop.
7.	Main rangefinder, in hood.	38.	Maintopmast.
8.	Multiple Lewis gun mount.	39.	Maintopgallantmast.
9.	Navigating bridge.	40.	Flagstaff.
10.	Control.	41.	Gaff.
11.	Tripod foremast.	43.	Crane for aircraft.
12.	Lower control top.	44.	After shelter deck.
13.	Director tower.	45.	Catapult.
14.	Access to platform.	46.	" X " turret.
15.	Platform.	47.	" Y " turret.
16.	Upper control top.	48.	Ensign staff.
17.	Tower.	49.	Sternwalk.
18.	Frame aerial for directional wireless.	50.	Stern.
19.	Yard.	51.	Quarterdeck (Q.D.).
20.	Charthouse.	52.	Main deck.
21.	Compass platform.	53.	Bulges.
22.	Bridge (in a flagship, Admiral's bridge).	54.	Workshop, etc.
23.	Signalling searchlights (S.L.).	55.	Floats.
24.	Flag deck or signal bridge.	56.	Boat boom.
25.	Platform.	57.	Paravane.
26.	Trunk of funnel.	58.	Forward shelter deck.
27.	Syren brackets.	59.	Breakwater.
28.	Steam pipes (actually, safety valve uptakes).	60.	do.
29.	Caging.	61.	Forecastle (F.X.)
30.	Funnel cap.	62.	Anchor in hawse pipe.
31.	Main searchlights.	63.	Bow.

ABBREVIATIONS USED IN FOLLOWING PAGES

AA. Anti-aircraft guns.
B.H.P. Brake horse power.
Boilers : D.E., double-ended.
   ,,   S.E., single-ended.
C.T. Conning tower.
D.C. Depth charge.
Dir. Con. Director controlled.
I.H.P. Indicated horse power.
K.C. Krupp cemented steel.
Length pp., between perpendiculars.
   ,,   o.a., over all.
   ,,   w.l., waterline.
M.G. Machine guns.
mm. Millimetres.
pdr. Pounder.
Q.D. Quarterdeck.
S.H.P. Shaft horse power.
S.L. Searchlight.
T.T. Torpedo tubes.

OUTSTANDING FEATURES OF A BRITISH FLOTILLA LEADER (H.M.S. FAULKNOR).

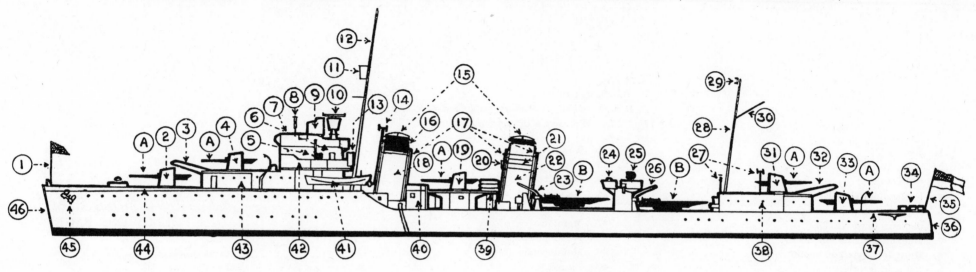

OUTSTANDING FEATURES OF A BRITISH ESCORT VESSEL (H.M.S. LEITH).

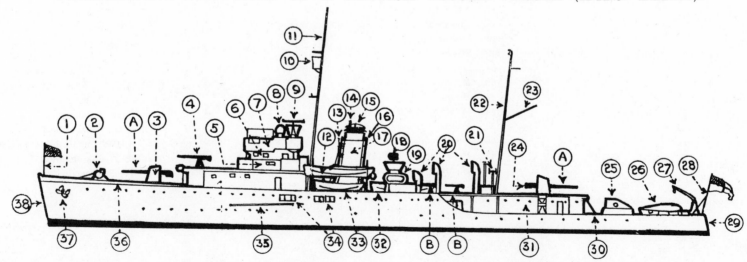

(FOR KEY TO VARIOUS NUMBERED PARTS, SEE OPPOSITE).

4

KEY TO DIAGRAM OF FLOTILLA LEADER (H.M.S. FAULKNOR).

A. A. A. A. A.   4·7 inch guns (in shields)   B. B.   Torpedo tubes (quadruple mounts)

1. Jackstaff.
2. No. 1 gun.
3. Blast screen.
4. No. 2 gun (superfiring).
5. Multi-machine gun.
6. Charthouse.
7. Navigating bridge.
8. Semaphore.
9. Control tower.
10. Rangefinder (R.F.).
11. Crow's nest (C.N.).
12. Foremast.
13. Flag rack.
14. Galley pipe.
15. Caps and caging.
16. Black top (indicating Flotilla Leader).

17. Steam pipes (safety valve uptakes).
18. Forefunnel.
19. No. 3 gun (on platform).
20. Syren brackets.
21. Funnel bands (indicating Flotilla).
22. After funnel.
23. Torpedo davit (port).
24. Compass on platform.
25. Searchlight (S.L.) on platform.
26. Torpedo davit (starboard).
27. Galley pipes.
28. Mainmast.
29. Navigation light.
30. Gaff.
31. No. 4 gun (superfiring).
32. Blast screen.

33. No. 5 gun.
34. Depth charges (D.C.).
35. Ensign staff.
36. Stern.
37. Quarterdeck (Q.D.).
38. After superstructure.
39. Floats.
40. Engineers' store.
41. Boats (in davits, port and starboard).
42. Signal bridge.
43. Forward superstructure.
44. Forecastle.
45. Anchor (in hawse pipe).
46. Bow (stem).

KEY TO DIAGRAM OF ESCORT VESSEL (H.M.S. LEITH).

A. A.   4·7 inch guns (in shields).   B. B.   3 pounder (saluting guns).

1. Jackstaff.
2. Windlass.
3. No. 1 gun.
4. 3 inch anti-aircraft (A.A.) gun (superfiring).
5. Signal deck.
6. Wheelhouse.
7. Navigating bridge.
8. Control.
9. Rangefinder (R.F.).
10. Crow's nest (C.N.).
11. Foremast.
12. Boats (in davits, port and starboard).
13. Syren brackets.

14. Galley pipe.
15. Cap and caging.
16. Steampipes (safety valve uptakes).
17. Funnel.
18. Searchlight (S.L.) on platform.
19. Float.
20. Ventilators (cowls).
21. Galley pipes.
22. Mainmast.
23. Gaff.
24. No. 2 gun.
25. Minesweeping winch.
26. High speed mine sweeps.

27. Davits (for sweeping gear).
28. Ensign staff.
29. Stern.
30. Quarterdeck (Q.D.).
31. After shelter deck.
32. Motor launch (in davits to starboard).
33. Boat.
34. Ventilation ports.
35. Boat boom.
36. Forecastle.
37. Anchor in hawse pipe.
38. Bow (stem).

BRITISH NAVAL ORDNANCE.

NOTE.—All details unofficial, but believed to be approximately correct.   (Particulars formerly given of some older marks of guns, no longer mounted in H.M. Ships, have been deleted.)

Calibre. ins.	Mark	Length of Bore in Calibres.	Weight of piece without B.M. (tons cwts. qrs.)	Weight of Projectile. (lbs.)	M.V. (f. s.)	M.E. (f. t.)	Weight of Full Charge. (lbs.)	REMARKS.
HEAVY B.L.								
16	I	45	103 10 0	2461	2953	..	640	"Nelson" and "Rodney."
15	I	42	97 3 0	1920	2450	84,070	428	Mounted in "Royal Sovereign," "Queen Elizabeth," "Hood," "Repulse," and "Erebus" classes.
14				1560				Mounted in "King George V" class.
13.5	VI	45	75 8 0	{ 1250 L. / 1400 H. }	2700	63,190	{ 293 L. / 297 H. }	
	V	45	74 18 1	..	2500	63,190	..	"Iron Duke."
MEDIUM B.L.								
8	I	50	16 10 0	256	3150	17,615	..	"Kent," "London," "Dorsetshire" and "York" classes.
6	XVIII	50	8 9 2	100	2800	..	28$\frac{5}{8}$	
	XVI	50	7 19 1	100	3100	6665	33	
	XII	45	6 14 2	100	2750	..	27$\frac{1}{2}$	Cruisers and Secondary Armament Battleships and Battle Cruisers.
	XI*	50	8 8 2	100	2937	5990	32$\frac{1}{12}$	
	XI	50	8 8 2	100	2937	5990	32$\frac{1}{12}$	
	VII	44.9	7 7 2	100	2493	5250	28$\frac{5}{8}$	Secondary Armament "Iron Duke."
5.5	I	50	6 1 0	82 / 85	2725	4222	22$\frac{1}{4}$	Breech mechanism of the Holmstrom type. Aircraft Carriers and Secondary Armament "Hood."
4.7	XII							Flotilla Leaders and Destroyers.
	II	40	3 1 0	48.5	2560	2205	..	AA. mounted in "Nelson" and "Rodney."
	I	45	3 1 0	50	3000	2800	11$\frac{3}{8}$	Mounted in Flotilla Leaders and Destroyers.
LIGHT B.L.								
4	XI	40	1 4 3	31	2100	..	..	
	IX*	44.35	2 1 1	31	2625	1934	7$\frac{11}{16}$	Secondary Armament, Battle Cruisers and Monitors.
	IX	44.35	2 1 1	31	2625	1934	7$\frac{11}{16}$	
	VIII	39.8	1 4 2	31	2287	..	5$\frac{3}{8}$	Earlier Destroyers.
MEDIUM Q.F.								
6	III	40	7 0 0	100	2025	..	13$\frac{1}{4}$	
4.7	VII	50	3 5 0	45	..	..	8$\frac{11}{16}$	
	V*	43.9	2 10 0	45	..	..	8$\frac{11}{16}$	
	V	43.9	2 10 0	45	..	..	8$\frac{11}{16}$	
4.5								Dual purpose. "Ark Royal," "Maidstone," "Forth."

BRITISH NAVAL ORDNANCE.

LIGHT GUNS.—(See Note on previous page.)

Calibre. ins.	Mark.	Length of Bore in Calibres.	Weight of piece without B.M.	Weight of Projectile.	M.V.	M.E.	Weight of Full Charge.	REMARKS.
			tons cwts. qrs.	lbs.	f. s.	f. t.	lbs.	

LIGHT Q.F.

Calibre. ins.	Mark.	Length of Bore in Calibres.	Weight of piece without B.M.	Weight of Projectile.	M.V.	M.E.	Weight of Full Charge.	REMARKS.
4	XVI							
	XII	40	1 6 0	31	2100	..	$5\frac{1}{8}$	Semi-automatic. Fixed ammunition. AA. mounting. Capital Ships, Cruisers and Aircraft Carriers.
	VII	40.5	1 4 4	31	2750	1970	$5\frac{5}{8}$	Do. do. do.
	V*	45	2 1 2	31	2625	1934	$5\frac{7}{8}$	Do. do. do.
	V	45	2 1 2	31	2625	1934	$7\frac{11}{16}$	Semi-automatic. } Earlier Destroyers and Submarines.
	IV	40	1 3 3	31	2225	1137	$5\frac{1}{4}$	Do.
	III	40	1 3 0	25	2456	1200	$3\frac{9}{16}$	D.A.M.S.
3	I	45	1 0 0	{ 16, 12½ }	2500	..	{ $2\frac{1}{8}$, $2\frac{1}{2}$ }	Semi-Automatic. Fixed ammunition. AA. mounting. Earlier Cruisers, Flotilla Leaders and Destroyers.
3	I	23	5 3	12½	1700	..	$1\frac{5}{16}$	Fixed ammunition.
3	I	40	11 2	12½	2197	..	2	Minesweepers, Sloops and Gunboats.
2.24	II	40	7 0	6	1735	..	ozs. $8\frac{3}{4}$	Fixed ammunition. Auxiliary patrol.
1.85	II	40	5 0	$3\frac{5}{16}$	1873	..	$7\frac{1}{4}$	Fixed ammunition. Hotchkiss. Saluting guns in all classes.
	I	50	6 0	$3\frac{5}{16}$	2575	152	$13\frac{3}{8}$	Fixed ammunition. Vickers. Auxiliary Patrol. Aircraft Carriers.
	II	39.37	1 3	2	2000	55.5	3	Automatic. AA. mounting. Cruisers, Flotilla Leaders and Destroyers.
	I	39.37	1 3	2	2000	55.5	3	

ANTI-SUBMARINE HOWITZERS, B.L.

Calibre. ins.	Mark.	Length of Bore in Calibres.	Weight of piece without B.M.	Weight of Projectile.	M.V.	M.E.	Weight of Full Charge.	REMARKS.
							lbs.	
11	I	8.5	1 14 2	200	..	..		
7.5	I	8.5	6 0	100	390	105.5	$1\frac{1}{4}$	

STICK BOMBS.

Gun.	Weight of Bomb.	Charge.	
4.7 in. Q.F.	{ 600, 500, 250, 200 }	3 lbs. 14 ozs.	
4 in. B.L. or Q.F.	{ 350, 200 }	2 lbs. 2 ozs. / 3 lbs. 4 ozs.	Mark IV. & VIII. / Mark V & IX.
12 pdr. 12 cwt. Q.F.	200	1 lb.	

Torpedoes.

No official details are available of the latest marks of torpedoes. Standard torpedo used is still the 21 inch heater type, though the *Nelson* and *Rodney* carry 24·5 inch torpedoes, which are discharged to port and starboard from submerged tubes forward. Increased size of latter type gives greater range and heavier explosive charge, but the extra weight and dimensions add to the difficulties of picking up and handling. On the other hand, the change of mounting to a position well forward of beam obviates the necessity for a bar to protect the torpedo while leaving the tube. All other tubes in ships of recent date are of the above-water pattern, each mounting carrying five tubes in the latest destroyers. Few modifications of the internal mechanism of torpedoes have been divulged, but running results are reported to show greatly increased efficiency and reliability.

18 inch torpedoes are used by the torpedo bombers of the Fleet Air Arm and some of the earlier motor torpedo boats.

Searchlights.

These are of 36 inch and 24 inch diameters. Most capital ships and cruisers now carry only four of the former size, with two 20 inch for signalling. Ship's supply voltage is reduced by resistances to that required by the arc. The arcs are mounted before parabolic mirrors. Carbons feed in automatically and are rotated constantly. The crater is kept at the correct focal distance from the mirror by a " third electrode ", thus ensuring a parallel beam. A carbon with a wiper action is used for striking the arc. Under normal conditions, no attention is required while burning until new carbons are needed. The barrels in which the lamp is mounted are fitted with iris shutters, and the light is controlled from the forebridge.

Mining.

Mark H.2 mine, as used in the later stages of the War, is still the standard pattern of contact mine laid by surface vessels, with modification for use by submarines. Weight is 650 lbs., positive buoyancy 400 lbs., diameter 38 inches. Six horns are fitted for detonating the charge. A spring-loaded switch renders the mine safe should the mooring wire break. This is in accordance with international law. Various patterns of sinkers are used with this mine, which allow mines to be moored at a set height above the sea bottom or depth below the surface.

Protective paravanes, of a design similar to that used during the War, are carried by all deep-draught ships, a modified pattern being used by destroyers as a high speed mine sweep.

Catapults.

Types experimented with and adopted have been the Carey ; Forbes ; R.A.E. (Royal Aircraft Establishment) ; and the Ransome & Rapier " Slider ". Performance aimed at in the earlier patterns was the launching into flight of aircraft up to a maximum weight of 7,000 lbs. at a speed of 45 m.p.h. with a travel of 34 ft. In later types, these figures have been improved to 8,000, lbs. 55–57 m.p.h. and over 50 ft. Power used is compressed air and/or cordite, transmitted either by a system of cables and pulleys or a series of multiple rams. The catapults are of (a) fixed or variable position and (b) fixed or variable lengths.

British Warship Builders.

In addition to the firms detailed below, the following shipyards have recently undertaken Admiralty orders for warships and/or Royal Fleet Auxiliaries : Ailsa Shipbuilding Co., Ltd., Troon ; Caledon Shipbuilding & Engineering Co., Ltd., Dundee ; Wm. Gray & Co., Ltd., West Hartlepool ; Furness Shipbuilding Co., Ltd., Haverton Hill on Tees ; Henry Robb, Ltd., Leith ; Philip & Son, Ltd., Dartmouth ; Ardrossan Dockyard Co., Ltd., Ardossan ; Lytham Shipbuilding Co., Ltd., Lytham ; Blyth Shipbuilding and Dry Dock Co., Ltd. ; Goole Shipbuilding & Repair Co., Ltd. ; Wm. Simons & Co., Ltd., Renfrew ; Lobnitz & Co., Ltd., Renfrew ; Hall, Russell & Co., Ltd., Aberdeen ; Charles Hill & Co., Ltd., Bristol ; John Lewis & Co., Aberdeen ; Fleming & Ferguson, Ltd., Paisley ; Smith's Dock Co., Ltd., South Bank-on-Tees ; Vosper, Ltd., Portsmouth ; British Power Boat Co., Ltd., Hythe, Southampton.

Note.—The headings give the abbreviated titles by which builders are mentioned on later Ship Pages. With a few exceptions, all details given below were kindly approved or furnished by the firms mentioned.

Cammell Laird.

CAMMELL, LAIRD & CO., Ltd. (Birkenhead and Tranmere). Area of yard, 108 acres. Six slips (longest 1000 ft.), six small slips. Seven graving docks, five small and No. 6, 708 × 80 ft. ; No. 7, 861 × 90 ft. Outer basin, 14¼ acres ; inner basin, 2¾ acres. Annual capacity, 100,000 tons *gross* and 400,000 H.P. output. Establishment consists of North Yard, where vessels up to 500 feet in length can be constructed, and the South Yard, in which are slips suitable for vessels between 600 and 900 feet in length. Builders of heavy armoured ships, cruisers, flotilla leaders, destroyers, submarines, &c., as well as of merchant vessels of all classes. Equipment of yard thoroughly up-to-date.

Clydebank.

JOHN BROWN & CO., Ltd. (Shipbuilding & Engineering Works, Clydebank, Glasgow). Area, 80 acres. River frontage, 1050 yards. Building berths : Five of 1,000 to 600 ft. in length, and three 600 to 450 ft. in length. Building berths are commanded by derricks, tower and gantry cranes ; two of berths are covered. Tidal basin : 5¼ acres in area, 35 ft. depth, L.W.O.S.T., with two entrances of 190 and 220 ft. width respectively. Basin commanded by two 150-ton cranes ; also four wharf cranes of 5 to 30 tons capacity. Builders of war and mercantile vessels of all types and the largest dimensions, inclusive of machinery and equipment. Steam engines of reciprocating type, Parsons and Brown-Curtis turbine types ; and Diesel oil engines.

Denny.

WM. DENNY & BROS., Ltd. (Leven Shipyard, Dumbarton). Area : 60 acres. Building berths up to 550 ft. in length. Two wet basins, one 475 ft., one 910 ft. Numerous cranes with lifts up to 110 tons. Destroyers, torpedo boats, escort vessels, surveying vessels, submarines and mercantile vessels built, with necessary machinery, &c.

Fairfield.

THE FAIRFIELD SHIPBUILDING & ENGINEERING CO., LTD. (GOVAN, GLASGOW). Area: 80 acres. Water front: 3,000 ft. 6 slips to build ships up to 1,000 ft. in length. Dock: 5½ acres with 270 ft. entrance. 250-ton crane. Wet basin: 900 ft. long. Naval and mercantile ships, engines, boilers, &c., of all types.

Hamilton.

WM. HAMILTON & CO., LTD. (PORT GLASGOW). Build minesweepers for the Royal Navy in addition to mercantile tonnage.

Harland & Wolff.

HARLAND & WOLFF, LIMITED. Shipbuilding, shiprepairing and engineering works at Belfast: 19 slips fully equipped to build the largest types of naval and mercantile vessels: 5 graving Docks in close proximity to the works. shipyard and shiprepairing works at Govan, Glasgow: 7 large slips and graving dock adjoining. Up-to-date engineering works at Finnieston, Glasgow. Engineering and ordnance works at Scotstoun, Glasgow. Large iron foundry at Govan, Glasgow: castings up to 100 tons. Modern and fully equipped ship and machinery repair works at London, Liverpool and Southampton. Shipyard for small craft and general engineering works at North Woolwich, London.

Hawthorn Leslie.

R. & W. HAWTHORN, LESLIE & CO., LTD. (HEBBURN YARD, HEBBURN-ON-TYNE). Nine slips up to 735 ft. long. One dock: 502¾ × 66 (entrance) × 23½ ft. on blocks; 26 ft. draught at quay at low water. Engine department of 200,000 I.H.P. per annum. Designers and builders of cruisers, destroyers and other warship types. Engine every type of war vessel.

Scotts'.

SCOTTS' SHIPBUILDING & ENGINEERING CO., LTD. (GREENOCK). Slips for eight large vessels; fitting-out basin; graving dock. Makers of heavy oil engines.

Stephen.

ALEX. STEPHEN & SONS, LTD. (LINTHOUSE, GOVAN, GLASGOW). Build cruisers, destroyers and torpedo craft; also mail, passenger and cargo steamers. Machinery: all types, 200,000 H.P. output per annum. Boilers: Scotch, cylindrical and all water-tube types. Six building berths for building ships up to 700 ft. long. Water front: 1,500 ft. Area of yard: 52 acres. Repairs of all classes to hulls and machinery.

Swan Hunter.

SWAN, HUNTER & WIGHAM RICHARDSON, LTD. (WALLSEND-ON-TYNE). Sixteen building berths up to 900 ft. in length, served by overhead electric cranes. Four of the largest berths covered in. Annual gross shipbuilding capacity, 150,000 tons. Engine works: 75,000 H.P. output per year.

The dry dock department includes a large repairing yard with three graving docks. Engine works build marine oil engines, marine steam turbines, Bauer-Wach exhaust turbines, and reciprocating steam engines. Total area of works: 80 acres. Water frontage: 4,000 ft.

Allied firms are the Wallsend Slipway & Engineering Co., Ltd., Wallsend; Barclay, Curle & Co., Ltd., of Whiteinch, Glasgow, Govan and Elderslie.

Thornycroft.

JOHN I. THORNYCROFT & CO., LTD. (WOOLSTON, SOUTHAMPTON). Builders of river gunboats, destroyers, light cruisers, merchant vessels up to 400 ft. Thirteen building berths, including three covered in. One hauling-up slip for ships up to 170 ft. long. Water frontage: 2,000 ft. opposite Southampton Docks. Specialities: Turbines, water-tube boilers, oil fuel gear. Workshops in Southampton Docks, adjacent to fitting-out dock for hull and machinery repairs. Total floor area: 25,000 sq. ft. Motor torpedo boats built at Hampton-on-Thames.

Vickers-Armstrongs.

(NAVAL YARD, BARROW-IN-FURNESS). Area of works: 121 acres. Thirteen building berths, of length respectively 800 ft.; 750 ft.; 700 ft.; 630 ft.; three of 600 ft.; three of 550 ft.; 450 ft.; 400 ft.; 350 ft.—the two latter being entirely under cover. Water frontage about 1,200 yards plus fitting-out quays about 1,000 yards. Building Berths fitted with modern Tower Cranes and covered Berths by Gantry Cranes. Fitting out Berths equipped with two 150-ton Giant Hammer-head cranes, 30-ton electric jib crane, Steam Derrick and Travelling Cranes, etc. Floating dock, 420 × 59½ ft., to lift 5,200 tons. Graving dock, 500 × 60 × 22 ft. Extensive shops fully equipped with the most modern machinery for the construction of steam and internal combustion engines, boilers, electric equipment, gun mountings, and every kind of naval and mercantile engineering work.

(NAVAL YARD, HIGH WALKER, NEWCASTLE-ON-TYNE). Area 83 acres. Opened 1913, equipped for the construction of both Warships and Mercantile Vessels. 10 Building Berths of lengths respectively 1,000 feet, 900 feet, 800 feet, two of 620 feet, five from 450 feet to 550 feet. Water frontage about 700 yards plus fitting-out quays about 800 yards. Building Berths fitted with modern Tower Cranes and fitting-out berth equipped with giant 250-ton Hammer Head Crane in addition to 30, 10, and 5-ton Travelling Cranes. Extensive Workshops fully equipped with the most modern machinery for Naval or Mercantile Ship construction, etc.

Also own the repairing establishment known as Palmers' Hebburn Co., Ltd., which includes the biggest graving dock on the N.E. coast. Agencies all over the world.

White.

J. SAMUEL WHITE & CO. LTD. (COWES). The oldest shipyard on the Admiralty list. Vessels up to 400 ft. in length, including light cruisers, flotilla leaders, destroyers, submarines, escort vessels, gunboats, patrol boats, high class passenger and cargo vessels, cross channel steamers, special service vessels, special craft for re-erection abroad, yachts, motor torpedo boats, pinnaces, and other small naval craft, high speed craft of all types. Seven building berths. Engine works for reciprocating engines and turbine engines of highest powers. Water-tube boilers (land and marine), " J. Samuel White " Diesel marine engines, " J. Samuel White " Diesel generating sets for marine service, " J. Samuel White " patent oil fuel installations for marine and land service, " Clinsol " clean-in-service strainers. Hammerhead 80-ton crane at fitting out quay.

Yarrow.

YARROW & CO., LTD. (SCOTSTOUN, GLASGOW). Area of yard: 16 acres. Water frontage: 750 ft. Six building berths, for ships up to 400 ft. long. Wet basin for fitting-out, 350 × 85 ft., served by 50-ton crane. Specialities are destroyers, fast yachts, vessels for shallow river navigation, both of stern-wheel type and of type propelled by screws working in tunnels, Yarrow water-tube boilers and Yarrow superheater, both for land and marine use. Also vessels propelled by internal-combustion motors. (Overseas Branch: Yarrows, Ltd., Victoria, B.C.)

(1) Home Fleet

2nd Battle Squadron.
NELSON (*Fleet Flagship of Home Fleet*)
RODNEY
RESOLUTION (*Rear-Admiral 2nd Battle Squadron*)
ROYAL OAK
ROYAL SOVEREIGN
RAMILLIES

Battle Cruiser Squadron
HOOD ((*Flag*)
REPULSE
RENOWN

2nd Cruiser Squadron.
SOUTHAMPTON (*Flag*)
NEWCASTLE
SHEFFIELD
GLASGOW
CUMBERLAND
EDINBURGH (to relieve *Southampton* as *Flag*)
BELFAST

Aircraft Carriers.	Attendant Destroyers.
ARK ROYAL	BEAGLE
(Vice-Admiral (A))	BOREAS
FURIOUS	

Destroyer Flotillas.
AURORA (Rear-Admiral (D), Home Fleet)

6th Flotilla.	7th Flotilla.	8th Flotilla.
SOMALI	JERVIS	FAULKNOR
(Capt. (D))	(Capt. (D))	(Capt. (D))
ASHANTI	JACKAL	FORTUNE
MASHONA	JERSEY	FIREDRAKE
ESKIMO	JAVELIN	(being FURY
TARTAR	JUPITER	re- FORESTER
PUNJABI		lieved FAME
MATABELE	ECHO	by FORESIGHT
BEDOUIN	ENCOUNTER	Jaguar FEARLESS
		Janus FOXHOUND
		Juno

Fleet Target Service.
CENTURION
GUARDIAN
SHIKARI
ST. CYRUS
BUCCANEER
BANDIT

2nd Submarine Flotilla.
FORTH (Captain (S))

MACKAY	CACHALOT	PORPOISE
NARWHAL	SEAHORSE	STARFISH

Drifters.
COLDSNAP (attached to *Nelson*)
CLOUD (*Ark Royal*)
FUMAROLE (*Cumberland*)
NOONTIDE (*Resolution*)
HARMATTAN (*Sheffield*)
WHIRLPOOL (*Rodney*)
HORIZON (*Royal Oak*)
SEABREEZE (*Royal Sovereign*)
HALO (*Furious*)
SUNDOWN (*Repulse*)
LUNAR BOW (*Southampton*)
MIST (*Forth*)
SHOWER (*Newcastle*)
SHEEN (*Glasgow*)
LEEWARD (*Hood*)

(2) Local Defence and Training Establishments, Patrol Flotillas, etc.

The Nore

Attached to Gunnery School.
PEMBROKE
MARSHAL SOULT

Cadets' Training Cruiser.
VINDICTIVE

Attached to Mechanical Training Establishment.
SANDHURST

Emergency Destroyers.

BRILLIANT	BLANCHE	BOADICEA

Devonport

Attached to Torpedo School.	Attached to R.N. Engineering College, Keyham.
MELPOMENE	CODRINGTON

Emergency Destroyers.	Aircraft Carrier.
ARDENT	HERMES
BASILISK	
BRAZEN	

Portsmouth

Attached to Navigation School.
ALRESFORD
SALTBURN

Gunnery Firing & Boys' Training Ship.
IRON DUKE

Gunnery and Torpedo School Cruiser.
DAUNTLESS

Drifter.
INDIAN SUMMER

Local Destroyer Flotilla.	Boom Defence Vessels.
KEMPENFELT	BARCOMBE
SARDONYX	BARRAGE
ANTELOPE	
ARROW	
VANOC	
EXMOUTH	
SCIMITAR	
WHITLEY (Escort Vessel)	

Attached to Gunnery School. (H.M.S. *Excellent*)

EXCELLENT	ST. FAGAN	ST. MARTIN
TEDWORTH	EREBUS	

Attached to Torpedo School. (H.M.S. *Vernon*)

ACASTA	ACHERON	AMAZON
SKATE	ANTHONY	NIGHTINGALE
M.T.B. 22	RINGDOVE	M.T.B. 100
M.T.B. 102	WILLOW	LINNET
PLOVER		HAWTHORN

5th Submarine Flotilla.

WINCHELSEA	DWARF	STERLET
SEAWOLF	SUNFISH	H. 43
L. 23	L. 26	UNDINE
THISTLE	TRITON	TRIUMPH
SEAL		

Reserve.

Group A.	Group B.	Group D.
OBERON	OSIRIS	H. 34
OTWAY	OSWALD	H. 44
OXLEY		H. 49

Rosyth

Boys' Training Ship.
CALEDONIA

Destroyer.
SABRE

Boom Defence Vessels.

BARBARIAN	BARFIELD	BOWNET
BARFAIR	BAYONET	MARTINET

Scapa Flow

BARBICAN	BRINE	PLANET
BARCROFT	BARRANCA	PLANTAGENET
BARLOW		

Clyde

BARMOUTH

Harwich

DUNNET

Dover

FALCONET

(3) Portland

Fishery Protection Flotilla.

HASTINGS	LEDA	COLNE
(Capt. F. P & M.)	BOYNE	DOON
PELICAN	MASTIFF	LILAC
GOSSAMER		

1st Minesweeping Flotilla.

HEBE (S.O.)	BRAMBLE	HAZARD
HUSSAR	SHARPSHOOTER	SALAMANDER
NIGER	SEAGULL	SPEEDY

6th Minesweeping Flotilla.

SYRINGA (S.O.)	CYPRESS	SYCAMORE
CEDAR	HOLLY	LAUREL
MAGNOLIA		

1st Anti-Submarine Flotilla.

BITTERN (S.O.)	WALPOLE	WALKER
VANQUISHER	KINGFISHER	KITTIWAKE
MALLARD	PUFFIN	SHELDRAKE
WIDGEON	SAPPHIRE	TOPAZE
TOURMALINE	TURQUOISE	BASSET

6th Submarine Flotilla.
TITANIA (Commander (S))

ACHATES	H. 32	H. 33
L. 27	SPEARFISH	STURGEON
SWORDFISH	ELFIN	UNITY
URSULA		

Flotilla Reserve: ALECTO

H. 28	H. 31	H. 50

Boom Working Vessel.
CORONET

(4) Reserve Fleet
(Portsmouth, Devonport and the Nore.)

Cruisers.

EFFINGHAM	COLOMBO	CALEDON
(*Flag*)	(S.O.R.F.)	(S.O.R.F.)
HAWKINS	CALYPSO	DRAGON
DURBAN	CARDIFF	DELHI
DUNEDIN	CERES	EMERALD
DANAE	DIOMEDE	
DESPATCH	CARADOC	
ENTERPRISE		

Aircraft Carriers.

ARGUS	COURAGEOUS

Anti-Aircraft Ships.

CAIRO	CALCUTTA	CURLEW

Destroyers.

MONTROSE	VERSATILE	WOLFHOUND
CAMPBELL	VIDETTE	ESCORT
BROKE	ELECTRA	VORTIGERN
KEPPEL	EXPRESS	VIMY
KEITH	VIMIERA	WHITSHED
ESK	VERITY	WESSEX
SALADIN	WINDSOR	WATCHMAN
VICEROY	WARWICK	STURDY
WILD SWAN	VENETIA	VISCOUNT
WREN	WOLVERINE	STRONGHOLD
WHITEHALL	ESCAPADE	WHIRLWIND
WITCH	VELOX	VESPER
ECLIPSE	WAKEFUL	WANDERER
VOLUNTEER		

Escort Vessels, Patrol Vessels and Minesweepers.

ROSEMARY	FOXGLOVE	LUPIN
P.C. 74	SPEEDWELL	SELKIRK
HALCYON	HARRIER	SKIPJACK
	VALOROUS	

Minelayer.	Seaplane Carrier.
ADVENTURE	ALBATROSS

Trawlers.

GARRY	LIFFEY	DEE
JAMES LUDFORD	KENNET	BLACKWATER
EDEN	FOYLE	

Drifter:
EBBTIDE

Surveying Vessels.

KELLETT	FITZROY

Maintenance Reserve.
(Rosyth)

Depôt Ships.

COCHRANE (S.O.)	GREENWICH

Cruiser.
CAPETOWN

Destroyers.

VANESSA	VANITY	VANSITTART
VENOMOUS	VERDUN	VIVACIOUS
WITHRINGTON	WIVERN	MALCOLM

Trawlers.

JASPER	AGATE	AMETHYST
CORNELIAN	PEARL	RUBY

(5) Miscellaneous Ships at Home Ports.

Battleships.

QUEEN ELIZABETH	VALIANT	REVENGE

Cruisers.

NORFOLK	LONDON	
FROBISHER	SUFFOLK	

Anti-Aircraft Ships.

COVENTRY	CURACOA	CARLISLE

Seaplane Carrier.
PEGASUS

Destroyers and Escort Vessels.

WORCESTER	VIVIEN	VETERAN
WOOLSTON	WINCHESTER	AMBUSCADE
WESTMINSTER	VEGA	VALENTINE
WALLACE	ROCHESTER	STORK

Submarine.
THAMES

Minesweeper.
BRITOMART

Trawlers.

LARCH	MYRTLE	OAK
TAMARISK		

Yachts.

VICTORIA & ALBERT	ENCHANTRESS

(6) Surveying Service.

CHALLENGER
ENDEAVOUR
FRANKLIN
GLEANER
HERALD
SCOTT
JASON
SCARBOROUGH

(7) Mediterranean Fleet

1st Battle Squadron.
WARSPITE (*Fleet Flagship*)
BARHAM (*Flag of V.A.C.*)
MALAYA

Aircraft Carrier.
GLORIOUS

1st Cruiser Squadron	Attendant Destroyer	3rd Cruiser Squadron
DEVONSHIRE (*Flag*)	BULLDOG	ARETHUSA (*Flag*)
SUSSEX		PENELOPE
SHROPSHIRE		

Destroyer Flotillas.
GALATEA (V.A. (D))
WOOLWICH

1st Flotilla	2nd Flotilla	3rd Flotilla	4th Flotilla
GRENVILLE	HARDY	INGLEFIELD	AFRIDI
(Capt. (D))	(Capt. (D))	(Capt. (D))	(Capt. (D))
GARLAND	HERO	IMOGEN	GURKHA
GIPSY	HEREWARD	ILEX	MOHAWK
GRAFTON	HOTSPUR	ISIS	SIKH
GALLANT	HAVOCK	IMPERIAL	COSSACK
GREYHOUND	HYPERION	INTREPID	MAORI
GLOWWORM	HASTY	ICARUS	ZULU
GRENADE	HOSTILE	IVANHOE	NUBIAN
GRIFFIN	HUNTER	IMPULSIVE	

(7) Mediterranean Fleet—continued.

1st Submarine Flotilla.   **1st M.T.B. Flotilla.**
MAIDSTONE (Capt. (S))   VULCAN
DOUGLAS   M.T.B. 1 to 6
CLYDE   M.T.B. 14 to 19
SEVERN
SALMON
SEALION
SHARK
SNAPPER

Netlayer.
PROTECTOR

Minelayer.
MEDUSA

Tug.
BRIGAND

Escort Vessels.
ABERDEEN   WESTON

Trawlers.
MOY   OUSE

Hospital Ship.
MAINE

Malta Reserve

Destroyers.
WOLSEY   WRESTLER

Minesweepers.
DUNOON (S.O.)   ALBURY   DUNDALK
MMS 1   MMS 2

Depôt and Repair Ships.
CYCLOPS   RESOURCE

Trawlers.
AMBER   BERYL   CORAL
JADE   MOONSTONE

Drifters.
LANDFALL   CRESCENT MOON   EDDY   SUNSET

Tug.   **Boom Working Vessel.**
ST. ISSEY   MAGNET

Alexandria Reserve.
FERMOY (S.O.M.S.)   ELGIN   PANGBOURNE (S.O.)
Egypt)   LYDD   SUTTON
SALTASH   ROSS

Gibraltar Reserve.
ACTIVE   WISHART   WRYNECK
ST. DAY   ST. OMAR

(8) East Indies

4th Cruiser Squadron.
GLOUCESTER   MANCHESTER   LIVERPOOL
(Flag of C. in C.)

Depôt Ship.
LUCIA

Red Sea Division.
EGRET (S.N.O.)   FLEETWOOD

Persian Gulf Division.
SHOREHAM (S.N.O.)   DEPTFORD   FOWEY

Trincomali.
BARNET   BARBETTE

(9) Africa

6th Cruiser Squadron.
NEPTUNE (Flag of C. in C.)

Escort Vessels.
BRIDGEWATER   MILFORD   LONDONDERRY
AUCKLAND

Minesweeping Trawlers.   **Sierra Leone**
MAPLE   REDWOOD   BARBROOK
BARCASTLE

(10) China

5th Cruiser Squadron.
KENT (Flag C. in C)   DORSETSHIRE
CORNWALL (Flag)   BIRMINGHAM

21st Destroyer Flotilla.
DUNCAN (Capt. (D))   DECOY   DEFENDER
DAINTY   DIANA   DELIGHT
DUCHESS   DARING   DIAMOND

Aircraft Carrier.
EAGLE

4th Submarine Flotilla.
MEDWAY (Capt. (S))   WESTCOTT   ODIN
OLYMPUS   ORPHEUS   OTUS
PANDORA   PARTHIAN   PERSEUS
PHOENIX   PROTEUS   RAINBOW
REGENT   REGULUS   ROYER
RORQUAL   GRAMPUS

2nd M.T.B. Flotilla.
M.T.B. 7 (S.O.)   M.T.B. 8   M.T.B. 9
M.T.B. 10   M.T.B. 11   M.T.B. 12

Escort Vessels.
FALMOUTH   FOLKESTONE   SANDWICH
GRIMSBY   LOWESTOFT   BIDEFORD

Yangtse Gunboats.
SCORPION   TERN   COCKCHAFER
(Rear-Admiral & APHIS   FALCON
S.N.O.,(Yangtse) CRICKET   GRASSHOPPER
GANNET   DRAGONFLY   MANTIS
GNAT   LADYBIRD   SCARAB
PETEREL   SANDPIPER

West River Gunboats.
TARANTULA (S.N.O.,   CICALA   MOTH
West River)   SEAMEW   ROBIN

Hong Kong.

Minelayer.
REDSTART

Destroyers.
THRACIAN   THANET   TENEDOS
SCOUT

    Boom Defence Vessels.
Tug.   BARLANE
ST. BREOCK   BARLIGHT

Singapore.

TERROR (Base Ship)
BARRICADE, BARRIER, FASTNET
(Boom Working Vessels)
ST. JUST (Tug)

In Reserve, 2nd Minesweeping Flotilla.
ABINGDON (S.O.)   ABERDARE   BAGSHOT
DERBY   HUNTLEY   HARROW
FAREHAM   STOKE   WIDNES

(11) America and West Indies

8th Cruiser Squadron.
BERWICK (Flag of   YORK   ORION
C. in C.)   AJAX   EXETER (Commodore,
South America Division)

Escort Vessels.
DUNDEE   PENZANCE

(12) New Zealand
(Under control of New Zealand Naval Board.)

Cruisers.
LEANDER (Commodore, New Zealand) ACHILLES

Escort Vessels.
LEITH   WELLINGTON

Ketch.
VIKING

Trawler.
WAKAKURA

(13) Royal Australian Navy
(Under control of Australian Naval Board.)

Cruiser Squadron.
CANBERRA (Rear-Admiral Commanding Australian Squadron.)
SYDNEY
HOBART
PERTH

Escort Vessels.
SWAN   YARRA

Destroyeys.
VENDETTA (Flotilla Leader)
VOYAGER   VAMPIRE

Depôt Ship.
PENGUIN

Surveying Ship.
MORESBY

In Reserve, Paid Off, etc.

Cruisers.
ADELAIDE   AUSTRALIA

Flotilla Leaders.
STUART   WATERHEN

(14) Royal Canadian Navy.
(Under control of Canadian Department of National Defence.)

Destroyers.
ST. LAURENT   FRASER   SAGUENAY
SKEENA   OTTAWA   RESTIGOUCHE

Training Ships.
VENTURE   SKIDEGATE

Minesweepers.
GASPÉ   FUNDY   COMOX
NOOTKA   ARMENTIÈRES

Ships Completing.

Destroyers.
KELLY   KELVIN   KIMBERLEY
KANDAHAR   KHARTOUM   KINGSTON
KASHMIR   KIPLING

Submarines.
TRIBUNE   TRIDENT   THETIS
(under salvage)

Patrol Vessels.
GUILLEMOT   PINTAIL   SHEARWATER

Ships Building and Authorised.

Battleships
KING GEORGE V, LION (V.-A., Tyne)
PRINCE OF WALES, Temeraire (Cammell Laird)
DUKE OF YORK, one of 1939 programme (Clydebank)
BEATTY (Fairfield)
JELLICOE (Swan Hunter)
One (1939 programme) not yet ordered.

Aircraft Carriers.
ILLUSTRIOUS, INDOMITABLE (V.-A., Barrow)
VICTORIOUS (V.-A., Tyne)
FORMIDABLE (Harland & Wolff)
IMPLACABLE (Fairfield)
INDEFATIGABLE (Clydebank)

Cruisers.
DIDO, Charybdis (Cammell Laird)
EURYALUS (Chatham)
NAIAD, Cleopatra (Hawthorn)
PHOEBE (Fairfield)
SIRIUS (Portsmouth)
BONAVENTURE, Scylla (Scotts)
HERMIONE, KENYA, Uganda (Stephen)
FIJI (Clydebank)
MAURITIUS, Jamaica (Swan Hunter)
NIGERIA, Gambia (V.-A., Tyne)
TRINIDAD (Devonport)
CEYLON (V.-A., Barrow)
Four (1939 programme) not yet ordered.

Minelayers.
Abdiel (White)
LATONA (Thornycroft)
Manxman (Stephen)
Welshman (Hawthorn)

Destroyers.
LAFOREY, LANCE (Yarrow)
LARNE, LIVELY (Cammell Laird)
LEGION, LIGHTNING (Hawthorn)
LOOKOUT, LOYAL, Milne, Marksman (Scotts)
Matchless, Meteor (Stephen)
Norman, Norseman (Thornycroft)
Nerissa, Nizam (Clydebank)
Noble, Nonpareil (Denny)
Marne, Martin (V.-A., Tyne)
Musketeer, Myrmidon, Napier, Nestor (Fairfield)
Two (Australia)

Submarines.
TAKU, Talisman (Cammell Laird)
TARPON, TUNA (Scotts)
TRIAD, TRUANT, Tetrarch (V.-A., Barrow)
TIGRIS, Torbay (Chatham)
Four (1939 programme) not yet ordered

Fast Escort Vessels.
Cattistock, Cleveland, Cotswold, Cottesmore (Yarrow)
Quorn, Southdown (White)
Tynedale, Whaddon (Stephen)
Pytchley, Quantock (Scotts)
Hambledon, Holderness, Mendip, Meynell (Swan Hunter)
Fernie, Garth (Clydebank)
Atherstone, Berkeley (Cammell Laird)
Eglinton, Exmoor (V.-A., Tyne)

Escort Vessels and Minesweepers.
BLACK SWAN, FLAMINGO (Yarrow)
Two minesweepers (Denny)
Erne, Ibis (Furness)
Blyth, Peterhead (Blyth)
Bangor, Blackpool (Harland & Wolff)
Polruan, Rye (Ailsa)
Rothesay, Tenby (Hamilton)
WARREGO, Parramatta (Australia)
Ten minesweepers (1939 programme) not yet ordered.

Depôt Ships.
TYNE (Scotts)
Hecla (Clydebank)
Adamant, Unicorn (Harland & Wolff)
Depot ship for M.T.B.'s (1939 programme) not yet ordered

River Gunboats.
One (White)

Boom Defence Vessels.
Barnehurst, Barnstone, and 2 more (Blyth)
KANGAROO (Australia)
Two (Lobnitz)

Trawlers.
ACACIA, ALMOND (Ardrossan)
ASH, BAY (Cochrane)
BIRCH, BLACKTHORN (Cook, Welton)
CHESTNUT, DEODAR (Goole)
ELM, FIR (A. & J. Inglis)
HAZEL, HICKORY (Henry Robb)
JUNIPER, MANGROVE (Ferguson Bros.)
OLIVE, PINE (Hall, Russell)
ROWAN, WALNUT, WISTARIA, WHITETHORN (Smiths Dock Co.)

Whalers.
Fifty-six (1939 programme) not yet ordered

Motor Torpedo Boats.
One (1936 programme) not yet ordered
Three (1938 programme) not yet ordered.
Six (1939 programme) not yet ordered
Twelve (for R.A.N.) not yet ordered

Oilers.
Three (1939 programme) not yet ordered.

Fleet Target Service Tug.
One (1939 programme) not yet ordered

Cable Ship.
One (1939 programme) not yet ordered

Royal Yacht.
One (1939 programme) not yet ordered

Hospital Ship.
One (Barclay Curle)

NAMES OF EXISTING WARSHIPS OF THE BRITISH EMPIRE, showing the number of ships which have borne each name and the date of its first being adopted by the Royal Navy.

Compiled from the records of the late Commander J. A. RUPERT-JONES, R.D., R.N.R., by T. D. MANNING,

ABBEYDALE (1st), 1937
ABDIEL (2nd), 1915
ABERDARE (1st), 1917
ABERDEEN (2nd), 1916
ABINGDON (1st), 1917
ACADIA (1st), 1913
ACASTA (3rd), 1797.
ACHATES (5th), 1573.
ACHERON (6th), 1803
ACHILLES (9th), 1744
ACTIVE (23rd), 1758
ADAMANT (3rd), 1779
ADELAIDE (7th), 1803
ADVENTURE (20th), 1594
ADVERSUS (1st), 1931
AFRIDI (2nd), 1907
AGATE (2nd), 1917
AJAX (8th), 1767
ALACHASSE (1st), 1931
ALBATROSS (12th), 1796
ALBURY (1st), 1917
ALDER (1st), 1939
ALDERSDALE (1st), 1937
ALECTO (4th), 1781
ALRESFORD (1st), 1918
AMAZON (9th), 1745
AMBER (2nd), 1917
AMBUSCADE (6th), 1746
AMETHYST (9th), 1793
ANTELOPE (13th), 1546
ANTHONY (2nd), 1417
APHIS (1st), 1915
APPLELEAF (1st), 1917
ARANMORE (1st), 1890
ARDENT (11th), 1764
ARETHUSA (8th), 1759
ARGENTEUIL (1st), 1916
ARGUS (11th), 1792
ARGYLE (3rd), 1776
ARK ROYAL (3rd), 1587
ARLEUX (1st), 1918
ARMENTIERES (1st), 1918
ARNDALE (1st), 1937
ARRAS (1st), 1918
ARROW (8th), 1821
ASHANTI (1st), 1936
ATHERSTONE (2nd), 1915
AUCKLAND (3rd), 1802
AURORA (9th), 1758
AUSTRALIA (3rd), 1886

BACCHUS (6th), 1806
BAGSHOT (1st), 1917
BANDIT (1st), 1937
BANGOR (1st), 1939
BARBARIAN (1st), 1937
BARBETTE (2nd), 1806
BARBICAN (1st), 1936
BARBROOK (1st), 1937
BARCASTLE (1st), 1937
BARCOMBE (1st), 1937
BARCROFT (1st), 1937
BARFAIR (1st), 1937
BARFIELD (1st), 1937
BARHAM (3rd), 1811
BARLANE (1st), 1937
BARLIGHT (1st), 1937
BARLOW (1st), 1937
BARMOUTH (1st), 1937
BARNEHURST (2nd), 1937
BARNET (1st), 1934
BARNSTONE (2nd), 1937
BARRAGE (1st), 1937

BARRANCA (1st), 1937
BARRICADE (1st), 1937
BARRIER (1st), 1937
BASILISK (10th), 1695
BASSET (1st), 1934
BAYONET (1st), 1937
BEAGLE (8th), 1804
BEATTY (1st), 1937
BEDOUIN (2nd), 1915
BEECH (1st), 1939
BELFAST (1st), 1936
BELGOL (1st), 1917
BELLECHASSE (1st), 1912
BERBERIS (2nd), 1915
BERENS (1st), 1921
BERKELEY (1st), 1939
BERNIER (1st), 1918
BERWICK (10th), 1679
BERYL (5th), 1915
BIDEFORD (5th), 1695
BIRCHOL (1st), 1917
BIRMINGHAM (2nd), 1912
BIRNIE (1st), 1921
BISHOPDALE (1st), 1937
BITTERN (7th), 1796
BLACKPOOL (1st), 1939
BLACK SWAN (1st), 1937
BLACKWATER (2nd), 1903
BLANCHE (12th), 1779
BLOODHOUND (4th), 1801
BLYTH (1st), 1939
BOADICEA (5th), 1797
BOARDALE (1st), 1937
BONAVENTURE (10th), 1489
BOREAS (6th), 1757
BOWNET (1st), 1938
BOXOL (1st), 1917
BOYNE (6th), 1692
BRADBURY (1st), 1915
BRAMBLE (8th), 1656
BRAMBLELEAF (1st), 1916
BRANT (1st), 1927
BRIDGEWATER (4th), 1655
BRIDLINGTON (3rd), 1918
BRIDPORT (1st), 1939
BRIGAND (1st), 1937
BRILLIANT (8th), 1696
BRINE (2nd), 1918
BRITOMART (6th), 1808
BROKE (2nd), 1914
BROOMDALE (1st), 1937
BRUCE (2nd), 1917
BUCCANEER (1st), 1937
BULLDOG (7th), 1782
BURGONET (1st), 1938

CACHALOT (2nd), 1915
CAIRNDALE (1st), 1938
CAIRO (2nd), 1916
CALCUTTA (5th), 1795
CALEDON (2nd), 1810
CALYPSO (10th), 1783
CAMPBELL (2nd), 1796
CANBERRA (1st), 1926
CAPETOWN (1st), 1918
CARADOC (2nd), 1846
CARDIFF (2nd), 1652
CARIBOU (1st), 1925
CARLISLE (3rd), 1693
CARTIER (1st), 1910
CASCADE (1st), 1918
CATTISTOCK (2nd), 1917
CEDAR (2nd), 1916

CEDARDALE (1st), 1938
CELEROL (1st), 1916
CENTURION (8th), 1650
CERBERUS (9th), 1758
CERES (6th), 1777
CEYLON (4th), 1805
CHALLENGER (8th), 1806
CHARYBDIS (5th), 1809
CHERRYLEAF (1st), 1917
CHERWELL (2nd), 1903
CHRYSANTHEMUM (2nd), 1917
CICALA (1st), 1915
CITADELLE (1st), 1932
CLEOPATRA (7th), 1779
CLEVELAND (4th), 1671
CLIVE (2nd), 1882
CLOUD (1st), 1918
CLYDE (8th), 1796
COCHRANE (2nd), 1905
COCKCHAFER (4th), 1795
CODRINGTON (1st), 1929
COLD SNAP (1st), 1918
COLNE (2nd), 1905
COLOMBO (1st), 1917
CORAL (1st), 1939
CORNELIAN (3rd), 1655
CORNFLOWER (1st), 1915
CORNWALL (6th), 1692
CORNWALLIS (7th), 1777
CORONET (1st), 1934
COSSACK (6th), 1805
COTSWOLD (2nd), 1917
COTTESMORE (2nd), 1917
COVENTRY (4th), 1658
CRUSADER (2nd), 1909
CUMBERLAND (9th), 1695
CURACOA (4th), 1809
CURLEW (11th), 1795
CYCLOPS (4th), 1779
CYPRESS (2nd), 1760

DAINTY (4th), 1589
DAISY (8th), 1855
DANAE (5th), 1759
DARING (7th), 1804
DAUNTLESS (5th), 1804
DECOY (5th), 1810
DEE (6th), 1814
DEFENDER (6th), 1797
DELHI (1st), 1917
DELIGHT (14th), 1583
DEPTFORD (8th), 1652
DERBY (2nd), 1916
DESPATCH (18th), 1692
DEVONSHIRE (7th), 1692
DIAMOND (14th), 1652
DIANA (12th), 1757
DIDO (5th), 1784
DIOMEDE (4th), 1781
DISTOL (1st), 1916
DOLLARD (1st), 1913
DOON (3rd), 1904
DORSETSHIRE (3rd), 1694
DOUGLAS (1st), 1917
DRAGON (18th), 1512
DRAGONET (1st), 1938
DRAGONFLY (3rd), 1906
DRUID (6th), 1760
DUCHESS (5th), 1652
DUKE OF YORK (7th), 1763
DUNCAN (5th), 1804
DUNDALK (1st), 1918
DUNDEE (3rd), 1915

DUNEDIN (2nd), 1917
DUNNET (1st), 1936
DUNOON (1st), 1918
DURBAN (2nd), 1918
DWARF (6th), 1826

EAGLE (20th), 1592
EBBTIDE (1st), 1924
EBONOL (1st), 1917
ECHO (11th), 1758
ECLIPSE (10th), 1715
EDDY (1st), 1918
EDEN (3rd), 1814
EDINBURGH (6th), 1707
EFFINGHAM (1st), 1917
EGLINTON (2nd), 1916
EGRET (3rd), 1919
ELDEROL (1st), 1917
ELECTRA (8th), 1806
ELFIN (3rd), 1847
ELGIN (2nd), 1814
ELMOL (1st), 1917
EMERALD (12th), 1762
ENCHANTRESS (7th), 1802
ENCOUNTER (5th), 1805
ENDEAVOUR (15th), 1652
ENTERPRISE (15th), 1709
EREBUS (5th), 1806
ERNE (6th), 1813
ESCAPADE (1st), 1933
ESCORT (7th), 1757
ESK (5th), 1813
ESKIMO (1st), 1936
ESTEVAN (1st), 1912
EURYALUS (5th), 1803
EXCELLENT (8th), 1787
EXETER (5th), 1680
EXMOOR (1st), 1939
EXMOUTH (4th), 1841
EXPRESS (8th), 1695

FALCON (28th), 1212
FALCONET (1st), 1937
FALMOUTH (12th), 1652
FAME (11th), 1653
FAREHAM (1st), 1917
FASTNET (2nd), 1904
FAULKNOR (2nd), 1914
FEARLESS (7th), 1794
FERMOY (1st), 1917
FERNIE (1st), 1939
FESTUBERT (1st), 1918
FIJI (1st), 1939
FIREDRAKE (5th), 1648
FITZROY (1st), 1919
FLAMINGO (2nd), 1876
FLEETWOOD (3rd), 1917
FLEURDELIS (1st), 1929
FOLKESTONE (7th), 1299
FORESIGHT (5th), 1570
FORESTER (11th), 1657
FORMIDABLE (5th), 1777
FORTH (4th), 1812
FORTOL (1st), 1917
FORTUNE (22nd), 1512
FOWEY (10th), 1696
FOXGLOVE (1st), 1914
FOXHOUND (7th), 1806
FOYLE (2nd), 1903
FRANCOL (1st), 1917
FRANKLIN (2nd), 1916
FRASER (2nd), 1916

FROBISHER (1st), 1916
FUMAROLE (1st), 1918
FURIOUS (5th), 1794
FURY (10th), 1779

GALATEA (7th), 1776
GALLANT (3rd), 1798
GAMBIA (1st), 1938
GANNET (8th), 1800
GARLAND (15th), 1242
GARRY (2nd), 1905
GARTH (2nd), 1917
GIPSY (5th), 1799
GIVENCHY (1st), 1918
GLASGOW (8th), 1707
GLEANER (7th), 1809
GLENCOE (1st), 1899
GLITTER (1st), 1918
GLORIOUS (1st), 1915
GLOUCESTER (10th), 1654
GLOWWORM (3rd), 1906
GNAT (4th), 1856
GOSSAMER (3rd), 1823
GRAFTON (7th), 1675
GRAMPUS (11th), 1740
GRASSHOPPER (8th), 1776
GREENWICH (6th), 1666
GRENADE (2nd), 1918
GRENVILLE (3rd), 1764
GREYHOUND (23rd), 1545
GRIFFIN (16th), 1656
GRIMSBY (2nd), 1916
GUARDIAN (2nd), 1783
GUAVA (1st), 1939
GUILLEMOT (2nd), 1916
GURKHA (3rd), 1888

HALCYON (5th), 1803
HALO (1st), 1918
HAMBLEDON (2nd), 1917
HARDY (8th), 1797
HARMATTAN (1st), 1918
HARRIER (9th), 1804
HARROW (1st), 1918
HASTINGS (6th), 1695
HASTY (6th), 1798
HAVOCK (7th), 1796
HAWKINS (1st), 1917
HAWTHORN (4th), 1546
HAZARD (8th), 1711
HEBE (7th), 1782
HECLA (7th), 1798
HERALD (6th), 1806
HEREWARD (2nd), 1913
HERMES (8th), 1796
HERMIONE (3rd), 1782
HERO (9th), 1759
HICKOROL (1st), 1917
HINDUSTAN (5th), 1795
HOBART (2nd), 1794
HOLDERNESS (2nd), 1916
HOLLY (5th), 1808
HOME (1st), 1900
HOOD (3rd), 1849
HORIZON (1st), 1918
HORNBEAM (1st), 1939
HOSTILE (5th), 1935
HOTSPUR (5th), 1810
HUNTER (16th), 1646
HUNTLEY (1st), 1918
HUSSAR (8th), 1757
HYPERION (2nd), 1807

IBIS (3rd), 1918
ICARUS (5th), 1814
ILEX (1st), 1935
ILLUSTRIOUS (4th), 1789
IMOGEN (6th), 1801
IMPERIAL (1st), 1935
IMPLACABLE (4th), 1805
IMPULSIVE (1st), 1935
INDEFATIGABLE (5th), 1784
INDIAN SUMMER (1st), 1918
INDOMITABLE (3rd), 1907
INDUS (4th), 1807
INGLEFIELD (1st), 1935
INTREPID (7th), 1747
INVESTIGATOR (9th), 1798
IRON DUKE (2nd), 1870
ISIS (7th), 1743
IVANHOE (3rd), 1913

JACKAL (7th), 1779
JADE (1st), 1939
JAGUAR (3rd), 1937
JAMAICA (7th), 1710
JAMES LUDFORD (1st), 1918
JANUS (9th), 1778
JASON (12th), 1673
JASPER (10th), 1808
JAVELIN (3rd), 1914
JELLICOE (1st), 1937
JENNET (2nd), 1539
JERSEY (6th), 1654
JERVIS (1st), 1937
JUNO (7th), 1757
JUPITER (6th), 1778

KANDAHAR (1st), 1937
KANGAROO (7th), 1795
KASHMIR (1st), 1937
KEITH (1st), 1929
KELLETT (1st), 1919
KELLY (1st), 1937
KELVIN (2nd), 1917
KEMPENFELT (2nd), 1915
KENNET (2nd), 1904
KENT (9th), 1652
KENYA (1st), 1937
KEPPEL (2nd), 1779
KHARTOUM (1st), 1937
KIMBERLEY (4th), 1918
KIMMEROL (1st), 1917
KING GEORGE V (2nd), 1911
KINGFISHER (14th), 1675
KINGSTON (4th), 1697
KIPLING (1st), 1937
KITTIWAKE (2nd), 1918
KOALA (1st), 1938
KOOKABURRA (1st), 1938
KURUMBA (1st), 1916
KYLE (1st), 1913

LABURNUM (2nd), 1915
LADYBIRD (1st), 1916
LADY GREY (1st), 1906
LADY LAURIER (1st), 1902
LAFOREY (2nd), 1913
LANCE (2nd), 1913
LANDFALL (1st), 1918
LARCH (1st), 1939
LARCHOL (1st), 1917
LARNE (4th), 1814
LASSO (2nd), 1915

LATONA (4th), 1781
LAUREL (13th), 1651
LAURENTIAN (1st), 1902
LAURIER (1st), 1937
LAWRENCE (3rd), 1350
LEANDER (6th), 1780
LEDA (6th), 1783
LEEWARD (1st), 1918
LEGION (2nd), 1913
LEITH (3rd), 1782
LIFFEY (4th), 1813
LIGHTNING (10th), 1691
LILAC (2nd), 1915
LILLOET (1st), 1908
LIMOL (1st), 1917
LINNET (11th), 1797
LION (17th), 1511
LIVELY (20th), 1709
LIVERPOOL (10th), 1741
LOCUST (4th), 1801
LONDON (10th), 1636
LONDONDERRY (1st), 1934
LOOKOUT (2nd), 1913
LOWESTOFT (6th), 1697
LOYAL (2nd), 1913
LUCIA (2nd), 1914
LUNAR BOW (1st), 1918
LUPIN (1st), 1915
LYDD (1st), 1918

MACDONALD (1st), 1937
MACKAY (1st), 1918
MADRAS (3rd), 1795
MAGNET (8th), 1807
MAGNOLIA (2nd), 1915
MAIDSTONE (8th), 1654
MAINE (2nd), 1908
MALASPINA (1st), 1913
MALAYA (1st), 1914
MALCOLM (1st), 1918
MALLARD (4th), 1801
MANCHESTER (1st), 1936
MANXMAN (2nd), 1915
MAORI (2nd), 1908
MAPLE (1st), 1939
MARAUDER (1st), 1938
MARKSMAN (2nd), 1915
MARNE (2nd), 1915
MARSHAL SOULT (1st), 1915
MARTIN (12th), 1651
MARTINET (1st), 1937
MASHONA (1st), 1936
MASTIFF (7th), 1797
MATABELE (1st), 1936
MATCHLESS (2nd), 1914
MAURITIUS (1st), 1937
MEDUSA (6th), 1788
MEDWAY (7th), 1693
MELPOMENE (6th), 1794
MENDIP (1st), 1939
METEOR (9th), 1797
MEYNELL (2nd), 1917
MILFORD (8th), 1660
MILNE (2nd), 1914
MINERVA (15th), 1759
MIST (1st), 1918
MIXOL (1st), 1916
MOHAWK (8th), 1798
MONTCALM (1st), 1904
MONTENOL (1st), 1917
MONTROSE (2nd), 1819
MOONSTONE (1st), 1939
MORESBY (2nd), 1915
MOSQUITO (12th), 1777
MOTH (2nd), 1906
MOY (2nd), 1904

MURRAY STEWART (1st), 1918
MUSKETEER (2nd), 1915
MYRMIDON (6th), 1781
MYRTLE (6th), 1807

NAIAD (3rd), 1797
NAPIER (2nd), 1915
NARWHAL (2nd), 1915
N. B. MACLEAN (1st), 1930
NELSON (8th), 1799
NEPTUNE (16th), 1683
NERISSA (3rd), 1916
NESTOR (3rd), 1781
NEWCASTLE (7th), 1654
NIGER (6th), 1759
NIGERIA (1st), 1937
NIGHTINGALE (10th), 1651
NIZAM (2nd), 1916
NOBLE (2nd), 1915
NONPAREIL (4th), 1580
NOONTIDE (5th), 1918
NORFOLK (4th), 1693
NORMAN (2nd), 1916
NORSEMAN (2nd), 1916
NORTHERN RANGER (1st), 1936
NUBIAN (3rd), 1903

OAK (3rd), 1652
OBERON (5th), 1805
OCEAN EAGLE (1st), 1919
ODIN (4th), 1807
OLCADES (1st), 1937
OLEANDER (1st), 1922
OLIGARCH (1st), 1937
OLNA (1st), 1921
OLWEN (1st), 1937
OLYMPUS (2nd), 1918
OLYNTHUS (1st), 1937
ONYX (8th), 1808
ORANGELEAF (1st), 1917
ORION (6th), 1787
ORPHEUS (7th), 1773
OSIRIS (4th), 1916
OSWALD (1st), 1928
OTTAWA (1st), 1938
OTUS (1st), 1928
OTWAY (2nd), 1914
OUSE (2nd), 1905
OXLEY (1st), 1925

PANDORA (10th), 1779
PANGBOURNE (1st), 1918
PARRAMATTA (3rd), 1909
PARTHIAN (6th), 1808
PATHAN (2nd), 1888
PEARL (14th), 1651
PEARLEAF (1st), 1917
PEGASUS (11th), 1598
PELICAN (21st), 1577
PEMBROKE (12th), 1655
PENELOPE (8th), 1778
PENAUIN (9th), 1751
PENZANCE (3rd), 1695
PERSEUS (5th), 1776
PERTH (2nd), 1918
PETEREL (8th), 1777
PETERHEAD (2nd), 1918
PETRELLA (1st), 1918
PETROBUS (1st), 1918
PETRONEL (1st), 1918
PHILOL (1st), 1916
PHOEBE (7th), 1795
PHOENIX (17th), 1546
PINTAIL (1st), 1937
PLANET (1st), 1937
PLANTAGENET (2nd), 1801

PLOVER (12th), 1652
PLUMLEAF (1st), 1917
POLRUAN (1st), 1939
PORPOISE (7th), 1777
PORTIA (7th), 1809
PRESIDENT (8th), 1646
PRESTOL (1st), 1917
PREVENTOR (1st), 1929
PRINCE OF WALES (12th), 1763
PROSPERO (2nd), 1837
PROTECTOR (5th), 1755
PROTEUS (2nd), 1777
PUFFIN (2nd), 1918
PUNJABI (1st), 1936
PUNNET (1st), 1939
PYTCHLEY (2nd), 1917

QUANNET (1st), 1939
QUANTOCK (1st), 1939
QUEEN ELIZABETH (1st), 1912
QUORN (2nd), 1917

RAINBOW (9th), 1586
RAMILLIES (5th), 1706
RAPIDOL (1st), 1917
REDSTART (2nd), 1918
REDWING (9th), 1806
REDWOOD (1st), 1939
REGENT (3rd), 1489
REGULUS (3rd), 1785
RELIANT (1st), 1933
RENNET (1st), 1939
RENOWN (10th), 1651
REPULSE (12th), 1595
RESOLUTION (17th), 1667
RESOLVE (1st), 1918
RESOURCE (4th), 1778
RESPOND (1st), 1918
RESTIGOUCHE (1st), 1938
RETORT (1st), 1918
REVENGE (10th), 1575
RINGDOVE (7th), 1806
ROBERT DUNDAS (1st), 1938
ROBERT MIDDLETON (1st), 1938
ROBIN (2nd), 1897
ROCHESTER (4th), 1693
RODNEY (7th), 1759
ROLLICKER (3rd), 1918
RORQUAL (2nd), 1915
ROSEMARY (1st), 1915
ROSS (2nd), 1795
ROTHESAY (1st), 1939
ROVER (11th), 1777
ROYAL SOVEREIGN (7th), 1635
ROYSTERER (1st), 1915
RUBY (11th), 1651
RYE (5th), 1696

SABRE (1st), 1917
SAFEGUARDER (1st), 1929
SAGONA (1st), 1912
SAGUENAY (1st), 1930
ST. ABBS (2nd), 1918
ST. BLAZEY (1st), 1918
ST. BREOCK (1st), 1918
ST. CLEARS (1st), 1918
ST. CYRUS (1st), 1918
ST. DAY (1st), 1918
ST. DOGMAEL (1st), 1918
ST. FAGAN (1st), 1918
ST. HELIERS (1st), 1918
ST. ISSEY (1st), 1918
ST. JUST (1st), 1918
ST. LAURENT (1st), 1937
ST. MARTIN (2nd), 1691

ST. MELLONS (1st), 1918
ST. MONANCE (1st), 1918
ST. OMAR (1st), 1918
SALADIN (1st), 1917
SALAMANDER (12th), 1544
SALMON (3rd), 1895
SALTASH (3rd), 1746
SALTBURN (1st), 1918
SANDPIPER (2nd), 1897
SANDWICH (10th), 1679
SAPPHIRE (11th), 1651
SARDONYX (1st), 1918
SAUREL (1st), 1929
SCARAB (1st), 1915
SCARBOROUGH (8th), 1691
SCIMITAR (1st), 1917
SCORPION (10th), 1746
SCOTOL (1st), 1917
SCOTT (3rd), 1915
SCOUT (14th), 1577
SCYLLA (4th), 1809
SEABREEZE (1st), 1918
SEAGULL (9th), 1795
SEAHORSE (13th), 1630
SEAL (2nd), 1897
SEALION (2nd), 1918
SEAMEW (4th), 1857
SEAWOLF (2nd), 1918
SELKIRK (1st), 1918
SERBOL (1st), 1917
SEVERN (9th), 1695
SHARK (1st), 1691
SHARPSHOOTER (5th), 1805
SHEARWATER (6th), 1808
SHEEN (1st), 1918
SHEFFIELD (1st), 1935
SHELDRAKE (7th), 1806
SHIKARI (2nd), 1918
SHOREHAM (4th), 1694
SHOWER (1st), 1918
SHROPSHIRE (1st), 1927
SIGNET (3rd), 1666
SIKH (2nd), 1917
SIRIUS (7th), 1786
SKATE (2nd), 1895
SKEENA (1st), 1929
SKIPJACK (5th), 1807
SLAVOL (1st), 1917
SNAPPER (7th), 1804
SOMALI (3rd), 1890
SONNET (1st), 1938
SOUTHAMPTON (5th), 1693
SOUTHDOWN (2nd), 1916
SPEARFISH (1st), 1935
SPEEDWELL (26th), 1559
SPEEDY (7th), 1782
SPHINX (7th), 1748
STARFISH (3rd), 1895
STERLET (1st), 1936
STEWART, WM. J. (1st), 1932
STOKE (1st), 1917
STORK (9th), 1652
STRONGHOLD (1st), 1918
STUART (1st), 1917
STURDY (2nd), 1912
STURGEON (3rd), 1894
SUFFOLK (7th), 1680
SUNDOWN (1st), 1919
SUNFISH (2nd), 1895
SUNSET (1st), 1918
SUSSEX (4th), 1652
SUTTON (1st), 1917
SWAN (24th), 1420
SWORDFISH (3rd), 1895
SYCAMORE (1st), 1935
SYDNEY (3rd), 1814
SYRINGA (3rd), 1917

TAKU (2nd), 1900
TALISMAN (3rd), 1912
TAMARISK (2nd), 1916
TARANTULA (1st), 1915
TARPON (2nd), 1916
TARTAR (14th), 1702
TEDWORTH (1st), 1916
TEMERAIRE (6th), 1694
TENBY (2nd), 1915
TENEDOS (4th), 1812
TERN (2nd), 1915
TERROR (9th), 1696
TETRARCH (2nd), 1916
THAMES (9th), 1758
THANET (2nd), 1917
THERMOL (1st), 1916
THETIS (13th), 1717
THISTLE (14th), 1808
THRACIAN (2nd), 1808
TIGRIS (4th), 1813
TITANIA (1st), 1915
TOIA (1st), 1919
TOPAZE (7th), 1793
TORBAY (5th), 1693
TOURMALINE (4th), 1875
TRIAD (2nd), 1915
TRIBUNE (7th), 1796
TRIDENT (7th), 1695
TRINIDAD (3rd), 1806
TRITON (9th), 1702
TRIUMPH (10th), 1561
TRUANT (2nd), 1918
TUNA (3rd), 1915
TURQUOISE (4th), 1876
TYNE (4th), 1814
TYNEDALE (2nd), 1915
TYRANT (1st), 1916

UGANDA (1st), 1938
ULNA (1st), 1909
UNDINE (5th), 1846
UNICORN (10th), 1544
UNITY (13th), 1665
URSULA (3rd), 1916

VALENTINE (2nd), 1418
VALIANT (3rd), 1759
VALOROUS (5th), 1804
VAMPIRE (1st), 1916
VANESSA (2nd), 1917
VANITY (1st), 1917
VANOC (1st), 1916
VANQUISHER (1st), 1916
VANSITTART (2nd), 1821
VARENNES (1st), 1911
VEGA (1st), 1916
VELOX (2nd), 1902
VENDETTA (1st), 1916
VENETIA (2nd), 1917
VENOMOUS (1st), 1918
VENTURE (4th), 1787
VERCHERES (1st), 1901
VERDUN (2nd), 1916
VERITY (1st), 1918
VERNON (6th), 1782
VERSATILE (1st), 1917
VESPER (2nd), 1916
VETERAN (6th), 1787
VICEROY (1st), 1916
VICTORIA AND ALBERT (3rd), 1842
VICTORIOUS (5th), 1785
VIDETTE (3rd), 1800
VIKING (3rd), 1909
VIMIERA (2nd), 1808
VIMY (1st), 1928

VINDICTIVE (5th), 1779
VISCOL (1st), 1916
VISCOUNT (1st), 1916
VIVACIOUS (1st), 1917
VIVIEN (1st), 1917
VOLUNTEER (3rd), 1801
VORTIGERN (1st), 1917
VOYAGER (1st), 1917
VULCAN (11th), 1691

WAKAKURA (1st), 1919
WAKEFUL (1st), 1917
WALKER (1st), 1917
WALLACE (1st), 1917
WALPOLE (2nd), 1917
WANDERER (7th), 1806
WAR AFRIDI (1st), 1919
WAR BAHADUR (1st), 1919
WAR BHARATA (1st), 1919
WAR BRAHMIN (1st), 1919
WAR DIWAN (1st), 1919
WAR HINDOO (1st), 1919
WAR KRISHNA (1st), 1919
WAR MEHTAR (1st), 1919
WAR NAWAB (1st), 1919
WAR NIZAM (1st), 1919
WAR PATHAN (1st), 1919
WAR PINDARI (1st), 1919
WAR SEPOY (1st), 1919
WAR SIRDAR (1st), 1919
WAR SUDRA (1st), 1919
WARREGO (2nd), 1911
WARSPITE (6th), 1596
WARWICK (5th), 1644
WATCHMAN (1st), 1917
WATERHEN (1st), 1917
WAVE (3rd), 1855
WELLINGTON (6th), 1810
WELSHMAN (2nd), 1901
WESSEX (1st), 1917
WESTCOTT (1st), 1917
WESTMINSTER (1st), 1917
WESTON (1st), 1931
WHADDON (1st), 1939
WHIRLPOOL (1st), 1918
WHIRLWIND (1st), 1917
WHITEHALL (1st), 1918
WHITLEY (1st), 1917
WHITSHED (1st), 1917
WIDGEON (5th), 1806
WIDNES (1st), 1917
WILD SWAN (2nd), 1876
WILLOW (1st), 1935
WINCHELSEA (6th), 1694
WINCHESTER (6th), 1693
WINDSOR (3rd), 1695
WISHART (1st), 1918
WITCH (1st), 1918
WITHERINGTON (1st), 1918
WIVERN (2nd), 1863
WOLFHOUND (1st), 1917
WOLSEY (1st), 1917
WOLVERINE (8th), 1798
WOOLSTON (1st), 1917
WOOLWICH (9th), 1677
WORCESTER (7th), 1651
WREN (3rd), 1653
WRESTLER (2nd), 1917
WRYNECK (1st), 1917

YARRA (2nd), 1909
YORK (9th), 1660
YPRES (1st), 1918

ZULU (2nd), 1909

WARSPITE (QUEEN ELIZABETH, VALIANT, to be similar).

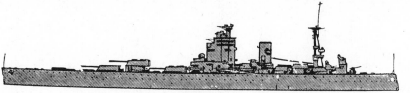

NELSON.
(RODNEY similar, but with catapult on " C " turret.)
(Foretops differ slightly.)

ROYAL SOVEREIGN.
(REVENGE heavier bridge and S.L. platform on mainmast)

BARHAM.

RESOLUTION.

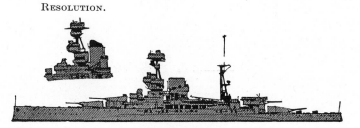

RAMILLIES.

HOOD.

MALAYA.

REPULSE.

RENOWN.

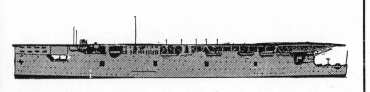

ARGUS.

IRON DUKE.

FURIOUS.

14

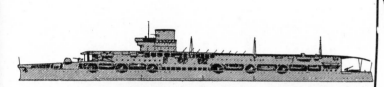

ARK ROYAL.
(Funnel since heightened)

CAIRO, CALCUTTA, CARLISLE, CURAÇOA

DANAE, DAUNTLESS, DRAGON.
(No. 3 gun abaft foremast.)

GLORIOUS.

CURLEW.
(COVENTRY as Part Sketch.)

DELHI group.
(Trawler bow.)
(DIOMEDE as Part Sketch.)

HERMES

CALEDON class.

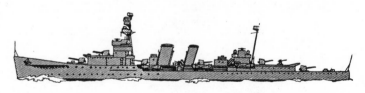

DUNEDIN.

CERES class.

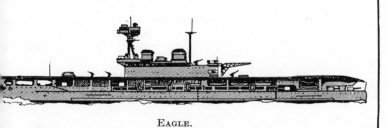

EAGLE.

COLOMBO, CAPETOWN.
(Trawler bow.)   (Reconstructing.)

ARETHUSA, GALATEA.
PENELOPE, also AURORA (with hangar between funnels)
as Part Sketch.

LEANDER *class*.
(NEPTUNE has shorter foremast and AJAX has hers stepped
slightly further aft.)

EXETER.

CUMBERLAND, *also* SUFFOLK, with high syren brackets.

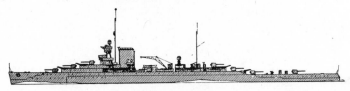

EFFINGHAM.
HAWKINS and FROBISHER being refitted.

YORK.

BERWICK.   CORNWALL.
AUSTRALIA, CANBERRA—R.A.N.
(*Also* KENT, without hangar and with sternwalk.)

VINDICTIVE.

ADVENTURE.

SOUTHAMPTON *class*.
(BIRMINGHAM has bow as ADVENTURE.)

ENTERPRISE.

LONDON *class*.

EDINBURGH, BELFAST.

EMERALD.

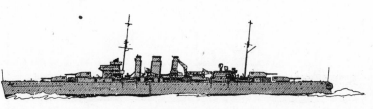

DORSETSHIRE *class*.

"A" AND "B" classes.
KEITH with C.N.
(In these and following classes, H.S.M.S. gear is sometimes absent.)

"E" AND "F" classes.
(Except ESK and EXPRESS.)
(Inset " D " class.)
KEMPENFELT, DUNCAN, with C. N.

ESK, EXPRESS.
(Note mainmast and whaler on fo'c'sle.)
(Carry reduced armament when serving as Minelayers.)

"G" AND "H" classes.
(HERO, HEREWARD and "I" class with enlarged forebridge.)
(Heights of funnels vary.)

TRIBAL class

JAVELIN class.

GRENVILLE.
(HARDY, INGLEFIELD, with tripod foremast.)

EXMOUTH, FAULKNOR.

CODRINGTON.
(Now has tall mainmast.)

CAMPBELL type.
(Mainmast now taller.)

BROKE type.
(All have tall mainmast.)

ADMIRALTY "S" class.

SKATE.

VETERAN *group.*
(WILD SWAN, tall mainmast; part sketch,
WITHERINGTON, WIVERN, WOLVERINE, WORCESTER.)

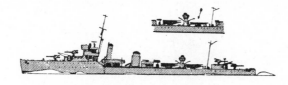

ADMIRALTY "W" *class.*
Short mainmast Admiralty "V" *classes.*
Part Sketch VIMY, VELOX, VERSATILE, VORTIGERN, VANOC.

CHALLENGER.

WISHART, WITCH.

VANSITTART *group.*

JASON, GLEANER.
(SCOTT, FRANKLIN have foremast before bridge and no
derrick post.)

AMAZON.

VICEROY, VISCOUNT

FOLKESTONE, SCARBOROUGH.

AMBUSCADE.

WHITLEY and other rearmed units.

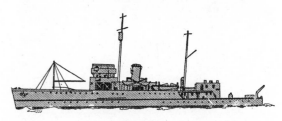

FITZROY.
(*Also* KELLETT with shorter foremast.)

ENDEAVOUR.

FALMOUTH.

HASTINGS, SHOREHAM *classes.*

PENZANCE.
BRIDGEWATER similar, but plain bow.

FLEETWOOD.

HALCYON *class.*

GRIMSBY *class.*

ENCHANTRESS.
(Gun before mainmast replaced by deckhouse.)

ABERDEEN.

ALRESFORD.

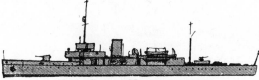

TWIN SCREW MINESWEEPERS.
("TOWN" *class.*)

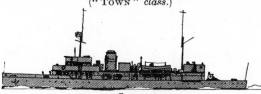

SALTBURN.

EGRET *class.*

BITTERN, STORK.

P.C.74.

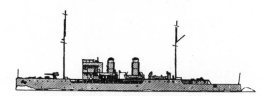

KINGFISHER *class.*
(Bridge now covered in.)

LUPIN, FOXGLOVE, ROSEMARY.
(Vary in details.)

ALBATROSS.

PEGASUS.

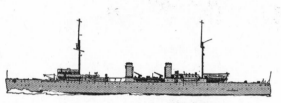

WOOLWICH.

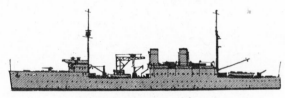

RESOURCE.

MEDWAY.

MAIDSTONE, FORTH

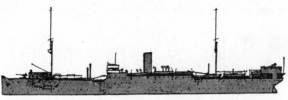

CYCLOPS.

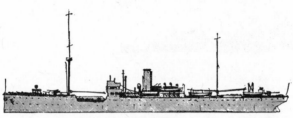

GREENWICH.

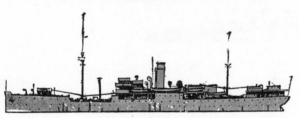

LUCIA.

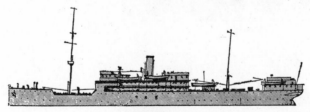

TITANIA.

ALECTO.

MERSEY *type*.
(Trawlers.)

DEE *type*.
(Trawlers.)

"TREE" *type*.
(Trawlers.)
(Vary in details.)

"GEM" *type*.
(Trawlers.)
(Vary in details.)

BASSET, *also* MASTIFF with fo'c'sle
extending abaft gun.

GUARDIAN.

PROTECTOR.

REDSTART, RINGDOVE.
(LINNET has cowl lower.)

VULCAN.

BARRICADE *class*.

BAYONET *class*.

Torpedo Boat 102.

Torpedo Boats 22, 24, 25.

Torpedo Boats 1—12, 14—19.

MMS 1, 2.

"H" cldss.

L 23, L 26, L 27.

Shark class.
(Shape of C.T. varies slightly.)

Starfish, Seahorse.
(Swordfish, Sturgeon as Part Sketch.)

Oberon.

Odin class.
Oxley, Otway. (With net cutter.)

Parthian class.

Rainbow class.

Thames class.

Narwhal group.
(Porpoise as Part Sketch.)

Triton class.

Unity class.

The following list of Pendant Numbers of Destroyers, Submarines, Minesweepers, Escort and Patrol Vessels has been furnished officially to "Fighting Ships" by the Admiralty.

Destroyers.

D Flag Superior.

Pendants.	Ship.
D 00	Stuart, R.A.N.
D 01	Montrose.
D 02	Inglefield.
D 03	Icarus.
D 06	Keith.
D 09	Imperial
D 10	Intrepid.
D 11	Impulsive.
D 16	Ivanhoe.
D 18	Kempenfelt.
D 19	Malcolm.
D 21	Wryneck.
D 22	Waterhen, R.A.N.
D 25	Warwick.
D 26	Watchman.
D 27	Walker.
D 28	Vanity.
D 29	Vanessa.
D 30	Whirlwind.
D 31	Voyager, R.A.N.
D 32	Versatile.
D 33	Vimy.
D 34	Velox.
D 36	Vivacious.
D 37	Vortigern.
D 38	Ambuscade.
D 39	Amazon.
D 41	Walpole.
D 43	Wessex.
D 44	Imogen.
D 46	Winchelsea.
D 47	Westcott.
D 48	Vidette.
D 53	Venetia.
D 54	Vanquisher.
D 55	Vesper.
D 56	Wolfhound.
D 59	Skeena, R.C.N.
D 60	Campbell.
D 61	Ilex.
D 62	Wild Swan.
D 63	Verity.
D 64	Vansittart.
D 65	Codrington.
D 66	Wivern.
D 67	Wishart.
D 68	Vampire, R.A.N.
D 69	Vendetta, R.A.N.
D 70	Mackay.
D 71	Volunteer.
D 72	Veteran.
D 74	Wanderer.
D 75	Venomous.
D 76	Witherington.
D 77	Whitshed.
D 78	Wolverine.
D 79	Saguenay, R.C.N.
D 83	Broke.
D 84	Keppel.
D 85	Shikari.
D 86	Thracian.
D 87	Isis.
D 88	Wren.
D 89	Witch.
D 90	Douglas.
D 91	Viceroy.
D 92	Viscount.
D 93	Verdun.
D 94	Whitehall.
D 96	Worcester.
D 99	Duncan.

F Flag Superior.

Pendants.	Ship.
F 00	Jervis.
F 01	Kelly.
F 03	Cossack.
F 07	Afridi.
F 12	Kashmir.
F 15	Loyal.
F 18	Zulu.
F 20	Gurkha.
F 21	Punjabi.
F 22	Jackal.
F 24	Maori.
F 26	Matabele.
F 28	Kandahar.
F 31	Mohawk.
F 32	Lookout.
F 33	Somali.
F 34	Jaguar.
F 36	Nubian.
F 37	Kelvin.
F 40	Lively.
F 43	Tartar.
F 45	Khartoum.
F 46	Juno.
F 50	Kimberley.
F 51	Ashanti.
F 53	Janus.
F 55	Lightning.
F 59	Mashona.
F 61	Javelin.
F 63	Larne.
F 64	Kingston.
F 67	Bedouin.
F 72	Jersey.
F 74	Legion.
F 75	Eskimo.
F 82	Sikh.
F 85	Jupiter.
F 87	Lance.
F 91	Kipling.
F 99	Laforey.

H Flag Superior.

Pendants.	Ship.
H 00	Restigouche, R.C.N.
H 01	Hotspur.
H 02	Exmouth.
H 03	Grenville.
H 04	Tenedos.
H 05	Greyhound.
H 07	Defender.
H 08	Eclipse.
H 09	Acasta.
H 10	Encounter.
H 11	Basilisk.
H 12	Achates.
H 14	Active.
H 15	Esk.
H 16	Daring.
H 17	Escapade.
H 18	Sabre.
H 21	Scimitar.
H 22	Diamond.
H 23	Echo.
H 24	Hasty.
H 26	Sardonyx.
H 27	Electra.
H 28	Sturdy.
H 29	Thanet.
H 30	Beagle.

H Flag Superior.

Pendants.	Ships.
H 31	Griffin.
H 33	Vanoc.
H 35	Hunter.
H 36	Antelope.
H 37	Garland.
H 38	Delight.
H 39	Skate.
H 40	Anthony.
H 41	Ardent.
H 42	Arrow.
H 43	Havock.
H 45	Acheron.
H 47	Blanche.
H 48	Fraser, R.C.N.
H 49	Diana.
H 50	Stronghold.
H 51	Scout.
H 53	Dainty.
H 54	Saladin.
H 55	Hostile.
H 59	Gallant.
H 60	Ottawa, R.C.N.
H 61	Express.
H 62	Faulknor.
H 63	Gipsy.
H 64	Duchess.
H 65	Boadicea.
H 66	Escort.
H 67	Fearless.
H 68	Foresight.
H 69	Foxhound.
H 70	Fortune.
H 74	Forester.
H 75	Decoy.
H 76	Fury.
H 77	Boreas.
H 78	Fame.
H 79	Firedrake.
H 80	Brazen.
H 83	St. Laurent, R.C.N
H 84	Brilliant.
H 86	Grenade.
H 87	Hardy.
H 89	Grafton.
H 91	Bulldog.
H 92	Glowworm.
H 93	Hereward.
H 95	Winchester.
H 97	Hyperion.
H 99	Hero.

Submarines.

Pendant Numbers.

Pendants.	Ship.
11	Thetis.
12	Clyde.
14	Porpoise.
15	Triton.
16	Rainbow.
17	Tarpon.
18	Triumph.
19	Starfish.
21	Oberon.
22	Sterlet.
23	L 23.
24	Thistle.
26	L 26.
27	L 27.
28	H 28.
29	Proteus.
31	H 31.
32	H 32.
33	H 33.
34	H 34.
35	Olympus.
36	Perseus.
37	Seal.
38	Taku.
39	Snapper.
41	Regent.
42	Pandora.
43	H 43.
44	H 44.
45	Narwhal.
46	Orpheus.
47	Seawolf.
48	Undine.
49	H 49.
50	H 50.
51	Otway.
52	Trident.
53	Triad.
54	Shark.
55	Oxley.
56	Grampus.
57	Severn.
58	Oswald.
59	Ursula.
61	Swordfish.
62	Rover.
62	Tigris.
65	Salmon.
66	Unity.
67	Osiris.
68	Truant.
69	Spearfish.
71	Thames.
72	Sealion.
73	Sturgeon.
74	Rorqual.
75	Parthian.
76	Tribune.
77	Tetrarch.
78	Talisman.
79	Torbay.
81	Sunfish.
83	Cachalot.
84	Odin.
88	Regulus.
92	Otus.
94	Tuna.
96	Phœnix.
98	Seahorse.

Escort and Patrol Vessels.

L Flag Superior.

Pendants.	Ship.
L 00	Valorous.
L 01	Bridgewater.
L 02	Wolsey.
L 04	Wryneck.
L 06	Sheldrake.
L 07	Bittern.
L 09	Cornwallis, R.I.N.
L 10	Wrestler.
L 12	Sandwich.
L 14	Rosemary.
L 15	Fowey.
L 16	Grimsby.
L 18	Flamingo.
L 19	Lupin.
L 21	Pintail.
L 23	Whitley.
L 26	Foxglove.
L 27	Hastings.
L 28	Penzance.
L 29	Vimiera.
L 30	Kittiwake.
L 31	Chrysanthemum.
L 32	Shoreham.
L 33	Vivien.
L 34	Falmouth.
L 36	Leith.
L 39	Shearwater.
L 40	Westminster.
L 41	Vega.
L 42	Mallard.
L 43	Bideford.
L 44	Parramatta, R.A.N.
L 47	Fleetwood.
L 49	Woolston.
L 50	Rochester.
L 51	Milford.
L 52	Puffin.
L 53	Deptford.
L 55	Winchester.
L 56	Enchantress.
L 57	Black Swan.
L 59	Lowestoft.
L 61	Auckland.
L 62	Widgeon.
L 64	Wallace.
L 65	Wellington.
L 67	Indus, R.I.N.
L 69	Valentine.
L 70	Kingfisher.
L 71	Pathan, R.I.N.
L 72	Weston.
L 73	Warrego, R.A.N.
L 74	Swan, R.A.N.
L 75	Egret.
L 76	Londonderry.
L 77	Yarra, R.A.N.
L 79	Clive, R.I.N.
L 80	Hindustan, R.I.N.
L 81	Stork.
L 83	Lawrence, R.I.N.
L 84	Dundee.
L 86	Pelican.
L 89	Guillemot.
L 91	Wakeful.
L 94	Windsor.
L 97	Aberdeen.

Minesweepers.

N Flag Superior.

Pendants.	Ship.
N 02	Hazard.
N 24	Hebe.
N 38	Skipjack.
N 42	Halcyon.
N 63	Gossamer.
N 68	Sharpshooter.
N 71	Harrier.
N 78	Niger.
N 81	Hussar.
N 85	Seagull.
N 86	Salamander.
N 87	Speedwell.
N 93	Leda.
N 99	Jason.

(Lion Class—4 Ships)

LION, TEMERAIRE, and 2 others (unnamed).

Displacement : *circa* 40,000 tons.

No official information available about these ships, which will be armed with 16 inch guns, and have a speed similar to *King George V* class.

Est.	Name.	Builder.	Machinery.	Ordered.	Laid down	To be Completed.
1938	Lion Temeraire	Vickers-Armstrongs (Tyne) Cammell Laird	V.-A. (Barrow) Cammell Laird	} 21/2/39	{ 4/7/39 1/6/39 }	1943
1939	1 ship 1 ship	Clydebank (Not announced)	Clydebank	16/8/39 /39	'39	1944

(King George V. Class—5 Ships)

KING GEORGE V. (Feb. 21, 1939), **PRINCE OF WALES** (May 3, 1939),

DUKE OF YORK (ex-*Anson*), (Sept. 16, 1939), **JELLICOE, BEATTY** (Nov. 11, 1939).

Displacement : 35,000 tons.

Aircraft : Probably 3

Guns : **10—14 inch.**

     16—5·25 inch.

(No torpedo tubes).

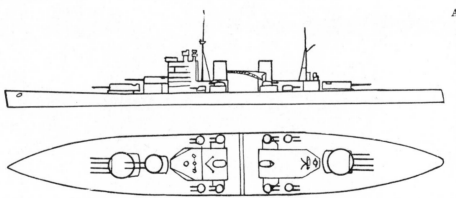

Armour :

Officially stated that design will include enhanced defence against air attack, including an improved distribution of deck and side armour, more elaborate sub-division, and an improved system of under-water protection.

Unofficial reports give weight of armour as over 14,000 tons, and water-line thickness as 16 inches.

Machinery : Parsons geared turbines. 4 shafts. Boilers : Admiralty 3-drum type. S.H.P. : 152,000 = over 30 kts. Oil fuel.

Gunnery Notes.—14 inch guns are a new model, with an effective range greater than the 15 inch mounted in earlier ships, as measured by the perforation of any given thickness of armour. Cost of fire control installation in each ship is £213,000.

Engineering Notes.—Improvements in boiler design have reduced boiler weights by about 15 per cent. as compared with *Nelson* and *Rodney.*

Est.	Name	Builder	Machinery	Laid down	To be Comptd.
1936	King George V Prince of Wales Duke of York	Vickers-Armstrongs (Tyne) Cammell Laird Clydebank	V.-A., (Barrow) Cammell Laird Clydebank	Jan. 1, 1937 Jan 1, 1937 May 5, 1937	}1940–41
1937	Jellicoe Beatty	Swan Hunter Fairfield	Wallsend Co. Fairfield	July 20, 1937 June 1, 1937	

(NELSON CLASS.)

NELSON (September 3rd, 1925), **RODNEY** (December 17th, 1925).

Displacement, 33,950 tons (*Nelson*), 33,900 tons (*Rodney*), (*full load*, about 38,000 tons).
Length, (*p.p.*) 660 feet, (*w.l.*) 702 feet, (*o.a.*) 710 feet. Beam, 106 feet. *Mean* draught, 30 feet.
Complement, as flagship, 1361; as private ship, 1314.

Guns :
  9—16 inch.
  12—6 inch.
  6—4.7 inch A.A.
  4—3 pdr.
  1—3 inch landing.
  22—Smaller.
(including multiple pompom on
  q.d.)
Torpedo tubes (*submerged*)
  2—24.5 inch.

Aircraft :
  1 recently carried in NELSON
    (handled by crane)
  2 with catapult (on "C" turret)
    in RODNEY.

Armour :
  Is largely con-
  centrated over
  guns and mag-
  azines in fore
  part of ship.
  Internal bulge
  protection.
  14" Belt ......
  16"—9" Turrets
  15" Barbettes.
  6¼" Deck ....

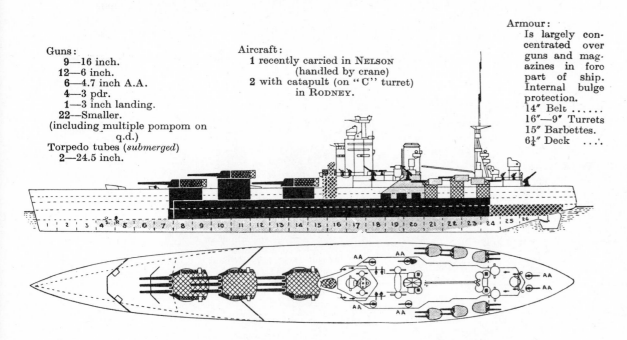

NELSON.

1934 *Photo, R. Perkins.*

Machinery : Brown-Curtis geared turbines. 2 shafts. Boilers : 8 Admiralty 3-drum type (with superheaters). Designed H.P. 45,000 = 23 kts. Oil fuel : 4,000 tons. Consumption : full speed, 16 tons per hour ; cruising speed, 2·7 tons per hour.

General Notes.—Both laid down under 1922-23 Estimates, being the last battleships designed by Sir E. Tennyson D'Eyncourt while D.N.C. They are reduced editions of the 48,000 ton battle-cruisers ordered in 1921 and cancelled under the Washington Treaty, in which 16 inch guns were to have been mounted in triple turrets. Designed to Treaty limits which could not be exceeded, and yet must be approached as closely as possible, weight estimation and economy was a far more important factor than in previous designs. The grouping of the main armament forward allows for a minimum length of armoured citadel with maximum protection to hull and magazines, and is con-sidered fully to compensate for the loss of fire astern. The design is therefore peculiar, in that it is governed more by constructional than tactical principles. By placing the boiler room abaft the engine rooms smoke inter-ference with the control positions is obviated. The bridge structure carries 16 inch, 6 inch and 4·7 inch directors, admiral's bridge, torpedo controls, signalling and navigating bridges, sea cabins and offices. Part of the material used in these two ships was originally ordered for the battle cruisers *Anson* and *Howe* (sister ships to *Hood*), construction of which was abandoned after the Armistice.
  High freeboard of these ships proved its value in combined Fleet Exercise of March, 1934, when an Atlantic gale made little difference to their efficiency as compared with *Royal Sovereign* and *Queen Elizabeth* classes.

Cost.—*Nelson* £7,504,055 ; *Rodney* £7,617,799. Cost of guns and turret armour approx. £3,000,000 ; engines, £490,000. Steering gear is of novel design and rudder can be swung over in 30 secs. at full speed. Accommodation is on generous lines and all living spaces have natural lighting and ventilation.

Gunnery Notes.—These are the only British warships mounting 16-inch guns. Arcs of fire of the 3 turrets reported to be 298, 330 and 250 degrees respectively. Elevation is 40° and range 35,000 yards. Cost of firing a triple salvo is £700. 6-inch guns have 60° elevation and can be used as A.A. They are the first power worked 6-inch in the Service. Special measures have been taken to protect personnel and instruments from the blast of the after 16-inch guns when fired abaft the beam at full elevation.

Armour Notes.—Citadel belt extends from first 16 inch to aftermost 6 inch turret, with thick armour deck over same area with specially designed hatches. Underwater protection is most efficient and the usual external bulges have been replaced by an alternative system of hull construction developed from a long series of experiments.

Name	Builder	Machinery	Laid down	Completed	Trials	Boilers
Nelson	Armstrong	Wallsend Co.	Dec. 28,	June, 1927	46,000 = 23·5	Admiralty
Rodney	Cammell Laird	Cammell Laird	1922	Aug., 1927	= 23·8	3-drum

NELSON.

1938 *Wright & Logan.*

NELSON (Showing crane). 1935, *R. Perkins.*

*(For particulars see
preceding page)*

RODNEY.

1939, *P. A. Vicary, Cromer.*

(ROYAL SOVEREIGN CLASS.)—All fitted as Flagships

ROYAL SOVEREIGN (29th April, 1915), **ROYAL OAK** (17th Nov., 1914), **RESOLUTION** (14th Jan., 1916), **RAMILLIES** (12th Sept., 1916), **REVENGE** (29th May, 1915).

Displacement, 29,150 tons, *about* 33,500 tons *full load.* Complement, 1009-1146.

Length (*p.p.*) 580 feet, (*w.l.*) 614½ feet, (*o.a.*) 620½ feet.† Beam, about 102½ feet. *Mean draught,* 28½ feet.

†*Revenge* 624½ feet (*o.a.*)

Guns :
8—15 inch, 42 cal.
12—6 inch, 50 cal.
8—4 inch AA.
4—3 pdr.
1—12 pdr. Field
5 M.G.
10 Lewis
(besides multi-M.G.)
Torpedo tubes (21 inch) :
4 *submerged* in *R. Oak,* 2 in *Revenge.*
Armour (H.T.) :
Deck. {
1″ Fo'xle over Battery
1½″—1½″ Upper .....
2″, 1½″, 1″ Main ......
2½″, 1″ (forw'd) } Lower
4″, 3″, 2½″ (aft) }
Special Protection :
1½″—1″ Torp. Prot. b.h.
between end barbettes.
(Also bulges, of varying types.)

Armour (K.C.) :
Vertical {
13″ Belt ....
6″—4″ Belt (ends) ....
1″ Belt (bow) ....
6″, 4″ Bulkheads (f. & a.)
6″ Battery ....
10″—7″ Barbettes .....
13″—5″ Gunhouses.....
6″—3″ C.T. Base ....
11″ C.T. (6″—3″ hood) .
6″ Fore com. tube ....
6″ Torp. con. tower ...
4″ Tube (T.C. tower) ..
}

Aircraft :
1 with catapult (on X turret), in *R. Oak* and RESOLUTION.

Note to Plan.—AA. guns now paired.

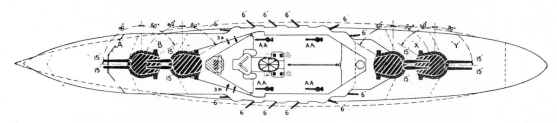

Machinery : Turbine, Parsons. Boilers : (see *Notes*). 4 shafts. Designed H.P. : 40,000 = under 22 knots *with* bulges. Oil fuel : *normal,* 900 tons ; *maximum,* 3,230 tons.

Gunnery Notes.—Much as *Queen Elizabeth* class. Battery differently disposed in these ships. 6 inch batteries are wet in head seas, but dwarf walls in battery retain water and it is rapidly drained away. 4 inch AA. mounted in place of former 3 inch AA. in 1924-25. Two superstructure 6 inch removed in 1927-28.

Armour Notes.—Thicknesses much as *Queen Elizabeth* class, but armour differently distributed. Barbettes 6″—4″ as they descend behind belt. Gunhouses, 13″ face, 11″ sides and rear ; crowns 5″. In these ships 2″ protective deck has a high 2″ slope behind belt, so that flat part of protection can be put on main deck and at top of belt, instead of a deck lower. Internal protection is very good, and with protective bulges, defence against underwater attack is very strong. All refitted with bulges, which in some ships extend almost up to battery.

Engineering Notes.—Designed to burn coal, but while building "all oil fuel" was adopted, so that 23 kts. would be secured with the resulting increase of H.P. Addition of bulges has brought speed down again to about 22 kts. Main Turbines are direct drive, cruising Turbines geared.

General Notes.—Begun under 1913-14 Estimates. *Revenge* first named *Renown. Ramillies* injured herself at launch and was delayed in completion. They are fine ships, but suffer rather from reduced freeboard. Searchlights on main mast removed 1922. Refits : *R. Sovereign,* 1927-28 ; *Royal Oak,* 1922-24 ; *Ramillies* and *Resolution,* 1926-27 ; *Revenge,* 1928 ; *Resolution,* 1930 ; *Royal Oak,* 1934-36 ; *Revenge,* 1936-37.

Cost.—*Royal Oak* £2,468,269, which was rather below average for the class.

26

RAMILLIES.   1939, *Wright & Logan.*

Appearance Notes.—*Resolution* has clinker screen to funnel. *R. Sovereign* retains pole mainmast and has very tall chart-house. *R. Oak* and *Ramillies* have deep bulges, extending almost up to battery. *Revenge* has pole mainmast with S.L. platform and short topmast, and extra heavy forebridge. *Royal Oak* has prominent square maintop. Details of bridge vary in each ship.

H.M.S. ROYAL OAK was torpedoed and sunk at Scapa Flow on October 14, 1939.

ROYAL OAK.   1936, *Wright & Logan.*

Name	Builder	Machinery	Laid down	Completed	Trials :—	Boilers
Royal Sovereign	Portsmouth Y.	Parsons	Jan.'14	May, '16	41,115 = 21·6	18 Babcock
Royal Oak	Devonport Y.	Hawthorn	Jan.'14	May, '16	40,360 =	18 Yarrow
Resolution	Palmer	Palmer	Nov.'13	Dec.,'16	41,406 =	18 Yarrow
Ramillies	Beardmore*	Beardmore	Nov.'13	Sept. '17	42,356 = 21·5	18 Babcock
Revenge	Vickers	Vickers	Dec.'13	Mar.,'16	42,962 = 21·9	18 Babcock

*Towed to Liverpool and completed by Cammell Laird & Co.

ROYAL SOVEREIGN.   1939, *Wright & Logan.*

RESOLUTION   1936, *Wright & Logan.*

REVENGE.   1939. *R. Perkins*

BRITISH—Battleships

Guns: (*Warspite*)
- 8—15 inch, 42 cal.
- 8—6 inch, 50 cal.
- 8—4 inch AA.
- 4—3 pdr.
- 5 M.G.
- 10 Lewis
  (besides multi-M.G.)

Aircraft:
- 4, with catapult.
  (Photos show positions.)

Armour:
Originally as for *Barham* (vide a later page) but has been modified extensively as a result of reconstruction. All are fitted with bulges.

(QUEEN ELIZABETH CLASS—1st 3 SHIPS.)
QUEEN ELIZABETH (16th Oct., 1913), WARSPITE (26th Nov., 1913), VALIANT (4th Nov., 1914).

Displacement, 30,600 tons (*about* 35,000 tons *full load*).   Complement, 1124-1184.   All fitted as flagships.

Length (*p.p.*), 600 feet; (*o.a.*) { 643¾ ft., except / *Valiant*, 639¾ ft. } (*w.l.*) 634½ feet.   Beam, 104 feet. { Mean draught, 30⅔ feet / Max. „   33½ „

WARSPITE.   1937, *Wright & Logan*.

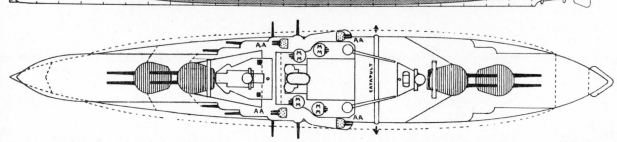

WARSPITE.   1937, *Wright & Logan*.

Machinery: Parsons geared turbine, but *Valiant* had Brown-Curtis before reconstruction. Geared cruising turbines in all ships. Boilers: Admiralty 3-drum type. Designed H.P.: 80,000 as reconstructed = 24 kts. Oil fuel: 650 tons *normal*, 3,400 tons *max*. Radius of action: *about* 4,400 miles.

General Notes.—First four begun under 1912 Estimates. *Malaya*, extra ship, gift of Federated Malay States. Cost, nearly £3,000,000 per ship. (*Q.E.*, £3,014,103; *Malaya*, £2,945,709; *Warspite*, £2,524,148.) *Q.E.*, *Barham* and *Warspite* have stern walks. Re-construction of this class, between 1925 and 1933, involved an expenditure of about £1,000,000 per ship; it included the remodelling of control top and bridgework and the trunking of the fore-funnel into the second. Two Torpedo tubes were removed. In 1934 *Warspite* and *Malaya* were taken in hand for further re-construction of an extensive character involving the provision of new turbines, additional protection, increased accommodation for aircraft and augmented AA. armament. In the case of the *Malaya*, the modernisation included about 60 per cent of ship's structure, but in the *Warspite* it was much more extensive. Cost of alterations, £2,362,000 (*Warspite*), £976,963, (*Malaya*). Both completed refits in 1937, when *Valiant* and *Queen Elizabeth* were in hand for similar renovation; former being re-engined by Fairfield, latter by Parsons.

Gunnery Notes.—15 inch guns and mountings designed for 20° elevation (increased to 30° when reconstructed). In *Warspite*, after main deck battery is now built in flush with ship's side.

Engineering Notes.—These ships steam splendidly, and can maintain a high average speed for long periods.

Appearance Notes.—As rebuilt, *Warspite* differs completely from former appearance, as will be seen by comparison with *Barham*.

28

Name.	Builder.	Machinery.	Laid down.	Completed.	Trials.	Boilers.
Queen Elizabeth	Portsmouth	Wallsend	Oct. '12	Jan., '15	75,130=	} Admiralty Type
Warspite	Devonport	Hawthorn	Oct. '12	Mar., '15	77,510=	
Valiant	Fairfield	Fairfield	Jan.'13	Feb.,'16	71,112=	
Barham	Clydebank	Clydebank	Feb.'13	Oct. '15	76,575=	24 Yarrow
Malaya	Elswick	Wallsend	Oct.'13	Feb.'16	76,074=	24 Babcock

WARSPITE.

1937, *Wright & Logan.*

MALAYA.

(Vide following page)

1937, *R. Perkins.*

WARSPITE.

1937, *Charles E. Brown.*

Guns:
  8—15 inch, 42 cal.
  12—6 inch, 50 cal.
  8—4 inch AA.
  4—3 pdr.
  5 M.G.
  10 Lewis.
    (besides multi-M.G.)

Torpedo tubes:
  2—21 inch in *Barham*.

Aircraft:
  4, with catapult, in *Malaya*.
  1, with catapult, in *Barham*.

Armour (K.C.): (*Barham*; *Malaya*'s protection has been modified and improved.)

Vertical {
  13″ on waterline ..
  6″—4″ over w.l. .. } Side
  6″—4″ (ends) ....
  6″, 4″ Bulkheads (f. & a.)
  6″ Battery ....
  10″—7″ Barbettes ......
  11″ Gunhouses ....
  6″—3″ C.T. base ......
  14″ C.T. (6″—2″ Hood) ..
  4″ Fore com. tube ....
  6″ Torpedo C.T........
}

Armour (H.T.):

Deck. {
  1″ Fo'xle (over battery).
  2″—1¼″ Upper ....
  1¼″ Main fwd. & aft. ..
  1″ Middle ....
  3″ (ends) } Lower.
  1 (amidships) }
}

Special Protec.
  2″—1″ Torp. pro. b'lkh'ds between end barbettes.

BARHAM (31st Dec., 1914),   **MALAYA** (18th Mar., 1915).

Displacement, 31,100 tons (*about* 35,100 tons *full load*).   Complement, 1124-1184.   All fitted as flagships.

Length (*p.p.*), 600 feet;   (*o.a.*) { 643¾ ft., except / *Malaya*, 639¾ ft. }   (*w.l.*) 634½ feet.   Beam, 104 feet. { *Mean* draught, 30⅔ feet. / *Max.* „ 33½ „ }

MALAYA.

1937, *R. Perkins*

Note to Plan.—Add catapult. 4-inch AA. guns are now paired.

BARHAM.

1938, *Wright & Logan*

Machinery: Parsons geared turbine in *Malaya*, Brown-Curtis direct drive in *Barham*. Geared cruising turbines in both. Designed H.P.: 75,000 = 25 kts. (reduced by fitting of bulges). Oil fuel: 650 tons *normal*, 3,400 tons *max*. Radius of action: *about* 4,400 miles.

Appearance Notes.—*Barham* has tripod mainmast and catapult on roof of X turret, flag deck extended aft to funnel and after shelter deck built up. *Malaya* has funnel encased by platforms and S.L. redistributed. Large hangar abeam of funnel, and new type (athwartship) catapult before mainmast.

For other notes and data concerning these two ships, see earlier page describing first 3 units of this class

Guns :
8—15 inch, 42 cal.
12—5·5 inch, 50 cal.
8—4 inch AA.
4—3 pdr.
5 M.G.
10 Lewis.
(besides multi-M.G.
Torpedo tubes (21 inch)
4 *above water* in pairs.
Aircraft :
1 to be added to equipment, with
catapult, when next refitted.

HOOD* (J. Brown & Co., Clydebank. Begun 1st Sept., 1916, Launched 22nd August, 1918, completed 5th March, 1920.)

Displacement, 42,100 tons (46,300 tons *full load*).   Complement, 1341.

Length $\left\{\begin{array}{l} \textit{p.p. } 810 \text{ ft.} \\ \textit{o.a. } 860 \text{ ft. 7 in.} \end{array}\right\}$ Beam *outside bulges* 105 ft. 2½ in.   Draught $\left\{\begin{array}{l} \textit{mean } 28\frac{1}{2}\text{ ft.} \\ \textit{max. } 31\frac{1}{2}\text{ ft.} \end{array}\right.$

*Fitted as Flagship'

Notes to Plan.—Combined thicknesses of side armour and
conning tower shown by dark patch in section 11.   Now
carries flagstaffs on both masts, with gaff on main.

Armour (K.C.) :
3″ Side (submerged) ..
12″, 7″, 5″ Side (amid-
ships) ....
6″—5″ Side (forward)..
6″ Side (aft)..........
5″—4″ Bulkh'ds (f. & a.)
12″ Barbettes ....
15″ Face ⎫ Turrets
12″—11″ Sides ⎭
11″ & 9″ C.T. ....
6″ C.T. Base ....
6″ Director tower ....
4″—3″ Torp. control
tower ....
1″ (H.T.) Shields to 5·5″
guns ....

Armour (H.T.) :
2″ Forecastle ....
1″ U.D. amidships ....
1½″—3″ Main deck ..
3″ M.D. over magazines
1½″—1″ L.D. forward
3″—1″ L.D. aft ......
3″ Director tower ....
5″ C.T. ....
3″ Torpedo control T.
5″ Turrets ....

Special protection (H.T.) :
1½″ and ¾″ Torp. pro. b'lk'd
over magazines, boiler and
engine rooms, bulges and
buoyancy spaces.

Vertical   *Decks.*   *Crowns.*

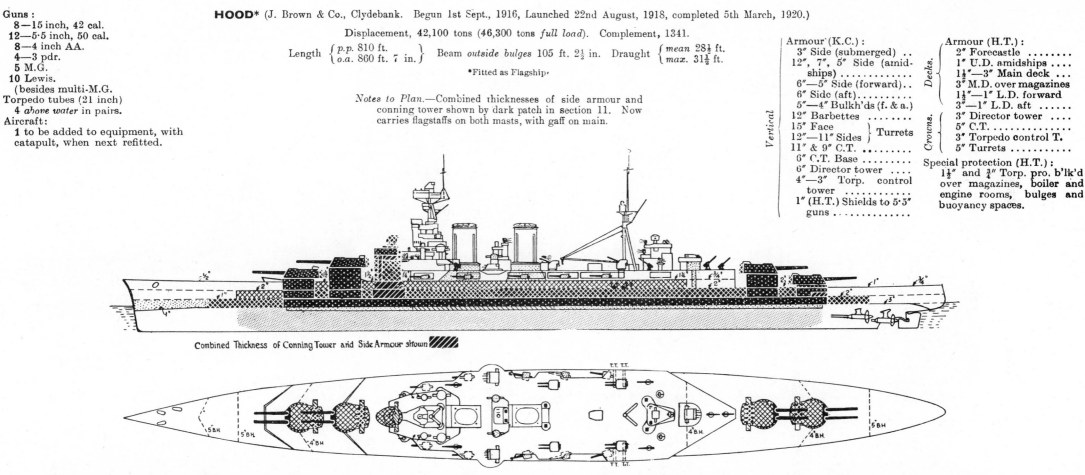

Combined Thickness of Conning Tower and Side Armour shown ⬛

Machinery (by Builders) : Brown-Curtis (all-geared) turbines.   4 shafts.   Boilers : 24 Yarrow (small tube).   Designed S.H.P. 144,000 = 31 kts.   Oil fuel : 1200 tons *normal*, 4,000 tons *maximum.*

Gunnery Notes.—Barbette heights over l.w.l. : A, 32 ft. ; B, 42 ft. ; X, 31¾ ft. ; Y, 21¾ ft. All turrets bear 150° on each beam. Designed to mount 16—5 5 inch, but the four after guns were removed before completion. Elevation of 15 inch guns, 30°. 8—36 inch controlled, and 4—24 inch signalling S.L. Guns, mountings, barbettes and ammunition = 5,300 tons.
Armour Notes.—Vertical side armour is backed by strong 2″—1″ H.T. plating, not included in thicknesses given. Area of 12″ armour at w.l., 562 ft. long by 9½ ft. deep. Gun houses. new type with flat crowns, small square sighting portscut low in face for laying over open sights. On roofs, armoured cases slightly wider than R.F. to allow R.F. to be traversed for fine adjustments. Barbettes, 6″—5″ as they descend through decks. C.T. is an enormous, elaborate, most expensive and ponderous structure : in upper stages, it consists of two shells, 12″ outer, 9″ inner, with narrow passage between. The slope inboard of hull side detracts from effects of plunging fire by virtual increase of armour thickness.   A perpendicular, dropped from topsides, just meets outer edges of bulges. which are of the improved "D'Eyncourt-Hopkinson" type. Total weight of armour and protection, 13,800 tons (equal to 33½ per cent. of load displacement).
Engineering Notes.—During world cruise, economical speed worked out at 288 miles in 24 hours on 180 tons of oil, i.e., 7½ tons an hour, ·625 ton per mile run.
Trials (unofficial figures).—At 42,200 tons, 151,000 S.H.P. = 32·07 kts. (run in bad weather, wind force 6 Beaufort scale) on Arran mile. At 44,600 tons, 31·89 kts. *mean* attained. On ⅔ power, 25 kts. easily secured.   Total weight of machinery (with water in boilers to working level) = 5,350 tons.

Notes on Original Design.—The original 1915 Design embodied same length and beam, but draughts were 25¼ feet *normal* = 36,300 ton., and 29 feet deep. Speed : 32 kts. Belt 8″, barbettes 9″, much thinner deck armour, and only 2—21 inch *submerged* T. T. Four ships ordered to this design April, 1916. In the design produced after Jutland (not approved till 1917), 5,000 tons extra protection was worked in. By use of small-tube boilers, 24.000 S.H.P. gained on *same* machinery weights as for *Renown* class.

General Notes.—Begun under Emergency War Programme. Originally, there were four ships in this class, *Anson, Hood, Howe, Rodney.* They were begun in the autumn of 1916, to meet the German Battle Cruisers, *Graf Spee, Mackensen, Ersatz Freya* and *Ersatz "A,"* which were laid down in 1916. Contractors were : *Anson* (Armstrong), *Howe* (Cammell Laird), *Rodney* (Fairfield), *Hood* (Brown). The enemy having ceased work on all his large ships, in 1917, *Anson, Howe* and *Rodney* were stopped in March, 1917, and dismantled to clear slips after the Armistice, but not before £860,000 had been expended on them. These ships were redesigned to meet the lessons of Jutland. In *Hood*, the outstanding feature is the huge areas covered by heavy armour, strong framing, &c.—in fact, the general scheme of protection is most comprehensive. Cost, *about* £6,025,000 = £145 per ton. General refit, 1929-30. Carried catapult and aircraft on quarterdeck in 1931.

HOOD (For particulars, see preceding page).

1939, *Wright & Logan.*

HOOD.

1939, *Wright & Logan.*

HOOD.

1939, *Wright & Logan.*

(RENOWN CLASS—1st ship)

RENOWN (March 4, 1916).

Displacement : 32,000 tons (37,400 tons *full load*).   Complement : 1,181/1,205.

Length : (*pp.*) 750 feet ; (*w.l.*), 787¾ feet ; (*o.a.*) 794 feet 1½ in.   Beam : 102⅔ feet.

Draught : 26⅔ feet (*mean*), 30¼ feet (*max.*).

Fitted as flagship.

Guns :
6—15 inch, 42 cal.
8—4·5 inch (dual purpose)
12—4 inch 40 cal.
18 smaller.
(No torpedo tubes.)

Aircraft :
4, with catapult.

Armour :
Originally as *Repulse*, on a later page ; but protection was considerably increased during 1936–39 reconstruction.

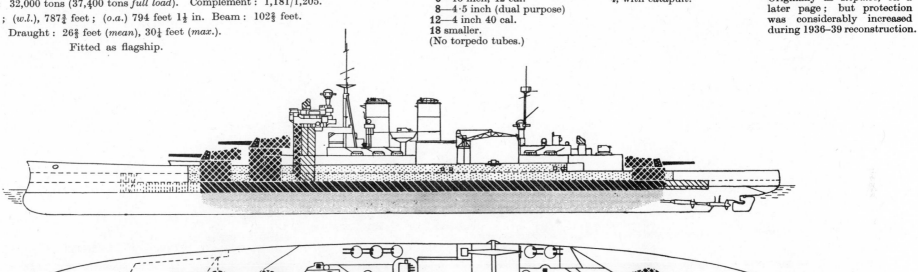

Machinery : Parsons geared turbines. 4 shafts. Boilers : 8 Admiralty 3-drum type (300 lb. working pressure). S.H.P. : 120,000 = 29 kts. Oil fuel : 1,000 tons *normal*, 4,289 tons *max.* Radius of action, *about* 3,650 miles.

General Notes.—This ship and *Repulse* were provided for under 1914 Navy Estimates, as battleships of *Royal Sovereign* class. After Falkland Islands battle they were re-designed as battle cruisers. Cost of *Renown*, £3,117,204. Refits : 1919–20, £100,738 ; 1921–22, £175,518 ; 1936–39 (complete reconstruction), £3,088,008.

Name.	Builder.	Machinery.	Begun.	Completed.	First Trials.
Renown	Fairfield	Fairfield	Jan. 25, 1915 (to new design)	Sept., 1916	126,300 = 32·68

RENOWN.

1939, *Wright & Logan.*

RENOWN.

1939, *Wright & Logan.*

RENOWN.

(For particulars, see preceding and following pages).

1939, *Wright & Logan.*

REPULSE.

1936, *Wright & Logan.*

REPULSE.

1936, *Wright & Logan.*

(RENOWN CLASS—2nd ship).

REPULSE (8th January, 1916).

Displacement, 32,000 tons (36,800 *full load*).   Complement, 1181/1205.

Length (*p.p.*) 750 feet.   (*w.l.*) 787¾ feet.   (*o.a.*) 794 feet 2½ in   Beam 102⅔ feet†   Draught, 27 feet (*mean*), 31¾ feet (*max.*)

Fitted as flagship.   †Outside bulges.   (See Armour Notes.)

Guns :

6—15 inch, 42 cal.
12—4 inch, 40 cal.
8—4 inch AA.
4—3 pdr.
1—12 pdr. Field
5 M.G.
10 Lewis
  (besides multi-M.G.)
Torpedo tubes (21 inch) :*
8 *above water* in pairs

   *See Torpedo Notes.

AIRCRAFT :

4, with catapult.

Armour (K.C.) :
9"— 6" Side (amidships)   ⎫
6"— 4" Side (within bow) ⎪ Lower
3" (stern)   ⎬ belt
4" Fore b'lkhead   ⎪
3" After b'lkh'd   ⎭
1½" Upper belt ....
7"—4" Barbettes .....
11"—7" Gunhouses.....
2" C.T. base (3" tube
  within)...........
10" C.T. ....
6" Sighting hood over
  C.T. ....
3" Torpedo C.T. ......

Vertical.

Armour (H.T.) :
1½"—1" Fo'xle ....
1⅞"—1½" Upper ....
3"—¾" Main (2" slopes)
2½" Bow   ⎫
3½"—3" Stern   ⎬ Lower
—" Barbettes   ⎭
3" C.T. and hood ....
1½" Torpedo C.T. .....
Special protection :
  Modified bulges......

Crowns   Decks

REPULSE.   1936, *Cribb.*

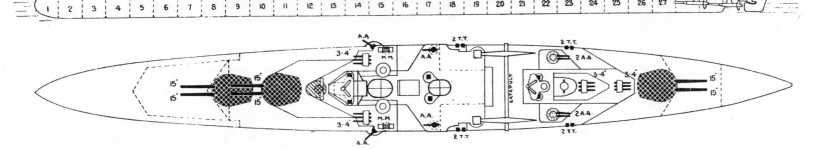

Machinery : Brown-Curtis turbines. 4 shafts. Boilers : 42 Babcock & Wilcox. Designed S.H.P. : 112,000. In service, present best speed *about* 29 kts. Oil fuel : 1,000 tons *normal*, 4,423 tons *maximum*. Radius of action, *about* 3,650 miles. Tactical diameter : 4⅓ times length (about 1,150 yards).

Gunnery Notes.—15-inch have range only limited by maximum visibility and director tower is under control tower on fore-mast. 4 inch triples have 2 director towers, and all guns can be worked from either tower or half the 4-inch from one tower. If towers are destroyed, 4-inch can work independently. 4-inch triples are clumsy and not liked. They are not mounted in one sleeve ; have separate breech mechanism ; gun crew of 23 to each triple.

Torpedo Notes.—*Repulse*, on 1919 re-fit, had 8 *above water* tubes in 4 twin mountings fitted on main deck above sections 18 and 23.

Armour Notes.—Armouring adapted from *Invincible* and *Indefatigable* classes. On re-fit 1919-20, *Repulse* re-armoured on w.l. with 9" K.C. and 6" K.C. between main and upper decks, extending over sections 8-27 on plans. Belt, *about* 9 ft. deep.

Name	Builder	Machinery	Begun*	Completed	Trials : H.P. kts.
Repulse	Clydebank	Clydebank	Jan.25,'15	Aug.,1916	119,025 = 31·7†

*To Battle Cruiser design.   †30 kts. on Arran mile after being re-armoured.

General Notes.—Cost of *Repulse*, £2,829,087 (not inclusive of all charges). Refits : 1918-22, £860,684 ; 1932-36, £1,377,748. (See also notes under *Renown*.)

ILLUSTRIOUS.   1939, *Sport & General.*

(ILLUSTRIOUS CLASS—6 Ships.)

ILLUSTRIOUS, (April 5, 1939,) **VICTORIOUS,** (Sept. 14, 1939), **FORMIDABLE,**
(August 17, 1939), **INDOMITABLE,** (Nov., 1939), **IMPLACABLE, INDEFATIGABLE.**

Displacement : 23,000 tons.   Complement : 1,600.

Length : 753 feet.   Beam :   feet.   Draught :   feet.

Guns :   Armour :
  16—4·5 inch (dual purpose).   Not reported.

Aircraft :

Machinery : Parsons Geared turbines. S.H.P. : 110,000 = over 30 kts. Boilers : 3-drum type.

Est.	Name	Builder	Machinery	Ordered	Begun	Completed
1936	*Illustrious*	V.-A., Barrow	Vickers-Armstrongs	13/1/37	27/4/37	
1936	*Victorious*	V.-A., Tyne	Wallsend Slipway	13/1/37	4/5/37	
1937	*Formidable*	Harland & Wolff	Harland & Wolff	19/3/37	17/6/37	To be 1940
1937	*Indomitable*	V.-A., Barrow	Vickers-Armstrongs	6/7/37	10/11/37	
	Implacable	Fairfield	Fairfield	11/10/38	2/39	
1939	*Indefatigable*	Clydebank	Clydebank	19/6/39		

ARK ROYAL   1938, *Wright & Logan.*

ARK ROYAL.   1938, *Wright & Logan.*

(*For particulars of above ship, see following page.*)

36

ARK ROYAL (April 13, 1937).

Displacement : 22,000 tons. (*About 27,000 tons full load.*)

Length (*pp.*) 685 feet ; (*o.a.*) 800 feet.   Beam : 94 feet.

Complement : 1,575

Draught : 22⅚ feet (*mean*).

Guns:

16—4·5 inch (dual purpose).
4—3 pdr.
6 multiple pompoms.
8 multiple M.G.

Aircraft :

60

Armour :

Not reported.

1938, *Wright & Logan.*

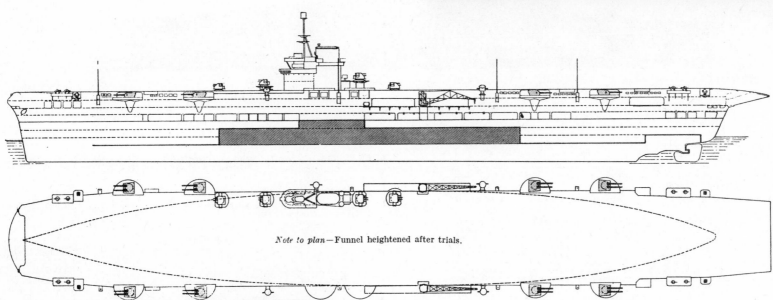

Note to plan—Funnel heightened after trials.

Machinery : Parsons geared turbines. S.H.P.: 102,000 = 30·75 kts.   (trials gave 31·75 kts.) 6 high pressure watertube boilers of 3-drum type.

General Notes.—Hangars are arranged on two decks, and are exceptionally roomy, with elaborate fire-fighting arrangements. 3 lifts for hoisting aircraft to flight deck. 2 hinged cranes for lowering and hoisting seaplanes. At night, navigating lights can be displayed by means of a special telescopic mast, rising from near centre of flight deck. Boats are stored in embrasures, out of which they can be run on a novel system. Accommodation for the numerous personnel is exceptionally good.   Total cost, £3,215,639.

Name.	Builder and Machinery	Ordered.	Begun.	Completed.
Ark Royal	Cammell Laird	12/3/25	16/9/35	16/11/38

(Courageous Class—2 Ships).

COURAGEOUS (5th February, 1916), **GLORIOUS** (20th April, 1916). (Late Cruisers.)

Displacement, 22,500 tons (*about* 26,500 tons *full load*). Complement, 748 (including R.A.F. personnel, 1216)

Length $\begin{cases} p.p. \ 735 \text{ ft.} \\ o.a. \ 786\frac{1}{4} \text{ ft.} \end{cases}$ Beam $\begin{cases} \cdot \text{(outside bulges), } 81\frac{1}{4} \text{ ft.} \\ \text{(across flight deck) 100 ft.} \end{cases}$ Draught $\begin{cases} mean \ 22\frac{1}{8} \text{ ft.} \\ max. \ 28\frac{1}{8} \text{ ft.} \end{cases}$

Guns :
16—4·7 inch (HA. or LA.)
4—3 pdr.
17 Smaller.

Aircraft :
(Official complement is 48 aircraft).

Armour :
3″ Side (amidships) ...
2″ Side (forward) ....
2″ (H.T.) Fore bulkhead
3″—1″ (H.T.) After Bulkhead ....
1½″ Side at upper deck level.
1″ Upper deck.......
1½″ Lower (stern, flat)
3″ Lower (stern, over rudder) ....
2″ Lower (on slopes) ..
Torpedo protection (H.T.)
Modified bulges 25 ft. deep ....
¾″ Inner screen to boiler and engine room vents.

COURAGEOUS.

1936, *Wright & Logan.*

Machinery : Parsons (all-geared) turbines. 4 shafts. Boilers : 18 Yarrow (small tube). Designed H.P. 90,000 = 30·5 kts. Oil fuel: *normal*, 3,550 tons ; *maximum*, 3,940 tons.

Armour Notes.—General scheme of armouring on Cruiser lines, the 3″ belt being built up of 2″ plating on 1″ shell plating. Decks round magazines thickened during completion.

Engineering Notes.—General arrangement of machinery as in "C" class cruisers. 4-shaft geared turbines and double helical gearing. Have done 32 kts. in service.

General Notes.—Emergency War Programme ships. Original cruiser design formulated by Lord Fisher in 1915, with a view to Baltic operations—hence the shallow draught. The lines are remarkably fine. On trials, *Courageous* met heavy weather and was driven into a head sea, straining her hull forward. Doubling plates were added here, and subsequent trials showed the defect had been overcome. *Glorious* strengthened in the same way a year later as a precautionary measure. First cost of *Glorious*, £2,119,066 ; but alterations added £2,137,374 to this. *Courageous* and *Glorious* taken in hand for conversion into aircraft carriers at Devonport (June, 1924 and Feb., 1924 respectively). Work on *Glorious* was started at Rosyth, but on that yard being closed she was towed to Devonport for completion. *Courageous* completed May 5, 1928, her conversion having cost £2,025,800. *Glorious* completed January, 1930. Both under refit, 1938–39.

Appearance Notes.—*Courageous* refitted 1936, with light tripod mast on superstructure. *Glorious* has had her quarter deck raised a deck higher than in *Courageous*, and has no charthouse before funnel. Tail of flight deck was extended aft to stern during refit, 1934–35.

H.M.S. Courageous was torpedoed and sunk on September 17, 1939.

Note to Plan.—3 pdr. guns mounted beneath flight deck forward. Carries 2 multiple A.A. mounts on forward flight deck and one immediately abaft island superstructure.

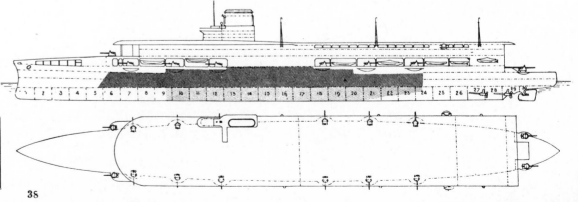

Name	Builder	Machinery	Begun	Completed	Trials
Courageous	Armstrong	Parsons	May, 1915	Jan., 1917	93,780 = 31·58
Glorious	Harland & Wolff, Belfast	Harland & Wolff	Mar., 1915	Jan., 1917	91,165 = 31·6

38

COURAGEOUS.   1936, *Wright & Logan.*

COURAGEOUS.   1936, *Cribb.*

GLORIOUS.   1935, *Cribb (added 1936).*

GLORIOUS.   1935, *Wright & Logan.*

In "Glorious" quarter deck has been raised flush with upper deck. and flight deck extended in a downward curve above it.

GLORIOUS.   1930 *Photo, Abrahams, Devonport.*

39

FURIOUS. (Before refit).

1932 *Photo, R. Perkins.*

1939, *Norman Parkinson, by courtesy of "The Bystander."*

FURIOUS (15 August, 1916). Late Cruiser.

Displacement, 22,450 tons. Complement, 748 (about 1,200 with R.A.F. personnel.)

Length, (p.p.) 735 feet, (o.a.) 786¼ feet. *Beam, 89¾ feet. Draught { mean 21⅔ feet. / max. 25 feet.

*Outside bulges.

Guns:
10—5·5 inch, 50 cal.
3—4 inch AA.
22 Smaller.
Aircraft:
(Official complement, 33)

Armour:
3″ Belt (amidships)................
2″ Belt (bow). ....
3″—2″ Bulkheads F. & A.........
1″ Decks (H.T. at stern)..........
3″—1½″ Decks (H.T. at stern)...
Anti-Torp. Pro.
Shallow bulges ....
1″ H.T. vertical. ....

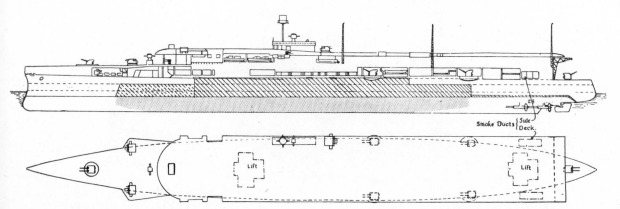

Smoke Ducts | Side Deck.

Lift   Lift

Machinery (by Wallsend Co.): Brown-Curtis (all geared) Turbines. 4 shafts. Boilers: 18 Yarrow.
Designed S.H.P. 90,000 = 31 kts. *Trials*: 90,820 = 30 kts. Oil fuel: 4010 tons.

Armour Notes.—3″ Belt consists of 2″ plating over 1″ shell plating, as in Light Cruisers.

General Notes.—Built under Emergency War Programme, by Armstrong Whitworth. Begun June, 1915; prior to completion, forward 18 inch turret suppressed and replaced by a forward flight deck. Completed July, 1917. Rebuilt between Nov., 1917 and March, 1918. Originally intended to be a modified *Courageous*, with 18 inch guns, forward and aft. During reconstruction, 1917–18, after 18 inch gun was removed and replaced by flight deck entailing removal of mainmast. Since conversion, she is said to be rather light, and is good now for 32–33 kts. Including cost of alterations, this ship is said to have absorbed over six million pounds. Underwent re-fit and alteration at H.M. Dockyards, Rosyth and Devonport, 1921–25, after which her appearance was completely altered, the funnel and mast being removed and a new hangar built forward. Smoke is discharged from vents at after end of hangar, or alternatively through flight deck, which measures 700 × 80 feet. Height of flight deck from water line is 75 feet. There are 2 hydraulic lifts from hangars to flight decks.

FURIOUS. (Particulars on preceding page. (Note that stern is painted *black*.) 1939, *Abrahams, Devonport*

EAGLE (Particulars on following page.) 1931 *Photo. R. Perkins.*

EAGLE (8th June, 1918), late Battleship.

Displacement, 22,600 (*deep load*, 26,400) tons.   Complement, 748.

Length $\left\{\begin{array}{l}(p.p.)\ 625\ \text{feet}\\(o.a.)\ 667\ \ \text{,,}\end{array}\right\}$ Beam $\left\{\begin{array}{l}92\frac{3}{4}\\105\frac{1}{6}\ (max.)\end{array}\right\}$ feet.* Draught $\left\{\begin{array}{l}24\ \text{feet }mean.\\27\ \text{feet }max.\end{array}\right\}$

* 100 feet, flight deck.

Guns
  9 —6 inch, 50 cal.
  4 —4 inch A.A.
  22 Smaller.

Aircraft :
  Official complement is 21.

Armour :
  ...″ Side (amidships)......
  ...″ Deck ....
Special protection :
  Bulges over about four-fifths of length, project-ing about 6 feet from side.

Bow view.   *Devonport.*

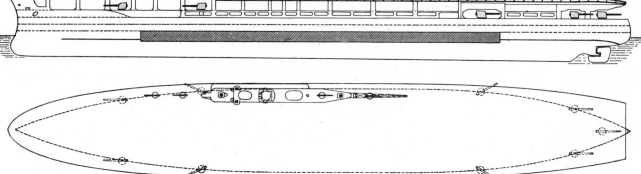

Machinery : Brown-Curtis (A.G.) turbines, by J. Brown & Co., Clydebank. Designed S.H.P. 50,000 = 24 kts. (No details available of trials). Boilers : 32 Yarrow. Oil fuel : *Normal*, 2500 tons ; *maximum*, 3750 tons.

General Notes.—Designed and begun by Armstrong Whitworth, February, 1913, for Chile, as *Almirante Cochrane*, a Dreadnought Battleship and sister to Chilean *Almirante Latorre*. All work on this ship ceased in August, 1914, and she lay on her slip until 1917, when her purchase was negotiated with the Chilean Government. Her design was modified to an Aircraft Carrier by Sir E. H. Tennyson d'Eyncourt. Commissioned for ship and flying trials with one funnel and no masts, 13th April, 1920. As a result of trials made off Scilly Islands, put in hand at H.M. Dockyard, Portsmouth, for modifications, November, 1920. Finally completed in 1924. Bought from Chile for £1,334,358, sums subsequently expended have raised total cost to £4,617,636 (Statement by First Lord, April 1927). Refit 1932.

EAGLE.   1927 *Photo, Cassar.*

HERMES (11th September, 1919).

Displacement, 10,850 tons *normal* (about 12,900 tons *full load*).   Complement, 664.

Length $\begin{cases} p.p. \ 548 \text{ feet} \\ o.a. \ 598 \ ,, \end{cases}$ Beam $\begin{cases} w.l \\ \text{outside bulges, 70 feet} \\ \text{over flight deck, 90 feet} \end{cases}$ Draught $\begin{cases} mean \ 18\frac{3}{4} \text{ feet.} \\ max. \ — \ ,, \end{cases}$

Guns :
6—5·5 inch, 50 cal.
3—4 inch AA.
18 Smaller.

Aircraft :
Official complement is 15.

Armour :
Not known—probably
of Light Cruiser
type.
Anti-Torpedo
Protection Bulges.

HERMES.

1934 *Photo, R. Perkins.*

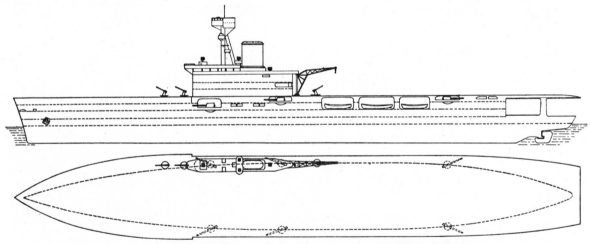

Machinery : Parsons (all geared) turbines.   Designed S.H.P. 40,000=25 kts.   2 shafts.
Boilers : Yarrow (small Tube).   Oil fuel : 1000 tons *normal*.   2000 tons *max.*

Name	Builder	Machinery	Ordered	Begun	Completed	Trials
Hermes	Armstrong Whitworth Devonport D.Y.*	Parsons	July, '17	15 Jan., '18	19/2/24	

* Towed here for completion, January, 1920.

General Notes.—Begun under Emergency War Programme   First vessel specially designed by Admiralty as an Aircraft Carrier.   Is a splendid sea boat, very steady, with remarkably little rolling propensity.

Can carry 20 sea or aeroplanes.   Special ventilation system to lessen danger of fire from petrol fumes. and new types of gear for handling, landing and flying-off aircraft.   Hangar aft, with electric lift from quarterdeck to flight deck, 'planes being wheeled out from hangar on to lift through an opening normally closed by shutters.   Transporter cranes fitted forward and aft.   Refit 1933-34.

1938, *R. Perkins.*

43

EXETER (July 18th, 1929). Devonport D.Y.

"Standard" displacement, 8390 tons. Complement, 600.

Length, 540 (*p.p.*), 575 (*o.a.*) feet.   Beam, 58 feet.   Draught, 17 feet (*mean*).

Guns :
  6—8 inch, 50 cal.
  4—4 inch AA.
  4—3 pdr.
  14 smaller.
Torpedo Tubes :
  6—21 inch (tripled).
Aircraft :
  2—with 2 catapults.

Armour :
  2″ Deck
  3″ C.T.
  2″—3″ Side at W.L.

EXETER.

1933 *Photo, R. Perkins*

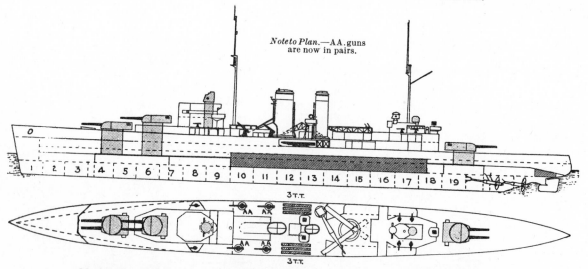

Note to Plan.—AA. guns are now in pairs.

3 T.T.

3 T.T.

Machinery : Parsons geared turbines. 4 shafts. Designed H.P. 80,000＝32 kts. Oil fuel: 1900 tons. Radius, 10,000 miles at 11–14 kts. Boilers : 8 Admiralty 3-drum type.

General Notes.—Designed by Sir William Berry and laid down at Devonport in August, 1928. Completed in May, 1931. Design is similar to *York*, with an increase in beam of 1 foot. Was to have had three raking funnels and catapult on raised turret, with masts spaced as in *York*, but the foremost funnel was trunked into the second in order to improve the habitability of the bridge and save space and weight. The catapult on the second turret having been dispensed with, the bridge has been lowered so that the director is only 60 feet above water. Note the absence of wings to the bridge and the searchlight arrangement similar to that in the *Nelson* class. The absence of rake to the masts and funnels, and the thickening of the second funnel by 4 feet enables her to be distinguished without difficulty from the *York*.

(*Forecastle plating now extends to second A A. gun on either side.*)

1931 *Photo, R. Perkins.*

44

YORK (July 17th, 1928). Palmers.

"Standard" displacement, 8250 tons. Complement, 600.

Length, 540 (*p.p.*), 575 (*o.a.*) feet. Beam, 57 feet.

Draught, 17 feet (*mean*).

Guns :
 6—8 inch, 50 cal.
 4—4 inch AA.
 4—3 pdr.
 14 smaller.
Torpedo Tubes :
 6—21 inch (tripled)

Aircraft:
 1, with catapult.

Armour :
 2" Deck
 3" C.T.
 2"—3" Side
 at W.L.

Note to Plan.—Catapult shown on "B" turret does not exist. The four 3 pdr. on after control platform are mounted singly and not as shown. 4 inch AA. guns should be shown in pairs.

YORK.

1933 *Photo, Cribb.*

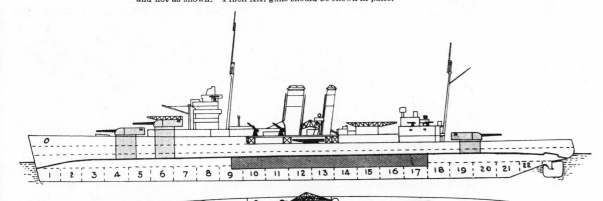

Machinery : Parsons geared turbines. 4 shafts. Designed H.P. 80,000 = 32·25 kts. Oil Fuel: 1900 tons. Radius, 10,000 miles at 11—14 kts. Boilers : 8 Admiralty 3-drum type.

General Notes.—Designed by Sir William Berry and marks the first attempt on the part of one of the Treaty Powers to break away from the 10,000 ton type of cruiser. To save 1,600 tons, two 8 inch guns were sacrificed, the resulting ship being little inferior to the 10,000 tonners, all things being considered. *York* was laid down at Messrs. Palmers' yard at Jarrow in May, 1927, and completed in June, 1930. The original design allowed for three funnels but during 1928 the plans were modified and the foremost funnel was trunked into the second. In order to clear the catapult shown in the plan on the second turret, the bridge was raised, and consequently the funnels. It has been found, however, that the turrets are too light for the catapult to be carried, so it and the derrick have been dispensed with. The reversion to the triple torpedo tubes is due to limitation of training space only.

YORK.

1933 *Photo, R. Perkins.*

(Dorsetshire Class—2 Ships).

DORSETSHIRE (January 29th, 1929). Portsmouth Dockyard.

NORFOLK (December 12th, 1928). Fairfield.

Displacement, 9,975 and 9,925 tons, respectively. Complement, 650.

Length, 590 (*p.p.*), 630 (*o.a.*) feet. Beam, 66 feet. Draught, 17 feet (*mean*).

DORSETSHIRE.   1937, *R. Perkins.*

Guns :
  8—8-inch, 50 cal.
  8—4-inch AA.
  4—3 pdr.
  16 smaller.
Torpedo Tubes :
  8—21-inch (quadrupled).

Aircraft :
  1, with catapult.

Armour :
  Similar to
  London
  class

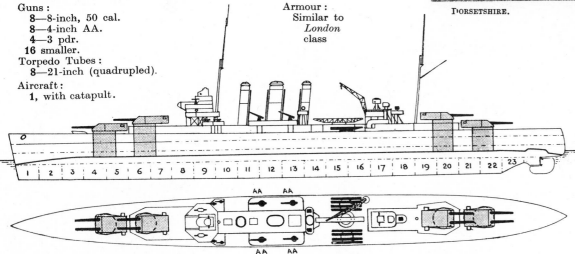

DORSETSHIRE, showing increased AA. armament.   1937, *R. Perkins.*

Note to Plan.—Crane is actually further forward than shown. AA. armament has been augmented, guns being paired.

Machinery : Parsons geared turbines. 4 shafts. Designed S.H.P. 80,000 = 32·25 kts. Oil fuel : 3200 tons. Boilers : 8 Admiralty 3-drum type. Machinery of *Dorsetshire* by Cammell Laird, *Norfolk* by Fairfield.

Engineering Notes.—Trials averaged 81,200 = 32·8 kts.

General Notes.—Designed by Sir William Berry and built under the 1926-27 Estimates. *Dorsetshire* begun September, 1927, and completed July, 1930 ; *Norfolk* in July, 1927, and completed in June. 1930. Two other ships of this class, *Surrey* and *Northumberland* were provided for under the 1926 Estimates, but were subsequently cancelled.

Appearance Notes.—Can be distinguished from *London* and *Kent* types by lower bridge and positions of AA. guns. Both ships have sternwalks.

NORFOLK.   1937, *R. Perkins.*

DEVONSHIRE.   1936, *R. Perkins.*

DEVONSHIRE.   1937, *R. Perkins.*

(LONDON CLASS—4 SHIPS.)

DEVONSHIRE (Oct. 22nd, 1927).
LONDON (Sept. 14th, 1927).
SHROPSHIRE (July 5th, 1928).
SUSSEX (Feb. 22nd, 1928).

Displacement: First pair, 9,850 tons ; second pair, 9,830 tons.
Complement, 650.

Length $\begin{Bmatrix} p.p. 595 \text{ feet} \\ o.a. 633 \text{ feet} \end{Bmatrix}$ Beam, 66 feet. Draught, 17 feet (*mean*)

Guns :
8—8 inch, 50 cal.
8—4 inch AA.
4—3 pdr.
14 smaller.
Torpedo tubes :
8—21 inch (quadrupled).
Aircraft :
1, with catapult.

Armour :
Similar to *Kent* class, without side armour or external bulges.
Note to Plan.—No crane on port beam. Large cabin added abaft bridge.

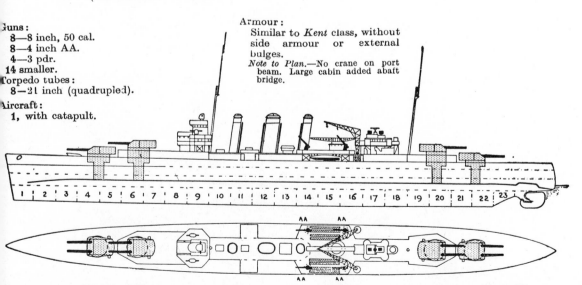

Machinery : Parsons geared turbines. 4 shafts. Designed S.H.P. 80,000 = 32·25 kts. Oil fuel : 3200 tons. Boilers : 8 Admiralty 3-drum type.

SHROPSHIRE.   1938, *Wright & Logan.*

Name	Builder	Machinery	Ordered	Begun	Completed	Trials	Est.
Devonshire	Devonport Y.	Vickers	1925 -26	16/3/26	19/3/39	Average : 81,200 = 32·8.	1925
London	Portsmouth Y.	Fairfield		22/2/26	5/2/29		
Shropshire	Beardmore	Beardmore		2/26	24/9/29		
Sussex	Hawthorn, Les.	Hawthorn		2/26	26/3/29		

General Notes.—All designed by Sir William J. Berry. Only one crane for aircraft (on starboard side).
Appearance Notes.—Higher bridges than *Dorsetshire* and *Norfolk*. Mainmast is stepped closer to " X " turret than in *Kent* class, and S.L. positions also differ.

CUMBERLAND. 1936, *Cribb*.

CUMBERLAND (SUFFOLK similar). 1936, *Wright & Logan*.

(For particulars of these ships, see following page).

KENT. 1938, *Medway Studios*.

CORNWALL (BERWICK similar). 1938, *R. Perkins*.

(Kent Class—5 Ships.)

BERWICK (March 30th 1926), **CORNWALL** (March 11th, 1926), **CUMBERLAND** (March 16th, 1926), **KENT** (March 16th, 1926), **SUFFOLK** (Feb. 16th, 1926).

Displacement : 10,000 tons, as refitted.

Complement, 679 (710 as flagship).

Length (*p.p.*) 590 feet, (*o a.*) 630 feet. Beam, 68¼ feet. Draught, 16¼ feet (*mean*)

Guns :
8—8 inch, 50 cal.
8—4 inch AA. (6 in *Suffolk*.)
20 Smaller

Torpedo tubes :
(Removed)

Aircraft :
3, with Catapult.

Armour :
3″–5″ Side at w.l.
3″—1½″ Deck over vitals
3″ C.T. ....
Bulges ....

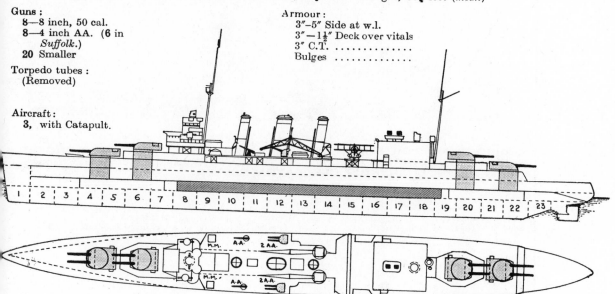

Note to Plan.—This represents *Cumberland* and *Suffolk ;* others vary as in photos, and plan of *Australia*, on a later page.

CORNWALL (BERWICK similar).   1938, *Wright & Logan.*

Machinery : Geared turbines (see table). 4 shafts. Designed S.H.P. 80,000 = 31·5 kts. Boilers : 8 Admiralty 3-drum type, with superheaters. Oil fuel : 3400 tons. Radius at full speed, 2300 miles ; at economical speed (11—14 kts.), 10,400 miles.

General Notes.—Built under 1924–25 Estimates ; designed by Sir Eustace Tennyson d'Eyncourt. Although on paper these ships appear to be inferior to foreign Treaty cruisers, in practice they are superior in sea-going qualities and have accommodation and habitability which is not equalled by any other cruisers. In addition, a considerable amount of weight has been expended in structural strength and internal protection. No attempt has been made to attain the high speeds which have been recorded by the *Tourville* and *Trento* types, the ideal aimed at being the ability to sustain the designed speed indefinitely and in all weathers, without exceeding the normal H.P. Actually over 34 knots has been maintained in service without in any way pressing the boilers. Two ships of the class, *Australia* and *Canberra*, were built for the Royal Australian Navy. Average cost is £1,970,000.

Gunnery Notes.—Exceptional elevation has been given to 8 inch guns, more than 65° having been observed. By means of an improved ammunition supply a rate of fire of four rounds per gun per minute can be maintained under director control. 8 inch broadside weighs 2,048 lbs. Total cost of armament £700,000 ; of firing a single broadside £408.

Armour Notes.—No side armour was included in original design, protection being afforded by a 3″–1½″ deck. External bulges are fitted and the internal subdivision is particularly well planned.

Engineering Notes.—Boiler pressure is 250 lbs.

Appearance Notes.—Mainmast stepped further forward than in *London* class S.L. positions also differ. *Kent* has a sternwalk.

Special Note.—All this class were reconstructed during 1935–38. Main alterations include the provision of a large hangar and additional aircraft, increased armour protection and modernisation of the anti-aircraft armament. To compensate for the additional weight so imposed, the *Cumberland* and *Suffolk* were cut down by one deck abaft the mainmast. This was not done in the *Cornwall*, *Kent* and *Berwick*.

Name	Builder	Machinery	Ordered	Begun	Completed	Trials	Turbines
Berwick	Fairfield	Fairfield		15/9/24	2/2/28	81,700 = 32·5	Brown-Curtis
Cornwall	Devonport Y.	Beardmore		9/10/24	2/28	(average of	Parsons
Cumberland	Vickers	Vickers	1924	18/10/24	1/28	results)	Parsons
Kent	Chatham Y.	Hawthorn		15/11/24	25/6/28		Parsons
Suffolk	Portsmouth Y.	Parsons		30/9/24	7/2/28		Parsons

(FIJI CLASS—13 SHIPS)

Will have 2 funnels and 2 masts.

FIJI (May 31, 1939), **KENYA** (Aug. 18, 1939), **MAURITIUS** (July 19, 1939), **NIGERIA** (July 18, 1939), **TRINIDAD** (Oct. 14, 1939), **CEYLON, GAMBIA, JAMAICA, UGANDA** and 4 more.

Displacement : 8,000 tons.

Length :   Beam :   Draught :

Guns :
12—6 inch.
8—4 inch AA.

(No plan available).

Machinery : Geared turbines.   Boilers : 3-drum type.   Speed : 33 kts.

Est.	Name	Builder	Machinery	Ordered	Begun	To be Completed
1937	Fiji	Clydebank	Clydebank	Dec., 1937	30/3/38	1940
	Kenya	Stephen	Stephen		18/6/38	
	Mauritius	Swan Hunter	Wallsend Slipway		31/3/38	
	Nigeria	V.-A., Tyne	Parsons		8/2/38	
	Trinidad	Devonport	Hawthorn Leslie		21/4/38	
1938	Ceylon	Stephen	Stephen	1939	1939	1942
	Gambia	Swan Hunter	Wallsend Slipway			
	Jamaica	V.-A., Barrow	V.-A., Barrow			
	Uganda	V.-A., Tyne	Parsons			
1939	4 Ships	(Still to be ordered)				

1939 *Illustration*

(DIDO CLASS—10 SHIPS).

DIDO (July 18, 1939), **EURYALUS** (June 6, 1939), **NAIAD** (Feb. 3, 1939), **PHOEBE** (March 25, 1939), **SIRIUS** (Nov., 1939), **BONAVENTURE** (April 19, 1939), **HERMIONE** (May 18, 1939), **CHARYBDIS, CLEOPATRA, SCYLLA.**

Displacement : 5,450 tons.

Length :   Beam :   Draught :

Guns :   Aircraft :   Armour :
10—5·25 inch (Unofficial).   **1,** with **1** catapult.   Similar to *Arethusa* class.

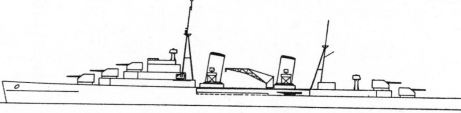

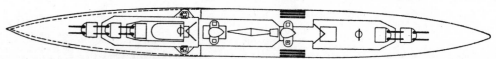

Machinery : Parsons single reduction geared Turbines.   4 shafts.   Speed : 33 kts.   Boilers : 3-drum type, working pressure 400 lbs.

Est.	Name	Builder	Machinery	Ordered	Begun	To be Completed
1936	Dido	Cammell Laird	Cammell Laird	21/3/37	20/10/37	1939-40
	Euryalus	Chatham	Hawthorn		21/10/37	
	Naiad	Hawthorn	Hawthorn		26/8/37	
	Phoebe	Fairfield	Fairfield		2/9/37	
	Sirius	Portsmouth	Scotts		6/4/38	
1937	Bonaventure	Scotts	Scotts		30/8/37	
	Hermione	Stephen	Stephen		6/10/37	
1938	Charybdis	Cammell Laird	Cammell Laird	18/8/38	9/11/38	1941
	Cleopatra	Hawthorn	Hawthorn		5/1/39	
	Scylla	Scotts	Scotts		19/4/39	

(EDINBURGH CLASS—2 SHIPS.)

EDINBURGH (March 31, 1938), BELFAST (March 17, 1938.)

Displacement : 10,000 tons.

Length : (pp.) 579 feet ; (o.a.) 613 ft. 6 in.   Beam : 63 ft. 4 in.   Draught : 17 ft. 3 in.

Guns :
12—6 inch.
12—4 inch AA.
4—3 pdr.
16 smaller.
(includes 2 Multiple
    pompoms and 2
    Multi-M.G.)

Aircraft : **3**, with **1** catapult.

Armour :
3″—4½″ side. Otherwise similar to *Southampton* type, but believed to be more extensive (see Notes).

Torpedo tubes :
6—21 inch (tripled).

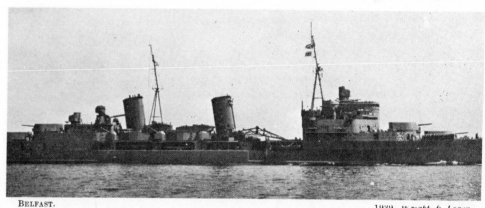

BELFAST.

1939, *Wright & Logan.*

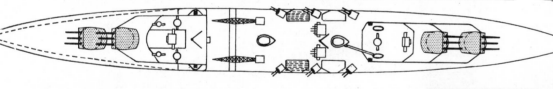

BELFAST.

1939, *Wright & Logan.*

Machinery : Parsons geared turbines.   S.H.P. : 80,000 = 32·5 kts.
    Boilers : 8 Admiralty 3-drum.

Est.	Name	Builder	Machinery	Ordered	Begun	To be Completed
1936 {	Edinburgh	Swan Hunter	Wallsend Slipway	15/8/36	29/12/36	} 1939
	Belfast	Harland & Wolff	Harland & Wolff	15/8/36	10/12/36	

Notes.—These two ships are reported to be very well protected, being designed (it is said) to withstand 8-inch shell fire.   Internal subdivision is exceptionally complete.

BELFAST.

1939, *courtesy Messrs. Harland & Wolff.*

(SOUTHAMPTON CLASS—8 SHIPS).

SOUTHAMPTON (ex-*Polyphemus*) (March 10, 1936),
NEWCASTLE (ex-*Minotaur*) (Jan. 23, 1936),
SHEFFIELD (July 23, 1936),
BIRMINGHAM (Sept. 1, 1936),
GLASGOW (June 20, 1936),
GLOUCESTER (Oct. 19, 1937),
LIVERPOOL (March 24, 1937),
MANCHESTER (April 12, 1937),

Displacement: 9,100 tons (Last 3: 9,400 tons). Complement: 700.
Length: (*pp.*) 558, (*w.l.*) 584 ft., (*o.a.*) 591 ft. 6 in. Beam: 61 ft. 8 in.
(last 3: 62 ft. 4 in.). Draught: 17 ft. (*mean*), except last 3 ships,
17 ft. 5 in. All are 20 ft. (*maximum*).

Guns:
  12—6 inch
   8—4 inch AA.
   1—3·7 inch howitzer.
   4—3 pdr.
  16 smaller.

Aircraft:
  3, with 1 catapult.

Tubes:
  6—21 inch (tripled).

Armour:
  1″—2″ Turrets.
  4″—3″ Side
  4″ C.T.

SOUTHAMPTON.

1937, *R. Perkins.*

(*Further photographs on following page*).

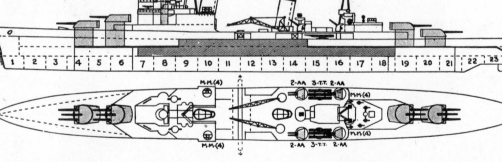

GLOUCESTER.

1939 *R. Perkins.*

Machinery: Parsons geared turbines. 4 shafts. S.H.P.: 75,000 = 32 kts. (Last 3: 82,500 = 32·3 kts.). Boilers: 8 Admiralty 3-drum. Oil fuel: 1,970 tons.

Est.	Name	Builder	Machinery	Ordered	Begun	Completed
1933	Southampton	Clydebank	Clydebank	1/6/34	21/11/34	6/3/37
	Newcastle	V.-A., Tyne	V.-A., Barrow	1/6/34	4/10/34	5/3/37
	Sheffield	Do.	Do.	17/12/34	31/1/35	25/8/37
1934	Glasgow	Scotts	Scotts	17/12/34	16/4/35	8/9/37
	Birmingham	Devonport	Clydebank	1/3/35	18/7/35	18/11/37
	Gloucester	Do.	Scotts	3/35	22/9/36	27/1/39
1935	Liverpool	Fairfield	Fairfield	3/35	17/2/36	25/10/38
	Manchester	Hawthorn	Hawthorn	3/35	28/3/36	4/8/38

Notes.—Built as a reply to the "*Mogami*" and "*Savannah*" classes, though the number of 6 inch guns is three less. Centre gun of each turret is mounted slightly further back than other two. Protection is somewhat better than in previous classes. Hangars form an extension aft of bridge structure, fore funnel being carried up between them. New type athwartship catapult mounted between funnels. Noteworthy features of these ships are the raking funnels and masts and the tripod masting.

BIRMINGHAM (Bow differs from rest of class).

1938, *Grand Studio, Malta.*

LIVERPOOL.

1938, " *Fighting Ships* "

NEWCASTLE, with catapult extended.

1937, *R. Perkins.*

(For particulars of all these ships, see preceding page.)

MANCHESTER. (Observe bridge details).

1938, *Wright & Logan.*

(ARETHUSA CLASS.—2 SHIPS).
ARETHUSA (March 6th, 1934).
GALATEA (August 9th, 1934).
Displacement, 5,220 tons.
(IMPROVED ARETHUSA CLASS—2 SHIPS).
PENELOPE (October 15th, 1935).
AURORA (August 20th, 1936).
Displacement, 5,270 tons.
Complement 450.

Length: (*p.p.*) 480 ft., (*w.l.*) 500 ft. Beam: 51 ft.
Draught: 13ft. 10in. (*mean*).

Guns :
6—6 inch.
8—4 inch AA.
2—3 pdr.
7 smaller guns.

Armour :
1″ turrets
2″ side

Torpedo Tubes :
6—21 inch in Triple mounts.

Aircraft :
1, with **1** catapult.

(Not carried at present by *Aurora*.)

Note to Plan.—Only one derrick as completed, on starboard side.

All now have 4 inch AA. in pairs. *Aurora* has superstructure between funnels.

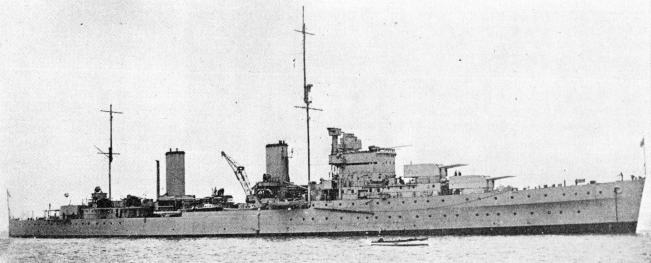

ARETHUSA.

1935, *Seward, Weymouth.*

Est.	Name	Builder	Machinery	Ordered	Begun	Completed
1931	*Arethusa*	Chatham	Parsons	1/9/32	25/1/33	Feb., 1935
1932	*Galatea*	Scotts	Scotts	21/2/33	2/6/33	Aug., 1935
1933	*Penelope*	Harland & Wolff	Harland & Wolff	8/3/34	30/5/34	Nov., 1936
1934	*Aurora*	Portsmouth	Wallsend	1/3/35	23/7/35	Nov., 1937

Machinery : Parsons geared Turbines. 4 shafts. S.H.P. 64,000=32·25 knots. Boilers : 4 Admiralty 3-drum type. Oil : 1,200 tons. Radius reported to be 12,000 miles at economical speed.

General Notes.—These ships may be said to bear the same relation to the *Leander* as the *York* class do to the *Kents*. Their tonnage is the minimum for oceangoing efficiency and the armament adequate to deal with likely convoy-raiders, bearing in mind that being relatively inexpensive they can be produced in numbers. The grouping of the AA. guns on the after superstructure instead of amidships should be noted, the multiple-mounts being on platforms below the bridge. Excepting for the two lifeboats all the boats are handled by the derrick, and the low bulwark amidships is to protect boats which cannot be carried higher as in *Amphion.* Funnels are stream-lined in order to take air current clear of aircraft between them.

Constructional Notes.—Weight reduction has been secured in these ships by the extensive use of electric welding for hull and internal subdivision, as well as by the employment of aluminium-covered plywood for cabin bulkheads and other light partitions, etc.

Engineering Notes.—A fluid flywheel enables power to be almost instantaneously switched over from main engines to cruising turbines. A reversion to two funnels is caused by the spacing of the boiler and engine rooms in two units, which obviates wholesale flooding of the boiler-rooms. Boiler temperature (with 300° superheat) is 650°.

Cost.—*Arethusa*, £1,251,161; *Galatea*, £1,210,733; *Penelope*, £1,290,787; *Aurora* £1,252,915.

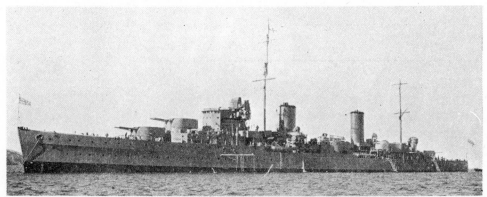

AURORA.

1938, *R. Perkins.*

(LEANDER CLASS—5 Ships.)

LEANDER (September 24, 1931).
ORION (Nov. 24, 1932).
NEPTUNE (Jan. 31, 1933).
ACHILLES (Sept. 1, 1932).
AJAX (March 1, 1934).

Displacement: *Leander*, 7,270 tons; *Orion*, 7,215 tons; *Neptune*, 7,175 tons: *Achilles*. 7,030 tons; *Ajax*, 6,985 tons. Complement, 550.
Length (*p.p.*) 530 feet; (*o.a.*) 554½ feet. Beam, 55ft. 2in. Draught (*mean*) 16 feet. *Ajax*, 522 (*p.p.*) × 55⅔ × 15½ feet (*mean*).

Guns :
    8—6 inch.
    8—4 inch AA. (4 in *Achilles*)
    4—3 pdr.
    10 Smaller Guns.

Armour :
    2″—4″ Side amidships.
    1″ Turrets.
    1″ Bridge.
    2″ Deck.

Torpedo Tubes :
    8—21 inch (quadrupled).

Aircraft :
    Leander, *Achilles*, 1, *Orion*, *Neptune*, *Ajax*, 2.
    (1 catapult in all).

NEPTUNE. (Observe shortened foremast).

1937 *R. Perkins.*

Note to Plan.—Crane is actually mounted on centre line, not as shown below, and AA. guns are paired.

NOTE.—*Achilles* and *Leander* lent to Dominion of New Zealand.

Machinery : Parsons I.R. geared Turbines. 4 shafts. Designed S.H.P. 72,000 = 32·5 kts. (made with designed H.P. on trials). Boilers : 4 Admiralty 3-drum type. Oil : 1,800 tons.

General Notes.—This class represents a return to moderate dimensions, compared with the thirteen ships of the 10,000 ton Treaty type. The eight guns in four turrets is a disposition of armament which is regarded by the gunnery branch as the best number and arrangement for satisfactory control, and superior in practice to nine guns in triple mountings as in the German *Köln* class. The 6-inch guns are of an entirely new model produced by the "auto-frettage" system instead of being wire wound. Forecastle plating extended aft and boats raised a deck since trials. Cost £1,500,000 to £1,600,000 apiece (*Ajax*, £1,480,097).

Est.	Name	Builder	Machinery	Ordered	Begun	Completed
1929	*Leander*	Devonport	Vickers-Armstrongs	18/2/30	8/9/30	23/3/33
1930	*Orion*	Do.	Do.	26/3/31	26/9/31	16/1/34
	Neptune	Portsmouth	Parsons	2/3/31	24/9/31	22/2/34
	Achilles	Cammell Laird	Cammell Laird	3/31	11/6/31	10/10/33
1931	*Ajax*	Vickers-Armstrongs	Vickers-Armstrongs	1/10/32	7/2/33	3/6/35

ORION.   (Observe extended forecastle plating.)   1937, *R. Perkins.*

EMERALD (19th May, 1920).

ENTERPRISE (23rd December, 1919).

Displacement, 7,550 and 7,580 tons, respectively.

(*Full load*, over 9,000 tons.)

Complement, 572.

Length $\left\{\begin{array}{l} p.p.\ 535\ feet \\ o.a.\ 570\ feet \end{array}\right\}$ Beam 54½ feet. Draught $\left\{\begin{array}{l} mean\ 16½\ feet. \\ max.\ \quad feet. \end{array}\right.$

Guns :
7—6 inch, 50 cal.
5—4 inch AA.
4—3 pdr.
9 smaller.

Armour (H.T.) :
3″ Side (amidships).
2½″—1½″ Side (bow).
2″ Side (stern).
1″ Upper Deck (amidships).
1″ Deck (over rudder).

Torpedo tubes (21 inch) :
16, quadrupled, *above water*.

Aircraft :
1 with catapult.

EMERALD.

1934 *Official Photo.*

Appearance Notes—Main differences are indicated in plan.

ENTERPRISE.

Note to Plan.—4-inch AA. guns amidships should be shown as pairs.

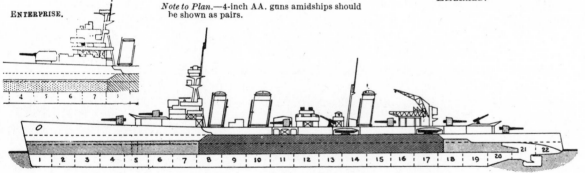

ENTERPRISE.

1936, *Medway Studios.*

Machinery : Turbines, 4 sets Brown-Curtis (geared). 4 shafts. Designed S.H.P. 80,000 = 33 kts. (light), 32 kts. (*full load*). Boilers : 8 Yarrow small tube. Fuel (oil only) : *normal*, 650 tons ; *maximum*, 1,746 tons.

Gunnery Notes.—Elevation of 6 inch, up to 40°. Heavy Director on foremast. R.F. on forward bridge.

Engineering Notes.—8 boilers in 4 w.t. compartments, part forward of amidships magazines and part abaft forward engine-room. This arrangement of boiler rooms is responsible for the somewhat unusual spacing of the funnels. On a full power trial in 1939, *Emerald* is reported to have exceeded 32 knots.

General Notes.—Begun under Emergency War Programme. A third ship, *Euphrates*, ordered from Fairfield Co., cancelled. They were designed early in 1918, to have a speed equal to that of any of the German Light Cruisers then existing or likely to be built. Cost of these ships was £1,617,062 for *Emerald* and £1,752,867 for *Enterprise*. Both ships refitted, 1934–36.

Name	Builder	Machinery	Ordered	Begun	Completed	Trials: H.P. kts.	Turbines
Emerald	*Armstrong	Wallsend	7/3/18	Sept. 23/18	Jan. 14/26	80450 = 32·9	Brown-Curtis
Enterprise	†Clydebank	Clydebank	7/3/18	June 28/18	Jan., '26	(*Enterprise* not tried).	Brown-Curtis

*Towed to Chatham D.Y. †Devonport D.Y. for completion.

(IMPROVED BIRMINGHAM CLASS—3 SHIPS.)

EFFINGHAM (8th June, 1921), **FROBISHER** (20th March, 1920), **HAWKINS** (1st Oct., 1917)

All fitted as Flagships.

Displacement, 9,550, 9,860 and 9,800 tons, respectively.

Complement, 712/749.

Length $\left\{\begin{array}{l}p.p.\ 565\ \text{feet}\\o.a.\ 605\ ,,\end{array}\right\}$ Beam $\left\{\begin{array}{l}w.l.\qquad\quad 58^*\ \text{feet}\\\text{outside bulges }65\quad ,,\end{array}\right\}$ Draught $\left\{\begin{array}{l}mean\ 17\frac{1}{4}\ \text{feet.}\\max.\ 20\frac{1}{2}\ ,,\end{array}\right.$

*Approximate.

Guns : (*Effingham*)
9—6 inch.
4—4 inch AA.
4—3 pdr.
10 smaller.

Torpedo tubes (21 inch)
4 *above water*

Aircraft :
To be added to equipment.

Armour (H.T. or Nickel) :
3″—2″ Side (amidships)
2½″—1½″ Side (bow) ..
2½″—2¼″ Side (stern) ..
1″ Upper deck (amids.)
1½″—1″ Deck over rudder (Hadfield) ..
3″ C.T. ....
Anti-Torpedo Protection :
Bulges, 5 ft. deep ...
Unpierced Bulkheads, below lower deck ...

EFFINGHAM.   1938, *Wright & Logan.*

EFFINGHAM.   1938, *R. Perkins.*

Machinery : Turbines, Brown-Curtis or Parsons (geared cruising). Designed S.H.P. in *Hawkins*, 55,000=29.5 kts. *Effingham* 58,000 = 29·5 kts. ; *Frobisher*, 65.000=30·5 kts. 4 shafts. Boilers : 10 Yarrow (small tube) except *Hawkins*, 8. Fuel : as completed, 1000 tons oil *normal*, 2150 *maximum*. *Hawkins*, as re-constructed, 2600 tons *maximum*. (Ships were originally intended to burn coal.)

Note.—All three ships are being reconstructed and rearmed. The *Vindictive*, a fourth ship of this class, has been demilitarised for use as a training ship, and will be found on a later page. *Raleigh*, of same type, was lost in August, 1922.

Name	Builder	Machinery	Begun	Completed	Turbines
Effingham	Portsmouth D.Y.	H. & Wolff	2 Ap., '17	July, '25	Brown-Curtis
Frobisher	Devonport D.Y.	Wallsend	2 Aug., '16	20 Sept. '24	Brown-Curtis
Hawkins	Chatham D.Y.	Parsons	June, '16	July 25. '19	Parsons

SPECIAL NOTE.—Up to date of outbreak of war rearmament of FROBISHER and HAWKINS had not been effected.

EFFINGHAM, showing AA. armament.   1939, *R. Perkins.*

("D" CLASS—8 Ships.)

DESPATCH (24th Sept., 1919), **DIOMEDE** (29th April, 1919),
DELHI (23rd Aug., 1918), **DUNEDIN** (19th Nov., 1918),
DURBAN (29th May, 1919), **DANAE** (26th Jan., 1918),
DAUNTLESS (10th April, 1918), **DRAGON** (29th Dec., 1917).

Displacement, 4,850 tons.

Length $\begin{cases} p.p. \text{ 445 feet} \\ w.l. \text{ 465}\frac{1}{2} \text{ ,,} \\ o.a. \text{ 472}\frac{1}{2} \text{ ,,} \end{cases}$ Beam, 46$\frac{1}{2}$ ft. Draught $\begin{cases} mean \text{ 14}\frac{1}{4} \text{ ft.} \\ max. \text{ 16}\frac{1}{2} \text{ ft.} \end{cases}$

Complements of all, 450/469.   All except first two fitted as Flagships.

Guns :
  6—6 inch, 50 cal
  3—4 inch AA.
  4—3 pdr.
  11 to 13 smaller.

Torpedo tubes (21 inch) :
  12 in 4 triple deck mountings.

Armour (H.T.) :
  3" Side (amidships) ...
  2", 1¾", 1½" Side (bow
    and stern) ....
  1" Upper deck (amids.)
  1" Deck over rudder ..
  (Hull and armour, 2940 tons.)

DUNEDIN. DIOMEDE has her forward forecastle 6 inch in gunhouse.   1939, *Wright & Logan.*

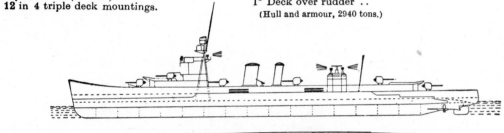

Machinery : Turbines (all-geared), Brown-Curtis or Parsons types. Designed S.H.P. 40,000 = 29 kts. 2 shafts. Boilers : 6 Yarrow (small tube). Oil fuel only : *normal,* 300 tons ; *maximum,* 1,050 tons. Machinery and engineering stores = 945 tons.

Name	Builder	Machinery	Ordered	Begun	Completed	Trials : H.P. kts.	Turbines
Diomede Despatch	Vickers* Fairfield*	Vickers Fairfield	Mar., 1918 Mar., 1918	June, 1918 July, 1918	24 Apr,1922 2 June,1922		Parsons Brown-Curtis
Delhi Durban	Armstrong Scotts*	Wallsend Scotts	Sept., 1917 Sept., 1917	29 Oct., '17 Jan., 1918	June, 1919 1 Sept. 1921	41,381=28·5† 41,026=	Brown-Curtis Brown-Curtis
Danae Dauntless Dragon Dunedin	Armstrong Palmer Scotts Armstrong	Wallsend Palmer Scotts Hawthorn	Sept., 1916 Sept., 1916 Sept., 1916 Sept., 1917	Dec., 1916 Jan., 1917 Jan., 1917 Nov., 1917	July, 1918 Dec., 1918 Aug., 1918 Oct., 1919	40,463= 42,808= 40,035= 41,268=29·19	Brown-Curtis Parsons Brown-Curtis Brown-Curtis

*Towed to following Dockyards for completion : *Despatch* to Chatham, *Durban* to Devonport, *Diomede* to Portsmouth.
† With PVs. out, and on deep draught.

DAUNTLESS.   1928 *Photo, Cribb.*

General Notes.—Emergency War Programme ships. Note that first three were ordered *before Carlisle* class. Design generally as *Ceres* class, but lengthened *about* 20 feet, to add a sixth 6-inch between foremast and first funnel; also triple tubes. Cost of *Delhi,* £840,182. Heavy director on foremast. *Dunedin* and *Diomede*, both served in New Zealand Division for over ten years. *Dauntless* badly damaged by grounding off Halifax Nova Scotia, July, 1928, and completely refitted 1929-30. *Danae, Delhi, Dragon,* all refitted 1929-30.

Cancelled Ships.—D*æ*dalus, D*a*ring, Desperate, Dryad (all ordered March ,1918).

CAPETOWN* (28th June, 1919), **COLOMBO*** (18th Dec., 1918).

Displacement, 4200 tons.

CARDIFF (ex-*Caprice*) (April 12, 1917). **CERES** (March 24, 1917).

Displacement, 4290 tons.   Complement, 400/437.

Length $\begin{cases} p.p. & 425 \text{ feet} \\ o.a. & 450 \text{ ,,} \end{cases}$ Beam, 43½ feet.   Draught $\begin{cases} mean & 14 \text{ feet 1 inch.} \\ max. & 16\frac{1}{4} \text{ ,,} \end{cases}$

Guns :
  5—6 inch, 50 cal.
  2—3 inch AA.
  2 to 4—3 pdr.
  9 to 11 smaller
Torpedo tubes (21 inch):
  above water, in 4 *double*
  mountings.

*Fitted as Flagships.

Armour (H.T.) :
  3″ Side (amidships) ...
  2¼″—1½″ Side (bow) ..
  2″ Side (stern) ......
  1″ Upper deck (amids.)
  1″ Deck over rudder ..
  (Harvey or Hadfield)
  3″ C.T. ....

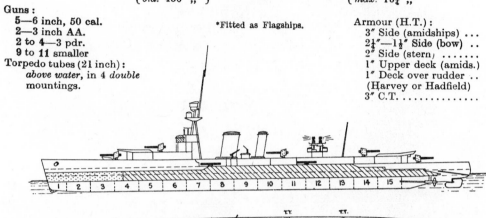

COLOMBO.   . 1926 *Photo, Grand Studio, Malta.*

Carlisle and *Capetown* originally had a hangar forward, but this has been removed and replaced by standard bridge work. Some now carry maintopmasts.

Name	Builder	Machinery	Begun	Completed	Trials H.P. kts.	Turbines
Cardiff	Fairfield	Fairfield	July, 1916	July, 1917	41,450 = 28·96	B-.Curtis A.G.
Ceres	Clydebank	Clydebank	Apr. 26, 1916	June, 1917	39,425 = 29·1	B-.Curtis A.G.
Capetown	Cammell Laird*	Cammell Laird	23 Feb.,'18	Feb., '22		Parsons
Colombo	Fairfield	Fairfield	Dec., 1917	June, '19		B.-Curtis

*Towed to Pembroke D.Y. for completion.

Machinery : Turbines (all-geared), see Table. 2 shafts in all. Designed S.H.P. 40,000 = 29 kts.
Boilers : Yarrow. Fuel (oil only) : 300 tons, *normal* ; *maximum*, 950 tons.

General Notes.—Emergency War Programme ships, ordered 1916–17. Very wet forward, to remedy which defect the later ships were given "trawler" bows. Heavy type director on foremast.

To distinguish : From "D" class Cruisers.—Absence of 6 inch between foremast and first funnel.

SPECIAL NOTE.

CAPETOWN and COLOMBO are to be rearmed as Anti-Aircraft Ships in due course.

CALYPSO.   1935, *R. Perkins.*

(CALEDON CLASS—3 SHIPS.)

CALEDON* (Nov. 25, 1916), **CALYPSO** (Jan. 24, 1917), **CARADOC** (Dec. 23, 1916).

Displacement : 4,180 tons.   Complement : 400/437.

Length $\begin{cases} p.p. \text{ 425 feet} \\ o.a. \text{ 450 feet} \end{cases}$ Beam : $42\frac{3}{4}$ feet.   Draught $\begin{cases} mean \text{ 14 ft. 1 in.} \\ max. \text{ } 16\frac{1}{4} \text{ feet.} \end{cases}$

* Fitted as Flagship.

Guns :
5—6 inch, 50 cal. (**Dir. Con.**)
2—3 inch AA.
4—3 pdr.
11 smaller
Torpedo tube (21 inch)
   8 *above water*, in 4 double
   mountings.

Armour : (H.T.)
3″ Side (amidships)
$2\frac{1}{4}″$—$1\frac{1}{4}″$ Side (bow)
$2\frac{1}{2}″$—2″ Side (stern)
1″ Deck
6″ C.T.
4″ Tube

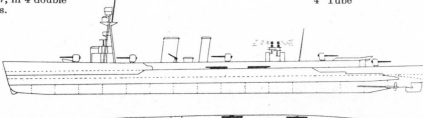

Machinery : Turbines (all-geared), Parsons. 2 screws. Designed S.H.P. : 40,000 = 29 kts.
Boilers : 8 Yarrow. Oil fuel : *normal*, 300 tons ; *maximum*, 935 tons.
Gunnery Notes.—Mark of 6-inch gun introduced in this class and mounted in later Cruisers has about 40° elevation.
Heavy type Director.

Name	*Builder*	*Machinery*	*Begun*	*Completed*	*Trials* H.P. kts.
Caledon	Cammell Laird	Cammell Laird	17/3/16	3/17	47 887 = 29
Calypso	Hawthorn Leslie	Hawthorn Leslie	7/2/16	21/6/17	43,312 = 29
Caradoc	Scotts	Scotts	2/16	6/17	41,196 = 29

General Notes.—Emergency War Programme. When new, they could make 29–30 kts. Are very wet forward, the fo'sle
6 inch being almost unfightable in a head sea. *Cassandra,* of this class, built by Messrs. Hawthorn Leslie, lost in Baltic
by mine, soon after Armistice was signed. *Caledon* refitted 1926–27, *Caradoc* 1927–28, *Calypso* 1929. All may
undergo further refits, 1940.

COVENTRY.   1936, *Wright & Logan.*

CURLEW.   1936, *Grand Studios, Malta.*

(COVENTRY CLASS—2 SHIPS, ex-CERES Type).

COVENTRY (ex-*Corsair*), (July 6, 1917), **CURLEW** (July 5, 1917).

Displacement, 4,290 tons.   Complement, 400.   Length (*p.p.*) 425 feet ; (*o.a.*) 450 feet.
Beam, $43\frac{1}{2}$ feet.   Draught, *mean* 14 feet 1 inch ; *max.* $16\frac{1}{4}$ feet.

Guns :
10—4 inch AA.
1—multiple pompom
10 smaller

Armour :
3″ Side (amidships)
$2\frac{1}{4}″$—$1\frac{1}{2}″$ Side (bow)
2″ Side (stern)
1″ Deck
3″ C.T.

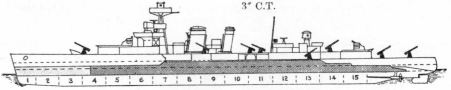

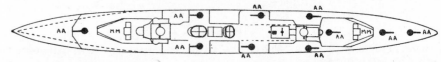

Machinery : All-geared Turbines, Brown-Curtis in *Coventry*, Parsons in *Curlew*. 2 Shafts.
Designed S.H.P. 40,000 = 29 kts. Boilers : Yarrow. Oil fuel : 300 tons *normal* ; 950 tons *maximum*.
Notes.—These two ships, originally sisters to *Cardiff*, were reconstructed and rearmed in 1935.

Name.	*Builder.*	*Machinery.*	*Begun.*	*Completed.*
Coventry	Swan Hunter	Wallsend	Aug., 1916	Feb., 1918
Curlew	Vickers	Vickers	Aug., 1916	Dec., 1917.

CAIRO (Nov. 19, 1918), **CALCUTTA** (July 9, 1918), **CARLISLE** (July 9, 1918),
CURACOA (May 5, 1917).

Displacement : 4,200 tons (except *Curacoa*, 4,290 tons).   Complement, 400.

Length (*pp.*) 425 feet ; (*o.a.*) 450 feet. Beam, 43½ feet. Draught, $14\frac{1}{3}$ feet *mean* ; 16¼ feet *max.*

Guns :
8—4 inch AA.
1 multiple pompom
Several smaller.

Armour :
    3″ Side (amidships)
    2¼″—1½″ Side (ends)
    1″ Deck
    3″ C.T.

CAIRO.

1939 *Wright & Logan.*

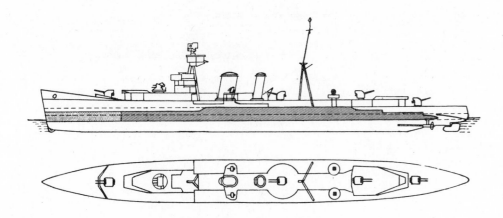

CAIRO.

1939, *Wright & Logan.*

Machinery : Parsons geared turbines in *Cairo* and *Calcutta*, Brown-Curtis in others. 2 shafts.
S.H.P. : 40,000 = 29 kts. Boilers : Yarrow. Oil fuel : 300 tons *normal*, 950 tons *maximum.*

Notes.—These ex-cruisers were all converted into Anti-Aircraft Ships in 1939.

Name.	Builder.	Machinery.	Begun.	Completed.
Cairo	Cammell Laird	Cammell Laird	28/11/17	24/9/19
Calcutta	Vickers	Vickers	10/17	21/8/19
Carlisle	Fairfield	Fairfield	10/17	11/11/18
Curacoa	Pembroke D.Y.	Harland & Wolff	7/16	2/18

Showing alteration to Stern.

1932 *Photo, R. Perkins.*

1937, B. R. Goodfellow, Esq. (added 1938).

(SPECIAL "CRUISER-MINELAYER" TYPE—1 SHIP.)

ADVENTURE (18th June, 1924).

"Standard" displacement, 6,740 tons. Complement, 400.

Length $\begin{cases} p.p., & 500 \text{ feet} \\ o.a., & 520 \text{ feet} \end{cases}$ Beam, 59 feet, (over bulges) Draught *mean*, 19¼ feet.

Armour :

Guns :
 4—4·7 inch. AA.
 4—3 pdr.
 18 smaller
No. of mines carried : 340.

Note to Plan.—Stern is now rounded, as in photos.
 A multiple pompom is now mounted on forward superfiring position

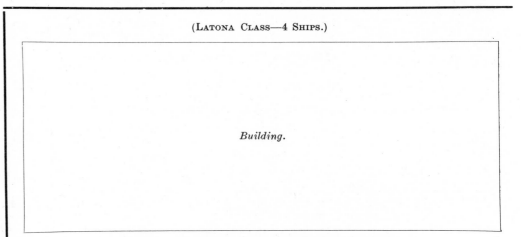

Machinery : Parsons geared turbines, with Diesel engines and electric drive for cruising purposes. 4 shafts. Designed S.H.P. 40,000 = 28 kts. Boilers : Admiralty 3–drum type. Fuel (oil only) : 1550 tons.

Notes.—Laid down at Devonport, Nov. 1922, and completed May, 1927. Originally had flat stern, which was rebuilt to present shape in 1932. Refitted 1939.

(LATONA CLASS—4 SHIPS.)

Building.

ABDIEL, LATONA, MANXMAN, WELSHMAN.

Displacement : 2,650 tons.

Length : 410 feet.   Beam :   **Draught**

Guns :
 Probably 4·7 inch.

Machinery : Parsons geared turbines. Boilers : Admiralty 3-drum type.

Notes.—First 3 laid down under 1938 Programme, *Welshman* under that for 1939.

Name.	Builder.	Ordered.	Begun.	Completed.
Abdiel	Stephen		/39	
Latona	Thornycroft	23/12/38	4/4/39	
Manxman	White		/39	
Welshman	Hawthorn	21/3/39	/39	

Funnel Markings.

(a) *Leaders.* Home and Mediterranean Fleets. Fore Funnel: 4 ft. black band round the top. In the case of single funnel Destroyers a 3 ft. black band round funnel as far as upper flotilla band.

(b) *Divisional Commanders.* Fore funnel: 2 ft. band 3 feet from the top.

Home Fleet—White
Mediterranean—Red or Black.
China—Black

In single funnel destroyers, a 2-ft. bar on both sides and parallel to axis of funnel, for a length of 6 ft. downwards from flotilla band. To be of same colour as upper band.

(c) *Flotillas.* Second (or only) funnel is as follows:

1st	Med.	— 1 Red
2nd	Med.	— 2 Red
3rd	Med.	— No marking
4th	Med.	— No marking
5th	Med.	— 1 black
6th	Home	— 1 white
7th	Home	— 2 white
8th	Home	— 3 white
9th	Home	— 1 black over 2 white
17th	Reserve	— 1 red over 2 white
19th	Reserve	— 1 white over 1 black
21st	China	— 2 white over 1 red

---

16 "Lightning" Class.

> Will be of modified *Javelin* design.

2 Yarrow: **Laforey** (LDR.), **Lance**
2 Cammell Laird: **Larne, Lively.**
2 Hawthorn: **Legion, Lightning.**
4 Scotts: **Lookout, Loyal, Milne** (LDR.), **Marksman.**
2 Fairfield: **Musketeer, Myrmidon.**
2 Stephen: **Matchless, Meteor.**
2 Vickers-Armstrongs (Tyne): **Marne, Martin.**

Displacement: 1,920 tons, except *Laforey, Milne,* 1,935 tons. Dimensions: Not advised. Guns: **6—4·7 inch,** several smaller. Tubes: **8—21 inch.** Machinery: Parsons geared turbines (by Parsons Co. in *Legion* and *Lively*). S.H.P.: 45,000 = 36·5 kts.

Name	Begun	Launch	Compl.	Name	Begun	Launch	Compl.
Lance	10/38			Legion	11/38		
Larne	12/38		⎱ To be	Lightning	11/38		⎱ To be
Lively	12/38		⎰ 1940	Lookout	11/38		⎰ 1940
Laforey	11/38			Loyal	11/38		

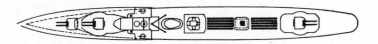

---

24 "Javelin" Class

JERVIS.   1939, *courtesy Messrs. Hawthorn Leslie (Builders).*

JERSEY.   1939, *Wright & Logan.*

2 Hawthorn: **Jervis, Kelly.** (both LEADERS).
4 Clydebank: **Jackal, Javelin** (ex-*Kashmir*), **Nerissa, Nizam.**
4 Denny: **Jaguar, Kandahar, Noble, Nonpareil.**
4 Fairfield: **Napier** (LEADER), **Juno, Kelvin, Nestor.**
2 Swan Hunter: **Janus, Khartoum.**
4 Thornycroft: **Kashmir** (ex-*Javelin*), **Kimberley, Norman, Norseman.**
2 White: **Jersey, Kingston.**
2 Yarrow: **Jupiter, Kipling.**

Displacement: 1,690 tons, except *Jervis, Kelly, Napier,* 1,695 tons. Complement: 183. Dimensions: 348 × 35 × 9 feet. Guns: **6—4·7 inch, 6** smaller. Tubes: **10—21 inch.** Machinery: Parsons geared turbines. S.H.P.: **40,000** = 36 kts. Boilers: 2 Admiralty 3-drum type.

Est.	Name	Begun	Launch	Compl.	Est.	Name	Begun	Launch	Compl.
	Jackal	24/9/37	25/10/38	13/4/39		Javelin	11/10/37	21/12/38	10/6/39
	Jaguar	11/37	22/11/38	/39		Kandahar	1/38	21/3/39	
	Juno	5/10/37	8/12/38	24/8/39		Kelvin	5/10/37	19/1/39	
1936	Janus	29/9/37	10/11/38	/39	1937	Khartoum	27/10/37	6/2/39	1939
	Kashmir	10/37	4/4/39	/39		Kimberley	1/38	1/6/39	
	Jersey	28/9/37	26/9/38	28/4/39		Kingston	6/10/37	9/1/39	
	Jupiter	20/9/37	27/10/38	16/6/39		Kipling	20/10/37	19/1/39	
	Jervis ⎱	26/8/37	⎧ 9/9/38	5/8/39					
	Kelly ⎰		⎩ 25/10/38	23/8/39					

16 " Tribal " Class

AFRIDI.

1938, *Wright & Logan.*

MOHAWK (Now carries Pendant No. F 31).

1938, *Wright & Logan.*

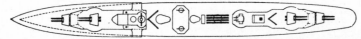

4 *Vickers-Armstrongs (Tyne)* : **Afridi, Cossack,** (both Ldrs.), **Eskimo, Mashona.**

2 *Fairfield* : **Gurkha, Maori.**
2 *Thornycroft* : **Mohawk, Nubian.**
2 *Stephen* : **Sikh, Zulu.**

2 *Scotts* : **Matabele, Punjabi.**
2 *Denny* : **Ashanti, Bedouin.**
2 *Swan Hunter* : **Somali, Tartar.** (both Ldrs.)

Displacement : 1,870 tons. Complement : 190 (as Leaders 219, or as Captain D., 226). Dimensions : 355½ × 36½ × 9 feet. Guns : 8—4·7 inch. Tubes : 4—21 inch. Machinery : Parsons geared turbines (by Parsons Co. in *Eskimo* and *Mashona* ; by Wallsend Co. in *Somali* and *Tartar* ; and by V.-A., Barrow, in *Afridi* and *Cossack*). S.H.P. : 44,000 = 36·5 kts. Boilers : 3 Admiralty 3-drum type. Cost averages just over £450,000 apiece.

Note.—*Afridi, Cossack, Somali* and *Tartar* are fitted as Leaders, though not classed as such. They do not differ in appearance from others.

Est.	Name	Begun	Launch	Compl.	Est.	Name	Begun	Launch	Compl.
1935	Afridi	9/6/36	8/6/37	3/5/38		Sikh	24/9/36	17/12/37	12/10/38
	Cossack		7/6/38			Matabele	1/10/36	6/10/37	25/1/39
	Mohawk	16/7/36	5/10/37	7/9/38		Punjabi		18/12/37	29/3/39
	Nubian	10/8/36	21/12/37	6/12/38		Ashanti	23/11/36	5/11/37	21/12/38
	Zulu	10/8/36	23/9/37	7/9/38	1936	Bedouin	1/37	21/12/37	15/3/39
	Gurkha	6/7/36	7/7/37	21/10/38		Eskimo	5/8/36	3/9/37	30/12/38
	Maori		2/9/37	2/1/39		Mashona			28/3/39
						Somali	26/8/36	24/8/37	12/12/38
						Tartar		21/10/37	10/3/39

8 " Intrepid " class

ICARUS. (Observe quintuple T.T. mounts).   Height of funnels now reduced.   1937, *Wright & Logan.*

Programme
1935
{
2 *Clydebank* : **Icarus, Ilex**
2 *Hawthorn Leslie* : **Imogen, Imperial**
2 *White* : **Impulsive, Intrepid**
2 *Yarrow* : **Isis, Ivanhoe**
}

Displacement : 1,370 tons. Complement : 145. Dimensions : 312 (*pp.*), 320 (*w.l.*) × 33 × 8½ feet (*mean*). Guns : 4—4·7 inch, **6** smaller. Tubes : **10**—21 inch. Machinery : Parsons geared turbines. S.H.P. : 34,000 = 36 kts. Boilers: 3 Admiralty 3-drum type, working pressure 350 lbs. Cost averages just over £320,000 apiece.

Note.—All this class are fitted for minelaying.

Name	Begun	Launched	Completed	Name	Begun	Launched	Completed
Icarus	3/36	26/11/36	3/5/37	Impulsive	3/36	1/3/37	29/1/38
Ilex	3/36	28/1/37	7/7/37	Intrepid	1/36	17/12/36	29/7/37
Imogen	1/36	30/10/36	2/6/37	Isis	2/36	12/11/36	2/6/37
Imperial	1/36	11/12/36	30/6/37	Ivanhoe	2/36	11/2/37	24/8/37

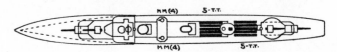

" I " *class* and GLOWWORM. ("G" and "H" *classes* as on following page.)

ILEX (Height of funnels now reduced).

1938, *Grand Studio.*

8 "Hero" and **8** "Greyhound" classes.

3 Admiralty Type Leaders.

HERO. Observe bridge and shortened funnels.   1939, *Wright & Logan.*

INGLEFIELD (HARDY similar; note light tripod foremast.)   1937, *Wright & Logan.*

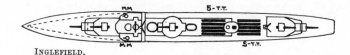

INGLEFIELD.

GREYHOUND.   1936, *Wright & Logan.*

Programme 1934	2 Denny: **Hasty, Havock**	Displacement, 1,340 tons.
	2 Vickers-Armstrongs (Tyne): **Hereward, Hero**	
	2 Scotts: **Hostile, Hotspur**	
	2 Swan Hunter: **Hunter, Hyperion**	
Programme 1933	2 Stephen: **Gallant, Grenade**	Displacement, 1,335 tons (except *Glowworm*, 1,345 tons).
	2 Fairfield: **Garland, Gipsy**	
	2 Thornycroft: **Glowworm, Grafton**	
	2 Vickers-Armstrongs (Barrow): **Greyhound, Griffin**	

Complement: 145. Dimensions: 312 (*pp.*), 320 (*w.l.*), 323 (*o.a.*) × 33 × 8½ feet (*mean*). Guns: **4**—4·7 inch, **6** smaller Tubes: **8**—21 inch (*Glowworm*, **10**). Machinery · Parsons geared turbines (by Parsons Co. in *Hereward* and *Hero* by Wallsend Co. in *Hunter* and *Hyperion*). S.H.P.: 34,000 = 36 kts. Boilers: 3 Admiralty 3-drum type. Oil fuel: 455 tons. Cost averages just over £300,000 apiece.

Name			Begun	Launch	Comp.	Name			Begun	Launch	Comp.
Gallant	..	..	15/9/34	26/9/35	25/2/36	Glowworm		..	15/8/34	22/7/35	22/1/36
Grenade		..	3/10/34	12/11/35	28/3/36	Grafton		..	30/8/34	18/9/35	20/3/36
Garland	..	..	22/8/34	24/10/35	3/3/36	Greyhound		..	20/9/34	15/8/35	31/1/36
Gipsy	..	..	5/9/34	7/11/35	22/2/36	Griffin		..	20/9/34	15/8/35	6/3/36
Hasty	..	..	4/35	5/5/36	11/11/36	Hostile		..	27/2/35	24/1/36	10/9/36
Havock	..	..	15/5/35	7/7/36	18/1/37	Hotspur				23/3/36	29/12/36
Hereward		28/2/35	10/3/36	9/12/36		Hunter		..	26/3/35	25/2/36	20/9/36
Hero				23/10/36		Hyperion		..		8/4/36	3/12/36

GRENVILLE.   1936, *Wright & Logan.*

1 Yarrow: **Grenville.** **2** Cammell Laird: **Hardy, Inglefield.**
Displacement: 1,485, 1,505, and 1,530 tons respectively. Complement: 175. Dimensions: *Grenville,* 319 (*pp.*), 327 (*w.l.*) × 34½ × 8¾ feet (*mean*); others, 326 (*pp.*), 334 (*w.l.*) × 34 × 8¾ feet (*mean*) in *Hardy,* 9 feet (*mean*) in *Inglefield.* Guns: **5**—4·7 inch, **6** smaller. Tubes: **8**—21 inch (quadrupled) in first two; **10**—21 inch (quintupled in *Inglefield.* Machinery: Parsons geared turbines. S.H.P.: 38,000 = 36·5 kts. (*Grenville,* 36·25). Boilers: 4 Admiralty 3-drum (of the side-fired type), 300 lbs. working pressure. Oil fuel: 470 tons (*Grenville*), 475 tons others. Cost: *Grenville,* £335,928; *Hardy,* £343,679; *Inglefield,* £354,303.

2 Admiralty Type Leaders.

EXMOUTH, FAULKNOR, GRENVILLE, HARDY.

EXMOUTH. 1935, *R. Perkins.*

1 *Portsmouth Dockyard:* **Exmouth.** 1 *Yarrow:* **Faulknor.**

Displacement : 1,475 and 1,460 tons, respectively. Complement : 175. Respective Dimensions : 332 (*w.l.*), 343 (*o.a.*) × 33¾ × 8⅝ feet (*mean*) ; 322 (*pp.*), 340 (*w.l.*) × 33¾ × 8⅛ feet (*mean*). Guns : 5—4·7 inch, **6** smaller. Tubes : **8**—21 inch (quadrupled). Machinery : Parsons geared turbines (By Fairfield in *Exmouth*). S.H.P. : 38,000 = 36·75 kts. Boilers : 4 Admiralty 3-drum type, 300 lbs. working pressure. Oil fuel : 490 tons. Cost : *Faulknor*, £330,239.

KEMPENFELT. 1932 *Photo, R. Perkins.*

1 *Vickers-Armstrongs (Barrow):* **Keith.** 1 *White:* **Kempenfelt.** 1 *Portsmouth Dockyard:* **Duncan.**

Displacement : 1400 tons (except *Kempenfelt*, 1390 tons). Dimensions : *Keith*, 312 (p.p.), 323 (o.a.) × 32¼ × 8½ (*mean*), 12 feet (*max.*). Others, 317¾ (*p.p.*), 326 (*w.l.*) × 33 × 8⅝ feet (*mean*). Guns : 4—4·7 inch, **6** smaller. Tubes : 8—21 inch (quadrupled). Machinery : Parsons geared turbines. S.H.P. : 36,000 = 35·75 kts. (*Keith*, 34,000 = 35·25 kts.). Boilers : Admiralty 3-drum type, 300 lbs. working pressure. Oil fuel : 470 tons. Complement : 175.

Appearance Note.—*Keith, Kempenfelt* and *Duncan* differ mainly from B and D type destroyers in having taller foremasts with crowsnests. They vary slightly in build of bridge. It is proposed to transfer *Kempenfelt* to Royal Canadian Navy.

Est.	Name	Begun	Launch	Comp.	Est.	Name	Begun	Launch	Comp.
1928	Keith	10/29	10/7/30	9/6/31	1932	Faulknor	31/7/33	12/6/34	24/5/35
1929	Kempenfelt	10/30	29/10/31	30/5/32	1933	Grenville	29/9/34	15/8/35	1/7/36
1930	Duncan	3/9/31	7/7/32	5/4/33	1934	Hardy	35	7/4/36	12/36
1931	Exmouth	16/5/33	7/2/34	31/10/34	1935	Inglefield	29/4/36	15/10/36	25/6/37

8 "Eclipse" and 8 "Fearless" classes.

FOXHOUND (and others except *Esk* and *Express*, which have light tripod aft). 1935, *R. Perkins.*

Plan of "E," "F," "G" and "H" classes (except GLOWWORM).

Programme 1932
{
2 *Cammell Laird.* **Fearless, Foresight.**
2 *Clydebank.* **Foxhound, Fortune.**
2 *White.* **Forester, Fury.**
2 *Vickers-Armstrongs (Tyne):* **Fame, Firedrake.**
}

Programme 1931
{
2 *Denny.* **Echo, Eclipse.**
2 *Scotts.* **Escapade, Escort.**
2 *Swan Hunter.* **Esk, Express.**
2 *Hawthorn Leslie.* **Electra, Encounter.**
}

Displacement : 1,375 tons *Eclipse* class and *Fearless* ; others, 1,350 tons.
Complement : 145.
Guns : 4—4·7 inch. **6** smaller.
Tubes : **8**—21 inch. 2 D.C. Throwers.

Dimensions : 318¼ (*p.p.*), 326 (*w.l.*), 329 (*o.a.*) × 33¼ × 8½ feet (*mean*). H.P. : 36,000 = 36 kts. Parsons geared Turbines (by Wallsend Co. in *Esk* and *Express* ; by Parsons Co. in *Fame* and *Firedrake* ; and by Builders in others), with exception of *Foxhound* and *Fortune*, which have Parsons L.P. and Brown-Curtis H.P. turbines. Boilers : 3 Admiralty 3-drum type, working at 300 lbs. pressure, with 200° superheat. Oil fuel : 480 tons.

General Note.—*Esk* and *Express* are fitted as mine-layers, have a light tripod aft to avoid shrouds and carry whaler on forecastle deck. Mount 2 guns less when acting as minelayers. Average cost approaches £300,000 apiece. Annual maintenance (direct expenditure), £41,000.

Engineering Notes.—Average speed of class on trials with designed horse power was 36·7 kts. Some reported to have reached 38 kts. Radius at 15 kts., 6,000 miles.

Name	Begun	Launch	Completed	Name	Begun	Launch	Completed
Fearless	17/7/33	12/5/34	22/12/34	Echo	20/3/33	16/2/34	25/10/34
Foresight	21/7/33	29/6/34	15/5/35	Eclipse	22/3/33	12/4/34	1/12/34
Foxhound	21/8/33	12/10/34	6/6/35	Escapade	30/1/34	3/9/34	
Fortune	25/7/33	29/8/34	27/4/35	Escort	30/3/33	29/3/34	6/11/34
Forester	15/5/33	28/6/34	29/3/35	Esk	23/3/33	19/3/34	2/10/34
Fury	19/5/33	10/9/34	18/5/35	Express	23/3/33	29/5/34	3/11/34
Fame	5/7/33	28/6/34	26/4/35	Electra	15/3/33	15/2/34	17/9/34
Firedrake	5/7/33	28/6/34	30/5/35	Encounter	15/3/33	29/3/34	9/11/34

8 "Defender" class

DELIGHT. (All *Defender* class similar; 3 inch AA. shown above has since been removed).   *Added 1935, Wright & Logan.*

Programme 1930
- 2 *Vickers-Armstrongs (Barrow)*: **Defender, Diamond.**
- 2 *Thornycroft*: **Daring, Decoy.**
- 2 *Fairfield*: **Dainty, Delight.**
- 2 *Palmers*: **Diana, Duchess.**

Special Note.—Four more ships of this type, formerly named *Comet, Crusader, Crescent* and *Cygnet*, were acquired by the Royal Canadian Navy in 1937 and 1938, and will be found on a later page.

Displacement :	1,375 tons.	Dimensions : 317¾ (*pp.*), 326 (*w.l.*) × 33 × 8½ feet (*mean*).	
Complement :	145.	H.P. : 36,000 = 36 kts.	
Guns :	4—4·7 inch. 6 smaller.	Parsons geared Turbines.	
Tubes	8—21 inch.	Boilers : 3 Admiralty 3-drum type. Oil : 470 tons.	

Name	Begun	Launch	Completed	Name	Begun	Launch	Completed
Defender	6/31	7/4/32	28/10/32	*Dainty*	20/4/31	3/5/32	3/1/33
Diamond	9/31	8/4/32	2/11/32	*Delight*	22/4/31	2/6/32	30/1/33
Daring	6/31	7/4/32	24/11/32	*Diana*	6/31	16/6/32	20/12/32
Decoy	6/31	7/6/32	4/4/33	*Duchess*	6/31	19/7/32	24/1/33
Basilisk	19/8/29	6/8/30	4/3/31	*Acasta*	13/8/28	7/8/29	11/2/30
Beagle	11/10/29	26/9/30	9/4/31	*Achates*	11/9/28	4/10/29	27/3/30
Blanche	31/7/29	29/5/30	2/31	*Acheron*	29/10/28	18/3/30	13/10/31
Boadicea	12/7/29	23/9/30	3/31	*Active*	10/7/28	9/7/29	9/2/30
Boreas	7/29	18/7/30	2/31	*Antelope*	11/7/28	27/7/29	20/3/30
Brazen	7/29	25/7/30	3/31	*Anthony*	30/7/28	24/4/29	14/2/30
Brilliant	9/7/29	9/10/30	2/31	*Ardent*	30/7/28	26/6/29	14/4/30
Bulldog	10/8/29	6/12/30	3/31	*Arrow*	20/8/28	22/8/29	14/4/30

8 "Beagle" class and 8 "Acasta" class

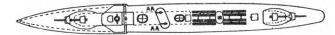

ACHERON. (All *Acasta* class similar). (Observe H.S.M.S. gear aft).   *1931 Photo, Cribb.*

Programme 1928
- 2 *Clydebank* : **Basilisk, Beagle.**
- 2 *Hawthorn Leslie* : **Blanche, Boadicea.**
- 2 *Palmers* : **Boreas, Brazen.**
- 2 *Swan Hunter* : **Brilliant, Bulldog.**

Displacement, 1360 tons.

Programme 1927
- 2 *Clydebank* : **Acasta, Achates.**
- 1 *Thornycroft* : **Acheron.**
- 2 *Hawthorn Leslie* : **Active, Antelope.**
- 2 *Scotts* : **Anthony, Ardent.**
- 1 *Vickers-Armstrongs (Barrow)* : **Arrow.**

Displacement : 1,350 tons.

Dimensions : 312 (*pp.*), 323 (*o.a.*) × 32¼ × 12 feet (*max.*), 8½ feet (*mean*). Guns : 4—4·7 inch, 6 smaller. Tubes : 8—21 inch on quadruple mounts. Machinery : Parsons geared turbines (by Parsons Co. in *Acheron*) in all except the *Acasta, Achates, Basilisk* and *Beagle*, which have Brown-Curtis H.P. turbines and Parsons L.P. 2 shafts. Designed S.H.P. : 34,000 = 35 kts. Boilers : 3 Admiralty 3-drum type, with superheaters (*see notes*). Oil fuel : 380 tons (except *Acheron*, 360 tons). Complement : 138.

General Notes.—A very successful class, all having exceeded designed speed with ease. Thus *Arrow* maintained 36·7 kts. with 34,119 H.P. for 6 hours, full power figures being those recorded at boiler capacity for this period. No short period spurts were included in the trials. *Acheron* is fitted with special 500 lb. pressure boilers, with a steam temperature of 750° F. In others of class, figures are 300 lbs. and 600° respectively. All have proved economical steamers, *Acasta* class averaging ·81 lb. (*Acheron* ·608 lb.) fuel per S.H.P. per hour, and *Beagle* class ·73 lb. per S.H.P. per hour.

Torpedo Note.—These are the first destroyers in which tubes are quadruply mounted.

BEAGLE. (All this class similar; no H.S.M.S. gear).   *1937, R. Perkins.*

1 "A" Type Leader.

CODRINGTON.

1930 *Photo, Abrahams, Devonport.*

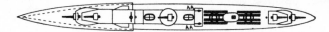

Codrington.

Built by Swan Hunter.   Laid down, 1928; launched, August 7, 1929.   Completed, **June, 1930.**

Displacement : 1540 tons standard. 2000 tons full load. Dimensions : $332 \times 33\frac{3}{4} \times 12\frac{1}{4}$ feet (*max.*), 9 feet (*mean*). Guns : 5—4·7 inch, **6** smaller. Tubes : **8**—21 inch on quadruple mounts. Machinery : Parsons geared turbines. 2 shafts. Designed S.H.P. : 39,000 = 35 kts. Boilers : 4 Admiralty 3-drum, working pressure 300 lbs., with superheaters. Oil fuel : 500 tons. Complement : 185.

2 "A" Type.

AMAZON.

Appearance Note.—Forecastle continues well abaft bridge in these 2 ships, distinguishing them from other classes.

AMAZON.

1935, *R. Perkins.*

1 *Thornycroft* : **Amazon** (Jan. 27th, 1926). Displacement : 1350 tons. Dimensions : $311\frac{3}{4}$ (*pp.*) $\times$ $31\frac{1}{2}$ $\times$ $9\frac{1}{4}$ feet (*mean* draught).

1 *Yarrow* : **Ambuscade** (Jan. 15th, 1926). Displacement : 1170 tons. Dimensions : 307 (*pp.*) $\times$ 31 $\times$ $8\frac{1}{4}$ feet (*mean* draught).

AMBUSCADE.

1935, *R. Perkins.*

Guns : 4—4·7 inch, **6** smaller. Tubes : **6**—21 inch in triple mounts. Machinery : Brown-Curtis turbines (all-geared type) H.P. and cruising ; Parsons L.P. Boilers : Admiralty 3-drum type, by Builders. Designed S.H.P. : 39,500 (*Amazon*), 33,000 (*Ambuscade*) = 37 kts. (made on trials). Superheated steam. Oil : *Amazon*, 433 tons ; *Ambuscade*, 385 tons. Complement : 138.

Notes.—Built under 1924–25 Estimates. All-steel bridges, higher freeboard and improved cabin accommodation are features of this and later types, which possess a larger radius of action than preceding classes. If necessary, induced ventilation can be supplied throughout the vessel, with a view to possible service in Tropics. *Ambuscade* laid down December 8th, 1924 ; *Amazon* in January, 1925. Both completed Sept., 1926. Cost : *Amazon*, £319,455 ; *Ambuscade*, £326,616.

14 Admiralty "Modified W."

WORCESTER. 7 BOATS, APPEARANCE AS ABOVE PHOTO :— Added 1939, Wright & Logan.

1 *Clydebank* : **Veteran.** 2 *Swan-Hunter* : **Whitshed, Wild Swan.**
4 *White* : **Witherington, Wivern, Wolverine, Worcester.†** (Completed by †Portsmouth D.Y.)
To distinguish.—Proportions of funnels reversed compared with other V's and W's. These boats have *thick* fore funnel
and *thin* after funnel. *No AA. guns abaft 2nd funnel.* 2 pdr. pom-poms *en echelon* between funnels. White
boats have plain S.L. tower without compass platform on fore side. *Witherington* and *Wivern*, only, have oval
after funnel, built in sideways. *Wild Swan* has tall mainmast.

WOLVERINE

WANDERER. 7 BOATS, APPEARANCE AS ABOVE PHOTO :—

WANDERER. 1937, R. Perkins.

1 *Beardmore* : **Vansittart.** 2 *Clydebank* · **Venomous** (ex *Venom*), **Verity.** 1 *Denny* : **Volunteer.**
1 *Fairfield* : **Wanderer.** 1 *Swan Hunter* : **Whitehall.** (Completed by Chatham D.Y.)
1 *Yarrow* : **Wren.** (Completed by Pembroke D.Y.)
To distinguish.—Difficult to distinguish from six tube V's. The short mainmast separates them from Admiralty W's.
Only distinctive feature is the 2—2 pdr. AA. guns abaft after funnel, *en echelon.* Only *Venomous* and *Verity* have
compass platform forward of S.L. tower. *Wren* has no caps to funnels.

General Notes for both Types.

Displacement : 1120 tons (1500 tons *full load*). Dimensions : 300 (*p.p.*), 312 (*o.a.*) × 29½ × 10¾ feet (*mean*) draught.
Guns : 4—4·7 inch (Dir. Con.), 2—2 pdr. pom-poms, 1 M.G., 4 Lewis. Tubes : 6—21 inch, in two triple mountings.
Machinery : Turbines (all-geared type)—all Brown-Curtis, but *Whitehall*, Parsons. Designed S.H.P. 27,000 =
34 kts.* 2 screws. Boilers : Yarrow, except *White* boats with White-Forster. Oil : 374-353/324-318 tons ;
Whitehall, 368/318. Complement, 134.
*Light load draught on *trials* ; on deep load 31 kts. with same S.H.P.
Notes.—Begun under War Emergency Programme, 1918, cost of completion of all comes under post-war Estimates. Differ
from preceding V's in armament.

		Begun.	Launch.	Comp.				Begun.	Launch.	Comp.
Veteran	..	30/8/18	26/4/19	13/11/19	Vansittart	..	..	1/7/18	17/4/19	5/11/19
Whitshed	..	6/18	31/1/19	11/7/19	Venomous	..	31/5/18	21/12/18	6/19
Wild Swan	..	7/18	17/5/19	14/11/19	Verity	..	17/5/18	19/3/19	17/9/19
Witherington	..	27/9/18	16/4/19	10/10/19	Volunteer	..	16/4/18	17/4/19	7/11/19
Wivern	..	19/8/18	16/4/19	23/12/19	Wanderer	..	1918	1/5/19	18/9/19
Wolverine	..	8/10/18	17/7/19	27/7/20	Whitehall	..	6/18	11/9/19	9/7/24
Worcester	..	20/12/18	24/10/19	20/9/22	Wren	..	6/18	11/11/19	2/23

2 Thornycroft "Modified W" Type.

WISHART (Rangefinder substituted for forward group of tubes). 1937, R. Perkins.

2 *Thornycroft* : **Wishart, Witch.** 1140 tons (1550 *full load*). Dimensions : 300 (*p.p.*), 312 (*o.a.*) × 30 ft.
7 in. × 10 feet. 11 ins. Guns : 4—4·7 inch (Dir. Con.), 2—2 pdr. pom-poms, 1 M.G., 4 Lewis. Torpedo
tubes : 6—21 inch (3 in *Wishart*). Machinery : Brown-Curtis turbines (all-geared type). 2 shafts. Boilers : 3
Thornycroft. Designed S.H.P. 30,000 = 35 kts. (light load draught on *trials*) and 32 kts. (deep load). Oil
fuel : 374/322 tons. Complement, 134.

General Notes.—Begun under Emergency War Programme. Differ from Admiralty "Modified W's" in dimensions.
H.P., speed and a few other details. *Witch* completed by Devonport D.Y.

To distinguish.—Big, flat-sided fore funnel, set well aft of bridges, both funnels nearly equal in height. Hull
stands high out of water. (Plans generally as for *Wolverine* in preceding column.)

		Begun.	Launch.	Comp.
Wishart	..	6/18	18/7/19	6/20
Witch	..	6/18	11/11/19	3/24

2 Thornycroft Leaders.

BROKE. 1937, R. Perkins.

2 *Thornycroft* : **Broke** (ex-*Rooke*), **Keppel.** Displacement : 1,480 tons. Dimensions : 318½ (*pp.*), 329 (*o.a.*) ×
31 ft. 9 in. × 12½ feet (*mean*), 14¾ (*max.*) draught. Guns : 5—4·7 inch B.L. (Dir. Con.), 1—3 inch AA., 2—2 pdr.
pom-pom, 1 M.G., 4 Lewis. Tubes : 6—21 inch in 2 triple deck mountings. Machinery : Brown-Curtis all geared
turbines. Designed S.H.P. : 40,000 = 36 kts. (Light load on *trials* ; on deep load, same S.H.P. = 31 kts.). 2
shafts. Boilers : Thornycroft. Oil : 550/250 tons (*Keppel*, 500/250). Complement : 183

General Notes.—Built under War Emergency Programme. Appearance almost exactly same as *Campbell* class,
but this pair have the usual big, flat-sided Thornycroft funnels. *Broke* was completed at Pembroke Dockyard,
Keppel at Portsmouth and Pembroke. No War Losses. *Cancelled* 1918 : *Saunders, Spragge, Barrington, Hughes.*
Scrapped : *Shakespeare, Spenser. Wallace*, of this type, rearmed as Escort Vessel, 1939, and will be found on a later
page.

		Begun.	Launch.	Comp.	Trials.		Cost.
Broke	..	10/18	23/4/20	13/12/24	35.6 (*mean*) 38 (*max.*)		£409,394
Keppel	..	11/18	16/9/20	15/4/25	36.1	,,	411,374

5 Campbell Class (Leaders).

CAMPBELL. 1932 *Photo, R. Perkins.*

4 *Cammell Laird:* **Campbell, Douglas, Mackay** (ex *Claverhouse*), **Malcolm.**
1 *Hawthorn Leslie:* **Montrose.**

Note.—Stuart, of this class transferred to R.A.N. *Bruce* scrapped. War loss *Scott.*

Displacement: 1530 tons. Dimensions: 320 (*p p.*), 332½ (*o.a.*) × 31¾ × 12¼ feet (*max.*), 9½ feet (*mean*) draught. Guns: **5—4·7** inch B.L. (Dir. Con.), **1—3** inch AA., **2—2** pdr. AA., **1** M.G., **4** Lewis. Tubes: **6—21** inch, in two triple mountings. Machinery: Parsons (all-geared) turbines in Cammell-Laird boats: Brown-Curtis in Hawthorn-Leslie boats. Designed S.H.P. 40,000=36·5 kts.* Boilers: Yarrow Oil fuel: 504/401 tons. Complement: 183.
*On *trials*, light load draught; on deep load, 31 kts. with same S.H.P.

9 Admiralty "W"

WARWICK. 1924 *Photo, Abraham*

1 *Clydebank:* **Watchman.***
2 *Denny:* **Walker.* Westcott.**
1 *Doxford:* **Walpole.**
1 *Fairfield:* **Wolfhound.**
2 *Hawthorn Leslie:* **Warwick.* Wessex.**
1 *Swan Hunter:* **Whirlwind.***
1 *White:* **Winchelsea.**

Note.—Vanquisher, although officially included in Admiralty "V" class in following column, is actually almost indistinguishable from Admiralty "W" type.

* Fitted as Mine Layers during War. Still have chutes at stern.

(Plans as for "6 tube V's" in following column.)

Displacement: 1100 tons. Dimensions: 300 (*p.p.*), 312 (*o.a.*) × 29½ × 10 ft. 10 ins. (*mean*), 11¼ (*max.*) draught. Guns: **4—4** inch (Mk. V. Dir. Con.), **2—2** pdr. pom-poms, **1** M.G., **4** Lewis. Torpedo tubes: **6—21** inch in two triple deck mountings. Machinery: "All-geared" turbines, Brown-Curtis in all except *Wryneck*, with Parsons. 2 shafts. Designed S.H.P.: 27,000 = 34 kts. (Light load draught on *trials;* on deep load at 1,480 tons, 31 kts. with same S.H.P.). Boilers: 3 Yarrow, except *Winchelsea* with White-Forster. Oil: *about* 368/322 tons. Complement: 134.

General Notes.—All Emergency War Programme. No War losses. *Waterhen* and *Voyager* transferred to R.A.N. *Walrus* ran ashore off Scarborough in Feb., 1938, and wreck was subsequently sold for scrapping. *Wakeful, Whitley, Wryneck, Westminster, Windsor, Wrestler, Winchester* all converted into escort vessels, 1938–39, and will be found on a later page.

To distinguish: From V's with 6 tubes: by taller mainmast.

		Begun	*Launch*	*Comp.*
Watchman	..	17/1/17	2/12/17	1/18
Walker	..	26/3/17	29/11/17	12/2/18
Westcott	..	30/3/17	14/2/18	12/4/18
Walpole	..	5/17	12/2/18	7/8/18
Wolfhound	..	4/17	14/3/18	27/4/18

		Begun.	*Launch.*	*Comp.*
Warwick	..	10/3/17	28/12/17	18/3/18
Wessex	..	23/5/17	12/3/18	11/5/18
Whirlwind	..	5/17	15/12/17	5/3/18
Winchelsea	..	24/5/17	15/12/17	15/3/18

13 Admiralty "V."

2 *Beardmore:* **Vanessa, Vanity.**
1 *Fairfield:* **Venetia.**
1 *Hawthorn Leslie:* **Verdun.**
2 *Stephen:* **Vidette, Vesper.**
1 *Yarrow:* **Vivacious.**
1 *Clydebank:* **Vanquisher.**

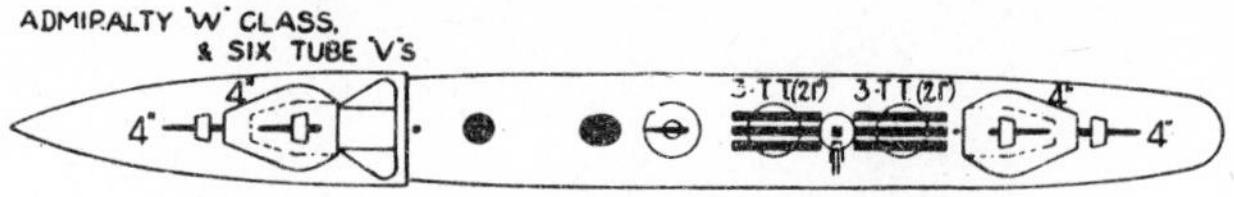

All above have 6—21 inch tubes in 2 triple deck mountings (1920 alteration).

To distinguish.—Identical now with "Admiralty W" class, but have *short* mainmasts (except *Vanquisher*, which has *high* mainmasts like "W" class, from which she is practically indistinguishable in appearance).

VANOC. 1936, *Wright & Logan.*

1 *Clydebank:* **Vanoc.**
1 *Beardmore:* **Vimy** (*ex-Vancouver*).
1 *Doxford:* **Velox.**
1 *Hawthorn Leslie:* **Versatile.**
1 *White:* **Vortigern.**

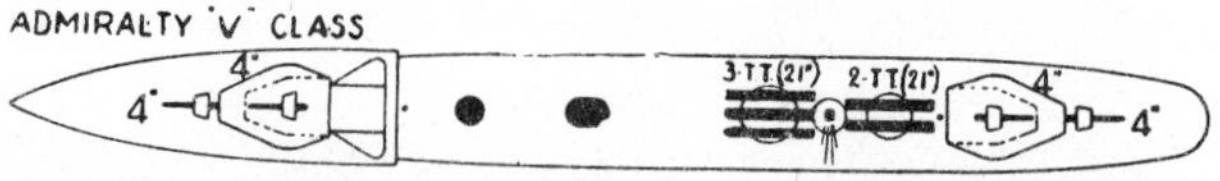

All above have *five* 21 inch tubes in one triple (forward) and one double (after) deck mountings (1920 alteration). All fitted as Mine Layers during War, some retain chutes at stern.

To distinguish.—The mixed T.T. mountings are special to these boats, and render them distinctive.

Displacements: 1090 tons (1480 tons *deep load*). Dimensions: 300 (*p.p.*), 312 (*o.a.*) × 29½ × 10 ft. 10 in. (*mean*), 11¾ (*max.*) draught. Guns: **4—4** inch (Mk. V. Dir. Con.), **1—2** pdr. pom-pom. **1** M.G., **4** Lewis. Torpedo tubes: As noted above. Machinery: "All-Geared" turbines: Brown-Curtis in all, except *Velox*, Parsons. 2 shafts. Designed S.H.P. 27,000 = 34 kts. (light load draught on *trials*) = 31 kts. (deep load draught). Boilers: 3 Yarrow in all, except *Vortigern* with White-Forster. Weight of machinery: 425 tons. Oil: 360/320 tons. Feed water: 20 tons + 7 for drinking. Complement: 134.

All Emergency War Programme.

Notes.—Minelayers: *Vimy, Velox, Versatile, Vortigern*, retain minelaying gear. *Vega, Vimiera, Vivien, Valorous, Valentine*, all converted into escort vessels.

		Begun.	*Launch.*	*Comp.*
Vimy	..	15/3/17	28/12/17	9/3/18
Vanessa	..	16/5/17	16/3/18	27/4/18
Vanity	..	28/7/17	3/5/18	21/6/18
Vanoc	..	20/9/16	14/6/17	8/17
Vanquisher	..	27/9/16	18/8/17	10/17
Velox ..	..	1/17	17/11/17	1/4/18
Venetia	..	1917	29/10/17	19/12/17

		Begun.	*Launch.*	*Comp.*
Verdun	..	13/1/17	21/8/17	3/11/17
Versatile	..	31/1/17	31/10/17	11/2/18
Vesper	..	27/12/16	15/12/17	20/2/18
Vidette	..	1/2/17	28/2/18	27/4/18
Vortigern	..	17/1/16	15/10/17	25/1/18
Vivacious	..	7/16	3/11/17	12/17
Tyne R.N.I.R.				

War Losses.—Vehement (Denny). *Verulam* (Hawthorn Leslie) and *Vittoria* (Swan Hunter) lost 1919 in Baltic operations *Valkyrie* mined during war and had to be almost entirely rebuilt at Chatham D.Y. *Valhalla* scrapped 1932; *Valkyrie, Vectis, Venturous, Violent*, 1936; *Vendetta* and *Vampire* transferred to R.A.N.

2 Thornycroft "V."

VICEROY. *Added 1935, Wright & Logan.*

2 *Thornycroft:* **Viceroy,**† **Viscount.** 1120 tons. Dimensions : 300 (*p.p.*), 312 (*o.a.*) × 30½ × 10¾ feet (*mean*) 11¾ feet (*max.*) draught. Guns : **4—4 inch** (Mk. V. DIR. CON.), **1—2 pdr. pom-pom, 1 M.G., 4 Lewis.** Tubes : **6—21 inch** in 2 triple deck mountings. Machinery : Brown-Curtis (all-geared) turbines. 2 shafts. Designed S.H.P. 30,000 = 35 kts.* Boilers : 3 Thornycroft. Oil fuel : 374/322 tons. Complement, 134.

* Light load draught on *trials* : on deep load at 1512 tons, 31 kts. with same S.H.P.

General Notes.—Emergency War Programme boats. Differ from Admiralty V design in dimensions, H.P. and speed. No War Losses.
To distinguish.—As Notes to *Wolsey* and *Woolston*, except in height of mainmast, which is *short*, in these two boats. (Plans as "6 tube V's.") † H.S. Sweeps.

| Viscount | .. | 12/16 | 29/12/17 | 3/18 | Viceroy | 12/16 | 17/11/17 | 1/18 |

1 "Admiralty R."

SKATE. (Pendant No. is now H 39). *1935, R. Perkins.*
1 *Clydebank :* **Skate.**

ADMIRALTY R CLASS
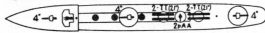

Displacement : 900 tons. Length (*p.p.*) 265 feet (*o.a.* 276 feet). Beam, 26¾ feet. *Mean* draught, 10½ feet. *Max.* draught, 15 feet. Guns : **3—4inch** (DIR. CON.), **1—2 pdr. pom-pom, 1 M.G., 4 Lewis.** Torpedo tubes : **4—21 inch** in pairs. Machinery : Brown-Curtis A.G. turbines. Designed S.H.P. 27,000 = 36 kts. 2 shafts. Boilers : 3 Modified Yarrow. Oil fuel : 301–285 tons. Complement, 98.
Note.—*Skate* has recently mounted only 2—4 inch, 2 T.T. forward, and minelaying chutes aft.

9 Admiralty "S."

THRACIAN as minelayer. (others similar). *1938, A. Hing.*

2 *Clydebank :* **Scimitar, Scout.**
3 *Hawthorn Leslie :* **Thanet, Thracian,**† **Tenedos.**
2 *Scott :* **Stronghold, Sturdy.**
2 *Stephen :* **Saladin, Sardonyx.**

.*Completed by Chatham D.Y. 1924 and †by Sheerness D.Y. 1922. Rest completed 1918-19.

Displacement : 905 tons. Dimensions : 265 (*pp.*) × 276 (*o.a.*) × 26¾ × 10⅜ feet (*mean*) draught. Guns : **3—4 inch** (Mk. IV DIR. CON. with 30° elevation), 5 smaller. Tubes : **4—21 inch** in pairs. Nearly all now fitted for minelaying. Machinery : Brown-Curtis turbines (all-geared type). Designed S.H.P. : 27,000 = 36 kts. 2 shafts. 3 Yarrow boilers. Oil : 301/254 tons. Complement : 98.

General Notes.—Emergency War Programme boats, but cost of completion of about 45 boats included in post-war Estimates. Design derived from "Admiralty Modified R" boats. Reported to be not quite so successful as the Admiralty R's. They are wet with sea on beam or bow ; they ride well in head seas, but throw spray over bridges. No War losses.

Scrappings, etc.—*Stonehenge* wrecked 1920. *Speedy* and *Tobago* lost 1922. *Saturn, Sycamore* (both Stephen) cancelled. *Stalwart, Success, Swordsman, Tattoo, Tasmania,* presented to Royal Australian Navy, 1918 and since scrapped. *Sikh* sold 1925, *Spear* 1926, *Tactician, Seabear, Simoon, Shark, Sparrowhawk, Splendid, Tilbury* sold 1930. *Trinidad, Tintagel, Seawolf, Scythe, Tara, Truant* sold 1931. *Sepoy, Sterling, Serapis, Somme* sold 1932. *Sesame, Sirdar, Stormcloud, Steadfast, Strenuous, Tribune, Seraph,* sold 1933. *Seafire, Senator, Serene,* sold 1935. *Scotsman, Shamrock, Spindrift, Turbulent, Swallow, Sportive, Trojan, Trusty, Searcher,* sold 1936–37. *Sabre* demilitarised 1936 for use as target ship, so is listed on a later page as is *Shikari,* employed as W/T control vessel for *Centurion.* Remainder of this class have been or are being fitted for service in Far East. *Saladin, Sardonyx, Stronghold, Sturdy,* all being altered as *Thracian.*

New Construction.

6 Motor Torpedo Boats are to be built under 1939 Programme; 3 more under 1938 Programme; and another has still to be ordered under that for 1936.

1 *Vosper*: **No. 103** (1939). Believed to be similar to *No.* 102 below.

1938, *courtesy Messrs. Vosper, Ltd.*

1 *Vosper*: **No. 102.** (1937). Displacement: 28 tons. Complement: 10. Dimensions: 68 × 14¾ × 3⅛ feet. Armament: 2—21 inch torpedo tubes, 2—20 mm. guns (twin mount, all-round firing positions). Machinery: 3 Isotta-Fraschini engines. B.H.P.: 3,000 = 47·8 kts. (light), 43·7 kts. fully loaded. Cost £22,529. (1937 Programme).

No. 22.

1939, *courtesy Messrs. Vosper (Builders).*

2 *Thornycroft*: **Nos. 24, 25.**
1 *Vosper*: **No. 22.**
Displacement: 32 tons. Length: 70 feet. Armament: 2—21 inch torpedo tubes, 2 M.G. AA. Machinery: 3 Isotta-Fraschini engines. B.H.P.: 3,450 = over 40 kts. (40 kts. can be maintained at ¾ throttle). 2 auxiliary cruising engines on wing shafts, which automatically turn over to main engines at 9 kts. Below that speed these engines can be used for silent approach. Are of a new design based on experience gained with *No.* 102. All laid down 1938 under programme for that year.

1 *White*: **No. 101.** (1937). Displacement: 22 tons. Dimensions: 67½ × 14½ × — feet. Armed with 21-inch torpedo tubes and guns in semi-enclosed mountings. Machinery: 3 Isotta-Franschini engines. Cost £36,700. (1936 Programme)

Torpedo Boats—*continued.*

1939, *P. A. Vicary.*

1 *British Power Boat* type : **No. 100** (ex-*M.M.S.* 51). Completed as a motor minesweeper, 1937, but since converted into a torpedo boat. No particulars furnished, but believed to be of same general design as *Nos.* 1 to 19 below. (1936 Programme).

No. 4.

1937, *R. Perkins.*

18 *British Power Boat* type : **Nos. 1** (ex-7), **2, 3, 4, 5, 6, 7** [1] (ex-13), **8, 9, 10, 11, 12, 14, 15, 16, 17, 18, 19** (ex-*No.* 1), (1936–38). Displacement : 18 tons. Complement : 7. Dimensions : $60 \times 13\frac{1}{4} \times 2\frac{3}{4}$ feet. Armament : Troughs for 2—18 inch torpedoes, and 8 Lewis guns. Machinery : 3 Napier Sealion engines. B.H.P. : 1,500 = 35 kts. Radius of action : 500 miles at 20 kts. Six of this class provided under 1935 Estimates; 3 under 1936, and 9 under 1937. Cost about £28,000 apiece.

Note.—It will be observed that there is no No. 13.

Miscellaneous Motor Vessels.

(For Motor Minesweepers, see a later page).

M.A.S.B. 1.

1939 *Fighting Ships*

5 *British Power Boat* type : M.A.S.B. **Nos. 2 to 6.** (1938–39). Built under 1938 Estimates. No particulars furnished

1 *British Power Boat* type : M.A.S.B. **No. 1.** Built under 1938 Estimates. No particulars available.

D.C.B. **No. 1.** (1937). Built by British Power Boat Co. No particulars furnished.

15 Triton class

TRIUMPH.

1939, *Wright & Logan.*

2 *Chatham Dockyard :* **Tigris, Torbay.**
6 *Vickers-Armstrongs :* **Triton, Triumph, Thistle, Triad, Truant, Tetrarch.**
4 *Cammell Laird :* **Thetis, Trident, Taku, Talisman.**
3 *Scotts :* **Tribune, Tarpon, Tuna.**

Displacement : *Triton,* 1,095/1,579 tons ; others, 1,090/1,575 tons. Complement : 53. Dimensions : 265 × 26½ × 12 feet. Guns : 1—4 inch, 2 smaller. Tubes : 10—21 inch. Speed : 15·25/9 kts.

Notes.—Officially described as " Patrol type " submarines, for general service. A return to moderate dimensions is the outstanding feature. Cost averages just under £350,000. *Thetis* foundered on trials, June 1, 1939, but is under salvage.

Est.	Name	Begun	Launch	Completed
1935	Triton	28/8/36	5/10/37	11/38
1936	Thetis	21/12/36	29/6/38	
	Tribune	3/3/37	8/12/38	39
	Trident	12/1/37	7/12/38	39
	Triumph	19/3/37	16/2/38	4/3/39
1937	Taku	18/11/37	20/5/39	
	Tarpon	5/10/37		
	Thistle	7/12/37	25/10/38	6/5/39
	Tigris	} 11/5/38		
	Triad			
	Truant	24/3/38	5/5/39	
	Tuna	13/6/38		
1938	Talisman	27/9/38		
	Tetrarch	24/8/38		
	Torbay	21/11/38		

6 Porpoise class (Minelayers.)

NARWHAL (Has recently had pendant number 05 painted on c.t.).

1936, *Wright & Logan.*

PORPOISE. (Only one of class with this type of forecastle).

1935, *R. Perkins.*

3 *Vickers-Armstrongs :* **Porpoise, Narwhal, Rorqual.**
2 *Chatham Dockyard :* **Grampus, Seal.**
1 *Scotts :* **Cachalot.**

Displacement : 1,520/2,157 tons, except *Porpoise,* 1,500/2,053 tons. Complement, 55.
Dimensions : 271½ × 25½ × 15 feet (*Porpoise,* 267 × 29⅜ × 13¾ feet) (*mean*).
Guns : 1—4 inch, 2 M.G. Tubes : 6—21 inch (bow).
Diesels of B.H.P. 3,300 = 15.75 kts. surface. (*Porpoise,* 15 kts.).
Electric motors, H.P. 1,630 = 8·75 kts. submerged.
Fuel : 136 tons.

Notes.—Very successful ships. Cost : *Grampus,* £408,112 ; *Narwhal,* £348,365 ; *Rorqual,* £350,639 ; *Cachalot,* £371,557 ; *Seal,* £430,862.

Est.	Name	Begun	Launch	Completed
1930	Porpoise	22/9/31	30/8/32	25/4/33
1933	Grampus	20 8/34	25/2/36	10/3/37
1933	Narwhal	29/5/34	29/8/35	11/3/36
1934	Rorqual	1/5/35	21/7/36	10/2/37
1935	Cachalot	12/5/36	2/12/37	15/8/38
1936	Seal	9/12/36	27/9/38	28/1/39

(Oceangoing Types.)

3 Thames class.

CLYDE.   1935, R. Perkins.

SEVERN.   1935, R. Perkins.

3 *Vickers-Armstrongs* : **Thames, Severn, Clyde.**
Displacement : 1,850/2,723 tons, except *Thames*, 1,805/2,680 tons.   Complement 60.
Dimensions : 325 × 28 × 13 feet (*Thames*, 13½ feet).   *Clyde*, 325 × 28½ × 13¾ feet
Guns : 1—4 inch, 2 M.G.   Tubes : **6**—21 inch (bow).   Electric motors, H.P. 2,500 = 10 kts. submerged.
Diesels, B.H.P. : 10,000 = 22·25 kts. on surface (*Thames*, 21·75).

Notes.—*Thames* was the first Diesel-driven submarine to exceed 21 kts., her actual designed speed. On trials she reached
22·5 kts. with designed horse power at 405 r.p.m. She subsequently made a passage from London to Venice at the
average speed of 17 kts. In 1938-39 she made a three months' cruise round Africa. Cost just over £500,000 each,
except *Clyde*, £459,886.

Est.	Name	Begun	Launch	Completed
1929	*Thames*	1/31	26/1/32	19/6/32
1931	*Severn*	27/3/33	16/1/34	2/35
1932	*Clyde*	15/5/33	15/3/34	4/35

4 Rainbow class

ROVER (Now has Pendant No. 62 on C.T.).   1935, *Wright & Logan.*
1 *Chatham Dockyard* : **Rainbow** (14 May 1930).
3 *Vickers-Armstrongs* : **Regent, Regulus, Rover** (All 11th June, 1930).

Displacement : 1475/2030 tons.   Dimensions : 260 × 28 × 13 ft. 10 in. (*mean*).   Armament : **1**—4 inch, 2 M.G.
8—21 inch tubes.   Designed H.P. 4400/1320 = 17·5/9·0 kts.   Fuel : 156 tons.   Complement, 50.

Laid down 1929 under 1928-29 Estimates. Two more boats, *Royalist* (Beardmore) and *Rupert* (Lairds) cancelled in
July, 1929.   *Regent* completed Sept. 1930 ; *Regulus*, Nov. 1930   *Rover*, Jan. 1931 ; *Rainbow*, Jan. 1932.

5 Parthian class

PERSEUS (Now has Pendant No. 06 on C.T.).   1930, *R. Perkins.*

1 *Chatham* : **Parthian** (June 22nd. 1929).
1 *Cammell Laird* : **Phœnix** (Oct. 3rd, 1929).
3 *Vickers-Armstrongs* : **Pandora** (*ex Python*) (Aug. 22nd, 1929), **Perseus** (May 22nd. 1929), **Proteus**
(July 23rd, 1929).

Displacement : 1475/2040 tons. Dimensions : 260 × 28 × 13¾ ft. (*mean*). Armament : 1—4 inch gun, 2 small 8—21 inch
tubes.   Designed H.P. $\frac{4400}{1350}$ = $\frac{17·5}{9}$ kts.   Fuel : 159 tons.   Complement, 50.

General Notes.—All laid down 1928 under 1927 Estimates. Generally resemble " O " type, with higher surface speed
and other improvements. Completed during 1930. *Poseidon* lost in collision June 9th, 1931.
Appearance Note.—Distinguishing letters are painted on c.t. of P. and R. types while serving on China Station.

6 Odin Class. (Oceangoing Types.)

OSWALD.   1930 *Photo, Cribb.*

1 *Chatham Dockyard :* **Odin** (May 5th, 1928).
2 *Beardmore :* **Olympus** (Dec. 11th, 1928), **Orpheus** (Feb. 26th, 1929).
3 *Vickers-Armstrong:* **Osiris** (May 19th, 1928). **Oswald** (June 19th, 1928), **Otus** (Aug. 31st, 1928).
Displacement : 1475/2038 tons. Dimensions : 260 (*p.p.*), 283½ (*o.a.*) × 28 × 13½ feet draught. Guns : 1—4 inch,
     2 M.G. Tubes : 8—21 inch (6 bow, 2 stern). Designed H.P. 4400/1320 = 17·5/9 kts. Oil fuel : 200 tons. Complement, 50.
Note.—Distinguishing letters are painted on C.T. of these submarines while serving on China Station.

3 Oberon Class.

Appearance Notes.—Three differing types of " O " series can be distinguished by shape of bows. *Oberon* has bow and
C.T. screen as shown in photo. *Otway* and *Oxley* are only units of this class with net cutters at bows.

OBERON.   1936, *Wright & Logan.*

1 *Chatham Dockyard :* **Oberon** (**Ex O.1.** Sept. 24th, 1926). Displacement 1311/1831 tons. Dimensions : 270 (*o.a.*)
     × 28 × 13½ feet (mean). H.P. : 2,950/1,350 = 15/9 kts. Fuel : 185 tons. Laid down March, 1924; completed,
     Dec. 31, 1926.
2 *Vickers-Armstrong;* **Oxley** (ex-*AO* 1, June 29th, 1926), **Otway** (ex-*AO* 2, Sept. 7th, 1926). Both completed in 1927.
     Otway, 1349/1872 tons, *Oxley,* 1354/1872 tons. Dimensions : 275 (*o.a.*) × 27¾ × 13½ feet (*mean*). H.P. $\frac{3000}{1350} = \frac{15·5}{9\ kts}$.
     Fuel : 195 tons.
2 latter completed in June–July, 1927, for the Royal Australian Navy and presented to the Royal Navy in 1931.
Following details are common to all 3 vessels : Complement, 54.

Guns : 1—4 inch, 2 M.G.
Tubes : 8—21 inch (6 bow and 2 stern).

OTWAY (OXLEY similar).   1935, *R. Perkins.*

3 L Class.

L 23.   1938, *Wright & Logan.*

3 *Vickers* (Completed by Dockyards) : **L 23, L 26, L 27,** (1918–19).

Admiralty saddle-tank type.

Displacement : 760/1,080 tons. Dimensions : 229 (*pp.*), 238½ (*o.a.*) × 23½ × 13¼ feet. Complement : 39. Armament:
     1—4 inch and 1 M.G., and 4—21 inch tubes. Machinery : 2 sets 12-cylinder solid injection Vickers type Diesels.
     H.P. : 2,400/1,600 = 17·5/10·5 kts. Fuel : 70 tons.

Notes.—All begun under Emergency War Programme, 1916. Equipment of these boats is extensive, e.g., refrigerating
     machinery for storage batteries, gyro compass with repeaters. 3 periscopes (one for night work), directional hydro-
     phones, &c. Breastwork revolves with gun. *L* 10 War loss. *L* 24 rammed off Portland, January, 1924. *L* 9
     foundered in a typhoon at Hong Kong, August, 1923, but was salved the following month ; since sold. Above 3
     submarines are the sole survivors of a once very numerous class. With the exception of *L* 55 in Soviet Navy.

(Seagoing Types.)

8 Shark class (Improved Swordfish design).

SUNFISH (Observe C.T.).

1937, *Wright & Logan.*

4 *Chatham Dockyard* : **Shark, Snapper, Sunfish, Sterlet.**
3 *Cammell Laird* : **Sealion, Salmon, Spearfish.**
1 *Scotts* : **Seawolf.**
Displacement : 670/960 tons. Complement : 40.
Dimensions : 193 (*pp.*), 202½ (*w.l.*) × 24 × 10½ feet (*mean*).
Guns : 1—3 inch, 1 M.G. Tubes : 6—21 inch (bow).
H.P. : 1,550/1,300 = 13·75/10 kts., except *Sunfish*, 1,900/1,300 = 15/10 kts. Fuel : 40 tons.

Notes.—Reputed to be very handy craft, capable of making a "crash-dive" in 30 seconds. Cost ranges between £230,000 and £245,000. Annual maintenance (direct expenditure only), £23,200.

Appearance Notes.—For differences, see silhouettes. *Seawolf* and later vessels have slightly lower freeboard at bow. *Sterlet* has C.T. of similar type to *Unity's*.

4 Swordfish class.

SWORDFISH, showing gun before C.T.

1937, *R. Perkins.*

4 *Chatham Dockyard* : **Swordfish, Sturgeon, Starfish, Seahorse.**
Displacement : 640/927 tons. Complement : 40.
Dimensions : 187 (*pp.*), 200¾ (*w.l.*) × 23½ × 10½ feet (*mean*).
Guns : 1—3 inch, 1 M.G. Tubes : 6—21 inch (bow).
H.P. : 1550/1300 = 13·75/10 kts.
Fuel : 44 tons.

SEAWOLF.

1936, *Wright & Logan.*

Est.	Name	Begun	Launch	Completed
1929	*Swordfish*	12/30	10/11/31	16/9/32
	Sturgeon	3/1/31	8/1/32	15/12/32
1930	*Starfish*	26/9/31	14/3/33	27/10/33
	Seahorse	14/9/31	15/11/32	26/7/33
1931	*Shark*	12/6/33	31/5/34	5/10/34
1931	*Sealion*	16/5/33	16/3/34	21/12/34
1932	*Snapper*	18/9/33	25/10/34	6/35
1932	*Salmon*	15/6/33	30/4/34	8/3/35
1933	*Seawolf*	25/8/34	28/11/35	12/3/36
1934	*Sunfish*	22/7/35	30/9/36	13/3/37
	Spearfish	23/5/35	21/4/36	9/12/36
1935	*Sterlet*	14/7/36	22/9/37	8/38

(Coastal Types.)
3 Unity Class.

UNDINE.

1938, *Wright & Logan.*

3 *Vickers-Armstrongs* : **Undine, Unity, Ursula.**
Displacement : 540/730 tons. Complement : 27. Dimensions : 180 × 16 × 12¾ feet. Armament : 6—21 inch. tubes, 1 small gun. Speed : 11·25/10 kts.

Programme	Name	Begun	Launched	Completed
1935	*Undine*	19/2/37	5/10/37	9/38
	Unity		16/2/38	11/38
	Ursula		16/2/38	22/12/38

Notes.—Built under 1936 Programme. Cost slightly over £200,000 apiece.

9 "H" Class.

H 33.

1939, *Wright & Logan.*

H 33, 34, are only ones of class with flat-topped C.T.; *H* 43, 44 have right angled instead of curved after screen to C.T.

3 *Vickers:* **H 28, H 31, H 32** (all 1918).
2 *Cammell Laird:* **H 33, H 34** (both 1918).
2 *Armstrong Whitworth:* **H 43, H 44** (both 1919).   (All used for training.)
2 *Beardmore:* **H 49, H 50** (both 1919).

Single-hull "Holland" (Electric Boat Co.) type modified by Admiralty. Displacement, 410/500 tons. Dimensions: 164½ (*p.p.*), 170 (*o.a.*) × 15¾ × 12¼ feet. Tubes: 4—21 inch bow. Machinery: 2 sets of Diesel engines, 8 cylinder, 4-cycle, air injection "H" type, developing 240 B.H.P. at 375 r.p.m., and built by Vickers, North British Diesel Co., Ruston & Hornsby, &c. Oil: 16 tons. D.H.P. 480/320 = 13/10·5 kts. 1 M.G. Complement, 22.

Notes.—All built under War Emergency Programme. Launching dates as above. First boat delivered January, 1918, and *H* 44 last, in March, 1920. *H* 29 sank in dock at Devonport, August, 1926, and disposed of in consequence. *H* 42 lost 1922.; *H* 47 sunk by collision with *L* 12, July, 1929. *H* 21, *H* 22, *H* 23, *H* 24, *H* 26, *H* 27, *H* 48, *H* 51, *H* 52 all scrapped.

Escort Vessels.

("HUNT" CLASS—20 SHIPS).

2 *Cammell Laird:* **ATHERSTONE, BERKELEY.**
4 *Yarrow:* **CATTISTOCK, CLEVELAND, COTSWOLD, COTTESMORE.**
2 *Vickers-Armstrongs* (*Tyne*): **EGLINTON, EXMOOR.**
2 *Clydebank:* **FERNIE, GARTH.**
4 *Swan Hunter:* **HAMBLEDON, HOLDERNESS, MENDIP, MEYNELL.**
2 *Scotts:* **PYTCHLEY, QUANTOCK.**
2 *White:* **QUORN, SOUTHDOWN.**
2 *Stephen:* **TYNEDALE, WHADDON.**

All laid down 1939, under Programme for that year.
Displacement: 900 tons.

Escort Vessels—*continued.*

(EX-DESTROYER TYPES—15 SHIPS)

Photo wanted.

WALLACE (Thornycroft, Oct. 26, 1918). Displacement: 1,480 tons. Dimensions: 318¼ (*pp.*), 329 (*o.a.*) × 31¾ × 12½ (*mean*), 14¾ feet (*max.*) draught. Guns: 4—4 inch H.A., 2 multi-M.G. Machinery: Brown-Curtis geared turbines. S.H.P.: = 25 kts. Boilers: Thornycroft. Oil fuel: 550 tons (*max.* stowage).

Note.—*Wallace* is attached to Mersey Division of R.N.V.R.

Photo wanted.

2 *Thornycroft:* **WOLSEY** (March 16, 1918), **WOOLSTON** (Jan. 27, 1918). Displacement: 1,120 tons. Dimensions: 300 (*pp.*), 312 (*o.a.*) × 30½ × 10¾ feet (*mean* draught). Guns: 4—4 inch H.A., 2 multi-M.G. Machinery: Brown-Curtis geared turbines. S.H.P.: = 25 kts. Boilers: 2 Thornycroft. Oil fuel: 374 tons.

WHITLEY.

1938, *Medway Studios.*

1 *Clydebank:* **WAKEFUL** (Oct. 6, 1917).
2 *Doxford:* **VEGA** (Sept. 1, 1917), **WHITLEY** (April 13, 1918).
1 *Palmer:* **WRYNECK** (May 13, 1918).
1 *White:* **WINCHESTER** (Feb. 1, 1918).
2 *Scotts:* **WESTMINSTER** (Feb. 24, 1918), **WINDSOR** (June 21, 1918).
2 *Swan Hunter:* **VIMIERA** (June 22, 1917), **WRESTLER** (Feb. 25, 1918).
1 *Denny:* **VALOROUS** (May 8, 1917).
1 *Yarrow:* **VIVIEN** (Feb. 16, 1918).
1 *Cammell Laird:* **VALENTINE** (March 24, 1917).
 Displacement: 1,090/1,100 tons. Dimensions: 300 (*pp.*), 312 (*o.a.*) × 29½ × 10¾ feet (*mean*). Guns: 4—4 inch H.A., 2 multi-M.G. Machinery: Brown-Curtis geared turbines in all except *Vega, Whitley, Vimiera, Wrestler, Valentine*, which have Parsons. S.H.P.: = 25 kts. Boilers: 2 Yarrow in all except *Winchester*, which has White-Forster. Oil fuel: 360–370 tons.

Notes.—All above vessels were originally destroyers of war design, but were rearmed as escort vessels in 1938–39.

4 Black Swan Class.

2 *Furness* : **ERNE, IBIS.** Ordered June, 1939, under that year's Estimates.

2 *Yarrow* : **BLACK SWAN** (July 7, 1939), **FLAMINGO** (April 18, 1939).

Building under 1937 Estimates.

Displacement : 1,250 tons.
Dimensions : not announced.
Guns : 8—4 inch AA., 5 smaller.
Machinery : Geared turbines (by Richardson, Westgarth & Co. in *Erne* and *Ibis*). S.H.P.: 3,600 = 19·25 kts. Boilers : 2, of 3-drum type.

Note.—Black Swan laid down June 20, 1938 ; *Flamingo*, May 26, 1938.

3 Egret Class

EGRET.

1938, *Wright & Logan.*

1 *White* : **EGRET** (May 31, 1938).
1 *Denny* : **AUCKLAND** (ex-*Heron*), (June 30, 1938).
1 *Thornycroft* : **PELICAN** (Sept. 12, 1938).

Displacement : 1,200 tons. Complement : 188.
Dimensions : 276 (*w.l.*) × 37½ × 8½ feet (*mean*).
Guns : 8—4 inch AA., 7 smaller.
Machinery : Parsons single reduction geared turbines. 2 shafts. S.H.P. : 3,600 = 19·25 kts.
Boilers : 2 Admiralty 3-drum type. Oil fuel.

Note.—Egret laid down July 21, 1937. *Auckland* in June, 1937, both under 1936 Estimates. *Pelican* in Sept., 1937, under those for 1937. First two completed in Nov., 1938, *Pelican* in April, 1939.

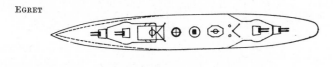

EGRET

BITTERN

3 Bittern Class.

BITTERN.

1938, *Wright & Logan.*

1 *Clydebank* : **ENCHANTRESS** (ex-*Bittern*), (Dec. 21, 1934). Displacement: 1,085 tons.
1 *White* : **BITTERN** (July 14, 1937). 1 *Denny* : **STORK** (April 21, 1936). Displacement : 1,190 tons.

Complement : 125.
Dimensions : 266 (*w.l.*) × 37 × 8½ feet (*mean*).
Guns : (*Enchantress*) 4—4·7 inch (Only 2 mounted), 4—3 pdr., 8 smaller.
(Others) 6—4 inch AA., 5 smaller.

Machinery : Brown-Curtis (*Enchantress*), and Parsons geared turbines (other two). S.H.P. : 3,300 = 18·75 kts. Boilers : 2 Admiralty 3-drum type. Oil : 270 tons.

Notes.—Enchantress laid down March 9th, 1934 ; completed April, 1935. Design allows for removal of deckhouse aft, provided for use as Admiralty yacht, in order to mount two more 4·7 inch guns when required. *Bittern* laid down in Aug., 1936 and completed March, 1938. *Stork* first completed as Surveying Vessel, but was relieved as such, and armed as Escort Vessel in 1939.
Cost of *Enchantress* was £169,175 ; of *Bittern*, £223,668 ; and of *Stork*, £159,366, exclusive of armament.
Estimates.—Enchantress, 1933 ; *Stork*, 1934 ; *Bittern*, 1935.

ENCHANTRESS.

1937, *R. Perkins.*

2 Aberdeen class

6 Grimsby class

ABERDEEN. 1936.

2 *Devonport Dockyard :* **ABERDEEN** (Jan. 22, 1936), **FLEETWOOD** (March 24, 1936).
   Displacement : 990 tons.   Complement, 100.
   Dimensions : 250 (*p.p.*), 262 (*w.l.*), 266 (*o.a.*) × 36 × 7½ feet (*mean*).
   Guns : **4**—4 inch AA., **9** smaller. (*Aberdeen*, only **2**—4 inch at present).
   Machinery : 2 sets Parsons geared turbines. S.H.P. : 2,000 = 16·5 kts.
   Boilers : 2 Admiralty 3-drum type.   Oil fuel : 280 tons.

Notes.—Built under 1934 Estimates. Are improvements on the *Grimsby* design, closely resembling Australian sloops *Yarra* and *Swan*. *Aberdeen* carries two 4 inch guns less than *Fleetwood*, in order to provide for extra accommodation required while attached to flagship of Mediterranean Fleet.

FLEETWOOD (Observe special armament). 1937, *R. Perkins.*

LOWESTOFT. 1934, *R. Perkins.*

GRIMSBY. 1938, *A. Hing.*

5 *Devonport Dockyard :* **GRIMSBY** (July 19, 1933), **LEITH** (Sept. 9, 1933), **LOWESTOFT** (April 11, 1934), **WELLINGTON** (May 29, 1934), **LONDONDERRY** (Jan. 16, 1935).
1 *Chatham Dockyard :* **DEPTFORD** (Feb. 5, 1935).
   Displacement : 990 tons.   Complement : 100.
   Dimensions : 250 (*p.p.*), 262 (*w.l.*), 266 (*o.a.*) × 34 × 7¼ (*mean*), 8¾ feet (*max*). *Deptford* and *Londonderry* are 36 × 7½ feet *mean*.
   Guns : **2**—4·7 inch, **1**—3 inch AA., **2**—3 pdr., **10** M.G. (**4**—3 pdr. in last 2 ships).
   Machinery : 2 sets Parsons geared turbines by J. S. White & Co., Ltd. S.H.P. : 2,000 = 16·5 kts. Boilers : 2 Admiralty 3-drum type. Oil fuel : 275 tons (280 in last two ships).

Notes.—Differ from earlier types in having AA. gun on superstructure forward. Built under following Estimates : 1931, *Grimsby, Leith ;* 1932, *Lowestoft, Wellington ;* 1933, *Londonderry, Deptford.* Cost from £160,000 to £175,000 each. All to be re-armed with six 4-inch guns on twin high-angle mountings, as opportunities occur.

PENZANCE.   1939, *P. A. Vicary, Cromer.*

HASTINGS as Fishery Patrol Vessel.   1937, *R. Perkins.*

FALMOUTH (With one 4 inch, as tender to China Station flagship).   1932 *Photo, R. Perkins.*

(2 BRIDGEWATER CLASS.)

2 *Hawthorn Leslie :* **BRIDGEWATER** (Sept. 14, 1928), **SANDWICH** (Sept. 28, 1928).
   Displacement : 1,045 tons.
   Dimensions : 250 (*pp.*), 266 (*o.a.*) × 34 × 8¼ feet (*mean*).

(2 HASTINGS CLASS.)

2 *Devonport :* **HASTINGS, PENZANCE** (both April 10, 1930).
   Displacement : 1,025 tons.
   Dimensions : 250 (*pp.*), 266 (*o.a.*) × 34 × 8 feet (*mean*).

(4 SHOREHAM CLASS.)

2 *Chatham :* **SHOREHAM** (Nov. 22, 1930). **ROCHESTER** (July 16, 1931).
2 *Devonport :* **FOWEY** (Nov. 4, 1930), **BIDEFORD** (April 1, 1931).
   Displacement : 1,105 tons.
   Dimensions : 250 (*pp.*), 266 (*o.a.*) × 34 × 9 feet.

(4 FALMOUTH CLASS.)

3 *Devonport :* **FALMOUTH** (April 19, 1932), **MILFORD** (June 11, 1932), **WESTON**
   (ex-*Weston-super-Mare*), (July 23, 1932).
1 *Chatham :* **DUNDEE** (Sept. 20, 1932).
   Displacement : 1,060 tons.
   Dimensions : 250 (*pp.*), 266 (*o.a.*) × 34 × 8¾ feet.

Following particulars apply to all : Guns : 2—4 inch AA., (*Hastings* and *Falmouth*, 1—4 inch),
9 to 13 smaller. *Hastings* fitted for minelaying. Machinery : Parsons impulse reaction turbines
(single reduction gearing). 2 shafts. 2 Admiralty 3-drum type boilers, pressure 250 lbs.
Designed S.H.P. : 2,000 = 16—16·5 kts. Oil : 275 tons. Designed for service abroad and
fitted for minesweeping. *Bridgewater* and *Sandwich* built under 1927 Estimates and both
completed March, 1929. Under 1928 Estimates : *Hastings, Penzance,* completed 1930–31.
Under 1929 Estimates : *Fowey, Shoreham, Bideford, Rochester,* completed 1931–32. Under
1930 Estimates : *Falmouth, Milford, Weston, Dundee,* completed 1932–33. Many of these ships
will in due course be rearmed with six 4-inch guns on twin high angle mountings.

(For 2 vessels of *Hastings* class (*Folkestone* and *Scarborough*) converted into Surveying Vessels, *vide*
   a later page.)

F

Escort Vessels—*Continued*
"FLOWER" CLASS

LUPIN.   1936, *P. A. Vicary, Cromer.*

(ARABIS TYPE.)

1 *Simons :* **LUPIN** (May, 1916).

1 *Richardson Duck :* **ROSEMARY** (Nov. 1915).

Displacement : 1,175 tons.
Complement : 98.
Dimensions : 267¾ (*o.a.*) × 33½ × 11 feet.

(ACACIA TYPE.)

1 *Barclay Curle :* **FOXGLOVE** (Mar., 1915).

Displacement : 1,165 tons.
Complement : 104.
Dimensions : 262½ (*o.a.*) × 33 × 11 feet.

Guns : *Foxglove,* 2—4 inch, **16** smaller ; Others, 1—4 inch, **12** smaller.
Machinery : 1 set Triple expansion. 1 shaft.
I.H.P. ; 2,000 = 16·5 kts. (*Foxglove,* 1,800 = 16 kts.)
Boilers : 2 cylindrical.
Coal : 130/200 tons = about 2,000 miles at 15 kts.
(*Lupin* is oil fired.)

Notes.—Others of this class are *President* (ex-*Saxifrage*) and *Chrysanthemum,* which are used as headquarters and drill-ships for London Division R.N.V.R. ; *Cornflower,* now Harbour Drillship for Hongkong R.N.V.R., and *Laburnum,* fulfilling a similar function at Singapore. *Lupin* employed as accommodation ship for boys, 1939.

Patrol Vessels.
3 GUILLEMOT CLASS.

> *Completing.*

2 *Denny :* **GUILLEMOT** (July 6, 1939), **PINTAIL** (Aug. 18, 1939).
1 *White :* **SHEARWATER** (April 18, 1939).

Displacement : 580 tons.
Guns : 1—4 inch AA.

Notes.—Laid down in August, 1938, under 1937 Estimates. Are understood to be an improvement on *Widgeon* design.

WIDGEON (Now carries Pendant No. L 62).   1938, *P. A. Vicary, Cromer.*

PUFFIN.   1936, *R. Perkins.*

1 *Fairfield :* **KINGFISHER** (Feb. 14, 1935.)
2 *Stephen :* **MALLARD** (March 26, 1936), **PUFFIN** (May 5, 1936.)
2 *Thornycroft :* **KITTIWAKE** (Nov. 30, 1936), **SHELDRAKE** (Jan. 28, 1937.)
1 *Yarrow :* **WIDGEON.** (Feb. 2, 1938).

Displacement : 510 tons (first 3), 530 tons (others).
Complement : 60.
Dimensions : 234 (*pp.*), 240 (*w.l.*), 243⅛ (*o.a.*) × 26½ × 6 feet (*mean*), except *Widgeon,* 26½ × 6½ feet.
Guns : 1—4 inch AA., 8 smaller.
Machinery : Parsons geared turbines.
S.H.P. : 3,600 = 20 kts. Boilers : 2 Admiralty 3-drum (250 lb. working pressure). Oil : 160 tons.

Note.—Are designed for coastal convoy service and are therefore of smaller steaming radius but higher speed than the larger escort vessels. In general conception they resemble "P" boats and will rely upon depth charges as their main offensive equipment. All can make their designed speed easily in service.
Kingfisher laid down June 1st, 1934 : completed June, 1935. Cost £93,288. *Mallard* and *Puffin* cost £214,379 for the pair.
Estimates.—Kingfisher, 1933 ; *Mallard* and *Puffin,* 1934 ; *Kittiwake* and *Sheldrake,* 1935 *Widgeon,* 1936

Patrol Vessels—*Continued*.

1926 *Photo, Abrahams & Sons, Devonport.*

P.C.74 (J. S. White & Co., 1918).
610 tons. Dimensions : 233 (*pp.*), 247 (*o.a.*) × 26¾ × 8 feet. Armament : **1**—4 inch, **24**—**30** D.C. Machinery : Brown-Curtis geared turbines. Boilers : White-Forster. 2 shafts. Designed S.H.P. : 3,500 = 20 kts. Oil : 164 tons *max.* Complement : 56.
General Notes.—Built under Emergency War Programme. Design converted or modified while building, to act as Submarine Decoy Vessel or "Q-boat." It was expected that, on account of shallow draught, torpedoes fired by U-boats would under-run *P.C.*-boats. To be discarded in 1939.

For another survivor of this type, see H.M.I.S. *Pathan.*

Minesweepers.

(BANGOR CLASS—20 ships).

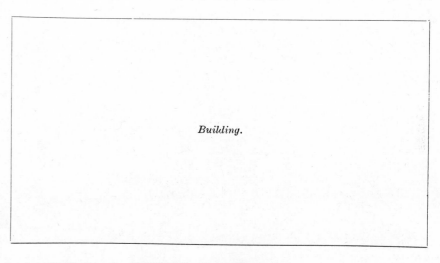

Building.

2 *Harland & Wolff (Govan)* : **BANGOR, BLACKPOOL.**

2 *Denny (machinery by Harland & Wolff)* : **BRIDLINGTON, BRIDPORT.**

2 *Blyth D.D. (machinery by White's Marine Engineering Co., Ltd.)* : **BLYTH, PETERHEAD.**

2 *Ailsa (machinery by Thornycroft)* : **POLRUAN, RYE.**

2 *Hamilton (machinery by J. S. White & Co.)* : **ROTHESAY, TENBY.**

(10 more to be ordered).

No particulars of these vessels have been released. Machinery believed to be triple expansion. Authorised under 1939 Estimates, and will ultimately replace old vessels of Improved "Hunt" Class.

Minesweepers
17 Halcyon class

Note.—For two Surveying Vessels of similar design (*Gleaner* and *Jason*), see a later page.

SHARPSHOOTER.   1938, *R. Perkins.*

HALCYON.   1934 *Photo, Wright & Logan.*

2 *Clydebank :* **HALCYON** (Dec. 20, 1933). **SKIPJACK** (Jan. 18, 1934).

2 *Thornycroft :* **HARRIER** (April 17, 1934), **HUSSAR** (Aug. 27, 1934).

4 *Hamilton :* **SPEEDWELL** (March 21, 1935), **GOSSAMER** (Oct. 5, 1937), **SPEEDY** (Nov. 23, 1938), **SPHINX** (Feb. 7, 1939).

2 *White :* **NIGER** (Jan. 29, 1936), **SALAMANDER** (March 24, 1936).

6 *Devonport Dockyard :* **HEBE** (Oct. 28, 1936), **SHARPSHOOTER** (Dec. 10, 1936), **LEDA** (June 8, 1937), **SEAGULL** (Oct. 28, 1937), **BRAMBLE** (July 12, 1938), **BRITOMART** (Aug. 23, 1938).

1 *Gray :* **HAZARD** (Feb. 26, 1937).
Displacement : 815 tons (*Hazard, Hebe, Sharpshooter,* 835 tons ; *Bramble, Britomart, Speedy, Sphinx,* 875 tons). Complement : 80.

Dimensions : 230 × 33½ × 7⅝ feet (*max.*), 6⅛ feet (*mean*), except *Gossamer, Leda, Seagull, Speedy, Sphinx, Bramble, Britomart,* 7¼ feet (*mean*).
Guns : 2—4 inch AA., 5 smaller.

Machinery : 2 sets 3-cylinder compound engines, fitted with poppet valves operated by rotary cam gear under totally enclosed forced lubrication system, in first 5 ; triple expansion in *Niger* and *Salamander;* geared turbines in others (by J. S. White & Co. in *Speedy, Sphinx*).

I.H.P. : 1,770 = 16·5 kts. (first 5) ; 2,000 = 17 kts. in *Niger and Salamander ;* 1,750 = 17 kts. in others. Boilers : 2 Admiralty 3-drum type. Oil fuel : 220 tons.

Notes.—Most of this class are named after minesweepers of 1914. Outstanding feature of earlier units is the novel machinery design. *Halcyon, Skipjack,* built under 1931 Estimates : *Harrier, Hussar,* under 1932 : *Speedwell,* 1933 : *Salamander, Niger,* 1934 : *Hazard, Hebe, Sharpshooter* 1935 : *Gossamer, Leda, Seagull,* 1936 ; *Bramble, Britomart, Speedy, Sphinx,* 1937. Cost averages over £100,000 each. *Seagull* was first rivetless ship built for the Royal Navy construction being entirely welded.

Minesweepers—continued.

SELKIRK. 1939, *R. Perkins.*

(IMPROVED "HUNT" CLASS—23 Ships.)

4 *Ailsa S.B. Co.:* **ABERDARE, ABINGDON, ALBURY, ALRESFORD.**
1 *Ardrossan Co.:* **BAGSHOT.**
3 *Clyde S.B. Co.:* **DERBY, DUNDALK, DUNOON.**
1 *Dunlop Bremner:* **FAREHAM.**
1 *Dundee S.B. Co.:* **FERMOY.**
2 *Eltringhams:* **HARROW, HUNTLY.**
1 *Fairfield:* **LYDD.**
2 *Lobnitz:* **PANGBOURNE, ROSS.**
3 *Murdoch & Murray:* **SALTASH, SALTBURN, SELKIRK.**
1 *Chas. Rennoldson:* **STOKE.**
1 *McMillan:* **SUTTON.**
2 *Simons:* **ELGIN, TEDWORTH.**
1 *Napier & Miller:* **WIDNES.**

All built under Emergency War Programme and launched between June, 1917 and Aug., 1919. Displacement, 710 tons; *except Tedworth,* 675 tons. Dimensions: 220 (*p.p.*), 231 (*o.a.*) × 28⅜ *Tedworth* 28 × 7½ ft. (*mean* draught). Machinery: Vertical triple expansion. 2 shafts. Yarrow boilers. Designed I.H.P. 2200 = 16 kts.; *except Tedworth,* 1800 = 16 kts. Coal: 185 tons = *about* 1500 miles at full speed (*Tedworth,* only 140 tons). Complement of all, 73. Guns: 1—4 inch, 1 smaller. *Tedworth,* none recently.

Notes.—All are stationed at Malta and Singapore, except *Selkirk* (in reserve), *Tedworth,* tender to Gunnery and Diving Schools, Portsmouth, and *Alresford* and *Saltburn,* tenders to Navigation School. There are various minor variations in these ships, *e.g.,* many have had deck houses built aft, &c. *Petersfield* lost 1932, *Marazion* scrapped 1933. *Forres, Caterham* and *Carstairs* scrapped 1934–35, *Tiverton* 1938. *Dunoon, Elgin* and *Lydd* on Disposal List, 1936, but decision reconsidered and ships refitted.

2 Motor Minesweepers.

M.M.S. 1. 1939, *Charles E. Brown.*

2 *Thornycroft:* **M.M.S. 1** and **2** (1937). Built at Hampton-on Thames. Wood.

Displacement: 52 tons. Dimensions: 75 × 14⅓ × 5 feet (*max.*). Complement: 11. Machinery: 3 Thornycroft Y. 12-cylinder petrol engines. 3 shafts. H.P.: 1,500 = 15 kts. (reduced to 10 kts. when sweeping). Radius: 18 hours at full speed.

Note.—Propellers are driven through S.L.M. oil-operated 2:1 reverse-reduction gears of the Modern Wheel Drive type.

River Gunboats.

A River Gunboat is building under 1939 Estimates by J. Samuel White & Co., Ltd.

DRAGONFLY 1939, *Courtesy of Messrs Thornycroft (Builders)*

DRAGONFLY (Dec. 8, 1938), **GRASSHOPPER** (Jan. 19, 1939), **LOCUST, MOSQUITO** (both building). Displacement: 585 tons. Complement: 74. Guns: 4 inch. Building under 1937 and 1938 Estimates, first pair by John I. Thornycroft & Co., Ltd., second pair by Yarrow & Co., Ltd.

1938, *Charles E. Brown.*

SCORPION (J. S. White & Co., Ltd., Dec. 20, 1937). Built under 1936 Estimates. Displacement: 700 tons. Complement: 93. Dimensions: 200 (*pp.*), 208¾ (*o.a.*) × 34⅔ × 5⅛ feet. Guns: 2—4 inch, 1—3·7 inch howitzer, 2—3 pdr., 10 smaller. Machinery: Parsons geared turbines. S.H.P.: 4,500 = 17 kts. Fitted for service as Flagship on Yangtse.

River Gunboats—continued.

1938, A. Hing.

ROBIN (March 7, 1934). Built by Yarrow. Displacement : 226 tons. Complement : 42. Dimensions : 150 × 26⅔ × 3 feet (*mean*). Guns : 1—3·7 inch Howitzer, 9 smaller. Machinery : 2 sets reciprocating. 1 Admiralty 3-drum type boiler. H.P. : 800 = 12·75 kts. Oil fuel : 41 tons.

SANDPIPER. (Now has mainmast). 1933 *Photo, courtesy of builders.*

SANDPIPER (June 9, 1933). Built by Thornycroft. Displacement : 185 tons. Complement : 40. Dimensions : 160 × 30⅔ × 2 feet (*mean*). Guns : 1—3·7 inch Howitzer, 9 smaller. Machinery : 2 sets Reciprocating, 2 shafts, 1 Admiralty 3-drum type boiler. H.P. : 600 = 11¼ kts.

River Gunboats—continued.

FALCON. 1931 *Photo, favour of Messrs. Yarrow.*

FALCON (1931) built by Messrs. Yarrow & Co., Ltd. Displacement : 372 tons. Complement : 55. Dimensions : 150 × 28⅔ × 5 feet (*mean*). Guns : 1—3·7 inch Howitzer, 2—6 pdr., 10 M.G. Machinery : Parsons geared turbines. Boilers, 2 Admiralty 3-drum type. S.H.P. : 2,250 = 15 kts. Fuel : 84 tons oil.

CICALA. 1938, A. Hing.

APHIS (1915), by Ailsa Co. **CICALA** (1915), **COCKCHAFER** (1915), **CRICKET** (1915), all by Barclay Curle. **GNAT** (1915), **LADYBIRD** (1915), both by Lobnitz. **MANTIS** (1915), **MOTH** (1915), both by Sunderland S.B. Co. **SCARAB** (1915), **TARANTULA** (1915), both by Wood, Skinner and Co. Displacement : 625 tons. Complement : 54–65. Dimensions : 237½ (*o.a.*) × 36 × 4 feet. Guns : 2—6 inch (*Tarantula,* 1—6 inch), 1—3 inch AA., 10 smaller. Machinery : Triple expansion. Twin screws in tunnels fitted with Yarrow's patent balanced flap. Boilers : Yarrow. Designed H.P. : 2,000 = 14 kts. Fuel : 35 tons coal, 54 tons oil. (*Moth,* 76 tons oil only).

Note.—Messrs. Yarrow & Co., Ltd., were solely responsible for the design of these vessels, which were built under their supervision during the War.

Cricket and *Mantis* to be discarded shortly.

River Gunboats—continued.

GANNET (1927) & **PETEREL** (1927), both designed and built by Messrs. Yarrow & Co., Ltd. Displacement, 310 tons. Dimensions : 177 (*w.l.*), 184⅔ (*o.a.*) × 29 × 3 ft. 2½ ins. draught. Guns : 2—3 inch AA., 8 M.G. Machinery : Geared turbines. Boilers : Yarrow. Designed H.P. 2250 = 16 kts. Fuel : 60 tons oil. Complement, 55.

TERN. *Added 1937, courtesy Arthur Sye, late R.N.*

SEAMEW (1927), **TERN** (1927), both designed and built by Messrs. Yarrow & Co., Ltd. Displacement, 262 tons. Dimensions : 160 (*w.l.*), 167½ (*o.a.*) × 27 × 5⅙ feet *max.* draught. Guns : 2—3 inch AA., 8 M.G. Armoured bridge and shields to guns. Machinery : Geared turbines. Boilers : Yarrow. Designed H.P. : 1,370 = 14 kts. Fuel : 50 tons oil. Complement : 55.

SCARAB. (GNAT identical.) *Photo added 1925.*
(TARANTULA has topmast *before* top.)

1937, *R. Perkins.*

1937, *Vicary, Cromer.*

PROTECTOR (Aug. 20, 1936). Laid down by Messrs. Yarrow & Co., Ltd., August 15, 1935, under 1934 Estimates. Completed end 1936. Displacement : 2,900 tons. Complement : 190. Dimensions : 310 (*pp.*), 338 (*o.a.*) × 50 × 11½ feet (*mean*). Guns : **1**—4 inch. Machinery : Parsons geared turbines. S.H.P. : 9,000 = 20 kts. Boilers : 2 Admiralty 3-drum type. Oil fuel : 690 tons. Cost : £326,230.

1939, *P. A. Vicary, Cromer.*

GUARDIAN (Chatham Dockyard, Sept. 1, 1932).

Displacement : 2,860 tons.   Complement : 181.
Dimensions : 310 × 53 × 12¼ feet (*max.*), 11⅙ feet (*mean*).
Guns : **2**—4 inch AA.
Machinery : Parsons geared turbines by Wallsend Co.
Boilers : 2 Admiralty 3-drum type.   H.P. : 6,500 = 18 kts.
Oil Fuel : 720 tons.

General Notes.—Designed for Net-laying and Fleet Photography work. The nets, sinkers and buoys are stowed to port and starboard, on the upper deck from just forward of the main-mast under the forecastle deck to the stern. The structure aft, placed on the deck spanning the nets, is the photographic cabin.

This ship is very beamy in relation to her length, the proportion being 1:6 only. She is intended for instructional purposes and the laying of special barrages to protect the fleet she accompanies. These are intended to be retrieved —a laborious job—and re-laid as requisite.

Laid down October 15, 1931 ; completed June 13, 1933.

1938, *R. Perkins.*

Cadets' Training Ship.

1937, *Wright & Logan.*

1933 *Photo, Cribb.*

IRON DUKE (ex-battleship), (Portsmouth, Oct. 12, 1912). Demilitarised under London Treaty, 1931–32, when B and Y turrets, conning tower, belt armour, and t.t. were removed, and boiler power reduced. Employed as Gunnery T.S. Present displacement (standard), 21,250 tons. Dimensions : 580 (*pp.*) × 90 × 26 feet. Guns : retained : **6—13·5 inch, 12—6 inch**, others being mounted temporarily in addition for trial purposes. Speed : 18 kts. Oil fuel only. Complement : 589 (exclusive of boys under training).

Target Service Ships. (*See also under Tugs, on a later page*).

1937, *Wright & Logan.*

Added 1938, *Wright & Logan.*

VINDICTIVE (ex-*Cavendish*) (Harland & Wolff, Jan. 17, 1918). Displacement : 9,100 tons Complement : 468 + 200 cadets. Dimensions : 565 (*pp.*), 605 (*o.a.*) × 58 × 20½ feet (*max.*). Armament reduced during reconstruction to convert ship from a cruiser to a training ship. Guns : 2—4·7 inch, 4—3 pdr., 1—2 pdr. pompom. Armour : 3″—1½″ side, 1″ deck, 3″ C.T. Machinery : Parsons geared turbines. 4 shafts. Boilers : 6 Yarrow (only 4 in use). S.H.P. : 25,000 = 23 kts.

Notes.—Built under Emergency War Programme as a cruiser of improved *Birmingham* class, completed as an aircraft carrier and renamed *Vindictive*, 1918. Converted into a cruiser again, 1923–25. Reconstructed as Cadets' training ship, 1936–37, at a cost of £280,000. Normal Complement of cadets is 200.

CENTURION (ex-battleship). (Devonport, Nov. 18, 1911). Standard Displacement : 25,500 tons. Dimensions : 555 (*p.p.*) × 89 × 30 feet. Speed (with oil fuel) : 16 kts. Complement : 250. Employed as wireless controlled target, for attack by guns up to 8-inch calibre. Is fitted with special relay equipment operated by wireless impulses from an attendant destroyer equipped with special plant. Signals of varying strength control different parts of the *Centurion's* mechanism. The helm can be moved over, the speed regulated and oil fuel fed to the boilers as requisite.

SHIKARI (Doxford, 1918), **SABRE** (Stephen, 1918). Demilitarised destroyers. Displacement : 905 tons. Dimensions : 265 (*pp.*), 276 (*o.a.*) × 26¾ × 10½ feet. Speed (originally), 36 kts. *Shikari* fitted with special W/T gear for control of *Centurion* ; *Sabre* employed as Torpedo Bomber Target.

 EREBUS.

1939, courtesy Messrs. Thornycroft.

EREBUS (19th June, 1916), TERROR (18th May, 1916).

Displacement, 7200 tons.   Complement, 315

Length, (p.p.) 380, (o.a.) 405 feet.   Beam, 88 feet.   Mean Draught, 11 feet.

Guns :
2—15 inch, 42 cal.*
8—4 inch in Terror.
2—3 inch (anti-aircraft)
10 smaller.
(12 in Erebus)
* H.A. elevation.

Armour :
4″ Bulkheads, F. & A.
8″ Barbette ....
13″—4¼″ Gunhouse ....

4″ Box citadel (over magazines) ......
6″ C.T. ....
1″ Fo'cle & upper decks
4″ Main deck (slopes)
2″ Main deck ....
1½″—¾″ Lower deck ..
Anti-torpedo pro.
bulges.

Machinery : Triple expansion. 2 shafts. Boilers : Babcock. Designed H.P. 6000 = 12 kts.
Fuel : 650 tons normal, 750 tons, maximum, oil only.

Gunnery Notes.—15 inch are high angle and can range up to 40,000 yards. Smoke screen apparatus fitted. Erebus has 15 inch removed from M. Ney.

Special Protection.—Bulges about 15 feet deep, sub-divided into 50 w.t.c.

Name	Builder and Machinery	Begun	Completed	Trials
Erebus	Harland & Wolff (Govan)	Oct., 1915	Sept., 1916	7244 H.P. = 14·1 kts.
Terror	Harland & Wolff (Belfast)	Oct., 1915	Aug., 1916	6235 H.P. = 13·1 kts.

General Notes.—Both Emergency War Programme. Erebus has a bow rudder fitted under forefoot. Terror is Base Ship at Singapore.

MARSHAL SOULT.

1923 Photo, Abrahams, Devonport.

MARSHAL SOULT (17th June, 1915).

Displacement, 6400 tons.   Complement, 280.

Length, 340 (p.p.), 355⅔ (o.a.) feet.   Beam, 90¼ feet.   Draught, 10½ feet.

Guns : 2—15 inch (DIR. CON.), H. A. elevation. Armour : 8″ Barbette, 13″—4¼″ Gunhouse ; 4″ Bulkheads fore and aft, 6″ C.T., 4″—1″ Box Citadel over Magazine, 1″ Fo'cle Deck, 2″—1½″ Upper Deck, Lower Deck 3″ at bow, 1½″ at stern, 1″ Navig. Position. Deep bulge Protection.

Machinery : 2 sets Diesel. 4 shafts. Designed H.P. 1500 = 6·7 kts. Fuel : 235 tons, maximum oil only.

Name	Builder	Machinery	Begun	Completed	Trials
M. Soult	Palmer	Vickers	Jan., 1915	Nov., 1915	1898 H.P. = 6·6 kts.

General Notes.—Emergency War Programme. Serves as Gunnery Training Ship at the Nore. Sister Ship M. Ney now Hulk Drake, at Devonport.

TERROR.

1934, Grand Studio, Malta.

1938, R. Perkins.

ALBATROSS (Feb. 21st, 1928).

Standard Displacement : **4,800** tons. Complement : **450**. Length : (*pp.*) **422** ft., (*o.a.*) **443¾** ft. Beam : **58** feet (**60⅝** feet *extreme*). Draught : **13¾** feet (*mean*), **16¼** feet (*max.*). Guns : **4**— 4·7 inch AA., **32** smaller. Accommodation for **9** seaplanes. (At present **6** Seagull S/R Amphibians are carried.) **1** Catapult. Machinery : Parsons geared turbines. **2** screws. Designed H.P. : **12,000** = **21** kts. Boilers : **4** Yarrow. Oil fuel : **997** tons.

General Notes.—Laid down at Cockatoo Yard, Sydney, in April, 1926, and completed at end of 1928. Cost £1,200,0 complete with armament and equipment. Trials, Dec., 1928, gave 22·5 kts. *maximum* with 12,910 H.P. Transferred to Royal Navy from Royal Australian Navy in 1938.

Building.

UNICORN. Fleet Air Arm Supply and Repair Ship. Laid down 1939 by Harland & Wolff under 1938 Estimates.

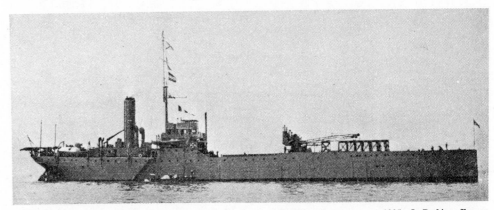

(Hein mat gear aft.)   1935, *J. Perkins, Esq.*

PEGASUS (ex-*Ark Royal*) (Blyth S.B. Co., 1914, purchased during construction 1914). **6,900** tons. Dimensions : **353½** (*p.p.*), **366** (*o.a.*) × **50⅚** × **17½** feet (*mean*). Guns : **10** M.G. and Lewis. I.H.P. : **3,000** = **11** kts. Machinery : Vertical triple expansion. **1** screw. Boilers : Cylindrical. Oil : **500** tons. Complement : **139**. Originally employed as a Seaplane Carrier. Now used in experimental work with aircraft landing rafts and catapults.

1938, R. Perkins.

ARGUS (2nd Dec., 1917). Late Liner.

" Queen Bee " Tender for training purposes.

Displacement, **14,000** tons. Complement, **373**.
Length, (*p.p.*) **535** feet (*w.l.*) **560** feet (*o.a.*) **565** feet.
Beam, **68** feet (excluding bulges).
Draught, **21** feet, *mean*.
Guns : **18** M.G. and Lewis.

Machinery (by builders) : Parsons turbines. **4** shafts. Designed S.H.P. **20,000** = **20** kts. Boilers : **12** cylindrical (**6** D.E. and **6** S.E.), with Howdens forced draught. Fuel : **2,000** tons oil.

General Notes.—Begun 1914, by Beardmore, for Italian Lloyd Sabaudo Line, as S.S. *Conte Rosso*. All work on her ceased in 1914. She was purchased in 1916 and converted to Aircraft Carrier. Completed September, 1918, at a cost of £1,307,615. Refitted 1925-26, and bulges added, extending from just forward of bridge to below exhaust fans aft. Again refitted in 1937 as a " Queen Bee " tender, and general anti-aircraft target service ship, flight deck being levelled at fore end and widened by 5 feet, tapering to a point forward. Accelerators have been fitted for throwing off target planes, of which 8 are carried.

A new Depot ship for Motor Torpedo Boats is to be built under 1939 estimates.

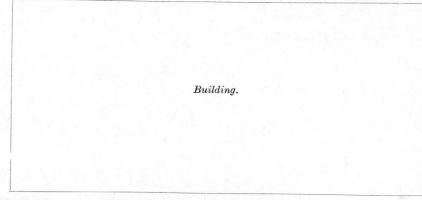

Building.

TYNE. Building by Scotts' S.B. & E. Co., Ltd., under 1937 Estimates. Displacement : 11,000 tons. Guns : – —4·5 inch. (Destroyer Depot Ship.)

Building.

ADAMANT. Building by Harland & Wolff, Ltd., Belfast, under 1938 Estimates. (Submarine Depot Ship).

MAIDSTONE

1938, *Wright & Logan.*

MAIDSTONE (Cct. 21, 1937), **FORTH** (Aug. 11, 1938). Both built at Clydebank. Displacement : 8,900 tons. Complement : 502 (including 64 repair staff and 43 as spare submarine crew). Dimensions : 497 (*pp.*), 531 (*w.l.*), 574 feet (*o.a.*) × 75 × 20 feet (*mean*). Guns : 8—4·5 inch, 2 multiple pompoms, 4—3 pdr., 4 smaller. Machinery : Brown-Curtis geared turbines. S.HP. : 7,000 = 17 kts. (Depot Ships for Submarines.)

Notes.—Maidstone ordered Aug. 17, 1936, under 1935 estimates and completed May 5, 1938 ; *Forth* laid down June 30, 1937 under estimates for that year, and completed May 14, 1939. Armament is notable, being the heaviest yet mounted in a British depot ship. Equipment includes a foundry ; coppersmiths', plumbers' and carpenters' shops ; heavy and light machine shops ; electrical and torpedo repair shops ; and plant for charging submarine batteries.

Building.

HECLA. Building by John Brown & Co., Ltd., Clydebank, under 1938 Estimates. (Destroyer Depot Ship).

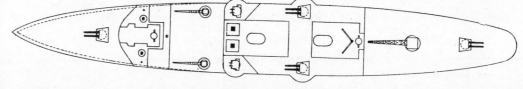

1935, *Wright & Logan.*

WOOLWICH (Fairfield, Sept. 20, 1934). Displacement : 8,750 tons. Complement : 350. Dimensions : 575 × 64 × 14⅗ feet (*mean* draught). Guns : **4**—4 inch AA., **10** smaller. Machinery : 2 sets single reduction geared turbines. 2 shafts. S.H.P. : 6,500 = 15 kts. Boilers : 4 Admiralty 3-drum type. Oil fuel : 1,170 tons. Authorised under 1932 Estimates. Laid down May 24, 1933, and completed June, 1935. Carries a full equipment of machine tools of the latest type, with a total motor H.P. exceeding 2,000. (Depot ship for Destroyers.)

1934 Photo, *Wright & Logan.*

RESOURCE (Vickers, Nov. 27, 1928). (Fleet Repair Ship).

Displacement : 12,300 tons. Complement : 450.
Dimensions : 500 (*p.p.*) × 83 × 22½ feet (*max.*).
Guns : **4**—4 inch AA., **4** smaller.
2 sets Parsons single reduction geared Turbines. H.P. : 7,500 = 15 kts.
4 Admiralty type 3-drum boilers, 235 lbs. pressure. Oil : 1,100 + 350 tons for other vessels.

1937, *Lieut. R. L. Jordan, R.N.*

MEDWAY. (Vickers, July 19, 1928). Laid down April, 1927, under 1926–27 Estimates, and completed in Sept., 1929. Displacement : 14,650 tons. Complement : 400. Dimensions: 545 (*p.p.*), 580 (*o.a.*) × 85 × 22$\frac{1}{12}$ feet (*max.*). Guns : **2**—4 inch, **4**—4 inch AA., **12** smaller. Has 2-shaft double-acting 2 stroke M.A.N. Diesel engines, total H.P. : 8,000 = 16 kts. Oil: 530 tons own fuel + 1,900 tons for submarines. Equipment includes a Foundry, Machine shop, Plate shop, Smithy, Torpedo shop, Plumber's shop, etc. Designed to mother 18 submarines.

1931 *Photo, Kestin Weymouth.*

TITANIA (Clyde S.B. Co., 1915, purchased 1915). 5,250 tons. Dimensions: 335 (*pp.*) × 46¼ × 18 feet 5 inches. I.H.P.: 3,200 = 14·5 kts. Coal: 498 tons. Complement: 249. Cyl boilers.

(Submarines.)

1937, R. Perkins.

LUCIA (Furness Withy & Co., 1907, ex German Prize, *Sprcewald*,* converted by Clyde S.B. Co., 1916). 5,800 tons. Dimensions: 367½ (*o.a.*) × 45 feet 2¼ ins. × 18⅝ feet. Guns: 2—3 pdr. AA. I.H.P. 2750 = 12·7 kts. Coal: 615 tons. Cyl. boilers. Complement, 262.

*Hamburg-Amerika Liner, captured by H.M.S. *Berwick*, September, 1914.

(Submarines.)

1935, R. Perkins.

CYCLOPS (ex-*Indrabarah*, Sir Jas. Laing & Co., 1905). 11,300 tons. Dimensions: 460 (*p.p.*), 477 (*o.a.*) × 55 × 21 ft. 2 in. Guns: 2—4 inch (mounted in bows). Machinery: Triple expansion. Designed H.P. 3500 = 13 kts. Coal capacity: 1595 tons. Complement, 266.

(Submarines.)

Note.—Depot Ship *Cochrane* (ex-*Ambrose*) is no longer in seagoing condition and has been deleted.

1921 *Photo, Gieves, Ltd.*

ALECTO (Laird, 1911). 935 tons. Dimensions: 190 (*p.p.*), 212 (*o.a.*) × 32½ × 11 ft. 1 in. (*mean*). Guns: none. Designed H.P. 1400 = 14 kts. Coal: 180 tons. Complement, 76.

(Submarines.)

Added 1935.

GREENWICH (Dobson & Co., completed by Swan Hunter. Purchased 1915). 8100 tons. Dimensions: 390 (*p.p.*), 402 (*o.a.*) × 52 × 19⅞ feet (*max.* draught). Guns: 4—4 inch, 1—3 inch AA. I.H.P. 2500 = 11 kts. Coal: 960 tons. Complement, 244. Cyl. boilers.

(Destroyers.)

Surveying Vessels

FRANKLIN (*Scott* similar)   1938, P. A. Vicary, Cromer.

(*For description of this ship, see following page*).

JASON. (GLEANER similar)
1938, *Wright & Logan.*

GLEANER (Wm. Gray & Co., June 10, 1937), **FRANKLIN** (Dec. 22, 1937), **JASON** (Oct. 6, 1937), (both by Ailsa Shipbuilding Co.), **SCOTT** (Caledon Shipbuilding & Engineering Co., Ltd., Aug. 23, 1938). Displacement : 830 tons. Complement : 80. Dimensions : 230 × 33½ × 7 feet (*mean*), 7¼ feet (*max.*). No guns. Machinery : Parsons geared turbines (by Thornycroft in *Franklin* and *Jason*, by Parsons in *Scott*). H.P. : 1,750 = 17 kts. Boilers : 2 Admiralty 3-drum type.

Note.—These vessels are of same type as later minesweepers of *Halcyon* class, modified for surveying purposes. *Gleaner* built under 1935 Estimates, *Franklin* and *Jason* under 1936, *Scott*, 1937. *Jason* and *Gleaner* are adapted for rapid conversion into Minesweepers when needed.

SCARBOROUGH.
1939, *R. Perkins.*

FOLKESTONE (Feb. 12, 1930), **SCARBOROUGH** (March 14, 1930). Both built by Swan Hunter Displacement : 1,045 tons. Dimensions : 250 (*pp.*), 266 (o.a.) × 34 × 9 feet. No guns. Machinery : Parsons geared turbines. 2 shafts. S.H.P. : 2,000 = 16 kts. 2 Admiralty 3-drum type boilers. Oil fuel : 275 tons. Built under 1928 Estimates as Escort Vessels, but now adapted for Surveying duties.

1932 *Photo, Wright & Logan.*

CHALLENGER (Chatham, June 1, 1931), built for research work by Fisheries Board, but taken over by Admiralty and employed on Surveying duties. Constructed at Chatham D.Y. Displacement : 1,140 tons, (*normal*, 1,250 tons). Complement : 84. Dimensions : 220 (o.a.), 200 (*pp.*) × 36 × 12½ feet (*mean*), 14¼ feet (*max.*). Triple expansion engines, oil fired. H.P. : 1,200 = 12½ kts. 1 shaft. Oil fuel : 340 tons. Has the exceptional radius of 9,000 miles.

KELLETT (*Fitzroy* has taller foremast.)
1924 *Photo.*

FITZROY (ex-*Pinner*, ex-*Portreath*), (1919), by Lobnitz & Co. **KELLETT** (ex-*Uppingham*), (1919), by Simons & Co. Converted Twin Screw Minesweepers of improved "Hunt Class." 800 tons. Dimensions : 231 (o.a.) × 28 ft. 7¼ in. × 7½ feet. Guns : 1—3 pdr. Machinery : Vertical triple expansion. 2 screws. I.H.P. : 2,200 = 16 kts. Boilers : Babcock or Yarrow. Coal : 185 tons. Complement : 87.

1924 *Photo, Abrahams, Devonport.*

ENDEAVOUR (Fairfield, 1912). 1280 tons. Dimensions : 241¼ (o.a.) × 34 ft. 2 in. × 11⅔ feet. Guns : 1—3 pdr., 1 M.G. H.P. 1100 = 13 kts. Coal : 220 tons. Complement, 139. Specially built for Hydrographic Duties.

1924 *Photo, Abrahams, Devonport.*

HERALD (ex *Merry Hampton*, 1918), built by Blyth S.B. Co. Converted Minesweeper of "24" (Racehorse) class. 1,320 tons. Dimensions : 276½ × 35 × 12 feet. Guns : 1—3 pdr. I.H.P. : 2,500 = 17 kts. Coal : 260 tons. Cylindrical Boilers. Complement, 132.

Note.—Was converted by Devonport D.Y., 1922–23. Sister ship *Moresby* transferred to R. Australian Navy, 1925. Will be relegated to harbour service on relief.

Building

2 *Ardrossan Dockyard :* **ACACIA, ALMOND.**
2 *Cochrane :* **ASH, BAY.**
2 *Cook, Welton & Gemmell :* **BIRCH, BLACKTHORN.**
2 *Goole S.B. & R. Co. :* **CHESTNUT, DEODAR.**
2 *A. & J. Inglis :* **ELM, FIR.**
2 *Henry Robb :* **HAZEL, HICKORY.**
2 *Ferguson Bros. :* **JUNIPER, MANGROVE.**
2 *Hall, Russell & Co. :* **OLIVE, PINE.**
4 *Smith's Dock Co. :* **ROWAN, WALNUT, WHITETHORN, WISTARIA.**

All ordered in July, 1939, under Estimates for that year. No particulars published, but will doubtless be of same general type as *Lilac* and *Alder* groups, below. Triple expansion engines.

Machinery supplied as follows : First pair, Plenty & Son ; second and fourth pairs, Amos & Smith ; third pair, C. D. Holmes & Co. ; fifth pair, Aitchison & Blair, Ltd. ; sixth pair, White's Marine Engineering Co. Remaining eight by builders.

BASSET (Now has foretopmast).   1937, *R. Perkins.*
MASTIFF similar, but slightly longer forecastle.

MASTIFF (Feb. 17, 1938). Laid down Jan. 27, 1937 by Messrs. Henry Robb, Ltd., under 1936 Estimates. Displacement : 520 tons. Dimensions : 150 (*pp.*), 163½ (*o.a.*) × 27⅙ × 8½ feet. Guns : **1—4** inch, 2 smaller. H.P. : 950 = 13 kts.

BASSET. (Henry Robb, Ltd., Leith, Sept. 28, 1935). Displacement : 461 tons (full load, 696 tons). Complement, 15. Dimensions : 150 (*pp.*), 160½ (*o.a.*) × 27½ × 10½ feet. Guns : **1—4** inch. Reciprocating engines and cylindrical boiler. I.H.P. : 850 = 12 kts. Fuel : 180 tons coal. Used for Anti-Submarine Training.

67 Trawlers were purchased under 1939 Supplementary Estimates. New names have not been announced, but former names and brief particulars of most of them are given below :

Arctic Ranger (501 tons gross ; built 1937), *Arsenal* (398, 1933), *Bandolero* (440, 1935), *Barnett,* (482, 1937), *Bedfordshire* (443, 1935), *Bengali* (455, 1937), *Brontes* (424, 1934), *Cambridgeshire* (443, 1935), *Canadian Prince* (455, 1937), *Cape Argona* (494, 1936), *Cape Chelyuskin* (494, 1936), *Cape Comorin* (504, 1936), *Cayton Wyke* (373, 1932), *Compton* (516, 1937), *Daneman* (516, 1937), *Davy* (449, 1936), *Derby County* (399, 1933), *Drangey* (434, 1935), *Hampshire* (425, 1934), *Huddersfield Town* (399, 1933), *Istria* (409, 1933), *Kelt* (455, 1937), *Kingston Alalite* (412, 1933), *Kingston Andalusite* (415, 1934), *Kingston Chrysolite* (448, 1935), *Kingston Cornelian* (449, 1934), *Kingston Galena* (415, 1934), *Kingston Olivine* (378, 1930), *Kirkella* (436, 1936), *Lady Beryl* (417, 1935), *Lady Elsa* (518, 1937), *Leeds United* (398, 1933), *Leyland* (452, 1936), *Loch Melfort* (440, 1934), *Loch Tulla* (423, 1934), *Lord Hotham* (464, 1936), *Lord Lloyd* (396, 1933), *Lord Plender* (396, 1933), *Lord Wakefield* (418, 1933), *Manchester City* (398, 1933), *Man o' War* (516, 1937), *Matabele* (440, 1935), *Mildenhall* (466, 1936), *Oriental Star* (427, 1934), *Pict* (462, 1936), *Quantock* (441, 1936), *Regal* (409, 1933), *St. Amandus* (400, 1933), *St. Andronicus* (399, 1933), *St. Arcadius* (403, 1933), *St. Attalus* (399, 1934), *Saon* (386, 1933), *Sindonis* (440, 1934), *Spaniard* (455, 1937), *Spurs* (399, 1933), *Stafnes* (454, 1936), *Stella Capella* (507, 1937), *Stella Dorado* (416, 1935), *Thornwick Bay* (437, 1936), *Turcoman* (455, 1937), *Vascama* (447, 1935), *Victorian* (440, 1935), *Warwick Deeping* (445, 1934), *Wellard* (514, 1937), *Westella* (413, 1934), *York City* (398, 1933).

Photo wanted

GUAVA (ex-*British Columbia*), (Richards Iron Works, Lowestoft, 1935). 134 tons *gross.* Ruston & Hornsby oil engine.

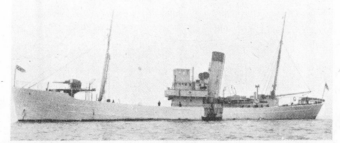

SAPPHIRE.   1936, *R. Perkins.*

6 *Smith's Dock Co., Ltd. :* **AGATE** (ex-*Mavis Rose*, 1934), **AMETHYST** (ex-*Phyllis Rosalie*, 1934), **SAPPHIRE** (ex-*Mildenhall*, 1935), **TOPAZE** (ex-*Melbourne*, 1935), **TOURMALINE** (ex-*Berkshire*, 1935), **TURQUOISE** (ex-*Warwickshire*, 1935). Displacement : First pair, 627 tons ; second pair, 608 tons ; third pair, 641 tons. Length : 157 to 160½ feet ; neam, 26⅔ feet. I.H.P. : 750 to 800 = 12 kts.

2 *Cook, Welton & Gemmell :* **PEARL** (ex-*Dervish*, 1934), 649 tons. 154½ × 25¼ feet. I.H.P. : 700 = 12 kts. **JASPER** (ex-*Balthasar*, 1932), 581 tons. Dimensions : 145 × 25 feet. I.H.P. : 600 = 12 kts.

All purchased in 1935. Average draught of all, about 12 feet. Guns : **1—4** inch ; also D.C. Used for Anti-Submarine training.

RUBY.   1936, *R. Perkins.*

2 *Cochrane & Sons :* **RUBY** (ex-*Cape Bathurst*, 1933), **CORNELIAN** (ex-*Cape Warwick*, 1933). Displacement : 568 tons. Dimensions : 152 × 25½ × 12 feet. Guns : 1—4 inch. D.C. carried. I.H.P. : 640 = 12 kts. Purchased 1935, and used for Anti-Submarine training.

      1937, *Wright & Logan.*

VULCAN (ex-*Mascot*, ex-*Aston Villa*), (Smith's Dock Co. Ltd., 1933). Purchased and converted, 1936. Displacement : 623 tons. Dimensions : 155 (*o.a.*) × 26½ × 12 feet. Reciprocating engines. I.H.P. : 678 = 11·5 kts. 1 cylindrical boiler. Depot Ship for Torpedo Boats.

Photo wanted.

2 *Cochrane :* **AMBER** (ex-*Cape Barfleur*, 1934), **CORAL** (ex-*Cape Duner*, 1935). Displacement : 700 tons.

3 *Cook, Welton & Gemmell :* **BERYL** (ex-*Lady Adelaide*, 1935) **JADE** (ex-*Lady Lilian*, 1933), **MOONSTONE** (ex-*Lady Madeleine*, 1934). Displacement : 615 tons. Of same general type as other "Gem" trawlers, above, and particulars similar.

LILAC.   1936, *Wright & Logan.*

7 *Cochrane & Sons :* **LILAC** (ex-*Beachflower*, 1930), 593 tons. **SYCAMORE** (ex-*Lord Beaverbrook*, 1930). 573 tons. 150½ × 25½ × 12 feet. **MAGNOLIA** (ex-*Lord Brentford*, 1930, (557) tons. 150¼ × 24½ × 12 feet. **CYPRESS** (ex-*Cape Finisterre*, 1930), 548 tons. **HAWTHORN** (ex-*Cape Guardafui*, 1930), 593 tons. **SYRINGA** (ex-*Cape Kanin*, 1930), **WILLOW** (ex-*Cape Spartivento*, 1930), Both 574 tons. All four of these, 140 × 24½ × 12 feet.

3 *Cook, Welton & Gemmell :* **CEDAR** (ex-*Arab*, 1933). 649 tons. 154½ × 25½ × 12 feet. **HOLLY** (ex-*Kingston Coral*, 1930). **LAUREL** (ex-*Kingston Cyanite*, 1930). Both 590 tons. 140¼ × 24½ × 11½ feet.

In all : Guns : 1—4 inch AA. D.C. carried. I.H.P. : 600 = 11 kts. (except *Cedar*, 700 = 11·5 kts.). All purchased 1935, and used for Minesweeping training.

ALDER.   1939, *R. Perkins.*

4 *Cochrane :* **ALDER** (ex-*Lord Davidson*, 1929). Displacement : 560 tons. **BEECH** (ex-*Lord Dawson*, 1929). 540 tons. **BERBERIS** (ex-*Lord Hewart*, 1928), 540 tons. **HORNBEAM** (ex-*Lord Trent*, 1929). 530 tons.

6 *Cook, Welton & Gemmell :* **LARCH** (ex-*St. Alexandra*, 1928), **MAPLE** (ex-*St. Gerontius*, 1929), **MYRTLE** (ex-*St. Irene*, 1928). All three 550 tons. **OAK** (ex-*St. Romanus*, 1928), **TAMARISK** (ex-*St. Gatien*, 1925), both 545 tons. **REDWOOD** (ex-*St. Rose*, 1928), 540 tons. Of same general design as other "Tree" trawlers, above, and particulars similar.

"DEE" TYPE.   1926 *Photo, Gieves Ltd., Portsmouth.*

DEE (ex-*T* 16, ex-*Battleaxe*).   **KENNET** (ex-*T* 17, ex-*Iceaxe*) **GARRY** (ex-*T* 13, ex-*Goldaxe*).   **LIFFEY** (ex-*T* 14, ex-*Stoneaxe*).

Ex-Russian Trawlers, designed and built by Smiths Dock Co., Ltd., 1916. Displacement : 393, 417, 407, and 373 tons, respectively. Dimensions : 130 (*pp.*) × 23½ × 13½ feet. I.H.P. : 525 = 10·5 kts. Coal : 140 tons.

EXCELLENT (Details of each vary slightly).   1935, *R. Perkins.*

Blackwater (ex-*William Inwood*).	**Foyle**	(ex-*Sonneblom*, ex-*Foyle*, ex-*John Edmund*).
***Boyne**	(ex-*William Jones*).	
***Colne**	(ex-*Isaac Chant*).	**James Ludford.**
***Doon**	(ex-*Fraser Evans*).	**Moy** (ex-*Alexander Hills*).
Eden	(ex-*Immortelle*, ex-*Eden*, ex-*Thomas Johns*).	**Ouse** (ex-*Andrew King*).
		Pembroke (ex-*Stour*, ex-*Daniel Fearall*.)
Excellent	(ex-*Nith*, ex-*Andrew Jewer*).	

All belong to "Mersey" type (designed by Messrs. Cochrane & Sons, Ltd., Selby, 1917–18). All built by Messrs. Cochrane except *Colne* and *James Ludford*, by Lobnitz. Displacement : 452 to 551 tons. Dimensions : 138½ (*pp.*) × 22¾ × 13½ feet. Triple expansion engines. 1 boiler. I.H.P. : 600 = 11 kts. Coal : 204 tons. *Moy, Ouse,* are employed on Fleet Target Service. Those marked * are rated as "Fishery Protection Trawlers," have black topped funnels, and carry 1—3 inch AA. Others mount 2—3 inch AA. *Pembroke* has 2—3 pdr.

PLANTAGENET. 1939, *courtesy Messrs. Lobnitz & Co., Ltd. (Builders).*

(BAYONET CLASS—11 SHIPS)

7 *Blyth DD. & S.B. Co.*: **BAYONET** (ex-*Barnehurst*), (Nov. 8, 1938), **FALCONET** (ex-*Barnham*), (Dec. 5, 1938), **BOWNET** (Jan. 19, 1939), **BURGONET** (March 14, 1939), **DRAGONET** (June 2, 1939), **SIGNET** (May 3, 1939), **SONNET.**
2 *Smith's Dock Co.*: **MAGNET** (ex-*Barnsley*), (Nov. 22, 1938), **MARTINET** (ex-*Barnstone*), (Dec. 8, 1938).
2 *Lobnitz*: **PLANET** (ex-*Barnwell*), (Dec. 26, 1938), **PLAN-TAGENET** (ex-*Barwood*), (Feb. 23, 1939). Authorised under 1937 and 1938 estimates.

Displacement: 530 tons. Dimensions: 135 × 30½ × 9 feet. Guns: 1—3 inch AA. Machinery: Triple expansion (By North-Eastern Marine Engineering Co., Ltd. in *Bownet, Burgonet, Dragonet*; by White's Marine Engineering Co., Ltd. in *Signet, Sonnet*). I.H.P.: 850 = 11·5 kts. Cylindrical boilers.

DUNNET. 1937, *courtesy D. Cochrane, Esq.*

DUNNET. (Lytham S. & E. Co., Ltd., August 5, 1936). Displacement: 385 tons. Complement, 15. Dimensions: 125 (*pp.*), 134¼ (*o.a.*) × 26½ × 9 feet (*max.*). Guns: 1—3 inch. Reciprocating engines and cylindrical boiler. I.H.P.: 350 = 10 kts. Fuel: 80 tons coal.

BARRAGE. 1938, *Wright & Logan.*

(Barricade Class—23 ships).

9 *Blyth D.D. & S.B. Co.*: **BARBARIAN** (Oct. 21, 1937), **BARBETTE** (Dec. 15, 1937), **BARBICAN** (March 14, 1938), **BARBROOK** (May 28, 1938), **BARCASTLE** (July 23, 1938), **BARNEHURST, BARNSTONE** and 2 more building. (Machinery by White's Marine Engineering Co., Ltd. in *Barbrook* and *Barcastle*, by North Eastern Marine Engineering Co., Ltd. in others).

2 *Hall, Russell & Co. (Aberdeen)*: **BARRAGE** (Dec. 2, 1937), **BARRANCA** (Jan. 18, 1938).

2 *Charles Hill & Co. (Bristol)*: **BARRICADE** (ex-*Ebgate*), (Feb. 7, 1938), **BARRIER** (ex-*Bargate*), (May 17, 1938).

2 *Goole S.B. & Repair Co.*: **BARCOMBE** (July 28, 1938), **BARCROFT.** Machinery by Amos & Smith, Ltd.

2 *John Lewis & Sons (Aberdeen)*: **BARFAIR** (May 31, 1938), **BARFIELD** (July 28, 1938).

4 *Lobnitz*: **BARLANE** (June 27, 1938), **BARLIGHT** (Sept. 10, 1938) and 2 more building.

2 *Simons*: **BARLOW** (Aug. 26, 1938), **BARMOUTH** (Oct. 11, 1938).

Built under 1935, 1936, 1937 and 1939 Estimates. Displacement: 730 tons. Dimensions: 150 (*pp.*), 173¾ (*o.a.*) × 32¼ × 9½ feet. Guns: 1—3 inch AA. Machinery: Triple expansion. I.H.P.: 850 = 11·75 kts. 2 boilers. Complement: 32.

Note.—Other boom defence craft which appear in the Navy List are without motive power.

Photo wanted

1 *Cook, Welton & Gemmell*: **JENNET** (ex-*Bunsen*, 1926), 358 tons *gross.*
3 *Cochrane*: **PUNNET** (ex-*Cape Matapan*, 1925), **RENNET** (ex-*Deepdale Wyke*, 1928), **QUANNET** (ex-*Dairycoates*, 1926). 321, 335 and 350 tons *gross*, respectively.

BARNET. 1934, *Grand Studio, Malta.*

BARNET (ex-*Earl Haig*). (Cochrane & Sons, Selby, 1919.) Purchased and converted, 1934. Displacement: 423 tons. Complement: 15. Dimensions: 138½ (*o.a.*) × 23¾ × 11¼ feet. Guns: 1—3 inch. Reciprocating engines and cylindrical boiler. I.H.P.: 600 = 11 kts. Fuel: 175 tons coal. Boom working vessel at Colombo.

1937.

FASTNET (ex-*Frobisher*). (Goole S.B. and Repairing Co., 1919). Purchased and converted, 1933. Displacement: 444 tons. Complement: 15. Dimensions: 147¾ (*o.a.*) × 23¾ × 12 feet. Guns: 1—3 inch. Reciprocating engines and cylindrical boiler. I.H.P.: 600 = 11 kts. Fuel: 175 tons coal. Boom working vessel at Malta.

Boom Defence Vessels—*continued*.

1939, *Wright & Logan*.

CORONET (ex-*Robert Cloughton*) (1917). Ex-Trawler, designed by Smiths Dock Co., Ltd., and built by Bow, McLachlan & Co., Ltd. Displacement : 429 tons. Dimensions : 125 (*p p.*) × 22½ × 12½ feet. I.H.P. 480 = 10·5 kts. Coal : 164 tons. Boom working vessel at Portland.

25 Drifters.

SEABREEZE. 1937, *R. Perkins*.

(All built of steel except those marked with an asterisk, which are believed to be wood. Those marked † are on Harbour Service List).

Cascade, Cloud, Cold Snap, Crescent Moon, *Ebbtide (ex-*C.D. 1*), *Eddy, *Fumarole, †Glitter, Halo, Harmattan, Horizon, Indian Summer, Landfall, Leeward, Lunar Bow, Mist, Noontide, †*Onyx* (ex-*C.D. 82*), *Seabreeze, Sheen, Shower, Sundown, Sunset, Whirlpool.* Also *Brine* (Purchased, 1938).

Displacement : 199 tons (except ex-*C.D.* type, 150 tons). Dimensions : 87 × 19¾ × 9½ feet. I.H.P. 270 = 9 kts. Guns : Usually 1—6 pdr. or 3 pdr. (Not mounted in peace time). Coal : 31-39 tons.

Coastal Minelayers.

LINNET. 1938, *Wright & Logan*.

LINNET (May 3, 1938), **REDSTART** (May 3, 1938), **RINGDOVE** (June 15, 1938). First built by Ardrossan Dockyard Co., Ltd. under 1936 Estimates, others by Henry Robb Ltd. under 1937 Estimates. Displacement : 498 tons. Complement : 24. Dimensions : 145 (*pp.*), 163¾ (*o.a.*) × 27⅙ × 8 feet. No guns. Machinery : Triple expansion, by Ferguson Bros. in *Linnet*, by White's Marine Engineering Co., Ltd. in others. I.H.P. : 400 = 10·5 kts. Two are Minelaying Tenders to *Vernon*, but *Redstart* is on China Station.

1937, *Wright & Logan*.

PLOVER (Denny, June 8, 1937). Displacement : 805 tons. Complement : 69. Dimensions : 180 (*pp.*), 195¼ (*o.a.*) × 37½ × 8⅙ feet. Guns : 2 M.G. Machinery : Triple expansion. I.H.P. : 1,400 = 14·75 kts. Laid down Oct. 7, 1936, and completed in Sept., 1937. Minelaying Tender to *Vernon*.

Coastal Minelayers—*continued*.

1937, *Wright & Logan*.

MEDUSA (ex-M 29),
MELPOMENE (ex-M 31), (Workman Clark.)

Launched and completed 1915. 535 tons. Complement : 52. Dimensions : 177 (*o.a.*) × 31 × 6¾ feet. Carry 52 mines. Machinery : Triple expansion. 2 shafts. Boilers : Yarrow. Oil fuel : 45 tons. H.P. : 400 = 10 kts.

Sister ship **MINERVA** still exists, though on disposal list.

Cable Vessels.

1 Cable Vessel to be built under 1939 Programme.

1938, *Wright & Logan*.

LASSO (March 17, 1938). Built by Messrs. Thornycroft under 1936 Estimates. Displacement : 903 tons. Dimensions : 180 (*pp.*), 205 (*o.a.*) × 35½ × 9¾ feet. No guns. Machinery : Triple expansion. I.H.P. : 1,100 = 13 kts. Tender to Anti-Submarine School, Portland.

KILMUN (1919). Built by Smith's Dock Co., Ltd. Displacement : 890 tons. Dimensions : 170 (*pp.*), 182 (*o.a.*) × 30 × 11¾ feet. No guns. Machinery : Triple expansion. I.H.P. : 700 = 10 kts. Boilers : Cylindrical. Coal : 330 tons. Tender to *Defiance* Establishment, Devonport.

1939, *courtesy Messrs. Vosper, Ltd.*

BLOODHOUND (Vosper, 1937). Displacement : 35 tons. Complement : 5. Dimensions : 68 × 19 × 3 feet. **1**—21 inch torpedo tube (3 torpedoes carried). Lorraine-Orion engines. H.P. : 1,600 = 25 kts. Tender to *Vernon*, used for torpedo practice. Built under 1937 Estimates.

1937, *Wright & Logan.*

DWARF. (1936). Built by Philip & Son, Ltd., Dartmouth. Displacement : 172 tons. Dimensions : 83½ (*pp.*), 91 (*o.a.*) × 19 × 6½ feet (*mean*), 7 feet (*max.*). No guns. 2 sets reciprocating engines and 1 cylindrical boiler. I.H.P. : 350 = 9·25 kts. Fuel : 16 tons coal. Tender to Submarine Headquarters, Portsmouth.

REDWING. 1934 *Photo, R. Perkins.*

ELFIN. 1935, *R. Perkins.*

REDWING (Oct. 19, 1933), **ELFIN** (Nov. 20, 1933). Both built by J. Samuel White & Co., Ltd., Cowes. Displacement : 225 and 222 tons respectively. Complement : 12. Dimensions : *Redwing*, 112 (*o.a.*) × 25 × 6⅔ feet ; *Elfin*, 108 (*o.a.*) × 25 × 6½ feet. No guns. 2 sets reciprocating engines and 1 cylindrical boiler. I.H.P. : 250 = 9·5 kts. Tenders to Torpedo School, Devonport, and Submarine Depot, Portland, respectively.

NIGHTINGALE. 1931 *Photo, Cribb.*

NIGHTINGALE (Sept. 30, 1931), **VERNON** (ex-*Skylark*), (Nov. 15, 1932). Both built at Portsmouth. Displacement : 298 and 302 tons, respectively. Complement : 15. Dimensions : *Nightingale*, 110 (*o.a.*) × 24½ × 7½ feet.; *Vernon*, 106¼ (*o.a.*) × 24½ × 7½ feet. No guns. 2 sets reciprocating engines and 1 cylindrical boiler. I.H.P. : 400 = 10 kts. Fuel : 15 tons coal. Mining tenders to *Vernon* Establishment.

23 Fleet Tugs.

1938, *courtesy Messrs. Fleming & Ferguson.*

BRIGAND (July 8, 1937), **BUCCANEER** (Sept. 7, 1937), **BANDIT** (Feb. 15, 1938), **MARAUDER** (Nov. 9, 1938). Built by Fleming & Ferguson, Paisley, under 1936, 1937 and 1938 Estimates. A fifth vessel of this type is to be built under the 1939 Estimates. Displacement : 840 tons. Complement : 36. Dimensions : 165 (*pp.*), 174 (*o.a.*) × 32 × 10⅔ feet. Guns : 1—3 inch AA. Triple expansion engines. 2 shafts. Designed H.P. : 3,000 = 16 kts.

Notes.—Fitted for salvage work, and have towing winches for work with battle practice targets.

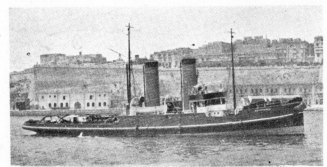

ROYSTERER. 1929 *Photo, N. T. Tangye, Esq.*

(*Resolve, Retort,* no Fx. deck).

5 ROLLICKER TYPE.

RESOLVE, RESPOND (both by Ayrshire D.Y. Co.). **RETORT** (Day, Summers & Co.), **ROYSTERER** (Thornycroft). **ROLLICKER** (Ferguson Bros.). Built 1918–19. Displacement : 1,400 tons. Dimensions : 175 × 34 × 17, (*maximum* draught). 2 screws. I.H.P. : 2,400 = 14 kts. Complement : 24.

Notes.—All on Harbour Service List.
Rollicker was transferred to Nigerian Government, but was reacquired by Admiralty in March, 1934.

Fleet Tugs—*continued.*

ST. ISSEY. 1929 *Photo, N. T. Tangye, Esq.*

14 "RESCUE" TYPE (SAINT CLASS).

ST. ABBS, ST. BLAZEY, ST. BREOCK, ST. CLEARS, ST. CYRUS, ST. DAY, ST. DOGMAEL, ST. FAGAN, ST. ISSEY, ST. JUST, ST. MARTIN, ST. MELLONS, ST. MONANCE, ST. OMAR. Built by various yards, 1918–19. Displacement : 820 tons. Dimensions : 135½ × 29 × 14½ feet (*maximum* draught), 1 screw. I.H.P. : 1,250 = 12 kts. Coal : 240 tons. Complement : 21.

Note.—*St. Cyrus, St. Fagan, St. Issey, St. Just, St. Martin,* employed for Target Towing, others on Harbour Service List, with exception of *St. Breock.* 2 tugs of this type, *Toia* (ex-*St. Boniface*) and *Ocean Eagle* (ex-*St. Arvans*), transferred to New Zealand and Canadian Governments, respectively. Others will be found in Brazilian, Iraqi, and Spanish Navies, and in commercial harbours such as Shanghai, Sydney, Fremantle, etc.

Petrol Carriers.

PETRONEL. 1934 *Photo, R. Perkins.*

PETROBUS, PETRELLA, (Dunlop, Bremner, 1918). Displacement : 1024 tons. Dimensions : 164 × 28 × 11½ feet. I.H.P. 500 = 9-10 kts. Deadweight capacity : 300 tons. Own oil : 50 tons. Cylindrical boilers. Complement, 16.

Water Carrier.

PETRONEL. Sister ship to *Petrobus* and *Petrella.*

Oilers.

3 Oilers of 3,500 tons are to be built under 1939 Estimates.

CAIRNDALE. 1939, *courtesy Messrs. Harland & Wolff.*

CAIRNDALE (ex-*Erato*, October 25, 1938), **CEDARDALE** (March 25, 1939). Built by Harland & Wolff and Blythswood S.B. Co., Ltd., respectively. Displacement : 17,000 tons. Complement : 40. Dimensions : 460 (*pp.*), 483 (*o.a.*) × 59 × 27½ feet (*mean*). Machinery : Burmeister & Wain 4-cycle Diesels. B.H.P. : 3,500 = 11·5 kts. Deadweight capacity : 12,000 tons.

BISHOPDALE. 1937, *courtesy Builders.*

2 *Swan Hunter* : **ABBEYDALE** (Dec. 28, 1936), **ARNDALE** (Aug. 5, 1937). Displacement : 17,210 tons.
1 *Cammell Laird* : **ALDERSDALE** (July 7, 1937). 17,231 tons.
1 *Lithgows* : **BISHOPDALE** (March 31, 1937). 17,357 tons.
2 *Harland & Wolff* (Govan) : **BOARDALE** (April 22, 1937), **BROOMDALE** (Sept. 2, 1937). 17,338 tons.
Following applies to all 6 : Complement : 40. Dimensions : 464₄ (*pp.*), 481½ (*o.a.*) × 62 × 27½ feet (*mean*). Machinery : Doxford Diesels in first 3, Burmeister & Wain in others. B.H.P. : 4,000 = 11·5 kts. Deadweight capacity : 11,650 tons. Own fuel : 850 tons.

1939, *Wright & Logan.*

OLEANDER (Pembroke D.Y., 1922), **OLNA** (Devonport D.Y., 1921). Displacement : 15,350 and 15,220 tons. Dimensions : 430 × 57 × 26¼ feet. Deadweight capacity : 10,000 tons. Triple expansion engines and cylindrical boilers. I.H.P.: 3,250 = 11 kts.

OLCADES. *Photo, Abrahams, Devonport (added* 1927).

OLCADES (ex-*British Beacon*), **OLIGARCH** (ex-*British Lantern*), (both Workman Clark, 1918), **OLYNTHUS** (ex-*British Star*), (Swan Hunter, 1917). Displacement : 15,030 tons (*Olcades*) and 15,003 tons (other two ships). Dimensions : 430 × 57 × 26¼ feet. Deadweight capacity : 9,000 tons. Triple expansion engines and cylindrical boilers. I.H.P. : 3,200 = 11 kts.

Added 1935, *Wright & Logan.*

OLWEN (ex-*British Light*), (Palmers, 1917). Displacement : 13,690 tons. Dimensions : 419½ × 54¼ × 26 feet. Deadweight capacity : 8,000 tons. Triple expansion engines and cylindrical boilers. I.H.P. : 3,150 = 10 kts.

WAR BAHADUR. *Photo, Abrahams, Devonport (added* 1927).

(Rigs vary considerably in these ships ; but all except *War Krishna* are more or less similar to above.)

WAR KRISHNA. *Photo, Abrahams, Devonport (added* 1927).

WAR AFRIDI (R. Duncan & Co., 1920), **WAR BAHADUR** (1918), **WAR MEHTAR** (1920), (both Armstrong) ; **WAR BRAHMIN** (1920), **WAR DIWAN** (1919), **WAR PINDARI** (1920), all three Lithgows ; **WAR BHARATA** (1920), **WAR NAWAB** (1919), **WAR NIZAM** (1918), **WAR SUDRA** (1920), all four Palmers ; **WAR HINDOO** (Hamilton, 1919) ; **WAR KRISHNA** (Swan Hunter, 1919); **WAR PATHAN** (1919), **WAR SIRDAR** (1920), both Sir J. Laing & Sons ; **WAR SEPOY** (W. Gray & Co., 1919). Displacement : from 11,660 to 11,681 tons. Dimensions : 400 × 52¼ × 25⅔ feet. Deadweight capacities vary from 6300 tons (*War Pindari*) to 8100 tons (*War Bahadur*). Triple expansion engines and cylindrical boilers. I.H.P. 3,000 = 10 kts.

LEAF Type. *Photo added* 1927.

APPLELEAF (ex-*Texol*) (Workman Clark), **CHERRYLEAF** (Sir R. Dixon & Co.), **PLUMLEAF** (ex-*Trinol*) (Swan Hunter). **BRAMBLELEAF** (Russell & Co.), **ORANGELEAF** (J. L. Thompson & Sons), **PEARLEAF** (W. Gray & Co.). All launched 1917. Displacements : from 12,270 to 12,370 tons. Dimensions : 405 × 54½ × 27½ feet. Triple expansion engines and cylindrical boilers. I.H.P. : 6,750 = 14 kts. Deadweight capacity : First three, 5,400 tons ; second three, 5,000 tons.

1920 *Photo, Coates, Harwich.*

MIXOL (Caledon S. B. & Eng. Co., 1916). **THERMOL** (Greenock D.Y. Co., 1916). 4326 tons. Dimensions : 270 × 38½ × 20¼ feet. I.H.P. 1200 = 11 kts. Oil : 150 tons. Deadweight capacity : 2000 tons.

CELEROL. 1938, *R. Perkins.*

BELGOL (Irvine's S.B. & D.D. Co.), **CELEROL** (Short Bros.), **FORTOL** (McMillan), **PRESTOL** (Napier & Miller), **RAPIDOL** (W. Gray), **SLAVOL** (Greenock D.Y. Co.). All launched 1917. Displacements : from 5,049 to 5,600 tons. Dimensions : 335 × 41½ × 20¼ feet. I.H.P. ; 3,375 = 14 kts. Own Oil : 300 tons. Cylindrical boilers. Complement : 39. Deadweight capacity : 2,000 tons.

Oilers—*continued.*

MONTENOL.   1939, *P. A. Vicary.*

FRANCOL (Earles S.B. Co.), **MONTENOL** (W. Gray), **SERBOL** (Caledon S.B. Co.) Displacements : 5,620, 5,049 and 5,600 tons, respectively. Other details as *Belgol* on preceding page. All launched 1917.

ELMOL.   1935, *R. Perkins.*

BIRCHOL, BOXOL (Barclay, Curle), **EBONOL** (Clyde S.B. Co.), **ELDEROL, ELMOL** (Swan Hunter), **LARCHOL, LIMOL** (Lobnitz), **HICKOROL** (McMillan). (All 1917). Displacements : from 2,365 to 2,410 tons. Dimensions : 220 × 34⅔ × 13½ feet. Triple expansion engines and cylindrical boilers. I.H.P. 700 = 9 kts. Own oil : 40 tons. Complement, 19. Deadweight capacity : 1000 tons.

DISTOL (W. Dobson & Co.), **PHILOL, SCOTOL** (Tyne Iron S.B. Co.), **KIMMEROL, VISCOL** (Craig, Taylor). (All 1916). Displacements : from 2,200 to 2,400 tons. Dimensions : 220 × 34⅔ × 12½ feet, otherwise as *Elmol* type, above.

Fleet Supply Ship.

1934 *Official.*

RELIANT (ex-*London Importer*). (Purchased, March, 1933.) Built by Furness Shipbuilding Co., 1923. Displacement : 17,000 tons. Gross tonnage : 7,938. Dimensions : 450½ (*p.p.*), 471½ (*o.a.*) × 58 × 30 feet (*max.*). 2 Brown-Curtis geared turbines. S.H.P. : 5,000 = 14 kts. 4 cylindrical boilers, 190 lbs. working pressure. Oil fuel : 2,170 tons.

Store Carriers.

ROBERT DUNDAS (July 28, 1938), **ROBERT MIDDLETON** (June 29, 1938). Both built by Grangemouth Dockyard Co., Ltd. Displacement : 900 tons. Complement : 17. Dimensions : 210 × 35 × 13½ feet (*mean*). Machinery : Atlas Polar Diesel by British Auxiliaries Ltd., Govan. 1 shaft. B.H.P. : 960 = 10·5 kts. Fuel : 60 tons. Deadweight capacity : 1,100 tons.

BACCHUS.   1936, *courtesy Builders.*

BACCHUS. (Caledon Shipbuilding & Engineering Co., Ltd., July 15, 1936). Displacement : 5,150 tons *standard*, 5,790 tons *full load*. Complement, 44. Dimensions : 320 (*pp.*), 337⅝ (*o.a.*) × 49 × 18 feet (*max.* draught). No guns. Machinery : Triple expansion. I.H.P. : 2,000 = 12 kts. 3 cylindrical boilers. Oil fuel : 643 tons. Equipped with distilling plant. Deadweight capacity : 3,300 tons.

Royal Yacht.

A new Royal Yacht is to be built under 1939 Navy Estimates.

VICTORIA AND ALBERT (1899). 4,700 tons. Dimensions : 380 (*p.p.*) × 40 × 18 feet (*mean* draught). Guns : 2—6 pdr. (bronze). H.P. 11,800 = 20 kts. Machinery : 2 sets triple expansion. Belleville boilers. Coal : *normal,* 350 tons; *maximum,* 2000 tons. Complement : 363.

Hospital Ships.

A new Hospital Ship was ordered from Messrs. Barclay, Curle & Co., Ltd. in August, 1939, under the Estimates for that year.

MAINE.   1935, *R. Perkins.*

MAINE (ex-Pacific Steam Navigation Company's s.s. *Panama*) (Fairfield Co., 1902). Purchased in 1920 and equipped for present duties. Displacement : 10,100 tons. Dimensions : 401⅙ × 58⅓ × 23½ feet. Machinery : Triple expansion. I.H.P. 4,000 = 13 kts. 2 D.E. and 2 S.E. boilers. Coal : 1,300 tons.

ROYAL AUSTRALIAN NAVY.

Australian Naval Board.

Commander-in-Chief: H. E. Brigadier-General the Rt. Hon. Lord Gowrie, V.C., G.C.M.G., C.B., D.S.O.

President: Minister of State for Defence, Brigadier G. A. Street, M.P.

1st Naval Member: Admiral Sir Ragnar Colvin, K.B.E., C.B.

2nd Naval Member: Commodore M. W. S. Boucher, D.S.O., R.N.

Finance and Civil Member: Mr. A. R. Nankervis.

Secretary: Hon. Paymaster Commander G. L. Macandie, C.B.E.

Liaison Officer, London: Paymr. Lieut.-Commander P. Perry, R.A.N.

Commanding Australian Squadron.

Rear-Admiral W. N. Custance, C.B.

Commonwealth Navy Estimates.

1936–37, £3,237,387. 1937–38, £3,316,000. 1938–39, £5,677,300.

Seagoing Personnel, 5,170 (to be raised to 6,770 by 1941).
Reserves, 5,066.

PENGUIN.

(Resembles **BAYONET** class of Royal Navy.)

KOOKABURRA.

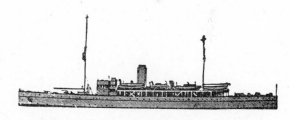

YARRA, SWAN.

PARRAMATTA, WARREGO.

AUSTRALIA, CANBERRA.
(Under reconstruction.)

MORESBY.

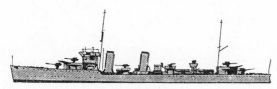

STUART.

"V" class.

ADELAIDE.

SYDNEY, HOBART, PERTH.

AUSTRALIA (17th March, 1927).   **CANBERRA** (31st May, 1927).

"Standard" displacement, 9,870 tons and 9,850 tons respectively. (13,630 *deep load*).
Complement, 679. (710 as flagship).

Length (*p.p.*) 590 feet, (*o.a.*) 630 feet.   Beam, 68¼ feet.   Draught, 16¼ feet (*mean*).

Guns :
  8—8 inch, 50 cal.
  8—4 inch AA.
  4—3 pdr.
  4—2 pdr. pom-poms.
  4 Machine, 8 Lewis.
Torpedo tubes :
  8—21 inch in quadruple
    mountings (being re-
    moved).

Aircraft : 1 in AUSTRALIA.

Armour :
  4″ Deck ....
  2″—1½″ Gun Houses ......
  3″ C.T. ....
  Bulges ....

AUSTRALIA.

Added 1937 courtesy Australian Naval Board.

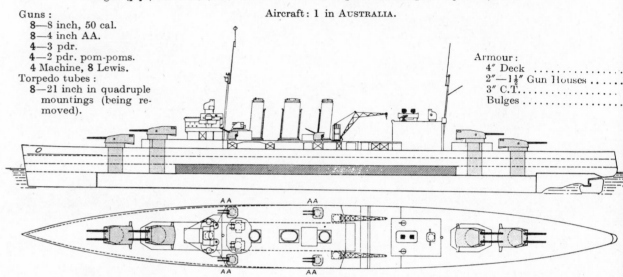

Note.—This plan represents H.M.S. CORNWALL as reconstructed.
Believed above ships will be altered on similar lines.
AUSTRALIA was taken in hand for this purpose at
Cockatoo Dockyard in 1938. When she is completed,
CANBERRA will also be reconstructed.

Machinery : Brown-Curtis geared turbines. 4 screws. Designed
S.H.P. 80,000 = 31·5 kts. Boilers : 8 Admiralty 3-drum type.
Oil fuel : 3,400 tons. Radius at full speed, 2,300 miles ; at economical
speed (11—14 kts.), 10,400 miles.

General Notes.—Sisters to *Kent* class, in British Navy Section. Designed by
Sir E. H. Tennyson d'Eyncourt. Laid down by John Brown & Co.. Ltd.,
Clydebank, in 1925, and completed in April and July, 1928, respectively.
(See also detailed notes under British *Kent* class, which apply to these two
ships.)

AUSTRALIA.

1935, *R. Perkins.*

104

PERTH (ex-*Amphion*), (July 27, 1934).

SYDNEY (ex-*Phaeton*.) (Sept. 22, 1934).

HOBART (ex-*Apollo*), (Oct. 9, 1934).

Displacement : 6,830 and 6,980 tons, respectively.

Complement : 550.

Dimensions : 530 (*p.p.*), 555 (*w.l.*) × $56\frac{2}{3}$ × $15\frac{2}{3}$ feet (*mean* draught).

Guns :	8—6 inch.	Aircraft :	Armour :
	8—4 inch AA.	1 with catapult.	1″ turrets.
	4—3 pdrs.		1″ bridges.
	10 smaller.		2—3″ side.
			2″ deck.

Tubes : 8—21 inch (quadrupled).

SYDNEY   1935, *Wright & Logan.*

Note to Plan.—Torpedo Tubes are above water, in position shown in photos, and AA. guns are in pairs.

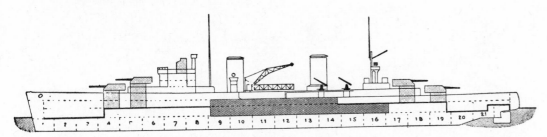

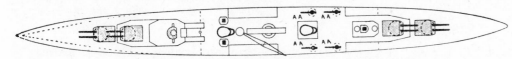

HOBART.   *Added 1939, Grand Studio.*

Machinery : 4 Parsons geared turbines. 4 shafts. S.H.P. : 72,000 = 32·5 kts. Boilers : 4 Admiralty 3-drum type. Oil : 1,725 tons.

Note.—Acquired for Royal Navy in 1934 and 1938, respectively. Sister ship *Amphion* to be taken over in 1939. Cost £1,422,727, and £1,434,579 respectively.

Est.	Name	Builder	Machinery	Ordered	Begun	Completed
1931	*Perth*	Portsmouth	Beardmore	1/12/32	26/6/33	7/36
1932 {	*Hobart*	Devonport	Beardmore	1/3/33	15/8/33	1/36
	Sydney	Swan Hunter	Wallsend	10/2/33	8/7/33	24/9/35

SYDNEY.   1935, *Wright & Logan.*

Cruiser.

ADELAIDE.

1939, *courtesy Australian Naval Board*

ADELAIDE (July, 1918).
Laid down at Sydney, Jan., 1915.   Completed, Aug., 1922.
Displacement, 5100 tons.   Complement, 470.
Length (*o.a.*), $462\frac{2}{3}$ feet.   Beam, $49\frac{5}{8}$ feet.   Draught, $15\frac{5}{6}$ feet (*mean*), $17\frac{3}{4}$—19 (*max*).

Guns :
8—6 inch, 50 cal.
3—4 inch AA.
4—3 pdr.
12—Smaller.

Armour :
2″ Deck (on slopes).
3″ (on sides) amidships.
$1\frac{1}{2}$″ (on sides) fore and aft.

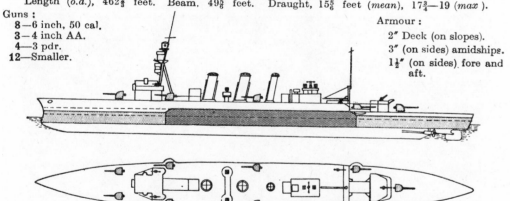

Machinery : Parsons turbines.   Boilers : Yarrow.   Designed S.H.P. : 25,000 = 25·5 kts.
Oil fuel : 1,412 tons.   2 shafts.

Notes.—Laid down at Cockatoo Dockyard, Sydney, in 1915 and completed in 1922.   Cost £1,271,782 to build.   Completely refitted 1938-9.

Gunnery Notes.—Electric Ammunition Hoists, dredger type.   Reported 6 inch guns have up to 40° elevation.

Escort Vessels.

(*See silhouette*).

PARRAMATTA (June 18, 1939), **WARREGO.**   Laid down at Cockatoo Dockyard, 1938, for completion in 1940.   Displacement : 1,060 tons.   Are of an improved *Yarra* type, with 2—4 inch A.A. in twin mounting in place of forward 4-inch, and a multiple M.G. in place of second 4-inch behind blast screen, which is omitted.   No 3-pdrs.

YARRA (Now mounts M.M.G. abaft S.L.).

1936, *courtesy Australian Naval Board.*

YARRA (March 28, 1935), **SWAN** (1936).   Displacement : 1,060 tons.   Complement, 100.   Dimensions : 250 (*p.p.*), 262 (*w.l.*), 266 (*o.a.*) × 36 × $7\frac{1}{2}$ feet (*mean*).   Guns : 3—4 inch AA., 4—3 pdr., 6 M.G.   Machinery : 2 sets Parsons geared turbines.   S.H.P. : 2,000 = 16·5 kts.   Boilers : 2 Admiralty 3-drum type.   Oil fuel : 275 tons.

Notes.—Laid down in 1934 and 1935, respectively, at Cockatoo Dockyard, Sydney.   *Yarra* completed Jan., 1936, *Swan* Jan., 1937.   Generally similar to H.M.S. *Deptford* but with an additional 4 inch gun.

Flotilla Leader.

Destroyers.

2 of the "Tribal" type are to be built at Cockatoo Dockyard, 1939-41.

4 "W" and "V" type.

VENDETTA.   *Added 1937 courtesy Australian Naval Board.*

Added 1937, courtesy Australian Naval Board.

Stuart (Hawthorn Leslie, Aug. 22, 1918).

Displacement : 1530 tons. Dimensions : $332\frac{1}{2}$ (*o.a.*) $\times$ $31\frac{3}{4}$ $\times$ $12\frac{1}{4}$ feet (*max.* draught)

Guns : **5**—4·7 inch, **1**—3 inch AA., **7** smaller.

Tubes : **6**—21 inch.

Brown-Curtis all-geared Turbines. H.P. 40,000 = 36·5 kts. Yarrow small tube boilers. Oil : 504 tons. Complement, 183. Transferred to R.A.N. 1932.

VAMPIRE.

1 *Palmer :* **Waterhen** (March 26, 1918); 1 *Stephen :* **Voyager** (May 8, 1918).   Displacement : 1100 tons.

1 *Fairfield :* **Vendetta** (Sept. 3, 1917); 1 *White :* **Vampire** (May 21, 1917). Displacement, 1,090 tons.

Dimensions : 312 (*o.a.*) $\times$ $29\frac{1}{2}$ $\times$ $10\frac{5}{8}$ feet (*mean* draught). Complement : 134.

Guns : **4**—4 inch, **5** smaller.

Tubes : **6**—21 inch.

Machinery : Brown-Curtis all-geared Turbines. H.P. : 27,000 = 34 kts. Yarrow boilers (except *Vampire*, White-Forster). Oil fuel : 360 tons. Transferred to R.A.N. 1932.

Notes.—*Vampire* is equipped internally as flotilla leader, having been so employed during the War, and has recently been so employed again.

Torpedo Boats.

It is proposed to construct 12 motor torpedo boats in Australia during 1939-40.

Depot and Repair Ship.

R.A.N. Official Photo, 1922.

PENGUIN (ex-*Platypus*) (Built at Clydebank. Begun Sept. 2nd, 1914; launched Oct. 28th, 1916; completed Mar., 1917.) 3455 tons. Dimensions: 310 (*w.l.*), 325 (*o.a*) × 44 × 15⅔ feet. (*max.* draught). Guns: *nil.* I.H.P. 3500 = 15½ kts. Two sets triple expansion reciprocating engines and 4 cylindrical return-tube boilers. 2 screws. Coal: 450 tons. Complement, 357. Serves as Destroyer Depot Ship and Fleet Repair Ship.

Surveying Vessel.

1935, courtesy of Paym. Com. A. J. White, R.A.N.

MORESBY (ex-*Silvio*, Barclay, Curle & Co., 1918). Ex-Minesweeper of "24" Racehorse class, converted by Pembroke D.Y., 1924–25. 1,320 tons. Dimensions: 276½ (*o.a.*) × 35 × 12 feet. Guns: 1—3 pdr. I.H.P.: 2,500 = 17 kts. Cylindrical boilers. Oil fuel: 230 tons (Converted from coal in 1935). Complement, 141.

Boom Working Vessels.

Building.

KOALA, KANGAROO Displacement: 730 tons. Dimensions: 150 (*p.p.*), 173¾ (*o.a.*) × 32⅙ × 9½ feet. Guns: 1—3 inch AA. Machinery: Triple expansion. I.H.P. 850 = 11·5 kts. 2 boilers. Oil fuel: 140 tons. Complement 32.

(See silhouette.)

KOOKABURRA (Oct. 29, 1938). Built at Cockatoo Dockyard. Displacement: 533 tons. Dimensions: 120 (*pp.*), 135 (*o.a.*) × 26½ × 10¼ feet. Guns: 1—3 inch AA. Machinery: Triple expansion. I.H.P.: 450 = 9·5 kts. Cylindrical boiler. Oil fuel: 82 tons.

Miscellaneous.

Added 1937, courtesy Australian Naval Board.

KURUMBA (Swan Hunter, Sept., 1916). Fleet Oiler. Displacement: 7930 tons (3978 tons *gross*). Complement, 44. Dimensions: 366 (*p.p.*), 378 (*o.a.*) × 45½ × 23½ feet (*max.* draught). Triple expansion engines and cylindrical boilers. 2 shafts. I.H.P.: 2,000 = 10 kts. Fuel: 950 tons oil.

CERBERUS (ex-*Kooronga*). Motor vessel. Displacement: 61 tons. Dimensions: 70 × 14 × 8½ feet. B.H.P.: 126 = 9 kts. Serves as tender to Flinders Naval Depot, Westernport.

ROYAL INDIAN NAVY.

Flag Officer Commanding R.I.N.: Vice-Admiral Herbert Fitzherbert, C.B., C.M.G.

Flags.—Vessels of R.I.N. fly same Ensign and pendant as H.M. Ships. The Indian flag is flown as a Jack. Flag Officer when afloat flies the flag appropriate to his naval rank.

Official Photos have been furnished by courtesy of the Flag Officer Commanding R.I.N.

Escort Vessels.

INDUS.   1935, *R. Perkins.*

INDUS (Hawthorn Leslie. Aug. 24, 1934). Displacement : (standard) 1,190 tons. Complement : 119. Dimensions : 296½ (*o.a.*) × 35½ × 8¾ feet (*mean* draught). Guns : 2—4·7 inch, 4—3 pdr., 11 smaller. Machinery : Parsons I.R. Turbines with single reduction gearing. 2 shafts. Boilers : 2 Admiralty 3-drum type, 250 lbs. pressure. S.H.P. : 2,000 = 16·5 kts. Oil fuel : 300 tons. Is a slightly enlarged edition of the *Grimsby* class, which she resembles closely, and has internal arrangements on similar lines to *Hindustan*, below.

HINDUSTAN.   1930 *Photo, favour of Messrs. Swan Hunter.*

HINDUSTAN. (Swan Hunter & Wigham Richardson). Laid down 1929, launched May 12, 1930 and completed October, 1930. Dimensions : 296½ (*o.a.*) × 35 × 8¾ feet (*mean*). Standard Displacement : 1190 tons. Complement, 119. Guns : 2—4 inch, 4—3 pdr., 10 smaller. Machinery : Parsons impulse reaction Turbines with single reduction gearing ; 2 shafts. 2 Admiralty 3-drum type boilers, 250 lbs. pressure. S.H.P. : 2000 = 16·5 kts. Oil : 275 tons. The internal arrangements have been designed with special care, making the ship most suitable for the Tropics, and the ventilation has been very carefully planned. The refrigerating plant is of the electrically driven CO_2 type. Is a slightly enlarged edition of *Hastings* class.

HINDUSTAN.

INVESTIGATOR.

INDUS.

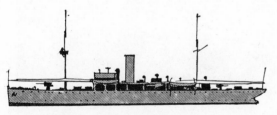

CORNWALLIS.

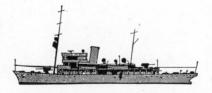

CLIVE.

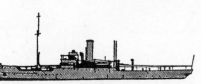

PATHAN.

LAWRENCE.

Escort Vessels.

1932 *Photo, Official.*

LAWRENCE (ex-Despatch Vessel, launched by Messrs. Beardmore, July 30th, 1919, completed December 27th, 1919). Standard displacement, 1,210 tons. Dimensions : 225 (*p.p.*), 241½ (*o.a.*) × 34 × 12 feet (*max.*) draught. Complement, 119. Guns : 2—4 inch, 4—3 pdrs., **12 smaller.** All-geared turbines. 2 screws. 2 Babcock boilers. S.H.P. 1900 = 15 kts. Oil : *normal,* 144 tons ; *max.,* 153 tons.

CLIVE (launched by Messrs. Beardmore, December 10th, 1919, completed April 20th, 1920). Standard displacement, 1,748 tons. Dimensions : 240 (*p.p.*), 262¼ (*o.a.*) × 38½ × 14 feet. Complement, 123. Guns : 2—4 inch, 4—3 pdrs., 12 smaller. All-geared turbines. 2 screws. 2 Babcock & Wilcox boilers. S.H.P 2,000 = 14·5 kts. Oil : 179 tons *normal,* and 199 tons *max.*

Escort Vessel.

CORNWALLIS (ex *Lychnis*) Hamilton, August, 1917. Escort Vessel of *Anchusa* class. 1,383 tons. Dimensions : 255¾ (*p.p.*), 266¼ (*w.l.*), 277¾ (*o.a.*) × 35 × 14½ feet. Guns : 3—4 inch, 4—3 pdrs. **12 smaller.** Machinery : 4-cyl. triple expansion vertical. Boilers : 2 cylindrical. 1 screw. Designed H.P. 2,500 = 16·5 kts. Coal : 260 tons. Complement, 119.

*Note.—*Cornwallis sold to Indian Government by the Admiralty, September 1921. Sister ship *Elphinstone* wrecked, Jan. 1925.

Patrol Vessel.

PATHAN.

1932 *Photo, Official.*

PATHAN (ex P.C. 69). Workman Clark. (1918). Standard displacement, 661 tons. Dimensions : 247½ × 26¼ × 9 feet. Turbines : S.H.P. 3500 = 20 kts. Oil, 164 tons. Guns : 1—4 inch, 2—3 inch. Complement, 66. (Used for training).

Surveying Vessel.

1933 *Photo, Official.*

INVESTIGATOR. Ex-cable ship *Patrick Stewart* (Simons, 1924). Displacement : 1,572 tons. Complement, 109. Dimensions : 226 (*pp.*), 247 (*o.a.*) × 37½ × 13½ feet (*mean* draught). No guns. Triple expansion engines. 2 shafts. H.P. : 1,137 = 12·5 kts. 2 cylindrical boilers. Oil fuel : 292 tons.

Trawler.

1932 *Photo, Official.*

MADRAS. (Burns & Co., Calcutta, 1919). Standard displacement : 413 tons. Complement, 23. Dimensions : 125 (*pp.*), 134 (*o.a.*) × 23¼ × 12 feet (*mean* draught). No guns. Machinery : Triple expansion, by Hawthorn Leslie. 1 shaft. H.P. : 460 = 10 kts. 1 cylindrical coal-fired boiler. Used for target towing.

STRAITS SETTLEMENTS

Motor Patrol Boats.

PAHLAWAN, PANGLIMA, PENINGAT, PANJI.
Photo and particulars of first two in Addenda.
Note.—Used for training of personnel, Straits Settlements Division, R.N.V.R.

NEWFOUNDLAND.

Transports, etc.

(All photos, courtesy H. A. Le Messurier, Esq.)

Added 1938.

CARIBOU (Nieuwe Waterweg Scheepsbouw Maatschappij, Rotterdam, 1935). 2222 tons *gross*. Dimensions : 266 × 41¼ × 18⅓ feet draught. Armament nil. I.H.P. 2800 = 14 kts. Machinery : Triple expansion. 1 screw. 2 S.E. boilers, working pressure 200 lbs. Coal : 411 tons. Complement, 42. Accommodation also provided for 180 passengers or 243 troops. Strengthened for ice navigation.

Added 1938.

NORTHERN RANGER. (Fleming & Ferguson, Paisley, 1936). 1,365 tons *gross*. Complement, 32. Dimensions : 220 × 36 × 16⅚ feet draught. Speed 11·5 kts. Coal : 270 tons. Strengthened for ice navigation.

111

Added 1938.

KYLE. (Swan Hunter, 1913). 1,055 tons *gross*. Complement, 34. Dimensions : 220 × 32 × 16⅔ feet draught. Speed : 13·5 kts. Strengthened for ice navigation.

Added 1938.

SAGONA. (Dundee Shipbuilding Co., Ltd., 1912). 808 tons *gross*. Complement, 26. Dimensions : 175 × 28¼ × 16½ feet draught. Speed : 11 kts. Strengthened for ice navigation.

DAISY. (J. Duthie Torry Shipbuilding Co., Aberdeen, 1912). Displacement : 510 tons, 248 tons *gross*. Complement, 16. Dimensions : 125 × 18 × 10 feet draught. Speed : 10 kts.

PORTIA.   *Added* 1938.

PORTIA, PROSPERO. (Murdoch & Murray, Port Glasgow, 1904). 978 tons *gross*. Complement, 32. Dimensions : 204 × 31 × 17 feet draught. Speed : 11·5 kts.

ARGYLE.   *Added* 1938.

ARGYLE, CLYDE, HOME. (A. & J. Inglis, Glasgow, 1900). 439 tons *gross*. Complement, 20. Dimensions : 154½ × 25 × 12 feet draught. Speed : 10 kts.

GLENCOE.   *Added* 1938.

GLENCOE. (A. & J. Inglis, Glasgow, 1899). 767 tons *gross*. Complement, 24. Dimensions : 208 × 30 × 16 feet draught. Speed : 11 kts.

ROYAL CANADIAN NAVY.

Chief of the Naval Staff under Minister of National Defence : Rear-Admiral P. W. Nelles, R.C.N.

Personnel : R.C.N., Officers, 150 ; Men, 1,822. R.C.N.R., 70 and 430. R.C.N.V.R., 138 and 1,678. Fishermen's Reserve of R.C.N.R., 40 skippers and 160 men.

Uniforms : As British Navy.

N.B.—(A = Atlantic, P = Pacific.)

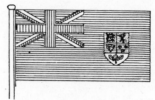

ENSIGN.

FRASER *class.*

ARMENTIÈRES.

SKEENA, SAGUENAY.

Minesweeping Trawlers.

> *Photo wanted.*
> *Understood to resemble* MASTIFF, *in British Navy Section.*

(P) **COMOX** (Burrard Dry Dock Co., Vancouver, B.C., Aug. 9, 1938). (A) **FUNDY** (Collingwood Shipyards, June 18, 1938). (A) **GASPÉ** (Morton Engineering & Dry Dock Co., Quebec, Aug. 12, 1938). (P) **NOOTKA** (Yarrows, Victoria, B.C., Sept. 26, 1938). Displacement : 460 tons (696 tons *full load*). Complement : 25 peace, 33 war. Dimensions : 150 × 27½ × 14½ feet. Guns : 1—4 inch. Machinery : Triple expansion. I.H.P. : 950 = 12·5 kts. Coal : 180 tons.

1932 *Photo, Official.*

(P) **ARMENTIÈRES** (1918). Ex-Trawler. Steel. 357 tons *gross*, 136 tons *net*. Dimensions : 130 × 25 × 14 feet. Guns : 1—3 inch. Speed : 10 kts. Complement : 18.

Note.—3 sister ships are in service of Department of Fisheries (see a later page).

4 "Fraser" class

Note.—It is proposed to acquire H.M.S. *Kempenfelt* for the Royal Canadian Navy. (Photo in British Navy Section.)

FRASER.

1932, *R. Perkins.*

Fraser (ex-*Crescent*), **St. Laurent** (ex-*Cygnet*), (both Vickers-Armstrongs, Sept. 29, 1931). **Ottawa** (ex-*Crusader*), **Restigouche** (ex-*Comet*), (both Portsmouth Dockyard, Sept. 30, 1931). Acquired from Royal Navy in 1937 and 1938. Displacement : 1,375 tons. Complement : 145. Dimensions : 317¾ (*pp.*), 326 (*w.l.*) × 33 × 8½ feet (*mean*). Guns : 4—4·7 inch, **7** smaller. Tubes : **8**—21 inch (quadrupled). Machinery : Parsons geared turbines. S.H.P. : 36,000 = 36 kts. Boilers : 3 Admiralty 3-drum type. Oil fuel : 470 tons. Laid down in 1930 and completed in 1932. (Plan as British *Defender* class.)

2 "Skeena" class.

SAGUENAY.

1932 *Photo, D. Trimingham, Esq.*

Saguenay (July 11, 1930) and **Skeena** (October 10. 1930), ordered in January, 1929, from Messrs. Thornycroft. Displacement : 1,337 tons. Dimensions : 309 (*pp.*), 321¼ (*o.a.*) × 32¼ × 10½ (*mean*), 12 feet (*max.*). Guns : 4—4·7 inch, 2—2 pdr. pom-pom, 5 M.G. Tubes : **8**—21 inch (quadrupled). H.P. : 32,000 = 35 kts Machinery : Parsons geared turbines. 3 Thornycroft boilers, with superheaters. Oil fuel : 440 tons Complement : 138.

Notes.—These ships exceeded 37 knots on trials with ease, and their running was marked by almost complete absence of vibration. Similar to British " A " class, but specially strengthened to withstand ice pressure. Laid down in 1929 and completed in 1931. Cost, with armament, about £670,000.

(Plan as British *Acasta* class.)

Training Ships.

1938, *D. Trimingham, Esq.*

VENTURE. (June 9, 1937). Auxiliary 3-masted Wooden Schooner. Displacement : 250 tons. Length : 110 feet (*w.l.*), 146 feet (*o.a.*) × 27 × 14 feet (*mean*). Machinery : Petter Diesel. B.H.P. : 120 = 7 kts. Radius : 1,000 miles ; carries water and provisions for 30 days. Sail area : 12,000 sq. feet. Complement : 40, including 24 boys under training.

Note.—This vessel was built for the R.C.N. by Meteghan Shipbuilding Co., Meteghan, N.S.

SKIDEGATE (1927). Motor launch. Dimensions : 47 × 13½ feet. Diesel engine. B.H.P. 80. Used for training Fishermen's Reserve organisation.

SOUTH AFRICA.

Motor Torpedo Boats.

2, of 70 ft. type, are to be built.

Minesweepers.

(*Photos in Addenda.*)

CRASSULA (Hall, Russell & Co., Aberdeen, 1935). 261 tons gross. Dimensions : 125½ × 23½ × 12 feet. Guns : 1—6 pdr. I.H.P. 480 = 11·5 kts. (ex-Trawler).

KOMMETJE (Nylands Värksted, Oslo, 1930). 252 tons gross. Dimensions : 115 × 23¾ × 11½ feet. Guns : 1—6 pdr. I.H.P. 550 = 12 kts.

Canadian Government Vessels

These form a potential reserve for the Royal Canadian Navy in time of war, though administered during peace by the several Departments named below. Guns, where provided, are dismounted and in store.

Department of Transport

ALBERNI (Sorel, Que., 1927). (Rebuilt, 1936). Steel. 502 tons *gross*. Complement : 24. Dimensions : 157·3 × 30·5 × 10·6 feet (depth). Machinery : Vertical fore and aft compound. I.H.P. : 360 = 8 kts. Coal : 270 tons. (Lighthouse and buoy service).

ARANMORE (W. B. Thompson, Dundee, 1890). Iron. 1,170 tons *gross*. Dimensions : 241½ × 34 × 15½ feet (depth). Machinery : Triple expansion. H.P. : 1,500 = 13 kts. Coal : 230 tons.

ARGENTEUIL (Sorel, Que., 1916). Steel. 165 tons *gross*. Complement, 13. Dimensions : 94 × 21 × 7 feet. Coal : 48 tons.

BELLECHASSE (Kingston S.B. Co., 1912). Steel. Displacement : 576 tons, 417 tons *gross*. Dimensions : 142¼ × 27 × 12 feet (depth). Machinery : Triple expansion. H.P. : 1,000 = 13 kts. Coal : 110 tons.

BERENS, BIRNIE (B.C. Yacht & Boat Builders Co., Victoria, 1921). Wood. 73 tons *gross*. Complement : 9. Dimensions : 66¼ × 18 × 9¾ feet (depth). Machinery : Semi-Diesel. B.H.P. : 100 = 8·5 kts. Fuel : 1,800 gallons.

BERNIER (ex-*Mardep*). (Davie S.B. & Repairing Co., Lauzon, Que., 1918). Steel. 317 tons *gross*. Complement : 19. Dimensions : 125 × 23 × 13½ feet (depth). Machinery : Triple expansion. I.H.P. : 500 = 9·5 kts. Coal : 100 tons.

BERTHIER (Sorel, Que., 1916). Steel. 368 tons *gross*. Complement : 20. Dimensions : 120 × 24 × 11·4 feet (depth). Machinery : Fore and aft compound. I.H.P. : 550 = 10·5 kts. Coal : 38 tons. (Ship Channel Service).

BRANT (Sorel, Que., 1927). Steel. 285 tons *gross*. Complement : 19. Dimensions : 124½ × 23 × 12 feet (depth). Machinery : Triple expansion. I.H.P. : 350 = 10 kts. Coal : 68 tons.

CITADELLE (Davie S.B. & Repairing Co., 1932). Steel. 431 tons *gross*. Complement : 13. Dimensions : 120½ × 30 × 13½ feet (depth). Machinery : Triple expansion. I.H.P. : 1,200 = 13 kts. Oil fuel : 74 tons.

DETECTOR (Sorel, Que., 1915). Steel. 584 tons *gross*. Complement : 23. Dimensions : 140 × 35 × 13 feet (depth). Machinery : Fore and aft compound. I.H.P. : 532 = 10·5 kts. Coal : 110 tons. (Ship Channel Service).

DOLLARD (Kingston S.B. Co., 1913). Steel. 761 tons *gross*. Dimensions : 178½ × 32 × 15¼ feet (depth). Machinery : Triple expansion. I.H.P. : 1,000 = 11 kts. Coal : 100 tons.

DRUID (Fleming & Ferguson, 1902). Steel. Displacement : 1,000 tons. Dimensions : 160 × 30 × 12½ feet (depth). Machinery : Triple expansion. H.P. : 800 = 10 kts. Coal : 100 tons.

ESTEVAN (Collingwood S.B. Co., 1912). Steel. Displacement : 2,100 tons, 1,161 tons *gross*. Dimensions : 212 × 38 × 15¼ feet (depth). Machinery : Triple expansion. I.H.P. : 1,500 = 12·5 kts. Coal : 350 tons.

FRONTENAC (Sorel, Que., 1930). Steel. 248 tons *gross*. Complement : 20. Dimensions : 108·8 × 24 × 10 feet (depth). Machinery : Vertical triple expansion. I.H.P. : 472 = 10 kts. Coal : 45 tons. (Ship Channel Service).

GRENVILLE (Polson Iron Works, 1915). Steel. 497 tons *gross*. Dimensions : 155 × 31 × 11 feet (depth). Machinery : Triple expansion. I.H.P. : 900 = 11·5 kts. Coal : 100 tons.

JALOBERT (Kingston Shipbuilding Co., Ltd., Kingston, Ont., 1911). Steel. 278 tons *gross*. Complement : 20. Dimensions : 107·5 × 23 × 11·9 feet (depth). Machinery : Vertical fore and aft compound. I.H.P. : 120 = 11 kts. Coal : 58½ tons. (Ship Channel Service).

LADY GREY (Vickers, 1906). Steel. Displacement : 1,080 tons. 733 tons *gross*. Dimensions : 172 × 32 × 16 feet (depth). Machinery : Triple expansion. I.H.P. : 2,300 = 14 kts. Coal : 200 tons. (Icebreaker).

LADY LAURIER (Fleming & Ferguson, 1902). Steel. Displacement : 1,970 tons, 1,051 tons *gross*. Dimensions : 215 × 34¼ × 17¼ feet. Machinery : Triple expansion. I.H.P. : 1,800 = 13 kts. Coal : 175 tons.

LANORAIE II (Sorel, Que., 1928). Steel. 177 tons *gross*. Complement : 13. Dimensions : 93·7 × 23 × 10 feet (depth). Machinery : Vertical fore and aft compound. I.H.P. : 336 = 10 kts. Coal : 30 tons. (Lighthouse and buoy service).

LAURENTIAN (ex-*King Edward*). (Cook, Welton & Gemmell, 1902). Steel. 355 tons *gross*. Dimensions : 149 × 24 × 11 feet (depth). Machinery : Triple expansion. I.H.P. : 520 = 11 kts.

MONTCALM (Napier & Miller, 1904). Steel. Displacement : 3,270 tons, 1,432 tons *gross*. Dimensions : 245 × 40½ × 15¾ feet. Machinery : Triple expansion. I.H.P. : 3,600 = 14 kts. Watertube boilers. Coal : 425 tons.

MURRAY STEWART (Port Arthur, Ont., 1918). Steel. 234 tons *gross*. Complement, 15. Dimensions : 119 × 26 × 15½ feet. Speed : 10 kts. Coal : 150 tons.

N. B. McLEAN (Halifax Shipyards, March, 1930). Steel. Displacement : 5,000 tons. 3,254 tons *gross*. Complement : 49. Dimensions : 260 × 60¼ × 28½ feet (depth). Machinery : Triple expansion. I.H.P. : 6,500 = 15 kts. Oil fuel : 1,322 tons. (Icebreaker).

OCEAN EAGLE (ex-*St. Arvans*), (Day, Summers & Co., 1919 ; rebuilt, 1927). Steel. 420 tons *gross*. Complement : 15. Dimensions : 135 × 29 × 14⅞ feet (*mean draught*). Machinery : Triple expansion. I.H.P. : 1,200 = 11·5 kts. Coal : 221 tons. (Tug).

ST HELIERS (Port Glasgow, 1919), (Re-built, St. John, N.B., 1930). Steel. 929 tons *gross*. Complement, 23. Dimensions : 190¼ × 29 × 16¼ feet. I.H.P. : 1,200 = 11·5 kts. Oil fuel : 110 tons.

SAFEGUARDER (ex-salvage vessel *Safeguard*). (Day, Summers & Co., 1914 ; rebuilt, 1929). Steel. 665 tons *gross*. Complement : 24. Dimensions : 160 × 29 × 15¾ feet (depth). Machinery : Triple expansion. I.H.P. : 1,350 = 13·5 kts. Coal : 110 tons.

SAUREL (Canadian Vickers, Oct. 30, 1929). Steel. 1,176 tons *gross*. Complement : 23. Dimensions : 200 × 42 × 19¼ feet (depth). Machinery : Triple expansion. I.H.P. : 3,000 = 17 kts. Oil fuel : 370 tons.

VARENNES (Sorel, 1911). Wood. 187 tons *gross*. Complement : 12. Dimensions : 85½ × 22¼ × 9½ feet (depth). Machinery : Compound. I.H.P. : 200 = 9 kts. Coal : 50 tons.

VERCHERES (Polson Iron Works, 1901 ; rebuilt, 1928). Steel. 157 tons *gross*. Complement : 14. Dimensions : 104 × 26¼ × 11 feet (depth). Machinery : Compound. I.H.P. : 60 = 8 kts. Coal : 50 tons.

Department of Mines and Resources.

ACADIA (Swan Hunter, 1913). Steel. Displacement : 1,710 tons. Complement : 49. Dimensions : 170 × 33¾ × 19 feet (depth). Guns : 1—4 inch, 2—3 inch. Machinery : Triple expansion. H.P. : 1,200 = 12 kts. Coal : 260 tons. (Surveying Service, Atlantic).

CARTIER (Swan Hunter, 1910). Steel. Displacement : 897 tons. Complement : 41. Dimensions : 164 × 29 × 13 feet. Guns : 3—3 inch. Machinery : Triple expansion. I.H.P. : 830 = 12 kts. Coal : 180 tons. (Surveying Service, Atlantic).

WILLIAM J. STEWART (Collingwood Shipyards, 1932). Steel. 1,295 tons *gross*. Complement : 57. Dimensions : 214 × 36 × 15 feet (depth). Machinery : Triple expansion. I.H.P. : 1,200 = 12 kts. Coal : 300 tons. (Surveying Service, Pacific).

Department of Lands (Manitoba)

BRADBURV (1915). Steel. Displacement : 500 tons, 394 tons *gross*. Complement : 13. Dimensions : 151 × 27¼ × 8 feet. Machinery : Triple expansion. (Employed on Fisheries Patrol, Lake Winnipeg).

Department of Fisheries

FISHERY PATROL VESSELS—

ARLEUX, ARRAS, GIVENCHY (all 1918). Steel. 357 tons *gross*. Complement : 18. Dimensions : 130 × 25 × 13 feet. Guns : 1—3 inch. Machinery : Triple expansion. I.H.P. : 480 = 10 kts. Coal : 140 tons.

MALASPINA (Dublin Dockyard Co., 1913). Steel. Displacement : 850 tons. Complement : 40. Dimensions : 162¼ × 27 × 13 feet (depth). Guns : 1—6 pdr. Machinery : Triple expansion. I.H.P. : 1,350 = 14·5 kts. Coal : 200 tons.

Royal Canadian Mounted Police (Marine Section)

CUSTOMS PATROL VESSELS—

ADVERSUS (1931). Composite. 156 tons *gross*. Complement : 14. Dimensions : 112 × 19 × 11 feet (depth). Diesel engines. B.H.P. : 365.

FLEURDELIS (Canadian Vickers, 1929). Steel. 316 tons *gross*. Complement : 23. Dimensions : 165 × 21 × 11 feet (depth). Winton engines of 1,800 B.H.P.

FRENCH (Davie S.B. & Repairing Co., 1938). Steel. 226 tons *gross*.

LAURIER, MACDONALD (1937). 201 tons *gross*. Dimensions : 113 × 21 × 10⅓ feet (depth).

(There are 8 smaller vessels, also used in Customs Patrol.)

New Construction.

An Icebreaker was ordered from the Davie Shipbuilding & Repair Co. in 1939 to replace LADY GREY, above.

NEW ZEALAND.

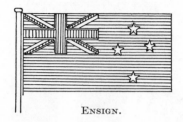

ENSIGN.

Commander-in-Chief—H. E. The Rt. Hon. Viscount Galway, G.C.M.G., D.S.O., O.B.E.

Naval Board.

President : The Minister of Defence, the Hon. Frederick Jones, M.P.
First Naval Member : Commodore H. E. Horan, D.S.C., R.N.
Second Naval Member and Chief Staff Officer : Commander A. B. Fanshawe, R.N.
Naval Secretary : Paymaster Captain N. T. P. Cooper, R.N.
Commanding N.Z. Division : Commodore J. W. Rivett-Carnac, D.S.C., R.N.

Minesweeping Trawler.
(It is proposed to acquire 3 more Trawlers).

ACHILLES.

1934 *Photo, R. Perkins.*

LEANDER.

1937, *R. Perkins.*

ACHILLES (1932), **LEANDER** (1931), 7,030 and 7,270 tons respectively. Guns : **8**—6 inch, **8**—4 inch AA., **4**—3 pdr., **8** smaller. 1 aircraft carried. (Full details of both ships will be found in Royal Navy section, on earlier pages. Both are lent to the New Zealand Government by the Admiralty, the former paying for their annual maintenance on the Station.)

Sail Training Vessel.
VIKING. Length, 67 feet. Ketch, attached to Training Depot at Auckland.

Note.—Escort Vessels *Leith* and *Wellington* and Surveying Vessel *Endeavour* (all described on earlier pages) are also attached to New Zealand Division for duty in the islands of the S. Pacific.

1937, *Nautical Photo Agency.*

WAKAKURA (ex-*T.R.*1). "Castle" type, similar to *Coronet*, in British Navy section.

Fleet Tug.
TOIA (ex-*St. Boniface*, ex-*St. Fergus*). Details as "Saint" class, in British Navy Section.

EIRE.

2 Thornycroft M.T.B. of 70 ft. type under construction. 1939.

ARGENTINA.

Flags.

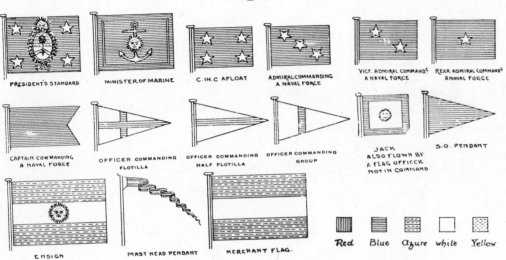

Insignia or Rank.

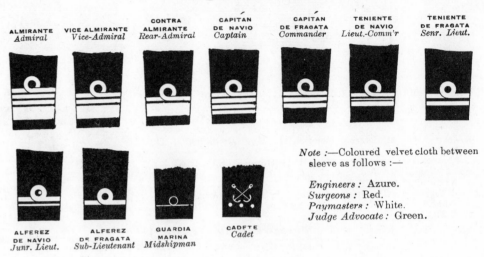

Notation.	Nominal Calibre.		Maker.	Length in Calibres.	Muzzle Velocity.	Weight A.P. Projectile.	Max. penetration against K.C. with capped A.P. at	
							5000 yards.	3000 yards.
	inches	c/m.		calibres.	ft. secs.	lbs.	inches.	inches.
Heavy	12	30·5	B	50	2900	870	19	23
Medium	10	25·4	A	40	2207	500	7	9½
	9·4	24	K	35	{2300 2133}	352	4½	6
	7·5	19	A	52	3116	200	...	...
Light	6	15	B	50	2600	105	...	8¼
	6	15	A	45	2500	100	3	4½
	6	15	A	40	2200	100	3	3¾
	4·7	12	A	45	2570	45	...	2¾
	4·7	12	A	40	2230	45	...	...
	4	10·16	B	50	2996	30	...	...

In the Maker's column A = Armstrong; B = Bethlehem; K = Krupp.
There are also Italian models of 4 inch and 3·9 inch guns.
The above details of Argentine Naval Ordnance have been officially revised.

Dockyards and Arsenals.

DÁRSENA NORTE. (Buenos Aires) Dry docks: (Eastern) 590½ × 65½ × 25 feet, and (Western) 492 × 65½ × 25 feet.

PUERTO BELGRANO (Bahia Blanca). Dry docks: (1) 657 × 84 × 32½ ft., (2) 683 × 114 × 43 ft.
RIO SANTIAGO. Dock, 672 × 114 × 36 feet. Two floating docks. (1) 1500 tons lift; (2) 300 tons lift.

Mercantile Marine.

(From "Lloyd's Register," 1939 figures.)
337 vessels of 312,970 tons, gross tonnage.

General Notes.

Minister of Marine : Vicealmirante Leon L. Scasso.
Chief of Naval Staff : Vicealmirante Julian Fablet.
Chief of Naval Commission (Europe) and Naval Attaché, London : Capitan de Navio José S. Zuloaga.
Personnel : 1,000 officers, 14,500 men.
Form of Address : Capitán de Navio ——, A.R.A. ——.

Note :—Coloured velvet cloth between sleeve as follows :—

Engineers : Azure.
Surgeons : Red.
Paymasters : White.
Judge Advocate : Green.

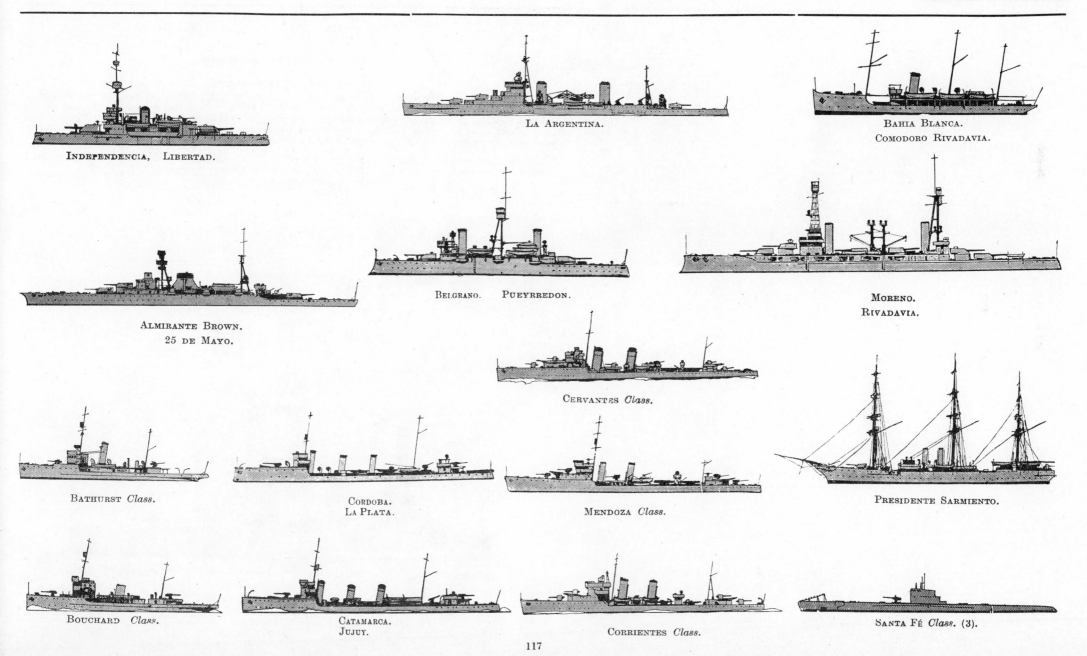

INDEPENDENCIA, LIBERTAD.

LA ARGENTINA.

BAHIA BLANCA.
COMODORO RIVADAVIA.

ALMIRANTE BROWN.
25 DE MAYO.

BELGRANO. PUEYRREDON.

MORENO.
RIVADAVIA.

CERVANTES *Class.*

BATHURST *Class.*

CORDOBA.
LA PLATA.

MENDOZA *Class.*

PRESIDENTE SARMIENTO.

BOUCHARD *Class.*

CATAMARCA.
JUJUY.

CORRIENTES *Class.*

SANTA FÉ *Class.* (3).

MORENO.   1937, *Official*.

New Construction.

The current Naval Programme, approved by Parliament in Sept., 1926, involved the expenditure of 75,000,000 gold pesos (£15,000,000) over the ten years 1927-1936. In addition to the extension of present dockyard facilities on the River Plate and at Puerto Belgrano, and the opening of a new yard at Mardel Plata, the construction of a number of ships to replace obsolete tonnage was provided for; but it has not been found possible to complete this programme in ten years.

So far, 3 cruisers, 12 destroyers, 3 submarines, 9 patrol vessels and 2 surveying vessels have been completed. Two escort vessels are under construction, and 5 more destroyers are projected.

(For particulars, see following page)

MORENO   1937, *R. Perkins*.

RIVADAVIA (26 Aug., 1911) & **MORENO** (23 Sept., 1911).

Standard displacement, 27,720 tons. *Full load*, over **31,000** tons. Complement, 1215.

Length (*w.l.*), 577½ feet. Beam, 95 feet. *Max.* load draught, 28 feet. Length (*over all*), 585 feet.

Guns (Bethlehem) :
12—12 inch, 50 cal.
12—6 inch, 50 cal.
4—3 inch AA.
4—3 pdr.
6 M.G.
(4 landing).
Torpedo tubes (21 inch) :
2 *submerged*
(broadside).

Armour (Krupp) : (*See notes.*)
11″—8″ Belt (amidships)
5″ Belt (bow) N.C.
4″ Belt (stern) N.C.
3″ Deck (slopes)
9″—8″ Side above belt..
12″—9″ Big gun turrets ..
6″ Secondary battery (N.C.)
12″ Conning Tower(forward)
9″ Do. (aft.)
Total weight: 7600 tons.

Machinery : Curtis geared turbines. 3 screws. S.H.P. 45,000 = 23 kts.
Boilers : 18 Babcock (converted to oil burning, 1924-25). Oil : 3,600 tons.
Nominal radius : 3930 miles at full speed, 8500 miles at 10 kts.

Note to plan:—
3 pdr. guns shown on top of B and X turrets, since replaced by rangefinders.

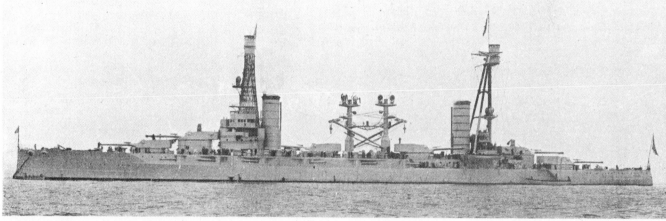

MORENO. (RIVADAVIA same appearance). 1937, R. Perkins.

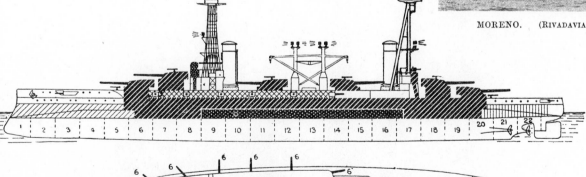

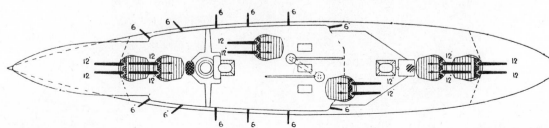

119

Gunnery Notes.—Heights of barbettes over normal draught w.l.: No. 1, 29½ feet; No. 2, 37½ feet; Nos. 3 and 4 (echelon), and No. 5, 29 feet; No. 6, 20 feet; 6 inch guns, 19½ feet above w.l. Arcs of fire : end barbettes, Nos. 1 and 6, 270°; Nos. 2 and 5 (super-firing), 300°; Nos. 3 and 4 (echelon) 180° own beam and 100° far beam. Director controls (U.S.) type installed during 1924—25 refits. Rates of fire are reported to be : 12 inch, 2 rounds a minute ; 6 inch, 8 ; 4 inch, 12.

Armour Notes.—Main belt is 8 feet deep, 4½ feet above water-line and 3½ feet below same at normal draught. It is 240 feet long, but 11″ section is only 2 feet deep from top edge of belt, and then tapers to 5″ on lower (under-water) edge. Belt under end barbettes is 10″ tapering to 5″ as main belt. Upper belt 400 feet long, 9″ lower edge, 8″ top edge, 6″ battery above this. Funnel bases, 1½″ nickel steel for 15 feet above deck. Protective decks, 1½″ upper, 3″ lower. Two Director stations behind upper belt at bases of C.T. communication tubes. Barbettes : bases are 9″ where exposed. Shields to these : 12″ port-plate, 9″ sides, 11″ back, 3″ roof.

Anti-Torpedo Defence.—3″ longitudinal wing bulkheads in way of machinery and magazine spaces. ¾″ nickel steel flats under magazines, boilers, and engine rooms. Total weight, 680 tons (included in 7,600 tons total weight of armour given above). 12—38-inch searchlights.

General Notes.—Built under 1908 Programme. Large refits in U.S.A., 1924—25.

Electric Engineering Notes.—Electric installation at 220 volts.

Name	Builder	Machinery	Laid down	Completed	Trials	Boilers	Best recent speed
Rivadavia Moreno	Fore River Co. N.Y. Ship-building	Fore River Co.	May. '10 July, '10	Dec., 1914 Mar., 1915	39,750 = 22·5	Babcock Babcock	

LA ARGENTINA (March 16, 1937).

(Specially designed as Training Cruiser).

Displacement: 6,000 tons *standard*, 7,500 tons full load. Complement, 556 + 60 cadets. Dimensions: 450 (*p.p.*), 500 (*o.a.*) × 56 × $16\frac{1}{2}$ feet (*max.*)

1938, courtesy Messrs. Vickers-Armstrongs, Ltd.

Guns:
9—6 inch.
*4—4 inch AA.
2—3 inch (field)
4—3 pdr.
8—2 pdr. AA.

Torpedo Tubes:
6—21 inch (tripled).

*Only 2 of these were mounted up to summer of 1939.

Aircraft :
2 Seagull Amphibians with 1 Catapult.

Armour :
2″ Deck.
2″ Gunhouses.
3″ Side.
3″ C.T.

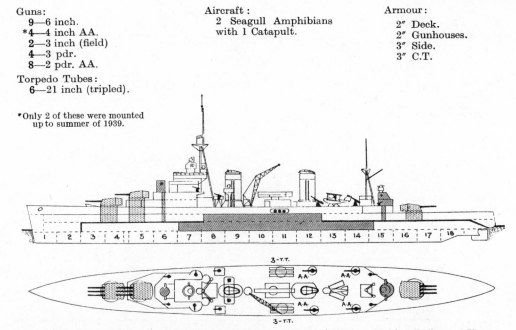

Machinery : Parsons geared turbines. 4 shafts. S.H.P. : 60,000 = 31 kts. Boilers : 4 Yarrow, working pressure 300 lbs. Oil fuel : 1,500 tons.

Note.—Laid down by Vickers-Armstrongs, Ltd., at Barrow, 1935, to replace *Presidente Sarmiento*, and delivered Jan. 31, 1939. Cost 6,000,000 gold pesos (about £1,750,000).

1938, Keith P. Lewis.

ALMIRANTE BROWN.

1931 *Photo, favour of Count C. de Grave Sells.*

ALMIRANTE BROWN (Aug. 25th, 1929). VEINTICINCO DE MAYO (Aug. 11th, 1929)

Standard displacement, 6800 tons. (*Full load about* 8600 tons.) Complement, 600.

Length, 533¼ feet. (w.l.) 545¾ (o.a.) Beam, 58 feet. Draught, 16¼ feet.

Guns :
  6—7·5 inch, 52 cal.
  12—3·9 inch, 47 cal. AA.
  6—40 m/m. pom-poms.
Torpedo tubes (21 inch) :
  6 *above water* (in triple
    mountings).

Armour :
  1″ Deck ....
  2″ Gun Houses ....
  2½″ C.T. ....
  2¾″ Side ....

Machinery : Geared Parsons turbines. **6** Yarrow boilers. S.H.P. 85,000 = 32 kts. Oil fuel : 1800 tons. **2** screws.

General Notes.—Both laid down 1927, *25 de Mayo* by Orlando at Leghorn, *Alm. Brown* by Odero at Sestri Ponente. Cost £1,225,000 each. Rig shown in plan was that originally proposed, but subsequently modified as in photos. A proposal to add aircraft to their equipment had not materialised up to 1939.

Gunnery Notes—AA. guns are in twin mountings similar to those in Italian *Trento* type.

VEINTICINCO DE MAYO.

1932 *Photos, Official.*

121

ARGENTINA—Coast Defence Ships

2 ex-Cruisers (*classed as Coast Defence Ships*).

BELGRANO.

1930 *Photo, courtesy of Ministry of Marine.*

BELGRANO (ex-*Varese*), (July 25, 1897), Orlando, Leghorn.

PUEYRREDON (ex-*Giuseppe Garibaldi*), (Sept. 25, 1897), Ansaldo, Sestri Ponente.

Displacement : 6,100 tons *standard*.
Dimensions : $328 \times 59 \cdot 7 \times 23 \cdot 5$ feet.

Guns : *Belgrano :* **2**—10 inch, **8**—4·7 inch, **4**—6 pdr., **2**—37 mm. A.A.
      Pueyrredon : **2**—10 inch, **8**—6 inch, **4**—6 pdr., **1**—37 mm. AA.

Armour : Terni. Belt 6″–3″. Deck 1½″–2″. Lower deck side 6″. Battery 6″. Barbettes 6″. Gunhouses 6″. C.T. 6″.

Machinery : 2 sets T. Exp. Boilers : 8 Yarrow. H.P. 13,000 = 18 kts. Oil fuel : 1,000 tons.

Notes—These old cruisers are officially rated as coast defence ships. They have been converted to oil fuel and had main deck battery removed, tripod mast fitted and Director firing installed. *Belgrano* completed 1930 by Odero. *Pueyrredon* refitted at Puerto Belgrano ; sister ships *Garibaldi* and *San Martin* scrapped 1934.

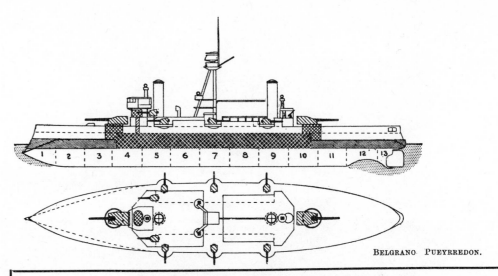

BELGRANO PUEYRREDON.

2 Coast Defence Ships. (Classed as *Canoneros*).

LIBERTAD.

1936 *Official (added* 1937)

INDEPENDENCIA (1891), **LIBERTAD** (ex-*Nueve de Julio*), (1890). Both built by Laird's, Birkenhead. Displacement, 2,595 tons. Complement, 196. Dimensions : 240 (*p.p.*) × 43 × 13 feet (*max.*). Guns : **2**—9·4 inch, 35 cal. (Krupp), **4**—4·7 inch, 40 cal. (Armstrong), **4**— 3 pdr. Armour (compound) : 8″ Belt (amidships), 2″ Deck (flat on belt), 8″ Bulkhead (forward), 6″ Bulkhead (aft), 8″ Barbettes and bases, 5″ Shields to big guns (fronts), 4″ Conning tower. Machinery : Compound vertical. 2 screws. Boilers : 4 double cylindrical. Designed H.P. 3,000 = 13 kts. Oil fuel : 170 tons. (Converted to burn oil, 1925–27).

7 Corrientes class

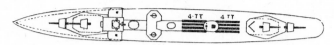

ENTRE RIOS   *1938, courtesy Messrs. Vickers-Armstrongs, Ltd.*

3 *Vickers-Armstrongs (Barrow)*: **Corrientes, Entre Rios, Buenos Aires,** (all Sept. 21, 1937).
2 *Cammell Laird*: **Misiones** (Sept. 23rd, 1937). **Santa Cruz** (Nov. 3, 1937).
2 *Clydebank*: **San Juan** (June 24, 1937). **San Luis** (Aug. 24, 1937).
Displacement; 1,375 tons standard. Complement, 130. Dimensions; 312 (*p.p.*), 320 (*w.l.*) 323 (*o.a.*) × 33 × 8½ feet (*mean draught*). Guns: 4—4·7 inch, 8 smaller. Torpedo tubes: 8—21 inch (quadrupled). Machinery: Parsons geared turbines. S.H.P.: 34,000 = 35·5 kts. Boilers: 3, of 3-drum type. Oil fuel: 450 tons.

Notes.—Generally similar to British *Greyhound* type. All laid down 1936 and completed March—Oct. 1938. Cost approaches £400,000 each. 5 more of this type are projected. Pendant Nos. are E 6, *Buenos Aires*; E 7, *Entre Rios*; E 8, *Corrientes*; E 9, *San Juan*; E 10, *San Luis*; E 11, *Misiones*; E 12, *Santa Cruz*.

TUCUMAN.   *1936, Official (added 1937).*

3 *White*: **Mendoza** (July 18th, 1928), **Tucuman** (Oct. 16th, 1928) and **La Rioja** (Jan. 26th, 1929). All laid down in June, 1927 for completion in June, 1929. Displacement, (*standard*) 1570 tons; (*deep load*) 2300 tons. Complement, 160. Dimensions: 332¼ (*w.l.*), 335 (*o.a.*) × 31¾ × 12¼ feet. Guns (Vickers-Armstrong): 5—4·7 inch, 1—3 inch AA., 2—2 pdr. Torpedo tubes: 6—21 inch, in triple deck mountings. 2 sets Parsons turbines, with single reduction gearing. Steam supplied at 250 lbs. from 4—3 drum water-tube boilers. H.P. 42,000 = 36 kts. 38 kts. maintained for 6 hours on trials by *Mendoza* and *Tucuman*; *La Rioja* touched 39·4 kts. without running machinery in excess of designed power. Oil fuel: 540 tons. Radius of action: 4,500 miles at 14 kts.

Note.—Pendant Nos. are: *Mendoza*, E 3; *La Rioja*, E 4; *Tucuman*, E 5.

JUAN DE GARAY   *1939, Official.*

Cervantes (ex *Churruca*, Cadiz, June 26th, 1925), **Juan de Garay** (ex-*Alcala Galiano*, Cartagena, Nov. 3rd, 1925). Purchased from Spanish Government, 1927. Displacement, 1,522 tons *standard* 2087 tons *full load*). Dimensions: 320 × 31¾ × 10½ feet. Guns: 5—4·7 inch, 1—3 inch AA., 4 M.G. Torpedo tubes: 6—21 inch, in triple deck mountings. 2 D.C. carried. Machinery: 2 sets Parsons geared turbines. S.H.P.: 42,000 = 36 kts. Oil fuel: 540 tons. Radius of action: 4,500 miles at 14 kts. Complement: 175.

Note.—Design generally resembles that of British *Scott* class. Pendant Nos. are E 1 and E 2, respectively.

SANTA CRUZ.   *1938, Keith P. Lewis.*

MENDOZA and CERVANTES *classes.*   *Plan by courtesy of Messrs. J. Samuel White & Co., Ltd,*

Destroyers.—*Continued.*

(The four following vessels are rated as *Destructores*.)

CATAMARCA.

1933 *Photo, Official.*

2 (*German*) type: **Cordoba** (Schichau, Nov. 1910). **La Plata** (Germania, Jan., 1911). 1000 tons. 295 × 29½ × 7½ feet. Armament: **3**–4 in. (Beth.), **2**–37 mm. AA. **4**—21 inch. tubes. 1 D.C. Thrower. Curtis (A.E.G.) turbines. Boilers: 5 Schulz-Thornycroft, altered to burn oil. Designed S.H.P. 28,000=26·5 kts. Oil: 200 tons. Endurance: 2700 miles at 15 kts., 715 miles at full speed. Trials (*max.*): *Cordoba*, 34·2; *La Plata*, 34·7. Complement: 99.

2 (*German*) type: **Catamarca** (Schichau, Jan., 1911), **Jujuy** (Germania. March. 1911). 997 tons. 288⅔ × 7¼ × 28 feet. Armament: **3** –4 inch (Beth.). **2**–37 mm. AA., **4**–21 inch tubes. 1 D.C. Thrower. Curtis (A.E.G.) turbines. Boilers: Schulz-Thornycroft, altered to burn oil. Designed S.H.P. 28,000=27·2 kts. Oil: 220 tons. Endurance: 3000 miles at 15 kts., 800 miles at full speed. Complement: 99.

Appearance Note.—*Cordoba* and *La Plata* have ram bow

3 Submarines.

SANTIAGO DEL ESTERO.

1936, *Official, (added* 1937).

3 *Cavallini* type: **Salta,** (Jan. 17, 1932), **Santa Fe,** (July 11, 1931), **Santiago del Estero.** (March 28, 1932). Ordered from Cantiere Navale Franco Tosi, Taranto, Oct., 1927. Displacement $\frac{775}{920}$ tons. Dimensions: 220 (*w.l.*), 226½ (*o.a.*) × 21 × 13 feet. 2 Tosi 6-cylinder Diesels. H.P.: 3,000 = 17·5 kts. *surface.* B.H.P.: 1,400 = 9 kts. *submerged.* Armament: **1**—4 inch, **1**—37 mm. AA. guns, **8**—21 inch tubes. Cost £206,000 each, fully equipped. General design resembles Italian *Mameli* type.

Note.—Are differentiated by numerals painted on conning towers.

3 Surveying Vessels

1928 *Photo, by courtesy of Mess:s. R. & W. Hawthorn, Leslie & Co., Ltd.*

COMODORO RIVADAVIA, (BAHIA BLANCA behind her).

BAHIA BLANCA (ex-*San Luis*) (Oct. 26, 1927). **COMODORO RIVADAVIA** (ex-*San Juan*) (Sept. 27, 1927). Both built by Hawthorn, Leslie & Co., Ltd., Hebburn-on-Tyne. Delivered Feb. 1928. Displacement, 970 tons. Dimensions: 207 (*o.a.*) × 33 × 11 feet draught. Complement, 92. Guns: Nil. Machinery: Single shaft Hawthorn-Werkspoor Diesel engine. B.H.P. 700 = 12 kts. 1 screw. 1 single ended Scotch boiler to supply steam to auxiliary machinery. Oil fuel 85 tons. Radius of action: 4000 nautical miles.

Surveying Vessels—*continued*.

1936, *Official*.

ALFEREZ MACKINLAY (Netherlands, 1914). 783 tons. Dimensions: $193\frac{3}{4} \times 28\frac{1}{4} \times 13$ feet. Guns: Nil. H.P. 520 = 10 kts. Used as Lighthouse Inspection Vessel.

Training Ship.

PRESIDENTE SARMIENTO (1898). Built at Birkenhead. 2850 tons. Complement 294. Dimensions: $251\frac{5}{12} \times 43\frac{1}{4} \times 23\frac{1}{4}$. Guns: 3—4·7 inch, 45 cal.; 1—4 inch, 2—6 pdr., 2—3 pdr. Torpedo tubes: 3 *above water*. Designed H.P. 2800 = 15 kts. Coal: 330 tons. Boilers: 1 Niclausse, 1 Yarrow, 2 cylindrical single-ended. Radius: 4500 miles at 10 kts.

Notes.—Sheathed and coppered. Has accommodation for 400 boys. Refitted by builders, 1926. Relieved as Training Ship in 1939 by *La Argentina*, but is still retained.

2 Escort Vessels

Building

MURATURE, KING. Laid down at Rio Santiago, 1938 and 1939, respectively; 2 more of this type projected. Displacement: 800 tons (*full load*). Dimensions: $252\frac{2}{3} \times 29 \times 8\frac{2}{3}$ feet. Machinery: Diesel. B.H.P.: 4,000 = 16 kts. To be attached to Naval College for seagoing training.

15 Patrol Vessels. (*Rastreadores*)

GRANVILLE   1938, *Official*.

BOUCHARD (March 20, 1936), **DRUMMOND** (June 19, 1936), **GRANVILLE** (Jan. 27, 1937), **SPIRO** (June 7, 1937), **COMODORO PY** (March 30, 1938), and **FOURNIER** (1939), all built at Rio Santiago Naval Yard; **ROBINSON, SEAVER** (both Aug. 18, 1938) by Hansen & Puccini at San Fernando; **PARKER** (May 2, 1937), by Sanchez Shipyard, San Fernando. All laid down 1935–37. Standard displacement: 450 tons; full load, 520 tons. Complement: 62. Dimensions: 164 (*pp.*), $180\frac{1}{2}$ (*o.a.*) × $23\frac{1}{2}$ × $6\frac{1}{2}$ feet (*max.* draught). Guns: 2—3·9 inch, 47 cal., 2—40 mm. AA., 2 D.C. Machinery: 2 sets M.A.N. 2-cycle Diesels. B.H.P.: 2,000 = 15 kts. Oil fuel: 50 tons. Radius of action: 3,000 miles at 10 kts.

Note.—These are the first Argentine warships to be built in local shipyards. They are named after distinguished naval officers.

PINEDO.   1936, *Official* (Added 1937.)

BATHURST (ex-*M* 1, ex-*M* 48), **JORGE** (ex-*M* 3, ex-*M* 52), **PINEDO** (ex-*M* 6, ex-*M* 79), **SEGUI** (ex-*M* 8, ex-*M* 90), **THORNE** (ex-*M* 9, ex-*M* 101), **GOLONDRINA** (ex-*M* 10, ex-*M* 105). All built in Germany, 1916–19. Former German minesweepers, purchased by the Argentine Government in 1922 for use as despatch vessels, and since converted to burn oil. Displacement: 500 tons. Complement: 50. Dimensions: 184 (*w.l.*), 192 (*o.a.*) × $24\frac{1}{4}$ × $7\frac{1}{2}$ feet (*max.* draught). Guns: 3—3 inch. Machinery: 2 sets vertical triple expansion. 1 shaft. I.H.P.: 1,850 = 16 kts. Boilers: 2 Schulz. Oil fuel: 105 tons.

Notes—*Segui* serves as Diving Tender, *Golondrina* as Admiralty Yacht. All are named after distinguished Argentine naval officers. *Py* scrapped, 1937, after foundering in dock; and *Fournier*, *King* and *Murature* removed from effective list.

River Monitors.

1918 *Photo, Official*.

PARANA (April, 1908) & **ROSARIO** (July, 1908). Both built by Armstrong. Displacement, 1055 tons. Complement, 142. Length, 240 feet. Beam, $32\frac{2}{3}$ feet. Draught, $7\frac{5}{12}$ feet. Guns: 2—6 inch Howitzers, 6—3 inch, 2—37 mm. AA., 4 M.G. Armour: 3" Belt (amidships), $1\frac{1}{2}$"—1" Deck, 3" Conning tower. H.P. 1600 = 15 kts. 2 Yarrow boilers. 2 screws. Coal: 120 tons. *Nominal* radius, 2400 miles at $10\frac{1}{2}$ kts.

Note.—These two vessels are remarkable in that their main armament consists of howitzers, 13 calibres in length.

ARGENTINA—Miscellaneous

Transports (*Transportes*).

Completing.

USHUAIA. Laid down at Rio Santiago in Jan., 1938. Displacement : 1,275 tons (*full load*). Dimensions : 211 × 31½ × 11½ feet. Machinery : 2 sets Diesels. B.H.P. : 1,200 = 12 kts. Fuel : 100 tons.

1939, Official.

PATAGONIA (Ostsee Werft, Stettin, 1925.) Displacement . 1,350 tons. Dimensions : 193½ × 27 × 13 feet. H.P. : 446 = 9·5 kts.

1932 Photo, Official.

CHACO (ex-*Rio Claro*, 1923), **PAMPA** (ex-*Rio Bueno*, 1923) (both built by Danziger Werft, Danzig). Displacement : 2,100 tons. Dimensions : 273 × 37 × 24 feet. H.P. 1,500 = 11 kts.

Note.—Chaco serves as Submarine Depot Ship.

Oilers (rated as Transports).

1939, Official.

PUNTA ALTA (Puerto Belgrano, 1937.) Displacement : 1,600 tons. Dimensions : 200 × 33½ × 11½ feet. Deadweight capacity : 800 tons.

1932 Photo, Official.

MINISTRO EZCURRA (Grangemouth Dockyard Co., Grange mouth. 1914). 2600 tons. Dimensions : 250 × 40 × 18¾ feet. H.P. 1243 = 10·5 kts.

Tug (*Remolcadores*).

TOBA.   *1928 Photo, by courtesy of Builders.*

MATACO (Jan. 24th, 1928), **TOBA** (Dec. 23rd, 1927). Both built by Hawthorn Leslie. (Completed March, 1928). 339 tons *gross*. Dimensions : 130½ (*p.p.*), 137 (*w.l.*) × 28½ × 13½ feet. H.P. : 1100 = 12 kts. 2 screws. Oil fuel.

1932 Photo, Official.

ONA, QUERANDI (Thornycroft, 1913). 345 tons *gross*. Dimensions : 130 × 28 × 12 feet. H.P. : 1200 = 12 kts.

AZOPARDO (ex-*Barstow*, Bethlehem Co., 1919). 437 tons *gross*. Dimensions : 164 × 27½ × 14 feet. H.P. 1800 = 14 kts.

BELGIUM.

Flags.

SHIPS BELONGING
TO THE STATE.

DIRECTEUR GÉNÉRAL
DE LA MARINE.

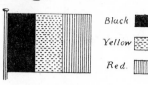

Black ▪
Yellow ▫
Red ▥

MERCANTILE MARINE

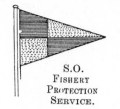

S.O.
FISHERY
PROTECTION
SERVICE.

PENDANT.

Uniforms.

Commandant.   Premier Lieutenant.   Lieutenant.

Mercantile Marine (1939) : 200 vessels of 408,418 tons.

Fishery Protection Vessels.

A new ship to replace the *Zinnia* was laid down at the Cockerill Yard at Antwerp in 1939. Displacement : 1,600 tons. Dimensions : 292 (*pp.*), 315½ (*o.a.*) × 33½ × 10¾ feet. Guns : 2—4·7 inch, 1—3 inch, several smaller. Fitted for minelaying and sweeping (stowage for 120 mines). **30** D.C. carried. To cost 30,000,000 francs.

ZINNIA.   1936, *courtesy Commandant Jean Baneux.*

ZINNIA (ex-British escort vessel of "Flower" class). (Swan Hunter, August, 1915). Purchased for Belgian Navy, June, 1920. Displacement ; 1,200 tons. Dimensions : 250 (*pp.*), 262½ (*o.a.*) × 33 × 11 (*mean*), 11¾ feet (*max.* draught). Guns : 1 M.G. on AA. mounting. Designed I.H.P. : 1,400 = 17 kts., but actually requires *about* 2,000 I.H.P. for this speed. 1 set, triple expansion engines. 1 shaft. Boilers : 2 cylindrical. Coal : 130 tons *normal* ; 250 tons *max.* = about 2,000 miles at 15 kts. Complement (as British ship) : 77.

Patrol Vessels.

A Fast Motor Patrol Vessel is to be built.

WIELINGEN.   1938, *W. A. Fuller, Esq.*

2 ex-German torpedo boats of the war-built "A" type, the **WIELINGEN** and **WEST DIEP,** still exist, and would be available for defence purposes in emergency. At present they are without armament, being employed for training personnel and on fishery protection duties.

Sail Training Ship.

For Photo, see Addenda.

MERCATOR (Ramage & Ferguson, Leith, Dec. 9, 1931). Barquentine. Displacement : 1,200 tons (770 tons *gross*). Complement : 80. Dimensions : 190½ × 34⅚ × 14 feet. Auxiliary Diesel. B.H.P. : 500 = 11 kts. Sail area : 13,584 sq. feet.

BULGARIA.

Note that the red of the flag is crimson.

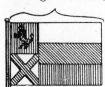

ENSIGN

MERCANTILE

[IIIII] = Red.   [☐] = White.   [⧄⧄] = Green.   [:::::] = Yellow.

Flags.

Jack: A white flag with a green saltire and superimposed over all the Cross of St. George.

Minister of War and Marine :—General Daskaloff.

Mercantile Marine : 14 steamers of 17,476 tons.

PENNANT

ENSIGN

PRESIDENT

MINISTER OF MARINE

ADMIRALTY

CHIEF OF STAFF

ADMIRAL

VICE ADMIRAL

REAR ADMIRAL

JACK

Blue

Yellow

Green

COMMODORE

CAPTAIN IN COMMAND OF FORCES

S.O. IN COMMAND OF FORCES

CAPTAIN OF PORT

Uniforms.

Almirante.	Vice-Almirante.	Contra-Almirante.	Capitão de Mar e Guerra.	Capitão de Fragata.	Capitão de Corveta.	Capititão Tenente.
(Admiral.)	*(Vice-Admiral.)*	*(Rear-Admiral.)*	*(Captain.)*	*(Commander.) (Senior.)*	*(Commander.) (Junior.)*	*(Lieut.-Commander.)*

SLEEVE BADGES.

Primeiro Tenente.	Sagundo Tenente.	Guard Marinha.	Reserve Officer.
(Lieut.)	*(Sub-Lieut.)*	*(Midshipman.)*	

Aviation.   Engineers.   Harbour Honorary Master.   Rank.

All have three buttons towards back of sleeves and across stripes. Deck, Engineer and Aviation Branches all have curl.   Other branches have not.

Caps :--As British Navy.

Minister of Marine :—Vice-Admiral Henrique Aristides Guilhem.
Chief of Naval Staff :—Vice-Admiral José Machado de Castro e Silva.
Chief of Naval Commission in Europe :—Captain José Maria Neiva.
Naval Agent (for Information) in London :—Engineer Captain Natal Arnaud.

Torpedo Boats.

4 *Creusot* boats: *Smyeli, Khrabri, Derzki, Strogi* (built in sections in France; reassembled at Varna, 1907-8). 100 tons. Dimensions : 126½ × 13¼ × 8¾ feet. Armament : 2—47 mm., 1 M.G., 2—18-inch torpedo tubes. Designed H.P. : 2,000 = 26 kts. 1 screw. Du Temple boilers. Coal : 27 tons. Complement : 23. Reported to be fitted for minesweeping.

Motor Patrol Boats.

Belomoretz (ex-French C 27), *Chernomoretz* (ex-C 80). Both purchased 1922. 77 tons. 3 sets of 220 B.H.P. standard petrol motors, totalling 660 B.H.P. = 17 kts. Petrol : 9 tons. Endurance : 700 miles at 10 kts. Guns : 1—47 mm., 2 M.G. Complement : 26. Are differentiated by the numerals 1 and 2, painted on bows.

Sail Training Vessels.

Simeon, Auxiliary motor schooner. 600 tons. Guns : 2—3 inch, 4—37 mm. B.H.P   70.
Assen, (1912). 240 tons. Guns : 2—65 mm., 1 M.G. H.P. : 120 = 7 kts.

Mercantile Marine.

(From " Lloyd's Register," 1939).   305 vessels of 487,820 gross tonnage.

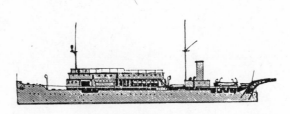

CARIOCA *class*

CEARÁ *(S/M. Depot Ship).*
(Double hulls at stern.)

ALMIRANTE SALDANHA

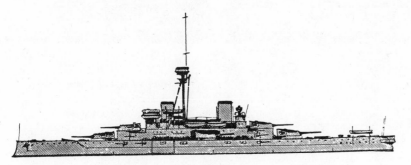

SÃO PAULO.
(Being re-constructed as Minas Geraes.)

MINAS GERAES.

BAHIA *class.*

Guns in Service.

ALAGOAS *class.*

MARANHÃO.

TAMOYO *class.*

HUMAYTÁ.

Nota-tion.	Calibre.		Length in calibres	Weight of A.P. shell.	Muzzle Velocity.	Max. penetration A.P. capped at K.C. at		Danger Space against average ships at			Service rounds per minute
						5000 yards.	3000 yards.	10,000 yards.	5000 yards.	3000 yards.	
	inch.	c/m.	cals.	lbs.	ft. secs.	inch.	inch.				
HEAVY	12	30·5	45	850	2800	...	...	...	...	...	2
LIGHT	4·7	12	40	45	2150	..	..	...	...	...	8
	4·7	12	45	48	2780						8
	4·7	12	50	45	2630	$1\frac{3}{4}$	3	153	55	11	
	4·7	12	45	48	2286						
	4	10	50	..							
	3	76	50	14	2560						

The 1936 programme of naval construction, to be spread over several years, includes :—

2 Cruisers
9 Destroyers
8 Submarines
6 Minelayers
3 Oil Tankers

Orders placed up to Oct. 1938 have included
9 Destroyers, 3 Submarines, 6 Minelayers and 2 Oilers.

I

MINAS GERAES (Sept. 10, 1908).
SÃO PAULO (April 19, 1909).

Normal Displacement : 19,200 tons.

Complement : 1,087 and 1,113, respectively.

Dimensions : 533 (*w.l.*), 500 (*p.p.*) × 83 × 25 feet (*max.*).

Guns (Armstrong) :

12—12 inch, 45 cal.
14—4·7 inch, 50 cal.
4—3 inch AA.
4—40 mm. AA.
8 M.G.

Armour (Krupp) :

9″ Belt ....
6″—4″ Belt (bow) N.C. ...
6″—4″ Belt (aft) N.C. .....
9″—6″ Upper belt ....
9″ & 3″ Bulkheads ....
9″ Battery (main deck) ...
9″—8″ Turrets (K.C.) ... .
12″ Conning tower (fore) ...
9″ Conning tower (aft) ...
8″—3″ Com. Tubes ....
1½″ Torp. Pro. Bulkh'd ...

MINAS GERAES (*re-constructing*).

1937, *courtesy Eng.-Capt. Natal Arnaud.*

Note to Plan.—Disregard apparent main deck battery in elevation. Number of 4·7 inch will be as given above, though exact arrangement has still to be reported.

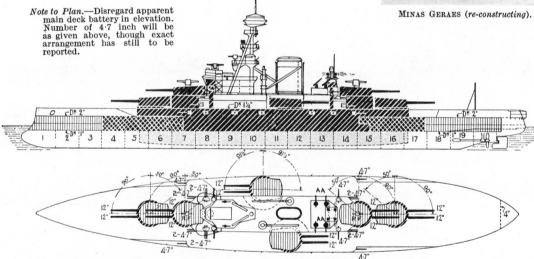

MINAS GERAES (*re-constructing*).

1937 *Official.*

Machinery : 2 sets triple expansion. 2 shafts. S.H.P. : 30,000 = 21 kts.

Boilers : 6 Thornycroft. Oil fuel only.

General Notes.—Both ships reconstructed and modernised, in 1934-39 and 1937-40, respectively.

Engineering Notes.—The former No. 1 stokehold was converted into four oil-fuel deep-tanks,—the space available between top of tanks and main deck being used as distilling plant, with all necessary auxiliaries. 12 side coal bunkers converted into wing oil-fuel tanks, there being 2 service oil tanks for each stokehold. All upper coal bunkers removed. Internal arrangements entirely changed, in accordance with the requirements of new uptakes. The whole Thornycroft supply includes :—main and auxiliary feed water pumps, oil fuel pumps, oil heaters and filters, teledep-installation, ventilating-plant, pipes, etc., etc.

Name.	Builder.	Machinery.	Laid down.	Completed.	Trials. 30 hour at ¼	Full power	Boilers.	Refit.
M. Geraes	Armstrong	Vickers	1907	Jan.'10			Thornycroft	1934-39
S. Paulo	Vickers	Vickers	1907	July '10	16,067=19·85	25,517=21·2	Babcock	1937-40

Cruisers (*Cruzadores*).

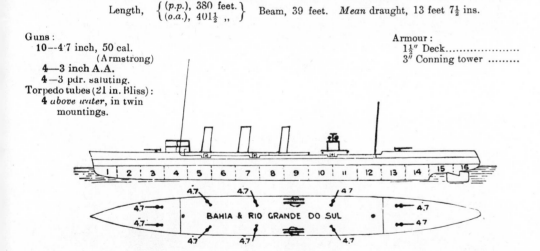

BAHIA
Added 1936, courtesy Eng. Capt. Natal Arnaud.

BAHIA (Jan., 1909), **RIO GRANDE DO SUL** (April, 1909).

Normal displacement 3150 tons.   Complement 368.

Length, $\left\{\begin{array}{l}(p.p.),\ 380\ \text{feet.}\\(o.a.),\ 401\frac{1}{2}\ ,,\end{array}\right\}$ Beam, 39 feet.   *Mean* draught, 13 feet $7\frac{1}{2}$ ins.

Guns :
10—4·7 inch, 50 cal.
   (Armstrong)
4—3 inch A.A.
4—3 pdr. saluting.
Torpedo tubes (21 in. Bliss) :
4 *above water*, in twin
   mountings.

Armour :
1½″ Deck....................
3″ Conning tower ....

BAHIA & RIO GRANDE DO SUL

Machinery : 3 Brown-Curtis geared turbines.   3 shafts.   Boilers : 6 Thornycroft oil-burning.
S.H.P 22,000 = 27 kts.   1926 *Trials* : H.P., 23,000 = 28·6.   Oil fuel : 640 tons.   Endurance:
about 2400 miles at 24 kts., 3092 miles at 18 kts., 6600 miles at 10 kts.

Gunnery Notes.—Fire control originally consisted of voice tubes from control stations to bridge and to plotting rooms
on second deck—thence to battery.   1 R.F. and 2 S.L.   1 S.L. over Chart house and 1 on after S.L. platform.
These arrangements have been improved, and Director system is now installed.

General Notes.—Built by Armstrong; engined by Vickers ; both begun 1908 (under 1907 Naval Programme) and
completed 1910.   Completely refitted 1925-26 by Companhia Nacional de Navegação Costeira, Rio, new engines
and boilers (to burn oil fuel) being installed by Messrs. Thornycroft.   Heating Surface 26,027 sq. ft.

1 + 9 (*building*) Destroyers

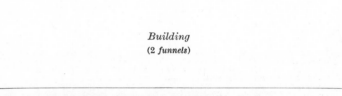

Building
Similar to British "Hero" class.

2 *Thornycroft* : **Jaguaribe, Juruena.**   (Aug. 1, 1939).
2 *White* : **Javary**, (July 17, 1939) **Jutahy.**
2 *Vickers-Armstrongs* : **Japura, Jurua.**
   } All laid down during 1938.

Displacement : 1,340 tons.   Dimensions : 323 (*o.a.*) × 33 × 8½ feet (*mean*).   Guns : 4—4·7 inch, 7 smaller.   Tubes :
8—21 inch (quadrupled).   Machinery : Parsons geared turbines.   S.H.P. : 34,000 = 35·5 kts.   Boilers : 3 of 3-drum
type.   Oil fuel : 450 tons.   Complement : 150.

Building
(2 *funnels*)

3 *U.S.A.* type : **Greenhaigh, Marcilio Dias, Mariz e Barros.**   Building at Ilha das Cobras, Rio de Janeiro,
with material imported from U.S.A.   Displacement : 1,500 tons.   Dimensions : 357 (*o.a.*) × 34⅜ × 9⅜ feet (*mean*).
Guns : 5—5 inch, 38 cal. (dual purpose), 4 M.G.   Tubes : 12—21 inch (quadrupled).   Machinery : Geared turbines
by General Electric Co.   S.H.P. : 42,800 = 36·5 kts.   4 high pressure watertube boilers of Express Type by Babcock
& Wilcox.   Oil fuel : 500 tons.   Radius : 6,000 miles.   Complement : 160.

Note.—These ships will be generally similar to *Mahan* class, of U.S. Navy.

Photo added 1923.

1 *Thornycroft* type.   **Maranhão** (ex H.M.S. *Porpoise*, 1913).   Displacement : 934 tons.   Dimensions : 265¼ × 26¼ × 9¼
(*minimum*), 10¼ (*maximum*) draught.   Guns : 3—4 inch. 1—2 pdr.   Tubes : 4—21 inch, in pairs.   Designed H.P.
22,500 = 28 kts.   Machinery : Parsons turbines.   Thornycroft boilers.   Oil : 250 tons.   Complement : 117.

Torpedo Boats.

1918 *Photo.*

6 Yarrow type: **Mato Grosso, Piauhy** (both 1908), **Rio Grande do Norte, Parahyba, Santa Catarina** (all 1909), **Sergipe** (1910). Displacement 560 tons (*full load,* 640 tons). Dimensions: 240 × 23¼ × 7⅝ feet (*Max.* draught). Armament: 2—4 inch, 4—3 pdrs., 2—18 in. tubes. Designed H.P. 8000 = 27 kts. Machinery: 2 sets triple expansion reciprocating. 2 double-ended Yarrow boilers. Majority of these boats retubed 1917-18. Coal: 140 tons. Nominal radius: 1600 miles at 15 kts. On acceptance trials with 6563 to 8877 H.P. they made 27·1 to 28·7 kts. No effective means of controlling fire of guns or torpedo tubes. Complement: 110.

Note.—Originally there were 10 vessels in this class, but *Alagoas, Para, Parana* and *Amazonas* have been scrapped.

Submarine Depot Ship and Salvage Vessel.

1917 *Photo, by courtesy of the Fiat-San Giorgio Co.*

CEARÁ (Spezia, 1915). Length (*p.p.*) 328 feet. Beam: 52 feet. Displacement and draught (with all stores) vary thus :
(*a*) with dock empty and dock-gate closed 4100 tons at 14 feet draught ; (*b*) with dock-gate open and dock flooded to float submarine in, 4130 tons at 14½ feet ; (*c*) with gate closed and submarine docked, 4560 tons at 15 feet ; (*d*) with gate closed and submarine under hydraulic pressure test in dock, 6460 tons at 20½ feet ; (*e*) with dock empty and gate closed and when raising submarines by double cranes at stern, 4615 tons at 15 feet. Machinery: 2 sets 6-cylinder, 2-cycle Fiat-Diesel engines. 4100 B.H.P. = 14 kts. Fuel: 400 tons (own bunkers) + 240 tons for submarines. Radius of action 400 miles at 10 kts. Guns: 4—4 inch, 2 smaller. Built by Fiat-San Giorgio Co. Completed 1916. Complement: 352.

Submarines.

TUPY. 1937, *courtesy Engineer Captain Natal Arnaud.*

3 *Odero-Terni-Orlando* type. **Tamoyo** (ex-*Ascianghi,* Feb. 14, 1937), **Tupy** (ex-*Neghelli,* Nov. 28, 1936), **Timbyra** (ex-*Gondar,* Dec. 30, 1936). Built at Spezia. Displacement : 620 tons on surface, 853 tons *submerged.* Dimensions : 197½ × 21 × 14½ feet. Armament : 1—3·9 inch, 47 cal., 2—13 mm. M.G., 6—21 inch torpedo tubes. Fiat Diesels. H.P. : 1,350/800 = 14/7·5 kts. Complement : 37. All three delivered in September, 1937. Are generally similar to Italian *Perla* type.

HUMAYTÁ. *Added* 1939, *courtesy W. H. Davis, Esq.*

1 *Ansaldo* type : **Humaytá.** Ansaldo San Giorgio Co., Spezia, April, 1927. Displacement: 1450 tons *surface,* 1884 tons *submerged.* Dimensions : 284¼ × 25½ × 14 feet. Fiat type Diesel engines. Designed H.P. $\frac{4900}{2200} = \frac{18 \cdot 5}{10}$ kts. Armament : 1—4·7 inch, 45 cal., 4—13 mm. AA., 6—21 inch tubes (4 bow, 2 stern). Similar in general design to Italian *Balilla* type (*vide* notes in Italian Section for further details). Ordered in 1926 and completed in 1927, but not delivered in Brazilian waters until two years later. Complement : 74.

Training Ship.

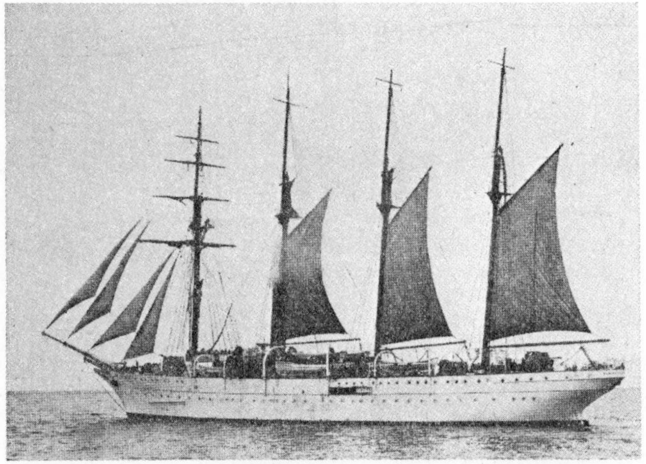

1934 *Photo, Courtesy Messrs. Vickers-Armstrongs.*

ALMIRANTE SALDANHA (Vickers-Armstrongs, Ltd., Barrow, Dec. 19, 1933). Displacement, 3,325 tons. Complement: 356 + 100 midshipmen and cadets. Dimensions: 262 (*pp.*), $307\frac{1}{4}$ (*o.a.*) × 52 × $18\frac{1}{4}$ feet (*mean* draught). Guns: 4—4 inch, 1—3 inch AA., 4—3 pdr., 1—13 mm. AA., 2 M.G. Torpedo tubes: 1—21 inch. Total sail area, 25,990 sq. feet. Auxiliary Diesel engine, B.H.P. 1,400 = 11 kts. (12 kts. reached on trials). Radius of action, 12,000 miles. Cost £314,500. Instructional minelaying gear is included in equipment.

Repair Ship

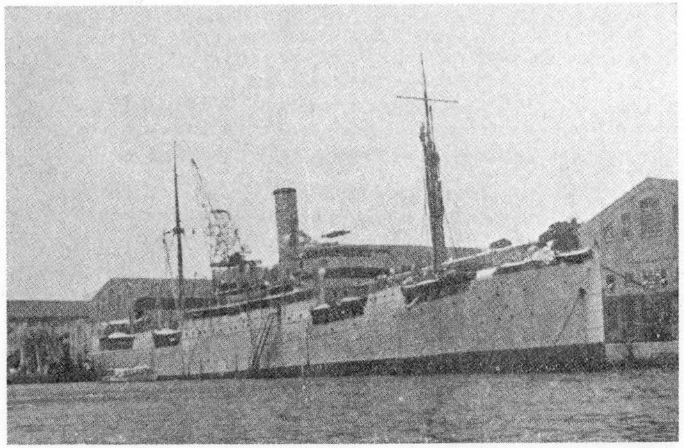

1938, *D. G. Lambert, Esq.*

BELMONTE (ex-German S.S. *Valesia*, Rostock, 1912). 5,227 tons *gross*. Dimensions: $364\frac{3}{4}$ × 51 × 15 feet. Guns: 4—4·7 in., 2—6 pdr. H.P.: 2,700 = 12 kts. Can take about 6,500 tons as cargo. Complement: 338.

River Monitors.

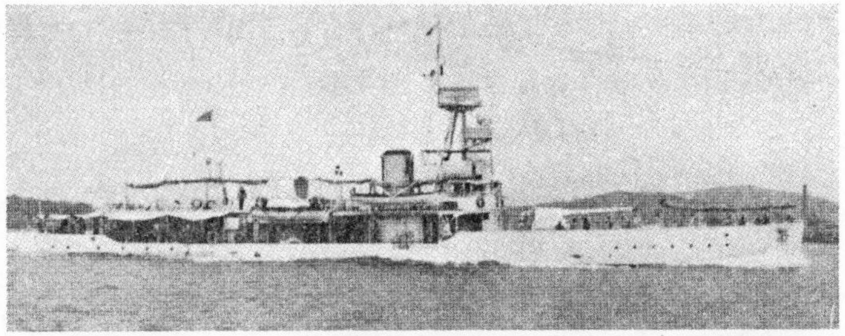

1938, *Courtesy Eng. Capt. Julio Regis Bittencourt*

PARNAHYBA (Sept., 1937). Laid down at Rio, June 11, 1936, and completed Nov., 1937. Displacement: 620 tons. Complement: 90. Dimensions: $180\frac{1}{2}$ (*o.a.*), $178\frac{1}{4}$ (*pp.*) × $33\frac{1}{2}$ × 5 feet (*max.* draught). Guns: 1—6 inch, 2—3·4 inch howitzers, 2—47 mm., 4 M.G. Armour: 3″ side and partial deck protection. Machinery: 2 sets vertical triple expansion by Thornycroft. 2 shafts. I.H.P.: 1,300 = 12 kts. Boilers: 2 of 3-drum type, working pressure 250 lbs. Oil fuel: 70 tons.

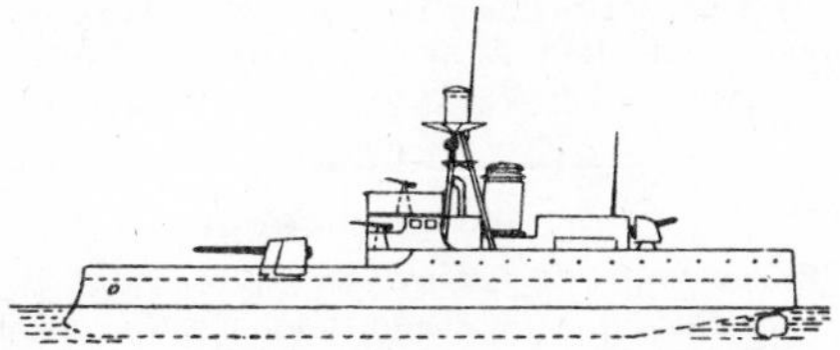

PARAGUASSÚ (ex-*Victoria*). Building at Rio. Displacement: 430 tons. Dimensions: $146\frac{1}{3}$ × $34\frac{3}{4}$ × 5 feet. Guns: 1—4·7 inch, 2—3·4 inch howitzers, 2—47 mm., 4 M.G. Machinery: 2 sets triple expansion, by J. S. White & Co., Ltd., Cowes. I.H.P. 1,100 = 13 kts. Boilers: 2 of 3-drum type. Oil fuel: 40 tons. Complement: 88.

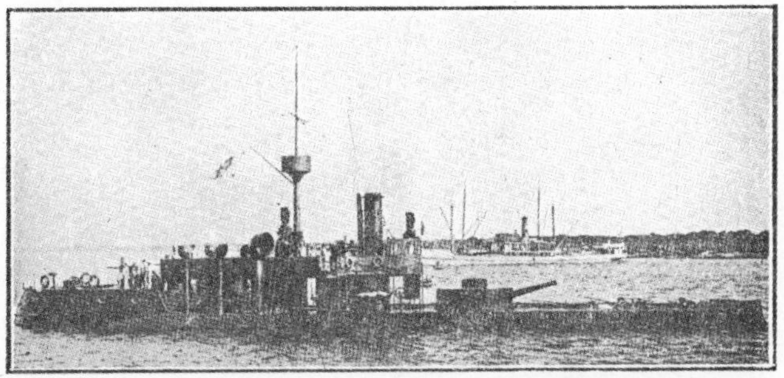

1910 *Photo, Abrahams.*

PERNAMBUCO (Rio, 1905, completed 1910). 470 tons. Dimensions: 146 × 24 × $5\frac{1}{4}$ feet. Guns: 2—4·7 inch, 2—3 pdr. Armour: 6·6″–4″ belt, 4″ deck, $3\frac{1}{2}$″ conning tower, 6″ turret. H.P.: 800 = 11 kts. 2 shafts. Coal: 45 tons. Took 20 years to build, having been laid down in 1890. Boilers renewed by Messrs. J. S. White & Co., Ltd., 1937. Complement: 81.

River Gunboats.

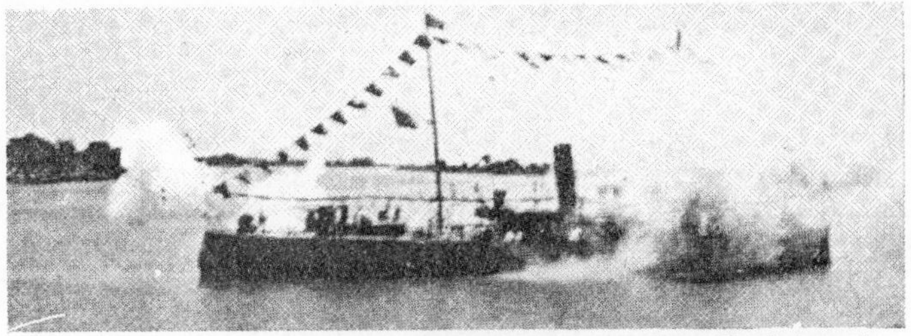

1937, *Courtesy Eng. Capt. Natal Arnaud.*

OYAPOCK (ex-*Amapa*). (Thornycroft, 1907). Displacement, 195 tons. Dimensions: 130 (*pp.*). 137 (*o.a.*) × 18 × 6 feet. Guns: 2—3 pdr., 2 M.G. Machinery: Triple expansion. 2 shafts. H.P.: 450 = 14 kts. 1 Babcock watertube boiler. Coal: 51 tons. Complement: 51.

AMAPA. Displacement: 290 tons. Dimensions: 104 × 24 × $10\frac{1}{2}$ feet. Guns: 2—57 mm., 6 M.G. Complement: 39.

Minelayers (Mineiros)

(*For photo, see Addenda*).

CAMOCIM, CANANÉA (Oct., 1938), **CARIOCA** (1938), **CABEDELO, CARAVELAS, CANAVIERAS.** All building at Rio. (First pair laid down on Nov. 6, 1937). Displacement: 552 tons. Dimensions: $188\frac{2}{3}$ × $25\frac{1}{2}$ × 8 feet (*mean*). Guns: 2—4 inch, 4 M.G. AA. 50 Mines. Machinery: 2 sets vertical triple expansion by Thornycroft. I.H.P.: 2,200 = 14 kts. (exceeded on trials). Oil fuel: 70 tons. Complement: 97.

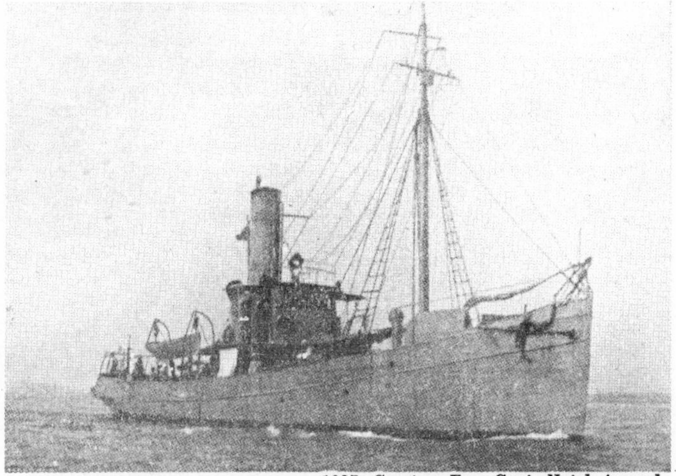

1937, *Courtesy Eng. Capt. Natal Arnaud*

ITAPEMERIM (ex-*Maria do Couto*). Displacement: 340 tons. Dimensions: 116 × 21 × 12 feet. Guns: 2—3 pdr. Mines: 30. Complement: 45.

ITACURUSSÁ (Ramage & Ferguson, Leith, 1901). Displacement: 210 tons. Dimensions: $95\frac{1}{4}$ (*pp.*), $102\frac{1}{3}$ (*o.a.*) × $19\frac{1}{2}$ × $10\frac{1}{3}$ feet (*max.* draught). Guns: 1—37 mm. Machinery: Reciprocating. I.H.P.: 110 = 10 kts. Coal: 35 tons. Complement: 45.

Surveying Vessels (*Navios Hydrograficos*).

1937, *Courtesy Eng Capt. Natal Arnaud*

JACEGUAY (ex-*Flecha*, ex-*H.M.S. Fairfield*), (Clyde Shipbuilding Co., 1919). Ex-minesweeper, purchased for use as a surveying vessel in 1937. Displacement : 710 tons. Dimensions : 231 (*o.a.*) × 28½ × 7½ feet. Guns : None reported. I.H.P. : 2,200 = 16 kts. Coal : 185 tons. Complement : 79.

1935, *Official.*

RIO BRANCO (ex-Canadian Government vessel *Margaret*). (Thornycroft, 1914). Displacement : 896 tons. Dimensions : 200 × 32 × 10 feet. Guns : 2—6 pdr. I.H.P. : 2,000 = 15 kts. Coal : 200 tons. Complement : 91.

1935, *Official.*

JOSÉ BONIFACIO (ex-*Itapema*, 1909), **VITAL DE OLIVEIRA** (ex-*Itauba*, 1910). Both built by Ailsa S.B. Co., Troon. Displacement : 1,300 tons. Dimensions : 270 × 42 × 14 feet. Guns : 2—4 inch, 2—6 pdr. H.P. : 540 = 9 kts. Complement : 152.

Oilers.

POTENGY (Papendrecht, March, 16, 1938). Displacement : 600 tons. Dimensions : 175½ (*pp.*), 178¾ (*o.a.*) × 24½ × 6 feet. Diesel engines. 2 shafts. B.H.P. : 550 = 10 kts. Complement : 19.

1938, *D. G. Lambert, Esq.*

MARAJÓ (ex-*Malistan*), (Bartram & Sons, Sunderland, 1924). Purchased 1936. Displacement : 7,930 tons; 5,553 tons *gross*. Dimensions : 400 × 52¼ × 25¼ feet (*mean*). Machinery : Triple expansion. H.P. : 3,100 = 10 kts. Complement : 92.

NOVAES DE ABREU (Rotterdam, 1918). Displacement, 500 tons. Dimensions : 140 × 23 × 12 feet. H.P. : 400 = 10 kts. Oil : 400 tons. Complement : 34.

Minesweepers.

IGUAPE (ex-*Salles de Carvalho*). (Wivenhoe, 1908). **ITAJAHY** (ex-*Rio Pardo*). (Geestemunde, 1908). Displacement : 150 tons. Dimensions : 85 × 19 × 9 feet. Guns : 1—47 mm., 2 M.G. I.H.P. : 350 = 10 kts. Complement : 28.

Tugs

L. PITTA.   1935, *Courtesy Eng. Capt. N. Arnaud.*

LAURINDO PITTA. (1910). Built by Vickers. Displacement : 514 tons. Dimensions : 130 × 26 × 15 feet. Machinery : Triple expansion, 2 shafts. I.H.P : 850 = 11 kts.

Seagoing Tugs (*Rebocadores*).—continued.

1935, *Official.*

ANNIBAL MENDONÇA (ex-*Times*, ex-*St. Keyne*). **D.N.O.G.** (ex-*Paraná*, ex-*St. Teath*). (1919). Displacement : 820 tons. Dimensions : 135 × 30 × 14½ feet. Guns : 2—3 pdr. I.H.P. : 1,200 = 12 kts. (present best speed, 10 kts.). Coal : 240 tons. Complement : 45.

H. PERDIGÃO.   1937, *Courtesy Eng. Capt. Natal Arnaud*

HEITOR PERDIGÃO, MUNIZ FREIRE. (1921). Displacement : 500 tons. Dimensions : 132 × 26 × 15 feet. Guns : 2—3 pdr. I.H.P. : 850 = 11 kts. Complement : 45.

Lighthouse Tenders (*Navios Pharoleiros*).

1935, *Official.*

MARIO ALVES, LAHMEYER, Displacement : 280 tons. Dimensions : 116¼ × 22¾ × 11 feet. Guns : 2 M.G. Complement : 38.

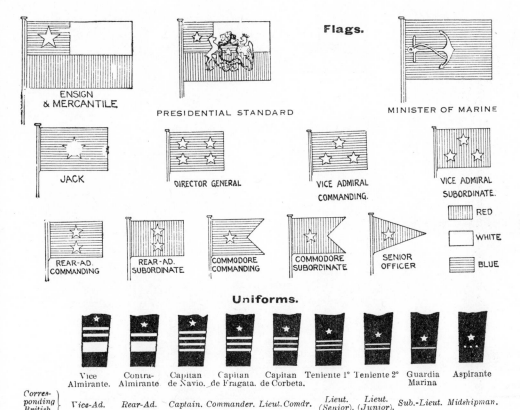

Flags.

ENSIGN & MERCANTILE

PRESIDENTIAL STANDARD

MINISTER OF MARINE

JACK

DIRECTOR GENERAL

VICE ADMIRAL COMMANDING.

VICE ADMIRAL SUBORDINATE.

RED

WHITE

BLUE

REAR-AD. COMMANDING

REAR-AD. SUBORDINATE

COMMODORE COMMANDING

COMMODORE SUBORDINATE

SENIOR OFFICER

Uniforms.

| Vice Almirante. | Contra-Almirante | Capitan de Navio. | Capitan de Fragata. | Capitan de Corbeta. | Teniente 1° | Teniente 2° | Guardia Marina | Aspirante |

Corresponding British or U.S. : Vice-Ad. Rear-Ad. Captain. Commander. Lieut.-Comdr. Lieut. (Senior). Lieut. (Junior). Sub.-Lieut. Midshipman.

Other Branches the same with colours as follows :—Engineers (blue), Paymasters (white), Doctors (red), Chaplains (purple).

Minister of National Defence : Sr. Guillermo Labarca.
Chief of the Naval Staff : Rear-Admiral E. Daroch S.
Chief of Naval Commission (London) : Vice-Admiral Juan T. Gerken.
Naval Attaché (London) :
Personnel : About 6000, all ranks.

Naval Bases.

TALCAHUANO. Two dry docks, 614 × 87 × 30½ feet and 800 × 116 × 36 feet respectively. One small floating dock, 216 × 42 × 15 feet. Gunnery, Torpedo, Submarine, and other Training Establishments here.

VALPARAISO. One small steel floating dock privately owned. 314 × 65 × 21 feet (4500 tons capacity). Staff College and Naval Academy for training of executive and Engineering branches here, also schools for Communications, Coast Artillery, Navigation, etc.

There is also a small steel floating dock at Mejillones.

Naval Ordnance. (All details unofficial.)

	Type*	Calibre. Inches.	Calibre. Cm.	Length (cals.)	Weight of Gun (tons.)	Weight of Proj. (lbs.)	Weight of Charge. (lbs.)	M.V (ft.-secs.)	M.E. (ft.-tons.)	Max. R.P.M.
HEAVY	A	14	35·6	45	85	1585	324	2500	..	2
MEDIUM	A	8	20·3	45	18·5	210	44	2650	10,226	4
	A	8	20·3	40	15	..	..	2582	..	..
	A	6	15·2	50	8¾	100	31	3000	6240	9
	A	6	15·2	40	6⅔ cwt.	100	18·3	2500	4334	8
	A	4·7	12	50	63½	45	10¾	2953	2721	12
	A	4·7	12	45	53	45	8	2552	2110	10
LIGHT	A	4	10·2	..	..	..	..	..	..	..

* A = Armstrong

14 inch, 45 cal., in *Alm. Latorre.*
8 inch, 40 cal., in *O'Higgins, B. Encalada.*

6 inch, 50 cal., in *Alm. Latorre* and *Chacabuco.*
6 inch, 40 cal., in *O'Higgins, B. Encalada.*
4.7 inch in *Serrano* class (6).
4.7 inch in *Chacabuco, G. Baquedano*
4 inch in *Alm. Lynch* class (2).

Torpedoes : 21 inch (heater), and 18 inch.   **Mines :** Similar to British pattern.

Mercantile Marine.

(From "Lloyd's Register" 1939 figures.)

106 vessels of 176,289 gross tonnage.

ELICURA *class*.

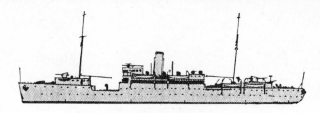

GENERAL BAQUEDANO.
(*Training Ship.*)

ARAUCANO.

ALMIRANTE LATORRE.

CHACABUCO.

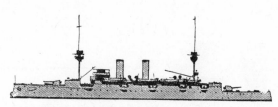

BLANCO ENCALADA.

GENERAL O'HIGGINS.

TORPEDO CRAFT.

SERRANO *class*.

ALM. LYNCH.   ALM. CONDELL.

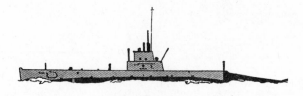

GUALCOLDA *class*.

O'BRIEN *class*.

ALMIRANTE LATORRE (ex British *Canada*, ex Chilean *Almirante Latorre*, ex *Valparaiso*, Nov., 1913). Standard displacement, 28,000 tons (over 32,000 *full load*). Complement, 1176.

Length (p.p.), 625 feet. (o.a.), 661 feet. Beam, 103 feet. { Mean draught, 28½ feet. } { Max. „ 30 „ }

Guns (Armstrong):
- 10—14 inch, 45 cal.
- 14—6 inch, 50 cal.
- 4—4 inch AA.
- 4—3 pdr.
- 12 M.G.
Torpedo tubes (21 inch):
- 4 *submerged*.
- 1 Catapult.

Armour :
Decks. {
- 1″ Shelter (over casemates)
- 1″ Fo'xle (over battery)
- 1½″ Upper (outside battery)
- 1½″ Main (aft)
- 1″ Protective
- 2″ (forward) } lower
- 4″ (aft) }
Torpedo Protec. :
- 2″—1½″ Bulkheads
  (mags., &c.) Sections
  6–8, 15, 19–21 on plans.

Armour :
Vertical. {
- 10″ Lower belt .... ▨
- 7″ Middle belt .... ▨
- 4½″ Upper belt .... ▨
- 6″– 4″ Belt (ends) ▦ ▥
- 4½″, 4″ B'lkh'ds (f. & a.) ▩
- 6″ Batteries ▩
- 10″ Barbettes .... ■•••
- 10½″–9″ Gunhouses •••• ▨
- 3″ C.T. base* ■
- 11″ C.T. (6″–3″ hood).. ■•••
- 6″ Fore com. tube .... ▩
- 6″ Torpedo C.T. ...... ▩
- 6″ Aft com. tube ..... ▩
  (Bulges)
*Not shown on plans.

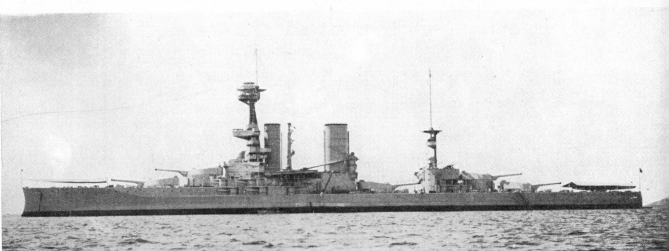

1933 *Photo, Official.*

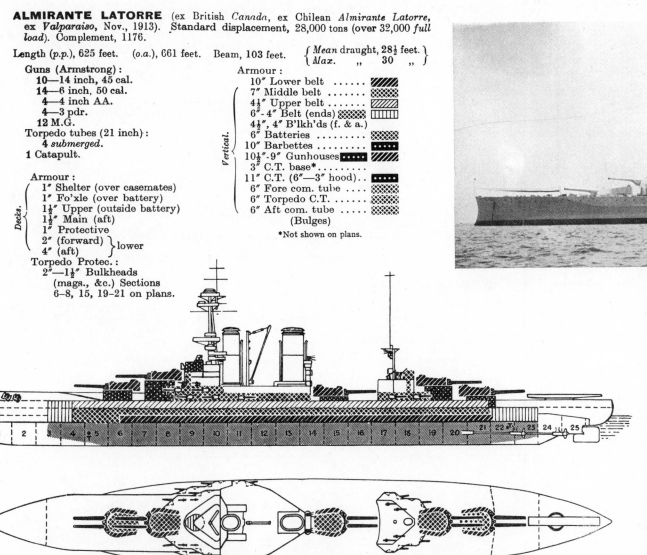

1931, *R. Perkins, Esq.*

Machinery : Turbine, 4-shaft : (L.P.) Parsons ; (H.P.) Parsons. Boilers : 21 Yarrow. Designed H.P. 37,000 = 22·75 kts. Oil : 4,300 tons. Endurance : 4,400 miles at 10 kts.

Gunnery Notes.—14-inch have a range only limited by *max.* visibility. Originally had 16—6 inch, but the 2—6 inch on upper deck, abeam of after funnel, were removed and ports plated over. Reason for removal was because guns were within a few feet from muzzle of " Q " turret 14-inch guns on extreme bearing and were damaged by blast. Anti-aircraft guns are mounted on after superstructure.

Armour Notes.—Barbettes, 6″ and 4″ as they descend behind belts.

Searchlights.—8—24 inch and 2—20 inch (signalling) Harrison lamp type burners.

General Notes.—Laid down for Chile by Armstrong, in Nov. 1911, as the *Valparaiso*, her name being altered afterwards to *Almirante Latorre*. Purchased for British Navy on outbreak of War and re-named *Canada*. Completed Sept., 1915. Additional protection, &c., added during War is said to have raised her *normal* displacement to over 30,000 tons. Re-purchased by Chile, April, 1920. Arrived at Devonport in summer of 1929 to be refitted in the dockyard under a special contract with new machinery supplied by Vickers-Armstrongs, Ltd. Bulges fitted, and masts and bridgework underwent slight modifications. The main topmast was raised to 60 feet, and controls fitted at the ends of the upper bridge : searchlights removed from bridge ; new turbines and oil fuel only installed. She returned to Chile early in 1931. A catapult is mounted on the quarterdeck. Her sister ship, *Almirante Cochrane*, was purchased for British Navy in 1917, re-named *Eagle*, and modified for service as an Aircraft Carrier. (See British Navy Section.)

Coast Defence Ship.

1938, *Official.*

HUASCAR (Laird, Birkenhead, 1865). Displacement : 1,870 tons. Complement : 135. Dimensions : 190 × 30½ × 16 feet. Guns : 2—8 inch, 3—4·7 inch, 4—47 mm.

Note.—As will be seen from above photograph, this ship (which was captured from Peru in 1879) has been reconditioned. She wears the flag of the Port Admiral at Talcahuano.

Cruisers.

New Construction

It is proposed to invite tenders from British and Continental shipyards in 1939 for 2 cruisers of 3,000 tons, to be armed with 5·5 inch or 6 inch guns, and to have a speed of 37 kts.

1933 *Photo, Official.*

GENERAL O'HIGGINS (Armstrong, 1897). 8,500 tons. Sheathed and coppered. Complement 700. Length (*p.p.*), 412 feet. Beam, 62¾ feet. *Max.* draught, 22 feet. Guns (Armstrong) : **4**—8 inch, 45 cal. **10**—6 inch, 40 cal., **13**—3 inch. (1 field), **4** M.G. Torpedo tubes (18 inch) : **2** *submerged.* Armour (Harvey-nickel) : 7″-5″ Belt (amidships), 2″ Deck (slopes), 7½″ Port plates to 8 inch gun turrets, 6″ Hoists to these, 6″ Gun houses to 6 inch guns, 6″ Casemates (6), 9″ Conning tower. Machinery : 2 sets triple expansion. 2 screws. Boilers : 30 Belleville (in 3 groups). Designed H.P. : 16,000 = 21·5 kts. (still steams very well and can do 20 kts.). Coal : *normal* 700 tons ; *maximum* 1,200 tons. Endurance : (*a*) 2,250 miles at 20 kts. ; (*b*) 6,000 miles at 10 kts. Large re-fit 1928–29.

1919 *Copyright photo, G. Allan, Valparaiso.*

CHACABUCO (Armstrong, 1898, purchased 1902). 4,500 tons. Complement 400. Length (*p.p.*), 360 feet. Beam, 46½ feet. *Maximum* draught, 17 feet. Guns (Armstrong) : 2--6 inch, 50 cal. **10**—4·7 inch, 40 cal., **5**—3 inch, **1**—3 pdr. Armour (Harvey-nickel) : 4½″ Deck (amidships), 1¾″ Deck (ends), 4½″ Fronts to 6 in. gun shields, 2½″ Sides to 6 in. gun shields, 2½″ Shields to 4·7 in. guns, 5″ Conning tower. Boilers, cylindrical. I.H.P. 15,500 = 24 kts. Still steams very well. 2 screws. Coal : *normal* 300 tons ; *maximum* 1,028 tons. Electric training and elevating gear to 6 inch guns. Laid down at Elswick, 1897, as a speculation. Completed 1902, and purchased by Chile.

Cruisers.—*Continued*

1937, *Official, courtesy Com. G. H. Trudgett.*

BLANCO ENCALADA (Armstrong, 1893). 4420 tons (sheathed and coppered). Complement 427. Length (*p.p.*), 370 feet. Beam, 46½ feet. *Maximum* draught, 19½ feet. Armament: 2—8 inch, 40 cal., 10- 6 inch, 40 cal., 5—3 inch, 1—1 pdr., 2 Maxims. Armour: 4″ Deck, 6″ Shields to 8″ guns, 6″ Conning tower. Boilers: cylindrical (retubed 1908-9). Designed H.P. 14,500= 22·75 kts. (only about 19 kts. now.) Coal: *maximum* 850 tons. Endurance: 5000 miles at 10 kts. Refitted, 1920, at Talcahuano.

Note.—Laid down Sept., 1892, launched a year later, and completed April, 1894.

Training Ship.

1919 *Copyright photo, G. Allan, Valparaiso.*

GENERAL BAQUEDANO (1898). 2500 tons, sheathed and coppered. Armed with 4—4·7 inch 40 cal., 4—6 pdr. I.H.P. 1500 = 13·75 kts. Belleville boilers (renewed 1924). Coal: 300 tons. Built by Armstrong, Whitworth & Co. Ld. (Refitted 1923-24.)

8 Destroyers.

SERRANO. 1937, *Official, courtesy Com. G. H. Trudgett.*

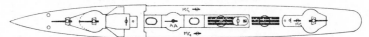

(*Plan by courtesy of Messrs. John I. Thornycroft & Co. Ltd.*)

6 Serrano Class.

6 *Thornycroft* type. **Serrano** (Jan. 25th, 1928), **Orella** (March 8th, 1928), **Riquelme** (May 28th, 1928), **Hyatt** (July 21st, 1928), **Aldea** (Nov. 29th, 1928), **Videla** (Oct. 16th, 1928). All laid down June-July, 1927. "Standard" displacement, 1090 tons; *full load*, 1430 tons. Dimensions: 288¼ (*p.p.*), 300 (*o.a.*) × 29 × 12⅝ feet (*maximum* draught). Guns: 3—4.7 inch, 1—3 inch AA, 3 M.G. 2 D.C. Throwers. Tubes: 6—21 inch, in triple deck mountings. Machinery: Geared turbines (Brown-Curtis h.p. and cruising, Parsons l.p.). Boilers: 3 Thornycroft, 3-drum type. S.H.P. 28,000 = 35 kts. Oil fuel: 320 tons. 2 screws. Provision made for carrying mines. Complement, 130.

Notes.—These destroyers are named after naval officers who distinguished themselves at the battle of Iquique in 1879. Plating is galvanised throughout, and the heavy hull scantlings reduce the stresses to even less than those allowed by British Admiralty practice. All exceeded their contract speed on trials. They have exceptionally good accommodation for vessels of their size, and are adapted for service in a wide range of climates. The contract, amounting to about £1,750,000, was awarded to Messrs. Thornycroft after intensive competition with many other yards, British and foreign.

2 Almirante Class.

ALM. LYNCH   1934 *Photo, Official.*

Now has two pairs of 21-inch torpedo tubes in centre line and superstructure abaft mainmast has been extended a considerable distance aft. Four 13 mm. AA. guns are mounted on topside, abaft S.L., as shown in plan below.

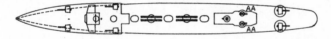

2 *White* : ***Almirante Lynch*** (1912), ***Al. Condell*** (1913). Dimensions: $320 \times 32\frac{1}{2} \times 11$ feet. *Normal* displacement: 1,730 tons. *Full load* : 1,850 tons. Armament : 6—4 inch, 4—13 mm. AA., 4—21 inch tubes. Designed H.P.: 30,000 = 31 kts. Turbines : Parsons. Boilers : 6 White-Forster. 3 shafts. Fuel : 427 tons coal + 80 tons oil = 2,750 miles at 15 kts. Trials : *Al. Lynch*, 31·8 kts. (6 hours) ; *Al. Condell*, 33·4 kts. Complement : 160.

Note to Illustration.—First letter of name painted on bow for identification purposes, *e.g.*, L = *Lynch*, C = *Condell*.

(Partially rearmed 1936.)

Submarines.

2 Submarines of 750 tons displacement, armed with 6 torpedo tubes and a 4-inch gun, are projected.

1930 *Photo, Courtesy of Messrs. Vickers-Armstrongs.*

3 *Vickers-Armstrongs* : ***Capitan O'Brien*** (October 2nd, 1928), ***Capitan Thompson, Almirante Simpson,*** (Jan. 15th, 1929). Displacement $\frac{1540}{2020}$ tons. Dimensions: $260 \times 28 \times 13\frac{1}{4}$ feet draught. H.P. $\frac{3000}{1300} = \frac{15}{9}$ kts. Fuel: 200 tons. Guns: 1—4·7 inch. Tubes: 8—21 inch (6 bow, 2 stern). Of same general design as British "O" type. All 3 laid down at Barrow-in-Furness, Nov. 15, 1927 : completed June 19, 1929 (*O'Brien*); Aug. 24, 1929 (*Thompson*); and Sept. 14, 1929 (*Simpson*).

GUALCOLDA.   1933 *Photo, Official.*

6 *Holland Type* (Electric Boat Co. design): ***Gualcolda*** (H 1.) ***Tegualda*** (H 2.) ***Rucumilla*** (H 3.) ***Guale*** (H 4. ***Quidora*** (H 5.) ***Fresia*** (H 6.) (Fore River Co., U.S.A., 1915-17). Displacements: $\frac{364}{435}$ tons. Dimensions: $150\frac{1}{4} \times 15\frac{3}{4} \times 12\frac{1}{4}$ feet, H.P. $\frac{480}{620} = \frac{12.75}{10.25}$ kts. Machinery: *for surface* 2 sets 210 H.P. Nelseco Diesel engines. Endurance : 2800 miles at 11 kts. *on surface* ; at 30 miles 5 kts. *submerged.* Oil: $17\frac{1}{2}$ tons. Torpedo tubes 4—18 inch (bow). Complement 22.

Notes.—These boats were originally *H 13* and *H 16—20* of the British *H 11—20* group of submarines, built by the Fore River Co., U.S.A., during 1915. The Admiralty intended to take them over and equip them with torpedo tubes at the Canadian Vickers Co. Yard at Montreal—provided that these boats could legally be delivered in an unarmed state. The U.S. Government decided the submarines could not leave any U.S. port, so long as the United States remained neutral, and all the boats were interned at Boston. They were released on the U.S. declaration of war, 1917. With the approval of the U.S. authorities, the above six boats were ceded to Chile by Great Britain, in part payment for the Chilean warships building in British yards in August, 1914, and appropriated for the British Navy. Names are those of Araucanian chiefs.

Added 1938, *Courtesy Commander G. H. Trudgett.*

MICALVI (ex-*Bostonlincs*, ex-*Bragi*) (Ostsee Werft, Stettin, 1925). Displacement 850 tons. (612 tons *gross*). Dimensions: 181½ × 28¾ × 11 feet.   Triple expansion engines.   I.H.P. 380 = 9·5 kts.

Added 1939, *Official.*

CONDOR. Iron and wood. Built in Marseilles, 1889. Large refit 1927.   Displacement: 145 tons. Dimensions: 102 × 18¾ × 9 feet.   Speed: 9 kts.   Coal: 20 tons. Employed as **Lighthouse Tender.**

(Most of the above vessels are employed on Surveying Service.)

Surveying Vessel.

A yacht is being acquired for conversion into a Surveying Vessel.

Building.

New Construction

1 vessel laid down at Valdivia, 1939. Displacement: 1,026 tons. Dimensions: 180 × 30 × 12 feet. Machinery: Reciprocating. I.H.P.: 900 = 12 kts. 1 boiler, 220 lbs. working pressure. Coal capacity: 125 tons.

ELICURA.   1931 *Photo, Official.*

ELICURA, LEUCOTON, OROMPELLO. All built by Maskin och Brobyggnads Co., Helsingfors, 1919. All were completed 1919.   530 tons.   Length (*o.a.*), 172·6 feet. Beam, 24·6 feet. *Maximum* draught, 11 feet. Guns: 2—3 inch.   I.H.P. 1400 = 14½ kts. speed.   2 sets triple expansion engines.   2 screws.   Boilers: 3 cylindrical.   Coal capacity: *Leucoton* 56 tons; *Elicura* and *Orompello*, 65 tons.   Complement, 42.   Refitted by Messrs. J. Samuel White & Co., Cowes, 1920.

YELCHO   1938, *Official.*

YELCHO (1906). Displacement: 467 tons. Dimensions: 128 × 23 × 9½ feet.   Speed: 12 kts.

Submarine Depot Ship.

1933 *Photo, Official.*

ARAUCANO (Vickers-Armstrongs, Barrow, Oct. 22, 1929). Displacement : 9,000 tons. Dimensions : 390 × 55 × 16½ feet draught. Guns : 2—4·7 inch, 2—3 inch AA. S.H.P. : 2,400 = 13 kts. Machinery : Parsons geared turbines. 1 screw. Coal : 670 tons. Has accommodation for 585, including crews of attached submarines. Laid down, March 1, 1929, and completed March, 1930. Has since had a seaplane added to her equipment.

Oilers.

RANCAGUA   1930 *Photo.*

MAIPO (Jan., 1930), **RANCAGUA** (Nov., 1929). Both built by Vickers-Armstrongs, Ltd., on the Tyne. Displacement : 7,715 tons (3,800 tons *gross*). Complement : 54. Dimensions : 365 × 49¾ × 22½ feet draught. Guns : 2—4·7 inch, 2 M.G. AA. I.H.P. : 4,800 = 15 kts. Machinery : Triple expansion. 2 screws. 4 S.E. boilers. Oil fuel : 725 tons. Laid down in March, 1929. Completed in March, 1930. Are distinguished by initials of names painted on bows.

Transports.

(A new transport of 3,000 tons cargo capacity is to be built or acquired.)

Photo wanted.

ABTAO (ex-*Sosua*) (Oslo, 1912). Displacement : 691 tons *standard*. Dimensions : 225 × 33½ × 18 feet. Machinery : Triple expansion. I.H.P. 1185 = 10 kts. 2 cylindrical boilers.

Seagoing Tugs (*Remolcadores*).

2 new tugs of 500 tons are to be built.

Photo wanted.

CONTRAMAESTRE BRITO (1937), **HUEMUL** (ex-*Vilumilla*) (1937). Both built at Valdivia. Displacement : 320 tons. Dimensions : 100 (*w.l.*) × 22 × 13 feet. Machinery : Reciprocating. I.H.P. : 650 = 12 kts. 1 boiler. Coal capacity : 35 tons.

Seagoing Tugs—*continued*.

1931 *Photo, Official.*

PILOTO SIBBALD (1916), built by Bow, McLachlan & Co., Paisley. Displacement : 1,100 tons. Dimensions : 141¾ × 28¾ × 11 feet. Machinery : Triple expansion. 2 screws. 2 cylindrical boilers. I.H.P. : 1,200 = 11½ kts. Coal capacity : 145 tons. Complement, 18. Possesses fire fighting and salvage equipment.

Note.—During the War this vessel was taken over by the British Navy, in which she served as the *Stoic.* Re-acquired by Chile in 1920.

SOBENES.   1931 *Photo, Official.*

SOBENES, CABRALES (1929), **COLOCOLO, GALVARINO** and **JANEQUEO** (1930) built by Bow McLachlan. Displacement : 790 tons. Dimensions : 126½ × 27 × 12 feet (*mean*). I.H.P. 1050 = 11 kts. Coal capacity : 130 tons.

CHINA.

Uniforms.

| Admiral. | Vice-Admiral. | Rear-Admiral. | Commodore. | Captain. | Commander. | Lieut.-Comm'r. | Lieut. | Sub-Lieut. 1st Class. | Sub-Lieut 2nd Class. |

Colour between stripes :—*Engineers* (none); *Surgeons*, red; *Paymasters*, white; *Ship Constructor*, purple; *Navigating Officers*, light indigo blue; *Ordnance*, Pink; *Wireless*, Mauve; *Bandmasters*, Green; *Judge Advocates*, Grey. All these branches *without* the curl or emblem over top stripe. *Aviation*, no colour between stripes, but Gold Eagle replaces emblem above stripe.

Minister of the Navy —Admiral S. K. Chen. *Vice-Ministers of the Navy* :—Vice-Admiral C. L. Chen, Vice-Admiral H. Y. Chen. *Naval Attaché, London* :—Capt. Y. H. Lung.

Flags.

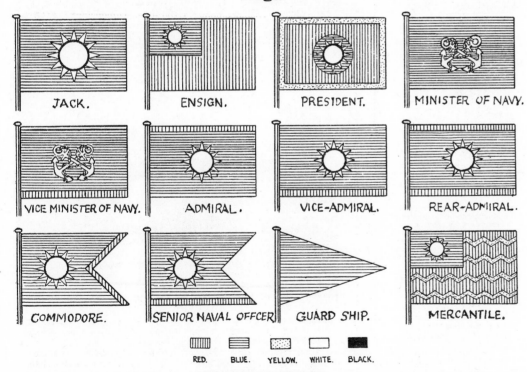

JACK.	ENSIGN.	PRESIDENT.	MINISTER OF NAVY.
VICE MINISTER OF NAVY.	ADMIRAL.	VICE-ADMIRAL.	REAR-ADMIRAL.
COMMODORE.	SENIOR NAVAL OFFICER	GUARD SHIP.	MERCANTILE.

| RED. | BLUE. | YELLOW. | WHITE. | BLACK. |

Mercantile Marine.

(From "Lloyd's Register" 1939 figures.)   173 Vessels of 258,432 *Gross* Tonnage.

SPECIAL NOTE

Pending the termination of hostilities between China and Japan, it has proved impossible to obtain a reliable list of the ships of the Chinese Navy that remain in service. But it is believed that the following have been destroyed or otherwise lost :

Cruisers : NING HAI, PING HAI (both salved and taken over by Japanese forces), HAI CHI, HAI CHOU, HAI SHEN, HAI YUNG, CHAO HO, YING SWEI, TUNG CHI.

Escort Vessels : YAT SEN (Refloated and taken over by Japanese Navy), HAI CHAO.

Gunboats : HSIEN NING, YUNG CHIEN, YUNG HSIANG, YUNG CHI (believed to have been taken over by Japan), CHU TAI, CHU YIU, CHU YU, KIANG LI, TA TUNG, TZE CHION.

Torpedo Boats : CHIEN KANG, TUNG AN, HU YING, and about 6 of motor type.

Patrol Boats : KIANG NING, WEI NING, SUH NING, WU NING, CHANG NING, CHENG NING, CHUNG NING.

Seaplane Carriers : TEH SHENG, WEI SHENG.

Surveying Vessels : CHIAO JIH, CHIN TIEN.

In addition, the following are reported to have been more or less seriously damaged :

Gunboats : MING CHUN, MING SEN, CHU KUAN.

Torpedo Boats : HU CHUN, HU PENG.

Patrol Boats : YI SHENG, SUI NING.

It is quite likely that there have been other losses, unrecorded. In the absence of full and authentic details, it has been decided to omit photographs and particulars of the few possibly surviving vessels from this issue of " Fighting Ships," with the exception of the following :

Motor Torpedo Boats.

Added 1938, courtesy Messrs. Thornycroft.

A number of M.T.B. of the Thornycroft type are still in existence. Dimensions: 55 × 11 feet. Complement, 5. Armament: 2 M.G., 2—18 inch Torpedoes. B.H.P. 1,000 = 45 kts.

A depôt ship for M.T.B., displacing 1,500 tons, and 1 or 2 patrol vessels are under construction at Hong Kong.

COLOMBIA.

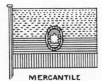

NAVAL	MERCANTILE

Red ▥
White ☐
Blue ▤
Yellow ▦

Destroyers. *(Fitted for Minelaying)*

ANTIOQUIA.   1933 *Photo, Sen. Henrique Seixas.*

2 *Yarrow type :* **ANTIOQUIA** (ex-*Douro*, June 9, 1932), **CALDAS** (ex-*Tejo*, Nov. 18, 1933). Both built at Lisbon for Portugal, and purchased in 1934. Displacement : 1,239 tons *standard*, 1,620 tons *full load*. Complement : 147. Dimensions : 319 (*pp.*), 322 (*o.a.*) × 31 × 11 feet *max.* draught. Guns : 4—4·7 inch, 3—40 mm. A.A. 2 Depth Charge throwers. Tubes : 8—21 inch, in quadruple mounts. Machinery : Parsons geared turbines. H.P. : 33,000 = 36 kts. Boilers : 3 Yarrow, working pressure 400 lbs. Oil fuel : 296 tons. Radius of action : 5,400 miles at 15 kts.

Gunboats.

1938, *W. H. Davis, Esq.*

MARISCAL SUCRE (ex-yacht *Flying Fox*, ex-*Winchester*). (Yarrow, 1909). *Standard* displacement : 125 tons. Dimensions : 160 (*pp.*), 165 (*o.a.*) × 15½ × 4 feet. Guns : 2—3 inch, 1 M.G. Machinery : Parsons turbines. 3 shafts. S.H.P. : 2,500 = 25 kts. Boilers : 2 Yarrow, 250 lb. w.p. Oil fuel : 17 tons.

Gunboats—*continued.*

BOGOTA (ex-Norwegian s.s. *Tonsberg I*, ex-*Helgoland*, ex-German minesweeper *M* 139). **CORDOBA** (ex-*Dinard*, ex-*Grille*, ex-*M* 158). Built by Joh. C. Tecklenborg A.G., and Nordseewerke A.G., respectively, 1919, and purchased in 1933. Displacement : 525 tons. Dimensions : 184 (*w.l.*), 192 (*o.a.*) × 24¼ × 7¼ feet. Guns : 1—3·5 inch, 2—3 inch, 2 M.G. Machinery : 2 sets triple expansion. H.P. : 1,850 = 16 kts. Boilers : 2 Schulz. 2 screws. Coal : 160 tons.

River Gunboats.

CARTAGENA

CARTAGENA (March 26, 1930), **SANTA MARTA** (April 16, 1930), **BARRANQUILLA** (May 10, 1930). All built by Yarrow & Co., Ltd. Displacement : 142 tons. Complement : 12. Dimensions : 130 (*p.p.*), 137¾ (*o.a.*) × 23½ × 2¾ feet *maximum* draught. Guns : 1—3 inch, 4 M.G. Machinery : 2 Gardner semi-Diesel engines. H.P. : 600 = 15·5 kts. 2 screws, working in tunnels. Fuel : 24 tons.

Notes.—These three vessels crossed the Atlantic under their own power without mishap, making the voyage from the Clyde to the Magdalena in 24 days with only one stop (St. Vincent). They represent an extraordinarily efficient type of shallow draft gunboat, incorporating many improvements on previous types. The designed speed has been exceeded on trial and is very high for this type of craft. Hull is of galvanised steel, and machinery spaces, cabins and magazines are of bullet proof plating. Ventilation and refrigerating plant designed to secure excellent habitability.

PRESIDENTE MOSQUERA. Sternwheel Gunboat. Displacement : 200 tons. Dimensions : 150 × 35 × 3½ feet. Guns : 2—37 mm.

A, B, C, D. (ex-*L.M.* 15, 17, 19, 20). (1918.) Bought in Germany, 1933. Displacement : 12 tons. Complement, 8. Dimensions : 57½ × 8¾ × 2¾ feet. 2 M.G. Machinery : Mercedes-Benz motors. B.H.P. 900 = 28 kts.

Nos. 1, 2, 3, 4 (Yarrow, 1913). 20 tons. Dimensions : 80 × 12½ × 3¼ feet. Guns : 1—1 pdr. H.P. : 160 = 12 kts. Fuel : 1800 galls. petrol = 2400 miles at 10 kts.

Coastguard Patrol Vessels.

JUNIN.   1938, *W. H. Davis, Esq.*

JUNIN (ex-*Boyaca*) (July 8, 1925), **CARABOBO** (August 8, 1925), **PICHINCHA** (Sept. 5, 1925). All built by Soc. Anon. des Chantiers et Ateliers de St. Nazaire (Penhoët), at Rouen. 120 tons. Dimensions : 100 × 20 × 8½ feet. Guns : 1—3 inch, 2 M.G. Triple expansion engines and oil-burning water-tube boilers by Messrs. Thornycroft. Speed : 13 kts.

Training Ship.

1938, *W. H. Davies, Esq.*

CUCUTA (ex-*Commercial Traveller*, ex-*Crofton Hall*). (Hamilton, Glasgow, 1913). Displacement : 5,378 tons *gross*. Dimensions : 405 × 52 × 26½ feet. Machinery : Triple expansion. I.H.P. : 3,000 = 10 kts. 4 boilers. Oil fuel.

Transports.

BOYACA (ex-*Bridgetown*, ex-*Lake Fillmore*). (Toledo Shipbuilding Co., 1920). Displacement : 3,000 tons, 2,559 tons *gross*. Triple expansion engines and oil-fired boilers.

MOSQUERA (ex-*Royal Highlander*, ex-*Royal Scot*). (Caledon Shipbuilding Co., Ltd., Dundee, 1910). Purchased 1933. Displacement : 3,500 tons, 1,726 tons *gross*. Guns : 2—3·5 inch. Triple expansion engines.

CUBA.

A Government dockyard is projected in Havana Bay, near the Tiscornia. To have a 4,000 ton Floating Dock. Naval Academy at Mariel to be transferred to vicinity of Dockyard.

Private Docks: At Havana, private floating dock (U.S. and Cuban Allied Works Engineering Corp.) 360×66×17½ feet (5,600 tons); also Havana Marine Co. has a slipway 3,000 tons capacity.

Chief of Naval Staff: Captain G. del Real.

Personnel: Officers, Line 65; Engineers 49, Paymasters 8, Surgeons 8, Judge-Advocates 2=132. Men 1050.

Mercantile Marine.

"Lloyd's Register," 1939 Figures.
39 vessels of 29,947 gross tonnage.

Flags.

(To distinguish jack from Chilean ensign, note that the positions of the colours are transposed.)

RED.
SKY BLUE

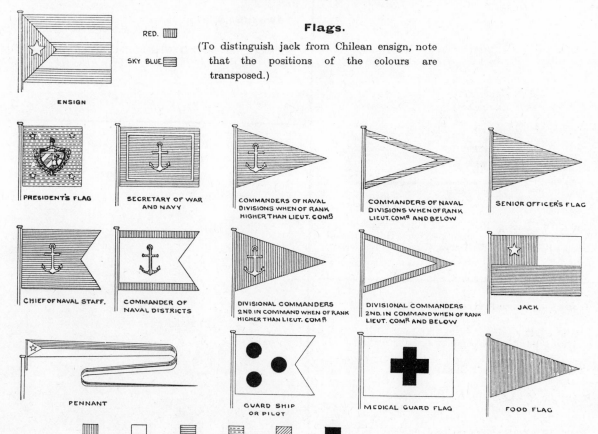

ENSIGN

PRESIDENT'S FLAG

SECRETARY OF WAR AND NAVY

COMMANDERS OF NAVAL DIVISIONS WHEN OF RANK HIGHER THAN LIEUT. COMᴰ

COMMANDERS OF NAVAL DIVISIONS WHEN OF RANK LIEUT. COMᴿ AND BELOW

SENIOR OFFICER'S FLAG

CHIEF OF NAVAL STAFF.

COMMANDER OF NAVAL DISTRICTS

DIVISIONAL COMMANDERS 2ND IN COMMAND WHEN OF RANK HIGHER THAN LIEUT. COMᴿ

DIVISIONAL COMMANDERS 2ND. IN COMMAND WHEN OF RANK LIEUT. COMᴿ AND BELOW

JACK

PENNANT

GUARD SHIP OR PILOT

MEDICAL GUARD FLAG

FOOD FLAG

Red   White   Blue   Azure   Green   Black

Uniforms

Insignia of Rank on Sleeves—Executives.

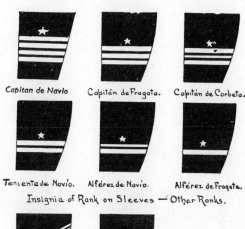

Capitan de Navio.   Capitán de Fragata.   Capitán de Corbeta.

Teniente de Navío.   Alférez de Navío.   Alférez de Fragata.

Insignia of Rank on Sleeves — Other Ranks.

Aspirante.
1-4 stripes acc. to years of training

Sub-Official.
(Radio-operator)

Blue shoulder pieces having stripes in same arrangement worn on white uniform and overcoat.

New Construction.

The following programme has been recommended, to involve an expenditure of 7,220,000 pesos, spread over a period of ten years :—

1 cruiser of 4,500—5,000 tons.
1 ,, ,, 2,500 tons.
8 gunboats of 900 tons.
8 ,, ,, 200 tons.

K

Escort Vessels (rated as Cruisers).
(Both reconstructed, 1936-7)

1937, *R. Perkins.*

CUBA (Cramp, Philadelphia, 10th August, 1911). 2055 tons. Dimensions: (*p.p.*) 260 × 39 × 14 feet. Armament: 2—4 inch, 6—3 inch, 4—6 pdr., 4—3 pdr., 2 machine. H.P.: 6000 = 18 kts. Babcock boilers. Coal: 250 tons.

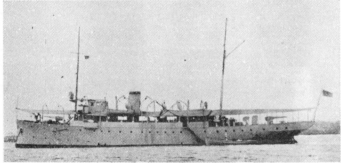

(*Training Ship.*)   1937, *W. H. Davis, Esq.*

PATRIA (Cramp, Philadelphia, 10th August, 1911). 1200 tons. Dimensions: 200 (*p.p.*) × 36 × 13 feet. Guns: 2—3 inch (Bethlehem), 4—6 pdr., 4—3 pdr., I.H.P.: 4000 = 16 kts. Babcock boilers. Coal: 150 tons.

Gunboats.

1921 *Photo. by courtesy of Captain J. Morales Coello.*

HABANA (1912) and **PINAR DEL RIO** (1912). Both wooden vessels of 80 tons, built at Havana. Dimensions: 100 × 18 × 6 feet. Guns: 1—1 pdr. I.H.P.: 200 = 12 kts. 1 screw. Coal: 20 tons.

Gunboats--*continued.*

DIEZ DE OCTUBRE (J. Samuel White, Cowes, 1911), **VEINTE Y CUATRO DE FEBRERO** (J. Samuel White, Cowes, 1911). 218 tons. Dimensions: 110 × 20 × 8 feet. Guns: 3—3 pdr. Speed: 12 kts. Coal: 50 tons.

1921 *Photo, by courtesy of Captain J. Morales Coello.*

BAIRE (Klawitter Yd., Danzig, 1906). 500 tons. Dimensions 196 × 23 × 9 feet. Guns: 4—3 inch, 2—3 pdr. H.P.: 1200 = 14 kts. Babcock boilers. Coal: 120 tons. (Used as Presidential Yacht.)

Coast Guard Patrol Vessels.

CAPITAN QUEVEDO (Havana, 1932). 115 tons. Guns: 1—3 inch AA., 2—1 pdr. Diesel engines. Speed: 12 kts.

GENERAL ZAGAS. 500 tons. Guns: 2—1 pdr.

MATANZAS (1912), **VILLAS** (1912). Details as *Habana* and *Pinar del Rio*; differ in appearance.

ENRIQUE VILLUENDAS (Chester. U.S.A., 1899). 178 tons. 132 × 20 × 9 feet. Guns: 2—3 pdr. I.H.P.: 600 = 16 kts. Coal: 55 tons.

Coast Guard Patrol Vessels—*continued.*

1937, *W. H. Davis, Esq.*

YARA (Middlesbrough, 1895). 449 tons. 155 × 26 × 13 feet. Guns: 2—6 pdr., 2—3 pdr. I.H.P.: 600 = 12 kts. Coal: 150 tons.

VEINTE DE MAYO (Glasgow, 1895). 203 tons. 141 × 18·5 × 10·5 feet. Guns: 2—3 pdr., 2—1 pdr. I.H.P.: 500 = 12 kts. Coal: 50 tons.

Transport.

COLUMBIA.   *Added 1939, Theo. N. Silberstein.*

(*Particulars wanted.*)

DENMARK.

Flags.

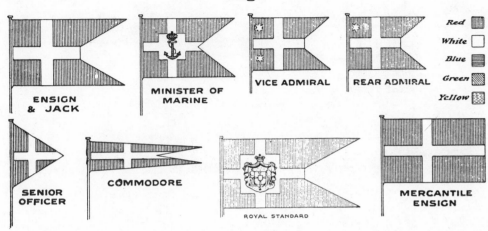

ENSIGN & JACK

MINISTER OF MARINE

VICE ADMIRAL

REAR ADMIRAL

Red	▦
White	☐
Blue	▤
Green	▨
Yellow	▦

SENIOR OFFICER

COMMODORE

ROYAL STANDARD

MERCANTILE ENSIGN

Note.—Division flag is pennant, otherwise as commodore.

Principal Naval Guns.

Bore :		Length in Calibres.	Make and Date of Model.		Weight of Gun.	Weight of Projectile.	Muzzle Velocity.	Mounted in :
ins.	cm.				metric tons.	lbs.	ft.-secs.	
9·4	24	43	Bofors	M. '06	24·5	352	2690	*P. Skram*
5·9	15	45	Bofors	M. '20	6·1	101	2740	*Niels Iuel*
5·9	15	50	Bofors	M. '06	7·5	112	2723	*P. Skram*
4·7	12	40	Danish		2·4	44	2526	*Ingolf*
3·4	8·7	50	Danish	M. '32				*Glenten class*
3·5	8·8	40	Bofors	M. '28				*Hvidbjörnen*

Torpedoes :—45 cm. heater type in all vessels except 1939 Torpedo Boats which will have 53·3 cm.

Insignia of Rank on Sleeves.

| Admiral. | Vice-Admiral. | Kontre-Admiral. | Kommandör. | Kommandör-kaptajn. | Orlogs-kaptajn. | Orlogs-kaptajn. | Kaptajn-löjtnant. | Sölöjtnant. 1' Grad. | Sölöjtnant. 2' Grad. | Kadet Ældste Klasse |

British or U.S.A.

| Admiral. | Vice-Admiral | Rear-Admiral. | Commodore. | Captain. | Commander. *(being replaced by fresh insignia as on right).* | Commander | Lieutenant-Commander. | Lieutenant. | Sub-Lieutenant. | Midshipman. |

Personnel : About 4000, all ranks.

Oversea Possessions : Greenland, Faröe Islands.

Minister of Defence : Alsing Andersen.

C. in C. and Director-General, Ministry of Marine : Vice-Admiral H. Rechnitzer.

Navy Estimates, 1938-39. Kr. 15,500,000.

Mercantile Marine.

From "Lloyd's Register" 1939.

709 Vessels of 1,176,173 tons gross.

Future Construction (1937).

The following programme of naval construction has been approved, to be spread over a period of 6 years :

- 2 Torpedo Boats
- 4 Submarines
- 3 Minesweepers

- 1 Minelayer
- 1 Patrol Vessel
- 1 Surveying Vessel

Note to pages following this.

All displacements are "Standard". Where measurement of length is not stated, it can be taken as between perpendiculars (*p.p.*). All draughts *max. load aft.* unless otherwise stated.

Danish warships are referred to officially with the prefix H.D.M.S.

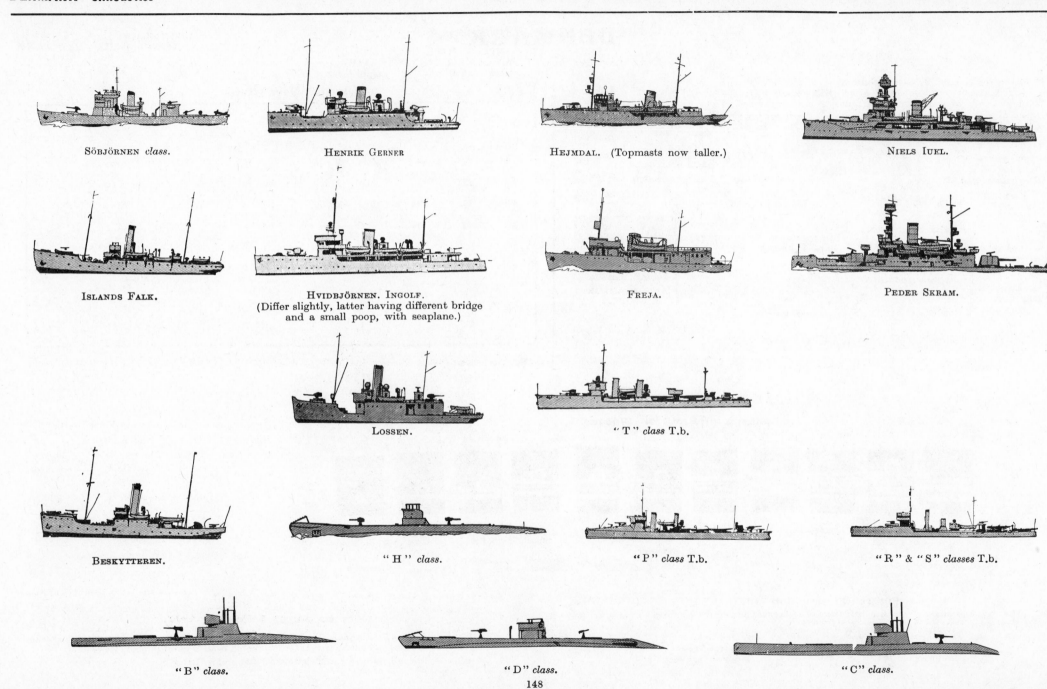

SÖBJÖRNEN *class.*

HENRIK GERNER

HEJMDAL. (Topmasts now taller.)

NIELS IUEL.

ISLANDS FALK.

HVIDBJÖRNEN. INGOLF.
(Differ slightly, latter having different bridge
and a small poop, with seaplane.)

FREJA.

PEDER SKRAM.

LOSSEN.

" T " *class* T.b.

BESKYTTEREN.

" H " *class.*

" P " *class* T.b.

" R " & " S " *classes* T.b.

" B " *class.*

" D " *class.*

" C " *class.*

New Construction

It is proposed to build 2 Coast Defence Ships of about 7,000 tons displacement, well protected, armed with 4—10 inch, 8—4 inch AA, and sundry smaller guns, and with a speed of 18 kts.

Guns (Bofors) :
  10—5·9 inch, 45 cal.
  2—6 pdr.
  10—20 mm. AA.
  14—8 mm. M.G.
Torpedo tubes (17·7 inch heater) :
  2 submerged (broadside).

Armour (Krupp) :
  $7\frac{3}{4}''$
  $7\frac{1}{2}''$ } Side (amidships
  $7''$ }   b - g) { ▨
  6″ Side (forward & aft.
       a - b and g - h) ▨
  $6\frac{1}{2}''$ Bulkheads (forward
       and aft.)
  3″ Uptake to funnel ..
  $6\frac{3}{4}''$ Conning Tower ...... ▨
  4″ Tubes to C.T. ....
  $1\frac{3}{4}''$ Gun shields ($\frac{1}{2}''$ at
       sides) ....
  $2\frac{1}{4}''$ Deck....................
  $2\frac{1}{2}''$ Deck (forward) ......

Machinery : Triple expansion. 2 screws. Boilers : 4 Yarrow (2 coal and 2 oil fired). I.H.P. 6,000 = 16 kts. Fuel : 250 tons coal + 240 tons oil. Endurance : about 5000 miles at 10 kts. Laid down Feb., 1914 ; first commissioned 23rd May, 1923.

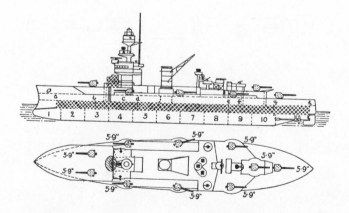

Note.—Modernised, 1935–36, and fitted with up-to-date fire control arrangement at a cost of about £150,000. To be used in future as seagoing training ship for midshipmen.

NIELS IUEL (July, 1918).
Built at Royal Dockyard, Copenhagen.
Displacement, 3,800 tons.   Complement, 365.

Length { (p.p.), $285\frac{1}{2}$ feet.   Beam, $53\frac{1}{2}$ feet.   Draught { mean $15\frac{3}{4}$ feet.
       { (o.a.), $295\frac{1}{4}$ feet.   { full load, aft., 17 feet.

1937, *R. Perkins.*

1936 *Official*

1936 *Official*

PEDER SKRAM (No longer has funnel bands)   1935, *Com. Steen Steensen, R.D.N.*

PEDER SKRAM (1908).

(Built at Royal Dockyard, Copenhagen.)

Displacement, 3,500 tons. Complement, 275.

Length (*p.p.*) 275 feet. Beam, 51 feet. Draught, 16½ feet.

Guns :
2—9·4 inch, 43 cal.
4—5·9 inch, 50 cal.
8—3 inch.
2—1 pdr.
4—20 mm. AA.
2—8 mm. AA.

Torpedo Tubes : 4 (see Notes below).

Armour (*see Notes*) :
7″ Side (amidships) ...
6″ Side (fore & aft) ...
2½″ Deck (forward) ...
2½″ Deck flat on belt.
7″ Turrets ... ...
6″ Casemates (KNC)...
7″ Bulkhead ... ...
7″ Conning tower ...

Machinery : 2 sets, triple expansion, 2 screws. 6 Thornycroft boilers. Coal (*maximum*) : 265 tons. I.H.P. 5,400 = 16 kts.

Gunnery Notes.—Guns are Bofors 1906 models.

Armour Notes.—Krupp armour. Belt is 7 feet deep, 3½ feet above and 3½ feet below water-line. It stops 20 feet from bow. Armoured deck is 3 feet above water-line.

Torpedo Notes.—All tubes 18 inch and submerged : 1 bow, 1 stern, 2 broadside.

Engineering Notes.—Trial : 5,400 = 16 kts. Endurance is about 2,000 miles at 10 kts., and 1,050 miles at 14¾ kts. On a steam trial in the summer of 1939 this old ship made 15·9 kts. with 5,900 I.H.P.

17 + 2 Torpedo Boats. (*Torpedobaade*)

Note.—Danish Torpedo Boats are numbered as follows :—

No.	Name	No.	Name	No.	Name
R 5	Sælen	S 4	Söhunden	T 5	Högen
R 4	Havkatten	S 3	Söridderen	T 4	Glenten
R 3	Nordkaperen	S 2	Stören	T 3	Laxen
R 2	Makrelen	S 1	Springeren	T 2	Hvalen
S 6	Narhvalen	P 1	Hvalrossen	T 1	Dragen
S 5	Havörnen	T 6	Örnen		

New Construction

1939, *Official Sketch*

2 Torpedo Boats laid down at Royal Dockyard, Copenhagen, 1939. Displacement : 710 tons. Dimensions : 279 (*pp.*) × 27⅓ × 8 feet. Guns : 2—4·7 inch, 4—40 mm. AA., 6—20 mm. Tubes : 6—21 inch. 60 Mines carried. Machinery : Geared turbines. 2 shafts. S.H.P. : 21,000 = 35 kts. Oil fuel : 100 tons. Complement : 100.

3 "T 4" Class.

GLENTEN.   1935, *Com. R. Steen Steensen, R.D.N.*

3 boats : *Glenten, Högen* (both 1933), *Örnen* (Oct. 19, 1934), all by Royal Dockyard, Copenhagen. 290 tons. Dimensions : 198¾ (*o.a.*) × 19½ × 7¾ feet. Armament : 2—3·5 inch, 2—20 mm. AA., 2—8 mm. AA., 2 D.C.T., 6—18-inch Tubes. Fitted for minelaying. Machinery : Danish Atlas geared turbines. S.H.P. : 6,000 = 27·5 kts. Oil : 40 tons. Complement : 55.

6 "S" Class.

STÖREN.   1930 *Photo, Com. R. S. Steensen, R.D.N.*

6 *Improved Ormen* class (similar to above): **Springeren (S1), Stören (S2), Söridderen** (ex-*Sölöven*) **(S3), Söhunden (S4), Havörnen** (ex-*Havhesten*) **(S5), Narhvalen (S6).** (All by Royal Dockyard, Copenhagen, launched 1916–17.) Guns: 2—6 pdr. AA., 1—18 inch tube in bow. After tube replaced by mine-sweeping gear. Details as " R " class above.

1 "P" Class.

(Serves as Gunnery School Tender; sometimes employed on fishery protection duties.)

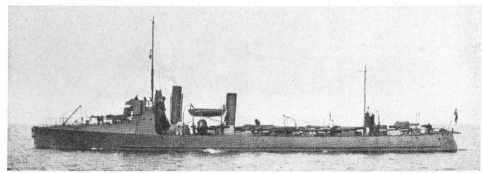

HVALROSSEN.   1922 *Photo, Com. R. S. Steensen, R.D.N.*

1 *Hvalrossen* type: **Hvalrossen, P1** (1913), built at Royal Copenhagen Dockyard. 169 tons. Dimensions: 148¼ (o.a.) × 17×7 feet. Guns: 1—3 inch (aft)., 1—8 mm. AA. 4—18 inch tubes. I.H.P. 3500 = 26 kts. Coal 29 tons. Compl. 33.

Note.—In sketch annexed, positions of double and single deck tubes should be transposed.

3 "T1" Class.

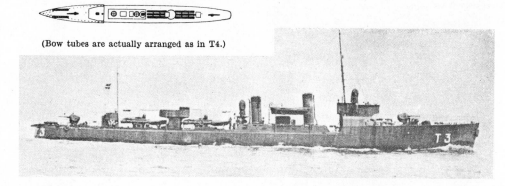

(Bow tubes are actually arranged as in T4.)

LAXEN.   1932 *Photo, Com. R. Steen Steensen, R.D.N.*

3 boats : **Dragen** (Dec., 1929), **Hvalen, Laxen** (both 1930), all by Royal Dockyard, Copenhagen. 290 tons. Dimensions: 198¾ (o.a.) × 19½ × 7¾ feet. Armament: 2—3 inch, 2—20 mm. AA., 2—8 mm. AA., 8—18-inch Tubes (2 in bow and 2 triples). Machinery: Geared turbines (Brown Boveri in *Dragen* and *Laxen*, Danish Atlas in *Hvalen*). S.H.P.: 6,000 = 27·5 kts. Oil: 40 tons. Complement: 51.

4 "R" Class.

HAVKATTEN.   1934, *Com. R. S. Steensen, R.D.N. (added 1935).*

4 *Improved Ormen* class : **Havkatten R4, Saelen R5,** (both launched 1919), **Makrelen R2, Nordkaperen R3,** (both launched 1918). All by Royal Dockyard, Copenhagen. Displacement, 110 tons. Complement, 26. Dimensions: 126½ (o.a) × 14 × 8¾ feet *max.* draught. Armament: 2—6 pdr., 30 cal. (anti-aircraft). 2—18 inch tubes (one bow, one deck, both *above water*), and two depth charge throwers. I.H.P. 2000 = 24·3 kts. Coal, 15 tons.

DENMARK—Submarines.

12 Submarines *(Undervandsbaade)*.

Note.—Danish Submarines are painted green, and numbered thus for identification purposes: *Ran* B9, *Triton* B10, *Galathea* B12, *Rota* C1, *Bellona* C2, *Flora* C3, *Daphne* D1, *Dryaden* D2; *Havmanden* H1, *Havfruen* H2, *Havkalen* H 3, *Havhesten* H4.

4 "H" Class.

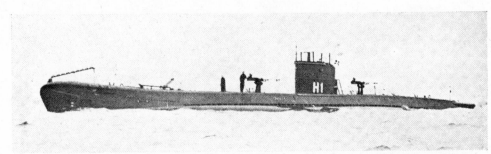

HAVMANDEN.

1939, *Com. R. Steen Steensen, R.D.N.*

4 *Navy* type **Havmanden** (June 6th, 1937), **Havfruen** (Nov. 6th, 1937), **Havkalen** (March 3rd, 1938) **Havhesten** (1939). Built at Royal Dockyard, Copenhagen. Displacement: 314/407 tons. Dimensions: 155¾ (*o.a.*) × 14½ × 9½ feet. Armament: 2—40 mm. AA., 2—8 mm. AA. 5—18-inch tubes (3 bow, 2 stern). B. & W. Diesels. B.H.P.: 1,200/450 = 15/7 kts. Complement: 20.

2 "D" Class.

DRYADEN.

1928 *Photo, Com. R. Steen Steensen, R.D.N.*

(Mast since struck.)

2 *Navy* type: **Daphne** (Dec., 1925), **Dryaden** (June 3, 1926). Built at Royal Dockyard, Copenhagen. Displacement: 301/381 tons. Dimensions: 160¾ (*o.a.*) × 16 × 8½ feet. Burmeister & Wain type Diesels. H.P.: 900/400 = 13·5/6·5 kts. Armament: 1—3 inch gun 1—20 mm. AA., 4 bow and 2 stern 18 inch tubes. *Daphne* completed 1926, *Dryaden* 1927. Complement: 25.

3 "C" Class.

FLORA.
(No mast now.)

1927 *Photo, Com. R. Steen Steensen, R.D.N.*

3 *Navy* type: **Bellona** (1919), **Flora** (1920), and **Rota** (1918). All built at Royal Dockyard, Copenhagen. Displacement: 300/369 tons. Dimensions: 155¾ (*o.a.*) × 14½ × 9½ feet. Armament: 1—6 pdr. AA., 4—18-inch torpedo tubes (3 bow, 1 stern). *Rota* has one deck tube in addition before C.T. Burmeister & Wain type Diesels. H.P.: 900/640 = 14/8 kts. Complement: 24.

3 "B" Class

GALATHEA.

1935, *Com. R. Steen Steensen, R.D.N.*

3 *Holland* type: **Galathea** (1916), **Ran** (1915), **Triton** (1915), all built at Royal Dockyard, Copenhagen. Displacement: 173/237 tons. Dimensions: 133¼ (*o.a.*) × 12¼ × 8 feet. Armament: 3—18-inch torpedo tubes (2 bow, 1 stern), 1—6 pdr. AA. gun. Burmeister & Wain type Diesels. H.P.: 450/340 = 13/6·5 kts. Complement: 14.

1939, *Com. R. Steen Steensen, R.D.N.*

FREJA (Dec. 22, 1938). Built at Royal Dockyard, Copenhagen. Displacement : 322 tons. Complement : 40. Dimensions : 124¾ (*pp.*), 134 (*o.a.*) × 25¼ × 7¼ feet. Guns : 2—3 inch, 2—20 mm. AA. (Not mounted when on Surveying Service.) Machinery : Triple expansion, 1 shaft. I.H.P. : 300 = 10·5 kts. Boilers : 1 cylindrical. Oil fuel : 15 tons. Classed as *Opmaalingsskib* (Surveying Vessel).

HVIDBJÖRNEN.   1936, *Com. R. Steen Steensen, R.D.N.*

HVIDBJÖRNEN (Royal Dockyard, Copenhagen, 1928). Displacement : 1,050 tons. Complement, 61. Dimensions : 196¾ (*p.p.*) × 32 × 13 feet (*mean* draught). Guns : 2—3·5 inch. Machinery : Double compound Lentz valve engine. 1 shaft. I.H.P. : 1,800 = 14·5 kts. 2 boilers (1 Babcock, 1 Thornycroft). Oil : 140 tons. Radius : 2,300 miles at 12 kts. On service in Icelandic waters. Classed as *Fiskeriinspektionsskib*.
Note.—The name of this ship means White Bear.

With seaplane added to equipment.   1938, *Com. R. Steen Steensen, R.D.N.*

INGOLF (Royal Dockyard, Copenhagen, 1933). Displacement : 1,180 tons. Complement : 66. Dimensions : 213¼ (*p.p.*), 226 (*o.a.*) × 35½ × 16 feet (*max.*). Guns : 2—4·7 inch, 2—6 pdrs./57 mm., 2—20 mm. AA., 2—8 mm. AA. Machinery : Triple expansion. 1 shaft. I.H.P. : 2,935 = 16·5 kts. Boilers : 2 Thornycroft. Oil : 170 tons. Radius : 5,300 miles at 12 kts. On service in Greenland waters. Visits Iceland occasionally. Classed as *Fiskeriinspektionsskib*.

(Topmasts now taller).   1935, *Com. R. Steen Steensen, R.D.N.*

HEJMDAL (Royal Dockyard, Copenhagen, Feb. 1, 1935). Displacement 705 tons. Complement : 40. Dimensions : 175 (*o.a.*) × 30 × 12 feet. Guns : 2—3 inch, 4—20 mm. AA., 2—8 mm. AA. Machinery : Triple expansion. 1 shaft. I.H.P. : 800 = 13 kts. Boilers : 2 cylindrical. Oil : 100 tons. Radius : 4,000 miles at 12 kts. Completed April, 1935. Classed as a Surveying Vessel, but also employed on Fishery Protection duties in Greenland waters and off the Färöes.

Fishery Patrol Vessels—*continued*.

1921 *Photo, Commdr. R. S. Steensen, R.D.N.*

ISLANDS FALK (Elsinore 1906). 730 tons. Complement, 64. 170·6 (*p.p.*), 183·6 (*o.a.*) × 29·3 × 16·9 feet. Guns : **2**—3 inch, 2—3 pdr. I.H.P. 1100 = 11·7 kts (*f.d.*) Cruising speed is 9 kts. Re-boilered 1921. Employed on North Sea Fisheries and Färoes.

Now has short Topmasts. To be replaced in near future.

1932 *Photo Commdr. R. S. Steensen, R.D.N.*

MAAGEN (Frederikssund, 1930). Wood. Displacement : 90 tons. Dimensions : 71½ (*o.a.*) × 16½ × 9½ feet. Guns : **1**—37 mm. 1 Tuxham motor. B.H.P. : 108 = 8 kts. Complement : 11.
On service in Greenland waters. Classed as Fishery Patrol Cutter (*Fiskeriinspektionsfartöj*).

1921 *Photo, Commdr. R. S. Steensen, R.D.N.*

BESKYTTEREN (1900). 415 tons. Comp. 47. 134 (*p.p.*), 142·5 (*o.a.*) × 24·8 × 12·5 feet. Guns : **1**—6 pdr., 2—8 mm. AA, I.H.P. 620 = 11 kts. (*f.d.*). Cruising speed is 9 kts. Re-boilered 1920. Employed in North Sea and inside Skaw. At certain seasons serves as midshipmen's training ship and aircraft tender.

TERNEN.   1938 *Official.*
TERNEN (Faaborg, 1937.) Wood. Displacement : 82 tons. Complement : 11. Dimensions : 68½ (*o.a.*) × 16¾ × 9¾ feet. Guns : **1**—37 mm. 1 Möller & Jochumsen Diesel engine. B.H.P. : 110 = 8 kts. Employed on fishery research and coastal surveying duties, Greenland. Classed as Surveying Tender (*Opmaalingsfartöj*).

Minesweepers.

SÖLÖVEN.   1939, *Com. R. Steen Steensen, R.D.N.*

SÖLÖVEN.   1939, *Com. R. Steen Steensen, R.D.N.*

SÖBJÖREN (Feb. 16, 1939), **SÖLÖVEN** (Dec. 3, 1938), **SÖULVEN** (1939). Laid down 1938, at Royal Dockyard, Copenhagen. Displacement : 270 tons. Complement : 47. Dimensions : 176½ (*o.a.*), 170 (*pp.*) × 20¾ × 6½ feet. Guns : **2**—3 inch, 4—20 mm. AA., 4—8 mm. AA., 2 D.C.T. Equipped for minelaying. Machinery : Geared turbine, 1 shaft. S.H.P. 2,200 = 19 kts. Boiler : 1 Thornycroft 3-drum type. Oil fuel : 30 tons.

Submarine Depôt and Repair Ship.

HENRIK GERNER.   1928 *Photo.*

HENRIK GERNER (Royal Dockyard, Copenhagen, 1927). Displacement : 463 tons. Dimensions : 160 (*o.a.*) × 27 × 9·3 feet. Guns : 2—3 inch, 2—8 mm. AA. 2 Burmeister & Wain 6-cylinder, 4-cycle Diesel engines of 900 combined B.H.P. = 13·2 kts. Oil : 45 tons. Complement : 46. Fitted for minelaying.

Minelayers (*Mineskibe*).

LINDORMEN, Building at Royal Dockyard, Copenhagen. Displacement : 614 tons. Complement : 58. Dimensions : 167¼ (*pp.*) × 29 × 8 feet. Guns : 2—3 inch, 3—20 mm. AA. Mines : 150. Machinery : Triple expansion. 2 shafts. I.H.P. : 1,200 = 14 kts. Boilers : 2 Thornycroft 3-drum type. Oil fuel : 35 tons. Will replace *Lossen.*

Photo, Ministry of Defence (added 1921).

LOSSEN (1910). 640 tons. Complement, **61.** 149⅓ (*pp.*) × 28 × 10 feet. Guns : 2—3 inch, 2—8 mm. AA. I.H.P. : 900 = 12 kts. Coal : 44 tons. 175 mines carried.

Mining Tenders (*Minefartöier.*)

1920 *Photo, Com. R. Steen Steensen, R.D.N.*

KVINTUS (1917), **SIXTUS** (1919), (Royal Dockyard, Copenhagen) **186** tons. Dimensions : 88·5 (*p.p.*) × 20·7 × 6·6 feet (*mean* draught). Guns : 2—1 pdr. Machinery : in each, 2 sets of Bergsund surface-ignition, heavy-oil motors and electric drive. B.H.P. 300 = 8 kts. Complement, 27. Carry 60 mines.

Royal Yacht (*Kongeskib*).

1936, *Commdr. R. S. Steensen, R.D.N.*

DANNEBROG (Royal Dockyard, Copenhagen, 1931). 1,130 tons. Complement : 57. Dimensions : 246 (*o.a.*) × 34 × 11⅕ feet. Guns : 2 M.G. Two Burmeister & Wain 8-cylinder, 2-cycle Diesels. B.H.P. : 1,800 = 14 kts.

Harbour Tender.

1930 *Photo, Com. R. Steen Steensen, R.D.N.*

DAMPBAAD A (ex-*Minekran I*) (1896). **96** tons. Dimensions : 72¼ (*o.a.*) × 16½ × 6½ feet. Guns : **2** machine. Speed : **7** kts. Complement : 18.

Torpedo Tender (*Torpedo Transportbaad*).

1920 *Photo Com. R. Steen Steensen, R.D.N.*

SLEIPNER (1882). 80 tons. 73 (*o.a.*) × 14¾ × 6 feet (**mean** draught). Guns : none. I.H.P. : 110 = 9 kts.

EGYPT.

A :—Royal Egyptian Navy.

A sum of £3,500,000 is to be expended over two years in the construction of a cruiser, 4 minesweepers and 6 torpedo boats, orders for which it is proposed to place with British yards.

British Naval Adviser : Captain G. T. Philip, D.S.C., R.N.

Mercantile Marine : (" Lloyd's Register " 1939 figures) 56 vessels of 109,825 tons gross.

B :—Coastguard and Fisheries Administration.

Transport.

1930 *Photo, Swan, Hunter.*

EL AMIRA FAWZIA (Swan, Hunter, July 8th, 1929). 2,640 tons. Dimensions : 275 × 36 × 14 feet. Guns : 2—3 pdr. Machinery : Triple expansion. H.P. : 2,130 = 14 kts. 2 screws. 2 S.E. boilers (working pressure, 180 lbs.). Oil fuel. Fitted as transport for 400 men and 40 horses. Normally employed on coasting service carrying passengers. Complement, 79.

Escort Vessel.

EL AMIR FAROUQ (Hawthorn, Leslie, 1926). 1441 tons. Dimensions : 247 × 34 × 13¼ feet. Guns : 1—6 pdr. 4 M.G. Machinery : Triple expansion. 2 screws. I.H.P. : 2,800 = 17 kts. 2 s.e. boilers, working pressure, 180 lbs. Oil fuel. Complement : 70.

Motor Patrol Vessels.

1939, *Official.*

RAQIB (Alexandria, 1938). Dimensions : 66 × 12½ × 4 feet. Guns : 1—37 mm. Machinery : 2 Otto Deutz 8-cyl. Diesel engines. 2 shafts. B.H.P. : 540 = 15 kts. Fuel : 520 gallons. Complement : 9.

AL SAREA (J. S. White & Co., Ltd., 1936). Dimensions : 55 × 11½ × 3⅙ feet. Guns : 1—37 mm. Machinery : 2 Kermath 12-cyl. petrol engines. H.P. : 900 = 35 kts. Fuel : 340 gallons. Complement : 9.

DARFEEL.

1939, *Official.*

DARFEEL, NOOR-EL-BAHR (Thornycroft, 1925). Displacement : 20 tons. Dimensions : 56 × 11 × 3½ feet. Guns : 1—37 mm. Machinery : 3 Thornycroft 6-cyl. petrol engines. 3 shafts. B.H.P. : 330 = 17 kts. Fuel : 600 gallons. Complement : 9.

Research Vessel.

1930 *Photo, Swan, Hunter.*

MABAHISS—Built by Swan, Hunter, and completed 1930. Displacement : 618 tons. Dimensions : 138 × 23½ × 13½ feet. Machinery : Triple expansion. 1 shaft. I.H.P. : 650 = 11 kts. 1 s.e. boiler. Fuel : Coal. Complement : 39.

C :—Ports and Lighthouses Administration.

Salvage Tug.

1936 *Official.*

PHAROS (1929). Displacement, 455 tons. Dimensions : 131 feet (*o.a.*) × 27 × 14 feet *depth*. I.H.P. 1,000 = 12 kts. Equipment includes 2—10 inch centrifugal pumps, capacity of each 500 tons per hour. (There are 2 smaller tugs, *Teir-el-Mina* and *Safaga*, 195 and 80 tons respectively.)

C:—Ports and Lighthouses Administration
—*continued*
Transports

SOLLUM.   1939, *Official.*

SOLLUM (ex-British Escort Vessel *Syringa*, of *Anchusa* class, built by Workman, Clark & Co., 1917). Displacement : 1,290 tons. Dimensions : $255\frac{1}{4}$ (*pp.*), $262\frac{1}{4}$ (*o.a.*) × 35 × 16 feet. Guns : 1—3 pdr. I.H.P. : 2,500 = 16 kts. 1 screw. Coal : 260 tons. Many alterations have been effected at considerable cost to fit this vessel for accommodation of Government officials on visits of inspection, etc., to Mediterranean coast. Complement : 77.

1939, *Official.*

NAPHTYS (Howaldt, Kiel, 1905). Displacement : 620 tons. Dimensions : $187\frac{3}{4}$ (*pp.*) × 35 × $8\frac{1}{2}$ feet. Machinery : Triple expansion. 1 shaft. I.H.P. : 360 = 7 kts. Complement : 47.

Coastal Motor Boats.

QAMAR	23 tons.	71 feet.	11 kts.
EL HOOT	24 tons.	46 feet.	7 kts.

Lighthouse Tender.

Foretopmast since struck.

AÏDA (A. & Ch. de la Loire, Nantes, 1911). 1428 tons *gross.* Dimensions : $246\frac{1}{3}$ × $31\frac{3}{4}$ × $13\frac{1}{2}$ feet draught. I.H.P. 1200 = 10 kts. 1 screw. Serves in Red Sea. Complement, 63.

D—Royal Yacht.

MAHROUSSA.   1927 *Photo, Cribb.*

MAHROUSSA. Iron. Built by Samuda Bros., Poplar, 1865. Reconstructed by A. & J. Inglis, Glasgow, 1905, and re-fitted 1919-20 at Portsmouth Dockyard. Displacement : 4561 tons. Dimensions : 400 (*p.p.*), 420 (*w.l.*), $477\frac{5}{6}$ (*o.a.*) × $42\frac{3}{4}$ × $17\frac{1}{4}$ feet draught. Machinery : 3 Parsons turbines. Boilers (new 1905) : 5 main and 1 auxiliary Inglis multitubular. 3 screws. S.H.P. 5500 = 16 kts. Oil : 346 tons. Complement, 164.

DOMINICAN REPUBLIC.

Coastguard Patrol Vessels (*Guardacostas*).

Three (ex-*CG.* 110, 144, 302). (1924). Purchased from U.S. Coast Guard in October, 1938. Wood. Displacement : 37 tons. Dimensions : 75 × 13¾ × 4 feet. Guns : 1—1 pdr. Machinery : Petrol engine. B.H.P. : 400 = 13·5 kts.

Transport.

PRESIDENTE TRUJILLO (ex-*Presidente Machado*, ex-*Comerio*, ex-*Guantanamo*, ex-*Registan*). (Wm. Gray & Co., Ltd., West Hartlepool, 1910). 3,349 tons *gross*. Dimensions : 350½ × 46½ × — feet. Guns : Not reported. Machinery : Triple expansion I.H.P. : 2,000 = 11 kts.

Presidential Yacht.

RAMSIS (ex-*Camargo*). (1928). 969 tons *gross*. Dimensions : 181½ (*w.l.*), 225 (*o.a.*) × 32½ × — feet. Guns : 2—3 pdr. Machinery : 2 sets Diesels.

ECUADOR

Personnel : About 400.

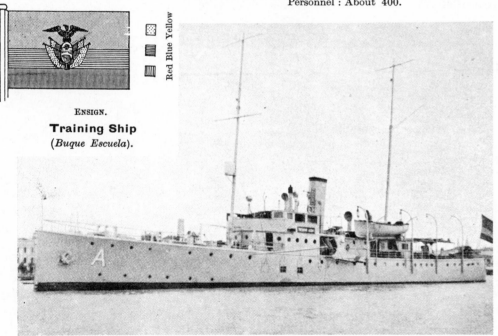

ENSIGN.

Red Blue Yellow

Training Ship
(*Buque Escuela*).

1936, *courtesy Lieut. L. F. Bouman*

PRESIDENTE ALFARO (ex-yacht *Ara*). (Camper & Nicholsons, Southampton, 1917). Purchased 1935. Displacement : 1,030 tons *Std.* Dimensions : 213 (*w.l.*) × 31¼ × 14½ feet. 2 Atlas Diesels. 2 shafts. B.H.P. 2,400 = 16 kts.

ESTONIA

Naval Uniforms.

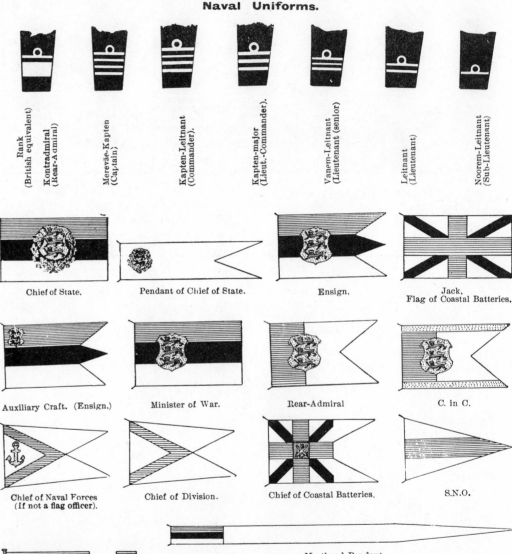

| Rank (British equivalent) | Kontradmiral (Rear-Admiral) | Merevāe-Kapten (Captain) | Kapten-Leitnant (Commander) | Kapten-major (Lieut.-Commander) | Vanem-Leitnant (Lieutenant (senior) | Leitnant (Lieutenant) | Noorem-Leitnant (Sub-Lieutenant) |

Chief of State. — Pendant of Chief of State. — Ensign. — Jack, Flag of Coastal Batteries.

Auxiliary Craft. (Ensign.) — Minister of War. — Rear-Admiral — C. in C.

Chief of Naval Forces (If not a flag officer). — Chief of Division. — Chief of Coastal Batteries. — S.N.O.

Masthead Pendant.

PALE BLUE.

BLACK.

WHITE.

MERCANTILE ENSIGN.

Commander-in-Chief of Fleet and Coast Defence : Captain V. Mere.
Chief of Naval Staff : Captain R. Linnuste.
Naval Officers and Men : 1600
Colour of Ships : Grey.
Mercantile Marine ("Lloyd's Register" 1939): 184 vessels of 200,410 gross tonnage.

Submarines.

LEMBIT.

1937, *Wright & Logan.*

Torpedo Boats.

Note.—The construction of a number of motor torpedo boats is projected. Number and design still to be settled.

One was ordered from Messrs. Thornycroft in Jan., 1939. Dimensions : 72 × 16 × — feet. 2—18-inch tubes. Machinery: 4 Y 12-cyl. engines. H.P. : 2,400 = over 40 kts.

1934 *Photo, Official.*

Sulev (ex-German *A*32). Built at Elbing, 1916. (Sunk off Estonian Coast, October, 1917, salved and refitted 1923.) Displacement, 228 tons. Dimensions : 165½ × 17½ × 6 feet. Guns : 2—3 inch, 50 cal. Torpedo tubes : 2—18 inch, in double deck mounting. Can carry 10 mines. Designed S.H.P. 3500 = 26 kts. Oil : 50 tons = 975 miles at 20 kts. Complement, 35. Main mast shortened 1932. Refitted, 1935.

KALEV.

1937, *courtesy Messrs. Vickers-Armstrongs (Builders).*

2 *Vickers-Armstrongs* type : **Kalev, Lembit** (July 7, 1936). Both built at Barrow. Displacement : 600/820 tons. Complement : 30. Dimensions : 190 (*o.a.*) × 24½ × 11½ feet. Armament : 1—40 mm. AA. gun, 4—21 inch Torpedo tubes (bow), 20 mines. Machinery : 2 Vickers Diesels. B.H.P. : 1,200 = 13·5 kts. on *surface.* Electric motors, H.P.: 450 = 8·5 kts. *submerged.* Radius of action, 2,000 miles at 10 kts.

Gunboats. (*Suurtükilaevad*)

1929 *Official Photo.*

LAINE (1915). 400 tons. Dimensions : 129 × 20 × 11½ feet. Guns : 2—75 m/m. Designed H.P. 350 = 12 kts. Coal : 30 tons. Complement, 25. (Refitted 1930).

1929 *Official Photo.*

MARDUS. Refitted 1921. 80 tons. Dimensions : 90 × 21 × 7 feet. Guns : 2—3 inch, 50 cal., 2 M.G. Designed H.P. 225 = 11 kts. Complement, 25. **In Reserve.**

Gunboats—*continued*.

1929 *Official Photo.*

*AHTI. Built 1908, refitted 1929. 144 tons. Dimensions : 90½ × 16½ × 6 feet. Guns : 2—47 m/m., 2 M.G. Designed H.P. 220 = 10 kts. Complement, 17.
*Stationed in Peipus Lake.

1929 *Official Photo.*

*TARTU. Paddle vessel. Refitted 1919. 108 tons. Dimensions : 128½ × 17½ × 2¾ feet. Guns : 2—47 m/m., 2 M.G. Designed H.P. 120 = 11 kts. Complement, 20. (Refitted 1931).
*Stationed in Peipus Lake.

Minelayers.

RISTNA. 1929 *Official Photo.*

RISTNA (1908), **SUUROP** (1907). Paddle Vessels. Refitted 1927. 500 tons. Dimensions : 198½ × 49½ (over paddle boxes) × 6½ feet. Guns : 1—3 inch, 50 cal., 1—1 pdr. Pom-Pom. Designed H.P. 750 = 12·5 kts. Complement, 40. Also fitted for use as Minesweepers.

VAINDLO. 1933 *Official Photo.*

KERI (ex-*Kalev*, ex-Russian *M.8*), **VAINDLO** (ex-*Olev*, ex-Russian *M.15*) (1914). 50 tons. Dimensions : 68½ × 15 × 4 feet. Guns : 1—57 m/m. Engines : 2 sets of petrol motors. Designed H.P. 80 = 9 kts. Complement, 10.

Minesweeper.

(See also *Ristna* and *Suurop*, on preceding page.)

1929 *Official Photo.*

TAHKONA (1919). 45 tons. Dimensions : $57\frac{1}{2} \times 10\frac{1}{2} \times 5\frac{1}{2}$ feet. Designed H.P. 150 = 12 kts. Complement, 8.

Coastguard Vessels.

KÕU. Refitted 1928. 100 tons. Dimensions : $87 \times 17\frac{1}{2} \times 8\frac{1}{2}$ feet. Guns : 1—50 m/m., 2 M.G. Designed H.P. 350 = 12 kts. Complement, 18.

1929 *Official Photo.*

ERILANE. Built 1915, refitted 1919. 25 tons. Dimensions : $53 \times 10 \times 5$ feet. 1 M.G. Designed H.P. 50 = 10 kts.

Icebreakers.

1939, *Official.*

SUUR TÕLL (ex-*Vainamoinen*, ex-*Volhynetz*, ex-*Tsar Mikhail Feodorovitch*, 1914) Displacement, 3,622 tons. Dimensions: $236\frac{1}{2} \times 57 \times 18\frac{3}{4}$ feet. H.P. 4,500 = 13.5 kts. **TASUJA** (1,100 tons), and **JURI VILMS** (200 tons), are in peacetime all under the control of the Government Shipping Department.

Tugs and Tenders.

1929 *Official Photo.*

KOMPASS (1918). 300 tons. Dimensions : $143 \times 21 \times 12$ feet. Designed H.P. 220 = 9 kts. Complement, 20. Fitted for cable laying.

Tugs and Tenders—*continued.*

JAAN POSKA. 1939, *Official.*

JAAN POSKA. 250 tons. Dimensions : $101 \times 21 \times 9\frac{1}{2}$ feet. H.P. 600 = 11 kts. Complement, 15. Commissioned in 1929 as a Tug-icebreaker.

SAKALA. 40 tons. Dimensions : $62 \times 11 \times 6\frac{1}{2}$ feet. Designed H.P. 40 = 8 kts. Complement, 6.

M.P. 10. 1939, *Official.*

M.P.10. 24 tons. Dimensions : $55\frac{1}{2} \times 9\frac{1}{2} \times 3\frac{1}{2}$ feet. Designed H.P. 100 = 13.5 kts. Complement, 6.

1929 *Official Photo.*

M.P.8., M.P.14., M.P.23. (1909). 12 tons. Dimensions : $53 \times 13 \times 6$ feet. Designed H.P. 55 = 9 kts. Complement, 6.

L

FINLAND.

Uniforms.

(a) = Finnish Rank ; (b) = British Rank.

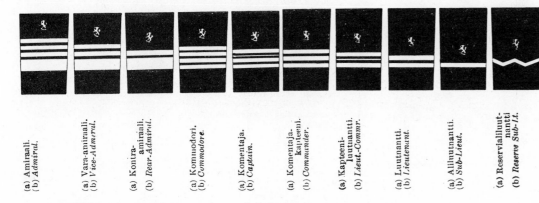

(a) Amiraali.	(a) Vara-amiraali.	(a) Kontra-amiraali.	(a) Komnodori.	(a) Komentaja.	(a) Komentaja-kapteeni.	(a) Kapteeni-luutnantti.	(a) Luutnantti.	(a) Alihutnantti.	(a) Reserviiliiluutnantti.
(b) Admiral.	(b) Vice-Admiral.	(b) Rear-Admiral.	(b) Commodore.	(b) Captain.	(b) Commander.	(b) Lieut.-Commr.	(b) Lieutenant.	(b) Sub-Lieut.	(b) Reserve Sub-Lt.

The figure over top stripe is the Lion of the Finnish Arms, as enlarged sketch reproduced herewith.   Colour of cloth between stripes :—

Engineers : purple ;   *Paymasters* : silver stripes and 1 silver star; *Surgeons*: red ; *Army officers in Naval Service* : green.   *Reserve* officers have wavy stripes as R.N.V.R.

Minister of Defence :   Juho Niukkanen.

Chief of Sea Forces :   Major-General V. L. R. Valve.

Chief of Staff :   Capt. R. Hakola.

Commanding Coastal Fleet :   Commodore E. A. Rahola.

Naval Attaché (*London*) :   Commander Holger Gröndahl.

Personnel : Active List, including Coastal Artillery, about 4,500 officers and men.

Wireless.

Marconi, Western Electric and Telefunken systems used.

Colour of Ships.

Grey.

Mercantile Marine.

(From "Lloyd's Register," 1939)

432 vessels of 625,531 *Gross* Tonnage.

Flags :—

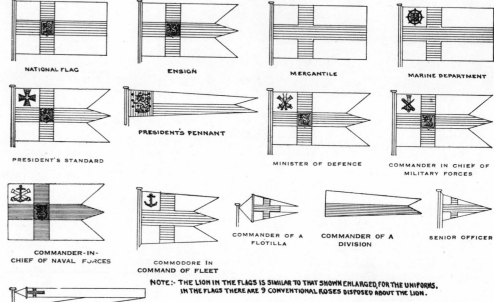

NOTE :- THE LION IN THE FLAGS IS SIMILAR TO THAT SHOWN ENLARGED FOR THE UNIFORMS. IN THE FLAGS THERE ARE 9 CONVENTIONAL ROSES DISPOSED ABOUT THE LION.

Red   White   Blue   Yellow

Naval Ordnance.

(Not all mounted afloat at present),

Calibre inches.	m/m.	Maker.	Length.	M.V.	Weight of A.P. projectile.
10	254	B	45	2788 fps.	495 lbs.
6	150	C	Howitzer	2601 ,,	91 ,,
4·7	120	A	41	2132 ,,	44 ,,
4·7	120	V	50	3001 ,,	44 ,,
4·7	120	C	45	2699 ,,	44 ,,
4·1	105	B	50	2952 ,,	35 ,,
4	102	C	60	2706 ,,	38·5 lbs.

A = Armstrong.   B = Bofors.   C = Schneider-Canet.   V = Vickers.

Note.—A gun factory was opened at Jyvaskyla in February, 1939.

VÄINÄMÖINEN. ILMARINEN.

AURA.

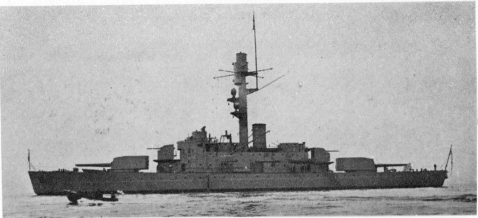

VÄINÄMÖINEN.   1937 *R. Perkins.*

VÄINÄMÖINEN (Dec. 20, 1930). **ILMARINEN** (July 9th, 1931)

Built by A. B. Crichton-Vulcan, Turku, (Åbo).
Displacement : 3,900 tons. Complement, 329.
Dimensions : 305 × 55½ × 14¾ feet.

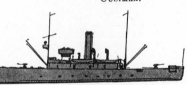

HÄMEENMAA.
UUSIMAA.

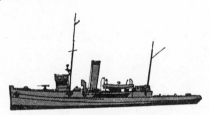

KARJALA.
TURUNMAA.

LOUHI.

SISU.

Guns :
  4—10 inch, 46 cal.
  8—4·1 inch AA.
  4—2 pdr. AA.

Armour :
  4″ Turrets
  ½″—¾″ Deck

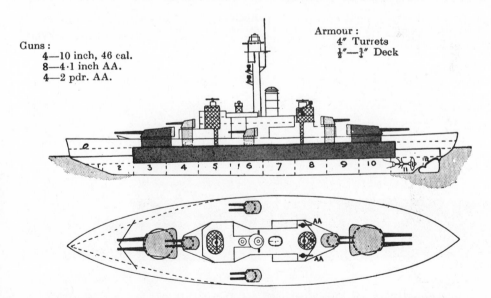

RAUTU. VILPPULA.

VESIKKO.

VETEHINEN *class.*

SAUKKO.

Machinery : Germania Diesels with electric drive, Leonard system, by Brown, Boveri & Co.
2 shafts. B.H.P. : 5,000 = 15·5 kts. Fuel : 93 tons.

Notes.—Laid down Aug.-Sept., 1929. Completed 1932 and 1933 respectively. Guns: Max. elevation of 10 inch
is 50°.

5 Submarines. (*Sukellusveneet*).

Vesikko (1933), built by A/B Crichton-Vulcan as a private speculation and taken over by Finnish Navy Jan. 1936. Displacement : 250/300 tons. Complement, 16. Dimensions : $134\frac{1}{2} \times 13 \times 13\frac{1}{2}$ feet. 1 M.G. Torpedo tubes : 3—21 inch. Machinery : Mannheim B.M.V. H.P. 700/180 = 13/7 kts. Fuel : 9 tons. Radius of action, 1,500/50 miles. Diving limit reported to be 50 fathoms.

1932 *Official Photo.*

1 boat : **Saukko** (1930). Laid down 1929 by Hietalahden Laivatelakka of Helsinki. Displacement : 100/136 tons. Complement, 13. Dimensions : $106\frac{1}{2} \times 13\frac{1}{2} \times 10\frac{1}{2}$ feet. 1 M.G. 2—18 inch torpedo tubes. 9 mines. Machinery : Germania Diesels. H.P. 200/150 = 9/6 kts. Radius of action, 375/45 miles.

VETEHINEN.   1932 *Official Photo.*

3 boats : **Vetehinen** (June 2, 1930), **Vesihiisi** (1930), **Iku-Turso** (1931). Built by A/B Crichton-Vulcan, Turku, Abo, the first keel being laid in Sept., 1926, other two early in 1927. Displacement : 490/715 tons. Complement, 27. Dimensions : $208\frac{1}{2}$ (*o.a.*) $\times 20\frac{1}{4} \times 10\frac{3}{4}$ feet. Torpedo Tubes : 4—21 inch (533 mm.). Guns : 1—3 inch, 1— M.G. Reported to carry 20 mines. Machinery : Atlas Diesels. H.P. 1,060/600 = 14/8 kts. Fuel : 20 tons. Radius of action : 1.500/75 miles. Diving limit, 40 fathoms.

4 Gunboats (*Tykkiveneet*)

KARJALA.   1934 *Photo.*

KARJALA (ex-Russian *Filin*, 1918), **TURUNMAA** (ex-Russian *Orlan*, 1916). Both built by Crichton A/B Turku. Ordered by late Imperial Russian Government, 1914. Displacement : 342 tons. Complement, 52. Length (*p.p.*) 154 feet (*o.a.*) 164 feet. Beam, 22½ feet. Designed load draught, 9½ feet. Guns : 2—3 inch, 3 M.G. Machinery : 2 sets triple expansion. Boilers : Normand. Designed I.H.P. : 1,000 = 15 kts. Coal capacity : 60 tons.

Notes.—" Borowski type " Patrol Vessels and generally sisters to Polish *K. Pilsudski* and *Gen. Haller*. *Turunmaa* is employed as Cadets' Training Ship.

UUSIMAA.   1934 *Photo*

UUSIMAA (ex-German *Beo*, ex-*Golub*, 1917), **HÄMEENMAA** (ex-German *Wulf*, ex-*Pingvin*, 1917). Built at Helsinki to order of late Imperial Russian Government. Displacement : 400 tons. Complement, 54. Dimensions : 160 (*p.p.*), 170½ (*o.a.*) × 24½ × 11 feet. Guns : 2—3·9 inch, 1—40 mm. AA., 3 M.G. Machinery : 2 sets triple expansion. Designed H.P. : 1,400 = 15 kts. Cylindrical boilers. Coal : 70 tons.

Note.—Sisters to Russian *Pionir* and *Kopchik*.

TURUNMAA. (Note funnel band.)   1932 *Official Photo.*

165

FINLAND—Minelayers and Minesweepers

Minelayers. (*Miinanlaskijat*).

2 Minelayers of 300 tons are projected.

1934 *Photo.*

LOUHI (ex-*M.*1, ex-Russian *Voin*, Kolomna, 1917). Displacement : 640 tons. Complement, 46. Dimensions : 151 (*p.p.*) 164 (*o.a.*) × 26¼ × 8½ feet. Guns : 2—3 inch, 2—40 mm. AA., 3 M.G. Machinery : 1 set triple expansion. Designed H.P. 1,000 = 11 kts. Coal : 39 tons. Carries 140 mines. (Is also employed as Submarine Depot Ship.)

RAUTU.   1924 *Photo, Commdr. Raninen.*

VILPPULA (ex-*T.*2, 1916) and **RAUTU** (ex-Russian *Murman*, 1917). Displacement : 268 tons. Complement, 35. Dimensions : 147⅔ (*o.a.*) × 20⅓ × 6½ feet. Guns : 1—3 inch, 2 M.G. Machinery : 2 sets triple expansion. Designed H.P. 450 = 12 kts. Boilers : Yarrow and Schulz respectively. Oil : 19 tons. Can carry 30 mines.

Minelayers.—*continued.*

POMMI (MIINA similar)   1933 *Photo.*

POMMI (ex-*M.* 7, 1916), **MIINA** (ex-*T.* 17, 1917). Built by Porin Konepaja O.Y., Pori. Displacement : 80 tons. Complement, 6. Dimensions : 65⅔ × 17 × 4 feet. Machinery : 2 sets of B.M.V. petrol motors. Designed I.H.P. 90 = 9 kts. Fuel : 1¼ ton.

LOIMU.   1934 *Photo.*

LOIMU (ex-*T.* 21, 1915), **LIESKA** (ex-*T.* 16, 1916), **PAUKKU** (ex-*T.* 15, 1916). Built by Porin Konepaja O.Y., Pori. Displacement : 60 tons. Complement, 6. Dimensions : 62¼ × 17 × 3⅔ feet. Machinery : 2 sets of B.M.V. petrol motors. Designed I.H.P. 60 = 7·5 kts. Fuel : 1¼ ton.

Minesweepers. (*Raivaajat*).

(*Of similar appearance to AF 2 on following page.*)

AHVEN, KIISKI, MUIKKU, SÄRKI, KUORE, LAHNA (Turun Veneveistämö Yard, 1936–37). Displacement : 17 tons. Complement, 8. Dimensions : 56⅓ × 12 × 4¼ feet. H.P. : 60 = 10·5 kts.

A.37. (*for description, see following column*)   1934.

Minesweepers
(continued).

HAUKKA.   *Photo* 1934.

A.F. 2   1934 *Photo.*

11 *boats :* **BVA., BVD., A.37, A.38, A.40, A.42, A.43, A.45, B.3, AF.2, HAUKKA.** Displacement: *BVA.—A.*45, 9 tons; *B.*3, 18 tons ; *AF.*2, 25 tons ; *Haukka,* 12 tons. Complement, 6. Dimensions : 53 × 11⅕ × 4 feet (first 8). Engines : Petrol motor. Designed I.H.P. : 45–60 = 8–9·5 kts.

Motor Torpedo Boats.
(*Moottoritorpedoveneet.*)

SYÖKSY.   1937.

4 boats : **Syöksy** (ex-*M.T.V.* 4), **Nuoli** (ex-*M.T.V.* 5), **Vinha** (ex-*M.T.V.* 6), and **Raju** (ex-*M.T.V.* 7). *Syöksy* and *Nuoli* built 1928 by Thornycroft, *Vinha* 1929 by Turun Veneveistämö, and *Raju* 1929 by Porvoon Veneveistämö. Displacement: 12 tons. Complement, 7. Dimensions : 55 × 11 × 3¼ feet. Guns : 2 Lewis. Torpedoes 2—17·7 inch. 2 D.C. I.H.P. 750 = 40 kts.

1 boat : **Isku** (ex-*M.T.V.* 3). Built by Porvoon Veneveistämö in 1926. Displacement : 11 tons. Dimensions : 54 × 11 × 3¼ feet. 2 M.G. Torpedoes : 2— 17·7 inch, carried in dropping gears. Machinery: 2 sets Fiat motors. I.H.P. 650 = 31 kts.

1924 *Photo, Commdr. Raninen.*

2 boats : **Sisu II.** (ex-*M.T.V.*1) **Hurja** ex-*M.T.V.* 2. (ex-*M.A.S.* 220, 221). Built for Royal Italian Navy by Flli. Orlando 1916 and purchased, 1920. Displacement : 13 tons. Complement, 7. Dimensions : 53 × 9½ × 4 feet. Guns · 2 M.G. on high angle mounts. Torpedoes · 2—17·7 inch (450 mm.). Machinery : 2 sets Isotta Fraschini motors. I.H.P. 500 = 26 kts.

Presidential Yacht.
(Appearance as Silhouette.)

AURA (ex-*Seagull*). (Göteborg, 1884). (Rebuilt 1929–30). 563 tons *gross*. Dimensions : 190½ × 25½ × 17½ feet. Machinery : Compound. I.H.P. : 574 = 12 kts. 2 boilers. Complement : 16.

Motor Patrol Boats.
(*Vartiomoottoriveneet.*)

VMV. 9   1935.

VMV. 1, 2, 5, 6 (1930–31). **VMV. 8–17** (1935). Built in Germany. Displacement : 30 tons. Dimensions : 82 × 13¾ × 3¼ feet. Guns : 1—20 mm. Machinery : Benzol motors in first 3, semi-Diesel in others. H.P. : 1,220 = 25 kts.

Sail Training Ship.
Koululaiva.)

1932 *Official Photo.*

SUOMEN JOUTSEN (ex-*Oldenburg*) (St. Nazaire, 1902). Purchased by Finnish Navy in 1931. Displacement : ·3,200 tons. Complement, 27 + 60 cadets. Dimensions : 316½ × 40⅞ × 16½ feet. Machinery : 2 auxiliary Diesels. H.P. 400 = 6 kts. Fuel : 40 tons.

Gunboats.
(On Lake Ladoga)

AALLOKAS (1935). Displacement: 300 tons. Dimensions: $108\frac{1}{4} \times 24\frac{1}{2} \times 10$ feet. H.P.: 500 = 10 kts. Fitted for ice breaking and used as Fishery Protection Vessel.

AUNUS.   1934 *Photo.*

AUNUS (Vulcan Yard, Turku, 1900). Displacement: 100 tons. Complement, 21. Dimensions: $83\frac{1}{3} \times 19\frac{1}{3} \times 7$ feet. Guns: 2—57 mm., 2 M.G. Machinery: 2 sets compound. Cylindrical Boiler. I.H.P. 260 = 10 kts. Coal: 12 tons.

YRJÖ (1895). Displacement: 290 tons. Complement, 19. Dimensions: $95 \times 20 \times 8$ feet. 1 M.G. Machinery: 1 set compound. Cylindrical Boiler. I.H.P. 200 = 8 kts. Coal: 11 tons.

VAKAVA. Ex-tug. Particulars wanted.

Submarine Depot Ship and Icebreaker.
(For appearance, see silhouette.)

SISU (Sandvikens, Sept. 24, 1938), Displacement: 2,000 tons. Dimensions: $194\frac{3}{4}$ (*w.l.*), $210\frac{1}{2}$ (*o.a.*) $\times 46\frac{1}{2} \times 16\frac{1}{4}$ feet. Guns: 2—3.9 inch, AA. Machinery: 3 sets Atlas Polar Diesels with electric drive. 2 shafts and a bow propeller. H.P.: 4,000 = 16 kts. Complement, 100.

Icebreakers.
(Jäänsärkijät)

OTSO (1936). Dimensions: $134\frac{1}{2} \times 35\frac{1}{2} \times 15\frac{1}{4}$ feet. H.P.: 1,800 = 13 kts. Oil fuel: 60 tons.

Added 1938, courtesy Messrs. Smit.

JÄÄKARHU (Smit, Rotterdam, 1926). Displacement: 4,825 tons. Dimensions: $246 \times 63 \times 21$ feet. Machinery: Triple expansion. 3 shafts. I.H.P.: 9,200 = 15 kts. 8 boilers. Oil fuel.

Added 1938, courtesy Messrs. Armstrong.

TARMO (ex-*Sampo II*), (Armstrong, 1907). Displacement: 2,300 tons. Dimensions: $210\frac{1}{2} \times 47 \times 18\frac{1}{6}$ feet. Machinery: Triple expansion. I.H.P.: 3,850 = 12 kts.

168

VOIMA (Sandvikens, 1917). Displacement: 2,070 tons. Dimensions: $210\frac{3}{4} \times 46\frac{1}{2} \times 16\frac{3}{4}$ feet. Machinery: Triple expansion. 1 shaft. I.H.P.: 4,100 = 13.5 kts.

Added 1938, courtesy Messrs. Armstrong.

SAMPO (Armstrong, 1898). Displacement: 1,850 tons. Dimensions: $202 \times 43 \times 18\frac{1}{4}$ feet. Machinery: Triple expansion. 2 shafts. I.H.P.: 3,000 = 12 kts. Complement, 43.

Illustrated in "Fighting Ships, 1919, p. 375.

APU (ex-*Avance*), (Howaldt, Kiel, 1899). Displacement: 800 tons. Dimensions: 136 (*pp.*), 144 (*o.a.*) $\times 35\frac{1}{2} \times 18$ feet. I.H.P.: 1,385 = 10 kts.

Illustrated in "Fighting Ships," 1919, p. 375.

MURTAJA (Stockholm, 1890). Displacement: 815 tons. Dimensions: $137\frac{1}{2} \times 36 \times 15\frac{1}{2}$ feet. H.P.: 1,130 = 11 kts.

Salvage Vessel.
(Pelastuslaiva).

(*Photo wanted.*)

MURSU (ex-*Stannum*, Kiel, 1902). 615 tons gross. Dimensions: $117\frac{1}{4}$ (*p.p.*), 131 (*o.a.*) $\times 41 \times 15$ feet. I.H.P. 500 = 8 kts. Purchased 1935 for re-equipment as a salvage vessel. Is fitted with special lifting gear for raising sunken submarines.

Uniforms.

Minister of Marine—Monsieur César Campinchi.

Naval Attaché (London)—Capitaine de Vaisseau C. L. M. C. Denis de Rivoyre.

Ass^t. Naval Attaché—Lieut. de Vaisseau L. Bedin.

Navy Estimates.

1937 : Frcs. 4,460,000,000.
1938 : Frcs. 4,650,000,000+1,500,000,000 Supplementary Credit. (2.5.38).
1939 : Frcs. 8,072,000,000+1,565,000,000 „ „

Personnel.

Estimates for 1938 : 4,868 Officers, 77,500 Men. To be increased to 85,000 in all by 1940

Flags.

Presidential Flag : Initials of the President worked in Gold letters on central (white) stripe of the Ensign, the letters and their dimensions being chosen by M. le Président.

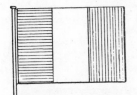

Ensign & Jack
(Minister of Marine).

Vice-Amiral
Chef d' Etat Major
Général
ou Inspecteur Général
des Forces Maritimes.

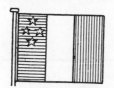

V.A. Comm. in Chief,
Préfet
Maritime de
Regions.

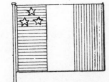

Autres Vice-Amiraux,
et Généraux de Division
en Mission Officielle,
ou pourvus d'un Com-
mandement en Chef.

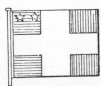

Contre-Amiral
et Général de Brigade
en Mission Officielle.

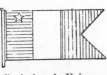

Capitaine de Vaisseau
Chef de Division
(independante ou en
sous ordre).

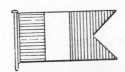

Capitaine de Vaisseau
Comm't un groupe de
bâtiments, ou
Major-Général
commandant la Marine.

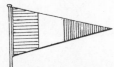

Capitaine de Frégate
ou de Corvette, Comm't
un groupe de bâtiments
ou commandant la Marine.

Comm't supérieur
temporaire de tout
grade.

Rouge Blanc Bleu

Note.—The ranks of Amiral de la Flotte, Amiral and Vice-Amiral d' Escadre were instituted in 1939.

      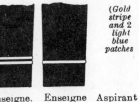

(Gold
stripe
and 2
light
blue
patches

| V.A. Chief of Staff. | V.A. in Command of Forces. | Vice-Amiral. | Contre-Amiral. | Capitaine de vaisseau.* | Capitaine de frégate.† | Capitaine de corvette. | Lieutenant de vaisseau. | Enseigne. | Enseigne 2e classe. | Aspirant |

Corresponding ⎱
to British ⎰

Vice-Ad. Rear-Ad. Captain. Commander. *Lieut.- Comm'der.* Lieut. *Lieut. (junior.)* Sub-Lieut. Midshipman

*Capitaine de Vaisseau, Chef de Division, has one star above the stripes.
†Only three of the Capitaine de frégate's stripes are gold : the second and fourth are silver.
Epaulettes with parade uniform are of the usual sort, *except that*—
A Vice-Admiral's epaulettes have the usual anchor and 3 stars.
A Rear-Admiral's „ „ „ „ 2 „
Caps are similar to British Navy in shape but badge differs, being more like Italian and there are stripes right round corresponding to rank. The cocked hat carries the tri-colour.

Torpedoes. (Details official).

Whitehead pattern, made at Toulon Torpedo Factory ; also at St. Tropez, where Whitehead marks are built by the Société Française de Torpilles Whitehead.

Date.	French Designation.	Diameter.	Length.		Charge.	Pressure in chamber.	Maximum range.
		inches.	feet.	ins.	lbs.	lbs. per sq. in.	metres
1919	55 c/m (D)	21·7	27		551	2420	15,000
1912	45 c/m	18	22	2	317	2420	8000
1912	40 c/m	15·7					

Notes.—All fitted with gyros. There are also 1923 and 1924 models of the *55 c/m* torpedo, with ranges up to 20,000 metres.

Mines.

Present types understood to include mainly 120 and 200 kg. types for laying by S/M ; 360 kilo Sautter-Harlé spherical and 700-kilo Breguet spherical types. Paravanes British marks.

Catapults.

Of compressed air type in all ships prior to *Algérie*. In that ship and all of later date explosive propellant is used.

General Notes.

COLOUR OF SHIPS : *Surface ships.*—Light grey (darker for Atlantic ships.)
Submarines.—Sea green or light grey.
EFFECTIVE LIFE OF SHIPS : Fixed in 1936 as—Battleships, 26 years ; Aircraft Carriers, 20 years ; Cruisers, 20 years ; Torpedo Craft, 16 years ; Submarines, 13 years. All reckoned from date of first commissioning for trials.

Washington Treaty standard has been adopted for regulation of displacements

Mercantile Marine.

(From "Lloyd's Register," 1939 figures.)
1,282 vessels of 2,952,975 gross tonnage.

NAVAL ORDNANCE.

(There are also a 15 inch (*Richelieu* class), 1932–33 models of 5·5, 5·1 and 3·9 inch, and a 3 inch AA. of 35 cal.)

Calibres (inches)	13·4	13	12	8	6·1	6	5·5			5·1		3·9	3·5	3	1·5
(mm.)	340	330	305	203	155	152	138			130		100	90	75	37
Modèle	1912	1933	1906–10	1924	1920	1930	1929	1923	1910	1924	1919	1917	1926	1924	1925
Longueur (en calibres)	45	52	45	50	50	55	50	40	55	40	40	45	50	50	50
Poids du canon (Kgs.)	66,280	..	54,020	20,716	8530	8128	4114	4113	5300	3875	4392	1565	1600	1095	158
Poids du projectile (Kgs.)	554	540	432	123	56	54	40	40	39	32	32	14	9·5	6	0·75
Poids de la charge (Kgs.)	151	..	126	47	19·6	17	..	9	11	8	8	4	3	2	0·25
Pression Kg./cm.	2800	..	2400	2750	3050	3200	..	2500	2500	2420	2420	2300	3200	2560	2400
Vitesse initiale m/sec.	794	1061	783	850	850	870	860	700	830	734	734	720	850	850	850

Battleships and Aircraft Carriers

DUNKERQUE. STRASBOURG.

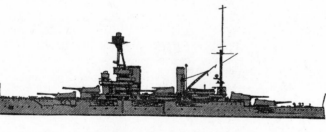

LORRAINE.

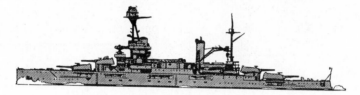

BEARN. Funnel on starboard side.

BRETAGNE. PROVENCE.

COMMDT. TESTE.

PARIS.

COURBET.

ALGÉRIE.

DUQUESNE, TOURVILLE.

EMILE BERTIN. (*Now has hangar before 2nd funnel*).

SUFFREN.

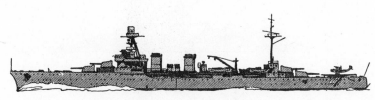

DUGUAY-TROUIN *class*.

JEANNE D'ARC.

COLBERT.

LA GALISSONNIÈRE *class*.
(Catapult now mounted on after turret).

LA TOUR D'AUVERGNE.

DUPLEIX.

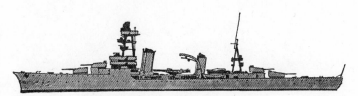

FOCH.

LA POMONE *class.*

SIMOUN *and* ADROIT *classes.*

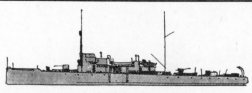

DILIGENTE.

CHACAL *class.*

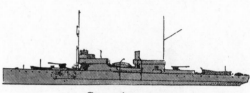

CONQUÉRANTE.
(ENGAGEANTE similar, but Yacht Bow).

LE FANTASQUE *class.*
(Now have control tower abaft second funnel).

GUÉPARD *type.*

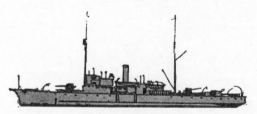

LURONNE.

SOMME.   YSER.

MOGADOR.
(VOLTA has forefunnel top similar to after funnel).

CASSARD *type.*

SUIPPE.   ANCRE.

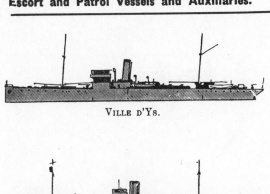

VILLE D'YS.

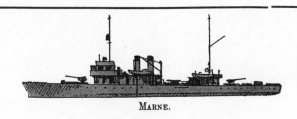

MARNE.

GRANIT *class*.

AMIRAL MOUCHEZ

AILETTE.

ARDENT *type*.

QUENTIN ROOSEVELT.

CH 1—4.

YPRES *class*.

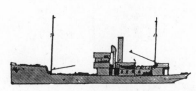

FAUVETTE II.

CH 106—115.

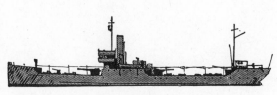

BOUGAINVILLE *class*.

ASTROLABE *class*.

LE GLADIATEUR.

ARRAS *class*.

DUBOURDIEU *class*.

LA PÉROUSE.

173

CASTOR.

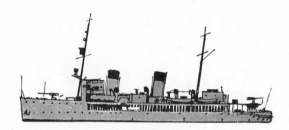

POLLUX.

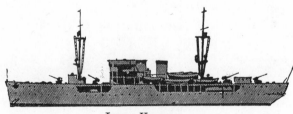

JULES VERNE.

SURCOUF.

SAPHIR *class.*

PASCAL *type.*
(REDOUTABLE, VENGEUR, as part sketch.)

REQUIN *class.*

SIRÈNE *group.*

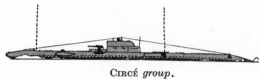

CIRCÉ *group.*

ARIANE *group.*

DIANE *class.* (A).

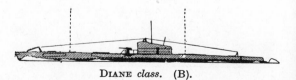

DIANE *class.* (B).

(RICHELIEU CLASS—4 SHIPS.)

RICHELIEU (Jan. 17, 1939), JEAN BART, CLEMENCEAU, GASCOGNE

Displacement : 35,000 tons.   Complement,

Length : 794 feet.   Beam, 108¼ feet.   Draught, 26½ feet (*mean*)

Guns :
  8—15 inch
  15—6 inch
  8—37 mm. AA.
  10—13 mm. AA.

Armour:
  9´—16″ Belt
  8″ Deck (upper and lower combined)
  (Total weight of armour, 15,000 tons ; of machinery, 3,000 tons.)

Aircraft :
  4, with 2 catapults

Note to Plan.—3.9 inch A.A. guns are not now to be mounted as shown.

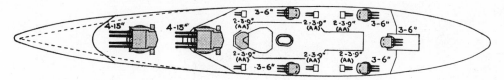

Machinery : Geared turbines. H.P. : 155,000 = over 30 kts. Boilers : 6 Indret.

General Notes.—These ships are designed to form a homogeneous squadron with the *Dunkerque* and *Strasbourg*. Percentage of displacement devoted to armour is higher even than in those two ships. *Jean Bart* built in Loire yard, but construction shared by Penhoët concern. *Richelieu* and *J. Bart* were both built in dry docks.

Programme :

	Name	Builder	Machinery	Laid down	Compl.
1935 {	Richelieu	Brest	Loire	22/10/35	To be 1940
	Jean Bart	{ Penhoët } { Loire }	Penhoët	1/1/37	„ 1941
1938 {	Clemenceau	Brest		17/1/39	} „ 1942-43
	Gascogne	{ Penhoët } { Loire }		End '39	

DUNKERQUE. 1937, R. Perkins.

DUNKERQUE. 1937, R. Perkins.

(Particulars of these ships will be found on following page.)

DUNKERQUE. 1938, Official.

STRASBOURG. (Bridge details differ from Dunkerque). 1938, courtesy M. Henri Le Masson.

DUNKERQUE (Oct. 2, 1935).   STRASBOURG (Dec. 12, 1936).

Standard Displacement, 26,500 tons.   Complement : 1,381.

Dimensions : Length (*w.l.*) 686 ; (*o.a.*) 702 feet. Beam : 101¾ feet. Draught : 28 feet (*mean*)

Guns :
- **8**—13 inch.
- **16**—5·1 inch (dual purpose).
- **4**—47 mm.
- **8**—37 mm. AA.
- **32**—13 mm. AA.

Aircraft : 4, with
1 catapult (on
q.d.).

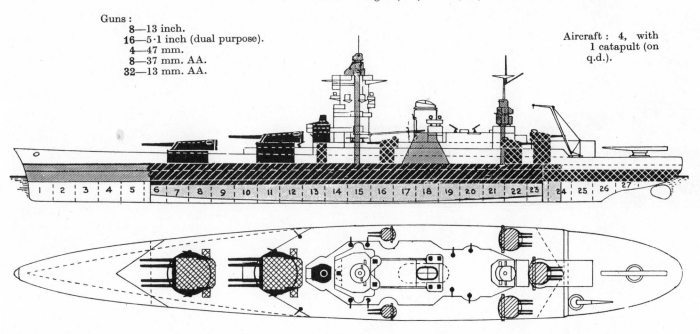

Armour :
- 14″ C.T.
- 14″ Turrets.
- 11″ Side (at w.l.).
- 7″ do. (at main deck).
- 1½″ Longitudinal Torpedo Bulkhead.
- Protective Decks :
- 5″ Upper.
- 2″ Lower.
- (Total weight of armour, *over* 10,000 tons.)

(Other illustrations on preceding and following pages).

Machinery : Parsons Geared Turbines. H.P. : 100,000 = 29·5 kts. (trials, 136,900 = 31·5).
Radius : 7500 miles at 15 kts. 6 Indret boilers.

General Notes.—These two ships are to replace the *France* (lost in 1922) and the *Océan*. Cost approximately Frcs. 700,000,000 each. Modelled on the *Nelson*, the quadruple turrets were finally adopted after a variety of other gun dispositions had been considered, this grouping having been selected for the pre-War ships of the *Normandie* and *Tourville* classes. The turrets are widely separated to localise the effects of shell fire and reduce blast on the tower when trained abaft the beam. Bridge structure is also modelled on that of *Nelson*. It includes a lift in its interior. The percentage of displacement devoted to protection is the highest yet recorded in any capital ship. A feature which does not show in illustrations is the extraordinary height between decks.

    Dunkerque was built in dry dock. Being too long for the dock, the stem piece was constructed separately and attached to hull after floating out.
    The construction of *Strasbourg*, although nominally by Penhoët, was shared by Ch. Loire.

Gunnery Notes.—13 inch guns fire projectiles of 1,200 lbs. weight. Rate of fire 3 rounds a minute. All-round loading position. Elevation 35°. 5·1 inch guns can fire with extreme elevation and are said to have an average rate of fire of 10 rounds per minute and a range of 11,000 yards when so discharged.

Name	Builder	Machinery	Laid down	Completed
Dunkerque	Brest	Loire	26/12/32	April 1937
Strasbourg	Penhoët	Penhoët	25/11/34	Dec. 1938

Distinctive features.—*Dunkerque* has 2 white bands around funnel, *Strasbourg* only 1 band.

DUNKERQUE.   1937, *R. Perkins.*

STRASBOURG.   1938, *Official.*

(*For particulars of these ships, see preceding page*).

DUNKERQUE.   1937, *R. Perkins.*

PROVENCE.

1936, *Courtesy M. Henri Le Masson.*

PROVENCE.

1935, *Courtesy of Mons. H. Le Masson.*

General Notes.—B., L. and P. belong to the 1912 programme, one of them being a replace ship for the *Liberté*, blown up September, 1911. Estimated cost, £2,908,000 per ship = £126 per ton. After the War tripod foremasts and directors were installed. All converted to partial oil burning, 1927–30. In 1932–35 all were extensively refitted, being given new 13·4 inch guns (originally ordered for *Normandie* class), additional AA. and machine guns, enhanced protection, and small-tube boilers, burning oil. All can now make 20 kts. continuously at sea.

(BRETAGNE CLASS—FIRST 2 SHIPS.)
BRETAGNE (April 21, 1913), PROVENCE (April 20, 1913).

Standard displacement, 22,189 tons.   Complement, 1,133 (+ 57 as Flagship).

Length (*waterline*), 541⅓ feet, *over all*, 544½ feet.   Beam, 88½ feet.   *Maximum* draught, 32 feet.

Guns:
10—13·4 inch, 45 cal.
14—5·5 inch, 55 cal. (M.'10).
8—3 inch AA, 60 cal.
7—47 mm.
16—13 mm.
Torpedo tubes (Removed)

Armour (chromo-nickel):
10¾″ Belt (amidships) ...
7″ Belt (ends) ....
Deck (*see Notes*) ....
10″—6″ Lower deck side
17″—10″ Turrets.........
11″ Turret bases (N.C.)
7″ Secondary battery ...
12½″ Conning tower ......

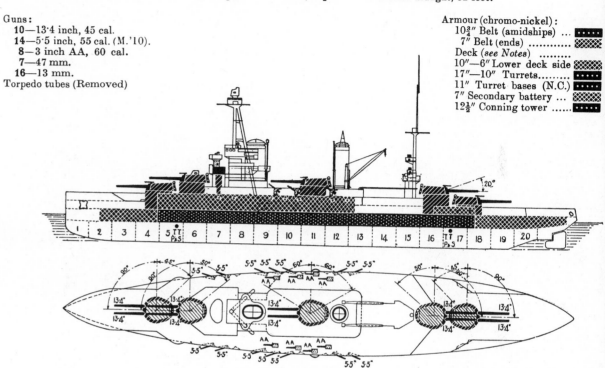

Machinery : Parsons turbine. 4 shafts. Boilers : Indret. Designed H.P. : 29,000 = 20 kts. (since increased). Oil fuel : 2,600 tons. Radius at 10 kts., over 7,000 miles.

Gunnery Notes.— Carry 100 rounds per gun for 13·4 inch and 275 per gun for the 5·5 inch. Janney electro-hydraulic mountings to big guns. Special cooling for magazines · temperature 27° Fahr. Magazines can be completely flooded inside ten minutes. Height of guns above l.w.l.: 1st turret, 30¼ feet; 2nd. 37¼ feet; 3rd, 33¼ feet; 4th, 28¼ feet; 5th, 21¼ feet. Arcs of training: Nos 1 and 5. 270°: Nos 2 & 4. 280°: No. 3. 120° either beam. Arcs of secondary guns: 120°. Big gun elevation increased from 18° to 23°: *max.* range is 23,000 metres. *Lorriane* has had turret removed amidships to make room for catapult.

Torpedo Notes.—8- 36″ and 2 - 30″ searchlights. 4—200 k.w. dynamos. Torpedoes: 24 carried. Also 30 blockade mines.

Armour Notes.—Turrets of maximum thickness at ports. instead of uniform thickness as in *Courbet* type. According to the 1917 Edition of "Flottes de Combat," the barbette shields are not of uniform design. Those for the end barbettes are 13·4″ thick, for the super-firing barbettes 9¼″ thick and for the central barbette 15¾″ thick. The double bottom is carried to the under side of protective deck. Main belt is 13¼ feet wide, 5₁²⁄₁₂ feet below and 7¼ above l.w.l. Battery 197 feet long with 7 in. bulkheads. Protective decks: lower 2″ slopes, 1¼″ flat. Upper, 1¼″ flat on top of belt.

Engineering Notes.—All now converted to oil fuel. 6 new Indret small tube type now supply turbines with steam, giving a large reserve of power beyond the designed figure.

Name	Builder	Machinery	Laid down	Com pleted	Trials	Turbines	Boilers	Best recent speed
Bretagne	Brest	La Seyne	July '12	Sept.'15		Parsons		22
Lorraine	Penhoët	Penhoët	Nov. '12	July '16	21·4 kts.	Parsons	Indret in all	22
Provence	Lorient	La Seyne	June '12	June '15		Parsons		20·5

179

*Unofficial.

BRETAGNE. AA. guns mounted singly. (Now has 2 black bands on after funnel.)

1934 *Official* (*added* 1935).

For particulars of BRETAGNE *see preceding page.*

BRETAGNE.

1935, *Capitaine M. Adam.*

180

BRETAGNE.

1935 *courtesy of Mons. H. Le Masson.*

(Bretagne Class—3rd Ship.)
LORRAINE (September 30, 1913).
Standard displacement : 22,189 tons.   Complement, 1,133 (+57 as Flagship).
Length (w.l.) 541⅓ feet, (o.a.) 544½ feet.   Beam, 88½ feet.   Max. draught, 32 feet.

(Now has 1 black band on after funnel.) 1936, *Official.*

Guns :
   8—13·4 inch
  14—5·5 inch, 55 cal.
   8—3·9 inch, 60 cal. AA.
   6—47 mm.
   8—37 mm. AA.
  12—13 mm.
   8 M.G.
Torpedo tubes (Removed)

Aircraft : 4

Armour (Chromo-nickel) :
  10¾″ Belt (amidships)
  7″ Belt (ends)
  3½″ Deck
  10″—6″ Lower deck side
  17″—10″ Turrets
  11″ Turret bases (N.C.)
  7″ Secondary Battery
  12½″ Conning tower

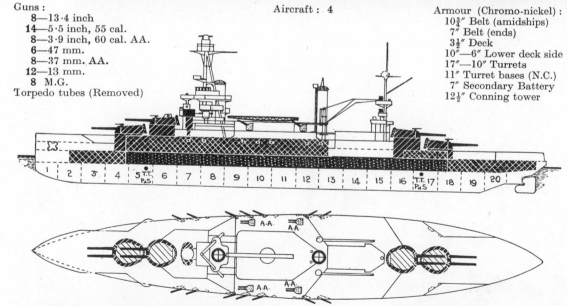

1937, *courtesy M. Henri Le Masson.*

Machinery : Parsons turbines. 4 shafts. Boilers : 6 Indret. S.H.P. : 43,000 = 21·4 kts.
(trials with new boilers). Oil fuel : 2,600 tons.
General Notes.—*Lorraine* was extensively reconstructed in 1934–35, centre turret being removed to make room for aircraft and catapult. For other particulars, vide sister ships *Bretagne* and *Provence*, on an earlier page.

FRANCE—Battleships

COURBET (Sept. 23, 1911), PARIS (Sept. 28, 1912).

Standard displacement, 22,189 tons. *Full load,* 25,850 tons. Complement, 1108.
Length (*pp.*) 541 feet, (*o. a.*) 551 feet. Beam, 92½ feet. *Maximum* draught, 32½ feet.

Guns (M. '06—10):
12—12 inch, 45 cal.
22—5·5 inch, 55 cal. (M. '10).
7—3 inch AA. (M. 1922).
2—47 mm. AA.
Torpedo tubes (18 inch):
4 submerged.

Armour: (Chromo-nickel):
10¾" Belt (amidships)......
7" Belt (bow) (N.C.) ...
7" Belt (aft) (N.C.) ......
2¾" Deck ....
10"—6" Lower deck side
12½" Turrets (N.C.)
11" Turret bases (N.C.) ..
7" Secondary battery ...
11¾" Conning tower (N.C.)

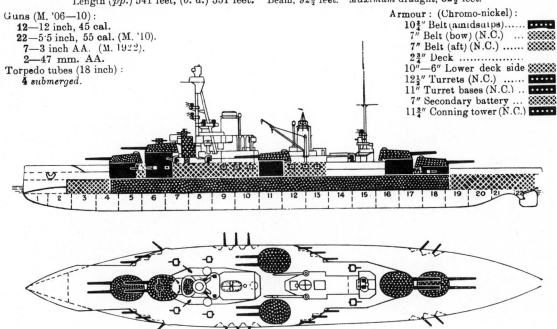

PARIS. (Observe 2 funnels forward and bridgework.)   1929 *Photo, M. Bar, Toulon*

Name	Builder	Machinery	Laid down	Completed	Trials Full power	Boilers	Best recent speed
Courbet	Lorient	St. N'z're (Ch. de l'Atlantique)	Sept., '10	Sept. '13	= 20·81	Belleville & small tube in each	16
Paris	La Seyne	F. & C. de la Méd	Nov., '11	Aug. '14	35,610 = 21·6		

General Notes.—Designed by M. Lyasse. Construction very fine and highly finished in details. Average cost about £2,475,000. *France,* of this class, foundered in Quiberon Bay, Aug., 1922. All this class have been reconstructed, 1928–1929. *Courbet* has been completely re-boilered at La Seyne (1929) with small tube boilers (originally ordered for *Normandie* class), and is now gunnery training-ship. *Paris* is attached to Torpedo School for sea training. *Océan,* of this type, has been demilitarised for training purposes. These two ships will be removed from effective list on completion of *Richelieu* and *Jean Bart.*

Machinery: Parsons turbine. 4 shafts. 24 Boilers: see Notes. H.P. 43,000 = 20 kts after refit. Coal: *normal,* 906 tons; *maximum,* 2700 tons; also 310 tons oil (two boiler rooms are fitted for oil burning).
*Endurance, 2700 at 18¾ kts.

Armour Notes —Belt, 13¼ feet wide; 7¾ feet of it above water, 5½ feet of it below. For about 325 feet it is 10¾". Upper belt, 7" thick forms redoubt for secondary battery. The 4—5·5 inch aft. are in casemates. Prot. decks: 2¾" curved from lower edge of belt to l.w.l. level. Above that a flat 1¾" deck from end to end on top of main belt. Above again is a 1⅕" splinter deck against aerial attack. Conning tower is in three stories. 10¾" communication tube. Two armoured fire control stations on top.

Gunnery Notes.—Amidship 12 inch 180°, the centre line turrets 270° each. The 5·5 inch 120°. Elevation of guns reported increased to give range of 24,000 metres. Height of guns above water: Turrets (1) 30½ feet, (2) 37¾ (amidships) 25 feet, (5) 28½ feet, (6) 21⅓ feet; upper deck battery, 5·5 inch, 21⅓ feet; main deck, 5·5 inch aft, 11⅔ feet. Ammunition carried: 100 for each 12 in., 275 for each 5·5 inch, 300 for each 3 pdr. Westinghouse refrigerators in magazines. 77°F.

Torpedo Notes.—8 searchlights (36 inch), also 2—30 inch. Carries 12 torpedoes and 30 blockade mines.

Engineering Notes.—Outer shafts: H.P. turbines; inner, L.P. Condensers (2): 32,076 sq. feet cooling surface. Turbines: 300 r.p.m. Belleville oil fuel system.

* Unofficial.

COURBET (Note AA. guns abreast of foremast.)

1939, *H. Emery, Toulon.*

BEARN (F. & Ch. de la Mediterranée, La Seyne).

Laid down January, 1914, as a battleship of the "*Normandie*" class. Launched April, 1920 construction having been suspended during the war; re-designed as an Aircraft Carrier (*Bâtimen Porte-Avions*), and conversion begun at La Seyne in August, 1923. Finally completed May, 1927.

Standard displacement : 22,146 tons; 25,000 tons *full load*.

Dimensions : 576 (*w.l.*), 560 (*p.p.*) 599 (*o.a.*) feet × 89 feet × 30½ feet (*max.* draught). (Extreme beam is 115½ feet.) Complement : (including air personnel) 875.

Guns :
8—6·1 inch.
6—3·9 inch. AA.
8— 37 mm. AA.
16 M.G.

Tubes :
4—21·7 inch

Aircraft : 36 (full complement, 40) (see Notes).

Note to Plan.—3·9 inch are now mounted behind shields, and flight deck is curved downward at bow.

Armour :
1" Main deck ....
1—2¾" Lower deck ....
1" Flight deck .. ..
3¼" Side armour to 6½ feet below w.l.

New Construction

JOFFRE, PAINLEVÉ. Building under 1938 Programme.

Joffre ordered April, 1938; *Painlevé* in 1939, both from Penhoët. Former laid down Nov. 26, 1938. Displacement : 18,000 tons. Dimensions : 774⅓ × 111½ × — feet. Guns : Probably 8—5·1 inch AA. Reported to be designed for a speed of 32 kts., and to accommodate 40 aircraft.

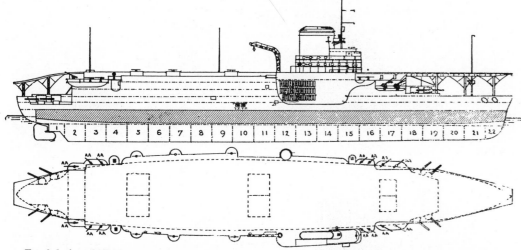

BÉARN after 1935 refit (note flight deck forward).　　　　1936, *Marius Bar, Toulon.*

Total designed H.P. 37,200 = 21·5 kts. Fitted with 2 turbines on inner shafts (for main propulsion) = 22,200 S.H.P. and 2 sets reciprocating engines on outer shafts (for cruising and manœuvring purposes only) = 15,000 I.H.P. This machinery was originally ordered for *Normandie*. 12 Du Temple-Normand small tube boilers. 4 screws. Oil fuel : 2,160 tons. Radius : 6,000 miles at 10 kts. Is capable of accommodating over 40 planes.

At a height of 51 feet from the waterline is the flight deck, 600 feet long. An external gangway at a level 3 ft. 9 in. lower allows personnel to move about clear of the flight deck. Underneath the flight deck is the central hangar, in which are housed 5 torpedo planes, 5 reconnaissance planes, and 7 fighter planes (part of the total of 36 carried). Under this hangar again, are workshops for assembling and repairs, and for accommodation of partially equipped planes. The hangar and workshops can be divided into two portions, by means of asbestos curtains.

Hangar and workshops are equipped with overhead transporter cranes for the rapid manipulation of heavy weights, and a special type of derrick (12 tons capacity, 33 feet radius) is fitted on the starboard side of ship, abaft funnel.

Planes are carried up to flight deck by means of three electric lifts, the smallest being 27 × 40 feet and the largest 50 × 50 feet. On a lift, forward, is a charthouse which can be raised above or dropped below flight deck.

Smoke is diluted with cold air to avoid eddies in surrounding atmosphere.

Other items of equipment comprise a special hot water service for filling radiators of seaplanes, and a pneumatic distributing system for conveying their fuel.

Stores carried include 3530 cubic ft. of petrol, under inert gas, and 530 cubic feet of oil.

It has been stated that owing to lack of space on flight deck, only about one fourth of the total number of planes carried can be employed simultaneously.

Trials.—On trial a speed of 21·5 kts. was reached with over 40,000 H.P.
(Refitted completely at La Seyne, 1935.)

BÉARN.　　　　1927, *Marius Bar, Toulon.*

ALGÉRIE, (Brest, May 21st, 1932).

Standard Displacement, 10,000 tons. Complement, 616. (629 as flagship.)
Length (*w.l.*) 610¼ feet ; (*o.a.*) 617 feet. Beam, 65⅔ feet. Draught, 24 feet. (*max.*)

1934 Photo, Capt. M. Adam.

Guns :

  8—8 inch (new model).
  12—3·9 inch AA.
  8—37 mm. AA.
  16—13 mm. AA.

Torpedo tubes :

  6—21·7 inch (tripled).

Machinery : 4 Rateau-Chantiers de Bretagne geared Turbines.

S.H.P. : 84,000 = 31 kts. Radius : 5,000 miles at 15 kts.

Boilers : 8 Indret. Fuel : 1,900 tons

Trials : Average of 86,000 = over 32 kts. Max. speed, over 33 kts.

Note to Plan.—There are actually 3 S.L. mounted on tower amidships.

Aircraft : 3.

Catapults : 2, of 3-ton type.

Armour :
  4¹⁄₃″ Vert. Side.
  3″ Deck.
  Internal bulges, with hull thickness of 1½″.
  (Total weight of Armour 2,000 tons.)

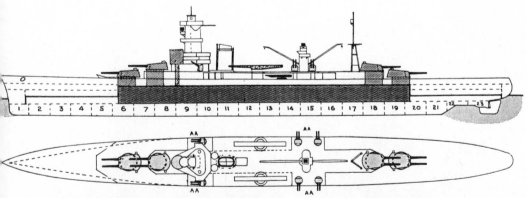

General Notes.—Laid down on March 13th, 1931 at Brest.   The design constitutes a distinct departure from the "Tin-clad" vogue, and is more along the lines of a modern edition of the armoured cruiser of thirty years ago, being a reply to the Italian *Zara* type. A novel distribution of internal armour has been introduced giving special anti-aerial and torpedo protection, while the big guns and hoists are adequately armoured instead of being mounted in gunhouses made up of thin plating with unarmoured hoists.   Speed has not been reduced as a result of these modifications and equals that of the *Foch* group but with less designed h.p. The 8 inch gun introduced in this ship, firing improved shells, has a greater range than the previous model. She was completed in 1934.

Aircraft Notes.—Unlike those of earlier cruisers, *Algérie's* catapults are of explosive type. Previously compressed air had been the motive power.

1938, D. W. Hargreaves, Esq.

SUFFREN (Note mainmast, bridge, and position of catapults).

1939, H. Emery, Toulon.

Note to Plan.—Dupleix is only ship of the 4 to have 3·5 in. guns in pairs.

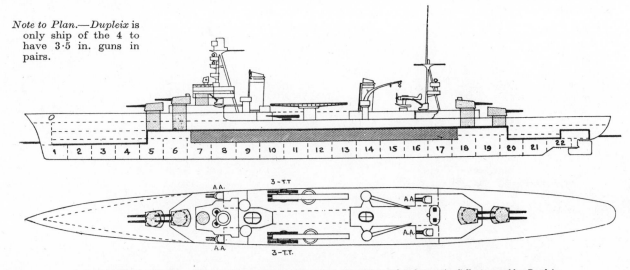

Appearance Notes.—Foch has different foremast from other ships. *Dupleix*, no fore-topmast. *Colbert* resembles *Dupleix*, but has fore-topmast. *Suffren* has pole mainmast and only one crane (with straight jib) and derrick post, instead of gooseneck cranes as in other ships of class. Bridgework also differs.

SUFFREN CLASS—4 SHIPS.

SUFFREN (May 3rd, 1927). COLBERT (April 20th, 1928).
FOCH (April 24th, 1929). DUPLEIX (October 9th, 1930).

Standard Displacement, 9,938 tons. Complement, 605.

Length (*p.p.*), 607 feet, (*o.a.*), 637 feet, (*Suffren*, 643 ; *Dupleix*, 636½ feet), Beam, 63½ feet, (*Suffren*, 65⅔ feet). Draught, 24½ feet (*max.*).

Aircraft : 3. (only 2 in *Suffren*)
Catapults : 2 of 3-ton type.

Guns :

8—8 inch
8—3·5 inch AA.
(*Suffren*, 8—3 inch AA.)
6—37 m/m. (*Suffren*, 8)
16 M.G.
Torpedo Tubes :
6—21·7 inch (tripled).

Armour :

Has a patch of thin armour over engine and boiler spaces, with 17 W.T. bulkheads carried right up to upper deck. Fitted with internal bulges.

Machinery : 3 Rateau-Chantiers de Bretagne geared turbines. Boilers : 9 Guyot (8 main and 1 auxiliary). Designed : S.H.P. 90,000=31·3 to 32·5 kts. 3 screws. Fuel : oil, 1800 tons. Auxiliary equipment driven through 3 Diesels (Renault type) with dynamos. Radius : 5000 miles at 15 kts.

Name	Builder	Machinery	Laid down	Completed	Trials
Suffren	Brest	A. & C. de	May, 1926	1930	98,300=33·7
Colbert	,,	Bretagne	June, 1927	1931	101,800=33·9
Foch	,,	in all	June, 1928	1931	119,000=34·1
Dupleix	,,		Oct., 1929	1932	

Are able to steam at 29 knots with half-power.

Cost : *Suffren*, 144 million. *Colbert*, 147 million francs. *Foch*, 156 million. *Dupleix*, 167 million francs.
*General Notes.—*Are modified editions of *Tourville* class in which about two knots have been sacrificed in order to gain better protection. At full speed *Foch* proved very successful, compared with *Lamotte-Picquet*, due to modified bow and stern lines.

*Gunnery Notes.—*Light AA. armaments vary in these ships, as will be gathered from figures given above.

DUPLEIX. *1932 Photo, Capt. M. Adam.*

DUPLEIX (No fore-topmast and tall mainmast).

1934 *Photo, Marius Bar.*

FOCH (Foremast differs from other ships).

1935, *Ganda.*

(*For particulars of these ships, see preceding page*)

COLBERT (Note position of catapult, bridgework, cranes, and mainmast).

1939, *H. Emery, Toulon.*

(TOURVILLE CLASS—2 SHIPS.)

DUQUESNE (Dec. 17th, 1925), **TOURVILLE** (Aug. 24th, 1926). Standard displacement, 10,000 tons (11,900 tons deep load). Complement, 605.

Length (*p.p.*), 607 feet; (*o.a.*), 626⅔ feet; Beam, 62⅓ feet. Draught, 23 feet (*max*).

TOURVILLE.

1935, *Ganda*.

Guns :
8—8 inch
8—3 inch AA.
8—37 m/m AA.
12—13 m/m AA.
Torpedo tubes (21·7 inch) :
6 (in triple mountings *above water*.)

Aircraft :
2, with catapult of 3-ton type.

Armour :
Practically nil except for thin gun-shields and a splinter-proof C.T.

Note to Plan.—Now rigged as in photo. There are no prominent ventilators amidships. T.T. are actually in line with derrick.

Machinery : 4 Rateau-Chantiers de Bretagne geared turbines. Boilers : 9 Guyot (8 main and 1 auxiliary). Designed S.H.P. : 120,000 = 33 kts. 4 screws. Oil : 1,800 tons. Radius : 5,000 miles at 15 kts. ; 700 at full speed.

Name	Builder	Machinery	Laid down	Completed	Trials
Tourville	Lorient	A. & C. de	14 April, 1925	1928	130,000 = 36·15
Duquesne	Brest	Bretagne	30 Oct., 1924	1928	135,000 = 35·3

General Note.—Above ships are practically enlarged copies of *Duguay-Trouin* design, with an improved form of hull and heavier armament.

Engineering Notes.—Boiler and engine rooms are arranged alternately, and not in two separate groups, as suggested in plans appearing elsewhere. *Tourville's* trial speed of over 36 kts. was obtained while running on normal displacement. Auxiliaries driven through 3 Diesels (Renault Type) with dynamo.

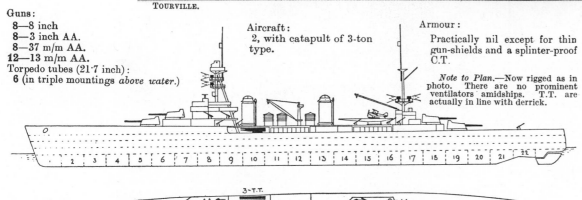

187

(DE GRASSE CLASS—3 Ships)

Reported to be of same general design as 7,600 ton cruisers of *La Galissonnière* class, but with increased speed.

JEAN DE VIENNE.   1937.

DE GRASSE, CHATEAURENAULT, GUICHEN.

Displacement : 8,000 tons.　　　　Complement : 580

Length :　　　Beam :　　　Draught :

Guns :　　　Aircraft : 4.　　　Armour :

9—6 inch.　　　　　　　Probably similar to *La Galissonnière*.

8—3·5 inch AA

8—13 mm. AA.

Tubes :

LA GALISSONNIÈRE.   1937

Machinery : Rateau-Chantiers de Bretagne geared turbines. Speed reported as 34 kts.

Estimates	Name	Builder	Machinery		Laid down	Completed
1937	De Grasse	Lorient	{	A. & C. de Bretagne	Nov. 1938	To be 1941
1938	Chateaurenault	F. & C. Med.		Builders	1939	
1938	Guichen	F. & C. Gironde			1939	

(*For particulars of above ships, see following page.*)

La GALISSONNIERE (Nov. 17, 1933). **JEAN de VIENNE** (July 31, 1935).

GLOIRE (Sept. 28, 1935). **MARSEILLAISE** (July 17, 1935). **MONTCALM** (Oct. 26, 1935). **GEORGES LEYGUES** (*ex-Chateaurenault*) (March 24th, 1936).

Displacement : 7,600 tons (9,120 tons *full load*).   Complement : 540.

Length : (*pp.*) 548 feet, (*o.a.*) 580¾ feet. } Beam : 57⅓ feet.
Draught : 17⅓ feet (*max.*).

Guns :	Aircraft :	Armour (unofficial) :
9—6 inch	4, with 1 Catapult.	4¾″—3″ Vert. Side.
8—3·5 inch AA.		2⅗″ Deck
8—13 mm. AA.		5½″ Turret faces.
Tubes :		2″ Turret sides.
4—21·7 inch		3¾″ C.T.

Note to Plan :—Catapult now mounted on after turret.

GEORGES LEYGUES. (*Marseillaise* has cranes alongside after funnel.)

1938, *M. Henri Le Masson.*

(Foremasthead details vary in these ships.)

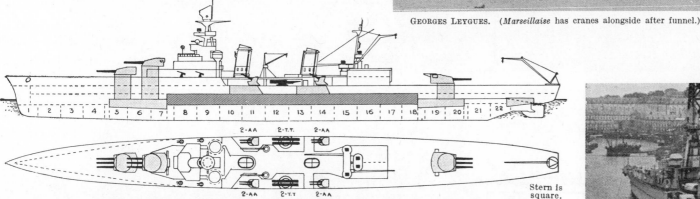

Stern is square.

Machinery : 2 Rateau-Chantiers de Bretagne (first 3 ships) or Parsons geared turbines. S.H.P. : 84,000 = 31 kts. Boilers : 4 Indret small tube. Fuel : 1,500 tons oil. Radius : 6,000 miles at 13 kts.

Programme	Name	Builder	Machinery	Laid down	Completed
1931	{ La Galissonnière	Brest	Ch. de	27.10.31	31.12.35
	Jean de Vienne	Lorient	Bretagne	12.31	15.4.37
1932	{ Gloire	F. C. Gironde			4.12.37
	Marseillaise	A. C. Loire	Builders		25.10.37
	Montcalm	F. C. Med.	in	1933	4.12.37
	{ G. Leygues	C. A. St. Nazaire	each		4.12.37
		(Penhoët)	case		

General Notes.—The delay in the construction of these ships was in part due to modifications having been introduced into the design, which is based on that of the *Emile Bertin* with additional protection which is said to be capable of resisting 6-inch shell. A feature of the design is the long quarter-deck. The bow flare is angled and not curved. The four later ships differ from *La Galissonnière* and *Jean de Vienne* in minor details. Altogether the design of these cruisers is a remarkably successful one, embodying the maximum advantage to be obtained from their relatively low displacement. Trials : *La Galissonnière* (8 hours) 96,000 = 35·42 ; *Jean de Vienne* has also exceeded 35 kts. ; *Montcalm*, 35·7 ; *Marseillaise*, 36·1. Sea speed about 30 kts. Fuel consumption reported to be exceptionally low in this class.

LA GALISSONNIÈRE, showing opening for Hein mat in counter.

1936 *Courtesy M. Le Mason.*

EMILE BERTIN, (Penhoët, St. Nazaire.) (May 9, 1933).

Displacement: 5,886 tons.   Complement: 567.   Length: (*p.p.*) 548 feet, (*o.a.*) 580¾ feet.   Beam: 51¾ feet.   Draught: 17¾ feet (*max.*).

1935, *courtesy Mons. H. le Masson.*

(Now has small oval hangar immediately forward of second funnel.)

Guns :
 9—6 inch.
 4—3·5 inch. AA.
 8—37 m/m. AA.
 8—13 m/m. AA.
Tubes :
 6—21·7 inch (tripled).
Mines : 200 (unofficial).

Aircraft :
 2, with catapult of 1½ ton type.

Armour : 1″–2″ Deck.

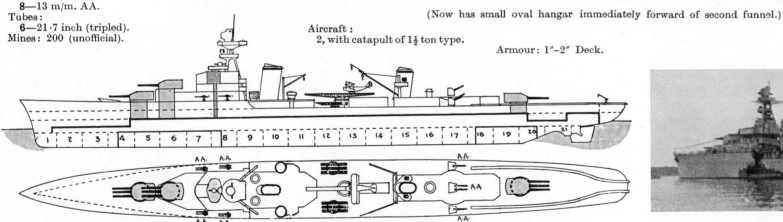

1934 *Photo, Capt. M. Adam.*

Machinery : Parsons geared Turbines. 4 shafts. S.H.P. : 102,000 = 34 kts. Boilers : 6 Penhoët.
Oil Fuel : 1,400 tons.

Notes.—Authorised under the 1930 Programme. Laid down 1931. Completed in 1934. The triple mounting makes its first appearance in the French Navy in this ship. Originally intended to be merely an improved *Pluton*, a new design was ultimately evolved, in which cruiser characteristics were in no way subordinated to minelaying considerations. On trials, the ship exceeded expectations, maintaining 37 kts. for an hour in a 13 ft. swell. Maximum power and speed on trials, 123,000 = 39·8 kts. Hull strengthened beneath turrets to permit salvo firing, 1935.

JEANNE D'ARC (Penhoët, St. Nazaire.) (Feb. 14th, 1930.)

Standard Displacement : 6,496 tons.   Complement : 505.
Length (*p.p.*), 525 feet ; (*o.a.*), 557¾ feet. Beam, 57½ feet. Draught, 17¾ feet (*mean*) ; 20⅔ feet (*max.*).

1934 *Photo.*

Guns :
8—6·1 inch.
4—3 inch AA.
4—37 m/m. (paired).
Tubes :
2—21·7 inch.

Aircraft :
2 (handled by crane)

Armour : Nil.
Protective deck and light plating to gunhouses and conning tower.

1937, *Wright & Logan.*

Machinery : Parsons geared turbines. 2 shafts. Designed H.P. : 32,500 = 25 kts. Boilers : 4 Penhoët. Oil : 1,400 tons. Radius : 5,000 miles at cruising speed (14—15 kts.).

General Notes.—Original design provided for 2 catapults, but as completed she is without any. Can accommodate 156 midshipmen and cadets and 20 instructional officers, in addition to ordinary complement. Authorised under 1927 Programme and laid down at Penhoët Yard, St. Nazaire in 1928. Completed in 1931.

Trials :—3 hours' full power : 39,200 H.P. = 27·03 kts. (*mean*), 27·84 kts. (*max.*).

191

LA TOUR D'AUVERGNE (ex-*Pluton*) (April 10th, 1929).
Displacement, 4,773 tons. Complement, 424.   Length, (*p.p.*) 472½ feet, (*o.a.*) 500⅓ feet.   Beam, 51 feet.
Draught, 17 feet (*mean*), 20 feet (*max.*).

1939, H. Emery, Toulon.

1939, H. Emery, Toulon.

Guns :
 4—5·5 inch.
 4—3 inch AA.
 2—37 mm. AA.
 12—13 mm. AA.
Mines: 290.

Note to Plan.
Now rigged as photos.

Armour : Nil.

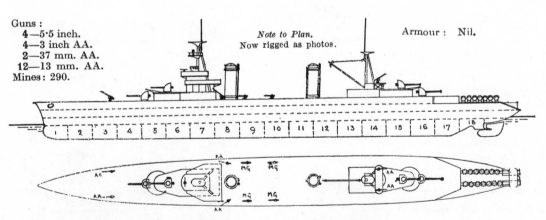

Machinery : 2 Breguet geared turbines. 2 shafts. S.H.P. : 57,000 = 30 kts. Trials : H.P. :
56,000 = 30·6 kts. Max. speed : 31·6 kts. Oil : 1,200 tons. Boilers : 4 small tube.

Note.—Authorised under 1925 Programme, laid down at Lorient Dockyard in April, 1928, and completed April, 1931.
In 1939 she was re-named and re-fitted for service as an additional seagoing training ship for midshipmen and cadets.

(DUGUAY-TROUIN CLASS—3 SHIPS.)

DUGUAY-TROUIN (14th Aug., 1923), **LAMOTTE-PICQUET** (21st March, 1924),
PRIMAUGUET (21st May, 1924).

Standard displacement, 7,249 tons. Normal displacement, 7,880 tons. (*Full load,* 9,350.) Complement, 577.
Length (*p.p.*) 575 feet, (*o.a.*) 594¾ feet. Beam, 57½ feet. Draught, 17¼ feet *mean* ; 20⅔ feet *maximum* at full load.

Guns:
8—6·1 inch, 50 cal.
4—3 inch AA.
2—3 pdr. (saluting).
1—1 pdr. (landing).
4 Machine.
Torpedo tubes (21·7 inch) :
12 (in triple mountings)
above water.

Note to Plan.—Catapult now mounted on quarterdeck. Gunhouses are flat-sided, not circular as shown. Fore-topmast struck.

Aircraft:
1, with catapult of 1½ ton type.

Armour :
Practically nil, except for thin gunshields, splinter-proof C.T., and double armoured deck.

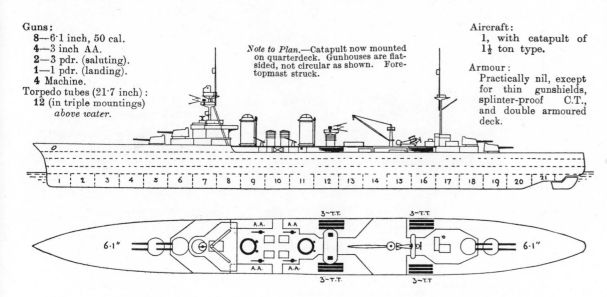

DUGUAY-TROUIN.

1939, *H. Emery, Toulon.*

Machinery : 4 Parsons geared turbines. Boilers : 8 Guyot. Designed S.H.P. 102,000 = 33 kts. 4 screws. Oil : 500 tons *normal,* 1500 tons *maximum.* Radius : 880 miles at 33 kts. ; 1290 at 30; 3000 at 20; 4500 at 15. Depth charges carried.

Gunnery Notes.—6·1 inch guns are 1920 model with ballistic powers superior to old marks of 7·6 inch. Range reported to be 28,000 yards, elevation 35°. Reason for adoption of this calibre is said to have been its uniformity with Army type 6·1 inch, simplifying munition supply, more particularly of gas and incendiary shells. Gunhouses are reported to be gas-tight, and to have a special method of ventilation by forced draught.

Engineering Notes.—Trial results tabulated are averages of 6 hours with full complement of fuel and stores. *Maximum* speed for 1 hour, 34·5 kts. All three ships maintained 30 kts. for 24 hours' continuous steaming at half power with full load, and have proved very economical. Heating surface, 13,209 sq. feet.

Torpedo Notes.—24 torpedoes carried (12 in tubes, 12 in magazine). In addition, 4—17·7 inch torpedoes are carried for picket boats.

Name.	Builder.	Machinery.	Laid down.	Completed.	Trials. (6 hours)	
Duguay-Trouin	Brest	F. & C. de la Méd.	4 Aug., '22	10 Sep. '26	116,235 = 33·6	
Primauguet	Brest	A & C. de la Loire	10 Aug.,'23	1 Oct. '26	116,849 = 33·06	
Lamotte-Picquet	Lorient	C. & A. de St. Nazaire (Penhoët).	17 Jan., '23	1 Sep. '26	115,100 = 33·04	

General Notes.—These ships have shown excellent sea-keeping qualities. *Primauguet* given a big refit at Lorient in 1937.

DUGUAY-TROUIN

1939, *H. Emery, Toulon.*

FRANCE—Destroyers

IDENTIFICATION MARKS, FRENCH FLOTILLAS

Torpilleurs : Coloured bands around fore funnel, thus :

Colour	1 Band	2 Bands	3 Bands
White	1st Divn.	7th Divn.	13th Divn.
Black	2nd ,,	8th ,,	
Yellow	3rd ,,	9th ,,	
Green	4th ,,	10th ,,	
Red	5th ,,	11th ,,	
Blue	6th ,,	12th ,,	

All carry white letter T on either bow, followed by two figures (or three in case of 10/13th Divisions). The first figure (or two figures) refers to number of Division, the last to vessel's rank in the Division.

Contre-Torpilleurs : Same arrangement, but letter X instead of T, and coloured bands around after funnel. In all cases the name, inserted in copper letters in a copper frame at the stern, is on a background painted in a colour corresponding with the funnel band.

12 Le Hardi class.

(Classed as *Torpilleurs*)

> *Photo wanted.*

LE HARDI.

2 *A. et C. de la Loire :* **Le Hardi, Mameluck.**
4 *F. et C. de la Gironde :* **Epée, Lansquenet, Aventurier, Opiniatre.**
6 *F. et C. de la Mediterranée* (*La Seyne*) : **Casque, Fleuret, Le Corsaire, Le Flibustier, Intrepide,**
  Téméraire.

Standard displacement : 1,772 tons. Complement : 175
Dimensions : $333\frac{1}{4} \times 32\frac{1}{2} \times 11$ feet (*mean*).
Guns : **6—5·1 inch, 4—37 mm. AA., 4—13 mm. AA.** Tubes : **7—21·7 inch.**
Machinery : Parsons geared turbines in all except *Fleuret* and 4 Gironde-built ships, which have Rateau-Chantiers de
  Bretagne. S.H.P. : 58,000 = 37 kts. Radius : 6,000 miles at 15 kts.

Note.—Cost of earlier ships averages Fcs. 84,000,000 each.

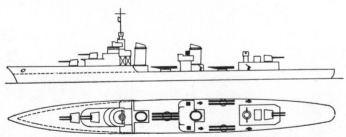

Programme	Name	Laid down	Launch	Completed	Programme	Name	Laid down	Launch	Completed
1932	Le Hardi	1936	4/5/38	1939	1937	Le Corsaire		3/38	
1935	Epée	1936	26/10/38			Le Flibustier		3/38	
	Fleuret	1936	27/7/38		1938	Aventurier		1939	
1936	Casque	1937	24/11/38			Opiniatre		1939	
	Lansquenet	1937	20/5/39			Intrepide		1939	
	Mameluck	1937	18/2/39			Téméraire		1399	

6 Mogador class.

(Classed as *Contre-Torpilleurs*)

MOGADOR.   1939, *Wright & Logan.*

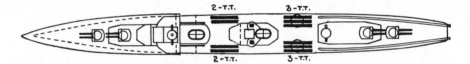

2 *Lorient :* **Mogador, Desaix.**
3 *Ch. de Bretagne :* **Volta, Hoche, Marceau.**
1 *At. et Ch. de France :* **Kléber**
Displacement : 2,884 tons. (About 3,500 tons full load.) Complement : 238.
Dimensions : $451 \times 41 \times 14\frac{3}{4}$ feet (*mean*).
Guns : **8—5·5 inch, 4—37 mm. AA., 4—13 mm. AA., 4 D.C.T.**
Tubes : **10—21·7 inch** (2 triple mounts and 2 pairs).
Machinery : Rateau-Chantiers de Bretagne geared turbines by Indret in *Mogador* and by A. & C. de Bretagne in *Volta*
  and *Marceau* ; Parsons in others. S.H.P. : 90,000 = 38 kts. Boilers : 6 Indret small tube. Oil fuel : 630 tons.

Gunnery Notes.—5·5 inch are of a new model, semi-automatic, and have a range of 25,000 yards. A rate of fire of 16
  rounds a minute can be maintained.

Programme	Name	Laid down	Launch	Completed
1932	Mogador	Dec. 1934	9/6/37	1/6/38
1934	Volta	Jan. 1935	26/11/36	15/9/38
1938	Desaix			
	Hoche		1939	
	Marceau			
	Kléber			

6 Fantasque Class. *1930 Programme.*

LE FANTASQUE.

1936, *favour Mons. H. Le Masson.*

Le Fantasque }	(Both March 15, 1934).	**Le Terrible**	(Nov. 29, 1933).
L'Audacieux }		**Le Triomphant**	(April 16, 1934).
Le Malin	(Aug. 17, 1933).	**L'Indomptable**	(Dec. 7, 1933).

Displacement: 2,569 tons (3,230 tons *full load*). Complement: 220.

Dimensions: 411½ (*p.p.*), 434⅚ (*o.a.*) × 39⅓ × 14 feet (*mean*).

Guns: 5—5·5 inch, 4—37 mm., 4—13 mm. AA., 4 D.C. throwers. Tubes: 9—21·7 inch (tripled).

Machinery: 2 sets geared turbines. Parsons in *Le Malin*, *Le Triomphant* and *L'Indomptable*, Rateau-Chantiers de Bretagne in others. S.H.P.: 74,000 = 37 kts. Boilers: 4 small tube. Oil fuel: 650 tons.

Builders: *Le Fantasque*, *L'Audacieux*, Lorient; *Le Malin*, *L'Indomptable*, F. Ch. de la Mediterranée, La Seyne; *Le Terrible*, Ch. Nav. Français, Blainville; *Le Triomphant*, Ch. de France, Dunkerque.

Notes.—On trials, *Le Terrible* is reported to have reached record speed of 45·25 kts. with 94,200 H.P. All the ships of this class exceeded 43 kts. and are excellent sea boats, able to maintain 37 kts. continuously.

Appearance Notes.—No mainmast in these ships, w.t. aerials being slung from brackets on second funnel. Very conspicuous control platform abaft the second funnel.

LE TERRIBLE.

1936, *courtesy Builders.*

MAILLÉ BRÉZÉ (all *Cassard* class now have tripod foremast).

1933 *Photo,* Capt. M. Adam.

MILAN, EPERVIER and 6 of CASSARD group (but twin after tubes in latter). Others of AIGLE class have tubes arranged as in GUÉPARD, in following columns.

12 AIGLE Class.

1927 Programme.

		Begun	*Launch*	*Completed*	*Trials*
Aigle	Ch. France	'29	19/2/31	1932	=38·67
Albatros	Ch. Loire	'29	28/6/30	1931	87,000 =41·9
Epervier	Lorient	6/30	14/8/31	1933	=42·6
Gerfaut	Ch. Bretagne	'29	14/6/30	1932	=42·78
Milan	Lorient	6/30	13/10/31	1933	83,000 =43·4
Vautour	F. C. Med. Havre	'29	26/8/30	1932	80,000 =40·2

Dimensions: 423¼ × 40 × 16 feet.

1928—29 Programme.

Cassard	Ch. Bretagne	11/30	8/11/31	1932	80,600 =43·4
Le Chevalier Paul	La Seyne	2/31	21/3/32	1934	=40·4
Maillé Brézé	Penhoët	10/30	9/11/31	1932	=42·0
Kersaint	Ch. Loire	9/30	14/11/31	1933	=39·1
Tartu	Ch. Loire	'30	7/12/31	1932	=41·02
Vauquelin	Ch. France	3/30	29/9/32	1933	=39·4

Dimensions: 424¼ × 39 × 15¾ feet.

All 12: Displacement: 2,441 tons. (3,090 tons full load.)

Complement: 220.

ARMAMENT: Guns: 5—5·5 inch, 4—37 m/m., 4—D.C. Throwers. Tubes: 6—21·7 inch (7 in *Epervier*, *Milan*).

Machinery: 2 sets geared turbines. Parsons in *Kersaint*, *Tartu*, *M. Brézé* *Milan*, *Albatros*, *Vautour* and *Ch. Paul*. Zoelly-Fives-Lille in *Aigle* and *Vauquelin*. Rateau-Ch. de Bretagne in *Epervier*, *Gerfaut* and *Cassard*. Boilers: 4 small tube, Yarrow or Penhoët.

S.H.P. 64,000 = 36 kts (68,000 = 37 kts. in *Milan* and *Epervier*).

Oil: 650 tons. Radius: 2,500—3,000 miles at 18 kts.

BISON.

Added 1937, *Grand Studio.*

(This ship was badly damaged by collision with *G. Leygues* in Feb., 1939.)

VAUBAN

1938, *Grand Studio.*

6 GUÉPARD Class.
1925 Programme.

	Builders.	Begun.	Launched.	Compl.	Max. Speed
Bison	Lorient	Feb. '27	29/10/28	1930	=40·6
Guépard			19/4/28	1929 69,100	=38·4
Lion	Ch. France	Apl.'27	5/8/29	1931	=40·4

Dimensions: 427 × 38¾ × 15½ feet.

1926 Programme.

Vauban	Ch. France	'27	1/2/29	1931	=40·2
Valmy	Penhoët	'27	19/5/29	1930 69,300	=39·8
Verdun	Ch. Loire	'27	4/7/28	1930 72,400	=40·1

Dimensions : 427 × 39 × 16½ feet.
All 6: Displacement: 2,436 tons. About 3,080 tons full load.
Complement: 209.
Guns : 5—5·5 inch. 4—37 m/m. 4—D.C. Throwers. Tubes : 6—21·7 inch.
S.H.P. 64 000 = 36 kts. Oil : 500-650 tons. Radius : 3,000 miles at 18 kts.
Turbines: Parsons in *Valmy, Verdun, Guépard* and *Bison.* Zoelly-Fives-Lille in *Vauban* and *Lion.*

Average speed at normal displacement and designed H.P.

Guépard 35·9 *Valmy* 37 *Verdun* 36·7 *Bison* 36·5

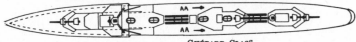

GUÉPARD CLASS.
Also AIGLE, ALBATROS, GERFAUT, VAUTOUR.

6 Chacal Class.

LEOPARD

1936, *Wright & Logan.*

1922 Programme

		Begun.	Launched.	Compl.	Trials.
Jaguar	Lorient		6/11/23	1926 52,000	=34·7
Panthère	Dockyard		28/10/24	1926	=35·5
Léopard ..	Ch. de Loire		29/9/24	1927	
Lynx ..	St. Nazaire	1922	25/2/25	1927	=35·5
Chacal ..	Penhoët		27/9/24	1926 52,000	=36·1
Tigre ..	Ch. de Bretagne Nantes.		2/8/24	1926 58,000	=36·7

Displacement : 2,126 tons ; 2,700 tons full load. Complement : 204.

Dimensions : 392¾ (*p.p.*), 416 (*o.a.*) × 37½ × 17½ feet (*max.*)

Guns : 5—5·1 inch. Oil : 250/550 tons.
8—13 mm. AA. Radius : 3,500 miles at 15 kts.
4—D.C. Throwers. 2,500 ,, ,, 18 ,,
Tubes : 6—21·7 inch. 900 ,, ,, full speed.

S.H.P. 55,000 = 35·5 kts. Breguet-Loire turbines (*Léopard* and *Lynx*).
Rateau-Ch. de Bretagne in other four. 5 small tube Du Temple boilers.

Average speed at normal displacement and H.P.

Jaguar 34·2   *Chacal* 34·7
Panthère 35·3   *Tigre* 35·9
Léopard 34·9   *Lynx* 34·5

Note to Plan:—Additional AA. gun positions not indicated.

Note.—Classified on a tonnage basis these ships, and those of *Guépard, Aigle, Fantasque* and *Mogador* classes, would rank as cruisers by Washington Treaty rules, being above 2,000 tons standard displacement. They are employed in divisions and not as flotilla leaders.

14 Adroit Class.

Le Mars.   1929 *Photo, M. Bar, Toulon.*

L'Adroit (April 1st, 1927).

Le Fortuné (Nov. 15, 1926), *Le Mars* (Aug. 28, 1926).

La Palme (June 30th, 1926), *La Railleuse* (Sept. 9th, 1926).

L'Alcyon (June 26th, 1926).   (Launched at Harfleur and towed to Bordeaux for completion.)

Basque (May 25th, 1929), *Bordelais* (May 23rd, 1928), *Boulonnais* (June 1st, 1927), *Brestois* (May 18th, 1927).

Forbin (July 17th, 1928), *Foudroyant* (April 24th, 1929), *Fougueux* (Aug. 4th, 1928), *Frondeur* (June 20th, 1929).

Displacement : 1,378 tons *standard* (*about* 1,750 *full load*). Dimensions : 330·9 × 32¼ × 9½ feet. Complement : 142. Guns : 4—5·1 inch, 2—37 m/m. AA. Torpedo tubes : 6—21·7 inch, in triple deck mountings. 16 Depth Charges carried. Machinery : 2 sets geared turbines of Zoelly type in *Adroit* and *Alcyon, Bordelais, Frondeur.* Rateau-Ch. de Bretagne in *Basque, Fougueux, Orage, Ouragan.* Parsons in remainder. H.P. : 32,000—35,000 = 32-33·5 kts. Other particulars similar to those of *Simoun* class, but slightly increased boiler power to give improved speed. On trials *Brestois* reached 34·5 kts., *Fougueux* 36·4 (both *max.*). *Basque,* 38,000 = 35 *max.*

Note.—Ordered under Programmes of 1924 (first six), 1925 (next four), and 1926 (last four). As compared with *Simoun* type, these vessels possess improved stability, higher rate of salvo firing, better aerial defence and lower fuel consumption. 5·1 inch guns said to possess a range of 19,000 yards, and can fire eight rounds a minute.

Name	Builders	Engines	Begun	Completed
L'Adroit	Ch. de France, Dunkerque	Fives, Lille	} 1925	1928
L'Alcyon	Ch. de la Gironde	Ch. de la Gironde		1927
Le Fortuné	Ch. Navals Français, Blainville	A. & Ch. de la Loire		Sept., 1927
Le Mars	Ch. Navals Français, Blainville	A. & Ch. de la Loire		April, 1927
La Palme	Ch. Dubigeon, Nantes	A. & Ch. de la Loire		1927
La Railleuse	Ch. Dubigeon, Nantes	A. & Ch. de la Loire		1927
Brestois	Ch. Navals Français, Blainville	A. & Ch. de la Loire	} Sept., 1926	
Boulonnais	Ch. Navals Français, Blainville	A. & Ch. de la Loire		1928-29
Basque	Ch. de la Seine Maritime	A. & Ch. de Bretagne		
Bordelais	Ch. de la Gironde, Bordeaux	Ch. de la Gironde		
Forbin	F. & Ch. de la Med., Havre	F. & Ch. de la Med.	} 1927	
Foudroyant	Dyle & Bacalan, Bordeaux			1929
Fougueux	A. & Ch. de Bretagne, Nantes	A. & Ch. de Bretagne		
Frondeur	Ch. Navals Français, Blainville	A. & Ch. de la Loire		

12 Simoun Class.

Simoun.   1930 *Photo, M. H. le Masson.*

1 *Chantiers de France (Dunkerque)*: **Bourrasque** (Aug. 5th, 1925).
2 *F. & Ch. de la Méditerranée (Havre)*: **Cyclone** (Jan. 24th, 1925), **Mistral** (June 6th, 1925).
2 *Ch. Navals Français (Blainville)*: **Orage** (Aug. 30th, 1924), **Ouragan** (Dec. 6th, 1924).
2 *A. & Ch. de St. Nazaire (Penhoët)*: **Simoun** (June 3rd, 1924), **Siroco** (October 3rd, 1925).
1 *Ch. Dubigeon*: **Tempête** (Feb. 21st, 1925).
3 *Ch. de la Gironde*: **Tramontane** (Nov. 29th, 1924), **Typhon** (May 22nd, 1924), **Trombe** (Dec. 29th, 1925).
1 *Dyle & Bacalan*: **Tornade** (March 12th, 1925).

Displacement : 1,319 tons *standard*, 1,727 tons *full load*. Dimensions : 326 (*pp.*), 347 (*o.a.*) × 33 × 13¾ feet. Complement : 138. Guns : 4—5·1 inch, 2—37 m/m. AA. Torpedo tubes : 6—21·7 inch, in triple deck mountings. Geared turbines of Rateau type in *Orage* and *Ouragan* ; Zoelly in *Typhon, Tramontane* and *Trombe* ; Parsons in other seven boats. H.P. : 33,000 = 33 kts. (over 34 reached on trials). Boilers : 3 small tube. 2 screws. Oil : 165 tons *normal,* 300 tons *max.* Radius : 3,000 miles at 15 kts.

Notes.—Authorised by Law of 18th August, 1922. 8 hours' trials : *Orage,* 34,000 = 33·8 kts. ; *Simoun,* 29,000 = 33·2 kts. (1 hour = 34·3) ; *Ouragan,* 35,000 = 34·4 ; *Bourrasque,* = 34·12 (36·4 for one hour) ; *Mistral* (12 hours), 34 kts. All completed 1926-27. It has been stated that these vessels lose their speed rapidly in a seaway, and that few, if any, of them can now make designed speed. All had funnels cut down by about 3 feet to improve stability, soon after completion.

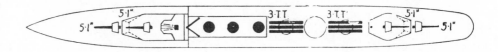

(Classed as *Torpilleurs Légers*)

14 Agile Class

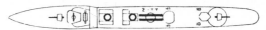

12 Pomone Class.

Building

LA FLORE.   1937, *Capt. M. Adam.*

5 *At. et Ch. de Bretagne :* **L'Agile, Le Fier, L'Alsacien, Le Breton, Le Savoyard,**
7 *At. et Ch. de la Loire :* **L'Entreprenant, Le Farouche, Le Corse, Le Tunisien, Le Normand, Le Parisien, Le Provencal.**
2 *F. et Ch. de la Mediterranéz :* **Le Nicois, Le Saintongeais.**
Displacement : 994 tons.
Dimensions : 295¼ × 30½ × 8½ feet.
Guns : 4—3·9 inch, 4—40 mm. AA. Tubes : 4—21·7 inch (paired).
Machinery : Geared turbines, Rateau-Chantiers de Bretagne in first five ; Parsons in others. S.H.P. : 28,000 = 34 kts.

Programme	Name	Laid down	Launch	Completed
1937	L'Agile Le Fier L'Entreprenant Le Farouche		1938	
1938	L'Alsacien Le Breton Le Savoyard Le Corse Le Tunisien Le Normand Le Parisien Le Provencal Le Nicois Le Saintongeais		1939	

12 boats : **La Melpomène** (Ch. de Bretagne, Nantes, 24 Jan. 1935)
La Pomone (Ch. de Loire, Nantes, 25 Jan., 1935)
La Flore (Ch. de Bretagne, Nantes, 4 May, 1935)
L'Iphigenie (Ch. de Loire, Nantes, 18 April, 1935)
La Poursuivante (At. et Ch. de France, Dunkerque, 4 Aug., 1936)
L'Incomprise (Ch. Worms, Rouen, April 14, 1937)
La Bayonnaise (Ch. Sud Ouest, Bordeaux, Jan. 28, 1936)
La Cordélière (Sept. 9, 1936) } (Augustin Normand)
Branlebas (April 12, 1937)
Bombarde (At. et Ch. de la Loire, St. Nazaire, March 23, 1936)
Baliste (At. et Ch. de France, Dunkerque, March 17th, 1937)
Bouclier (Ch. Worms, Rouen, Aug. 9. 1937)

Displacement: 610 tons (700 tons *full load*). Complement, 92.

Dimensions: 245½ (*p.p.*), 264¾ (*o.a.*) × 26 × 9½ feet (*mean* draught).

Guns : 2—3·9 inch, 2—37 m/m., 2 Twin M.G.

Tubes : 2—21·7 inch.

Machinery : Parsons geared turbines in all except *La Cordelière, L'Incomprise, Bouclier, Branlebas* which have Rateau—Bretagne Type.

H.P. 22,000 = 34·5 kts. (exceeded on trials.)

Oil fuel : 90 tons.

Radius : 1,800 at 18 kts. ; 700 at 35 kts.

Provided for under 1931 and 1932 Programmes.

First 4 completed during 1936, second 4 in 1937, third 4 in 1938.

LA POMONE.   1937, *courtesy M. Le Masson.*

Motor Torpedo Boats.
(*Vedettes Torpilleurs à Moteurs*)

VTB 8.   1938, *Official*

VTB 15–40. Authorised or building under 1938 Programme. May not all be of same type. Four boats have been ordered from Jouett, Sartrouville, to have Lorraine engines, and eight more ordered elsewhere are to be similarly engined. It is possible that experimental orders may also be placed with English builders.

VTB 11, 12, 13, 14, building under 1937 and 1938 Programmes. Displacement: 28 tons. 2—18 inch Torpedo Tubes. H.P.: 2,000 = 45 kts. No other particulars advised, except that they are of same general type as *VTB 8*, below.

VTB 8 (A. C. Loire and Silbur Meulan). 19 tons. Dimensions: 62½ × 13 × 95 feet. Two 12-cylinder motors. H.P.: 2,200 = 46 kts. (50 kts. on trials). Armament: 2—M.G., 2—18 inch Torpedoes fired from twin closed Tubes, stern first, or carried externally in side gears. Reported to be an exceptionally handy craft, able to turn in her own length, and a good sea boat.

Note.—Earlier vessels now disarmed and relegated to harbour training service and reckoned non-effective. *VTB 9* was lost on August 7, 1939.

SURCOUF.   1935

Submarines.

1932 *Photo.*

SURCOUF (showing hangar open and AA guns.)   1936, *M. Le Masson.*

Surcouf (November 18, 1929. Cherbourg). Displacement: 2,880/4,300 tons. Complement: 150. Dimensions: 361 × 29½ × 23½ feet. Guns: 2—8 inch, 2—37mm. AA., 4 M.G. Tubes: 10—21·7 inch. 22 Torpedoes carried. Aircraft: 1 Small Seaplane. Machinery: Sulzer Diesels. B.H.P.: 7,600 = 18 kts. *surface* (19 kts. on *trials*). Electric Motors, H.P.: 3,400 = 10 kts. *submerged*. Radius: 12,000 miles at 10 kts. Diving limit: over 70 fathoms.

Notes.—Is the largest submarine in the world, representing an experimental type not likely to be repeated. Designed as a corsair and carries the heaviest guns allowed by Treaty. Can dive in 2 minutes. The Torpedo armament appears to be disposed as follows : 2 in bows, 4 revolving in pairs before C.T., and 4 abaft it. Trials included an endurance cruise of 5,000 miles from Cherbourg to Agadir, Dakar and Konakri in Nov., 1932, and submergence for a period of 60 hours. She did not officially enter into service until 1934. Sea speed does not exceed 16 kts. Designed by M. Roquebert under 1926 Programme.

5 Morillot Class

(Building.)

Roland Morillot, La Praya, La Guadeloupe, La Martinique, La Réunion. First 2 laid down at Cherbourg in May, 1937 and 1938, under 1934 and 1937 Programmes, respectively. Others building under 1938 Programme. Displacement: 1,605/2,100 tons. Dimensions: $302\frac{1}{2} \times 27\frac{1}{4} \times 14$ feet. Guns: 1—3·9 inch, 2—13 mm. AA. (twin mount). Tubes: **10**—21·7 inch. Diesels H.P.: 12,000 = 23 kts. *surface*. Electric motors, H.P. = 10 kts. *submerged*.

AGOSTA   1936

30 Redoutable Class.

MONGE.   1935, *Ganda.*

VENGEUR.   1930 *Photo, favour of M. of Marine.*

30 *Roquebert type.*

1924 Programme.
Redoutable (Feb. 24th, 1928) } Cherbourg.
Vengeur (Sept. 1st, 1928)

1925 Programme.
Pascal } (July 19th, 1928), Brest.
Pasteur
Henri Poincaré } (April 10th, 1929), Lorient.
Poncelet
Fresnel (June 8th, 1929), St. Nazaire (Penhoët).
Archimede (Sept. 6th, 1930), Ch. Nav. Fr. Blainville.
Monge (June 25th, 1929), La Seyne.

1926 Programme.
Actéon (April 10th, 1929) } A. C. Loire.
Acheron (Aug. 6th, 1929)
Argo (April 11th, 1929), Ch. Dubigeon, Nantes.
Achille } (May 28th, 1930) Brest.
Ajax

1927 Programme.
Persée (May 23rd, 1931), C. N. F. Blainville.
Protée (July 31st, 1930), F. C. Havre.
Pégase (July 28th, 1930), A. C. Loire.

1928 Programme.
L'Espoir (July 18th, 1931) } Cherbourg.
Le Glorieux (Nov. 29th, 1932)
Le Centaure } (Oct. 14th, 1932), Brest.
Le Héros
Le Conquerant (June 26th, 1934), A. C. Loire.
Le Tonnant (Dec. 15th, 1934), La Seyne.

1930 Programme.
Agosta (Apl. 30th, 1934)
Beveziers (Oct. 14th, 1935) } Cherbourg.
Ouessant (Nov. 30, 1936)
Sidi-Ferruch (July 9, 1937)
Sfax (Dec. 6th, 1934) } A. C. Loire.
Casabianca (Feb. 2nd, 1935)
(ex *Casablanca*)

1939 Replacement,
Phénix (building.)

Displacement: 1,384 tons *surface*; 2,080 tons *submerged* for first two; remainder 1,379 tons *surface*: 2,060 tons *submerged*. Dimensions: $302\frac{1}{2} \times 27 \times 16$ feet. Diesels: 2 sets Sulzer or Schneider-Carel type, H.P. 6,000 = 17 kts. Vessels of 1930 Programme, H.P. 8,400 = 18 kts. Electric motors of H.P. 2,000 = 10 kts. *submerged*. 1 auxiliary Diesel, H.P. 750. 2 shafts. Armament: 1—3·9 inch AA, 2 M.G. (first two have 1—37 mm. AA. and 1 M.G. as secondary armament), 11—21·7 inch tubes, including 2 sets of revolving tubes in triple and quadruple mountings, the latter at the stern. Complement: 67.

Radius of action = 30 days' cruising.

Notes.—Have proved very successful vessels. *Vengeur* and *Redoutable* performed a cruise to the West Indies in 1930 without mishap, and were able to make 19 kts. easily without being pressed. A longer unescorted cruise was that of *Glorieux* and *Héros* from Toulon to Saigon in 1935, a distance of 14,350 miles for the round voyage. Even longer cruises were made 1937-38, by other units, to the West Indies, Indo-China and the South Atlantic. *H. Poincaré* maintained an average of 17·6 kts. for 48 hours on trials. 1927 and 1928 boats reached 19 kts. and with 6,500 H.P., and *Agosta* with 8,600 H.P. was able to do 20·5 kts. *Promethee* lost on trials, July 8, 1932 *Phénix* lost in Indo-Chinese waters, June 15, 1939, and a new vessel of same name ordered in replacement.

15 Aurore Class.

Building

1 *Toulon* : **Aurore**   1 *Schneider* : **Antigone**
5 *Normand* : **La Bayadère, La Creole, Artemis, Gorgone, Hermione**
4 *Ch. Worms* : **L'Africaine, La Favorite, Andromaque, Armide**
4 *Ch. Dubigeon* : **Andromède, Astrée, Clorinde, Cornélie**
Displacement : 893/1,170 tons.
Dimensions : 241 × 21¼ × 11½ feet.
Guns : 1—3·9 inch, 2—13 mm. AA. Tubes : 9—21·7 inch.
Machinery : Schneider Diesels in *Aurore, Antigone, L'Africaine, La Favorite* ; Sulzer type in others.
H.P. : 3,000/1,400 = 17/9 kts.

Programme	Name	Laid down	Launch Completed	Programme	Name	Laid down	Launch	Completed
1934	*Aurore*	1936	26/7/39		*Antigone*			
1937	*L'Africaine*	1938			*Artemis*			
	La Favorite				*Gorgone*			
	La Bayadere				*Hermione*			
	La Creole			1938	*Andromaque*		1939	
					Armide			
					Andromede			
					Astrée			
					Clorinde			
					Cornélie			

10 Saphir Class (Minelayers).

TURQUOISE.   *1930 Photo, A. Ganda.*

10 *Normand-Fenaux* type : **Saphir** (Dec. 20th, 1928) ; **Turquoise** (May 16th, 1929) ; **Nautilus** (Mar. 21st, 1930) ; **Rubis** (Sept. 30th, 1931) ; **Diamant** (May 18th, 1933) ; **Perle** (July 30th, 1935) ; **Emeraude** (laid down 1937) ; **Agathe, Corail, Escarboucle,** (all 3 laid down 1939). All built at Toulon. Displacement : 669 tons *on surface* ; 925 *submerged*. Dimensions : 216¼ × 23¾ × 16 feet. Machinery : 2 sets Vickers-Normand 4-cycle Diesels. B.H.P. : 1,300 = 12 kts. *Submerged* H.P. : 1,000 = 9 kts. Armaments : 1—3 inch AA., 5—21·7 inch tubes, **32** minelaying chutes, arranged on Normand-Fenaux system. Carry **6** torpedoes and **32** mines of 460 lbs. weight. *Saphir* and *Turquoise* 1925 Programme, *Nautilus* 1926, *Rubis* 1927, *Diamant* 1928–29, *Perle* 1930, *Emeraude* 1937, remaining three 1938. Complement : 40. Radius of action : 2,500 miles *surface* ; 850 miles *submerged*.

Note.—Mines are stowed in wells in outer ballast tanks, with direct release arrangement.

9 Requin Class.

NARVAL.   *1938, Official.*

9 *Fuzier-Roquebert* type : **Requin** (19th July, 1924), **Morse** (11th Nov., 1925), **Narval** (9th May, 1925), **Souffleur** (Oct. 1st. 1924), **Caïman** (3rd March, 1927), (all Cherbourg), **Dauphin** (1925), **Espadon** (28th May, 1926), (both Toulon), **Marsouin** (Dec. 27th, 1924), **Phoque** (16th March, 1926), (both Brest). 974 tons (*on surface*) 1441 tons (*submerged*). Dimensions : 257½ (*p.p.*) × 23 × 17¾ feet. Complement : 51. Machinery : 2 Diesel motors, of Sulzer or Schneider-Carel type, each 1450 H.P. Total 2900 H.P. = 16 kts. Electric drive : 248 " D " type batteries, 1800 H.P. = 10 kts. Radius : 7000 miles at 9 kts. (*on surface*), 105 miles at 5 kts. (*submerged*). Endurance : equal to 30 days' cruising. Guns : 1—3·9 inch, 2 M.G. AA. Torpedo tubes : 10—21·7 inch (4 bow and 2 stern submerged ; 4 above water, revolving in pairs before and abaft C.T.). 32 torpedoes (24 of 1922 model, 8 of 1919 model) carried by *Caïman, Espadon, Phoque* ; 16 by others.

Notes.—*Requin, Souffleur, Morse, Narval, Marsouin, Dauphin* begun as Q 115—120 of 1922-1923 Programme. Other three came under Coast Defence Vote of June 30, 1923. All completed 1926-27. Freeboard about 7 feet. Can dive with safety to 100 metres (say, 55 fathoms). On commissioning, *Requin* carried out a 5,000 mile cruise, occupying 31 days in African waters, without mishap of any kind.

(All this class modernised, with complete refit of hull and machinery, 1935–37.)

Second Class
22′ Diane Class.

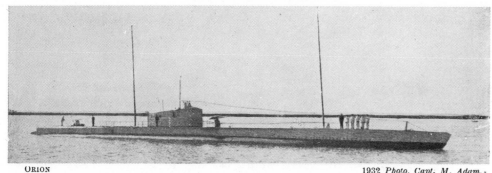

ORION

1932 Photo, Capt. M. Adam.

All are of same general type with minor differences, reflected in appearance, according to builders. (See note and photographs.)

1926 PROGRAMME
Argonaute (May 23rd, 1929) ⎫ Schneider
Aréthuse (Aug. 8th, 1929) ⎭
Diane (May 13th, 1930) ⎫ Normand
Méduse (Aug. 26th, 1930) ⎭

1927 PROGRAMME
Amphitrite (Dec. 20th, 1930) Normand
Antiope (Aug. 19th,1930) ⎫ Worms
Amazone (Dec. 28th, 1931) ⎭
Atalante (Aug. 5th, 1930) Schneider

1928 PROGRAMME
Orphée (Nov. 10th, 1931) Normand
Oréade (May 23rd, 1932) Worms
Orion (April 21st, 1931).. Loire
Ondine (May 4th, 1931)..Dubigeon

1929 PROGRAMME
La Psyché (Aug. 4th, 1932) Normand
La Sybille (Jan. 28th, 1933) Worms
La Vestale (May 25th, 1932) ⎫ Schneider
La Sultane (Aug. 9th, 1932) ⎭

1930 PROGRAMME
Minerve (Oct. 23, '34) Cherbourg
Junon (Sept. 15th, 1935) Normand
Venus (April 6th, 1935) Worms
Iris (Sept. 23rd, 1934) Dubigeon

1936 PROGRAMME
Cérès (Dec. 9th, 1938). Worms
Pallas (Aug. 25th, 1938) Normand

Displacements : *Argonaute, Aréthuse, Atalante, La Vestale, La Sultane,* 565/800 tons; *Diane, Méduse, Amphitrite, Antiope, Amazone, Oréade, Orphée, La Psyché, La Sybille,* 571/809 tons; *Orion, Ondine,* 558/787 tons; *Minerve, Junon, Venus, Iris,* 597/825 tons; *Cérès, Pallas,* 662/858 tons. Complement: 48. Dimensions: *Argonaute, Aréthuse, Atalante,* 208 × 21 × 13¾ feet; *Orion, Ondine,* 219 × 22 × 15 feet; *Cérès, Pallas,* 221 × 18½ × 15 feet; remainder, 211 × 20 × 13¾ feet' Armament: 1—3 inch AA. 1 M.G., 8—21·7 inch tubes in first 16 boats; but 7—21·7 inch and 2—15·7 inch in remaining 6, which have latter tubes mounted on either side of a larger tube in after triple group. Machinery: 2 sets Diesels, of Schnieder-Carel type in *Argonaute, Aréthuse, Atalante, La Vestale, La Sultane, Cérès, Pallas;* Vickers-Normand in *Diane, Méduse, Amphitrite, Amazone, Antiope, Orphée, Oréade, La Psyché, La Sybille, Minerve, Junon;* Sulzer in *Orion, Ondine.* B.H.P.: 1,300 to 1,800 = 14 kts. *surface.* Electric motors. H.P.: 1,000 = 9 kts. *submerged.* Radius: 3,000 miles at 10 kts. *surface;* 78 miles at 5 kts. *submerged.*

Notes.—Designs of these submarines are by Normand, Loire-Simonot (*Orion* and *Ondine*) and 1930-36 batch by Ministry of Marine.

MÉDUSE, LA SULTANE, LA PSYCHÉ, AMAZONE.

1936, courtesy M. Henri Le Masson.

This picture gives an excellent idea of the variations in appearance.

ATALANTE

Added 1937, Ganda.

10 Sirene Class.

SIRÈNE.

1927 *Official Photo.*

3 *Simonot* type, built by A. & C. de la Loire, St. Nazaire: **Näiade** (Oct. 20, 1925), **Sirène** (August 6, 1925), **Galatee** (Dec. 18, 1925). Displacement: 552 tons surface, 780 tons submerged. Dimensions: 210 (p.p.) × 21 × 14¾ feet. Machinery: 2 sets 2-cycle Sulzer Diesels, B.H.P. 1,300 on *surface,* = 14 kts. 1,000 submerged = 7·5 kts. Complement, 40.

Following particulars apply to all 11. Complement: 40. 140 to 144 "D" type electric batteries. Speed: 14 kts. on *surface*, 7·5 kts. *submerged*. Radius: *surface*, 2,000 miles at 10 kts.; *submerged*, 90 miles at 5 kts. Endurance equal to 20 days' cruising. Can dive to 45 fathoms. Guns: **1**—3 inch AA., **2** M.G. Torpedo tubes (21·7 inch): **7**. 13 torpedoes carried. Cost stated to be Frs. 8,500,000 each.

Notes.—*Ariane, Calypso, Circé, Naïade, Ondine, Sirène,* were laid down as *Q.121—126* of 1922-23 Programme; others under Coast Defence Vote of Sept. 30, 1923. *Nymph,* of this type, scrapped in 1939.

ARIANE.

1927 *Official Photo.*

3 *Normand-Fenaux* type, built by C. & A. Augustin Normand, Le Hâvre: **Ariane** (August 6, 1925), **Danaë** (Sept. 11, 1927), **Eurydice** (May 31, 1927). Displacement: 576 tons *surface*, 765 tons *submerged*. Dimensions: 216½ (p.p.) × 20½ × 13½ feet. Machinery: 2 sets 4-cycle Diesels, Vickers-Normand type. Electric motors by Schneider et Cie. 1,200 B.H.P. on *surface* = 14 kts. 1,000 *submerged*—7.5 kts. Complement, 40.

Note.—This type is reported to have given great satisfaction in service. A fourth boat, *Ondine*, lost by collision with a Greek steamer, October 3rd, 1928.

DORIS

1929 *Photo, M. Bar, Toulon.*

Schneider-Laubeuf type, built by Schneider et Cie, Chalon-sur-Saône: **Circé** (Oct. 29, 1925), **Calypso** (Jan. 1926), **Doris** (Nov 25, 1927), **Thetis** (June 30, 1927). Displacement: 548 tons *surface*, 764 tons *submerged*. Dimensions 204½ (p.p.) × 21½ × 12¾ feet. Machinery: 2 sets 2-cycle Schneider-Carels Diesels, 1,250 B.H.P. = 14 kts. H.P. 1000 = 7·5 kts. *submerged.*

Minelayers (*Mouilleurs de Mines*).

Note.—10 submarines of *Saphir* class are also fitted for minelaying.

CASTOR.

1930 *Photo, M. Bar.*

CASTOR (ex-Russian Icebreaker *Kozma Minin*) (Swan Hunter, 1916). Displacement: 3,150 (*standard*) tons. Dimensions: 236 (*pp.*), 248 (*o.a.*) × 57 × 19 feet (*mean*), 22 feet (*max*). 3 sets triple expansion engines. 6 S.E. boilers. I.H.P.: 6,400 = 14·5 kts. Coal: 686 tons. Carries 368 mines. Armament: **4**—3·9 inch, **2**—37 mm. AA. Complement: 167. Radius: 4,500 miles at 10 kts.

POLLUX.

1930 *Photo, courtesy of Ministry of Marine.*

POLLUX (ex-Russian Icebreaker *Ilya Murometz*) (Swan Hunter, 1915). Displacement: 2,461 (*standard*) tons. Dimensions: 200 (*p.p.*), 211 (*o.a.*) × 50½ × 20 feet. Triple expansion engines. 6 cylindrical boilers. I.H.P.: 4,000 = 14 kts. 2 screws. Coal: 367 tons. Carries 236 mines. Armament: **4**—3·9 inch, **2**—37 mm. AA. Complement: 162. Radius: 2,300 at 8 kts., 1,470 miles at 14 kts.

Note.—Both these vessels were converted into Mine Layers by Lorient Dockyard, 1928-29.

Netlayer.

1935 *courtesy Mons. H. Le Masson.*

1935, *A. Ganda.*

LE GLADIATEUR (April 10, 1933). Displacement : 2,293 tons. Complement : 132. Dimensions : 370¾ × 41½ × 11½ feet. Guns : 4—3·5 inch AA., 6 M.G. Machinery : 2 Parsons turbines. S.H.P. : 6,000 = 18 kts. 2 Indret boilers. Oil : 399 tons.

Notes.—Laid down at Lorient, 1932, under 1930 Programme. Completed 1934. Trials : S.H.P. 7,700 = 21 kts.

Training Ships (ex-Battleships, demilitarised).

1938, *Official.*

L'OCÉAN (ex-*Jean Bart*), (Sept. 22, 1911). Displacement : 22,189 tons. Dimensions : 541 × 92 × 32½ feet. Guns : 12—12 inch, 22—5·5 inch, 7—3 inch AA., 2—47 mm. AA. H.P. : 28,000 = 20 kts. Was originally a sister ship of *Courbet* and *Paris*, on an earlier page.

1938, *Official.*

CONDORCET (April, 1909). Displacement : 17,597 tons. Dimensions : 475¾ × 84½ × 30 feet. Guns : 4—12 inch, 12—9·4 inch, 2—3 inch AA. H.P. : 22,500 = 16 kts.

COMMANDANT TESTE. (F. et C. de la Gironde, Bordeaux, April 12th, 1929.)

Standard Displacement : 10,000 tons (about 11,500 tons *deep load*). Length : 512¾ feet (*pp.*), 558 feet (*o.a.*). Beam : 71½ feet (88½ feet, extreme). Draught : 22¾ feet. Complement : 686.

Guns :
12—3·9 inch AA.
8—3 pdr. AA.
12 M.G.
Aircraft : 26
Catapults : 4

Armour :
2″ (H.T.?) side at waterline.
1½″ protective deck over engine and boiler spaces.

Note to Plan.—3·9 inch AA. abeam of funnel are at deck level.

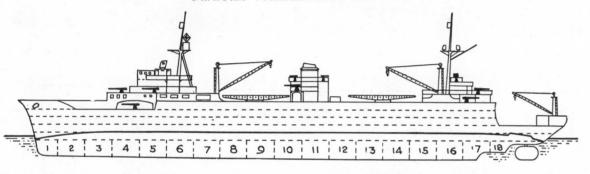

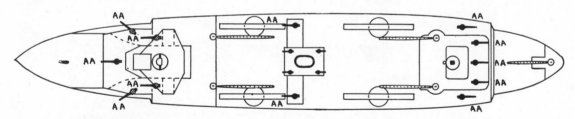

Machinery : 2 Schneider-Zoelly geared turbines. 2 screws. 4 Yarrow-Loire boilers (mixed firing). S.H.P. 21,000 = 20·5 kts. Radius of action : 6000 miles at 10 kts. Fuel :— Oil 290, coal 720 tons. Trials : Average speed of 21·77 kts. maintained for 3 hours.

Notes.—This vessel is intended to act as a tender to *Béarn*, and as a reserve from which aircraft supplies can be drawn by cruisers which carry planes. Authorised under 1926 Programme, she was ordered in May, 1927, and completed in 1931. She carries 4 catapults, Penhoët 3-ton type, with accommodation for 26 seaplanes in a hangar measuring 275 × 88½ × 23 feet high.

1934, *Nautical Photo Agency (added 1935).*

1933 *Photo, Leslie H. Howard, Esq.*

FRANCE—Escort Vessels

(Classed as *Avisos Coloniaux*).

BOUGAINVILLE Class—8 Ships.

Special Note.—For two more ships of this design (*Beautemps-Beaupré* and *Lapérouse*), see under Surveying Vessels.

2 *Ch. Gironde :*	**BOUGAINVILLE** (April 21, 1931).
	RIGAULT DE GENOUILLY (Sept. 18, 1932).
3 *Ch. Sud-Ouest :*	**DUMONT D'URVILLE** (March 21, 1931).
	SAVORGNAN DE BRAZZA (June 18. 1931).
	AMIRAL CHARNER (Oct. 1, 1932).
3 *Ch. Provence :*	**D'ENTRECASTEAUX** (June 22, 1931).
	D'IBERVILLE (Sept. 23, 1934).
	VILLE D'YS (Laid down 1937).

DUMONT D'URVILLE.   1932 *Photo, Official.*

Displacement : 1,969 tons *standard*; 2,156 tons *normal*. Complement : 136.

Dimensions : 340 × 41⅜ × 14¾ feet.

Guns : 3—5·5 inch, 4—37 mm. AA., 6 or 8 M.G. Stowage for 50 mines. 1 seaplane carried.

Machinery: 2 sets Diesels—Sulzer in *D'Iberville, Dumont d'Urville, Ville d'Ys* and *Savorgnan de Brazza ;* Schneider-Burmeister in other 4 ships. S.H.P. : 3,200 = 15·5 kts.

Radius : 9,000 miles at 10 kts. Fuel Oil : 60 tons. Diesel Oil : 220 tons.

Notes.—First two were authorised in 1927 ; two in 1928, three in 1930, and one in 1937. Those built by At. & Ch. du Sud-Ouest, Bordeaux (except *Charner*) have Sulzer Diesels, made by the At. & Ch. de la Loire and F. & Ch. de la Mediterranée, respectively. Those built by La Société d'Exploitation des Chantiers de la Gironde, Bordeaux, and Ch. & At. Provence, Port de Bouc, are engined with Burmeister & Wain Diesels manufactured by Schneider.

These vessels are designed for tropical service, with a special arrangement for circulation of cool air, and auxiliary plant is electrically driven through 3 Diesel groups 125 kws. each and 2 auxiliary petrol groups 22 kws. each. All are fitted as flagships. Hulls, roofs and bridges are protected against bullets and splinters.

They have proved most efficient and reliable in service. On trials, *Am. Charner* averaged 17·86 kts., maximum 18 9 kts. *Dumont d'Urville* averaged 17·2 kts. *Sav. de Brazza,* 18·1 kts. *D'Entrecasteaux,* 17·5 kts. Consumption at 10 kts. averages 26·55 lbs. per mile.

SAVORGNAN DE BRAZZA.   1934 *Photo.*

(Classed as *Ariso*)

1921 *Photo, Com. R. Steen Steensen, R.D.N.*

VILLE D'YS (ex-*Andromède*), Swan, Hunter & Wigham Richardson, Wallsend-on-Tyne, June, 1917.

Displacement : 1,121 tons. Complement : 103.

Dimensions : 255¼ (*p.p.*), 272½ (*o.a.*) × 39⅓ × 16½ feet.

Guns : 3—3·9 inch, 2—3 inch, 2—47 mm.

Machinery : 1 set 4-cyl. triple expansion. I.H.P. : 2,500 = 17 kts.

Boilers : 2 cylindrical. Coal : 270 tons = 2,400 miles at 10 kts.

Note.—Generally same build as British escort vessels of " Flower " class. Built under 1916 War Programme to replace *Rigel,* lost. Begun for British Navy as *Andromeda,* and turned over to French Navy. Now employed on Newfoundland fisheries services. Will be scrapped by the time new ship of same name (above) is ready for service.

AMIRAL CHARNER.   1935, *Canda*

(Classed as *Avisos-Dragueurs*.)

(ÉLAN CLASS—26 SHIPS.)

CDT. BORY.

1939.

8 *Lorient Dockyard :* **CHAMOIS** (April 19, 1938), **CHEVREUIL** (June 17, 1939), **ÉLAN** (July 27, 1938), **LA SURPRISE** (ex-*Bambara*) (June 17, 1939), **GAZELLE** (June 17, 1939), **ANNAMITE** (June 17, 1939), **LA CURIEUSE, LA MOQUEUSE.**

4 *At. et Ch. de France, Dunkerque:* **COMMANDANT BORY** (Jan. 26, 1939), **COMMANDANT DELAGE** (Feb. 25, 1939), **L'IMPETUEUSE** (Aug. 17, 1939), **LA BOUDEUSE** (Sept., 1939).

3 *Ch. Dubigeon, Nantes :* **COMMANDANT DUBOC** (Jan. 16, 1938), **LA CAPRICIEUSE** (April 19, 1939), **COMMANDANT DOMINÉ** (ex-*La Rieuse*) (May 2, 1939).

7 *Ch. et At. de Provence, Port de Bouc :* **COMMANDANT RIVIÈRE** (Feb. 16, 1939), **LA BATAILLEUSE, AMIRAL SÉNÉS, ENSEIGNE BALLANDE, MATELOT LEBLANC, RAGEOT DE LA TOUCHE.**

3 *not allotted :* **LA FURIEUSE, LA JOYEUSE, LA TROMPEUSE.**

Standard displacement : 630 tons, except 3 fitted for Colonial service (*Chevreuil, Gazelle, Annamite*) which are 647 tons. Complement :

Dimensions : 256 × 27¾ × 7¾ feet.

Guns : 2—3·9 inch AA., 8 M.G.
Machinery : 4 sets Sulzer Diesels. 2 shafts. B.H.P. : 4,000 = 20 kts.

*Note.—*Élan built under 1934 Programme ; *Chamois, Chevreuil* and *Gazelle* under 1935 ; *Commandant* series (except *Cdt. Dominé*) under 1936 ; last 7 under 1938, and remainder under 1937. First 8 laid down during 1936, others (except last 7) in 1937. *Chamois* is tender to Navigation School, and differs slightly in appearance from others of class.

(Classed as *Dragueurs de Mines*)
*Note.—*12 trawlers are to be acquired as *Dragueurs Auxiliares* under 1938 Estimates.

MEULIÈRE.

1936, *M. Le Masson.*

GRANIT, MEULIÈRE, (1918). 354 tons. Dimensions : 189 (*o.a.*) × 26 × 7½ feet. Machinery : Triple expansion. I.H.P. : 550 = 12 kts. Guns : 1—65 m/m. Coal : 73—90 tons. Complement : 63.

Porphyre scrapped 1932 ; *Mica* and *Quartz*, 1938.

(Classed as *Avisos*.)

SUIPPE ; ANCRE has same appearance.

1930 *Photo.*

ANCRE (Lorient D.Y. Jan., 1918).
SUIPPE (Lorient D.Y. April, 1918).
Displacement : 604 tons. Complement : 107. Dimensions : 250—262 × 28½ × 10¾ feet.
Guns : 4—3·9 inch, 1—9 pdr. AA., 2 M.G. Designed H.P. : 5,000 = 20 kts.
Machinery : 2 sets geared turbines. Boilers : 2 du Temple. 2 screws.
Oil fuel : 140 to 145 tons = 4,000 miles at 10 kts.

*Note.—*Ancre is tender to Navigation School.

COUCY (Some have foremast abaft funnel).

1933 *Photo, R. Perkins, Esq.*

("ARRAS" CLASS.—11 SHIPS.)

3 built at Navy Yards :—
ARRAS (July, 1918), **YPRES** (ex-*Dunkerque*), (July, 1918). Both built by Brest D.Y.
 BELFORT (March, 1919), by Lorient D.Y.

8 built by Private Yards :—
LASSIGNY (July, 1919) and **LES ÉPARGES** (September, 1919), both by Ch. de Bretagne, Nantes. **TAHURE** (——, 1919), by Ch. de la Loire, St. Nazaire. **COUCY** (June, 1919), **ÉPINAL** (August, 1919), and **VAUQUOIS** (August, 1919), all three by Ch. de St. Nazaire, Penhoët. **AMIENS** (May, 1919), and **CALAIS** (Nov., 1919), both by F. et C. de la Med., La Seyne.

Avisos. Standard displacement : 644 tons. Dimensions : 246 × 31 × 12½ feet. Guns : 2—5·5 inch, 1—3 inch AA., 2 M.G. Carry depth charges. Fitted with from two to four searchlights. Designed S.H.P. : 5,000 = 20 kts. Machinery : 2 sets Parsons (geared) turbines. 2 screws. Boilers : 2 Normand or Guyot du Temple oil-burning (small tube). Fuel : 200 tons oil = Endurance : 1,000 miles at 17 kts. ; 3,000 at 11 kts. Complement : about 110.

Notes.—5·5 inch guns reported to be M.1910 (and perhaps M.1916), but *Epinal* is armed with two 5·5 inch guns rebored to fit Army shells. 5·5 inch have large degree of elevation ; *max.* range 17,000 metres. They are very roomy and comfortable ships for their size, and their high bows make them very dry in head seas. But with sea on the beam they are said to roll ' like old boots " (*comme des veritables-sabots*), owing to heavy topweight of guns, superstructure, etc. These vessels can make their speed on light draught in good weather, but in a seaway they drop down to 13 kts. Built under Programme VI and VII of 1917 and mostly completed 1919–21, though *Reims* was not finished till 1924. *Ypres* and *Les Éparges* employed on surveying duties ; *Belfort* is Seaplane Tender, with a crane aft. Each has 1—3 inch gun only.

Bar-le-Duc lost, December 1920; *Baccarat, Montmirail,* scrapped 1933 ; *Béthune, Epernay,* 1934 ; *Craonne, Liévin, Lunéville, Mondement, Péronne, Toul, Vimy, Vitry-le-Francois,* 1935 ; *Remiremont,* 1936 ; *Bapaume, Révigny,* 1937 ; *Nancy, Reims, Laffaux,* 1938.

1924 *Photo. A. Dussau, Toulon.*

AILETTE. The 3·9 inch guns are concealed within lidded ports at angles of superstructure. AA. gun on forecastle.

AILETTE (Brest D.Y., March, 1918).
 Displacement : 492 tons. Complement : 107.
 Dimensions : 229½ × 27¼ × 10 feet.
 Guns : 4—3·9 inch, 1—9 pdr. AA., 2 M.G. S.H.P. : 5,000 = 20 kts. 2 sets geared Turbines.
 Boilers : 2 du Temple. 2 screws. Oil : 140 tons = 4,000 miles at 10 kts. 1,400 miles at 15 kts.
 Is now employed on Fishery Protection duties, though rated as *Aviso*.

1921 *Photo, M. Bar, Toulon.*

"DUBOURDIEU" TYPE.— 2 *Avisos*.

DUBOURDIEU (April, 1918), **ENSEIGNE HENRY** (Nov., 1918). *Standard* displacement : 453 tons. Dimensions : 213¼ (*o.a.*) × 27 × 10 feet (*max.* draught). Guns : 1—5·5 inch, 1—3·9 inch. S.H.P. : 2,000 = 17·4 kts. Machinery : 2 sets of Breguet de Wooch turbines. 2 screws. Boilers : 2 Du Temple-Guyot. Oil : 143 tons = 1,985 miles at full speed. Complement : 74.

Notes.—Built under 1917–18 War Programme. Completed June, 1919—May, 1920. Sixth boat of this class, *Décrès,* cancelled. Originally rated as " Anti-Submarine Gunboats " (*Canonnières Contre Sousmarins*). In build they are like *Arras* class. *Dubourdieu* employed on Surveying Service. *Ens. Henry,* originally named *Dumont-D'Urville,* is tender to Boy Artificers Training Establishment, Lorient. *Duperré, Ducouedic* and *Duchaffault* scrapped.

ENGAGEANTE. *Conquérante* similar, but straight stem.   1935.

DILIGENTE. (Straight stem. No funnel).   *Added* 1939, *H. Emery, Toulon.*
LURONNE. (Yacht stem and thin funnel).

CONQUERANTE (Brest D.Y., 1917), **DILIGENTE** (Brest D.Y., 1916), **ENGAGEANTE** (Brest D.Y., 1917), **LURONNE** (Brest D.Y., 1917). Displacement: 315 tons, except *Conquerante*, 374 tons, and *Luronne*, 265 tons. Dimensions: *Conquerante*, 217¾ × 26 × 9¼ feet; *Diligente, Engageante*, 217¾ × 23 × 9¼ feet; *Luronne*, 197½ × 23½ × 9½ feet. Guns: 2—3·9 inch. Carry D.C. and may also be equipped as Minesweepers. B.H.P.: *Conquerante*, 1,500 = 17 kts.; others, 900* = 15 kts. Machinery: 2 sets 450* B.H.P. Sulzer*-Diesel engines. Oil: 30 tons = 3,000 miles at 10 kts., 1,600 miles at 15 kts. Complement: 54.

Notes.—Generally the same design as the *Ardent* type (steam-driven) boats in next column, but above 3 boats have Diesel engines. All built under 1916 War Programme, except *Luronne*, of 1917 Programme. *Chiffonne, Friponne, Impatiente* and *Mignonne* sold to Rumania, January, 1920; *Bouffonne, Vaillante* and *Surveillante* scrapped.

* *Luronne* has two Fiat type Diesel engines of 325 B.H.P., total H.P. 650, which are reported to have given a speed of 13·8 kts. She is employed as tender to the training establishment for boy artificers at Lorient.

1921 *Copyright Photo, M. Bar, Toulon.*

(ARDENT type—4 Steam-engined boats.)

AUDACIEUSE (Port de Bouc, 1917).   **ETOURDI** (Lorient D.Y., 1916).
DÉDAIGNEUSE (Bordeaux, 1916).   **TAPAGEUSE** (Port de Bouc, 1916).

Displacement: 265 tons. Dimensions: 197½ × 23½ × 9½ feet. Guns: 2—3·9 inch, 1—3 pdr. *or* 1 M.G. Carry D.C. Machinery: Reciprocating. I.H.P.: 1,200 = 15 kts. Du Temple or Normand boilers. Fuel: 85 tons coal = 3,000 miles at 10 kts., 1,600 miles at full speed. Complement: 65.

Notes.—Note that masts are stepped well to starboard of the centre-line. *Moqueuse* wrecked, 1923. *Curieuse* condemned, 1926. *Belliqueuse* and *Emporté,* 1927. *Malicieuse* and *Éveillé,* 1932. *Inconstant,* 1933. *Agile, Alerte, Ardent, Capricieuse, Sans Souci,* 1935; *Batailleuse* and *Impetueuse,* 1937; *Gracieuse,* 1938. *Etourdi* differs from remainder of class, displacing 310 tons, with armament of 2—5·5 inch and 1—3 inch AA. H.P. 1500 = 16·5 kts.

YSER (*Marne* has 2 funnels.)   1920, *Photo, M. Bar, Toulon.*

MARNE (Lorient D.Y., Nov., 1916).   **YSER** (Rochefort D.Y., Jan., 1917).
SOMME (Brest D.Y., March, 1917).

Rated as *Avisos, 2e classe*

Though the design of these Despatch Vessels is uniform, the latitude allowed to the building yards has resulted in differing appearances.

Displacement, 576 tons (*Marne* 601 tons). Dimensions: 256 (*o.a.*) × 29¼ × 11 feet. Armament: 4—3·9 inch, 2—65 m/m. in all. Designed I.H.P.: 4,000 = 20·5 kts. (5,000 = 21 in *Marne*). Machinery: 2 sets geared turbines. Boilers: 2 du Temple. 2 screws. Oil fuel: 135 tons, 145 tons in *Marne*. Radius: 4,000 miles at 10 kts. Complement: 107. All built under 1916 War Programme.

Note.—*Aisne, Meuse, Oise,* scrapped, 1938. Others laid up and to be discarded later.

+-----------------------------+
| Building. |
+-----------------------------+

6 *Ch. de Normandie (Fécamp) :* **CH 41** (May 1, 1939), **CH 42, CH 43, CH 44, CH 45, CH 46, CH 47, CH 48.** Building under 1937 Programme (except last pair, 1938). Wood. Displacement : 126 tons. Dimensions : × × feet. Guns : 1—3 inch. Diesel engines. B.H.P. : 1,100 = 16 kts. Specially designed for alternative use with Seaplanes.

+-----------------------------+
| Photo wanted. |
+-----------------------------+

4 *Ch. Worms :* **CH 13, CH 14, CH 15, CH 16.** *Not yet allotted :* **CH 17—21.**
4 *At. et Ch. de France :* **CH 9, CH 10, CH 11, CH 12.**
4 *F. et C. de la Mediterranée :* **CH 5** (April 3, 1939), **CH 6** (July 18, 1939). **CH 7, CH 8.**
Above 17 all ordered under 1937 Programme, except *CH 17—21,* which are 1938. Steel. Displacement : 107 tons. Dimensions : 121⅓ × 16½ × feet. Guns : 1—3 inch. M.A.N. Diesels. B.H.P. : 1,100 = 16 kts.

CH 3.

1936, *M. H. le Masson.*

4 *Ch. Bretagne* type : **CH 1, CH 2, CH 3, CH 4.** All launched at Nantes, 1934. Standard Displacement : 148 tons. Dimensions : 157½ × 17¾ × 5½ feet. Guns : 1—3 inch, 2 M.G. Depth charges carried. Sulzer-Diesels in CH 1 and 3, M.A.N. in CH 2 and 4. B.H.P. : 2,400 = 20 kts. Are fitted for mine-sweeping. On Trials CH 1 averaged 22·5 kts. with 2,624 H.P., others doing as well or better. All exceeded 20 kts. with ¾ power.

1930 *Photo.*

Note.—Funnels are slightly staggered, the foremost being to port and after one to starboard of the centre-line.
3 *Normand type* boats : **CH 106** (Normand, Le Havre, 1918–21). **CH 107** and **CH 115** (respective builders unknown).* 128 tons. Dimensions : 136⅝ (*p.p.*), 142 (*o.a.*) × 17⅛ × 8½ feet (*max. draught*). Guns : 1—3 inch, 2 M.G. Designed I.H.P. 1300 = 16·5 kts. Triple expansions engines. 2 Normand boilers. Coal : 24 tons, except in *CH 107,* 28 tons. Complement, 32. Contract for 2 other boats with Normand cancelled 1918. *CH 101* swamped and sunk off Spanish Coast, December, 1920.
*Built by Chantiers de la Loire, Nantes, Chantiers Dubigeon, Nantes.
Note.—Former *CH 111* and *CH 112* have been given respective names of *Commandant Bourdais* and *Avalanche* and adapted for service as river gunboats in Indo-China.

1920 *Photo, H. Freund, Brest.*

6—100 *foot type :* **C 25, 51, 56, 74, 95, 98.** Built by U.S. Navy Yards and smaller ship-building firms, 1917–18, for U.S. Navy as *SC5—SC404,* but contracts transferred to French Government. *Designed* displacement : 54 tons. *Standard* figure, 60 tons. Dimensions : 105 (*p.p.*), 110 (*o.a.*) × 15½ × 7½ feet (*maximum* draught). Machinery : 3 sets of 220 B.H.P. Standard petrol motors, totalling 660 B.H.P. = 17 kts. Petrol : 2,400 gallons = 900 miles at 10 kts. Armament : 1—3 inch (14 pdr.) field gun converted to naval mounting, but some have one of smaller calibre. Carry depth charges. Complement : 19.

C 96 lost December, 1931, *C 91* sunk by bombs from Spanish aircraft in October, 1937. Many others scrapped.

MYTHO.

1934, *Courtesy of Mons. H. Le Masson.*

MYTHO, TOURANE (Saigon, 1933). Displacement : 95 tons (*Standard*). Complement : 16. Dimensions : 114¾ × 17½ × 3 feet. Guns : 1—3 inch Howitzer, 2—37 mm., 2 M.G. 1 Mortar (Army pattern). Machinery : 2 Diesels. H.P. : 250 = 10 kts. Radius : 560 miles at 10 kts.

VIGILANTE.

1924 *Photo, A. Dussau, Toulon.*

ARGUS, VIGILANTE (1922, Toulon, D.Y.). 218 tons. Dimensions : 170 (*o.a.*) × 25¼ × 4 feet (*max.*). Guns : 2—3 inch, 2—37 m/m., 4 M.G. I.H.P. : 550 = 12 kts. 2 screws and 2 boilers. Bullet-proof plating over conning position and W/T cabinet. Ammunition carried : 300 rounds per 14 pdr., and 50,000 cartridges. Complement : 42.

FRANCIS-GARNIER.

1930 *Photo, by favour of M.Henri le Masson.*

FRANCIS-GARNIER (Dec. 7, 1927). River Gunboat, for Lower Yangtse, ordered 1926 from Chantiers Navals Français, Blainville. Displacement, 639 tons. Complement, 103. Dimensions : 196¾ × 33¾ × 7¼ feet. Guns : 2—4 inch, 1—3 inch AA, 2—2 pdr., 4 M.G. 2 sets triple expansion, H.P. 3200 = 15 kts. 2 Du Temple boilers. Oil fuel : 100 tons. Completed in 1929.

BALNY.

Photo added 1927, courtesy M.Henri Le Masson.

BALNY (1920). Built by Chantiers de Bretagne, Nantes. 201 tons. Dimensions : 167¼ × 23 × 4½ feet. Guns : 1—3 inch, 2—1 pdr., 4 M.G. Reciprocating engines. H.P. : 920 = 14 kts. 2 Foubé w.t. boilers. Coal : 45 tons. Complement : 49.

River Gunboats—*continued.*

AVALANCHE (ex-*C.112*), **COMMANDANT BOURDAIS** (ex-*C.111*). (1921). 128 tons. Dimensions: 142 × 17 × 8¼ feet. Guns: 1—3 inch, 2 M.G. Triple expansion engines. I.H.P.: 1,300 = 16·5 kts.

Note.—Ex-submarine chasers adapted for present service in Indo-China. Appearance as illustration on an earlier page.

1920 Photo, Ch. de Bretagne.

DOUDART DE LAGRÉE (1909). 183 tons. Dimensions: 167¼ × 22½ × 4¼ feet. Guns: 1—3 inch (field type), 2—37 mm., 4 M.G. Reciprocating engines. H.P.: 900 = 14 kts. 2 Fouché w.t. boilers. Coal: 45 tons. Complement: 59. Built by Chantiers de Bretagne, Nantes.

Submarine Depot Ship.

Photo 1932, Official.

JULES VERNE (Lorient, Feb. 3, 1931). Displacement: 5,747 tons. Complement: 259. Dimensions: 377½ (*p.p.*), 400¼ (*o.a.*) × 56½ × 19 feet. Guns: 4—3·5 inch AA., 4—37 mm. AA. 2 sets Sulzer-Diesels. 2 shafts. B.H.P.: 7,000 = 16 kts. Equipped for the supply and maintenance of a flotilla of 6 submarines, with accommodation for their personnel, numbering 265, in addition to ship's own complement.

Q. ROOSEVELT.   *1937 M. Davenport, Esq.*

(On North Sea Fishery Protection Service.)

QUENTIN ROOSEVELT (ex-*Flamant*, Rochefort D.Y., December, 1916). Despatch Vessel of 585 tons. Dimensions: 154 × 27½ × 14½ feet. Guns: 1—3 inch., 1—3 pdr. I.H.P. 1100 = 13 kts. Coal: 100 tons = 1500 miles at 10 kts. Complement, 53. Was begun 1913, stopped 1914–16 and completed April, 1918.

Note.—Escort vessel *Ville d'Ys* and patrol vessel *Ailette*, recorded on earlier pages, are also employed on Fishery Protection duties.

Target Ship

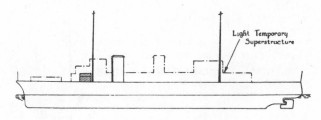

IMPASSIBLE.

IMPASSIBLE (Lorient, June 17, 1939). Displacement: 2,450 tons. Dimensions: 328 × 39⅓ × 13 feet. S.H.P.: 10,000 = 20 kts. Ordered, Feb., 1937, under 1936 Programme, and laid down, May 23, 1938. Will be controlled by wireless.

Fishery Protection Vessels.

FAUVETTE II (1916). 315 tons. Dimensions: 131¼ (*p.p.*), 142¾ (*o.a.*) × 24 × 12 feet. No Guns. I.H.P.: 500 = 10 kts. Coal: 120 tons. Complement, 23.

1935.

PRIMEVÈRE (1912). 490 tons. Dimensions: 116 × 22 × 14 feet. No Guns. H.P. 450 = 8·5 kts. 1 screw. Coal: 30 tons.

Surveying Vessels.

Usually commissioned for the six months April—November, and reduced to Reserve during other six months of the year.

Notes.—3 patrol vessels, *Dubourdieu, Les Eparges* and *Ypres*, employed on this service, will be found on other pages

BENGALI, CORMORAN, GOELAND, IBIS, MOUETTE, PELICAN. Of a new Type. To be built under 1938 Programme to replace 6 oldest existing Surveying Vessels.

Building or authorised.

BEAUTEMPS-BEAUPRÉ (A. et C. de la Gironde). Laid down 1937. **LAPÉROUSE.** 2,000 tons. Sister ships to escort vessel *Ville d'Ys*, but with reduced armament. 2 B. & W. Diesels by Penhoët. B.H.P.: 3,200 = 15·5 kts.

1937, Capt. M. Adam.

AMIRAL MOUCHEZ (Aug. 3, 1936). Laid down at Cherbourg, Jan. 1935. Displacement: 719 tons. Dimensions: $203\frac{1}{2} \times 33\frac{1}{4} \times 11$ feet. Guns: 1—3 inch. (In war time, provision is made for mounting 2—3.9 inch). 1 Sulzer Diesel. B.H.P.: 800 = 12 kts. Complement: 81.

Photo wanted.

PRESIDENT THEODORE TISSIER (Ch. Worms, 1933). (Taken over by Navy in 1938). Displacement: 1,240 tons. Dimensions: 166 × 29 × 16 feet. Machinery: M.A.N. Diesel, 7 cyl., single stroke, 4 cycle. B.H.P.: 800 = 11 kts. Fuel: 250 tons. Has a remarkable radius, equal to 100 days continuously at 10 kts. Equipped with modern deep sea sounding apparatus.

Surveying Vessels—*continued.*

1935.

LAPÉROUSE (launched 21st November, 1919). 781 tons. Dimensions: $196\frac{2}{3}$ (*p.p.*) $\times 27\frac{3}{4} \times 17\frac{3}{4}$ feet. Guns: 1—3 inch AA. Triple expansion engines. I.H.P.: 1,100 = 11 kts. 2 w.t. boilers. Oil: 132 tons. Complement, 104. Ex-Navy Transport of the *Coëtlogon* class, built at Brest D.Y., and lengthened when transferred to surveying service. Reboilered in 1938.

1921 Photo, M. Bar.

ASTROLABE (ex-*Mauviette*), **GASTON RIVIER** (ex-*Ortolan*), **OCTANT** (ex-*Pivert*), **ESTAFETTE** (all 1918), **SENTINELLE** (1920). 460 tons. Dimensions: $142\frac{3}{4} \times 24 \times 13$ feet. Guns: 1—47 mm. I.H.P.: 450 = 10 kts. Coal: 120 tons. Complement: 32.

CHIMÈRE (ex-*Zelée*, ex-*Huron*) (1901). Ex-Tug of 613 tons. I.H.P.: 880 = 14 kts.

Aircraft Tenders.

Note.—The patrol vessel *Belfort* and the small transport *Hamelin* (described on other pages) are also fitted for service as Aircraft Tenders, their official rating being *Ravitailleurs d'Aviation.*

Building.

SANS SOUCI, SANS PAREIL, SANS PEUR, SANS REPROCHE (ex-*Sans Crainte*). Building under 1937 Programme. All laid down Aug., 1938, first pair by At. et Ch. de la Loire, second pair by Penhoët. Displacement: 1,172 tons. Guns: 1—3 inch. Machinery: Sulzer Diesels. Speed: 15 kts.

1938, Official

PÉTREL Nos. 1, 2, 3, 4, 5, 6, 7, 8 (1932–33). Displacement: 80 tons. Dimensions: $87 \times 14\frac{2}{3} \times 3$ feet. Machinery: Diesel. H.P.: 270 = 11·5 kts. Stationed at various points around the coast.

Oilers (*Transports Pétroliers*).

SAONE, SEINE, LIAMONE, MEDJERDA. Building by At. et Ch. de France, Dunkerque, under 1938 Programme. Displacement: 19,250 tons (*full load*), 14,800 tons *deadweight.* Cargo capacity: 11,000 tons. Dimensions: $525\frac{3}{4} \times 72 \times$ — feet. Machinery: Parsons geared turbines. S.H.P.: 14,750 = 18 kts. Rated as *Petroliers Rapides.*

Oilers.—*continued.*

BUILDING OR COMPLETING

ADOUR (Oct. 9, 1938), **LOT** (June 19, 1939), **TARN** (Sept., 1939), **CHARENTE, MAYENNE, BAISE.**
Adour built by Stë. Provencale des Constructions Navales, La Ciotat, next pair by At. et Ch. de France, Dunkerque, next pair by Ch. Worms, Le Trait. *Baise* still to be ordered. Displacement : 4,220 tons ; 7,400 tons *deadweight*. Dimensions : 433 × 52½ × 20¾ feet. Guns: 2—3·9 inch. Machinery : Parsons geared turbines. H.P. : 5,200 = 15 kts. Radius : 10,000 miles at 13-14 kts. Provided for under 1936, 1937 and 1938 Programmes, and rated as *Ravitailleurs d'Escadre.*

PHOTO WANTED

ETHYLENE (July 8, 1937). Displacement : 1,950 tons, 1,200 tons *deadweight* capacity. Dimensions : 202 × 40 × feet. H.P. : 900 = 10·5 kts. (Rated as *Batiment de Servitude.*)

1935, *Capitaine M. Adam.*

NIVÔSE. (Deutsche Werft A.G., Hamburg, 1931). Purchased in 1934. Displacement : 8,500 tons *standard*, 14,160 tons deadweight. Dimensions : 467 × 62 × 28¾ feet. Guns : 2—3·9 inch, 2—37 mm. AA. Machinery : Quadruple expansion. 1 shaft. I.H.P. : 3,400 = 11 kts. Capacity for 14,500 tons.

VAR. 1932 *Photo, Capt. M. Adam.*

VAR (1931), **ELORN** (1930). Both built by Deutsche Werft A.G., Hamburg, on War Reparations account. Displacement : 5,482 tons *standard*. Full load, 15,150 tons. Complement : 75. Dimensions : 436¼ (*p.p.*), 456 (*o.a.*) × 61¾ × 26 feet. Guns : 2—3·9 inch, 2—1 pdr. AA., 2 B. & W. Diesels. H.P. : 4,850 = 13·5 kts. Capacity : 9,600 tons, arranged as in *Le Mékong* and *Le Niger.*

LE MÉKONG. 1929 *Photo by favour of M. Henri le Masson.*

LE MÉKONG, bv Ch. & At. de St. Nazaire (Penhoët) (Aug. 31, 1928), **LE NIGER,** by Ch. & At. Maritimes du Sud-Ouest, Bordeaux (March 14, 1930). Displacement : 5,482 tons *standard*; 15,150 tons *full load*. Dimensions : 436¼ (*p.p.*), 456 (*o.a.*) × 61¾ × 26 feet *mean* draught. Guns : 2—3·9 inch, 2—1 pdr. 2 sets Burmeister & Wain Diesel engines. H.P. : 4,850 = 13·5 kts. (6,000 on trials). Capacity of tanks : 33,900 cubic metres. Dead weight : 9,600 tons, of which oil fuel absorbs 9,000 ; distilled water, 500 ; lubricating oil, 100. Complement, 76.

1928 *Photo, R. Perkins.*

LE LOING (At. & Ch. de la Seine Maritime, Le Trait, 4th April, 1927). Displacement : 3,481 tons *standard* ; 9,900 tons full load. Dimensions : 503½ × 50½ × 25 feet. Guns : 2—3·9 inch, 2—3 inch AA. 2 sets 4-cycle single-acting Diesel engines by Burmeister & Wain. H.P. : 4,100 = 13·5 kts. (exceeded on trials). Carries 5,900 tons oil. Constructed on Isherwood system. Complement, 70.

AUBE. 1921 *Photo, H. Freund.*

AUBE (July, 1920), **DURANCE** (1920), **RANCE** (July, 1921), all by Lorient D.Y. 1,055 tons. Complement, 70. Dimensions : 242¾ × 38 × 15¾ feet. Guns : 2—3 inch AA. Machinery : Breguet turbines. S.H.P. : 1,000 = 10 kts. Radius : 1,580 miles at 10 kts. Capacity for 1,500 tons of oil.

1921 *Photo, H. Freund.*

DORDOGNE (ex-*San Isidoro*, Armstrong, 1914). Displacement, 7,333 tons. 15,160 tons D.W. Carries 13,000 tons oil. Dimensions : 530 × 66½ × 29 feet. Guns : 2—6·1 inch. H.P. 4,150 = 11·7 kts. Refitted in 1937.

Oilers.—*continued.*

1920 *Photo H Freund.*

GARONNE (1911). 3,533 tons. Dimensions : 394 × 50¾ × 27¼ feet. Guns : 2—3·9 inch. H.P. 2,600 = 11 kts. Carries 5,800 tons oil as cargo. Complement, 65.

(Now painted light grey.) 1931 *Photo.*

RHÔNE (1910). 2,785 tons. Dimensions : 369 × 45 × 25 feet. H.P. : 2,100 = 11 kts. Carries 4,000 tons oil as cargo. Complement : 57.

Transports, Supply Ships (*Soutiens d'Escadre*) **and Refrigerator Ships** (*Navires Frigorifiques*).

1935, *courtesy Mons. H. Le Masson.*

GOLO (F. & C. de la Gironde, Bordeaux, July 8, 1933). Displacement : 2,152 tons *standard* ; deadweight capacity : 1,300 tons. Dimensions : 274¾ (*p.p.*), 294½ (*o.a.*) × 44⅓ × 15¾ feet. Guns : 2—3 inch, 2—37 mm. AA. Machinery : 2 Burmeister & Wain Diesels by Penhoët. B.H.P. : 1,850 = 12·5 kts. (13 kts. on trials.) Has Yourkevitch special hull form.

AUSTRAL 1938, *Capt. M. Adam.*

AUSTRAL (ex-*Léon Poret*), **BOREAL** (ex-*Remy-Chuinard*). (La Ciotat, 1927). Purchased 1937, and converted into Refrigerator Ships. Displacement : 2,270 tons. Dimensions : 208 × 33½ × 15 feet. Guns : 1—3 inch. Machinery : Triple expansion. H.P. : 1,200 = 11 kts. Oil fuel.

1936, *Capt. M. Adam* (added 1937).

AUDE (ex-*Chateau Lafite*). (Ch. de la Seine Maritime, 1924). Displacement : 1,820 tons. Deadweight capacity : 3,360 tons. Dimensions : 279¾ × 39½ × 20½ feet. Machinery : Triple expansion. I.H.P. : 1,700 = 10 kts.

CHAMPLAIN (April, 1919), **ALLIER** (ex-*Primauguet*, April, 1919), both by Brest D.Y. 521 tons. Complement : 40. Dimensions : 167⅓ × 26¼ × 13¾ feet. Guns : 1—3 inch. H.P. : 1,100 = 10 kts. Coal : 80 tons.

FORFAIT. 1927 *Photo, H. Freund.*

COËTLOGON. 1930 *Photo, M. Bar.*

COËTLOGON (June, 1919), **FORFAIT** (1920), **HAMELIN*** (1920), by Ch. de Bretagne, Nantes. 622 tons. Dimensions : 168 × 26 × 17 feet. Guns : 2—3·9 inch, 1 M.G. I.H.P. : 1,200 = 12 kts. Triple expansion engines. 1 screw. 2 cylindrical boilers. Coal : 80 tons. 850 miles endurance.

* Usually employed as seaplane tender.

JEANNE ET GENEVIÈVE (1917). 620 tons. Dimensions 147 × 24 × 12½ feet.

Transports de Personnel

POULMIC.   1939, *Captain M. Adam.*

LANVEOC, POULMIC (F. et C. de la Mediterranée, Graville, 1937). Displacement : 350 tons. Dimensions : 121⅓ × 26½ × 10 feet. Diesel engine. H.P. : 540 = 12 kts.

Fleet Tugs
(All fitted with reciprocating engines.)

Photo Wanted

BUFFLE (May 4, 1939). Laid down 1938 by A. & C. de Bretagne. Displacement : 1,115 tons. Complement : 32. Dimensions : 167⅓ × 33 × — feet. Machinery : 2 sets Triple expansion. I.H.P. : 2,000 = 12 kts.

Building.

ACTIF, APPLIQUE, ATTENTIF, CÉPET, COTENTIN, CHAMPION, TÉBESSA. All laid down 1938, *Actif* by Ch. de la Loire, Nantes, *Tébessa* by F. & C. de la Méditerranée, La Seyne, *Cépet* and *Cotentin* by Ch. Dubigeon, Nantes, others by F. & C. de la Gironde, Bordeaux. Displacement : 672 tons. Dimensions : 114¾ × 27¾ × feet. Machinery : Triple expansion. I.H.P. : 1,000 = 11 kts.

Fleet Tugs—*continued.*

VALEUREUX (1930). Of similar type to above.

FORT, TENACE (1933). Displacement : 600 tons. H.P. : 1,000 = 13 kts.

LABORIEUX (1930). Displacement : 876 tons. I.H.P. : 2,000 = 11 kts.

SIX-FOURS (1920). Displacement : 590 tons. I.H.P. : 1,500 = 10 kts.

FAISAN (1919), **PAON** (1918), **PIGEON** (1918). Displacement : 767 tons. I.H.P. : 800 = 11 kts.

HIPPOPOTAME (1918), **MAMMOUTH** (1918), **MASTODONTE** (1919), **RHINOCEROS** (1918). Displacement : 954 tons. I.H.P. : 1,800 = 12 kts.

ATHLETE (1918), **LUTTEUR** (1919). Displacement : 590 tons. I.H.P. : 750 = 9 kts.

HERON II ((1918). Displacement : 667 tons. I.H.P. : 850 = 10·5 kts.

PINGOUIN, PINTADE (1917). Displacement : 700 tons. I.H.P. : 700 = 10 kts.

RAMIER (1917). Displacement : 685 tons. I.H.P. : 750 = 10 kts.

NESSUS (1913). Displacement : 590 tons. I.H.P. : 1,500 = 12 kts.

SAMSON (1906). Displacement : 650 tons. I.H.P. : 1,000 = 11 kts.

GOLIATH (1903). Displacement : 1,127 tons. I.H.P. : 1,450 = 11 kts.

CYCLOPE (1901). Displacement : 650 tons. I.H.P. : 1,000 = 13 kts.

Sailing Vessels.
(Used for training purposes)

Building.

LA GRANDIÈRE. Building, to replace *Zélee*, below, for service on Pacific Station. Funds originally voted for construction of river gunboat *Jouffroy d'Abbans* (not to be built) have been appropriated for this purpose.

L'ETOILE   1936, *M. Le Masson.*

LA BELLE-POULE, L'ÉTOILE. Both built by Chantiers de Normandie (Fécamp), 1932. Displacement : 227 tons. Dimensions : 128 (*o.a.*) × 23⅔ × 11¾ feet. Accommodation for 3 officers, 30 cadets, 5 petty officers, 12 seamen. Machinery : Sulzer-Diesels. B.H.P. : 120 = 6 kts.

ZÉLÉE (purchased 1931). 197 tons. Dimensions : 151 × 29½ × 10 feet. Auxiliary Diesel. B.H.P. : 90 = 7 kts. Guns : 1—3 pdr. For service in Oceania and Tahiti.

ALOUETTE (1929). 44 tons. Dimensions : 60 × 20⅓ × 10 feet.

MESANGE (1921). 60 tons. Dimensions : 56¾ × 21½ × 10 feet.

MUTIN (1927). 54 tons. Dimensions : 36¼ × 20 × 10¾ feet.

Chief of Admiralty : Grossadmiral Dr. (h.c.) E. Raeder.

Naval Attaché, London : Kapitän z. See L. Siemens.

Uniforms.

INSIGNIA OF RANK ON SLEEVES

| Grossadmiral and Generaladmiral. (*Admiral of the Fleet.*) | Admiral. (*Vice-Ad.*) | Vizeadmiral. (*Vice-Ad.*) | Konteradmiral. (*Rear-Ad.*) | Kapitän zur See (*Captain.*) & Fregattenkapitän (*Commander*) | Korvettenkapitän. (*Lieut.-Com.*) | Kapitänleutnant. (*Lieut., senior.*) | Oberleut. z. See. (*Lieut., junior.*) | Leutnant z. See. (*Sub-Lieut.*) |

Flaggoffiziere. — Stabsoffiziere. — Subalternoffiziere.

NOTE.—In above sketch, a *star* should replace devices which appear in the 5 junior ranks.

Uniforms and distinguishing marks of rank are the same for officers of all branches of the service ; but in place of the star on the sleeve, which distinguishes the military branch, there is worn by :

    Engineer Officers, a pinion wheel
    Medical Officers, the rod of Æsculapius   } As in sketches above.
    Accountant Officers, the winged staff of Hermes

The difference between a *Kapitän zur See* and a *Fregattenkapitän* is indicated by stars on the shoulder straps.

Kommodores wear the same sleeve stripes as a *Kapitän zur See*, but with the cords and shoulder bands of a Flag Officer.

Flags.

ENSIGN

NATIONAL FLAG AND JACK

STATE SERVICE FLAG (Fleet Auxiliaries)

NATIONAL FLAG FOR MERCHANT SHIPS COMMANDED BY NAVAL RESERVE OFFICERS

FÜHRER'S STANDARD

C-IN-C. OF NAVY

ADMIRAL

VICE ADMIRAL

REAR ADMIRAL

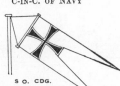

(a) COMMODORE WHEN FLOWN FROM MAIN MAST
(b) SENIOR OFFICER WHEN FLOWN FROM UPPER SIGNAL YARD

S O. CDG. MINESWEEPING DESTROYER OR SUBMARINE FLOTILLAS

COMMANDER OF A FLOTILLA

PENNANT

WHEN FLOWN FROM MAIN MAST, BUT LEADER'S PENNANT WHEN FLOWN FROM UPPER SIGNAL YARD

Black	■
White	□
Yellow	▦
R	⊞

Naval Guns.

Calibre		Usual Naval Designation.	Length in cals.	Date of Model.	Weight of Gun.	Weight of A.P. shot.	Initial Velocity.	Maximum penetration, direct impact against K.O. at			Danger space against average ships at			Approximate Muzzle Energy.
								9000 yds.	6000 yds.	3000 yds.	10,000	5000	3000	
inch.	c/m.				tons.	lbs.	foot-secs.	in.	in.	in.	yards.	yards.	yards.	foot tons.
15	38·1	...		'36	...	670	...	...	...	...	...	...	...	...
11	28			'28										
11	28		40	'01	32·2	661·4	2756	6	10	14	150	450	740	31,600
8	20.3													
5·9	15		50		5·5		3084	...	...	...	...	...	...	6,690
5·9	15		45	'09	5	101·4 {|	...	...	...	...	...	200	420	5,990
5	12.7						2920	...	...	5	...			
4·1	10·5		45	'16		38·2	...	...	...	...	...	...	...	...
4·1	10·5		50	'28										
4·1	10·5		A.A.											
3·5	90		A.A.											

Brass cartridge cases to all guns.

11 inch, 40 cal., M. '01 in *Schlesien* and *Schleswig-Holstein.*

Lesser guns : 3·4 inch (88 m/m) firing 22 lb. projectiles in modern and 15 lb. in old models.

A.A. guns : 4·1 inch, 3·5 inch on H.A. mounts ("Flak").

Projectiles : Guns of 11 inch and over fire A.P., Ersatz A.P., H.E., and common shell.

All models have the recoil utilized to return the gun to firing position for pieces over 5.9 inch. In 5.9 in. springs are employed. German guns have a lower muzzle pressure than normally obtains.

Personnel.

Total personnel, 1938, 75,000 officers and men. (Since increased)

Colour of Ships.

Light Grey, *except* Sail Training Ships, which are white with yellow superstructures.

Mercantile Marine.

(From "Lloyd's Register." 1939 figures.)
2,466 vessels of 4,492,708 gross tonnage.

Navy Estimates.

Later figures not communicated.
{
1930-31, 191,597,200 marks
1931-32, 191,855,550 „
1932-33, 187,339,400 „
1933-34, 186,243,200 „
}

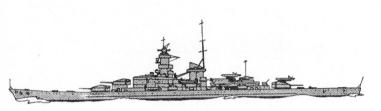

GNEISENAU

ADMIRAL HIPPER *class.*

LEIPZIG
(Mainmast now taller and a different type of crane fitted.)

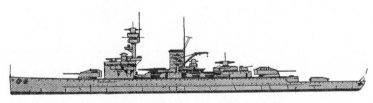

SCHARNHORST.

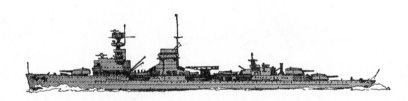

NÜRNBERG.
(Mizzenmast since added and funnel modified.)

DEUTSCHLAND.

KÖLN *Class.*
(Insets : KÖNIGSBERG left ; KARLSRUHE right).

SCHEER.
SPEE.

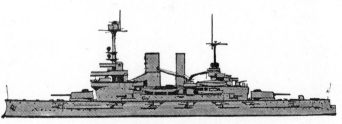

SCHLESIEN.
SCHLESWIG-HOLSTEIN.

EMDEN.

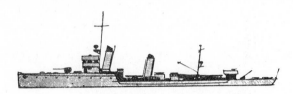

G 7. 8. 10. 11.
(T 23 similar but no Torpedo Tubes.)

C. van Bevern.

T 196.

E. Jungmann class.

Wolf Class.
(Möwe Class as part sketch.)

L. Maass Class.

D. von Roeder class.
(Some have straight bow and S.L. low on mast.)

Tanga.

Erwin Wassner.

Isar, Lech.

Grille.

Saar.

Tsingtau.

Brummer.

Bremse.

Königin Luise, Hai, F 1, F 2, F 4, F 5, F 7—10

"M" Class.
(JAGD, PELIKAN and others, no mainmast.)

M 1–24

ELBE, WESER.

MEMEL.

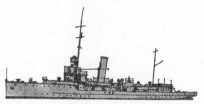

NAUTILUS *Type.*
(Also FRAUENLOB with taller mainmast.)

NETTELBECK.

METEOR.

LAUTING.

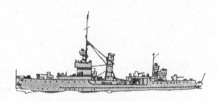

FUCHS.

DRACHE.

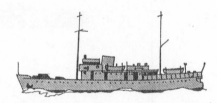

PAUL BENEKE.

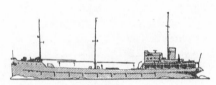

MOSEL.

HAVEL.

NORDSEE.

STRAHL.

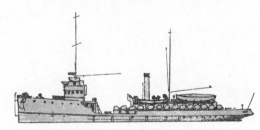

M.T. 1, 2.
(Now have AA. gun on fo'c'sle.)

SUNDEVALL.

HELA.

TRAWLERS
(vary in details.)

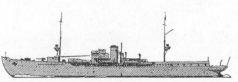

WEICHSEL.

U 1 *Class.*
(Coastal type.)

U 27 *Class.*
(Medium type.)

U 25, 26.
(Oceangoing type.)

Launch of TIRPITZ.   1939, *Wide World Photos.*

Bismarck Class—4 ships.

BISMARCK (Feb. 14, 1939), **TIRPITZ** (April 1, 1939), "**H**" and "**I**" (building).

Standard displacement : 35,000 tons.   Complement :

Length (*w.l.*), 729⅓ feet.   Beam, 118 feet.   Draught, 26 feet (*mean*).

Guns :   Aircraft :   Armour :
  8—15 inch   **4,** with 2 catapults.   Not reported.
  12—5·9 inch

Machinery : Geared turbines. 2 shafts. High pressure water-tube boilers. Designed speed : Probably 30 kts.

Name.	Builder.	Laid down.	Completed.
Bismarck	Blohm & Voss	1936	
Tirpitz	Wilhelmshaven	1936	
H	Deutsche Werke	1937	
I	Wilhelmshaven	1938	

Notes.—Apparently *Bismarck* will have a straight stem, and *Tirpitz* one of the overhanging type. It has been reported that "*H*" and "*I*" may be 40,000-ton ships, but confirmation of this is lacking.

SCHARNHORST.   1939.

GNEISENAU.   *Differences* : Bow, funnel, stepping of foremast.   1939, *W. Schäfer.*

(Scharnhorst Class—2 ships)

SCHARNHORST (October 3, 1936).
GNEISENAU (December 8, 1936).

Standard displacement: 26,000 tons. Complement: 1,461.
Length (*w.l.*) 741½ feet. Beam, 98½ feet. Draught, 24⅔ feet (*mean*).

Guns:

    9—11 inch.
    12—5·9 inch.
    14—4·1 inch A.A.
    16—37 mm. AA.

Aircraft: 4

Catapults : 2
(No torpedo tubes.)

Armour : (Unofficial)

    12″—13″ Belt amid-
       ships, 3″—4″ ends.
    12″ Turrets.
    6″ Decks.

Note to Plan.—Hangar between funnel
   and after superstructure.

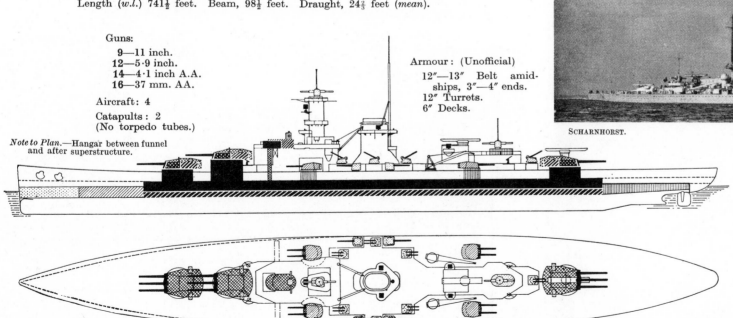

SCHARNHORST.   1939, *W. Schäfer.*

Machinery : Geared turbines, combined with Diesels for cruising speeds. 3 shafts. High pressure water tube boilers. Designed speed : 27 kts., considerably exceeded on trials.

Name.	Builder.	Laid down.	Completed.
Scharnhorst	Wilhelmshaven	} 1934	{ 7 Jan.,1939
Gneisenau	Deutsche Werke		{ 21 May,1938

General Notes.— Names commemorate those of 2 cruisers sunk at the Battle of the Falklands, Dec. 8, 1914.

Gunnery Notes.—11 inch calibre was accepted for these ships in order to allow a greater proportion of weight to protection.

Special Note.

One of these 3 ships was damaged by air bombs on September 4, 1939.

(Deutschland class—3 ships.)

DEUTSCHLAND (May 19th, 1931.)

ADMIRAL SCHEER (April 1st, 1933.)

ADMIRAL GRAF SPEE (June 30th, 1934.)

Standard displacement, 10,000 tons. Complement, 926.

Length, 593 (*w.l.*). 609¼ (*o.a.*) feet. Beam, 67½ feet (*Deutschland*), 69½ (*Scheer*), 70⅖ (*Spee*). Draught, 21⅓.

Guns :
 6—11 inch
 8—5·9 inch.
 6—4·1 inch AA.
 8—3 pdr. AA.
 10—M.G.
Torpedo tubes :
 8—21 inch (*above water*).
Aircraft:
 2, with catapult.

Note to Plan.—This relates only to *Deutschland*. Later ships vary as shown in separate plan.

Armour : (In *Scheer*, average thickness of armour is slightly less, but it is spread over a larger area.)
 Belt—4″ with 1½″ internally.
 Turrets : 4″ bases.
  5½″ faces.
  2—3″ sides.
 C.T. 5″
  2″ roof.
 Deck 1½″—2¼″
  3″ over magazine.
 External bulges.

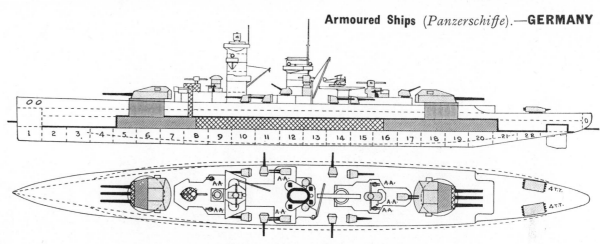

Plan of ADMIRAL SCHEER and ADMIRAL GRAF SPEE.

Note—Following alterations in appearance were effected in 1937. 2 new cranes have replaced the former one ; a small deckhouse has been added at base of catapult ; derrick posts have been cut down and S.L. rearranged on a platform around upper part of funnel. There is a pole mast on after director.

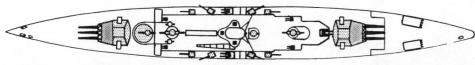

Machinery : 8 sets M.A.N. Diesels, of 6,750 H.P. each. 2 shafts. Total H.P. : 54,000 = 26 kts. Fuel : 1,200 tons. Radius : 10,000 miles at 15 kts.

General Notes.—These are the first ships of such size to have electrically welded hulls and to be propelled by Diesel engines. By these means a saving in weight of 550 tons is said to be effected. Are officially rated as " Armoured Ships " (*Panzerschiffe*), and popularly referred to as " Pocket Battleships." Actually , they are equivalent to armoured cruisers of an exceptionally powerful type. Cost £3,750,000 = £375 per ton.

Gunnery Notes.—The 11 inch guns are a new Krupp model, firing a 670 lb. projectile, with a range of 30,000 yards and an elevation of 60°.

Machinery Note.—8 sets compressorless double-acting two-stroke M.A.N. Diesels each of 6,750 B.H.P. at 450 r.p.m. Each group of four drives a single propeller shaft through Vulcan gear, which reduces speed to 250 r.p.m. Net weight of engines about 17·6 lb. per b.h.p. excluding Vulcan drive, shafting, propeller and air reservoirs. Total weight of whole plant about 48·5 lb. per b.h.p. Electrically welded plate framing employed for the first time. It is stated that Diesels have operated satisfactorily in service, without undue vibration or noise from exhaust ; but unofficial reports suggest that they have not entirely answered expectations in these respects.

AD. SCHEER.

1935.

(*Additional photographs will be found on following page*)

Name.	Builder.	Laid down	Completed.
Deutschland	Deutsche Werke	5/ 2/29	1/4/33
Ad. Scheer	Wilhelmshaven	25/ 6/31	12/11/34
Ad. Graf Spee	Wilhelmshaven	1/10/32	6/1/36

SPEE (Now as in detail view).   1937, *R. Perkins*.

DEUTSCHLAND.

SPEE.   1938, *A. Klein*.

1938, *Schäfer*

Aircraft Carriers.

(*Flugzeugträger.*)

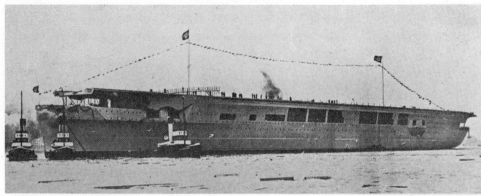

Launch of GRAF ZEPPELIN.   *Added* 1939, *Wide World Photos.*

GRAF ZEPPELIN (Deutsche Werke, Kiel, Dec. 8, 1938) and **" B "** Both laid down in 1936, under the Programme for that year. *Standard* displacement : 19,250 tons.

Length: 820¼ feet.   Beam : 88½ feet.   Draught : 18⅓ feet (*mean*).

Guns :   Aircraft : 40.   Armour :
  16—5·9 inch   Casemates for 5·9 inch
  10—4·1 inch AA.   guns. No bulges. Also
  22—37 mm. AA.   *see* notes.

(*For Plan, see Addenda.*)

Machinery : Geared turbines.   Speed : 32 kts.

Notes.—Flight deck reported to measure 790 × 88½ feet. Sides appear to be armoured for two-thirds of length amidships, and to a lesser extent as far as bow, which is of bulbous form. Will have island superstructure on starboard side.

HIPPER.   1939, *Dr. Erich Gröner.*

Heavy Cruisers (*Schwere Kreuzer*).

(HIPPER CLASS—5 SHIPS).

HIPPER.   1939.

HIPPER.   1939.

BLÜCHER (June 8, 1937), **ADMIRAL HIPPER** (Feb. 6, 1937), **PRINZ EUGEN** (Aug. 22, 1938), **SEYDLITZ** (Jan. 19, 1939), **LÜTZOW** (July 1, 1939). *Standard* displacement : 10,000 tons. Complement :

Dimensions : 639¾ × 69¾ × 15½ feet (first 2 ships) ; others, 654½ × 71 × 15 feet.

Guns :   Aircraft : 3.   Armour :
  8—8 inch   5″ Vert. Side.
  12—4·1 inch AA.   Catapult : 1.   (Unofficial)
  12—37 mm. AA.

Torpedo Tubes :   *Plan in Addenda.*
  12—21 inch (tripled).

Machinery : Geared turbines. 3 shafts. High pressure watertube boilers. S.H.P. : 80,000 = 32 kts.

Programme	Name	Builder	Laid down	Completed
1935	Blücher	Deutsche Werke	1935	8.39
	Hipper	Blohm & Voss	1935	29.4.39
1936	Prinz Eugen	Germania	1936	To be 1940
	Seydlitz	Deschimag		
	Lützow	do.		

225

P

NÜRNBERG (Now has cinder screen to funnel)

1936, *Renard*.

(*Leichte Kreuzer*).

"M", "N", "O" and "P". *Standard* displacement: 8,000 tons. Armed with 5·9 inch guns. First pair laid down in 1937 and 1938; second pair begun early in 1939.

NÜRNBERG (Deutsche Werke, Kiel, Dec. 8, 1934.)
Standard Displacement: 6,000 tons.   Complement: 656.

Dimensions: 557¾ (*p.p.*), 603 (*o.a.*) × 54 × 14¼ feet (*mean* draught).

Guns:
9—5·9 inch, 50 cal.
8—3·5 inch AA.
8—3 pdr. AA.
4 M.G.

Torpedo Tubes:
12—21 inch, *above water*
(tripled).

Aircraft:
2, with catapult.

Armour:
3″—4″ Vert. Side.
2″ Gunhouses.
3″ C.T.
Side armour is more extensive than in *Leipzig*, both horizontally and vertically but average thickness is slightly less.

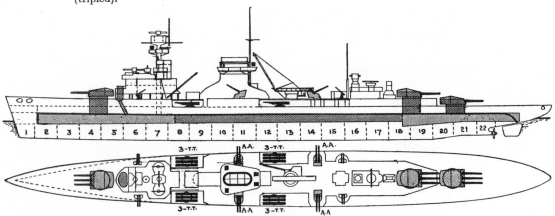

Machinery: Geared turbines. S.H.P.: 60,000, with Diesels of 12,000 B.H.P. for cruising. Speed: 32 kts. 3 shafts. Boilers: 6 Marine type.

Other details understood to be generally similar to *Leipzig*, of which she is a slightly improved edition. Laid down early in 1934 and commissioned at beginning of November, 1935.

NÜRNBERG.

1938, *Ferd. Urbahns*.

LEIPZIG (Wilhelmshaven, Oct. 18, 1929).

Standard Displacement: 6,000 tons.

Dimensions: 544 (*p.p.*) 580 (*o.a.*) × 53½ × 15¾ ft.

Complement: 615.

Guns:
9—5·9 inch, 50 cal.
6—3·5 inch, AA.
8—3 pdr. AA.
4 M.G.
Torpedo tubes:
12—21 inch, *above water*
(tripled).
Aircraft:
2, with catapult.

Armour:
3"—4" Vert. Side.
2" Gun houses.
2" C.T.

LEIPZIG. (A different type of crane has since been fitted).

1938, *Schäfer.*

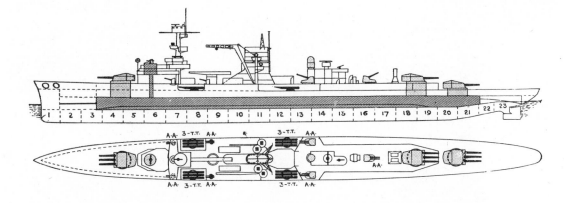

Machinery: Geared turbines, 60,000 S.H.P. with Diesel engines of 12,000 B.H.P. Speed: 32 kts. Triple screws (centre—system " Helix "). Boilers: 6 " Marine " type (modified Schulz-Thornycroft), double-ended oil burning. Centre shaft Diesel driven: can be used for cruising or combined with turbines to give full speed. Radius of action with Diesel engines at 14·5 kts: 3,800 miles; with turbines at 14·5 kts.: 3,200 miles = 7,000 miles. Radius could be greatly augmented if all bunkers were filled with Diesel fuel only. Fuel: 1,200 tons + 378 tons Diesel fuel.

Machinery Notes.—Variable pitch propeller on inner shaft, which "feathers" when Turbines only are used. Under Diesels alone, wing shafts are spun by 500 b.h.p. motors through spur gearing from centre shaft, thus obviating loss of 3,000 b.h.p. if they were allowed to turn idly. Plant is four 7-cyl. M.A.N. two-stroke double-acting compressorless Diesels. Engine speed = 600 r.p.m. Four engines to each shaft, through Vulcan hyd. clutches and reducing gear, giving shaft speed of 400 r.p.m. Weight of machinery, including scavenging blower and its driving engine, and auxiliaries to propelling plant = 12·1 lb. per b.h.p. (5·5 kg.). Turbines are Germania type.

General Notes.—Laid down at Wilhelmshaven April 18th, 1928. Completed in 1931. Modified *Königsberg* design with after turrets in centre-line and uptakes trunked into one funnel: fitted with bulges below water-line which are to be filled with oil fuel and are designed to improve speed lines rather than to act as a means of protection.

(See note above)

1935, *courtesy "Taschenbuch der Kriegsflotten"*

(Königsberg Class—3 Ships.)

KÖNIGSBERG (March 26th, 1927), **KARLSRUHE**
(August 20th, 1927), **KÖLN** (May 23rd, 1928).

Displacement, 6000 tons.   Complement, 571.

Length, 554 feet 5½ inches (*w.l.*), 570 feet (*o.a.*),

Beam, 49 feet 10½ inches.

Designed draught, 17 feet 9 inches.

Guns :

   9—5·9 inch, 50 cal.
   6—3·5 inch AA.
   8—3 pdr. AA.
   4 M.G.

Armour :

   3″—4″ Vert. Side
   2″ Gun Houses
   3″ C.T.

Torpedo tubes :
   12—21 inch, *above
water*, tripled.

Aircraft : 2, with catapult.

(Removed temporarily from *Köln* and another ship, 1938.)

KARLSRUHE.   (Now has twin AA. guns as in sister ships).   1936, *Renard.*

Machinery : Geared turbines, with 10 cyl. 4-stroke Diesel engines for cruising purposes.
Boilers : Schulz-Thornycroft. Designed H.P. : 65,000 = 32 kts. Fuel : 1,200 tons oil + 300 tons
Diesel fuel. Radius : at 14 kts., 5,500 miles ; at 10 kts., 10,000.

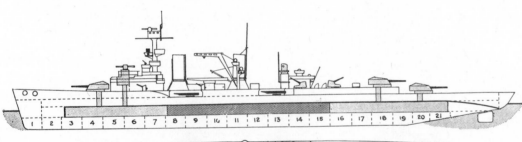

KÖNIGSBERG.   *August*, 1939.

Name	Building Yard	Begun	Completed	Trials	Boilers	Best recent speed
Königsberg	Wilhelmshaven	12/4/26	Spring, 1929		6 Schulz-Thorny-croft	32·2
Karlsruhe	Deutsche Werke, Kiel	27/7/26	Autumn, 1929			
Köln	Wilhelmshaven	7/8/26	Jan. 1930			

General Notes.—Every possible expedient for saving weight has been employed in these ships.   A very high grade of
steel was selected, and electric welding has taken the place of riveting.

   Königsberg is a gunnery training ship.

Gunnery Notes.—3—5·9 inch can fire simultaneously at rate of 6 salvoes a minute, and range to 20,000 yards.
Disposition of after turrets is governed by arrangement of ammunition handling rooms.

Engineering Notes.—Designed horse-power of turbines is 63,000, and of Diesels, 2,000.

   Königsberg originally had Schichau Diesels, but these have been replaced by Germania type.

KÖLN, with aircraft gear removed.   1938, *Ferd. Urbahns.*

EMDEN (Wilhelmshaven, 7th January, 1925).

Standard displacement, 5,400 tons.   Complement, 534.

Dimensions : 493¾ (*w.l.*), 508½ (*o.a.*) × 47 × 17½ feet (*mean* draught), 21 feet (*max.*).

Guns :
8—5·9 inch 45 cal.
3—3·5 inch AA.
4—M.G.
Torpedo tubes :
4—19·7 inch (*above water*).

Armour :
3″—4″ Vert. Side   ....
2″ Gun Houses   ....
3″ C.T.

1937, *Renard.*

EMDEN.

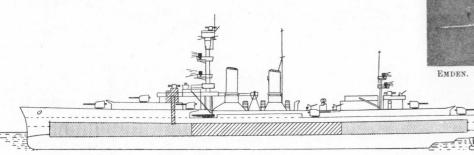

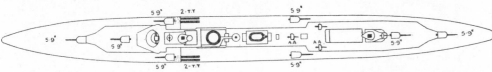

Machinery : Geared turbines.   Boilers : 10 Schulz-Thornycroft "Marine" type (Converted to oil-burning 1934).   Designed H.P. 46,500 = 29 kts.   Oil fuel : 1,260 tons.

Engineering Notes.—Designed to maintain a speed of 27·5 kts. in fair weather.   Revs. per minute : 2435 H.P. turbines. 1568 L.P. turbines, geared down to 295 R.P.M. on propellers.   On trials designed speed was slightly exceeded with 46,500 H.P.

General Notes.—The tubular foremast is about 5 feet in diameter.   Masting modified and second funnel heightened, 1926–27.   *Emden* was designed for foreign service, particular attention being paid to accommodation.   Laid down in December, 1921, commissioned 15th October, 1925.   Now used as sea-going training ship for cadets.

Destroyers.

D. von ROEDER.

1938 *Schäfer.*

K. GALSTER (W. HEIDKAMP similar).

1939, *Schäfer.*

14 *Roeder* class : **Diether von Roeder** (1937), **Hans Lüdemann** (1937), **Hermann Künne** (1937), **Karl Galster, Wilhelm Heidkamp, Anton Schmidt,** and 8 more.   Laid down 1936–38.   Standard displacement : 1,811 tons.   Dimensions : 384 × 38¼ × 9½ feet.   Guns : 5—5 inch. 4—37 mm. A.A.   Tubes : 8—21 inch quadrupled.   Speed : 36 kts.   *D. von Roeder* (Pendant No. 51) commissioned Aug. 29, 1938 ; *H. Lüdemann* (53), Oct. 8, 1938 ; and *H. Künne* (52), Jan. 12, 1939 ; *K. Galster* (42), March 21, 1939 ; *W. Heidkamp* (43) and *A. Schmidt* (41) later in 1939.

Note.—First 6 built by Deschimag, Bremen, under 1936 Programme.

Destroyers—*continued*

16 Maass Class.

T. RIEDEL.   *1937, Renard.*

M. SCHULTZ.   *1937, Schafer.*

4 *Deutsche Werke* : **Leberecht Maass, Georg Thiele, Max Schultz, Richard Beitzen** (all 1935).

5 *Germania*: **Paul Jacobi, Theodor Riedel, Hermann Schoemann, Bruno Heinemann, Wolfgang Zenker** (All 1936)

4 *Deschimag* : **Hans Lody, Bernd Von Arnim, Erich Giese** (all 1936), **Erich Koellner** (1937).

3 *Blohm & Voss* : **Friedrich Ihn** (1935), **Erich Steinbrinck** (1936), **Friedrich Eckoldt** (1937).

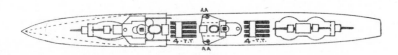

Standard Displacement : 1,625 tons. Complement : 283. Dimensions : 374 × 37 × 9¼ feet.
Guns : 5—5 inch, 4—37 mm. AA. Tubes : 8—21 inch, quadrupled.
Machinery : Geared turbines. S.H.P. = 40,000 = 36 kts. High pressure watertube boilers.

Note.—Notable feature of these torpedo craft is the first appearance in German flotillas of quadruple torpedo tubes.
First of class were laid down in autumn of 1934, latest in autumn of 1935. All authorised under 1934 Programme, and completed by end of 1938 or early 1939. Pendant Numbers, as so far allotted : *L. Maass*, fitted as leader, has none. *R. Beitzen*, 11 ; *M. Schultz*, 12 ; *G. Thiele*, 13 ; *P. Jacobi*, 21 ; *T. Riedel*, 22 ; *H. Schoemann*, 23 ; *E. Steinbrinck*, 31 ; *F. Eckoldt*, 32 ; *F. Ihn*, 33 ; *B. von Arnim*, 81 ; *E. Giese*, 62 ; *E. Koellner*, 83 ; *W. Zenker*, 61 ; *H. Lody*, 82 ; *B. Heinemann*, 63. The first figure in each case refers to the flotilla, the second to position of ship therein.

Torpedo Boats.

30 boats: **T1—T18** (completing), **T19—30** (building), (*T*11 launched in March, 1939 and *T*13 on June 15, 1939). *Standard* displacement : 600 tons. Dimensions : 267 × 28¼ × 6¼ feet. Guns : 1—4·1 inch, 2—37 mm. Tubes : 6—21 inch (tripled). Speed : 36 kts. First 12 laid down 1936. Some building by F. Schichau, Elbing, others by Deschimag, Bremen, under 1935–1938 programmes.

LUCHS.   *1939, Renard, Kiel.*

6 *Wilhelmshaven Yard* : **Iltis, Wolf** (both Oct. 12th, 1927), **Jaguar, Leopard, Luchs, Tiger** (all March, 1928). Laid down 1927. Standard Displacement : 800 tons (1,000 tons deep load). Dimensions : 292 (*p.p.*), 304 (*o.a.*) × 28 × 9 feet. Guns : 3—5 inch, only in *Leopard, Luchs* ; 3—4·1 inch in others ; and in all, 2—1 pdr. AA. T.T. : 6—21 inch (tripled parallel). Designed S.H.P. : 25,000 = 34 kts. Geared turbines and Schulz-Thornycroft boilers. Oil fuel : 330 tons. Complement : 123. Are of same general type as *Möwe* class, with minor improvements . *Jaguar* employed as Gunnery School Tender.

FALKE.   *1939, Dr. Erich Gröner.*

6 *Wilhelmshaven Yard* : **Möwe** (March 4th, 1926), **Albatros, Greif, Seeadler** (all three July 15th, 1926), **Falke, Kondor** (both Sept. 22nd, 1926). Standard Displacement : 800 tons (960 tons deep load). Dimensions : 277¾ × 27½ × 9¼ feet draught. Guns : 3—4·1 inch, 50 cal., 2—1 pdr. AA. T.T. : 6—21 inch (tripled parallel). Geared turbines. 3 Schulz-Thornycroft boilers. Designed S.H.P. 24,000 = 33 kts. (exceeded on trials). Oil fuel : 320 tons. Complement, 121.

Notes.—Laid down under 1924 and 1925 Programmes, as *W* 102-107. *Möwe* commissioned October 1st, 1926, others passed into service during 1927, replacing old destroyer *T* 175 and the worn-out torpedo boats of *T* 149 type. Have longitudinal framing and double bottom to hull. Guns said to elevate to 80°. The cost of these vessels is extraordinarily high, working out at about £215 per ton.

Identification letters, painted on bows : Aᴛ, *Albatros* ; Fᴋ, *Falke* ; Gʀ, *Greif*; Iᴛ, *Iltis* ; Jʀ, *Jaguar* ; Kᴏ, *Kondor*; Lᴘ, *Leopard* ; Lᴜ, *Luchs* ; Mö, *Möwe* ; Sᴇ, *Seeadler* ; Tɢ, *Tiger* ; Wʟ, *Wolf*.

WOLF and MÖWE types.

MÖWE has pointed stern.

SPECIAL NOTE.

Seven of the Submarines on this page were destroyed during September, 1939.

15+11 Oceangoing type.

11 Vessels of this type are building under the 1939 Programme. Guns: 1—4·1 inch.

24+17 Seagoing type.

17 Vessels of this type are building under the 1939 Programme. Guns: 1—3·5 inch.

U 37   1938, *Schäfer.*

1938, *Schäfer.*

U 45—55. (Germania, 1938); ***U 69—71*** (1939). Displacement: 517 tons. Complement: 35. Dimensions: 213½ × 19½ × 13 feet. Armament: 1—3·5 inch, 1—1 pdr. A.A., 5—21 inch tubes (4 bow, 1 stern). H.P.: 2,100 = 16·5/8 kts. First 7 laid down early in 1937, others begun by end of year. *U* 45 commissioned June 25, 1938. *U* 46, Nov. 2, 1938; *U* 47, Dec. 7, 1938; *U* 51, Aug. 6, 1938; *U* 52, Feb. 4, 1939; *U* 53, June 24, 1939.

U 41   1939, *Dr. Erich Gröner.*

U 37—44 (Deschimag, 1938), ***U 64—68*** (1939). Displacement: 740 tons. Complement: 40. Dimensions: 244½ × 20½ × 13½ feet. Armament: 1—4·1 inch 45 cal., 2—1 pdr. A.A., 6—21 inch tubes (4 bow, 2 stern). H.P.: 3,200 = 18·5/8 kts.

Notes.—U 37 completed Aug. 4, 1938; U 39, Oct. 24, 1938; U 39, Dec. 10, 1938. These vessels may be minelayers.

U33   1936, *Schäfer.*

U 32.   1937, *Schäfer.*

U 27 to ***U 36*** (1936). Standard displacement: 500 tons. Complement, 35. Dimensions: 206⅔ × 19½ × 13 feet. Armament: 1—3·5 inch, 1—1 pdr. A.A.; 5—21 inch tubes (4 bow, 1 stern). H.P. 2,000 = 16·5/8 kts.

Notes.—Laid down under 1935 and 1936 Programmes and completed during 1936–37. *U* 33—36 built by Germania, *U* 27—32 by Deschimag.

No.	Launch	No.	Launch
U 27	12/8/36	U 32	25/2/37
U 28	14/7/36	U 33	11/6/36
U 29	29/8/36	U 34	17/7/36
U 30	8/4/36	U 35	29/9/36
U 31	25/9/36	U 36	4/11/36

U 25   1936, *Schäfer.*

U 25 (Feb. 14, 1936), ***U 26*** (March 14, 1936). Built by Deschimag, Bremen. Standard displacement: 712 tons. Complement, 40. Dimensions: 233 × 20½ × 13½ feet. Armament: 1—4·1 inch 45 cal. gun, 1—1 pdr. A.A.; 6—21 inch tubes (4 bow, 2 stern). H.P. 2,800 = 18/8 kts.

Notes.—Both laid down in 1935, under programme for that year. Commissioned April 6 and May 11, 1936, respectively.

32 Coastal type.

U 16.

1936, *Renard, Kiel.*

U 59.

1939, *Schäfer.*

U 1 to **U 24** (1935–36), **U 56** to **U 63** (1938). *Standard* displacement: 250/330 tons. Complement: 23. Dimensions: $136\frac{1}{2} \times 13 \times 12\frac{3}{8}$ feet. Armament: **1**—1 pdr. AA., **3**—21 inch torpedo tubes. H.P.: 700 = 13/7 kts. Diving limit reported to be 50 fathoms.

Appearance Note.—Of those so far reported, identification numbers are painted in *black* on C.T. of U 1—6, and in *white* on C.T. of later boats

No.	Builder	Begun	Launch	Comp.	No.	Builder	Begun	Launch	Comp.
U 1			15/6/35		17			14/11/35	
2			1/7/35		18	Germania		7/12/35	
3	Deutsche		19/7/35		19		1935	21/12/35	
5	Werke,		31/7/35		20			14/ 1/36	
4	Kiel		14/8/35		21			13/ 7/36	1936
6		1935	21/8/35	1935	22	Deschimag,	1936	29/ 7/36	
7			29/6/35		23	Bremen		28/ 8/36	
8			16/7/35		24			24/ 9/36	
9			30/7/35		56			26/11/38	
10	Germania, Kiel.		13/8/35		57			29/12/38	
11			27/8/35		58			4/2/39	
12			11/9/35		59	Deutsche	1938	39	
U 13			9/11/35	1935	60	Werke		39	
14	Deutsche	1935	28/12/35		61			15/6/39	
15	Werke		15/ 2/36	1936	62			39	
16			28/ 4/36		63			39	

U 18 sunk by collision, Nov. 1936, but was salved shortly afterwards.

Escort Vessels
(*Geleitboote*)

HAI

1937, *Renard, Kiel.*

F 1, F 2, KÖNIGIN LUISE (ex-*F 3*), **F 4, F 5, HAI** (ex-*F 6*), **F 7, F 8, F 9, F 10**.
Standard displacement: 600 tons. Complement: 124. Dimensions: 241 (*pp.*), $249\frac{1}{3}$ (*o.a.*) $\times 28\frac{3}{4} \times 8\frac{1}{4}$ feet (*mean* draught). Guns: 2—4·1 inch, 50 cal. ; 4—37 mm. A.A., 2—1 pdr. AA. Also D.C. Throwers. Machinery: Geared turbines. S.H.P.: 9,000 = 28 kts. High pressure boilers. Oil fuel. Built under 1934 Programme, and completed during 1935–36. Are fitted for minelaying. *Hai* now rated as *Flottentender*, *Königin Luise* as leader of escort vessels.

No.	Builder.	Begun	Launch	No.	Builder	Begun	Launch
F 1			1/3/35	7	Blohm & Voss,	1935	25/5/35
2			2/4/35	8	Hamburg		25/7/35
K. Luise	Germania,	1934	1/3/35	9	Wilhelmshaven	1934	11/5/35
4	Kiel		2/7/35	10			
5			14/8/35				
Hai			1/10/35				

Motor Torpedo Boats.
(*Schnellboote*)
S 26—37, under construction or projected.

S 8

1939, *Renard, Kiel*

20 boats : **S 6—25** (Lürssen, Vegesack, 1933–38). Displacement : 62 tons. Length : (*o.a.*) 93 feet. Armament : 2—19·7 inch T.T., 1—1 pdr. AA. Machinery : High speed M.A.N. Diesels or Daimler Benz petrol engines. H.P. : 2,400 = 30–36 kts. Complement : 17.

Notes.—All these boats are of wood or composite section U-form, exceptionally stout and seaworthy.

Note.—A third gunnery training ship is projected.

(*Both fitted for Minelaying.*)

1936 *Renard.*

1933 *Photo, Official*

1936 *Schäfer.*

1934 *Photo*

BRUMMER (Deschimag, Bremen, May 29, 1935.)

Standard Displacement : 2,410 tons.   Complement, 214.

Dimensions : $354\frac{1}{3} \times 44\frac{1}{3} \times 11\frac{1}{2}$ feet.

Guns : **4**—3·5 inch AA. (new model), **2**—3·5 inch AA. (of older pattern), **4**—3 pdr. AA. (Number and calibre of guns likely to vary from time to time.)

Machinery : Geared turbines. High pressure w.t. boilers. Speed : 20 kts. (in service), but believed capable of considerably more.

Notes.—Laid down 1934 under current programme : commissioned Feb. 8, 1936. Used as AA. gunnery training ship. In emergency she would become a combatant unit of fleet. Unofficial reports suggest that she is not an unqualified success. She spent several months of 1936 in dockyard hands, undergoing repairs and alterations.

BREMSE (Wilhelmshaven, Jan. 24, 1931.)

Standard Displacement, 1,460 tons.   Complement, 192.

Dimensions : $318\frac{1}{4}$ (*w.l.*), $339\frac{1}{2}$ (*o.a.*) $\times 31 \times 9\frac{1}{2}$ feet.

Guns : **4**—5 inch, **2**—20 mm. AA. (Modified at times for testing other calibres.)

Machinery : 8 M.A.N. double acting, 2 stroke, geared Diesels. 2 shafts. Designed H.P. : 25,000 = 27 kts. Oil fuel :

Note.—Boat derricks are arranged to handle heavy targets in a seaway. Her 27 knots will permit of high speed towing —a necessary provision in modern gunnery practice. She is extremely noisy when under way. Laid down, 1929 : completed, 1931.

Engineering Notes.—Machinery comprises eight 8-cyl. M.A.N. two-stroke engines of 600 r.p.m. reduced by Vulcan gearing to shaft speed of 400 r.p.m. Four engines to each shaft (twin screw). Total 26,000 S.H.P. Height of engines 8ft. 6in. from top to centre of shaft. Machinery power per litre is 7·38 b.h.p. against 5·14 b.h.p. per litre in *Deutschland.*

Training Ships (*Schulschiffe*).

(ex-Battleships)

SCHLESIEN.

1937, *R. Perkins.*

SCHLESIEN (May 28, 1906), SCHLESWIG-HOLSTEIN (Dec. 17, 1906).

Displacement, 13,040 tons.　　　Complement, 718.

Length $\begin{cases} (w.l.)\ 413 \\ (o.a.)\ 419 \end{cases}$ feet.　Beam, $72\frac{1}{5}$ feet.　*Mean* draught, $25\frac{1}{4}$ feet.

Guns :
　4—11 inch, 40 cal.
　10—5·9 inch, 45 cal.
　4—3·5 inch AA.
　4 M.G.
Torpedo tubes :
　　(*Removed*)

Armour :
　$9\frac{1}{2}''$ Belt (amidships) ......
　4″ Belt (ends) ....
　$3''$—$1\frac{1}{2}''$ Deck ....
　11″ Barbettes ....
　10″ Turrets to these, 8″
　　lower deck (side) ....
　$6\frac{3}{4}''$ Battery..............
　12″ Conning tower (fore) ....
　6″　　,,　　,,　　(aft) ...

Note to plan.—Now mounts 4—3·5 inch AA. at end of superstructure abaft mainmast. Upper deck 5·9 inch guns and torpedo tubes removed.

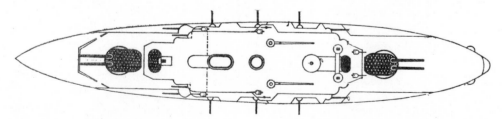

Machinery : 3 sets 3 cylinder triple expansion. 3 screws.　　Boilers : 12 Schulz-Thornycroft.
　Designed H.P. 17,000/19,300 = 18 kts.　Coal : 436 tons.　　Oil fuel : 1,130 tons.　*Nominal*
radius : 5900 miles at 10 kts.

Notes.—*Schlesien* and *Schleswig-Holstein*, built by Schichau, Danzig, 1904–08, and Germania, Kiel, 1905–08, respectively. Both were reconstructed and partially re-armed in 1926–28, and were converted into Cadets' Training Ships in 1935–36. Latter ship took part in operations at Danzig in September, 1939.

Depot and Repair Ships.

Note.—2 Depot Ships for Torpedo Craft and 1 for Submarines are under construction.

VALDEMAR KOPHAMEL (May 16, 1939). Built at Kiel. **WILHELM BAUER** (Dec. 20, 1938). Built by Howaldtwerke, Kiel. Depot Ships for Submarines.

Now has S.L. on superstructure abaft mainmast.

1934, *Schäfer.*

SAAR (Deutsche Werke, Kiel, April 5, 1934).

Standard displacement : 2,710 tons.　　Complement : 214.
Dimensions : $308 \times 44\frac{1}{4} \times 14$ feet.
Guns : 3—4·1 inch, 4 M.G.　Machinery : Linke-Hofmann-Busch Diesels.　2 shafts.
B.H.P. : 3,700 = 16 kts.　　Fuel : 336 tons.

Note.—*Saar* is at present attached to Submarine School. Classed as *Unterseebootsbegleitschiff.*

1935, *Renard.*

TSINGTAU (Blohm & Voss, Hamburg, June 6, 1934).

Standard displacement : 1,970 tons.　　Complement : 143.
Dimensions : $278\frac{3}{4} \times 44\frac{1}{4} \times 12\frac{3}{4}$ feet.
Guns : 2—3·5 inch AA., 4 M.G.　Machinery : Linke-Hofmann-Busch Diesels.　2 shafts.
B.H.P. : 4,100 = 17·5 kts.　　Fuel : 182 tons.
Depot ship for Motor T.B. Classed as *Schnellbootsbegleitschiff.*

Depot Ships—*continued.*

1939, *Schäfer.*

ERWIN WASSNER (ex-*Gran Canaria*), (Hamburg, 1938). 3,866 tons *gross.* Dimensions : 379¾ × 54¾ × — feet. Machinery : Geared turbines. 1 shaft. I.H.P. : 5,000. Submarine Depot Ship.

Note.—A sister ship, the *Santa Cruz*, is also reported to have been acquired.

1939, *Schäfer.*

MEMEL (1937). Displacement : 998 tons. Speed : 13 knots. Parent Ship of "Weddigen" Submarine Flotilla.

1939, *Schäfer.*

TANGA (Neptun Werft, Rostock, 1938). Classed as *Schnellbootsbegleitschiff.*

Photo wanted.

MARS (ex-*Samoa*, ex-*Altair*), (Emden, 1937). 2,414 tons *gross.* Dimensions : 324¼ × 46¾ × — feet. Machinery : Quadruple expansion. Speed : 11 kts. Tender to Gunnery School.

LECH. 1939, *Dr. Erich Gröner.*

ISAR (ex-*Puma*), **LECH** (ex-*Panther*), (Bremer Vulkan, Vegesack, 1930). Displacement : 3,850 tons. Dimensions : 319 × 45½ × 13 feet. Machinery : Triple expansion. H.P. : 2,000 = 12 kts. Both purchased 1938 for use as Submarine Depot Ships.

1937, *Schäfer.*

WEICHSEL (ex-*Syra*), (Howaldt, Kiel, 1923). Displacement : 3,974 tons. Dimensions : 309¼ × 44 × 13½ feet. Guns : 4—20 mm. AA. Machinery : Triple expansion. H.P. : 1,400 = 10·5 kts. Coal : 425 tons. 2 watertube boilers. Complement, 135. (Depot Ship for Submarines.)

Note.—Purchased in summer of 1936 and rebuilt at Stettin.

1938, *Schäfer.*

DONAU (ex-*Nicea*), (Lübeck, 1922). Displacement : 3,886 tons. Dimensions : 287½ × 41½ × 14 feet. Guns : 4—20 mm. AA. Machinery : Triple expansion. H.P. : 1,150 = 10 kts. Coal : 335 tons. 2 watertube boilers. Complement, 135. (Depot Ship for Submarines.)

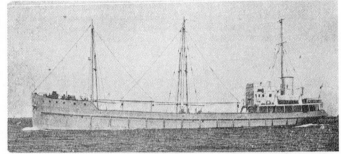

1937, *Schäfer.*

MOSEL (ex-*Frieda*). (Hamburg, 1921). Displacement : 796 tons. Guns : 2—20 mm. AA. Speed : 9 kts. Complement, 34. Further particulars wanted. (Depot Ship for Submarines.)

Photo wanted.

WARNOW (ex-*Vorwärts*). 726 tons *gross.* Speed : 13 kts. Further particulars wanted.

Minesweepers.

(*Minensuchboote*)

M 7   1939, *Ferd. Urbahns.*

M 1—M 36. Displacement : 600 tons. Complement : 82. Guns :
2—4·1 inch, 2—37 mm. Machinery : Triple expansion.
Speed : 17 kts. Coal : 150 tons. All laid down during 1936
and 1937 under 1935–37 Programmes.

Builders of these vessels are : H. C. Stülcken Sohn, Hamburg ;
Schichau, Elbing ; Stettiner Oderwerke, Stettin ; and Lübecker
Flenderwerke, Lübeck.

Notes.—*M* 1 commissioned Sept. 1938 ; *M* 2–8 all completed by end Jan. 1939.
M 20 was launched June 16, 1939.

M. 117.   1934 *Photo, Schäfer.*

19 vessels :—

M 157	M 122	M 104	M 85	M 61
M 145	M 117	M 102	M 84	TAKU (*ex*-M146)
M 132	M 111	M 98	M 75	WACHT(*ex*-M133)
M 126	M 110	M 89	M 72	

Built 1916–1920. Displacement : 525 tons. Dimensions : 184
(*w.l.*), 192 (*o.a.*) × 24¼ × 7¼ feet. Guns : 1—4·1 inch, 1 M.G.
Engines : 2 sets triple expansion. Boilers : 2 watertube
"Schulz." I.H.P. : 1,850 = 16 kts. 2 screws. Coal : 145–160
tons. Complement : 51.

Note.—Sundry other units of this class have been given names on appropriation
for various special services, vide later pages. One of above vessels is reported
to have been lost in the Baltic on September 10, 1939.

Tenders.

New Construction.

A new Fleet Tender (to be named *Hela*) was laid down in 1938.
Ex-*Geleitboot Hai* (on an earlier page) is rated as a Fleet Tender.

NETTELBECK.   1939, *Schäfer.*

NETTELBECK (ex-*Zieten*, ex-*M* 138, Tecklenborg, Feb. 17,
1919). Displacement : 550 tons. Dimensions : 184 × 34 ×
7½ feet. Guns : 1—4·1 inch, 2—1 pdr. AA. 2 sets Diesel
engines. B.H.P. : 840 = 12 kts. Complement : 40. Fuel :
90 tons.

VON DER GRÖBEN (ex-*M* 107, 1919). Of similar type to
Nettelbeck.

Note.—Ex-Minesweepers converted for service as *Räumbootsbegleitschiffe* in 1934
and 1938, respectively.

1936, *Schäfer.*

DRACHE (Germania, 1908). 790 tons. Dimensions : 176 × 31¾
× 10½ feet. Complement : 66. Guns : 6—4·1 inch.
1—20 mm. AA. Machinery : Geared turbines. High pressure
watertube boilers. Oil fuel. Speed believed to exceed 18 kts.
since 1936 refit.

Note.—Rated as Gunnery School Tender (*Artillerieschulboot.*)

Tenders—*continued.*

FUCHS.   *Added* 1939, *Schäfer.*

FUCHS (ex-*M* 130, 1919). Displacement : 525 tons. Dimensions : 184 × 24 × 7¼ feet. Guns : 3—3·5 inch AA. Machinery :
2 sets triple expansion. Boilers : 2 Schulz w.t. 2 screws.
I.H.P. : 1,850 = 16 kts. Coal : 160 tons. Complement : 49.

Note.—On occasions mounts 2—4·1 inch instead of 3—3·5 inch guns, being
Gunnery School Tender.

BROMMY.   1938, *Schäfer.*

BROMMY (ex-*M* 50, 1916). Displacement : 480 tons. Dimensions : 180½ × 24 × 7½ feet. Guns : 1—4·1 inch. Machinery :
2 sets triple expansion. 2 shafts. I.H.P. : 1,800 = 16·5 kts.
Boilers : 2 Schulz w.t. Coal : 145 tons.

Note.—Rated as *Räumbootsbegleitschiff.*

GAZELLE. (Described in following column).   1938, *Schäfer.*

HAVEL. 1939, *Schäfer.*

HECHT (ex-*M* 60, 1917), **JAGD** (ex-*M* 82, 1917), **DELPHIN** (ex-*M* 108, 1919), **ACHERON** (ex-*M* 113, 1918) **FRAUENLOB** (ex-*M* 134, 1919), **GAZELLE** (ex-*Hela*, ex-*M* 135, March 15, 1919), **HAVEL** (ex-*M* 136). Ex-Minesweepers of 525 tons. Complement : 49. Dimensions : 184 × 24¼ × 7¼ feet. Guns : 1—4·1 inch in some, none in others. Machinery : 2 sets triple expansion. 2 shafts. I.H.P. : 1,850 = 16 kts. Boilers : 2 Schulz w.t. Coal : 160 tons. *Acheron, Havel* classed as Submarine Tenders (*Unterseebootstender*). *Frauenlob*, Station Tender. *Delphin*, Gunnery School Tender. *Hela, Hecht, Jagd* classed as Fleet Tenders.

PELIKAN (ex-*M*. 28) 1934 *Photo, Schäfer.*

PELIKAN (ex-*M*.28, 1916). Displacement : 500 tons. Complement : 49. Dimensions : 180½ × 24 × 7½ feet. Guns : 1—4·1 inch. Machinery : 2 sets triple expansion. 2 shafts. I.H.P. : 1,800 = 16·5 kts. Boilers : 2 Schulz w.t. Coal : 145 tons. Classed as *Versuchsboot.*

NAUTILUS. 1938, *W. A. Fuller.*

STÖRTEBEKER. 1938, *Schäfer.*

STÖRTEBEKER (ex-*M* 66, 1918), **NAUTILUS** (ex-*M* 81, 1919), **ARKONA** (ex-*M* 115, 1918), **OTTO BRAUN** (ex-*M* 129). Displacement : 525 tons. Complement : 49. Dimensions : 184 × 24¼ × 7¼ feet. Guns : 1—4·1 inch, 1 M.G. Machinery : 2 sets triple expansion. 2 shafts. I.H.P. : 1,850 = 16 kts. Boilers : 2 Schulz w.t. Coal : 160 tons. All classed as *Versuchsboote.*

1939, *Schäfer.*

STRAHL (ex-*Latona*, ex-*Soneck*, 1902). Displacement : 1,643 tons. Complement : 35. Dimensions : 235 × 33½ × 11½ feet. Machinery : Triple expansion. I.H.P. : 800 = 10 kts. 1 cyl. boiler. First commissioned Oct. 20, 1936. Classed as *Versuchsschiff.*

1939, *Schäfer.*

NORDSEE (Atlas Werke, Bremen, 1914). 830 tons. Complement, 46 Dimensions : 175¾ × 30¾ × 12 feet. Armament : Nil. Machinery : Triple expansion. H.P. : 1,680 = 12 kts. 2 screws. Coal : 105 tons. Well deck built up 1923. Tender to Navigation School.

1939, *Schäfer*.

PAUL BENEKE (ex-*Admiral*), (Memel, 1936). Displacement : 460 tons. Dimensions : 165 (*o.a.*), 156 (*w.l*) × 25 × 10½ feet. No guns. Diesel engine. 1 shaft. B.H.P. : 800 = 12·5 kts. Complement : 30. Navigation School Tender.

1939, *Dr. E. Gröner*.

DAHME (ex-trawler *Carsten Rehder*) (1936). 475 tons *gross*. Dimensions : 186 × 26¼ × 13 feet. Machinery : Triple expansion. Submarine School Tender.

NIXE.   1935 *Photo*.

NIXE (ex-*Fiora*, Harburg, 1914). Displacement : 108 tons. Dimensions : 96¾ × 16¼ × 5½ feet. Machinery : 2 Daimler 4-cylinder 4-stroke benzol engines. 2 screws. H.P. : 200 = 13 kts. Fuel : 10 tons. Complement : 13. (Purchased 1916.) Used as Commander-in-Chief's yacht, Kiel.

M·T 1   1930 *Photo*.

MT1 (ex-*Heppens*), **MT**2 (ex-*Mariensiel*). Both launched 1917 at Neptun Yard, Rostock. Displacement : 550 tons. Dimensions : 164 × 30½ × 7½ feet. Armament : **1** M.G. Machinery : 2 screws triple expansion. Boilers : 2 single-ended coal-burning Schulz-Thornycroft. 2 screws. Designed H.P. : 375 = 10 kts. Radius : 1,200 miles at 7 kts. Coal : 37 tons. Complement : 47. Classed as *Sperrübungsfahrzeuge*. (Minelaying tenders.)

C 21   1938, *Schäfer*.

C 21—C 24 (1935–37). Displacement : 120 tons. Speed : 9 kts. Minelaying Tenders.

A, B (building), **C, D** (projected).

Notes.—There are also C 3, 5, 9-11, 13, 14, 16 (1906–15), old steamers of 75–80 tons, belonging to the Blocking Division.

1939, *Dr. Erich Gröner*.

ORKAN (ex-*Welle*, ex-*Grille*, ex-*Star of Eve*, ex-*Von der Goltz*). (Hamburg, 1916.) Purchased 1927. Displacement : 470 tons. Complement : 22. Dimensions : 120 × 24 × 12½ feet. H.P. : 400 = 10 kts. Coal : 65 tons.

No'e.—Sank in heavy weather, 1937, but salved and refitted. Used for recovery of practice Torpedoes. Classed as *Torpedobergungsdampfer*, and flies State Service Flag.

SPREE (ex-*Spreeufer*, ex-*Seeadler*, ex-*Ada*), (1918). Dimensions : 127¼ × 22½ × — feet. Machinery : Triple expansion. Tender to Submarine School.

TAUCHER   1935, *Renard*.

TAUCHER (Stulcken & Sohn, Hamburg, 1935). Displacement : 195 tons. Complement : 17. Dimensions : 88½ × 22⅓ × 6¼ feet. Diesel engine. H.P. : 60 = 6·5 kts. No armament. Diving School Tender (*Taucherfahrzeug*).

T 196 (Observe AA. guns added aft).
C. VAN BEVERN has no deckhouse between funnels or abaft mainmast.

1938, Schäfer.

1 *Krupp Germania*, **T196** (ex-*V196*).
1 *Vulkan*, **CLAUS VAN BEVERN** (ex-*T* 190 ex-*V* 190). } launched 1911.　　Big refit 1927-28.

Displacement : 755 tons. Dimensions : *T* 196, 242¾ × 26½ × 10¾ feet ; *T* 190, 241½ × 26 × 10½ feet. Armament : 1—4·1 inch, 45 cal., 2 M.G. AA. Machinery : Germania turbines in *T* 196 ; A.E.G. Vulcan type in *T* 190. Designed H.P. : *T* 196, 18,200 = 32·5 kts. ; *T* 190, 18,000 = 30·5 kts. Present best speed, 25 kts. Fuel : *T* 196, 204 tons ; *T* 190, 198 tons. 3 Schulz-Thornycroft boilers (oil burning). Complement : 99.
Notes.—*T* 196 classed as *flottentender*. *C. van Bevern* experimental tender (*Versuchsboot*).

G 7.
4 *Krupp-Germania* : **G 7, G 8** (both 1911), **G 10, G 11** (both 1912).

1938, courtesy Dr. Erich Gröner.

Displacement : 760 tons. Dimensions : 247¾ × 25 × 10½ feet. Armament : 1—4·1 inch, 45 cal., 2 M.G. AA. Torpedo tubes : 3—19·7 inch in *G* 8, *G* 10 ; 3—21 inch and 1—19·7 inch in others. 2 sets Satz-Germania turbines. Designed H.P. : 16,000 = 31 kts. (now about 25 kts.) 3 Schulz-Thornycroft boilers (oil burning). Oil fuel : 173 tons. Complement : 85.
G 7, *G* 8, *G* 10, *G* 11 lengthened 14¾ feet during alterations 1928-31. Triple tubes abaft mast. Single tube between funnels in *G* 10, *G* 11. Used as training tenders (*Torpedoschulboote*) and will be discarded in near future.

T 156.

1938, courtesy Dr. Erich Gröner.

EDUARD JUNGMANN (ex-*T 153*), *T 155, 156, 157, 158* (Vulcan, 1907–8).

Displacement : 660 tons. Dimensions : 237 × 25½ × 10½ feet (*max.* draught).
Guns : **1 M.G.** in all but *T* 153.
Machinery : Triple expansion. Designed H.P. : 10,900 = 30 kts. (now only 22 kts.) Oil : 181 tons. Complement, 87.
Note.—*E. Jungmann* used as Gunnery School Tender, others as tenders to submarines.

1938, courtesy Dr. Erich Gröner.

T 23 (Schichau, March 29, 1913). 640 tons. Dimensions : 233 × 24⅓ × 9¾ feet. Armament : 2 M.G. Designed S.H.P. : 15,700 = 31 kts. Schichau turbines. Fuel : 71 tons oil. Complement, 92. Used as Submarine Tender.

Patrol Vessels. (*Vorpostenboote*)

FRITHJOF.   1937, *Schäfer.*

(All similar except *Hagen*, in which deckhouse extends further aft.)

BEOWULF (ex-*Joh. Vester*, ex-*Beowulf*), **FREYR** (ex-*Glücksburg*) **FRITHJOF** (ex-*N. Ebeling*, ex-*Frithjof*), **HEIMDALL** (ex-*Lauenburg*), **SIGFRID** (ex-*Esteburg*, ex-*Sigfrid*), **WOTAN** (ex-*Augustenburg*), **HAGEN** (ex-*Anton Palm*, ex-*Gustav Harms*), **HILDEBRAND** (ex-*Seelöwe*, ex-*Wilhelm Grünhage*), **HUGIN** (ex-*Gorch Fock*, ex-*Hugin*), **MUNIN** (ex-*Ditmar Koel*, ex-*Munin*), **ODIN** (ex-*Österreich*), **VOLKER** (ex-*Niedersachsen*), (1912–21). Ex-Trawlers, acquired 1937. Displacement : 496 tons. Dimensions vary from 117 × 22 × 11 to 136 × 24 × 11½ feet. Guns : 1—3·5 inch, 3—1 pdr. AA. Machinery : Triple expansion. I.H.P. : 400 = 10 kts.

Fishery Protection Vessels. (*Fischereischutzboote*).

WESER (ELBE similar).   1939, *Dr. Erich Gröner.*

ELBE, WESER (both launched Jan. 24, 1931 at Wilhelmshaven). Displacement : 600 tons. Dimensions : 157½ × 27¼ × 10¼ feet. Armament : 1—3·5 inch, 1 M.G. Machinery : 2 sets Linke-Hofmann-Busch 6-cylinder 4-stroke Diesel engines. 2 screws. Designed H.P. 1600 = 15 kts. Radius : 7000 miles at 11 kts. Complement : 48.

Surveying Vessels (*Vermessungsschiffe*).

HOOGE (1938). Particulars wanted.

SUNDEVALL.

SUNDEVALL (ex-*Johann Wittenborg*, ex-*M 109*), (1919). Displacement : 525 tons. Complement : 49. Dimensions : 184 × 24¼ × 7¼ feet. Guns : Not known. Machinery : 2 sets triple expansion. 2 shafts. I.H.P. : 1,850 = 16 kts. Boilers : 2 Schulz. Coal : 160 tons.

NORDEROOG (ex-*Peilboot II*) and **SÜDEROOG** (ex-*Peilboot V*), built 1911–12, serve as Coastal Surveying Craft.

1939, *Dr. Erich Gröner.*

METEOR (Danzig, Jan. 18, 1915). 1,200 tons. Complement : 111. Dimensions : 219⅓ × 33½ × 12½ feet. Guns : 1—3·5 inch. Machinery : 2 sets 8 cyl. 4-stroke Diesels. 2 screws. H.P. : 2,200 = 14·5 kts. Completed June, 1925, and converted to Diesel propulsion in 1934.

Target Service Ships (*Zielschiffe*).

1937, *Schäfer.*

HESSEN (ex-Battleship). (1903). Reconstructed 1936–37 as a wireless-controlled target ship. Displacement : 13,200 tons. Dimensions : 400¼ × 73 × 23½ feet. H.P. : 16,000 = 20 kts. Oil fuel and automatically fired boilers.

1934 *Photo.*

ZÄHRINGEN (ex-Battleship), (1901), reconstructed 1927–28 for use as a wireless controlled target ship on similar lines to British *Centurion*. Displacement : 11,800 tons. Dimensions : 393½ × 68⅛ × 25 feet. H.P. 5,000 = 13 kts. 2 screws. Oil fuel and automatically fired boilers. Complement : 104.

1939, *Dr. Erich Gröner.*

PFEIL (ex-*T 139*, 1906). Ex-Torpedo Boat. Displacement : 530 tons. Classed as *Schnellschlepper.*

Target Service Ships—*continued.*

BLITZ (KOMET similar). 1939, *Schäfer.*

BLITZ (ex-*T.* 185, Vulcan, 1910), **KOMET** (ex-*T* 151, Vulcan, 1907). Ex-Torpedo boats, used for wireless target control and classed as *Fernlenkboote.* Displacement : 637 and 675 tons, respectively.

LUDWIG PREUSSER (Lürrsen, Vegesack, 1938). Tug used for target towing and wireless control.

Mine Transports.

(Manned by mercantile personnel.)

LAUTING. 1937, *Schäfer.*

LAUTING, RHEIN (both Oderwerke), **OTTER** (Schichau, Elbing) (1934). *Standard* displacement : 1,253 tons. Speed : 9·5 kts. Complement : 40. Other particulars wanted.

Admiralty Yacht.

(Officially classed as *Aviso.*)

1935, *Renard.*

GRILLE (Blohm & Voss, Hamburg, Dec. 15, 1934). Standard displacement : 2,560 tons. Complement, 240. Dimensions : $377\frac{1}{4} \times 44\frac{1}{4} \times 11\frac{1}{4}$ feet. Guns : **3**—4·1 inch, 2—37 mm. AA., **4** M.G. Geared turbines. S.H.P. : 8,000 = 20 kts. High pressure watertube boilers. Oil fuel : tons. Commissioned May 20, 1935, and used for Training duties with destroyers and submarines and as Tender to Signal School.

Motor Launches.

(Classed as *Räumboote.*)

R 26. 1939, *Dr. Erich Gröner.*

R 39. 1939, *Dr. Erich Gröner.*

20 boats : **R 17—40** (Travemünde and Weser Yards, 1935–38). Displacement : 90 tons. Guns : 2—1 pdr. AA. Machinery : 2 M.W.M. Diesels with Voith-Schneider propellers. B.H.P. : 1,800 = 18 kts. Complement, 17.

R 16. 1935 *Photo.*

16 boats : **R 1—16** (Lürssen, Vegesack, and other Weser Yards, 1930–35). Displacement : 45 tons. Length : 85 feet. Armament : **1**—1 pdr. AA. Machinery : 2 M.W.M. Diesel engines. 2 shafts. Designed H.P. : 600 = 18 kts. Complement, 15.

Note.— R 8 is fitted with Voith-Schneider propellers.

UZ (S) 18.

1 BOAT : **UZ (S) 18** (1929). Displacement : 26 tons. Dimensions : $70 \times 13\frac{3}{4} \times 3\frac{1}{4}$ feet. Armament : none. Machinery : 3 sets 6 cylinder 4-stroke benzol engines. 3 screws. Designed H.P. : 720 = 27 kts. (Now much less). Fuel : 3 tons. Complement : 8.

Note.—Now relegated to Harbour service.

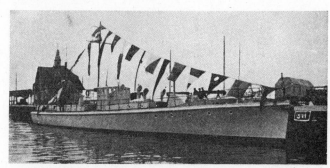

1930 *Photo.*

(Classed as *Bewachungsfahrzeuge*).

2 boats : **UZ 32, 33** (1919–20). 60 tons. Dimensions : $101\frac{1}{2} \times 14\frac{1}{3} \times 4$ feet. Machinery : 2 Benz 6-cylinder, 4-stroke benzol engines. H.P. : 500 = 14 kts. 2 screws. Fuel : $8\frac{1}{2}$ tons. Complement, 17.

Oilers.

(All fly State Service Flag, and are manned by mercantile personnel.)

Completing.

FRANKEN (Deutsche Werke, June 8, 1939). 2,000 tons *d.w.* Diesel engines.

1939, *Dr. Erich Gröner.*

INSEL POEL. Particulars wanted.

SAMLAND   *Added* 1938 *courtesy Dr. E. Gröner.*

SAMLAND (ex-*Hansa*), (Schichau, 1929). Displacement : 10,111 tons. Dimensions : 413 × 52⅔ × — feet. I.H.P. : 2,100.

WOLLIN   1938, *courtesy Dr. Erich Gröner.*

WOLLIN (Reiherstieg, Hamburg, 1916). Displacement : 3,429 tons. Dimensions : 246 × 36 × — feet. Machinery : Triple expansion. I.H.P. : 600 = 9·5 kts.

Added 1938.

BRÖSEN (Howaldt, Kiel, 1915). Displacement : 2,498 tons *standard.* Dimensions : 233 × 34½ × 16 feet. Machinery : Triple expansion. I.H.P. : 250 = 8 kts.

NORDERNEY. Displacement : 1,110 tons. Speed : 7 kts.

Sail Training Ships. (*Schulschiffe*)

HORST WESSEL.   1936

HORST WESSEL (June 13, 1936), **ALBERT LEO SCHLAGETER** (Oct. 31, 1937). Both built by Blohm & Voss, Hamburg. *Horst Wessel* begun Feb. 15, 1936, and completed Sept. 17, 1936. Displacement : 1,634 tons. Complement : 289, including 200 midshipmen. Dimensions : 265¾ (*pp.*), 295¼ (*o.a.*) × 39⅓ × 15¾ (*mean*), 16½ feet (*max.* draught). Machinery : M.A.N. auxiliary Diesels. B.H.P. : 700 = 10 kts. Sail area, 21,530 sq. feet.

1939, *Schäfer.*

GORCH FOCK (Blohm & Voss, Hamburg, 1933). Displacement : 1,354 tons. Dimensions : 200 (*pp.*), 241⅔ (*o.a.*) × 39⅓ × 15 feet. M.A.N. auxiliary Diesels. H.P. : 500 = 8 kts. Fuel : 25 tons. Sail area : 19,376 sq. ft. Complement, 255.

Note.—20 per cent. of the cost of this vessel was defrayed by public subscription organised after the loss of the *Niobe*, the previous sail training ship of the German Navy.

ASTA, ORION. Small sailing yachts used for coastal training. Officially classed as *Segelfahrzeuge bei den Stationen.* Latter vessel was built at Travemünde and commissioned April 22, 1936.

The following River Force (including many ex-Austrian and ex-Czechoslovakian vessels) is maintained on the Danube, being known officially as the Donauflottille, Linz (where its headquarters are situated). It is manned by naval personnel.

River Patrol Vessels

ALBERICH (ex-*Remus*), (Linz Shipyard, 1938). Displacement: 240 tons. Dimensions: $160\frac{3}{4}$ (*w.l.*), $167\frac{2}{3}$ (*o.a.*) $\times 25 \times 3\frac{2}{3}$ feet. Guns: 2—1 pdr. AA. Machinery: 2 Sulzer Diesels. 2 shafts, triple rudder and Kort nozzle. B.H.P.: $560 = 12$ kts. Fuel: 20 tons. Classed as *Schlepper* (Tug). Date is probably that of conversion to present service.

*Ex-***PRESIDENT MASARYK** (1930). Displacement: 200 tons. Complement: 50. Dimensions: $150 \times 20 \times \cdot5$ feet. Guns: 4—3 inch AA., 10 M.G. Machinery: 2 sets turbines. S.H.P.: $1,600 = 16\cdot8$ kts. Oil: 45 tons.

1938, courtesy Dr. E. Gröner.

BIRAGO (ex-Hungarian *Siofok*, ex-Austro-Hungarian *Czuka*). Laid down Jan. 1915 as patrol vessel "K" at the Ganz-Danubius Shipyard, Budapest. Completed and commissioned March 1, 1916. Purchased by Austria in Aug. 1929. Displacement, 60 tons. Complement, 18. Dimensions: $118 \times 15 \times 2\frac{2}{3}$ feet. Protected by bullet-proof belt of chrome steel. Guns: 1—61 mm., 26 cal., 1—1 pdr. AA., 1 M.G. Machinery: Reciprocating. I.H.P.: $800 = 12$ kts.

6 boats (1936–37). Displacement: 48 tons. Complement: 24. Guns: 1—47 mm., 2 M.G. Speed: 21 kts.

9 boats. Displacement: 21 tons. Guns: 1—3 inch, 2 M.G. Machinery: High speed Diesels. B.H.P.: $1,600 = 33$ kts. (?)

Motor Launches. (*Flussräumboote.*)

1938, courtesy Dr. E. Gröner.

F.R. 1—12, (1938). Rated as River Minesweeper. Particulars wanted.

(There are also a number of new fast motor boats, rated as *Flusschnellboote*).

F.H.R. 1—6 (ex-Austrian *Krems, Murr, Salzach, Enns, Drau*) (1933–35). Steel. Dimensions: $46 \times 10 \times 2\frac{1}{2}$ feet. 2 M.G. 2 sets Diesels. 2 shafts. H.P.: 200. Complement: 6. Rated as Auxiliary River Minesweepers.

GAZELLE. Of similar design to above vessels, but $30 \times 7\frac{1}{2} \times 2$ feet.

There are also several steel launches of single screw type. Dimensions: $21\frac{3}{4} \times 7\frac{1}{2} \times 1\frac{2}{3}$ feet. 2 M.G. 1 motor. Complement, 7.

Note.—Apart from the foregoing vessels, many other craft, mostly small launches, have been transferred to the Danube Flotilla from other organisations, such as the Police, Hitler Youth, etc. A number of additional units are under construction. These include the *Brünhild* and *Kriemhild* (rated as *Begleitschiffe*) ; *Uta* (*Versorgungsschiff*); *Nothung* (*Bereisungsboot*); *Nibelung* and *Schildung* (*Motorboote*).

Special Note.

It is probable that some of the Polish River Flotilla on the Vistula have been added to the above total during September, 1939.

GREECE.

Flags.

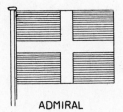

ADMIRAL

Vice-Admiral's flag similar, but has a white ball in upper left canton.

Rear-Admiral's has a white ball in each left canton.

CAPTAIN COMMANDING A DIVISION

Sky Blue

White

ENSIGN AND MERCANTILE

SENIOR OFFICER

Personnel :—About 6,300 (conscript, 18 months or enlistment).
Minister of Marine :—General Metaxas.
Chief of General Naval Staff :—Rear-Admiral A. Sakellariou.
Naval Attaché, London : Captain S. Matessis.

Uniforms.

| 1 | 2 | 3 | 4 | 5 | 6 | 7 | 8 | 9 |

(1) **Navarkhos** *Admiral.*
(2) Andinavarkhos. *Vice-Admiral.*
(3) Yponavarkhos. *Rear-Admiral.*
(4) Ploiarkhos. *Captain.*
(5) Andiploiarkhos. *Commander.*

(6) Plotarkhis. *Lieutenant-Commander.*
(7) Ypoploiarkhos. *Lieutenant.*
(8) Anthipoploiarkhos. *Sub-Lieut.*
(9) Simæophoros. *Act. Sub-Lieut.*

Other branches without curl :—
Constructors: *black velvet.*
Paymasters: *scarlet velvet.*
Surgeons: *purple velvet.*
Apothecaries: *green velvet.*
Aviation: *light green velvet.*
Dockyard: *black.*

With curl :—
Engineers : *violet velvet.*

Tonnage.

At Standard Displacement.

Mercantile Marine.

From " Lloyd's Register " 1939
607 vessels of 1,780,666 Tonnage.

Naval Ordnance

Nominal Calibre In.	mm.	Maker and Date		Length in Calibres	Weight of Gun	Weight of Projectile	Muzzle Velocity Foot-sec.	Muzzle Energy Foot-tons
					Tons	lb.		
9·2	233·4	A.	1906	45	27·2	380	2,725	18,550
7·5	190·5	A.	1906	45	14	200	2,888	11,746
6	152·4	A.	1910	50	9	100	2,986	6,238
5	127·8	R.	1938	45	3·65	62	2,756	3,180
4·7	120	T.	1929	50	3	48	3,117	2,200
4	102	B.	1910	50	2·6	33	2,998	1,937
3·5	88	K.	1907	30	1	18	2,500	1,000
3 H.A.	76·2	V.	1924	50	1·1	12·8	2,789	675
3	76	A.	1908	40	14 cwt.	12·8	2,297	459
2·6	66	S.	1905	30	12 cwt.	9	2,000	400
1·58 H.A.	40	T.	1917	39	5 cwt.	2	2,000	55
1·46 H.A.	37	R.	1938	60	3 cwt.	1·38	2,756	

A = Armstrong ; T = Terni ; B = Bethlehem ; V = Vickers ; K = Krupp ; S = Skoda ;
R = Rheinmetall ; H.A. = High Angle.

New Construction Programme.

12 Destroyers to be built between 1937 and 1940. 2 Submarines also projected.
Though tenders have been invited for some of these ships, only 2 destroyers have so far been built.

PLEIAS.

ARES.

HELLE.

VASILEVS GEORGIOS 1.
VASILISSA OLGA

AVEROFF.

HYDRA *class*.

PERGAMOS *class*.

KIOS *class*.

AIGLI *class*.

AETOS *class*.

ASPIS, NIKI.

THYELLA.
SPHENDONI.

KATSONIS *class*.

NEREUS *class*.

245

Cruiser.

AVEROFF.

1937, *R. Perkins.*

AVEROFF (March, 1910).

Displacement, 9,450 tons.   Complement, 670.

Length (*over all*), 462 feet.   Beam, 69 feet.   *Maximum* draught, 24⅔ feet.

Guns (Armstrong):
4—9·2 inch. 45 cal.
8—7·5 inch. 45 cal.
16—3 inch (14 pdr.)
2—3 inch AA. (Vickers).
4—40 mm. AA.
2 M.G.
Torpedo tubes (removed)
Searchlights :
2—36 inch.

Armour (Terni) :
8" Belt (amidships) ......
3¼" Belt (ends) ....
2" Deck ....
7"—6" Upper belt .
4" Upper belt (ends) ......
8" Main barbettes (N.C.)....
6½" Turrets (N.C.) ....
7" Citadel ....
7" Second'ry turrets (N.C.)
7" Conning tower ....

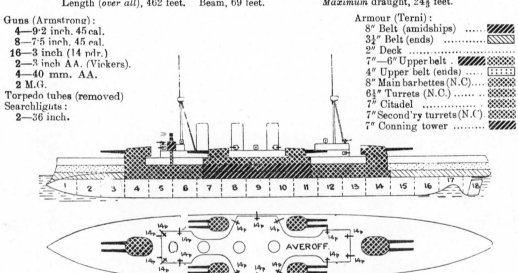

Machinery : 2 sets 4 cylinder triple expansion. 2 screws. Boilers : 22 Belleville. Designed H.P. 19,000 = 22·5 kts.   Trials : 21,500 = 23·9.   Coal : *normal* 660 tons ; *maximum* 1500 tons = 7125 miles at 10 kts. ; 2489 miles at 17¾ kts. Built by Orlando.

Gunnery Notes.—All big guns hydraulically controlled. 2—3 inch AA. guns mounted on after superstructure.
General Notes.—Cost £950,750. Sister to Italian *Pisa*. Reboiled and completely refitted by Forges et Ch. de la Mediterranée, at La Seyne 1925-27, the alterations effected including the installation of new heavy type tripod foremast with director tower, additional rangefinders and searchlights, AA. guns. new boats, etc., at a cost of £140,000.

Minelayer (ex-Cruiser).

HELLE.

1931 *Photo, Official.*

HELLE (ex-Chinese *Fei Hung*, May, 1912).

Displacement, 2115 tons.   Complement, 232.

Length (*over all*), 322 feet.   Beam, 39 feet.   Draught, 14 feet.

Guns (Armstrong) :
3—6 inch.
4—6 pdr.
2—66 mm. AA.
Torpedo tubes (18 inch) :
2 *above water.*

110 *Mines carried.*

Armour (steel):
2" Deck on slopes ...
2" Deck on flat.........

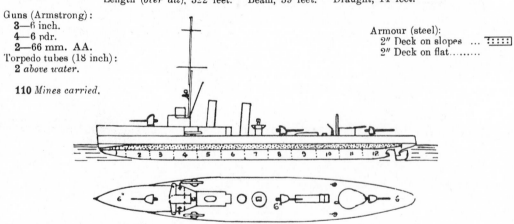

Machinery : 3 Parsons geared turbines. 3 screws. Boilers : 3 Yarrow. Designed H.P. 7500 = 20·5 kts. Oil : *normal* 600 tons = 7000 miles at 10 kts.

Name	Builder	Machinery	Laid down	Completed	Trials : 4 hours.	Full Power.	Boilers	Best recent speed
Helle	N.Y. Shipblg.	N.Y. Shipblg.	1910	Nov.,'13	7500=20·3	8650=21	Yarrow	

General Notes.—Built as the *Fei Hung* for China. Purchased 1914. Originally fitted with Thornycroft boilers, mixed coal and oil burning. Now converted to oil fuel only. Original turbines have also been replaced, and vessel equipped for mine-laying, 1926-28. This cruiser has been completely transformed by the reduction of her armament, 4 broadside guns being removed and main battery arranged on centre-line, as well as by the removal of the old poop and other heavy weights. The whole of this work was carried out by the F. & Ch. de la Mediterranée, La Seyne, costing £130,000. On fresh trials 21 kts. with full mine load ; 21½ kts. without mines.

4 Vasilevs Georgios class.

4 Hydra class.

1939 *Official.*

HYDRA.

1932 *Photo, Official.*

4 *Yarrow* type: **Vasilevs Georgios I** (March 3, 1938), **Vasilissa Olga** (June 2, 1938), and 2 more (building). Displacement: 1,350 tons. Dimensions: 312 (*pp.*), 320 (*w.l.*) × 33 × 8½ feet (*mean*). Guns: **4**—5 inch, **4**—37 mm. AA., **3** M.G. Tubes: **8**—21 inch. Machinery: Parsons geared turbines. S. H. P.: 34,000 = 36 kts. Boilers: 3 Yarrow 3-drum type. Complement: 150.

HYDRA.

1938, *Grand Studio.*

Notes.—The first pair were laid down at Scotstoun in February, 1937, and were delivered in February, 1939. The second pair were laid down in the Royal Hellenic Naval Yard, their machinery and boilers to be supplied by Messrs. Yarrow & Co., Ltd., towards the end of 1939.

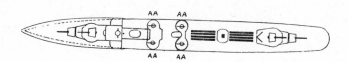

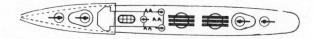

4 *Odero* type: **Hydra** (Oct. 21, 1931), **Kondouriotis** (Aug. 29, 1931), **Spetsai, Psara** (1932). All built at Genoa. Displacement: 1,350 tons, 2,050 tons *deep load.* Dimensions: 303 × 32 × 12½ feet, *max.* draught. Armament: **4**—4·7 inch, **3**—40 mm. AA., **6**—21 inch tubes. All fitted to carry 40 mines. Machinery: 2 sets Parsons geared turbines. 3 Express type boilers. S.H.P.: 40,000 = 39·5 kts. Oil: 630 tons. Cost about £272,000 each. Radius: 5,800 miles at 20 kts. Complement: 156.

Trials: 4 hrs. *Hydra* 39·9.   *Spetsai* 40·9.   *Kondouriotis* 40·75 kts.   *Psara* 40·13 kts.
       Max.   „   41·7.   „   41·5.   „   41·8 kts.   „   41·10 kts.

4 Aetos Class.

AETOS.

1931 *Official Photo.*

4 *Cammell-Laird* type : **Aetos, Ierax, Leon, Panther** (all launched 1911). 1013 tons *normal,* 1300 *full load.* Dimensions : 293 × 27¾ × 8½ feet, *normal* draught; *full load* draught, 10 feet. Armament : 4—4 inch (Bethlehem), 2—2 pdr. Pom-poms. Tubes : 6—21 inch, in triple deck mountings. All four vessels are fitted for mine-laying, and carry 40 mines each. 3 searchlights. S.H.P. : 19,750 = 32 kts. Combined Parsons and Curtis turbines. 4 Yarrow boilers. Oil : 260 tons. These were 4 boats, *San Luis, Santa Fé, Tucuman* and *Santiago,* built for Argentina. Purchased by Greece, Oct., 1912. Reconstructed and re-boilered by Messrs. J. S. White & Co., Ltd., E. Cowes, 1924-25, at a cost of £110,000 each.

General Notes.—The refit of these destroyers has proved a great success, the original speed being exceeded by 2 kts.

2 Thyella Class.

THYELLA.

1931 *Official Photo.*

2 *Yarrow* type : **Thyella, Sphendoni** (1906-07). 305 tons. Dimensions : 220¼ × 20¼ × 6 feet, *mean* draught ; *max.* draught, 9 feet. Armament : 2—3·5 inch Krupp, 1—2·7 inch AA. 2 tubes (18 inch). Speed : 30 kts. Coal : 80 tons. Endurance : 1140 to 1250 miles at 15 kts. · Complement, 70.

Notes.—Both refitted 1926-28. Present speed 29 kts. Full load displacement is 390 tons.

2 Niki Class.

NIKI

ι931 *Official Photo.*

2 *Vulkan Stettin* type : **Aspis** (1906), **Niki** (1905). 275 tons. Dimensions : 220¼ × 20¼ × 6 feet, *mean* draught; *max.* draught, 9 feet. H.P. : 6,700 = 30 kts. Armament : 2—3·5 inch Krupp, 1—2·7 inch AA., 2 tubes (18 inch). Coal : 90 tons. Complement : 70. Endurance : 1,140 to 1,250 miles at 15 kts.

Note.—Both underwent a thorough refit, 1928-29. Present speed 29 kts.

4 Aigli Class.

AIGLI.

Added 1931 Official.

4 *Vulkan* type : **Aigli, Alkyone, Arethousa, Doris,** (all launched 1913). 145 tons. Dimensions : 147¾ × 9¼ × 4 feet. Armament : 2—6 pdr. Bethlehem, 2—18 inch tubes. I.H.P. 2600 = 25 kts. (about 24 kts. best speed now). Trials : *Aigli* 26·2, *Doris* 25·7. Coal : 25 tons.

Note.—These four boats were completely refitted, 1926-30.

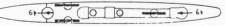

(Should show only one Tube in centre line forward).

248

PERGAMOS. (Now has tall foremast and stump mainmast.)   1922 *Photo, Official.*

2 *Ex-Austrian* boats : **Pergamos** (ex-95 F), **Prousa** (ex-92 F).   Built by Ganz-Danubius Yard, Fiume (1914-1915). 241 tons.   Dimensions : 188¼ × 19 × 5 feet *max.* draught.   H.P. 5000 = 28 kts.   2 turbines.   2 Yarrow boilers (1 coal and 1 oil).   Fuel : 21 tons coal + 31 tons oil.   Guns : 1—11 pdr. Skoda.   3—18 inch Tubes. Complement, 25.

Note.—These boats underwent a general refit at Piraeus, 1926.   Original speed exceeded.

KYZIKOS.   1932 *Official Photo.*

3 *Ex-Austrian* boats : **Kyzikos** (ex-98 M), **Kios** (ex-99 M), **Kidonia** (ex-100 M).   Built at Monfalcone (1914). 241 tons.   Dimensions : 197 × 18 × 4·9 feet *max.* draught.   Machinery details as *Pergamos* type, above. Armament ; 1—11 pdr. Skoda. 2—18 inch Tubes.

Note.—All three boats underwent a general refit at Piraeus 1926.   Original speed exceeded.

Submarines.

Note:—2 submarines are to be ordered under 1937–1940 Construction Programme.

4 Glafkos Class.

GLAFKOS.   1938, *Grand Studio.*

4 *Simonot* type.   **Nireus** (Dec., 1927), **Proteus** (Oct. 24th, 1927), **Triton** (April 4th, 1928), all built by At. & Ch. de la Loire, at Nantes, **Glafkos** (1928), by Chantiers Navals Français, at Blainville.   Displacement : 700/930 tons (metric).   Dimensions : 225 (*p.p.*) × 18·8 × 13·7 feet.   Machinery (supplied by At. & Ch. de la Loire) : On *surface*, 2 sets 2-cycle Sulzer-Diesels, totalling 1420 B.H.P. for 14 kts. : *submerged* 1200 B.H.P. for 9¼ kts. Oil fuel : 105 tons.   Endurance on *surface* : normal 1,500 miles, *maximum* 4,000 miles ; both at 10 kts.   When *submerged*, 100 miles at 5 kts.   Armament : 1—3·9 inch, 1—3 pdr. AA., 6—21 inch internal bow tubes, 2—21 inch internal stern tubes.   Stowage for 10 torpedoes, 150 rounds of 4 inch ammunition.   Complement, 41.   *Maximum* depth of submergence : 45 fathoms.   Approximate cost £119,000 each.   Pendant Nos. (painted on C.T.) are : *Proteus,* Y3   *Nireus,* Y4   *Triton,* Y5   *Glafkos,* Y6.

2 Katsonis Class.

KATSONIS.   1938, *Grand Studio.*

2 *Schneider-Laubeuf* type.   **Katsonis** (20 March, 1926), by Ch de la Gironde, at Bordeaux ; **Papanicolis** (Nov. 1926), by At. & Ch. de la Loire, at Nantes.   Displacement : 576/775 tons.   Dimensions : 204¼ (*p.p.*) × 17¼ × 11 feet.   On *surface*, 2 sets of 2-cycle Machinery : Schneider-Carels Diesels, totalling 1300 B.H.P. for 14 kts.   *Submerged,* 1000 B.H.P. for 9¼ kts.   Endurance, on *surface* : normal 1500 miles, *maximum* 3500 miles, both at 10 kts. ; when *submerged*, 100 miles at 5 kts.   Armament : 1—3·9 inch, 1—3 pdr. AA., 2—21 inch internal bow tubes, 2—21 inch external bow tubes, 2—21 inch external stern tubes.   Stowage for 7 torpedoes, 100 rounds of 4 inch ammunition. Complement, 39.   *Maximum* depth of submergence : 45 fathoms.

Identification Note.—Submarines are differentiated by letters and numerals painted on side of conning tower, i.e. *Katsonis,* Y1, *Papanicolis,* Y2.

Mine Layers.

Photo wanted.

1931 *Official photo.*

1931 *Official photo.*

ALIAKMON (ex-*Lord Merrivale*, 1926), **NESTOS** (ex-*Lord Bradbury*, 1925), **STRYMON** (ex-*Cape Otway*, 1925), **AXIOS** (ex-*Cape Grisnez*, 1919). Ex-trawlers, built by Cochrane & Sons, Ltd., Selby. Dimensions : 138¾ × 23¾ × 13½ feet. Armament : 1—37 mm. AA., 40 mines. Machinery : Triple expansion. I.H.P. : 600 = 11 kts. Also fitted for minesweeping.

PARALOS (Rotterdam, 1925). Displacement : 395 tons. Dimensions : 150 × 22 × 10½ feet. I.H.P. 550 = 13 kts. Coal : 35 tons. Carries 52 mines. Used in peace time as a despatch vessel.

TENEDOS (Glasgow, 1906). Displacement : 460 tons. Dimensions : 142 × 24 × 10 feet (*mean* draught). I.H.P 560 = 13 kts. Coal : 40 tons. Carries 40 mines. Employed as a despatch vessel.

PLEIAS.   1931 *Official Photo.*

1931 *Official photo.*

PLEIAS (Soc. Italiana Ernesto Breda, Mestre Yard, Venice, 28th April, 1926). Displacement : 520 tons. Dimensions : 162 × 27 × 12½ feet. I.H.P. 1000 = 14 kts. Coal : 90 tons. Carries 50 mines. Normally this ship is employed as a Lighthouse Tender.

KORGIALENIOS (Rotterdam, 1916). Displacement : 380 tons. Dimensions : 150 × 21½ × 10 feet (depth). I.H.P. 550 = 13½ kts. Coal : 35 tons. Carries 50 mines. Employed as a despatch vessel.

Training Ship.

ARES.   1932 *Photo, Official.*

ARES (Forges et Chantiers de la Méditerranée, La Seyne, Jan. 28th, 1927). Steel Barquentine. Displacement : 2200 tons. Dimensions : 208 (*p.p.*) × 39½ × 18 feet. Guns : 4—3 inch. Auxiliary steam engine (reciprocating) I.H.P. 1000 = 10 kts. 2 oil-fired Babcock & Wilcox boilers. Fitted with lecture rooms, workshops and accommodation for 100 Naval Cadets and 150 Boys. Total complement : 419. Carries an exceptionally full equipment of boats for training purposes.

Note.—On trials, H.P. 1144 = 11·38 kts.

Motor Torpedo Boats.

To be completed 1940.

T3, T4 (Vosper, Portsmouth, 1939). Displacement : 32 tons. Length : 70 feet. Armament : 2—21 inch torpedo tubes, 1—20 mm. AA. gun. Machinery : 3 Isotta-Fraschini engines. H.P. : 3,450 = over 40 kts.

Added 1938, courtesy Messrs. Thornycroft.

T1, T2. Thornycroft 55 ft. type (1929). Two motors each 375 H.P. = 37 kts. (40 kts. reached on trials.) 2 Lewis guns, 2—18 inch torpedoes, 4 D.C.

Fleet Repair and Submarine Depôt Ship.

1938 *Grand Studio*

HIFAISTOS (ex-*Khios*) (ex-German Cargo Ship *Marie Reppel*, Rostock, 1920). *Gross* tonnage, 4549. Dimensions : 360½ × 50 × 23 feet. I.H.P. 2500 = 11½ kts. Guns : 4—4 inch AA. Converted into a Repair Ship by Messrs. Palmers, Jarrow-on-Tyne, 1925. Fitted with up-to-date workshops and plant.

Oiler.

Photo wanted.

ARGO (ex-*Solna*, ex-*Granlund*, ex-*Corbis*, ex-*War Ranee*), (Swan Hunter, 1918). Displacement : 11,715 tons ; 8,350 tons *deadweight*. Dimensions : 400 × 52¼ × 25½ feet. Machinery : Triple expansion. I.H.P. : 2,176 = 11 kts. 3 boilers. Fuel capacity : 2,200 tons.

HUNGARY.

(Danube Flotilla.)

ENSIGN

FLAG OFFICER

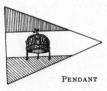

PENDANT

Principal Base.—Budapest.

Under Law XIV of 1922 the Royal Hungarian Honvéd River Force (Magyar Királyi Honvéd Folyamerök) was established for police purposes on the Danube, under the control of the Ministry of the Interior.

Colour of Ships : Khaki, and Green below waterline.

Insignia of Rank.

Vezérkapitany.	Fökapitany.	1 Törzs-	2 Törzs-	Kapitany.
(*Rear-Admiral.*)	(*Captain, senior.*)	kapitany. (*Captain, junior.*)	kapitany. (*Commander.*)	(*Lieut.- Commander.*)

Föhajónagy.	Hajónagy.	Gyakornok.
(*Lieut.*)	(*Sub-Lieut.*)	(*Midshipman.*)

Without curl, and with colour between stripes :—
Surgeons : Black velvet.
Engineers : Cherry-coloured cloth.
Constructors : Cherry-coloured velvet.
Paymasters : Red cloth.
Musical Directors : Violet cloth.

Uniform Cap.
Badge is a golden anchor surrounded by a laurel wreath and surmounted by the Holy Crown of Hungary.

4 River Patrol Boats.

(Ex-Austro-Hungarian.)

DEBRECEN.   (Masts now of equal height.)   1925 *Official Photo.*

DEBRECEN (ex-*Komaron*, ex-Austro-Hungarian *Lachs*), (Ganz-Danubius Yard, Budapest, 1918). Displacement : 140 tons. Dimensions : $149\frac{1}{4} \times 19\frac{1}{2} \times 3\frac{1}{4}$ feet *mean* draught. H.P. 1400 = 15 kts. A.E.G. turbines. 2 Yarrow boilers. Tunnel screws. Guns : 2—3 inch, 2 M.G. 1 S.L. Oil fuel : 18 tons Complement, 44. Refitted 1924.

1933 *Photo, Official.*

GYOR (ex-Austro-Hungarian *Stöhr*).
(Ganz-Danubius Yard, Budapest, 1918).
Refitted 1928.

Details as *Debrecen* above.

SZEGED.   1925 *Official Photo.*

SZEGED (ex-*Bregainica*, ex-Austro-Hungarian *Wels*, 1915),
KECSKEMÉT (ex-Austro-Hungarian *Viza*, 1916). Both built at Ganz-Danubius Yard, Budapest. Displacement : 133 tons. Dimensions : $144\frac{1}{2} \times 16\frac{1}{2} \times 3\frac{1}{4}$ feet *mean* draught. H.P. 1100 = 15 kts. A.E.G. turbines. 2 Yarrow boilers. Tunnel screws. Guns : 2—3 inch, 2 M.G. 1 S.L. Oil fuel : 18 tons. Complement, 44. *Szeged* refitted 1921, *Kecskemét,* 1923.

Depôt Ship.

1934 *Photo, Official.*

CSOBANC (Ganz-Danubius Yard, Budapest, 1928).
300 tons. Dimensions : $132 \times 18 \times 4\frac{1}{2}$ feet.
H.P. 180 = 8 kts. 2 Diesels. Tunnel screws.
Oil : 8 tons. Complement, 18.

In addition to the above, there are a number of small Motor Launches and Guard Boats.

HAITI.

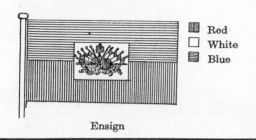

Red
White
Blue

Ensign

Patrol Vessels.

No. 2.   1937, *W. H. Davis, Esq.*

Nos. 1 and 2. Employed on Coastguard Service. Particulars wanted.

ICELAND.

Red
White
Blue

National Flag.

Fishery Protection Vessels.

(All photos by courtesy of Commander R. Steen Steensen, R.D.N.)

ÆGIR (April 25, 1929). Built by Burmeister & Wain, Copenhagen. 500 tons. Complement: 25. Guns: 1—57 mm. Diesel engines. Speed, 14 kts.

THOR (ex-German trawler *Senator Schaffer*). Built by Wollheim, Stettin, 1922, and purchased 1931. 300 tons. Complement: 18. Guns: 1—57 mm. I.H.P. 450 = 10 kts.

VIFIL. Motor vessel of 150 tons. Guns: 1—47 mm. Speed, 8·5 kts

IRAQ

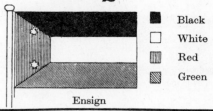

Black
White
Red
Green

Ensign

Patrol Vessels.

1937, *courtesy Messrs. Thornycroft (builders).*

4 *Thornycroft* type: Nos. 1, 2, 3, 4 (1937). 67 tons. 100 × 17 × 3 feet-(*mean* draught). Guns: 1—3·7 inch howitzer, 4 M.G., 2—3 inch trench mortars. 2 Thornycroft Diesels of 6-cylinder type. H.P.: 280 = 12 kts. Protected by bullet-proof plating. First launched April 16, 1937; all delivered by summer.

Royal Yacht.

1937, *courtesy Messrs. G. L. Watson (designers).*

(Ex-*Sans Peur*, ex-*Restless*). (Clydebank, 1923). Displacement: 1,025 tons. Dimensions: 186 × 29½ × — feet. Machinery: Triple expansion. 2 shafts. I.H.P.: 850 = 13 kts. 1 oil-fired boiler.

Tug.

ALARM (ex-*St. Ewe*). (Murdoch & Murray, 1919). Displacement: 820 tons. Dimensions: 135 × 30 × 14½ feet. I.H.P.: 1,200 = 12 kts. Coal: 240 tons. (May have been converted to oil firing.)

IRAN

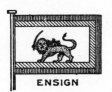

ENSIGN

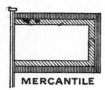

MERCANTILE

Personnel : 850 officers and men.

Escort Vessels.

BABR. Added 1936.

PALANG. 1932 *Photo, favour of the " Motorship."*

BABR (Aug., 1931), **PALANG** (Nov., 1931). Built by Cantieri Navali Riuniti, Palermo. Displacement : 950 tons. Dimensions : 204¾ (*pp.*) × 29¼ × 10 feet. Guns : 3—4 inch. 2 M.G. Machinery : 2 sets Fiat Diesels. Oil fuel : 120 tons. H.P. : 1,900 = 15 kts. Complement : 85.

Gunboats

SIMORGH 1931 *Photo.*

CHAROGH (July 26, 1931), **SIMORGH** (August 3, 1931), **KARKAS** (August 3, 1931), **CHAHBAAZ** (August 3, 1931). Laid down in 1930 at Cant. Nav. Riuniti (Palermo) (*Chahbaaz*), and Cant. Partenopei (Naples) (other 3). Displacement : 331 tons. Dimensions : 170 (*pp.*) × 22 × 6 (*mean*) feet. Guns : 2—3 inch, 2—37 mm. AA. Machinery : 2 sets Fiat Diesels. H.P. : 900 = 15·5 kts. Radius : 3,000 miles at 8 kts.

HOMAY (1931). Built in Italy. Displacement : 700 tons. No other particulars received. (Existence of this ship has been questioned.)

SHAHIN (ex-*Pahlavi*, ex-*Fatiya*, ex-*FM* 24). (Einswarden, 1917). Ex-German minesweeper, purchased 1923 for £4,000. Displacement : (*normal*) 170 tons. Dimensions : 132½ (*w.l.*) × 19¾ × 4 feet *normal* draught. Guns : 1—3 pdr. Machinery : 2 sets triple expansion. Oil fuel : 35 tons. I.H.P. : 800 = 16 kts. (after alterations). Complement : 44.

Imperial Yacht. (*Caspian Sea*)

CHAHSEVAR (1936). Built by N.V. Boele's Scheepwerven, Bolnes, Netherlands. 530 tons. Dimensions : 176½ × 25⅓ × 10½ feet. 2 sets Diesels by Gebr. Stork, of Hengelo. B.H.P. : 1,300 = 15 kts.

Patrol Boats.

1936

AZERBAIJAN, GEHLANI, MAZENDERAN, (Cant. Nav. Riuniti, Palermo, 1935). Displacement : 28 tons. Dimensions : 68½ × 12½ × 3½ feet. Guns : 1—37 mm. Machinery : Diesel. 2 shafts. B.H.P. : 300 = 14 kts.

Tug.

1936

NEYROU (Cant. Nav. Riuniti, Ancona, Dec. 9, 1934). Particulars wanted.

Uniforms.

Note.—A five pointed silver star (or gold in the case of flag officers) is worn on lapel of coat.

INSIGNIA OF RANK ON SLEEVES·

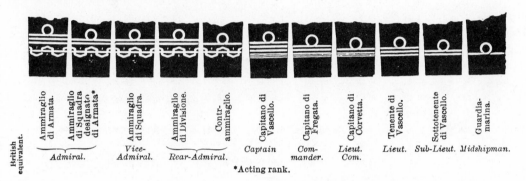

British equivalent.	Ammiraglio di Armata.	Ammiraglio di Squadra designato di Armata*	Ammiraglio di Squadra.	Ammiraglio di Divisione.	Contr-ammiraglio.	Capitano di Vascello.	Capitano di Fregata.	Capitano di Corvetta.	Tenente di Vascello.	Sottotenente di Vascello.	Guardia-marina.
	Admiral.		Vice-Admiral.	Rear-Admiral.		Captain	Com-mander.	Lieut. Com.	Lieut.	Sub-Lieut.	Midshipman.

*Acting rank.

The rank of Grande Ammiraglio (four stripes) equivalent to Admiral of the Fleet can only be conferred for special merit on flag officers who have commanded fleets in time of war.

Lesser ranks are : Aspirante ; Allievo dell' Accademia Navale (*Naval Cadet*).

Other branches distinguished by following Colours : Armi Navali (*Ordnance Constructors*), yellow-brown ; Genio Navale (*Naval Constructors* and *Engineers*), dark purple ; Sanitario (*Doctors*), blue ; Commissariato (*Paymasters*), red ; Chemists, green ; Harbour Masters, grey-green.

Note.—All officers under arms on duty wear a blue sash over right shoulder, ending in a blue knot at left hip ; worn with belt. Officers on staff duty wear it on opposite shoulder, with or without belt. Tropical white tunic has insignia of rank on shoulder straps, with stars to correspond with number of stripes. Senior lieutenants wear a piece of gold under the stars of shoulder strap.

Navy Estimates
{
1935-36.   1,304,881,000 lire Italian
1936-37.   1,609,891,000 „   „
1937-38.   1,857,891,000 „   „
1938-39.   2,013,000,000 „   „
1939-40.   2,703,000,000 „   „
}
Excluding Supplementary Credits.

Total Personnel : Officers, 4,143.   Men, 70,500.

Minister of Marine : S. E. Benito Mussolini.

Secretary of Marine Ministry : Ammiraglio di Armata Domenico Cavagnari.

Deputy Chief of Naval Staff : Ammiraglio di Squadra Inigo Campioni.

Naval Attaché, London : Contrammiraglio Bruno Brivonesi.

Asst. Naval Attaché : Capitano del Genio Navale Ernesto Trenchi.

Form of Address : Capitan di Vascello—, R.N.—

Flags.

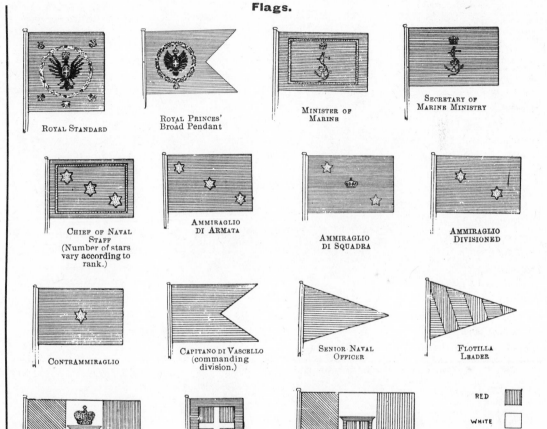

ROYAL STANDARD

ROYAL PRINCES' Broad Pendant

MINISTER OF MARINE

SECRETARY OF MARINE MINISTRY

CHIEF OF NAVAL STAFF (Number of stars vary according to rank.)

AMMIRAGLIO DI ARMATA

AMMIRAGLIO DI SQUADRA

AMMIRAGLIO DIVISIONED

CONTRAMMIRAGLIO

CAPITANO DI VASCELLO (commanding division.)

SENIOR NAVAL OFFICER

FLOTILLA LEADER

ENSIGN

JACK

MERCANTILE ENSIGN

RED
WHITE
BLUE
YELLOW
GREEN

Mercantile Marine.

From "Lloyd's Register" 1939 figures.

1,235 vessels of 3,448,453 gross tonnage.

ITALY.

OFFICIAL TABLE OF NAVAL ORDNANCE. (Revised, 1931.)

Official Designation.— Calibre mm length cal.	381/40	254/45	254/45	203/54	203/50	190/45	152/53	152/50	152/45	120/50	120/50	120/45	102/45	102/35	100/47	76/50	76/45	76/40	76/17
Mark A=Armstrong, V=Vickers An=Ansaldo, S=Schneider. Mark O.T.O.=Odero-Terni-Orlando.	V.	A	V.	An.	S.-An.	A., V.	An. O.T.O.	A.	S.	An.	A., V.	A.	S.-A.	S.	O.T.O.	A., V.	S.	A.	S.
Date of introduction.	1917	1907	1906	1929	1924	1908-1906	1927-29	1918	1911	1926.	1909	1918	1917	1914-15	1929	1909	1911	1916	1912
Designation by Calibre, c/m.	38.1	25.4	25.4	20.3	20.3	19.05	15.24	15.24	15.24	12	12	12	10.2	10·2	10.0	7.62	7.62	7.62	7.62
Calibre, in inches	15	10	10	8	8	7.5	6	6	6	4.75	4.75	4.75	4	4	3.9	3	3	3	3
Lengths — Total, in feet		39.07	38.715	36.545	34.593	29.22	27.83	25.94	23.42	19.57	20.38	18.38	15.715	12.247	15.721	13.271	11.722	10.292	4.593
Lengths — Rifled Bore, in inches		358.4	370.5	358·66	—	281.7	—	256.6	219.2	—	204.64	174.64	150.74	114.29	12.365	126	107.2	101.57	44.88
Lengths — Powder Chamber, in inches		74.91	74.91	64.66	—	51.65	—	44.6	44.6	—	28.64	35.03	27.16	23.50	3.112	22	25.4	—	—
Lengths — Bore, in calibres		35.84	37.05	—	—	37.5	—	42.77	36.54	—	43.31	36.96	37.53	28.46	15.371	42	35.73	28.42	14.96
No. of Grooves		60	70	52	52	44	44	36	56	36	36	36	40	32	26	28	2⅜	16	24
Twist of Rifling, in calibres		30	00–30	—	30	00–30	30	33	36	30	30	30	—	—	30	30	35.9	33	22
Total Weight, in tons	82	34.49	35.339	19.170	20.800	14.478	7.700	8.100	7.025	3.00	3.662	4.035	2.327	1.200	2.020	1.122	0.698	0.660	0.104
Firing Charge — Armour-piercing projectile lb.		185	185	110.994	103.19	70.987	43	—	—	19	—	—	—	—	—	—	—	—	—
Firing Charge — Common Shell H.E., lb.		185	185	—	—	70.987	—	32.79	30.64	—	14.66	9.589	9.479	6.50	10.319	3.02	3.571	2.281	0.529
Weight — Armour-piercing projectile, lb.		494	494	275.573	260	200.39	103.5	—	—	50.5	—	—	—	—	—	—	—	—	—
Weight — Shell H.E., lb.		489.8	489.8	—	—	498.5	—	110.22	103.61	—	48.74	48.74	30.31	30.31	30.318	14.05	14.05	13.954	11.68
Weight — Shrapnel, lb.		—	—	—	—	—	—	—	—	—	—	—	—	—	—	—	—	—	11.68
Bursting Charge — Armour-piercing projectile, lb.		4.37	4.37	—	—	2.332	—	—	—	—	—	—	—	—	—	—	—	—	—
Bursting Charge — Shell H.E., lb.		29.86	29.86	—	—	11.706	—	5.996	7.528	—	2.711	2.711	2.866	2.866	—	1.102	1.102	—	0.782
Bursting Charge — Shrapnel, lb.		—	—	—	—	—	—	—	—	—	—	—	—	—	—	—	—	—	0.165
Muzzle Velocity, in ft. secs.		2788.77	2788.77	3031.180	2743.20	2788.77	2785	2854	2723	2786	2788	2460	2788	2460	2438.40	2460	2460	2214	1230
Muzzle Energy — Total tons per sq. inch		17.71	17.71	—	—	17.98	—	18.37	16.86	—	18.37	15.75	18.37	18.37	—	—	18.37	15.75	12.47

Note.—German 5·9 in. and Austrian 3·9 in. are retained in ex-enemy cruisers and destroyers. There is also a new 15 inch, and an O.T.O. model 12·6 inch.

15 inch in *Littorio* class.
12.6 ,, *Cesare* class.
10 ,, 45 cal. *S. Giorgio*
8 ,, 53 ,, *Zara* class and *Bolzano*.
8 ,, 50 ,, *Trento* classes.
7.5 ,, 45 ,, *San Giorgio*.
6 ,, 53 ,, *Condottieri* class and later types.
4.7 ,, 50 ,, *Quarto* and *Navigatori* class.
3.9 ,, 47 ,, *Trento, Zara,* and *Condottieri* classes.

Displacement.

Now given in English Tons, "Standard" calculation.

Directors, Rangefinders, &c.

Supplied by the Galileo and S. Giorgio Companies, of Florence and Genoa, respectively. Rangefinders are of a new model both co-incident and stereoscopic, of 5 and 7.20 metres base for main armament and 3 metres for secondary guns.

Programmes

	1934	1935	1936	1937	1938	1939
Capital Ships	*Littorio* *Vittorio Veneto*	—	—	—	*Impero* *Roma*	—
Cruisers	—	—	—	—	12 *Regolo*	2
Escort Vessels	*Eritrea* 4 *Orsa*	—	—	—	—	—
Destroyers	—	4 *Oriani*	12 *Aviere*			
Torpedo Boats	*S. Turr*	10 *Vega*	16 *Partenope*			(Number not specified)
Submarines	*Foca* *Zoea*	10 *Perla* 2 *Argo*	10 *Adua*	9 *Marcello* 3 *Brin* 7 *Adua* 1 *Atropo* (Number not specified)		
M.T.B.	—	—	25			

Torpedoes.
Supplied by Silurificio Italiano di Fiume.
Cal. 533·4 mm. *Length,* 7·2 m. *Charge* 250 kg. *Speed,* 4,000 m. = 50 kts.
6,000 = 43 kts., 8,000 = 39 kts., 10,000 = 34 kts., 12,000 = 30 kts.

GORIZIA.

CONDOTTIERI *class.* "A" *type.*

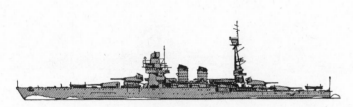

CAVOUR. CESARE.

ZARA. FIUME.

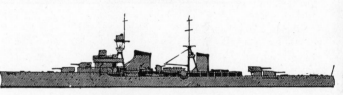

CONDOTTIERI *class.* "B" *type.*

(*Reconstructing*).
(Will probably resemble *Cavour* type).

DORIA. DUILIO.

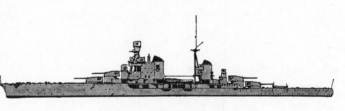

POLA.

CONDOTTIERI *class.* "C" and "D" *types.*
(former with thinner after funnel).

BOLZANO.

CONDOTTIERI *class.* "E" *type.*

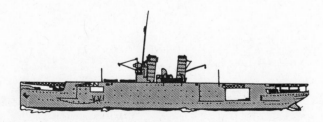

MIRAGLIA.

TRENTO. TRIESTE.

R

BARI.

E. GIOVANNINI.

S. TURR.

ORSA class. (Approx.)

ALBATROS.

GRECALE class.

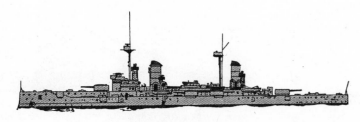

SAN GIORGIO.

SPICA class.

DARDO and FOLGORE classes.

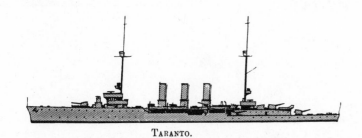

TARANTO.

A. ORIANI class.
(AVIERE class similar).

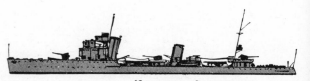

NAVIGATORI class.

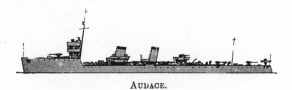

Audace.

Mirabello *class*.

Abba and Insidioso *classes*.

Curtatone *class*.

Leone *class*.

Sella *class*.

Sirtori, Cosenz, & Generali *classes*.

Palestro *class*.

Borea
class.

Sauro and Borea *classes*.

Cortellazzo *class*.

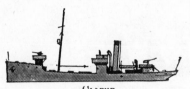

CIRENE.

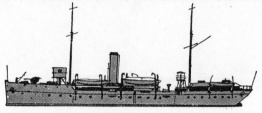

CABOTO.

AURORA.

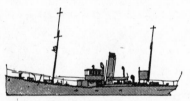

PALMAIOLA, *etc.*

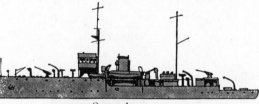

OSTIA *class.*

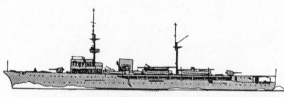

ERITREA.

BERTA *class.*

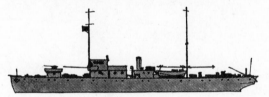

FASANA *class.*

CROTONE.
VIESTI.

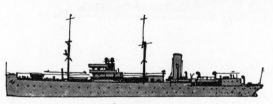

QUARNARO.

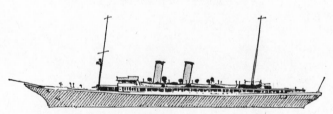

SAVOIA.

PACINOTTI
VOLTA.

H *class.*

X 2, X 3.

Settembrini *class.*

Delfino *class.*

Corridoni *class.*

Santarosa *class.*

Pisani *class.*

Mameli *class.*

Balilla *class.*

Glauco *class.*

Fieramosca.

Archimede *class.*

Micca.

Calvi *class.*

Foca *Class.*

Argo *class.*

Argonauta *class.*
(Sirena and Perla *classes* similar.)

The following list of distinctive letters, painted on bows of destroyers, torpedo boats and allied types, has been furnished officially to "Fighting Ships" by the courtesy of the Ministry of Marine. Apparent duplication of certain letters is due to the fact that vessels in question differ noticeably in appearance.

A A	ALBATROS	C I	CASCINO, CALIPSO	L C	LINCE	P O	POERIO
A B	ABBA	C L	CAIROLI, CLIO	L E	LEONE	P R	PRESTINARI, PROCIONE
A C	ACERBI, ALCIONE	C M	CALATAFIMI	L F	LA FARINA		
A D	ANDROMEDA, AUDACE	C N	CAMICIA NERA	L I	LIBECCIO	P S	PERSEO PESSAGNO
		C O	CENTAURO	L M	LA MASA		
A E	ARIEL	C P	CALLIOPE	L N	LANCIERE	P T	PALESTRO
A F	ALFIERI	C R	CRISPI	L P	LUPO		
A I	ASCARI	C S	CASSIOPEA, COSENZ	L R	LIRA	R C	RICASOLI
A L	AQUILONE, ALDEBARAN			M A	MANIN	R I	RIBOTY
		C T	CASTORE, CURTATONE	M B	MONZAMBANO		
A N	ANTARES			M D	MEDICI	S A	SAETTA
A O	AIRONE	C Z	CORAZZIERE	M I	MIRABELLO	S C	SCIROCCO
A P	ALPINO			M L	MAESTRALE	S E	SELLA
A R	ARTIGLIERE	D A	DARDO	M N	MONTANARI	S F	SCHIAFFINO
A S	ASTORE	D M	DA MOSTO	M O	MALOCELLO	S G	SAGITTARIO
A T	ALTAIR	D N	DA NOLI	M S	MISSORI	S I	SIRIO
A U	ARETUSA	D R	DA RECCO	M T	MOSTO	S L	SOLFERINO
A V	AVIERE	D V	DA VERAZZANO			S M	SAN MARTINO
		D Z	DEZZA	N B	NEMBO	S P	SPICA
B G	BERSAGLIERE			N C	NICOTERA	S R	SIRTORI
B O	BALENO	E R	EURO	N L	NULLO	S T	STRALE, STOCCO
B R	BOREA	E S	ESPERO			S U	SAURO
B S	BASSINI			O A	ORIANI		
B T	BATTISTI	F B	FABRIZI	O N	ORIONE	T A	TARIGO
		F C	FUCILIERE	O R	ORSINI	T B	TURBINE
C A	CANOPO, CARINI	F G	FOLGORE	O S	ORSA	T I	TIGRE
C B	CARABINIERE	F L	FULMINE	O T	OSTRO	T U	TURR
C C	CIRCE	F R	FRECCIA				
C D	CASTELFIDARDO, CARDUCCI	G B	GIOBERTI	P A	PAPA, PANTERA	U S	USODIMARE
		G E	GENIERE	P E	PEPE		
C E	CANTORE, CLIMENE	G N	GRANATIERE,	P G	PEGASO	V G	VEGA
		G R	GRECALE	P I	PIGAFETTA	V I	VIVALDI
C F	CONFIENZA	G V	GIOVANNINI	P L	PILO, PLEIADI		
C G	CIGNO	L A	LAMPO	P N	PANCALDO, PARTENOPE	Z E	ZENO
C H	CHINOTTO	L B	LIBRA			Z F	ZEFFIRO

SUBMARINE RECOGNITION LETTERS. Painted on Conning Tower.

A A	AMETISTA	C A	CAGNI	G A	GALVANI	M O	MOCENIGO	S I	SIRENA
A D	ADUA	C C	CARACCIOLO	G E	GEMMA	M P	MALASPINA	S N	SANTAROSA
A G	ARGONAUTA	C L	CAPPELLINI	G I	GUGLIELMOTTI	M R	MANARA	S P	SALPA
A H	ARCHIMEDE	C N	COLONNA	G L	GALILEI	M S	MOROSINI	S Q	SQUALO
A L	ALAGI	C O	CORALLO	G M	G. MAMELI	M U	MEDUSA	S R	SCIRE
A M	AMBRA	C R	CORRIDONI	G N	GIULIANI	N A	NAIADE	S T	SETTEMBRINI
A N	ANFITRITE	C V	CALVI	G O	GONDAR	N E	NEREIDE	T C	TURCHESE
A O	ARGO	D A	DAGABUR	G P	G. DA PROCIDA	N G	NEGHELLI	T E	TEMBIEN
A R	ARADAM	D E	DESSIE	G T	GALATEA	N I	NANI	T I	TOSELLI
A S	ASCIANGHI	D L	DELFINO	G U	GLAUCO	N R	NARVALO	T L	TORRICELLI
A T	ATROPO	D M	DIAMANTE	I A	JALEA	O A	OTARIA	T O	TOTI
A X	AXUM	D N	DES GENEYS	I N	JANTINA	O C	ONICE	T P	TOPAZIO
B A	BANDIERA	D O	DANDOLO	I R	IRIDE	O N	ONDINA	T R	TRICHECO
B C	BARACCA	D S	DIASPRO	L A	LAFOLE	P C	P. CAPPONI	T S	T. SPERI
B E	BERILLO	D U	DURBO	L V	L. DA VINCI	P L	PERLA	T T	TARANTINI
B G	BRAGADINO	E M	E. MILLO	L Z	LIUZZI	P N	PISANI	T Z	TAZZOLI
B H	BIANCHI	E O	EMO	M A	MACALLE	P R	PROVANA	U R	UARSCIEK
B I	BAGNOLINI	F A	FERRARIS	M C	MICCA	R S	R. SETTIMO	U S	UEBI-SCEBELI
B L	BALILLA	F B	F. DI BRUNO	M E	MENOTTI	R U	RUBINO	V L	VELELLA
B N	BAUSAN	F R	FIERAMOSCA	M H	MALACHITE	S B	S. BON	V N	VENIERO
B O	BARBARIGO	F O	FOCA	M I	MILLELIRE	S C	SCIESA	Z A	ZAFFIRO
B R	BRIN	F S	FISALIA	M L	MARCELLO	S D	SMERALDO	Z E	ZOEA
B U	BEILUL	F Z	FINZI	M N	MARCONI	S E	SERPENTE		

(LITTORIO CLASS—4 SHIPS.)

LITTORIO (Aug. 27, 1937,) **VITTORIO VENETO** (July 25, 1937), **IMPERO** (building), **ROMA** (building). *Standard* displacement : 35,000 tons. Complement : 1,600. Length : 754¼ (*pp.*), 762½ (*w.l.*), 775 feet (*o.a.*). Beam : 106½ feet. Draught : 28 feet (*mean*), 30½ feet (*max.*).

Guns :   Aircraft : **3**   Armour :
   9—15 inch.   9″—12″ Belt.
  12—6 inch, 55 cal.
  12—3·5 inch AA.
  40 M.G. AA.

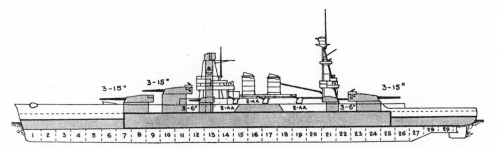

Machinery : Parsons geared turbines. 4 shafts. S.H.P. : 130,000 = 30 kts. High pressure water-tube boilers of 3-drum type. Oil fuel.

Name.	Builder and Machinery	Laid down.	Completed.
Littorio	Ansaldo	28 Oct., 1934	
Vittorio Veneto	} C.R.D.A., San Marco, Trieste]	28 Oct., 1934	} To be '39
Roma		18 Sept., 1938	
Impero	Ansaldo	14 May, 1938	

Notes.—Designed by Engineer Inspector-General Umberto Pugliese. Above information is all official, and plan is based on reliable data. First two ships were intended to have been completed before the end of 1938, but it is not likely that they will be ready until at least a year later.

CONTE DI CAVOUR. (Described on following page.)   1937.

(CAVOUR CLASS—4 SHIPS.)

CONTE DI CAVOUR (Aug. 10, 1911), **GIULIO CESARE** (Oct. 15, 1911). Both reconstructed 1933–37.

CAIO DUILIO (April 24, 1913), **ANDREA DORIA** (March 30, 1913). Undergoing similar reconstruction, 1937–39.

Standard displacement (as reconstructed): 23,622 tons (over 25,000 full load). Complement: 1,198. Dimensions: 597 (*w.l.*), 611½ (*o.a.*) × 92 × 30 feet (*mean draught*).

Guns : (First pair)
10—12·6 inch.
12—4·7 inch.
8—3·9 inch AA.
36—M.G., AA.

(2nd pair)
10—12·6 inch
12—5·3 inch
10—3·5 inch
39—M.G., AA.

Aircraft :
4, with 2 catapults.

Armour (originally, now improved over magazines, machinery and boiler spaces):
9¾″–8″ Belt (amidships)
5″ Belt (ends)
9½″ Barbettes
11″ Turrets to these
11″ Conning tower (fore)

CESARE.   1938, *courtesy Dott. Ing. L. Accorsi.*

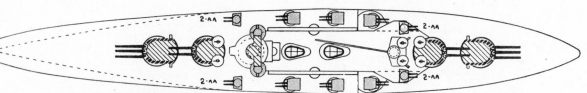

CESARE.   1938, *Grand Studio.*

Machinery : Belluzzo geared turbines. 2 shafts. S.H.P. : 75,000 = 27 kts. 8 boilers of 3-drum type. Oil fuel : 2,000 tons.

Note.—These ships were originally of entirely different appearance, with a main armament of **13—12 inch** guns, in 3 triple and 2 double turrets and a secondary battery of 6-inch guns. Cost of reconstruction, Lit. 300,000.000 for the first two.

A fifth ship of this class, *Leonardo da Vinci*, blew up at Taranto on Aug. 2, 1916.

Gunnery Note.—12·6 inch guns, first mounted in these 4 ships, are of the latest Terni model, which has given remarkably successful results in proof tests.

Name	Builder	Machinery	Laid down	Completed	Rebuilt by
Cavour	Spezia	Orlando	10/8/10	Jan. 15	Cant. Riuniti dell' Adriatico
Cesare	Ansaldo	Ansaldo	23/6/10	29/11/13	Cant. Nav. del Tirreno
Doria	Spezia	,,	24/3/12	Mar. 16	Cant. Riuniti dell' Adriatico
Duilio	Castellammare	,,	25/4/12	May 15	Cant. Nav. del Tirreno

CAVOUR. (*Another view on preceding page.*)   1938, *J. R. Potts, Esq.*

(MODIFIED " TRENTO " TYPE.)

BOLZANO. Ansaldo, Sestri-Ponente. (Aug. 31, 1932),

Standard displacement, 10,000 tons. Complement, 723.
Length 627 (*p.p.*), 637½ (*w.l.*), 646¼ (*o.a.*). Beam 68 feet.
Draught 18¾ feet (*mean*).

BOLZANO

1935, *Sig. F. Cianciafara.*

Guns :
  8—8 inch. 54 cal.
  12—3·9 inch. 47 cal.
  10—37 mm. AA.
  8—13 mm. AA.
Torpedo tubes :
  8—21 inch.

Aircraft :
  2, with 1 catapult (amidships)

Armour (unofficial)
  2¾″ side amidships.
  3″ Turrets.
  3″ C.T.
  2″ Deck.

Note to Plan:—Aftermost pair of 3·9 inch on either side removed, and 4—13 mm. AA. substituted. T.T. are mounted on either side, amidships.

BOLZANO.

1934 *Photo. Sig. F. Cianciafara.*

Machinery : 4 Parsons geared turbines, S.H.P. 150,000 = 36 kts. 4 shafts. 10 Ansaldo 3-drum boilers (300 lbs. pressure). Oil fuel : 3,000 tons.

General Notes.—Laid down under 1929 Programme as a third unit of the *Trento* class, but differs from these in dimensions and in having a forecastle deck, besides various alterations in rig, bridgework, etc. She resembles *Trento* in sacrificing a certain amount of protection for an additional 3·5 kts. compared with *Zara*—a modern rendering of the " battle cruiser " role applied to cruisers. Speed on 8 hrs. trial = 38 kts. *Max.* 39 kts. The bridge structure has been " stream-lined " to flush the funnel in order to minimise back draught at full speed, which drove the funnel fumes into the bridge. Laid down June 1930, completed Aug., 1933.

(ZARA CLASS.—4 SHIPS.)

ZARA, FIUME (Both Apl. 27th, 1930), **GORIZIA** (Dec. 28, 1930), **POLA** (Dec. 5, 1931).

Standard displacement, 10,000 tons. Complement, 705.

Length (*p.p.*) 589¼; (*o.a.*) 599½ feet. Beam, 67⅔ feet. Draught, 19½ feet.

Guns :
  8—8 inch, 54 cal.
  12—3·9 inch, 47 cal.
  10—37 mm. AA.
  8—13 mm. AA.
Torpedo tubes :
  Nil.

Aircraft :
  2, with catapult.

Armour :
  5½″ Side ....
  5″ Turrets ....
  4½″ Transverse Bulkheads
  3″ C.T. ....
  2″ Deck ....

ZARA.   1932 *Photo.*

Note to Plan:—Aftermost pair of 3·9 inch on either side removed, and 4—13 mm. AA. substituted.

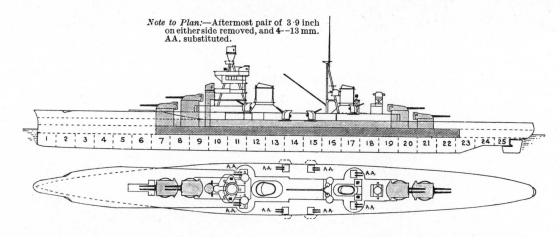

Machinery : 2 Parsons geared turbines. S.H.P.: 95,000 = 32 kts. 2 shafts. Oil fuel : 1,450 tons *normal*, 2,200 tons *maximum.* Radius : 3,200 miles at 25 kts. 8 boilers, 3-drum type, 300 lbs. pressure.

General Notes.—Zara, Fiume laid down under 1928 Programme, *Gorizia* under that for 1929, *Pola*, 1930.

Name	Builder	Machinery	Laid down	Completed	Trials 8 hours.
Fiume	Stab. Tecnico Odero-Terni- Orlando	Stab. Tecnico Odero-Tern - Orlando	Apr. '29	Nov. 1931	33·1
Zara			July '29	Oct. 1931	34·2
Pola			Mar. '31	Dec. 1932	33·9
Gorizia			Mar. '30	Dec. 1931	33·8

POLA.   1935, *Sig. F. Cianciafara*

Observe how bridge structure has been built in flush with funnel to obviate back draught which drew fumes down on to bridge at high speed.

(Trento Class.—2 Ships.)

TRENTO (Orlando, Leghorn, Oct. 4th, 1927).

TRIESTE (Stab. Tecnico, Trieste, Oct. 24th, 1926).

Standard displacement, 10,000 tons.   Complement, **723**.

Length (*p.p.*), 624, (*w.l.*) 636½. (*o.a.*), 645 feet.

Beam, 67½ feet. *Mean* draught, 19 feet.

TRENTO.

1933 *Photo, Official.*

To differentiate, note that in *Trieste* the lower fore top encloses all the mast legs. Also, these ships have differently marked fore funnels.

Guns :
  8—8 inch, 50 cal.
  12—3·9 inch, 47 cal.
  18 smaller AA.
Torpedo tubes (21 inch) :
  8, *above water*, on main deck.

Aircraft: **2**, with catapult.

Note to Plan:—
  Aftermost pair of 3·9 inch on either side removed, and 4—13 mm. AA. substituted.

Armour :
  3″ Side amidships
  2″ Turrets
  3″ C.T.
  2″ Deck

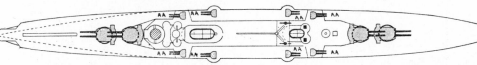

Plan revised 1934.

Machinery : 4 Parsons geared turbines. 4 shafts. S.H.P. : 150,000 = 35 kts. 12 3-drum boilers (300 lbs. pressure).   Oil fuel : 3,000 tons.

General Notes.—Laid down under 1923-24 Programme. *Trento*, 8/2/25 ; *Trieste*, in June, 1925. Carry three scouting seaplanes, equipped for bombing. Design modified during construction. They were originally to have had hangar amidships, but this idea has been abandoned and a catapult installed on forecastle. In the revised design, after C.T. is dispensed with, AA. armament redistributed, and additional mast control tops added. These ships are believed to be much more lightly constructed than British *Kent* class, in order to attain a high speed. Completion dates : *Trento*, April, 1929 ; *Trieste*, March, 1930.

Gunnery Notes.—8 inch reported to be remarkably powerful weapons with exceptional range. *Maximum* elevation is 45°.

Engineering Notes.—Trials in August, 1928, are said to have given consumption of 68 tons of oil per hour. *Maximum* figure, *Trento*, 38·7 kts. Displacement was 11,000 tons (*normal*) at the time. Average trial figures : *Trento*, 146,640 = 36·6 kts. *Trieste*, 124,761 = 35·6 kts. Weight of engines is about 33 lbs. per S.H.P.

TRIESTE.

1932 *Lt. A. E. T. Christie, R.N.*

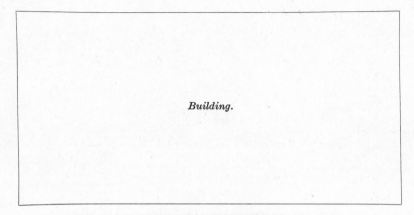

Building.

(Ciano Class—2 Ships)

AMMIRAGLIO COSTANZO CIANO and another.

Displacement : 8,000 tons.   Complement : 600.

Length :   Beam :   Draught :

Guns :   Aircraft :   Armour :
10—6 inch, 55 cal.   4   Believed to be somewhat
more extensive than in
Garibaldi type.

Machinery : Geared turbines.

Note.—Laid down 1939 under Programme for that year.

Building.   Will have 2 funnels.

(Regolo Class—12 Ships)

ATTILIO REGOLO, SCIPIONE AFRICANO, CAIO MARIO, CLAUDIO TIBERIO, PAOLO EMILIO, CORNELIO SILLA, OTTAVIANO AUGUSTO, POMPEO MAGNO, ULPIO TRAIANO, VIPSANIO AGRIPPA, CLAUDIO DRUSO, GIULIO GERMANICO.

Displacement : 3,362 tons.   Complement :

Length : (*w.l.*) 444¼ feet.   Beam : 44¾ feet.   Draught : 13 feet (*mean*).

Guns :   Armour :
8—5·3 inch   Practically *nil*.
6—65 mm. AA.
14 M.G. AA.
Torpedo Tubes :
8—21 inch.

Mines : Equipped for laying.

Machinery : 2 sets geared turbines. 2 shafts. S.H.P. : 120,000 = 41 kts. Oil fuel.

Name.	Builder.	Laid down.	Completed.
A. Regolo	} O.T.O., Leghorn	1939	
Scip. Africano			
Caio Mario			
C. Tiberio	O.T.O., Spezia	1939	
P. Emilio	} Ansaldo	1939	
C. Silla			*To be*
O. Augusto	} Riuniti, Ancona	1939	*1941*
Pompeo Magno			
U. Traiano	Riuniti, Palermo	1939	
V. Agrippa	} Tirreno	1939	
C. Druso			
G. Germanico	Navalmeccanica, Castellammare	1939	

(Condottieri Class—"E" Type.)

(GARIBALDI CLASS—2 SHIPS.)

GIUSEPPE GARIBALDI, LUIGI DI SAVOIA DUCA DEGLI ABRUZZI

(Both April 21, 1936.)

Standard displacement: 7,874 tons (9,000 tons full load).

Complement, 600.

Length: 593 (*w.l.*), 613¾ feet (*o.a.*). Beam, 61 feet. Draught, 17 feet (*mean*).

Guns:
- 10—6 inch, 55 cal.
- 8—3·9 inch, 47 cal.
- 8—37 mm. AA.
- 8—13 mm. AA.
- 2 D.C.T.

Torpedo tubes:
- 6—21 inch (tripled).

Mines:
- Equipped for Minelaying.

Aircraft:
4, with 2 catapults.

Armour: (*Unofficial*)
- 1½″—3″ Vert. Side.
- 1½″ Deck.
- 1″ Turrets.
- 1″ C.T.

LUIGI DI SAVOIA DUCA DEGLI ABRUZZI on trials.

1937.

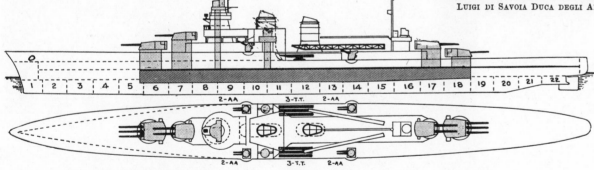
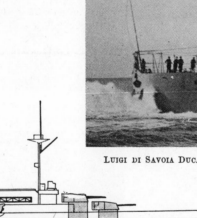

Machinery: Parsons geared turbines. 2 shafts. Designed S.H.P.: 100,000 = 35 kts. Boilers: 8, of 3-drum type. Oil fuel: 1,200 tons.

Name	Builder	Laid down	Completed
G. Garibaldi	C.R. dell' Adriatico	Dec. 1933	1937
Luigi di Savoia	Odero–Terni–Orlando	Dec. 1933	1937

Notes.—These ships represent yet a further expansion of the original "Condottieri" design. The 6-inch guns are a new model, more powerful than the 53 cal. weapons with which previous cruisers have been armed. *Duca degli Abruzzi* reported to have reached 38 kts. on trials.

L. DI SAVOIA DUCA DEGLI ABRUZZI

1938, *courtesy Dott. Ing. L. Accorsi*

(CONDOTTIERI CLASS.—" D " TYPE.)

(EMANUELE FILIBERTO CLASS—2 SHIPS.)

EUGENIO DI SAVOIA (March 16, 1935).
EMANUELE FILIBERTO DUCA D'AOSTA (April 22, 1934).

Standard displacement : 7,283 tons. (About 8,500 tons full load.)

Complement : 551

Dimensions : 592 (*w.l.*) 610¼ (*o.a.*) × 57⅓ × 16⅓ feet (*mean* draught).

Guns : **8**—6 inch, 53 cal.	Aircraft : 3 with 1 catapult.
6—3·9 inch, 47 cal. AA.	
8—37 mm. AA.	Armour : (*Unofficial*)
8—13 mm. AA.	1½"–3" Vert. side.
2 D.C.T.	1½" Deck.
Torpedo Tubes : **6**—21 inch (tripled).	1" Turrets.
	1" C.T.

Mines : Equipped for Minelaying.

Note to Plan.—Torpedo tubes are tripled, not paired, as shown.

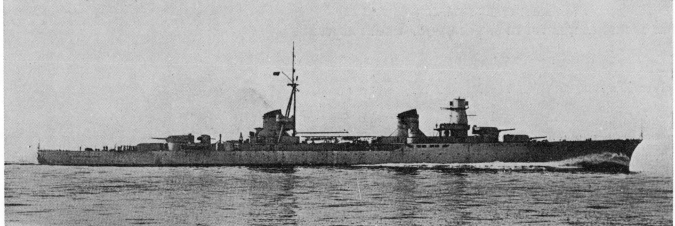

EMANUELE FILIBERTO DUCA D'AOSTA   1935

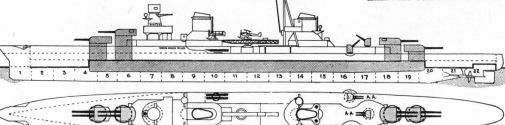

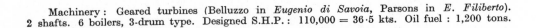

Machinery : Geared turbines (Belluzzo in *Eugenio di Savoia*, Parsons in *E. Filiberto*). 2 shafts. 6 boilers, 3-drum type. Designed S.H.P. : 110,000 = 36·5 kts. Oil fuel : 1,200 tons.

EMANUELE FILIBERTO DUCA D'AOSTA.   1936

Name	Builders	Laid down	Completed
E. di Savoia	Ansaldo	Jan., 1932	Jan., 1936
E. F. Duca d'Aosta	Odero-Terni-Orlando	Jan., 1932	July, 1935

General Notes.—These two ships are enlarged editions of the *Montecuccoli* class. Reported to be very lightly constructed.

EUGENIO DI SAVOIA   1937

(CONDOTTIÈRI CLASS—" C " TYPE.)

RAIMONDO MONTECUCCOLI (Ansaldo, Sestri Ponente, August 2, 1934).

MUZIO ATTENDOLO (Cant. Riuniti dell' Adriatico, San Marco, Trieste, September 9, 1934).

Standard displacement : 6,941 tons (about 8,000 tons full load). Complement, 522.

Dimensions : $575\frac{1}{4}$ (*pp.*), 577 (*w.l.*), $597\frac{3}{4}$ (*o.a.*) × $54\frac{1}{2}$ × $14\frac{3}{4}$ feet (*mean* draught).

Guns : **8**—6 inch, 53 cal.
      6—3·9 inch, 47 cal. AA.
      8—37 mm. AA.
      8—13 mm. AA.
      2 D.C.T.

Aircraft : 3, with catapult.

Torpedo Tubes : **4**—21 inch.

Mines : Equipped for laying.

Armour :
Similar to " B " type of this class, but side armour decidedly thicker at w.l.

MUZIO ATTENDOLO   1936

R. MONTECUCCOLI   1937

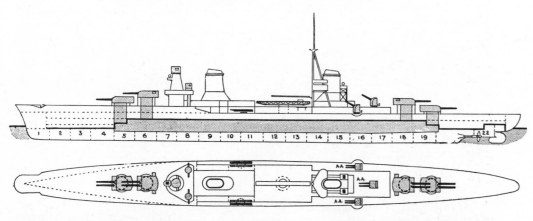

Machinery : Belluzzo and Parsons turbines, respectively. 2 shafts. 6 boilers of 3-drum type. S.H.P. : 106,000 = 37 kts. Oil fuel : 500/1,200 tons.

Note—These ships were laid down in October and September, 1931, respectively, under 1930 Programme, but construction was held up pending alterations to their plans. The simple tower forward marks the abandonment of the former tiers of bridgework and tripod mast and a Gagnotto catapult amidships replaces the fixed pattern in previous classes. Note the grouping of the AA. guns aft. Completed in July and August, 1935, respectively. *R. Montecuccoli* made 39·4 kts. on trials, without stores or ammunition on board.

M. ATTENDOLO.   1939, *courtesy Dott. Ing. L. Accorsi.*

("Condottieri" Class—"B" Type, 2 Ships.)

LUIGI CADORNA (Cant. Riuniti dell' Adriatico, San Marco, Trieste, Sept. 30, 1931).

ARMANDO DIAZ (Odero-Terni-Orlando, July 10, 1932).

Displacement : 5,008 tons. Complement : 500.
Dimensions : 547 (*w.l.*), 554½ (*o.a.*) × 50⅕ × 14 feet (*mean*) draught.

Guns :	Aircraft :
8—6 inch 53 cal.	2, with Catapult.
6—3·9 inch AA.	
8—37 mm. AA.	
8—13 mm. AA.	
2 D.C.T.	

Torpedo Tubes : 4—21 inch.

Mines: Equipped for laying.

Armour :
Thin plating only on Side, Turrets, and Decks.

LUIGI CADORNA.

1934 (added 1935) *Sig. F. Cianciafara.*

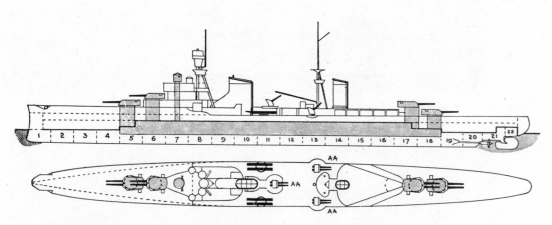

ARMANDO DIAZ

1935, *Sig. F. Cianciafara.*

Machinery :
2 Parsons Geared Turbines. 2 shafts.
H.P. 95,000 = 37 kts. (On trials at 5,500 tons displacement *Diaz* made a mean speed of 39·78 kts. with 106,000 H.P.)

Oil : 500/1,000 tons. 6 boilers of 3-drum type.

Radius : 2,500 miles at 25 kts.

General Note.—Laid down September and July, 1930, and completed in August and April, 1933, respectively. Are modified *Bande Nere* type with reduced upper works, different arrangement of rig and funnels, and altered positions of AA. guns. There is a fixed catapult training to starboard on the platform between the funnel and after turret, where aircraft are also stowed.

ARMANDO DIAZ

1933 *Photo.*

("Condottieri" Class—"A" Type, 4 Ships.)

GIOVANNI DELLE BANDE NERE (April 27, 1930).
BARTOLOMEO COLLEONI (December 21, 1930).
ALBERTO DI GIUSSANO (April 27, 1930).
ALBERICO DA BARBIANO (August 23, 1930).

Displacement : 5,069 tons.   Complement : 500.
Dimensions : 547 (w.l.) 555½ (o.a.) × 50⅖ × 14¼ feet (*mean* draught).

Guns :   Aircraft : 2 with catapult

8—6 inch, 53 cal.
6—3·9 inch AA.
8—37 mm. AA.   Armour :
8—13 mm. AA.   Side, Deck, Turrets.
2 D.C.T.   Thin plating only.

Torpedo Tubes (21 inch) :
4 *above water* (paired).

Mines : All except *Giussano* equipped for laying.

GIOVANNI DELLE BANDE NERE.

1933 *Photo, L.U.C.E.*

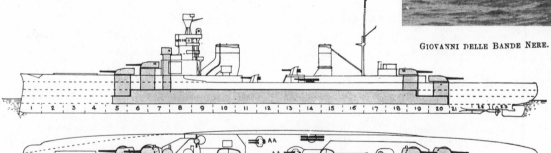

Machinery : 2 Geared Belluzzo turbines. 2 shafts. H.P.: 95,000 = 37 kts. 6 Boilers of 3-drum type. Oil : 500/1,000 tons. Radius : 2,500 miles at 25 kts.

Name	Builder	Machinery	Laid down	Completed	Trials 8 hrs.
Bande Nere	Castellammare	Trieste	Oct. '28	Apr. '31	39·0 kts.
Colleoni	Ansaldo	Ansaldo	June '28	Feb. '32	40·9 „
Barbiano	Ansaldo	Ansaldo	April '28	June '31	39·74 „
Giussano	Ansaldo	Ansaldo	Mar. '28	Feb. '31	38·95 „

General Notes.—This class were built as a reply to the French destroyers of the *Lion* type, over which they have every advantage. They represent a type of cruiser capable of overtaking the fastest destroyer. On trials the *A. da Barbiano* reached 42·04 knots at 5,607 tons, and maintained 39·74 knots for 8 hours with her full armament aboard. (Dec., 1930). Their appearance is particularly striking, with their lofty bridgework, squat funnels, and general effect of aggressiveness. The fire control top is 95 feet over water. A catapult of the Magaldi type is fitted along the forecastle. The policy of placing an order for three ships at once with one firm resulted in various constructional economies. All the Ansaldo ships were launched with their masts and funnels in place and proceeded on trials very soon after taking the water.

ALBERICO DA BARBIANO

1935, *Bassan.*

1937, *Official.*

BARI (ex-German *Pillau*, ex-Russian *Muraviev Amurski*, April, 1914).

Standard displacement, 3,248 tons. *Normal* displacement, 4,600 tons. Complement, 398.

Length $\begin{Bmatrix} 435\frac{1}{2}w.l. \\ 444 \ o.a. \end{Bmatrix}$ Beam, 44½ feet. $\begin{cases} Mean \ \text{draught, } 13\frac{1}{2} \text{ feet.} \\ Max. \quad \text{,,} \quad 19 \text{ feet.} \end{cases}$

Guns (German):
8—5·9 inch, 42 cal., S.A.
3—3 inch AA.
3 M.G.
Torpedo tubes removed.
Can carry 120 mines.

Armour:
3¼″ side.....................
1½″ Deck (on slopes).....
¾″ Deck (bow) ....
3″ Deck (over rudder) ...
4″ Conning tower ....

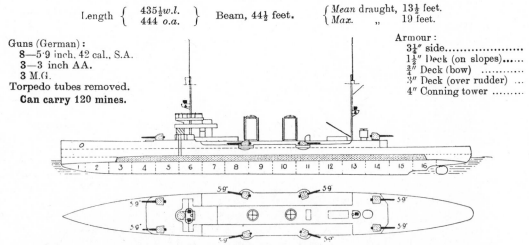

Machinery: Parsons turbines. 2 screws. Designed H.P.: 21,000 = 27 kts. Boilers: 4 (renewed). Oil fuel: 1300 tons = 4,500 miles at 10 kts.

General Notes.—Built by Schichau, Danzig, April, 1913—December, 1915. A sister ship, *Elbing*, sunk in the Battle of Jutland. Both vessels were seized by Germany on outbreak of war with Russia, for whom they were originally laid down. *Bari* taken over by Italy, 1920. Refitted for Colonial service, 1937, when number of funnels was reduced from three to two.

(Forefunnel now removed.) 1930 *Photo, Capt. Mateo Mille.*

TARANTO (ex-German *Strassburg*, Aug. 24, 1911).

Standard displacement, 3184 tons. *Normal* displacement, 4550 tons; 5100 tons *full load.* Complement, 445.
Length (*p.p.*) 440⅓ feet (*w.l.,*) 446½ feet. (455 *o.a.*) Beam, 44 feet. *Mean* draught, 12⅛ feet. (*Max.* 16⅔)

Guns (German):
7—5·9 inch, 43 cal.
2—3 inch A.A.
3 M.G.
Torpedo tubes removed.
Can carry 120 mines.
Aircraft: 1

Armour:
2½″ Belt (amidships).....
2¼″ Belt (ends) ....
2″ Deck (amidships).....
4″ Conning tower ....

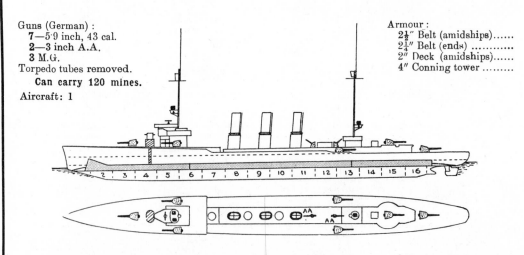

Machinery: 4 Parsons turbines. 2 screws. Boilers: 14 Schulz-Thornycroft. Designed H.P. 13,000 = 21 kts. Coal: *normal,* 880 tons; *maximum,* 1330 tons. Oil: 130 tons.

Notes.—Laid down for German Navy at Wilhelmshaven, April, 1910; completed December, 1912. Taken over by Italy, 1920. 4 boilers are oil burning. Refitted for Colonial service, 1937

Escort Vessel.

(Classed as *Nave Coloniale*.)

1937, *W. H. Davis, Esq.*

ERITREA (Castellammare, Sept. 20, 1936). Standard displacement, 2,172 tons (2,500 tons full load). Dimensions : 251½ (*w.l.*), 274 (*o.a.*) × 43⅔ × 11½ feet (*mean* draught). Guns : 4—4·7 inch, 4—37 mm. AA., 2—13 mm. AA. Fitted for minelaying. Machinery : 2 Fiat Diesels, with electric drive to 2 Marelli motors. H.P. : 8,000 = 20 kts. Fuel : 320 tons.

Notes.—Ordered May 8 1935 .and laid down July 25 following. Designed by Engineer Major-General Icilio d'Esposito.

Coast Defence Ship (ex-Cruiser)

(as re-constructed) 1939, *Signor Aldo Fraccaroli*

SAN GIORGIO (Castellammare D.Y. July, 1908).

Displacement : 9,232 tons. Complement, 726.

Dimensions : 430 (*pp.*) 462¼ (*o.a.*) × 69 × 22¾ (*mean*) 24 (*max.*) ft.

Guns :
- 4—10 inch, 45 cal.
- 8—7·5 inch, 45 cal.
- 8—3·9 inch, 47 cal.
- 4— M.G. AA.

Armour Terni :
- 8″ Belt (amidships)
- 2¼″ Belt (ends)
- 1¾″ & 1½″ Decks
- 7″ Lower deck redoubt
- 8″ Main barbettes
- 5¼″ Turrets to these
- 7″ Citadel
- 6¼″ Secondary turrets
- 9¾″ Conning towers (4)

Machinery : (Ansaldo). 2 sets 4 cylinder triple expansion. 2 shafts. Boilers : (New in 1937), 8 (4 oil-burning). Designed H.P. : 18,000 = 22 kts. Fuel : 1,570 tons. Radius : 6,270 miles at 10 kts. ; 2,640 miles at 20 kts. Laid down July, 1905. Completed July, 1910. Trials.—H.P. 19,595 = 23·2 kts.

Gunnery Notes.—All guns electrically controlled. Central pivot mountings. Fore 10 inch, 31 feet above waterline ; after 10 inch, 22 feet ; 7·5 inch guns 22 feet above water.

A sister ship, *San Marco*, has been converted into a Wireless-controlled Target Ship, as noted on a later page.

(All fitted for Minelaying).

12 Aviere Class.

CAMICIA NERA.   *1938, Courtesy Dott. Ing. L. Accorsi*

6 *Odero-Terni-Orlando :* **Aviere** (Sept. 20, 1937), **Artigliere** (Dec. 12, 1937), **Ascari** (July 31, 1938), **Camicia Nera** (Aug. 8, 1937), **Corazziere** (May 22, 1938), **Geniere** (ex-*Pontiere*), (Feb. 27, 1938)
2 *Riuniti, Ancona :* **Alpino** (Sept. 18, 1938), **Fuciliere** (July 31, 1938).
2 *Riuniti, Palmero :* **Bersagliere** (July 3, 1938), **Granatiere** (April 24, 1938).
2 *Tirreno :* **Carabiniere** (July 24, 1938), **Lanciere** (Dec. 18, 1938)

Displacement : 1,620 tons (*standard*), about 1,900 tons full load. Complement : 165. Dimensions : 339 (*w.l.*), 350 (*o.a.*) × 38⅓ × 10¾ feet (*mean*). Guns : 4—4·7 inch, 50 cal., 6—37 mm. AA., 2—13 mm. AA., 2 D.C.T. Torpedo tubes : 6—21 inch (tripled). Machinery : 2 sets geared turbines (Parsons in O.T.O. boats, Belluzzo in others). 2 shafts. S.H.P. : 48,000 = 39 kts. 3 boilers of 3-drum type. Oil fuel : 250 tons. All laid down Jan.—May, 1937.

4 Oriani Class.

G. CARDUCCI.   *1938, Grand Studio.*

4 *Odero-Terni-Orlando :* **Vittorio Alfieri** (Dec. 20, 1936), **Giosue Carducci** (Oct. 28, 1936), **Vincenzo Gioberti** (Sept. 19, 1936), **Alfredo Oriani** (July 30, 1936). All ordered 1935. *Oriani* laid down Oct. 1935, others early in 1936. *Standard* displacement : 1,729 tons (about 1,950 tons full load). Dimensions : 341 (*w.l.*), 350⅓ (*o.a.*) × 33⅓ × 11¼ feet (*mean*), 12 ft. (*max.*). Guns : 4—4·7 inch, 50 cal., 8—37 mm. AA., 4—13 mm. AA. 2 D.C.T. Torpedo tubes : 6—21 inch (tripled). Machinery : 2 sets Parsons geared turbines. 2 shafts. S.H.P. : 48,000 = 39 kts. 3 boilers of 3-drum type. Oil fuel : 250 tons. Complement : 157

4 Grecale class.

GRECALE.   1936.

LIBECCIO.   1936.

2 *Riuniti, Ancona :*—**Maestrale** (April 15, 1934), **Grecale** (June 17th, 1934).

2 *Tirreno :*—**Libeccio** (July 7th, 1934), **Scirocco** (April 22nd, 1934).

Displacement : 1,449 tons. Complement, 153. Dimensions : 333⅓ (*w.l.*), 350 (*o.a.*) × 33⅓ × 10 feet. Guns : 4—4·7 inch, 50 cal., 8—37 mm. AA., 4—13 mm. AA. Tubes : 6—21 inch. Machinery : 2 sets Parsons geared turbines. 2 shafts. S.H.P. 44,000 = 38 kts. 3 boilers of 3-drum type. Oil fuel : 250 tons.
Built under 1930 Programme. Laid down end 1931 and completed 1934. Are enlarged editions of the *Dardo* class with the same general design.

ORIANI
TYPE.

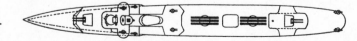

(All fitted for Minelaying).

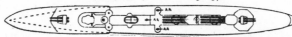

4 Folgore Class

4 Dardo Class

BALENO.

1935, *Bassan.*

STRALE. Now has cinder screen to funnel.

1932 *Photo, Official.*

2 *Partenopei*: **Folgore** (Apl. 26th, 1931), **Lampo** (July 26th, 1931).

2 *Quarnaro*: **Baleno** (Mar. 22nd, 1931), **Fulmine** (Aug. 2nd, 1931).

Displacement : 1,220 tons (*standard*). Dimensions : 309 (*pp.*), 315¼ (*o.a.*) × 30¼ × 10¼ feet.
Guns : 4—4·7 inch, 50 cal., 4—37 m/m. AA., 4—13 m/m. AA. Tubes : 6—21 inch, tripled.
Machinery : 2 sets Belluzzo geared turbines. 2 shafts.
S.H.P. 44,000 = 38 kts. 3 boilers of 3-drum type.
Oil : 225 tons. Complement, 150.
All ordered 1929, laid down 1930 and completed 1932.

2 *Odero*: **Dardo** (Sept. 6th, 1930), **Strale** (Mar. 26th, 1931).

2 *Tirreno*: **Freccia** (Aug. 3rd, 1930), **Saetta** (Jan. 17, 1932).

Displacement : 1,206 tons *standard*, 1,450 tons *normal*. Dimensions : 302¼ (*pp.*), 315 (*o.a.*) × 32 × 9½ feet.
Guns : 4—4·7 inch, 50 cal., 4—37 m/m. AA., 4—13 m/m. AA. Tubes : 6—21 inch, tripled.
Machinery : 2 sets Parsons geared turbines. S.H.P. 44,000 = 38 kts. 3 boilers of 3-drum type. Oil fuel : 225 tons.
Complement, 150. All ordered 1928. *Freccia* completed 1931, others 1932.

Dardo class.—As first designed these boats had two funnels and a straight bow, resembling *Turbine* in profile.
During construction the design was changed, the uptakes being trunked into one stack, and the bridge and upper-works modified, while the bows were given an overhang. After launching further modifications were made, the tripod foremast was abolished, control platforms and a searchlight tower were added to the bridgework and the funnel raised.

FOLGORE.

1937, *Official*

SAETTA. Cinder screen now probably added to funnel.

Added 1937, *Official.*

(All fitted for Minelaying.)

12 "Navigatori" class

A. USODIMARE.   1939.

2 *Ansaldo* : **Luca Tarigo** (Dec. 9th, 1928), **Lanzerotto Malocello** (March 14th, 1929).
2 *Odero* : **Ugolino Vivaldi** (Jan. 9th, 1929), **Antoniotto Usodimare** (May 12th, 1929).
2 *Tirreno* : **Leone Pancaldo** (Feb. 6th, 1929), **Antonio da Noli** (May 21st, 1929).
2 *Riuniti* (Ancona) : **Emanuele Pessagno** (August 12th, 1930), **Nicoloso da Recco** (Jan. 5, 1930).
4 *Quarnaro* : **Nicolo Zeno** (Aug. 11, 1928), **Giovanni da Verazzano** (Dec. 15th 1928),
    Alvise da Mosto. (July 1st, 1929), **Antonio Pigafetta.** (Nov. 10th, 1929.)

Displacement : 1,628 tons, *standard* ; 2,010 tons *deep load*. Dimensions : 352 (*o.a.*), 351 (*p.p.*) × 33½ × 16¾ feet.
    Guns : 6—4·7 inch, 50 cal. 4—37 m/m. AA. 6—13 m/m. AA. Tubes : 4—21 inch, paired. Some carry 50 mines.
Machinery and boilers : 2 Parsons turbines and 4 Odero boilers in *L. Tarigo, L. Malocello, U. Vivaldi, A. Usodimare,
L. Pancaldo, A. da Noli, E. Pessagno.* 2 Belluzzo turbines and 4 modified Yarrow boilers in *N. Zeno, G. da Verazzano,
A. Pigafetta, A. da Mosto* ; 2 Tosi turbines and 3 boilers of 3-drum type in *N. da Recco.*
S.H.P. 50,000 = 38 kts.
    On trials, *A. da Mosto* attained speeds of from 44 to 45 kts. with 71,000 H.P. Complement, 185.

Notes.—All ordered 1926, and laid down in 1927, except last pair, which were begun in 1928.

A. DA MOSTO.   *Added 1937, Bassan.*

8 "Turbine" Class.

OSTRO.   1939, *courtesy Dott. Ing. L. Accorsi.*

4 *Ansaldo* : **Borea** (Jan. 1927), **Espero** (Aug. 31st, 1927), **Ostro** (Jan. 2nd, 1928), **Zeffiro** (27th May, 1927).
    2 *Odero* : **Aquilone** (Aug. 3rd, 1927), **Turbine** (21st April, 1927). 2 by Cant. del Tirreno, Riva Trigoso :
    Euro (July 7th, 1927), **Nembo** (27th Jan., 1927).

All ordered or laid down 1924-25. Displacement : first four 1,073 tons. Remainder 1,092 tons. Dimensions : 299½ (*p.p.*),
307½ (*o.a*) × 30½ × 10¾ feet. Parsons geared turbines. 3 Express boilers, with superheaters. S.H.P. 40,000 = 36 kts.
Guns : 4—4·7 inch, 45 cal., 4—37 mm. AA., 2—13 mm. AA. Tubes : 6—21 inch, in triple deck mountings. Oil :
270 tons. Complement, 142.

Mean speed on trials : *Euro* 38·9 ; *Aquilone* 39·5 ; *Borea* 36·5 ; *Espero* 38·4 ; *Nembo* 38·4 ; *Turbine* 39·6.

EURO.   1937, *Pucci.*

4 "Sauro" class.

(All fitted for Minelaying).

3 Leone Class.

D. MANIN.

1935, *Bassan.*

2 *Odero* : **Cesare Battisti** (11th Dec., 1926), **Nazario Sauro** (12th May, 1926).
2 *Quarnaro* : **Daniele Manin** (24th June, 1925), **Francesco Nullo** (Oct., 1925). All designed by Odero
and laid down 1924. Displacement : 1058 tons *standard*. Dimensions: 295¼ × 30½ × 10½ feet. Parsons geared turbines.
3 Express oil-fired boilers, with superheaters. S.H.P. 36,000 = 35 kts. Guns : 4—4·7 inch, 4—37 mm. AA.,
2—13 mm. AA. Tubes : 4—21 inch, in twin deck mountings. 30 mines carried. Oil : 230 tons. Complement, 142.

Mean trial figures : *Sauro* 37,000 = 36·5 *Battisti* 41,280 = 37 *Nullo* 45,000 = 37 : *Manin* 41,800 = 36·8.

Sauro and *Sella* classes

TIGRE.

1935, *Bassan.*

4 "Sella" class.

F. CRISPI.

1935, *Bassan.*

4 *Pattison* : **Francesco Crispi** (Oct., 1925), **Giovanni Nicotera** (24th June, 1926), **Bettino Ricasoli**
(29th Jan., 1926), **Quintino Sella** (25th April, 1925). All laid down 1922-23. 935 tons *standard*. Dimensions : 275½
× 27 × 9¾ feet. Guns : 4—4·7 inch (45 cal.), 2—40 m/m. AA., 2 M.G. Torpedo tubes : 4— 21 inch in two pairs.
Machinery : Turbines (Belluzzo in *Crispi*, Parsons in others). S.H.P. 36,000 = 35 kts. 3 Thornycroft boilers.
Oil fuel : 200 tons *normal*, 255 tons *max*. Radius : 2,750 miles at 15 kts. Complement, 120.

Mean speeds on trials : *Crispi* 38·6, with H.P. : 35,540, 39·4 *max*. ; *Sella* 37·3, with H.P. : 35,090, 38·6 *max*. *Crispi*
re-engined, 1937.

LEONE.

Added 1936.

3* *Ansaldo* : **Leone, Pantera, Tigre** (1923). 1526 tons (*standard*), 2283 tons (*full load*). Dimensions **37**
(*o.a.*), 359½ (*p.p.*) × 34 × 11·5 feet (*mean*). Guns : 8—4·7 inch (45 cal.), 2—40 mm. AA., 4 M.G. Tubes : 4—21
inch. Designed S.H.P. : 40,000 = 34 kts. (Trials, 50,000 = 35 kts.). Best recent speeds, 33 kts. or less. 2 Parsons
turbines (geared). 4 Yarrow oil-burning boilers. 2 screws. Oil fuel : 200 tons *normal*, 400 tons *max*. Carry 60
mines (*normal stowage*), or 100 (*maximum*). Complement, 201.

*Leopardo and *Lince* cancelled.

Notes.—Internally these ships are most elaborately fitted. Each is equipped with a different system of fire-control—
British, Italian and German respectively. 4·7 inch guns are paired very closely—only 1 foot apart. *Max.*
elevation : 30°. Special apparatus for smoke screen production is fitted on starboard quarter of each.

2 Mirabello class.

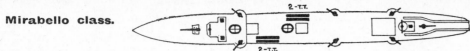

4 Orsa class.

ORIONE completing   1937, *W. H. Davis, Esq.*

2 *Riuniti* (*Palermo*) boats : **ORIONE** (April 22, 1937), **ORSA** (March 21, 1937).
2 *Napoletani* boats : **PEGASO** (Dec. 8, 1936), **PROCIONE** (Jan. 1, 1937).
Standard displacement : 855 tons. Dimensions : $274\frac{1}{4}$ (*p.p.*), 279 (*w.l.*), $292\frac{3}{4}$ (*o.a.*) $\times$ 31 $\times 11\frac{1}{4}$ (*max.*), 8 feet (*mean* draught). Guns : 2—3·9 inch, 47 cal., 8 M.G., 6 D.C.T. Tubes : 4—18 inch, paired. Machinery : Tosi geared turbines. 2 shafts. S.H.P. : 16,000 = 28 kts. 2 boilers of 3-drum type.

Notes.—Ordered 1935, and laid down early in 1936. Were originally rated as Escort Vessels (*Avvisi Scorta*).

                                        1926 *Photo, Capitan M. Mille.*
Height of Fore-funnel reported to have been increased as in *Leone* class.
2 *Ansaldo* type : **Carlo Mirabello** (1914), **Augusto Riboty** (1915).   1383 tons.   Dimensions : 331·4 (*p.p.*) $\times$ 32 $\times$ 10·6 feet (*mean*).   Guns : 8—4 inch, 2—40 mm. AA., 2 M.G.   Tubes : 4—18 inch.   Carry 100 mines.   Designed S.H.P. 35,000 = 35 kts.   Made 33·75 and 35·03 kts. on *trials* respectively. 4 Yarrow oil-burning boilers.   2 Parsons geared turbines. 2 screws. Oil fuel ; *normal* 200 tons, *maximum* 350 tons. Endurance : 2840 miles (15 kts.), 500 miles (full speed). Complement, 145.

16 "Partenope" Class.
(*All fitted for Minelaying*)

LUPO.   1939, *Sig. Aldo Fraccaroli.*
4 *Napoletani* boats : **Partenope** (Feb. 27, 1938), **Polluce** (Oct, 24, 1937), **Pallade** (Dec. 19, 1937), **Pleiadi** (Sept. 5, 1937.)
4 *Quarnaro* boats : **Libra** (Oct. 3, 1937), **Lince** (Jan. 15, 1938), **Lira** (Sept. 12, 1937), **Lupo** (Nov. 7, 1937).
8 *Ansaldo* boats : **Airone** (Jan. 23, 1938), **Alcione** (Dec. 23, 1937), **Aretusa** (Feb. 6, 1938), **Ariel** (March 14, 1938), **Calipso** (June 12, 1938), **Calliope** (April 15, 1938), **Circe** (June 29, 1938), **Clio** (April 3, 1938).
Standard displacement : 679 tons. Complement : 94. Dimensions : $254\frac{3}{4}$ (*w.l.*), 267 (*o.a.*) $\times$ 26 $\times 7\frac{3}{4}$ feet (*mean*). Guns : 3—3·9 inch, 6—37 mm. AA., 2—13 mm. AA., 2 D.C.T. Tubes : 4—18 inch, paired in all *except* Quarnaro boats, which have tubes arranged as in later units of *Spica* class. Machinery : 2 sets Tosi geared turbines. 2 shafts. S.H.P. : 19,000 = 34 kts. 2 boilers of 3-drum type. All laid down Oct., 1936—March, 1937.

                                        1938, *courtesy Dott. Ing. L. Accorsi.*
Albatros (Cantieri Riuniti, Palermo, May 27, 1934).   Displacement : 340 tons. Dimensions : $231\frac{1}{2} \times 22\frac{1}{2} \times$ 6 feet.   Guns : 2—3·9 inch, 47 cal., 4—37 mm. AA., 4 D.C.T. Tubes : 2—18 inch. Machinery : 2 Belluzzo geared turbines. 2 shafts. S.H.P. 4,000 = 24·5 kts. 2 boilers of 3-drum type.
Note.—This vessel was originally classed as a Submarine Chaser (*Cacciasommergibili*).

16 "Spica" class.

(All fitted for Minelaying)

PERSEO.

1938, *Cav. Angelo Priore.*

VEGA.

1937, *W. H. Davis, Esq.*

2 *Napoletani* boats : **Spica** (March 11, 1934), **Astore** (April 22, 1934).
4 *Riuniti* (*Ancona*) boats : **Centauro** (Feb. 19, 1936), **Climene** (Jan. 7, 1936), **Castore** (Sept. 27, 1936), **Cigno** (Nov. 24, 1936).
2 *Tirreno* boats : **Canopo** (Oct. 10, 1936), **Cassiopea** (Nov. 22, 1936).
4 *Quarnaro* boats : **Sirio** (Nov. 14, 1935), **Perseo** (Oct. 9, 1935), **Sagittario** (June 21,1936), **Vega** (July 12, 1936).
4 *Ansaldo* boats : **Altair** (July 26, 1936), **Antares** (July 15, 1936), **Aldebaran,** (July 19, 1936), **Andromeda.** (June 28, 1936).

Standard displacement : *Spica* and *Astore*, 638 tons ; Riuniti and Tirreno boats, 652 tons ; Quarnaro and Ansaldo boats, tons. Respective lengths (*o.a.*) 263½, 267, and 269 feet. Beam : 27 feet. Respective draughts : 7½, 7½ and 7 feet (*mean in all*). Complement : 94. Guns : 3—3·9 inch. 47 cal., 6—37 mm. AA., 2—13 mm. AA., 2 D.C.T. Tubes : 4—18 inch, arranged as shown in plans below. Machinery : 2 Tosi geared turbines. 2 shafts. S.H.P. : 19,000 = 34 kts. (exceeded on trials). 2 boilers of 3-drum type. Oil fuel.

Name	Laid down	Compl.	Name	Laid down	Compl.
Spica	May 1933	June 1935	Altair		
Astore		May 1935	Antares	Oct. 1935	1936
Centauro	May 1934	1936	Aldebaran		
Climene		Apr. 1936	Andromeda		
Perseo	Nov. 1934	Feb. 1936	Sagittario	Nov. 1935	1937
Sirio			Vega		
Canopo	Dec. 1935		Castore	Mar. 1936	1937
Cassiopea		1936	Cigno		

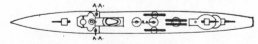

SPICA, ASTORE, CENTAURO, CLIMENE.

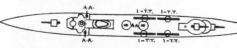

Other boats of SPICA class, also LIBRA, LINCE, LIRA, LUPO. of PARTENOPE class.

4 "Curtatone" class.

(Fitted for Minelaying)

CURTATONE.

1934 *Photo, Official.*

4 *Orlando* type : **Calatafimi** (17th March, 1923), **Castelfidardo** (1923), **Curtatone** (1922), **Monzambano** (6th August, 1923). 966 tons (1190 *full load*). Dimensions 262½ × 24⅔ × 8½ feet. Guns : 4—4 inch, 2—3 inch AA. Tubes : 4—18 inch. 10 Mines. S.H.P. 22,000 = 32 kts. Trials : H.P. 27,500 = 34 kts. 4 Thornycroft boilers. Oil fuel. 2 Zoelly turbines. Complement, 105.
Mean speeds on trials : *Curtatone* 36·6 *Castelfidardo* 35·5 *Calatafimi* 33·3 *Monzambano* 33·5.

4 "Palestro" class.

(Fitted for Minelaying)

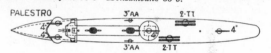

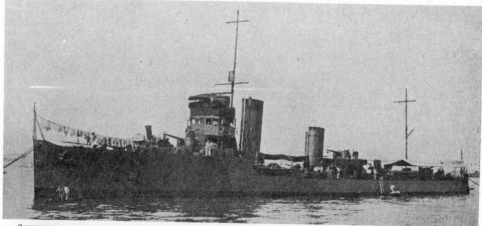

SOLFERINO.

1935, *Bassan.*

4 *Orlando* type : **Confienza** (1920), **Palestro** (1919), **San Martino** (1920), **Solferino** (1920). 862 tons *standard* (1076 *full load*). Dimensions : 256½ (*p.p.*) × 24⅔ × 8½ feet (*mean*). Guns : 4—4 inch, 45 cal., 2—3 inch, 40 cal. AA., 4 M.G. Tubes : 4—18 inch in twin deck mountings. 10 mines carried. 2 Zoelly turbines. Designed S.H.P. 22,000 = 32 kts. 4 Thornycroft boilers. 2 screws. Oil : 170 tons. Complement, 105.
Mean speeds on trials : *Palestro* 32·4 ; *Solferino* 31·9 ; *S. Martino* 31·1 ; *Confienza* 32·2.

6 "Generali" class (*Minelayers*).

GENERALE M. PRESTINARI.   1936.

6 *Oa.* type: *Generale Achille Papa* (1921), ***Generale Antonio Cantore*** (April, 1921), ***Generale Antonino Cascino*** (1922), ***Generale Antonio Chinotto*** (1921), ***Generale Carlo Montanari*** (1922), ***Generale Marcello Prestinari*** (1922). Displacement: 635 tons. Dimensions : 237·9 × 23·9 × 9 feet. Guns : 3—4 inch, 45 cal., 2—3 inch AA., 2 M.G. Tubes : 4—18 inch in two twin deck mountings. Tosi Turbines. S.H.P. 18,000 = 33 kts. (*about* 30 kts. best speed now). 4 Thornycroft boilers. Oil : 150 tons. Complement, 105. Radius : 2200 miles at 14 kts.; 600 miles at 33 kts.

1925 *Photo, by courtesy of the Ministry of Marine.*

1 *Pattison* type: ERNESTO GIOVANNINI (1921). *Standard* displacement : 182 tons. Dimensions : 170½ × 19 × 5⅔ feet (*mean*). Guns : 2—4 inch, 35 cal., 2 M.G. Tubes : 2 18 inch, paired. Fitted for minelaying. Machinery : Triple expansion. 2 shafts. Designed H.P. : 2,400 = 23 kts. (Trials : 3,262 = 23·7 kts.) 2 boilers. Oil fuel : 40 tons. Radius : 900 miles at 20 kts.

Notes.—Originally classed as an Escort Vessel. Another ship of this class, *E. Rosso*, was burned on stocks and hull scrapped, while 4 others have been placed on disposal list.

7 "Cosenz" class.

Deck Plan of COSENZ class (*Generali* class similar, but only 1—4 inch on forecastle).

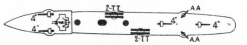

E. COSENZ   1925 *Photo, Pucci.*

7 *Odero* type: *Enrico Cosenz* (ex-*Agostino Bertani*), ***Giacomo Medici, Giuseppe La Farina,*** and ***Nicola Fabrizi*** (all 1917); ***Angelo Bassini, Giacinto Carini, Giuseppe La Masa,*** (all 1916). 635 tons (810 *full load*). Dimensions: 238 (*p.p.*) × 24 × 9·2 feet (*mean*). Guns : 4—4 inch, 2—3 inch, AA. 4 M.G. Tubes (in all): 4—18 inch. in two twin-deck mountings. No mines carried. S.H.P. 15,500 = 32 kts. (On trials made 34·1 kts. Now good for *about* 30 kts.) Fuel : 150 tons. Complement, 100. 2 Tosi turbines 4 Thornycroft oil-burning boilers. 2 screws. Endurance : 1700 miles (15 kts.), 470 miles (full speed) *Benedetto Cairoli* of this class. lost during War.

4 "Sirtori" class.

G. ACERBI.   1935, *Bassan.*

4 *Odero* type: *Giuseppe Sirtori, Francesco Stocco, Giovanni Acerbi, Vincenzo Orsini* (all 1916). Displacement : 669 tons *Standard* Dimensions : 238 (*p.p.*) × 24 × 9·2 feet (*mean*). Guns : 6—4 inch, 35 cal., 2—40 m/m. AA. 4 M.G. Tubes : 4—18inch, in twin mountings. 2 Tosi turbines. S.H.P. 15,500 = 30 kts. 4 Thornycroft oil-burning boilers. 2 screws Radius : 1700 miles at 15 kts., 470 miles at 33 kts. Fuel : 150 tons. Complement, 100. Carry 10 mines.

7 "Abba" class.

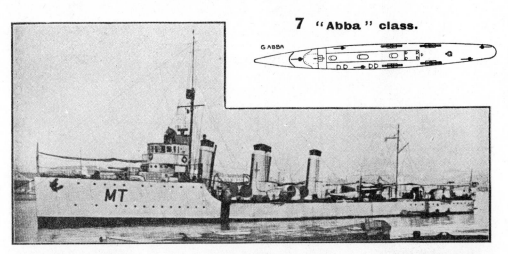

ANTONIO MOSTO.

1925 Photo, Bassan.

2 *Pattison* boats : **Fratelli Cairoli**, (*Ex-Francesco Nullo*), **Antonio Mosto** (both 1914).
5 *Odero* boats : **Rosolino Pilo, Giuseppe Abba, Simone Schiaffino, Giuseppe Dezza** (*Ex-Pilade Bronzetti*), (all 1914), **Giuseppe Missori** (1915). 615 tons. Dimensions : 236.2 (*p.p.*) × 24 × 8·8 feet (*mean*). Guns : 5—4 inch, 2—40 m/m. AA. 4 M.G. Tubes : 4 single 18 inch. Made about 31·8 kts. on trials. 2 Tosi turbines and 4 Thornycroft oil-burning boilers. 2 screws. Endurance : 1700 miles 15 (kts.) 440 miles (full speed). S.H.P. 15,500 = 32 to 33·8 kts. except 2 Pattison boats, S.H.P. 14,500=30·8 kts. Fuel : 150 tons. Complement, 94.

1 "Audace" class.

Now used as Control Vessel to the Target Ship *San Marco*.

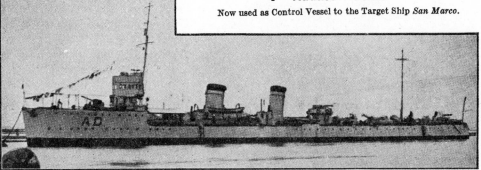

AUDACE. (*New and up-to-date photo wanted*).

1925 Photo, Bassan.

1 *Yarrow* type : **Audace** (ex-Japanese *Kawakaze*, Scotstoun, Glasgow 1915). 629 tons (over 1000 tons *full load*). Dimensions : 275 (*p.p.*), 283 (*o.a.*) × 27½ × 9½ feet (*max.*). Guns : 7—4 inch, 2—40 m/m. AA. 4 M.G. Tubes : 4 - 18 inch, in two twin mountings. Fuel : 252 tons. 2 sets Brown-Curtis turbines and 3 Yarrow large-tube oil-burning boilers Endurance : 2,180 miles (15 kts.), 560 miles (full speed). S.H.P. 22,000 = 31 kts. Complement, 113.

Note —This boat must not be confused with *Audace* built in 1912-13 by Orlando. The Orlando *Audace* was sunk during the War, and the Japanese *Kawakaze* (closely resembling the lost *Audace*) was purchased by Italy and re-named *Audace*

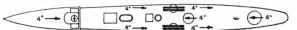

Classed as M.A.S. (*Motoscafi Anti-Sommergibili*)

1938.

Stefano Turr (Cant. Costruz. Mecc. e Aeronautica, Pisa, May 9, 1935). *Standard* displacement: 59 tons. Dimensions: 105 (*o.a.*) × 18 × 2⅔ feet. Guns : 3 M.G. AA. Tubes : 4—18 inch. Machinery : 4 Fiat high speed 4-stroke Diesels. 2 shafts. H.P. : 3,000 = 34 kts. (actual speed reported to be under 30 kts.)

Note.—It is reported that this vessel is being re-engined with Isotta-Fraschini petrol motors.

M.A.S. 507.   1938, *added* 1939.

1938.

53 *Baglietto* type : Nos. **451, 452, 501-551** (1936-39). Displacement : 20 tons (*average*). Dimensions : 65¾ (*pp.*), 69 (*o.a.*) × 14¾ × 4½ feet. Armament : 2—18 inch torpedo tubes (side firing), **1** or **2** M.G. AA., 5 D.C. Machinery : 2 Isotta-Fraschini petrol engines. H.P. : 2,000 = 47 kts. Petrol : 1¼ ton. Radius : 260 miles.

1937.

4 S.V.A.N. boats : **M.A.S. 438—441** (1935). 35½ tons. Speed : 36 kts.

284

1935, *Official.*

1935, *Official.*

8 S.V.A.N. boats : **M.A.S. 423, 424, 426, 430, 432, 433, 434, 437,** (1923-30). Displacement : 13½ to 14 tons. 2 M.G., 2 T.T., 5 D.C. Length over 50 feet. H.P. : 1,500 = 40 kts.

1 Baglietto boat : **M.A.S. 431.** (1931) 15 tons. Of similar type to above.

1919 *Photo.*

5 boats "Tipo A" : **M.A.S. 204, 206, 210, 213, 216,** (S.V.A.N., Ansaldo, Orlando, Baglietto, etc., 1916-19). 12 tons. Length : 52½ feet. Motors (Isotta Fraschini) : 400 to 500 B.H.P. = 26 kts. Guns : 2 M.G., 2 Torpedo tubes or dropping gears. Some carry mines.

Ocean-going types *(Sommergibili Oceanici)*

Particulars and numbers of Submarines to be built under 1939 Programme have not been announced)

4 St. Bon Class.

Building or Completing.

4 *Adriatico :* **Ammiraglio Saint Bon, Ammiraglio Cagni, Ammiraglio Caracciolo, Ammiraglio Millo.** Displacement : 1,461/—— tons. Dimensions : 288¾ × 25½ × 17 feet. Guns : 2—3·9 inch, 4 M.G. Tubes : 14—18 inch. Machinery : Fiat Diesels. B.H.P. : 4,600 = 18 kts.

Note.—All belong to 1938 Programme. A remarkable feature of this type is the reversion to a smaller pattern of torpedo tube.

4 Liuzzi Class.

Building or Completing.

4 *Tosi :* **Console Generale Liuzzi, Alpino Bagnolini, Reginaldo Giuliani, Capitano Tarantini.** Displacement : 1,031/—— tons. Dimensions : 252½ × 23 × 13¾ feet. Guns : 2—3·9 inch, 4 M.G. Tubes : 8—21 inch. Machinery : Tosi Diesels. B.H.P. : 3,500 = 18 kts.

Note.—All belong to 1938 Programme. First 3 laid down in 1938, *Tarantini* in 1939.

6 Marconi Class.

Building or Completing.

2 *Adriatico :* **Guglielmo Marconi,** (July 27, 1939), **Leonardo da Vinci.**

4 *Odero-Terni-Orlando :* **Michele Bianchi, Luigi Torelli, Alessandro Malaspina, Maggiore Baracca.** Displacement : 1,036/—— tons. Dimensions : 251 × 22¼ × 15¼ feet. Guns : 2—3·9 inch, 4 M.G. Tubes : 8—21 inch. Machinery : Adriatico Diesels. B.H.P. : 3,600 = 18 kts.

Notes.—Built under 1938 Programme.

2 Cappellini Class.

Completing.

2 *Odero-Terni-Orlando :* **Comandante Cappellini** (May 14, 1939) **Comandante Faa di Bruno** (June 18, 1939). Displacement : 951/1,270 tons. Dimensions : 239½ × 23¾ × 15 feet. Guns : 4—3·9 inch, 4 M.G. Tubes : 8—21 inch. Machinery : Fiat Diesels. B.H.P. : 3,000 = 17 kts.

Notes.—Built under 1938 Programme. Appear to be a modified version of *Marcello* design.

9 " Marcello " Class.

Photo wanted.

9 *Adriatico*: **Dandolo, Marcello, Mocenigo** (all Nov. 20, 1937), **Barbarigo** (June 12, 1938), **Emo** (June 29, 1938), **Morosini** (July 28, 1938), **Nani** (Jan. 16, 1938), **Provana** (March 16, 1938), **Veniero** (Feb. 14, 1938).
Displacement: 941/1,260 tons. Dimensions: 235 (*w.l.*), 239½ (*o.a.*) × 23⅝ × 15½ feet (*mean*). Guns: 2—3·9 inch, 2—13 mm. AA. Tubes: 8—21 inch. 2 Sulzer Diesels by builders (except *Mocenigo* and *Veniero*, which have Fiat Diesels) and 2 electric motors. H.F.: 3,000/800 = 17/9 kts. Diving Limit, 58 fathoms.

3 " Galvani " Class.

Photo wanted.

3 *Tosi* boats **Brin** (April 3, 1938), **Galvani** (May 22, 1938), **Guglielmotti.** (Sept. 11, 1938).
Displacement: 896/1,247 tons. Dimensions: 228¾ (*w.l.*), 231⅓ (*o.a.*) × 22½ × 13½ feet (*mean*). Guns: 1—3·9 inch. 2 13 mm. AA. Tubes: 8—21 inch. 2 Tosi Diesels and 2 electric motors. H.P.: 3,000/840 = 17/9 kts. Diving limit, 60 fathoms.

3 Foca Class.
(Minelayers).

FOCA.   1938, *courtesy Dott. Ing. L. Accorsi.*

3 *Tosi* boats: **Foca** (June 26, 1937), **Zoea** (Dec. 5, 1937), **Atropo** (Nov. 20, 1938).   First two laid down at Taranto in January and February, 1936, respectively, *Atropo* in 1937. Displacement: 1,109/1,533 tons (*Atropo*, 1,121 tons). Dimensions: 253¾ (*w.l.*), 266¾ (*o.a.*) × 23½ × 12½ feet (*Atropo*, 255¼ × 23⅓ × 15½ feet). Guns: 1—3·9 inch, 47 cal., 2 13 mm. AA. Tubes: 6—21 inch (bow).   2 mine-discharging chutes. Fiat Diesels (except *Atropo*, which has Tosi) and 2 electric motors. H.P.: 2,880/1,250 = 16/8 kts. *Atropo* reached 58 fathoms in diving trials.

3 " Calvi " Class.

(Improved " BALILLA " design.)

G. FINZI.   1937.

G. FINZI.   1937.

3 *Odero-Terni-Orlando* type: **Pietro Calvi** (March 31, 1935).   **Enrico Tazzoli** (Oct. 14, 1935).   **Giuseppe Finzi** (June 29, 1935).
Standard displacement: 1,332/1,965 tons.   Complement, 66.
Dimensions: 272 (*w.l.*), 276½ (*o.a.*) × 25¼ × 13 feet (*mean*).
Guns: 2—4·7 inch, 45 cal., 4—13 mm. AA. Tubes: 8—21 inch (6 bow, 2 stern).
2 Fiat Diesels.   H.P.: 4,400/1,800 = 17/8¾ kts.
Radius: *Surface*: 13,500 miles at 9 kts; *submerged*: 80 miles at 4 kts.

Notes.—Laid down 1932, under 1930 Programme.   Normal diving limit, 55 fathoms (reached on trials at Spezia).

2 " Glauco " Class.

For appearance, see Silhouette.

2 *Bernardis* type: **Glauco** (Jan 5, 1935), **Otaria** (March 20, 1935), (Cant. Riuniti dell' Adriatico, Trieste).
Displacement: 863/1,167 tons.   Complement, 48.   Dimensions: 239½ × 23½ × 14½ feet.   Guns: 2—3·9 inch, 47 cal., 2—13 mm. AA. Tubes:; 8—21 inch. Machinery: 2 sets Fiat Diesels. H.P. 3,000 = 17 kts.   2 motors H.P. 1,400 = 8·5 kts. *submerged.*

1 Minelaying Type

1936.

1 *Cavallini* type: **Pietro Micca** (Cant. Nav. Franco Tosi, Taranto, March 31, 1935). Displacement: 1,371/1,883 tons. Complement, 66. Dimensions: 296¼ (*o.a.*) × 25¼ × 17½ feet. Guns: 2—4·7 inch, 45 cal., 4—13 mm. AA. Mines: 40. Tubes: 6—21 inch.(in bow.) Machinery: Tosi Diesels. H.P. 3,000/1,600 = 15·5 kts. *surface*, 8·5 kts. *submerged*.

4 "Archimede" class.

G. FERRARIS.

1935, *Sig. F. Cianciafara.*

4 *Cavallini* type: **Archimede** (Dec. 10th, 1933), **Galileo Galilei** (March 19th, 1934), **Evangelista Torricelli** (May 27th, 1934), **Galileo Ferraris** (April 11th, 1934). Built by Cant. Nav. F. Tosi, Taranto. Displacement: 880/1,231 tons. Dimensions: 231⅓ × 22⅓ × 13 feet. Complement, 50. Guns: 2—3·9 inch, 47 cal., 2—13 mm. AA. Tubes: 8—21 inch. Machinery: 2 Tosi Diesels. H.P. 3,000 = 17 kts. 2 Ansaldo Motors H.P. 1,300 = 8·5 kts. *submerged*.

E. FIERAMOSCA.   1932 *Photo, Official.*

1 *Bernardis* type: **Ettore Fieramosca** (April 15th, 1929). Laid down August, 1926, by Cantiere Navale Franco Tosi, Taranto. 1,340 tons *surface* displacement, 1,788 tons *submerged*. Complement, 64. Dimensions: 270¼ (*o.a.*) × 27⅓ × 14¾ feet (*mean*). Guns: 1—4·7 inch, 45 cal., 4—13 mm. AA. 8—21 inch tubes. Can carry a small seaplane. Machinery: 2 sets Tosi Diesels. B.H.P. 5,500 = 19 kts.*surface*. Electric motors, H.P. 2,000 = 10 kts. *submerged*. Fuel: 150 tons.

4 "Balilla" Class.

E. TOTI.   1939, *courtesy Dott. Ing. L. Accorsi.*

D. MILLELIRE.   1935, *Sig. F. Cianciafara*

4 *Odero* type: **Balilla** (20th Feb., 1927), **Antonio Sciesa,** (Aug 12th. 1928), **Enrico Toti,** (14th April, 1928), **Domenico Millelire** Sept. 19th. 1927). Built at Spezia by Odero-Terni Co. *Surface* displacement, 1,368 tons; *submerged*, 1,874 tons. Dimensions: 282 (*o.a.*) × 24½ × 14 feet *mean* draught. Guns: 1—4·7 inch, 45 cal., 4—13 mm. AA. Tubes: 6—21 inch (4 bow, 2 stern). Complement: 64. Machinery: 2 sets Fiat Diesels, of H.P: 4,400 = 17·5 kts. *on surface*; electric motors of H.P.: 2,200 = 9·5 kts. *submerged*. Fuel: 140 tons.

Note.—Above submarines are designed for deep diving, and are of exceptionally strong construction. The design of these boats embodies a number of innovations, such as the placing of the Diesel engines and electric motors much further forward than usual; the elimination of bow hydroplanes; novel distribution of ballast tanks: and an improved form of hull. In consequence, an unprecedented degree of safety, both in diving and manœuvring is claimed for this type. They were laid down early in 1925. *Millelire* reached a depth of 66 fathoms in diving trials May 1928, and in 1930 remained submerged off the mouth of the Gambia for 36 hours. In 1934 *Toti* and *Sciesa* cruised right round Africa (15,000 miles) in 5½ months.

2 "Argo" Class.

VELELLA   *1937, W. H. Davis, Esq.*

2 *Adriatico* boats : **Argo**, (Nov. 24, 1936), **Velella** (Dec. 18, 1936). Laid down at Monfalcone, Sept., 1935. Displacement : 676/857 tons. Dimensions : 195¾ (*w.l.*), 206¾ (*o.a.*) × 22½ × 10½ feet (*mean*). Guns : 1—3·9 inch, 47 cal., 2 M.G. AA. Tubes : 6—21 inch (bow). Fiat Diesels and 2 electric motors. H.P. : 1,350/800 = 14/8 kts.

27 "Perla" Class.

DESSIE   *1938, courtesy Dott. Ing. L. Accorsi.*

1937 Programme :
5 *Odero-Terni-Orlando* : **Beilul,** (May 22, 1938), **Durbo,** (March 6, 1938), **Lafole,** (April 10, 1938). **Scire,** (Jan. 6, 1938). **Tembien,** (Feb. 6, 1938).
2 *Tosi* : **Uarsciek,** (Sept. 19, 1937), **Uebi Scebeli,** (Oct. 3, 1937).

1936 Programme :
4 *Odero-Terni-Orlando* : **Ascianghi** (Dec. 5, 1937), **Gondar** (Oct. 3, 1937), **Macalle** (Oct. 29, 1936), **Neghelli** (Nov. 7, 1937).
4 *Adriatico* : **Adua** (Sept. 13, 1936), **Alagi** (Nov. 11, 1936), **Aradam** (Oct. 18, 1936), **Axum** (Sept. 27, 1936).
2 *Tosi* : **Dagabur, Dessie** (both Nov. 22, 1936.)

1935 Programme :
6 *Adriatico* : **Berillo** (June 14, 1936), **Corallo** (Aug. 2, 1936), **Diaspro** (July 5, 1936), **Gemma** (May 21, 1936), **Perla** (May 1, 1936), **Turchese** (July 19, 1936).
4 *Odero-Terni-Orlando* : **Ambra** (May 28, 1936), **Iride** (July 30, 1936), **Malachite** (July 15, 1936), **Onice** (June 15, 1936.)

Displacement : 620/853 tons, *except* O.T.O. vessels, 615, and Tosi, 613 tons. Dimensions : 195 (*w.l.*), 197½ (*o.a.*) × 21 × 13 feet (*mean*). *Corallo, Turchese,* and 4 of *Adua* group, Adriatico-Sulzer Diesels ; *Ambra, Malachite,* and Tosi boats, Tosi Diesels ; all the remainder have Fiat type. Armament, horsepower, and speed same as *Sirena* class (following). Diving limit : 50 fathoms.

Note.—Brazilian submarines *Tamoyo, Timbyra* and *Tupy* were originally units of this class, and first bore the respective names *Ascianghi, Gondar* and *Neghelli.*

12 "Sirena" Class.

DIAMANTE   *1935, Sig. F. Cianciafara.*

6 *Adriatico* : **Sirena** (Jan. 26, 1933), **Naiade** (March 27, 1933), **Nereide** (May 25, 1933) **Anfitrite** (Aug. 5, 1933), **Galatea** (Oct. 5, 1933), **Ondina** (Dec. 2, 1933).
2 *Tosi* : **Diamante** (May 21, 1933), **Smeraldo** (July 23, 1933).
2 *Odero-Terni-Orlando* : **Ametista** (April 26, 1933), **Zaffiro** (July 28, 1933).
2 *Quarnaro* : **Rubino** (March 29, 1933), **Topazio** (May 15, 1933).

Displacement : 590/787 tons. Dimensions : 194½ (*w.l.*), 197½ (*o.a.*) × 21 × 12 (*mean*). 13¾ feet (*max.*). Guns : 1—3·9 inch 47 cal., 2—13 mm. AA. Tubes : 6—21 inch. Machinery : 2 sets Fiat Diesels in all except Tosi and Quarnaro vessels, which have 2 sets Tosi Diesels. H.P. 1,350/800 = 14/8·5 kts. Complement 41.

5 Argonauta Class. *(Bernardis type).*

Special Note—Two of the submarines of this class are understood to have been acquired by the Spanish Nationalist Government and renamed *Mola* and *Sanjurjo.* Their exact identities have still to be satisfactorily established, but it is thought they may be the *Salpa* and *Serpente.*

ARGONAUTA.   *1935, Sig. F. Cianciafara.*

3 *Adriatico* : **Argonauta** (Jan 19, 1931), **Fisalia** (May 2, 1931), **Medusa** (Dec. 12, 1931).
2 *Tosi* : **Serpente** (Feb. 28, 1932), **Salpa** (May 8, 1932).
2 *Odero-Terni-Orlando* : **Jalea** (June 15, 1932), **Jantina** (May 16, 1932).

Displacement : 599/778 tons. Dimensions : 200½ (*w.l.*), 201¾ (*o.a.*) (except Tosi boats 218 *o.a.*) × 18½ × 14½ feet. Guns · 1—4 inch, 35 cal., 2—13 mm. AA Tubes : 6—21 inch. Machinery : 2 sets. Fiat Diesels in *Argonauta, Fisalia, Jalea, Jantina* 2 sets Tosi Diesels in *Serpente, Salpa*; 2 sets Adriatico type in *Medusa.* H.P. 1,200/800 = 14/8·5 kts. Complement, 41.

Coastal—*continued*

2 "Settembrini" Class.

LUIGI SETTEMBRINI.

1935, *Sig. F. Cianciafara.*

2 *Cavallini* type: **Luigi Settembrini,** (Sept. 28, 1930), **Ruggiero Settimo** (March 29, 1931), (Cant. Nav. F. Tosi, Taranto). 798 tons *surface* and 1,134 tons *submerged.* Complement, 48. Dimensions: 225¼ (*w.l.*), 226⅔ (*o.a.*) × 25¾ × 11½ feet (*mean*). 2 Tosi Diesels. H.P. 3,000 = 17·5 kts. Electric motors, H.P. 1,400 = 9 kts. *submerged.* Guns: 1—4 inch, 2—13 mm. AA. Tubes: 8—21 inch. Radius: 9,000 miles at 8 kts. *surface*, 80 miles *submerged.*

2 "Corridoni" Class (*Minelayers*).

F. CORRIDONI.

Added 1935, *Official.*

2 *Bernardis* type: **Marcantonio Bragadino** (July 3rd, 1929), **Filippo Corridoni.** (March 30th, 1930). Both by Cant. Nav. F. Tosi, Taranto. Displacement: 803 tons *surface*, 1,051 tons *submerged.* Complement, 47 Dimensions: 232½ (*w.l.*), 234⅔ (*o.a.*) × 20 × 13¼ feet (*mean*). 2 Tosi Diesels of H.P. 1,500 = 14 kts. *surface* speed. Electric motors of 1,000 H.P. = 8 kts. *submerged.* Guns: 1—4 inch, 2 M.G. Tubes: 4—21 inch. 2 mine-launching chutes. 24 mines.

4 "Santarosa" Class.

SANTAROSA.

1934 *Photo, Pucci.*

4 *Bernardis* type: **Santorre Santarosa** (Oct. 22nd, 1929), **Ciro Menotti** (Dec. 29th, 1929), (both Odero-Terni Co., Spezia); **Fratelli Bandiera** (Aug. 7th, 1929), **Luciano Manara** (Oct. 5th, 1929), (both Cant. Nav. Triestino, Monfalcone).

Displacement: 815 tons on *surface*, 1,078 tons *submerged.*. Complement, 48. Dimensions: 227½ (*w.l.*), 229 (*o.a.*) × 23⅜ × 13½ feet (*mean*). 2 Fiat Diesels. H.P. 3,000 = 17·5 kts. *surface*; electric motors, B.H.P. 1,300 = 9 kts. *submerged.* Guns: 1—4 inch, 3—13 mm. AA. Tubes: 8—21 inch. Are an improvement of *Pisani* design. Ordered 1928, and completed 1930.

4 "Squalo" Class.

TRICHECO.

1934 *Photo, Pucci.*

4 *Bernardis* type: ordered 1928 from Cant. Nav. Triestino, Monfalcone: **Delfino** (April 27, 1930), **Narvalo** (March 15, 1930), **Squalo** (Jan. 15, 1930), **Tricheco** (Sept. 11, 1930).
Names translated are respectively *Dolphin, Swordfish, Shark, Walrus.*
Displacement: 810/1,077 tons. Complement, 48. Dimensions: 229 × 18¾ × 16¼ feet. Machinery: 2 sets Fiat Diesels, H.P. 3 000 = 16·5 kts. 2 electric motors. H.P. 1,400 = 9 kts. Guns: 1—4 inch, 2—13 mm. AA. Tubes: 8—21 inch. *Delfino* has dived to 58 fathoms.

T

Coastal—*continued*.

4 "Pisani" class.

VITTOR PISANI.　　　　　　　　　　　　　　　　　　　　　1930 *Official Photo.*

M. COLONNA.　　　　　　　　　　　　　　　　　　　　　1930 *Official Photo.*

4 *Bernardis* type : **Vittor Pisani** (Nov. 24, 1927), **Giovanni Bausan** (March 24, 1928), **Marcantonio Colonna** (Dec. 26, 1927), **Ammiraglio des Geneys** (Nov. 14, 1928). Ordered from Cantiere Navale Triestino, Monfalcone, 1924-25. Displacement : 791 tons *on surface*, 1,040 tons *submerged*. Dimensions : 223 × 19 × 14 feet. Machinery : 2 Tosi Diesels, H.P. : 2,700 = 17·5 kts. *on surface.* Electric motors of 1,200 H.P. = 9 kts. *submerged.* Guns : 1—4 inch, 2—13 mm. AA Tubes : 6—21 inch. Complement, 46.

4 "Mameli" class.

G. MAMELI.　　　　　　　　　　　　　　　　　　　　　1928 *Official Photo.*

4 *Cavallini* type : **Goffredo Mameli** (ex-*Masaniello*, 9th Dec., 1926), **Pier Capponi** (19th June, 1927), **Tito Speri** (May 25, 1928), **Giovanni da Procida** (April 1, 1928). Ordered from Cantiere Navale F. Tosi, Taranto, 1924-25. Displacement : 770 tons *on surface.* 994 tons *submerged.* Dimensions : 213¼ × 21¼ × 13 feet. 2 Tosi Diesel 8-cyl 4-cycle engines. H.P. : 3,000 = 17 kts. *on surface.* Electric motors of 1,100 H.P. = 9 kts. *submerged.* Guns : 1—4 inch, 2—13 mm. AA. Torpedo tubes : 6—21 inch. Complement, 46.

Note.—In March, 1929, *G. Mameli* dived to a depth of 64 fathoms during trials, remaining submerged for 20 minutes, and in March, 1930, to 58 fathoms for 1 hour.

5 "H" Class

H. 2.　　　　　　　　　　　　　　　　　　　　　1931 *Photo.*

5 *Electric Boat Co.* design : **H1, H2** (1916), **H4, H6, H8** (1917), by Canadian Vickers Co., Montreal. Displacement: 336 tons *on surface* 434 tons *when submerged.* Dimensions : 150¼ × 15¾ × 12¼ feet. 4—18 inch bow tubes. Machinery : 2 Nelseco Diesel engines *on surface* ; 2 Electric Dynamic Co. motors *when submerged.* H.P. 480 = 13 kts. *on surface,* H.P. 620 = 11 kts. *when submerged.* Radius: 3,000 miles at 9 kts *on surface.* 130 miles at 2 kts. *when submerged.* Complement, 22. Oil: 18 tons. *H*5 War loss. *H*3, *H*7 scrapped.

2 "X" Class (*Minelayers*).

X 3.　　(Gun since removed).　　　　　　　　　　　　　1928 *Photo, Pucci.*

2 *Bernardis* type : **X2, X3** (Ansaldo, Sestri Ponente, 1916). Displacement : 389 tons *on surface* ; 453 tons *submerged.* Dimensions : 140 × 18 × 13 feet. 1 M.G. Torpedo tubes : 2—18 inch. Carry 18 mines in 9 discharge chutes. Machinery : 2 Sulzer Diesels *on surface* ; 2 Ansaldo electric *submerged.* 660 H.P. = 10 kts. *on surface* ; 320 H.P. = 7·9 kts. *when submerged.* Carry 18 tons of fuel. Radius : 1,360 miles at 6·5 kts. *on surface* ; 96 miles at 4 kts. *when submerged.*

Seaplane Carrier. (*Nave Appoggio Aerei.*)

G. MIRAGLIA.   1939, *courtesy Dott. Ing. L. Accorsi.*

G. MIRAGLIA.   (Observe bulge.)   1935, *Bassan.*

GIUSEPPE MIRAGLIA (ex-*Citta di Messina*, 20th December, 1923). Displacement : 4,880 tons. Dimensions : 377 × 49 × 17 feet. Guns : 4—4 inch. A.A., 4—M.G. Parsons geared turbines. 8 Yarrow boilers. I.H.P. : 12,000 = 21 kts. Oil Fuel : 440 tons. Complement : 180. Reconstructed at Spezia D.Y., 1924–27. Carries 4 large and 16 smaller planes, with usual facilities for repairs and renewals and 2 catapults (forward and aft) for launching planes.

Minelayers. (*Navi Posamine.*)

Note.—Cruisers *Bari, Taranto*; Surveying Vessel *Cariddi*, certain Transports and Water Carriers, all Destroyers and 8 Submarines are fitted for minelaying.

LEGNANO.   1934.

4 *Ostia* type : **AZIO** (May 4th, 1927), **LEGNANO** (May, 1926), **LEPANTO** (May 22nd, 1927), **OSTIA** (1925). All ordered 1924, the first three from Cant. Nav. Riuniti, Ancona, the fourth ship from Cant. Nav. Triestino, Monfalcone. Displacement : 615 tons (*full load*, 850 tons). Dimensions : 204 × 28½ × 8½ feet. H.P. : 1,500 = 15 kts. Oil fuel in first 3, coal in *Ostia*. Guns : 2—4 inch, 35 cal., 1—3 inch AA., 2 M.G. First three have an effective radius of 3,500 miles. All fitted for sweeping if required. 80 mines carried.

Note.—2 more ships of this class (*Dardanelli* and *Milazzo*) were sold to Venezuela in 1938.

BUCCARI.   1928 *Photo, Pucci.*

4 *Fasana* type : **BUCCARI** (1926), **DURAZZO** (1st April, 1926), **FASANA** (1924), **PELAGOSA** (1926). All built at Castellammare. 531 tons. Dimensions : 192 (*p.p.*) × 32 × 5·7 feet. Engines : 2 sets Fiat Diesels, together 700 B.H.P. = 10 kts. Guns : 1—3 inch AA. Carry 54 mines.

Minelayers—continued.

R.D. 1. (C.N.R., Ancona, 1938). 188 tons. Dimensions: $109\frac{1}{2} \times 21\frac{2}{3} \times 7\frac{1}{2}$ feet. Guns: 1—3 inch. Diesel engines. 1 shaft. H.P.: 450 = 10 kts.

> *Photo wanted.*

ALBONA (1919), **LAURANA** (1920), **ROVIGNO** (1919), (ex-Austrian Minesweepers *M.T.* 130—132). Built at Ganz-Danubius Yard. 113 tons. Guns: 1—3 inch. Machinery: Triple expansion. H.P.: 280 = 11 kts. 1 Yarrow oil-fired boiler.

RD 31.   *1928 Photo, Pucci.*

39 small tugs, of *ca.* 150 tons, bearing various numbers, RD 4 to 57, are also fitted for minesweeping. Majority are H.P. 800 = 13 kts. Most armed with 1—3 inch AA.

Gunboats (*Cannoniere*).

VIESTI   *1926 Photo, by courtesy of Ministry of Marine.*

CROTONE (ex-*Abastro*, ex-German *M* 120), **VIESTI** (ex-*Meteo*, ex-German *M* 119.) Built at Neptun Yard, Rostock, 1918, and taken over by Italy in 1919. Displacement: 359 tons. Dimensions: 182 (*w.l.*), 192 (*o.a.*) $\times 23\frac{1}{2} \times 7$ feet. Guns: 2—4 inch. Machinery: Triple expansion. 2 shafts. I.H.P. 1600 = 14 kts. 2 water-tube boilers. Coal: 125 tons.

Mine Sweepers (*Dragamine*)

> *Photo wanted.*

VEDETTA, VIGILANTE (Adriatico, 1937). Displacement: 70 tons. Dimensions: $85\frac{1}{2} \times 14 \times 4\frac{1}{4}$ feet. Guns: 1—3 inch. Machinery: 2 Diesel motors. B.H.P.: 400 = 12·3 kts.

G. BERTA.   Added 1936.

GIOVANNI BERTA (ex-*Triglia*), **GIUSEPPE BIGLIERI** (ex-*Dentice*), **MARIO SONZINI** (ex-*Acciuga*), **PELLEGRINO MATTEUCCI** (ex-*Merluzzo*). All built 1924, the first by Schiffbau Ges. Unterweser, the other 3 by Deutsche Werft. *Standard* displacement: 620 tons. Dimensions: $138\frac{3}{4} \times 24\frac{1}{4} \times 12\frac{1}{4}$ feet. Guns: 2—3 inch, except *G. Berta*, which now has 1—3 inch, 1 M.G. Machinery: Triple expansion. 1 shaft. H.P.: 450 = 9 kts. (*P. Matteucci* is officially rated as a transport.)

Gunboats—(continued)

1933 *Photo, Capt. Dante Solimbergo, R.I.N.*

ERMANNO CARLOTTO (Shanghai Dock & Engineering Co. 1921). Shallow-draught river gunboat. 180 tons. Dimensions: 160 × 24½ × 2¾ feet. Guns: 2—3 inch AA., 6 M.G. Designed H.P.: 1,100 = 14 kts. 2 Yarrow boilers. Complement: 60. Oil: 56 tons. Twin screws in tunnels.

PALMAIOLA. *1925 Photo, by courtesy of the Ministry of Marine.*

PALMAIOLA (ex-*Mary*) (Hull, 1902). 472 tons. Dimensions: 133 × 19½ × 12 feet. H.P.: 380 = 8·5 kts. Guns: 1—3 inch AA. Complement: 80. (Purchased, 1916).

Photo wanted.

VALOROSO (ex-*Bayard*) (Glasgow, 1908). Purchased in 1915. 338 tons. Guns: 1—3 inch AA., 1 M.G. H.P. 477 = 10 kts.

Gunboats—continued.

The following were all acquired from Japan, 1917. Some carry minesweeping gear.

Added 1936.

ALULA (ex-*G* 23, ex-*Sekijyo Maru*, Osaka, 1912). 308 tons. Dimensions: 131½ × 21 × 9¾ feet. Guns: 1—3 inch AA. H.P.: 500 = 13 kts. Complement: 27.

PORTO CORSINI (ex-*G* 15, ex-*Fumi Maru*). (Osaka, 1912). 280 tons. Guns: 2—3 inch AA. H.P.: 300 = 9 kts. Complement: 24.

RIMINI (ex-*G* 16, ex-*Fuku Maru*). (Osaka, 1912). 319 tons. Guns: 1—3 inch AA. H.P.: 350 = 9.5 kts. Complement: 24.

GALLIPOLI. *1929 Photo, by courtesy of Ministry of Marine.*

GALLIPOLI (ex-*G* 31, ex-*Hakata Maru No.* 8). (Osaka, 1911). 310 tons. Guns: 2—3 inch AA. H.P.: 350 = 10 kts. Complement: 24.

OTRANTO (ex-*G* 36, ex-*Sumiye Maru*, ex-*Mariveles*). (Middlesbrough, 1911). 290 tons. Guns: 2—3 inch AA. H.P. 550 = 9·5 kts. Complement: 24.

Gunboats—continued.

CIRENE. *1925 Photo, by courtesy of the Ministry of Marine.*

CIRENE (ex-*G* 13, ex-*Hoyo Maru*). (Kobe, 1912). 383 tons. Guns: 2—3 inch AA., 1 M.G. H.P.: 300 = 9 kts.

Target Ship. (*Nave Bersaglio*).

1936, *Official.*

SAN MARCO (Castellammare, Dec., 1908). Ex-armoured cruiser converted into a wireless controlled target ship. Displacement: 8,600 tons. Dimensions: 430 (*p.p.*), 462¼ (*o.a.*) × 69 × 22¾ feet. Armament removed. Machinery: Parsons turbines. 2 shafts. S.H.P. 13,000 = 18 kts. 8 Blechynden boilers.

Note.—Old Torpedo boat *Audace* serves as control vessel.

Royal Yacht.

SAVOIA.   1937, W. H. Davis, Esq.

SAVOIA (ex-*Citta di Palermo*, 1st September, 1923).   5280 tons. Dimensions: 390 (*w.l.*) × 49 × 17 feet.   Guns: 4—3 inch AA.   2 sets Parsons geared turbines.   8 Yarrow boilers, oil-fired.   I.H.P.: 12,000 = 22 kts.

Note.—Built at Spezia and reconstructed by Cant. Nav. Riuniti, Palermo, as a yacht.

Admiralty Yacht (Classed as *Cannoniera*).

1936

AURORA (ex-*Marechiaro*, ex-Austrian *Taurus*, ex-*Nirvana*). (D. & W. Henderson & Co., Glasgow, 1904).   Reconstructed 1928.   Displacement: 935 tons.   Dimensions: 261 (*o.a.*) × 30 × 14 feet (*mean*).   Guns: 2—57 mm.   Machinery: Parsons geared turbines.   2 shafts.   2 Thornycroft boilers.   H.P.: 3,255 = 14·7 kts.   Oil: 117 tons.

Training Ships (*Navi Scuola*).

1932 *Photo, Capt. Ferratti.*

AMERIGO VESPUCCI (March 22, 1930).   Built at Castellammare.   Displacement: 3,543 tons.   Dimensions: 229·6 × 51 × 22 feet.   Guns: 4—3 inch AA., 2 M.G.   Machinery: Two Fiat Diesels, with electric drive to 2 Marelli motors.   1 shaft.   H.P.: 1,900 = 10·5 kts.   Sail area: 22,600 sq. feet.   Complement: 400 + 150 midshipmen.

C. COLOMBO.   1928 *Photo, Capitan M. Mille.*

CRISTOFORO COLOMBO (April 4, 1928).   Built at Castellammare.   Displacement: 2,787 tons.   Dimensions: 218 (*p.p.*) × 48½ × 20¾ feet.   Guns: 4—3 inch AA., 2 M.G.   Machinery: 2 Tosi Diesels with electric drive to 2 Marelli motors.   H.P.: 1,600 = 10 kts.   2 shafts.   Fuel: 103 tons.   Sail area: 18,700 sq. feet.   Radius: 6,000 miles at 8 kts.

Notes.—C. Colombo usually depends on sail power, machinery being treated as auxiliary.   Hull, masts and yards, are all of steel.   Loud speakers and echo sounding gear form part of her equipment.   About 140 midshipmen and cadets (or an equal number of boys) are usually carried.

Submarine Depot Ships.
(*Navi per appoggio sommergibili.*)

1932 *Photo.*

ALESSANDRO VOLTA (ex-*Caprera*, 1921).
ANTONIO PACINOTTI (ex-*Citta di Sassari*, 1922).
Both reconstructed at Castellammare D.Y., 1924–25.   2,727 tons. Dimensions: 288¾ × 36 × 15 feet.   Guns: 4—3 inch AA. Zoelly geared turbines.   H.P.: 7,500 = 19 kts.   2 cylindrical oil-fired boilers in *Pacinotti*, 4 in *Volta*.

(Now has black-topped funnel).   1920 *Photo, A. Boo, Cheefu.*

SEBASTIANO CABOTO (Palermo, 1912).   Displacement: 778 tons.   Complement, 104.   Dimensions: 196·8 × 31·8 × 9 feet.   Guns: 6—3 inch.   4 M.G.   H.P., 1200 = 13 kts. (formerly classed as a Gunboat).

Repair Ship (*Nave Officina*)

Official 1928 *Photo.*

QUARNARO (Scoglio Ulivi Yard, Pola, July 30, 1924).   7,185 tons.   Dimensions: 374 × 48½ × 20 feet.   Guns: 3—4 inch AA.   Machinery: Triple expansion.   1 shaft.   H.P. 2,300 = 11·5 kts.   3 cylindrical boilers, oil-fired.

Submarine Salvage Vessels.

(*Navi per salvataggio Sommergibili.*)

ANTEO (Smulders, Schiedam, 1912). Special Salvage Ship for Submarines. 1,252 tons. Dimensions : 164 × 78¾ × 6¾ feet. I.H.P., 720 = 8 kts. 2 screws. 2 cyl. boilers. 2 cranes, each lifting 200 tons.

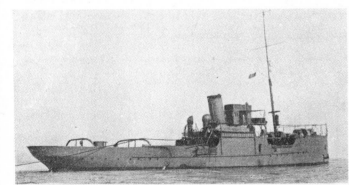

TITANO.   *Added* 1936.

TITANO (Ansaldo, 1913). 828 tons. Guns : 1—3 inch. Machinery : Triple expansion. H.P. 1,850 = 14 kts. 2 screws. 2 Thornycroft boilers. Coal : 160 tons.

Salvage Vessels (*Navi Salvataggio*)

Added 1936.

TESEO (ex-*Semper Paratus*, ex-H.M.S. *Buttercup*). (Barclay, Curle & Co., Glasgow, 1915.) 1,250 tons. Dimensions : 265 × 33½ × 11 feet. Guns : 2—3 inch. Machinery : Triple expansion. 1 shaft. H.P. 2,300 = 16 kts. 2 cylindrical boilers. Coal : 250 tons.

Note.—This ship was purchased in 1932. Former vessel of same name was1 on Dec. 13, 1931.

CICLOPE.   *1930 Photo, Capitan M. Mille.*

CICLOPE (Pattison, Naples, 1903). 1050 tons. Guns : 1—3 inch. H.P. : 1,900 = 13·5 kts. 2 shafts. 2 Thornycroft boilers.

Surveying Vessels (*Navi Idrografiche*).

AM. MAGNAGHI.   *1929 Photo, Capitan M. Mille, Sp.N.*

AMMIRAGLIO MAGNAGHI (Odero, Aug., 1914). 1,506 tons. Complement : 137. Dimensions : 229½ (*pp.*), 273 (*o.a.*) × 37½ × 12½ feet. Guns : 4—3 inch. I.H.P. : 950 = 10·5 kts. Machinery : 2 sets vertical triple expansion. Boilers: 4 cylindrical. (Was originally laid down as a Passenger Steamer).

1938, added 1939, courtesy Dott. Ing. L.Accorsi.

CARIDDI (ex-*G* 21, ex-*Nishiso Maru No.* 1). (Kawasaki Co., Kobe, 1911; purchased 1917.) 330 tons. Guns : 1—3 inch. H.P. 450 = 10 kts. Is fitted for minelaying.

Lighthouse Tenders

(Naviglio addetto al servizio fari.)

Mostly ex-Trawlers, purchased during 1917.

RICCARDO GRAZIOLI LANTE (ex-*Abisso*, ex-*Falco*, ex-*Petrel*), (J. Duthie Torry Co., Aberdeen, 1912). Displacement : 295 tons. Dimensions : 139¾ × 22 × 9 feet. Guns : 2—3 inch. Machinery : Triple expansion. 1 shaft. I.H.P. : 550 = 12 kts. 1 cyl. boiler.

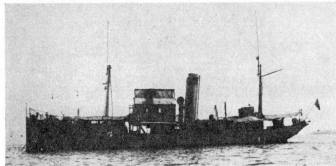

1928, *Pucci.*

DANTE DE LUTTI (ex-*G 34*, ex-*Tomiye Maru*). (Mitubisi, Nagasaki, 1911). Displacement : 266 tons. Dimensions : 118 × 21 × 8½ feet. Guns : 2—3 inch. Machinery : Triple expansion. 1 shaft. I.H.P. : 400 = 12 kts. 1 cyl. boiler.

MARIO BIANCO (ex-*G 24*, ex-*Fukuhaku Maru No. 6*, ex-*Yoshida Maru No.1*). (Kawasaki, Kobe, 1911). Displacement : 258 tons. Dimensions : 109 × 23 × 8 feet. Guns : 2—3 inch. Machinery : Triple expansion. 1 shaft. I.H.P. : 340 = 11·5 kts. 1 cyl. boiler.

SCILLA. *Added* 1939, *courtesy Sig. Aldo Fraccaroli.*

SCILLA (ex-*Panaria*, ex-*Fantasma*, ex-*Lord Charles Beresford*). (A. Hall & Co., Aberdeen, 1904 ; purchased 1916). Displacement : 350 tons. Guns : 1—3 inch. Machinery : Triple expansion. 1 shaft. H.P. : 450 = 9 kts.

Lighthouse Tenders—*continued*

LIDO (Castellammare, 1907). Displacement : 226 tons. Dimensions : 116 × 21⅓ × 7 feet. Guns : 1—3 inch. Machinery : Triple expansion. 1 shaft. I.H.P.: 550 = 12 kts. Babcock boiler.

LEVANZO (ex-*Tiburon*, ex-*Nankeen*), (Scott & Sons, Bowling, 1906). Displacement : 226 tons. Dimensions : 122 × 21⅓ × 7½ feet. Guns : 2—3 inch. Machinery : Triple expansion. 1 shaft. I.H.P. : 500 = 11 kts. 1 cyl. boiler.

Research Ships *(Navi Posacavi).*

1932 *Photo, Official.*

GIASONE (Cantiere Breda, Venice, 1929). Displacement : 1,191 tons. Dimensions : 210 (*pp.*), 251 (*o.a.*) × 33¾ × 13 feet. Guns : 2—3 inch AA. Machinery : Triple expansion. 2 shafts. Boilers : 2 water tube. H.P. : 2,500 = 15 kts.

CITTA DI MILANO. 1929 *Official Photo.*

CITTA DI MILANO (ex-*Grossherzog von Oldenburg*). (Schichau, Elbing, 1905). 5,295 tons. Dimensions : 332¾ (*o.a.*), 305 (*pp.*) × 41⅓ × 22 feet. Guns : 2—37 mm. AA. Triple expansion engines. 3 cylindrical boilers. H.P. : 1,500 = 11 kts. (Originally intended for cable laying.)

Transports *(Navi Trasporto).*

BUFFOLUTO. 1928 *Photo, Pucci.*

PANIGAGLIA (10th July, 1923), **BUFFOLUTO** (1924), **VALLELUNGA** (1924). All built by Ansaldo San Giorgio, Spezia. 915 tons. Dimensions : 184½ (*o.a.*), 172¼ (*p.p.*) × 29½ × 11 feet. Guns : 2—3·9 inch, 47 cal., 1 M.G. Triple expansion engines. 2 Thornycroft boilers. H.P. : 1,400 = 11 kts. Radius at this speed, 960 miles. Classed as "*Navi Trasporto Munizioni.*" Fitted for minelaying.

Photo wanted.

TRIPOLI (Odero, 1922). 2,460 tons. Dimensions : 205¾ (*o.a.*) × 31¾ × 15 feet. Guns : None at present. Triple expansion engines. H.P. : 600 = 8·5 kts.

CHERSO. (Recently employed in Surveying Service) 1928 *Photo, Pucci.*

CHERSO (ex-*Amalfi*) **LUSSIN** (ex-*Marsala*). (A. G. Neptun, Rostock, 1912). Displacement : 3,988 tons. Dimensions : 300 × 41 × 17½ feet H.P. : 1,100 = 10·5 kts. Guns : 4—4·7 inch. 2—3 inch AA. Classed as "*Navi Trasporto Materiale.*" Cargo : 3,000 tons.

Transports—continued

Photo Wanted

ASMARA (ex-*Nasina*, ex-*Meissonier*). (Russell, Glasgow, 1915). Purchased 1935. Displacement : 6,850 tons. Dimensions : 454¾ × 55¾ × 23¾ feet. Machinery : Quadruple expansion. 2 shafts. H.P. 4,300 = 12·5 kts. 4 cyl. boilers. Classed as *Nave Frigorifere.*

Photo Wanted

ENRICHETTA (ex-*Presto*, ex-*Alberto Fassini*, ex-*Kossuth Ferencz*). (J. L. Thompson & Co., Sunderland, 1907). Displacement : 8,360 tons. Dimensions : 399 × 50 × 22 feet. Machinery : Triple expansion. H.P. 1,500 = 9·5 kts. 2 cyl. boilers.

Note.—There are a number of smaller transports, of the coasting type, not worth inclusion here.

Petrol Carrier (*Navi Cisterna per Benzina*).

STIGE   *Added* 1936.

STIGE (Spezia Dockyard, 1924). 1,343 tons. Dimensions : 173¼ × 30½ × 13 feet. Guns : 1—4·7 inch, 1—3 inch. Tosi Diesels. H.P. : 650 = 8 kts.

Distilling Ship (*Nave Distillatrice*),

1934 *Photo.*

CITTA DI SIRACUSA (Odero, 1910). 3,593 tons. Dimensions : 363½ (*o.a.*) × 42¼ × 16½ feet. Guns : 2—3 inch AA. Machinery : Triple expansion. Boilers : 10 cylindrical. H.P. : 12,000 = 20 kts. Is fitted with Ansaldo distilling plant to produce 190 tons of fresh water daily.

Oilers (*Navi Cisterna per Nafta*).

1928 *Photo, by courtesy of Ministry of Marine.*

TARVISIO (Castellammare, April 11, 1927). 10,915 tons. Dimensions : 372½ × 59 × 22¾ feet. Guns : 4—4·7 inch, 2—3 inch AA. Parsons turbines. 3 oil-fired cylindrical boilers. H.P. : 2,600 = 10 kts. Cargo : 8,000 tons. Protective arrangements as *Brennero* in a later column.

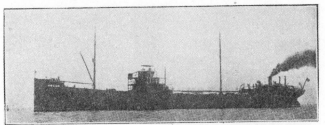

URANO.   *Photo added* 1927.

URANO (Deutsche Werke, Kiel, 1922). Built under War Reparations account. 10,550 tons. Dimensions : 414¾ × 54 × 23½ feet. Guns : 2—4·7 inch, 2—3 inch AA., 2 M.G. Diesels. 2 shafts. H.P. : 2,000 = 11 kts. Cargo : 8,000 tons.

Oilers—continued.

PROMETEO.   1936.

PROMETEO (ex-*Ostia*). (Stab. Tecnico Triestino, 1920). 1,080 tons. Dimensions : 179½ × 26¼ × 11 feet. Guns : 2—3 inch AA. Triple expansion engines. 1 Yarrow oil-fired boiler. H.P. : 600 = 10 kts.

BRENNERO.   1925 *Photo, by courtesy of Ministry of Marine.*

BRENNERO (Societa Esercizi Bacini, Riva Trigoso, 1921). Displacement : 9,790 tons (7,400 tons *d.w.c.*). Dimensions : 343½ × 59 × 24½ feet. Guns : 4—4·7 inch, 45 cal., 2—3 inch AA. Magazines are well protected. I.H.P. : 2,600 = 10·9 kts. (for trials), 9·5 (in service). Triple expansion engines. 1 screw. 2 Yarrow oil-fired boilers. Protection : " Pugliese " type bulges, with central " shock-absorbing " cylinders.

NETTUNO.   1928 *Photo, by courtesy of Ministry of Marine.*

GIOVE, NETTUNO (Cant. Nav. Riuniti, Palermo, 1916).
9,540 tons. Dimensions : 416½ × 51½ × 24 feet. Guns :
Giove, 2—4·7 inch, 2—3 inch AA.; *Nettuno,* 3—4·7 inch,
2—3 inch AA. Triple expansion engines. 4 Yarrow oil-fired
boilers. H.P. : 4,200 = 14 kts. Cargo : 6,000 tons oil fuel.

NIOBE.   1929 *Photo, by courtesy of Ministry of Marine.*

NIOBE (ex-German *Sylt,* Reiherstieg Yard, Hamburg, 1916).
3,160 tons. Dimensions : 263⅓ × 37½ × 15 feet. Triple expansion engines. 2 Oil-fired cylindrical boilers. H.P. : 1,000 =
11 kts. Guns : 3—3 inch AA. Cargo capacity : 2,000 tons.

CERERE.   1929 *Photo, by courtesy of Ministry of Marine.*

CERERE (ex-*Baltrum,* Kiel, 1915). 2,530 tons. Dimensions:
246⅛ × 34½ × 14½ feet. Guns : 2—3 inch AA. Triple expansion engines. 2 coal-fired cylindrical boilers. H.P.: 800 =
10 kts. Capacity : 1,500 tons.

COCITO   1939, *courtesy Dott. Ing. L. Accorsi.*

COCITO, LETE (Riva Trigoso, 1914–15). 1,165 tons. Dimensions : 168⅓ × 30½ × 11 feet. Guns : 3—3 inch AA. Tosi
Diesels. H.P. 750 = 10 kts. Cargo : 760 tons.

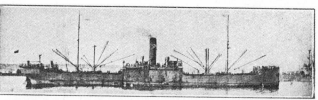

BRONTE (Orlando, 1904). 8,238 tons. Complement, 79.
Dimensions : 391 × 47 × 23 feet. Guns : 2—3 inch, 2—3 inch
AA. With full cargo : 3,700 I.H.P. = 11·5 kts. ; with reduced
cargo 4,300 I.H.P. = 14·5 kts. Triple expansion engines.
2 screws. 2 cylindrical boilers. Carries 6,000 tons. Own fuel :
550 tons. *Sterope* (sister ship), lost during War.

1936, *Pucci.*

MARTE (ex-Austrian *Vesta*) (Armstrong, 1892). 4,695 tons.
Dimensions : 301 × 37½ × 20 feet. Guns : 2—3 inch AA.
Triple expansion engines. 2 coal-fired cylindrical boilers.
I.H.P. : 1,200 = 10 kts.

Water Carriers (*Navi Cisterna per Acqua*).

ISONZO.   1938, *courtesy Sig. F. Cianciafara.*

ISONZO (June 9, 1937), **PO, VOLTURNO** (1936). *Po* built by
C. N. Riuniti, Ancona, other 2 by Tirreno. Displacement : 3,336
tons. Dimensions : 265¾ × 38¾ × 16¾ feet. Guns : 2—4·7
inch. 4 M.G. AA. Machinery : Triple expansion. 1 shaft.
H.P. : 1,700 = 11·5 kts. Oil-fired watertube boilers.
Capacity : 2,000 tons.

Water Carriers—*continued,*

SCRIVIA, TIRSO (Tirreno, 1937). 1,086 tons. Dimensions: 174 × 33 × 11½ feet. 4 M.G. (Fitted for Minelaying.) Fiat Diesels. H.P.: 600 = 9·5 kts.

GARIGLIANO   1937.

GARIGLIANO (Tirreno, 1934), **SESIA** (Adriatico, 1933). 1,050 tons. Dimensions: 213¼ × 33 × 11½ feet. 4 M.G. (Fitted for minelaying). Fiat Diesels. 2 shafts. H.P. 600 = 9·5 kts.

METAURO, SILE (Quarnaro, 1933), **SEBETO** (Venice, 1933). Displacement: 592 tons. Dimensions: 119 × 26¼ × 10½ feet. Tosi Diesels. H.P.: 400 = 9 kts.

ARNO, BRENTA (Odero-Terni, 1929). 635 tons. Dimensions: 138¾ × 26 × 10 feet. Fiat Diesels. H.P.: 350 = 9 kts.

BORMIDA, MINCIO (Venice, 1929). 645 tons. Dimensions: 138⅛ × 26¼ × 10 feet. Tosi Diesels. H.P.: 350 = 9 kts.

1930 *Photo, Capitan M. Mille.*

ADIGE (Castellammare, 1928). 780 tons. Dimensions: 154 × 31½ × 7½ feet. 4 M.G. (Fitted for minelaying.) M.A.N. Diesels. 2 shafts. H.P.: 280 = 8 kts.

Water Carriers—*continued.*

1939, *courtesy Dott. Ing. L. Accorsi.*

TICINO (Vulkan, Hamburg, 1924). 2,588 tons. Dimensions: 244 × 36 × 15½ feet. Guns: 2—3 inch. M.A.N. Diesels. 1 shaft. H.P.: 620 = 9·5 kts.

DALMAZIA.   1929 *Official Photo.*

DALMAZIA (Fiume, 1922), **ISTRIA** (Fiume, 1923). Displacement: 2,900 tons. Dimensions: 260 × 32½ × 15¼ feet. Guns: 1—4·7 inch, 1—3 inch AA. Triple expansion engines. 2 shafts. 2 Thornycroft oil-fired boilers. H.P.: 1,450 = 10 kts. Cargo: 1,800 tons. Both built at Quarnaro Yard.

Water Carriers—*continued.*

PAGANO

PAGANO, VERDE (Spezia Dockyard, 1921). 1,432 tons. Dimensions: 173⅓ × 30½ × 14 feet. Fiat Diesel engines. B.H.P.: 400 = 7·5 kts. Guns: 1—4·7 inch, 1—3 inch AA. Capacity: 950 tons.

1936

FLEGETONTE (Riva Trigoso, 1915). Sister ship to Oilers *Cocito* and *Lete*. 1,162 tons. Guns: 3—3 inch AA. Tosi Diesels. H.P.: 700 = 9 kts. Capacity: 750 tons.

FRIGIDO (ex-*Fukuju Maru*). (Osaka, 1912.) (Purchased, 1916.) 398 tons. Dimensions: 116½ × 21½ × 10 feet. 2 M.G. Triple expansion engines. 1 cylindrical boiler. H.P. 221 = 9 kts.

Note.—There are a number of smaller water carriers not worth listing here.

Tugs. (*Rimorchiatori*)

4 vessels (building). 389 tons. H.P. : 1,000 = 12 kts.

Added, 1936.

POLIFEMO (ex-*Einigkeit*, 1916). Salvage Vessel and Tug. 1,035 tons. H.P.: 1,250 = 12 kts. Thornycroft boiler.

RAPALLO, TAORMINA (1937). 276 tons. Guns : 1—3 inch. H.P. : 650 = 10 kts.

NEREO (1936). 340 tons. Guns : 1—3 inch. H.P. : 900 = 11 kts.

TINO   1936

SALVORE, TINO, PANTELLARIA, PORTO FERRAIO, PORTO TORRES, PORTO CONTE, PORTO ERCOLE, PORTO QUIETO, PORTO SDOBBA, PORTO FOSSONE, PORTO VENERE, PORTO BUSO, PORTO RECANATI, PORTO SALVO, PORTO PISANO, MISENO, PALINURO (1929–1937). 223 to 226 tons. Guns : 1—3 inch. H.P. : 600 = 11 kts.

Tugs—*continued.*

ATLANTE.   1936

ATLANTE (1928), **ERCOLE** (1928), **AUSONIA** (1920). 355 tons. Guns : 1—3 inch. H.P. : 900 = 11 kts.

FAVIGNANA.   1936

FAVIGNANA (1918). 320 tons. Guns : 2—3 inch. H.P. : 560 = 10 kts.

1936

MONTECRISTO (Danzig, 1916). 340 tons. H.P. : 500 = 10 kts. Guns : 1—3 inch.

Tugs—*continued.*

L. F. MARSIGLI.   1929 *Official Photo.*

LUIGI FERDINANDO MARSIGLI (ex-*Tremiti*, 1916), **LUNI** (1914), **MARITTIMO** (1915), **EGADI** (1915). 337 tons. Guns : 1—3 inch. H.P. : 975 = 12 kts.

1936

LIPARI (1917). 250 tons. H.P. : 500 = 10 kts. Guns : 1—3 inch.

PORTO EMPEDOCLE (1914). 330 tons. Guns : 1—3 inch. H.P. 500 = 11 kts.

Note.—There are a great many small tugs not worth listing here.

Minister of the Navy: Vice-Admiral Zengo Yoshida.

Chief of Naval Staff: Admiral Prince Hiroyasu Fushimi, G.C.V.O.

Naval Attaché, London: Capt. T. Kondo.

Assistant Naval Attachés, London: Commander K. Matsunaga, Lieut.-Commander M. Genda.

Flags.

1 *Standard of H.I.M. the Empress.*—A forked flag with a gold chrysanthemum on a red ground (as sketch for Imperial Standard).

2 *Standard of H.I.H. the Crown Prince.*—As Imperial Standard, but the chrysanthemum is enclosed in a square white border set a little distance within edges of flag.

3 *Imperial Princes and Princesses.*—A square white flag, with red border run round edges of flag and gold chrysanthemum in centre.

4 *Duty Flag.*—As transport flag, but *white* stripes over *red* ground.

5 *Repair Ship Flag.*—As transport flag, but with red stripes along upper and lower edges of flag, instead of across centre.

6 *Pendant for Men of War.*—Usual narrow triangulated shape, with Rising Sun next to hoist, as in Commodore's broad pendant.

Navy Estimates.

(excluding Supplementary Credits).

1937-38, Yen 683,958,292   1938-39, Yen 680,383,351   1939-40, Yen 826,752,432

Personnel: About 107,000, all ranks.

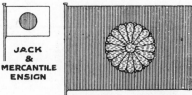

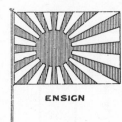

ENSIGN

JACK & MERCANTILE ENSIGN

IMPERIAL STANDARD

MINISTER OF THE NAVY

Red

White

Gold

Blue

ADMIRAL

VICE ADMIRAL

REAR ADMIRAL

COMMODORE

SENIOR OFFICER

TRANSPORT

Mercantile Marine.

(From "Lloyd's Register," 1939 figures).

2,337 vessels of 5,629,845 gross tonnage.

Personnel and Uniforms.

INSIGNIA OF RANK—EXECUTIVE OFFICERS—SLEEVES.

CAP.

The cap is the same as the British (but without gold embroidery in the senior ranks).

CAP BADGE.

Sho-i Ko-hosei. Midshipman.   Small anchor, surrounded by cherry leaves and blossom

Executive Branch:	Tai-sho.	Chu-sho.	Sho-sho.	Tai-sa.	Chu-sa.	Sho-sa.	Tai-i.	Chu-i.	Sho-i
Corresponding British:	*Admiral.*	*Vice-Ad.*	*Rear-Ad.*	*Captain.*	*Commander.*	*Lieut. Com.*	*Lieutenant.*	*Sub-Lieut.*	*Acting Sub-Lieut.*

Sho-i *Acting Sub-Lieut.* Has a stripe half the width of a Sho-i.

BAND between stripes. (BRANCHES, with but after Executive).

Violet   Kikwan (*Engineer*) (with executive rank and curl. Titles as above with the prefix Kikwan).

Red   Gun-i (*Doctor*).

White   Shukei (*Paymaster*).

Brown   Zosen (*Constructor*).

    Zoki (*Engineer-Constructor*). } with curl, as Executive.

Purple–Brown   Zohei (*Gun Constructor*).

Blue   Suiro (*Hydrographer*).

The senior officer of any branch on board the ship always carries the affix "*cho.*" Thus: Ho-jitsu-cho (*Gunnery*), Sui-rai-cho (*Torpedo*), Ko-kai-cho (*Navigator*), Gun-i-cho (*Senior Doctor*), Shukei-cho (*Senior Paymaster*).

Undress is a military tunic (dark blue) with the sleeve insignia of rank in black braid only, with curl, and with collar insignia of rank and branch.

NOMENCLATURE OF JAPANESE WARSHIPS.

The system of nomenclature now being used is thus:—

Battleships: Named after Provinces and Mountains.

Aircraft Carriers: Named after Mountains, Dragons, and Birds.

Cruisers: Named after Rivers and Mountains.

Destroyers (First Class): Meteorological Names in poetic style.

Destroyers (Second Class): Named after Trees, Flowers and Fruits.

Torpedo Boats: Named after Birds.

Colour of Ships: Dark grey usually. Since 1934 submarines of the 18th and 29th Flotillas have been painted black, presumably as an experiment.

Principal Naval Guns.

Notation.	Calibre.	Length in calibres.	Model.	Weight of Gun.	Weight of A.P. shot.	Maximum Initial Velocity.	Maximum penetration firing AP capped at K.O.		Danger space against average ship, at			Service rate of Fire. Rounds per minute.
							5000 yards.	3000 yards.	10,000 yards.	5000 yards.	3000 yards.	
	inches.			tons.	lbs.	F. S.	inches.	inches.				
HEAVY.	16	45	K.M.	105	...	2600	...	•••	...	...	...	...
	14	45	V	82	1400	...	...	...	...	...	...	...
		50										
MEDIUM.	8	45	A	17½	250	2740	7	10	110	425	600	1·2
	8	40	A	15½	250	2580	5½	7½	100	400	580	1·2
	6	45	('04)	8½	100	3000	4½	6½	75	250	475	...
	6	50	V	8	100	3000	4½	6½	75	250	475	6
	6	40	A	6½	100	2500	3	4½	65	210	435	7
	6	40	A	6	100	2220	2½	4	35	150	360	8
	5·5	50	...	6¼	82	2725	...	...	...	...	...	12
	4·7	45	...	...	...	...	...	...	...	...	...	...
	4·7	40	A	2	45	2150	...	2½	...	...	...	8
	4·7	32	A	1¾	36	1938	...	...	...	...	...	8·6
LIGHT	3	...	...	...	14	...	...	...	...	...	...	...
	3	40	...	2	12	2200	...	...	...	...	...	...
AA	3	40	...	...	13	...	...	...	...	...	...	...

In the Model column A = Armstrong; V = Vickers; K.M. = Kure Arsenal and Muroran Steel Works.

There are also mounted in recent ships : 6·1 inch (*Mogami* class) 6 inch, 50 cal. K.M.; 5 inch, 50 cal. AA., 1927 K.M.; 4·7 inch, 50 cal. AA.; and various marks of 4 inch and 3 inch.

(All details tabulated above are unofficial.)

Second Fleet Replenishment Law, 1933. (First Law completed at end of 1937.)

2 cruisers of 8,500 tons	4 submarines	1 repair ship
2 aircraft carriers of 10,000 tons	6 submarine chasers	2 oilers
14 destroyers	1 submarine depot ship	3 aircraft tenders
16 torpedo boats		

The Second Replenishment Law also includes the strengthening of the Fleet Air Arm by a further 8 squadrons between 1934–37, giving a total of 39 squadrons in 1937.

Third Replenishment Law, 1937.

4 battleships, 1 or 2 aircraft carriers, and a number of cruisers, destroyers and submarines. To be completed at end of 1942.

Fourth Replenishment Law, 1939.

To involve the expenditure of Yen 1,700,000,000 (of which Yen 1,200,000,000 will be on new construction) up to end of 1945.

Japanese Alphabet. Read name from right to left in syllables made by consonants (down) and vowels· (across), in names painted on sides of smaller ships.

	A	E	I	O	U	YA	YO	YU	WA
	ア	エ	イ	オ	ウ	/	/	/	/
B	バ	ベ	ビ	ボ	ブ	ビャ	ビョ	ビュ	/
D	ダ	デ	ヂ	ド	ツ	ヂャ	ヂョ	ヂュ	/
G	ガ	ゲ	ギ	ゴ	グ	ギャ	ギョ	ギュ	グヮ
H	ハ	ヘ	ヒ	ホ	フ	ヒャ	ヒョ	ヒュ	/
K	カ	ケ	キ	コ	ク	キャ	キョ	キュ	クヮ
M	マ	メ	ミ	モ	ム	ミャ	ミョ	ミュ	/
N	ナ	ネ	ニ	ノ	ヌ	ニャ	ニョ	ニュ	/
P	パ	ペ	ピ	ポ	プ	ピャ	ピョ	ピュ	/
R	ラ	レ	リ	ロ	ル	リャ	リョ	リュ	/
S	サ	セ	シ	ソ	ス	シャ	ショ	シュ	/
T	タ	テ	チ	ト	ツ	チャ	チョ	チュ	/
W	ワ	エ	ヰ	ヲ	/	/	/	/	/
Y	ヤ	/	/	ヨ	ユ	/	/	/	/
Z	ザ	ゼ	ジ	ゾ	ズ	ジャ	ジョ	ジュ	/

N = ン

Hosyo.

Mutu. Nagato.

Hiei.

Akagi.

Hyuga. Ise.

Haruna. Kirisima. Kongo.

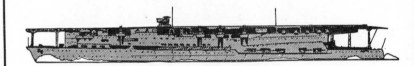

Kaga.

Huso. Yamasiro.

Ryuzyo.

Soryu.

303

ex-Ping-Hai.

ex-Ning-Hai.

Yubari.

Mogami *class.*

Kasuga.

Hurutaka.
Kako.

Kinugasa.
Aoba.

Nati.   Asigara.
Myoko.   Haguro.

Atago.   Maya.
Tyokai.   Takao.

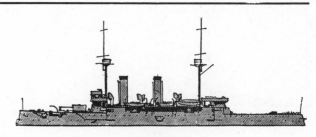

Tokiwa.

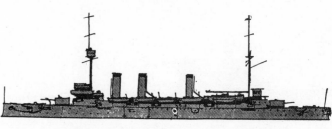

Aduma.

Yakumo.

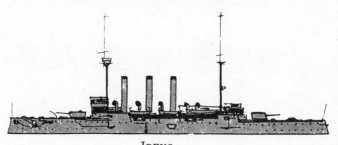

Idumo.
Iwate.

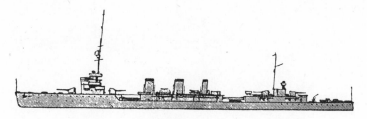

TATUTA.
TENRYU. (Now fitted with tripod foremast)

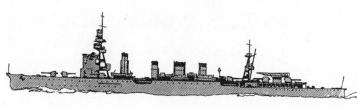

NAKA.

S.C. 3 (1 and 2 similar).

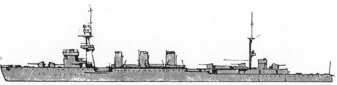

KISO. TAMA. OI.
KITAKAMI.

SENDAI and ZINTU.

S.C. 51-53

KUMA

TIDORI and OTORI *classes*.

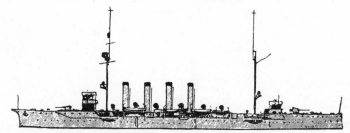

NATORI *class*.
(Some have spoon bows).

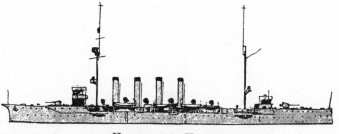

HIRADO. YAHAGI.

MINESWEEPERS Nos. 1—6. (5 and 6 only with tripod.)

MOMO *class*

U

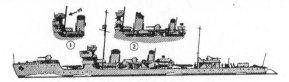

WAKATAKE *class.*

(Inset 1, KAYA *class.* Inset 2, HASU and KURETAKE.)

HUBUKI *class*

(Some have no shields to tubes; others a more slender first funnel.)

SIRATAKA.

HIBIKI *class*

YAEYAMA.

AKIKAZE *class.*

SIGURE *class.*

(HATUHARU *class* similar.)

KAMOME. TUBAME.

KAMIKAZE *class.*

(NAMIKAZE, NOKAZE and NUMARAZE similar.)

ASASIO *class.*

NATUSIMA *class.*

MUTUKI *class.*

(Note bow and amidships t.t.)

KAGERO *class.*

MINESWEEPERS 13 to 16.

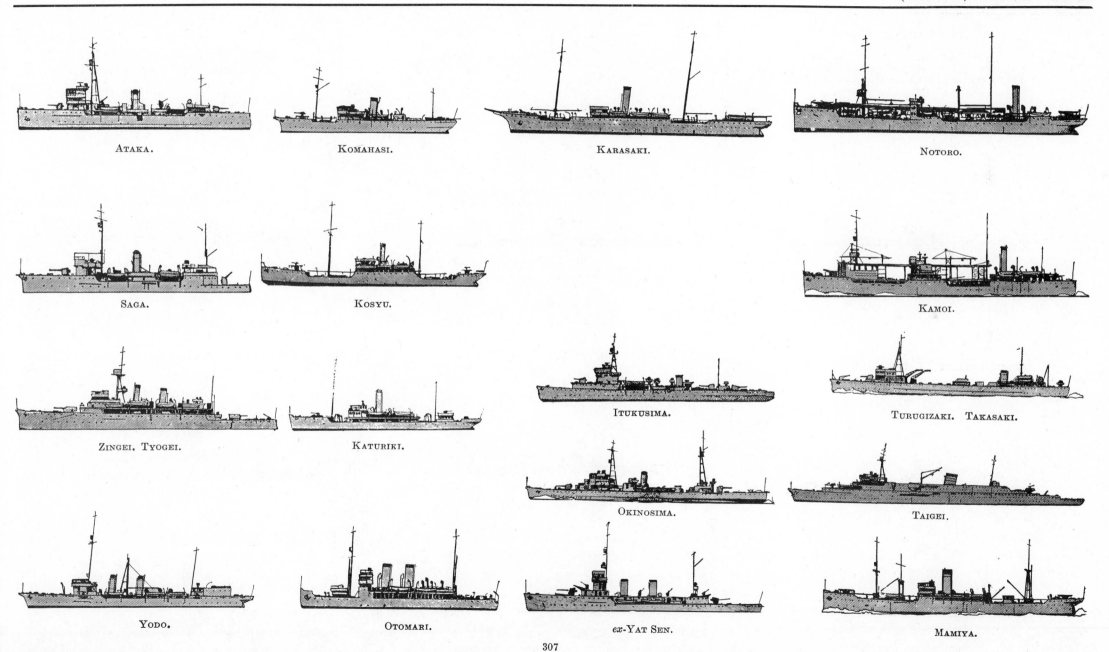

ATAKA.

KOMAHASI.

KARASAKI.

NOTORO.

SAGA.

KOSYU.

KAMOI.

ZINGEI. TYOGEI.

KATURIKI.

ITUKUSIMA.

TURUGIZAKI. TAKASAKI.

OKINOSIMA.

TAIGEI.

YODO.

OTOMARI.

ex-YAT SEN.

MAMIYA.

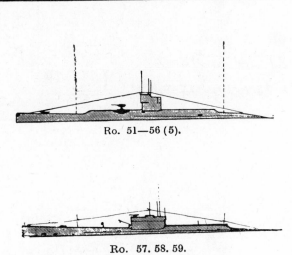

Ro. 51—56 (5).

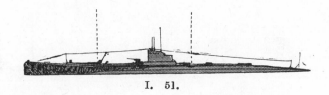

I. 51.

Ro. 57. 58. 59.

Ro. 26. 27. 28.

I. 52.

Ro. 30—32.

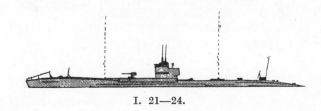

I. 21—24.

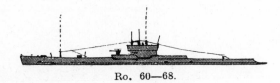

Ro. 60—68.

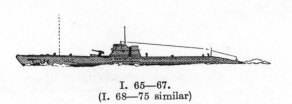

I. 65—67.
(I. 68—75 similar)

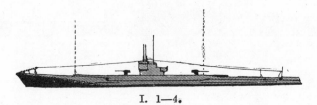

I. 1—4.

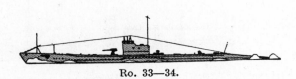

Ro. 33—34.

I. 53—64.
(Deck flush from bow to C.T.)

New Construction.

Four new battleships are believed to have been laid down during 1938-39, at Kure, Yokosuka, Kawasaki and Mitubisi yards. It is reported that they are ships of over 40,000 tons, armed with eight or nine 16 inch guns and with a speed in the region of 30 kts.

MUTU.

1938, *added* 1939.

(NAGATO CLASS—2 SHIPS).

NAGATO (Nov. 9th, 1919), **MUTU** (May 31st, 1920).

Standard displacement, 32,720 tons.

$$\text{Complement,} \left\{ \begin{array}{l} 74 \text{ officers} \\ 1{,}258 \text{ men} \end{array} \right\} = \textbf{1{,}332.}$$

$$\text{Length,} \left\{ \begin{array}{l} p.p., 660\tfrac{2}{3} \text{ feet.} \\ o.a., 700 \text{ feet approximate.} \end{array} \right\} \begin{array}{l} \text{Beam, 95 feet.} \\ \text{Draught, 30 feet } max. \end{array}$$

NAGATO.

1937

Guns (Japanese):
8—16 inch, 45 cal.
20—5.5 inch, 50 cal.
8—5 inch A.A.
7 M.G.
Torpedo tubes (21 inch):
6 *submerged*.
Searchlights: 8.

Aircraft: 3.

Armour: (*unofficial*)
13″ *or* 12″ Belt ... .
8″—4″ Ends ....
3½″ Deck ....
7″ deck above magazines, boilers and engine rooms.
14″ Turrets ....
  ″ Battery ....
12″ Conning tower ...
(Bulges and other special anti-torpedo protection.)

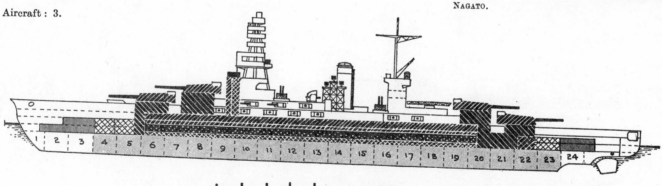

Plans revised 1936

Machinery : Geared turbines. 4 shafts. Boilers : 21 Kanpon. Designed H.P. : 80,000 = 23 kts. Oil fuel : about 4,500 tons.

Notes.—Both built at Naval Yards as shown in table. Extensively reconstructed at same yards in 1934-36, being given bulges and triple bottoms for protection against torpedo attack, new machinery, aircraft, increased deck protection and increased elevaton of 16-inch guns. Trial speed after reconstruction and reboilering reported as 26 kts.

Name	Builder	Machinery	Laid down	Completed	Trials	Boilers
Nagato	Kure	Kure	28 Aug., 1917	25 Nov., 1920	84,000 = 23·5	Kanpon
Mutu	Yokosuka	Yokosuka	1 June, 1918	24 Oct., 1921	= 23·4	

ISE (Nov. 12, 1916),

HYUGA (Jan. 27, 1917).

Standard Displacement, 29,990 tons.   Complement, 1,360.

Length (*p.p*). 640 feet.   Beam, 94 feet.   *Max.* draught, 28⅔ feet.   Length (*o.a.*), 683 feet.

Guns (Japanese):   Aircraft : 3.
    12—14 inch, 45 cal.
    18—5·5 inch, 50 cal.
    8—5 inch, AA.
    7—M.G.
Torpedo tubes (21 inch):
    4 *submerged.*

Armour (Japanese):
12″—8″ Belts . . . .
5″—3″ Belt (Ends)
2½″—1¼″ Decks . .
12″—8″ Turrets . .
6″ Battery. . . . . .
12″—6″ C.T. . . . .

ISE.   1937.

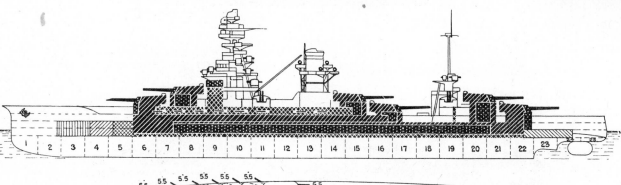

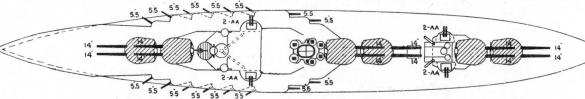

Machinery : Brown-Curtis turbines in *Ise* ; Parsons turbines in *Hyuga*. 4 shafts. Boilers : 24 Kanpon.* Designed H.P. 45,000 = 23 kts. Oil fuel : 4,500 tons.

*General Note concerning boilers of these and certain other ships: "Kanpon" is a Japanese Admiralty type of W.T. boiler, resembling Yarrow type, with Japanese modifications.

Name	Built by	Machinery	Laid down	Completed	Trials. H.P. = kts.
Ise	Kawasaki Co.	Kawasaki Co.	10.5.15	15.12.17	= 23 3.
Hyuga	Mitubisi Co.	Mitubisi Co.	6.5.15	30.4.18	

HYUGA.   1938, *added* 1939.

HYUGA.   1938, *added* 1939.

HUSO (March 28th, 1914),

YAMASIRO (Nov. 3rd, 1915).

Standard Displacement, 29,330 tons.

Complement, 1243 and 1272, respectively.

Length $\left\{\begin{array}{l}\text{(p.p.) 630 feet.}\\\text{(o.a.) 673 feet.}\end{array}\right\}$ Beam, 94 feet. *Max.* draught, 28½ feet.

Guns (Japanese):
12—14 inch, 45 cal.
16—6 inch, 50 cal.
8—5 inch AA.
26 machine.
4 landing.
Torpedo tubes (21 inch):
2 *submerged*.

Aircraft:
1, with catapult—on turret amidships in *Huso* and on q.d. in *Yamasiro*.

Armour:
12″–8″ Belt (amidships)
5″, 4½″, 4″ Belt (bow)
4″ Belt (stern) ....
8″ Upper belt ....
6″ Battery ....
12″–8″ Barbettes ....
12″–8″ Gunhouses ....
12″ & 6″ C.T. ....
(Bulkheads 12″ to 4″)
2″ & 1¼″ Decks ....
—″ Roofs $\left\{\begin{array}{l}\text{Gunhouses}\\\text{C.T. ......}\end{array}\right\}$

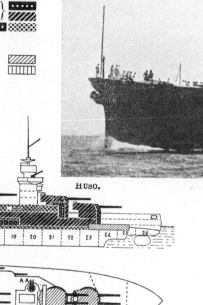

HUSO.

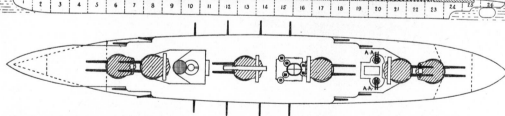

Machinery: Brown-Curtis turbines. 4 shafts. Boilers: Kanpon. Designed H.P. 40,000 = 22·5 kts. Fuel: 5000 tons oil.

General Notes.—Both ships were thoroughly reconstructed 1932-33 and altered in profile. The replacing of the 24 Miyabara boilers by (?) 8 Kanpon has enabled the forward boiler room to be converted to other uses, and there is now only one funnel fitted with an anti-flare top. The base of the foremast has been enlarged and fitted with wings, and the tripod mainmast is replaced by a tower base on which AA guns are mounted. No. 3 turret in *Huso* only now bears forward, and has a catapult on the crown, while additional searchlights have been grouped around the funnel. A large amount of additional armour and anti-torpedo structure has been worked into the ships, but details are lacking. Formerly 14 inch guns were reported as having an elevation of 25°, but this has probably now been increased.

Name.	Builder.	Machinery.	Laid down	Completed	Trials. H.P. = kts.		Turbine.	Boilers	Best recent speed
Huso	Kure	Kawasaki	11 3.12	8.11.15	46,500 = 23.		Curtis	Kanpon	
Yamasiro	Yokosuka	Kawasaki	20.11.13	31. 3.17	...	...	Curtis	Kanpon	

1934 *Photo.*

YAMASIRO.

1936 *Official.*

(KONGO CLASS—4 SHIPS.)

KONGO (May 18th, 1912).
HIEI (Nov. 21, 1912).

Employed as Seagoing Training Ships.

HARUNA
(Dec. 14th, 1913),
KIRISIMA
(Dec. 1st, 1913).

Standard displacement, 29,330 tons. Complement, 980.

Length $\begin{cases} (p.p.)\ 653\frac{1}{2}\ \text{feet.} \\ (o.a.)\ 704\ '' \end{cases}$ $\begin{cases} Kirisima \quad \text{Beam, 95 feet.} \\ Kongo \qquad \ '' \quad 92\ '' \\ Hiei \qquad\quad\ '' \quad 92\ '' \\ Haruna \qquad '' \quad 95\ '' \end{cases}$ $\begin{array}{l}\textit{Max. draught, } 27\frac{1}{2}\ \textit{feet} \\ \textit{Mean, } 20\frac{3}{4}\ \textit{feet.} \end{array}$

Aircraft: 3

Guns (*see Notes*) :
- 8—14 inch, 45 cal.
- 16—6 inch, 50 cal.
- 8—5 inch AA.
- 4 machine.
- 4 landing.

Torpedo tubes (21 inch) :
- 4 submerged.

Hiei :
- 6—14 inch.
- 16—6 inch.
- 4—5 inch AA.
- 4—3 inch AA.

Note to Plan.—
.5 inch AA.
now in twin
mounts.

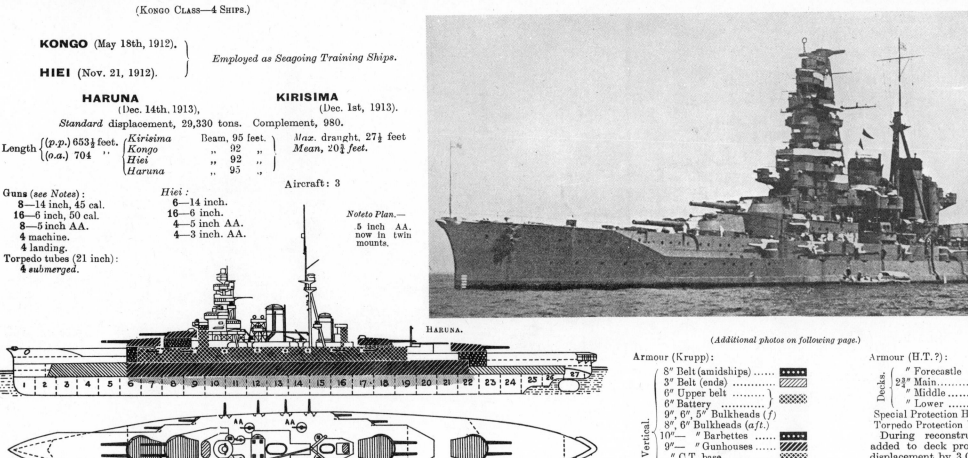

HARUNA.

1934 (added 1935).

(*Additional photos on following page.*)

Armour (Krupp) :

Vertical. $\begin{cases} 8''\ \text{Belt (amidships)} \dots \text{▦} \\ 3''\ \text{Belt (ends)} \dots \text{▨} \\ 6''\ \text{Upper belt} \dots \\ 6''\ \text{Battery} \dots \end{cases}$ ⎱ ▦
$9'',\ 6'',\ 5''\ \text{Bulkheads } (f)$
$8'',\ 6''\ \text{Bulkheads } (aft.)$
$10''—\quad''\ \text{Barbettes} \dots \text{■}$
$9''—\quad''\ \text{Gunhouses} \dots \text{▨}$
$\dots''\ \text{C.T. base} \dots \text{▦}$
$10''\ \text{C.T. (} ''\ \text{hood)} \dots \text{▦}$
$''\ \text{Fore comm. tube} \dots$
$6''\ \text{Torpedo con. tower} \dots \text{▦}$
$''\ \text{Tube (C.T. tower)} \dots$

Armour (H.T. ?) :

Decks. $\begin{cases} ''\ \text{Forecastle} \dots \\ 2\frac{3}{4}''\ \text{Main} \dots \\ ''\ \text{Middle} \dots \\ ''\ \text{Lower} \dots \end{cases}$

Special Protection H.T.
Torpedo Protection Bulkheads.
During reconstruction 4'' was
added to deck protection, raising
displacement by 3,000 tons.

These Notes are not from any official data.

Machinery : Parsons 4-shaft (in *Haruna* only, Curtis 4-shaft) turbines. Designed H.P. : 64,000 = 26 kts. (*Hiei*, 13,800 = 18 kts.). Boilers : See *Notes*. Fuel : About 4,500 tons oil.

Name	Builder	Machinery	Laid down	Completed	Trials F.P.	Turbine	Boilers	Re-fit
Hiei	Yokosuka	Mitubisi	4,11,11	4.8.'14		Parsons	Kanpon	1936
Kongo	Vickers	Vickers	17.1.11	16.8.'13		Parsons	Kanpon	1926
Haruna	Kawasaki	Kawasaki	16.3.12	⎱19.4,'15		Curtis	Kanpon	1926
Kirisima	Mitubisi	Mitubisi	17.3.12	⎰		Parsons	Kanpon	1925

General Notes.—*Kongo* 1910–11 Programme, others 1911–12 Programme. Designed by Sir George Thurston. For *Haruna* 30% of material was imported and erected in Japan. 3 planes added to equipment, 1927. All 4 refitted 1926–30, and bulges added, reducing speed by over a knot. Funnels altered on conversion to oil fuel only. *Kongo* completely rebuilt, 1935–37, being given additional protection against torpedo and aircraft attack. *Hiei*, de-militarised for Training purposes, reported to be in hand for re-armament, but this is not officially admitted.

Gunnery Notes.—In *Kongo* guns are Vickers models ; but in other three ships all calibres are of Japanese manufacture. *Kongo* has combined Vickers (hydraulic) and Janney-Williams (electric) manœuvring systems for her barbettes ; there is also a small auxiliary hydraulic installation, generally used for cleaning purposes, which can be used in emergency for working the 14-inch guns.

Armour Notes.—Main belt is 12' 5'' deep. 8'' thick, and extends between Barbettes Nos. 1 and 4. Upper belt between Barbettes Nos. 1 and 3, 6'' thick, and carried up to forecastle deck. Bulkheads : Main belt is closed by diagonal bulkheads of 8''—6'' aft and by a 6''—5'' bulkhead forward. Upper belt closed by 6'' bulkhead aft and 9''—6'' bulkhead forward. There is also a narrow 3 inch strip of armour, 2 feet 6 inch deep under whole length of main belt ; this is not shown on plans.

Anti-Torpedo Protection Notes.—Internal sub-division by longitudinal and cross bulkheads. Extra protection given by armour to all magazine spaces. Port and starboard engine rooms are divided by an unpierced longitudinal bulkhead along keel-line.

Torpedo Notes.—Tubes are twin submerged type, at varying levels, some being only 6 feet below waterline. Except in the case of the tubes in wake of No. 3 Barbette, Starboard Tube is before Port Tube. *Kongo* has combined hydraulic and electrically-operated tubes. In *Haruna*, tubes are Armstrong 21-inch side-loading, hydraulically operated.

Engineering Notes.—In *Kongo*, and *Kirisima* Parsons turbines have H.P. rotors on outboard shafts and L.P. on inner shafts with astern turbines aft and in same casing. Reconstruction included new Kanpon boilers.

For particulars of these ships, see preceding page

HIEI as demilitarised. 1933 *Photo.*

KONGO (funnels of equal height). 1938, *added* 1939.

KIRISIMA. 1935.

Aircraft Carriers.

(SORYU Class—3 SHIPS)

SORYU (HIRYU similar, but with light tripod mast abaft bridge on starboard side) 1939.

SORYU (Dec. 23, 1935).

HIRYU (Nov. 16, 1937).

SYOKAKU (June 2, 1939).

Displacement : 10,050 tons.

Dimensions : $688\frac{1}{2} \times 68\frac{1}{3} \times 16\frac{1}{2}$ feet (*mean* draught).

(*For plan, see Addenda*).

Guns :
  12—5 inch AA. (paired).
  4—S.L.

  Machinery : Geared turbines. 4 shafts. S.H.P. : 60,000 = 30 kts. 8 Kanpon boilers.

Reported unofficially to have accommodation for 30 to 40 aircraft, and to be fitted with gyro-stabilisers.

Note.—Former names mean *Blue Dragon* and *Flying Dragon* respectively. *Syokaku* (meaning *Crane*) was originally reported building under name of *Koryu.* It is possible that she is of a new and much larger design, as one report suggests her length to be over 800 feet.

Name	Builder	Laid down	Completed
Soryu	Kure	20/11/34	29/12/37
Hiryu	Yokosuka	8/7/36	
Syokaku	Yokosuka	11/12/37	

1933 *Photo, Official.*

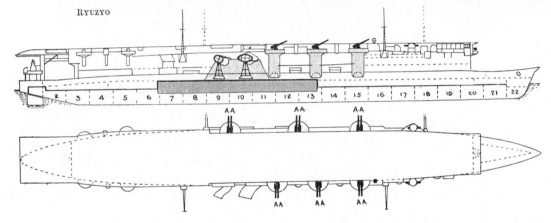

RYUZYO

RYUZYO (April 2, 1931).

Displacement : 7,100 tons.   Complement : 600.

Length : 548 feet.   Beam : 60½ feet.   Draught : 15⅓ feet.

Guns : 12—5 inch AA.   24 M.G.   24 aircraft carried (unofficial).

Machinery : Geared turbines.   Kanpon Boilers.   S.H.P. 40,000 = 25 kts.

Laid down Nov. 26, 1929.   Completed May 9, 1933.

Note.—Smoke discharge is arranged through 2 funnels projecting from starboard side. This ship, though completed at Yokosuka Naval Yard, was actually laid down and launched at the Yokohama Dock Company's establishment.

RYUZYO.

1934 *Photo, Official.*

KAGA (17th Nov., 1921).

Displacement, 26,900 tons.

Length (*p.p.*) 715 feet.

Beam 102¾ feet.

Draught 21⅓ feet.

KAGA.

Added 1939

1938

Guns : **10**—8 inch.
12—4·7 inch AA.
28—M.G.

Aircraft : **60** (Maximum capacity ; normal complement is unofficially reported to be 30.)

Armour :
    On side and gunhouses, thickness doubtful.

Machinery : Brown-Curtis geared turbines. Designed S.H.P. 91,000 = 23 kts. Oil : 5,300 tons.
    12 Kanpon boilers. 4 shafts.

Notes.—Originally laid down July 19, 1920, as a battleship of 39,000 tons, under the 1917 "Eight-Four" Fleet Law. As a result of the Washington Treaty, she was converted into an aircraft carrier, forming part of the 1923 Shipbuilding Programme, and was completed March 31, 1928. She was laid down and launched at the Kawasaki Co.'s yard at Kobe, but was towed to Yokosuka for completion as an aircraft carrier. Smoke was formerly discharged through huge trunks on both sides, extending for nearly half the length of the ship and turning outboard towards the stern, but these were removed in course of 1935–36 refit at Saseho.

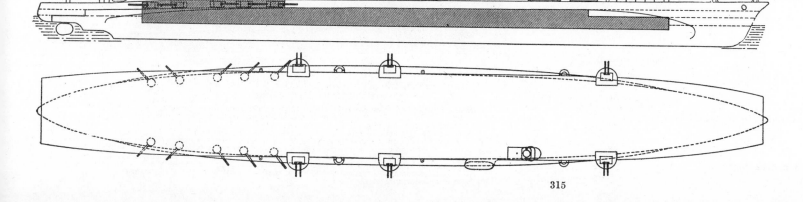

AKAGI (Kure Naval Yard, April 22nd, 1925).

Displacement : 26,900 tons.   Length (*p.p.*), 763 feet.   Beam, 92 feet.   Draught, 21¼ feet.

1930 *Photo.*

Under refit at Saseho, 1937, island superstructure being added and upper flight deck extended over bows.

Guns :
  10—8 inch.
  12—4.7 inch AA.
  22—MG

Aircraft : (Unofficial)
  30 to 50 (see *Notes*)

Armour :
  ″ Side.
  ″ Gunhouses.

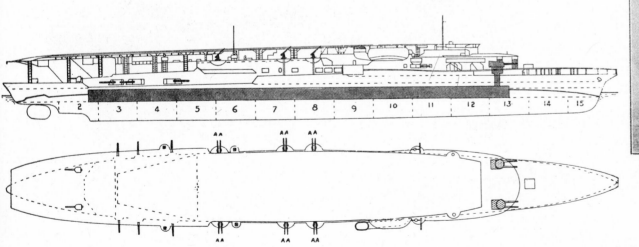

Turrets forward now raised a deck higher

AKAGI.   1929 *Photo, Lieut. de Vaisseau Lafa*

Machinery : Geared turbines.   S.H.P. : 131,200=28·5 kts.   19 Kanpon boilers
Fuel : Coal 2100 tons, Oil 3900 tons.   4 shafts.

Notes.—Originally laid down on Dec. 6th, 1920, as a battle cruiser of 42,000 tons, under 1917 " Eight Four " Fleet Law.   As a result of the Washington Treaty, she was converted into an aircraft carrier, forming part of 1924 Programme.   Completion date, March 25, 1927.   Funnels are arranged on starboard side so that the foremost (which is internally divided into four) is trunked outward and downward amidships, while the second projects slightly above flight deck abaft of the first.   Though she has accommodation for 50 planes, only about 30 are carried normally. There are 2 aircraft lifts on starboard side, one abaft funnels and a smaller one right astern.
Sister ship, *Amagi*, laid down at Yokosuka Dockyard, and launched late in 1922, was so badly damaged by earthquake and fire, September, 1923, that her construction was abandoned, and *Kaga's* hull was appropriated to replace her.

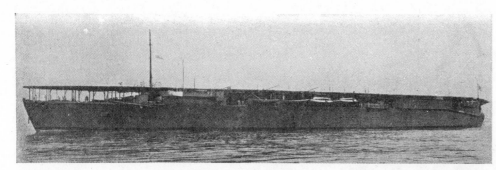

HOSYO.   *Added* 1935.

HOSYO with funnels lowered to horizontal position.   1932 *Photo.*

HOSYO (Asano Co., Turumi, November 13, 1921). Displacement: 7,470 tons. Dimensions:
510 (*p.p.*) × 62 × 20¼ feet. Guns: 4—5·5 inch. 2—3 inch AA.
Machinery: 2 geared turbines. S.H.P.: 30,000 = 25 kts. 8 Kanpon boilers. Fuel: Oil
only, 550 tons. Can carry 26 aircraft with all accessories, etc., though normal complement seldom
exceeds 20. (Unofficial). Sperry gyro-stabiliser fitted. 2 searchlights.

(Plan reversed to illustrate funnel arrangement.)

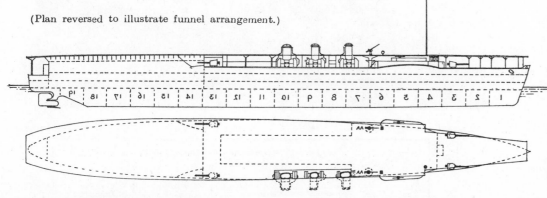

Note.—Laid down December 16, 1919; completed December 27, 1922. The building of a second ship of this type (to
have been named *Syokaku*) was cancelled owing to Washington Treaty.

ATAGO.   1933 *Official Photo.*

MAYA.   1933 *Photo.*

(For particulars of above ships, see following page).

MAYA.

(*Additional views on preceding page.*)

1932 *Photo.*

(ATAGO CLASS—4 SHIPS).

ATAGO (June 16th, 1930), **TAKAO** (May 12th, 1930),
TYOKAI (April 5, 1931), **MAYA** (Nov. 8, 1930).

Standard displacement, 9,850 tons.
Complement, 692.
Length : 630 (*p.p.*), 650 (*o.a.*) feet.   Beam : 62⅓ feet.   Draught : 16⅔ feet (*mean*).

Guns:
10—8 inch, 50 cal.
4—4·7 inch AA.
8—47 mm. AA.
4 M.G.
Torpedo tubes (21 inch) :
8 *above water*.

Armour (unofficial) :
3-4″ Side.....................
3″ Deck ....
3″ Turrets ....
Aircraft :
4, with 2 catapults.

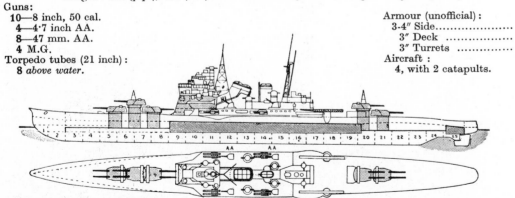

ATAGO.

1932 *Photo.*

Machinery : Geared turbines. Boilers : 12 Kanpon. S.H.P. 100,000 = 33 kts. *max.* (32 kts.
at deep load). Oil : 2,000 tons. Radius at 14–15 kts. : 14,000 miles.

Notes :—Provided for under 1925 and later Programmes. Triple hull, designed to give greatest possible protection against
submarines. Vertical and deck protection over boiler and machinery spaces is 410 feet long. Guns are a new model
with very high muzzle velocity. Cost £2,200,000 each.

Name	Builder	Machinery	Laid down	Completed
Atago	Kure	Kure	6/27	30 March 1932
Takao	Yokosuka	Yokosuka	28/4/27	31 May 1932
Tyokai	Mitubisi	Mitubisi	26/3/28	30 June 1932
Maya	Kawasaki, Kobe	Kawasaki	4/12/28	30 „ 1932

ASIGARA.

ASIGARA.

(All 4 photos, R. Perkins).

ASIGARA.

ASIGARA.

(NATI CLASS—4 SHIPS.)

NATI (June 15th, 1927), **MYOKO** (April 16th, 1927), **ASIGARA** (April 22nd, 1928), **HAGURO** (March 24th, 1928).

Standard displacement, 10,000 tons.

Complement, 692.

Length (*p.p.*), 630 feet, (*o.a.*), 640 feet.   Beam, 62⅓ feet.   Draught, 16½ feet (*mean*).

MYOKO   1935 (*Added* 1936)

Guns :
10—8 inch, 50 cal.
6—4·7 inch AA. (8 in *Asigara*)
8—47 mm. AA.
2—M.G.
Torpedo tubes (21 inch) :
8 *above water*. (quadrupled).

Note io plan : T.T. actually are slightly further aft than shown, above section 18.

Armour (unofficial) :
3″ Side ....
2·3″ Deck ....
3″ Turrets ....

Aircraft : 4 with 2 Catapults.

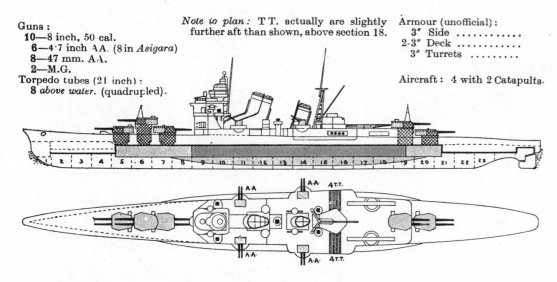

Machinery : Geared turbines.   Boilers : 12 Kanpon.   S.H.P. 100,000 = 33 kts. *max.* (32 kts. at deep load).   Oil : 2,000 tons.   Radius at 14-15 kts. : 14,000 miles.

Notes.—Provided for under 1923 and later Programmes.   Triple hull, designed to give greatest possible protection against submarines.   Vertical and deck protection over boiler and machinery spaces is 410 feet long.   Guns are a new model with very high muzzle velocity.   Cost £2,200,000 each.
All 4 ships extensively refitted 1934-36, fore funnel being heightened, after control structure extended, anti-aircraft armament augmented and torpedo tubes rearranged in quadruple mountings.

Name	Builder	Machinery	Laid down	Completed	Trials
Nati	Kure	Kure	26/11/24	26 Nov. 1928	
Myoko	Yokosuka	Yokosuka	25/10/24	31 July. 1929	
Asigara	Kawasaki Kobe	Kure	11/4/25	20 Aug. 1929	
Haguro	Mitubisi	Yokosuka	16/3/25	25 April. 1929	

MYOKO.   1938, *B. R. Goodfellow, Esq.*

(KAKO CLASS—4 SHIPS.)

KAKO (April 10, 1925), **HURUTAKA** (Feb. 25, 1925),

KINUGASA (Oct. 24th, 1926), **AOBA** (Sept. 25th, 1926).

Standard Displacement, 7,100 tons. Complement, 604.

Length (*w.l.*) 580 feet. (*o.a.*) 595 feet. Beam : 50¾ feet.
Draught: 14¾ feet (*mean*).

Aircraft : **2**, with catapult

Guns :
 6—8 inch.
 4—4·7 inch AA.
 10—M.G
Torpedo tubes (21 inch):
 8 or 12, *above water.*
 (quadrupled in first pair)

Armour : (Unofficial)
 2″ Side amidships ....
 2″ Deck ....
 1½″ Turrets ....
 (Bulges added, 1938–39)

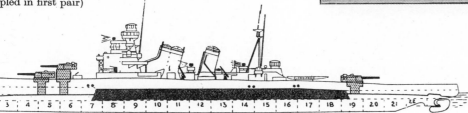

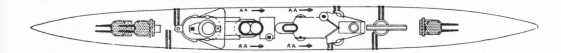

Machinery : Geared turbines. Boilers : 12 Kampon (10 oil, 2 mixed). S.H.P. : 95,000 =
33 kts. (said to have been considerably reduced by addition of bulges). Fuel : 1,400 tons oil ; 400
tons coal.

Name	Builder	Machinery	Laid down	Completed	Trials
Kako	Kawasaki, Kobe	Kawasaki	17 Nov., 1922	20 July, 1926	
Hurutaka	Mitubisi, Nagasaki	Mitubisi	5 Dec. 1922	31 Mar., 1926	
Kinugasa	Kawasaki, Kobe	Kawasaki	23 Jan., 1924	30 Sept., 1927	
Aoba	Mitubisi, Nagasaki	Mitubisi	4 Feb., 1924	20 Dec., 1927	

Notes.—Provided for under 1922 and 1923 Programmes. Noteworthy features introduced in these ships are the undulating
deck line, unusual bridgework and masts, trunked and heavily raked funnels and angled hull form. As originally
completed with six single turrets, *Kako* and *Hurutaka* proved deficient in seakeeping qualities. They were therefore rebuilt at Kure on similar lines to two later ships in 1938–39.

AOBA.

1927 *Photo (added* 1928).

AOBA.

KINUGASA.

1934 *Photo.*

x

New Construction.

It is reported that 5 cruisers of 7,000 tons are under construction. Possibly the **Katori** (Mitubisi, Yokohama; June 17, 1939) is one of these; but it is equally likely that this vessel and a sister ship building at the same yard, are of a smaller type—perhaps Minelayers.

(6 Mogami Class.)

MIKUMA (May 31st, 1934) **MOGAMI** (March 14th, 1934), **SUZUYA** (Nov. 20th, 1934), **KUMANO** (Oct. 15th, 1936), **TONE** (Nov. 21st, 1937), **TIKUMA** (March 19, 1938)

KUMANO   1938.

Standard displacement : 8,500 tons.

Complement :

Length (*p.p.*), 625 feet, (*o.a.*) 639¾ feet; Beam, 59¾ feet; Draught, 14¾ feet (*mean*). Last two ships, 614¼ × 63 × 14¾ feet.

Guns :
15—6·1 inch.
(*Tone, Tikuma*, 12—6·1 inch)
8—5 inch AA.
6 M.G.

Aircraft :
4, with 2 catapults.

Torpedo Tubes :
12—21 inch, *above water*
(in triple mounts)

Armour: (Unofficial)
2″ Deck.

Searchlights :
3

Name	Builder	Machinery	Begun	Completed
Mikuma	Mitubisi	Mitubisi	24 Dec., 1931	29 Aug., 1935
Mogami	Kure		27 Oct., 1931	28 July, 1935
Suzuya	Yokosuka		11 Dec., 1933	31 Oct., 1937
Kumano	Kawasaki	Kawasaki	5 April, 1934	31 Oct., 1937
Tone	Mitubisi	Mitubisi	1 Dec., 1934	20 Nov., 1938
Tikuma	Mitubisi	Mitubisi	1 Oct., 1935	

General Notes.—First four laid down under Fleet Replenishment Law of 1931; remaining two under Law of 1933. *Mogami* and *Mikuma*, though delivered complete on dates named above, did not join the fleet until more than a year later, various modifications having to be made as the result of trials. *Suzuya* and *Kumano's* official completion date uncertain. Trials began in July, 1937. Progress of *Tone* believed to have been delayed by alteration of original design to incorporate improvements adopted as the result of experience with *Mikuma* and *Mogami*. Armament of last two ships was reduced to save top weight.

Appearance Notes.—*Mogami* has one and *Mikuma* two white bands around funnel. There are other small differences in appearance as completed.

Machinery : 4 sets geared turbines. 4 shafts.
Boilers : 10 Kanpon in first 2 ships ; 8 in others. Designed H.P. : 90,000 = 33 kts.

MIKUMA   1939

The following ex-Chinese ships have been salved and taken over by the Imperial Japanese Navy. New names not reported.

ex-**NING HAI** (Harima S.B. Co., Japan. 1931).

ex-**PING HAI** (Kiangnan Dock Co., Shanghai. 1932).

Displacement, 2500 tons. Complement 340.

Dimensions 350 (*p.p.*) 360 (*o.a.*) × 39 × 13 feet.

Guns:
 6—5·5 inch.
 6—3·5 inch, Krupp A.A.
  Ping Hai, only 3.
 8—M.G.
Tubes:
 4—21 inch.
Aircraft:
 2

Armour:
 Thin plating on gun houses
 and side amidships.
 1″ deck.

NING HAI.

1934 *Photo.*

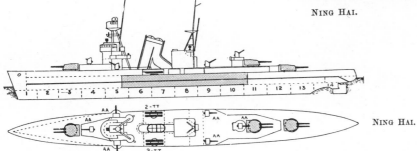

NING HAI.

Machinery: Geared turbines.   H.P. 9500 = 22¼ kts. (*Trials*, 10,500 = 24 kts.) Coal fired.

PING HAI.

1937, *Courtesy Admiral S. K. Chen.*

General Notes.—This design is an exceedingly ingenious production, displaying considerable originality. One plane is stowed in hangar at base of main mast. *Ping Hai*, though laid down on July 9, 1931, was not completed till late in 1936, construction having been suspended in 1933. Machinery and main armament of these ships were supplied from Japan.

PING HAI.

1937, *Courtesy Admiral S. K. Chen.*

PING HAI.

(ZINTU CLASS—3 SHIPS.)

ZINTU (8th Dec., 1923), **NAKA** (24th March, 1925),

SENDAI (30th Oct., 1923).

Standard displacement, 5195 tons. Complement, 450.

Length (*p.p.*), 500 feet; (*o.a.*) 535 feet. Beam, 46¾ feet.
Draught, 15 feet 10½ in.

Guns :
  7—5·5 inch, 50 cal.
  2—3 inch, 13 pdr., 40 cal.
  AA.
  6 M.G.
Torpedo tubes :
  8—21 inch, *above water*.

Aircraft : 1, with catapult

Armour : (Unofficial)
  2″ Side (amidships) ....
  2″ C.T. ....

Note to Plan.—Now carry catapult in position shown in photos.

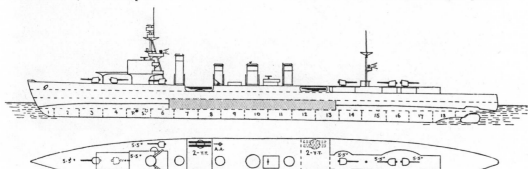

SENDAI. Note 3rd funnel appears taller than 2nd and 4th.   1939.

NAKA. (Aftermost gun now mounted nearer stern.)   1935 *appearance*.

Machinery : 4 geared turbines. 4 shafts. Boilers : 12 Kanpon. Designed S.H.P. 70,000 = 33 kts. Fuel : 300 tons *coal*. 1200 tons *oil*.

Name	Builder	Machinery	Begun	Completed	Trials
Zintu	Kawasaki, Kobe	Kawasaki	4 Aug., '22	31 July, '25	
Sendai	Mitubisi, Nagasaki	Mitubisi	16 Feb., '22	29 Apr., '24	
Naka	Yokohama Dock Co.	Mitubisi	10 June, '22	30 Nov., '25	

General Notes.—Slightly enlarged and improved editions of *Natori* class on following page. The launch of *Naka* was delayed by earthquake of Sept., 1923. Catapult fitted 1929. Foremost boiler is fitted for mixed firing.

ZINTU.   1938, *Official, courtesy of Navy Dept., Tokyo.*

"Natori" Class (6 Ships).

ISUZU (29th Oct., 1921).   **NAGARA** (25th April, 1921).

NATORI (16th Feb., 1922).   **YURA** (15th Feb., 1922).

KINU (29th May, 1922).   **ABUKUMA** (16th March, 1923).
Standard displacement, 5170 tons.   Comp., 438.
Length (*p.p.*) 500 feet, (*o.a.*) 535 feet.   Beam, 46¾ feet.
Draught, 15 feet 10½ in.

ISUZU. (*Yura* similar).   1934 (*added* 1935).

Guns :—
  7—5·5 inch, 50 cal.
  2—3 inch, 13 pdr. 40 cal.
  AA.
  2 M.G.
Torpedo tubes : (21 inch)
  8 (*above water*).
Aircraft:
  1, with catapult.

Armour :   (Unofficial)
  2″ Side (amidships).
  2″ C.T.

Machinery : 4 geared turbines. 4 shafts. Boilers : 12 Kanpon,
8 oil and 4 coal burning.   Designed S.H.P. : 70,000 = 33 kts.
Fuel : 350 tons coal, 1,150 tons oil.

KINU.   Aug. 1937.

Plan : Details generally as *Kuma*. Formerly had aircraft hangar forward but this has been removed from most if not all of class.

Name	Builder	Machinery	Begun	Com-pleted	Trials (*unofficial*)
Isuzu	Uraga Dock Co.	Mitubisi	10 Aug., '20	15/8/23	
Nagara	Saseho	Kawasaki	9 Sept., '20	21/4/22	
Natori	Mitubisi, Nagasaki	Mitubisi	14 Dec., '20	15/9/22	65,000 = 33.4
Kinu	Kawasaki Co., Kobe	Kawasaki	17 Jan., '21	10/11/22	
Yura	Saseho	Kawasaki	21 May, '21	20/3/23	
Abukuma	Uraga Dock Co.	Mitubisi	8 Dec., '21	26/5/25	

General Notes.—Commencement authorised by 1919 Naval Programme. Cost of each ship is said to be £1,250,000. Completion of ABUKUMA was delayed owing to earthquake damage at Uraga Yard in Sept., 1923.

NATORI and ABUKUMA (showing catapult mounted between guns Nos 5 and 6).   1934 *Photo*

KUMA CLASS—5 SHIPS.

KUMA (July 14th, 1919),   **TAMA** (Feb. 10th, 1920),

OI (July 15th, 1920),

KITAKAMI (July 3rd, 1920),   **KISO** (Dec.14th, 1920).

Standard displacement, 5100 tons. Complement, 439.
Length (*p.p.*) 500 feet, (*o.a.*) 535 feet. Beam, 46¾ feet. *Mean* draught, 15¾ feet.

Guns :
  7—5·5 inch, 50 cal.
  2—3 inch (13 pdr.), 40 cal.
  2 M.G.
Torpedo tubes (21 inch):
  8 *above water*.
Searchlights :
  3—30 inch.
Mines:
  80 can be carried
Aircraft : 1.

Armour (*unofficial*) :
  2″ (H.T.) Side (amidships)......
  2″ C.T. ....

KUMA (fitted with anti-flare tops to funnels).   *1935 Official.*

Note to Plan.—Apparent rake shown in plan does not exist. Foremast control tops now as in photos.

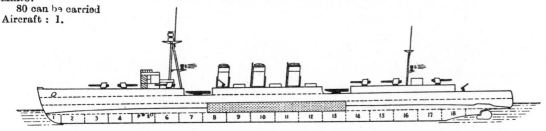

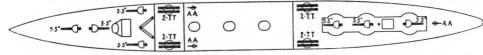

Ahead : **3**—5·5 inch.   Broadside : **6**—5·5 inch, **4**—21 inch T.T.   Astern : **1**—5·5 inch.

Machinery : Geared Parsons or Curtis Turbines. 4 shafts. Boilers : 12 Kanpon, 10 oil fuel, 2 mixed firing. Designed H.P. 70,000 = 33 kts. Fuel : *normal*, 350 tons ; *maximum*, about 1500 tons = 8500 miles at 10 kts.

Name	Builder	Machinery	Laid down	Completed	First Trials.	Boilers.
Oi	Kawasaki	Kawasaki	24/11/19	3/10/21		
Kitakami	Saseho	Kawasaki	1/9/19	15/4/21		
Kiso	{ Mitubisi Nagasaki }	Mitubisi	10/6/19	4/5/21	—34	All 12 Kanpon.
Kuma	Saseho	Kawasaki	29/8/18	31/8/20		
Tama	{ Mitubisi Nagasaki }	Mitubisi	10/8/18	29/1/21		

General Notes.—*Kuma* and *Tama* begun under the 1917 Naval Programme ; *Oi, Kitakami, Kiso* under 1918 Programme. Completion of *Oi* delayed by failure of one of her engines when she was running trials at end of Dec., 1920. Said to be very efficiently sub-divided and the general scheme of protection has been developed since the war. Fuel supply is somewhere above the average = 6,000 miles at 15 kts., and between 1,000 and 1,100 miles at full speed. No official data published concerning trials, but are reported to have averaged about 64,500 H.P. and about 33 kts. Cost about £1,000,000 each. An aeroplane was added to the equipment of these ships in 1927.

KISO.   *1938, B. R. Goodfellow, Esq.*

KUMA   *1937.*

1928 *Photo.*

YUBARI (5th March, 1923).

Standard displacement, 2890 tons. Complement, 328.
Length (*p.p.*), 435 feet. Beam, 39½ feet. Draught, 11 feet 9 ins.

Guns:
  6—5 5 inch, 50 cal
  1—3 inch AA.
  2—M G
Torpedo tubes (21 inch):
  4 (*above water*).
Mines:
  Storage for 34.
Searchlights : 2

Armour (unofficial):
  2″ side (H.T.)

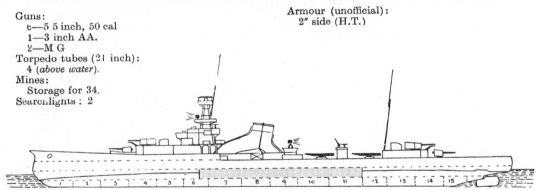

Machinery : Geared Turbines. 3 shafts. Boilers : 8 Kanpon
(coal and oil-burning). Designed S.H.P. : 57,000 = 33 kts. Fuel :
820 tons.

Note.—Laid down on 5th June, 1922, at Saseho Dockyard. Completed July 31, 1923.

Torpedo Notes.—Tubes are arranged so that they can be trained on either broadside.

Engineering Notes.—Machinery was built by Saseho Dockyard.

TENRYU.

1939.

(1916 Programme)
(TENRYU CLASS—2 SHIPS.)

TATUTA (29th May, 1918)   **TENRYU** (11th Mar., 1918)
Standard displacement, 3230 tons. Complement, 332.
Length (*o.a.*) 468 feet (*p.p.*), 440 feet. Beam : 40¾ feet. *Mean* draught : 13 feet.

Guns :
  4—5·5 inch, 50 cal.
  1—3 inch (13 pdr.) 40 cal. AA
  2 M.G.
Torpedo tubes : (21 in.)
  6 *above water* in two triple
  U.D. mountings.
Searchlights :
  2—30 inch.
Mines :
  May be carried.

Armour (unofficial) :
  2″ or 1½″ (H.T.) Side
    amidships ....
  —″ Deck (H.T.) at
    ends ....
  —″ C.T. ....

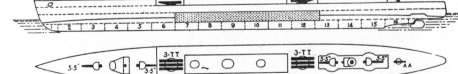

Machinery : Curtis and Parsons turbines, respectively. 3 shafts. Boilers : 10 Kanpon.
Designed H.P. : 51,000 = 31 kts. Fuel : Coal and oil, 900 tons = 6,000 miles at 10 kts. (unofficial).

Name	Builder	Machinery	Laid down	Completed	2nd Period	Trials
Tatuta	Saseho	Kawasaki	24/7/17	31 Mar.,'19	1927—35	51,000 = 33 kts.
Tenryu	Yokosuka	Mitubisi	17/5/17	20 Nov.,'19	1927—35	

Old Cruisers (used as Training Ships).

YAHAGI.   1931 *Photo.*

HIRADO (June 29th, 1911),   **YAHAGI** (Oct. 3rd, 1911).
Standard displacement 4400 tons.   Complement, 452.
Length (*p.p.*), 440 feet; (*o.a.*), 475 feet.   Beam, 46½ feet.   *Max.* draught, 17⅔ feet.
Guns : 8—6 inch, 50 cal., 2—3 inch, 2—3 inch AA., 2 M.G.   Torpedo tubes (18 inch) : 3 above *water* (363 tons).   Armour : 3″ Deck (amidships), 3″ Deck (ends), 4″ Conning tower (139 tons). Weight of hull, etc., 2,278 tons.   Machinery : *Hirado*, Curtis turbines (2 shafts) ; *Yahagi*, Parsons turbines (4 shafts).   Boilers : 6 Kanpon.   Designed H.P. : 22,500 = 26 kts.   Coal : *normal* 500 tons ; *maximum* 900 tons + 300 oil = 10,000 miles at 10 kts.   Both now used for training purposes.

Name	Builder	Machinery	Laid down	Com- pleted	Third Period	Trials H.P. = kts.	Boilers
Hirado	Kawasaki Co.	Kawasaki Co.	10/8/10	17/6/12	1928-36	....	Kanpon
Yahagi	Mitubisi	Mitubisi	20/6/10	27/7/12	1928-36	27,408 = 26·8	in all.

Escort Vessel (ex-Chinese).

1931 *Photo, Official.*

*ex-***YAT SEN** (1930).   Displacement: 1,650 tons.   Dimensions : 275 (*o.a.*), 252 (*p.p.*) × 34 × 11 feet. Complement: 173.   Guns : 1—6 inch, 1—5·5 inch, 4—3 inch AA., 2—3 pdr., 4 M.G.   H.P. 4000=20 kts.   Coal : 280 tons.
Note.—This vessel was stranded near Nanking on Sept. 25, 1937.   Subsequently refloated and added to Japanese fleet.

Seaplane Carriers.

(For photo of MIDUHO, *see Addenda)*

TITOSE (Nov. 29, 1936), **TIYODA** (Nov. 19, 1937), **MIDUHO** (May 16, 1938).   *Standard* displacement : 9,000 tons.   Dimensions : 577½ × 61⅚ × 19 feet (*mean*).   Guns : 4—5 inch AA. (paired) in first two ; 6—5 inch AA. in *Miduho*.   Machinery : Geared turbines.   H.P. : 15,000 = 20 kts. (*Miduho*, 9,000 = 17 kts.   Built under Second Fleet Replenishment Law, *Titose* having been laid down on Nov. 26, 1934, *Tiyoda* on December 14, 1936, and *Miduho* on May 1, 1937, the first two at Kure and the *Miduho* at Kawasaki, Kobe.

Note.—A number of merchant vessels have been fitted out as temporary Seaplane Carriers in connection with the operations in China.

KAMOI. (Now has crane aft.)   1924 *Photo, Official.*

KAMOI (New York S.B. Co., June 8, 1922).   *Standard* displacement : 17,000 tons (10,222 tons *gross*).   Dimensions : 496 (*w.l.*), 478½ (*p.p.*) × 67 × 27⅔ feet.   Guns : 2—5·5 inch, 2—3 inch AA.   Machinery : G.E. (Curtis) turbines and electric drive.   Boilers : 4 Yarrow.   S.H.P. : 8,000 = 15 kts.   Fuel : 2,500 tons coal.   Laid down Sept. 14, 1921 and completed Sept. 12, 1922. Converted from a tanker 1932–33.   The first Japanese warship to have electric drive installed. Reported to carry from 10 to 16 aircraft, former being normal complement.

1932 *Photo.*

NOTORO (Kawasaki Co., Kobe, May 3, 1920).   *Standard* displacement : 14,050 tons (8,000 tons *gross*).   Complement : 155.   Dimensions : 455 (*pp.*), 470¾ (*o.a.*) × 58 × 26½ feet.   Guns : 2— 4·7 inch, 2—3 inch AA.   Reciprocating engines.   H.P. : 5,850 = 12 kts.   Oil Fuel : 1,000 tons. Converted from a tanker of the *Erimo* class (*vide* a later page).   Laid down Nov. 24, 1919 and completed Aug. 10, 1920.   Reported to carry from 8 to 16 aircraft, latter figure presumably representing maximum stowage.

328

YAKUMO.

(Deckhouse since added abaft foremast). 1929 *Photo.*

YAKUMO (Vulcan Co., July 8, 1899). Displacement : 9,010 tons. Complement : 698. Length : (*pp.*) 409 feet ; *over all*, 434 feet. Beam : $64\frac{1}{4}$ feet. *Mean* draught : $23\frac{3}{4}$ feet. Guns : 4—8 inch, 40 cal., 8—6 inch, 40 cal., 4—3 inch, 4 S.L. Torpedo tubes (18 inch) : 2 *submerged*. Armour (Krupp) : 7″ Belt (amidships), $3\frac{1}{2}$″ Belt (ends), $2\frac{1}{2}$″ Deck (slopes), 6″ Turrets (N.C.), 6″ Turret bases (N.C.), 5″ Lower deck side, 6″ Casemates (8), 10″ Conning tower. (Total weight, 2,040 tons.). Machinery : 2 sets vertical triple expansion. 2 screws. Boilers : 6 Yarrow. I.H.P. : 7,000 = 16 kts. Coal : *normal*, 550 tons ; *max.*, 1,200 tons. Employed as Midshipmen's Training Ship, and speed reduced. Full armament (not mounted at present) includes 12—6 inch.

1931 *Photo, Official.*

ADUMA (St. Nazaire, June 24, 1899). Displacement : 8,640 tons. Complement : 644. Length : (*w.l.*) 430 ; (*o.a.*) $452\frac{1}{2}$ feet. Beam : $59\frac{1}{2}$ feet. *Max.* draught : 25 feet. Guns (Armstrong) : 4—8 inch, 40 cal., 8—6 inch, 40 cal., 4—3 inch, 1—3 inch AA. Torpedo tubes : 4 *submerged*. Armour (Krupp mostly) : 7″ Belt (amidships), $3\frac{1}{2}$″ Belt (ends), $2\frac{1}{2}$″ Deck (on slopes), 6″ Turrets and bases (H.N.), 6″ Casemates (H.N.), 5″ Side above belt. (Total weight, 2000 tons.) Machinery : 2 sets vertical triple expansion. 2 screws. Boilers : 24 Belleville. Designed H.P. : 17,000 = 21 kts. Coal : *normal*, 600 tons ; *maximum*, 1,200 tons. Good for about 16 kts. now.

IDUMO. 1938, *Official, courtesy of Navy Dept., Tokyo.*

IDUMO (Sept. 19, 1899), and **IWATE** (March 29, 1900). Built by Armstrong. Displacement : 9,180 tons. Complement : 658. Length (*p.p.*), 400 feet ; (*o.a.*) 434 feet. Beam : $68\frac{1}{2}$ feet. *Max.* draught : $24\frac{1}{4}$ feet. Guns (Armstrong) : 4—8 inch, 40 cal., 8—6 inch, 40 cal., 1—3 inch AA., 4–3 inch, 3 M.G., 4 S.L. Torpedo tubes : 4 *submerged*. Armour (Krupp) : 7″ Belt (amidship), $3\frac{1}{2}$″ Belt (ends), $2\frac{1}{2}$″ Deck (slopes), 5″ Lower deck (redoubt), 6″ Turrets and bases, 6″ Casemates. 14″ Conning tower. (Total 2100 tons.) Machinery by Humphrys & Tennant : 2 sets 4-cylinder triple expansion. 2 screws. Boilers : Belleville in *Idumo* ; 6 Yarrow in *Iwate*. *Idumo*, I.H.P. : 14,700 = 20·75 kts. *Iwate*, I.H.P. : 7,000 = 16 kts. Coal : *normal* 550 tons ; *maximum*, 1,400 tons. Begun at Elswick 1898–99, and completed 1900–01. *Iwate* used as seagoing Training Ship. Full armament (not mounted in peace time) includes 14—6 inch guns.

KASUGA. *Photo* 1931.

KASUGA (October 22, 1902). Displacement : 7,080 tons. Complement : 595. Length (*waterline*) : 357 feet. Beam : 61 feet 11 ins. *Maximum* draught : $25\frac{1}{4}$ feet. Guns (Armstrong) : 1—10 inch, 2—8 inch, 45 cal., 4—6 inch, 45 cal., 4—3 inch, 1—3 inch AA., 2 M.G. Torpedo tubes (18 inches) : 4 *above water* (in casemates). Armour (Terni) : 6″ Belt (amidships), $4\frac{1}{2}$″ (ends), $1\frac{1}{2}$″ Deck (on slopes), $5\frac{1}{2}$″ Turrets and bases, 6″ Lower deck side and battery, $4\frac{1}{2}$″ Lower deck bulkheads and Battery bulkheads, $4\frac{3}{4}$″ Conning tower. 4 Searchlights. Machinery : 2 sets 3-cylinder vertical triple expansion. 2 screws. Boilers : 12 Kanpon. Designed H.P. : 13,500 = 20 kts. (Now much less) Coal : *normal*, 650 tons ; *maximum*, 1,200 tons.

Note.—Kasuga (ex-*Rivadavia*, ex-*Mitra*) built by Ansaldo ; purchased from Argentina, 1904. Full armament includes 14—6 inch guns.

Meanings of names of Destroyers. (Supplied officially to "Fighting Ships.")

N.B.—Many of these names are poetical in conception ; and where adequate translation is not possible the English version should be taken merely as an approximate indication of the meaning of the names.

KAGERO class.

Siranui	.. ..	Phosphorescent foam (literally, "Unknown fires")
Kagero	.. ..	Gossamer.
Kurosio	..	Black tide.
Oyasio	..	Parent tide.
Hatukaze	..	Early breeze.
Hayasio	..	Fast running tide.
Yukikaze		Snowstorm.
Natusio	..	Summer tide.
Isokaze	..	Shore breeze.

ASASIO class.

Asasio	..	Morning tide.
Arasio	..	Rough tide.
Osio	..	High tide.
Mitisio	..	Tide running full.
Asagumo	..	White clouds of the morning.
Yamagumo		White clouds on the hillsides.
Minegumo		White clouds on the mountain peak.
Natugumo		White clouds of summer.
Kasumi	..	Haze (literally, "Mist of flowers").
Arare	..	Hail

SIGURE class.
1ST CLASS.

Yamakaze	..	Wind from the hills.
Suzukaze	..	Cool breeze of summer.
Kawakaze	..	Wind on the river.
Umikaze	..	Sea breeze.
Siratuyu	..	White dew.
Sigure	..	Autumn shower.
Murasame	..	Scattered showers.
Yudati	..	Evening thunder shower in summer.
Harusame	..	Spring shower.
Samidare	..	Early summer rain.

HATUHARU class.

Hatuharu	..	First days of spring.
Nenohi	..	A day of New Year celebrations in old Japan.
Wakab	..	Fresh verdure (young leaves shooting).
Hatusimo	..	First frost of the season.
Ariake	..	Dawn (still the moon remains in the sky).
Yugure	..	Evening.

HUBUKI class.

Hubuki	..	Blizzard (snowstorm).
Sirayuki	..	White snow.
Hatuyuki	..	First snow of the season.
Murakumo	..	Cloud clusters.
Sinonome	..	Dawn.
Usugumo	..	Fleecy clouds.
Sirakumo	..	White clouds.
Isonami	..	Waves on the beach.
Uranami	..	Waves in the bay.
Ayanami	..	Waves whose beauty suggests figures woven in silk.
Sikinami	..	Waves chasing one another.
Asagiri	..	Morning mist.
Yugiri	..	Evening mist.
Amagiri	..	Mist in the sky.
Sagiri	..	Mist.
Oboro	..	Haziness diffusing moonlight.
Akebono	..	Daybreak.
Sazanami	..	Ripples.
Usio	..	Tide.
Akatuki	..	Dawn.
Hibiki	..	Echo.
Ikaduti	..	Thunder.
Inaduma	..	Lightning.

MUTSUKI class

Mutuki, Kisaragi, Yayoi, Uduki, Satuki, Minaduki, Humiduki, Nagatuki, Kikuduki. These are poetical names for January, February, March, April, May, June, July, and September (two examples), respectively.

Mikaduki	..	New moon.
Motiduki	..	Full moon.
Yuduki	..	Evening moon.

KAMIKAZE and MINEKAZE classes.

Kamikaze	..	Divine wind.
Asakaze	..	Morning breeze.
Harukaze	..	Spring breeze.
Matukaze	..	Wind among the pine trees.
Hatakaze	..	Wind which causes the flapping of a flag.
Oite	..	Fair wind (i.e., favourable wind).
Hayate	..	Squall.
Asanagi	..	Morning calm.
Yunagi	..	Evening calm.
Akikaze	..	Autumn wind.
Yukaze	..	Evening breeze.
Hokaze	..	Wind on the sail.
Siokaze	..	Wind springing up at the turn of the tide.
Tatikaze	..	Wind caused by the stroke of a sword.
Namikaze	..	Wind on the waves.
Numakaze	..	Wind over the marsh.
Nokaze	..	Wind over the field.
Nadakaze	..	Wind on the open sea.
Simakaze	..	Wind on the island.
Sawakaze	..	Wind from the swamp.
Hakaze	..	Wind of a bird's flight.
Yakaze	..	Wind of an arrow's flight.

WAKATAKE class.
2ND CLASS.

Wakatake	..	Young bamboo.
Kuretake	..	Certain variety of bamboo.
Sanae	..	Rice seedling.
Asagao	.:	Morning glory.
Yugao	..	Bottle gourd.
Huyo	..	A species of rose.
Karukaya	..	Sage.

KAYA and MOMO classes.

Kaya	..	Tumion (strong-scented yew).
Kuri	..	Chestnut.
Nire	..	A species of elm.
Nasi	..	Pear.
Take	..	Bamboo.
Aoi	..	Hollyhock.
Kiku	..	Chrysanthemum.
Hagi	..	Bush-clover.
Kaki	..	Persimmon.
Susuki	..	Pampas grass.
Tuga	..	Japanese hemlock-spruce.
Hudi	..	Wistaria.
Asi	..	Reed.
Tuta	..	Japanese ivy.
Hasu	..	Lotus.
Hisi	..	Water caltrop (water-nut).
Sumire	..	Violet.
Yomogi	..	Fellon-herb.
Tade	..	Knotweed.
Yanagi	..	Willow.
Momo	..	Peach.
Hinoki	..	Japanese cypress.

12, Kagero class.

> *Building or completing.*
> *Will have 2 funnels and 2 light tripod masts.*

Kagero, Siranui, Kurosio, Oyasio, Hatukaze, Natusio, Yukikaze, Isokaze, Hayasio, and
3 more.
Displacement : 2,000 tons. Length : 361 feet.
Guns : 6—5 inch, 2 M.G. Torpedo tubes : 8—21 inch.
Machinery : Geared turbines. 2 shafts. S.H.P. : 45,000 = 36 kts. Boilers : Kanpon.

Name.	Builder.	Laid down.	Launch.	Completed.
Kagero	Maiduru	July, 1937	Sept. 28, 1938	1939
Siranui	Uraga	Aug. 30, 1937	June 28, 1938	1939
Kurosio	Hudinagata	1937	Oct. 25, 1938	
Oyasio	Maiduru	1938	Nov. 29, 1938	
Hatukaze	Kawasaki	1938	Jan. 24, 1939	
Natusio	Hudinagata	1938	Feb. 23, 1939	
Hayasio	Uraga	1938	April 19, 1939	
Yukikaze	Saseho	1938	March 24, 1939	
Isokaze	Saseho	1938	June 19, 1939	

10 Asasio class.

ASAGUMO.   1938.

Asasio, Arasio, Osio, Mitisio, Asagumo, Yamagumo, Minegumo, Natugumo, Kasumi, Arare.
Displacement : 1,500 tons. Complement : 190.
Dimensions : 356 × 33½ × 9 feet.
Guns : 6—5 inch, 2 M.G. Torpedo Tubes : 8—21 inch.
Machinery : Geared turbines. 2 shafts.
S.H.P. : 38,000 = 34 kts.
Boilers : 3 Kanpon. Oil fuel : About 400 tons.

10 Sigure class.

KAWAKAZE.   1937.

SAMIDARE.   1937.

*Sigure, Siratuyu, Murasame, Yudati, Harusame, Samidare, Yamakaze, Suzukaze
Kawakaze, Umikaze.*
Displacement : 1,368 tons. Complement : 180.
Dimensions : 335½ × 31¾ × 9½ feet (*mean*).
Guns : 5—5 inch 2 M.G. Torpedo tubes : 8—21 inch (quadrupled).
Machinery : Geared turbines. S.H.P. : 37,000 = 34 kts.
Boilers : 3 Kanpon. Oil fuel : About 400 tons.
Notes.—It is reported that the guns of these and later destroyers have nearly 90° elevation, so they may be regarded
as " dual purpose " guns.

6 Hatúharu class.

HATUSIMO.   (Plan as *Sigure* class, but 6 T.T. in triple mounts).   1937.

Ariake, Nenohi, Hatuharu, Hatusimo, Wakaba, Yugure.

Displacement : 1,368 tons *standard*. Complement, 180.
Dimensions : $337\frac{3}{4} \times 32\frac{1}{2} \times 8\frac{3}{4}$ feet (*mean* draught).
Guns : 5—5 inch, 2 M.G. Torpedo tubes : 6—21 inch.
Machinery : Geared turbines. S.H.P. 37,000 = 34 kts.
Boilers : 3 Kanpon. Oil fuel : About 400 tons.

Notes.—As the result of the capsizing of the torpedo boat *Tomoduru*, the design of these destroyers was modified, the number of torpedo tubes being reduced and forward guns paired. A high percentage of electric welding was used.

Name	Builder	Laid down	Launch	Completed
Hatuharu	Saseho	May 14, 1931	Feb. 27, 1933	Sept. 30, 1933
Nenohi	Uraga	Dec. 15, 1931	Dec. 22, 1932	Sept. 30, 1933
Wakaba	Saseho	Dec. 12, 1931	Mar. 18, 1934	Oct. 31, 1934
Hatusimo	Uraga	Jan. 31, 1933	Nov. 4, 1933	Sept. 27, 1934
Ariake	Kawasaki	Jan. 14, 1933	Sept. 23, 1934	Mar. 25, 1935
Yugure	Maiduru	April 9, 1933	May 6, 1934	Mar. 30, 1935
Siratuyu	Saseho	Nov. 14, 1933	April 5, 1935	Aug. 20, 1936
Sigure	Uraga	Dec. 9, 1933	May 18, 1935	Sept. 7, 1936
Murasame	Hudinagata	Feb. 1, 1934	June 20, 1935	Jan. 7, 1937
Yudati	Saseho	Oct. 16, 1934	June 21, 1936	Jan. 7, 1937
Harusame	Maiduru	Feb. 3, 1935	Sept. 21, 1935	Aug. 26, 1937
Samidare	Uraga	Dec. 19, 1934	July 6, 1935	Jan. 29, 1937
Yamakaze	Uraga	May 25, 1935	Feb. 21, 1936	July 30, 1937
Suzukaze	Uraga	July 9, 1935	Mar. 11, 1937	Aug. 31, 1937
Kawakaze	Hudinagata	April 25, 1935	Nov. 1, 1936	April 30, 1937
Umikaze	Maiduru	May 4, 1935	Nov. 27, 1936	May 31, 1937
Asasio	Saseho	Sept. 7, 1935	Dec. 16, 1936	Aug. 31, 1937
Arasio	Kawasaki	Oct. 1, 1935	May 26, 1937	Dec. 20, 1937
Osio	Maiduru	Aug. 5, 1936	April 19, 1937	Oct. 31, 1937
Mitisio	Hudinagata	Nov. 5, 1935	Mar. 15, 1937	Oct. 31, 1937
Asagumo	Kawasaki	Dec. 23, 1936	Nov. 5, 1937	Mar. 31, 1938
Yamagumo	Hudinagata	Nov. 4, 1936	July 24, 1937	Jan. 15, 1938
Minegumo	Hudinagata	Mar. 22, 1936	Nov. 4, 1937	April 30, 1938
Natugumo	Saseho	July 1, 1936	May 26, 1937	Feb. 10, 1938
Kasumi	Uraga	Dec. 1, 1936	Nov. 18, 1937	, 1938
Arare	Maiduru	Mar. 5, 1937	Nov. 16, 1937	, 1938

23 Hubuki Class.

(A) "Amagiri" type. 11 Vessels.

URANAMI.   1933 *Photo.*

ASAGIRI.   1933 *Photo.*

(AMAGIRI, AKEBONO, AYANAMI, OBORO, SAGIRI, SAZANAMI, SIKINAMI, USIO, YUGIRI similar, with collar ventilators around funnels, and bridge control tower level with funnel caps, which in all this class (23) are anti-flare fittings.)

Hubuki	**Uranami**	**Ayanami**	**Yugiri**	**Akatuki**
Sirayuki	**Sinonome**	**Asagiri**	**Usio**	**Hibiki**
Hatuyuki	**Usugumo**	**Amagiri**	**Oboro**	**Ikaduti**
Murakumo	**Sirakumo**	**Sagiri**	**Akebono**	**Inaduma**
	Isonami	**Sikinami**	**Sazanami**	

Authorised under 1926 and subsequent sections of the Fleet Replenishment Law   1700 tons (2125 tons full load)

Dimensions : $371\frac{1}{2} \times 33\frac{3}{4} \times 9\frac{3}{4}$ feet (*mean*). Armament : 6—5 inch, 50 cal., 4 AA. M.G. and 9—21 inch tubes.

Machinery : Parsons geared turbines. Boilers : 4 Kanpon. H.P. 40,000 = 34 kts. Oil : 420 tons. Complement, 197.

Notes :—*Hibiki* was the first rivetless ship in the Japanese Navy. *Miyuki* (built by Uraga Co.) lost by collision in 1934.

Hubuki Class—*continued*

(B) "Hibiki" type. **4** Vessels.

IKADUTI.   *1937 (added 1938)*

(AKATUKI, HIBIKI, INADUMA, similar with small fore funnel, high bridge, and big flat-sided shields to Torpedo Tubes.)

(C) "Sinonome" type. **8** Vessels.

SIRAKUMO (note shields to Tubes).   *1932 Photo.*

HUBUKI.   *1933 Photo.*

(HATSUYUKI, ISONAMI, MURAKUMO, SINONOME, SIRAKUMO, SIRAYUKI, USUGUMO, similar with smaller bridge and cowls abreast funnels.)

12 Mutuki Class.

UDUKI.   *Photo 1933.*

UDUKI.   *Photo added 1927.*

12 boats ; **Mutuki** (ex-No. 19), (by Saseho), **Kisaragi** (ex-No. 21), (by Maiduru), **Yayoi** (ex-No. 23), (by Uraga Dock Co.), **Uduki** (ex-No. 25), (by Isikawazima Co.), **Satuki** (ex-No. 27), (by Hudinagata Co.), **Minatuki** (Uraga Dock Co.), **Humituki** (Hudinagata Co.), **Nagatuki** (Isikawazima Co.), **Kikutuki** (Maiduru), **Mikaduki** (Saseho), **Motiduki** (Uraga Dock Co.), **Yuduki** (Hudinagata Co.), (ex-Nos. 28–34). Enlarged editions of *Kamikaze*. Built under 1923, 1924 and 1925 sections of Navy Law. 1,315 tons. Dimensions : 320 (*p.p.*) × 30 × 9 feet (*max.* draught). Armament : 4—4·7 inch, 50 cal., 2 AA. M.G. and 6—21 inch tubes (in triple deck mountings). 3 S.L. Machinery : Parsons 2-shaft turbines, 4 Kanpon boilers. Designed H.P. : 38,500 = 34 kts. Oil : 350 tons. Endurance : 4,000 miles at 15 kts. Complement, 150.

9 Kamikaze Class.

ASAKAZE.　　　　　　　　　　　　　　1934 *Photo.*

9 *boats :* **Kamikaze** (ex-No. 1) and **Asakaze** (ex-No. 3) (both by Mitubisi Z.K.), **Harukaze** (ex-No. 5), **Matukaze** (ex-No. 7), **Hatakaze** (ex-No. 9), (all three by Maiduru D.Y.), **Oite** (ex-No. 11), (by Uraga Dock Co.), **Hayate** (ex-No. 13), (by Isikawazima Co.), **Asanagi** (ex-No. 15), (by Hudinagata Co.), **Yunagi** (ex-No. 17), (by Saseho).

Built under 1922 and 1923 Sections of Navy Law. 1270 tons. Dimensions: 320 (*p.p.*) × 30 × $9\frac{7}{12}$ feet (*max. draught*). Armament : 4—4·7 inch, 50 cal., **2** AA. M.G. and 6—21 inch torpedo tubes. 2 S.L. Machinery : Parsons 4-shaft turbines. 4 Kanpon boilers. Designed H.P. 38,500 = 34 kts. Oil : 350 tons. Endurance: 4000 miles at 15 kts. Complement, 148.

Name	Builder	Laid dn.	Launch.	Compl.	Name	Builder	Laid dn.	Launch.	Compl.
Hubuki	Maiduru	19/6/26	15/11/27	10/8/28	Yugiri	Maiduru	1/4/29	12/5/30	3/12/30
Sirayuki	Yokohama	19/3/27	20/3/28	18/12/28	Amagiri	Isikawazima	28/11/28	27/2/30	10/11/30
Hatuyuki	Maiduru	12/4/27	29/9/27	30/3/28	Sagiri	Uraga	28/3/29	23/12/29	31/1/31
Murakumo	Hudinagata	25/4/27	27/9/27	10/5/28	Oboro	Saseho	29/11/29	8/11/30	31/10/31
Sinonome	Saseho	12/8/26	26/11/27	25/7/28	Akebono	Hudinagata	25/10/29	7/11/30	31/7/31
Usugumo	Isikawazima	21/10/26	26/12/27	26/7/28	Sazanami	Maiduru	21/2/30	6/6/31	19/5/32
Sirakumo	Hudinagata	27/10/26	27/12/27	28/7/28	Usio	Uraga	24/12/29	17/11/30	14/11/31
Isonami	Uraga	18/10/26	24/11/27	30/6/28	Akatuki	Saseho	17/2/30	7/5/32	30/11/32
Uranami	Saseho	28/4/27	29/11/28	30/6/29	Hibiki	Maiduru	21/2/30	16/6/32	31/3/33
Ayanami	Hudinagata	20/1/28	5/10/29	30/4/30	Ikaduti	Uraga	7/3/30	22/10/31	15/8/32
Sikinami	Maiduru	6/7/28	22/6/29	24/12/29	Inaduma	Hudinagata	7/3/30	25/2/32	15/11/32
Asagiri	Saseho	12/12/28	18/11/29	30/6/30					

Name.	Begun.	Launch.	Comp.	Name.	Begun.	Launch.	Comp.
Minatuki	24/3/25	25/5/26	22/3/27	Mutuki	21/5/24	23/7/25	25/3/26
Humituki	20/10/24	16/2/26	3/7/26	Kisaragi	3/6/24	5/6/25	21/12/25
Nagatuki	16/4/25	6/10/26	30/4/27	Yayoi	11/1/24	11/7/25	28/8/26
Kikutuki	15/6/25	15/5/26	20/11/26	Uduki	11/1/24	15/10/25	14/9/26
Mikaduki	21/8/25	12/7/26	7/5/27	Satuki	1/12/24	25/3/25	15/11/25
Motiduki	23/3/26	28/4/27	31/10/27				
Yuduki	27/11/26	4/3/27	25/7/27				
Kamikaze	15/12/21	25/9/22	28/12/22	Hayate	11/11/22	23/3/25	21/12/25
Asakaze	16/2/22	8/12/22	16/6/23	Asanagi	5/3/23	21/4/24	29/12/24
Harukaze	16/5/22	18/12/22	31/5/23	Yunagi	17/9/23	23/4/24	24/4/25
Matukaze	2/12/22	30/10/23	5/4/24				
Hatakaze	3/7/23	15/3/24	30/8/24				
Oite	16/3/23	27/11/24	30/10/25	Minekaze	20/4/18	8/2/19	29/3/20
				Okikaze	22/2/19	3/10/19	17/8/20
Akikaze	7/6/20	14/12/20	1/4/21	Hokaze	30/11/20	12/7/21	22/12/21
Yukaze	14/12/20	28/5/21	24/8/21	Siokaze	15/5/20	22/10/20	29/7/21
Namikaze	7/11/21	24/6/22	11/11/22	Tatikaze	18/8/20	31/3/21	5/12/21
Numakaze	10/8/21	25/2/22	24/7/22	Nokaze	16/4/21	1/10/21	31/3/22
Nadakaze	9/1/20	26/6/21	30/9/21	Sawakaze	7/1/18	7/1/19	16/3/20
Simakaze	5/9/19	31/3/20	15/11/20	Hakaze	11/11/18	21/6/20	16/9/20
				Yakaze	15/8/18	10/4/20	19/7/20

15 Akikaze class.

MINEKAZE

SIMAKAZE　(Observe funnel tops.)　　　　　1934 *Photo.*

NUMAKAZE (NAMIKAZE and NOKAZE similar).　　　1937.

15 *Akikaze* class: **Akikaze** and **Yukaze** (both by Mitubisi Z.K., Nagasaki); **Minekaze, Okikaze, Hokaze, Siokaze, Tatikaze, Namikaze, Numakaze, Nokaze, Nadakaze, Simakaze.** All by Maiduru. **Sawakaze, Hakaze** and **Yakaze** all built by Mitubisi Co., at Nagasaki. Displacement : 1215 tons. Dimensions : 320 (*p.p.*), $336\frac{1}{2}$ (*o.a.*) × $29\frac{1}{2}$ × $9\frac{1}{2}$ feet (*mean* draught). Armament : 4—4·7 inch, 45 cal., 2 M.G. (AA.), and 6—21 inch torpedo tubes. 2—30 inch searchlights in Maiduru built vessels : only **1** in others. Designed S.H.P. : 38,500 = 34 kts. Machinery : Parsons 4 shaft turbines and 4 Kanpon boilers. Oil : 315 tons. Complement : *Sawakaze*, 145, others 148. *Sawakaze* belongs to the 1917 Programme ; *Nadakaze, Simakaze, Hakaze* and *Yakaze* to the 1918 Programme. Remainder authorised under 1919 and 1920 sections of the 1918–24 Navy Law.

2nd Class Destroyers. (1000 to 600 tons)

7 Wakatake Class.

KURETAKE.

1936 (added 1938). B. R. Goodfellow, Esq.

7 *Wakatake* class: **Wakatake** (ex-No. 2) and **Kuretake** (ex-No. 4), (both by Kawasaki Co., Kobe): **Sanaye** (ex-No. 6 by Uraga Dock Co.); **Asagao** (ex-No. 10) and **Yugao** (ex-No. 12), (both by Isikawazima Co.); **Huyo** (ex-No. 16) and **Karukaya** (ex-No. 18), (both by Hudinagata Co.).

Built under 1921 Naval Programme. Displacement: 820 tons. Complement: 110. Dimensions: 275 × 26½ × 8¼ feet. Guns: 3—4·7 inch, 45 cal., 2 M.G. Tubes: 4—21 inch (paired). Machinery: Parsons geared turbines. 2 shafts. S.H.P. 21,500 = 31·5 kts. 3 Kanpon boilers. Oil: 275 tons.

All originally bore numbers only. Names were conferred on August 1st, 1928. *Sawarabi* lost off Formosa, Dec. 5, 1932.

Name.	Begun.	Launch.	Comp.	Name.	Begun.	Launch.	Comp.
Wakatake	13/12/21	24/7/22	30/ 9/22	Yugao	15/5/22	14/4/23	31/5/24
Kuretake	15/3/22	21/10/22	21/12/22	Huyo	16/2/22	23/9/22	16/3/23
Sanaye	5/4/22	15/2/23	5/11/23	Karukaya	16/5/22	19/3/23	20/8/23
Asagao	14/3/22	4/11/22	10/5/23				

KARUKAYA.

1937.

19 Kaya Class (12 Kaya + 7 Asi).

HASU (Observe forefunnel).

1936, *Official*, added 1937.

TUGA (painted white).

1936, *Official*, added 1937.

12 *Kaya* class: **Kaya** (Yokosuka), **Kuri** and **Nire** (Kure), **Nasi**, **Take**, **Aoi** and **Kiku** (Kawasaki Co., Kobé), **Hagi** and **Kaki** (Uraga Co.), **Susuki** and **Tuga** (Isikawazima Co.), **Hudi** (Hudinagata Co. Osaka). 770 tons. Dimensions: 275 (*p.p.*) × 26 × 8 feet. Armament: 3—4.7 inch, 45 cal., 2 M.G. (AA). 4—21 inch torpedo tubes in two twin-deck mountings. 1—30 inch searchlight. Designed S.H.P.: 17,500 = 31·5 kts., *except Hagi, Susuki, Hudi.* 21,500 = 31·5 kts. Machinery: Parsons direct drive turbines. 3 Kanpon boilers. 2 shafts. Oil: 275 tons. Endurance: 3,000 miles at 15 kts. Complement, 110. Built under 1918–19 Programme.

7 *Asi* class: **Asi** and **Tuta** (Kawasaki Co.), **Hasu** and **Hisi** (Uraga Dock Co.), **Sumire** and **Yomogi** (Isikawazima Co.), **Tade** (Hudinagata Co., Osaka). All details as *Kaya* class, but 2 searchlights carried and S.H.P. 21,500 = 31.5 kts. Begun under 1920 Naval Programme.

Notes.—*Warabi*, of this class, lost by collision, Aug. 24, 1927. *Momi* scrapped, 1932. *Kaya, Nasi, Take* reported to have been relegated to harbour training duties

(For details of launch dates, etc., see following column.)

Destroyers—continued.

3 Momo Class.

MOMO

YANAGI.

1920 Photo, Seward, Weymouth.

3 *Momo* class : **Yanagi** (1917) and **Momo** (1916), both built at Saseho: **Hinoki** (1916), built at Maiduru. Displacement : 755 tons. Dimensions : 275 (o.a.) × 25 × 7¾ feet. Armament : 3—4·7 inch, 2 M.G., 1 small AA. gun, and 6—18 inch tubes in two triple mountings. One searchlight. Machinery : 3 sets Curtis turbines and 4 Kanpon boilers. Designed H.P. : 16,000 = 31·5 kts. Fuel : 92 tons coal, 212 tons oil. Complement : 109. Built under the 1915 Naval Programme. *Enoki* and *Nara* of this class converted into Minesweepers, 1930, and afterwards scrapped. *Maki, Keyaki, Kuwa, Tubaki*, scrapped. *Kasi*, transferred to Manchukuo. First two have H.P. : 17,500 = 31·5 kts.

Name.	Begun.	Launch.	Comp.	Name.	Begun.	Launch.	Comp.
Kaya	23/12/18	10/6/19	28/3/20	*Kiku*	20/1/20	13/10/20	10/12/20
Kuri	5/12/19	19/3/20	30/4/20	*Hagi*	28/2/20	29/10/20	20/4/21
Nire	5/9/19	22/12/19	31/3/20	*Kaki*	27/2/19	20/10/19	2/8/20
Nasi	2/12/18	26/8/19	10/12/19	*Susuki*	3/5/20	21/2/21	25/5/21
Take	2/12/18	26/8/19	25/12/19	*Tuga*	5/3/19	17/4/20	20/7/20
Aoi	1/4/20	9/11/20	31/12/20	*Hudi*	6/12/19	27/11/20	31/5/21
Asi	15/11/20	3/9/21	29/10/21	*Sumire*	24/11/20	14/12/21	31/3/23
Tuta	16/10/20	9/5/21	30/6/21	*Yomogi*	26/2/21	14/3/22	19/8/22
Hasu	2/3/21	8/12/21	31/7/22	*Tade*	20/12/20	15/3/22	31/7/22
Hisi	10/11/20	30/5/21	23/3/22				

12 + 8 (Building) Torpedo Boats.

SAGI.

1938.

16 *Otori* class : **Otori, Hiyodori, Hayabusa, Kasasagi, Kizi, Kari, Sagi, Hato,** and 8 others not yet named, laid down 1937–38.

Displacement : 595 tons *standard*. Dimensions : 263 × 26 × 6¾ feet. Guns : 3—4·7 inch, 1 M.G. Torpedo tubes ; 3—21 inch. 1 S.L. Machinery : Parsons geared turbines. 2 shafts. S.H.P. : 9,000 = 28 kts. Boilers : Kanpon Oil fuel.

Notes.—Authorised by 2nd Fleet Replenishment Law, 1933. Design modified in consequence of capsizing of *Tomoduru*.

Torpedo Boats—continued.

HATUKARI.

1935.

4 *Tidori* class : **Tidori, Tomoduru, Hatukari, Manaduru.** Displacement : 527 tons. Dimensions : 254 × 24 × 6 feet. Guns : 3—4·7 inch, 1 M.G. Tubes : 2—21 inch. Machinery : Parsons geared turbines. H.P. : 7,000 = 26 kts.

Notes.—Built under 1931 Programme. After the capsizing of *Tomoduru* in March, 1934, these vessels were altered extensively to improve stability, armaments being reduced to lessen top weight.

Name.	Builders.	Begun.	Launch.	Completed.
Tidori	Maiduru	13/10/31	1/4/33	20/11/33
Manaduru	Hudinagata	22/12/31	11/7/33	31/11/34
Tomoduru	Maiduru	11/11/32	1/10/33	24/2/34
Hatukari	Hudinagata	6/4/33	19/12/33	15/7/34
Otori	Maiduru	8/11/34	25/4/35	10/10/36
Hiyodori	Isikawazima	26/11/34	25/10/35	20/12/36
Hayabusa	Yokohama Dock	19/12/34	28/10/35	7/12/36
Kasasagi	Osaka Iron Wks.	4/3/35	28/11/35	15/1/37
Kizi	Mitui (Tama)	24/10/35	26/1/37	31/7/37
Kari	Yokohama Dock	11/5/36	20/1/37	20/9/37
Sagi	Harima	20/5/36	30/1/37	31/7/37
Hato	Isikawazima	28/5/36	25/1/37	7/8/37

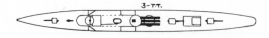

TIDORI class (*Otori* similar, but only 2 tubes).

MEANINGS OF NAMES OF TORPEDO BOATS.

Tidori	Dotterel Plover.	Hayabusa	Peregrine falcon.
Manaduru	White-naped crane.	Kasasagi	Magpie.
Tomoduru	Flight of cranes.	Kizi	Pheasant.
Hatukari	First wild goose of the season.	Kari	Wild goose.
Otori	Japanese stork.	Sagi	Snowy Heron.
Hiyodori	Brown-eared bulbul.	Hato	Dove.

336

Submarines (*Sensuikan*).

Now divided into 4 groups, Oceangoing, Seagoing, Minelaying and Coastal.

(a) Oceangoing

16 "I 9" Class.

> *Building.*

I 9—I 24 building under 1937 Programme, *I* 16 at Kure (*I* 18 was launched at Saseho, on Nov. 12, 1938). No other particulars received, but believed to be vessels of about 1,500 tons *surface* displacement. Some may be larger, evolved from design of *I* 6.

3 "Improved I5" Type.

> *Photo wanted.*

1 *boat*: *I 6* (Kawasaki, March 31, 1934). Displacement: 1,900/2,500 tons. Dimensions: 309½ (*pp.*), 343½ (*o.a.*) × 29¾ × 15¼ feet. Guns: 1—5 inch, 2 M.G. A.A. Tubes: 6—21 inch. 2 sets Diesels. H.P.: 6,000=17 kts. *surface*. *Submerged*, 9 kts. Completed 1935,

2 *boats*: *I 7* (Kure, July 3, 1935), *I 8* (Kawasaki, July 20, 1936). Displacement: 1,950/2,600 tons. Dimensions 356½ (*o.a.*) × 29¾ × 14½ feet (*mean* draught). Guns: 2—5·5 inch., 2 M.G. A.A. Tubes: 6—21 inch. 1 S.L. 2 sets Kanpon Diesels. H.P.: 6,000 = 17 kts., *surface*. *Submerged*, 9 kts.

Note.—These 2 vessels were laid down Sept. 12 and Oct. 1, 1934, respectively. *I* 7 completed March 31, 1937, *I* 8 on Dec. 5, 1938.

1 Experimental Boat.

I 5 (Number on bow is that of flotilla).   1939.

I 5. (Kawasaki, June 19th, 1931). Displacement: 1,955/2,500 tons. Dimensions: 320 × 30¼ × 15¾ feet. Guns: 1—5 inch., 2 M.G. A.A. Tubes: 6—21 inch. Machinery: Diesels, 6,000 H.P. = 17 kts. *surface*. Motors H.P. 1,800 = 9 kts.

Note.—Differs mainly from I 1—4 in calibre of gun and in having a seaplane with folding wings housed in a hangar in two tubular sections on either side of superstructure abaft C.T., instead of a second gun. Fuselage, floats and engine are stowed in one section, wings in the other. (It is possible that this experimental equipment has since been removed). Laid down Oct. 30, 1929, and completed July 31, 1932.

4 Kawasaki Boats.

I 1.   1926 *Photo, by courtesy of Navy Department.*

4 *boats*: *I 1* (*ex*-No. 74, Oct., 1924), *I 2* (*ex*-No. 75, Feb. 23., 1925), *I 3* (*ex*-No. 76, June 8, 1925), *I 4* (May 22, 1928). All by Kawasaki, Kobe. Displacement: 1,955/2,480 tons. Dimensions: 320 × 30¼ × 15¾ feet. Guns: 2—5·5 inch, 2 M.G. A.A. Tubes: 6—21 inch. Machinery: Diesels, H.P. 6,000 = 17 kts. *surface*. Motors H.P. 1,800 = 9 kts. Design is based in its main features on the *ex*-German Submarine *O* 1 (*ex-U* 125). First three authorised by 1922 Programme, and completed 1926. *I* 1 carried out a test cruise of 2,500 miles with complete success. *I* 4, laid down at Kawasaki in April, 1926, built under direct superintendence of Naval Construction Department and completed in Dec., 1929.

(b) Seagoing.

8 Kaigun Type.

I 71.   1936, *Official.*

5 *boats*: *I 71* (Kawasaki, Aug. 25, 1934), *I 72* (Mitubisi, April 6, 1935), *I 73* (Kawasaki, June 20, 1935), *I 74* (Saseho, March 28, 1937), *I 75* (Mitubisi, Sept. 16, 1936). Displacement, dimensions, etc., as preceding group below, but armed with 1—4·7 inch gun, 6—21 inch tubes.

3 *boats*: *I 68* (Kure, June 26, 1933), *I 69* (Mitubisi, Kobe, Feb. 15, 1934), *I 70* (Saseho, June 14, 1934). *Surface* displacement: 1,400 tons. Dimensions: 331½ × 27 × 13 feet. Guns: 1—4 inch, 1 M.G. Tubes: 6—21 inch. 2 sets Diesels. H.P.: 6,000 = 20 kts., *surface*. *Submerged* 9 kts.

I 71 completed Dec. 24, 1935. *I* 72, *I* 73 both completed Jan. 7, 1937. *I* 74 in 1938, *I* 69, *I* 70 in 1935, and *I* 68 in 1934. All reported to have a radius of action of 16,000 miles.

Seagoing—continued.

3 Kaigun Type.

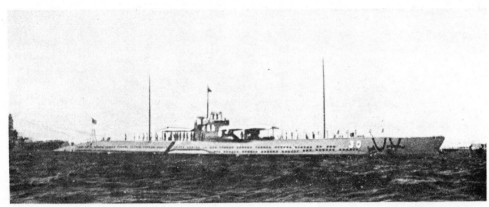

I 65.   1933 *(added 1935).*

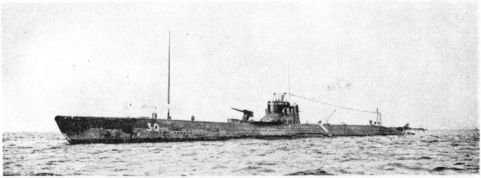

I 65.   1935.

3 *boats:* I **65** (Kure, June 2, 1931), I **66** (Saseho, June 2, 1931), I **67** (Mitubisi, April 7, 1931). Displacement : 1,638/2,100 tons. Dimensions : 321½ × 27 × 16 feet, Guns : 1—4 inch, 1 M.G, Tubes : 6—21 inch. 2 sets Diesels. H.P. 6,000 = 19 kts. *surface. Submerged* speed, 9 kts.

11 Kaigun Type.

I 55.   1928 *Photo.*

I 61.   1930 *Official.*

11 boats : I **53** (ex-*No.* 64, Kure, Aug. 5, 1925), I **54** (ex-*No.* 77, Saseho, March 15, 1926), I **55** (ex-*No.* 78, Kure Sept. 2, 1925), I **56** (Kure, March 23, 1928), I **57** (Kure, Oct. 1, 1928), I **58** (Yokosuka, Oct. 3, 1925), I **59** (Yokosuka, March 25, 1929). I **60** (Saseho, April 24, 1929), I **61** (Mitubisi, Nov. 12, 1927), I **62** (Mitubisi. Nov. 29, 1928), I **64** (Kure, Oct. 5, 1929). Displacement : 1,635/2,100. Dimensions : 331 × 26 × 16 feet (except I 61, 62, 64, which are 321½ × 25½. Armament : 1—4·7 inch, 1 M.G., 8—21 inch tubes (except I 61, 62, 64, which have only 6 tubes). Machinery : 2 sets Diesels. B.H.P. : 6,000 = 19 kts. Electric motors, H.P. : 1,800 = 9 kts. Believed begun under 1923-25 Programmes. Cruising radius is undoubtedly very large, 16,000 miles being reported. They are supposed to be capable of crossing the Pacific and returning without refuelling. This design is the fruit of experience gained with I 51 and I 52.

Note.—I 63 sunk by collision in Bungo Channel, Feb. 2, 1939.

Seagoing—(continued)

2 Kaigun Experimental Type.

1926 *Photo.*

I 52 (ex-*No.* 51, Kure, June 12, 1922). Built under 1920 Programme. Displacement : 1,390/2,000 tons. Dimensions : 331 × 25 × 17 feet. Armament : 1—4·7 inch, 1 M.G., 8—21 inch tubes. H.P. : 6,000/1,800. Speed : 19/9 kts. Completed in May, 1925.

I 51 (ex-44).

Photo added 1927.

I 51 (ex-*No.* 44, Kure, Nov. 29th, 1921). Laid down under 1920 Programme as an experimental boat. Displacement : 1,390/2,000 tons. Dimensions : 300 × 29 × 15 feet. Armament : 1—4·7 inch, 1 M.G., 8—21 inch tubes. 2 Sets Sulzer Diesels. H.P. : 5,200 = 17 kts. Electric motors, H.P. : 1,800 = 9 kts. Completed June, 1924.

(c) Minelaying.

4 Kawasaki Boats

I 122.

1930 *Photo.*

I 121.

1927 *Photo, by courtesy of Navy Dept.*

4 boats : **I 121** (ex-*I* 21, ex-48) (March 30, 1926), **I 122** (ex-*I* 22, ex-49) (Nov. 8, 1926), **I 123** (ex-*I* 23, ex-50) (March 19, 1927), **I 124** (ex-*I* 24) (Dec. 12, 1927), all by Kawasaki Co., Kobe, the first probably laid down under 1919 Programme. Displacement : 1,142/1,470 tons. Dimensions : 279½ × 24¾ × 14¼ feet. Armament : 1—5·5 inch, 4—21 inch tubes, 42 mines. Machinery : Diesels, H.P. : 2,400 = 14 kts. Electric motors, H.P. : 1,200 = 9·5 kts. I 22 and I 23 completed at Kure, owing to temporary suspension of business by Kawasaki Co. Construction of I 24 completed at Kawasaki by Naval Construction Dept. Design believed to be based on German *U B* types.

(d) *Coastal* from 500 to 1000 tons.

2 Kaigun type.

RO. 33.   1937.

2 *boats*: **Ro. 33** (Kure, Oct. 10, 1934), **Ro. 34** (Mitubisi, Dec. 12, 1935). Displacement, 700/—tons. Dimensions 239½ × 22 × 12 feet. Armament : 1—3 inch AA., 4—21 inch tubes (believed all in bow). H.P. : 2,600/— = 16/9 kts.

9 Mitubisi Type.

RO. 64.   *Photo added* 1926.

9 boats : **Ro. 60** (ex-*No. 59*), **Ro. 61** (ex-*No. 72*), **Ro. 62** (ex-*No. 73*), **Ro. 63** (ex-*No. 84*), **Ro. 64—68.** All built by Mitubisi, Kobe, 1923–25. Displacement : 988/1,300 tons. Dimensions : 250 (*p.p.*) × 24 × 13 feet. Guns : 1—3 inch, 1 M.G. Torpedo tubes : 6—21 inch. Vickers Diesels H.P. 2,400 = 16 kts. Motors : 1,800 H.P. = 10 kts. Fuel : 75 tons. Complement : 48.

Notes.—Built under 1920–22 Programmes. Apparently an enlargement of the *Ro. 51—59* type. Completed—*Ro. 60* 1923 ; *Ro. 61—63*, 1924 *Ro. 64* and 68, 1925 ; *Ro. 65* and 67, 1926 *Ro. 66*, 1927.

6 Mitubisi-Vickers type.

RO. 58.   (*Ro. 57* and 59 same.)   (Note absence of step forward.)   *Photo added* 1926.

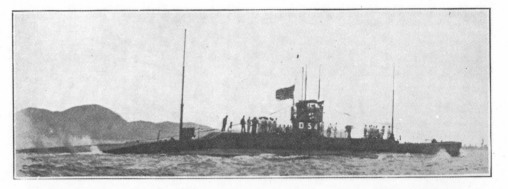

RO. 54.   *Photo added* 1927.

6 boats : **Ro. 51** (ex-*No. 25*), **Ro. 53, Ro. 56,** (ex-*No. 30*), **Ro. 57** (ex-*No. 46*), **Ro. 58** (ex-*No. 47*), **Ro. 59** (ex-*No. 57*). (Mitubisi, Kobe, 1919–22.) Displacement : First five, 893/1,082 tons ; remaining three, 889/1,082 tons. Dimensions : 232 × 23½ × 13 feet. (Ro. 57—59, 250 feet) Guns : 1—3 inch AA. Torpedo tubes : 6—18 inch in *Ro.* 51 and 54—56 ; 4—21 inch in *Ro.* 53 and 57—59. H.P. : 2,400/1,200 = Speed 17/9 kts. Fuel : 65 tons. Complement : 48. Endurance : *About* 7,500 miles *on surface.*

Notes.—Gun mounted on extended C.T. in *Ro.* 57—59. Begun under 1917–18 and 1919 Programmes. Completed 1920–23. *Ro.* 52 scrapped April, 1932.

3 Kawasaki Boats (Minelayers).

1926 *Photo, by courtesy of Navy Department.*

3 boats: **Ro. 30-32** (ex-*Nos.* 69—71). (Kawasaki Co., Kobe, 1923—26). Dimensions: 243½ (*p.p.*) × 20 × 12 feet. Displacement: 655/1,000 tons. Guns: 1—4·7 inch, 1—3 pdr. Torpedo tubes: originally carried 5—21 inch, now 4—21 inch, and are fitted as minelayers. H.P.: 1,200/1,200 = 13/10 kts.

Notes.—Built under 1919 Programme, and completed 1923-24 *Ro.* 31. (ex-*No* 70) sank during trials at Kobe, August, 1923, but was salved and rebuilt. *Ro.* 30 and *Ro* 32 both completed during 1924. *Ro.* 31 completed at Kure, 1927, owing to financial crisis at Kawasaki Yard.

3 Kaigun Type.

Ro. 26.

1926 *Photo, by courtesy of Navy Department, Tokyo.*

3 boats: **Ro. 26** (ex-*No.* 45, Saseho, Oct. 18, 1921), **Ro. 27** (ex-*No.* 58, Yokosuka, July 22, 1922), **Ro. 28** (ex-*No.* 62, Saseho, April 13, 1922). Displacement: 746/1,000 tons Dimensions: 243½ × 20 × 12 feet. Guns: 1—3 inch AA. Torpedo tubes: 4—21 inch. 2 sets of Sulzer Diesels. H.P.: 2,600 = 16 kts Electric motors, H.P.: 1,200 = 9 kts. Complement: 40.

Notes.—Built under 1919 Programme and completed 1923-24.

Submarine Chasers.

Photo wanted.

Nos. 4 (Osaka Iron Works, Sept. 13, 1938), **5** (Mitubisi, Yokohama, July 28, 1938), **6** (Turumi Steel Works, Feb. 6, 1939), **7** (Turumi, 1939), **8** (Tama Works, Aug. 9, 1938), **9** (Mitubisi, Yokohama, 1938), **11** (Turumi Steel Works, 1939). Nos. 10 and 12 believed to be building. Displacement: 270 tons. No other particulars received, but are believed to differ in certain respects from No. 3, next page.

No. 53.   1938.

No. 51 (June 9, 1937), **No. 52** (Aug. 25, 1937), both by Turumi Steel Works; **No. 53** (July 15, 1937), by Osaka Iron Works.

Displacement: 170 tons. Dimensions: 146 × 15⅓ × 5½ feet. Armed with D.C. and **1** AA. gun. Machinery: Diesel (except No. 53, reported to be steam turbine). H.P.: 3,000 = 23 kts.

Submarine Chasers—*continued*.

No. 3 (Asano Co., June 6, 1936). Displacement : 270 tons. Dimensions : 179 × 18⅓ × 6½ feet. H.P. : 2,500 = 20 kts. Armed with D.C. and 4 M.G.

No. 2.   1935.

No. 1 (Uraga Dock Co., Dec., 1933), **No. 2** (Isikawazima, Dec., 1933). Displacement : 300 tons. Dimensions : 210½ × 19¾ × 5 feet. Machinery : Diesel. H.P. : 3,400 = 24 kts. Armed with Depth Charges and 4 M.G.

Minesweepers.

Photo wanted.

No. 7 (Tama Works, June 16, 1938)   **No. 9** (Maiduru, Sept. 10, 1938)
No. 8 (Uraga Dock Co., May 28, 1938).   **No. 10** (Isikawazima Co., Sept. 22, 1938).
   Displacement : 630 tons. Dimensions : 226 × 25¾ × 7⅔ feet. Guns : 3—4·7 inch, 2 M.G.
   Speed : 20 kts.

No. 11 (Uraga Dock Co., Dec. 28, 1938).   **No. 12** (Isikawazima Co., Feb. 18, 1939).
   Believed to be similar to above, but no particulars received.

No. 13.   1935.

No. 13 (Hudinagata S.B. Co., March 30, 1933).   **No. 16** (Tama Works, March 30, 1934).
No. 14 (Osaka Iron Works, May 20, 1933).   **No. 17** (Osaka Iron Works, Aug. 3, 1935).
No. 15 (Hudinagata S.B. Co., Feb. 14, 1934).   **No. 18** (Tama Works, Sept. 19, 1935).

   Nos. 13—16 : Displacement : 492 tons. Dimensions : 232¼ × 25 × 6 feet. *Nos.* 17, 18 :
   Dimensions : 218 × 25⅓ × 6½ feet.
   In all : Guns : 2—4·7 inch, 2 M.G. Machinery : Triple expansion. H.P. 3,200 = 20 kts.,
   except *Nos.* 17, 18, only 19 kts.

   Notes.—All built under First Fleet Replenishment Law of 1931.

Minesweepers—*continued.*

MINESWEEPER No. 6 (Tripod foremast in this one and No. 5).

1930, *Photo.*

MINESWEEPER No. 1.

1938, *Official, courtesy of Navy Dept., Tokyo.*

Nos. 1 (Harima S.B. Co., March 6, 1923), **2** (Tama Works, March 17, 1923), **3** (Osaka Iron Works, March 29, 1923), **4** (Saseho, April 24, 1924), **5** (Tama Works, Oct. 30, 1928), **6** (Osaka I.W., Oct. 29, 1928). All provided by 1920–28 Fleet Replenishment Law. 615 tons. $235 \times 26\frac{1}{3} \times 7\frac{1}{2}$ feet. Guns : 2—4·7 inch, 1—3 inch AA., 2 D.C. throwers. Complement : 87. Triple expansion engines. 3 Kanpon boilers. H.P. : 4,000 = 20 kts.

Minelayers (*Husetukan*).
First Class (over 1,000 tons).

1937.

OKINOSIMA (Harima S.B. Co., Nov. 15, 1935.) *Standard* displacement : 4,400 tons. Dimensions : $386\frac{1}{2} \times 51\frac{1}{2} \times 16\frac{1}{2}$ feet (*mean*). Guns : 4—5·5 inch, 4 M.G. Geared turbines. S.H.P 9,000 = 20 kts. 4 Kanpon boilers.

Note.—Laid down Sept. 27, 1934, and completed Sept. 30, 1936. Name is that of an island off which the Battle of the Japan Sea was fought in 1905.

YAEYAMA (Now painted white).

1933 *Photo, Official.*

YAEYAMA (Kure, October 15, 1931). *Standard* displacement : 1,135 tons. Complement : 150. Dimensions : $280\frac{1}{2} \times 34\frac{1}{2} \times 8$ feet. Guns : 2—4·7 inch AA., 2 M.G. Machinery : 2 sets triple expansion, H.P. : 4,800 = 20 kts. 2 Kanpon boilers. Fuel: Mixed firing.

Note.—Is also fitted for laying anti-submarine nets. Laid down Aug. 2, 1930, and completed Aug. 31, 1932.

ITUKUSIMA (May 22nd, 1929).

Standard displacement, 1,970 tons ; *normal*, 2,020 tons.

Dimensions, 328 × 42 × 10 feet.   Complement, 235.

Guns :   Armour: Nil.
 3—5·5 inch, 50 cal.
 2—3 inch AA.

Mines :
 250 large or 500 small.
Depth charge throwers :
 1—each side amidships.

General Notes.—Laid down by Uraga Co., in Feb. 1928, and completed Dec. 1929.   Is the first experimental Diesel-driven ship in the Japanese Navy.   Design suggested by H.M.S. *Adventure* of which she is a small edition.   First searchlight shown in plan has been replaced by a 6 ft. anti-aircraft range-finder.   Officers' cabins in superstructure deck under fore gun and bridge.   Upper deck is for mine stowage, 4 lines of minelaying rails extending from forecastle to stern.   Two outer lines start abaft of bridge and extend to the wing-ports at stern.   There is a single line on the forecastle from starboard bow to gun for transport back to store of picked-up practice mines.   Two sizes of mines can be carried and number stowed varies as the type—roughly twice as many of the smaller size.

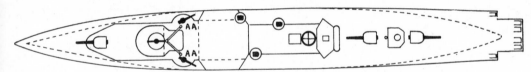

Machinery : 3 sets Diesel engines.   B.H.P. 3,000 = 16 kts.   3 shafts.   Radius of action is 5,000 miles at 16 kts.

1930 *Photo.*

1920 *Photo, Navy Dept., Tokyo.*

KATURIKI (Kure, Oct., 1916). 1,540 tons. Dimensions : 240 × 39 × 14 feet. Guns : **3**—3 inch. Machinery : 2 sets triple expansion. H.P. : 1,800 = 13 kts. Built under 1915–16 Programme. Fitted with 4 gallows for sweeps. Reported to carry 150 mines.

SIRATAKA.

1939

SIRATAKA (Isikawazima Co., Tokyo, 25th January, 1929). Displacement : **1,345 tons** *standard* ; **1,405 tons** *normal.* Dimensions : 260 × 38 × 9 feet. Guns : **3**—4·7 inch AA., **1** M.G. Machinery : 2 sets triple expansion. Boilers : 2 Kanpon. H.P. 2,200 = 16 kts.

Notes.—Also fitted for anti-submarine netlaying. Was laid down on Nov. 24, 1927, and completed April 9, 1929. *Sirataka* means White Hawk.

1930 *Photo.*

TOKIWA (Armstrong, July 6, 1898) 9,240 tons. Dimensions : 408 (*pp.*), 442 (*o.a.*) × 67¼ × × 24¼ feet. Guns : **2**—8 inch, 40 cal., **8**—6 inch, 40 cal., **2**—3 inch, **1**—3 inch AA. Armour : 7″ belt, tapering to 3½″, 2″ deck, 6″ turret, 6″ casemates. Machinery : 2 sets triple expansion. Boilers : 16 Miyabara. H.P. : 18,000 = 21¼ kts. Coal : 1,400 tons. Originally a cruiser.

Note.—*Tokiwa* means Evergreen. After turret removed 1929, when she was adapted for minelaying.

Minelayers, Second Class (*Husetutei*)

> Photo wanted.

SOKUTEN (Mitubisi, April 27, 1938), **SIRAKAMI** (Isikawazima, June 25, 1938). Displacement: 720 tons. Dimensions: $239 \times 25\frac{3}{4} \times 8\frac{1}{3}$ feet. Guns: Probably 2—4·7 inch. Machinery: 2 sets Diesels. H.P.: 3,600 = 20 kts. 1 S.L.

NASAMI

1936, *official.*

NATUSIMA

1934, *Official.*

NATUSIMA (Isikawazima S.B. Co., March 24, 1934).
SARUSIMA (Yokohama Dock Co., Dec. 16, 1933).
NASAMI (Harima Co., March 26, 1934).

Displacement: 443 tons. Dimensions: $225 \times 24\frac{1}{2} \times 5\frac{1}{2}$ feet. Guns: 2—3 inch AA., 1 M.G. Machinery: 2 sets Diesels. H.P.: 2,300 = 19 kts, except *Sarusima*, H.P.: 2,100 = 18 kts.

TUBAME.

1931 *Photo.*

(*Kamome* similar but 2 white bands on funnel).

TUBAME (now has 1 white band on funnel as in upper photo).

1930 *Photo, Navy Dept., Tokyo.*

KAMOME (Osaka Ironworks, 27th April, 1929), **TUBAME** (Yokohama Dock Co., 24th April, 1929), Displacement: 450 tons *standard*, 570 tons *normal.* Dimensions: $206\frac{2}{3} \times 23\frac{1}{2} \times 6\frac{1}{3}$ feet. Guns: 1—3 inch A.A., 1 M.G. H.P. 2,500 = 19 kts. Also equipped for netlaying.

Notes.—Both laid down in 1928. Meanings of names are as follows: *Kamome*—Seagull. *Tubame*—Swallow.

Gunboats.

FUSIMI (Hudinagata, March 26, 1939). Particulars wanted.

ATAKA (Now has tripod foremast, as in silhouette).   1936, *Official*.

ATAKA (ex-*Nakoso*). (Yokohama Dock Co., April, 1922). 725 tons. Complement: 118. Dimensions: 222 × 32 × 7½ feet. Guns: 2—4·7 inch, 2—3 inch AA. Machinery: Triple expansion. Designed H.P.: 1,700 = 16 kts. Boilers: 2 Kanpon. Authorised under 1920–28 Fleet Law, laid down 1921, and completed 1922. Equipped for submarine salvage work.

ex-*Yung Chi* (Kiangnan, Shanghai, 1915). 860 tons. Complement: 140. Dimensions: 205 × 29½ × 11½ feet. Guns: not known. I.H.P. 1,350 = 13 kts

1936 *Official*.

SAGA (Saseho, 1912). 685 tons. Complement, 99. 210 × 29½ × 7¼ feet. Guns: 1—4·7 inch, 3—3 inch AA., 6 M.G. Machinery: Triple expansion, 3 screws. Boilers: 2 Kanpon. Designed H.P. 1600 = 15 kts. Coal: *maximum* 400 tons. Completed Nov., 1912.

River Gunboats.

ATAMI.   1937.

ATAMI (Tama Works, March 30, 1929), **HUTAMI** (Hudinagata Co., Nov. 20, 1929). Displacement: 170 tons. Dimensions: 148⅔ × 20⅔ × 3 feet. Guns: 1—3 inch AA., 6 M.G. H.P.: 1,200 = 16 kts. Machinery: 2 sets triple expansion. Boilers: 2 Kanpon. Completed 1929 and 1930 respectively.

SETA.   1937.

HIRA (March 24, 1923, Mitubisi, Kobe).
HQDU (April 19, 1923, Mitubisi, Kobe).
KATADA (July 16, 1923, Harima S.B. Co.).
SETA (June 30, 1922, Harima S.B. Co.).

Displacement: 305 tons. Dimensions: 180 × 27 × 3⅓ feet. Guns: 2—3 inch AA., 6 M.G. Machinery: 2 sets triple expansion. Boilers: 2 Kanpon (mixed firing). Designed H.P.: 2,100 = 16 kts. Authorised under 1920–28 Fleet Law. Laid down 1922 and completed 1923.

347

River Gunboats—*continued*.

1937.

TOBA (1911). 215 tons. Complement: 59. Dimensions: 180 × 27 × 2⅔ feet. Guns: 2—3 inch AA., 6 M.G. H.P.: 1,400 = 15 kts. Coal: 80 tons. Built at Saseho.

River Patrol Vessel.

KOTAKA (Dec., 1929). 55 tons. Dimensions: 98½ × 16 × 2 feet. Guns: 3 M.G. Machinery: 2 Diesels. H.P.: 400 = 15 kts. Laid down September, 1929 at Tama Works, and completed January, 1930.

Note.—A number of smaller patrol vessels, with Diesel propulsion, similar to the Manchukuo *Emin* type, are also in service on the Yangtse.

Repair Ship.

Completing.

AKASI (Saseho, June 29, 1938). Displacement: 9,000 tons. Dimensions: $500 \times 67\frac{1}{4} \times 18\frac{2}{3}$ feet. Guns: 4—5 inch AA., 12 M.G. Machinery: 2 sets geared turbines. S.H.P.: 10,000 = 19 kts. First big repair ship built for the Imperial Japanese Navy, and the largest vessel ever launched at Saseho. Laid down Jan. 18, 1937, under Second Fleet Replenishment Law.

Submarine Depot Ships (*Sensui Bokan*).

Similar to *Taigei*, below, but funnel nearer foremast.

TURUGIZAKI (Yokosuka June 1, 1935), **TAKASAKI** (Yokosuka, June 19th, 1936). Standard displacement: 12,000 tons. Dimensions: $660\frac{1}{4} \times 59\frac{1}{2} \times 21$ feet. Guns: 4—5 inch. H.P.: 13,000 = 19 kts. Both built under Second Replenishment Law of 1933, and completed during 1938.

1936.

TAIGEI (Yokosuka, Nov. 16, 1933). Displacement: 10,000 tons. Dimensions: 647 (*w.l.*), 689 (*o.a.*) $\times$ 59 $\times$ 17 feet. Guns: 4—5 inch AA., 12 M.G. 4 sets Diesels. H.P.: 13,000 = 20 kts. Complement: 413. 3 Aircraft included in equipment, with 2 catapults.

Notes.—Laid down April 12, 1933; completed March 31, 1934. *Taigei* means Great Whale.
Reported to roll badly owing to light draught.

Submarine Depot Ships—*continued.*

TYOGEI (2 steam pipes to first funnel).   1934 *Photo.*

ZINGEI. (Now has white band round first funnel).   *Photo added* 1926.

ZINGEI (May 4, 1923), **TYOGEI** (March 24, 1924). Both by Mitubisi Co., Nagasaki. 5,160 tons. Dimensions: $380 \times 53 \times 19\frac{1}{2}$ feet (*mean*), $22\frac{2}{3}$ (*max.*). Geared turbines. 2 shafts. *Zingei*, 6 Kanpon boilers; *Tyogei*, 5. H.P.: 7,000 = 16 kts. Guns: 4—5·5 inch, 2—3 inch AA., 2 M.G. 2 searchlights. Each equipped to carry 1 seaplane. Both laid down in 1922; completed in August 1923 and August 1924, respectively.

Zingei—Swift swimming Whale.   *Tyogei*—Long Whale.

Submarine Depot Ships—*continued*.

1937.

KOMAHASI (Saseho, May 21, 1913). 1,125 tons. Dimensions: 227 × 35 × 17¾ feet. Guns: 2—3 inch, 1—3 inch AA. H.P.: 1,200 = 13·9 kts. Was originally built as a Naval Transport. Laid down Oct. 7, 1912, and completed Jan. 20, 1914.

KARASAKI (ex-*Ekaterinoslav*, 1896, captured 1904). 9,570 tons. Dimensions: 419 (*p.p.*), 440 (*o.a.*) × 49¾ × 17¼ feet (*max. draught*). Armament: 1—3 inch, 1—3 inch AA., 1—3 pdr. H.P.: 2,900 = 12·5 kts. (Was originally the Russian Volunteer Fleet *s.s. Ekaterinoslav*, built by Hawthorn, Leslie & Co., Hebburn-on-Tyne.)

Oilers (Officially rated as Transports).

SIRIYA.

Photo added 1927.

NARUTO.

1932.

IRO, SIRIYA, TURUMI, NARUTO, HAYATOMO, ONDO, SATA, ERIMO and SIRETOKO.

Displacement: 14,050 tons. (8,000 tons *gross*). Dimensions: 470⅔ (*o.a.*), 455 (*p.p.*) × 58 × 26½ feet. Guns: 2—5·5 inch. 2—3 inch AA., *except Erimo and Siretoko*, 2—4·7 inch, 2—3 inch AA. Reciprocating engines. 4 cylindrical boilers, (except *Naruto*, 6 Miyabara). I.H.P.: 5,850 = 12 kts. Fuel: 8,000 tons oil as cargo and 1,000 tons oil for own bunkers. Complement: 155–157.

Name.		Builder.	Begun.	Launch.	Comp.
Erimo	..	Kawasaki Co., Kobe.	3/5/20	28/10/20	16/12/20
Siretoko	..		16/2/20	17/7/20	20/9/20
Ondo	..		15/3/22	21/10/22	12/3/23
Iro ..	..	Osaka I.W.	2/9/21	5/8/22	30/10/22
Turumi	..		10/3/21	29/9/21	14/3/22
Sata	..	Yokohama Dock Co.	6/3/20	28/10/20	24/2/21
Siriya	..		7/4/21	12/11/21	8/2/22
Hayatomo	..	Kure	14/3/22	4/12/22	18/5/24
Naruto	..	Yokosuka	11/4/22	30/1/23	30/10/24

Oilers—*continued*.

1920 *Photo, Navy Dept., Tokyo.*

SUNOSAKI (Yokosuka D.Y., June, 1918). 8,800 tons. Dimensions: 400 × 50 × 23 feet. Guns: 2—4·7 inch, 2—3 inch AA. H.P.: 6,000 = 14 kts. Carries 5,000 tons oil. Built under 1916–17 Programme.

Colliers (rated as Transports).

NOZIMA.

1933 *Photo*.

(*Note Is passing "Akagi" seen over well decks.*)

NOZIMA (Feb. 3, 1919), **MUROTO** (Oct. 23, 1918). Both built by Mitubisi Co., Kobe. 8,215 tons. Dimensions: 345 × 50 × 23·9 feet. Guns: 2—4·7 inch. H.P.: 2,500 = 12·5 kts. Coal: 877 tons. Built under Special 1918–19 Programme.

Fleet Supply Ship.

MAMIYA. (4 legs to mainmast). *Photo added* 1935.

MAMIYA (Kawasaki Co., Kobe, 26 Oct., 1923). Displacement : 15,820 tons. Dimensions : 475 × 61 × 28 feet. Guns : 2— 5·5 inch, 2—3 inch AA. Triple expansion engines. 8 Kanpon boilers. H.P. : 10,000 = 14 kts. Complement, 195.

Ice Breaker.

OTOMARI. *Photo added* 1925 *by courtesy of the Ministry of Marine.*

OTOMARI (Kawasaki Co., Oct. 3, 1921). 2,330 tons. Dimensions : 200 × 50 × 18½ feet. Guns : 1—3 inch. Reciprocating engines. 5 cylindrical boilers. H.P. : 4,000 = 13 kts.

Miscellaneous Repair, Depot and Training Ships.

1929 *Photo.*

ASAHI (March, 1899). Ex-battleship of 11,441 tons standard displacement rendered non-effective. Dimensions : 425¼ (*o.a.*) × 75¼ × 27¼ feet. Machinery : 2 sets vertical triple expansion. 2 screws. 4 cylindrical boilers (replacing original Bellevilles). Present speed 18 kts. The name of this ship means " Rising Sun." She has no armament.

SIKISIMA (Nov., 1898). Ex-battleship of 11,275 tons. No guns.

HUZI (March, 1896). Ex-battleship of 9,179 tons. No guns.

Note.—Cruisers *Hirado, Yahagi* and *Oi,* and Coast Defence Ships *Yakumo, Iwate* and *Kasuga* are employed as seagoing training ships.

Surveying Vessels.

1937.

YODO (Kobe, 1907). 1,320 tons. Complement : 182. D¹mensions : 280 (*pp.*), 305½ (*o.a.*) × 32 × 11 feet. Guns : 2—3 inch, 2 M.G. Armour : 2½″ deck. Torpedo tubes : 2—18 inch. Machinery : 2 sets 4-cyl. triple expansion. Designed H.P. : 6,500 = 22 kts. Boilers : 4 Miyabara. Coal : 340 tons + 80 tons oil. Completed by Kawasaki, April, 1908, and officially rated as a gunboat.

1920 *Photo, Navy Dept., Tokyo.*

KOSYŪ (ex-German S.S. *Michael Jebsen,* built by Howaldt, Kiel, 1904, and captured 1914). 2,080 tons. Dimensions : 252½ × 36 × 12¼ feet. Guns : 2—3 inch. H.P. : 800 = 10 kts. Ice-breaking stem.

LATVIA.

Flags.

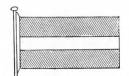
MERCANTILE.

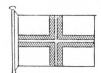
ENSIGN.

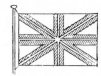
JACK.

ADMIRAL.

COMMANDER-IN-CHIEF OF FORCES.

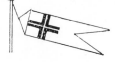
CAPTAIN COMMANDING NAVAL FORCES

Colour of Ships : Light grey.
Personnel : About 450 permanent + 200 yearly conscripts.
Minister of War : General T. Balodis.
Commanding Officer, Naval Forces : Captain T. Spade.

Naval Uniforms.

Admiralis
Rear-Admiral

Juras Kapteinis
Captain

Komand Kapteinis
Commander

Kapteinis
Lt. Commander

Virsleitnants
Lieutenant

Leitnants
Sub-Lieutenant

Mercantile Marine.

(From "Lloyd's Register," 1939 figures.)

93 vessels of 191,848 tons *gross*.

2 Submarines.

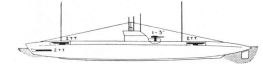

1927 *Photo, A. & Ch. de la Loire (Builders).*

RONIS

2 *Loire-Simonot* type : **Ronis** (At. & Ch. de la Loire, Nantes, July 1st, 1926), **Spidola** (Ch. & At. Augustin Normand, Havre, Oct. 6th, 1926). Displacement : $\frac{390}{514}$ tons. Dimensions $180\frac{1}{2} \times 15 \times 10$ feet. Armaments: 1—3 inc AA., 2 M.G., 6—17·7 inch tubes (2 fixed bow, other 4 in revolving twin mounts.) Machinery: sets Sulzer Diesels. H.P. $\frac{1300}{700}$. Speed : $\frac{14}{9·25}$ kts. Oil Fuel: 19 tons. Radius : $\frac{1600}{85}$ miles at $\frac{14}{9}$ kts. Diving limit, 28 fathoms. Complement, 28.

---

1 Gunboat.

1926 *Official Photo.*

VIRSAITIS (ex-German Minesweeper *M* 68, Neptun Werft, Rostock, 1917). Reconstructed at Riga, 1921-22, after being sunk during War. Displacement : 525 tons. Dimensions : 184 (*w.l.*) $\times 24\frac{1}{4} \times 7\frac{1}{4}$ feet. Guns : 2—3·4 inch. AA., 2—57 mm., 4 M.G. 1 S.L. H.P. 1850 = 17 kts. Coal : 120 tons. Complement, 69.

---

2 Minesweepers.

IMANTA.

1927 *Photo, Messrs. Normand (Builders).*

VIESTURS (Chantiers Dubigeon, Nantes, May 27th, 1926), **IMANTA** (Normand, Havre, Aug. 11th, 1926). Displacement : 255 tons. Dimensions : $160 \times 21 \times 5$ feet. Guns : 1—3 inch AA., 4 M.G. Provision for 30 mines. Machinery : 2 sets triple expansion. H.P. 750 = 14 kts. Fuel : 30 tons. Complement, 39.

Note.—These two vessels were designed for the Latvian Navy by Ch. & At. Augustin Normand.

Submarine Depot Ship.

1936, *Official.*

VARONIS (1908). Displacement : 250 tons. Dimensions : 95½ × 21½ × 12 feet. I.H.P. : 425 = 10 kts. (Originally an icebreaker.)

Icebreaker.

1939 *Official.*

KRISJANIS VALDEMARS (Beardmore, 1925). Displacement 2,800 tons. Dimensions : 196½ × 55⅔ × 22 feet. Machinery : Triple expansion. I.H.P. : 5,200 = 15 kts. Coal : 350 tons. Complement : 55.

Surveying Vessel.

1936, *Official.*

HIDROGRAFS (ex-*Weichsel*, built by J. W. Klawitter, Danzig, 1918). Displacement : 600 tons. Dimensions : 126¼ × 23¼ × 13½ feet. Machinery : Triple expansion. Speed : 10 kts.

Gunnery Tender.

ARTILLERISTS (1910). Displacement: 150 tons. Dimensions : 74½ × 17½ × 8½ feet. I.H.P.: 350 = 9 kts.

LITHUANIA.

Ensign.

Minister of Defence : Colonel Stasys Dirmantas.

Patrol Vessel.

1936 *Official, by courtesy of Lithuanian Legation.*

PREZIDENTAS SMETONA (ex-German minesweeper *M* 59). (Geestemunde, 1917.) (Reconstructed.) Displacement : 500 tons. Complement, 48. Dimensions : 184 (*w.l.*), 193 (*o.a.*) × 24¼ × 8½ feet (*max.* draught). Guns : 2—3 inch, 3 M.G. Machinery 2 sets triple expansion. 2 shafts. I.H.P. : 1,800 = 16 kts. Boilers : 2 Schulz. Coal : 160 tons.

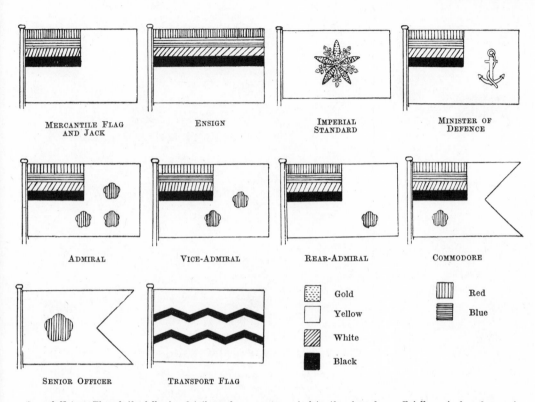

MERCANTILE FLAG AND JACK

ENSIGN

IMPERIAL STANDARD

MINISTER OF DEFENCE

ADMIRAL

VICE-ADMIRAL

REAR-ADMIRAL

COMMODORE

	Gold		Red
	Yellow		Blue
	White		
	Black		

SENIOR OFFICER

TRANSPORT FLAG

General Notes.—Though the following details are by no means complete, they have been officially revised, and present the first comprehensive record of the Manchukuo Navy that has yet been presented. Most of the vessels listed appear to be river craft. Several have their bows strengthened against floating ice. Some of those built in Japan were re-launched at Kharbin. In the past, much confusion has arisen through ships being referred to at different times by their Manchukuo, Japanese and Chinese names.

Insignia of Rank.

Shang-Chiang	*Chung-chiang*	*Shao-chiang*	*Shang-hsiao*	*Chung-hsiao*	*Shao-hsiao*	*Shang-wei*	*Chung-wei*	*Shao-wei*
Admiral	Vice-Admiral	Rear-Admiral	Captain	Commander	Lieut.-Commander	Lieut.	Sub-Lieut.	Acting Sub-Lieut.

Other branches have distinguishing colours between stripes as follows:

> Engineers (*Lun-chi*), Purple.
> Surgeons (*Chun-i*), Red.
> Paymasters (*Chun-hsu*), White.
> Constructors (*Tsao-hsin*), Green.

Destroyer

Added 1939.

Hai Wei (ex-*Kasi*), (Maiduru, 1916). Acquired from Japan in 1937. Displacement : 755 tons. Dimensions : 275 (*o.a.*) × 25 × 7¾ feet. Guns : 3—4·7 inch, 3 M.G. Torpedo tubes : 6—18 inch (tripled). 1 searchlight. Machinery : 3 sets Curtis turbines S.H.P.: 16,000 = 31·5 kts. Boilers : 4 Kanpon. Fuel : 212 tons oil and 92 tons coal. Complement: 109.

TING PIEN. 1935.

TING PIEN, CHIN JEN (Harima Co., 1935). *Standard* Displacement : 290 tons. Complement, 70. Dimensions : 195 × 29 × 3 feet. Guns : 2—4·7 inch AA., 3 M.G. Machinery : Diesels. B.H.P. : 680 = 13 kts.

Note.—Japanese versions of these names are *Teiken, Shinjin.*

YANG MIN. 1935.

SHUN TIEN. 1936, *Official.*

SHUN TIEN, YANG MIN (Harima Co., 1934). *Standard* Displacement : 270 tons. Complement, 70. Dimensions : 183 × 29 × 3 feet. Guns : 2—4·7 inch AA., 3 M.G. Machinery : Diesels. B.H.P. : 680 = 12·5 kts.

Note.—Japanese renderings, *Junten, Yomin.*

TATUNG. 1936, *Official.*

LIMIN. 1936, *Official.*

TATUNG, LIMIN (Mitubisi, 1933). Displacement, 65 tons. Complement, 20. Dimensions : 100 × 16 × 2½ feet. Guns : 3 M.G. Machinery : Diesels. B.H.P. : 240 = 10·5 kts.

Note.—Japanese names, *Daido, Rimin.*

```
                Photo wanted.
```

CHIMIN (Harbin, 1934). 20 tons. Dimensions : 65 × 11 × 2 feet. Guns : 2 M.G. Machinery : Diesel. B.H.P. : 80 = 8·5 kts.

EMIN. 1935.

PUMIN, EMIN, HUIMIN. 1934 *Official, added* 1936.

EMIN, HUIMIN, PUMIN (Kawasaki Co., 1933). Displacement : 15 tons. Dimensions : 56 × 11 × 2½ feet. Guns : 3 M.G. Machinery : Diesels. B.H.P. : 80 = 8·5 kts.

Note.—Japanese names, *Eimin, Keimin, Fumin.*

LISUI (ex-German gunboat *Vaterland*), (Schichau, Elbing, August 26, 1903.) Displacement : 350 tons (*full load ?*). Complement, 50. Dimensions : 164 × 26¼ × 2½ feet. Guns : 2—57 mm., 2 M.G. Machinery : Triple expansion. I.H.P. : 1,380 = 13 kts. (*trials*), present speed under 7 kts. Boilers : Schulz. Coal : 80 tons.

Note.—Japanese name, *Risui.*

Gunboats—*continued*.

1936, *Official*.

CHIANG TUNG (ex-Russian, 1903 ?). Displacement : 250 tons. Dimensions : 150 × 18¼ × 3 feet. Guns : 1—3 inch, 4 M.G. Speed : 4·5 kts. (Needs re-boilering.)

Note.—Japanese name, *Kotsu*. It is possible that this may be *ex-Mongol*, but dimensions as given above disagree.

Added 1935.

CHIANG CHING, CHIANG PIEN (both ex-Russian, 1897–1900). Displacement : 360 tons. Dimensions : 164 × 31½ × 3¼ feet. Guns : 1—3 inch, 4 M.G. Present speed, 7 to 7·5 kts.

Note.—Japanese names, *Kosei, Kohei*.

LICHI (ex-Russian, 1895). (Photo wanted.) Displacement : 362 tons. Dimensions : 158 × 42¾ × 3½ feet. Guns : 1—3 inch, 4 M.G. Present speed about 7·5 kts.

Note.—Japanese name, *Risei*.

Patrol Vessels.

Note.—These vessels are under the authority of the Police organisation, and are not part of the Navy.

HAIFENG. 1934 *Official, added* 1936.

HAIFENG, HAILUNG (Kawasaki Co., 1933.) Displacement : 200 tons. Dimensions : 143 × 20 × 5 feet. Guns : 2—3 inch, 2 M.G. Machinery: 2 sets Diesels. Speed: 14 kts. Strengthened for ice navigation.

Note.—Japanese names, *Kaiho, Koiryin*.

1934 *Official, added* 1936.

HAI KUANG, HAI JUI, HAI JUNG, HAI HUA (All Kawasaki, 1933.) Displacement : 45 tons. Dimensions : 85 × 12¾ × 3 feet. Guns : 1—57 mm., 2 M.G. Speed : 12 kts.

Note.—Japanese names, *Kaiko, Kaizui, Kaiei, Kaikwa*.

Surveying Vessel.

(Name not reported). Launched in Japan during 1935. Dimensions : 56 (*o.a.*) × 14½ ×   feet. Machinery : 2 Kermath Diesels.

Note.—It is probable that other ships exist, but the foregoing are the only ones whose identity has been established. Names reported include *Shuan An, Shuan Kai, Tierhaipien, Tsifuhaipien, Jurasen, Shuntsu, Kokei, Konei, Suikai, Haiwang*. It is possible that some of these are transports. Information on this subject will be welcomed.

Special Note.

Two old gunboats, names reported as *Hi Ryu* (or *Hi Ma*), 200 tons, and *Hai Yen*, 56 tons, were seized at Taku on July 29, 1937, and towed to Dairen. It is believed they have been added to the Manchurian Navy.

ENSIGN

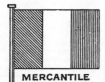

MERCANTILE

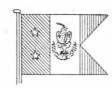

SECRETARY OF WAR AND
NAVY DEPTS.

OFFICER COMMANDING
A DIVISION.

Minister of War and Marine : General Quiroga.

Chief of Naval Staff : Rear-Admiral O. P. Blanco.

Personnel : 436 officers, 1,481 men.

Mercantile Marine (1939) :
56 vessels of 38,373 tons *gross.*

Escort Vessel. (Classed as *Transporte*).

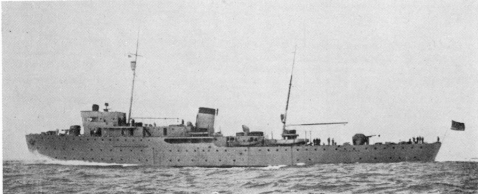

DURANGO.

1935, added 1936, *courtesy Capitan M. Mille.*

DURANGO (Union Naval de Levante, Valencia, June 28, 1935).

Standard displacement : 1,600 tons. Dimensions : 282 × 40 × 10 feet.

Guns : 2—4 inch. 4—25 mm. AA. (twin mounts) 4—13 mm. AA. (twin mounts)

Machinery : Parsons geared turbines. 2 shafts. S.H.P. : 6,500 = 20 kts. Yarrow boilers.

Accommodation for 40 officers, 450 men, 80 horses. Designed primarily as an armed transport, this vessel carries a weaker armament than *Potosi* class. A sister ship, the *Zacatecas,* was taken over by the Spanish Navy on completion and re-named *Calvo Sotelo.*

Escort Vessels.
(Classed as *Cañoneros*).

GUANAJUATO.

1936, *favour A. E. Kimberley, Esq.*

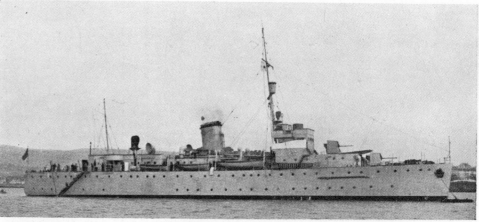

QUERÉTARO.

1935, added 1936, *courtesy Capitan M. Mille.*

GUANAJUATO (May 29, 1934), **QUERÉTARO** (June 29, 1934). (Both Societa Español de Construccion Naval, Ferrol), **POTOSI** (S.E. de C.N., Matagorda, Cadiz, August 24, 1934).

Standard displacement : 1,300 tons.

Dimensions : 260 × 37¾ × 10 feet.

Guns :

3—4 inch

4—25 mm. AA. (twin)

4—13 mm. AA. (twin mounts)

Machinery : Parsons geared turbines. 2 screws. S.H.P. : 5,000 = 20 kts. Yarrow boilers.

Note.—Guanajuato and *Potosi* are on Pacific Coast, *Querétaro* on Atlantic.

Escort Vessels—*continued*.

1925 *Photo, by courtesy of Captain Julio Morales Coello, C.N.*

PROGRESO (Odero, 1907). 1,590 tons. Dimensions: 230 × 36½ × 11 feet. Guns: 4—6 pdr. H.P. 1400 = 13 kts. Coal: 209 tons. (Classed as a Transport.) Refitted, 1937–38.

1938, *courtesy A. J. Wohler, Esq.*

NICOLAS BRAVO (Odero, 1903). 1227 tons. Dimensions: 242 × 34 × 9¾ feet. Guns: 2—4 inch, 4—6 pdr. H.P. 3000 = 12·25 kts. 2 screws. Oil fuel: 226 tons. Complement, 130.

(Classed as a Gunboat.)

Gunboats

(Classed as *Guardacostas*).

1935, *courtesy of Capitan M. Mille.*

10 *vessels :* Nos. **G** 20–29 (Compania Euskalduna de Construccion, Bilbao,) 1934–35. Displacement: 130 tons (*standard*), 180 tons (*full load*). Dimensions: 147½ (*p.p*), 153 (*w.l.*) × 16½ × 5¼ feet (*mean*). M.A.N. Diesels. H.P.: 3000 = 26 kts. 2 screws. Guns: 2—25 mm. AA. (twin mount), (forward), 4—13 mm. AA. (aft), (quadruple mount). Complement: 21.

Note.—Though of British design, these vessels were built in Spain, with German engines and bullet-proof hull plating, and armed with French guns.

Patrol Vessels (*Guardacostas*).

VERACRUZ.   1938, *courtesy A. J. Wohler, Esq.*

MAZATLAN, ACAPULCO (ex-*Salinas*), **VERACRUZ.**
All are ex-trawlers purchased in Canada 192(Built 1918. 486 tons. Dimensions: 133 × 24 × 13½ feet Guns: 1—6 pdr., 2 M.G. I.H.P. 557 = 8 kts. Coal: 208 tons.

Veracruz refitted, 1937-38.

Vessels under control of Free Ports Department.

COAHUILA, JALISCO (Cramps, Philadelphia, 1916). 2,876 tons *gross*. Displacement: 5,794 tons. I.H.P. 1,350 = 10·5 kts. Oil fuel.

Note.—Above ships are available for transport service when required.

NETHERLANDS.

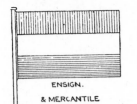

ENSIGN.
& MERCANTILE

ADMIRAL
OF THE
FLEET

ADMIRAL

VICE-ADMIRAL

REAR-ADMIRAL

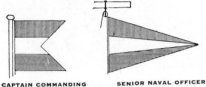

CAPTAIN COMMANDING
DIVISION

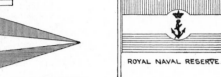

SENIOR NAVAL OFFICER

ROYAL NAVAL RESERVE.

JACK

PRINCE CONSORT

ROYAL STANDARD
H.M. THE QUEEN

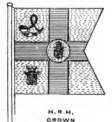

H.R.H.
CROWN
PRINCESS.

MINISTER OF DEFENCE

Officers commanding Flotillas fly a
yellow pendant with black letter
D in centre, from signal yard.

Notes to Flags.

Royal Standard ⎱
H.R.H. The Crown Princess ⎰ — Colours of these are *Nassau* blue (*dark* blue) and *dark* orange.
Governor-General of Netherland Indies : A broad pendant (Red, White, Blue) above Ensign.
Governors of Surinam and of Curaçao : Three white balls replace stars, in flag of Vice-Admiral's type.

Netherlands Uniforms.   7

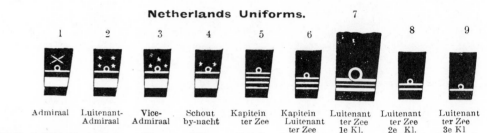

1	2	3	4	5	6	7	8	9
Admiraal	Luitenant-Admiraal	Vice-Admiraal	Schout by-nacht	Kapitein ter Zee	Kapitein Luitenant ter Zee	Luitenant ter Zee 1e Kl.	Luitenant ter Zee 2e Kl.	Luitenant ter Zee 3e Kl

Corresponding ⎱ Admiral ⎰ Admiral — Vice-Admiral — Rear-Admiral — Captain — Commander — Lieut.-Commander — Lieutenant — Sub.Lieut.
to British ⎰ of the Fleet

In relative ranks (all with " curl ") :
   Doctors   have insignia 5 to 9 in gold, with staff of Æsculapius on collar.
   Paymasters   „   5 to 9 in silver.
   Engineers   „   5 to 9 in gold, and are to be distinguished by the badge of a torch, crossed by two arrows, on the collar, instead of the usual anchor.
Flying Officers are of ranks 7, 8 and 9, and are to be distinguished by the badge of an aeroplane propeller on collar instead of the usual anchor. R.N. Reserve Officers are of ranks 5, 6, 7, 8, and 9 and wear no special distinguishing mark.

Notes.

All displacements are " Standard."

Personnel : About 11,750 all ranks, navy and marine infantry, including Officers, both at home and in E. Indies. To be increased to 15,000.

Oversea Possessions : Dutch East Indies (Sumatra, Java, Borneo, etc.) ; Dutch Guiana (Surinam), Curaçao, Bonaire, Aruba, Saba, St. Eustatius and St. Martin.

Minister of Defence : Lieut.-Col. A. Q. H. Dijxhoorn.   *Chief of the Naval Staff* : Vice-Admiral

Naval Attaché, London : Lieut.-Com. A. de Booy.   J. Th. Furstner.

Form of Address : HR. Ms. " (Name of Ship) "   *Chief of Naval Dept., E. Indies* : Vice-Admiral H. Ferwerda.

Colour of Ships : Greyish Blue, *except* Submarines, painted Dark Green in home waters and Black in E. Indies.

Netherland warships are referred to officially as H.N.M.S.

Naval Guns

	Cal. inch	Cal. cm.	Official Mark No.	Length, cals.	Weight of Shell	Initial Vel. ft. secs.	K = Krupp, B = Bofors, F = Wilton-Fijenoord
HEAVY	11	28	—	42½	595	2920	*Soerabaja*, K.
MEDIUM	5·9	15	11	50	101½	2953	Twin mounting. *Tromp* class, A.A., F.
	5·9	15	10	50	101½	2953	Single, *De Ruyter*, A.A., F.
	5·9	15	9	50	101½	2953	Turrets, *De Ruyter*, A.A., F.
	5·9	15	7, 8	50	101½	2953	*Flores* class, *Johan Maurits*, B.
	5·9	15	6	50	101½	2953	*Java, Sumatra*, K.
	4·7	12	7, 8	50	53	2444	Twin mounting. *W. van der Zaan* New destroyers, A.A., F.
	4·7	12	6	50	53	2950	*Van Kinsbergen*, A.A., F.
	4·7	12	4, 5	50	53	2950	Destroyers, B. and F.
	4·7	12	2, 3	40	52	2231	*Gelderland*, gunboats, K.
LIGHT	4·1	10·5	1	50	39¾	2897	*Brinio* class, semi-automatic, K.
	3·5	8·8	1, 2, 3	45	22	2625	Submarines, A.A., B. and F
	3·	7·5	6, 7, 8, 9	52	13	2936	A.A., B.
	3·	7·5	5	18	13	1148	Submarines, B.
	3·	7·5	4	30	13	2034	Torpedo boats, *Jan v. Amstel* class, K.
	3·	7·5	2, 3	40	13	2231	K.
	3·	SA. 7·5	4, 5	52	13	2936	A.A. semi-automatic, B.
	3·	SA. 7·5	1, 2, 3	52	13	2936	Semi-automatic, K.
	2·	SA. 5·	—	52	3·9	2936	*Hadda* class, K.
	1·5	4	3, 5	60	2·	2953	Twin mount, A.A., automatic, B. (No. 5 in submarines.)
	1·5	4	1, 2	40	2·	1975	Single mount, AA., automatic, B.
	1·4	3·7	—	30	1·	1358	

Mercantile Marine.

From " Lloyd's Register " 1939 figures.
1,532 Vessels of 2,972,871 gross Tonnage.

Defence Estimates, 1939.

Naval Construction	46,616,980 florins.	
Ordinary and other Expenses	181,987,418 „	(Navy and Army).
Non-military Expenses	5,092,622 „	
	233,697,020 „	

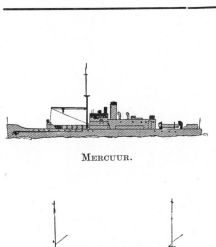

MERCUUR.

VAN MEERLANT.
DOUWE AUKES.
(HYDRA, MEDUSA, similar).

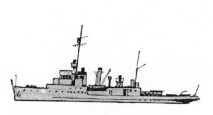

PRO PATRIA.

MINE SWEEPERS.
A.B.C.D.

C. DREBBEL.

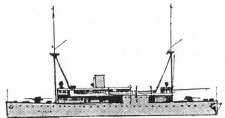

KRAKATAU.

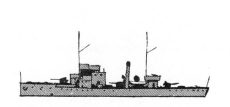

FRISO, BRINIO, GRUNO.

SOERABAJA.

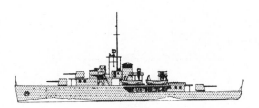

JOHAN MAURITS VAN NASSAU.

DE RUYTER.

NAUTILUS.

W. VAN DER ZAAN.

SOEMBA and FLORES.

TROMP, HEEMSKERCK.

VAN KINSBERGEN.

JAN VAN AMSTEL *class*.

JAN VAN BRAKEL.

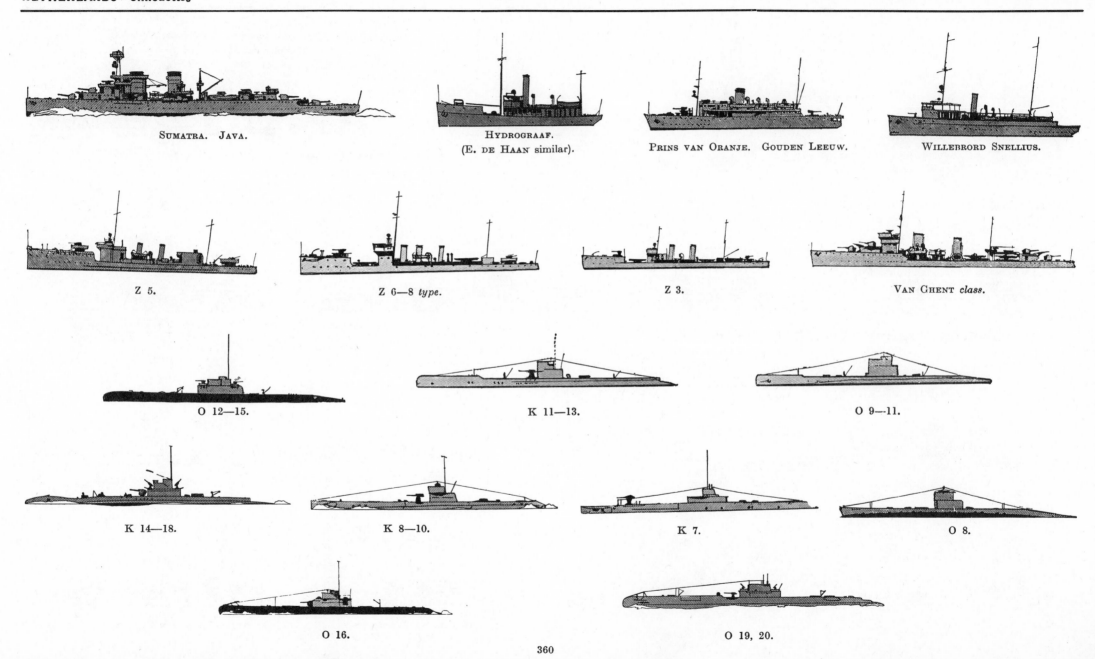

SUMATRA. JAVA.

HYDROGRAAF.
(E. DE HAAN similar).

PRINS VAN ORANJE. GOUDEN LEEUW.

WILLEBRORD SNELLIUS.

Z 5.

Z 6—8 type.

Z 3.

VAN GHENT class.

O 12—15.

K 11—13.

O 9—11.

K 14—18.

K 8—10.

K 7.

O 8.

O 16.

O 19, 20.

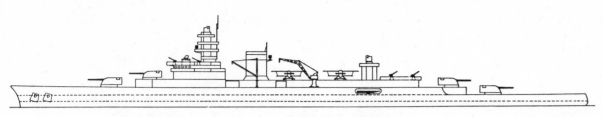

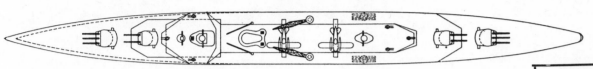

(Officially rated as Flotilla Leaders.)

TROMP (May 24, 1937), **HEEMSKERCK** (building.)

Displacement : 3,350 tons *standard* ; 4,215 tons *full load.*

Complement : 309.

Length, (*p.p.*) 426½ feet ; (*o.a.*) 433 feet. Beam, 40¾ feet. *Maximum* draught, 15 feet.

Guns : (Bofors)
6—5·9 inch, 50 cal.
8—40 mm. AA. (2 pdr.) (twin mounts)
4—12·7 mm. AA. (twin mounts)
4—D.C.T.

Torpedo Tubes :
6—21 inch (tripled).

Aircraft :
1, handled by derrick.

Armour :
2″–2½″ Vert. Side
1½″ Deck.

DE ZEVEN PROVINCIEN, KIJKDUIN.

Displacement : 8,350 tons.
Dimensions : 607 (*o.a.*) × 55¾ × — feet.
Guns : (Wilton-Fijenoord).
10—5·9 inch
14—40 mm. AA.
8—12·7 mm. AA.
Torpedo Tubes :
6—21 inch
Machinery : Parsons geared turbines. S.H.P. : 78,000 = 33 kts. Boilers : 6, of 3-drum type.

Aircraft : 2.
Catapults : 2.

Armour :
3″–4″ side
(Weight of armour is considerably greater than in *De Ruyter.*)

Notes.—Both ships ordered Feb., 1939, from Wilton-Fijenoord, and Rotterdam Dry Dock Co., respectively, for completion in 1941. Machinery of both supplied by K. M. de Schelde.

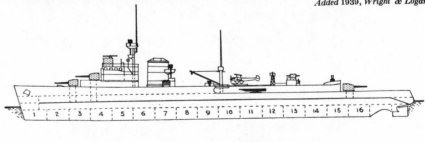

Added 1939, Wright & Logan

Machinery : Parsons geared turbines. 2 shafts. Designed H.P. : 56,000 = 33 kts. (34·5 on trials). Boilers : 4 Yarrow. Oil : 860 tons.

Notes.—*Tromp* authorised in 1931, and laid down 17 January, 1936, by Nederlandsche Scheepsbouw Mij., Amsterdam, having been designed by Directeur van Scheepsbouw 't Hooft. Machinery by Werkspoor. Much aluminium employed in internal construction. Cost 7,700,000 gulden. Was originally to have been a flotilla leader of 2,500 tons but design was expanded to present dimensions. She replaced *Hertog Hendrik* when completed in May, 1938. *Heemskerck* laid down Oct. 31, 1938 by same builders as replacement of former ship of that name.

Gunnery Notes—The 5.9 inch guns have 60° elevation and can be used as AA. weapons.

TROMP.

1938 *Werner Crone.*

DE RUYTER (Wilton-Fijenoord Co., Rotterdam, May 11, 1935).
Displacement : 6,450 tons *standard*, 7,548 tons *full load*.
Complement : 435.

Length : 551 (*p.p.*), 557¾ (*o.a.*) feet. Beam : 51¼ feet. Draught :
16½ feet (*mean*), 19¼ feet (*max.*).

Guns : (Wilton-Fijenoord)
7—5·9 inch, 50 cal.
10—40 mm.   AA. (twin mounts).
8—12·7 mm. AA. (twin mounts).
8—M.G.

Aircraft :
2, with catapult.

Armour :
2″—3″ side.
1¼″ deck.
1″ control positions.

1936, *W. Crone.*

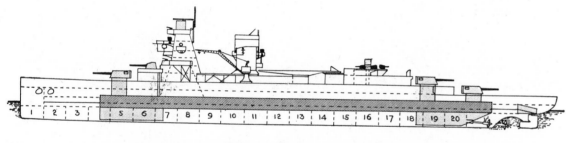

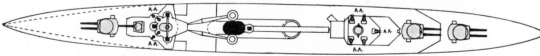

Machinery : 2 sets Parsons geared turbines. 2 shafts. S.H.P. : 66,000 = 32 kts. 6 Yarrow boilers,
working pressure 400 lbs. Oil : 1,000 tons. Radius of action : 5,000 miles at 12 kts.

1936, *W. Crone.*

General Notes.—This ship was laid down in November, 1933, completed in May, 1936, and placed in full commission
Oct. 4, 1936. A considerable amount of electric welding was used in her construction. Echo sounding gear and
loud speakers for transmitting orders are included in equipment.

Armour Notes.—Belt begins 85 feet from the bows and ends 65 feet from the stern, and is 13 feet wide.

Aircraft Note.—Carries two Fokker C. 11 W. type seaplanes, fitted with Wright Cyclone engines, on platform abaft funnel.

Gunnery Notes.—All the 5·9 inch guns elevate to 60° and can be used as anti-aircraft weapons.

Engineering Notes.—Under tropical conditions a speed of 33 knots has been realised, only a knot below the original
trial figure.

DE RUYTER.

1936, *courtesy Wilton-Fijenoord (Builders).*

362

JAVA (Aug. 6th, 1921) & SUMATRA (Dec. 29th, 1920).

Displacement, 6670 tons.
Complement, 287 + 238 natives = 525.
Length (o.a.), 509½ feet. Beam, 52½ feet. Max. draught, 18 feet.

Guns (Bofors) :
10—5·9 inch (50 cal.) "No. 6."
8—40 mm. AA. (Sumatra, 6).
4—2 pdr. saluting.
6—12.7 mm. AA.
Torpedo tubes :
None.
Mines : 12.
Searchlights : 6—47 inch.
Paravanes : 4.
Range Finders : 4.

Aircraft : 2.

Armour (Coventry) :
2"—3" Belt ....
Deck { 1" flat
{ 2" slopes
4" Gun shield faces
(much thinner at
sides and roof)
2" Funnel bases ...
5" Conning tower

JAVA.

1935, courtesy Ir. R. F. Scheltema.

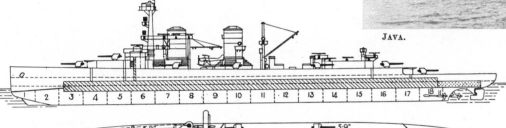

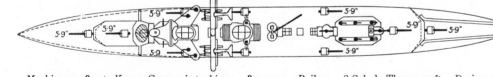

Machinery : 3 sets Krupp-Germania turbines. 3 screws. Boilers : 8 Schulz-Thornycroft. Designed H.P., 72,000 = 31 kts. Fuel, oil only : *normal*, 1000 tons ; *maximum*, 1200 tons. Radius of action : 4800 miles at 12 kts., 3600 miles at 15 kts.

JAVA.

1937, R. Perkins.

Name	Builder	Machinery	Laid down	Completed	Trials	Boilers	Best recent speed
Sumatra	Nederlandsche Scheepsbouw Maatschappij. Amsterdam	Krupp, Germania	July,'16	Nov. 1925	82,000 = 31.8	Schulz	30·3
Java	K. M. de Schelde, Flushing	Krupp, Germania*	May,'16	May 1925	73,000 = 31·5 (St. Abbs, 7/7/25)	Schulz	

* Contracted for, June, 1917.

General Notes.—The German design of these ships remains more evident than ever as the result of a big refit completed in 1935. Mainmast has been dwarfed to the stature of a derrick post and stepped in a fresh position, further forward, while a new tubular foremast, with director tower and searchlight platform, has been installed. Flag deck now extends along both sides of the fore funnel, 2 M.G. being mounted on each wing.

Of the two, the *Java* is decidedly the more successful ship As the outcome of recurring engine-room troubles, a fire in 1929 and a stranding in 1931, the *Sumatra* has spent a large proportion of her life in dockyard hands. But after last refit she exceeded 28 kts. with four-fifths power at full load displacement, under tropical conditions.

Gunnery Notes.—5·9 inch guns elevate to 25–30°. Electric hoists.

Armour Notes.—C.T. divided into gunnery control and navigation compartments. 3" belt is 392½ feet long. Towards stern and over steering gear, belt is narrower for a length of 42½ feet, and is only 2" thick.

SUMATRA.

1936.

1937, *Official.*

SOERABAJA, (*ex-De Zeven Provincien*) (March, 1909).

Displacement : 5,644 tons.   Complement : 180 + 300 cadets and boys.

Length (*o.a.*), 333 feet.   Beam, 56 feet.   *Maximum* draught, 20¼ feet.

Guns (Krupp):	Armour (Krupp) :
2—11 inch, 42½ cal.	6″ Belt (amidships)
2—3 inch, 55 cal. S.A. "No. 1."	4″ Belt (ends)
6—40 mm. A.A.	2″ Deck (on slopes)
6 machine.	9¾″ Main Barbettes (N.C.)
Torpedo tubes :	9¾″ Shields
None.	4″ Small Barbettes
	7¾″ Conning tower (N.C.)

Machinery : 2 sets triple expansion. 2 screws. Boilers : 3 Yarrow. Designed H.P. : 8,000 = 16 kts. (Trials : 8,516 = 16·3 kts.) (with 8 boilers). Fuel now oil only.

Notes.—Main belt is 7 feet wide. Laid down Feb., 1908 at Amsterdam D.Y. No longer included in active list. Renamed Oct. 21, 1936, and fitted out as a Training Ship. Stationed in E. Indies.

Gunnery Training Ships.

1939, *Werner Crone.*

VAN KINSBERGEN (January 5, 1939). *Standard* displacement : 1,760 tons (2,100 tons *full load*). Complement : 190. Dimensions : 338 (*o.a.*) × 38 × 11 feet.

Guns :	Armour :
4—4·7 inch.	To be given slight protection,
4—40 mm. AA. (twin mounts).	probably confined to armoured
4—12·7 mm. AA. (twin mounts).	deck and C.T.

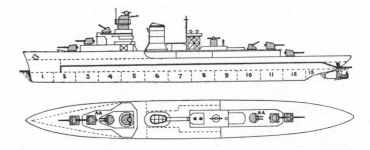

Machinery : Geared turbines by Gebr. Stork. S.H.P. : 16,000 = 25·5 kts. Boilers : 2 Yarrow

Note.—Ordered Nov. 1936 from Rotterdam Dry Dock Co. Relieved *Gelderland* when completed, in August, 1939.

Gunnery Training Ships—*continued.*

WITTE DE WITH. *Added 1935, W. Crone, Den Helder.*

4 *Yarrow* type; **Van Galen** (June 28, 1928), **Witte de With** (Sept. 11, 1928), both by Mij. Fijenoord. **Banckert** (1929), **Van Nes** (March 20, 1930), both by Burgerhouts. Displacement: 1,316 tons *standard*, 1,650 tons *full load*. Complement: 120. Dimensions: 307 (*pp.*), 322 (*o.a.*) × 31¼ × 10 feet (*max.* draught). Guns: 4—4·7 inch, 50 cal., 1—3 inch AA. 4—40 mm. AA., 4—12·7 mm. AA., 1 M.G., 4 D.C.T. Tubes: 6—21 inch (tripled). Machinery: Hochdruck geared turbines. 2 shafts. S.H.P.: 31,000 = 36 kts. Boilers: 3 Yarrow, 400 lbs. pressure. Oil: 330 tons.

GELDERLAND. *1932 Photo.*

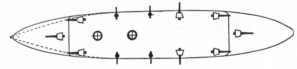

Gelderland (1898). 3,512 tons.
Guns: 8—4·7 inch, 4—3 inch.
2—37 mm., 7 M.G.
1—40 mm.

(Paid off into Reserve, 1939).

Reboilered 1934–35, and can make 16 kts.

EVERTSEN. *1935, Grand Studio, Malta.*

4 *Yarrow* type: **Van Ghent** (ex-*De Ruyter*) (Oct. 23, 1926), built by K. M. de Schelde, Flushing: **Evertsen** (Dec. 29, 1926), **Kortenaer** (June 30, 1927), **Piet Hein** (April 2, 1927), all three by Burgerhouts, Rotterdam. Displacement: 1,310 tons *standard*, 1,640 tons *full load*. Complement, 129. Dimensions: 307 (*p.p.*), 322 (*o.a.*) × 31¼ × 10½ feet *max.* draught. Guns: 4—4·7 inch, 50 cal., 2—3 inch AA., 4—12·7 mm. AA., 2 M.G., 4 D.C.T. 24 mines, with double laying gear. Tubes: 6—21 inch. Machinery: Parsons geared turbines. 2 shafts. S.H.P.: 31,000 = 36 kts. *light*, 34 kts in *loaded* condition. Boilers: Yarrow, 250 lbs. pressure. Oil: 300 tons. On trials, at 80 per cent of full load displacement, speeds of from 35 to 36 kts. were realised without difficulty.

Identification letters—VG - Van Galen.   EV—Evertsen.   KN—Kortenaer.   PH—Piet Hein.
GT—Van Ghent.   WW—Witte de With.   BK—Banckert.   VN—Van Nes.

Appearance Notes.—First four boats have S.L. abeam of fore funnel. Later ones have S.L. *en echelon* between funnels.

8 + 4 (*Building*) Destroyers (*Jagers*)

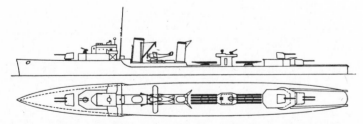

Gerard-Callenburgh, Tjerk Hiddes, Philips Van Almonde, Isaäc Sweers. Laid down 1938, two by K. M. de Schelde and two by Rotterdam Dry Dock Co. Displacement: 1,628 tons. Dimensions: 348¾ × 33¾ × 11½ feet. Guns: 5—4·7 inch, 8—40 mm. AA., 8—12·7 mm. AA., 3 D.C.T. Tubes: 8—21 inch (quadrupled). Fitted for minelaying. 1 Fokker seaplane carried. Machinery: Geared turbines by Werkspoor. 2 shafts. S.H.P.: 45,000 = 36 kts. Boilers: 3 Yarrow.

Notes.—Hulls are very largely welded. Completion expected in 1940.

12 + *32* **Torpedo Boats** (*Torpedobooten*).

(All the old T.B. are relegated to subsidiary duties in harbour, etc.)

1932 *Photo.*

3 boats, **Z8, Z7, Z6** (K. M. de Schelde and Fijenoord, 1915). 263 tons. Dimensions : 193 × 19⅔ × 5¼ feet. Guns : 2—3 inch, " No. 4," 2 Machine. Torpedo tubes: 4—17·7 inch (one twin and 2 single deck mountings). Designed H.P. : 5,000 to 5,500 = 27 kts. (made about 27·4 on trials). Machinery: Reciprocating. Boilers fitted to burn coal or oil. Carry 80 tons coal + 7 tons oil. Radius of action : 425 miles at 20 kts. Complement : 48. Completed 1916.

Z3 similar to above.

1933 *Photo.*

Z3 (Ned. Scheepsb, Mij., Amsterdam, 1916-17.). 277 tons. Dimensions : 201 × 20¼ × 6 feet. Guns : 2—3 inch, " No. 4," 2 machine. Torpedo tubes: 4—17·7 inch (one twin deck mounting + 2 single ditto). Designed S.H.P. 5500=27 kts. Curtis type turbines. Boilers fitted to burn coal or oil. Carry 72 tons coal + 9·4 tons oil. Radius of action : 425 miles at 20 kts. Compl. 48.

G13.   1919 *Photo, Fotopersbureau " Holland," Amsterdam.*

3 boats ('12-'14): **G 16, G 15** (Fijenoord Co., Rotterdam, 1914.) **G 13** (K. M. de Schelde, Flushing, 1913), 180 tons. Dimensions : 162·4 × 17 × 4·6 feet. Armaments : 2—3 inch, " No. 4," 3—17·7 inch deck tubes. Designed H.P. : 2,600 = 25 kts. (26 kts. on trials). Coal : 44 tons. Complement : 27.
G 13. used as Stokers' Training Ship. G 15. used as Tender.

Z5.   1932 *Photo.*

Z 5 (De Schelde, Vlissingen, 1913). 263 tons. Dimensions : 193 × 19·8 × 5·6 feet. Guns : 2—3 inch, 2 M.G. I.H.P. : 3,000 = 22 kts. Oil fuel : 100 tons. Complement : 34.

Notes.—Originally as *Z* 8. Refitted for patrol work 1932, with lengthened forecastle ; foremost boiler removed : additional bunker space. Is employed as a Tender.

Motor Type.

T.M. 51 (1939), by British Power Boat Co., Ltd. Wood. Displacement : 32 tons (37 tons *full load*). Dimensions : 70 (*o.a.*) × 20 × 4¼ feet. Armament : 2—20 mm. guns, 4—18 inch tubes, 6 D.C. Machinery : 3 Rolls-Royce Merlin petrol engines. H.P. : 3,000 = 42·5 kts. Complement : 9.
19 more of this type are being built by Werf Gusto, Schiedam.
T.M. 3 (Soerabaja, 1937-38) and 11 more, building. Steel. Displacement : 15 tons. Dimensions : 61 × 12¾ × 4 feet. Armament : 4 M.G., 2—18 inch tubes, and D.C. Machinery : 3 petrol engines. H.P. : 1,260 = 38 kts. Complement : 6.

21 + 9 (building) Submarines

Notes.—Formerly " *O* " numbers were for Home Service ; " *K* " numbers for East Indies, but this distinction no longer holds good. Displacements given are *standard*. All are double-hull design except *K 7*.

7 boats : **O 21, O 22** (both by K. M. de Schelde), **O 23, O 24** (both by Rotterdam Dry Dock Co.), **O 25** (by Wilton-Fijenoord), **O 26, O 27** (both by Rotterdam Dry Dock Co.). All laid down during 1937–38, for completion in 1940. Displacement : 888/1,380 tons. Complement : 38. Dimensions : 255 × 21½ × 13 feet. Armament : 1—3·5 inch gun, 2—40 mm. AA., 1—12·7 mm. AA., 8—21 inch tubes. 2 Sulzer Diesels, by K. M. de Schelde. B.H.P. : 5,200 = 19·5 kts. Submerged B.H.P. : 1,000 = 9 kts. All were originally to have been given " K " numbers. To be completed 1940–41.

O 19.   1939, *Werner Crone.*

2 *Minelaying* type: **O 19** (ex-*K* 19), (Sept. 22, 1938), **O 20** (ex-*K*20), (Jan. 31, 1939). Laid down in 1936 by Wilton-Fijenoord at Schiedam. Displacement : 967/1,468 tons. Complement : 38. Dimensions : 264¾ × 23¼ × 12¾ feet. Armament : 1—3·5 inch gun, 2—40 mm. AA., 1—12·7 mm. AA., 8—21 inch tubes, 40 mines. 2 Sulzer Diesels by K. M. de Schelde. B.H.P. : 5,000 = 20 kts. *surface.* *Submerged* B.H.P. : 1,000 = 9 kts. Due for completion in 1938.

1937, *courtesy Ir. R. F. Scheltema.*

1 boat : **O 16** (Kon. Mij. de Schelde, Jan. 27, 1936). Displacement : 896/1,200 tons. Dimensions : 254½ × 21½ × 13 feet. Guns : 1—3·5 inch, 2—40 mm. AA. Tubes : 8—21 inch (4 bow, 2 stern, 2 deck). 2 M.A.N. Diesels. H.P. 3,200/860 = 18/9 kts. Complement, 38.

O 12.   1932 *Photo, Chef. Kreuger.*

3 boats : **O 12,** (1930), **O 13,** (Nov. 8, 1930), **O 14** (1931). All by K. M. de Schelde. Ordered 1927–28. Displacement : 546/704 tons. Dimensions : 198¼ (*o.a.*) × 17¾ × 11¾ feet. 2 Sulzer Diesels. H.P. : 1,800/600 = 15/8 kts. (Trials gave 16 kts. *surface* easily.) Armament : 5—21 inch tubes (4 bow, 1 stern), 2—40 mm. AA. guns, mounted in watertight tube in C.T. Radius : 3,500 miles at 10 kts. *on surface ;* 26 miles at 8 kts. *submerged.* Complement : 31.

1 boat : **O 15** (Fijenoord, 1931). (Ordered 1929). Similar to above, but M.A.N. Diesels.

Note.—O 12 and O 14 made the passage from the Netherlands to the East Indies in 1937 with only one port of call.

K 17.   1933 *Photo.*

3 boats : **K 14** (July, 1932), **K 15** (Dec., 1932), **K 16** (April, 1933). Ordered 1929–30, Rotterdam Dry Dock Co.

2 boats : **K 17** (July, 1932), **K 18** (Sept., 1932). Ordered 1929–30, M. Fijenoord.

Displacement : 771/1,008 tons (first 3) ; 782/1,024 tons (last 2). Dimensions of all : 242¼ (*o.a.*) × 25 × 12⅝ feet. H.P. 3,200/1,000 = 17/9 kts. Armament : 8—21 inch tubes (4 bow, 2 stern, 2 deck), 14 Torpedoes carried, 1—3·5 inch gun, 2—40 mm. AA. Radius : 3,500 miles at 11 kts., 26 miles at 8·5 kts. Complement : 38. Diving limit : 44 fms.

Note.—On Trials these boats made 19 kts. K 18 accomplished a record passage for an unescorted submarine, from the Netherlands to the East Indies via South America and Western Australia, a distance of 23,000 miles. She proved herself an excellent sea-boat.

O 9.

1926 *Photo, Ir. R. F. Scheltema.*

K 10.

1926 *Photo, Ir. R. F. Scheltema.*

O 11.

1926 *Photo, by courtesy of Chief of Staff, The Hague.*

3 *Navy* (Home Service) type : **O 11** (M. Fijenoord, 19th March, 1925), **O 10** (Nederlandsche Scheepsbouw, 30th July, 1925), **O 9** (K. M. de Schelde, 1925). Displacement : 483 tons *on surface*, 647 tons *submerged*. Dimensions : 179¼ (*o.a.*) × 17¼ × 11⅜ feet. Engines : 2 sets Sulzer Diesels, total H.P. 900 = 12 kts. *on surface.* Submerged speed : 8 kts. Armament : 1—3·5 inch, 1 M.G., and 5 torpedo tubes (2—21 inch and 2—17·7 inch in bow ; 1—17·7 inch in stern). 10 torpedoes carried. Provided for under 1917 Programme. Complement, 29. Diving limit, 33 fathoms.

1925 *Official Photo, by courtesy of Chief of Naval Staff, The Hague.*

3 *Navy* type : **K 13** (Dec., 1924), **K 12** (Nov., 1924), **K 11** (April, 1924), all by M. Fijenoord, Rotterdam. Displacement : 611 tons *on surface*, 815 tons *submerged*. Dimensions : 218¾ (*o.a.*) × 19 × 12½ feet. Engines : 2 sets, M.A.N. Diesels, each 1,200 B.H.P. = 15 kts. *surface* speed (17 kts. reached on trials.) *Submerged* speed : 8 kts. Armament : 1—3·5 inch, 1—12·7 mm., 2—21 and 4—17·7 inch tubes (2 of each calibre in bow, 2—17·7 inch in stern). 12 Torpedoes carried. Complement, 31. Provided for under 1918 Naval Programme. Diving limit 33 fathoms.

Note.— K 13 completed the voyage from Amsterdam to Soerabaja, via the Panama Canal, unescorted, without mishap. Period occupied was from May 27 to Dec. 12, 1926.

K 8, 9, 10.

1925 *Photo, by favour Ir. R. F. Scheltema.*

3 *Electric Boat Co.* design : **K 10** (May, 1922), **K 9** (1922), and **K 8** (1922) all by K. M. de Schelde. Displacements : 521 tons on *surface*, 712 tons *submerged*. Dimensions : 210¼ (*o.a.*) × 17¾ × 11⅜ feet. Armament : 1—3·5 inch, AA., 1—12·7 mm. AA., 4—17·7 inch tubes (2 bow, 2 stern). Machinery : K 8 has two sets of M.A.N. Diesels, H.P. : 1,800, while K 9 and K 10 have 2 Schelde-Sulzer type, H.P. : 1,500, for a *surface* speed of 15 kts. (16 reached on trials.) Electric motors B.H.P. : 630 = 9·5 kts., *submerged* speed. Endurance about 3,500 miles at 11 kts. on *surface*, 26 miles at 8·5 kts., *submerged*. Complement : 31. Diving limit, 22 fathoms.

K 5 (of same type, now scrapped).   1921 *Photo by courtesy of the Chief of Naval Staff, Batavia.*

1 *Hay-Denny* type: **K 7** (Mar. 8, 1920), (M. Fijenoord, Rotterdam). Displacement: 507/639 tons. Dimensions: 177 (*p.p.*), 188 (*o.a.*) × 16½ × 12½ feet. Machinery: 2 sets Sulzer Diesels. H.P.: 1,200 = 13·5 kts. *surface.* *Submerged* speed: 8 kts. Guns: 1—3 inch, 1—12·7 mm. AA. Tubes: **6**—17·7 inch (2 bow, 2 stern, 2½ deck). Begun 1916, completed 1922. Diving limit: 22 fathoms.

O 8. (Now has C.T. screen).   1918 *Photo, Fotopersbureau "Holland."*

1 *Holland* type: **O 8** (ex-British submarine *H 6*), built by Canadian Vickers Co., Montreal, 1915, wrecked on Schiermonnikoog Island, Jan., 1916, salved Feb., 1916, interned at Nieuwediep, and subsequently purchased by Dutch Government. Displacements: 343 tons on *surface*, 433 tons *submerged*. Dimensions: 146½ (*p.p.*), 151½ (*o.a.*) × 15⅓ × 12¾ feet. Armament: 4—18 inch tubes (all bow). Guns: 1—37 mm., 1 M.G. Machinery: 8 cyl. Nelseco* Diesels H.P. 480 = 11·5 kts. on *surface; submerged* speed 8 kts. Fuel: 16 tons oil carried. Complement, 26.

*"Nelseco" is trade mark for engines manufactured by the New London Ship & Engine Co., Groton, Conn., U.S.A. Their engines are the German M.A.N. (Nuremberg) type built under licence.

Armoured Gunboats (*Kanonneerbooten*).

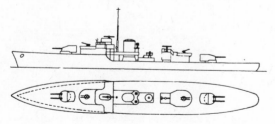

7 Gunboats are to be built, three of which were ordered in 1938 (2 from Smit, Rotterdam, 1 from Gusto, Schiedam). Displacement: 1,268 tons. Dimensions: 255½ × 33½ × 9⅝ feet. Guns: 4—4·7 inch, 4—40 mm. AA., 4—12·7 mm. AA., 2 D.C.T. Machinery: Burmeister & Wain Diesels by P. Smit Jr. B.H.P.: 3,500 = 18 kts.

Note.—These vessels will be exceptionally well protected for their size. The fourth vessel of this type will be laid down in 1940.

BRINIO. (*Friso* similar, but has thinner and taller funnel.)   1934 *Photo.*

GRUNO   1934 *Photo.*

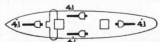

BRINIO (1912), **FRISO** (1912), **GRUNO** (1913). All built by Amsterdam D.Y. 540 tons. Complement: 52. Dimensions: 172¼ (*o.a.*) × 28 × 9¼ feet *max.* draught. Armament: 4— 4·1 inch semi-automatic, 1—12·7 mm. AA., 2 M.G. Armour: 2″ belt, ⅔″ deck, 2″ conning tower. Machinery: 2 sets Diesel engines. (All were re-engined, 1934–35, with Sulzer Diesels in *Brinio* and *Gruno*, M.A.N. in *Friso*). B.H.P.: 1,500 = 14 kts. Oil: 34 tons. Complement: 63. These vessels are intended to guard mine fields.

Escort Vessels (Classed as *Kanonneerbooten*).

Mine Layers (*Mijnenleggers*).

(Serving in W. Indies.)   1939, *courtesy W. H. Davis, Esq.*

JOHAN MAURITS VAN NASSAU (Aug. 20, 1932). Built at Flushing. Displacement: 1,520 tons. Dimensions: 258 × 38 × 12·3 feet. Guns: 3—5·9 inch, 2—40 mm. AA., 4—12·7 mm. AA., 4 M.G. H.P.: 2,100 = 15 kts. Oil: 273 tons. Complement: 124.

Note.—Has electrically welded armoured deck and ordinary balanced rudder, but otherwise is merely an enlarged edition of *Flores* type, below.

1939, *Ben G. Kool, Den Helder.*

WILLEM VAN DER ZAAN (Dec. 15, 1938). Laid down 1937 by Netherland Dry Dock Co. *Standard* displacement: 1,300 tons. Complement: 92 as minelayer, 130 as training ship. Dimensions: 229⅔ (*pp.*), 247 (*o.a.*) × 36¼ × 11 feet. Guns: 2—4·7 inch, 50 cal., 4—40 mm. AA. (twin mounts), 4—12·7 mm. AA. (twin mounts). (120 mines). Machinery: 2 sets triple expansion. H.P.: 2,200 = 15·5 kts. Boilers: 2 Yarrow. During peace time is employed as Seagoing Training Ship for Cadets and Midshipmen. Equipment includes a seaplane and derrick.

One minelayer (N. V. Boele's Scheepwerven, Bolnes, June 24, 1939). Displacement: 555 tons. Dimensions: 163 × 28½ × 11 feet. Machinery: Diesel. B.H.P.: 1,150 = 14 kts.

1929 *Photo, by courtesy of Chief of Naval Staff.*

KRAKATAU (Soerabaja D.Y., 1924). Displacement, 982 tons. Dimensions: 213 × 34½ × 10½ feet. Guns: 2—3 inch AA., 4 M.G. H.P.: 2,500 = 15·5 kts. Complement: 91. Reconstructed 1928, after funnel being removed. Foundered in 1932 through stern mine ports being left open while steaming at full speed in shallow water. Salved and refitted same year.

SOEMBA.   1926 *Photo, by courtesy of Chief of Naval Staff.*

FLORES (15th Aug., 1925), **SOEMBA** (24th Aug., 1925). Built at Rotterdam by M. Fijenoord and Wiltons, respectively. Displacement: 1457 tons. Dimensions: 248 × 37½ × 11¾ feet. Guns: 3—5·9 inch, 1—3 inch AA., 4—12·7 mm., AA., 4 M.G. Machinery: 2 sets triple expansion, H.P. 2000 = 15 kts. 4 Yarrow boilers. Oil: 285 tons. Complement, 132.

Note.—These Vessels have a 1″ armoured deck and C.T. They are fitted with Flettner rudders, and have accommodation for a seaplane.

PRINS VAN ORANJE.   1932 *Photo.*

PRINS VAN ORANJE (Aug., 1931), **GOUDEN LEEUW** (Sept., 1931). Both built by N. V. Scheepsbouw Mij. De Maas, Slikkerveer. Displacement: 1,291 tons. Dimensions: 216 × 36 × 11 feet. Guns: 2—3 inch AA., 2—40 mm. AA., 2—12·7 mm. AA., 2 M.G. H.P.: 1,750 = 15 kts. Complement: 121.

PRO PATRIA.   1926 *Photo, by courtesy of Chief of Naval Staff.*

PRO PATRIA (Soerabaja D.Y., July 21, 1922). Displacement, 537 tons. Dimensions: 154 × 28¼ × 9¼ feet. Guns: 1—3 inch A.A., 2 M.G. H.P.: 650 = 10 kts. Complement: 61. (Serving at present as depot ship for torpedo craft.)

Mine Layers—continued.

VAN MEERLANT. 1926 *Photo, by courtesy of Chief of Naval Staff.*

DOUWE AUKES. 1933 *Photo.*

VAN MEERLANT (Nov. 24th, 1920), **DOUWE AUKES** (Feb. 23rd, 1922). First built under 1917 Naval Programme and the second under 1918 Naval Programme, by Werf Gusto, Schiedam. **687 tons.** Dimensions : $180\frac{1}{2} \times 28\frac{1}{2} \times 10\frac{1}{2}$ feet. Guns : 3—3 inch AA., 2—12·7 inch AA., 2 M.G. Twin screws. Engines : 2 sets triple exp. surface condensation. I.H.P. 1000 = 13 kts. Coal : 115 tons. Complement, 60.

Of the same type as *Hydra* and *Medusa* (see next column), but faster. 2 steam winches for handling mines and double laying gears.

Mine Layers—continued.

1918 *Photo, Fotopersbureau " Holland."*

HYDRA (1911) & **MEDUSA** (1911). Both built at Amsterdam D.Y. 593 tons. Complement, 53. Dimensions: $163 \times 29\frac{1}{2} \times 9$ feet. Guns : 2—3 inch AA., 1—3 inch S.A., 2—12·7 mm. AA., 1 M.G. Designed H.P. : 800 = 12 kts. Coal : 72 tons. Radius of action : 1,440 miles at 6 kts.

Note.—*Hydra* sank off the " Wielingen " Light Ship by collision with T.B. *Z 3*, Feb., 1921 ; salved April, 1921 and again in service.

SERDANG (1897), 680 tons. About $173\frac{1}{4} \times 31\frac{1}{4} \times 12$ feet average. Armament : 2—1 pdr., 4 M.G. H.P. : 1,290 = 13 kts. Coal : 150 tons. Complement : 97 (55 Europeans, 42 natives). Double minelaying gear fitted. Serves as seagoing tender to Torpedo School.

Mine Sweepers.

6 to be built. Displacement : 383 tons. Complement : 49. Dimensions : $210 \times 22\frac{1}{2} \times 6\frac{1}{4}$ feet. Guns : 4—40 mm. AA. **60** D.C. carried. Machinery : Parsons geared turbines. S.H.P. : 5,500 = 24 kts.

A. VAN DER HULST. 1938, *Ir. R. F. Scheltema.*

JAN VAN AMSTEL (Aug. 27, 1936), **PIETER DE BITTER** (Oct. 29, 1936), both by Smit, Rotterdam ; **ABRAHAM CRIJNSSEN** (Sept. 22, 1936), **ELAND DUBOIS** (Oct. 24, 1936), both by Werf Gusto, Schiedam ; **PIETER FLORISZ** (May 11, 1937), by Smit ; **JAN VAN GELDER** (April 17, 1937), **ABRAHAM VAN DER HULST** (May 27, 1937), both by Werf Gusto. 4 more of this type were ordered from Smit in 1939. Displacement : 525 tons. Complement : 46. Dimensions : $183 \times 25\frac{1}{2} \times 7$ feet. Guns : 1—3 inch 55 cal. in first 4, 40 cal. in others, 4—12·7 mm. AA., 1 M.G. H.P. : 1,690 = 15 kts. Oil fuel : 110 tons. Are also equipped for mine laying.

Notes.—All reached 16 kts. on trials. Are lettered on side with 2 initials of each surname A to H. *William van Ewijck*, of this class, lost through striking a mine off Terschelling, Sept. 8, 1939.

1934 *Photo.*

A, B, C, D. (Willemsoord D.Y., Den Helder, 1929–30). Displacement : 179 tons. Dimensions : $140\frac{1}{2} \times 19\frac{3}{4} \times 5$ feet. **2** M.G. H.P. : 700 = 14·5 kts. Oil : 40 tons. Complement : 30.

Mine Sweepers—*continued*.

1934 *Photo*.

M 1 (Van der Kuyk en Ree, Rotterdam), 238 tons. **M 2** (Koopman, Dordrecht), 205 tons. **M 3, 4** (v.d. Schuyt, Papendrecht), both 230 tons. Completed and taken over in 1916. Steel. Dimensions : 92 × 20½ × 10 feet. Speed : 10 kts. Guns : 1 machine. Complement : 16.

Submarine Depot and Repair Ship.

CORNELIS DREBBEL (1915). 668 tons. Dimensions : 166·8 × 32·8 × 6·8 feet. Guns : 1—1 pdr. Diesel engines. 3 shafts. B.H.P. : 170 = 6 kts. Oil fuel : 71 tons. Complement : 73. Built by Werf Conrad, Haarlem.

Fishery Protection Vessels.

1938.

JAN VAN BRAKEL (K. M. de Schelde, Feb. 8, 1936). Displacement : 740 tons, *standard*, (*full load* 955 tons). Dimensions : 181½ × 30 × 10 feet *mean*, 13 feet *max*. Guns : 2—3 inch, 1—37 mm., 4—12·7 mm. AA. Fitted for minelaying. Machinery : Triple expansion. 2 shafts. H.P. : 1,600 = 15 kts. 2 Yarrow boilers. Oil fuel. Complement : 65.

1930 *Photo, by courtesy of Ministry of Defence.*

NAUTILUS (Oct. 30th, 1929). Built by Rotterdam Dry Dock Co. Displacement : 800 tons. Dimensions : 180½ (*p.p.*), 191½ (*o.a.*) × 31 × 11½ feet. Guns : 2—3 inch, 1—37 mm., 2—40 mm. AA. H.P. : 1,350 = 14 kts. Oil : 138 tons. Complement : 50. (This vessel is used on Fishery Protection duties. She is fitted to carry mines. 3 inch guns not mounted at present.)

River Gunboats. (*Rivierkanonneerbooten*)

(Mostly employed as Harbour Tenders, or for Training purposes. Reported several have been rearmed with 1—3 inch and 2—12·7 mm. AA.).

HEFRING. 1921 *Photo, Ir. R. F. Scheltema.*

BRAGA, HEFRING, TYR, FREIJR Are old iron twin-screw Gunboats, built 1876–79. 240 tons. Complement : 34–30. Dimensions : 91·5 to 91·8 (*o.a.*) × 26·9 × 7·8 to 8·1 feet (*max.* draught). Guns : In *Braga*, *Hefring*, 1—4·7 inch, 2—1 pdr., 1 machine. In *Freijr*, 1—3 inch, 2—12·7 mm. AA. In *Tyr*, 3—1 pdrs., 1 M.G. H.P. : 100 to 170 = 7 to 8 kts. Coal : 30 tons.

1920 *Photo, Ir. R. F. Scheltema.*

BALDER (1878), **THOR** (1877), **VIDAR, BULGIA** and **HADDA** (1879), ex-gunboats of 223–244 tons. Complement, 34–36. Guns : 2—4 pdr. in *Balder, Hadda*, 2—1 pdr. in *Vidar* and *Thor* ; 1 M.G. in all four. Speed : 7 kts. Coal : 30 tons. Double mine laying gears in all.

Salvage Vessel.

CASTOR (Soerabaja, 1915). Displacement : 670 tons. Complement : 43. Dimensions : 163 × 32¾ × 10 feet. Machinery : Diesel. B.H.P. : 500 = 8·5 kts. (Was formerly a Lighthouse Tender).

Surveying Vessels.

1939, courtesy F. W. Endert, Esq.

WILLEBRORD SNELLIUS (Fijenoord Co., Aug. 14th, 1928.) Displacement: 930 tons. Dimensions: 190 (p.p.). 203½ (o.a.) × 31¾ × 11¼ feet. H.P. 525 = 10·5 kts. Oil 190 tons. Guns: 1—3 inch, 2—1 pdrs., 2 M.G. Complement: 85.

Eilerts de Haan.

1932 Photo, Chef Kreuger.

EILERTS DE HAAN (25th June, 1919). Fijenoord Co. Rotterdam. 312 tons. Dimensions: 147·3 × 21·9 × 7 feet. No guns. Designed H.P. 600 = 12 kts. Coal: 44 tons. Complement, 18. Begun under 1915 Naval Programme. Completed May, 1921.

Surveying Vessels—*continued.*

1936

TYDEMAN (Soerabaja D.Y., 1916). 1,160 tons. Dimensions: 226·4 × 32·8 × 11·8 feet. Guns: 1—3 inch, 2—1 pdrs., 2 M.G. Diesels. H.P.: 700 = 10 kts. 2 screws. Oil: 194 tons. Complement: 104.

HYDROGRAAF (1911). 300 tons. Dimensions: 132·7 × 21·9 × 9·6 feet. Guns: none. I.H.P. 360 = 9 kts. Coal: 30 tons. Complement, 18. (Similar in appearance to above).

Fleet Supply Ship.

1939, courtesy F. W. Endert, Esq.

ZUIDERKRUIS (1923). 2,660 tons. Dimensions: 256 × 36¾ × 14¼ feet. Machinery: Triple expansion. 2 shafts. I.H.P.: 1,600 = 12·5 kts. Complement: 97. (Was formerly a cable ship attached to Gouvernementsmarine.)

Oiler.

1 building at Wimpen. Displacement: 6,900 tons. Dimensions: 410 × 53 × 24 feet. Guns: 2—4·7 inch, 2—40 mm. AA. Machinery: Werkspoor Diesel. B.H.P.: 7,000 = 16·5 kts.

Sail Training Ship.

1938.

URANIA. Schooner used for training of cadets in seamanship.

Tenders.

1939, Ir. R. F. Scheltema.

(*Rated as Torpedo Transport*)

MERCUUR (Feb. 26, 1936). Displacement: 265 tons *standard*, 284 tons *full load*. Dimensions: 137½ (p.p.), 140 (o.a.) × 23 × 9 feet No guns. H.P. 325 = 12 kts.

MOK I (Den Helder, 1939). Displacement: 177 tons. Dimensions: 114 × 20½ × — feet. Machinery: 2 Diesels. B.H.P.: 400 = 12 kts. (Communication tender.)

MOK II (1939). Displacement: 83 tons. Dimensions: 88½ × 16½ × — feet. Machinery: 1 Diesel with Voith-Schneider propeller. B.H.P.: 230 = 11 kts. (Communication tender).

D I (Den Helder, 1939). Displacement: 49 tons. Dimensions: 72 × 14½ × — feet. Machinery: 2 Kromhout-Gardner Diesels. B.H.P.: 120 = 10 kts. (Diving tender). There is also a Torpedo Recovery Tender (British Power Boat Co., 1938), of 6 tons, 37½ feet long, with two petrol motors, H.P. 400 = 34 kts.

Vessels in Netherland East Indies.

1. The following ships of the Royal Netherland Navy are stationed in East Indies : *De Ruyter, Java, Tromp,* 8 destroyers; *K7* to *K18; O16, O19, O20; TM3* and others of this type; *Flores, Soemba, Krakatau, Pro Patria, Serdang, Prins van Oranje, Gouden Leeuw;* Minesweepers *A, B, C, D, Jan van Amstel, Pieter de Bitter, Abraham Crijnssen, Eland Dubois; Snellius, Tydeman, Soerabaja, Zuiderkruis, Castor.*
2. To the Naval Department in the East Indies is also attached the "Gouvernementsmarine," a civil force, which is the property of the East Indies Government, and in peace time is used for Customs and Police Duties, &c. Most vessels mount one or two 3 inch guns. The personnel is enlisted in the Naval Reserve and the ships are destined for auxiliary duties with the fleet in time of war.

New Construction

4 Patrol Vessels laid down at Soerabaja, 1939. Displacement : 328 tons. Dimensions : $205 \times 20 \times 6\frac{1}{2}$ feet. Guns : **1—**3 inch, **4—**40 mm. AA. Machinery : Diesel. B.H.P. : 5,000 = 24 kts.

(2 more of above type and 2 others of another design are projected.)

Photo wanted.

FAZANT, REIGER (Soerabaja, 1930–31). Displacement : 624 tons. Complement : 40. Dimensions : $156\frac{3}{4} \times 27\frac{1}{2} \times 9\frac{1}{4}$ feet. I.H.P. : 525 = 12 kts.

MEREL (Soerabaja, 1927). Similar to above, but 592 tons and $152\frac{1}{4}$ feet in length.

Height of masts is being reduced.   1937, W. Crone.
(Fitted for minelaying).

RIGEL (Nederlandsche Dok Mij, 1929). Displacement : 1,631 tons. Dimensions : $221\frac{1}{2}$ (*pp.*), $242\frac{3}{4}$ (*o.a.*) $\times 36\frac{1}{4} \times 10$ feet. Guns : 2—3 inch, 2—12·7 mm. AA. Machinery : Triple expansion. H.P. : 1,400 = 12·5 kts. Complement : 63. Specially fitted for use of the Governor-General of East Indies.

*Note.—*Another vessel of similar type to *Rigel* is to be laid down in 1939.

AROE.   1939, *courtesy F. W. Endert, Esq.*

AROE, BANTAM, BOEROE, BOGOR, CERAM, CHERIBON, DIGOEL (1937). Displacement : 200 tons. Dimensions : $104 \times 18 \times 8\frac{1}{2}$ feet. Machinery : Diesel. B.H.P. : 350 = 12 kts.

AREND.   1933 *Photo.*

AREND (May 21, 1929), **VALK** (Oct. 19, 1929). Both built by Fijenoord Co. for fishery protection duties in East Indies. Displacement : 1,011 tons. Dimensions : $229\frac{2}{3}$ *p.p.*, 236 *o.a.* $\times 29\frac{1}{2} \times 9\frac{1}{4}$ feet. H.P. : 3,350 = 18 kts. Guns : 2—3 inch., 2 M.G. Complement : 61. Equipment includes a seaplane (not carried in peace time).

*Note.—*Meaning of these names is " Eagle " and " Falcon."

1939, *courtesy F. W. Endert, Esq.*

SIRIUS, WEGA (Gorinchem, 1922). Displacement : 1,015 tons. Complement : 50. Dimensions : $182\frac{1}{2} \times 31 \times 10\frac{3}{4}$ feet. I.H.P. : 900 = 12·8 kts. (trials).

(*Of similar type.*)
FOMALHOUT (Soerabaja, 1923). Displacement : 1,000 tons. Complement : 55. Dimensions : $186 \times 31 \times 11$ feet. I.H.P. : 855 = 13·4 kts. (trials).

GEMMA.   *Official Photo, added* 1934.

GEMMA (A. F. Smulders, Schiedam, 1918). Displacement : 845 tons. Dimensions : $175 \times 29\frac{1}{2} \times 10\frac{1}{2}$ feet. I.H.P. : 800 = 12 kts. Complement : 44.

ERIDANUS (Soerabaja, 1919). Displacement : 996 tons. Dimensions : $185\frac{1}{3} \times 29\frac{1}{2} \times 11\frac{1}{2}$ feet. Otherwise as *Gemma.*

ALBATROS. *Official Photo, added 1934.*

ALBATROS (1912). Built at Vlissingen. Displacement: 892 tons. Dimensions: $164 \times 31 \times 10\frac{3}{4}$ feet. I.H.P.: 1,140 = 12·4 kts. Complement: 47.

Lighthouse Service.

POOLSTER (Tanjong Priok, Feb. 3, 1939). Displacement: 1,600 tons. Dimensions: 216 (*w.l.*), 245 (*o.a.*) × $39\frac{1}{4}$ × 10 feet. Machinery: Diesel. B.H.P.: 1,250 = 12 kts.

ZEEMAN *Official Photo, added 1934.*

HOOFDINSPECTEUR ZEEMAN (Amsterdam, 1909). Displacement: 780 tons. Dimensions: 164 (pp.) × $30\frac{1}{4}$ × $10\frac{1}{2}$ feet. I.H.P.: 860 = 11 kts. Complement: 43.

DENEB. *Official Photo, added 1931.*

CANOPUS. *Official Photo, added 1934.*

DENEB (1915). **CANOPUS** (1914).

BELLATRIX (1914).

Displacement: 773 tons. Dimensions: $175 \times 29\frac{1}{2} \times 10$ feet. I.H.P.: 800 = 12·3 kts. Complement: 45. All built at Rijks-Marinewerf, Amsterdam.

ALDEBARAN (1913). Displacement: 892 tons. Dimensions: $175 \times 27 \times 11\frac{1}{2}$ feet. Otherwise as above three. Built at Soerabaja.

ORION (Soerabaja, 1912). Displacement: 1,062 tons. Complement: 71. Dimensions: $183\frac{1}{2} \times 29\frac{1}{2} \times 12$ feet. I.H.P.: 1,380 = 14 kts.

POLLUX. 1939, *courtesy F. W. Endert, Esq.*

POLLUX (Amsterdam, 1922). Displacement: 946 tons. Complement: 48. Dimensions: $182\frac{1}{2} \times 31\frac{1}{4} \times 10\frac{1}{4}$ feet. I.H.P.: 550 = 12 kts.

NICARAGUA

NICARAGUA — ENSIGN.

Patrol Boat.

For appearance, vide photo of this type in the U.S. Coast Guard section.

Ex-**C.G. 274** (1924). Purchased from U.S. Coast Guard, 1938. Wood. Displacement: 37 tons. Dimensions: $75 \times 13\frac{3}{4} \times 4$ feet. Guns: 1—1 pdr. Machinery: Petrol engine. B.H.P.: 400 = 13·5 kts.

NORWAY.

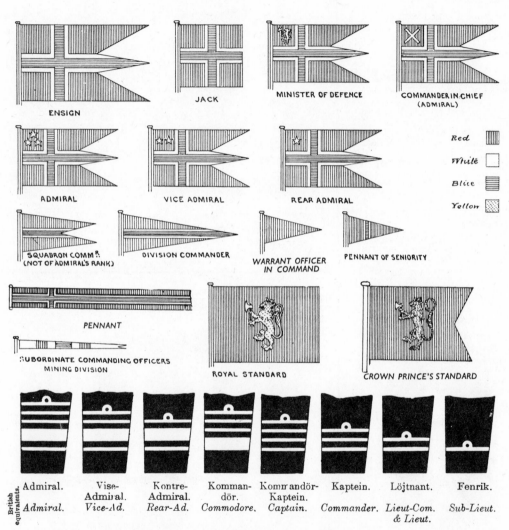

ENSIGN

JACK

MINISTER OF DEFENCE

COMMANDER IN CHIEF (ADMIRAL)

ADMIRAL

VICE ADMIRAL

REAR ADMIRAL

Red

White

Blue

Yellow

SQUADRON COMMᴿ (NOT OF ADMIRAL'S RANK)

DIVISION COMMANDER

WARRANT OFFICER IN COMMAND

PENNANT OF SENIORITY

PENNANT

SUBORDINATE COMMANDING OFFICERS MINING DIVISION

ROYAL STANDARD

CROWN PRINCE'S STANDARD

| British equivalents. | Admiral. *Admiral.* | Vise-Admiral. *Vice-Ad.* | Kontre-Admiral. *Rear-Ad.* | Komman-dör. *Commodore.* | Kommandör-Kaptein. *Captain.* | Kaptein. *Commander.* | Löjtnant. *Lieut-Com. & Lieut.* | Fenrik. *Sub-Lieut.* |

In relative rank Doctors have the same *without curl*, and a *red* passe poil above upper stripe.
   ,,   ,,   Paymasters ,,   ,,   ,,   ,, *blue* ,,   ,,   ,,
   ,,   ,,   Warrant Officers ,,   ,, and with various branch marks above upper stripe.

Modern Guns (Armstrong and Bofors). (Details officially revised 1930.)

Nota-tion.	Designation		Length in calibres	Model. *	Weight of Gun.	Weight of A.P. shot.	Initial velocity	Max. penetration firing A P. capped at K.C.		Danger Space against average warship, at			Nom. Rounds per minute.
								5000 yards.	3000 yards.	10,000 yards	5000 yards.	3000 yards.	
MEDIUM.	c/m. 20·9	inches. 8·2	44	A	tons. 18½	lbs. 309	ft. secs. 2300	6½	9¼	100	405	594	4
	14·91	5·9	46	A	7	100	2625	3	4½	67	215	440	8
	12	4·7	44	B	2½	46	2625	...	...	...	...	...	10
	12	4·7	44	A	2¾	44	2570	...	...	...	...	...	10
LIGHT.	10·16	4	40	B	2	32	2545						20
	7·6	3	50	B	1	12	2820	...	...	...	...	...	...
	7·6	3	40	A	⅗	12	2210						...
	7·6	3†	28	B	⅖	12	1640						...
	7·6	3†	21	B	⅓	12	1500						...
	4	1·57	60	B	⅕	2	2790						...
	2	·8	70	O	1/17	·31	2725	...	...	...	...	...	...
	2	·8	60	O	1/17	·31	2460	...	...	...	...	...	...

* B = Bofors.   A = Armstrong.   O = Oerlikon.   † Anti-Aircraft.   There is also a 3 pdr. AA. gun.

Minister of Defence.—Mr. F. R. Monsen.   *Commander in Chief.*—Rear-Admiral H. E. Diesen.

Colour of Ships : Coast Defence Ships, Destroyers, Torpedo Boats, Gunboats, &c., all light grey.

General Notes.—Personnel : About 850 permanent, 700 yearly conscripts, all seafaring men in reserve.

Mercantile Marine.—(From " Lloyd's Register," 1939). 1,990 Vessels of 4,834,902 gross Tonnage.

Navy Estimates.—1938–39, Kr. 16,101,276 + 19,699,900 Extraordinary expenditure. Total, Kr. 35,801,176.

        1937–38, Kr. 14,673,556 + 4,199,900 Extraordinary expenditure. Total, Kr. 18,873,456.

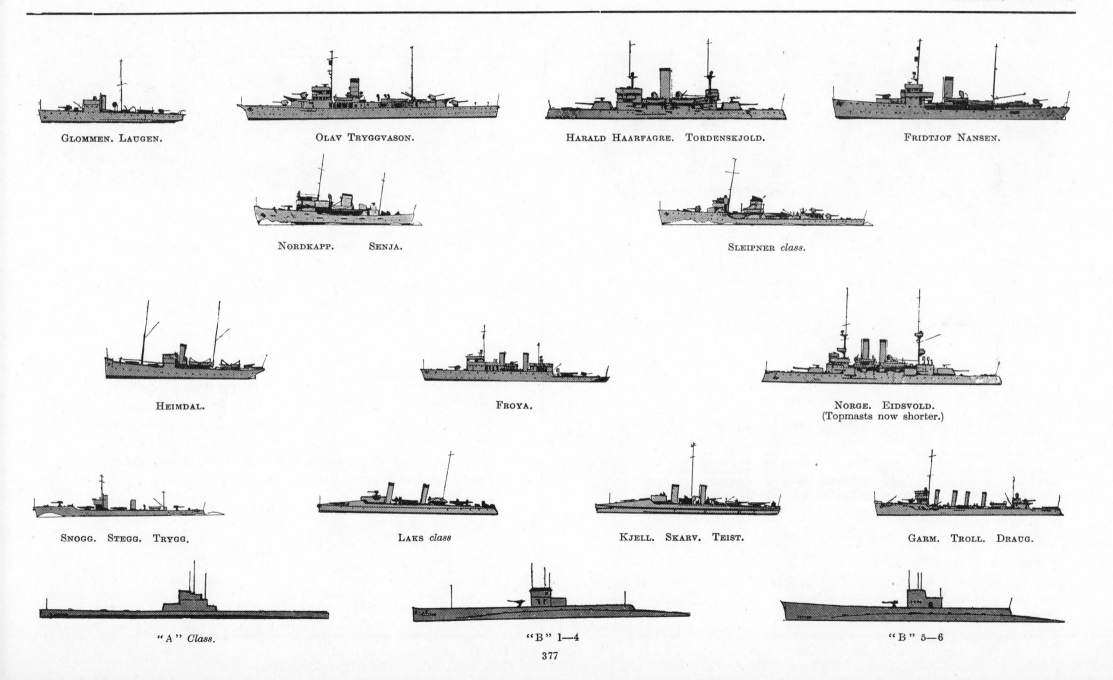

GLOMMEN. LAUGEN.

OLAV TRYGGVASON.

HARALD HAARFAGRE. TORDENSKJOLD.

FRIDTJOF NANSEN.

NORDKAPP. SENJA.

SLEIPNER *class*.

HEIMDAL.

FROYA.

NORGE. EIDSVOLD.
(Topmasts now shorter.)

SNOGG. STEGG. TRYGG.

LAKS *class*

KJELL. SKARV. TEIST.

GARM. TROLL. DRAUG.

"A" *Class*.

"B" 1—4

"B" 5—6

1933 *Photo, Official.*

TORDENSKJOLD.

1933 *Photo, Official.*

NORGE (March, 1900), **EIDSVOLD** (June, 1900).

Displacement, 4166 tons.   Complement, 270.

Length (*p.p.*), 290 feet.   Length (*over all*), 301¼ feet.   Beam, 50½ feet.   *Max.* draught, 17⅔ feet.
Mean draught 16½ feet.

HARALD HAARFAGRE (Jan., 1897), **TORDENSKJOLD** (March, 1897).

Displacement, 3858 tons.   Complement, 249.

Length (*p.p.*), 279 feet.   Length (*over all*), 304 feet.   Beam, 48½ feet.   *Maximum* draught,
17⅔ feet.   *Mean* draught, 16½ feet.

Note to Plan.—Forebridge now built up as in photo.

Guns :
  2—8·2 inch, 44 cal.
  6—5·9 inch, 46 cal.
  8—3 inch 12 pdr.
  2—3 pdr. AA.

Armour (Krupp) :
  6″ Belt..............
  2″ Deck slopes ...
  8″ Turrets ....
  6″ Bases ....
  5″ Casemates (NC)
  6″ Conning tower

Guns (Armstrong) :
  2—8·2 inch, 44 cal.
  6—4·7 inch, 44 cal.
  6—3 inch 12 pdr.
  2—3 inch AA.
  2—1 pdr. (Hotchkiss)

Armour (Harvey) :
  7″ Belt (amidships)
  4″ Belt ends ......
  2″ Deck (flat on belt)
  8″ Bulkheads ......
  8″—5″ Turrets ...
  6″ Bases of turrets
  6″ Conning tower

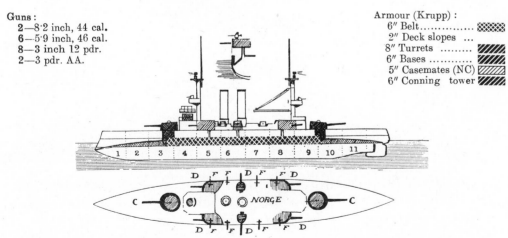

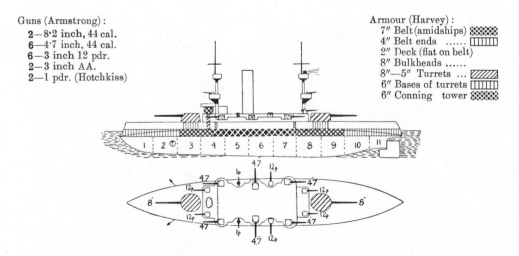

Machinery : Triple expansion. 2 shafts. Boilers : 6 Yarrow. Designed H.P. : 4,500 = 16·5 kts. Coal : 590 tons.

Notes.—Built by Armstrong. Completed 1900–1901. Machinery by Hawthorn, Leslie & Co. Excellent seaboats, and still good for 15 kts. On plans C = 8·2 inch guns ; D = 5·9 inch ; F = 3 inch 12 pdr. guns.

Machinery : Triple expansion. 2 shafts. Boilers : 3 cylindrical. Designed H.P. : 4,500 = 16·9 kts. (made 17·2 on *trial*, 1897–8). Coal : 550 tons.

Notes.—Built by Armstrong, and completed 1897–8. Engined by Hawthorn, Leslie & Co. Belt is 174 feet long by 6½ feet deep. Excellent seaboats, good for 14 kts. still.

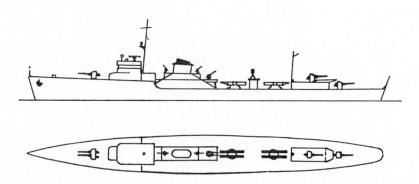

2 Destroyers were laid down at Horten, in April, 1939. Displacement: 1,220 tons *standard*. Complement: 130. Dimensions: 300 (*pp.*), 319 (*o.a.*) × 32¾ × 9 feet. Guns: 4—4·7 inch, 2—40 mm. AA., 2—12·7 mm. Tubes: 4—21 inch (paired). Machinery: De Laval geared turbines. S.H.P.: 30,000 = 34 kts. Oil fuel: 300 tons. To be completed in 1943.

SLEIPNER. 1937, *Official*.

Sleipner (May 7, 1936), *Aeger* (Sept., 1936), *Gyller* (July 2, 1938), *Odin* (Jan. 17, 1939), *Tor* (1939), *Balder* (1939). *Standard* displacement: 597 tons. Complement: 72. Dimensions: 236¼ (*pp.*), 243¾ (*o.a.*) × 25½ × 7 feet (*mean*), 9 feet (*max.*). Guns: 3—4 inch, 1—40 mm. AA., 2 M.G., 4 D.C.T. Fitted for minelaying. Torpedo tubes: 2—21 inch, paired (except *Gyller*, 4). Machinery: 2 De Laval geared turbines. 2 shafts. Designed H.P.: 12,500 = 32 kts. 3 water-tube boilers, working pressure: 450 lbs. Oil fuel: 100 tons. All built at Horten except *Tor*, for which contract was placed with Fredrikstad Mekaniske Verksted in 1938.

SLEIPNER *class* (GYLLER has 4 tubes.)

DRAUG

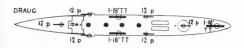

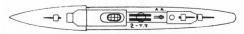

GARM

Garm (1913), *Draug* (1908), and *Troll* (1910). All built at Horten. 540 tons. Dimensions: 227 × 23¼ × 8¾ feet. Armament: 6—3 inch, 3—18 in. tubes. H.P. 7500 (8000 in *Garm*) = 27 kts. Reciprocating engines in last two, turbines in *Garm*. Coal: 105 tons. Complement, 76.

Photo, by favour of "Flottes de Combat"

3 boats: *Snøgg, Stegg, Trygg* (Horten, 1916-17). 220 tons. Dimensions: 173·9 × 18 × 5·2 feet. Guns: 2—3 inch. Tubes: 4—18 inch. Fitted for minelaying. Designed H.P. 3,500 = 25 kts. Fuel capacity: 30 tons oil. Complement: 33.

4 Motor Torpedo Boats ordered from Vosper, Ltd., Portsmouth, 1939. Length: 60 feet. Machinery: 2 Isotta-Fraschini petrol engines. H.P.: 2,200 = over 40 kts. Complement: 10.

4 Motor Torpedo Boats ordered from British Power Boat Co., Ltd, 1939. Displacement: 24 tons Dimensions: 63 × 18½ × 4 feet. Armament: 2—18 inch tubes, 2 M.G. Machinery; 2 Rolls-Royce Merlin engines. H.P.: 2,200 = 40 kts. Complement: 8

SKARV.   1925 *Photo, by favour of the Ministry of Defence.*

3 boats; *Kjell* (1912), 94 tons: *Skarv, Teist* (Karl Johans Verksted, Horten, 1907–08). 92 tons. *Skarv, Teist,* 2—3 pdr. guns. *Kjell* 1—3 inch. In all three boats, 3—18 inch tubes, one bow and two deck aft. Speed of all three boats, 25 kts. H.P. 1,700. Coal: 16 tons. Complement, 21.

6 boats: *Laks, Sild, Sael, Skrei* (1900). 90 tons and 21 kts.   1934 *Photo, Official.*
        Brand, Storm (1899). 20 kts. 79 tons.

All armed with 2—1 pdr. guns and 2—18 inch tubes on deck. Complement, 19. Built by Karl Johans Verksted, Horten. H.P. 1,000. Coal: 17 tons.

GRIB, JO, LOM, ÖRN, RAVN, as above photo.   1918 *Photo, Wilse, Oslo.*

5 boats: *Grib, Jo, Lom* (1906) and *Örn, Ravn* (1904). All 70 tons, and about 22–23 kts. Guns: 2—1 pdr. but *Lom* has 2—3 pdr. Complement, 16.
Note.—All above 5 boats have 2—18 inch tubes, viz., 1 bow and 1 deck. All built in Norway.

        1918 *Photo, Wilse. Oslo.*

2 boats: *Hauk, Falk* (1903), 63 tons; 2—1 pdr. and 1 bow torpedo tube. 20 kts., Complement, 14. Built in Norway. Fitted as minesweepers.

HVAS.   1934 *Photo, Official.*

2 boats: *Hvas, Kjœk* (1900), 64 tons; Guns: 2—1 pdr. 1 bow tube, 19 kts. Complement, 14. Fitted as minesweepers.

5 boats: *Kvik, Djerv, Dristig* (1897–98), 67 tons. *Blink, Lyn* (1896), 45 tons. All three boats 19 kts. speed. *Djerv* and *Dristig* fitted for minesweeping. Guns: 2—1 pdr. Complement: 14 for all. Built in Norway.

9 Submarines *(Undervandsbaater).*

2 new submarines are to be built at Horten.

B 2.   *1925 Photo, by favour of the Ministry of Defence.*

6 *Electric Boat Co.* design : **B 1** (1923), **B 2** (Oct. 1, 1924), **B 3** (1926), **B 4** (May 1, 1927), **B 5** (June 17, 1929), **B 6** (August, 1929), (all built at Horten). 420 tons *on surface*, 545 tons *submerged.* H.P. : 900 = 14¾ kts. *on surface,* 700 = 11 kts. *when submerged.* Dimensions : 167⅓ × 17½ × 11½ feet. Sulzer type Diesel engines, built at Horten. Electric motors built in Norway. Armament : 1—3 inch, 4—18 inch torpedo tubes (2 bow, 2 stern). Complement : 23 Laid down 1915. B 1 completed 1923, and reported to have been very successful, maintaining a speed of 14·5 kts. on trial. B 2 completed in 1924, B 3 in 1926, B 4 in 1927. B 5, B 6 both laid down in Dec., 1925, and completed in 1929 and 1930 respectively.

A 4.   *Photo added 1924.*

3 *Krupp-Germania* type : **A4–A2** (all 1914). 250 tons *on surface,* 335 tons *submerged.* H.P. 700 = 14¼ kts. *on surface* 380 = 9 kts. *submerged.* Complement, 15. Dimensions : 152⅓ × 16¼ × 9¼ feet. Surface engines : Krupp-Diesel. 3—18 inch tubes, 2 bow 1 stern. 4 torpedoes carried.

Minelayers.

     1937, Capitaine M. Adam.

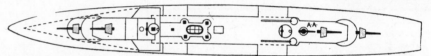

OLAV TRYGGVASON (Horten, 1933). Displacement : 1,596 tons (*full load,* 1,924 tons). Complement, 128. Dimensions : 304 (*p.p.*) 319 (*o.a.*) ×37½×12 feet (*mean*), 18⅔ feet (*max.* draught). Guns : 4—4·7 inch, 1—3 inch AA., 2—3 pdr., 2 M.G. Stowage for 280 mines, which can be laid from ports under counter. Machinery : 2 De Laval geared turbines, with 2 sets Sulzer Diesels and electric drive for cruising purposes. 2 shafts. S.H.P. 6,000 = 20 kts. (made on 6 hours' trial). 3 water-tube boilers. Fuel : 200 tons including Diesel oil. Radius of action, 3,000 miles at 14 knots.

Note.—Employed as cadets' training ship ; can accommodate 65 cadets in addition to complement shown above.

FROYA.   *1930 Photo, by courtesy of the Ministry of Defence.*

FROYA (1916). 760 tons. Complement, 78. Dimensions : 248·7 × 27 × 8·2 feet. Guns : 4—4 inch, 1—3 inch, AA. 2—1 pdr. Tubes : 2—18 inch deck. Designed H.P. 7000 = 22 kts. Coal : 95 tons + 60 tons oil. Carries 160 mines.

Minelayers—*continued*.

GLOMMEN. 1921 *Photo, by courtesy of the Ministry of Defence.*

GLOMMEN (1917), **LAUGEN** (1917). Both Akers Yard, Oslo. 335 tons. Complement : 39. Dimensions : 137·8 × 27·9 × 6·2 feet. Guns : 2—3 inch. Designed H.P. : 170 = 9·5 kts. Coal : 21 tons. Each carries about 50 mines.

Name.	Date.	Tons.	Crew.	Guns.	Speed kts.
Tyr	1888	281	44	1—4·7 in., 1—12,+2—1 pdr.	10·5
Gor	1885	276	44	1—4·7 in., 1—12,+2—1 pdr.	10·5
Vidar ...	1881	254	41		9·5
Brage ...	1876			1—4·7 in., 1—3,+2—1 pdr.	8·5
Nor	1878	254	38		8·5
Vale	1878	233	41	1—4·7 in. 3—1 pdr.	8
Uller ...	1874				

Fishery Protection Vessels.

1931 *Photo, Comm. Steen Steensen.*

FRIDTJOF NANSEN (Horten, 1931). Displacement : 1,300 tons (full load, 1,700 tons). Complement, 70. Dimensions : 239·3 × 34·7 × 16·7 feet. Guns : 2—4 inch, 2—3 pdr. I.H.P. 2,000 = 15 kts. Coal : 150 tons + 95 tons oil.

(Wrecked in 1933, but salved in following year and refitted in 1936).

Fishery Protection Vessels—*continued*.

NORDKAPP 1937 *Official.*

NORDKAPP (Aug. 18, 1937), **SENJA** (Aug. 25, 1937). (Horten). *Standard* displacement : 243 tons (275 tons *full load*). Complement : 22. Dimensions : 130½ × 21½ × 7½ feet. Guns : 1—47 mm. 2 Sulzer Diesels, with electric drive. 1 shaft. H.P. : 830 = 13·75 kts. Fuel : 30 tons.

Photo, Wilse, Oslo.

HEIMDAL (1892). 640 tons. Complement, 62. Length, 181 feet. Draught, 13 feet. Guns : 4—3 inch. H.P. 625 = 12 kts. Coal : 92 tons.

MICHAEL SARS (1900) 300 tons. 126 × 23 × 11 feet. Guns : 2—3 pdr. Speed : 10 kts. Complement : 27.

Minesweepers.

OTRA (Aug. 5, 1939), **RAUMA** (1939). Built by Nylands Verksted, Oslo. Displacement : 320 tons. Dimensions : 167 × 23 × 6 feet. Guns : 1—40 mm. AA., 2—12·7 mm. Machinery : 2 sets triple expansion. I.H.P. : 900 = 13·5 kts. 1 watertube boiler. Complement : 23.

Submarine Depot Vessel.

1934 *Photo, Official.*

SARPEN (1860). (Rebuilt, 1918). 187 tons. Guns : 2—9 pdr., 1—1 pdr. Speed : 9 kts.

Transport (*Transportskib.*)

1918 *Photo, Wilse, Oslo.*

FARM (1900). 300 tons. Complement, 32. Guns : 2—9 pdr., 2—1 pdr. Speed : 9 kts.

PARAGUAY.

Ensign & Mercantile

Capitán de Navio.   Capitán de Fragata.   Capitán de Corbeta.   Teniente 1°.   Teniente 2°.   Guardia Marina.

Minister of War: General Nicolás Delgado.
Director of Naval Department: Commander D. M. Aponte.

1932 *Photo, Official.*

CAPITAN CABRAL (Werf-Conrad, Haarlem, 1907). 180 tons. Complement, 47. Dimensions: 98·4 (*p.p.*)×23·5×6 feet. Guns: 1—3 inch Vickers, 2—37 mm. Vickers. H.P. 300 = 12·5 kts. Wood.

River Gunboats

HUMAITA.   1932 *Photo, Official.*

HUMAITA, PARAGUAY (both 1930). Built by Odero, Genoa. Displacement: 745 tons (865 tons full load). Dimensions: 230 × 35 × 5½ feet *draught.* Guns: 4—4·7 inch, 3—3 inch AA., 2—40 mm. AA. H.T. Armour: ½″ side amidships, ⅓″ deck, ¾″ C.T. Parsons turbines and oil-fired boilers. H.P.: 3,000 = 18·5 kts. Oil: 240 tons. Radius: 1,700 miles at 16 kts. Complement: 86. Completed 1930.

Note—Mines are included in the equipment of these vessels.

TACUARI.   1932 *Photo, Official.*

TACUARI (T. & J. Hosking, 1910). 150 tons. Complement: 54. Dimensions: 129·2 (*p.p.*)×24·8×6 feet. Guns: 2—3 inch Vickers, 2—3 inch Armstrong, 2—37 mm. Vickers. H.P. 300 = 10 kts. Wood.

National Flag.
Mercantile flag the same but
without centre device.

Pendant.　　　　Jack.　　President.　　Minister of　　Chief of Staff.
　　　　　　　　　　　　　　　　　　　　Marine.

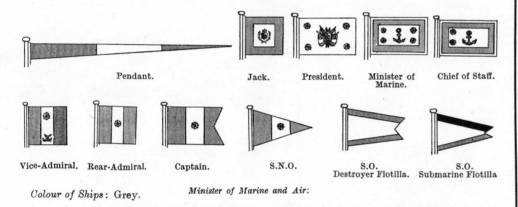

Vice-Admiral.　Rear-Admiral.　　Captain.　　　　S.N.O.　　　　　S.O.　　　　　　S.O.
　　　　　　　　　　　　　　　　　　　　　　　　Destroyer Flotilla.　Submarine Flotilla.

Colour of Ships: Grey.　　　　*Minister of Marine and Air*:

Uniforms.　(Device is a radiant sun, *without* circle round it as shown below.)

As Contra-Almirante but with 2 thin stripes							

Vice-　　Contra-　Capitán　Capitán　Capitán　Teniente　Teniente　Alferez
Almirante.　Almirante.　de Navio.　de Fragata.　de Corbeta.　1°.　　2°.　　de Fragata.
Vice-　　*Rear-*　*Captain.*　*Commander.*　*Commander.*　*Lieut.*　*Lieut.*　*Sub.*
Admiral.　*Admiral.*　　　*Senior.*　*Junior.*　*Comm'r.*　　　　*Lieutenant.*

All branches have the same insignia : Engineers are distinguished from doctors who wear respectively,
instead of the Rising Sun, a propeller and a caduceus.

Mercantile Marine, 1939 : 32 vessels of 39,894 tons *gross*.

Form of Address : Capitan de Navio don—— B.A.P.——.

ALM. GRAU (COR. BOLOGNESI similar, but no poop).

ALMIRANTE GUISE.

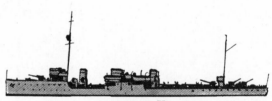

ALMIRANTE VILLAR.

T. RODRIGUEZ.

R. 1—4.

Cruisers.

CORONEL BOLOGNESI. The *A. Grau* is identical *except* that she has a poop.

ALMIRANTE GRAU (March 27, 1906) & CORONEL BOLOGNESI (Sept. 24, 1906).

Displacement: 3,200 tons. Complement, 315.

Length (*p.p.*), 370 feet. Beam, 40½ feet. *Maximum* draught, 14¼ feet.

Guns (Vickers):
2—6 inch, 50 cal.
6—3 inch (14 pdr.).
2—3 inch AA.
4—20 mm. AA. Japanese
5—M.G.
Torpedo tubes (18 inch):
2 *submerged*.

Note to Plan.—After bridge (with S.L.) extends almost full width of ship.

Armour:
1½" Deck (amidships) = ▨
3" Conning tower ... ▨
3" Gun Shields ... ▨

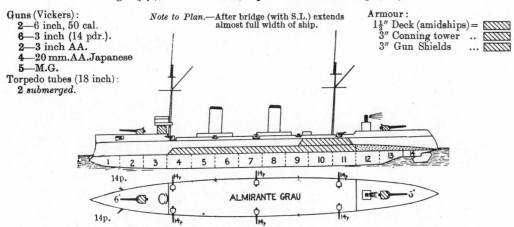

Machinery: 4 cylinder vertical triple expansion. 2 screws. Boilers: 8 Yarrow (new in 1934). Designed H.P. 14,000 = 24 kts. Oil: *normal*, 500 tons; Endurance: 3,700 miles at 10 kts.

General Notes.—Built and engined by Messrs. Vickers, Ltd., about 1905–07. Refitted at Balboa, boilers being re-tubed and modified for oil burning, 1923–25. Both reboilered by Yarrow, 1934–35. Both ships are now good for 23·5 kts. at sea. *Grau* is at present employed as fleet flagship.

Gunnery Notes.—Italian Giradelli type training indicators are believed to have been added to gunnery equipment 2 after 3 inch (14 pdr.) guns replaced by new ones of Japanese manufacture, 1936.

2 Destroyers.

(Both captured from Soviet Navy by British Cruisers and Destroyers in the Baltic, in December, 1918, and transferred to Estonia, from whom they were purchased in 1933.)

1929 *Photo.*

Almirante Guise (ex *Lennuk*, ex-Russian *Avtroil*). Launched at Tallinn by Reval Shipbuilding Co., 1915, completed 1917. Displacement: 1,785 tons. Dimensions: 344½ × 31¼ × 11·8 feet. Guns: 5—4 inch, 60 cal., 2—20 mm. AA., 3 M.G. Torpedo tubes: 9—18 inch, in 3 triple deck mountings. Designed to carry and lay 80 mines. Designed S.H.P. 32,000 = 30 kts. A.E.G. Curtis turbines. Oil fuel: 450 tons = 2,400 miles at 15 kts. Complement, 142.

Note.—This vessel was built to the design of Chantiers et Ateliers Augustin Normand, Le Havre.

(Plans of these 2 ships as those of Russian *Karl Marx* and *Uritski* types, respectively.)

1935.

Almirante Villar (ex-*Vambola*, ex-Russian *Spartak*, ex-*Mikula Mcklei*). Launched by Putilov Works, Petrograd, 1915, and completed 1918. Displacement: 1,550 tons. Dimensions: 315·7 × 30¼ × 12·15 feet. Guns: 4—4 inch, 60 cal., 2—20 mm. AA., 3 M.G. Torpedo tubes: 9—18 inch, in 3 triple deck mountings. Designed to carry and lay 80 mines. Designed S.H.P. 32,000 = 30 kts. A.E.G. Curtis turbines. Oil fuel: 420 tons = 2,500 miles at 15 kts. Complement, 142.

BB

PERU

Torpedo Boat.

Photo by courtesy of Messrs. Schneider et Cie

1 *Schneider-Creusot:*—**Teniente Rodriguez** (1909, ex-*Actée*). 490 tons. Dimensions: 212×21·3×14¾ feet. H.P. 8,600=28 kts. (present best speed 25 kts.). Schneider-Zoelly turbines, du Temple boilers (retubed 1922). Coal: 100 tons = 1,200 miles at 10 kts. Armament: 6—65 mm., 2—20 mm. AA., 3—18 inch tubes. Complement 60. This vessel is regularly employed in the Training of Cadets. She was built as a French warship, but was acquired by Peru on completion in 1911.

Motor Launches.

Built in U.S.A. Length 90 feet. Further particulars wanted.

Submarines.

R1.

1927 *Photo by courtesy of Electric Boat Co.*

R1.

Official Photo, 1927.

4 *Electric Boat Co.* design : **R 1** (April, 1926), **R 2** (May, 1926), **R 3** (April 21, 1928), **R 4** (May 10, 1928). Built by Electric Boat C°, Groton, Conn. *Surface* displacement : 576 tons. *Submerged* displacement : 682 tons (exclusive of non-watertight parts), 755 tons (inclusive of such parts). Dimensions : 186¼ (*o.a.*), 178½ (*pp.*) × 17½ × 15 feet. 2 Nelseco Diesel engines, together H.P. : 880 = 14·5 kts. Electric motors of 1,000 B.H.P. = 9·5 kts. Radius of action : 8,000 miles. Guns : 1—3 inch. Tubes : 4—21 inch (bow). Complement : 30.

Note.—R 1, R 2, on delivery, completed an unescorted trip from Connecticut to Callao, without mishap, arriving in good order. R 3, R 4 delivered in summer of 1928. R 1 ,R 2 were refitted at builders' yard in 1935, R 3 and R 4 in 1936.

Depot Ship (Classed as Cruiser).

LIMA. 1935, *Official.*

LIMA (ex-*Socrates*, Kiel, 1880). 1,790 tons. Dimensions : 250 × 35 × 15 feet (*mean*). H.P. : 2,000 = 14 kts. Coal : 300 tons. Guns : 3—4 inch, 4—3 pdr., 2—20 mm. AA., 2 M.G. Believed equipped for minelaying. Complement: 150.

Note.—This Ship was completely refitted 1927-8 and can now make her designed speed. Radius is 3,000 miles at 10 kts.

River Gunboats (Upper Amazon Flotilla).

1935, *Official.*

AMAZONAS, LORETO (1934). Designed and built by Electric Boat Co., Groton, Conn. Displacement : 250 tons (*standard*). Length : 153¼ feet. Guns : 4—3 inch AA., 2—20 mm. AA., 2 M.G. Machinery : Diesel. H.P. : 750 = 15 kts. Complement : 35.

NAPO (Yarrow, 1920). Steel. 98 tons. Dimensions : 100 (*p.p.*) 101½ (*o.a.*) × 18 × 3 feet. Guns : 4—47 mm. (3 pdr.), 2—37 mm., 2—20 mm. AA., 4 M.G. Machinery : Triple expansion. H.P. : 250 = 12 kts. Yarrow boilers. Fuel : 380 cubic feet wood. Complement : 22.

River Gunboats—*continued.*

AMERICA. 1935, *by courtesy of Ministry of Marine.*

AMERICA (1904). Steel. 240 tons. Dimensions : 133 × 19½ × 4½ feet. Guns : 2—65 mm., 3—47 mm. (3 pdr.), 2—20 mm. AA. I.H.P. : 350 = 14 kts. Coal : 42 tons. Complement : .

1935, *Official.*

IQUITOS (1875). Rebuilt 1896. 50 tons. Dimensions : 77 × 12 × 7½ feet. Guns : 4—37 mm., 2—20 mm., 2 M.G. Speed : 7·5 kts.

1935, *Official.*

CAHUAPANAS (1896). 30 tons. Dimensions : 65 × 12½ × 3½ feet. 2 M.G. Speed : 7 kts.

River Gunboats—*continued.*

CORONEL PORTILLO (ex-*San Pablo*). 49 tons net. Dimensions : 80⅓ × 16¼ × 4 feet. Guns : 2. Compound engines. Speed : under 7 kts.

Note.—*Iquitos, Cahuapanas* and *Cor. Portillo* are all converted merchant vessels.

Oiler.

PARIÑAS (ex-*Sjömand*). (Thornycroft, 1921). 2,820 tons *gross.* Dimensions : 300 × 44 × 21½ feet. Machinery : Turbines. I.H.P. : 1,600 = 10 kts. Oil : 560 tons. Tanks : 4,300 tons.

Transport.

RIMAC (ex-*Eten*, ex-*Rhakotis*). (Blohm & Voss, Hamburg, 1907). 6,848 tons *gross.* Dimensions : 485½ × 53 × 26 feet. I.H.P.: 3,200 = 12 kts. Coal : 1,600 tons.

POLAND.

Flags.

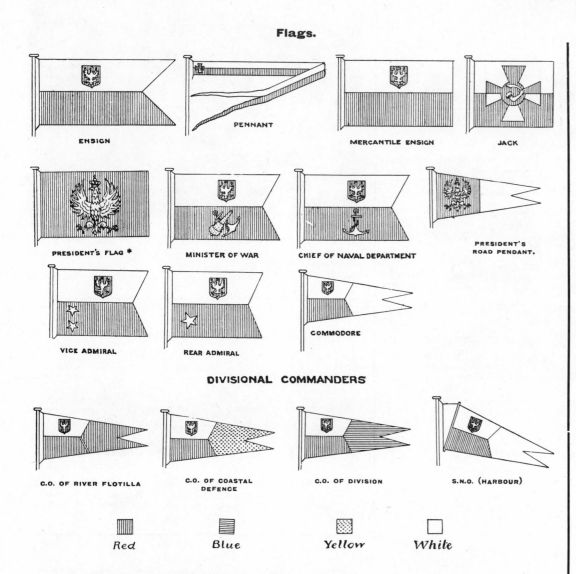

ENSIGN

PENNANT

MERCANTILE ENSIGN

JACK

PRESIDENT'S FLAG *

MINISTER OF WAR

CHIEF OF NAVAL DEPARTMENT

PRESIDENT'S ROAD PENDANT.

VICE ADMIRAL

REAR ADMIRAL

COMMODORE

DIVISIONAL COMMANDERS

C.O. OF RIVER FLOTILLA

C.O. OF COASTAL DEFENCE

C.O. OF DIVISION

S.N.O. (HARBOUR)

Red   Blue   Yellow   White

Note.—The Emblem in the centre of the Jack is a flesh-coloured arm holding a steel-blue scimitar with gold hilt. The covering over shoulder of the arm is pale blue and has a gold-tasselled fringe.

* President's flag now has a crenated border.

Minister of War.—Lieut.-General T. Kasprzycki.

Chief of the Naval Department.—Rear-Admiral J. Swirski.

Chief of Naval Staff.—Captain K. Korytowski.

Navel Attaché, London.—Commander T. Stoklasa.

Personnel.—400 officers, 4,000 men : total, 4,400.

Colour of Warships.—Grey-green.

Uniforms.

a) = Polish Rank.   *(b)* = Equivalent British Rank.

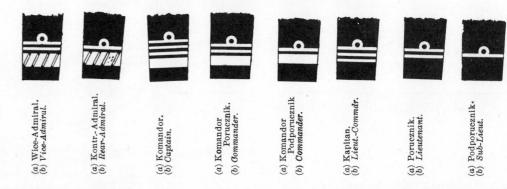

(a) Wice-Admiral.
(b) Vice-Admiral.

(a) Kontr.-Admiral.
(b) Rear-Admiral.

(a) Komandor.
(b) Captain.

(a) Komandor Porucznik.
(b) Commander.

(a) Komandor Podporucznik
(b) Commander.

(a) Kapitan.
(b) Lieut.-Commdr.

(a) Porucznik.
(b) Lieutenant.

(a) Podporucznik.
(b) Sub-Lieut.

Arsenals, Shipbuilders, &c.

Naval base and dockyard at Gdynia.

Naval College is temporarily established at Bydgoszcz.

Mercantile Marine.

Lloyd's Register figures (1939) :
63 ships of 121,630 tons *gross*.

JASKÓLKA *class*

GRYF.

POMORZANIN.

MAZUR

WILK *class.*

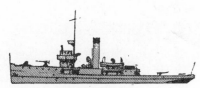

GENERAL HALLER,
KOMENDANT PILSUDSKI

ORZEL, SEP

BURZA
WICHER

BLYSKAWICA. GROM.

4 **Destroyers** (*Niszczyciele*).

BLYSKAWICA. 1937, *R. Perkins.*

BLYSKAWICA. 1937, *R. Perkins.*

Blyskawica (Oct. 1, 1936), ***Grom*** (July 20, 1936). Built by J. Samuel White & Co., Ltd., Cowes. *Standard* displacement : 2,144 tons. Complement : 180. Dimensions : 357 (*pp.*), 374 (*o.a.*) × 37 × 10¼ feet. Guns : **7—4·7 inch, 4—47 mm. AA. 4** M.G. Tubes : **6—21 inch** (tripled). **2** D.C.T. Fitted for minelaying. Machinery : Parsons geared turbines. 2 shafts. H.P. : 54,000 = 39 kts. Boilers : 4 of 3-drum type, 385 lbs. pressure with 200° of superheat. Bows strengthened for ice navigation.

Note.—Names of these ships mean " Lightning " and " Thunderbolt," respectively. Both completed 1937. Trials exceeded designed speed.

Destroyers—*continued.*

ORZEL.   1939, *Official.*

Orzel (Jan. 15, 1938), ***Sep*** (Oct. 17, 1938). Laid down, 1936, by K. M. de Schelde, Flushing, and by Rotterdam Dry Dock Co., respectively. Displacement: 1,110/1,473 tons. Complement: 56. Dimensions: 273½ (*pp.*), 275½ (*o.a.*) × 22 × 13 feet. Guns: 1—3·5 inch, 2—40 mm. AA. Torpedo tubes: 8—21 inch. Fitted for minelaying. Machinery: 2 Sulzer Diesels. B.H.P.: 4,740/1,000 = 19/9 kts.

Note.—These names mean Eagle and Vulture respectively. *Orzel* was paid for by funds subscribed by the Polish Navy League. *Sep* interned at Stockholm, September, 1939.

BURZA.   1937, *R. Perkins.*

Burza (April 16th, 1929), ***Wicher*** (July 10th, 1928). Both laid down by Chantiers Navals Français, Blainville, Nov. 1st, 1926, and Feb. 19th, 1927, respectively. Displacement: 1540 tons. Dimensions: 344 (*w.l.*), 351 (*o.a.*) × 29 × 9¾ feet draught. Guns: 4—5·1 inch, 2—47 mm. AA., 4 M.G. Torpedo tubes: 6—21 inch, in triple deck mountings. Machinery: Geared turbines (supplied by At. & Ch. de la Loire). H.P. 35,000 = 33 kts.

Notes.—Design of these vessels follows closely that of French *Simoun* class. Meanings of names are: *Burza*, Squall; *Wicher*, Hurricane. Completed 1930. Are to be distinguished by initial letters of names painted on bows.

Submarines. (*Okrety Podwodne*)

Building

WILK.   1930 *Photo, by courtesy of Messrs. Augustin Normand.*

3 *Normand-Fenaux* type: ***Rys*** (At. & Ch. de la Loire, Nantes), April 22, 1929, ***Zbik*** (Ch. Navals Français, Blainville, June 14, 1930), ***Wilk*** (Ch. & At. Augustin Normand, Le Havre, April 12, 1929). Displacement: $\frac{980}{1250}$ tons. Dimensions: 246 × 16 × 13 feet. Guns: 1—3·9 inch, 1—1·5 inch AA. Torpedo tubes: 6—20·8 inch. Mines carried: **38.** 2 sets Vickers-Normand Diesels, H.P. 1800 = 14 kts. on *surface*. Electric motors, B.H.P. 1200 = 9 kts. *submerged.* Radius of action: 3500 miles on *surface* at 10 kts., 100 miles *submerged.* Diving limit: 44 fathoms. Carry **10** torpedoes and **38** mines.

Notes.—Meanings of names are as follows: *Rys*, Lynx; *Wilk*, Wolf; *Zbik*, Wild Cat. *Wilk* is prototype of the class, and all were built to Normand plans. Are distinguished by initials of names, painted on C.T. *Rys* and *Zbik* were both interned in Sweden, September, 1939.

2 *Normand* type: To be laid down by Ch. & At. Augustin Normand, Le Havre, Sept., 1939, and At. & Ch. de la Loire, Nantes, October, 1939. Displacement: 1,175/1,550 tons. Dimensions: 284½ × 22½ × 13¾ feet. Armament: Probably similar to *Orzel* type, below. Machinery: 2 sets Sulzer 2-cycle Diesels. B.H.P. 5,400/1,000 = 19/9 kts.

Minelayer (*Stawiaczmin*).

1938, *Official.*

GRYF (Ch. & At. Augustin Normand, Le Havre, Nov. 29, 1936). Laid down November, 1934, and completed February, 1938. Displacement : 2,227 tons. Complement : 205. Dimensions 337¾ × 44½ × 28 feet.
Guns : 6—4·7 inch. 4—40 mm. (twin mounts). Stowage for 300 mines. Machinery : 2 sets Sulzer Diesels. H.P. : 6,000 = 20 kts.

Note.—*Gryf* is also used as Seagoing Training Ship for Cadets. Her name means Griffin.

1938, *courtesy C. & A. Augustin Normand* (*Builders*).

Gunboats (*Kanonierki*).

Kom. Pilsudski (Gen. Haller of similar appearance). 1938, *Official.*

KOMENDANT PILSUDSKI ⎫ (Crichton, Abö, Finland, 1918-19.) ⎧ Completed Jan., 1921.
GENERAL HALLER ⎭ ⎩ „ 1920.

Displacement : 342 tons. Complement, 60. Length, (*p.p.*) 154¼ feet, (*o.a.*) 164½ feet. Beam, 22¾ feet.
Designed load draught, 7 ft. 7 in. Guns : 2—12 pdr., 2—3 pdr.
Machinery : 2 sets triple expansion. 2 screws. Boilers : Normand. Designed I.H.P., 1000 = 15 kts. at 120 r.p.m. Coal capacity : 50 tons *normal* = 700 miles at full speed.

Notes.—Belong to a Class of four vessels originally ordered for the Russian Navy. The above two purchased from Finland ; the remaining two added to Finnish Navy as *Karjala* and *Turunmaa* (*q.v.*).

Torpedo Boats (*Torpedowce*).

2 Motor Torpedo Boats were ordered in Jan., 1939, from J. Samuel White & Co., Ltd., Cowes. Displacement : 39 tons.
Dimensions : 75 × 16½ × 4½ feet. Machinery : Isotta-Fraschini petrol engines. Complement : 9. (13 more M.T.B. projected).

1938, *Mr. Geo. Rutkowski.*

1 *ex-German* boat : **Mazur** (ex-German *V 105*). Built by Vulkan, Hamburg, 1914-15. Displacement : 349 tons *normal*, 421 tons *full* load. Dimensions : 205½ × 20½ × 7½ feet. Guns : 4—3 inch, 2 M.G. Tubes : 2—17·7 inch. H.P. 6,000 = 30 kts., *on trials* 5,500 = 28 kts. Fuel : 59·7 tons coal + 16·2 tons oil = 640 miles at 20 kts. Complement, 74.

Note.—*Mazur* was completely rebuilt in 1937. Transferred to Poland, Nov. 4th, 1920.

Surveying Vessel (*Okret Pomiarowy*).

Photo 1933, Official.

POMORZANIN (ex *Mewa*). Buil, 1917. *Normal* Displacement: 170 tons (203 tons *full load*). Dimensions: (*p.p.*) 131¼, (*w.l.*) 132½, (*o.a.*) 140¾ × 19⅔ × 4 feet *normal* draught, 5 feet "medium load" draught. Guns: **1**—3 pdr., **2** M.G. Machinery: 2 sets triple expansion I.H.P. 700 = 13 kts. speed. Coal: 20 tons *normal;* 34·6 tons *full load.* Oil: 4 tons. Complement, 44.

Notes.—Ex-German "F. M. Boot," *i.e.* flat-bottomed Mine "searcher." Purchased by Poland, 1921, and converted into a surveying vessel in 1932.

Training Ship.

(*Okret Szkolny*)

ISKRA. *1932 Photo, Official.*

ISKRA (1917). Auxiliary 3-masted Schooner, purchased in Netherlands, 1927. Displacement: 560 tons. Dimensions: 127¾ × 25 × 9¾ feet. H.P. 130 = 7·5 kts. Sea-going Tender to Naval College. Complement (including cadets), 58.

Transport (*Transportowiec*).

WILJA. *1932 Photo, Official.*

WILJA (ex-*Laurent Schiaffino*, ex-*Le Bourget*, ex-*Tinos*, ex-*Hilda Horn*, ex-*Ganelon*). (Flensburg, 1906). Displacement: 8,400 tons, (3,570 tons *gross*.) Dimensions: 341 × 48¾ × 19½ feet. I.H.P.: 1,350 = 10 kts. Complement: 53. Coal: 600 tons.

Minesweepers (*Wylawiaczemin*).

MEWA. *1938, Official.*

JASKÓLKA (Sept. 13, 1934), **MEWA** (1935), **CZAJKA** (April 10, 1935), **RYBITWA** (April 26, 1935), **CZAPLA** and **ZURAW** (both Aug. 22, 1938). Displacement: 183 tons. Dimensions: 139½ × 21⅓ × 5½ feet. Guns: 1—3 inch. Diesel engines. B.H.P.: 1,040 = 15 kts. Complement, 30.

Notes.—First pair built at Gdynia, second pair at Modlin. Respective meanings of names are: Swallow, Seagull, Plover, Tern, Heron, Crane.

Tugs.

1934 Photo, Official.

SMOK (1921). Displacement: 655 tons. Dimensions: 128 × 27·5 × 10·9 feet. Designed—I.H.P. 1,000. Speed: 12·5 kts.

LECH. *Photo 1933, Official.*

LECH (1903). Displacement: 280 tons. Dimensions: 96 × 20·8 × 11·3 feet. Designed—I.H.P. 560. Speed: 12 kts.

Tugs—continued.

KAPER. 1939, Official.

KRAKUS. 1939, Official.

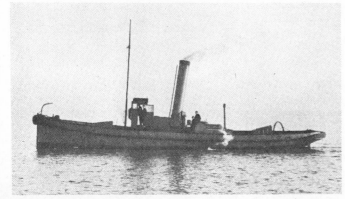

SOKOL. 1939 Official.

Tugs—continued.

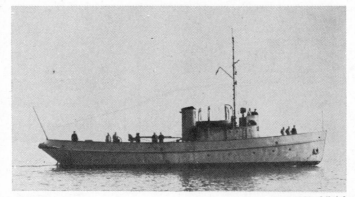

NUREK. 1939, Official.

River Gunboats. (Kanonierki Rzeczni)

Photo wanted.

NIEDOSCIGNIONA, NIEZWYCIEZONA (Both 1934).
Displacement: 38 tons. Dimensions: $75\frac{1}{2} \times 13 \times 2$ feet.
Guns: 1—40 mm., 1—32 mm., 1—13 mm. Machinery:
Diesel. B.H.P.: 450 = 11 kts.

Note.—These names mean "Incomparable" and "Invincible," respectively.
A third vessel of this type is projected, to be named Nieuchwytny.

HETMAN CHODKIEWICZ. 1924 Official Photo.

**ADMIRAL SIERPINEK, GENERAL SOSNKOWSKI,
GENERAL SIKORSKI, HETMAN CHODKIEWICZ,
ADMIRAL DICKMAN, GENERAL SZEPTYCKI.**
Displacement: 100-200 tons. Guns: 2—3 inch, 4 M.G.
Armour plated. Speed, 8 kts. Complement, 38.

393

River Monitors (Monitory Rzeczne).

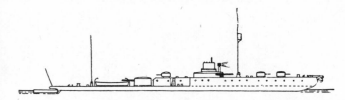

WILNO (1925), **KRAKOW** (1925). Both built by Zieleniewski,
Krakow. Displacement: 70 tons. Dimensions: $115 \times 20 \times 1\frac{1}{4}$ feet normal draught. Guns: 1—4·1 inch, 3—3 inch, 3 M.G.
Armour: Not reported. Machinery: 2 sets Diesel engines.
H.P.: 140 = 9 kts. Complement: 35.

Note.—4·1 inch is reported to be a howitzer.

HORODYSZCZE and PINSK. Official Photo, 1922.

WARSZAWA (1920), **HORODYSZCZE** (1920), **TORÚN**
(1920), **PINSK** (1920). "Armoured Monitors" built by Gdansk
Shipyard, 1920, for service on the Vistula. Displacement: 110 tons
normal, 135 deep load. Dimensions: $113\frac{1}{4}$ (o.a.) $\times 16\frac{1}{2} \times 2\frac{1}{3}$ feet
normal draught, $2\frac{2}{3}$ feet deep load. Guns: 2—4·1 inch, 5 M.G.
Armour: $\frac{1}{3}''$ side amidships, $\frac{1}{2}''$ turrets, —" C.T. Machinery: 3
sets 60 B.H.P. Daimler motors totalling 180 B.H.P. = 9·1 kts.
Petroleum fuel, 5 tons normal, 10 tons max. capacity = 1500 miles
at 8 kts. Complement, 34.

River Motor Boats.

45 boats. 7-13 tons. 10 kts. Guns: 1—1 pdr., 2 M.G.

ENSIGN

JACK

KEY

RED   GREEN

MINISTRO DA MARINHA

MAIOR
GENERAL DA
ARMADA

CHEFE DO
ESTADO MAIOR
NAVAL

CONTRA-ALMIRANTE
COMANDANTE
EM CHEFE

CONTRA-
ALMIRANTE
DEBAIXO
DE ORDENS

INSPECTOR DA MARINHA
OU QUALQUER OFFICIAL
GENERAL EM SERVICO
DE INSPECÇÃO

DIRECTOR GERAL
DA MARINHA

INTENDENTE DA
MARINHA NO
ALFEITE

CAPITÃO DE MAR E GUERRA COMANDANTE
DE FORZA NAVAL DEBAIXO DE ORDENS OU
COMANDANTE SUPERIOR DE NAVIOS NO
PORTO DE LISBOA

CAPITÃO DE FRAGATA
OU CAPITÃO TENENTE
COMANDANTE DE
FLOTILHA OU
ESQUADRILHA

COMODORO

COMANDANTE
MAIS ANTIGO
NUMA REUNIAO
ACIDENTAL
DE NAVIOS

Naval Uniforms:

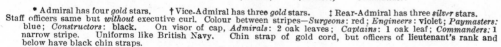

British rank.	Almirante.*	Vice-almirante.†	Contra-almirante.‡	Capitão de mar e guerra.	Capitão de fragata.	Capitão-tenente.	Primeiro tenente.	Segundo Tenente.	Guarda marinha.
	Admiral.	Vice-Admiral.	Rear-Admiral.	Captain.	Commander. (Senior.)	Commander. (Junior.)	Lieut.-Commander.	Lieut.	Midshipman

* Admiral has four *gold* stars.   † Vice-Admiral has three *gold* stars.   ‡ Rear-Admiral has three *silver* stars.
Staff officers same but *without* executive curl. Colour between stripes—*Surgeons*: red; *Engineers*: violet; *Paymasters*:
blue; *Constructors*: black.   On visor of cap, *Admirals*: 2 oak leaves; *Captains*: 1 oak leaf; *Commanders*: 1
narrow stripe.   Uniforms like British Navy.   Chin strap of gold cord, but officers of lieutenant's rank and
below have black chin straps.

Minister of Marine: Commander Manoel Ortins de Bettencourt.

Chief of the Naval Staff: Vice-Admiral Botelho de Sousa.
Personnel: 719 officers and 5,550 men.   *Colour of ships:* Light grey.
Mercantile Marine: (From "Lloyd's Register," 1939 figures) 266 vessels, *gross* tonnage, 269,118.
Navy Estimates, 1939: Escudos 228,810,164.

Mode of address: N.R.P. "———". (Navio da Republica Portuguesa).   *Displacements:* Standard.

FARO.   LAGOS.

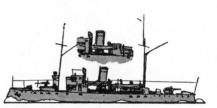

DIU *class.*
(*Inset:* BEIRA.   IBO).

SADO

VOUGA *class.*

REPUBLICA.   C. ARAUJO.

GONÇALVES ZARCO.   GONÇALO VELHO.

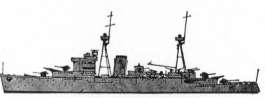

PEDRO NUNES.
JOÃO DE LISBOA.

AFONSO DE ALBUQUERQUE.
BARTOLOMEU DIAS.

TAMEGA.

DELFIM.   ESPADARTE.   GOLFINHO.

1st class. *(Avisos de 1a Classe.)*

AFONSO DE ALBUQUERQUE.

1935, *Courtesy of the builders.*

B. DIAS.

1936, *courtesy Eng. Lieut.-Com. Aluino Martins da Silva.*

AFONSO DE ALBUQUERQUE (May 28, '34). **BARTOLOMEU DIAS** (Oct. 10, '34).
R. & W. Hawthorn Leslie & Co.

Displacement : (*standard*), 1,811 and 1,816 tons, respectively ; (*full load*), 2,473 and 2,478 tons, respectively.

Complement : 189 (peace), 229 (war). Dimensions : $326\frac{3}{4} \times 44\frac{1}{4} \times 12\frac{1}{2}$ feet (*mean*).

Guns :　　　　　　　　　　　　　　　　　Aircraft : 1.

4—4·7 inch, 50 cal.
2—3 inch AA.
4—40 mm. AA.
2 D.C.T.

Fitted to carry 40 mines.

B. DIAS.

1937, *R. Perkins.*

Machinery : Parsons geared turbines. S.H.P.: 8,000 = 21 kts. Oil fuel : 660 tons. Radius : 8,000 miles at 10 kts. 2 Yarrow boilers.

Notes.—Original contract placed with Odero-Terni-Orlando, 1931, cancelled 1932, and design modified by new builders when fresh contract was made. Both ships made 22 kts. on trials without being pressed. They are differentiated by the white band around funnel of *B. Dias.*

2nd Class (*Avisos de 2a Classe*).

GONÇALO VELHO (*Zarco* distinguished by white band on funnel). 1933 *Photo, Courtesy of builders.*

GONÇALVES ZARCO (Nov. 28, 1932), GONÇALO VELHO (Aug. 3, 1932).

R. & W. Hawthorn Leslie & Co.

Displacement : (*Standard*), 966 tons; (*full load*), 1,436 tons.

Complement : 128.

Dimensions : 250 (*p.p.*), 268 (*o.a.*) × 35½ × 11¼ feet (*mean*).

Guns :
  3—4·7 inch, 50 cal.
  2—40 mm. AA.
  2—D.C.T.

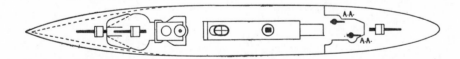

Machinery : Parsons geared turbines. S.H.P. : 2,000 = 17·5 kts. 2 screws. Boilers : 2 Yarrow. Radius : 9,831 miles at 11 kts. Oil : 335 tons *normal*, 470 tons *maximum*. Trials : 4 hours full speed = 17·4 kts.

Note.—Both vessels laid down October 9, 1931.

JOÃO DE LISBOA.   (Observe funnel band).   1938, *Capitaine M. Adam.*

PEDRO NUNES.   1936, *courtesy Eng. Lt.-Com. Aluino Martins.*

PEDRO NUNES (1933), JOÃO DE LISBOA (ex-*Infante D. Henrique*). (May 21, 1936).

Displacement : (*Standard*), 1,107 and 1,108 tons, respectively; (*full load*), 1,217 and 1,238 tons, respectively. Complement : 112/138.

Dimensions : *J. de Lisboa*, 234⅓ (*p.p.*), *P. Nunes*, 223 (*p.p.*) × 32¾ × 9⅓ feet (*mean*), 10½ feet (*max.*)

Guns :
  2—4·7 inch, 50 cal.
  4—40 mm. AA.
  2—D.C.T.

Note to Plan.—Secondary armament is actually as stated, 4—40 mm. AA.

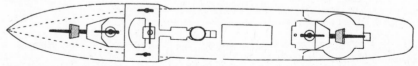

Machinery : 2 sets M.A.N. 8 cyc. Diesels. B.H.P. : 2,400 = 16·5 kts. Radius : 8,850 miles at 12 kts., 4,800 at 16 kts. Oil : 110 tons *normal*, 126 tons *max.*

Notes.—Both built at the Naval Arsenal, Lisbon. *P. Nunes* laid down early in 1930. Unlike her sister ship, she is not part of ten-year programme introduced that year.

Escort Vessels 2nd class—*continued.*

REPUBLICA. (Note white band on first funnel.)   1933, *Eng. Lt.-Com. Aluino Martins, P.N.*

REPUBLICA (ex-H.M.S. *Gladiolus*, launched Oct. 1915, by Chas. Connell & Co., Scotstoun.) Displacement : 963 tons *standard*, 1,258 tons *full load*. Dimensions : 255¼ (*pp.*), 267¾ (*o.a.*) × 33½ × 11 (*mean*), 11¾ feet (*max.* draught). Guns : 2—4 inch (Vickers), 2—3 inch A.A (Armstrong), 4—3 pdr. (Hotchkiss, 2 M.G. I.H.P. : 2,362 = 16·4 kts. Machinery : 1 set 3-cyl. triple exp. Boilers : 2 cylindrical. 1 screw. Coal : 295 tons (present normal stowage) = about 5,000 at 15 kts. Complement : 137. Built under British Emergency War Programme as a unit of the *Azalea* group of " Flower Class " Sloops. Sold to Portugal 1920. Refitted 1928–30 for Colonial Service.

1933, *Eng. Lt.-Com. Aluino Martins, P.N.*

CARVALHO ARAUJO (ex-H.M.S. *Jonquil*, launched May, 1915, by Chas. Connell & Co., Scotstoun.) Displacement : 916 tons *standard*, 1,210 tons *full load*. Dimensions : 250 (*pp.*), 262½ (*o.a.*) × 33 × 11 (*mean*), 11¾ feet (*max.* draught). Guns : as *Republica* above and also 2 Thornycroft type depth charge throwers. I.H.P. : 2,242 = 17·25 kts. Speed machinery, boilers, &c., as *Republica*. Built under British Emergency War Programme as a unit of the *Acacia* group of " Flower Class " Sloops. Sold to Portugal, 1920. Refitted 1928–30 for Colonial Service. In 1937 adapted for use as a Surveying Vessel. Complement as such : 90.

Note.—This ship is named after a Portuguese naval officer killed in action with a German submarine during the Great War.

6 Destroyers (*Contra-Torpedeiros*).

3 authorised for construction in 1939. Displacement : 1,400 tons.

TEJO.   1936, *Courtesy Eng. Lieut.-Com. Aluino Martins da Silva.*

5 *Yarrow* type : **Dão** (July 27, 1934), **Vouga** (Jan. 25, 1933), **Lima** (May 29, 1933), **Tejo** (May 4, 1935), **Douro** (Aug. 16, 1935). Displacement : 1,239 tons *standard*, 1,588 tons *full load*. Complement : 163 *normal*, 184 *full*. Dimensions : 319 (*pp.*), 322 (*o.a.*) × 31 × 11 feet (*mean draught*). Guns : 4—4·7 inch, 50 cal., 3—40 mm. AA., 2 D.C.T. Torpedo tubes : 8—21 inch, quadrupled. Mine rails fitted and 20 mines carried.

Machinery : Parsons geared turbines. S.H.P. 33,000 = 36 kts. 3 Yarrow boilers (400 lbs. pressure). Oil : 296 tons *normal*, 345 tons *maximum*. Radius : 5,400 miles at 15 kts. Trials gave speeds of from 36·65 to 37 kts. with ample margin of power and boiler capacity.

Note.—Two earlier ships of this class, originally named *Douro* and *Tejo*, were sold to Colombia, fresh ships with these names being built to replace them. All built at Lisbon except *Vouga* and *Lima*, constructed on the Clyde by Messrs. Yarrow, as were machinery and boilers of all five.

Distinguishing letters on bows :   D—Dão   L—Lima   V—Vouga
D R—Douro   T—Tejo

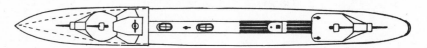

VOUGA   1933, *courtesy Messrs. Yarrow.*

Destroyers (*continued*).

TAMEGA.   1938, *courtesy E. H. Garrett, Esq.*

1 *Yarrow* type : **Tamega** (Jan. 1922) by Lisbon D.Y.   524 tons (670 tons *full load*).   Dimensions : 240 × 23½ × 7⅞ feet, *max*. draught.   Armament : **1**—4 inch, **2**—3 inch.   **4**—18 inch Torpedo tubes (paired)   Parsons turbines : 11,000 = 27 kts.   3 Yarrow boilers.   Coal : 146 tons = 800 miles at 15 kts.   Complement, 80.

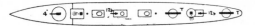

(Note.—Now has twin TT mountings.)

Torpedo Boat (*Torpedeiro*).

SADO.   1933 *Photo, Eng. Lt.-Com. Aluino Martins, P.N.*

1 Ex-Austrian boat : **Sado,** (ex-*F* 89).   (Ganz-Danubius Co., Porto Re, Fiume, 1913–15.   Displacement : 195 tons *standard*, 250 tons *full load*.   Dimensions : 188·3 × 19 × 8 feet *max*. draught.   Guns : **1**—56 mm. Skoda, **1**—57 mm. Hotchkiss.   Tubes : **4**—18 inch paired.   Designed S.H.P. : 5,000 = 28 kts. (made 31 kts. when new).   Turbine engines and 2 Yarrow boilers.   Fuel : 20 tons coal + 34 tons oil.   Complement : 46.

3 Submarines (*Submersiveis*).

3 authorised for construction in 1939.   Displacement : 900 tons.

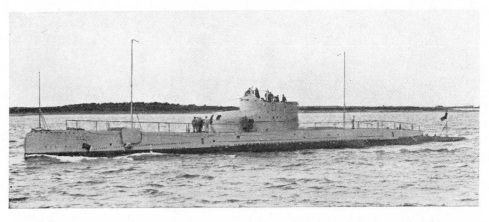

DELFIM.   1934 *Photo Messrs. Vickers Armstrongs.*

3 *Vickers-Armstrongs* type : **Delfim** (May 1, 1934), **Espadarte**, **Golfinho** (both May 30, 1934).

Displacement : 813/1,125 tons.   Dimensions : 227·2 × 21·3 × 12·7 feet.
Armament : **1**—4 inch, **2** M.G.   Tubes : **6**—21 inch (4 bow, 2 stern).   12 torpedoes carried.
Machinery : Vickers Diesels, B.H.P. 2,300 = 16·5 kts.   Motors H.P. 1,000 = 9·25 kts.   Radius : 2,080 miles full speed, 5,000 miles at 10 kts. ; *submerged* = 8 miles at full speed and 110 miles at 4 kts.
Complement, 36.

Notes.—All three laid down at Barrow, 9th March, 1933, and completed 1935.   Distinguished by initial letters of names painted on C.T.

Motor Torpedo Boats.

6 M.T.B. are projected.

Gunboats (Canhoneiras).

ZAIRE. 1933 Photo, Eng. Lt.-Com. Aluino Martins, P.N.

DIU (Oct., 1929), **ZAIRE** (ex-*Goa*, Feb. 26, 1925), **IBO** (1911). **MANDOVI** (1917). All built at Lisbon D.Y. Displacement : 403 tons *standard*, 500 tons *full load*. Dimensions : 147⅔ × 27¼ × 7 feet. Guns : 2—3 inch 40 cal. (Armstrong), 2—47 mm. (except *Mandovi*, which has only 4—47 mm.). H.P. : 700 = 13 kts. Coal : 85 tons. Radius : 3,200 miles at 9 kts. Machinery : Triple expansion. 2 shafts. Boilers : Cylindrical in *Ibo*, 2 Yarrow in others. Complement : 67.

Identification letters : *Diu*, none ; *Ibo*, I ; *Zaire*, Z ; *Mandovi*, M.

Fishery Protection Vessels.
(*Canhoneiras da Fiscalização da Pesca*)

NEW CONSTRUCTION.

2 vessels, building at Lisbon. Displacement : 250 tons (*full load*). Complement : 25. Dimensions : 134½ (*p.p.*), 139¾ (*o.a.*) × 21⅓ × 7 feet (*max.*). Guns : 4—25 mm. AA. in twin mounts : Machinery : M.A.N. Diesel. 2 shafts. B.H.P. : 2,600 = 18 kts. Fuel : 25 tons. Radius of action : 2,500 miles at cruising speed, 850 miles at full speed.

(4 more of these vessels are projected.)

LAGOS. 1933 Photo, Mr. Henrique Seixas.
Now has white band round funnel to distinguish from FARO).

FARO, LAGOS (1927). Built at Lisbon D.Y. Displacement : 300 tons. Dimensions : 120 (*p.p.*), 130½ (*o.a.*) × 22 × 10½ feet. Guns : 2—47 mm. H.P. : 650 = 13 kts. 1 Yarrow boiler. 1 screw. Radius : 2,000 miles at 7·5 kts. Oil : 42 tons. Complement : 55.

Fishery Protection Vessels—(*continued*).

LIDADOR. 1933, Eng. Lt.-Com. Aluino Martins, P.N.

LIDADOR (Laird, Birkenhead, 1884). Iron. 201 tons. Dimensions : 113¾ (*p.p.*), 115 (*o.a.*) × 20 × 6½ feet. Guns : 2 Hotchkiss 47 mm. Machinery : 2 sets 2 cyl. Comp. H.P. : 400 = 11 kts. 2 screws. 1 cyl. Boiler. Coal : 40 tons = 1,528 miles at 7 kts. Complement : 40. Classed as a Tug, she is employed on Fishery Protection duties.

PORTUGAL—Miscellaneous
River Gunboats (Lanchas-Canhoneiras).

1938, Eng. Lieut.-Com. Aluino Martins da Silva.

MACAU (Yarrow, 1909). 95 tons. $119\frac{2}{3} \times 19\frac{3}{4} \times 2$ feet. Guns: 2—6 pdr., 3 machine. H.P. 250=11·8 kts. Boilers: 1 Yarrow. Complement: 24. On China Station.

1933 Photo, Mr. Henrique Seixas.

TÉTE (1918). 100 tons. Guns: 2—20 mm., 2 M.G. H.P.: 200 = 9 kts. Employed on Zambesi River.

River Gunboats—continued.

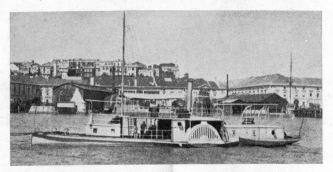

1933 Photo, Eng. Lt.-Com. Aluino Martins, P.N.

RIO MINHO (Lisbon D.Y., 1904). 38 tons. Paddlewheel. $80\frac{3}{4} \times 13 \times 2$ feet. H.P.: 64 = $7\frac{1}{2}$ kts. Guns: 1—1 pdr., 1 M.G. Complement: 68 are nominally borne on her books, the majority of these ranks and ratings being actually at various shore stations on the Portuguese bank of the river Minho, for fisheries inspection, customs duties, &c.

Patrol Vessel (Patrulha).

1933 Photo, Eng. Lt.-Com. Aluino Martins, P.N.

LINCE (Orlando, 1911). 78 tons. $88\frac{1}{2} \times 14 \times 6$ feet. 2 sets semi-Diesels. B.H.P.: 300 = 12 kts. 2 screws. Complement: 20. Attached to Torpedo Training School.

400

Mining Tenders (Lança-minas).

1933 Photo, Mr. Henrique Seixas.

VULCANO (Thornycroft, 1910). 129 tons. $110 \times 19\frac{1}{2} \times 7\frac{1}{4}$ feet. H.P.: 500 = 13 kts. 2 screws. Thornycroft boiler. Complement: 27. Employed in Diving and Torpedo instruction, mounting 3 Torpedo Tubes for this purpose, besides Mine-dropping gear forward.

1933 Photo, Mr. Henrique Seixas.

MINEIRO (1892). 77 tons. $58\frac{1}{2} \times 13\frac{1}{2} \times 7$ feet. I.H.P.: 150 = 8 kts. 2 screws. Coal: 10 tons. Complement, 18.

Lighthouse Tender. (Navio Balizador).

1934 Photo, Official.

ALMIRANTE SCHULTZ (Penhoët, 1929). 529 tons. Complement: 48. Dimensions: $131\frac{1}{4} \times 31 \times 10\frac{3}{4}$ feet. 2 sets Rateau. Diesels. H.P.: 350 = 11 kts. Fuel: 21 tons.

Surveying Vessels (*Navios Hidrograficos*).

Note.—Escort Vessel *Carvalho Araujo*, on an earlier page, is serving temporarily as a Surveying Vessel.

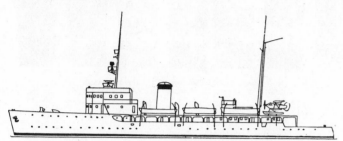

A new Surveying Vessel was laid down May 5, 1939, at the new Naval Dockyard at Alfeite, opposite Lisbon. Displacement : 960 tons (1,140 tons *full load*). Dimensions : 206¾ (*pp.*), 215⅔ (*o.a.*) × 32⅕ × 9½ feet (*mean*). Machinery : 2 sets triple expansion by McKie & Baxter, Ltd., Paisley. I.H.P. : 1,200 = 12·5 kts. Boilers : 2 of 3-drum type by J. Samuel White & Co., Ltd. Oil fuel. Radius : 5,000 miles. 1 seaplane carried.

1937, *Eng. Lt.-Com. Aluino Martins, P.N.*

BEIRA (Lisbon, 1910). Ex-gunboat, adapted for Surveying in 1936. 403 tons. Dimensions : 147¼ × 27¼ × 7 feet. Guns : 2—65 mm., 2—47 mm. Machinery : Triple expansion. 2 shafts. H.P. : 700 = 13 kts. Boilers : Cylindrical. Coal : 85 tons. Radius : 3,200 miles at 9 kts. Complement : 34.

Surveying Vessels—*continued*.

1933 *Photo, Mr. Henrique Seixas.*

BERRIO (S.A. At. et Ch. Loire, 1897). 350 tons. Guns : nil. Compound engines. H.P. 1,070 = 10 kts. Coal : 103 tons. Complement : 68. Ex-Fleet Tug. Employed on Portuguese E. African Coast.

Oiler

1 building at Alfeite. Displacement : 7,000 tons. Capacity : 3,500 tons. Dimensions : 410 × 50¾ × 18 feet. Guns : 1—3·9 inch AA. Machinery : B. & W. Diesel. B.H.P. : 2,500 = 12 knots.

Transport (*Transporte*).

1933 *Photo, Eng. Lt.-Com. Aluino Martins, P.N.*

GIL EANES (ex-*Lahneck*) (Joh. C. Tecklenborg, 1914). 2,769 tons. Dimensions : 278 × 41 × 16·8 feet. Guns : 2—47 mm. H.P. : 2,000 = 11 kts. 1 screw. Cylindrical boilers. Employed as Hospital Ship on Fishery Service.

Training Ship (*Navio-Escola*).

1933 *Photo, Eng. Lt.-Com. Aluino Martins, P.N.*

SAGRES (ex-*Flores*, ex-*Max*, ex-*Rickmer Rickmers*). (Bremerhaven, 1896). Displacement : 3,116 tons (1,980 tons *gross*). Dimensions : 263½ × 40⅓ × 19 feet. Guns : 4—57 mm. Machinery : 2 sets Krupp Diesels. B.H.P. : 700 = 8 kts. 2 screws. Complement : 181 (+ 196, personnel under training). Captured German sailing vessel, adapted as a naval training ship, 1924–27 ; auxiliary motors fitted in 1931.

ROUMANIA.

FLAGS

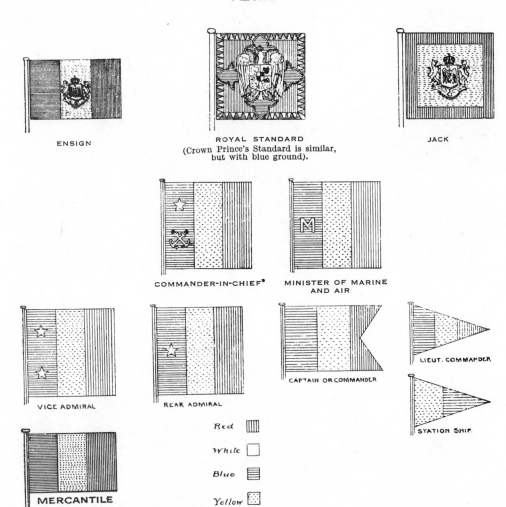

ENSIGN

ROYAL STANDARD
(Crown Prince's Standard is similar,
but with blue ground).

JACK

COMMANDER-IN-CHIEF*

MINISTER OF MARINE
AND AIR

VICE ADMIRAL

REAR ADMIRAL

LIEUT. COMMANDER

CAPTAIN OR COMMANDER

STATION SHIP.

MERCANTILE

Red

White

Blue

Yellow

* When the C. in C. is a Vice-Admiral, as at present, this flag carries two stars and crossed anchors.

Uniforms.

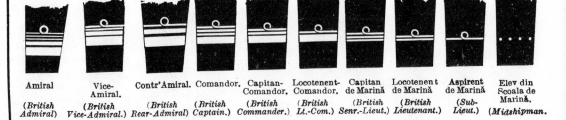

Amiral	Vice-Amiral.	Contr'Amiral.	Comandor.	Capitan-Comandor.	Locotenent-Comandor.	Capitan de Marină	Locotenent de Marină	Aspirent de Marină	Elev din Scoala de Marină.
(British Admiral)	(British Vice-Admiral.)	(British Rear-Admiral)	(British Captain.)	(British Commander.)	(British Lt.-Com.)	(British Senr.-Lieut.)	(British Lieutenant.)	(Sub-Lieut.)	(Midshipman.

There is also the rank of Admiral of the Fleet, held only by the King, (as Admiral, but 4 thin stripes).

Stripes are gold (except Paymasters, who wear silver) with curl for all branches. Colour of silk between, above and below stripes :—Executive, black ; Engineers, violet ; Surgeons, dark red, almost purple in colour : Constructors, light blue ; Apothecaries, green ; Musical Director, light grey.

ADMINISTRATION.

Minister of Marine (and Air) : General Paul Teodorescu, A.d.C.

Secretary-General : Contr' Amiral Alexandru Gheorghiu.

Commander-in-Chief and Director General of the Navy : Vice-Amiral Petre I. Bărbuneanu.

Naval Attaché, London : Captain Gheorghe St. Dumitrescu, C.V.O.

Mercantile Marine 1939: 35 vessels of 111,678 gross tonnage.

Colour of Ships : Light grey.

Personnel : 250 officers, 3,000 men.

Form of Address : " N.M.S." (" Nava Majestații Sale ").

Silhouettes.

LT. LEPRI REMUS *class* (4).

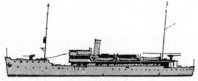

CONSTANTA.

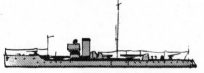

SBORUL.

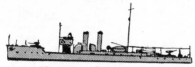

NALUCA. SMEUL.

LUCEAFARUL.

REGELÈ FERDINAND
REGINA MARIA.

MARASTI. MARASESTI.

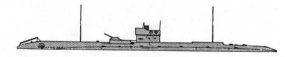

DELFINUL.

(1) **Black Sea Division** (*Divizia de Mare*). **4 Destroyers** (*Distrugătoăre*).

REGELÈ FERDINAND   (Note band around fore funnel)   1935.

REGINA MARIA. (Note band around after funnel.)   1937, *R. Perkins.*

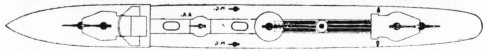

2 *Thornycroft type:* **Regelè Ferdinand** (Dec. 2nd, 1928), **Regina Maria** (March 2nd, 1929). Laid down at Pattison Yard, Naples, in June, 1927, to design of Messrs. Thornycroft. Displacement 1900 tons. Dimensions: 334½ × 31½ × 11½ feet. Parsons geared turbines by Stabilimento Tecnico Triestino. H.P. 48.000 = 35 kts. Radius: 3000 miles at 15 kts. Armament: **5**—4·7 inch, 50 cal., Bofors, **1**—3 inch, AA., Bofors, **2**—2 pdr. pom-pom, **6**—21 inch torpedo tubes (tripled), 50 mines. Firing Director of Siemens type. Cost per ship, without armament £205,000: completed 1930. Complement, 212.

Note.—*Regina Maria* refitted at Malta, 1938.

Destroyers.—*continued.*

1932.

2 *Pattison type*: **Marasti** (ex-Italian *Sparviero*, 1919), and **Marasesti** (ex-Italian *Nibbio*, 1918). 1391 tons *normal* (1723 tons *full load*). Dimensions : 309¼ (*p.p.*) × 31 × 11½ feet. Guns : 5—4·7 inch, 2—3 inch, 40 cal. AA. 2 M.G. Tubes : 4—17·7 inch in twin deck mountings. Searchlights : 1—36 inch. Designed S.H.P. 45,000 = 34 kts. Trials : *Marasesti*, 48,020 S.H.P.=38·04 kts., 2 Tosi turbines. 2 screws. 5 Thornycroft oil burning boilers. Oil : 260 tons=1700 miles (15 kts.), 380 miles (full speed). Complement : 139.

Notes.—Belong to class of 4 Destroyers, *Vifor, Viscol, Vârtej, Vijelia*, ordered for Roumanian Navy about 1913. Were requisitioned for Italian Navy during war and re-named *Aquila, Falco, Nibbio, Sparviero*. Last two re-purchased by Roumania 1920, and renamed after actions fought in 1917. Refitted and rearmed at Galatz and Naples, 1925-26.

Submarine Depot Ship (*Navă Bază*).

1931.

CONSTANTA) November 8, 1928). Laid down at the Quarnaro Yard, Fiume, August 15, 1927, completed in 1931. Displacement : 1,350 tons. Dimensions : 255¾ × 37 × 13¼ feet. 2 sets Diesels. B.H.P. : 1,000 = 13 kts. Radius : 12,000 miles. Guns : 2—4 inch, 2 M.G. 3 sets generating sets. H.P. : 136. Fitted with engineering and torpedo shops ; bakery ; torpedo loading room ; salvage, diving and submarine signalling apparatus.

3 Torpedo Boats. (*Torpiloare*).

1934.

1 Ex-Austrian boat : **Sborul** (ex-*81T*), (Stab Tecnico Triestino, Trieste, 1913-14). Displacement : 262 tons. Dimensions : 189½ × 19 × 5 feet. Guns : 2—11 pdr. ; Torpedo tubes : 4—17·7 inch. Designed S.H.P. 5000=28 kts. (24 best speed now) Turbine engines and Yarrow boilers. Fuel : 18 tons coal + 24 tons oil. *Sborul* means Flight.

NALUCA.   1935.

2 Ex-Austrian boats : **Naluca** (ex- *82F*), **Smeul** (ex-83F), (Ganz-Danubius Co., Porto Ré, Fiume, 1913-14.) 260 tons. Beam, 19 feet. Guns : 2—11 pdr., 2 M.G. No tubes, 1—16·5 inch S.L. Fuel : 20 tons coal + 34 tons oil, other details as *Sborul* above. *Smeul*=Dragon. *Naluca*=Phantom.

Submarine.

Note.—2 more submarines are building in the Naval Dockyard at Galatz.

1 *Quarnaro* boat : **Delfinul.** (June 22, 1930). Displacement : 650/900 tons. Dimensions : 225 × 19¼ × 12 feet. Speed 14/9 kts. Guns : 1—4 inch, 35 cal. Tubes : 8—21 inch. Completed 1931, but not taken over by Roumania until April, 1936.

(Black Sea) Gunboats (*Canoniere*).

STIHI EUGEN.

1935.

LOCOTENENT LEPRI REMUS (ex-French *Chiffonne*, Lorient D.Y. launched 1917).
LOCOTENENT-COMANDOR STIHI EUGEN (ex-French *Friponne*, Lorient D.Y., launched 1916).
SUBLOCOTENENT GHICULESCU (ex-French *Impatiente*, Brest D.Y., launched 1916).
CĂPITAN DUMITRESCU C. (ex-French *Mignonne*, Brest D.Y., launched 1917).
Displacement: 400, 450, 350, 390 tons respectively. Length: 189½ to 199¾ ft. Beam: 22 ft. 7 in. Draught: first pair, 9¼ ft.; second pair, 7¾ ft. Guns: 2—3·9 inch. 2 M.G. S.L.: 2—15·7 inch. Engines: 2 sets of Sulzer Diesel motors. B.H.P. 900 = 15 kts. Fuel carried: 30 tons oil = 3000 miles (10 kts.), 1600 miles (15 kts.) Complement, 50.

Notes.—Purchased from French Navy, 9th January, 1920. Entered service 15th Jan., 1920. Are differentiated by coloured rings around crowsnest. Names are those of naval officers killed in action. 1916-18.

Royal Yachts.

LUCEAFARUL. *Added 1937, courtesy Messrs. G. L. Watson & Co., (Designers).*

LUCEAFARUL (ex-*Nahlin*). (Clydebank, 1930). Purchased 1937. Displacement, 2,050 tons. Dimensions: 250 (*w.l.*), 296 (*o.a.*) × 36 × — feet. Machinery: 4 Brown Curtis geared turbines. 2 shafts. S.H.P.: 4,000 = 17·5 kts. Oil fuel.
TAIFUN (J. Samuel White & Co. Ltd., Cowes, 1938). Wood. 34 tons Thames measurement. Dimensions: 54 × 12½ × 3 feet. Machinery: 2 petrol motors. 2 shafts.

(2) Danube Division (*Divizia de Dunăre*).

Monitors (*Monitoare*).

Note.—With exception of *Bratianu* class, all are named after Roumanian provinces acquired after the Great War.

(Now has 2 white bands around funnel. Has flush deck forward.)

BUCOVINA (ex-Austro-Hungarian *Sava*, launched 1915). Displacement, 550 tons. Dimensions: 190¼ × 33·8 × 4¼ feet. Guns: 2—4.7 inch, 45 cal. Skoda (paired in single turret forward) + 2—4.7 inch, 10 cal. howitzers (fortress type, singly mounted in pits with cupola protection), 2—66 m/m. (AA., twin-mounted in turret), 2—47 m/m., and 6 M.G. 1—24 inch searchlight. Armour: 1½″ Belt and Bulkheads, 1″ Deck, 2″ C.T., 2″ Turret and Cupolas. 3 magazines with water-jackets and electric-controlled refrigerators. Designed H.P. 1600 = 12 kts. Boilers: Yarrow. Fuel: 75 tons, oil *only*. Complement, 90 to 100. Built under 1914-15 Austro-Hungarian Naval Programme, completed 1915. Interned at Novi Sad 1919-20 and handed over by Yugo-Slavs at Orsova early in 1921. Sister ship, *Drava*, now unit of Yugo-Slav Danube Flotilla.

BASARABIA (ex-Austro-Hungarian *Inn*, launched 1915). Displacement, 590 tons. Dimensions 203¼ (*o.a.*) × 34½ × 4¼ feet. Guns: 2—4.7 inch, 45 cal. + 3—4.7 inch, 10 cal. howitzers, 2—47 m/m., 9 M.G. Armour: 1½″ Belt and Bulkheads, 1″ Deck, 2″ Turret and Cupolas, 2″ C.T. Designed I.H.P. 1500 = 12 kts. Boilers: Yarrow. Fuel: 70 tons, oil *only*. Complement, 100. Built under Austro-Hungarian 1912 Naval Programme; interned at Novi Sad 1919-20, handed over by Yugo-Slavs at Orsova early in 1921. Sister ship *Vardar*, now unit of Yugo-Slav Danube Flotilla is shown above.

(Danube) Monitors—*continued.*

L. CATARGIU. 1934

ION C. BRĂTIANU (1907), **MIHAIL KOGĂLNICEANU** (1907), **ALEXANDRU LAHOVARI** (1908), and **LASCĂR CATARGIU** (1907). Displacement : 680 tons. Complement, 110. Dimensions : 208¼ × 33¾ × 5¼ feet. Guns (Skoda) : 3—4.7 inch, 35 cal. (2—4.7 inch howitzers removed during the War), 1—3 inch. AA., 2—47 m/m., 2 M.G. 1—30.7 inch searchlight. Armour : 3″ Belt, 3″ Deck, 3″—2″ Turrets. H.P. 1800 = 13 kts. Coal : 60 tons. Built by Stabilimento Tecnico Triestino, at Trieste, in sections, re-erected at Galatz. Deck cabins, military masts and howitzers removed during the War, and funnel modified. All named after nineteenth century Roumanian statesmen.

1922 *Photo.*

ARDEAL (ex-Austro-Hungarian *Temes*, 1904). Displacement : 450 tons. Complement, 80 to 90. Dimensions : 183½ × 31¼ × 3¾ feet. Guns : 2—4.7 inch, 35 cal., 1—3.5 inch AA., 2—47 m/m., 4 M.G. Armour : 1½″ Belt, 3″ and 1½″ Turrets, 1½″ Bulkheads, 1″ Deck. H.P. 1400 = 10 kts. Fuel capacity : 60 tons. Was originally built as a sister-ship to *Sava*, of Yugo-Slav Navy. While serving on Danube as Austro-Hungarian *Temes*, she was sunk in October, 1914, but was raised in June, 1916, and entirely rebuilt 1916-17 ; she is thus, compared with others of the same original design, a practically new Monitor. Re-entered service April, 1917. Interned at Novi Sad, 1919-20 ; handed over at Orsova by Yugo-Slavs early in 1921. Easily identified by her tall, thin funnel and raised gun aft, mounted during reconstruction, 1916-17. No other Monitor exists with this arrangement, except Yugo-Slav *Morava*, and her guns are not all in turrets.

Note.—*Ardeal* is the Roumanian name for the province of Transylvania.

(Danube) Patrol Vessels (*Vedete*).

1922.

No. 3, (ex-*Căpitan Romano Mihail*) **No. 7,** (ex-*Locotenent Călinescu Dimitrie*), (Thames Iron Works, 1906). Displacement : 50 tons. Dimensions : 100 × 13 × 2¾ feet. Armament : 1—47 m/m. Skoda 1 machine. 1—20 inch S.L. 2 screws. H.P. : 550 = 18 kts. Oil fuel : 7½ tons. Complement : 20. Differentiated by large coloured numerals on funnels. Their two twin funnels, ram bows and round tunnel sterns make their recognition easy. *Capt. V. Mârăcineau* mined 1916, and 4 others scrapped. All were originally named after Army officers who fell in the War of Independence, 1877-

(Black Sea) Sail Training Ship. (*Vas Scoală*)

(For photo, see Addenda.)

MIRCEA (Blohm & Voss Hamburg, Sept. 22, 1938). Displacement : 1,604 tons. Dimensions : 239½ (o.a.), 267⅓ (*with bowsprit*) × 39⅓ × 16½ feet. Auxiliary M.A.N. 6-cylinder Diesel. B.H.P. : 500 = 9·5 kts. Sail area : 18,830 sq. ft. Complement : 83 + 140 junior officers for training. Laid down April 30, 1938, and delivered March 29, 1939.

Minelayers (*Puitoare de Mine*)

AMIRAL MURGESCU (Galatz, June 14, 1939) and another (building). *Standard* displacement : 812 tons. Complement : 78. Dimensions : 252½ (o.a.) × 29½ × 8¼ feet (*mean* draught). Guns : 2—4 inch (dual purpose), 2—37 mm. AA., 2 D.C.T. Mines : 135. Machinery : 2 Krupp Diesels. B.H.P. : 2,100 = 16 kts. Radius of action : 3,400 miles at 12 kts.

RUSSIA.

UNION OF SOCIALIST SOVIET REPUBLICS.

It is extremely difficult to secure accurate information regarding the Russian Navy, but the particulars given in these pages were revised and compared with data from reliable sources in 1939.

Displacements of more important ships are standard.

Minister of War and Marine.—Marshal K. E. Voroshilov.

Komissar for Navy.—Admiral Nikolai Kuznetsov.

Naval Flags.

NATIONAL FLAG.

JACK.

COMMANDER IN CHIEF.

CHIEF OF STAFF.

OFFICER COMMANDING NAVAL FORCES.

SENIOR FLAG OFFICER.

JUNIOR FLAG OFFICER.

COMMODORE

SENIOR OFFICER AFLOAT.

PENDANT.

COMMANDER OF FLOTILLA.

	Red
	Blue
	Black
	Green
	Yellow
	White

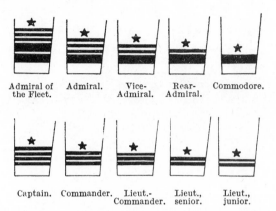

Admiral of the Fleet. Admiral. Vice-Admiral. Rear-Admiral. Commodore.

Captain. Commander. Lieut.-Commander. Lieut., senior. Lieut., junior.

Distribution of Fleet.

Reports from Japanese sources indicate that the Soviet Fleet based on Vladivostok includes 70 submarines, over 50 motor torpedo boats and a number of patrol vessels of various types. "Fighting Ships" has secured independent evidence which goes far to support these figures.

Most of these vessels are believed to have proceeded to their present station by way of North East Passage.

Personnel: 23,600 (about 10,000 seagoing). These figures have been largely increased.

Modern Naval Guns (Obukhoff).

Designation.		Length in Calibres.	Weight of Guns.	Weight of A.P. Shot.	Initial Velocity (approximate).	Maximum Penetration with A.P. Capped Shell against K.C. Armour.			Danger Space against average warship at			Usual Rounds per minute.
						10,000 yds.	5000 yds.	3000 yds.	10,000 yards.	5000 yards.	3000 yards.	
C.M.	inch.	calibres.	tons.	lbs.	f.s.	in.	in.	in.	yards.	yards.	yards.	
30·5	12	52	48·2	714	3000	...	14½	20	...	...	...	...
18.0	7.1	55										
	6	45	7½	89	2900	...	4¼	6	60	250	485	3
	6	45	7	89	2600	...	3¼	5	50	200	430	3
13.0	5.1	55/60	...	...	...	...	...	...	...	...	...	...
12.0	4.7	50	2¼	46	2600	...	...	...	...	...	...	about 4
10·2	4	...	...	...	...	...	...	...	...	...	...	...
10.0	3·9	60	...	...	·	...	...	...	...	...	...	...
7·5	3	60	14 cwt.	13½	2700	...	...	...	...	...	...	...
6·3	2·5	35	12 „	13¼	2600	...	...	...	...	...	...	...

Mercantile Marine.

From "Lloyd's Register," 1939 figures, 716 vessels of 1,315,766 *gross* tonnage.

(B)—*Baltic.* **(BS)**—*Black Sea.* **(C)**—*Caspian.*

PARISKAYA-KOMMUNA. (B.S.)
(Now has tripod foremast, and may have catapult.)

KIROV *class.* (B) and (B.S.)

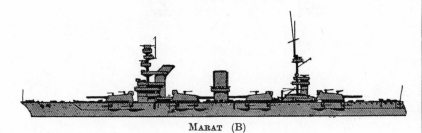

MARAT (B)

PROFINTERN, CHERVONAYA UKRAÏNA. (B.S.)

KRASNI-KAVKAZ. (B.S.)

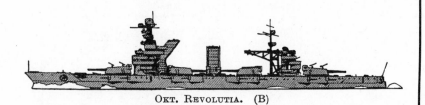

OKT. REVOLUTIA. (B)

MARTI (B)

KOMINTERN. (B.S.)

(**B**)—*Baltic.*   (**BS**)—*Black Sea.*   (**C**)—*Caspian.*

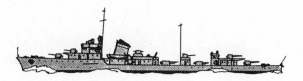

STREMITELNI *class.*

FRUNZE. (B.S.)

MARTINOV *class.* (B)

SHTORM *class.* (B)

PETROVSKI *class.* (B.S.)

KONSTRUKTOR. (B)

LENINGRAD *class.* (B)

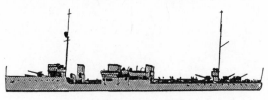

STALIN *class.* (B)
(No tripods.)

TASHKENT.

RYKOV. (B)
(Observe tripods.)

MARKIN *class.* (C)

ZHELESNIAKOV *class.* (B)

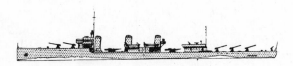

KARL MARX *class.* (B)

ex-YAKOV SVERDLOV (B)

(**B**)—*Baltic.*   (**BS**)—*Black Sea.*   (**C**)—*Caspian.*

Dzerjinski *type* (Far East).

Znamya-Sozialisma. (B.S.)

Trevolev.(B) Leningrad Soviet.(B)
(Vary in details.)

Svir.

Fugas *class* (B. and Far East).

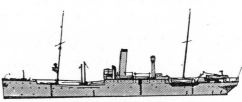

Serp-i-Molot (B)

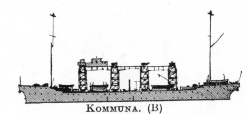

Kommuna. (B)

Vorovsky (Far East).

25 Oktiabrya. (B)

Krasni-Azarbaijan. (C)
Lenin. (C)

Deviatoe-Yanvarya. (B) Pervoe-Maya. (B.S.)

Komsomoletz. (B)

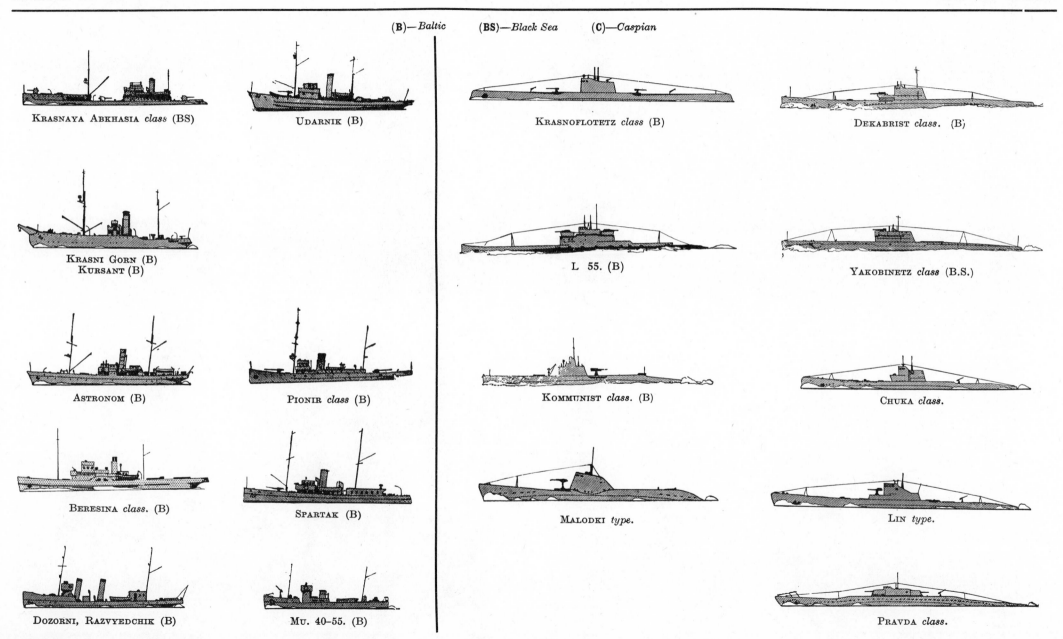

(B)—*Baltic*   **(BS)**—*Black Sea*   **(C)**—*Caspian*

KRASNAYA ABKHASIA *class* (BS)

UDARNIK (B)

KRASNOFLOTETZ *class* (B)

DEKABRIST *class.* (B)

KRASNI GORN (B)
KURSANT (B)

L 55. (B)

YAKOBINETZ *class* (B.S.)

ASTRONOM (B)

PIONIR *class* (B)

KOMMUNIST *class.* (B)

CHUKA *class.*

BERESINA *class.* (B)

SPARTAK (B)

MALODKI *type.*

LIN *type.*

DOZORNI, RAZVYEDCHIK (B)

MU. 40–55. (B)

PRAVDA *class.*

MARAT.

1935, *Nautical Photo Agency.*

New Construction

3 ships of 35,000 tons *projected*. Approximate dimensions 820 × 100 feet. To be armed with 9—16 inch and 12—6 inch guns: Though it has been reported that the first ship, to be named *Tretii International*, will be laid down at Leningrad in 1939, guns, armour and boilers having been ordered abroad, there is no reliable information on the subject. A naval mission under Admiral Isakov has visited the United States in connection with the purchase of the necessary material.

(For particulars of ships illustrated here, see following page.)

MARAT.

1937, *R. Perkins.*

OKT. REVOLUTIA.

1935 *Nautical Photo Agency.*

PARISKAYA-KOMMUNA (ex-*Sevastopol*, June, 1911),

MARAT (ex-*Petropavlovsk*, Sept., 1911),

OKTIABRSKAYA-REVOLUTIA (ex-*Gangut*, October, 1911).

Standard displacement, 23,016, 23,606 and 23,256 tons, respectively; *full load*, over 26,000 tons. Complement, 1125.

Length *over all*, 619 feet. Beam, 87 feet. *Mean* draught, 27½ feet.

MARAT. 1937, *R. Perkins.*

Guns :
12—12 inch, 52 cal.
16—4·7 inch, 50 cal.
10—3 inch AA. (*Marat*, 6).
1—3 pdr.
8 Machine.

Torpedo tubes (18 inch) :
4 *submerged*.

Aircraft :
1 (No catapult except in *Par.-Kom*).

Armour (Krupp) :
8¾″ Belt (amidships) ...
5″-2″ Belt (ends)
3″-4″ Internal belt (*see notes*)
3″ Deck
12″-10″ Turrets
8″ Turret bases
6″ Battery
10″ Conning tower

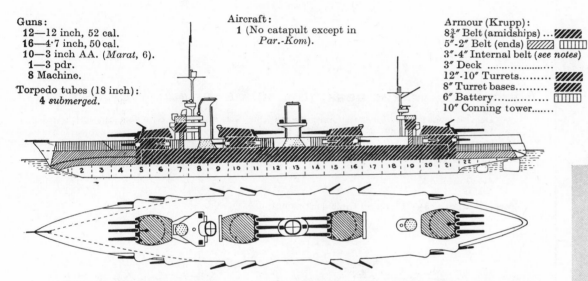

Machinery : Parsons turbine. 4 screws. Boilers : 25 Yarrow. Designed H.P. 42,000 = 23 kts. Coal *normal*, 1,000 tons ; *maximum*, 3000 tons. Also 1,170 tons oil. Radius of action : 900 miles at 23 kts., 4,000 miles at 16 kts.

Gunnery Notes.—The port plate above each gun is in the form of a hinged flap, allowing each 12-inch gun to elevate to 30—40° *maximum*. Arcs of fire : End triple 12-inch barbettes, 310° ; central barbettes, 130° *each beam* ; aft group of 4—4·7 inch, 90° ; other 4·7 inch, 85°.

Armour Notes.—Belt is about 15 feet wide, 5 feet of it below water, uniform thickness. There is a *secondary 3″-4″* internal belt 11 feet inboard above protective deck, extending between the end barbettes. The space between main belt and internal belts is divided up into w.t. compartments.

Name	Builder	Machinery	Laid down	Com- pleted	Trials : Full power	Boilers	Best recent speed
Marat	} Baltic Works	Baltic Works	June,'09	Jan. '14 }	About 50,000 = 23·4	Yarrow	18
P.Kommuna		Franco- }	June,'09	Jan. '15 }			16
Okt. Revolutia	Galernii	Rus. Works }		Jan. '14 }			18

General Notes.—The late Gen. Vittorio Cuniberti prepared the original designs for this type. The Ministry of Marine afterwards altered the plans to include Russian ideas of armouring, ice-breaking bows and other special features. Further, to obtain a higher speed, hull design is relatively lighter than in contemporary battleships of other fleets. Said to be most unhealthy, insanitary and badly ventilated. *Pariskaya-Kommuna* proceeded to Black Sea early in 1930 in company with *Profintern*. General condition reported to be unsatisfactory, and official explanation of her remaining in Black Sea is that she could not face the return passage. But she has since undergone an extensive refit.
A fourth ship of this type, *Mihail Frunze*, is understood to have been scrapped.

PARISKAYA-KOMMUNA (Now has tripod foremast, aircraft and catapult). 1930 *Photo.*

Aircraft Carriers.

KRASNOYE ZNAMYA and another (projected).
Displacement : 12,000 tons. Complement : .
Dimensions : Not reported.

Guns :
   12—4 inch.
Machinery :
   Geared Turbines

Aircraft : 40.

Speed : 30 kts.

(Both to be laid down at Leningrad in 1939-40.)

Photo wanted

STALIN (ex-*Krasnaya Bessarabia*, ex-*Admiral Kornilov*), (Oct. 4, 1937).
Displacement : 9,000 tons. Complement :
Dimensions : Not reported.

Guns :
   Not reported.

Aircraft :
   22.

Machinery : Geared turbines. Speed : 30 kts.

Note.—Laid down at Nikolaiev, 1914, as a cruiser, and construction suspended until 1929, when she was re-designed as an aircraft carrier and extensive alterations put in hand. Completed in 1939.

Cruisers.

Note.—3 cruisers of 8,000 tons with an armament of 9—6 inch guns are said to be projected.

(Kirov Class—4 Ships)

Photo wanted.

KIROV (1936), **MAXIM GORKI** (1937), **KUBYSHEV** (*building*), **ORJONIKIDZE** (*building*).
Displacement : 8,500 tons. (Also reported as 7,800 tons *standard*). Complement : 624.
Length : over 600 feet. Beam : 60 feet. Draught : 21 feet (*max.*).

Guns :
   6—7·1 inch.
   4—4 inch AA.
   4—37 mm. AA.
   4 M.G.

Aircraft : 2 or 3.

Armour :
   2″—3″ Side.
   2″ Deck.
   3″ Gunhouses.
   3″ C.T.

Torpedo tubes : 6—21 inch (in triple deck mountings).

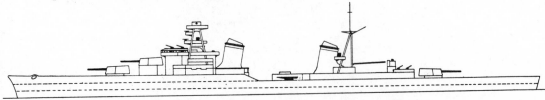

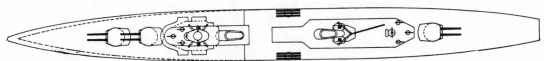

Machinery : Geared turbines with Diesels for cruising speeds. 4 shafts. H.P. : 100,000 = 35 kts.

Notes.—Design and technical direction of construction said to have been furnished by Ansaldo. *Kubyshev* has also been reported under name of *Voroshilov*. Supposition that these four ships are the re-designed hulls of the *Admiral Butakov, Admiral Spiridov, Admiral Greig* and *Admiral Istomin* appears to be unfounded.

Name.	Builder.	Machinery.	Laid down.	Completed.
Kirov	Baltic Works		1934	Aug., 1937
M. Gorki	Baltic Works	Possibly	1934	1939
Kubyshev	Marti Yard, Nikolaiev	Italian	1935	} To be
Orjonikidze	Marti Yard, Nikolaiev		1935	} 1940

KRASNI KAVKAZ (ex-*Admiral Lazarcv*, June, 1916. Nikolaiev).

1934 *Photo, favour of R. I. T. Falkner, Sub.-Lieut., R.N.*

Displacement : 8,030 tons. Complement : 624.

Length, 530 feet. Beam, 50½ feet. Draught, 20⅓ feet.

Guns :
4—7·1 inch.
4—4 inch AA.
4—37 mm. AA.
4 M.G.

Aircraft :
1, with catapult.

Tubes :
12—21 inch (tripled)

Mines : 100.

KRASNI KAVKAZ.

Correction to Plan.— Torpedo Tubes are tripled. Only 1 S.L. abaft after funnel.

Armour :
2″–3″ Side.
1″ Deck.
3″ Gunhouses.
3″ C.T.

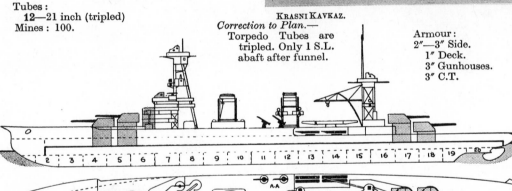

Machinery : Parsons Turbines. H.P. : 55,000 = 30 kts. Boilers : 13 Yarrow. Coal : 540 tons.
Oil : 690 tons = 3,700 miles at 14 kts.

Note.—Laid down in 1914, the construction of this ship was held up for many years. As completed, *Krasni Kavkaz* mounts an entirely different armament from *Profintern* and *Chervonaya Ukraina*, to which she was originally to have been a sister. She is said to be fitted for minelaying.

KRASNI KAVKAZ.

1934 *Photo, Herr Torsten Hallonblad.*

415

PROFINTERN (ex-*Sovnarkom*, ex-*Klara Zetkin*, ex-*Svietlana*, June, 1915. Reval).

CHERVONAYA UKRAÏNA (ex-*Ad.Nakhimov*, October, 1915. Nikolaiev).

Displacement, 6,600 and 6,934 tons, respectively. Complement, 624. Length, 507¾ feet. Beam, 50⅓ feet. Draught, 18⅓ feet.

Guns :
15—5·1 inch, 55 cal.
8—4 in. AA.
4 machine.
Torpedo Tubes: (21 inch)
12 in Triple Mounts.
Mines : 100.

Aircraft :
2, handled by crane.

CHERVONAYA UKRAÏNA.

1934 *Photo, Sig. F. Cianciafara.*

Note to Plan—Now carry T.T. above sections 9 and 13.

Armour :
2″ Side.....................
1″ Deck ....
3″ Gun shields ....
3″ Conning tower ... .

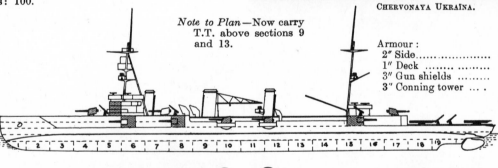

Machinery : Brown Curtis or Parsons turbines. Boilers: 13 Yarrow. H.P. 50,000 = 29·5 kts. Coal: 540 tons. Oil: 690 tons. Radius of action: 470 miles at full speed, 3700 at 14 kts.

General Notes.—Built under the 1912 Naval Programme and laid down in 1913. Construction was held up for many years, *C. Ukraïna* being the first to be completed in December, 1924, followed by *Profintern* in January, 1925. *Profintern* towed to Leningrad for completion 1918. Proceeded to Black Sea, 1930, staying for repairs at Brest and Naples, where it is reported that her condition was very unsatisfactory and that only minor repairs would be undertaken. Have always been described as having 3 inch armour for full length over main and lower decks, but from inspection it appears that there is no special side armour; apparently the hull is built of thicker plating than usually obtains. Armour has therefore been deleted from above plan and exact protection is uncertain. *Profintern* refitted, 1937.

416

CH. UKRAÏNA

Added, 1935.

KOMINTERN

Photo added 1925.

(Employed as Seagoing Training Ship.)

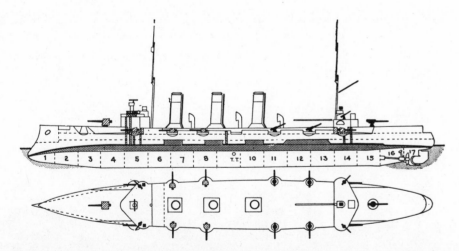

KOMINTERN (ex-*Pamiat Merkuria*, ex-*Kagul*, June, 1905). 6,338 tons. Dimensions : 436 × 54 × 20½ feet. Complement, 573. Guns : 10—5.1 inch, 8—3 inch AA., 2 M.G. Torpedo tubes : 2—18 inch (*submerged*). Armour : 1″—3″ deck, turrets and casemates. Machinery : Triple expansion. 2 screws. Boilers : 16 Normand. Designed H.P., 19,500 = 23 kts. Coal : *normal* 700 tons, *maximum* 1,100 tons. Refitted and rearmed. Present best speed under 20 kts.

Note.—Old cruiser *Avrora* still exists, but is no longer a seagoing ship, being employed as a stationary training establishment at Kronstadt.

Cruiser-Minelayer.

(*Photo wanted.*)

MARTI (ex-*Shtandart*, 1895).

Displacement : 3,500 tons. Complement :
Length : 370 feet (*w.l.*). Beam : 52½ feet. Draught : 20 feet (*mean*).

Guns :
    4—5.1 inch.
    4—37 mm. AA.

Armour :
    2″ Deck.

Mines :
    300.

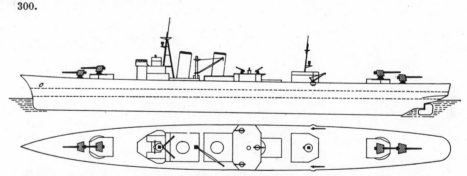

Machinery : Geared turbines. Speed : 25 kts. Oil fuel.

Note.—This ship is the former Imperial yacht, laid down at Copenhagen in 1893, and converted into a minelayer at Leningrad in 1935–37.

9 Stremitelni Class.

8 Leningrad Class.

LENINGRAD.   1937, *courtesy H. C. Bywater, Esq.*

Stremitelni (1936), ***Smetlivi*** (1937), ***Gordi*** (1937), ***Gromki*** (1938), ***Grosni, Grosovoi, Gnievni, Gremiastchi Grosiastchi,*** (all building). Built at Leningrad. Displacement: 1,400 tons *standard.*
Dimensions: Not reported. Guns: 5—5·1 inch, 55 cal., 4—37 mm., 4 D.C.T. Tubes: 6—21 inch (tripled).
Machinery: Geared turbines. S.H.P.: 90,000 = 38 kts. Boilers of 3-drum type. Oil fuel.
Notes.—These vessels were originally reported as belonging to *Leningrad* class, and were supposed to be identical with *Kharkov, Kiev, Stalinsk, Moskva, Perekop* and *Volochaevka.* They are said to be much better sea boats than *Leningrad* type, having less top weight. They are of Odero-Terni-Orlando design.

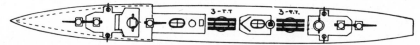

8 *French* type : ***Leningrad*** (1935), ***Minsk*** (1936). Both built at Leningrad. ***Moskva*** (1937), ***Kharkov*** (1937),
Kiev (1938), ***Perekop, Stalinsk, Volochevka.*** All built in Black Sea yards. Displacement:
2,900 tons (3,500 *full load*). Dimensions: 459½ × 40 × 14 feet. Guns: 5—5·1 inch 55 cal., 4—37 mm. AA., 4
D.C.T. Tubes: 6—21 inch (tripled). Fitted for minelaying. Machinery: Geared turbines. S.H.P.: 90,000 =
36 kts. Watertube boiler is of 3-drum type. Oil fuel.

Note.—*Leningrad* reported to have made 39·3 kts. on trials. These ships resemble French *contretorpilleurs* of recent
design, and their construction is understood to have been supervised by French technical experts. Reported to
be very poor sea boats.

TASHKENT (on trials).   1939, *courtesy Dott. Ing. L. Accorsi.*

Tashkent (Odero-Terni-Orlando, Leghorn, Nov. 21, 1937). Displacement: 2,895 tons. Dimensions: 457⅞ × 45
× 11¼ feet. Guns: 6—5·1 inch, 55 cal., 6—45 mm. AA., 6 M.G. 4 D.C.T. Tubes: 9—21 inch (tripled). Fitted
for mine-laying. Machinery: Geared turbines. 2 shafts. S.H.P.: 95,000 = 39 kts. (Claimed to have made 45·8
kts. on 6 hours trials with 110,000 S.H.P., but this was before guns were mounted). Water-tube boilers of 3-
drum type. Oil fuel.

Note.—Design reported to be of an unusually light type, to obtain highest possible speed.

1928 *Photo.*

Frunze (ex-*Bistri*, 1915). (Refitted and rearmed 1928.) 1,300 tons. Complement, 156. Dimensions: 321¼ × 30¼
× 12¼ feet. Armament: 4—3·9 inch, 1—3 inch AA., 1 M.G., 9—18 inch tubes, 80 mines Boilers: 4 Thornycroft.
2 screws. Oil: 350 tons. H.P.: 23,000 = 25 kts.

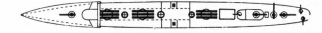

2 Karl Marx Class.

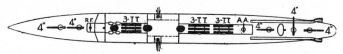

KARL MARX (Now has deckhouse aft).   1932.

2 *Reval Shipbuilding Co.*: **Karl Marx** (ex-*Isyaslav*), **Kalinin** (ex-*Priamislav*) (1914). 1354 tons. Dimensions: 344½ × 31¼ × 9¾ feet. Guns: 5—3·9 inch, 1—3 inch AA., 2 M.G. *Kalinin* only 4—3 9 inch. Torpedo tubes: 6—18 inch in *K. Marx*, 9—18 inch in *Kalinin*. 60 mines. Machinery: Parsons turbines. Designed H.P.: 32,700 = 33 kts. (Trials reported to have given 32 kts., but present figure only 28 kts.). Normand boilers. Oil: 450 tons. Complement: 167.

Notes.—These vessels were built to the designs of Chantiers et Ateliers Augustin Normand, Le Havre and laid down in 1912. *K. Marx* completed 1923, but *Kalinin* was not completed till 1927. Former vessel was reconstructed, 1935–37.

1937.

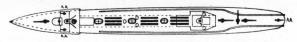

ex-Yakov Sverdlov (ex-*Novik*). Built 1910–12. Rebuilt and re-armed 1931. Displacement: 1,271 tons. Dimensions: 336 × 31 × 9½ feet. 3 A.E.G. turbines .S.H.P.: 36,500 = 32 kts. 6 Vulcan boilers. Oil: 400 tons. Complement: 112. Guns: 4—3·9 inch, 3—37 mm. AA., 1 M.G. 9—18 inch tubes.

Note.—Recent alterations include enlarged bridge, tripod foremast, extended forecastle, and shifting of after-super-structure, and main mast. Employed on cruiser duties. Trials, 1915 = 35·7 kts. Reported to have been re-named, 1937, but new name not advised.

4 Petrovski Class.

SHAUMYAN.   1935, J. Weinberg.

1935, J. Weinberg.

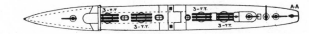

4 boats: **Felix Dzerzhinski** (ex-*Kaliakria*, 1918), **Nezamojnik** (ex-*Zante*, 1917), **Petrovski** (ex-*Korfu*, 1917), **Shaumyan** (ex-*Levkos*, 1917). All built at Nikolaieff. 1,323 tons (*Petrovski*, 1,308 tons). Dimensions: 303½ × 29¼ × 9 feet. Armament: 4—3·9 inch, 1—3 inch AA., 1—37 mm. AA., 12—18 inch tubes, in triple mountings. Originally designed to carry 80 mines of pre-war pattern, but will now have 45 of heavier type. Turbine engines. Oil fuel only: 390 tons. S.H.P.: 29,000 = 33 kts. (Actual speed considerably less.) Complement: 161. *Nezamojnik* not completed till 1923, and *Petrovski* and *Shaumyan* till 1925. *Dzerzhinski* sunk in 1918, but salved in 1925 and refitted.

9 Uritski Class

ENGELS (Observe funnel tops).   1937.

EX-RYKOV (Observe tripod masts).   1932.

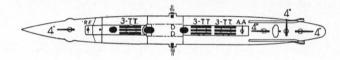

LENIN.   1936.

6 Leningrad Metal Works : *Uritski* (ex-*Zabiaka*, 1914); *Volodarski* (ex-*Pobieditel*, 1914); *Artem* (ex-*Zinoviev*, ex-*Azard*), *Engels* (ex-*Desna*), *Stalin* (ex-*Samson*), *Rykov* (ex-*Kap. Kern*). All 1914–15.

3 Putilov Works, Leningrad : *Karl Liebknecht* (ex-*Kap.-Lt. Belli*), *Volkov* (ex-*Trotski*, ex-*Leit. Ilyin*), *Lenin* (ex-*Kap. 2r. Isylmettiev*). All 1914–15.

Displacement : 1,150 to 1,417 tons. Dimensions : 314¾ to 321½ × 30½ × 9¾ feet. Complement : 157. Guns : 4—3·9 inch, 1—3 inch AA., 1 M.G. Torpedo tubes : 9—18 inch (tripled). All carry mines. Machinery : Turbines. S.H.P. : 30,000 = 28 to 30 kts. Thornycroft boilers. Oil fuel : 400 tons. All laid down under 1912 Programme, and mostly completed after War. *Rykov* and *K. Liebknecht* were not commissioned till 1927 and 1928, respectively.

Appearance Notes.—These destroyers vary in appearance according to builders. Those constructed by Leningrad Metal Works mostly have slanting funnel tops. *Stalin* has been reconstructed and differs from rest of class in appearance. *Rykov* reported to have been re-named, 1937 but new name not advised. *Uritski* was reconstructed in 1937.

Torpedo Boats
15 Shtorm Class (rated as Escort Vessels).

    1934 *Photo.*

SHTORM, SHKVAL, SMERTCH, URAGAN, TAIFUN, SIKLON, GROZA, METEL, VIKHR, VIYUGA, GROM, BURIYA, TUCHA, SNIEG, PURGA (1932–6). Displacement : 740 tons. Complement : 72. Dimensions : 238 (*pp.*) × 24 × 10 feet. Guns : 2—3·9 inch, 4—40 mm. AA., 2 M.G., 2 D.C.T. Tubes : 3—18 inch (tripled). 50 Mines carried. Machinery : Geared turbines. 2 shafts. H.P. : 13,200 = 29 kts.

Note.—Reported to be poorly constructed and to roll heavily, owing to excessive tophamper. Last 3 vessels believed to be a trifle bigger than the rest.

3 Markin class.

BABINSKI RABOTCHI.

Photo, Dmitri Novik (added 1929).

3 "*Markin*" class, named ***Alfater*** (ex-*Turkmenetz-Stavropolski*). ***Markin*** (ex-*Ükraina*) ***Babinski Rabotchi*** (ex-*Voiskovoi*) (all 1904). Built by Lange's Yard, Riga. 580 tons. Dimensions : 240 × 23¾ × 7¼ feet. Designed H.P. 6200 = 25 kts. Boilers : 4 Normand. Coal : 50 tons *normal*, 135 tons *full load*. Complement, 88–85. Armament : 3—3·9 inch, 1—1 pdr., 2 M.G., and 2—18 inch tubes. Carry 16 mines.
Present Speeds : *Markin*, 23 kts. *Alfater*, 20 kts. *Babinski Rabotchi* probably less. All three are in Caspian Sea.

KONSTRUKTOR.

1932 Photo.

1 *Kondratenko* type : ***Konstruktor*** (ex-*Sibirski-Strelok*, Helsinki, 1906). 625 tons. Dimensions : 246 × 27½ × 8¼ feet. Guns : 3—3·9 inch, 2—4 pdr. AA. Tubes : 1—18 inch. 50 mines. H.P. : 7,300 = 25 kts. Coal : 215 tons. Complement : 101.
(Serving as Leader of Minesweepers, Baltic.)

2 Zhelesniakov class.

2 *Zhelesniakov* class, named ***Sladkov*** (ex-*Vsadnik*). (Krupp 1905), ***Zhelesniakov*** (ex-*Amuretz*. Riga, 1905), 710 tons. Dimensions : first ship, 233 × 24·2 × 7·5 feet, second, 233 × 23·6 × 7·8 feet. Designed H.P. : 6,500 and 6,200 respectively = 25 kts. Coal : 205 tons. Complement : 105. Guns : 3—3·9 inch, 1—3 pdr., 1—1 pdr. AA. 4 M.G. Tubes : 3—18 inch. Carry 25 mines.
Note.—Present best speeds : 22–24 kts.

Torpedo Boats—Motor Type

In Baltic.   1937.

In Far East.   1937.

Total number uncertain, but is at least 130. Displacement varies from 6 to 35 tons. Majority are of Italian M.A.S. type. Usual armament, 2 torpedoes. Machinery of Italian design. Distributed between Baltic, Black Sea and Far East. The latest type, of which 12 were built under licence at Marti Yard, Leningrad, in 1937, are of 11 tons with a speed of 42 kts. Others have been completed recently in Black Sea yards. Distinctive numbers are painted on C.T.'s of all those observed.
Names reported from the Black Sea are :
Beshumni, Besposhadni, Bestrashni, Bezupretchni, Biedovi, Bodri, Buini, Pilki, Pritki, Pronzitelni, Protchni, Serditi, Silni, Smieli, Zavietni, Zhivuchi, Zorki.

These are probably motor launches, built in U.S.A., 1915-16.

150 + 20 *(building)* Submarines *(Podrodniya Lodki.)*

Note.—Above total is only approximate, and may well be less than the real one, as list below does not pretend to be exhaustive. At Vladivostok, in 1936, in addition to a large number of coastal submarines of the 200-ton type described below, 17 units of *Chuka* and/or *Dekabrist* class were observed, bearing numerals between 100 and 127. Number at that port has since been increased considerably according to Japanese accounts. Many of these submarines are believed to be minelayers.

15 (or more) Nalim Class.

> *Photo. wanted.*

15 boats : **Nalim** (*N* 1), (1937), and at least 14 more. Displacement : 1,080/1,320 tons. Guns : **1**—4 inch, 45 cal., **1**—1 pdr. AA. Tubes : **6**—21 inch. Reported to have exceptionally high surface speed (20/9 kts.).

7 (or more) Pravda Class.

> *Photo wanted. For appearance, see silhouette.*

7 boats : **Pravda** (*P* 1), **Sviezda** (*P* 2), **Iskra** (*P* 3), and at least 4 more. Built 1936. Displacement : 1,200/1,800 tons. Dimensions unknown. Guns : **2**—4 inch, 45 cal., **1**—37 mm. AA. Torpedo tubes : **8**—21 inch. Said to be quite a successful type, capable of rapid diving.

8 Garibaldietz Class.

> *Photo wanted.*

Adriatico design boats : **Garibaldietz** (*B* 4), **Chartist** (*B* 5), **Karbonari** (*B* 6). and 5 more. Completed 1933–35. Displacement : 1,039/1,335 tons. Guns : **1**—4 inch, 45 cal., **1** M.G. Tubes : **6**—21 inch. Speed : 14/8·5 kts. In Black Sea.

5 Yakobinetz Class.

YAKOBINETZ   *1935, J. Weinberg.*

5 boats : **Yakobinetz** (No. 11), **Revolutioner** (No. 12), **Spa.takovetz** (No. 13), and 2 others. Completed 1931. Displacement : 959/1,370. tons. Dimensions : 284 × 23½ × 16½ feet. Guns : **1**—4 inch AA., **1**—37 mm. AA., **2** M.G. Torpedo Tubes : **8**—21 inch. H.P. 2,600/1,200 = 15/8 kts. In Black Sea.

22 Dekabrist Class.

1937, courtesy " Taschenbuch der Kriegsflotten "

DEKABRIST *type.*   1935.

22 boats : **Dekabrist** (*L* 1), **Narodovoletz** (*L* 2), **Krasnogvardietz** (*L* 3), and at least 19 others. Earlier units built at Baltic Yard, Leningrad 1929–30. Displacement : 896/1,318 tons. Complement : 44. Dimensions : 279 × 23 × 16½ feet. Guns : **1**—4 inch AA., **1**—37 mm. AA., **2** M.G. Torpedo tubes : **8**—21 inch (6 bow, 2 stern). H.P.: 2,500/1,200 = 15/8 kts. *Surface* radius : 7,000 at 9 kts. *B 3* (believed to be of this class) sank during exercises in Gulf of Finland, July, 1935 ; reported to have been salved. Another vessel of this type reported lost on trials.

1 special boat : **Komsomolka** (1933). Displacement : 889/1,312 tons. Guns : **1**—4 inch, 45 cal., **1**—1 pdr. AA. Tubes : **6**—21 inch. Other particulars believed to be similar to *Dekabrist*. Built by subscription from Communist Youth movement. Used for training.

24 Lin Class.

> *Photo wanted. Appearance as silhouette.*

24 boats : **Lin** (305) and at least 7 more (306–312) are in service. Displacement : about 500 tons. Guns : **1**—1 pdr. AA. Tubes : **4**—21 inch. *Surface* speed : 19 kts. (Many more of this class under construction.) Reported to be designed for coast defence purposes.

16 Chuka Class.

CHUKA *type.*

1937.

16 (or more) boats : **Chuka** (301), **Okun** (302), **Yorch** (303), **Makrel** (304) and 12 others. Built 1935–37. Over 600 tons displacement. Guns : 1—1 pdr. AA. Tubes : 4—21 inch. Reported to be minelayers. Are numbered from 301 to 304 and 313 to 324 (possibly higher), the latter series being of a slightly improved design.

40 "Malodki" Type.

1938, *courtesy M. Henri Le Masson.*

About 40 boats : Of a small design, about 200 tons *surface* displacement. Built 1928–30. Those in Baltic numbered M 70—103. Armed with 1 M.G. and 2 Torpedo tubes. " Malodki " is an abbreviation of *Maliya Lodki,* meaning small submarines. Can be easily transported by rail, but have a very limited radius of action. *M* 91, of this type, lost in Gulf of Finland, Nov., 1937.

The following is a list of names that have been reported without type being ascertained : *Blücher, Budenni, Orlov, Komsomeletz, Sviezdochka, Bezbojnik, Frunzovetz, Leninetz, Sverdlovetz, Stalinetz, Bezvirnik, Mudrovetz, Profilski Ukraina, Krasni Spania.* Some of these are reported as of considerable size, others as of smaller design. Doubtless all belong to one or other of the various types enumerated above ; but there are a good many more under construction, design of which has not been ascertained.

3 Bolshevik Class.

KRASNOARMEYETZ No. (4). (Since reconstructed.) 1930, *Comm. R. Steen Steensen.*

3 *Bubnov* type : **Bolshevik** (ex-*Ryss*), **Krasnoflotetz** (ex-*Yaguar*), **Krasnoarmeyetz** (ex-*Leopard*). All built by Nobel & Lessner, Reval, 1915–16. Displacement : 650/784 tons. Dimensions : 223 × 14⅔ × 12⅔ feet. Guns : 1—3 inch, 1 M.G. Tubes : 4—18 inch. Dropping gears : 8. H.P. : 500/900 or 2,400/900. Speed : 10/9 or 18/10 kts.

Note.—*Rabotchi* (No. 9) was sunk in the Baltic May 25, 1931. Since raised and scrapped. *Tovarich* (No. 3) sunk by collision with *Marat* in August, 1935. *Komissar* and *Kommunar* paid off for scrapping, 1938. *Krasnoflotetz* (No. 5) and *Krasnoarmeyetz* (No. 4) both reconstructed during 1937 (vide silhouette). All this class used only for training.

1 ex-British **"L.55."** (Fairfield, 1918). Displacement : 870/1,139 tons Dimensions : 220½ (*p.p*), 235 (*o.a.*) × 23½ × 13¾ feet. Guns : 2—3 inch, 1 M.G. Tubes : 6—21 inch, all in bows. Machinery : 2 sets 12-cylinder solid injection. Vickers type Diesel engines. Oil : 78 tons. B.H.P. : 2,400/1,600 = 17·5/10·5 kts. Lost in the Baltic, 1919, salved 1928, repaired, and put into service October 9, 1931. Sunk in same month by collision with a merchant vessel, but now again in service though only used for training purposes. Present speeds not above 14/9 kts.

4 Metallist Class.

1930 *Photo.*

(All boats now carry identification numbers, as above).

4 *Electric Boat Co.* design: **Politrabotnik** (ex-*AG* 26), 1916–1924; **Metallist** (ex-*AG* 21), 1916–1918; **Kommunist** (ex-*AG* 24), 1916–1922; **Marxist** (ex-*Kamenev*, ex-*AG* 25), 1916–1922. Displacement: 375—467 tons. H.P.: 480 = 12 kts. *on surface*, 320 = 8 kts. *submerged*. Guns: 1—6 pdr., 4—18 inch tubes. Dimensions: 150¼ × 15¾ × 15¼ feet. Used for training in Black Sea. Dates given are those of laying down and completion.

Patrol Vessels.

> *Photo wanted.*

CHEKA, KAPSIUL, PARAVAN, VEKHA. These 4 vessels proceeded to Vladivostok via the Suez Canal in the spring of 1939. Particulars not so far reported, but are fitted for minesweeping. Displacement reported as 383 tons.

PODSEKATEL, STRELA. These 2 proceeded to Vladivostok via the Panama Canal in the summer of 1939. No information as to type.

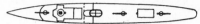

Patrol Vessels—*Continued.*

KIROV.

Added 1935.

2 *Ansaldo* type: **DZERZHINSKI** (ex-*P.S.* 8), (Aug. 19, 1934), **KIROV** (ex-*P.S.* 26), (Sept. 18, 1934). Built by Ansaldo. *Standard* displacement: 810 tons. Complement: 120. Dimensions: 249⅓ (*pp.*), 262½ (*o.a.*) × 27¼ × 16¾ feet. Guns: 3—4 inch, 4—40 mm. AA. Fitted for mine-laying. Machinery: 3 Fiat and Tosi Diesels respectively. 3 shafts. H.P.: 4,800 = 20 kts. (Trials: H.P.: 5,400 = 21 kts.) Fuel: 44 tons. (In Far East.)

Photo added 1933.

5 *Schichau* type (Old T.B. with tubes removed): **Martynov** (ex-*Vnushitelni*), **Artemiev** (ex-*Vinoslivi*), **Roshal** (ex-*Ing. Mech. Dmitriev*), **Shemchushni** (ex-*Ing. Mech. Sveriev*), **Ossoaviakhim** (ex-*Vnimatelni*). All built by Schichau, 1905. Displacement: 375 tons. Dimensions: 210 × 24 × 8¼ feet. Guns: 2—3 inch, 4 M.G. May also carry mines. H.P.: 6,200 = 28 kts. (15—20 kts. present speed). Coal: 125 tons. Complement: 69.

1 *Normand* type: **Krepki** (La Seyne, 1905). Displacement: 324 tons. Dimensions: 185 × 21 × 7 feet. Guns: 1—3 inch, 5—3 pdr., 2 M.G. H.P.: 5,600 = 26 kts. (now much less). Coal: 100 tons. Used as a patrol vessel on Lake Ladoga.

Patrol Vessels—*continued.*

MATROS. (Another view in Addenda).   1939, *Associated Press.*

FUGAS, MINREP, MATROS, PROVODNIK, VZRYF, ZAPAL (1935–36). Displacement: 500 tons. Dimensions: not reported. Guns: 1—3·9 inch, 2—37 mm. AA. Fitted for minesweeping. Machinery: Diesel. 2 shafts. Speed: 16 kts.

Note.—These are the vessels previously known as *P.S.* 1 to 6. Initials *P.S.* stand for *Pogranitchni Storoshevoi,* meaning Frontier Patrol.

Added 1938.

Nos. 200–212 (1937–38). Motor vessels, similar to Finnish V.M.V. type. Guns: 2—47 mm. Speed: 25 kts. or more.

River Gunboats.

1911

(Now have tripod masts and control tops.) (Amur Flotilla.)

LENIN (ex *Shtorm*), SUN-YAT-SEN (ex-*Shkval*), KRASNI-VOSTOK (ex-*Viyuga*), SVERDLOV (ex-*Uragan*), CHICHERIN (ex-*Vikhr*) (1910). 950 tons. Complement: 104. Dimensions: 233 × 42 × 4½ feet. Guns: 2—6 inch, 2—4·7 inch, 6 M.G. Armour: 4½″ turrets. Machinery: Nobel-Lessner Diesels. H.P.: 1,000 = 11 kts.

KRASNI-AZARBAIJAN.   1931 *Photo.*

KRASNI - AZARBAIJAN (ex-*Trotsky,* ex-*Ardagan*). LENIN (ex-*Kars*). (Both 1909). 630 tons. Guns: 2—4·7 inch, 2—4 inch, 4 M.G. Diesel: 1,000 H.P. = 11 kts. Complement, 126. (Both in Caspian Sea.)

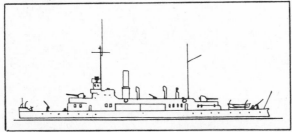

KRASNOYE ZNAMIYA (ex-*Sibiriak*), BIEDNOTA (ex-*Vogul*) PROLETARI (ex-*Buriat*), RABOTCHI (ex-*Kalmuk*), (1907) 190 tons. Dimensions: 164 × 27 × 2 feet. Guns: 2—4·7 inch, 2 M.G. H.P. 500 = 11 kts. Fuel: 145 tons. (Amur Flotilla.)

Surveying Vessel.

(*Appearance as Silhouette.*)

ASTRONOM (1918). Dimensions: 143 × 21 × 12 feet. Designed H.P.: 220 = 9 kts. Complement: 20.

Minelayers.

Note.—Many Torpedo Craft are equipped as minelayers, as detailed on an earlier page. See also *Marti,* on an earlier page.

NEW CONSTRUCTION.

2 Minelayers of 700 tons are building at Nikolaiev.

MINER (ex-*Yastreb,* ex-*Bore*), (1918). 350 tons. Dimensions: 164 × 23 × 9½ feet. H.P.: 1,000 = 12 kts. Otherwise as *Pionir* type.

Photo wanted.
For appearance, see silhouette.

KRASNOYE ABKHASIA, KRASNI AJARISTAN, KRASNAYA GRUSIA, KRASNI KRIM (1916). Displacement: 1,100 tons. Guns: 2—5·1 inch, 2—3 inch AA., 2 M.G. (Some reported to mount 3—5·1 inch.) 248 mines carried. H.P.: 640 = 9 kts.

Appearance as silhouette.

YAUSSA, BERESINA, KUBAN (1916–17). 1165 tons. Guns: 2—37 mm. AA. 90 mines. Paddle propulsion. H.P.: 500 = 10 kts.

PIONER.   1932 *Photo.*

PIONER (ex-*Korchun*), KOPCHIK (1915). 400 tons. Dimensions: 154 × 25 × 10 feet. Guns: 2—4 inch, 1—1 pdr. AA. 70 mines. H.P.: 1,150 = 14 kts.

Minelayers.—continued.

1932 photo.

SPARTAK (ex-*Tsaritsa*). (Sandvikens, 1913.) Displacement: 250 tons. Dimensions: $132\frac{3}{4} \times 21\frac{1}{3} \times 11$ feet. Guns: **1—3 inch.** H.P.: **740 = 12 kts.**

1932 Photo.

DEVIATOË YANVARYA (ex-*Volga*, 1905). 1711 tons. Dimensions: $229 \times 45 \times 13$ feet. Complement, 266. Armament: **4—3 inch.** Carries 236 mines H.P. 1600 = 13 kts. Babcock boilers. Coal: 160 tons. Present best speed, 10 kts.

PERVOE MAYA (ex-*Dunai*, 1891). 1620 tons. Complement, 234. Dimensions: $203\frac{1}{3} \times 32\frac{2}{3} \times 14\frac{3}{4}$ feet. Guns: **3—3 inch** 2 M.G. H.P.: **1,500 = 13 kts.** Coal: 130 tons. Carries 250 mines. Present efficiency questionable.

Minelayers.—continued.

DVADSATPYATAVO OKTIABRYA (ex-*Narova*, ex-*General Admiral*, 1873). Displacement: 4,250 tons. Dimensions: $284\frac{1}{2} \times 48 \times 22$ feet. Guns: **4—3 inch, 4 M.G.** 600 mines. H.P.: **4,500 = 9 kts.** (Minelaying Training Ship.)

Fishery Protection Vessels.

1924 Photo, Abrahams, Devonport.

VOROVSKY (ex-*Yaroslavna*, ex-yacht *Lysistrata*, built by Denny, Dumbarton, 1900). 2089 tons (yacht measurement), 1900 tons (registered). Dimensions: 285 (*p.p.*), 319 (*o.a.*) $\times$ 40 $\times$ 18 feet. Engines: Triple expansion. 2 screws. H.P. 3500 = 18 kts. Guns: **2—4·7 inch., 2—3 pdr., 2 M.G.** Complement: 127. (In Far East.)

BAKAN (1896). 885 tons. Dimensions: $180 \times 25 \times 11$ feet. Guns: **2—3 inch.** I.H.P.: **3,800 = 11 kts.**

Minesweepers.

N. 1—6 (1934–35). 200 tons. Guns: **1—3 pdr., 1 M.G.** Diesel engines. Speed: 16 kts.

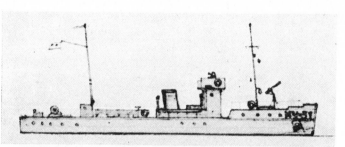

M.U. 40—54. Small craft attached to Mining School as Tenders. Diesel-driven.

JALITA (1926). 359 tons. } In Black Sea.
DOROTEA (1924). 443 tons. }
Each armed with **2—3 inch** guns.

IJORA (ex-*Plamya*), **PATRON** (Middlesbrough, 1913–14). 500 tons. Dimensions: $146 \times 24\frac{1}{2} \times 10$ feet. Guns: **2—3 inch.** H.P.: **650 = 11 kts.**

MIKULA. 1931, (added 1936).

ZMEYA, YAKORI, SPARTAK, KRAMBOL MIKULA, NEVOD (1914–17). Ex-tugs of 185 tons. Guns: **1—3 inch,** 2 M.G. H.P.: **550 = 10 kts.**

DOZORNI, RAZVYEDCHIK (1904). 100 tons. Guns: **1—37 mm., 1 M.G.** Speed: 16 kts.

Minesweepers—*continued.*

1932 *Photo.*

KLIUZ, UDARNIK (1916). Displacement : 268 tons. Complement : 35. Dimensions : $147\frac{2}{3}$ (*o.a.*) $\times 20\frac{1}{3} \times 6\frac{1}{2}$ feet. Guns : 1—3 inch, 2 M.G. Machinery : Triple expansion. I.H.P. : 450 = 12 kts.

Note.—*Udarnik* is also reported to be of a larger type, displacing 500 tons.

Water Carriers.

VODOLEI II (1905). Built at Sandvikens. 660 tons. 9·5 kts.
VODOLEI I (1907). 730 tons. 9·5 kts.

Salvage Vessel (ex-Gunboat).

Photo added, 1922.

ZNAMYA SOZIALISMA (ex-*Teretz*, 1887). 1295 tons. Compl. 135. Guns : 3—5·1 inch, 2—3 inch. H.P. 1,500 = 11 kts. Coal : 220–237 tons.

Training Ships.

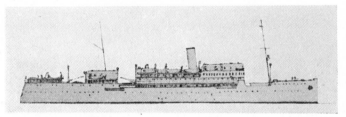

Added 1938.

SVIR (ex-Rotterdam Lloyd liner *Patria*), (K. M. de Schelde, Flushing, 1919). 9,686 tons *gross*. Dimensions : $480\frac{1}{2} \times 57\frac{1}{4} \times 29$ feet. Guns : 4—37 mm. Machinery : Single reduction geared turbines. Speed : 15 kts. Seamen's Training Ship.

(Since reconstructed.)

KOMSOMOLETZ (ex-*Okean*, Howaldt, 1902). 11,900 tons. Guns : 4—3 pdr. H.P. 11,000 = 18 kts. Coal : 1600 tons. Boilers : 6 Belleville, 6 Niclausse, 3 Yarrow, 2 Thornycroft. Complement, 700.

Training Ships—*continued.*

TREVOLEV. 1931 *Photo.*

TREVOLEV (ex-*Voin*, 1893, rebuilt 1930). 1280 tons. Guns : 4—3 inch. Speed : 9 kts. Submarine Training headquarters.

LENINGRADSKI SOVIET (ex-*Vierny*, 1895, rebuilt 1926). Similar to *Trevolev* in main features. Attached to Navigation School.

Added 1938.

POLARNAIA SVIEZDA (1890). Displacement : 3,640 tons. Dimensions : $315\frac{1}{2} \times 46 \times 17\frac{1}{2}$ feet. No guns. Machinery : Triple expansion. I.H.P. : 5,000 = 15 kts. Reboilered 1936. May burn oil fuel now. Used as Training Ship for artificers and stokers. (Ex-Imperial Yacht, rebuilt 1936–37.)

Depôt Ships.

1931 *Photo.*

KOMMUNA (ex-*Volkhov*, Putilov, 1913). 2400 tons. Dimensions : 315 × 69 × 11¾ feet. Diesel engines. H.P. 1200 = 10 kts. Radius 3600 miles. Can raise 1000 tons.

Note.—Carries all essential stores for submarines (oil fuel, reserve accumulators, &c.), and has compressed air, distilling and charging plant, workshops, &c.

SMOLNY (ex-*Tosno*) (Hull, 1907). 3200 tons. Dimensions : 318 × 41 × 18 feet. H.P. 1,200 = 13 kts. (only good for 10 kts. now). Guns : 4—3 pdr. Coal : 390 tons. Depôt Ship for Submarines.

KRASNI KUBANETZ (ex-*Kubanetz*, 1887). 1295 tons Sister to *Znamya Sozialisma*, described under Gunboats.

KRASNI KOMANDIR (ex-*General Brusilov*).

Note.—There is also a Depôt Ship for M.T.B., name unknown. She is a single-funnelled converted cargo vessel.

Oilers.

ZHELESNOROSHNIK. 2,000 tons. 10 kts.
METALLIST (ex-*Tamara*), (1898). 1,530 tons. 10 kts.
GORNYAK (ex-*Tatiana*), (1898). 1,575 tons.

Repair Ships.

(Now has derrick on forecastle).

KRASNI GORN (ex-*Kama*, 1911). 1982 tons. Dimensions : 237¾ × 36 × 12 feet. I.H.P. 1250 = 10 kts. Coal : 170 tons.

Photo added 1929.

SERP-I-MOLOT (ex-*Angara*), (1900). 5,920 tons. Dimensions : 352 × 46 × 24 feet. I.H.P. : 2,000 = 12 kts. Coal : 1,057 tons.

Icebreakers.

Note.—Most of these icebreakers are immensely strong in framing and scantlings, with exceptionally thick plating, and decks strengthened to permit of guns being mounted in war time.

> *Building.*

SERGEI KIROV, VALERIAN KUBYSHEV. Built at Leningrad. Displacement : 12,000 tons. Dimensions : 357½ × 69¼ × 23½ feet. Machinery : Diesel-electric. B.H.P. : 12,000. 3 shafts (2 stern, 1 bow). Radius : 12,000 miles. 2 aircraft carried.

L. KAGANOVICH   1939, *Midshipman T. B. Healey, R.N.R.*

LAZAR KAGANOVICH (April 30, 1937), **SCHMIDT** (building), **YOSIF STALIN** (Aug. 14, 1937), **VIATC-HESLAV MOLOTOV** (March 8, 1939). First pair built at Nikolaiev, second pair at Baltic Works, Leningrad. Displacement : 11,000 tons. Dimensions : 351 × 75½ × 22 feet. Machinery : 3 sets triple expansion. 3 shafts (2 stern, 1 bow). H.P. : 10,050 = 15·5 kts. 9 boilers. Coal : 4,000 tons. 3 aircraft, 1 catapult included in design, though not seen in above photo. *L. Kaganovich* is in Far East.

> *Building.*

FRIEDRICH ENGELS (ex-*Max Holtz*), **JEAN JAURÈS** (ex-*Bela Kuhn*). Both built at Leningrad. Dimensions : 347¼ × 48½ × 20 feet. Machinery : M.A.N. Diesel. B.H.P. : 1,800.

> *Photo wanted.*

SEVMORPUTI (Marti Yard, Leningrad, May 20, 1937). 6,000 tons *gross*. Speed : 11·5 kts.

Added 1938, courtesy Messrs. Armstrongs.

KRASSIN (ex-*Sviatogor*). (Armstrong, 1917). Displacement: 8,700 tons. 5,168 tons *gross*. Dimensions: 297 (*w.l.*), 323¼ (*o.a.*) × 71 × 26 feet. Machinery: 3 sets triple expansion. I.H.P.: 10,000 = 15 kts. 10 single-ended boilers. Coal: 3,200 tons. Complement: 190. (Stationed in Arctic).

1938, E. Iwanow.

LENIN (ex-*Aleksandr Nevski*). (Armstrong, 1917). Displacement: 5,600 tons. 3,375 tons *gross*. Complement: 122. Dimensions: 273 (*w.l.*), 281 (*o.a.*) × 64 × 19 feet. Machinery: 3 sets triple expansion. 3 shafts. H.P.: 8,000 = 19 kts. 8 boilers. (Arctic).

Added 1938, courtesy Messrs. Swan, Hunter.

STEFAN MAKAROFF (ex-*Kniaz Pojarski*), (Swan, Hunter, 1916). *Standard* displacement: 3,150 tons. 2,432 tons *gross*. Dimensions: 236 (*pp.*), 248 (*o.a.*) × 57 × 22 feet. Machinery: 3 sets triple expansion. 3 shafts. I.H.P.: 6,400 = 14·5 kts. 6 boilers. Coal: 700 tons. (Black Sea).

Added 1938, courtesy Messrs. Swan, Hunter.

DOBRINA NIKITICH (Swan, Hunter, 1916). *Standard* displacement: 2,460 tons. 1,664 tons *gross*. Dimensions: 200 (*pp.*), 211 (*o.a.*) × 50½ × 20 feet. Machinery: Triple expansion. 2 shafts. I.H.P.: 4,000 = 14 kts. 6 boilers. Coal: 370 tons. (Far East).

Added 1938, courtesy Messrs. Swan, Hunter.

SADKO (ex-*Lintrose*), (Swan, Hunter, 1913). 1,166 tons *gross*. Dimensions: 255 × 37½ × 21 feet. Machinery: Triple expansion. 1 shaft. I.H.P.: 3,500 = 14 kts. 4 boilers. (Arctic).

Note.—This ship was sunk during the War off the Arctic coast of Russia, where she lay for many years until raised and refitted.

(Photo wanted).

MALYGIN (ex-*Solovei Budimirovitch*, ex-*Bruce*). (Napier & Miller, 1912). 1,553 tons *gross*. Dimensions: 250½ × 36 × 17½ feet. Machinery: Triple expansion. 1 shaft. I.H.P.: 3,000 = 15 kts. (Arctic).

Added 1938, courtesy Vickers-Armstrongs, Ltd.

FEODOR LITKE (ex-*Kanada*, ex-*Earl Grey*). (Vickers, 1909). Displacement: 3,400 tons. 2,357 tons *gross*. Dimensions: 250 (*pp.*), 265 (*o.a.*) × 47½ × 17¾ feet. Machinery: Triple expansion. 2 shafts. I.H.P.: 6,000 = 17 kts. (Baltic).

(*Photo wanted*).

ALEKSANDR SIBIRIAKOFF (ex-*Bellaventure*), **GEORGEI SEDOFF** (ex-*Beothic*), **VLADIMIR RUSSANOFF** (ex-*Bonaventure*). All built 1909, first two by D. & W. Henderson & Co., third by Napier & Miller. 1,132 tons *gross*. Dimensions: 240½ × 36 × 16½ feet. Machinery: Triple expansion. 1 shaft. I.H.P.: 2,000 = 13·5 kts. (Arctic).

Note.—In 1939 *G. Sedoff* achieved a record latitude in her ice-bound drift northward.

Photograph in "*Fighting Ships*," 1921, p. 607.

ERMAK (Armstrong, 1898). Displacement: 7,875 tons. 4,817 tons *gross*. Dimensions: 305 × 71 × 25 feet. Machinery: Triple expansion. 3 shafts. I.H.P.: 7,000 = 15 kts. Coal: 3,000 tons. (Baltic). Complement: 112.

Added 1938, courtesy Messrs. Burmeister & Wain.

DAVIDOFF (ex-*Krasni Oktiabr*, ex-*Nadiejni*). (Burmeister & Wain, 1897). 1,212 tons *gross*. Dimensions: 184 × 43 × — feet. Machinery: Compound. I.H.P.: 2,200 = 13 kts. (Far East).

(*Photo wanted*).
Of similar appearance to *Davidoff*.

TRUVOR (ex-*Sleipner*). (Burmeister & Wain, 1896). Displacement: 1,450 tons. 1,000 tons *gross*. Dimensions: 165 × 40 × — feet. Machinery: Compound. I.H.P.: 1,900 = 13 kts. (Baltic).

(There are a large number of smaller icebreakers of insufficient importance to warrant their inclusion here.)

Transports.

KURSANT (ex-*Krasni Leningrad*, ex-*Sukhona*), (1910), **OKA, MESEN** (1911). Appearance similar to *Krasni Gorn*, on an earlier page, and particulars identical. First ship employed recently as Cadets' Training Ship. All strengthened for ice navigation.

TAIMYR.   *Added* 1938.

TAIMYR (1909). Displacement: 1,290 tons. Speed: 10.5 kts. (Strengthened for ice navigation).

SPANISH NAVY.

Flags.

MINISTER OF MARINE.

VICE-ADMIRAL.

REAR-ADMIRAL.

DIVISIONAL CAPTAIN.   DIVISIONAL COMMANDER.   SENIOR OFFICER

 DARK BLUE

RED

YELLOW

MAUVE

Minister of Marine—Admiral Don Juan Cervera

Naval Attaché (London)—

Personnel.

Officers: 1,686.   Departmental Officials: 1,666.   P.O.'s and men: 15,447.   Marines: 1,619.

| Vice-Almirante. *Vice-Admiral* | Contra Almirante. *Rear-Admiral.* | Capitán de **Navio** *Captain.* | Capitán de Fragata. *Commander.* | Capitán de Corbeta. *Lieutenant-Commander.* | Teniente de Navio. *Lieutenant.* | Alferez de Navio. *Sub-Lieutenant.* |

Other branches, *without a star*, have distinguishing colours as follows:—

Engineers	...	*green.*	Astronomical	...	*green brown.*
Constructors	...	*blue.*	Pharmacists.	...	*yellow.*
Surgeons.	...	*red.*			
Paymasters	...	*white.*			

Training Establishments.

Shore Establishments are:—For Executive Officers, Naval School (*Escuela Naval Militar*), San Fernando.   For Engineering Branch and Cadets, Ferrol.   For Accountant Officers, Cartagena.

Naval Ordnance.

Nota-tion.	Nominal Calibre.		Model.	Length in calibres	Weight of Gun.	Weight of A.P. shell.	Initial velocity	Max. penetration A.P. capped direct impact at K.C. at		Danger Space against average ship, at			Rounds per minute.
								5000 yards.	3000 yards.	10,000 yards.	5000 yards.	3000 yards.	
HEAVY	c/m. 30·5	inches. 12	V'09	50	tons. 66	lbs. 850	ft. secs. 3010	inches. 17	inches. 20	...	...	...	2
	20·3	8	V.	50	15	256	3000	...	...	...	...	...	6
MEDIUM	15·2	6	✢V.	50	7¾	100	3100	...	8¾	...	...	...	10
LIGHT	12	4·7	V.	45	3·1	48·5	2788	...	...	...	..	...	·12
	10·2	4	V.	50	2·1	31	30·30	...	...	...	...	..	15
	7·6	3	V.										
	7·6	3	A.										

V = Vickers.   A = Armstrong.

✢ Arsenal de Carraca.

Colour of Ships.
Light grey.

Mercantile Marine.
From "Lloyd's Register," 1939 figures.   824 vessels of 913,898 gross tonnage.

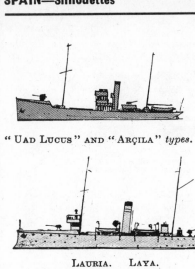

"Uad Lucus" and "Arçila" types.

Alcazar. Larache. Tetuan.

Canovas del Castillo Canalejas. Dato.

Tofiño. Malaspina.

Mar Cantabrico. Mar Negro.

Lauria. Laya.

Canarias.

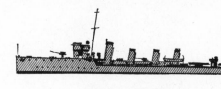

Almirante Cervera.

Navarra.

Calvo Sotelo

Alm. Antequera class.

Libertad. Miguel de Cervantes.

Mendez Nuñez.

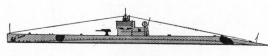

T.B's.

Churruca class.

Ceuta. Melilla.

Alsedo. Velasco. Lazaga.

Jupiter class.

Huesca. Teruel.

"C" class.

"B" class.

NOTE—The old battleship **JAIME PRIMERO** (15,452 tons) is still in existence, but is reported to be unfit for sea service.   As it is improbable that she will again become effective, she is omitted from the present edition of "Fighting Ships."

CANARIAS.

1939.

1st Class Cruiser

(Crucero de la Clase).

CANARIAS (May 28th, 1931).

Displacement: 10,000 tons *standard* (12,230 tons *full load*). Complement, 765.

Length, 636 feet.

Beam, 64 feet.

Draught, 17⅓ feet (*mean*).

Guns:
8—8 inch.
8—4.7 inch AA.
8—2 pdr. pom-pom AA.
Torpedo tubes (21 inch):
12 (*above water*, tripled).

Aircraft:
2, with catapult

Armour:
2"—1½" Side
1" Turrets
4" Magazines

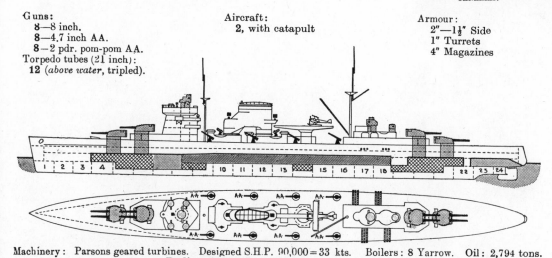

Machinery: Parsons geared turbines. Designed S.H.P. 90,000 = 33 kts. Boilers: 8 Yarrow. Oil: 2,794 tons.
Radius: 8000 miles at 15 kts.

General Notes.—Designed by Sir Philip Watts, laid down at Ferrol, August 15, 1928, and completed in 1935. Sister ship *Baleares* torpedoed and sunk, March 6, 1938.

Gunnery Note.—Maximum elevation of 8-inch guns is 70°.

CANARIAS (Mainmast now much lower).

1936, *Mr. G. L. Blowers, R.N.*

LIBERTAD (ex-**Principe Alfonso**) (Jan. 3rd, 1925), **ALMIRANTE CERVERA** (Oct. 16th, 1925), and **MIGUEL DE CERVANTES** (May 19th, 1928).

Normal Displacement, 7,850 tons.   *Full load,* 9,237 tons.

Length, 575 feet, (*p.p.*)   579½ feet, (*o.a.*)   Beam, 54 feet.

Draught, *mean* 16½ feet, *deep load* 20½ feet.

Complement, 564.

Guns :
- **8**—6 inch, 50 cal.
- **4**—4 inch, 45 cal. AA.
- **2**—3 pdrs. AA.
- **1** Machine.

Tubes :
- **12**—21 inch (tripled) in revolving mounts on upper deck.

Armour :
- 3″ Side (amidships.) ....
- 2″ Side (forward.) ....
- 1½″ Side (aft.) ....
- 1″ Deck. ....
- 2″ (H.T. ?) over rudder. ?........
- 6″ Conning tower. ?..............

MIGUEL DE CERVANTES.

1939, *Associated Press.*

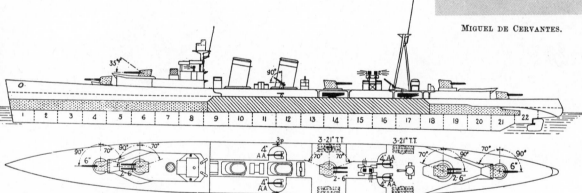

Machinery : Parsons Geared Turbines.   4 screws.   Boilers : 8 Yarrow (large tube). Designed S.H.P. 80,000 = 33 kts.   Fuel capacity : 500 tons oil, *normal* ; 1650 tons oil, *maximum.* Endurance : 5000 at 15 kts., 1200 at *full power.*

Name	Builder	Machinery	Laid down	Completed	Trials	Boilers
Libertad Alm. Cervera M. de Cervantes	Ferrol D.Y.	S. E. C. N.	Aug. '22 25 Nov. '22 Apr. '26	Dec. '25 May '27 1931	83000 = 34·7.	Yarrow

Notes.—Laid down by S.E.C.N. at Ferrol D.Y., under Navy Law of 17th Feb., 1915.   Cost estimated at about 8122 pesetas a ton.

Designed under direction of late Sir Philip Watts, K.C.B., Director of Sir W. G. Armstrong, Whitworth & Co., Ltd., for Spanish Government.   Are practically modifications of British " E " class, with second, third and fourth gun positions paired and beam guns omitted.

ALM. CERVERA.

1939.

Observe tripod foremast and s.l. around after funnel.

1932 *Photo, Capitan M. Mille.*

MENDEZ NUÑEZ (3rd March, 1923).

Normal Displacement: 4650 tons.   (*full load*, 6043 tons).   Complement, 320
Length, (*p.p.*) 440 feet, (*o.a.*) 462 feet.   Beam, 46 feet.   Draught, 14⅓ feet *mean* 19 feet *max.*

Guns :
6—6 inch, 50 cal.
4—3 pdr. AA.
4 machine.
(1—12 pdr. landing.)
Torpedo Tubes (21 inch) :
12 *above water* (triple mountings).

Armour :
3″ Side amidships ....
2½-1¼″ Side (ends) ....
1″ Deck ....
6″ C.T. ....
″ Director tower........... ....

Note to plan—Now has tripod foremast.

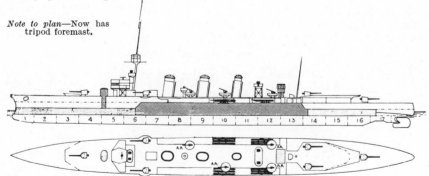

Machinery : Parsons (geared) turbines. 4 screws. Boilers : 12 Yarrow (6 oil burning, 6 mixed firing). Designed H.P. 45,000 = 29 kts. Coal : *normal*, 250 tons ; *maximum*, 787 tons + 492 tons oil. Radius : 5000 miles at 13 kts. *Blas de Lezo*, wrecked July 11, 1932, was a sister ship.

Name	Builder	Machinery	Laid down	Completed	Trials	Boilers
Nuñez	Ferrol D.Y.	S. E. C. N.	28 Sept.'17	1924	43,776 = 29·28	Yarrow

1939

NAVARRA, (ex-*Republica* ex-*Reina Victoria Eugenia*) (21st April, 1920).

Displacement, 5502 tons.   6348 tons *full load*.   Complement, 404.
Length (*p.p.*) 440 feet, (*o.a.*) 462 feet.   Beam, 50 feet.   Mean draught, 15¾ feet, *max.*, 21¼ feet.

Guns (Vickers) :
6—6 inch, 50 cal.
4—3 pdr. AA.
1—12 pdr. (Field)
4 Machine
Torpedo tubes : (21 inch).
4 *above water*
(twin mountings).

Armour (Nickel and H.T.) :
3″ Side ....
2½-1¼″ Ends (......
3″ Deck ....
6″ Conning tower

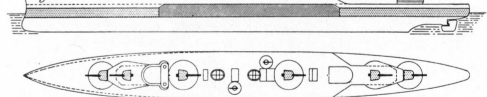

Machinery : Parsons turbines. 2 screws. Boilers : 12 Yarrow (oil burning), in 3 rooms. Designed H.P. : 25,500 = 25·5 kts. Oil fuel : 1,200 tons. Radius : 4,500 miles at 15 kts.

Gunnery Notes.—6 inch are Vickers models, built at La Carraca.

Torpedo Notes.—Above water tubes are behind lidded ports on main deck below bridge.

Name	Builder	Machinery	Ordered	Laid down	Completed	Trials	Boilers	Best recent speed
Navarra	Ferrol D.Y.	S. E. C. N.	Aug. '14	Mar. '15	15 Jan., '23	8 hours: 26,049 = 25·77 4 hours: 28,387 = 26·9	Yarrow	

General Notes.—Built under Navy Law of July 30, 1914. Refitted and reboilered at Cadiz, 1937-38, changes involved being reduction of funnels from 3 to 2, removal of 3 guns of main armament, new bridgework and masts.

Destroyers (*Destructores*).

14 Churruca class.

1926 *Photo, by courtesy of the Ministry of Marine.*

ALM. ANTEQUERA.   1935, *courtesy Capitán M. Mille.*

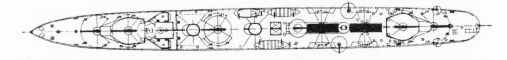

First Group (5).

SANCHEZ BARCAIZTEGUI (July 24, 1926), **JOSÉ LUIS DIEZ** (Aug. 25, 1928), **LEPANTO** (Nov. 7, 1929), **ALCALÁ GALIANO** (April 12, 1930), **ALMIRANTE VALDÉS** (Sept. 8, 1930). Appearance as above photo.

All built at Cartagena by S.E. de C.N. Displacement : 1,650 tons *normal*, 2,087 tons *full load*. Dimensions : 320 (*pp.*), 333 (*o.a.*) × 31¾ × 17 feet *max*. draught. Complement : 175. Guns : 5—4·7 inch, 1—3 inch AA., 4 M.G. 2 D.C. Throwers. Torpedo tubes : 6—21 inch (tripled). Machinery : 2 sets Parsons geared turbines. 2 shafts. S.H.P. : 42,000 = 36 kts. Boilers : 4 of 3-drum type. Oil fuel : 540 tons. Radius : 4,500 miles at 14 kts.

Notes.—Design generally follows that of British flotilla leaders of *Scott* class. Two earliest ships of this class, originally named *Alcalá Galiano* and *Churruca*, were sold to Argentina, 1927, new units bearing same names being built to replace them. *Alm. Juan Ferrandiz* and *Ciscar* sunk in Civil War, Sept., 1936 and Oct., 1937, respectively, but latter ship was salved and refitted in 1938–39. *Churruca* torpedoed by submarine.

Following initials are painted on bows : *Sanchez Barcaiztegui*, SB : *José Luis Diez*, JD ; *Lepanto*, LP ; *A. Galiano*, AG ; *Ciscar*, CC. ; *Alm. Valdés*, AV ; *Alm. Antequera*, AA ; *Alm. Miranda*, AM ; *Gravina*, GR ; *Escaño*, ES ; *Ulloa*, UL ; *J. Juan*, JJ.

Second Group (7).

ALMIRANTE ANTEQUERA (Dec. 29, 1930), **ALMIRANTE MIRANDA** (June 20, 1931), **GRAVINA** (Dec. 24, 1931), **ESCAÑO** (June 28, 1932), **ULLOA** (July 24, 1933), **JORGE JUAN** (March 28, 1933), **CISCAR** (Oct. 26, 1933). All as above photo. Details as in preceding column.

Third Group (2).

ALAVA, LINIERS. Laid down at Cartagena by S.E. de C.N., 1936. Of same general design as 2nd group, but armament as follows : Guns : 4—4·7 inch, 4—25 mm. AA. (twin mounts). Torpedo tubes : 8—21 inch (quadrupled). The 4·7 inch guns will be of a new and greatly improved model, elevating to 45°.

Destroyers—*continued.*

3 Alsedo Class.

ALSEDO.   1928 *Photo, Abrahams & Sons, Devonport.*

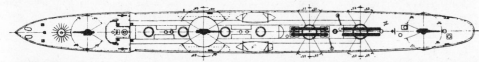

3 *Alsedo* class: **Alsedo** (Oct. 26, 1922), **Velasco** (1923), **Lazaga** (March, 1924). All built at Cartagena. Displacement: 1,145 tons (*normal*), 1,315 tons (*full load*). Dimensions: 275 (*p.p.*), 283 (*o.a.*) × 27 × 15 feet. (*max.*) Parsons geared turbines. 4 Yarrow boilers. H.P. 33,000 = 34 kts. (36 kts. reached on trials). Fuel: 272 tons oil only. Radius: 2,500 miles at 15 kts. Guns: 3—4 inch, 40 cal., 2—2 pdr. anti-aircraft. Torpedo tubes: 4—21 inch in 2 twin deck mountings. Complement, 70.

Notes.—Provided under Law of 1915. First of class laid down about June, 1920. Design resembles British *Nimrod* type. *Lazaga* was originally known as *Juan Lazaga*. Are distinguished by initial letters painted on bows, viz., *Alsedo*, A; *Lazaga*, L *Velasco*, V.

MELILLA.   1939.

2 *Pattison* type: **Ceuta** (ex-*Falco*, 1919). Displacement: 1,286 tons. **Melilla** (ex-*Aquila*, 1916.) Displacement: 1,407 tons. Dimensions: 309½ (*w.l.*), 310⅔ (*o.a.*) × 31 × 9 feet (*mean*) in *V.C.*, 10 feet in *V.M.* Guns: 4—4·7 inch, 45 cal., 2—3 inch, 2 M.G. AA. Tubes: 4—18 inch. 50 mines carried. 2 Tosi turbines. 2 shafts. S.H.P.: 40,000 = 34 kts. 5 Thornycroft boilers. Oil fuel: 260 tons *max*. Radius: 1,700 miles at 15 kts. Complement: 150.

Note.—Sister ships to *Marasti* and *Marasesti*, in Roumanian Navy, for which they were built. Taken over by Italy in 1915 and sold to Spanish Government in 1937.

Destroyers—*continued.*

TERUEL.   1925, *Pucci.*

2 *Ansaldo* type: **Huesca** (ex-*Guglielmo Pepe*), **Teruel** (ex-*Alessandro Poerio*), (both 1914). Displacement: 845 tons, 1,028 tons (*full load*). Dimensions: 267¾ (*w.l.*), 281¾ (*o.a.*) × 26½ × 8 feet (*mean*). Guns: 5—4 inch, 4 M.G. AA. Tubes: 4—18 inch. Fitted for minelaying. Parsons turbines. 2 shafts. S.H.P.: 20,000 = 32 kts. 3 Yarrow boilers. Oil fuel: 180 tons. Radius: 2,930 miles at 15 kts. Complement: 137.

Note.—These 2 destroyers were purchased from Italy by Spanish Government in 1937.

Torpedo Boats (*Torpederos*).

Oviedo, Toledo, Badajoz, C. Perez. Particulars wanted. May be of German motor type.

No. 11.   1931 *Photo, Capitán M. Mille.*

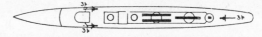

11 *Vickers-Normand.* Numbered **3** (1912), **7** (1914), **9, 14,** (1915), **16** (1916), **17-19, 20,** (1918), **21, 22** (1919) 177 tons. Dimensions: 164×16½×6½ feet (*max.* draught). Armament: 3—3 pdr., 3—18 in. tubes, twin amidships and single aft. H.P. 3750 = 26 kts. Parsons turbines and Normand boilers. Coal: 33 tons. 3 screws (Nos. 1—7). 2 screws (Nos. 8—22). Complement, 31. 24 boats sanctioned under Law of the 7th January, 1908, but Nos. 23 and 24 were abandoned 1919. No. 22 completed 1921. All are fitted for minelaying. Nos. 1, 4, 5, 11, scrapped 1931; 6, 8, 10, 12, 13, 15, scrapped 1932; No. 2 lost in Sept. 1937.

Note.—TB 14, 16, 17, 19, and 20 are now used and rated as Minelayers. No. 18 condemned to be scrapped 1935, but since recommissioned.

13 + 3 (building) Submarines (Submarinos)

A submarine named **Tabaldo Aguilar** is also reported to exist. She may be one of those below, re-named.

None launched up to date of publication.

3 *Admiralty* type; **D 1 D 2, D 3,** All under construction at Cartagena. Displacement: 1,050/1,375 tons. Dimensions: 275½ × 21¾ × 13½ feet (*mean*). H.P.: 5,000/1,350 = 20·5/9·5 kts. Tubes: 6—21 inch (4 bow, 2 stern). Guns: 1—4·7 inch, 4—2 pdr. Diving limit, 50 fathoms. Radius *on surface*: 9,000 miles.

For appearance, see photo of *Argonauta* in Italian section.

2 *Italian Bernardis* type: **Mola, Sanjurjo** (1933). Displacement: 599/778 tons. Complement: 41. Dimensions: 200½ (*w.l.*), 201¾ (*o.a.*) × 18½ × 14½ feet (*max.*) Guns: 1—4 inch, 35 cal., 2—13 mm. AA. Tubes: 6—11 inch. H.P.: 1,200/800 = 14/8·5 kts.

Note.—These 2 submarines were purchased from Italy by Spanish Government in 1937. Original names not yet ascertained.

C 2.   *1933 Photo, Capitán Mateo Mille.*

6 *Electric Boat Co.* design: Built at Cartagena; **C 1** (March 28, 1927), **C 2** (May 4, 1928), **C 3** (Feb. 20, 1929), **C 4** (July 6, 1929), **C 5, C 6** (both Dec. 28, 1929). Displacement: 915 tons *on surface*, 1,290 tons *submerged*. Dimensions: 247 (*o.a.*) × 20¾ × 13½ feet. Machinery: 2 sets 6-cylinder Vickers Diesel engines. H.P.: 2,000 = 16 kts. (*surface*), 8½ kts. (*submerged*). Guns: 1—3 inch AA. Torpedo tubes: 6—21 inch (4 bow, 2 stern). Diving limit, 45 fathoms, (reached) by C 1 on trials in 1928. Complement: 40.

Notes.—About Sept. 1930 C 1 was named **Isaac Peral.** The number is retained. C 3 was sunk at Malaga in Dec., 1936, but was salved some months later and towed to Cadiz for refit

1933 Photo, Capitán M. Mille.

5 *Electric Boat Co.* design: **B1** (1921), **B2** (1922), **B3** (1922), **B4** (1922), **B5** (1923), all laid down at Cartagena, July, 1916. Displacements: 556 tons *on surface*, 836 tons *submerged*. Dimensions: 205 (*p.p.*), 210½ (*o.a.*) × 18½ × 11½ feet. Machinery: *on surface*, 2 sets 8-cyl. Nelseco Diesel engines, totalling 1,400 B.H.P. = 16 kts.; when *submerged*, electric motors and batteries of 850 H.P. = 10—10½ kts. Trial results for class averaged $\frac{16\cdot8}{10\cdot7}$ kts. Guns: 1—3 inch. Torpedo tubes: 4—18 inch. Provided for by Law of 17th February, 1915. Complement, 28. Radius *on surface*, 8,000 miles at 10½ kts.; *submerged*, 125 miles at 4½ kts.

Note.—B 6 (shown in above photo) was sunk during Civil War, September, 1936. Several of this class reported to be incapable of deep diving.

Minelayers.

EOLO, TRITÓN. Laid down by S.E. de C.N. at Ferrol, 1936. Displacement 1,500 tons. Dimensions: 278 × 38½ × 10 feet. Guns: 4—4 inch, 4—40 mm. AA., 4—13 mm. AA. Stowage for 70 mines. Speed: 18·5 kts. Design resembles Mexican *Queretaro* type.

JÚPITER.   *1938, J. R. Potts, Esq.*

JUPITER (Sept. 14, 1935), **VULCANO** (Oct. 18, 1935), **MARTE** (June 19, 1936), **NEPTUNO** (Dec. 19, 1937. All built at Ferrol. Displacement: 2,000 tons. Dimensions: 302¾ (*pp.*), 315 (*o.a.*) × 41½ × 11½ feet. Guns: 4—4·7 inch, 4—40 mm. AA. (twin mounts), 4—7 mm. AA., 2 D.C. Throwers. Machinery: 2 sets Parsons geared turbines. Yarrow boilers. H.P.: 5,000 = 18·5 kts. Fuel: 280 tons. Stowage for 264 mines. Complement: 123.

Escort Vessels, rated as 1st Class Gunboats.

(Cañoneros de 1ª Clase).

(For appearance see Silhouette).

CALVO SOTELO (ex-*Zacatecas*) (Echavarrieta y Larrinaga, Cadiz, August 27, 1934). Displacement : 1,600 tons. Dimensions : 282 × 40 × 10 feet. Guns : Originally 2—4 inch, 4—25 mm. AA., 4—13 mm. AA. (May have been increased to 4—4 inch.) Machinery : Parsons geared turbines. 2 shafts. S.H.P. 6,500 = 20 kts. Yarrow boilers.

Note.—This ship was completing for the Mexican Navy in 1936, when she was acquired by the Spanish Government.

LAYA. 1925 *Photo, W. A. Fuller, Esq.*

LAURIA (1912), **LAYA** (1910). 800 tons. Complement : 126–129. Dimensions : 213¾ × 30 × 9½ feet (*max.*) draught. Guns : 4—4 inch, 2—3 pdr. AA. Designed H.P. : 1,100 = 14 kts. Made 13·8 to 14·6 kts on trial. Yarrow boilers. Coal : 148 tons. Radius : 3,000 at 10 kts. Built under Navy Law of Jan. 7, 1908, at Cartagena.

DATO. 1939, *Official.*

CANOVAS DEL CASTILLO (Jan. 21, 1922), **CANALEJAS** (Dec. 1, 1922), **DATO** (1923). Built by S.E.C.N., at Cartagena. Displacement : 1,314 tons. Complement : 220. Dimensions : 236⅓ (*p.p.*), 251⅓ (*o.a.*) × 33¾ × 11¾ feet. Guns : 4—4 inch, 2—3 pdr. AA., 2 pom-poms (for landing). No torpedo tubes. Machinery : 2 sets triple expansion. Boilers : 2 Yarrow. Designed I.H.P. : 1,700. Speed : 15 kts. Fuel : 324 tons coal *or* oil = 6,500 miles at 10·5 kts. Provided for by Law of Feb. 17, 1915, and ordered Jan., 1920. *C. de Castillo* and *Canalejas* completed 1923, *Dato* completed 1924. Were originally named *Antonio Canovas del Castillo*, *José Canalejas* and *Eduardo Dato*, but names have since been shortened.

9 Coastguard Gunboats.

(Ex-trawlers, purchased in England and France, 1922.)

Note.—Many more trawlers were requisitioned and armed by both sides during the Civil War.

Photo added 1925 by courtesy of Messrs. Cochrane & Sons, Ltd.

1 *Special type* : **UAD KERT** (ex-*Rother*, ex-*Anthony Aslett*, Cochrane & Sons, Ltd., Selby, 1917). Displacement : 640 tons. Complement, 39. Dimensions : 123¾ (*p.p.*) × 23½ × 15¾ feet. Guns : 2—3 inch. I.H.P. 500 = 9·5 kts. Coal : 200 tons.

2 " *Mersey type* " **ARCILA** (ex-*William Doak*, Goole S.B. & Rep. Co., 1918). **XAUEN** (ex *Henry Cramwell*, Lobnitz, 1918). Displacement : 510 tons and 768 tons respectively. Complement, 39. Dimensions : 138½ (*p.p.*), 148 (*o.a.*) × 23¾ × 15¾ feet. (*Xauen*, 17 feet). Guns : 2—3 inch. I.H.P. 500 = 10 kts. Coal : 200 tons.

1925 Photo, W. A. Fuller, Esq.

3 "*Castle type*" : **UAD LUCUS** (ex-*Ness*, ex-*Alexander Palmer*, Smith's Dock Co., Ltd. 1917), **UAD MARTIN** (ex-*Erne*, ex-*John Chivers*, Bow, McLachlan & Co., 1917), **UAD MULUYA** (ex-*Wareney*, ex-*James Conner*, W. Harkness & Co. Ltd., 1917). Displacement : 420 tons (*average*). Complement : 39. Dimensions : 125 (*pp.*) × 23½ × 15½ feet. Guns : 1—3 inch. I.H.P. 500 = 9·5 kts. Coal : 200 tons.

Coastguard Gunboats – (*continued*).

ALCÁZAR.   *1925 Photo, W. A. Fuller, Esq.*

LARACHE.   *1922 Photo.*

3 "*French type*" (builders not reported): **ALCÁZAR** (ex-*Rengagé*), **LARACHE** (ex-*Poilu*), **TETUÁN** (ex-*Grognard*). Displacement : 400 tons. Complement : 41. Dimensions : 134½ × 23½ × 11¾ feet. 1—3 inch. *Alcázar* has 2—3 pdr. in addition. I.H.P. : 425 = 10 kts. Coal : 80 tons.

Fishery Protection Vessels (*Guardapescas*).

CONDESTABLE ZARAGOZA, CONTRAMAESTRE CASTELLÓ, MAQUINISTA MACIAS, CABO DE IA. MA. GARCIOLO, TORPEDISTA HERNANDEZ, MARINERO CANTE, FOGONERO BAÑOBRE, MARINERO JARANA (1910). Displacement : 150 tons. Dimensions : 79⅓ × 19½ × 9 feet. Guns : 1—6 pdr. H.P. : 300 = 11 kts.

Surveying Vessels (*Buques Planeros*).

TOFIÑO   *1934 Photo, Capt. Mateo Mille.*

MALASPINA (ex-*Bausá*) (Matagorda, Cadiz, Sept. 13, 1935), **TOFIÑO** (Ferrol, Aug. 21, 1933). Both built by S.E. de C.N. Displacement : 1,200 tons. Complement, 130. Dimensions : 224 × 35 × 11 feet. Guns : 1—3 pdr. Machinery : Reciprocating. H.P. 850 = 12·5 kts. 2 Yarrow boilers. Fuel : 190 tons. 1 Seaplane carried in each.

Training Ships (*Buques Escuelas*).

1931 Photo.

JUAN SEBASTIAN DE ELCANO. (Echevarrieta Yard, Cadiz, 5th March, 1927), completed 1928. Four-masted Schooner. Displacement at ¾ load : 3420 tons. Dimensions : 269¼ (*p.p.*), 308½ (*o.a.*) × 43 × 23 feet *full load* draught. Guns : 4—6 pdr. 1 Sulzer Diesel motor of 800 H.P. = 9·5 kts. 1 screw. Oil : 230 tons. Endurance : 10,000 miles at 9·5 kts. Complement : 224 + 80 cadets.

Training Ships—continued.

GALATEA.   Photo, Manuel I. Codoner, Esq., 1927.

GALATEA (ex-Barque *Clarastella*, 1896). Purchased in Italy, 1922. 2,713 tons. Dimensions : 243 × 38¾ × 17¾ feet. Guns : 4—6 pdr. 2 auxiliary Diesel motors, combined H.P. : 900 = 8·5 kts. Fuel : 46 tons. T.S. for boys.

River Patrol Boat

1936, Capitán M. Mille.

CABO FRADERA. Displacement : 44 tons. Complement, 11. Dimensions : 74⅔ × 14½ × 4¼ feet. Guns : 1—42 mm. H.P., 120 = 10 kts. Engaged in patrol of River Miño (Minho) on Portuguese frontier.

Motor Launches.

FALANGE, REQUETE. Particulars wanted.

Submarine Salvage Vessel.

(Buque para salvamento de submarinos.)

1921 Photo, Capitán M. Mille.

(Attached to S/M. Station, Cartagena.)

KANGURO (1916). Double hulled type, with interior docking space. Built by Werf Conrad, Haarlem, Netherlands. Displacement : 2,707 tons. Dimensions : 295¼ × 65½ × 14½ feet or (with submarine docked), 20 feet. Can dock submarine up to 151 feet long. Salvage power : Can raise 650 tons, from 27¼ fathoms. H.P. : 1,000 = 10 kts. (9·53 trials). Fuel : 150 tons = 2,448 miles at economical speed. Guns : 4—42 mm.

Fleet Oiler.

1935 Photo, Capitán M. Mille.

PLUTÓN (ex-*Campilo*) (Valencia, 1931). Purchased in Dec., 1934. Displacement : 7,500 tons (in light condition). Dimensions : 342½ × 53¾ × 19½ feet. 2 sets B. & W. Diesels, built in Barcelona. H.P. : 2,530 = 13·5 kts.

Sea-going Tugs (*Remolcadores*).

CICLOPE (ex-*St. Clement*, purchased 1922.) Built by Crichton & Co., 1918. Displacement : 800 tons. 136 × 29 × 16½ feet. Guns : 1—3 inch. H.P. 1200 = 12¼ kts. Coal : 240 tons.
GALICIA (ex-*R.5*). Displacement : 350 tons. 100½ × 21 × 11 feet. H.P. 550 = 10 kts. Guns : 1—3 inch.
CARTAGENERO (ex-*H.S. 78*), **FERROLANO** (ex-*H.S. 80*), **GADITANO** (ex-*H.S. 82*). Built by Crichton & Co., South Saltney, Chester, 1918. Displacement : 300 tons. 83½ × 21½ × 10½ feet. Guns : 1—6 pdr. H.P., 420 = 10 kts.

Note.—There are a number of smaller tugs in service.

Transports (*Transportes*).

MAR CANTABRICO   1938, J. R. Potts, Esq.

MAR CANTABRICO, MAR NEGRO (Cia. Euskalduna, Bilbao, 1930). 6,632 tons *gross*. Dimensions : 404¼ × 54¼ × 25¾ feet. Guns : 4—5·9 inch, 8—40 mm. AA. Machinery : Diesels. B.H.P. 4,500 = 15 kts.

CONTRAMAESTRE CASADO.
1929 Photo, Capitán M. Mille.

CONTRAMAESTRE CASADO (Armstrong Naval Yard, launched Oct. 26, 1920). Displacement : 7,275 tons. Complement : 107. Dimensions : 320 (*p.p.* and *w.l.*) 332¼ (*o.a.*) × 45 × 23⅓ feet. Guns : 4—42 mm. Machinery : 1 set triple expansion. Boilers : 3 cyl. (Howden f.d.). 1 screw. I.H.P. : 2,000 = 10·5 kts. Coal : 826 tons.

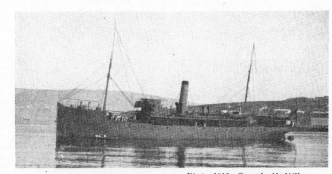

Photo (1919), Capitán M. Mille.

ALMIRANTE LOBO (1909). 2,505 tons. Dimensions : 259½ × 38 × 14 feet. Guns : 2—42 mm. Designed H.P. : 1,170 = 12 kts. Coal : 289 tons. *Nominal* radius : 4,540 miles at 10 kts. Complement : 69.

ROYAL SWEDISH NAVY.

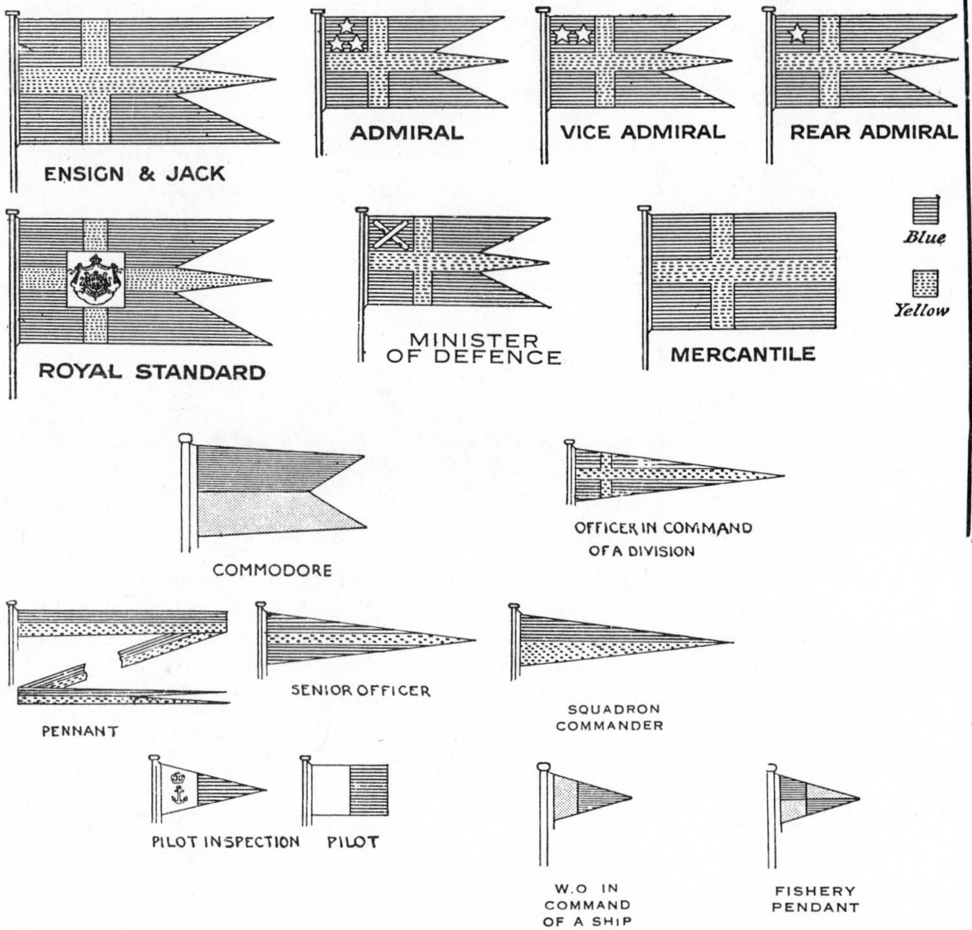
ENSIGN & JACK
ADMIRAL
VICE ADMIRAL
REAR ADMIRAL
ROYAL STANDARD
MINISTER OF DEFENCE
MERCANTILE
Blue
Yellow
COMMODORE
OFFICER IN COMMAND OF A DIVISION
PENNANT
SENIOR OFFICER
SQUADRON COMMANDER
PILOT INSPECTION
PILOT
W.O IN COMMAND OF A SHIP
FISHERY PENDANT

Note.—The blue is azure in every case but last 3 pendants.

Administration.

Minister of Defence : Hr. P. E. Sköld, M.P.
Commander-in-Chief of the Navy (including Coast Artillery) : Vice-Admiral C. F. Tamm.
President of the Navy Technical and Administrative Board : Rear-Admiral K. G. Bjurner.
Commander-in-Chief of the Fleet : Rear-Admiral Count Gösta Ehrensvärd.
Naval Attaché (London) : Captain N. J. Wesström.

INSIGNIA OF RANK ON SLEEVES.

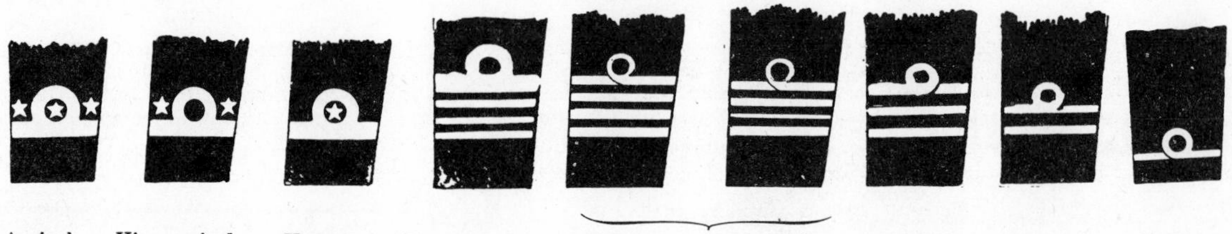

	Amiral.	Vice amiral.	Konter-amiral.	Kommendör.	Kommendörkapten av: 1 graden.	Kommendörkapten av: 2 graden.	Kapten.	Löjtnant.	Fänrik
British equivalent	*Ad-miral.*	*Vice-Ad.*	*Rear-Ad.*	*Commodore.*	*Captain. (Senior)*	*Captain. (Junior)*	*Commander & Lieut.-Com.*	*Lieutenant.*	*Sub-Lieut*

Paymasters have similar stripes with *white* braid following uppermost stripe.
Other branches have stripes with triangular curl, and colour between stripes as follows :—
Constructors and Engineers, *purple blue ;* Doctors, *scarlet.*

Personnel : Active List, *about* 5500 officers and men. Total for Reserves cannot be estimated, as it is dependent on conscription, but includes 700 officers.

Modern Swedish Guns (Bofors).

(Details furnished by Bofors).

Designation (cm.)	Designation (inches)	Length in calibres	Model	Weight of gun (tons)	Weight of A.P. shot (lbs.)	Initial velocity (ft. secs.)	
28·3	11	45	'12	44·2	672¼	2,850	Sverige *class*
21·0	8·3	45	'98	18·0	275⅛	2,460	Oscar II, Äran *class*
15·2	6·0	55	'30	10·0	101¼	2,950	Gotland
15·2	6·0	50	{'03 '12}	7·8	100	2,790	Oscar II, Sverige *class*
15·2	6·0	44	'98	6·0	100	2,460	Äran *class*, Fylgia
12·0	4·7	46	{'24 '34}	3·0	46⅓	2,625	{Ehrensk öld *class* Göteborg *class*}
12·0	4·7	50	'11	3·9	46⅓	2,825	Clas Fleming
12·0	4·7	45	'94	2·8	46⅓	2,430	Örnen *class*
10·5	4·1	41	'25	1·2	35⅕	2,300	Draken *class*
7·5	3·0	60	'26	1·3	12⅛	2,780	Gotland
7·5	3·0	50	'24	1·1	12⅛	2,660	Sverige class, Dristigheten, Valen
4·0	1·6	60	{'31 '36}	0·22	2⅕	2,950	
4·0	1·6	43	'32	0·17	2⅕	2,300	
2·5	1·0	64	'32	0·06	½	2,950	

Torpedoes.

21 in., and 18 in. Torpedoes manufactured at Karlskrona.

Colour of Ships.

Light Grey all over, excepting S/ms and some training ships. Displacements "Standard."

Navy Estimates.

1937–38: 38.000,000 kronor.
1938–39: 49,364,000 „
1939–40 : 70,000,000

Mercantile Marine.

From "Lloyd's Register," 1939 figures.
1238 vessels of 1,581,919 gross tonnage.

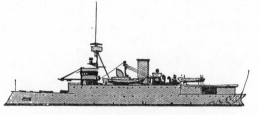

SVEA

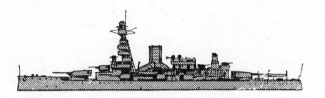

GUSTAF V.

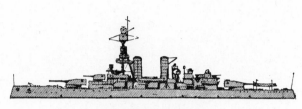

DROTTNING VICTORIA.

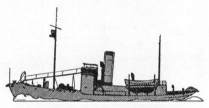

STARKODDER, STYRBJÖRN.

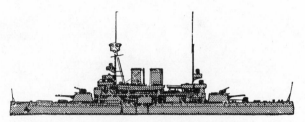

MANLIGHETEN, TAPPERHETEN, WASA.
(ÄRAN reconstructing)

JÄGAREN class.

ÖRNEN. JACOB BAGGE.
(Topmasts now shorter; *J. Bagge*, no mainmast.)

CLAS FLEMING.
(Now reconstructing).

SVERIGE.
(Now reconstructing).

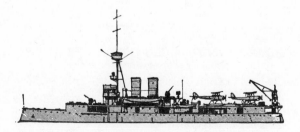

DRISTIGHETEN.

FYLGIA.

Oscar II.
(Now reconstructing).

Gotland.

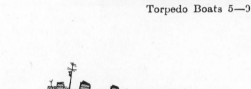

Torpedo Boats 5—9

Ehrensköld.   Nordenskjöld.
Klas Horn.   Klas Uggla (with pole abaft second funnel).

Wale *class*

Göteborg.   Stockholm.

Wrangel.   Wachtmeister

Bävern *class*.

Delfinen *class*.

Draken *class*.

Hajen *class*.

New Construction

(1939 Programme)

Coast Defence Ships (rated as Battleships).

(*Plan and illustration in Addenda.*)

Two ordered in 1939, from Kockums Mek. Verkstad A/B, Malmö, and Götaverken, Göteborg, respectively.
Displacement: 8,000 tons. Dimensions: $426\frac{1}{2}$ (*pp.*), $436\frac{1}{4}$ (*w.l.*) × 64 × $18\frac{3}{4}$ feet.
Guns: 4—10 inch, 6—4·7 inch AA., 8—40 mm. AA.
Speed: 23 kts.
To cost 37,000,000 kronor apiece.

Rated as Battleships (*Pansarskepp*)

SVERIGE (Götaverken, Göteborg. May 3, 1915).
DROTTNING VICTORIA (Götaverken, Göteborg. Sept. 15, 1917).
GUSTAF V (Kockums Mek. Verkstads A/B., Malmö. January 18, 1918).

Displacement : 7,080, 7,120 and 7,275 tons, respectively. Complement : 450.

Length (*w.l.*) { *Sverige*, 392·8 feet. / *D.V.* & *G.V*, 396·6 feet } Beam, 61 feet. *Max.* draught, 22 feet.

Guns (Bofors) :
4—11 inch 45 cal.
6—6 inch, 50 cal. (*Dr. Vic.*, 8)
4—3 inch, AA.
4—40 mm. AA. } (*Dr. Vic.*, 2—57 mm.,
8—25 mm. AA. } and 3—25 mm)
6—M.G. AA.

Armour : (Carnegie and Bofors).
8″ Belt (amidships)......
6″—3″ Belt (ends)...
1⅝″ Deck (slopes) ......
4″ Redoubt..............
8″ Big gun turrets......
6″ Barbettes ....
5″—2½″ Small turrets
7″ Conning tower ......

1938, *Registrator Ossi Janson.*

GUSTAF V. AND DR. VICTORIA.

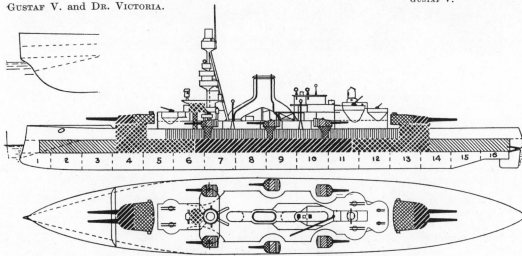

DROTTNING VICTORIA.

1937, *R. Perkins.*

Machinery : In *Sverige*, Curtis turbines by Kockum Co., 4 screws ; in *Gustaf V* and *Drottning Victoria*, Westinghouse geared turbines by the Motala Company. 2 shafts. Boilers : 6 Yarrow (coal and mixed firing) and 2 Penhoët (oil burning) in *Gustaf V* and *Dr. Vic.* ; 4 Penhoët (oil burning) in *Sverige*. Designed S.H.P. : 20,000 in *Sverige* ; 22,000 in *D. Victoria* and *Gustaf V* = 22·5 kts. Trials : 23 to 23·6 kts. Fuel : *Sverige*, 550 tons oil ; other 2 ships, 360 tons coal + 273 tons oil.

Gunnery Notes.—11 inch guns load in 17 seconds. Turrets somewhat cramped ; are divided by partition bulkheads.

Armour Notes.—11 inch gun shields are 8″ on fore side, 4″ on side, 4¾″ rear. Smaller gunshields are 5″ front, 3′ sides.

General Notes.—Appearance originally as *Drottning Victoria* but with light tripod foremast. *Sverige* refitted 1926 and given heavier foremast ; *Dr. Victoria* similarly refitted 1927. *Gustaf V* reconstructed 1929–30 when funnels were trunked into one and upperworks considerably remodelled. In *Sverige* fore funnel was inclined aft to clear the bridgework and second funnel retained, and after superstructure altered, 1932–33. *Drottning Victoria* was reconstructed in 1934–35, when 6 of her original 12 boilers were changed for 2 oil-fired boilers. *Gustaf V* was similarly modernised in 1936–37, and her armament modified. *Sverige* was taken in hand for modernisation in 1938 and will not be ready for sea again until 1940.

GUSTAF V.

1938, *Official.*

OSCAR II (Being refitted with new foremast).

1930 *Photo, by courtesy of Ministry of Defence.*

OSCAR II (June 6 1905).

Displacement, 4,320 tons. Complement, 339.

Length (*w.l.*) 313⅔ feet. Beam, 50½ feet. *Maximum* draught, 18 feet.

Guns (Bofors):
2—8·3 inch, 44 cal.
8—6 inch, 50 cal.
4—57 mm. A.A.
2—25mm. A.A.
(Fitted for minelaying.)

Armour (Krupp):
6″—4″ Belt (amidships)
2″ Deck (slopes)
6″ Bulkheads
4″ Lower deck redoubt
7½″—5″ Big gun
″ turrets (N.C.)
7″ Hoists to these
5″—2½″ Small tur-
rets (N.C.)
7″ Conning tower

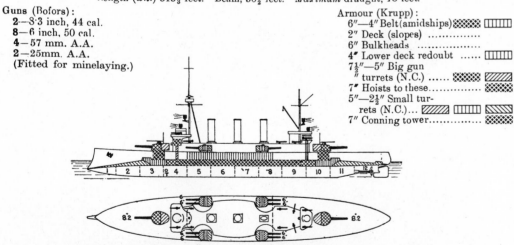

Machinery : 2 sets 4 cylinder triple expansion. 2 screws. Boilers : 10 Yarrow (8 coal-fired, 2 oil). Designed H.P. : 9,000 = 18·3 kts. Coal : *normal* 350 tons ; *maximum* 500 tons = 2,950 miles at 10 kts.

Notes.—Four searchlights carried—one on each bridge, and one on each mast. Built by Lindholmens Verkstads, Göteborg 1903–07. On Trial : 9,400 = 18·96 kts. To be refitted, 1939.

MANLIGHETEN (ÄRAN rebuilt, with only 1 funnel and 1 mast).

1926 *Photo, Cribb.*

(ÄRAN CLASS—4 SHIPS).

ÄRAN (Aug., 1901), WASA (May 29, 1901), TAPPERHETEN (Nov. 7, 1901) & MANLIGHETEN (Dec. 1, 1903).

Displacement, 3415, tons. Complement, 301.

Length, (*w.l.*) 287 feet. Beam, 49¼ feet. *Maximum* draught, 16¼ to 17¾ feet.

Guns (Bofors) :
2—8·3 inch, 44 cal.
6—6 inch, 45 cal.
10—6 pdr.* { *Äran,* 4—57 mm.
1—1 pdr. { AA., 2—25 mm. AA.
Torpedo tubes (18 inch) :
submerged (Armstrong).

Manligheten only
8—6 pdr.

Armour (Krupp) :
7″ Belt (amidships)
1″ Deck (flat on belt)
7″ Bulkheads
7½″—5″ Turrets
7½″ Supports
5″—2½″ Small turrets (N.C.)
4″ Hoists, etc.
7″ Conning tower

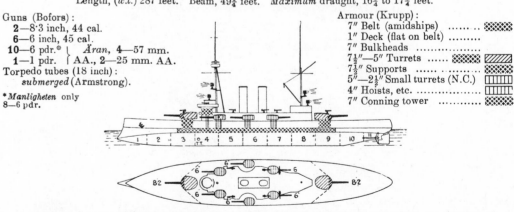

Machinery : 2 sets triple expansion. 2 screws. Boilers : 8 Yarrow (coal-fired), *Manligheten* has 2 oil-fired in addition. Designed H.P. : 7,400 = 17 kts. Coal : *maximum,* 300 tons. Endurance : 2,000 at 10 kts.

Notes.—Where built : *Äran,* Lindholmens, Göteborg ; *Wasa,* Bergsund, Stockholm ; *Tapperheten* and *Manligheten,* Kockums, Malmö. Completed : *Äran, Wasa,* 1902 ; *Tapperheten,* 1903 ; *Manligheten,* 1904.

(Classed as *Flygplankryssare*).

GOTLAND. (Götaverken. Sept. 14, 1933).

Displacement: 4,775 tons.   Complement, 480.

Length, (*w.l.*) 426½ feet, (*o.a.*) 472½ feet.   Beam, 50½ feet.   *Max.* draught, 18 feet.

Guns: (Bofors).
6—6 inch, 50 cal. (1930 Model).
4—3 inch A.A. (1928 Model).
4—25 mm. A.A.
4—M.G.
Torpedo tubes :
(in triple deck mountings).
6—21 inch.

Aircraft :
8 Hawker Osprey (space to stow 11).
Armour :
1⅛″—2″ Side
2″ Deck
⅝″—1⅛″ vertical Bulkheads.
1⅛″—2″ Turrets
1⅛″ Uptakes ....
1⅛″—2″ Hoists and supports
2″ Conning Tower ....
Mines :
Fitted for laying.

1936, *R. Perkins.*

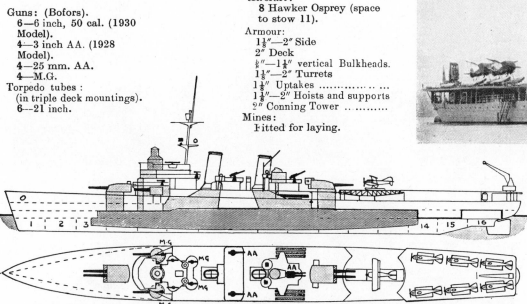

Machinery : 2 sets De Laval geared turbines. 2 shafts. Designed S.H.P. : 33,000 = 27 kts. (Trials, 34,000 = 28 kts.) Boilers : 4 Penhoët. Oil Fuel : 600 tons *normal*, 800 tons *max.*

General Notes.—The first cruiser designed to act as an aircraft carrier, and represents a well-conceived and exceedingly useful type of warship. Laid down Dec., 1927. Cost exceeded £900,000, by date of completion (Dec., 1934).

Gunnery Notes.—6 inch guns can be elevated to 60°. Range is 26,000 yds.

Aircraft Notes.—Each plane is mounted on a launching trolley, which can be driven by its own motor on to a catapult and connected up to launching mechanism. By this system aircraft can be launched at intervals of 2 minutes. Catapult is of compressed air type.

1935

1936. *R. Perkins.*

1936. *R. Perkins.*

Armoured Cruiser (*Pansarkryssare*).

(Under reconstruction; will be altered as plan).

FYLGIA (Dec. 20, 1905).

Standard Displacement, 4,700 tons.   Complement, 341.

Length (*w.l.*), 377⅔ feet.   Beam, 48½ feet.   *Max.* draught, 20⅔ feet.

Guns (Bofors).
8—6 inch, 50 cal.
4—57 mm. AA.
4—40 mm. AA.
2 M.G. AA.

Torpedo tubes (21 inch) :
2 *above water* (singles)

Armour (Krupp) :
4″ Belt ……… ……
2″ Deck (slopes) ……
5″—2″ Turrets ▨▨
4″ Hoists and supports
4″ Conning tower……

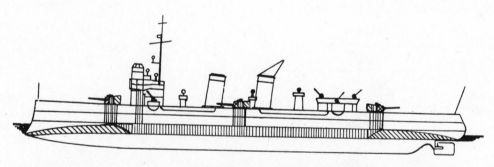

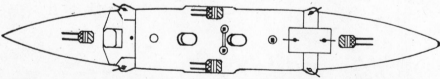

Machinery : 2 sets 4 cylinder triple expansion. 2 shafts. Boilers : 4 Penhoët. Designed
H.P. : 13,000 = 21·5 kts. Oil fuel.

General Notes.—Laid down by Bergsund Co., Stockholm, in 1903, and completed 1907. Under refit, 1939–40, and will be
altered as shown in plan. Will become Cadets' Training Ship in 1940.

Destroyers (*Jagare*).

4 Göteborg class.

(*Fitted for Minelaying.*)

GÖTEBORG.   1936 *courtesy Commander T. Hagman.*

MALMÖ.   1939, *courtesy Eriksberg Verkstad (Builders).*

1 *Götaverken* (*Göteborg*) : **Göteborg** (Oct. 14, 1935).
2 *Karlskrona* : **Stockholm** (March 24, 1936), **Karlskrona** (June 16, 1939).
1 *Eriksberg* (*Göteborg*) : **Malmö** (Sept. 22, 1938).

Displacement : 1,040 tons (1,200 tons *full load*). Complement : 130. Dimensions : 304 (*w.l.*), 310½ (*o.a.*) × 29½ × 9 feet
(*mean*), 12 feet (*max.*). Guns : 3—4·7 inch, 4—1 pdr. A.A. (*Karlskrona* and *Malmö*, 6—1 pdr. AA.). Torpedo tubes :
6—21 inch (tripled). Machinery : De Laval geared turbines. S.H.P. : 32,000 = 39 kts. (*Malmö* exceeded 42 kts.
with full load on trials). 3 boilers by Penhoët.

Notes.—First pair laid down in 1933, and completed 1936 and 1937 respectively. Second pair laid down 1936. *Malmö*
completed in 1939.

4 Ehrensköld class.

(fitted for Minelaying).

KLAS UGGLA. (*Klas Horn* similar).

1933 *Photo, Official.*

EHRENSKÖLD (Now No. 1). (*Nordenskjöld* similar).

1930, *Registrator Ossi Janson.*

Ehrensköld (Sept 25, 1926), **Nordenkjöld** (June 19, 1926). Built by Kockums M.V., Malmö, and Göta-verken, Göteborg, respectively. Displacement: 940 tons. Dimensions: 293 (*w.l.*) × 29¼ × 12½ feet (*max.* draught). **Klas Horn** (June 13, 1931), **Klas Uggla** (June 18, 1931). Laid down 1928, by Kockums M.V. and at Karlskrona D.Y., respectively. Displacement: 1,020 tons. Dimensions: 297 (*w.l.*) × 29¼ × 12¼ feet (*max.* draught). Armament: 3—4·7 inch and 2—40 mm. AA. guns ; 6—21 inch torpedo tubes in triple deck mountings. Machinery : De Laval geared turbines. S.H.P. : 24,000 = 35 kts. 3 boilers by Penhoët. Fuel (oil only) : 150 tons. Radius of action : 600 miles at full speed ; 1,600 miles at 20 kts. Complement : 125. Estimated cost : Kr. 7,150,000 each. First pair laid down 1924, completed in 1927 and refitted in 1939. Second pair completed in 1932.

Pendant numbers: *Ehrensköld* (1).   *Nordenskjöld* (2).   *Göteborg* (5).

                    Klas Horn (3).   *Klas Uggla* (4).   *Stockholm* (6).

2 Wrangel class.

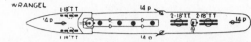

WRANGEL.

1939, *courtesy Swedish Navy League, " Sveriges Flotta."*

2 *Wrangel* class : **Wrangel** and **Wachtmeister** (Lindholmens Verkstad, Göteborg, both 1917). 465 tons. Dimensions : 232¾ × 22 × 9¼ feet. Armament : 4—3 inch, 3 M.G., and 6—18 inch torpedo tubes in two twin-deck mountings and two single mountings, P. and S. in forecastle. Machinery : De Laval geared turbines. Designed S.H.P. : 11,000 (*n.d.*), 13,000 (*f.d.*) = 34 kts. Reported to have attained 34·8 kts. on trials. Boilers : 4 Yarrow. Oil : 103·5 tons. Complement : 81. Completed early 1918. Pendant numbers are 9 and 10, respectively.

6 Hugin and Wale classes.

VIDAR.

1928, *Registrator Ossi Janson.*

2 *Hugin* class : **Hugin** (1911), **Munin** (1912). 360 tons. Dimensions : 215¼ × 20¾ × 8¼ feet. Guns : 4—3 inch, 2 machine. Torpedo tubes : 4—18 inch. Machinery : A.E.G. Vulcan turbines. S.H.P. : 10,000 = 31 kts. Boilers : 4 Yarrow. Fuel : 90 tons coal + 1½ tons oil. Endurance : 800 miles at 15 kts. *Hugin* built by Götaverken, Göteborg, and *Munin* by Kockums M.V., Malmö. Distinctive numbers : *Hugin* 7, *Munin* 8.

4 *Wale* class :—**Wale** (1907), **Ragnar** (1908), **Sigurd** (1908), **Vidar** (1909). 360 tons. Dimensions : 215¼ × 20¾ × 9 feet. Armament : *Wale*, 2—3 inch, 4—6 pdr., 2 machine ; other boats, 4—3 inch, 2 machine ; 4—18 inch tubes in all. S.H.P. : 8,000 = 30·5 kts. 4 Yarrow boilers. Coal : 84 tons. Radius of action : 920 miles at 15 kts. *Sigurd* built by Lindholmens Verkstad, Göteborg, other 3 by Kockums M.V., Malmö. Hull on Thornycroft lines. Distinctive numbers : *Wale*, 3 ; *Vidar*, 4 ; *Ragnar*, 5 ; *Sigurd*, 6. Only *Munin* and *Vidar* have charthouse on bridge.

(a) Sea-going Types.

SJÖLEJONET.

1939, *Official.*

6 *Sjölejonet* class : **Sjölejonet** (July 25, 1936), **Sjöhunden** (Nov. 26, 1938), **Sjöbjörnen** (Jan. 15, 1938). and 3 more (ordered 1939). All by Kockums Mek. Verkstad A/B., Malmö. Displacement : 580/760 tons. Dimensions : 204 × 20½ × 11 feet. Guns : 2—40 mm., 2 M.G. AA. Tubes : 6—21 inch (3 bow, 1 stern and 2 deck aft). Fitted for minelaying. B.H.P. : 3,000/—— = 15/10 kts. Complement : 32.

DELFINEN.

1936, *courtesy Swedish Navy League, " Sveriges Flotta."*

3 *Delfinen* class : **Delfinen** (Dec. 20, 1934), **Nordkaparen** (Feb. 9, 1935), **Springaren** (April 27, 1935). All built by Kockums M.V., Malmö. Displacement : 540/720 tons. Dimensions : 199 × 20½ × 11 feet. Guns : 1—4·1 inch, 1—57 mm. AA. Tubes : 4—21 inch (3 bow, 1 stern). Fitted for minelaying. Speed : 15/10 kts. Complement : 28.

DRAKEN.

1929 *Photo.*

3 *Draken* class : **Draken** (1926), **Gripen** (1928), **Ulven** (1930), all Karlskrona D.Y. Displacement : 667/850 tons. Dimensions : 213¼ × 21 × 11¾ feet. Armament : 1—3 inch AA., 1—25 mm. AA., 4—21 inch tubes. H.P. : 2,800/—— = 15/9 kts. Radius : 5,600 miles at 10 kts. *surface.* Complement : 32.

1937, *Registrator Ossi Janson.*

Valen (May 6, 1925), built at Karlskrona Naval Dockyard. Fitted for laying mines on the Normand-Fenaux system. Displacement : 501/730 tons Dimensions : 186 × 23¼ × 10 feet. Guns : 1—3 inch, 1—25 mm. AA. Tubes : 4—21 inch. B.H.P. : 2,800 = 15/9 kts. Complement : 28.

(b) Coastal Types.

U1, U2, Ordered 1939 from Kockums Mek. Verkstad. A/B., Malmö, and Stockholm Naval dockyard respectively. Displacement : 350/—— tons. Tubes : 4—21 inch

UTTERN.

1930, *courtesy Swedish Navy League, "Sveriges Flotta."*

3 *Bävern* class : **Bävern, Illern,** (1921), **Uttern** (1922), built by Kockums M.V., Malmö. Displacement : 429/640 tons. Dimensions : 185 × 18½ × 10 feet. H.P. : 2,800 = 15 kts. *on surface;* 9 kts. *submerged.* Guns : 1—6 p.dr. AA., 1 M.G. Tubes : 4—21 inch (bow). 8 torpedoes carried. Radius 3,000 miles at 15 kts. *surface,* 54 miles at 6 kts. *submerged.* Complement : 28.

HAJEN.

1924, *Official Photo.*

3 *Hajen* class : **Hajen** (1917), **Sälen** (1918), **Valrossen** (1918), built by Kockums M.V., Malmö. Displacement : 392/600 tons. Dimensions : 171 × 16½ × 11½ feet. Guns : 1—6 pdr. AA. Tubes : 4—18 inch. H.P. 2,800/ —— = 15/9 kts. Complement : 26.

Distinctive letters, painted on C.T., are : Bv, *Bävern* ; De, *Definen* ; Dk, *Draken* ; Gr., *Gripen* ; Hj, *Hajen* ; In, *Illern* ; Nd, *Nordkaparen* ; Sä, *Sälen* ; Sb, *Sjöbjörnen* ; Sh, *Sjöhunden* ; Sj, *Sjölejonet* ; Sp, *Springaren* ; Ut, *Uttern* ; Uv, *Ulven* ; Va, Valen ; Wa, Valrossen.

Aircraft Depot Ship (*Flygmoderfartyg*).

1936, *Miss Hjördis Karlsson.*

DRISTIGHETEN (Lindholmens Verkstad, Göteborg, 1900). Displacement : 3,270 tons. Dimensions : 285 × 48½ × 17 feet. Guns : 4—3 inch AA., 2—25 mm. AA., 4 M.G. AA. H.P. : 5,000 = 16 kts. Coal : 310 tons. Is an old battleship converted into an Aircraft Tender and Depot Ship in 1930. Carries 3 aircraft, and is fitted for minelaying.

Minelayer (*Minkryssare*)

Reconstructed, 1939. Lengthened 20 feet and completely modernised.

CLAS FLEMING (1914). Displacement : 1,570 tons. Complement : 175. Dimensions : 263 × 34 × 14 feet. (Being lengthened 20 feet.) Guns : 4—4·7 inch, 50 cal., 4 M.G. Machinery : Diesel-turbine installation by Götaverken.

6 Minesweepers (*Minsvepare*)

ARHOLMA.

1939, *courtesy " Sveriges Flotta."*

ARHOLMA (April 27, 1937), **LANDSORT** (Nov. 26, 1937). Both built at Karlskrona. Displacement : 375 tons *standard*, 442 tons *full load*. Complement : 37. Dimensions : 180¾ (*w.l.*), 186 (*o.a.*) × 24¾ × 7 feet *max.* Guns : 2—3 inch, 1—25 mm. AA., 2 D.C.T. Machinery : De Laval geared turbines. S.H.P. : 3,200 = 19 kts. Oil fuel : 60 tons.

STYRBJÖRN.

Added 1936, courtesy " Sveriges Flotta."

STARKODDER (ex-*Graham*, 1925), **STYRBJÖRN** (ex-*Klo*, 1923). Ex-whalers, built in Norway, purchased in 1935. Displacement : 375 and 350 tons, respectively. Dimensions : 99¾ × 23 × 14 feet, and 104 × 22 × 14 feet, respectively. Guns : 1—37 mm. Machinery : Reciprocating. I.H.P. : 750 = 15 kts.

MINESWEEPER 1.

1938, *Official.*

Nos. 1 and **2** (Ekensberg Varv, Stockholm, 1936). Displacement : 61 tons *standard*, 64 tons *full load*. Complement, 11. Dimensions : 97¾ (*w.l.*), 100¾ (*o.a.*) × 14 × 3½ feet *max.* Guns : 2—8 mm. AA. Machinery : Diesels. B.H.P. 600 = 16 kts. Fuel : 3 tons.

Note.—Completed in February and May, 1938, respectively.

6 Motor Torpedo Boats. (*Motortorpedbåtar*)

T 3, T 4 (1939), by Vosper, Ltd., Portsmouth. Length: 60 feet. Machinery: 2 Isotta-Fraschini motors. H.P.: 2,200. Complement: 10.

T 1, T 2, (1939), by British Power Boat Co., Ltd., Hythe, Southampton. Displacement: 24 tons. Length: 63 feet. Machinery: 2 Rolls-Royce-Merlin motors. H.P.: 2,200. Petrol: 3·7 tons. Complement: 10.

Added 1938, courtesy Messrs. Thornycroft.

Nos. 3 and 4. Built by Messrs. Thornycroft, at Hampton-on-Thames, 1925. Usual 55-ft. type C.M.B. with smoke screen apparatus. 11 tons. 1 M.G., 2—18 inch torpedoes. H.P.: 750 = 41 kts.

5 Torpedo Boats. (*2 kl. torpedbåtar*)

Nos. 5, 6, 7, 8, 9, (1906-08). Displacement, 50 tons. Dimensions: 106×12¾×6½ feet. Armament: 1—1 pdr., 2—18 inch tubes. H.P. 800= 21 kts. Coal: 11 tons. Complement, 14.

Patrol Boats (*Vedettbåtar*).

KAPAREN   *1935, Official.*

4 boats. **JÄGAREN** (Dec., 1932), **KAPAREN** (March 3, 1933), **SNAPPHANEN** (Nov. 2, 1933), **VÄKTAREN** (April 25, 1934). All built at Karlskrona. Displacement: 292 tons. Complement, 37. Dimensions: 177 × 19½ × 8¼ feet. Guns: 2—3 inch, 2—25 mm. AA. 2 D.C.T. Machinery: De Laval geared turbines. S.H.P.: 3,600 = 24 kts. Vanson boilers. Oil fuel: 50 tons. Identification Nos. 21 to 24, respectively.

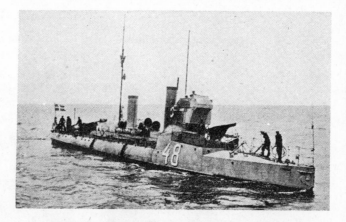

1930, courtesy Swedish Navy League, " Sveriges Flotta."

16 ex-Torpedo boats, **VEGA, VESTA, POLARIS, PERSEUS, REGULUS, RIGEL, ANTARES, ARCTURUS ALTAIR, ARGO, CASTOR, POLLUX, IRIS, THETIS, ASTREA, SPICA** (1908-1911). Displacement: 105 tons. Dimensions: 127 × 14½ × 9 feet. Guns: 1 or 2—57 mm. 1—18 inch torpedo tube. H.P.: 2,000 = 25 kts. All built by Karlskrona D.Y., Bergsunds Verkstad, Stockholm, or Götaverken, Göteborg, to designs of Ch. & At. Augustin Normand, Le Havre. Identification Nos. 39 to 54.

Patrol Boats—*continued.*

No. 32. (Since scrapped).   *1928, Registrator Ossi Janson.*

7 boats. **Nos.** 27 (ex-*Blixt*), 28 (ex-*Meteor*), 30 (ex-*Orkan*), 33 (ex-*Virgo*), 34 (ex-*Mira*), 35 (ex-*Orion*), 36 (ex-*Sirius*), by Karlskrona D.Y. and Bergsunds Verkstad, (1898–1903). 90 tons. H.P.: 1,300 = 23 kts. Fuel: 13–20 tons. Guns: 2—1 pdr., 1—15 inch tube. Complement: 15–18. All are ex-Torpedo boats. Mostly laid up in dockyards.

Tenders (rated as *Vedattbåtar*)

(Two new 67½ feet Tenders with Diesel engines are building at Kalmar.)

Nos. 74–76 (1933). Displacement : 28 tons. Complement : 7. Dimensions : 69½ × 12½ × 5 feet. Guns : 1—37 mm. AA. Machinery : Diesel. B.H.P. : 92 = 11 kts.

Nos. 71–73 (1932). Displacement : 25 tons. Length : 63¼ feet. Otherwise similar to *Nos. 74–76*.

SÖKAREN.   1939, *Registrator Ossi Janson.*

SÖKAREN, SVEPAREN, SPRÄNGAREN (1918, Motala Co.). 160 tons. Dimensions : 85·3 × 23 × 9·8 feet. H.P. 400 = 11 kts. Guns : 1—6 pdr. Complement : 18. Identification Nos. are 16, 17, 18, respectively, which have been painted on bows.

1926 *Photo, by courtesy of the Ministry of Defence.*

No. 19 (1914). 55 tons. Guns : 1—1 pdr., 1 M.G. Speed : 10 kts. (oil motor). Used as an Aircraft Tender.

Nos. 10, 11, 12, 14, 15 (1907–9). Displacement : 50 tons. Complement : 16. Dimensions : 106¼ × 13 × 6½ feet. Guns : 1—37 mm. Machinery : Triple expansion. I.H.P. : 700 = 16 kts. Yarrow boiler. Coal : 11 tons. (Ex-Torpedo Boats).

Nos. 41, 45 (1902). Displacement : 54 tons. Complement : 11. Dimensions : 70¾ × 16 × 6 feet. Guns : 1—37 mm. Machinery : Triple expansion. Speed : 11 kts.

Depot Ships (*Moderfartyg*).

A Submarine Depot Ship was laid down in 1939 for completion in 1941. Displacement : 2,600 tons *full load*. Dimensions : 305 (*pp.*), 329 (*o.a.*) × 43¼ × 13¼ feet. Guns : **40** mm. and **25** mm. AA. Machinery : Diesel. Speed : 11 kts. Complement : 120 + 223 submarine personnel.

JACOB BAGGE.   1936, *Registrator Ossi Janson*

ÖRNEN.   1936, *Registrator Ossi Janson.*

JACOB BAGGE (1898), **ÖRNEN** (1896), Displacement : 750 tons. Dimensions : 220 × 27 × 9 feet. Machinery : Triple expansion. Designed H.P. 4,000 = 20 kts. Coal : 100 tons. Guns : 2—4·7 inch, 4—6 pdr.

General Notes.—To distinguish between these ships compare relative positions of foremast, bridges, and fore funnel. *Örnen* has cut-away stern and mainmast. Both employed as Depot and Training Ships, though officially rated as *Torpedkryssare.*

Depot Ships—*continued.*

SVEA.   1933 *Photo, Official.*

SVEA. Old Coast Defence Battleship built by Lindholmen Co., 1886, rebuilt 1904 and 1921. 2,840 tons. Dimensions : 248·4 × 48·5 × 16·4 feet. Guns : 2—6 pdr. (*AA*), 2 M.G. Armour : 11¾″–8″ Belt, 2″ Decks. 2 screws. 6 cyl. boilers. I.H.P. 4,650 = 15 kts. Coal : 220 tons. Fitted as a depot ship for Submarines.

Note.—Old coast defence ships *Niord* and *Göta*, also serving as depot ships, are no longer illustrated here, as they are purely harbour service vessels.

Ice Breakers (*Isbrytarfartyg*)

1938 *Registrator Ossi Janson.*

YMER (1933). Built by Kockums M.V.A/B., Malmö, Displacement : 3,465 tons (4,350 tons *full load*). Dimensions : 246 (*pp.*), 257 (*o.a.*) × 63¼ × 21 feet. Guns : 4—3 inch AA., 2—40 mm. AA., 4—25 mm. AA. Machinery : 6 Atlas Diesels driving electric generators. H.P. : 9,000 = 16·5 kts. Complement : 44.

Note.—Ymer was first large icebreaker to be given Diesel electric propulsion.

1933, *Registrator Ossi Janson.*

ATLE (1926). Displacement : 1,750 tons. Dimensions : 194½ (*pp.*), 207 (*o.a.*) × 55¾ × 20½ feet. H.P. : 4,000 = 16 kts. Complement : 44.

Training Ships (*Övningsfartyg*).

1930, *courtesy Swedish Navy League, " Sveriges Flotta."*

NAJADEN (1897). }
JARRAMAS (1900). } 350 tons.

Mining Tenders.

(Manned by Coast Artillery personnel.)

No. 1 (1937). 200 tons.
No. 9 (1912). 120 tons. 9 kts.
Nos. 7, 8 (1904–5). 109 tons. 7·5 kts.
Nos. 5, 6 (1885–93). 108 tons. 6·5 kts.
No. 3 (1879). 99 tons. 6·5 kts.

Oiler. (*Tankfartyg*)

1933 *Registrator Ossi Janson.*

BRÄNNAREN (1933). Built by Kockums M.V.A/B., Malmö. Displacement : 1,100 tons. Dimensions : 165 (*pp.*), 173 (*o.a.*) × 29 × 12 feet. Machinery : Atlas Diesels. H.P. : 500 = 10 kts.

Fishery Patrol Vessel (*Fiskebevakningsfartyg*).

SVENSKSUND.   1936, *Registrator Ossi Janson.*

SVENSKSUND (1891). 360 tons. Guns : 2—6 pdr. H.P. 400 = 12½ kts. Coal : 50 tons. Officially rated as a Gunboat (*Kanonbat*).

ROYAL THAIAN NAVY.

Flags.

"TRAIRANGA".
NATIONAL FLAG.

NAVAL ENSIGN.

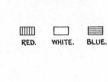

NAVAL JACK.

RED.   WHITE.   BLUE.

ADMIRAL OF THE FLEET'S FLAG.—A blue flag with a white elephant, and in the upper canton next the staff two yellow anchors crossed surmounted by the Thai crown.

ADMIRAL'S FLAG.—A blue flag with a white elephant in the centre.

VICE ADMIRAL'S FLAG.—The same as the Admiral's flag but with a white "Chakra" in the upper canton next the staff.

REAR ADMIRAL'S FLAG.—The same as the Admiral's flag but with two white "Chakras" near the staff.

Personnel: 4726.   Officers: 352.

Minister of Defence: Colonel Luang Bipul.

Commander-in-Chief of Navy: Eng. Captain Phya Vicharn Chakrakich.

Mercantile Marine.

14 steamers of 9,186 tons gross (Bureau Veritas figures).

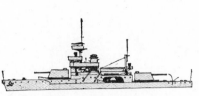

SUKHODAYA.   RATANAKOSINDRA.

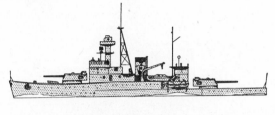

AYUTHIA, DHONBURI.

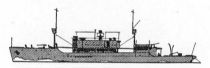

Nos. 1 and 2.

MEKLONG, TACHIN.

T.B. 1, 2, 3, 4

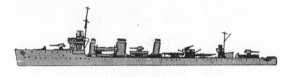

PHRA RUANG.

SUA KHAMRONSINDHU.
SUA TAYARNCHOL (similar without fourth funnel).

BALI, SUGRIB, MONGKUT.

ANGTHONG.

KANTAN *class.*

CHNAO PHYA.

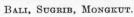

MACHANU *class.*

TRAD *class.*

455

Cruisers.

Two Cruisers were laid down by the Cantieri Riuniti dell' Adriatico, Trieste, in October, 1938. Displacement reported as 4,200 tons: Dimensions : $482\frac{1}{4} \times 47 \times 13\frac{3}{4}$ feet. Guns : 6—6 inch, 6—3 inch AA., 10 M.G. Torpedo Tubes : 6—18 inch. Geared turbines S:H.P : 45,000 = 30 kts.

DHONBURI   1938.

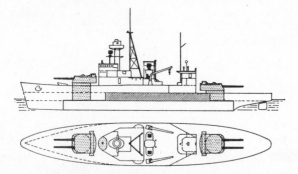

AYUTHIA (July 21, 1937), **DHONBURI** (Jan. 31, 1938). Both laid down by Kawasaki Co., Kobe, in 1936. Displacement : 2,265 tons. Dimensions : $252\frac{2}{3} \times 47\frac{1}{4} \times 13\frac{3}{4}$ feet. Guns : 4—8 inch, 4—3 inch AA., 4—20 mm. AA. Machinery : 2 sets M.A.N. Diesels. B.H.P. : 5,200 = 16·5 kts.

Note.—Apparently these ships are an expansion of *Ratanakosindra* design.

SUKHODAYA.   1930 *Photo, by courtesy of Messrs. Vickers-Armstrongs.*

RATANAKOSINDRA.   1926 *Photo, by courtesy of Messrs. Armstrongs.*

SUKHODAYA (Vickers Armstrongs, Nov. 19, 1929).

RATANAKOSINDRA (Armstrong, April 21, 1925). 1000 tons. 160 (*p.p.*), 173 (*o.a.*) × 37 × $10\frac{3}{4}$ feet. Guns : 2—6 inch, 4—3 inch AA. Protection : Side $2\frac{1}{2}''$ (amidships), $1\frac{1}{4}''$ ends, nickel steel. Barbette rings, $2\frac{1}{2}''$ nickel steel. C.T. $4\frac{3}{4}''$ cast steel armour. Upper deck, $\frac{3}{4}''$ to $1\frac{1}{4}''$ high tensile steel. 2 screws. Vertical triple expansion engines. H.P. 850 = 12 kts. 2 oil-burning water-tube boilers, working pressure 225 lb. Oil : 102 and 96 tons respectively. Complement : 103.

Ratanakosindra laid down 29th Sept., 1924, and completed August, 1925. *Sukhodaya* completed 1930.

Destroyer.

PHRA RUANG

1921 *Photo, by courtesy of J. Bailey, Esq.*

PHRA RUANG

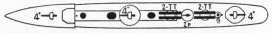

Phra Ruang (ex-British *Radiant*, launched by Thornycrofts, Nov., 1917. Purchased during July, 1920). 1,035 tons. Dimensions: 274 (*o.a.*), 265 (*p.p.*), × 27½ × 11 feet (*max.* draught) and 8½ feet (*mean*). Guns: 3—4 inch 1—3 inch AA., 1—2 pdr., 1 M.G. Tubes: 4—21 inch, in two twin deck mountings. Machinery: Brown-Curtis (all geared) turbines. Designed S.H.P.: 29,000 = 35 kts. (39·67 trials). 3 Yarrow boilers. Oil fuel: *about* 285 tons (*max.*). Complement, 100.

Submarines.

BLAJUNBOL, SINSAMUDAR. 1938.

4 *Mitubisi* type: **Machanu, Vilun** (both Dec. 24, 1936), **Blajunbol, Sinsamudar** (both May 14, 1937). *Standard* displacement: 370 tons. Dimensions: 167⅓ × 13½ × 12 feet. Armament: 5 tubes, 1 M.G. Speed 14·5/8 kts. Complement: 24.

Notes.—First pair laid down on April 6, 1936, second pair Oct. 1, 1936. 4 more are projected.

Torpedo Boats.

PUKET. 1936.

TRAD. 1936, *courtesy Commander R. Steen Steensen.*

9 *Adriatico* type: **Trad** (No. 11) (Oct. 26, 1935), **Puket** (No. 12) (Sept. 28, 1935), **Patani** (No. 13) (Oct. 16, 1936), **Surasdra** (No. 21) (Nov. 28, 1936), **Chandraburi** (No. 22) (Dec. 16, 1936), **Rayong** (No. 23) (Jan. 11, 1937), **Chunphorn** (No. 31) (Jan. 18, 1937), **Cholburi** (No. 32) (Feb. 10, 1937), **Songkla** (No. 33) (Feb. 9, 1937). *Standard* displacement: 470 tons. Dimensions: 219 (*p.p.*), 223 (*o.a.*) × 21 × 7 feet *max.* draught. Armament: 3—3 inch AA., 2—20 mm. AA., 4—8 mm., 6—18 inch tubes (2 single, 4 paired). Parsons geared turbines. H.P.: 9,000 = 31 kts. Radius: 1,700 miles at 15 kts. Complement: 70.

Notes.—First 2 laid down Feb. 8, 1935 by Cantieri Navali Riuniti dell'Adriatico, Monfalcone, for delivery by end of 1935. Armament supplied by Vickers-Armstrongs, Ltd. First boat reached 32·54 kts. on trials with 10,000 H.P. All delivered by summer of 1937.

Torpedo Boats—*continued.*

TAKBAI.   1937.

KANTAN (No. 7), **KLONGYAI** (No. 5), **TAKBAI** (No. 6) (Isikawazima Co., March 26, 1937), and 2 more building. Displacement: 110 tons *standard*, 135 tons *full load*. Complement: 25. Dimensions: 131½ × 15½ × 4 feet. Guns: 1—3 inch, 2—20 mm. Tubes: 2—18 inch. Machinery: Geared turbines. 2 shafts. Speed: 19 kts. 2 water tube boilers. Oil fuel.

Notes——First 3 completed June 21, 1937.

Motor Type.

Added 1938, courtesy Messrs. Thornycroft.

4 *Thornycroft* type: Nos. **6** to **9** (1935). 16 tons. B.H.P. 950=40 kts. 2 M.G., 2 torpedoes, 2 D.C.
5 *Thornycroft* type: Nos. **1** to **5** (1922). 11 tons. 55 × 11 feet. B.H.P.: 750 = 37 kts. (40 kts. *extreme*). Petrol carried: 300 gallons *normal*, 500 *max.* 4 Lewis guns, 2 torpedoes, 2 D.C. Complement, 5.

Escort Vessels (Training Ships).

MEKLONG.   1937.

TACHIN.   1937.

TACHIN (July 24, 1936), **MEKLONG** (Nov. 27, 1936), both by Uraga Dock Co. Displacement: 1,400 tons. Dimensions: 269 × 34½ × 10⅓ feet (*mean*). Guns: 4—4·7 inch, 2—20 mm. AA. Tubes: 4—21 inch (paired). H.P.: 2,500 = 17 kts. Fitted for minesweeping. Complement (as training ships), 155.

Both delivered in June, 1937. (2 more of this type were to be begun in 1939.)

Despatch Vessel.

SAMET (ex-*Pi-Sua-Nam.*) Displacement: 165 tons. Dimensions: 100 × 20 × 8½ (*mean* draught) feet. H.P.: 210 = 9½ kts. Complement: 25.

Training Ship.

CHAO PHYA.   1921 *Photo, by courtesy of Messrs. Thornycroft.*

CHAO PHYA (ex-British Twin Screw Minesweeper *Harant*, built by Eltringhams, S. Shields, Nov., 1918, purchased 1923 and reconstructed by Messrs. Thornycroft). Displacement, 840 tons. Dimensions: $220 \times 28\frac{1}{2} \times 7\frac{1}{2}$ feet. Machinery: Vertical triple expansion. Boilers: Yarrow, converted to burn oil. I.H.P. 2200 $= 16$ kts. Oil: 160 tons. Complement, 65.

Fishery Protection Vessels.

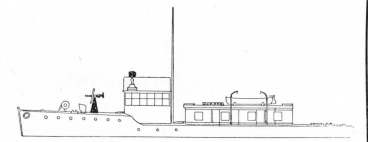

3 buil' in Royal Dockyard, Bangkok, 1936. (A fourth projected.) Displacement : 50 tons.

Guns : 1—37 mm.

Oilers.

1938.

SUMUI (Hakodate Dock Co., April 18, 1936), and another projected. Displacement : 1,854 tons *standard*. Dimensions: $240 \times 39 \times$ feet. 2 Sulzer Diesel engines. B.H.P. $2,141 = 12$ kts.

Minelayers.

1936.

BANGRADIAN (No. 1), (1936), **NONSARAI** (No. 2), (July 22, 1936). Cant. Nav. Riuniti dell' Adriatico, Monfalcone. (A third vessel reported building at Cant. Nav. Riuniti, Ancona.) Displacement : 368 tons *standard*, 408 tons *full load*. Complement : 55. Length : Under 200 feet. Guns : 2—3 inch AA. Diesel engines of Burmeister & Wain type. Speed : 12 kts.

Transports.

1938.

PANGAN, SICHANG (Harima Co., Japan, Nov. 10, 1937). Displacement : 650 tons. Machinery : Diesel. Other details wanted. Completed in January, 1938.

Transports—*continued*.

1919 *Photo, J. Bailey, Esq.*

ANGTHONG (ex-*Maha Chakri*), (Kawasaki Co., Kobé, Japan, 1918). About 2,400 tons *gross*. Complement : 199. Length : 298 feet (*w.l.*), 335 feet (*o.a.*). Beam : 40 feet. Draught : feet. Guns : Not known. Machinery (*see Notes*) : 2 sets triple, exp. Boilers : 4 (type unknown) coal and oil burning. I.H.P. : about 2,000 = 15 kts. Oil fuel : 200 tons = 2,000 miles endurance. 2 screws.

Notes.—The hull of the old Royal Yacht *Maha Chakri* was sold to the Kawasaki Co. in 1917, but the engines and other fittings were removed, overhauled and renovated for installation in the above ship, which is now rated as a transport, and used also as Depot Ship for Submarines.

1921 *Photo, J. Bailey, Esq.*

CHANG (ex-*Vides Kichkar*, ex-*Buk*, ex-*Lycidas*, Ritson & Co., Maryport, 1902). 850 tons. $176 \times 27\frac{1}{6} \times 10$ feet. H.P. : $780 = 9$ to 10 kts.

CUONG (ex-*Pra-Yom*). Displacement : 190 tons. Dimensions : $110 \times 18 \times 8$ (*mean draught*) feet. H.P. : $225 = 10$ kts. Complement : 30.

Also 3 ex-N.D.L. steam lighters, re-named *Chen Thale, Han Thale, Leu Thale*, built by Hongkong and Whampoa Dock Co. About $160 \times 27 \times$ — feet, 440 tons *gross*. Nom. H.P. 60 – 8 kts. speed. Seized during the war and now used for various purposes, including occasional surveying duties.

TURKISH FLEET.

Colour of Ships: Grey.

Flags.

ENSIGN AND JACK.

PRESIDENT'S STANDARD.

COMMANDER-IN-CHIEF.

COMMANDER OF NAVAL BASE.

OR AMIRAL.*

TÜM AMIRAL.

TUG AMIRAL.

COMMODORE. †

SENIOR OFFICER (AT YARDARM)

SENR. OFFICER (SUBORDINATE)

*(Kor Amiral has three balls.) † Commodore 1st class has 3 balls, if Albay 2, and if Yarbay 1.

| Or Amiral. | Kor Amiral. | Tüm Amiral. | Tuğ Amiral. | Albay. |

| Yarbay. | Binbaşi. | Yüzbaşi | Ustegmen. | Tegmen. | Astegmen. |

Admiral of the Fleet	..	Büyük Amiral
(Non-existent in peacetime)		
Admiral	..	.. Or Amiral
Vice Admiral	..	.. Kor Amiral
Rear Admiral (Senior)	..	Tüm Amiral
Rear-Admiral (Junior)	..	Tuğ Amiral
Captain (Senior)	..	.. Albay
Captain (Junior)	..	.. Yarbay
Commander	..	.. Binbaşi
Lieutenant-Commander	..	Ön Yüzbaşi
Lieutenant ..	..	.. Yüzbaşi
Sub-Lieutenant	..	.. Ustegmen
Acting Sub-Lieutenant	..	Teğmen
Midshipman	..	.. Asteğmen

Minister of National Defence : General N. Tinaz.
Under-Secretary for Navy : Captain Hüsnü Gökdenizer.
Naval Attaché, London : Lieut.-Commander S. Cakir.

Mercantile Marine.

(From "Lloyd's Register," 1939 figures). 185 Vessels of 224,461 gross tonnage.

KEMAL REIS *class*

AYDIN REIS.

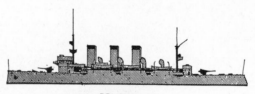

MECIDIYE.

TINAZTEPE. ZAFER.

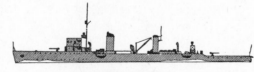

BERK, PEYK.

ERKIN.

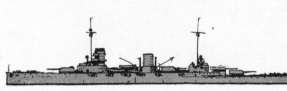

YAVUZ.

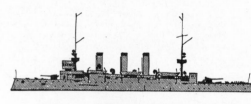

HAMIDIYE.

ADATEPE. KOCATEPE.

DUMLUPINAR. SAKARYA.

1 INÖNÜ, 2 INÖNÜ

BATIRAY.

GÜR.

YAVUZ (ex-German *Goeben*,) (Blohm & Voss, March, 1911).

Standard Displacement, 23,100 tons.   Complement, 1,300 (as Flagship).

Length (*w.l.*), 610¼ feet.   Beam, 96 ft. 10 in.   Draught (*max. load*), 26 ft. 11 in.

Guns :
10—11 in. 50 cal.
10—5·9 in. 45 cal.
2—3·5 in. 45 cal.
4—3.5 inch A.A.
4 M.G.
(1 landing)
Torpedo tubes (19·7 in.) :
2 *submerged*.

Anti-Torp. Pro. :—
2″—1″ deep H.T. Steel B.H., between extreme barbettes : Minute internal subdivision.

Armour (Krupp) :
10½″ Belt (amidships) tapers to 6″ at top and 5″ below
3¾″ Belt (bow and stern)
9″—8″ Barbettes . . . .
8″ Gunhouses . . . .
5″ Battery . . . .
10″ Fore C.T.   3″ Roof . .
8″—3″ Double com. tube
8″ After C.T. . . . .
6″—3″ Com. tube . . . . . .
3″—1″ Decks . . . .

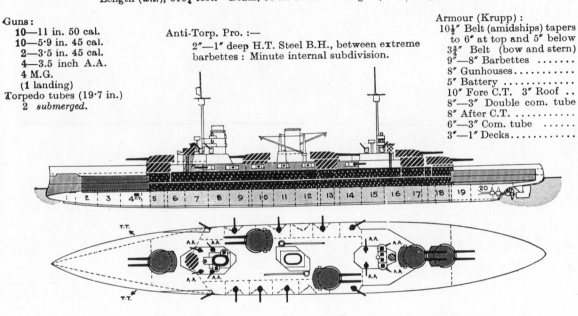

YAVUZ   1936, *Grand Studio, Malta.*

Machinery : Parsons turbine, 4 shaft, direct drive.   Boilers : 24 Schulz-Thornycroft (German "Marine Type.")   Designed H.P. : nominally 52,000 = 25·5 kts.   Coal : *normal* about 1,000 tons ; *maximum* 3,050 tons.

1934 *Photo, Official.*

Engineering Notes.—Endurance is (*a*) 5,350 miles at 10 kts., (*b*) 2,370 miles at a continuous *max.* sea-going speed of 23 kts. She made 26·8 knots on Trials for 6 hours, and 27·1 kts. for 4 hours, on Mar. 17, 1930.

General Notes.—Laid down, August, 1909, by Blohm & Voss, Hamburg, under 1909 German Navy Programme, as a sister to German *Moltke*.   Completed, July, 1912.   Transferred to the Turkish Navy in 1914, and during the war was twice mined, striking 5 mines in all.   A contract was signed in December, 1926, with the Chantiers de St. Nazaire (Penhoët), for the repair and refit of this battle-cruiser at Ismid ; the work was considerably delayed owing to a floating dock proving unequal to her weight, and completion was not reached till 1930.

Destroyers. (*Torpedo Muhnbi*)

2 *Vickers-Armstrongs*: **Demirhisar, Sultanhisar.**
2 *Denny*: **Gayret, Muavenet.**
   Displacement: 1,360 tons. Dimensions: 312 (*pp.*) × 33 × 8½ feet (*mean*). Guns: **4**—4·7 inch, **7** smaller. Tubes: **8**—21 inch. Machinery: Parsons geared turbines. S.H.P.: 34,000 = 35·5 kts. Boilers: 3, of 3-drum type. Oil fuel: 450 tons. Complement: 150.

Note—All 4 ordered 1939.

ADATEPE.   1932 *Photo, Official.*

2 *Ansaldo* boats: **Kocatepe** (Feb. 7, 1931) and **Adatepe** (March 19, 1931). Built at Sestri Ponente,
   Displacement: 1,250 tons (*standard*),
                 1,650 tons (*full load*).
   Dimensions: 321½ (*pp.*) 328⅝ (*o.a.*) ×30¾ ×9½ feet (*mean*).
   Guns: **4**—4·7 inch, 50 cal., **2**—40 m/m AA. and **2**—20 mm. AA.
   Tubes: **6**—21 inch in triple mountings.
   Parsons geared turbines. S.H.P. 40,000 = 38 kts.
   3 Thornycroft boilers with superheaters.
   Oil, 360 tons. Complement, 149.
   These boats are of Ansaldo design and are named after mountains near Smyrna associated with Turkish military glories.

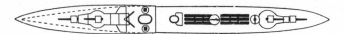

KOCATEPE.   1935.

ZAFER.   1933 *Photo, Official.*

2 *C.N. del Tirreno* boats: **Tinaztepe** (July 27, 1931). **Zafer** (Sept. 20, 1931). Built at Riva Trigoso.
   Displacement: 1,206 tons (*standard*).
                 1,610 tons (*full load*).
   Dimensions: 307 (*pp.*), 315 (*o.a.*) × 30½ × 10¾ feet.
   Guns: **4**—4·7 inch, 50 cal., **2**—40 m/m AA., **2**—20 mm. AA.
   Tubes: **6**—21 inch in triple mountings.
   Parsons geared turbines. S.H.P. 35,000 = 36 kts.
   3 Thornycroft boilers with superheaters.
   Oil: 450 tons. Complement, 149.
   These boats are of Italian design and generally resemble the Italian "Turbine" class.

TINAZTEPE.   1933 *Photo, Official.*

Old Cruisers (*Muhafazali Kruvazör*).

1932 *Photo, Official*

HAMIDIYE (ex-*Abdul Hamid*, Armstrong, Sept., 1903). 3830 tons. Complement, 302. Dimensions : 368 × 47½ × 16 feet (*mean* draught). Guns : **2**—5·9 inch, 45 cal. Krupp, **8**—3 inch 50 cal. (Krupp). Armour : 4″ Deck. Machinery : 2 sets 4-cylinder triple expansion. 2 screws. Boilers : Cylindrical. Designed H.P. : 12,000 = 22 kts. (*forced* draught). Present best speed about 16–18 kts. Coal : 750 tons. Endurance : 5,000 miles at 10 kts. At present serves as Training Ship for Naval Cadets.

1932 *Photo, Official.*

MECIDIYE (ex-Russian *Prut*, ex-Turkish *Medjidieh*, July 25, 1903). 3,500 tons. Complement : 330. Dimensions : 330 × 42 × 17½ feet (*max.* draught). Guns (as re-armed) : **6**—5·1 inch (Vickers), **4**—3 inch, 50 cal. (Schneider), **2** M.G. Deck, 1″. H.P. : 12,000 = about 18 kts. now. Babcock and Wilcox boilers. Coal : 600 tons. Endurance : 4,700 miles at 10 kts. Built by Cramps, Philadelphia. (Refitted and reboilered 1930.)

Notes.—Mined and sunk in Black Sea, April, 1915. Salved, repaired and re-fitted at Nikolaieff for Russian Navy, 1915–16 Seized by Austro-German Armies at Sevastopol, 1918, and returned to Turkish Navy.

Submarines.
Ordered March, 1939.

4 *Vickers-Armstrongs* (*Barrow*) : **Burak Reis, Murat Reis, Oruç Reis, Uluç Ali Reis.** Displacement : 683/970 tons. Dimensions : 193 (*pp.*), 202½ (*w.l.*) × 24 × 10½ feet (*mean*). Guns : **1**—3 inch, **1** M.G. Tubes : **6**—21 inch. H.P. : 1,550/1,300 = 13·75/10 kts. Fuel : 40 tons.

4 "AY" Class.

Photo wanted.

3 *Germania* type : **Atilay** (May 19, 1939), **Yildiray** (Aug. 26, 1939), (both built at Istanbul), **Saldiray** (Germania, Kiel, July 23, 1938). All laid down 1937. Displacement : 934/1,210 tons. Dimensions : 262½ × 21 × 14 feet. Guns : **1**—4 inch, **1**—20 mm. AA. Tubes : **6** (4 bow and 2 stern). 2 sets Burmeister & Wain Diesels. H.P. : 3,500 = 20/9 kts. Diving limit : 55 fathoms. Complement :

1939, *Dr. E. Gröner.*

1 *Germania* minelaying type : **Batiray** (Germania, Kiel, March 28, 1939). Displacement : 1,044/1,357 tons. Dimensions : 282 × 22½ × 14 feet. Other details as above, except Complement : 47.

1935, *courtesy of Capitán M. Mille.*

1 *German* design : **Gür** (Echavarrieta y Larrinaga, Cadiz, 1932). Purchased 1934 and delivered in Jan. 1935. Displacement : 750/960 tons. Dimensions : 237½ × 20½ × 13½ feet. Armament : **1**—4 inch, **1**—20 mm. AA. guns, **6**—21 inch tubes (4 bow, 2 stern). 14 torpedoes carried. 2 sets M.A.N Diesels. H.P. ——, speed. 20/9 kts. Radius : 6,400 miles at 9½ kts. on *surface*; 1,880 miles at 18½ kts. on *surface*; 101 miles at 4 kts. *submerged*. Diving limit, 44 fathoms. Complement : 42.

Note.—Many of the parts for this submarine were made in the Netherlands.

DUMLUPINAR.

1936, *Grand Studio.*

1 *Bernardis* minelaying type : **Dumlupinar** (4 March, 1931). Built by Cantiere Navale Triestino, Monfalcone. Displacement : 920/1,150 tons. Dimensions : 223 × 19 × 14 feet. Armament : 1—4 inch gun , 1 M.G., 6—21 inch tubes (4 bow, 2 stern). 48 mines carried. Machinery : M.A.N. Diesels. H.P. : 3,000 = 17·5 kts. *on surface.* Electric motors of 1,000 H.P. = 9 kts. *submerged.* Complement : 47.

1 *Bernardis* type : **Sakarya** (Cant. Nav. Triestino, Monfalcone, Feb. 2, 1931). Displacement : 750/940 tons. Dimensions : 196 (*p.p.*) × 22½ × 13 feet. Guns : 1—4 inch, 1—20 mm. AA. Tubes : 6—21 inch. M.A.N Diesels. H.P. : 1,600 = 16 kts. *surface* Electric motors. H.P. : 1,100 = 9·5 kts. *submerged.* Radius : 4,000 miles at 10 kts. Complement : 41.

2 Inönü Class.

BIRINCI INÖNÜ

1936, *Grand Studio.*

2 *Fijenoord* type : **Birinci Inönü** (February 1, 1927, **Ikinci Inönü** (March 12, 1927). Built by Fijenoord Co., Rotterdam. Displacement : 505/620 tons. Dimensions : 192½ × 19 × 11½ feet. 2 sets M.A.N. Diesels. H.P. : 1,100 = 13·5/8·5 kts. Guns : 1—3 inch, 1—20 mm. Tubes : 6—17·7 inch (4 bow, 2 stern). Complement : 29.

Note.—These two names refer to the first and second Turkish victories gained at Inönü, in Asia Minor.

Yachts.

1938.

SAVARONA (Blohm & Voss, 1931). Displacement : 5,750 tons. Dimensions : 349½ (*w.l.*), 408½ (*o.a.*) × 53 × 20½ feet (*mean*). Guns : 2—3 pdr. Machinery : 6 geared turbines. 2 shafts. S.H.P. : 10,750 = 21 kts. 4 watertube boilers, 400 lbs. working pressure. Oil fuel. Radius : 9,000 miles at 15 kts. Equipment includes Sperry gyro-stabilisers. Is probably the most sumptuously fitted yacht afloat. Complement : 79.

1937 " *Yavuz.*"

ERTUĞRUL (Armstrong, 1903). 964 tons. Dimensions: 260 (*pp.*) × 27⅓ × 11½ feet. Guns : 8—3 pdr. Machinery : Triple expansion by Hawthorn Leslie. H.P. : 2,500 = 21 kts. Boilers : Cylindrical.

Note.—Above yachts are not part of Turkish Navy in peace time, but come under Public Works Department.

Motor Torpedo Boats.

1931 Photo.

3 *S.V.A.N.* Type: **DOĞAN, MARTI, DENIZKUSU.**
Built at Venice, 1930–31. 32 tons. Dimensions: 69 × 13¾ × 4 feet. 2—18 inch torpedoes. 1—3 inch gun, 1 M.G., 8 D.C. H.P.: 1,500 = 34 kts.

Minelayers.

SIVRIHISAR, YÜZBAŞI HAKKI. Displacement: 350 tons. Machinery: 2 sets Atlas Polar Diesels. B.H.P.: 1,200. Laid down by Thornycroft, 1939.
ATAK (Gölcük,   , 1938). Believed to be of same type.

1938, courtesy Dott. Ing. L. Accorsi.

NUSRET (ex-*Yardim*, ex-*Nusret*, Germania, Kiel, 1912). 365 tons. Dimensions: 132 × 22 × 8¼ feet. H.P.: 1,200 = 15 kts. Guns: 2—57 mm. Can carry 25 mines.

Note.—This vessel laid the minefield in the Dardanelles on which *H.M.S. Irresistible* and *Ocean,* and the French battleship *Bouvet,* were lost on March 18, 1915.

1938, courtesy Dott. Ing. L. Accorsi.

UYANIK (ex-*Intibah*, ex-*Warren Hastings*, Port Glasgow, 1886). Iron. 616 tons *gross.* Dimensions: 202 × 30 × 12 feet. H.P. 1670 = 12 kts. 2 screws. Carries 50 mines.

Note.—Completely refitted in 1933. Originally a Salvage Tug.

Mine Sweepers.

ISA REIS   *Added 1937, " Yavuz."*

3 *La Seyne* type: **KEMAL REIS** (Feb., 1912), **HIZIR REIS** (Feb., 1912) and **ISA REIS** (Dec., 1911). 413 tons. Dimensions: 154¼ × 25¾ × 4¼ feet. Guns: 3—47 mm., 2—3 pdr., 2 M.G. H.P.: 850 = 14 kts. Refitted, 1923. The 2 forward guns, shown above in sponsons, are now mounted on forecastle in *Isa Reis.*

Torpedo Gunboats (*Torpedo Muhribi*).

PEYK.   *Added 1939, courtesy Dott. Ing. L. Accorsi.*

BERK (ex-*Berkisatvet*) (1907), **PEYK** (ex-*Peykisevket*) (Nov., 1906). Built at Krupps' Germania Yard, Kiel. 775 tons. Dimensions: 262½ × 27⅔ × 9½ feet. Guns: 2—3·9 inch, 4—6 pdr. Torpedo tubes: 3—18 inch. Designed H.P. 5100 = 22 kts. Coal: 240 tons. 25 mines carried. Complement, 105.

Note.—*Berkisatvet* was mined and had her stern rebuilt during the Great War. *Peykisevket* was torpedoed by British Submarine E 11, August, 1915, but was beached and salved. *Berk* being refitted as *Peyk*, 1939.

Submarine Depot Ship.

1938, courtesy Dott. Ing. L. Accorsi.

ERKIN (ex-N.D.L. liner *Trier*), (Weser, Bremen, 1923). Purchased in July, 1936. Displacement : 16,800 tons. 9,415 tons *gross*. Dimensions : 458½ × 57½ × 28 feet. Machinery : Triple expansion. I.H.P. : 4,200 = 12·5 kts.

Surveying Vessel.

1937, "Yavuz."

AYDIN REIS (St. Nazaire, June, 1912). Refitted in 1925. 502 tons. Dimensions : 178½ × 27⅝ × 8 feet. No Guns. Boilers : Babcock. H.P. : 1,025 = 14 kts.

Seagoing Tug.

1937, "Yavuz."

AKIN (ex-*Rasit*, ex-*Cow-Whale*), (Smith's Dock Co., 1915). Ex-Admiralty whaler, purchased 1926. Displacement : 336 tons. Dimensions : 139¾ × 25 × 6½ feet. Machinery : Triple expansion. 1 shaft. H.P. : 1,000 = 12 kts. Coal : 60 tons. Complement : 26. Fitted with deep sea diving apparatus, with which a depth of 115 fathoms has been reached.

Motor Launch.

Photo, Messrs. J. I. Thornycroft & Co.

1 *Thornycroft* type : **MÜLÂZIM HAYATI** (ex-*No.* 14), (1911). Dimensions : 62 × 11 × 2½ feet. Guns : 2 M.G. 140 H.P. Thornycroft petrol motor = 11 kts. Bullet-proof steel over conning position and engines.

Oiler.

1938, courtesy Dott. Ing. L. Accorsi.

GÖLCÜK (Gölcük Dockyard, Ismit, Nov. 4, 1935). Displacement : 1,255 tons. Deadweight capacity : 750 tons. Dimensions : 185 × 31⅓ × 10 feet. Machinery : B. & W. Diesel. H.P. : 700 = 12·5 kts.

Collier.

1938, courtesy Dott. Ing. L. Accorsi.

ULKU (ex-*Silvergray*, ex-*Julius Kessler*), (Duluth, Minn., 1920). Purchased in 1931. Displacement : 5,000 tons. 2,412 tons *gross*. Dimensions : 251 × 43½ × 21 feet (*mean*). Machinery : Triple expansion. H.P. : 1,250 = 10 kts.

UNITED STATES NAVY.

UNIFORMS.

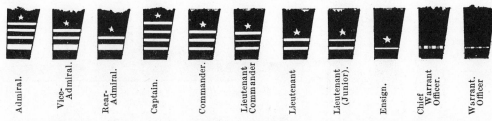

Admiral. — Vice-Admiral. — Rear-Admiral. — Captain. — Commander. — Lieutenant Commander. — Lieutenant. — Lieutenant (Junior). — Ensign. — Chief Warrant Officer. — Warrant Officer.

Note.—Lieutenants, junior grade, have 1½ stripes. Chief Warrant Officers one stripe broken with blue. Line Warrant Officers have one half stripe broken with blue. Staff Warrant Officers under Chiefs have no sleeve mark. Engineers same as Line Officers (interchangeable). Other branches than executive wear no sleeve star, but have following badges of branch over top stripe.

Carpenter. — Machinist. — Medical. — Supply. — Construction. — Boatswain.

Civil Engineer. — Gunner. — Pay Clerk. — Line. — Electrician. — Radio-Electrician.

FLAGS.

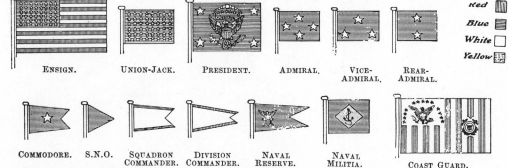

ENSIGN. — UNION-JACK. — PRESIDENT. — ADMIRAL. — VICE-ADMIRAL. — REAR-ADMIRAL.

Red | Blue | White | Yellow

COMMODORE. — S.N.O. — SQUADRON COMMANDER. — DIVISION COMMANDER. — NAVAL RESERVE. — NAVAL MILITIA. — COAST GUARD.

Commander in Chief : Franklin D. Roosevelt.
Acting Secretary of the Navy : Charles Edison.
Assistant Secretary of the Navy :
Chief of Naval Operations : Admiral Harold R. Stark.
Asst. Chief of Naval Operations : Rear-Admiral Robert L. Ghormley.
General Board : Rear-Admirals W. R. Sexton, J. W. Greenslade, F. J. Horne, E. J. King, C. S. Freeman.

Personnel U.S.N. and Marine Corps : 138,903 officers and men. Reserves : Officers, 14,790, Men, 55,464.

Naval Attaché, London : Captain Alan G. Kirk.

Principal Guns in the U.S. Fleet.

(Officially revised, 1929.)

Built at Washington Gun Factory, proved at Indian Head, Dahlgren, Va., and Potomac Range.

Notation	Nominal Calibre.	Mark or Model.	Length in Calibres.	Weight of Gun.	Weight of A.P. Shot.	Serrice Initial Velocity.	Maximum penetration firing capped A.P. direct impact against K.C. armour.			Muzzle Energy.
							9000	6000	3000	
	inch.			tons.	lbs.	ft. secs.	in.	in.	in.	ft-tons.
HEAVY	16	II	50	128	2100	2800	...	...	...	...
	16	I	45	105	2100	2600	...	...	...	98,531
	14	IV	50	81	1400	2800	...	...	...	76,087
	14	I	45	63⅓	1400	2600	18	...	...	...
	12	VII	50	56·1	870	2900	11·0	13·9	17·5	50,783
	12	VI	45	53·6	870	2700	10·6	13·3	16·6	44,020
	12	V	45	52·9	870	2700	9·8	12·3	15·5	44,020
	8	IX	55	19·7	250	3000	...	...	...	16,240
	8	VI	45	18·7	260	2750	4·4	6·1	8·6	13,630
	8	V	40	18·1	260	2500	4·0	5·3	7·5	11,264
MEDIUM	6	XII	53	10	105	3000	...	...	...	6,551
	6	VIII	50	8·6	105	2800	2·3	3·2	5·2	5,707
	6	VI	50	8·3	105	2600	2·2	2·9	4·7	4,920
	6*	IX	45	7·0	105	2250	2·1	2·5	3·8	3,685
	6*	IV. VII	40	6·0	105	2150	2·1	2·4	3·6	3,365
	5	VII	51	5·0	50	3150	1·4	1·8	3·4	3,439
	5	VI	50	4·6	50	3000	1·4	1·7	3·2	3,122
	5	V & VI	50	4·6	60	2700	1·6	2·0	3·5	3,032
	5*	II, III, IV	40	3·1	50	2300	1·4	1·7	2·6	1,834
LIGHT and AA.	4*	IX	50	3·0	33	2900	...	...	..	1,926
	4*	VIII	50	2·9	33	2800	1·2	1·5	2·6	1,794
	4*	VII	50	2·6	33	2500	1·2	1·4	2·2	1,430
	4*	III,IV,V,VI	40	1·5	33	2000	...	1·2	1·7	915
	3§	X	50	1·15	13	2700	...	...	...	657
	3	V, VI, S-A	50	1·0	13	2700	...	0·8	1·2	658
	3*	II, III	50	0·9	13	2700	...	0·8	1·2	658

(There are a 6 inch, 47 cal.,* a 5 inch, 38 cal., 1932, and a 5 inch 25 cal. AA.)

* = Brass cartridge case. § Anti-aircraft gun.

All guns use nitro-cellulose.

Naval Appropriation : 1938–1939 $546,866,494. 1939–1940, $773,049,151.

Mercantile Marine.

("Lloyd's Register," 1939, figures.)

Total *gross* tonnage, including Great Lakes and Philippines, 3,375 vessels of 12,003,028 tons.

NEW YORK.
(TEXAS, Platform above foretop).

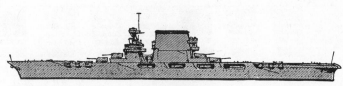

SARATOGA (with thick vertical stripe down middle of funnel).
LEXINGTON.

ARKANSAS.

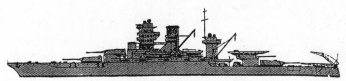

NEW MEXICO *class*.

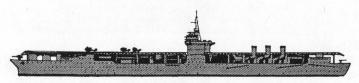

RANGER.

PENNSYLVANIA.   ARIZONA.

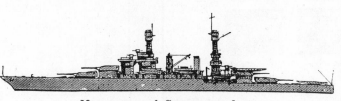

MARYLAND and CALIFORNIA *classes*.

YORKTOWN.
(ENTERPRISE same but without Y on funnel.)

OKLAHOMA.

NEVADA.

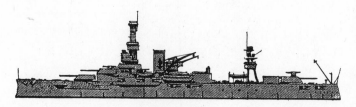

WYOMING.

LANGLEY.

PENSACOLA *class.*

INDIANAPOLIS.

NEW ORLEANS *class.*
(Some have thinner funnels).

HOUSTON. AUGUSTA. CHICAGO.

PORTLAND.

OMAHA *class.*

CHESTER. NORTHAMPTON. LOUISVILLE.

BROOKLYN *class.*

FARRAGUT *class.* (Part sketch, DEWEY)

PORTER *class.*
(Some have clinker screen to forefunnel.)

MAHAN *class.*
(Some lack clinker screen to fore funnel).

DUNLAP.   FANNING.

CONNOR.   STOCKTON.

SOMERS *class*, 381, 383, 394–396.

GRIDLEY *class.*
(Some have S.L. platform between T.T.)

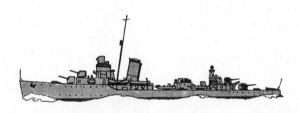

MAURY *class*, 397–408.

Flush Deckers.

Light Mine Layers.

470

" BIRD " *class.*
(*Minesweepers.*)

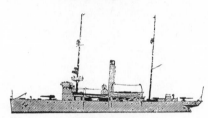

SACRAMENTO.

ASHEVILLE *class.*

CHARLESTON, ERIE

EAGLE boats.

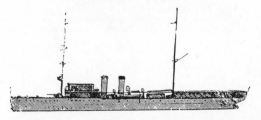

ISABEL.

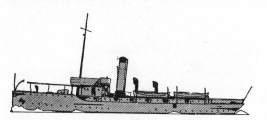

Pamlico

Chelan *class*.

Unalga.

Haida *class*.

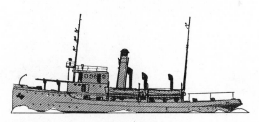

Shawnee.

G. W. Campbell *class*.
(Seaplane carried aft in some.)

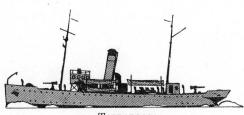

Tallapoosa.
(Ossipee similar).

Algonquin *class*.

Northland.

471

WRIGHT.

BUSHNELL.

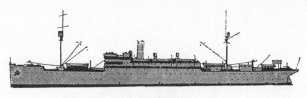

BRIDGEPORT.

PATOKA.

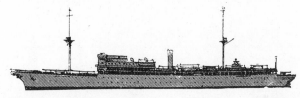

HOLLAND.
(Topmasts now shortened).

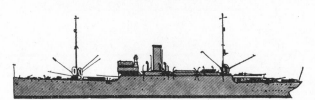

CAMDEN.

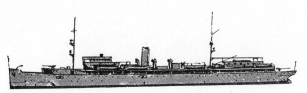

BEAVER.

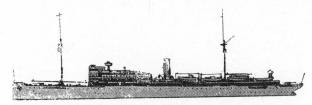

WHITNEY *class.*

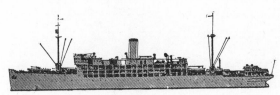

CANOPUS.

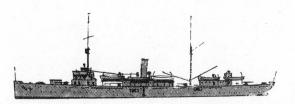

MELVILLE.

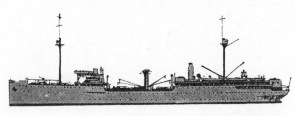

MEDUSA.

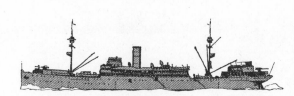

BLACK HAWK.

ALTAIR *class.*

Oglala.

Aroostook.

S.C. boats.

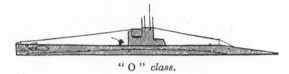

"O" class.

Barracuda class.

Dolphin.

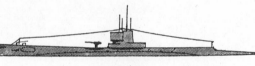

"R" class.

Argonaut.

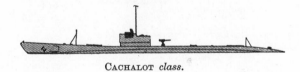

Cachalot class.

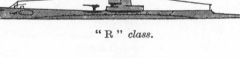

S. 1, 3, 6-41

Narwhal class.

Pike class.
(Perch class similar).

S. 22, 42-47.

Sargo class.

S. 48.

The United States Fleet.

Commander-in-Chief, United States Fleet
PENNSYLVANIA (*Flag*)
Note : HOUSTON (*Relief Flag*)

Battle Force, U.S. Fleet

Commander, Battle Force, U.S. Fleet
CALIFORNIA (*Flag*)

Battleships, Battle Force, U.S. Fleet

Commander, Battleships, Battle Force, U.S. Fleet

WEST VIRGINIA (*Flag*)

Batdiv One	Batdiv Two
Combatdiv One	Combatdiv Two
ARIZONA (F)	TENNESSEE (F)
NEVADA	OKLAHOMA
PENNSYLVANIA (FF)	CALIFORNIA (FF)
Batdiv Three	Batdiv Four
Combatdiv Three	Combatdiv Four
IDAHO (F)	WEST VIRGINIA (F)
MISSISSIPPI	COLORADO
NEW MEXICO	MARYLAND

Cruisers, Battle Force, U.S. Fleet

Commander, Cruisers, Battle Force, U.S. Fleet

HONOLULU (*Flag*)

Crudiv Three	Crudiv Eight	Crudiv Nine
Comcrudiv Three	Comcrudiv Eight	Comcrudiv Nine
CONCORD (F)	PHILADELPHIA (F)	HONOLULU (F)
CINCINNATI	BROOKLYN	PHOENIX
MILWAUKEE	SAVANNAH	BOISE (RFF)
OMAHA	NASHVILLE	ST. LOUIS [2]
TRENTON [1]		

[1] Assigned temporary duty flagship Squadron 40-T.
[2] To join during second quarter.

Destroyers, Battle Force, U.S. Fleet

Commander, Destroyers, Battle Force, U.S. Fleet
DETROIT (*Flag*)

Destroyer Flotilla One

Commander, Flotilla One, Destroyers, Battle Force, U.S. Fleet

RALEIGH	..	Flagship
DOBBIN	..	Tender for Squadrons One and Three
WHITNEY	..	Tender for Squadrons Two and Nine
Destroyer Squadron One	..	PHELPS, *Flag*
Destroyer Squadron Two	..	PORTER, *Flag*
Destroyer Squadron Three	..	CLARK, *Flag*
Destroyer Squadron Nine	..	McDOUGAL, *Flag*

Destroyer Squadron One

COMDESRON ONE

PHELPS (*Flag*)

Desdiv One	Desdiv Two
Comdesdiv One	Comdesdiv Two
DEWEY (F)	AYLWIN (F)
HULL	DALE
MACDONOUGH (RF)	FARRAGUT (RF)
WORDEN	MONAGHAN

Destroyer Squadron Two

COMDESRON TWO

PORTER (*Flag*)

Desdiv Three	Desdiv Four
Comdesdiv Three	Comdesdiv Four
DRAYTON (F)	CUSHING (F)
FLUSSER	PERKINS
LAMSON (RF)	PRESTON (RF)
MAHAN	SMITH

Destroyer Squadron Three

COMDESRON THREE

CLARK (*Flag*)

Desdiv Five	Desdiv Six
Comdesdiv Five	Comdesdiv Six
CASSIN (F)	CASE (F)
CONYNGHAM	SHAW
DOWNES (RF)	CUMMINGS (RF)
REID	TUCKER

Destroyer Squadron Nine

COMDESRON NINE

McDOUGAL (*Flag*)

Desdiv Seventeen	Desdiv Eighteen
Comdesdiv Seventeen	Comdesdiv Eighteen
SOMERS (F)	DAVIS (F) [2]
WARRINGTON	JOUETT [2]
WINSLOW [1]	SAMPSON [2]

[1] Until Desron Eight is formed in fourth quarter.
[2] Will join in first quarter fiscal year 1940.

Destroyer Flotilla Two

Commander, Flotilla Two, Destroyers, Battle Force, U.S. Fleet

DETROIT	..	Flagship
ALTAIR	..	Tender for Squadrons Four and Six
MELVILLE	..	Tender for Squadrons Seven, Eight, Twelve and Division Nineteen.
Destroyer Squadron Four	..	SELFRIDGE, *Flag*
Destroyer Squadron Six	..	BALCH, *Flag*
Destroyer Squadron Seven	..	MOFFETT, *Flag*
Destroyer Squadron Eight	..	WINSLOW, *Flag*
Destroyer Squadron Twelve	..	MOFFETT, *Flag*
Destroyer Division Nineteen	..	RATHBURNE, *Flag*

Destroyer Squadron Four

COMDESRON FOUR

SELFRIDGE (*Flag*)

Desdiv Seven	Desdiv Eight
Comdesdiv Seven	Comdesdiv Eight
HENLEY (F)	MUGFORD (F)
HELM	RALPH TALBOT
BLUE (RF)	JARVIS (RF)
BAGLEY	PATTERSON

Destroyer Squadron Six

COMDESRON SIX

BALCH (*Flag*)

Desdiv Eleven	Desdiv Twelve
Comdesdiv Eleven	Comdesdiv Twelve
GRIDLEY (F)	DUNLAP (F)
CRAVEN	BENHAM [1]
MAURY (RF)	FANNING (RF)
McCALL	ELLET [1]

[1] Will join in first quarter, fiscal year 1940.

Destroyer Squadron Seven [1]

COMDESRON SEVEN

MOFFETT (*Flag*) [2]

Desdiv Twenty-four [3]	Desdiv Twenty-eight [4]
Comdesdiv Twenty-four	Comdesdiv Twenty-eight
PERRY (F)	SOUTHARD (F)
WASMUTH	CHANDLER
ZANE (RF)	HOVEY (RF)
TREVER	LONG

[1] To be discontinued in fourth quarter.
[2] To be assigned as Flag Desron Twelve in fourth quarter.
[3] To remain in Desbatfor as separate division when Desron Seven is discontinued.
[4] Reduced commission in fourth quarter and to remain in Desbatfor for assignment to duty Training Naval Reserves on West Coast.

Destroyer Squadron Eight [1]

COMDESRON EIGHT

WINSLOW (*Flag*)

Desdiv Nine	Desdiv Ten
Comdesdiv Nine	Comdesdiv Ten
LANG (F)	MAYRANT (F) [2]
STACK [2]	TRIPPE [2]
STERETT (RF)	RHIND (RF)
WILSON	ROWAN

[1] To be organized in fourth quarter.
[2] Will not join in fiscal year 1940.

Destroyer Squadron Twelve [1]

COMDESRON TWELVE

MOFFETT (*Flag*) [2]

Desdiv Twenty-five	Desdiv Twenty-six
Comdesdiv Twenty-five	Comdesdiv Twenty-six
ANDERSON (F)	MUSTIN (F)
HAMMANN	RUSSELL
HUGHES (RF)	O'BRIEN (RF) [3]
SIMS [3]	WALKE [3]

[1] Will be organized in fourth quarter.
[2] To be assigned when Desron Seven is discontinued in fourth quarter.
[3] Will not join in fiscal year 1940.

Destroyer Division Nineteen [1] [2]

COMDESDIV NINETEEN

RATHBURNE (F)
TALBOT
DENT (RF)
WATERS

[1] In reduced commission.
[2] Operates with under-water sound training school.

Aircraft, Battle Force, U.S. Fleet

Commander, Aircraft, Battle Force, U.S. Fleet

YORKTOWN (*Flag*)

Carrier Division One	Carrier Division Two
Comcardiv One	Comcardiv Two
SARATOGA (F)	YORKTOWN (F)
LEXINGTON	ENTERPRISE

Minecraft, Battle Force, U.S. Fleet

Commander, Minecraft, Battle Force, U.S. Fleet
OGLALA (*Flag*)

Mine Squadron One

Mindiv One	Mindiv Two
Comindiv One	Comindiv Two
PRUITT (F)	TANAGER (F)
PREBLE	QUAIL
SICARD	LARK
TRACY	WHIPPOORWILL

Scouting Force, U.S. Fleet

Commander, Scouting Force, U.S. Fleet
INDIANAPOLIS (*Flag*) [1]
[1] Assigned to Crudiv Six for tactical purposes.

Cruisers, Scouting Force, U.S. Fleet

Commander, Cruisers, Scouting Force, U.S. Fleet
CHICAGO (*Flag*)

Crudiv Four	Crudiv Five
Comcrudiv Four	Comcrudiv Five
NORTHAMPTON (F)	CHICAGO (F)
HOUSTON (RFF) [2]	CHESTER
PENSACOLA	LOUISVILLE
SALT LAKE CITY	PORTLAND

Crudiv Six
Comcrudiv Six
MINNEAPOLIS (F)
ASTORIA
NEW ORLEANS
SAN FRANCISCO [3]

[2] Relief flag for Commander-in-Chief, U.S. Fleet.
[3] To join in second quarter when relieved as flag of Crudiv Seven by WICHITA.

Aircraft, Scouting Force, U.S. Fleet

Commander, Aircraft, Scouting Force, U.S. Fleet

MEMPHIS (*Flag*)
REUBEN JAMES (AVP) .. Reports in third quarter. Wing assignment will be made later.

Note.—Tenders assigned Patrol Wings as listed below.

(1) *Patrol Wing One*

WRIGHT (AV)	..	Seaplane Tender (Flag Compatwing 1)
AVOCET (AVP)	..	Seaplane Tender, Small
PELICAN (AVP)	..	Seaplane Tender, Small

(2) *Patrol Wing Two*
Fleet Air Base, Pearl Harbor

LANGLEY (AV)	..	Seaplane Tender (Flag Compatwing 2)
SWAN (AVP)	..	Seaplane Tender, Small
CHILDS (AVP)	..	Seaplane Tender, Small

(3) *Patrol Wing Three*
Fleet Air Base, Coco Solo

LAPWING (AVP)	..	Seaplane Tender, Small (Flag Compatwing 3)
SANDPIPER (AVP)	..	Seaplane Tender, Small

(4) *Patrol Wing Four*

TEAL (AVP)	..	Seaplane Tender, Small
WILLIAMSON (AVP)	..	Seaplane Tender, Small (Flag Compatwing 4)

(5) *Patrol Wing Five*
Fleet Air Base, Sitka

GANNET (AVP)	..	Seaplane Tender, Small (Flag Compatwing 5)
THRUSH (AVP)	..	Seaplane Tender, Small
OWL (AM) [1]	..	Minesweeper serving as Seaplane Tender, Small

[1] OWL assigned additional duty Fifth Naval District.

Atlantic Squadron, U.S. Fleet

Commander, Atlantic Squadron, U.S. Fleet

NEW YORK (*Flag*)
RANGER

Batdiv Five [1]	Crudiv Seven
Combatdiv Five	Comcrudiv Seven
NEW YORK (F)	SAN FRANCISCO (F) [3]
ARKANSAS	QUINCY
TEXAS (RF)	TUSCALOOSA
WYOMING [2]	VINCENNES
	WICHITA (F) [4]

[1] In reduced commission.
[2] Classed as an AG—operates with Batdiv Five.
[3] To join Crudiv Six, Scouting Force in second quarter.
[4] Joins in second quarter, relieves SAN FRANCISCO as flagship.

Destroyer Squadron Ten

COMDESRON TEN

DECATUR (*Flag*)

Desdiv Twenty-One	Desdiv Twenty-Two	Desdiv Twenty-Seven [1]
HOPKINS	LEARY	BORIE
REUBEN JAMES [7]	SCHENCK	BROOME
BARRY	FAIRFAX	SIMPSON
GOFF	MANLEY [2]	TRUXTUN

Desdiv Twenty-Nine	Desdiv Thirty
BADGER [3]	ROPER
JACOB JONES [3]	HAMILTON
HERBERT [4]	BABBITT
DICKERSON [5]	CLAXTON [6]

Destroyer Squadron Ten—continued.

[1] In reduced commission.
[2] Converted to an AG. Operates with Desron Ten.
[3] Assigned duty with Squadron 40-T.
[4] To relieve BADGER in Squadron 40-T in second quarter, fiscal year 1940.
[5] To relieve JACOB JONES in Squadron 40-T in second quarter, fiscal year 1940.
[6] Assigned duty at U.S. Naval Academy.
[7] To be converted to an AVP and assigned to Airscofor in third quarter, fiscal year 1940.

Submarine Force, U.S. Fleet

Commander, Submarine Force, U.S. Fleet

RICHMOND (*Flag*)
LITCHFIELD

Submarine Base, New London

SUBMARINE SQUADRON TWO

Commander, Submarine Base, New London, and Commander, Submarine Squadron Two.

FALCON (*Submarine Rescue Vessel*)

Subdiv Four	Subdiv Eight [1]
Comsubdiv Four	Comsubdiv Eight
(SS91) R—14 (F)	(SS129) S—24 (F)
(SS79) R—2	(SS126) S—21
(SS81) R—4	(SS130) S—25 [2]
(SS87) R—10	(SS131) S—26
(SS88) R—11	(SS134) S—29 [2]
(SS90) R—13 (FF)	(SS135) S—30

[1] In commission in reserve at New London.
[2] To join in first quarter, fiscal year 1940.

Experimental Division One

SEMMES (*Experimental Vessel*)
(SS125) S—20
(SS127) S—22

Submarine Squadron Three

Submarine Base, Coco Solo

Commander, Submarine Squadron Three, and Submarine Base, Coco Solo

MALLARD (*Submarine Rescue Vessel*)
Subdiv Eleven
Comsubdiv Eleven
(SS155) S—44 (FF)
(SS153) S—42 (F)
(SS154) S—43
(SS156) S—45
(SS157) S—46
(SS158) S—47

Submarine Squadron Four

Submarine Base, Pearl Harbour

Commander, Submarine Squadron Four, and Submarine Base, Pearl Harbor

BEAVER [1]	..	Tender
KEOSANQUA	..	Tender
SEAGULL	..	Tender
WIDGEON	..	Submarine Rescue Vessel

Subdiv Seven	Subdiv Twelve	Subdiv Thirteen [3]
Comsubdiv Seven	Comsubdiv Twelve	Comsubdiv Thirteen
(SS128) S—23 (F)	NAUTILUS (F)	SHARK (F)
(SS123) S—18	ARGONAUT (FF)	CACHALOT
(SS130) S—25 [2]	DOLPHIN	CUTTLEFISH
(SS134) S—29 [2]	NARWHAL	PIKE
(SS139) S—34		PORPOISE
(SS140) S—35		TARPON

[1] To proceed to San Diego to tend Subdiv Fourteen about 15 September, 1939.
[2] To be transferred to Subdiv Eight in first quarter, fiscal year 1940 and placed in commission in reserve.
[3] To be reorganized as shown under note at foot of "Unassigned" group, about 1 April, 1940.

Submarine Squadron Six

(Normally operates with Battle Force)
Commander, Submarine Squadron Six

PERCH	..	Flag
HOLLAND	..	Tender
ORTOLAN	..	Submarine Rescue Vessel

Subdiv Fourteen [1]	Subdiv Fifteen	Subdiv Sixteen [2]
Comsubdiv Fourteen	Comsubdiv Fifteen	Comsubdiv Sixteen
PERCH (FF)	SNAPPER (F)	SARGO (F)
PERMIT	SALMON	SAURY
PICKEREL (F)	SEAL	SCULPIN
PLUNGER	SKIPJACK	SPEARFISH
POLLACK	STINGRAY	SQUALUS
POMPANO [2]	STURGEON	SWORDFISH

Experimental Division Two [3]
(SS132) S—27
(SS133) S—28

[1] To be reorganized as shown under "Note" below and assigned to Asiatic Fleet.
[2] Upon reporting.
[3] Operating with Underwater Sound Training School.

Unassigned

Four new submarines, due for commissioning in fiscal year 1940, operating under the Chief of Naval Operations.

SEADRAGON
SEALION
SEARAVEN
SEAWOLF

Note.—About 1 April, 1940 Subdivs Thirteen and Fourteen will be reorganized as shown below. At that time Subdiv Thirteen as reorganized will remain assigned to Subron Four at Pearl Harbor. Subdiv Fourteen as reorganized assigned about 1 April, 1940 to Subron Five, Asiatic Fleet.

Subdiv Thirteen	Subdiv Fourteen
Comsubdiv Thirteen	Comsubdiv Fourteen
SHARK (F)	PERCH (F)
CACHALOT	PORPOISE
CUTTLEFISH	PIKE
PLUNGER	TARPON
POLLACK	PICKEREL
POMPANO	PERMIT

Base Force U.S. Fleet

Commander, Base Force, U.S. Fleet

ARGONNE .. Flag
RIGEL .. (*AD*) Also Receiving Ship, San Diego

Train, Base Force

Commander, Train

ARGONNE (*Flag*)
Fleet Training Base, San Clemente
Fleet Air Base, San Pedro
Destroyer Base, San Diego

ANTARES	(AG)	BRAZOS	(AO)
ARCTIC	(AF)	CUYAMA	(AO)
BRIDGE	(AF)	KANAWHA	(AO)
UTAH	(AG)	NECHES	(AO)
RELIEF	(AH)	CIMARRON	(AO)
BOBOLINK	(AM)	NEOSHO	(AO)
BRANT	(AM)	PLATTE [1]	(AO)
GREBE	(AM)	MEDUSA	(AR)
KINGFISHER	(AM)	VESTAL	(AR)
PARTRIDGE	(AM)	ALGORMA	(AT)
RAIL	(AM)	KALMIA	(AT)
ROBIN	(AM)	PINOLA	(AT)
TERN	(AM)	SONOMA	(AT)
TURKEY	(AM)	NAVAJO [1]	(AT)
VIREO	(AM)	SEMINOLE	(AT)

[1] Will join in fourth quarter.

Mobile Target Division One, Base Force

Comtardiv One

DORSEY	(DD) (F)
ELLIOT	(DD)
BOGGS	(AG)
LAMBERTON	(AG)

Asiatic Fleet

Commander-in-Chief, Asiatic Fleet

AUGUSTA (*Flag*)
MARBLEHEAD
ASHEVILLE
ISABEL
TULSA

Yangtze Patrol.	South China Patrol
Comyangpat	*Comsopat*
LUZON (F)	MINDANAO (F)
GUAM	
OAHU	
TUTUILA	

Destroyers, Asiatic Fleet

Destroyer Squadron Five.

Commander, Destroyer Squadron Five

PAUL JONES	..	Squadron Leader
BLACK HAWK	..	Tender

Desdiv Thirteen	Desdiv Fourteen
Comdesdiv Thirteen	Comdesdiv Fourteen
WHIPPLE (F)	STEWART (F)
ALDEN (RF)	BULMER (RF)
BARKER	EDSALL
EDWARDS, J. D.	PARROTT

Desdiv Fifteen
Comdesdiv Fifteen
PEARY (F)
FORD, J. D. (RF)
PILLSBURY
POPE

Submarine Squadron Five.

Commander, Submarine Squadron Five.

CANOPUS .. Flag
PIGEON .. Submarine Rescue Vessel
Subdiv Ten
Comsubdiv Ten
(SS142) S—37 (F)
(SS141) S—36
(SS143) S—38
(SS144) S—39
(SS145) S—40
(SS146) S—41
Subdiv Fourteen [1]
Comsubdiv Fourteen
PERCH (F)
PORPOISE
PIKE
TARPON
PICKEREL
PERMIT

[1] To be assigned about 1 April, 1940. Subdiv Fourteen assigned to Asiatic Fleet as eventual replacements for vessels of Subdiv Ten which are obsolete and approaching decommissioning. Subdiv Fourteen may be sent out in sections if necessary to fit overhaul schedules.

Train, Asiatic Fleet

Mindiv Three
BITTERN
FINCH

Aircraft Detachment.

HERON (AVP) .. Seaplane Tender, Small

Auxiliaries

PECOS (F)

Special Service Squadron.

Commander, Special Service Squadron

CHARLESTON (F)
ERIE (RF)
TATTNALL
J. FRED TALBOTT

Naval Transportation Service

CHAUMONT
HENDERSON
SANTA RITA
NITRO
PYRO
RAMAPO
SALINAS
SIRIUS
TRINITY
VEGA
CAPELLA

Special Duty

ACUSHNET	5th Naval District
ALLEGHENY	4th Naval District
BAGADUCE	11th Naval District
BUSHNELL	Survey Duty
CORMORANT	Bureau of Ordnance
CUYAHOGA	Special duty
DAHLGREN	Engineering Experimental, under Chief of Naval Operations
GOLDSTAR	Station Ship, Guam
*HANNIBAL	Surveying duty
KEWAYDIN	5th Naval District
MONTCALM	Guantanamo
NAPA	16th Naval District
ONTARIO	Station Ship, Samoa
ORIOLE	13th Naval District
PENGUIN	Guam
POTOMAC	Special duty
SAGAMORE	3rd Naval District
SUNNADIN	14th Naval District
UMPQUA	6th Naval District
WANDANK	1st Naval District
WOODCOCK	15th Naval District

*When SANTA INEZ is acquired HANNIBAL will be decommissioned.

SHIP NOMENCLATURE.

Battleships will be named after States; heavy and light cruisers after large cities; aircraft carriers after historical naval vessels or battles; destroyers after officers and enlisted men of the Navy and Marine Corps, Secretaries of the Navy, Members of Congress and inventors.

Submarines will be named after fish; minesweepers after birds; gunboats after small cities; river gunboats after islands; submarine tenders after pioneers in submarine development; repair ships after mythological characters; oilers after rivers; cargo ships after stars; destroyer tenders after natural areas of the United States; large seaplane tenders after sounds; small seaplane tenders after bays, straits and inlets; ocean-going tugs after Indian tribes; and harbour tugs after Indian chiefs and words of the Indian dialect.

(IOWA CLASS—2 Ships).

IOWA, NEW JERSEY.

Standard displacement : 45,000 tons.
Complement :
Length, 880 feet (*over all*). Beam, 108][feet.
Draught, 36 feet (*max.*).
Guns : **9**—16 inch
  12—5 inch, 51 cal.
Aircraft : 4. Catapults : 2.
Armour : Not reported.
Machinery : Geared turbines. Designed Speed :
  Over 30 kts. (35 kts. reported unofficially).
  Cost : Believed to be in the region of
  $100,000,000 apiece.

Notes.—Both ordered under 1939 Programme, and to be built
  by New York and Philadelphia Navy Yards, respectively.

(WASHINGTON CLASS—6 Ships)

NORTH CAROLINA, WASHINGTON, INDIANA, MASSACHUSETTS, ALABAMA, SOUTH DAKOTA.

Standard displacement : 35,000 tons. Complement :
Length : 750 feet. Beam : 108 feet. Draught : 36 feet (*mean*).

Guns :   Armour : (Unofficial)
  9—16 inch.   16″ Belt amidships.
  12—5 inch, 51 cal.   6″ Upper Deck.
  8—5 inch, 25 cal. AA.   4″ Lower Deck.

Aircraft : 4   Catapults : 2

Note to Plan.—This is believed to represent with accuracy the design as proposed at the date of laying down of the *North Carolina*; but it is quite likely that further modifications may be made in the course of construction, and that the appearance of the ships when completed may vary from that shown here. For example, it is possible that the 5 inch 25 cal. AA. guns may not be in gunhouses, as shown below.

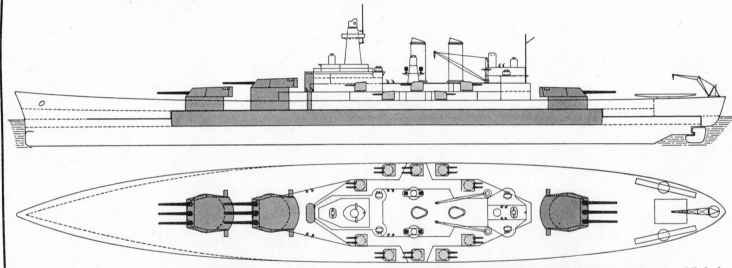

Machinery : Geared turbines. 4 shafts. Designed speed : 28 kts. (30 kts. expected). Watertube boilers of a new pattern. Oil fuel.

General Notes.—Delays in laying down these ships have been due to changes in design, late delivery of materials and necessity for extending and strengthening building slips. Ships are to be fully 35 per cent. welded. Engine room will be arranged on a novel plan to save weight. Cost estimated at $64,741,300 for *N. Carolina*, $65,815,200 for *Washington*, $52,794,000 for *S. Dakota*, $49,540,000 for *Indiana*, and $49,815,000 for *Massachusetts*. Last 3 figures exclude cost of armament.

Programme	Name	Builder	Machinery	To replace	Laid down	To be completed
1936	N. Carolina	New York Navy Yard	Westinghouse Co.	Arkansas	Oct. 27, 1937	Nov., 1941
	Washington	Philadelphia Navy Yard	Westinghouse Co.	Texas	June 14, 1938	Oct., 1942.
1938	Indiana	Newport News Co.	Westinghouse Co.	New York	Ordered Dec. 15, 1938	
	Massachusetts	Bethlehem Corpn (Quincy)	Builders	Nevada		1943
	Alabama	Norfolk Navy Yard	Westinghouse Co.	Oklahoma	Ordered Jan. 1, 1939	
	S. Dakota	New York S.B. Corpn.	Builders	Pennsylvania	July 5, 1939	

(MARYLAND CLASS—3 SHIPS.)

COLORADO (March 22nd, 1921), **MARYLAND** (March 20th, 1920), and **WEST VIRGINIA** (Nov. 19th, 1921).

Standard displacement, *Colorado*, 32,500 tons. *Maryland*, 31,500. *W. Virginia*, 31,800 tons. *Full load*, 33,590 tons. Complement, 1407.

Complement of *W. Virginia* as fleet flagship, 1486.

Length (*w.l.*), 600 feet. (*o.a.*), 624 feet. Beam, 97½ feet.

Mean draught, 30½ feet 29⅜ feet and 30 feet respectively. *Max.* draught of all, 35 feet.

Guns :
  8—16 inch, 45 cal. Mk. I.
  12—5 inch, 51 cal.
  8—5 inch (AA.) Mk. X.
  4—6 pdr. (saluting).
  2—1 pdr.
  2—M.G.
  11—M.G., AA.
Torpedo tubes (removed)
Aircraft: 3
Catapults :
  1 on "X" Turret.
  1 on Quarter Deck.

Armour :
  16"—14" Belt.............. ▮
  8" Belt (aft) .... ▨
  3" Deck (ends)............ ▧
  16"—9" Funnel bases ... ▮
  18"—9" Turrets .... ▮
  16" Conning tower and tube.................... ▮
  3½" upper and 2½" lower armour decks.

MARYLAND (Observe new main topmast).   1938, *Theo. N. Silberstein.*

Special Note.—It is proposed that provision shall be made in the near future for the modernisation of this class.

Gunnery Notes.—Maximum elevation of 16 inch 30° ; Maximum range at this elevation unofficially stated to be 33,300 yards. Turrets electrically manœuvred and with electric hoists. Excepting increase of calibre to 16 inch, otherwise as Notes for *Tennessee* Class. New director system installed, 1923. Main control is at a height of 120 feet above sea level.

Armour Notes. As for *California* and *Tennessee.*

Anti-Torpedo Protection.—Ferrati type triple hull and minute internal subdivision by longitudinal and transverse unpierced bulkheads.

Engineering Notes.—" Electric Drive " is identical with that for the *California* Class but in these ships, electric installation has been extended. Part of steam generated in boilers is diverted for running six auxiliary turbo-generators, supplying current to anchor gear, workshop lathes, refrigerating plant, bakeries, &c. Guns are also electrically manœuvred, ammunition hoists are electric. In fact, every possible item of equipment, even down to potato peelers and ice-cream freezers, is run by electric power. Estimated weight of machinery, 2002 tons. Heating surfaces as *Tennessee* on a later page.

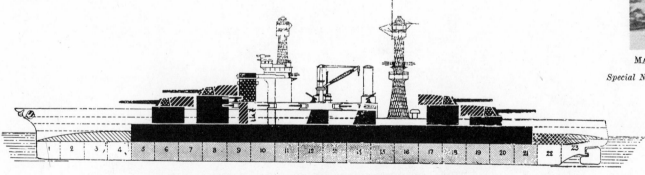

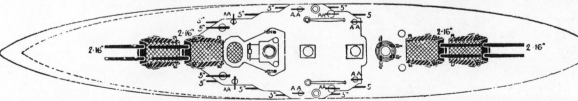

Name	Builder	Machinery	Laid down	Completed	Trials	Boilers	Best recent speed
Colorado	New York S.B. Co.	Westinghouse Co.	May '19	Aug.,'23	37,480 = 20·67	Babcock	
Maryland	Newport News	Gen. Elec. Co.	Apl.,'17	July '21	36,167 = 21·07	Babcock	21
W. Virginia	Newport News	Gen. Elec. Co.	Apl.,'20	Dec. '23	= 21·1	Babcock	

General Notes.—Authorised 1916 as *No. 45 (Colorado), No. 46 (Maryland),* and *No. 48 (W. Virginia). W. Virginia* and *Maryland* both fitted as Flagships. Except for change in primary armament, and slight increase in displacement, they are identical in nearly all respects with *California* class. *Washington* of this type scrapped before completion under Naval Treaty of 1922.

Machinery: In *Colorado* Westinghouse turbines and electric drive; in *Maryland* and *W. Virginia*, G.E. turbines and electric drive. Designed S.H.P. 27,300 = 21kts. cf. trials. 4 shafts. Boilers: 8 Babcock & Wilcox. Fuel (oil only): *normal* 2500 tons ; *maximum* 4000 tons (unofficial figures).

W. Virginia.

1935, *Bear Photo Service.*

W. Virginia—bow view.

1924 *Photo Abrahams.*

California.

1939

(CALIFORNIA *class*—2 ships.)

CALIFORNIA (Nov. 20th, 1919) and **TENNESSEE** (April 30th, 1919).

Displacement : *Standard* 32,600 and 32,300 tons, respectively. *Full load,*
35,190 tons. Complement : 1,480.

Length $\begin{cases} (w.l.)\ 600\ \text{feet.} \\ (o.a.)\ 624\ \text{feet.} \end{cases}$ Beam 97½ feet. $\begin{cases} Mean\ \text{draught, }30\tfrac{1}{2}\text{ feet, and }30\tfrac{1}{3}\text{ ft. resp.} \\ Max.\ \ ,,\ \ 35\tfrac{1}{2}\text{--}35\text{ feet, resp.} \end{cases}$

Guns :
  12—14 inch, 50 cal., Mk. IV.
  12—5 inch, 51 cal.
  8—5 inch, 25 cal. AA.
  4—6 pdr. (saluting).
  2—1 pdr.
  2 M.G.
  11 M.G. AA.
Torpedo tubes (removed).

Aircraft : 3
Catapults :
  1 on " X " turret.
  1 on Q.D.
Armour :
  14″ Belt ....
  8″ Belt (aft) ....
  3″ Deck (ends) ....
  15″—9″ Funnel bases ...
  18″—9″ Turrets........ ...
  16″ Conning tower and
      tube ....
  3½″ upper 2½″ lower armour
     decks

CALIFORNIA.

1930, *Official Photo*

Special Note.—It is proposed that provision shall be made in the near future for the modernisation of these 2 ships.

Gunnery Notes.*—The 14 inch mounted in separate sleeves ; elevation, up to 30°. Maximum **range stated to be over 35,000 yards. Main guns controlled from upper storey and 5 inch from lower storey of masthead tops. Fire control arrangements being modernised, 1937.

**Armour Notes.*—Internal subdivision by unpierced bulkheads developed to the utmost degree below waterline.

Engineering Notes.—Current generated is quarter-phase ; turbine speed is controlled by mechanical governors ; and control is located in one small room. Four alternating current motors, one to each propeller shaft, supplied by current at 3,400 volts, from 2 turbo-generators. *California* has squirrel-cage winding for starting and wound-rotor for running ; but *Tennessee* has wound-rotors for both purposes. Motors are designed for 24 and 36 poles. Oil for trials : 1,467 tons and 187 tons feed water. Estimated weight of machinery : *California*, 1,805 tons ; *Tennessee*, 2,045 tons. Heating surface : 50,984 sq. ft. for Bureau Express boilers in *California* ; 41,768 sq. ft. + 4,168 sq. ft. (superheated, for Babcock boilers in *Tennessee*. Each boiler is in a separate w.t. compartment. Boiler rooms are abeam of engine rooms (4 to port, 4 to starboard), and boilers are under central control. Turbines are in tandem on centre line. On *trials*, *Tennessee* brought to rest from full speed within 3 minutes ; tactical diameter : 700 yards (full helm, both screws turning forward).

Machinery : *California*, G. E. turbines and electric drive. *Tennessee*, Westinghouse turbines and electric drive. 4 shafts in both ships. Boilers : 8 Bureau Express type in *California*. 8 Babcock and Wilcox in *Tennessee*. Designed H.P. : 26,800 = 21 kts. Fuel (oil only) : *normal* 2,200, *maximum* 3,328 tons.

Name	Builder	Machinery	Laid down	Completed	Refit	Trials	Boilers	Best recent speed
California	Mare Island Y.	G. E. Co.	Oct.,'16	Aug '21		21·46	Express	
Tennessee	New York Yard	Westinghouse Co.	May,'17	June'20		30,908 = 21·01	Babcock	

General Notes.—Authorised 1915 as No. 43 (*Tennessee*) and 44 (*California*). The above design is practically identical with *New Mexico* class as originally completed. *California* fitted as Flagship.

U.S.A.—Battleships

(NEW MEXICO CLASS—3 ships.)

IDAHO	New York Shipbuilding Co.	(June 30th, 1917),
MISSISSIPPI	Newport News	(January 25th, 1917).
NEW MEXICO	New York Navy Yard	(April 23rd, 1917),

Displacement Standard { *Idaho* and *New Mexico* } 33,400 tons. { *Mississippi* 33,000 tons. } Complement, 1323

Length { *waterline*, 600 feet. *over all*, 624 feet. } Beam, 106¼ feet { *Mean* draught, Mississippi 29¼ ft. ; others 2⋅½ feet. *Max.* „ 34 feet

Guns :
12—14 inch, 50 cal., Mk. IV.
12—5 inch, 51 cal.
8—5 inch (A.A.), 25 cal.
4—3 pdr. (saluting) in *Idaho ;*
4—6 pdr. in others
12—M.G. AA.

Aircraft : 3

Catapults :
1 on " X " turret.
1 on quarter deck.

Armour :
14″ Belt (amidships) ...... ▮
8″ Belt (aft)......... ...... ▨
*″ Deck ends ...... ◪
15″—9″ Funnel base ...... ▨
18″–9″ Turrets ▮ ▰ •••• ▨
16″ Conning tower & tube ▮

*(Reported as 6″ upper and 4″ lower over vital areas)

NEW MEXICO

1934 *Photo, Official.*

(Note differences in funnels of these 3 ships.)

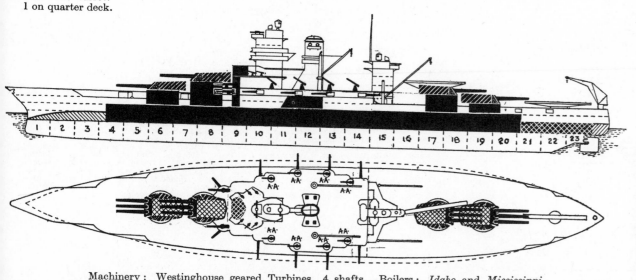

Machinery : Westinghouse geared Turbines. 4 shafts. Boilers : *Idaho* and *Mississippi,* 6 Bureau Express ; *New Mexico,* 4 White-Forster. Designed H.P. : 40,000 = 21·5 kts. Fuel : Oil only, 2,200 tons (pre-alterations figures). Since modernisation speed has been raised to 22–23 kts.

Name	Builder	Machinery Builders	Laid down	Completed
Idaho	N.Y.S.B. Co.	„	20/1/15	24/3/19
Mississippi	Newport News Co.	„	5/4/15	18/12/17
New Mexico	N.Y. Navy Yard	„	14/10/15	15/8/18

MISSISSIPPI.

1934 *Photo, Mr. L. Sprague de Camp.*

480

IDAHO.

1936, *O. W. Waterman*

MISSISSIPPI.

Added 1935, courtesy of U.S. Naval Institute, Annapolis, Md.

ARIZONA.

(Observe difference in height of C.T. compared with *Pennsylvania*.)

1935, *O. W. Waterman*

PENNSYLVANIA.

1934 *Photo, Mr. L. Sprague de Camp.*

HH

(PENNSYLVANIA CLASS—2 SHIPS).

PENNSYLVANIA (16th March, 1915) & **ARIZONA** (19th June, 1915)·
Standard Displacement, 33,100 and 32,600 tons respectively.

Length $\left\{\begin{array}{l} w.l.\ 600\ \text{feet} \\ o.a.\ 608\ \text{feet} \end{array}\right\}$ Beam, 106 feet, 3 in. $\left\{\begin{array}{l} \textit{Mean}\ \text{draught, 28 feet in } \textit{Penn-} \\ \textit{sylvania}\text{; 5 ins. less in} \\ \textit{Arizona.} \\ \textit{Maximum}\ \text{draught, } 33\frac{1}{2}\ \text{feet.} \end{array}\right.$

Complement, 1358.

Guns :

12—14 inch, 45 cal.
12—5 in., 51 cal.
8—5 in. (AA.), 25 cal.
4—3 pdr. (saluting).
(Torpedo tubes removed).

Aircraft : 3

Catapults :

1 on "X" Turret
1 on quarter deck.

Armour :

14″ Belt (amidships)	....
8″ Belt (aft)	....
3″ Deck (ends)	....
15″–9″ Funnel base	....
18″–9″ Turrets	
16″ Conning tower & tube ...	
(Total, 8072 tons.)′	
6″ deck amidships (4″ upper, 2″ lower).	

PENNSYLVANIA. (Funnel since heightened.)

1933 *O. W. Waterman.*

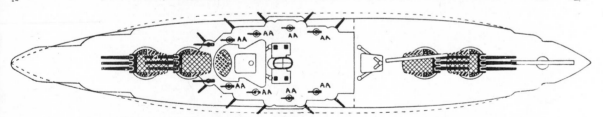

Machinery : *Pennsylvania*, Curtis turbines, L.P. ahead and astern, H.P. astern. *Arizona*, Parsons turbines, L.P. ahead and astern, H.P. astern. In both ships: Westinghouse geared turbines, H.P. ahead and cruising. 4 shafts. Boilers : *Arizona*, 6 Bureau Express. *Pennsylvania*, 1 Bureau Express, 5 White-Forster. Designed H.P. 32,000 = 21 kts. (unaffected by modernisation). Fuel : Oil only, *normal* 2,322 tons (694,830 gallons).

PENNSYLVANIA, showing heightened funnel. 1937

Name	Builder	Machinery	Laid down	Completed	Trials Full Power : 12 hrs.	Tons Fuel per day		
						10—	15—	19—kts.
Pennsylvania	Newport News	Newport News	Oct.'13	June,'16	29,366 = 21·05	65/—	90/—	—/—
Arizona	New York Yard	New York Yard	Mar.'14	Oct. '16	33,376 = 21	76/—	167/174	—/309

General Notes.—*Pennsylvania* authorised 1912, as *No. 38*, *Arizona* 1913, as *No. 39*. Both ships are enlarged and improved *Nevadas*. They have proved excellent sea boats, very steady gun platforms, and have proved to be very economical ships. Both ships have undergone extensive reconstruction which has cost $14,800,000. Battery raised a deck and AA. armament increased ; tripods fitted, funnel moved further aft ; bulges and increased internal protection ; additional bridges, and catapults fitted. In appearance differ from *Nevada* and *Oklahoma* in having higher conning tower and bridge which reaches funnel level.

Armour Notes.—Generally as for *Nevada* class. Increase of armour weight due to increased internal protection against submarine explosions and greater length of belt. Armour for each triple barbette, 226¼ tons. *Arizona* has cement backing to belt, instead of teak, and armoured fire-control tops.

Gunnery and Fire Control Notes.—14 inch guns mounted in single sleeve, and can be fired as one piece. *Max.* range at 15° elevation reported to be 21,000 yards. Triple positions weigh about 650 tons each (guns, mountings and armour). Turrets are capable of putting 2—3 salvoes a minute through a target at short range practice. Breech blocks worked by hand power. Interior of the shields to 14 inch guns very roomy and well arranged.

(NEVADA CLASS—2 SHIPS).

OKLAHOMA (March 23rd, 1914) & **NEVADA** (July 11th, 1914).

Standard Displacement 29,000 tons. Complement, both **1301**.

Length { *waterline*, 575 feet. } Beam, 107 ft. 11 in. *Mean* draught 27½ feet.
{ *over all*, 583 feet. } *Maximum* draught 32½ feet.

Guns :
10—14 inch, 45 cal.
12—5 inch, 51 cal.
8—5 inch, 25 cal. AA.
4—3 pdr. (saluting) in *Oklahoma*.
4—6 pdr. in *Nevada*.
8—M.G.

(Torpedo tubes removed.)

Aircraft: **3.**
Catapults :
1 on " X " Turret.
1 on quarter deck.

Armour :
13½" Belt (amidships) ....
8" Belt (aft) ....
13½" Bulkheads ....
13½" Funnel base ....
3" Deck (ends) ....
18"—9" Triple turrets .. }
16"—9" Double turrets... }
16" Conning tower and tube .....
(Total weight, 7664 tons.)
5" Deck (amidships). (3" upper and 2" lower).
(Bulges fitted).

NEVADA.   (To distinguish from *Oklahoma*, observe mainmasthead.)   1935, *O. W. Waterman.*

Note to Plan.—Now has S.L. Platforms abeam of funnel.

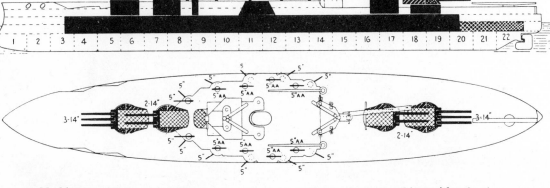

Special Note:

The alterations effected to *Oklahoma* and *Nevada* include substitution of tripod for cage masts, and installation of a deck house, on which, **8**—5 inch, 25 cal. guns are mounted. The 5 inch 51 cal. torpedo defence battery is raised from the main deck to the forecastle deck. The funnel is moved aft slightly. Cost of alterations $7,000,000 per ship. The addition of bulges has made them unwieldy at low speeds.

Armour Notes.—Main belt is 400 feet long by 17¼ feet wide; 8¼ feet of it being below *l.w.l.* Lower edge is 8". The ends are unarmoured; the battery also. Plates are applied in vertical strakes. Two protective decks, upper 3" flat, lower 1½" flat, 2" on slopes. Barbette bases are 13¼" thick, but turrets are only 4½" where below protective deck and behind belt. Barbette shields; 18" port plate for triple positions, 16" port plate for twin positions, 10" sides, 9" back, 5" roof. Sighting slits in conning tower closed by splinter-proof shutters. There is a signalling station protected by 16" armour behind conning tower. These ships marked a new era in naval construction, being the first to embody the "everything or nothing" idea in the matter of protection. No bulkhead between 14 inch guns.

Gunnery Notes.—Guns in the triple turrets in one sleeve, can be fired as one piece. Elevation has been increased to 30.°

Engineering Notes.—Cylinders of *Oklahoma* are H.P. 36·5 inch, I.P. 59·5 inch, L.P. (2) 78 inch. Stroke, 48 inch. Total heating surface, 45,080 sq. feet. Weight of machinery, *Nevada*, 1,860 tons; *Oklahoma*, 1,933 tons. Electric installation in both is 4 generating sets of 300 k.w., 125 volts, 2,400 amp. each Boilers are in 6 compartments and occupy less than 80 feet of length. Boilers are large tube "Express" type. No superheaters in either ship. Electric-driven f.d. blowers proved too unreliable, and were replaced by steam turbine-driven blowers. All oil fuel carried in double bottom; no wing tanks.

Name	Builder	Machinery	Laid down	Completed	Trials : (Full Power—12 hrs.)	Tons fuel per day:		
						10 kts.	15 kts.	19 kts.
Oklahoma	N.York S.B.Co	N.Y. S.B. Co.	Oct. '12	May,'16	21,703 = 19·68	77	143	278
Nevada	Fore River Co.	Fore River	Nov.'12	Mar. '16	23,312 = 20·28	{ 50·5† 77§	132·5† 149§	— 210§

†Cruising turbines. §Main turbines.

General Notes.—Authorised 1911 as No. *36* (*Nevada*), *37* (*Oklahoma*).

Machinery : Oklahoma, Triple expansion, 4 cylinder; *Nevada*, Parsons turbines with reduction gear. Both: 2 shafts. Boilers: 6 Bureau Express. Designed H.P.: 25,000 = 20·5 kts. Fuel: Oil, 598,400 gallons (2,000 tons), *maximum capacity.* Radius of action : 4,000 miles at full speed, 10,000 miles at 10 kts.

*Unofficial Notes.

OKLAHOMA.

1936, *Wright & Logan.*

OKLAHOMA

1936, *Wright & Logan.*

NEW YORK.

1934 *Photo, Mr. L. Sprague de Camp.*

NEW YORK.

1936 *Photo, O. W. Waterman.*

484

(Texas Class—2 Ships.)

NEW YORK (Oct. 30th, 1912) and **TEXAS** (May 18th, 1912).

Displacement, { *Standard*, 27,000 tons. *Full load*, 30,000 tons. } Complement, 1314.

Length (*waterline*), { 566 feet. } Length (*over all*), { 573 feet. } Beam, 106 feet.

Mean draught, 26ft.
Max. ,, 31¼ ft.

Guns :
10—14 inch, 45 cal.
16—5 inch, 51 cal.
8—3 inch AA., Mk. III.
4—3 pdr. (saluting).
2—1 pdr.
8 M.G.
2 landing.
(Torpedo tubes removed).

Aircraft: 3.
Catapults:
1 on turret amidships.

Armour (Midvale) :
12" Belt (amidships)......
6" Belt (ends) ....
3" Deck (since increased)
9"—6"Upper Belt
14"—8" Turrets...
12" Barbettes.............
6" Battery ....
12" C.T. ....
(Bulges fitted 1926-27).

TEXAS   (To distinguish from *New York*, note forward control top.)   1938, *Wright & Logan*.

The alterations effected in the Battleships of the *Arkansas*, *Texas* classes, include oil burning installation, anti-aircraft defence, increased underwater protection and improved aircraft handling arrangements. All carry catapults. Displacement increased by nearly 3,000 tons.

Gunnery Notes.—New fire control system installed 1926 with tripod foremast. *New York* now has four M.G. in each masthead top.

Engineering Notes.—Builders of turbine engines in the U.S. refused to adopt the standards laid down by the Navy Department. Accordingly, in these ships. reciprocating engines were reverted to, to show the turbine builders that the Navy Department was determined to have turbines built to official specification, or else the older type of engines would be taken up again. Cylinders: H.P. 39", I.P. 63", L.P. (2) 83". Stroke: 48". Weight of machinery: *Texas* 1971 tons: *N.Y.* 2048 tons, both exclusive of electric lighting equipment. Electrical installation : 4 sets each of 300 k.w., 125 volts. 2400 amps., by General Electric Co. Both ships converted to oil burning, and will have main engines and boilers renewed.

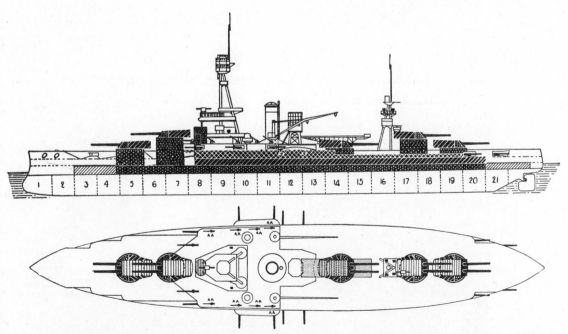

Machinery : Vertical triple expansion, 4 cylinder. 2 shafts. Boilers : 6 Bureau Express. Designed H.P. 28,100 = 21 kts. Oil : 5200 tons. Present speed 19 kts.

Name	Builder	Machinery	Laid down	Com-pleted	Trials : Full Power.	Boilers	Best recent speed
Texas	Newport News	Newport News	Apl.,'11	Mar.,'14	19·77	Bureau Express	19
New York	New York Yard	New York Yard	Sept.,'11	Apl.,'14	20·23		

General Notes.—Authorised 1910 as *No. 34 (N.Y.)* and *35 (Texas)*. Both ships fitted as flagships. They are slow since refit, hard to handle and bad sea boats in rough weather—wet and rolling so that waves ride the bulges into the amidships casemate. To be replaced in due course by new battleships *Washington* and *Indiana*.

(ARKANSAS CLASS)

ARKANSAS (N.Y. Shipbuilding Co. Jan. 14th, 1911).

Displacement, $\left\{\begin{array}{l}\textit{Standard,} \text{ 26,100 tons.} \\ \textit{Full load,} \text{ 29,000 tons.}\end{array}\right\}$ Complement, 1330.

Length $\left\{\begin{array}{l}(w.l.),\ 555\frac{1}{2}\text{ feet.} \\ (o.a.),\ 562\text{ feet.}\end{array}\right\}$ Beam, 106 feet.　Mean draught, 26 feet.
　　　　　　　　　　　　　　　　　　　　Max.　　,,　　32　,,

Guns :
　12—12 inch, 50 cal.
　16—5 inch, 51 cal.
　8—3 inch AA., Mk. III.
　4—3 pdr. (saluting).
　(Torpedo tubes removed).

Aircraft : 3
Catapults :
　1 on 3rd turret.

Armour (Midvale) :
　11"—9" Belt amidships $\}$
　5" Belt (ends) ....
　12"—9" Turrets.........$\}$
　11" Turret bases ....
　6½" Battery ....
　12" Conning tower........
　(Bulges fitted 1926-27)

1927 *Official Photo.*

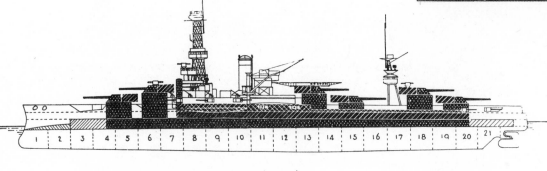

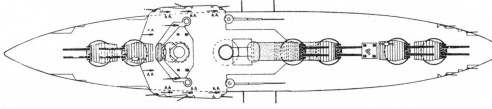

Machinery : Parsons turbines.　4 shafts.　Boilers : 4 White-Forster.　Designed H.P. 28,000 = 20·5 kts.　Oil : 5,100 tons.　Present speed 19·2 kts.

General Note.—Laid down Jan. 1910 and completed Sept. 1912.　Underwent extensive alterations and refit 1925-27 when displacement was increased by 3,000 tons.　To be replaced by new battleship *North Carolina.*

A sister ship **WYOMING** has been de-militarised according to the terms of the Naval Treaty.　Nos. 3, 4, 5 turrets removed.　She is employed as a Training Ship (vide a later page).

1934 *Photo, R. Perkins*

Recognition Letters of U.S. Aircraft Carriers

(painted prominently on after end of flight deck):

RANGER, RNGR.   LEXINGTON, LEX.   SARATOGA, SARA.

ENTERPRISE, EN ; YORKTOWN, YT.

ENTERPRISE (Oct. 3, 1936). HORNET (building).
YORKTOWN (April 4, 1936).

Displacement : 19,900 tons. Complement, 2,072 (including flying
personnel).

Length : 761 feet (*w.l.*), 809½ feet (*o.a.*). Beam, 83¼ feet.
Draught, 21⅔ feet (*mean*).

Guns :	Aircraft :
8—5 inch 38 cal. AA.	83 (space for over 100).
16—1·1 inch M.G. A.A.	Armour : A patch of side
16 smaller M.G.	armour over machinery
	and boiler spaces, and
	a heavy protective deck.

YORKTOWN (Note "Y" on funnel).   1939.

Note to Plan.—This shows starboard beam to illustrate details of funnel, etc.

ENTERPRISE.   1938, *Official, courtesy "Our Navy."*

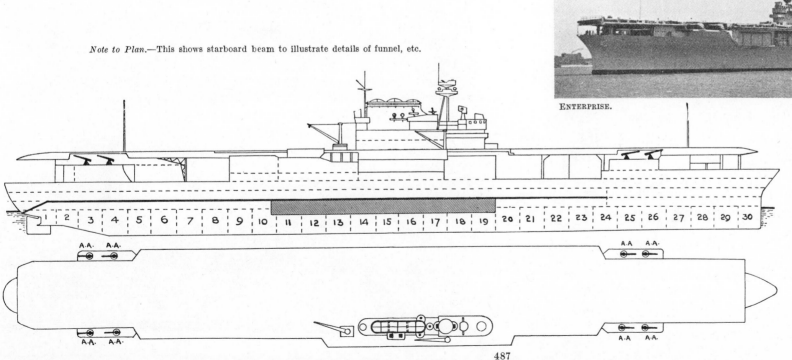

Machinery : Geared turbines. S.H.P.: 120,000
= 34 kts. (exceeded on trials). Boilers : 9
Babcock & Wilcox Express type.

Name	Builder	Laid down	Completed
Enterprise	Newport	16 July, 1934	18 July, 1938
Yorktown	News Co	21 May, 1934	1938
Hornet		Sept. 1939	1942

General Notes.—Owing to serious mechanical defects,
involving replacement of the reduction gearing and
over 1,200 boiler tubes, completion of *Yorktown* was
postponed until late in 1938. *Enterprise* was
similarly delayed. Cost over $21,000,000 apiece,
without armament. *Hornet* ordered end March, 1939.
To cost $31,800,000.

Aircraft Notes.—Aircraft can be catapulted from hangar
deck as well as from flight deck, thus increasing the
number that can be put into the air at short notice.

WASP (Bethlehem S.B. Corporation, Quincy, April 4, 1939). Laid down April 1, 1936, under 1935–36 Programme. Displacement: 14,700 tons. Dimensions: 688 (*w.l.*), 739 (*o.a.*) × $80\frac{1}{5}$ × 20 feet (*mean*) draught. Guns: **8**—5 inch 38 cal. AA., **40** smaller. Will carry 75 aircraft. Machinery: Parsons I.R. turbines. Speed: 30 kts. Boilers: Yarrow (by Bethlehem Co.). To cost $20,737,000 exclusive of armament. Will have hull on lines of *Ranger*, but funnel and island superstructure more like *Enterprise*.

RANGER.

Added 1935, courtesy U.S. Naval Institute.

RANGER (Newport News S.B. Co., Feb. 25, 1933). Displacement: 14,500 tons. Complement (including flying personnel): 1,788, of whom 162 are commissioned officers. Dimensions: 728 (*w.l.*), 769 (*o.a.*) × $80\frac{1}{12}$ × $19\frac{2}{3}$ ft. (*mean*).

Guns:
8—5 inch 25 cal. AA.
40 smaller

Aircraft:
72, of which 4 squadrons are bomber fighters, the remainder amphibians. Maximum capacity, 120. (unofficial).

Armour:
1″ Flight Deck
Double Hull and internal subdivision, but no side armour beyond small patch shown.

Note to Plan.—Guns shown on forecastle and q.d. now mounted on superstructure over sections 6 and 26—27, as shown in 1936—37 photos.

Added 1937, O. W. Waterman.

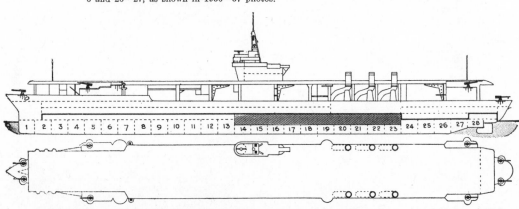

Machinery: Geared Turbines (high pressure Curtis; low pressure Parsons). 2 shafts. S.H.P.: 53,500 = $29\frac{1}{4}$ kts. Boilers: 6 Babcock & Wilcox sectional Express.

General Notes.—Laid down Sept. 26, 1931. Completed June 4, 1934. Trials: 58,700 = 30·35 kts. (*max.*). The six funnels can be lowered to horizontal position as in *Langley*.

With funnels lowered.

1936, O. W. Waterman.

488

LEXINGTON (3rd Oct., 1925.)

SARATOGA (7th April, 1925.)

Displacement, 33,000 tons. *Full load* about 40,000 tons.
Complement (including flying personnel): 1,899, of whom
169 are Commissioned Officers.
Length (*w.l.*) 830 ; (*pp.*), 850 ft. ; (*o.a.*) 888 ft.
Beam, 105½ ft. (*extreme*).
Draught, 24 feet 2 inches (*mean*). 32 feet (*max.*)

Guns :
8—8 inch, 55 cal.
12—5 inch AA., 25 cal.
4—6 pdr. saluting.
8—50 cal. M.G.

Aircraft :
Lexington 90.
Saratoga 79.
Catapult, 1.

Armour :
Unofficially reported to have
6″ Belt, 600 feet in length,
and 3″ deck. Triple hull and
bulge protection.

SARATOGA.

1936, *O. W. Waterman*

Engineering Notes.—Each boiler 11,250 H.P. Steam pressure, 295 lbs. to sq. inch. Fuel consumption estimated at 2000 tons daily under full power. Machinery is the most powerful ever installed in a warship ; it is all controlled, so far as main engines are concerned, from one central position. There are eight propelling motors of 22,500 H.P. (two to each of the four shafts), speed 317 R.P.M. On trials, it is stated that 97% of designed speed was obtained with 85% of designed power. *Lexington* did the voyage from San Diego to Honolulu (2,228 miles) at an average speed of 30·7 kts. A speed of 34·5 kts. was maintained for one hour by the latter ship with S.H.P 210,000. Average displacement of both ships on trials was about 39,000 tons.

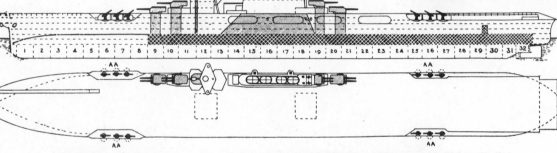

Machinery : G.E. turbines, electric drive. Designed S.H.P.: 180,000 = 33·25 kts. Boilers : *Lexington*, 16 Yarrow ; *Saratoga*, 16 White-Forster. 4 shafts. Oil fuel : 7,000 tons.

LEXINGTON, showing altered shape of bow.

1939.

Name	Builder	Machinery	Laid down	Completed	Trials	Boilers
Lexington	Fore River S.B. Co.	Gen. Elec. Co.	8/1/21	Dec.'27	153,600 = 33·04	Yarrow
Saratoga	New York S.B. Co.	Gen. Elec. Co.	25/9/20	Nov.'27	158,375 = 33·42	White-Forster

Special Note.—It is intended to reconstruct these 2 ships at a cost of $15,000,000 for the two. They will be modernised as regards AA. and gas defence, damage control and aircraft operation. Flight deck to be widened at the bow by 60 ft. A bulge to be built along port side, nearly the full length of the ship and adding 2½ feet to the beam, to balance the weight of the island superstructure. This will make it possible to utilise the full quantity of oil fuel carried, instead of retaining some as ballast. This will increase deadweight by 450/500 tons, but decrease displacement by about 2,000 tons, as ship will stand higher out of water.

General Notes.—These two ships were originally authorised in 1916 for construction as Battle Cruisers of 35,300 tons, with *seven* funnels and boilers disposed on two deck levels. After the War, plans were to a large extent re-cast, v. F.S. 1919–1921 Editions. Total cost, with aircraft, was over $45,000,000 each.

As Aircraft Carriers it is believed the waterline protection is retained and that deck protection has been heavily reinforced. The general lines of the hull remain unaltered, and the special system of underwater protection is also adhered to. Flight deck is 880 feet long, from 85 to 90 feet in width, and 60 feet above waterline. 8-inch guns have 30° elevation and range to 28,000 yards. Depth of hull from keel to flight deck is 74¼ feet, and funnel rises 79 feet above flight deck.

Handling of Aircraft.—The Landing Net is placed just before the recessed stern portion of the Flight Deck ; it is about 100 feet long. Before it is a large T-shaped lift for moving aircraft from Flight to Hangar Deck. There is another and similar T-shaped lift abeam of the mast and C.T. At the bow is a catapult, 155 feet in length, capable of launching the heaviest aircraft into the air at flying speed with a travel of 60 feet. Before the C.T. and abaft the Navigating Officers' Deck House, and right over to starboard beam, are powerful derricks for lifting seaplanes and flying boats from the water. As a result of experiments with *Langley*, certain modifications were made enabling planes to land safely on deck in any weather.

LEXINGTON. (Platform added around funnel top)

1936, *O. W. Waterman*

U.S.A.—Heavy Cruiser.

WICHITA (Nov. 16, 1937).

Displacement : 10,000 tons (*estimated*).   Complement : 551.

Length, 600 feet (*w.l.*), 614 feet (*o.a.*).   Beam, 61¾ feet.   Draught, 19⅚ feet (*mean*).

Guns :
9—8 inch, 55 cal.
8—5 inch AA.
2—3 pdr.
10 smaller

Aircraft :
4
Catapults :
2

Armour :
1½″ Side (fore and aft)
5″ Side (amidships)
3″ + 2″ Decks
5″—6″ Turret faces
3″ Turret sides and backs
8″ C.T.

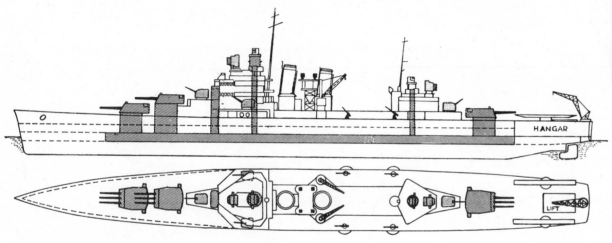

Machinery : Westinghouse geared turbines. 4 shafts. S.H.P. : 100,000 = 32·5 kts. Boilers : 8 Babcock & Wilcox. Fuel : 1,650 tons.

Notes.—Though originally to have been a unit of *Minneapolis* class, this ship was completed as a modified *Brooklyn* with 8 inch guns.

Name	Builder	Machinery	Laid down	Completed
Wichita	Philadelphia Navy Yard	Westinghouse Co.	Oct. 28, 1935	March, 1939

Appearance Note.—5 inch guns had not all been mounted when above photos were taken. A more recent view will be found in Addenda.

NEW ORLEANS

(MINNEAPOLIS CLASS—7 SHIPS)

ASTORIA (Dec. 16, 1933).
MINNEAPOLIS (Sept. 6, 1933).
NEW ORLEANS (April 12, 1933).
TUSCALOOSA (Nov. 15, 1933).
SAN FRANCISCO (March 9, 1933).
QUINCY (June 19, 1935).
VINCENNES (May 21, 1936).

Displacement: 9,950 tons, except *Tuscaloosa*, 9,975, *Vincennes*, 9,400 and *Quincy*, 9,375 tons.

Complement, 551.

Dimensions: 574 (*w.l.*), 588 (*o.a.*) × $61\frac{3}{4}$ × $19\frac{5}{12}$ feet (mean), $23\frac{1}{2}$ (max.).

Quincy and *Vincennes*: 569 (*w.l.*), 588 (*o.a.*) × $61\frac{5}{6}$ × $18\frac{2}{3}$ feet (mean).

Guns:
9—8 inch, 55 cal.
8—5 inch AA.
2—3 pdr.
10—Smaller.

Torpedo Tubes:
None
Aircraft: 4.
Catapults: 2.

Armour
$1\frac{1}{2}''$ Side (fore and aft).
5″ Side (amidships between sections 10—17).
3″+2″ Decks.
5″—6″ Turret faces.
3″ Turret sides and backs.
8″ Conning Tower.

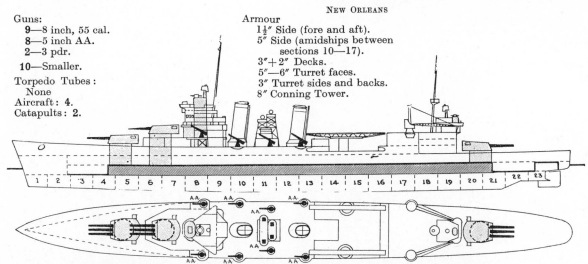

ASTORIA.

Machinery: Parsons geared turbines in *Tuscaloosa, Quincy, Vincennes* ; Westinghouse in others. 4 shafts. S.H.P.: 107,000 = 32·7 kts. (32 kts. in 2 later ships). 8 Babcock & Wilcox boilers.

Fuel: 1,650 tons.

General Notes.—In this class, the forecastle deck has been extended to the second funnel with a slight lowering of the freeboard ; the bow form altered and overhang dispensed with ; bridges raised and pole rig substituted for tripods ; AA. guns re-distributed : hangars moved aft and extended to shelter deck, all the boats excepting the lifeboats being stowed on top to avoid interference with the AA. guns. These ships possess better protection than the *Portland* class as armour has been distributed to better advantage on the new design. The utmost economy has been effected in construction, electric welding having been employed extensively and weight saved in every direction even to the extent of using aluminium paint internally. 8 inch guns and mountings are of a lighter model and the weight so saved has been put into armour. There is a certain amount of plating on the bridgework, not shown in the plan. Cost, $15,000,000 apiece.

Gunnery Notes.—8 inch guns elevate to 45°

491

Name	Builders	Machinery	Laid down	Completed
Astoria	Puget Sound Navy Yard	Westinghouse Co.	1/9/30	1/6/34
Minneapolis	Philadelphia Navy Yard	Do.	27/6/31	20/6/34
New Orleans	New York Navy Yard	Do.	14/3/31	18/4/34
Tuscaloosa	New York S.B. Corp.	N.Y.S.B. Corp.	3/9/31	17/8/34
San Francisco	Mare Isld. Navy Yard	Westinghouse Co.	9/9/31	23/4/34
Quincy	Bethlehem Fore River	Bethlehem Corp.	15/11/33	9/6/36
Vincennes	Bethlehem, Fore River	Do.	2/1/34	24/2/37

TUSCALOOSA.

1935, *O. W. Waterman.*

(*For particulars of these ships, see preceding page.*)

NEW ORLEANS.

1934 *Photo, Hr. Registrator Ossi Janson.*

QUINCY

1936 *Official.*

(Funnels in this ship and *Vincennes* are slightly thinner than in preceding ships.)

(PORTLAND CLASS—2 SHIPS).

PORTLAND (May 21, 1932). (Bethlehem S.B. Co., Quincy.)

INDIANAPOLIS (Nov. 7, 1931). (New York S.B. Co.)

Standard Displacement : 9,800 and 9,950 tons respectively. Complement : 551.

Dimensions : *Indianapolis*, 584 (*w.l.*), $610\frac{1}{4}$ (*o.a.*) × 66 × $17\frac{1}{3}$ feet (*mean*). *Portland*, 582 (*w.l.*), $610\frac{1}{4}$ (*o.a.*) × 66 × $17\frac{1}{12}$ feet (*mean*).

PORTLAND. (Fore funnel since heightened).

1933 *Photo, Official.*

Guns :	Aircraft :	Armour :
9—8 inch, 55 cal.	4 and 5, respectively.	3″—4″ Vert. Side
8—5 inch AA.	Catapults : 2.	2″+2″ Decks. } Not Official.
2—3 pdr.		$1\frac{1}{2}$″—3″ Turrets.
10—Smaller		
Torpedo tubes :		
None.		

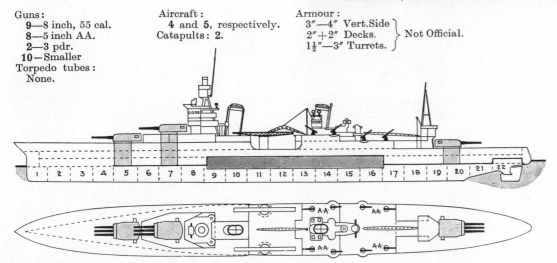

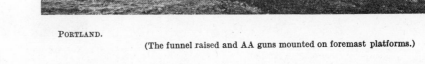

Machinery : Parsons geared turbines. 4 shafts. S.H.P. 107,000 = 32·7 kts. 8 White-Forster boilers in *Indianapolis*, 8 Yarrow in *Portland*.

General Notes.—These ships follow the general design of the *Augusta* class with alterations in weight distribution to improve stability. Some 40 tons of plating has been spread over the bridge work, which is higher than in *Augusta*, with a 30 feet reduction in the height of the masthead control top. *Portland* laid down Feb. 17, 1930, completed Feb. 23, 1933. *Indianapolis* laid down March 31, 1930, and completed November 15, 1932.

Portland said to be a bad roller; *Indianpolis* unaccountably is not. Machinery of both ships supplied by builders.

PORTLAND. 1934 *Photo.*
(The funnel raised and AA guns mounted on foremast platforms.)

(NORTHAMPTON CLASS—6 ships).

AUGUSTA (Feb. 1st, 1930). **CHESTER** (July 3rd, 1929). **CHICAGO** (Apr. 10th, 1930).
HOUSTON (Sept. 7th, 1929). **LOUISVILLE** (Sept. 1st, 1930). **NORTHAMPTON** (Sept. 5th, 1929).

Standard displacement, 9,050 tons.* Complement, 611.

✱ Dimensions : 569 (*w.l.*), 600¼ (*o.a.*) × 66 × 16⅓ feet (*mean*), 23 feet (*maximum*).

Guns :
9—8 inch, 55 cal.
4—5 inch AA.
2—3 pdr.
8—M.G.
Torpedo tubes :
Removed.

✱Chester 9,200 tons, 570 ft. (*w.l.*),
16½ feet (*mean*).
Chicago 9,300 tons, 572 ft. (*w.l.*),
16⅔ ft. (*mean*).

Aircraft : 4
Catapults : 2
Armour :
3″ Vert. Side.
2″ + 1″ Deck.
1½″ Gunhouses.

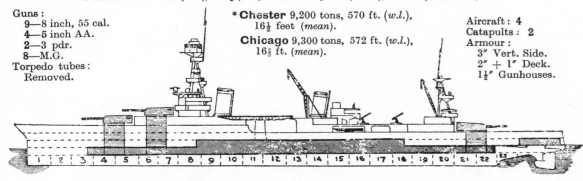

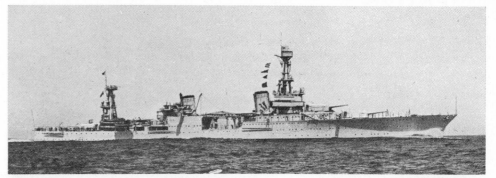

CHICAGO (*Augusta* similar; *Houston* has a small clinker screen.)   1938, *O. W. Waterman.*

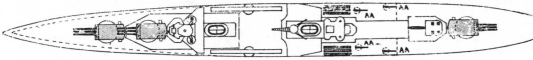

Machinery : Parsons geared turbines. 4 shafts. Designed S.H.P. 107,000 = 32·7 kts. 8 White-Forster boilers. Radius : 13,000 miles at 15 kts. Fuel : 1,500 tons.

General Notes.—Authorised 1926–27 under Act of December, 1924, as Nos. 26–31. The previous class having worked out at 9,100 tons only, the dimensions were increased and a forecastle deck added. Weight was saved by reducing and re-grouping the armament, while a certain amount of extra protection was provided. Because of vibration in the *Pensacola* the hull was stiffened to try and overcome this defect. Owing to the centre of gravity being placed too low, they were inclined to roll at low speed until fitted with bigger bilge keels. Four planes are carried inside the large hangars amidships, which can accommodate six aircraft if required. *Houston, Augusta* and *Chicago* are fitted as flagships and extra accommodation has been secured by extending the forecastle aft to the catapult. When first completed, *Augusta* suffered from a cracked sternpost, due to a defect in the casting, but this has been replaced.

Gunnery Notes.—Elevation of 8 inch guns, 45°. Control very accurate.

Engineering Notes.—Heating surface, 95,040 sq. feet. Machinery weighs 2,161 tons. 4 Turbo generator sets ; 250 kilo-watts each ; 120—240 volts ; built by General Electric Co. There are 4 boiler rooms.

Special Note.—Torpedo Tubes have been removed and additional AA. guns mounted on the hangar. *Chicago's* modernisation completed Dec., 1935.

CHESTER   (Now as *Northampton* below, but with clinker screen to fore funnel.)   1933 *Photo, O. W. Waterman.*

Name	Builders	Machinery	Laid down	Completed	Trials
Augusta	Newport News Co.	N.N. Co.	2/7/28	Jan., 1931	33·11
Chester	New York S.B. Cpn.	N.Y.S.B.C.	6/3/28	June, 1930	33·04
Chicago	Mare Island Navy Yard	G.E. Co.	10/9/28	March, 1931	—
Houston	Newport News Co.	N.N. Co.	1/5/28	June, 1930	33·02
Louisville	Puget Sound Navy Yard	P.S.N.Y.	4/7/28	March, 1931	32·74
Northampton	Bethlehem S.B. Co., Quincy	Bethlehem	12/4/28	May, 1930	33·10

NORTHAMPTON. (Observe raised fore funnel and short foretopmast.) (*Chester, Louisville,* similar.)   1935, *O. W. Waterman.*

Heavy Cruisers—*continued.*

(PENSACOLA CLASS).

PENSACOLA (April 25th, 1929), **SALT LAKE CITY** (Jan. 23rd, 1929).

Displacement, 9,100 tons.

Complement, 612.

Length (*w.l.*) 558 feet; o.a., 585½ feet. Beam, 65¼ ft.

Mean draught (at *normal* displacement), 16 ft. 2 in. *Max.* draught, 22 ft.

Guns :
10—8 inch, 55 cal.
4—5 inch, 25 cal. AA.
2—3 pdr.
Torpedo tubes : Removed.
Aircraft : 4.
Catapults 2.

Armour :
3″ side.
2″+1″ deck.
1½″ gunhouses.

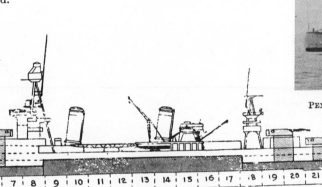

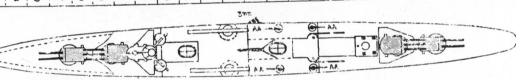

PENSACOLA. To distinguish, note position of main topmast.

1935 *Photo, O. W. Waterman.*

Machinery : 4 sets of Parsons geared Turbines. Cramp type, with de Laval single reduction gearing. 4 shafts. Designed S.H.P. 107,000 = 32·7 kts. 8 White-Forster boilers, working pressure reported as 300 lbs. per square inch. Radius of action : 13,000 miles at 15 kts. Fuel : 1500 tons.

General Notes.—Laid down under Act of December 18, 1924. Tons per inch immersion, 60·7. Utmost economy in weights practised in design and construction. Aluminium alloy fittings replacing steel and aluminium paint is used internally. Welding has been employed wherever possible instead of riveting.   They suffer from lack of freeboard, but no longer vibrate, although they roll at low speeds. Above 20 kts. they are extremely steady even in bad weather.

Gunnery Notes.—The 8 in. 55 cal. guns. have an elevation of 45° : fore control station at the mast head is about 120 feet above w.l. : the after control is abaft second funnel, and AA. control on fore bridge.

Engineering Notes.—Heating surface, 95,000 square feet. Machinery weighs 2,161 tons. Can steam at 30 kts. with 60 per cent H.P. There are 2 engine and 2 boiler rooms, the outboard shafts coming from the foremost engine rooms.

SALT LAKE CITY.

1935, *Official.*

Name	Builders	Machinery	Laid down	Completed	Trials
Pensacola Salt Lake City	New York N. Yd. New York S.B. Cpn.	} N.Y.S.B. Cpn. {	Oct. 1926 June 1927	6 Feb., '30 11 Dec., '29	=32·66 107,746=32·78

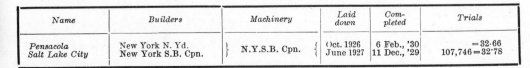

(CLEVELAND CLASS—2 Ships).

CLEVELAND, COLUMBIA.

Displacement : 8,000 tons.   Complement :

Length, 580 feet.   Beam, 58 feet.   Draught, not reported.

Guns :   Aircraft :   Armour :
  12—6 inch   3 or 4
  (Unofficial reports)

(No particulars released.)

Machinery : Geared turbines. Designed speed *about* 33 kts.

Notes.—Authorised for construction under 1939 Programme. One ship will probably be built in a Navy Yard and one by contract.

(ATLANTA CLASS—4 Ships).

ATLANTA, JUNEAU, SAN DIEGO, SAN JUAN.

Displacement : 6,000 tons.   Complement :

Length, 541 feet.   Beam, 52 feet.   Draught, not reported.

Guns :   Aircraft :   Armour :
  9—6 inch   2 or 3   3½″ Side
    or   2″ Deck
  12—5 inch

Torpedo Tubes :
  6—21 inch
  (in triple deck mountings)

Alternative designs, providing for main armaments as above, are reported to have been under consideration. In either case guns would be tripled.

Machinery : Geared turbines. Designed speed : 38 kts.

Name	Builders	Machinery	Laid down	Completed
Atlanta Juneau S. Diego S. Juan	Federal S.B. Co., Kearny Bethlehem Corpn., Quincy	Builders	All ordered April, 1939	*To be* 1942

Notes.—All belong to 1938 Programme. Are believed to be designed to act as flagships of Destroyer Flotillas. Cost will exceed $13,000,000 apiece, without armament.

BROOKLYN CLASS (9 SHIPS)

BROOKLYN (Nov. 30, 1936), **PHILADELPHIA** (Nov. 17, 1936), **SAVANNAH** (May 8, 1937), **NASHVILLE** (Oct. 2, 1937), **PHOENIX** (March 12, 1938), **BOISE** (Dec. 3, 1936), **HONOLULU** (Aug. 26, 1937), **HELENA** (Aug. 27, 1938), **ST. LOUIS** (April 15, 1938).

Displacement : 9,700 tons (*Brooklyn* and *Philadelphia*), 9,475 tons (*Savannah*), 9,650 tons (*Honolulu*), others estimated as 10,000 tons.
Complement : 868 (*Helena* and *St. Louis*, 888). Dimensions : 600 (*w.l.*) × 61½ × 19¾ feet (*mean*).

All now mount a 1-pdr. saluting gun on top of each turret.

HONOLULU. 1938, *Theo. N. Silberstein*.

HONOLULU. 1938, *Wright & Logan*.

Guns: **15**—6 inch, 47 cal.
8—5 inch, 25 cal. AA.
4—3 pdr.
5—1 pdr.
3 M.G.
(*Helena* and *St. Louis* will mount 5-in. guns in pairs behind shields.)
Aircraft : **4** (see *Notes*).

Armour : (Unofficial)
1½″—4″ Side.
3″ + 2″ Decks.
3″—5″ Gunhouses.
8″ C.T.

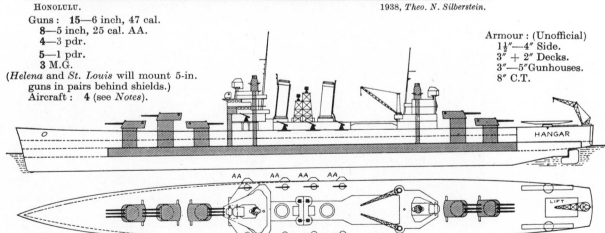

HONOLULU. 1938, *Wright & Logan*.

Machinery : Geared turbines. 4 shafts. S.H.P. : 100,000 = 32·5 kts. Boilers : 8 Babcock & Wilcox Express type. Oil fuel : 2,100 tons. Radius : 14,500 miles at 15 kts.

Note.—The first four of this class were ordered under the Emergency Programme of 1933 : the next three under the provisions of the " Vinson Bill "; and the last pair under the 1935–36 Programme. They are a reply to the Japanese " Mogami " class. Cost approaches $17,000,000 apiece. *Helena* and *St. Louis* are of a slightly modified design.

Aircraft Note—The hangar included in hull right aft is a completely new departure. It is provided with a lift and can accommodate 8 aircraft, though 4 is normal peace complement. Presence of this hangar accounts for very wide flat counter and high freeboard aft, which is also utilised to give after guns higher command. The two catapults are mounted as far outboard as possible and the revolving crane is placed at the extreme stern.

Name	Builders	Machinery	Laid down	Completed
Brooklyn	New York Navy Yd.		12/3/35	18/7/38
Philadelphia	Philadelphia Navy Yd.		28/5/35	28/7/38
Savannah	New York S.B. Corp.		31/5/34	30/8/38
Nashville	Do.	Builders in each case	24/1/35	25/11/38
Phœnix	Do.		15/4/35	18/3/39
Boise	Newport News Co.		1/4/35	1/2/39
Honolulu	New York Navy Yd.		10/9/35	7/9/38
Helena	New York Navy Yd.		9/12/36	/39
St. Louis	Newport News Co.		10/12/36	/39

(OMAHA CLASS—10 SHIPS.)

OMAHA (Dec. 14th, 1920), **MILWAUKEE** (Mar. 24th, 1921),
RALEIGH (Oct. 25th, 1922), **DETROIT** (June 29th, 1922),
CONCORD (Dec. 15th, 1921), **TRENTON** (April 16th, 1923),
MEMPHIS (April 17th, 1924), **RICHMOND** (Sept. 29th, 1921),
MARBLEHEAD (Oct. 9th, 1923), **CINCINNATI** (May 23rd, 1921).

Displacement: 7,050 tons. Complement: 458.

Dimensions: 550 (*w.l.*), 555½ (*o.a.*) × 55⅓ × 13½ feet (*mean*), 20 feet (*max*).

Guns:
10 —6 inch, 53 cal. Mk. XII.
(12—6 inch in *Concord, Memphis,
Milwaukee, Omaha, Trenton*).
4 —3 inch, 50 cal. AA.—6 in
Cincinnati and *Concord*.
2 —3 pdr. (saluting).
8—M.G. AA.

Armour:
3″ Side ....
1½″ Upper Deck .....

Torpedo tubes (21 inch):
6 (tripled) *above water*.
Aircraft : 4.
Catapults : 2.

CINCINNATI.

1937, *O. W. Waterman.*

Appearance Note.—Foretopmast removed in some to provide for 4 AA. M.G. in control top.

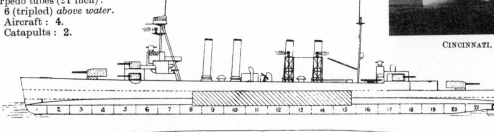

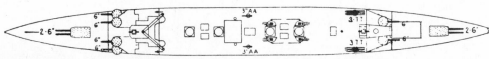

Machinery : Turbines (see Table for types), with reduction gears.   Designed S.H.P. 90,000 = 35 kts.
4 screws. Boilers : see Table. Fuel : oil only ; *about* 2,000 tons (300,000 gallons). Radius of action :
10,000 miles at 15 knots, 7,200 at 20 kts.

Name.	Built and Engined by	Laid down	Com-pleted	Trials	Turbines.	Boilers	Heating Surface (sq. ft.)
Omaha	Todd Co., Tacoma	6 Dec. '18	Feb. '23	94,290 = 34·87	Westghs.	12 Yarrow	
Milwaukee	" "	13 Dec. '18	June '23	90,060 = 34·64	"	12 Yarrow	90600
Cincinnati	" "	15 May '20	Dec. '23	94,290 = 34·44	"	12 Yarrow	
Raleigh	Bethlehem Co., Quincy	16 Aug. '20	Feb. '24	97,722 = 34·63	Curtis	12 Yarrow	90084
Detroit	" "	10 Nov. '20	July '23	97,375 = 34·63	"	12 Yarrow	
Richmond	Wm. Cramp & Sons	16 Feb. '20	June '23	95,000 = 34·2	Parsons	12 White-F	
Concord	" " "	29 Mar. '20	Nov. '23	92,772 = 33·48	"	12 White-F	
Trenton	" " "	18 Aug. '20	April, '24	33·91	"	12 White-F	90840
Marblehead	" " "	4 Aug. '20	Sept. '24	95,950 = 34·42	"	12 White-F	
Memphis	" " "	14 Oct. '20	Jan. '25	34·43	...	12 White-F	

Gunnery Note:—Max. range is 22,000 yards; effective at 18,000 yards.

MARBLEHEAD (Now mounts only 10—6 inch).

1935, *Official.*

Note.—All U.S. Destroyers carry Depth Charges and Smoke Screen apparatus.

Destroyers—U.S.A.

24 Benson Class. (1937–39 *Programmes*)

Building.

2 *Bethlehem (Fore River)*: **Benson, Mayo.**

6 *Bath Iron Works Corpn.*: **Gleaves, Niblack, Eberle, Grayson, Woolsey, Ludlow.**

6 *Boston Navy Yard*: **Lansdale, Madison, Gwin, Meredith, Wilkes, Nicholson.**

4 *Charleston Navy Yard*: **Hilary P. Jones, Livermore, Swanson, Ingraham.**

2 *Puget Sound Navy Yard*: **Charles F. Hughes, Monssen.**

4 *Federal S.B. & D.D. Co.*: **Kearny, Plunkett, Edison, Ericsson.**

Standard displacement: 1,630 tons. Otherwise similar to *Sims* class below, but possibly with 6—5 inch guns arranged in 3 pairs and 10 tubes in quintuple mounts.

Name	No.	Laid down	Launched	Completed	Name	No.	Laid down	Launched	Completed
Sims	409	15/7/37	8/4/39	1/8/39	H. P. Jones	427	16/11/38		
Hughes	410	15/9/37	17/6/39		C. F. Hughes	428	3/1/39		
Anderson	411	15/11/37	4/2/39	8/39	Livermore	435	17/7/39		
Hammann	412	17/1/38	4/2/39	8/39	Eberle	430	12/4/39		
Mustin	413	20/12/37	8/12/38		Plunkett	431	1/3/39		
Russell	414	20 12/37	8/12/38		Kearny	432	1/3/39		
O'Brien	415	31/5/38	2/9/39		Gwin	433	1/6/39		
Walke	416	31/5/38	2/9/39		Meredith	434	1/6/39		
Morris	417	7/6/38	1/6/39		Grayson	429	6/3/39		
Roe	418	23/4/38	21/6/39		Monssen	436	15/7/39		
Wainwright	419	7/6/38	1/6/39		Woolsey	437			
Buck	420	6/4/38	22/5/39		Ludlow	438			
Benson	421	16/5/38			Edison	439			
Mayo	422	16/5/38			Ericsson	440			
Gleaves	423	16/5/38			Wilkes	441			
Niblack	424	8/8/38			Nicholson	441			
Madison	425	19/12/38			Swanson	443			
Lansdale	426	19/12/38			Ingraham	444			

12 Sims Class (*1936 Programme*)

ANDERSON.   1939.

2 *Newport News Co.*: **Mustin, Russell,**
2 *Federal S.B. & D.D. Co.*: **Anderson, Hammann.**
2 *Bath Iron Works Corpn.*: **Hughes, Sims.**
2 *Boston Navy Yard*: **O'Brien, Walke.**
2 *Norfolk Navy Yard*: **Morris, Wainwright.**
1 *Charleston Navy Yard*: **Roe.**
1 *Philadelphia Navy Yard*: **Buck.**

Standard displacement: 1,570 tons. Dimensions not reported. Guns: 5—5 inch, 38 cal.. several smaller. Tubes: 12 —21 inch (quadrupled). Machinery: Parsons geared turbines. S.H.P.: 44,000 = 36·5 kts. Boilers: 4 Express. Oil fuel: 400 tons. Cost about $5,500,000 apiece.

Note.—This type combines the most successful features of *Craven* and *Mahan* classes. Reversion to 12 tubes understood to have been due to desire for higher freeboard abaft forecastle. General arrangement similar to *Dunlap* and *Fanning*, but with a single funnel. *Hammann* is reported to have made 39 knots on trials.

22 Craven Class (1934–35 Programmes)

BLUE.   1937, courtesy "Our Navy."

ELLET.   1939.

4 *Bethlehem S.B. Corpn., Fore River*: **Gridley, Craven, Maury, McCall.**
5 *Norfolk Navy Yard*: **Bagley, Blue, Helm, Rowan, Stack.**
4 *Boston Navy Yard*: **Mugford, Ralph Talbot, Mayrant, Trippe.**
1 *Mare Island Navy Yard*: **Henley.**
3 *Puget Sound Navy Yard*: **Patterson, Jarvis, Wilson.**
3 *Federal S.B. & D.D. Co.*: **Benham, Ellet, Lang.**
1 *Philadelphia Navy Yard*: **Rhind.**
1 *Charleston Navy Yard*: **Sterett.**

Standard displacement: 1,500 tons. Complement: 172. Dimensions: 334 (*w.l.*), 341⅔ (*o.a.*) × 34¾ × 9⅗ feet (*mean*) Guns: **4**—5 inch, 38 cal. (dual purpose), 4 M.G. Tubes: **16**—21 inch (quadrupled). Machinery: Parsons geared turbines. S.H.P.: 42,800 = 36·5 kts. Boilers: 4 Express type (except *Gridley* and *Craven*, 4 Bethlehem Yarrow). Oil fuel: 400 tons. Radius: 6,000 miles. Cost ranges from $3,400,000 to $3,750,000.

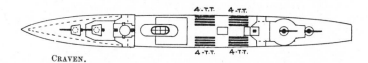

CRAVEN.

Notes.—Many of this class have exceeded designed speed on trials. *Ellet* and *Lang* are said to have approached 40 kts. Several ships were delayed in delivery through difficulties with high pressure and superheated installations.

2 Dunlap Class (1934 Programme)

DUNLAP.   1937, Mr. James Downey.

Plan as MAHAN class

DUNLAP.   1937, Mr. James Downey.

2 *United Dry Docks*: **Dunlap, Fanning.**

Standard displacement: 1,490 tons. Dimensions: 334 (*w.l.*), 341⅔ (*o.a.*) × 34¾ × 9⅗ feet (*mean*). Guns: **5**—5 inch, 38 cal. (dual purpose), 4 M.G. Tubes: **12**—21 inch (quadrupled). Machinery: Parsons geared turbines. S.H.P.: 42,800 = 36·5 kts. Boilers: 4 Express type. Oil fuel: 400 tons. Radius: 6,000 miles.

Name	No.	Laid down	Launched	Completed
Dunlap	384	10/4/35	18/4/36	7/7/38
Fanning	385	10/4/35	18/9/36	4/8/38

Name	No.	Laid down	Launched	Completed	Name	No.	Laid down	Launched	Completed
Gridley	380	3/6/35	1/12/36	30/6/38	Ellet	398	3/12/36	11/6/38	18/4/39
Craven	382	3/6/35	25/2/37	29/7/38	Lang	399	5/4/37	27/8/38	26/5/39
Bagley	386	31/7/35	3/9/36	10/8/38	McCall	400	17/3/36	20/11/37	19/12/38
Blue	387	25/9/35	27/5/37	10/8/38	Maury	401	24/3/36	14/2/38	17/1/39
Helm	388	25/9/35	27/5/37	16/9/38	Mayrant	402	15/4/37	14/5/38	/39
Mugford	389	28/10/35	31/10/36	23/9/38	Trippe	403	15/4/37	14/5/38	/39
Ralph Talbot	390	28/10/35	31/10/36	23/9/38	Rhind	404	22/9/37	28/7/38	/39
Henley	391	28/10/35	12/1/37	12/9/38	Rowan	405	25/6/37	5/5/38	/39
Patterson	392	22/7/35	6/5/37	11/10/38	Stack	406	25/6/37	5/5/38	/39
Jarvis	393	21/8/35	6/5/37	25/10/38	Sterett	407	2/12/36	27/10/38	/39
Benham	397	1/9/36	16/4/38	18/4/39	Wilson	408	22/3/37	12/4/39	/39

5 **Somers Class.** *(1934-35 Programmes).*

WARRINGTON.

1938, *Lieut. L. F. Bouman.*

SOMERS.

1938, *Wright & Logan.*

2 *Federal S.B. & D.D. Co.:* **Somers, Warrington.**
3 *Bath Iron Works Corpn.:* **Sampson, Jouett, Davis.**
Displacement ; 1,850 tons. Complement : 198. Dimensions : 371 (*w.l.*) × 36⅛ × 10¼ feet (*mean* draught). Guns : **8**—
  5 inch, 38 cal., **8**—1 pdr., **2** M.G. Tubes : **12**—21 inch. Machinery : Geared turbines. S.H.P. : 52,000 = 37 kts.
  4 Babcock & Wilcox high pressure boilers. Oil fuel : *circa* 500 tons. Cost averages over $5,000,000 each. In the
  case of *Somers* this includes a special air-conditioning plant.

Name	No.	Laid down	Launched	Completed	Name	No.	Laid down	Launched	Completed
Somers	381	27/6/35	13/3/37	30/6/38	*Davis*	395	28/7/36	30/7/38	16/12/38
Warrington	383	10/10/35	15/5/37	12/8/38	*Jouett*	396	26/3/36	24/9/38	7/3/39
Sampson	394	8/4/36	16/4/38	3/10/38					

8 **Porter Class** *(1933 Programme)·*

PHELPS.

1939, *O. W. Waterman.*

WINSLOW.

1938, *O. W. Waterman.*

4 *New York S.B. Corpn.:* **Porter, Selfridge, McDougal, Winslow.**
4 *Bethlehem S.B. Corpn., Fore River :* **Phelps, Clark, Moffett, Balch.**
Displacement : 1,850 tons (*Phelps* and *Clark* as completed, 1,805 tons ; *Balch* and *Moffett*, 1,825 tons). Complement :
  175. Dimensions : 371 (*w.l.*), 381 (*o.a.*) × 36⅛ × 10¼ to 10⅚ feet (*mean* draught). Guns : **8**—5 inch, 38 cal., **8**
  —1 pdr., **2** M.G. Tubes : **8**—21 inch. Machinery : Geared turbines. S.H.P. : 50,000 = 37 kts. (Trials, 39 kts.).
  4 Babcock & Wilcox high pressure boilers. Oil fuel : *circa* 500 tons. Cost approaches $4,000,000 each.

Name	No.	Laid down	Launched	Completed	Name	No.	Laid down	Launched	Completed
Porter	356	18/12/33	12/12/35	2/7/37	*Phelps*	360	2/1/34	18/7/35	26/2/36
Selfridge	357	18/12/33	18/4/36	26/10/37	*Clark*	361	2/1/34	15/10/35	20/5/36
McDougal	358	18/12/33	17/7/36	12/10/37	*Moffett*	362	2/1/34	11/12/35	28/9/37
Winslow	359	18/12/33	21/9/36	19/10/37	*Balch*	363	16/5/34	24/3/36	5/10/37

16 Mahan Class (1933 Programme)

8 Farragut Class (1932 Programme.)

PERKINS. 1939, *O. W. Waterman.*

AYLWIN. 1939.

CUMMINGS. 1938, *O.W. Waterman.*

DALE. 1937, *O. W. Waterman.*

2 *Bath Iron Works Corpn.* **Drayton, Lamson**
2 *Boston Navy Yard :* **Case, Conyngham.**
2 *United Dry Docks :* **Mahan, Cummings.**
2 *Federal S.B. and D.D. Co. :* **Flusser, Reid**
2 *Philadelphia Navy Yard :* **Cassin, Shaw.**
2 *Norfolk Navy Yard :* **Tucker, Downes.**
2 *Puget Sound Navy Yard :* **Cushing, Perkins.**
2 *Mare Island Navy Yard :* **Smith, Preston.**

Standard displacement : 1,500 tons (except *Mahan,* 1,450 tons ; *Cummings, Cushing, Perkins,* 1,465 tons. *Drayton, Lamson, Flusser, Reid, Smith, Preston,* 1,480 tons). Dimensions : 334 (*w.l.*), 341½ (*o.a.*) × 34⅞ × 9 ft. 8 in. (*Mahan*), 9 ft. 9 in. (1,465 and 1,480-ton ships), 9 ft. 10 in. others, (*mean*) ; all about 17 feet *max.* Guns : 5—5 inch, 38 cal. (dual purpose), 4 M.G. Tubes : 12—21 inch (quadrupled). Machinery : Geared turbines. S.H.P. : 42,800 = 36·5 kts. Boilers : 4 Express type. Oil fuel : 400 tons. Radius : 6,000 miles. Cost ranges from $3,400,000 to $3,750,000.

Name	No.	Laid down	Launched	Completed	Name	No.	Laid down	Launched	Completed
Mahan	364	12/6/34	15/10/35	16/11/36	Cassin	372	1/10/34	28/10/35	6/4/37
Cummings	365	26/6/34	11/12/35	26/1/37	Shaw	373	1/10/34	28/10/35	20/4/37
Drayton	366	20/3/34	26/3/36	1/6/37	Tucker	374	15/8/34	26/2/36	30/3/37
Lamson	367	20/3/34	17/6/36	4/1/37	Downes	375	15/8/34	22/4/36	26/3/37
Flusser	368	4/6/34	28/9/35	1/12/36	Cushing	376	15/8/34	31/12/35	10/12/36
Reid	369	25/6/34	11/1/36	4/1/37	Perkins	377	15/11/34	31/12/35	10/12/36
Case	370	19/9/34	14/9/35	19/3/37	Smith	378	27/10/34	20/2/36	31/12/36
Conyngham	371	19/9/34	14/9/35	10/4/37	Preston	379	27/10/34	22/4/36	23/1/37

1 *Bethlehem S.B. Corpn., Fore River :* **Farragut.**
2 *New York Navy Yard :* **Hull, Dale.**
1 *Bath Iron Works Corpn. :* **Dewey.**
2 *Boston Navy Yard :* **MacDonough, Monaghan.**
1 *Philadelphia Navy Yard :* **Aylwin.**
1 *Puget Sound Navy Yard :* **Worden.**

Standard displacement : 1,395 tons (except *Farragut,* 1,365 tons ; *Dewey,* 1,345 ; *Aylwin,* 1,375 ; *Worden,* 1410 tons.) Length, (*o.a.*), 341½ feet ; (*w.l.*), 331 feet (except *Farragut,* 330 ; *Dewey,* 329 feet). Beam, 34¼ feet. *Mean* draught, 8⅜ feet (except *Farragut,* 8¼ feet; *Dewey,* 8¹⁄₁₂ feet ; *Aylwin,* 8¾ feet). *Maximum* draught, 15¼ feet. Complement, 162. Guns : 5—5 inch, 38 cal. (dual purpose), 4 M.G. Tubes : 8—21 inch (quadrupled). Machinery : Geared turbines. S.H.P. 42,800 = 36·5 kts. (Max. trial speed reported to be 41 kts.) Boilers : 4 Yarrow (by Bethlehem), high pressure. Oil fuel : 400 tons. Radius : 6,000 miles. Cost ranges from $3,400,000 to $3,750,000.

Name	No.	Laid down	Launched	Compl.
Farragut	348	20/9/32	15/3/34	18/6/34
Dewey	349	16/12/32	28/7/34	3/10/34
Hull	350	7/3/33	31/1/34	24/5/35
MacDonough	351	15/5/33	22/8/34	28/6/35
Worden	352	29/12/32	27/10/34	1/3/35
Dale	353	10/2/34	23/1/35	19/7/35
Monaghan	354	21/11/33	9/1/35	30/8/35
Aylwin	355	23/9/33	10/7/34	1/5/35

502

153 boats (Flush Deckers).

Present Employment: *Childs* and *Williamson* are now Seaplane Tenders, and *Manley* is employed on transport duties. They are listed on later pages. *Reuben James* has been selected for conversion into a Seaplane Tender in 1940.

Special Note.

Numerals preceding name are the Official Pendant Number, which is painted on the bows of each ship. Numeral in parentheses after name refers to Builder (see list below).

Builders :—

1. Newport News S.B. Co.
2. Wm. Cramp & Sons.
3. Bath Iron Works.
4. Bethlehem S.B. Corpn., Quincy.
5. ,, ,, Squantum.
6. New York S.B. Corpn.
7. Bethlehem S.B. Corpn., Fore River.
8. Navy Yard, Mare Island.
9. Navy Yard, Norfolk.
10. Union Iron Works.
11. Seattle Con. and D.D. Co.
12. Navy Yard, Charleston.

1st Group (5 ships):

Name	Laid down	Launched	Compl.
232 *Brooks* (6)	11/6/18	24/4/19	18/6/20
234 *Fox* (6)	25/6/18	12/6/19	17/5/20
233 *Gilmer* (6)	25/6/18	24/5/19	30/4/20
231 *Hatfield* (6)	10/6/18	17/3/19	16/4/20
235 *Kane* (6)	3/7/18	12/8/19	11/6/20

Displacement: 1,190 tons, *standard*. Complement, 122. Dimensions: 310 (*w.l.*), $314\frac{1}{3}$ (*o.a.*) × $30\frac{5}{8}$ × $9\frac{1}{4}$ feet (*mean* draught), $13\frac{1}{2}$ feet (*max.*). Guns: **4**—5 inch, 51 cal., **1**—3 inch, 23 cal. AA. Tubes: **12**—21 inch (tripled). Machinery: Westinghouse geared turbines. 2 shafts. S.H.P. 26,000 = 35 kts. Boilers: 4 White-Forster. Total heating surface, 27,500 sq. ft. Oil fuel: 375 tons.

2nd Group (2 ships):

Name	Laid down	Launched	Compl.
208 *Hovey* (2)	719/18	26/4/19	2/10/19
209 *Long* (2)	23/9/18	26/4/19	20/10/19

Same as 1st Group, except 6—4 inch, 50 cal. guns, in twin mountings. Parsons geared turbines.

3rd Group (42 ships):

Name	Laid down	Launched	Compl.
211 *Alden* (2)	24/10/18	7/6/19	24/11/19
246 *Bainbridge* (6)	27/5/19	12/6/20	9/2/21
213 *Barker* (2)	30/4/19	11/9/19	27/12/19

3rd Group—*continued.*

Name	Laid down	Launched	Compl.
248 *Barry*((6)	26/7/19	28/10/20	28/12/20
215 *Borie* (2)	30/4/19	4/10/19	24/3/20
210 *Broome* (2)	8/10/18	14/5/19	31/10/19
222 *Bulmer* (2)	11/8/19	22/1/20	16/8/20
206 *Chandler* (2)	19/8/18	19/3/19	5/9/19
341 *Decatur* (8)	15/9/20	29/10/21	9/8/22
219 *Edsall* (2)	15/9/19	29/7/20	26/11/20
216 *John D. Edwards* (2)	21/5/19	18/10/19	6/4/20
228 *John D. Ford* (2)	11/11/19	2/9/20	30/12/20
247 *Goff* (6)	16/6/19	2/6/20	19/1/21
249 *Hopkins* (6)	30/7/19	26/6/20	21/3/21
107 *Hulbert* (9)	18/11/18	28/6/19	27/10/20
236 *Humphreys* (6)	31/7/18	28/7/19	21/7/20
245 *Rbn. James* (6)	2/4/19	4/10/19	24/9/20
230 *Paul Jones* (2)	23/12/19	30/9/20	19/4/21
242 *King* (6)	28/4/19	14/10/20	16/12/20
250 *Lawrence* (6)	14/8/19	10/7/20	18/4/21
336 *Litchfield* (8)	15/1/19	12/8/19	12/5/20
220 *MacLeish* (2)	19/8/19	18/12/19	2/8/20
223 *McCormick* (2)	11/8/19	14/2/20	30/8/20
237 *McFarland* (6)	31/7/18	30/3/20	30/9/20
159 *Noa* (9)	18/11/18	28/6/19	15/2/21
239 *Overton* (6)	30/10/18	10/7/19	30/6/20
218 *Parrott* (2)	23/7/19	25/11/19	11/5/20
226 *Peary* (2)	9/9/19	6/4/20	22/10/20
340 *Perry* (8)	15/9/20	29/10/21	7/8/22
227 *Pillsbury* (2)	23/10/19	3/8/20	15/12/20
225 *Pope* (2)	9/9/19	23/3/20	27/10/20
173 *Wm. B. Preston* (9)	18/11/18	9/8/19	23/8/20
243 *Sands* (6)	22/3/19	28/10/19	10/11/20
221 *Simpson* (2)	9/10/19	28/4/20	3/11/20
207 *Southard* (2)	18/8/18	31/3/19	24/9/19
224 *Stewart* (2)	9/9/19	4/3/20	15/9/20
240 *Sturtevant* (6)	23/11/18	29/7/20	21/9/20
339 *Trever* (8)	12/8/19	15/9/20	3/8/22
229 *Truxtun* (2)	3/12/19	28/9/20	16/2/21
338 *Wasmuth* (8)	12/8/19	15/9/20	16/12/21

* *Dahlgren* re-engined, 1938; speed being increased considerably. Third and fourth funnels have been combined in one large casing, and tubes removed.

3rd Group—*continued.*

Name	Laid down	Launched	Compl.
217 *Whipple* (2)	12/6/19	6/11/19	23/4/20
337 *Zane* (8)	15/1/19	12/8/19	15/2/21

Same as 1st Group, except **4**—4 inch, 50 cal. guns. Parsons or Westinghouse geared turbines; Four White-Forster or Normand boilers. H.P. 24,200, 25,000 or 26,000 = 35 kts. T.H.S. 27,500 or 27,000 sq. ft.

4th Group (31 ships):

Name	Laid down	Launched	Compl.
258 *Aulick* (4)	3/12/18	11/4/19	26/7/19
196 *G. E. Badger* (1)	24/9/18	6/3/20	21/7/20
269 *Bailey* (5)	3/6/18	5/2/19	27/6/19
267 *Ballard* (5)	3/6/18	7/12/18	5/6/19
256 *Bancroft*((4)	4/11/18	21/3/19	30/6/19
251 *Belknap* (4)	31/7/18	14/1/19	28/4/19
197 *Branch* (1)	25/10/18	19/4/19	3/4/20
186 *Clemson* (1)	11/5/18	5/9/18	17/11/19
*187 *Dahlgren* (1)	8/6/18	20/11/18	6/1/20
199 *Dallas* (1)	25/11/18	31/5/19	30/4/20
265 *Edwards* (5)	20/4/18	10/10/18	24/4/19
260 *Gillis* (4)	27/12/18	29/5/19	3/9/19
188 *Goldsborough* (1)	8/6/18	20/11/18	26/1/20

4th Group—*continued.*

Name	Laid down	Launched	Compl.
266 *Greene* (5)	3/6/18	2/11/18	9/5/19
198 *Herndon* (1)	25/11/18	31/5/19	17/4/20
194 *Hunt* (1)	20/8/18	14/2/20	8/6/20
255 *O. Ingram* (4)	15/10/18	28/2/19	27/6/19
263 *Laub* (5)	20/4/18	25/8/18	17/3/19
191 *Mason* (1)	10/7/18	8/3/19	28/2/20
253 *McCalla* (4)	25/9/18	28/3/19	19/5/19
252 *McCook* (4)	11/9/18	31/1/19	30/4/19
264 *McLanahan* (5)	20/4/18	22/9/18	5/4/19
274 *Meade* (5)	23/9/18	24/5/19	8/9/19
254 *Rodgers* (4)	25/9/18	26/4/19	22/7/19
190 *Satterlee* (1)	10/7/18	21/12/18	22/12/19
268 *Shubrick* (5)	3/6/18	31/12/18	3/7/19
273 *Swasey* (5)	27/8/18	7/5/19	31/7/19
270 *Thornton* (5)	3/6/18	22/3/19	15/7/19
193 *A. P. Upshur* (1)	20/8/18	14/2/20	21/5/20
257 *Welles* (4)	13/11/18	8/5/19	2/9/19
195 *W. C. Wood* (1)	24/9/18	6/3/20	25/6/20

Same as 3rd Group, except 311 feet water-line length. Curtis or Westinghouse geared turbines. Four White-Forster or Yarrow boilers. H.P. 25,000 or 27,000 = 35 kts. T.H.S. 27,500 or 27,540 sq. ft.

Borie. 1935, *O. W. Waterman.*

5th Group (41 ships):

Name	Laid down	Launched	Compl.
128 *Babbitt* (6)	19/2/18	30/9/18	24/10/19
126 *Badger* (6)	9/1/18	24/8/18	29/5/19
149 *Barney* (2)	26/3/18	5/9/18	14/3/19
153 *Bernadou* (2)	4/6/18	7/11/18	19/5/19
151 *Biddle* (2)	22/4/18	3/10/18	22/4/19
150 *Blakeley* (2)	26/3/18	19/9/18	8/5/19
148 *Breckinridge* (2)	11/3/18	17/8/18	27/2/19
131 *Buchanan* (3)	29/6/18	2/1/19	20/1/19
140 *Claxton* (8)	25/4/18	15/1/19	13/9/19
155 *Cole* (2)	25/6/18	11/1/19	19/6/19
134 *Crowninshield* (3)	5/11/18	24/7/19	6/8/19
116 *Dent* (2)	30/8/17	23/3/18	9/9/18
157 *Dickerson* (6)	25/5/18	12/3/19	3/9/19
117 *Dorsey* (2)	18/9/17	9/4/18	16/9/18
152 *Du Pont* (2)	2/5/18	22/10/18	30/4/19

5th Group—*continued.*

Name	Laid down	Launched	Compl.
146 *Elliot* (2)	23/2/18	4/7/18	25/1/19
154 *Ellis* (2)	8/7/18	30/11/18	7/6/19
78 *Evans* (3)	28/12/17	30/10/18	11/11/18
93 *Fairfax* (8)	10/7/17	15/12/17	6/4/18
145 *Greer* (2)	24/2/18	1/8/18	31/12/18
133 *Hale* (3)	7/10/18	29/5/19	12/6/19
141 *Hamilton* (8)	8/6/18	15/1/19	7/11/19
160 *Herbert* (6)	9/4/18	8/5/19	21/11/19
130 *Jacob Jones* (6)	21/2/18	20/11/18	20/10/19
118 *Lea* (2)	18/9/17	29/4/18	30/9/18
158 *Leary* (6)	6/3/18	18/12/18	5/12/19
76 *Philip* (3)	1/9/17	25/7/18	24/8/18
113 *Rathburne* (2)	12/7/17	27/12/17	24/6/18
147 *Roper* (2)	19/3/18	17/8/18	15/2/19
159 *Schenck* (6)	26/3/18	23/4/19	30/10/19

U.S.A—Destroyers, etc.

5TH GROUP—*continued.*

	Name	Laid down	Launched	Compl.
114	Talbot (2)	12/7/17	20/2/18	20/7/18
156	J. Fred Talbott (2)	8/7/18	14/12/18	30/6/19
142	Tarbell (2)	31/12/17	28/5/18	27/11/18
125	Tattnall (6)	1/12/17	5/9/18	26/6/19
135	Tillman (12)	29/7/18	7/7/19	30/4/21
127	Twiggs (6)	23/1/18	28/9/18	28/7/19
144	Upshur (2)	19/2/18	4/7/18	23/12/18
132	Aaron Ward (3)	1/8/18	10/4/19	21/4/19
115	Waters (2)	26/7/17	9/3/18	8/8/18

5TH GROUP—*continued.*

	Name	Laid down	Launched	Compl.
75	Wickes (3)	26/6/17	25/6/18	31/7/18
143	Yarnall (2)	12/2/18	19/6/18	29/11/18

Displacement : 1,090 tons *standard.* Dimensions : 309 (*w.l.*), 314⅓ (*o.a.*) × 30½ × 8⅔ feet (*mean* draught), 12 ft. (*max*). Armament as Groups 3 and 4. Parsons geared turbines ; Four White-Forster, Normand or Thornycroft boilers. H.P. 24,200, 26,000 or 27,000 = 35 kts. T.H.S.: 27,048, 27,000 or 27,500 sq. ft.

HOVEY & LONG HAVE 3 TWIN 4 INCH MOUNTS.
BROOKS CLASS HAVE 5 INCH GUNS. In each case after mount is placed on fantail

(Stern) 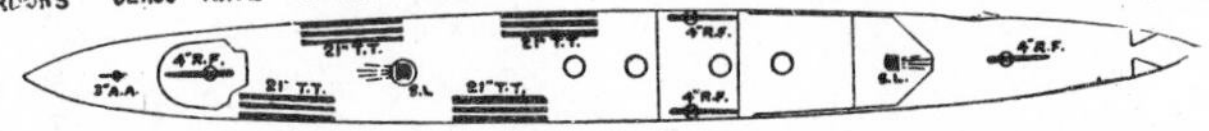   (Bow)

J. FRED TALBOTT. (5th and 6th groups like this),   1938, *Theo. N. Silberstein.*

6TH GROUP (30 ships):

	Name	Laid down	Launched	Compl.
184	Abbot (1)	5/4/18	4/7/18	18/7/19
106	Chew (10)	2/1/18	26/5/18	12/12/18
85	Colhoun (7)	19/9/17	21/2/18	12/6/18
167	Cowell (7)	15/7/18	23/11/18	17/3/19
109	Crane (10)	7/1/18	4/7/18	18/4/19
164	Crosby (7)	23/6/18	28/9/18	24/1/19
169	Foote (7)	7/8/18	14/12/18	21/3/19
82	Gregory (7)	25/8/17	27/1/18	31/5/18
183	Haraden (11)	30/3/18	4/7/19	6/6/19
178	Hogan (10)	25/11/18	12/4/18	1/10/19
181	Hopewell (1)	19/1/18	8/6/18	21/3/19
179	Howard (10)	9/12/18	26/4/19	28/1/20
170	Kalk (7)	17/8/18	21/12/18	29/3/19
138	Kennison (8)	14/2/18	8/6/18	2/4/19
137	Kilty (8)	15/12/17	25/4/18	17/12/18
79	Little (7)	18/6/17	11/11/17	5/4/18
175	Mackenzie (10)	4/7/18	19/9/18	25/7/19
168	Maddox (7)	20/7/18	27/10/18	10/3/19
90	McKean (10)	12/2/18	4/7/18	25/2/19

6TH GROUP—*continued.*

	Name	Laid down	Launched	Compl.
161	Palmer (7)	29/5/18	18/8/18	22/11/18
89	Ringgold (10)	20/10/17	14/4/18	14/11/18
88	Robinson (10)	31/10/17	28/3/18	19/10/18
103	Schley (10)	29/5/18	28/3/18	20/9/18
81	Sigourney (7)	25/8/17	16/12/17	14/5/18
180	Stansbury (10)	9/12/18	16/5/19	8/1/20
83	Stringham (7)	19/9/17	30/3/18	2/7/18
162	Thatcher (7)	8/6/18	31/8/18	14/1/19
182	Thomas (1)	23/3/18	4/7/18	25/4/19
139	Ward (8)	15/5/18	1/6/18	24/7/18
108	Williams (10)	25/3/18	4/7/18	1/3/19

Displacement : 1,060 tons *standard.* Dimensions : 309 (*w.l.*), 314⅓ (*o.a.*) × 30½ × 8⅓ feet (*mean* draught), 12 ft. (*max*). Armament as in 3rd, 4th and 5th Groups. Curtis, Parsons or G.E. Curtis turbines. Four Thornycroft, Yarrow or Normand boilers. H.P. 24,200, 25,000 or 27,000 = 35 kts. T.H.S.: 27,000, 27,540 or 28,000 sq. ft. Oil fuel : 300 tons.

STOCKTON (CONNER similar)   1919 *Photo.*

7TH GROUP (2 Ships):

	Name	Laid down	Launched	Compl.
72	Conner (2)	16/10/16	21/8/17	12/1/18
73	Stockton (2)	16/10/16	17/7/17	26/11/17

7TH GROUP—*continued.*

Displacement : 1,020 tons *standard.* Dimensions: 308 (*w.l.*), 315½ (*o.a.*) × 30⅔ × 7¼ feet (*mean* draught). Armament as in 3rd, 4th, 5th, and 6th Groups. Parsons turbines. Four White-Forster boilers. H.P. 18,000 = 30 kts. T.H.S.: 21,500 sq. ft. Oil fuel : 290 tons.

---

8 Light Minelayers (*ex-Destroyers*)

3 *Bath Iron Works* : **Preble, Pruitt, Sicard.**   1 *Cramp* : **Tracy.**

Displacement : 1,190 tons, *standard.* Dimensions : 310 (*w.l.*), 314⅓ (*o.a.*) × 30⅔ × 9¼ feet (*mean* draught), 13½ feet (*max*.). Guns : 4—4 inch, 50 cal., 1—3 inch, 23 cal. AA. Torpedo tubes removed. Machinery : Parsons geared turbines. 2 shafts. S.H.P.: 25,200 = 35 kts., except *Tracy*, 27,000 = 35 kts. Boilers : 4 Normand (except *Tracy*, 4 White-Forster). Total heating surface, 27,000 sq. feet (except *Tracy*, 27,500 sq. feet). Oil fuel : 375 tons.

Note.—Converted to present service from destroyers of 3rd group (above) in 1937.

Name	No.	Laid down	Launched	Completed	Name	No.	Laid down	Launched	Completed
Preble	DM 20	12/4/19	8/3/20	19/3/20	Sicard	DM 21	18/6/19	20/4/20	1/5/20
Pruitt	DM 22	25/6/19	2/8/20	2/9/20	Tracy	DM 19	3/4/19	12/8/19	9/3/20

Light Mine Layers—*continued*.

1921 *Photo.*

4 *Newport News S.B. Co.:* **Ramsay, Gamble, Breese, Montgomery.**

Ex-Flush Deck Destroyers, converted 1920–21. Identification Numbers: *Breese, DM* 18 ; *Gamble, DM* 15 ; *Montgomery, DM* 17 ; *Ramsay, DM* 16.

Displacements: 1,160 tons *standard* (1,284 *full load*). Dimensions: 309 (*w.l.*), 314 ft. 4 in. (*o.a.*) × 30 ft. 6 in. × 9 ft. (*mean* draught), 9 ft. 10 in. (*full load* draught aft).

Guns : 4—4 inch, 50 cal., 1—3 inch, 23 cal. AA. Torpedo tubes : Removed on conversion.

Mines carried : Unofficially reported to carry 80 Mark IV mines, for which magazines, deck rails and chutes have been fitted.

Machinery (*about* 486 tons) : Curtis geared turbines. 4 Yarrow or Thornycroft boilers—27,540 sq. ft. heating surface. 2 screws. Designed S.H.P. : 27,000 = 35 kts. Fuel : 283 tons oil. Complement : 128.

Motor Torpedo Boats.

Building.

PT. 1, 2, 3, 4. Wood. Length : 59 feet. First pair ordered from Fogal Boat Yard, Inc., second pair from Fisher Boat Works Co.

Building.

PT. 5, 6. Wood. Length : 81 feet. Ordered from Higgins Ind., Inc.

Notes.—First four to be delivered in five months from June, 1939, last pair in 7½ months from same date.

Submarines. *Note.*—All U.S. Submarines are painted black.

Fleet Submarines—Cruiser Type.

6 Grampus Class (1939 Programme).

Building.

3 *Electric Boat Co.*: **Gar, Grampus, Grayback.**
2 *Portsmouth Navy Yard*: **Grayling, Grenadier.**
1 *Mare Island Navy Yard*: **Gudgeon.**

Displacement : 1,475 tons. Believed to be slightly improved editions of *Thresher* class.

6 Thresher Class (1938 Programme).

Building.

3 *Electric Boat Co.*: **Tambor, Tautog, Thresher.**
2 *Portsmouth Navy Yard*: **Triton, Trout.**
1 *Mare Island Navy Yard*: **Tuna.**

Displacement : 1,450 tons. Other particulars as *Sargo* class, below, except Tubes : **10**—21 inch (6 bow, 4 stern). Machinery : G.M. Diesels in first 3, Fairbanks-Morse in others, with all-electric drive. Differ from *Sargo* type in silhouette, hull form, and internal lay-out. *Tambor* laid down 16/1/39, *Tautog* 1/3/39, *Thresher* 27/4/39, *Tuna* 19/7/39.

10 Sargo Class (1936–37 Programmes).

SAURY.   1939.

5 *Electric Boat Co.*: **Sargo, Saury, Seadragon, Sealion, Spearfish.**
4 *Portsmouth Navy Yard*: **Sculpin, Searaven, Seawolf, Squalus.**
1 *Mare Island Navy Yard*: **Swordfish.**

Displacement : 1,450/—— tons. Complement : 55. Dimensions : 300 (*w.l.*), 310 (*o.a.*) × 27 × 13¾ feet (*mean*). Guns : 1—3 inch, 50 cal., 1 M.G. AA. Tubes : 8—21 inch (4 bow, 2 stern). Machinery : H.O.R. Diesels in first 5, G.M. (Winton) in others.

Name and No.	Laid down	Launched	Completed	Name and No.	Laid down	Launched	Completed
Sargo (187)	12/5/37	6/6/38	7/2/39	*Sculpin* (190)	7/9/37	27/7/38	
Saury (188)	28/6/37	20/8/38	3/4/39	*Squalus* (191)	18/10/37	14/9/38	
Spearfish (189)	9/9/37	29/10/38	17/7/39	*Searaven* (195)	9/8/38	21/6/39	
Seadragon (193)	18/4/38	21/4/39		*Seawolf* (196)	27/9/38	17/8/39	
Sealion (194)	20/6/38	25/5/39		*Swordfish* (192)	27/10/37	1/4/39	

Notes.—Cost about $5,000,000 each. *Squalus* foundered May 23, 1939, but has since been salved.

6 Salmon Class.

SEAL. 1938, *Official.*

3 *Electric Boat Co.:* **Salmon, Seal, Skipjack.**
2 *Portsmouth Navy Yard:* **Snapper, Stingray.**
1 *Mare Island Navy Yard:* **Sturgeon.**

Displacement: 1,450/2,198 tons (first 3), 1,445 tons (others). Dimensions: 298 (*w.l.*) × 26 × $14\frac{1}{4}$ feet (*mean*). Guns: **1**—3 inch, 50 cal., **1** M.G. AA. Tubes: **8**—21 inch (4 bow, 4 stern). H.O.R. Diesels (except *Snapper*). Complement 55.

Name and No.	*Laid down*	*Launched*	*Completed*	*Name and No.*	*Laid down*	*Launched*	*Completed*
Salmon (*S1*)	15/4/36	12/6/37	/38	*Snapper* (*S4*)	23/7/36	24/8/37	1/3/38
Seal (*S2*)	25/5/36	25/8/37	/38	*Stingray* (*S5*)	1/10/36	6/10/37	30/6/38
Skipjack (*S3*)	22/7/36	23/10/37	/38	*Sturgeon* (*S6*)	27/10/36	15/3/38	2/9/38

6 Perch Class.

PLUNGER. 1938, *O. W. Waterman.*

3 *Electric Boat Co.:* **Perch, Pickerel, Permit** (ex-*Pinna*).
2 *Portsmouth Navy Yard:* **Plunger, Pollack,** 1 *Mare Island Yard:* **Pompano.**

Displacement: 1,330/1,998 tons (except *Plunger* and *Pollack*, 1,335 tons). Complement: 50. Dimensions: 290 (*w.l.*), $300\frac{1}{2}$ (*o.a.*) × 25 × $13\frac{1}{4}$ feet (*mean* draught). Guns: **1**—3 inch, 50 cal., **1** M.G.AA. Tubes: **6**—21 inch. Winton Diesels in first 3, with G.E. motors; Fairbanks-Morse Diesels and Elliott motors in *Plunger* and *Pollack*; H.O.R. (modified M.A.N.) Diesels and Allis-Chambers motors in *Pompano*. Cost averages $2,400,000 each.

Name and No.	*Laid down*	*Launched*	*Completed*	*Name and No.*	*Laid down*	*Launched*	*Completed*
Perch (*P5*)	25/2/35	9/5/36	4/6/37	*Plunger* (*P8*)	17/7/35	8/7/36	31/3/37
Pickerel (*P6*)	25/3/35	7/7/36	26/1/37	*Pollack* (*P9*)	1/10/35	15/9/36	28/4/37
Permit (*P7*)	6/6/35	5/10/36	17/3/37	*Pompano* *P10*)	14/1/36	11/3/37	4/12/37

4 Pike Class.

PORPOISE. 1937, *O. W. Waterman.*

2 *Portsmouth Navy Yard:* **Pike, Porpoise.**

Displacement: 1,310/1,934 tons. Dimensions: 283 (*w.l.*), 301 (*o.a.*) × 25 × 13 feet (*mean*). Winton Diesels. Elliott motors.

2 *Electric Boat Co.:* **Shark, Tarpon.**

Displacement: 1,315/1,968 tons. Dimensions: 287 (*w.l.*), 298 (*o.a.*) × 25 × $13\frac{1}{3}$ feet (*mean*). Winton Diesels, with electric drive. Elliott motors. First all-welded submarines in U.S. Navy.

Both types: Complement: 50. Guns: **1**—3 inch, 50 cal. Tubes: **6**—21 inch. Speed reported to exceed 20 kts.

Name and No.	*Laid down*	*Launched*	*Compl.*	*Name and No.*	*Laid down*	*Launched*	*Compl.*
Porpoise (*P1*)	27/10/33	20/6/35	15/1/36	*Shark* (*P3*)	24/10/33	21/5/35	25/1/36
Pike (*P2*)	20/12/33	12/9/35	17/4/36	*Tarpon* (*P4*)	22/12/33	4/9/35	12/3/36

CUTTLEFISH. 1935, *O. W. Waterman.*

Cachalot (**C.1** ex-*V*.8) Portsmouth Navy Yard. Laid down Oct. 21, 1931. Launched Oct. 19, 1933. Completed March 1, 1934. **Cuttlefish** (**C.2** ex-*V*.9) Electric Boat Co. Laid down Oct. 7, 1931. Launched Nov. 21, 1933. Completed June, 1934.

Respective displacements: 1,110 and 1,120/1,650 tons. Complement, 45. Dimensions: 260 (*w.l.*), $271\frac{1}{3}$ (*o.a.*) × $24\frac{3}{4}$ × $12\frac{5}{6}$ feet (*Cachalot*); 25 × $12\frac{3}{8}$ (*Cuttlefish*). Machinery: 2 sets Winton Diesels. H.P.: 3,100/800 = 17/9 kts. Armament: **1**—3 inch AA. Tubes: **6**—21 inch. All-welded construction. Guns mounted abaft C.T. No external torpedo stowage.

Note.—Owing to design of original engines (with direct drive) having proved unsatisfactory, *Cachalot* and *Cuttlefish* were given new machinery under 1936 Programme.

DOLPHIN. 1935, *O. W. Waterman.*

Dolphin (**D.1** ex-*V*.7) Portsmouth Navy Yard. Laid down June 14, 1930. Launched March 8, 1932. Completed Oct. 14th, 1932.

Displacement: 1,540/2,215 tons. Complement, 63. Dimensions: 307 (*w.l.*), 319 (*o.a.*) × $27\frac{1}{6}$ × 13 feet. M.A.N. Diesels, H.P.: 4,200 = 17 kts. *surface.* Electric motors, H.P.: 875 = 8 kts. *submerged.* Guns: **1**—4 inch, 50 cal., Tubes: **6**—21 inch + 3 Torpedoes stowed externally.

NAUTILUS. *Added*, 1938, *Wide World Photos.*

Narwhal (**N.1** ex-*V*.5) (Dec. 17, 1929), **Nautilus** (**N.2** ex-*V*.6) (March 15, 1930). Laid down at Portsmouth and Mare Island Navy Yards, respectively, May 10 and August 2, 1927. Machinery for both vessels built at New York Navy Yard. Displacement: 2,730/3,960 tons. Dimensions: 371 (*o.a.*), 349 (*w.l.*) × $33\frac{1}{4}$ × $15\frac{1}{4}$ feet (*mean*). Armament: **2**—6 inch, **6**—21 inch tubes. M.A.N. Diesels, H.P. 5,450 = 17 kts. *surface.* Westinghouse electric motors, H.P. 2,540 = 8·5 kts. *submerged.* Complement, 88. Estimated cost: Hull and machinery, $5,350,000 armament, $1,020,000. Authorised 1916 as Nos. 167–168. Completed in July and Oct., 1930, respectively.

Note.—Also carry eight external Torpedo Stowage Tubes, two each side fore and aft under the half-deck amidships. Neither vessel can exceed 14 kts. with present engines, which it is proposed to replace in 1939–40.

Fleet Submarines—Minelaying Type.

1928 *Official Photo.*

1929 *Official Photo.*

Fleet Submarines.

BONITA.   1935, *O. W. Waterman.*

BARRACUDA.   1935, *Bear Photo Service.*

Argonaut (A.1 ex-*V*.4) (Portsmouth Navy Yard, Nov. 10th, 1927). Machinery by Brooklyn Navy Yd. Displacement : 2,710/4,080 tons. Dimensions : 358 (*w.l.*), 381 (*o.a.*) × 33½ × 15½ feet. Armament : 2—6 inch guns, 4—21 inch tubes, **60** mines. Diesels of 3,175 S.H.P. Speed 14·6/8 kts. Complement, 89. Is an improved edition of *Barracuda* in other respects. Estimated cost : Hull and machinery, $5,300,000 ; armament, etc., $850,000. Authorised 1916, as No. 166, laid down May 1, 1925, and completed May 28, 1928.

Note.—It was stated officially in Jan. 1938, that, owing to defects in engine design, the *Argonaut's* speed does not exceed 13 knots. It is therefore intended to replace the existing engines. At the same time the latest system of Torpedo control will be installed.

3 *Bureau* design : **Barracuda** (ex-*V*.1), **Bass** (ex-*V*.2), **Bonita** (ex-*V*.3). Built at Portsmouth Navy Yard. Displacement : 2,000/2,506 tons. Complement : 75. Dimensions : 326 (*w.l.*), 341½ (*o.a.*) × 27 $\frac{1}{2}$ × 14½ feet. Guns : 1—3 inch AA., 2 M.G. Tubes : **6**—21 inch. 16 torpedoes carried. Machinery : 2 sets Busch–Sulzer Diesels aft for main drive. H.P. : 6,700 = 18·75 kts. on *surface.* Also 2 sets M.A.N. auxiliary Diesels forward driving generators supplying current to electric motors, H.P. : 2,400 = 8 kts. *submerged.* Latter combination can be used for cruising on surface with electric drive. Radius of action : 12,000 miles. Designed speed never realised in service.

Name & No.	Laid down	Launched	Compl.		Name & No.	Laid down	Launched	Compl.
Barracuda (B 1)	20/10/21	17/7/24	1/11/24		*Bonita* (B 3)	16/11/21	9/6/25	17/6/26
Bass (B 2)	20/10/21	27/12/24	26/9/25					

U.S.A.—Submarines

Fleet Submarines—*continued.*

Note on S Class.— An official report in 1925 stated that " experience in manœuvres indicates that these vessels cannot be considered as a satisfactory type of fleet submarines."

S 22.   1939, *W. H. Davis, Esq.*

6 *Electric Boat Co.* design : **S 42—S 47** (1923-24). 850/1,126 tons. All contracted for by Electric Boat Co.; hulls sub-contracted for by Bethlehem S.B. Co., Quincy. Authorised 1916-18. Displacement : 850/1,126 tons. Dimensions : 225¼ × 20⅜ × 15 feet. Guns : **1**—4 inch, 50 cal. Tubes : **4**—21 inch. **12** Torpedoes carried. Engines : Two sets 600 B.H.P., 8 cylinder, 4 cycle Nelseco. Motors : 2 sets each 750 H.P. Elect. Dy. Co. Speed : 14·5/11 kts. Oil : 11,463—46,363 gallons. Complement : 38.

1 *Bureau* design : **S 48** (1921). By Lake T. B. Co. 1000/1458 tons. Dimensions : 266 (*w.l.*), 267 (*o.a.*) 21⅜ × 13½ feet. Guns : 1—4 inch, 50 cal. Tubes : **5**—21 inch (4 bow, 1 stern). 14 torpedoes carried. Engines 2 sets M.A.N. (N.Y.) 4 cycle 6 cyl. = total B.H.P. 2000. Motors : 2 sets each 750 h.p. Speed 14·5/11 kts. Crash dive in 60 secs. *Max.* dive limit : 200 feet. Divided into 6 watertight compartments. Double hull amidships, single hull at ends. 3 periscopes. Oil : 23,411 gallons *normal*, 44,305 *max.* Rad : 8,000 at 10 kts. Authorised 1916. Complement: 38.

Note.—S 48 is stated to have been re-engined in 1929 with two new motors of 1000 H.P. each, oil storage being increased at same time. She was undergoing an extensive refit at Cristobal in 1938.

24 *Electric Boat Co.* design : **S 1, S 18** (1918), **S 20—41** (1918-22). All contracted for by Electric Boat Co., and sub-contracted for as follows : S1 by Fore River S.B. Co., S 18—S 29 by Bethlehem S.B. Co., Quincy, S 30—S 41 by Bethlehem S.B. Co., San Francisco. 800/1,062 tons. Dimensions : 219½ × 20⅜ × 15 feet. 2 sets of 600 B.H.P. Nelseco Diesel engines. Motors : 2 sets 750 H.P. Ridgeway or Electric Dynamic Co. (S 1). Oil : 11,511/41,921 gallons. Have large radius of action *on surface.* Armament : **1**—4 inch gun and **4**—21 inch bow tubes (**12** torpedoes carried). Authorised : S 1 (1916, as No. 105), S 18—21 (1916-17 as Nos. 123—126), S 22—41 (1916-17, as Nos. 127 —146). S 1 experimentally fitted, 1923 to carry a small seaplane in a cylindrical tank abaft C.T.

Note.—S 30 built at expense of Philippines Government. S 19 scrapped, 1937. S 20 used for experimental work.

S 14.   1929 *Official Photo.*

3 " *Bureau design* " boats : **S 11—13** (1919-21) ; all by Portsmouth Ny. Yd Dimensions : 231 × 21⅝ × 13½ feet. Displacement : 790/1,092 tons. Guns : **1**—4 inch, 50 cal. Tubes : **5**—21 inch (**14** torpedoes carried). Engines : 2 sets of 4-cycle " Bureau Design " M.A.N. (6 cyl.) type, each 1,000 B.H.P. Motors : 2 sets 600 H.P. Westinghouse. Oil : 19,271/36,950 gallons. Speed : 15/10·5 kts. Completed 1919-23. S 4 sunk by collision with Coast Guard Destroyer, *Paulding*, on Dec. 17, 1927 ; salved and brought in to port March, 1928. After being used for some time as a special vessel for experimental purposes, she was discarded and scuttled off Hawaii in 1936. Other numbers scrapped.

4 *Bureau* design : **S 14 - S 17** (1919—20). All by Lake T.B. Co. Dimensions : 231 × 21⅝ × 13 feet = 790 /1092 tons. Guns : 1—4 inch, 50 cal. Tubes · **4**—21 inch (12 torpedoes carried). Engines : 2 sets M.A.N (N.Y.) 4 cycle 6 cyl. = B.H.P. 2,000. Motors : 2 sets each 600 H.P. Westinghouse. Speed, 14/12·25 kts Complement, 38. Oil, 19,271/36,950 gallons.

Coastal Submarines.

Building.

1 *Electric Boat Co.:* **Mackerel.**
1 *Portsmouth Navy Yard :* **Marlin.**
Displacement : 800 tons. Machinery : Nelseco Diesels, Electric Dynamic motors. Provided for under 1939 Programme.

Official, added 1935.

19 *Electric Boat Co.* design : **R 1—7, 9—20** (1917-19). All contracted for by Electric Boat Co. and sub-contracts assigned as follows : R 1—7, 9—14, by Fore River S.B. Co., R 15—20 by Union I.W. San Francisco. Displacement : 530/680 tons. Dimensions : 186 × 18 × 14½ feet. Armament : 1—3 inch, 50 cal. gun, **4** torpedo tubes (8 torpedoes carried). Engines : 2 sets of 440 B.H.P. (400 r.p.m.) 6-cyl. 4-cycle Nelseco Diesel. Fuel : 7,691/18,880 gallons. Motors : 2—467 H.P. Electric Dynamic Co., with Cutler-Hammer Co. magnetic controllers. Batteries : Electric Storage Co. Type 31-WLL. Authorised 1916 as Nos. 78—97. Completed 1918-19.

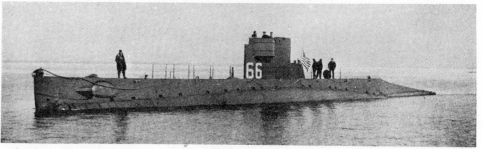

O 6.   1920 *Photo.*

8 *Electric Boat Co.* design : **O 2—O 4** and **O 6—O 10** (1917-18), viz. O 2 by Puget Sound Navy Yard ; O 3, O 4 and O 6—O 10 contracted for by Electric Boat Co. and sub-contracted for by Fore River Co. Dimensions : 172½ × 18 × 14½ feet. 480/624 tons. 1—3 inch, 23 cal. AA. gun. **4** torpedo tubes (8 torpedoes). Engines : 2 sets of 440 B.H.P. (400 r.p.m.) 6-cyl. 4-cycle Nelseco Diesel engines. 14·5/11 kts. 10,089/21,897 gallons. Motors : 2—370 H.P. in O 2, by New York Navy Yard ; in others, by Electric Dynamic Co., all with Cutler-Hammer Co. magnetic controller. Gould storage batteries, Type 29-WLL in O 2. Electric Storage Co., Type 49-WLL in others. Electric batteries weigh 65 tons. Radius of action : 3,500/3,000 miles, at 11 kts. *on surface.* Authorised 1915, as Nos. 62—71. Completed 1918.

Note.—O 5 wrecked, Oct. 28, 1923, and not considered worth repair after salvage. O 1 converted into an experimental vessel, 1937, and discarded following year.

Patrol Vessels—Submarine Chasers.

PC 451. Steel. Length, 170 feet (*o.a.*) Building by Defoe Boat and Motor Works.
PC 449, 450. Wood. Length, 110 feet (*o.a.*). Building by Luders Marine Construction Co. and American Car and Foundry Co., respectively.

EAGLE 17.

1919 *Photo, by courtesy of the Ford Motor Co., Detroit.*

"EAGLES" 19, 27, 32, 38, 48, 55, 56, 57, 58. Launched 1918–19, by Ford organisation. Displacement : *standard*, 430 tons, *full load* 615 tons. Complement : 61. Dimensions : Length, 200 feet (*p.p. and o.a.*). Beam, 25½ feet. *Mean* draught, 7¼ feet ; *full load*, 8½ feet. Armament : 2—4 inch, 50 cal. ; 1—3 inch AA., 2 M.G. Carry **12** depth charges. Machinery : Poole geared Turbine. 2 Bureau Express boilers. 1 screw. Designed H.P. : 2,500 = 18 kts. Fuel : 105 tons coal + 45 tons Oil. Endurance : 3,500 miles at 10 kts.

SC. 200.

1919 *Photo.*

SC 64, 102, 103, 185, 192, 229, 231, 330, 412, 428, 432, 437, 440. Built 1917–19 by various Navy Yards and private contractors. Displacement : 75 tons *standard*, 85 tons *full load*. Wooden hulls. Length : 105 feet (*p.p.*), 110 feet (*o.a.*). Beam : 14 ft. 9 in. *Mean* hull draught, 5 ft. 6 in., *full load* aft, 5 ft. 8 in. Armaments : 1—3 inch, 23 cal., M.G. and D.C. Machinery : 3 sets of 220 B.H.P. Standard petrol motors = 17 kts. 2,400 gallons Petrol = 900 miles at 10 kts. Complement : 26.

Training Ship.

1938, *Wright & Logan.*

WYOMING (May 26, 1911). Displacement : 19,700 tons (*standard*). Dimensions : 555½ (*w.l.*) × 93 × 23½ feet (*mean* draught). Guns : 6—12 inch, 50 cal. ; 16—5 inch, 51 cal.; 8—3 inch AA., 4—6 pdr. Parsons turbines. White-Forster boilers. H.P. 28,000 = 21 kts. Built by Cramps, sister to *Arkansas*, described on an earlier page. Demilitarised under terms of the London Naval Treaty, and bulges removed. H.P. and speed given above were prior to conversion. Best speed now is 18 kts.

Target Ships.

1934 *Photo.*

UTAH (New York S.B. Corpn., Dec. 23, 1909). Ex-battleship employed as wireless controlled target ship. *Standard* displacement : 19,800 tons. Dimensions : 512 (*w.l.*) × 106 × 22½ feet (*mean* draught). Parsons turbines. White-Forster boilers. Speed originally was 21 kts.

LAMBERTON, BOGGS. Ex-destroyers, now classed as Mobile Targets.

Escort Vessels, rated as
Patrol Vessels—Gunboats.

ERIE.   1936, R. Perkins.

CHARLESTON (Feb. 25, 1936). Built at Charleston Navy Yard.
ERIE (Jan. 29, 1936). Built at New York Navy Yard.
Standard displacement : 2,000 tons. Dimensions : 308 (*w.l.*),
$328\frac{1}{2}$ (*o.a.*) × $41\frac{1}{3}$ × $11\frac{1}{2}$ feet (*mean* draught). Guns: **4**—
6 inch, 2—quad. M.G. AA., 2—3 pdr. Protection : 1″ side
at waterline (3″ over vital spaces) ; 3″ C.T. ; 1″ shields
and bridge ; 2″ + 1″ decks. Machinery : Geared turbines.
2 shafts. S.H.P. : 6,200 = 20 kts.

Notes.—Ordered 1933 under Emergency Programme. Laid down in Oct. and Dec.,
1934, and completed in Oct., 1936. 6 inch guns are 47 cal. new model.

TULSA.   1925 *Photo, by courtesy of the Navy Dept.*

TULSA (Charleston, N.Y., 25th August, 1922). **ASHEVILLE**
(Charleston, N.Y., July, 1918). Displacement. 1270 tons (*full
load*, 1760 tons). Complement, 185. Length (*pp.*) 225 feet,
(*o.a.*) $241\frac{1}{4}$ feet. Beam, $41\frac{1}{4}$ feet. *Mean* draught, $11\frac{1}{3}$ feet. Guns :
3—4 inch, 50 cal., 2—3 pdr. **3**—1 pdr. Machinery : Parsons
turbine with reduction gear. 1 screw. Boilers : 3 Bureau
(modified Thornycroft). Designed H.P. 800 = 12 kts. Fuel, 180
tons coal + 440 tons oil.

1939, *Photo.*

SACRAMENTO (Feb., 1914). Displacement, 1140 tons. Complement, 153. Length (*waterline*), 210 feet. Beam, $40\frac{5}{6}$ feet.
Mean draught, $11\frac{1}{2}$ feet. Guns : 3—4 inch, 50 cal. ; 2—3 pdr. ;
2—1 pdr. Machinery : 1 set triple expansion. Boilers : 2 Babcock.
H.P. 950 (trials 1022 = 12·78 kts.). Coal : *maximum*, 428 tons.
Built by Cramps. Completed, 1914, and being refitted for
service on Great Lakes.

Patrol Vessels—River Gunboats (PR).

GUAM.   1928 *Official Photo.*

GUAM (May 28, 1927), **TUTUILA** (June 14, 1927). Displacement : 370 tons *standard*. 150 (*w.l.*), $159\frac{1}{2}$ (*o.a.*)
× 27 × $5\frac{1}{4}$ feet *mean* draught (fresh water), 6 feet
(*max.*). Freeboard at side (main deck): Forward, 6 ft. 3 in.;
amidships, 3 ft. 5 in.; aft, 4 ft. 2 in.
Triple expansion engines, $\dfrac{12 \times 18 \times 29}{16}$, revs. 320. H.P. 1950
= 14·5 kts. Oil fuel : 75 tons. Guns : 2—3 inch. 23 cal.,
behind shields, **10** M.G. Complement, 63 *Guam*, 58 *Tutuila*.

1929 *Official Photo.*

OAHU (Nov. 26, 1927). Displacement : 450 tons *standard*.
Complement : 65. 180 (*w.l.*), 191 (*o.a.*) × 28 × $5\frac{1}{4}$ (*mean*)
$6\frac{1}{2}$ (*max.*). Freeboard at side (main deck): Forward, 7 ft.
$9\frac{1}{2}$ in. ; amidships, 3 ft. $9\frac{1}{2}$ in. ; aft. 4 ft. 6 in. Triple expansion
engines, $\dfrac{13\frac{1}{4} \times 22 \times 34}{16}$, revs. 320. H.P. : 2,250 = 15 kts.
(Trials, 17·73 kts.). Oil fuel : 103 tons. Guns : 2—3 inch,
50 cal. AA., **10** M.G.

Note.—Sister ship *Panay* sunk by Japanese aircraft, Dec. 12, 1937.

LUZON.   1929 *Official Photo.*

LUZON (Sept. 12, 1927), **MINDANAO** (Sept. 28, 1927).
Displacement : 560 tons *standard*. Complement, 82 and 78,
respectively. 198 (*w.l.*), $210\frac{3}{4}$ (*o.a.*) × 31 × $6\frac{1}{2}$ (*mean*) 7 (*max.*).
Freeboard at side (main deck): Forward, 10 ft. 7 in.;
amidships, 5 ft. 7in.; aft, 5ft. 10 in.
Triple expansion engines, $\dfrac{15 \times 23 \times 36\frac{1}{4}}{18}$, revs. 320. H.P.
3,150 = 16 kts. Oil fuel : 173 tons. Guns : 2—3 inch, 50 cal.
AA., **10** M.G.
Above 5 gunboats authorised 1924 and laid down 1926 by
Kiangnan Dock and Engineering Works, Shanghai. Com-
pleted, 1928.
The following characteristics are common to all :—2 Thornycroft
oil-burning boilers, 250 lbs. working pressure. 2 shafts.

Patrol Vessel (Ex-Yacht).

ISABEL.   1927 *Photo.*

ISABEL (Bath I.W., 1917, taken over 1917). 710 tons*. Dimensions : 230 (*w.l.*) × 26 × 8·6 feet. Guns : 2—3 inch, 50 cal., 2—3 inch, AA 6 smaller. S.H.P. 8400 = 26 kts. Parsons turbine and 2 Normand boilers. Fuel : 216½ tons oil. Complement, 99.

Note.—Was fitted and classed as a Destroyer during the World War.

* Full load is 938 tons.

Presidential Yacht

1937 *courtesy Winton Engine Corpn.*

POTOMAC (ex- U.S. Coast Guard patrol boat *Electra*). (1934). Displacement, 370 tons. Dimensions : 165 × 25¼ × 8½ feet. Machinery : Winton Diesels. H.P. 1,300 = 16.5 kts.

Aircraft Tenders.

Note.—Minesweepers *Avocet, Heron, Lapwing, Swan, Thrush, Gannet, Pelican, Teal* and *Sandpiper*, are now officially rated as Aircraft Tenders (small type) for Patrol Planes.

Building.

CURTISS, ALBEMARLE. Laid down April 25, 1938, and 1939, by New York S.B. Corpn. under 1937 and 1938 Programmes respectively. Displacement : 8,625 tons.

4 smaller Seaplane Tenders, **BARNEGAT, BISCAYNE, CASCO, MACKINAC,** of 1,695 tons displacement are to be built under 1938 and 1939 Programmes at Puget Sound Navy Yard.

(*Classed as Seaplane Tender.*)   1939, *O. W. Waterman*

WRIGHT (ex-Emergency Fleet Corporation Hull *No. 680,* "Type B," launched at Hog Island, April 28th, 1920). Conversion effected by Tietjen & Lang Dry Dock Co., Hoboken, 1920-21. 8,675 tons. Dimensions : 448 (*p.p.* and *o.a.*) × 58 × 27⅝ feet *max.* draught. Guns : 2—5 inch, 51 cal., 2—3 inch, 50 cal. AA., 4 M.G. AA. Designed S.H.P. 6000 = 15 kts. G.E. Curtis geared turbines and 6 Babcock & Wilcox boilers. Oil : 1629 tons. Complement, 311. Fitted as flagship.

Aircraft Tenders—*continued.*

1937 *Official*

LANGLEY (ex-Fleet Collier *Jupiter*, launched Aug. 24th, 1912, converted 1920-21).

Displacement, 11,050 tons. Complement, 341 (excluding flying personnel).

Length, $\begin{cases} w.l. \ 519 \\ o.a. \ 542 \ \text{feet.} \end{cases}$ Beam, $65\frac{1}{2}$ feet. Draught $\begin{cases} Mean, \ 17 \ \text{feet 3 in.} \\ Max., \ 24 \ \text{feet.} \end{cases}$

Guns :
4—5 inch, 51 cal.

Aircraft :
2 (Observation type).

Machinery.—G.E. turbines and electric drive. 2 shafts. Boilers : 3 double-ended cylindrical and 1 auxiliary. S.H.P. (on first trials as Fleet collier) 7152 = 14·99 kts. *Max.* fuel capacity : oil only, 2300 tons.

Engineering Notes.—First large ship of U.S.N. built with electric drive and Melville-McAlpine reducing gear. This system of propulsion proved so successful, that it was adopted for Capital Ships. Two horizontal smoke ducts on port side with hinged extensions which can be lowered. Fitted with Sperry gyro-stabiliser.

General Notes.—Begun at Mare Island N. Yd., October, 1911, and completed as Fleet Collier, 1913. So served till March, 1920, when she was placed out of commission for conversion by Norfolk Navy Yd. into an Aircraft Carrier. In 1937 she was further modified and reclassed as an Aircraft Tender.

CHILDS (1920), **WILLIAMSON** (1919). Ex-destroyers. Displacement : 1,190 tons. Dimensions : 310 (*w.l.*), $314\frac{1}{3}$ (*o.a.*) × $30\frac{2}{3}$ × $9\frac{1}{4}$ feet (*mean* draught). Guns : 2—4 inch, 50 cal., 2 M.G. AA. Machinery : Westinghouse geared turbines. S.H.P. : 26,000 = 35 kts. Boilers : 4 White-Forster.

Note : These 2 vessels are distinguished by numerals 14 and 15 painted on bows.

1934 *Official.*

PATOKA (1919). Displacement : 5,375 tons. Dimensions : $463\frac{1}{4}$ (*p.p.*) × 60 × $26\frac{1}{4}$ feet (*mean* draught). Complement : 156. Guns : 2—5 inch, 2—3 inch AA. Machinery : Quadruple expansion. I.H.P. : 2,900 = 10·5 kts. Boilers : 3 S.E. Oil fuel : 1,109 tons. *Patoka*, though classed as an oiler, is fitted with a mooring mast for airships. Equipment includes workshops for repair of aircraft and storage for petrol.

Mine Layers.

TERROR. Displacement : 6,000 tons. To be built at Philadelphia Navy Yard, under the 1938 Programme. Guns : 6 or 8 —5 inch.

1932 *Photo, Official.*

AROOSTOOK (Cramps, 1907. Ex-S.S. *Bunker Hill*, of Eastern Steamship Corpn., purchased 1917 and converted by Boston N.Yd. into Mine Planter). All details as *Oglala*. Boilers : 8 S.E. H.P. 7000 = 20 kts. Has been employed as Aircraft Tender. Now out of commission.

1932 *Photo, Official.*

OGLALA (Cramps, 1907. Ex-*Shawmut*, ex-S.S. *Massachusetts*, of Eastern Steamship Corpn., purchased 1917 and converted by Boston N.Yd. into Mine Planter). 4,200 tons. Dimensions : 395 (*o.a.*) × $52\frac{1}{6}$ × $14\frac{1}{2}$ feet (*mean*). Guns : 1—5 inch, 51 cal., 2—3 inch AA, 2—6 pdr., 4—1 pdr. Reciprocating engines and 4 S. E. boilers. 2 screws. H.P. and speed uncertain. Oil : 607 tons. Complement : 373. Now out of commission.

Auxiliaries—Destroyer Tenders.

DIXIE (May 27, 1939). Laid down March 17, 1938, by New York S.B. Corpn., under 1937 Programme.

PRAIRIE. Laid down Dec. 7, 1938, by same builders, under 1938 Programme. Displacement : 9,450 tons. Dimensions : 520 (*w.l.*) × 73¼ × — feet.

DOBBIN.   *1925 Official Photo, U.S. Navy Dept.*

WHITNEY (Boston N.Yd., Oct. 12th, 19?3), **DOBBIN** (Philadelphia N.Yd., May 5th, 1921). 8,325 tons. Dimensions : 460 (*p.p.*), 483⅝ (*o.a.*) × 61 × 24¼ feet (*mean* draught). Guns : 8—5 inch, 4—3 inch AA., 2—6 pdr. Torpedo tubes, for testing purposes : 2—21 inch. Parsons geared turbines. Boilers : 2 Bureau Modified Thornycroft. 1 screw. Designed S.H.P. 7000 = 16 kts. Oil : 1107 tons. Complement, 589. Equipped to serve as Depot, Repair and Hospital Ship for 18 Destroyers. Possess special anti-torpedo protection. Generally sister ships to *Holland*, Tender to Submarines. Both fitted as flagships.

ALTAIR.   *1927 Official Photo.*

ALTAIR (1919), **DENEBOLA** (1919), **RIGEL** (1918). 6,250 tons. Dimensions : 423¾ × 54 × 20 feet. Guns : 4—5 inch, 51 cal., 4—3 inch AA., 2—6 pdr. Curtis geared turbines. Boilers : 3 single-ended. S.H.P. 2500 = 10·5 kts. Oil : 1097 tons. Complement, 284 to 590. All three built by Skinner & Eddy Corporation, Seattle.

Destroyer Tenders—*continued.*

Official, added 1935.

MELVILLE (1915). 5,250 tons. Complement, 574. Dimensions : 400 (*p.p.*) × 54½ × 20 feet (*mean* draught). Guns : 8—5 inch (51 cal.), 1—3 inch AA., 2—3 pdr. Torpedo tubes : 1—18 inch. Machinery : Parsons geared turbines. 2 Thornycroft boilers. H.P. (estimated) 4006 = 15·09 kts. Fuel : 930 tons *oil*. Built by New York S.B. Co.

1934 Photo.

BLACK HAWK (Cramp, 1913, ex-Grace Steamship Co. S.S. *Santa Catalina*, taken over 1917). 5,600 tons. Dimensions : 404½ (*p.p.*) × 53¾ × 19¾ feet. Guns : 4—5 inch, 2—3 pdr., 2—1 pdr. Machinery : Quadruple expansion. Boilers : 3 single-ended. I.H.P. 3400 = 13 kts. Oil : 2108 tons. Complement, 685.

Destroyer Tenders—*continued.*

1920 Photo, Seward, Weymouth.

BRIDGEPORT (Vegesack, Germany, 1901, ex-North German Lloyd S.S. *Breslau*, seized 1917). 7,175 tons. Dimensions : 429¼ (*p.p.*) × 54¼ × 24¾ feet. Guns : 8—5 inch, 4—3 inch 50 cal. AA. Machinery : Quadruple expansion. Boilers : 2 double-ended and 2 single-ended. I.H.P. 3600 = 12·5 kts. Coal : 1060 tons. Complement, 552.

Auxiliaries—Submarine Tenders.

FULTON. Displacement : 9,250 tons. Laid down July 19, 1939 at Mare Island Navy Yard, under 1938 Programme.

1937, O. W. Waterman.

HOLLAND (Puget Sound N. Yd., April 12, 1926). Begun April 11th, 1921, completed 1926. 8,100 tons. Dimensions : 460 (*p.p.*), 513 (*o.a.*) × 61 (*extreme*) × 22¾ feet (*mean* draught). Guns : 8—5 inch, 4—3 inch AA., 2—6 pdr. Torpedo tubes : 1—21 inch, *submerged.* Parsons geared turbines. 1 screw. Boilers : 2 Bureau Modified Thornycroft. Designed S.H.P. 7,000 = 16 kts. Oil : 1050 tons. Complement, 398. Generally sister ship to *Whitney* and *Dobbin*, Destroyer Tenders.

Submarine Tenders—*continued.*

Note.—Obsolete Cruiser *Alton*, ex-*Chicago*, Submarine Barracks at Pearl Harbour. Various Minesweepers of " Bird " class serve as Submarine Tenders at New London, Hampton Roads ; Coco Solo, and Pearl Harbour.

ARGONNE. 1930 *Photo, Lt.-Com. H. A. Gosnell, U.S.N.*

ARGONNE (Hog Island, 1920). 8,400 tons. Dimensions : 448×58×24⅔ feet *max.* draught. Guns : 4—5 inch, 51 cal., 4—3 inch, 50 cal. AA., 2—6 pdr. Curtis geared turbines. 1 screw. Boilers : 6 Babcock. S.H.P. 6000 = 15 kts. Oil fuel : 1473 tons. Complement, 344.

1926 *Official Photo.*

CANOPUS (New York S.B. Co., 1919). 5,975 tons. Dimensions : 373¾ × 51½ × 21½ feet. Guns : 2—5 inch, 51 cal., 4—3 inch AA., 2—3 pdr. Machinery: Quadruple expansion. 1 screw. Boilers : 4 single-ended. H.P. 3858 = 13 kts. Oil : 1277 tons. Complement, 317.

Auxiliaries—Submarine Tenders—*continued.*

BEAVER. 1935, *courtesy of U.S. Naval Institute, Annapolis, Md.*

BEAVER (Newport News, 1910, purchased 1918). 4,670 tons. Dimensions : 380 (*o.a.*) × 47 × 22⅔ feet (*max.* draught), Guns : 4 —5 inch, 2—1 pdr. 1 screw. Boilers : 6 single-ended. I.H.P. 4500 = 16·5 kts. Fuel : 530 tons oil fuel. Complement, 350.

1935, *Bear Photo Service.*

CAMDEN (Flensburger S. B. Co., 1900, ex-German-Australian s.s. *Kiel*, seized 1917). Displacement : 6,075 tons. Dimensions : 403⅔ (*o.a.*) × 48 × 22½ feet. Guns : 4—4 inch, 2—3 pdr., 2—1 pdr. Boilers : 4 Babcock. I.H.P. 2550 = 12 kts. Coal : 975 tons. Complement, 378.

Auxiliaries—Ammunition Ships.

PYRO. 1924 *Official Photo.*

NITRO, PYRO (both launched Dec. 16th, 1919, at Puget Sound N.Yd.). 7,025 tons. Dimensions : 460 × 61 × 21 feet. Guns : 4—5 inch, 2—3 inch AA. Boilers : 4 Babcock. S.H.P. 6700 = 13·3 kts. (*N.*), 13·2 kts. (*P*). Parsons (geared) turbines. 2 screws. Fuel capacity : 1078 tons coal (*Nitro*), 1493 tons oil (*Pyro*). Fitted with plant for powder testing and cooling, also large cold storage capacity for meat, in addition to ammunition-carrying spaces. Complement, 195.

Auxiliaries—Miscellaneous.

(Experimental Vessel).

SEMMES (1918). Ex-destroyer of Flush Deck type. Displacement : 1,190 tons. Dimensions : 311 (*w.l.*), 314½ (*o.a.*) × 30⅔ × 13½ feet (*mean* draught). No guns mounted. Machinery : Westinghouse geared turbines. S.H.P. : 26,000 = 35 kts. Boilers : 4 White-Forster.

Auxiliaries—Store Ships.

ARCTIC.   1926 *Official Photo.*

ARCTIC (1919), **BOREAS** (1919), **YUKON** (1920). 4,980 tons. Dimensions : 416½ × 53 × 26½ feet. Guns : 2—5 inch, 51 cal., 4—3 inch AA. (not always carried). Parsons geared turbines in *Arctic* and *Yukon*, Curtis in *Boreas*. Designed H.P. 2800 = 11 kts. Boilers : 4 Heine, except *Yukon*, 3 single-ended. Oil : 1794 tons. Complements : 166 (*Y*), 180 (*B*), 211 (*A*).

1935, *Bear Photo Service.*

BRIDGE (Boston N.Yd., May 18th, 1916). 5,000 tons. Complement, 212. Dimensions : 423 × 55¼ × 20⅔ feet (*mean draught*). Guns : 4—5 inch, 50 cal., 1—3 inch AA., 2—3 pdr. Boilers : 2 White-Forster. H.P. 4000 = 14 kts. Reciprocating engines. 2 screws. Fuel : 1000 tons *oil*. Fitted with towing winch, and has been employed as target towing vessel.

Auxiliaries—Repair Ships.

VULCAN. Displacement : 9,100 tons. Building by New York Shipbuilding Corporation under 1939 Programme.

1925 *Photo, W. W. Stewart, Esq.*

(Pacific Fleet.)

MEDUSA (Puget Sound N.Yd., April 16th, 1923). 8,125 tons. Dimensions : 460 × 70 × 20 feet. Guns : 4—5 inch, 51 cal., 2—3 inch AA., 2—6 pdr., 4—30 cal. Parsons geared turbines. Designed S.H.P. 7000 = 16 kts. 2 Bureau Modified Thornycroft boilers. Oil : 1834 tons. Complement, 466 (including an exceptionally full technical staff).

Note.—The *Medusa* was specially designed with a view to the execution of permanent as well as temporary repairs. She carries two 8 ton derricks, besides one 20 ton, one 10 ton and two 8 ton shear legs. Machinery is installed aft. Equipment includes a medical and hospital section.

VESTAL.   1935, *Bear Photo Service.*

PROMETHEUS (Mare Island N.Yd., 1908). **VESTAL** (New York N. Yd., 1908). Displacement 6,625 tons. Dimensions : 450 × 60 × 18 feet. Guns : 4—5 inch, 50 cal., 1—3 inch AA., 4—30 cal. Machinery : Triple expansion. Boilers : *Prometheus*, 6 Babcock ; *Vestal*, 2 White-Forster. H.P. 7,500 = 16 kts. Oil : *Prometheus*, 872 tons ; *Vestal*, 928 tons. Complement : 466. (Both re-engined in 1937).

Auxiliaries—Colliers.

NEREUS.   *Photo added* 1921.

NEREUS (1913), **PROTEUS** (1912). 6,275 tons. Dimensions : 522 × 62 × 27⅔ (*mean*). 2 screws. Boilers : 3 double-ended. H.P. 7000 = 14 kts. Fuel capacity (deadweight to designed draft) : 10,500 tons cargo fuel, Bunker capacity, 2,000 tons. *Maximum* cargo capacity (close stowage) : 11,800 tons coal + 1125 tons oil *or* 10,100 tons coal + 3050 tons oil. Guns : 4—4 inch, 50 cal. Complement, 181.

Auxiliaries—Oilers.

CIMARRON (Jan. 7, 1939), **NEOSHO** (April 29, 1939), **PLATTE** (July 8, 1939). Displacement : 8,000 tons (16,375 tons deadweight). Complement : 64. Dimensions : 525 (*w.l.*), 553 (*o.a.*) × 75 × 29⅝ feet. Machinery : Geared turbines. S.H.P. : 13,000 = 18 kts. (*Cimarron* trials, 19·28 kts.). Radius reported to be 18,000 miles. Cargo capacity exceeds 6,000,000 gallons. Provided for under 1938 Programme.

SALINAS.   1939.

RAPIDAN (1919), **SALINAS** (1920), **TIPPECANOE** (1920), **RAMAPO** (1919), **SAPELO** (1919), **SEPULGA** (1920), **TRINITY** (1920). 5,375 tons. Dimensions : 463¼ (*p.p.*) × 60 × 26¼ feet (*mean draught*). Quad. Exp. reciprocating engines † 3 S. E. boilers. I.H.P. 2900 = 10·5 kts. Guns : 2—5 inch, 51 cal., 2—3 inch AA. *Max.* cargo capacity : 11,145 tons oil fuel. Own fuel : 1109 tons oil. Complement, 107.

†Curtis turbine in *Trinity* and *Tippecanoe.*

Auxiliaries—Oilers—continued.

Photo wanted.

KAWEAH (1919), **LARAMIE** (1920), **MATTOLE** (1920), 4,410 tons. Dimensions: 446 (o.a.) × 58 × 25½ feet. Guns: 2—5 inch, 51 cal., 2—3 inch AA. Reciprocating engines and 3 S. E. boilers. H.P. 2800 = 11 kts. Cargo capacity, 8850 tons. Own fuel, 1288 tons. Complement, 107.

KANAWHA (& MAUMEE). 1935, *Bear Photo Service*.

BRAZOS (and remainder). 1927 *Official Photo*.

CUYAMA (1916), **MAUMEE** (1915), **KANAWHA** (1914). 4,990 tons. Complement: 249—475.

BRAZOS (1919), **NECHES** (1920), **PECOS** (1921), 5,400 tons. Complements: 227—317. Dimensions: 475⅔ (o.a.) × 56 × 26⅔ feet (mean). Guns: 4—5 inch, 51 cal., 2—3 inch. Machinery: Vert. triple expansion. H.P.: 5,200 = 14 kts.; except *Maumee*, 6 cyl. 2-cycle Diesels, H.P.: 5,000 = 14 kts. Boilers: 4 Ward in *Neches* and *Pecos*, 4 B. & W. in others, except *Maumee*, 2 B. & W. Cargo capacity: 7,850 tons. Own fuel: 820 tons. *Cuyama, Kanawha, Maumee,* have towing winches.

Auxiliaries—Cargo Ships.

SANTA RITA (1929). Ex-Grace liner, purchased 1939. Displacement: 6,000 tons. Dimensions: 380 × 53 × 21½ feet. Machinery: Diesel. 2 shafts. B.H.P.: 4,700 = 14 kts. Oil fuel: 1,484 tons.

ANTARES (1919). 5,050 tons.

REGULUS, GOLD STAR (*ex Arcturus*) (1920). 4,860 tons.

CAPELLA (1920), **SIRIUS** (1919), **SPICA** (1919), **VEGA** (1919). 4,070 tons. Dimensions: 401 × 54 × 24½ feet. Guns: 2—5 inch, 51 cal., 4—3 inch AA. Curtis geared turbines. 3 Babcock boilers. H.P. 2500 = 11·5 kts. Oil: 1222 tons. Complement, 106.

Antares flagship Training Squadron, Scouting Fleet, Atlantic, and is fitted as Target Repair Vessel, carrying special photographic apparatus for recording results of target practice.

Auxiliaries—Hospital Ship.

1935 *Official*.

RELIEF (Dec., 1919, Philadelphia N.Y.). 7,275 tons. Dimensions: 460 (p.p.) × 61 × 19½ feet. Designed H.P. 5250 = 16 kts. Parsons geared turbines. 2 screws. 3 Babcock and Wilcox boilers. Oil: 1951 tons. Complement, 397.

Auxiliaries—Transports.

1935, *Bear Photo Service*.

CHAUMONT (Hog Island, 1920). 8,300 tons. Dimensions: 448 × 58 × 23 feet. Guns: *Nil.* 1 screw. G.E. Curtis geared turbines. Boilers: 6 Babcock. S.H.P. 6000 = 15 kts. Oil: 1473 tons. Complement, 249.

MANLEY (1917). Ex-destroyer. Displacement: 1,020 tons. Dimensions: 308 (w.l.), 315½ (o.a.) × 20⅔ × 7½ feet (mean draught). Guns: 4—4 inch, 50 cal. Machinery: Parsons geared turbines. S.H.P.: 18,000 = 32 kts. Boilers: 4 Normand.

1935, *Bear Photo Service*.

HENDERSON (1916). 7,750 tons. Complement, 424. Dimensions: 483⅝ (o.a.) × 61 × 20 feet (mean draught). Guns: 8—5 inch, 51 cal., 2—3 inch, 2—3 pdr., 2—1 pdr. H.P. 4000 = 14 kts. Reciprocating engines. Boilers: 3 Babcock. 2 screws. Fuel: 1400 tons *oil.* Has Sperry gyro. stabilisers. To take 2000 men and 32 horses.

FLEET AUXILIARIES.

Auxiliaries—Fleet Tugs.

Note.—Other and Smaller Tugs attached to Naval Districts, rated as "Harbor Tugs."

CHEROKEE, NAVAJO, SEMINOLE. Displacement: 1,150 tons. Building under 1938 Programme, by Bethlehem New York Plant, Staten Island. Diesel engines. All three laid down Dec., 1938.

PINOLA. 1932 *Photo, Official.*

ALGORMA, BAGADUCE, IUKA, KALMIA, KEOSANQUA, KEWAYDIN, MAHOPAC, MONTCALM (ex-*Kineo*), **NAPA, PINOLA, SCIOTA, SUNNADIN, TATNUCK, UMPQUA, WANDANK.** All launched 1919-20. 795 tons. **ALLEGHENY** (1917), **SAGAMORE** (1917). 735 tons. Dimensions: 149⅓ (*p.p.*) × 30 × 11¾/12⅓ feet (*mean*). Guns: 2—3 inch AA. I.H.P. 1800 = 13 to 14 kts. Oil: 279 tons.

TAMAROA. 1931 *Photo.*

CAHOKIA, TAMAROA (1919). **BAY SPRING** (1920). 510 tons. Dimensions: 151¼ × 27½ × 10½ feet. Guns: 2—1 pdr. Speed: 11 kts. Oil fuel.

UNDAUNTED (1917). 475 tons. Dimensions: 143 (*o.a.*) × 28 × 15 feet. Guns: 1—3 inch AA. I.H.P.: 1,000 = 11·5 kts. Oil fuel: 329 tons.

Auxiliaries—Fleet Tugs—*continued.*

ACUSHNET (1908). Steel, 1 screw. 645 tons. Dimensions: 152 × 29 × 13 feet. Speed: 12·5 kts.

SONOMA (1912) and **ONTARIO** (1912). 1,030 and 1,080 tons. Dimensions: 175 (*p.p.*) × 34 × 12½ feet (*mean*). Guns: 1—3 inch, 1—3 inch AA. Speed: 13 kts. Coal: 440 tons (*average*).

GENESEE (ex-*Monocacy*, 1905, bought 1917). 745 tons. Guns: 2—3 inch. I.H.P. 1000 = 15 kts. Coal: 286 tons.

Mine-Sweepers.

Notes.—*Avocet, Heron, Lapwing, Thrush, Gannet, Pelican, Sandpiper, Swan,* and *Teal* are all classed as Aircraft Tenders (small type) for Patrol Planes; each carries a seaplane aft. *Seagull, Quail,* have been used as Submarine Tenders; *Redwing* has been transferred to Coast Guard (see a later page); *Falcon, Mallard, Chewink, Ortolan, Pigeon, Widgeon* classed as Submarine Rescue Vessels; *Whippoorwill* at Pearl Harbor.

RAVEN, OSPREY. Laid down June 28, 1939, under 1938 Programme at Norfolk Navy Yard. Displacement: 650 tons. Fairbanks Morse Diesel engines.

ORTOLAN. 1935, *Bear Photo Service.*

("BIRD" CLASS—41 BOATS.)

LAPWING, OWL, ROBIN, CHEWINK, CORMORANT, GANNET (all built by Todd S. B. Co., Tebo Yacht Basin, Brooklyn, N. Y.). **TANAGER, ORIOLE, GREBE, MALLARD, ORTOLAN, PEACOCK** (all built by Staten Id. S. B. Co., N. Y.). **AVOCET, BOBOLINK, LARK, PIGEON** (all built by Baltimore D. D. & S. B. Co.). **PELICAN, FALCON, SEAGULL, TERN** (all built by Gas Engine & Power Co., Morris Heights. N. Y.). **TURKEY, WOODCOCK, QUAIL, PARTRIDGE** (all built by Chester S. B. Co.). **SANDPIPER, WARBLER, VIREO, WILLET** (all built by Philadelphia Navy Yard). **SWAN, WHIPPOORWILL, BITTERN** (all built by Alabama

Fleet Auxiliaries—U.S.A.

Mine-Sweepers—*continued.*

S. B. & D. D. Co., Mobile). **WIDGEON, TEAL, BRANT** (all built by Sun S. B. Co., Chester). **KINGFISHER, RAIL** (both built by Puget Sound Navy Yard). **EIDER, THRUSH** (both built by Pusey & Jones, Wilmington). **FINCH, HERON** (both built by Standard S. B. Co., N. Y.). **PENGUIN** (built by New Jersey D. D. & T. Co., Elizabethport).

All built 1918-19. Displacement: 840 tons except *Chewink*, 960 tons; *Falcon, Mallard, Ortolan, Pigeon, Widgeon*, all 1,060 tons. Dimensions: 187⅞ *o.a.* × 35½ × 8⅚ to 10½ feet (*mean* draught). Guns: 2—3 inch AA. Machinery: 1 set triple expansion and 2 B. & W. boilers. Designed I.H.P. 1400 = 14 kts. Oil fuel only: 275 tons. Complement, 52 to 90 (according to employment of ship).

Surveying Ships.

BUSHNELL. 1919 *U.S. Navy Photo.*

BUSHNELL (Seattle Constrn. and D.D. Co., 1915). 2,900 tons. Complement: 217. Dimensions: 350½ × 45⅔ × 15 feet (*mean* draught). Guns: 4—5 inch (51 cal.). Machinery: Parsons turbines with reduction gear. Boilers: 2 Yarrow. H.P. (*on trials*) 2617 = 14·15 kts. Fuel: 728 tons *oil*. (Ex-Submarine Tender).

HANNIBAL. 1934 *Photo.*

HANNIBAL (ex-S.S. *Joseph Holland*). (Sunderland, 1898). Ex-Fuel Ship 2,160 tons. Dimensions: 274 × 39¼ × 15½ feet. Guns: 1—6 inch, 40 cal., 2—3 inch AA. Complement, 163. H.P. 1100 = 9 kts. Coal: 855 tons. (Being replaced by ex-Grace liner *Santa Inez*, sister ship to *Santa Rita*, recorded on preceding page.)

Notes.

Officially Revised, 1939, from materials furnished by courtesy of the Commandant, U.S. Coast Guard, Treasury Department, Washington, D.C Photos also official unless otherwise acknowledged.

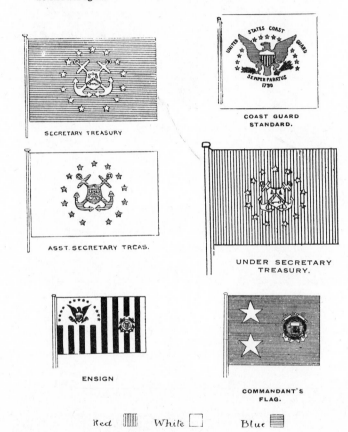

COAST GUARD STANDARD.

SECRETARY TREASURY

ASST. SECRETARY TREAS.

UNDER SECRETARY TREASURY.

ENSIGN

COMMANDANT'S FLAG.

Red [image] White [image] Blue [image]

I.—ESTABLISHMENT.

The U.S. Coast Guard was established by the consolidation of the Revenue-Cutter Service and the Life Saving Service by the Act of Congress approved 28 January, 1915. This act constituted the Coast Guard as a part of the military forces of the United States, " which shall operate under the Treasury Department in time of peace and operate as a part of the Navy in time of war or when the President shall so direct."

II.—DUTIES.

1. The Principal duties of the Coast Guard are the enforcement of the maritime laws of the United States and the saving of life and assistance to vessels in distress.

2. Law enforcement duties, performed for all departments of the government, include those relating to customs, movements and anchorage of vessels, immigration, quarantine, neutrality, navigation and other laws governing merchant vessels and motor boats, safety of life on navigable waters during regattas, oil pollution, sponge fisheries, protection of game and the seal and other fisheries in Alaska, protection of bird reservations established by Executive Order and the suppression of mutinies.

3. Life saving and assistance duties include the maintenance of coastal stations and communication lines on the continental coasts of the United States, the conduct of the International Ice Patrol, derelict destruction, winter cruising on the Atlantic coast, the extension of medical aid to fishing vessels, the Bering Sea Patrol, and flood relief work. In its humanitarian duties the Coast Guard renders aid and assistance to vessels in distress irrespective of nationality and extends its protection, if needed, to all shipping within the scope of its operations.

4. In time of war the Coast Guard operates as a part of the Navy. A military organization was adopted at the time the service was established in 1790, before the establishment of the Navy Department. This organization has been continued since that date for the purpose of maintaining the general efficiency of the operation of the service in its law enforcement duties in time of peace. The executive action under which the Coast Guard operates as a part of the Navy in time of war is similar in effect to a measure of mobilization. In this respect the Coast Guard is a potential reserve force for the Navy. No personnel are normally assigned or equipped as land troops. Vessels are prepared in emergencies to equip landing forces with small arms and machine guns; stations are similarly prepared to undertake emergency police duties in a more limited sense, because of the smaller units involved, but in both cases these duties would be incidental to the primary purpose of the service, the enforcement of civil law and the saving of life and property.

III.—ADMINISTRATION.

Secretary of the Treasury : The Honorable Henry Morgenthau, Jun.
Assistant Secretary of the Treasury * : The Honorable Stephen B. Gibbons.
Headquarters : (Washington, D.C.)
Commandant : Rear-Admiral R. R. Waesche.
* The Assistant Secretary has immediate supervision of the Coast Guard.

IV.—ORGANIZATION.

(a) The United States and its coastal waters are divided into nine divisions, each being under the command of a division commander operating directly under Coast Guard Headquarters in Washington. These divisions in turn include thirteen districts for the operation of 241 Coast Guard (Life Saving) Stations and the vessels and shore establishments assigned.

(b) The following training, repair, and supply establishments are maintained :
(1) Coast Guard Academy, New London, Connecticut. Four year course for cadets (entry by competitive examination).

(2) Coast Guard Receiving Unit and the Coast Guard Institute, New London, Connecticut. Training and educational courses for enlisted ratings.

(3) Coast Guard Depot, Curtis Bay, Maryland. Construction of life-boats, etc. Repair of vessels.

(4) Coast Guard Stores, Brooklyn, New York, and San Francisco, California. Supply depots for ships and stations.

V.—PERSONNEL.

(Total authorised complement : 10,188.)
Ranks : Rear Admiral (2).
Engineer-in-Chief (Ranks as Captain) (1).

	Line	Engineering	Constructor	District Commander
Captain	23	8	—	—
Commander	46	13	1	—
Lieutenant Commander ..	87	—	2	12
Lieutenant	173	—	2	4
Lieut. (j.g.) & Ensign ..	372	—	—	—

Professors : 5 (ranks from Lieut. to Commander)
Chief Warrant Officers : 393. Warrant Officers : 148.
Petty Officers and Men : 8,896. (Enlist for three years ; pay as U.S. Navy.)
Uniforms of officers and men are similar to those of U.S. Navy, but commissioned officers wear a gold shield on the sleeve instead of a star, and cap device is a gold spread-eagle, the talons grasping a horizontal foul anchor. A silver shield is mounted on the eagle's breast. Men of C.G. wear a shield on the sleeve.

VI.—VESSELS.

The vessels in commission on 1 July, 1939, consisted of 36 cruising cutters, 12 harbour tugs, 17 165-ft. patrol boats, 32 125-ft. patrol boats, 1 100-ft. patrol boat, 9 80-ft. patrol boats, 46 75-ft. patrol boats, 2 72-ft. patrol boats, 2 65-ft. patrol boats, 8 miscellaneous patrol boats, 8 special craft, 100 picket boats and about 1,800 life, station and small boats of various types.

VII.—AVIATION.

Air Stations in commission : 8. Location : Salem, Mass. ; Charleston, S.C. ; New York, N.Y. ; Miami, Fla. ; St. Petersburg, Fla. ; Biloxi, Miss. ; San Diego, Calif. ; Port Angeles, Wash. ; Elizabeth City, N.C. ; San Francisco, Calif.

VIII.—U.S. MARITIME SERVICE.

The establishment of the U.S. Maritime Service was authorized in June, 1938, as a part of the U.S. Maritime Commission. The administration of the Service is under the immediate supervision of the Commandant of the Coast Guard. The organization maintains training stations for unlicensed personnel at New York City and Oakland, California, and for licensed personnel at New London, Conn. and Oakland, California.

The training ships *American Seaman*, *Northland*, *Joseph Conrad*, and *Tusitala* are operated by the Service, the latter two being square-rigged ships.

Enrolment in the Maritime Service is limited to licensed and unlicensed personnel of the merchant marine who have been at least two years on American vessels.

Cruising Cutters.

GEO. W. CAMPBELL   1938, *Official.*

Observe seaplane   1939, *Official.*

GEORGE W. CAMPBELL .. *Stapleton, N.Y.*

SAMUEL D. INGHAM .. .. *Port Angeles, Wash.*

WILLIAM J. DUANE .. .. *Oakland, Calif.*

ROGER B. TANEY .. .. *Honolulu, T.H.*

All laid down May 1, 1935 at Philadelphia Navy Yard and launched June 3, 1936.

ALEXANDER HAMILTON .. *Oakland, Calif.*

JOHN C. SPENCER .. .. *Cordova, Alaska*

Both laid down at New York Navy Yard, Sept. 11, 1935, and launched Nov. 10, 1936, and Jan. 6, 1937, respectively.

GEORGE M. BIBB .. .. *Norfolk, Va.*

Laid down at Charleston Navy Yard, Aug. 15, 1935 and launched Jan. 14, 1937.

Standard displacement : 2,000 tons. Dimensions : 308 (*w.l.*), 327 (*o.a.*) × 41 × 11¼ feet (*mean draught*), 12¼ feet (*max.*). Guns : 2—5 inch, 2 quad. M.G. AA., 2—6 pdr. (with provision for mounting 2 extra 5 inch if needed). 1 Seaplane carried in some, with only one 5 inch gun. Westinghouse geared turbines. 2 shafts. S.H.P.: 6,200 = 20 kts. 2 wt. boilers. Fuel : 572 tons. Feed water : 143 tons, fresh water : 109 tons. Cruising radius : 8,000 miles at 12·5 kts.

Cruising Cutters—*continued.*

COMANCHE.   1935, *Official.*

Name.	Station.	Name.	Station.
ALGONQUIN	*Portland, Me.*	**ONONDAGA**	*Astoria, Oregon*
COMANCHE	*Stapleton, N.Y.*	**TAHOMA**	*Cleveland, Ohio*
MOHAWK	*Cape May, N.J.*	**ESCANABA**	*Grand Haven, Mich.*

All launched 1934 except *Escanaba,* 1932. Steel, strengthened for icebreaking. First 3 built by Pusey & Jones Corpn., Wilmington, Del., second 3 by Defoe Works, Bay City, Mich. Displacement : 1,005 tons. Complement : 60. Dimensions : 165 (*o.a.*) × 36 × 13⅛ feet. Guns : 2—3 inch, 50 cal., 2—6 pdr. Machinery : Turbines with double reduction gear. S.H.P: 1,500 = 13·5 kts. Radius : 5,000 miles. Approximate average inclusive cost, $584,000 each. These ships are reported to be very successful in service, making good headway through ice nearly 2 feet thick.

Cruising Cutters—*continued.*

CAYUGA.   1937, *Hr. Registrator Ossi Janson.*

CAYUGA (Oct. 8, 1931). *Boston, Mass.* Built by United D.D. Co., Staten Island, N.Y. Steel. Displacement : 1,975 tons. Dimensions : 250 (*o.a.*) × 42 × 16 feet. Turbo-Electric engines (1 main, 2 auxiliary). H.P.: 3,220 = 16 kts. 2 Babcock & Wilcox boilers. Oil fuel : 335 tons. Guns : 2—5 inch, 2—6 pdrs. Radius : 8,000 miles.

CHELAN.   1929 *Photo.*

Name.	Station.	Name.	Station.
ITASCA	*San Diego, Calif.*	**CHELAN** ..	*Boston, Mass.*
SEBAGO ..	*Norfolk, Va.*	**CHAMPLAIN**	*Stapleton, N.Y.*
SARANAC	*Galveston, Texas*	**MENDOTA** ..	*Norfolk, Va.*
SHOSHONE	*Oakland, Calif.*	**PONTCHARTRAIN**	*Stapleton, N.Y.*

Built 1930 by Gen. Eng. & Dry Dock Co., Oakland.

TAHOE *New Bedford, Mass.* Built 1928–29 by Bethlehem Shipbuilding Corporation at Quincy, Mass.

All similar to *Cayuga* above, but *Pontchartrain* has only 2—6 pdrs.

Cruising Cutters—continued.

NORTHLAND. (Rig modified). 1936.

NORTHLAND (Newport News Shipbuilding Co., 1927). Built of steel, hull being of exceptionally massive construction, to withstand ice pressure. Forefoot cut away to above w.l. Displacement: 2065 tons. Dimensions: 216 (o.a.) × 39 × 15 feet (mean draught). Two 6-cyl. 4-cycle Diesel engines with electric drive. Total B.H.P. 1200 = 11 kts. 1 screw. Guns: 2—6 pdr. Built for Bering Sea Patrol, but now used as a seagoing training ship. (Oakland, Calif.).

1938, Official.

SHAWNEE (1922). Steel. 900 tons. Dimensions: $158\frac{1}{4}$ × 30 × 14 feet. Guns: 2—1 pdr. Built by Union Con. Co., Oakland, Cal. Refitted completely, 1938. (Eureka, Calif.)

Cruising Cutters—continued.

TAMPA.

Name.				Station.
HAIDA	..	..	..	Juneau, Alaska.
MODOC	..	..	..	Wilmington, N.C.
MOJAVE	..	..	..	Miami, Fla.
TAMPA	..	..	..	Mobile, Ala.

All built 1921. Steel, 1 screw. 1780 tons. Dimensions: 240 × 39 × $16\frac{1}{2}$ feet. Guns: 2—5 inch, 1—3 inch AA., 2—6 pdr. S.H.P. 2600 = 15 kts. Machinery: Turbo-electric (General Electric Curtis Turbine).
All built by Gen. Eng. & Dry Dock Co., Oakland, Cal.

(For appearance, v. photo under "Auxiliaries—Mine Sweepers," in U.S. Navy Section.)

REDWING (1919.) Ex-Navy Minesweeper, taken over 1924. Steel, 1 screw. Standard displacement: 840 tons. Dimensions: $187\frac{5}{8}$ × $35\frac{1}{2}$ × $12\frac{1}{2}$ feet (mean draught). Speed: 12·8 kts. Guns: 2—3 inch, 23 cal., 2—1 pdr. (Port Angeles, Wash).

1920 Photo.

OSSIPEE (1915). Steel, 1 screw. 997 tons. Dimensions: $165\frac{5}{6}$ × 32 × $11\frac{3}{4}$ feet. Speed: 12 kts. Guns: 2- 3 inch, 2—6 pdr., 2—1 pdr. Strengthened for ice navigation. (Sault Ste. Marie, Mich.).

Cruising Cutters—continued.

1920 Photo.

TALLAPOOSA (1915). Steel, 1 screw, 964 tons. Dimensions: $165\frac{3}{4}$ × 32 × 11 feet, Speed: 11·8 kts. Oil fuel only. Guns: 2—3 inch, 50 cal., 2—6 pdr. (Savannah, Ga.).

1919 Photo, U.S. Navy Publicity Bureau.

UNALGA (1912). Steel, 1 screw. 1181 tons. Dimensions: 190 × $32\frac{1}{2}$ × 14 feet. Speed: 12 kts. Guns: 2—6 pdr. (San Juan, Puerto Rico).

Cruising Cutters—*continued.*

PAMLICO (1907). Steel, twin screw. 451 tons. Dimensions : 158 × 30 × 5⅔ feet. Speed : 9·3 kts. Guns : 2—6 pdr. (*Newbern, N.C.*)

Special Craft.

1938, *Official*

PEQUOT (ex-Minelayer *General Samuel M. Mills*, built 1909, transferred from War Department 1922). Steel, 1 screw. 950 tons. Dimensions : 166½ × 32½ × 11⅓ feet. 12 kts. (*Boston, Mass.*)

Harbour Craft—Tug Type (14).

Detailed to larger Maritime Ports to enforce Customs and Navigation Laws and the regulation of the anchorage and movements of vessels.

NAUGATUCK   1939, *Official*

ARUNDEL (June 24, 1939), **MAHONING** (July 22, 1939), **NAUGATUCK, RARITAN** (both March 23, 1939) Former pair built by Gulfport Works, Port Arthur, Texas ; latter pair by Defoe Works, Bay City, Mich. Displacement : 328 tons. Dimensions : 110 × 26½ × 10½ feet (*mean draught*). Machinery : Diesel-electric. S.H.P. : 1,000 = 12 kts. Strengthened for icebreaking. Respective Stations : *New York* (former pair), *Boston* and *Philadelphia*.

Note.—These 4 vessels are an improvement on design of *Hudson* class. Reported to be better sea boats.

TUCKAHOE.   1935, *Official.*

Calumet, Navesink, Tuckahoe, (Built at Charleston Navy Yard.) **Hudson** (Built at Portsmouth Navy Yard). All launched 1934. Steel. Displacement : 290 tons. Dimensions : 110½ × 24 × 10½ feet. Diesel engines. 1 shaft. H.P.: 800 = 12 kts. Radius : 2,000 miles. (*New York*).

Harbour Craft—*continued.*

Davey (1908). Steel, 1 screw. 182 tons. Dimensions : 92½ × 19 × 10½ feet. Guns : *Nil*. Speed : 10·5 kts. (*New Orleans, La.*)

Guthrie (1895). Iron, 1 screw. 149 tons. Dimensions : 88 × 17½ × 9 feet. Speed : 11 kts. (*Boston*).

MANHATTAN.   1938, *Official.*

Manhattan (1918). Steel, 1 Screw. Ice Breaker, Salvage Vessel, Tug and Fire Float. 406 tons. Dimensions : 120¼ × 24 × 11¾ feet. Speed : 9·5 kts. Guns : 2—1 pdr. (*New York, N.Y.*)

Winnisimmet (1903). Steel, 1 screw. 182 tons. Dimensions : 96½ × 20½ × 9 feet. Speed : 12 kts. (*Baltimore*).

AB 26.   1937 *Official.*

A.B. 25, 26 (Boston, Mass., 1936). Wood, sheathed. Displacement : 72 tons. Dimensions : 63½ × 19 × 5 feet. Diesel engine. 1 shaft. H.P. : 300 = 10 kts.

There are also 40 anchorage and boarding vessels, known as AB. boats and bearing numbers with the prefix AB, from 1 to 68, employed on harbour duties.

U.S.A.—Coast Guard

Patrol Boats.

ARGO. (AURORA, CALYPSO, DAPHNE, PERSEUS have only one funnel.)   1933 *Photo*.

17—165 ft. steel Patrol Boats.

					Station.
Argo ..	..	..	..	..	Newport, R.I.
Aurora	..	..	..	..	San Pedro, Cal.
Calypso	..	..	..	..	Baltimore, Md.
Daphne	..	..	..	..	Oakland, Cal.
Galatea	..	..	..	..	Stapleton, N.Y.
Hermes	..	..	..	..	San Pedro, Cal.
Icarus	..	..	..	..	Stapleton, N.Y.
Perseus	..	..	..	..	San Diego, Cal.
Thetis	..	..	..	..	Boston, Mass.
Ariadne	..	..	..	..	Oakland, Cal.
Atalanta	..	..	..	..	Seattle, Wash.
Cyane	..	..	..	..	Ketchikan, Alaska
Dione	..	..	..	..	Norfolk, Va.
Nemesis	..	..	..	..	St. Petersburg, Fla.
Nike	..	..	..	..	Pascagoula, Miss.
Pandora	..	..	..	..	Key West, Fla.
Triton	..	..	..	..	Gulfport, Miss.

Built during 1931–34. 337 tons. Dimensions : 165 × 25¼ × 8½ feet. Guns : 1—3 inch, 23 cal., 2—1 pdr. Winton Diesel engines. 2 shafts in some, 1 in others. H.P. : 1,300 = 16·5 kts.
Note.—*Electra*, of this class, renamed *Potomac* and converted into Presidential Yacht.

Patrol Boats—*continued*.

1939, *Official*.

32—125 ft. steel Patrol Boats: ***Active, Alert, Antietam, Cahoone, Colfax, Crawford, Diligence, Dix, Ewing, Faunce, Frederick Lee, General Greene, Harriet Lane, Jackson, Kimball, Legare, Marion, McLane, Morris, Pulaski, Reliance, Rush, Tiger, Travis, Vigilant, Woodbury, Yeaton, Agassiz, Bonham, Boutwell, Cartigan, Nemaha*** (1926-27). Displacement : 220 tons. Dimensions : 125 × 23½ × 6¾ feet. Guns : 1—3 inch, 23 cal. H.P. 300 = 14 kts. All being re-engined, and after refit vary considerably from original appearance.

Kimball and *Yeaton* employed on training duties.

Patrol Boats—*continued*.

FORWARD.   1934 *Photo, Official*.

2—100 ft. steel Patrol Boats: ***Forward, Nansemond.*** (Defoe Boat & Motor Works, Bay City, Mich., 1925–26). Displacement : 210 tons. Dimensions : 99⅔ × 23 × 8 feet. Guns : 1—3 inch, 23 cal. Diesel engines. 2 shafts. Speed : 10 kts.

Patrol Boats—continued.

1937 *Official.*

9—80 ft. Patrol Boats : **CG** 406—414. (Jacksonville, Fla. 1937). Wood. Displacement : 52 tons. Dimensions : $80\frac{1}{4} \times 15\frac{2}{3} \times$ 4 feet. Guns : 1—1 pdr. 4 petrol engines. 2 shafts. H.P. : 1,600 = 25 kts.

1932 *Photo.*

6—78 ft. Patrol Boats : **CG** 400—405. (Newport News, 1931). (*West Coast and Honolulu*). Wood. Displacement : 43 tons. Guns : 1—1 pdr. H.P. : 1,070 = 21·7 kts.

Patrol Boats—continued.

CG 182.   *Photo added* 1927.

46—75 ft. Patrol Boats : **CG**—119 to **CG**—283. (1924–25). Wood. Displacement : 37 tons. Dimensions : $75 \times 13\frac{3}{4} \times$ 4 feet. Petrol engine. H.P. : 400 = 13·5 kts. Guns : 1— 1 pdr.

Note.—A boat of this type, *CG* 274, was sold to Nicaragua in 1938. Three more CG 110, 144, 302, have been acquired by the Dominican Republic.

1937 *Official.*

2—72 ft. Patrol Boats : **CG** 440, 441. (Annapolis, Md., 1937). Wood. Displacement : 27 tons. Dimensions : $72 \times 14\frac{1}{6} \times$ $3\frac{3}{4}$ feet. 4 petrol engines. 2 shafts. H.P. : 1,600 = 34 kts. (*Norfolk, Va.*)

(Of similar appearance to *CG* 440).

2—65 ft. Patrol Boats : **CG** 442, 443. (Long Beach, Calif., 1937). Wood. Displacement : 30 tons. Dimensions : $65 \times 14 \times$ $3\frac{3}{4}$ feet. 4 petrol engines. 2 shafts. H.P. : 1,600 = 28 kts. (*San Francisco*).

Training Ships.

1939, *Official.*

AMERICAN SEAMAN (ex-*Edgemoor*), (1919). 7,038 tons *gross*. Dimensions : $409\frac{1}{2} \times 54\frac{1}{4} \times 27$ feet. Machinery : Geared turbines. 1 shaft. H.P. : 2,500 = 11 kts. Accommodation for 210 ratings under training.

JOSEPH CONRAD (ex-*Georg Stage*), (Copenhagen, 1882). 182 tons *gross*. $110\frac{1}{2} \times 25\frac{1}{4} \times$ — feet. H.P. : 160.

PHILIPPINES.

Motor Torpedo Boats.

Q III   1939, *Central Press.*

4 *Thornycroft type :*

Q III (1939). Dimensions : $65 \times 13\frac{1}{4}$ feet. 3 Thornycroft R.Y. 12 type 12-cyl. engines. B.H.P. : 1,800 = 39 kts. (41 kts. exceeded on trials). 2—18 inch tubes, 2 M.G. and D.C.

Q I (1938), **Q IV, Q V** (1939). Dimensions : 55×11 feet. B.H.P. : 1,200 = 40 kts.

URUGUAY.

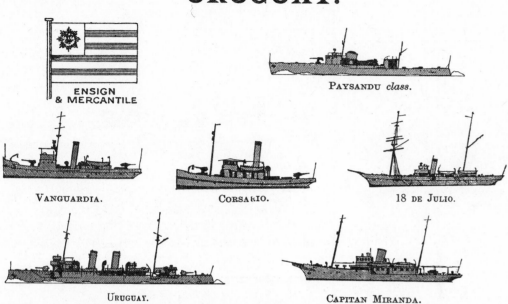

ENSIGN & MERCANTILE

VANGUARDIA.

PAYSANDU *class.*

CORSARIO.

18 DE JULIO.

URUGUAY.

CAPITAN MIRANDA.

Minister of War and Marine : General don Alfredo Campos.
Director of Navy : Rear-Admiral don Gustavo Schroder. *Personnel :* 938.
Form of Address : Capitan de Navio Don ——, R.O.U.——
Mercantile Marine : (Official figures, 1939) 247 vessels of 35,952 tons *gross.*

Patrol Vessels.

RIO NEGRO.

1939, *Official.*

PAYSANDU (July 21, 1935), **RIO NEGRO** (Aug. 22, 1935), **SALTO** (Aug. 11, 1935). All built by Cantieri Navali Riuniti, Ancona. *Standard* displacement : 180 tons. Complement, 51. Dimensions : $137\frac{1}{2} \times 19 \times 5\frac{1}{3}$ feet. Guns : 2—3 inch, 2—47 mm. AA., 2 M.G. 2 sets Diesels. B.H.P. 1,000 = 17 kts. Fuel : 18 tons. Radius : 4,000 miles at 10 kts.

Training Ships.

1936, *Nautical Photo Agency.*

URUGUAY (Vulkan, Stettin, 1910). Displacement : 1,150 tons. Complement : 125. Dimensions : $278\frac{3}{4}$ (*pp.*) $\times 30\frac{5}{6}$ $\times$ 12 feet (*max.* draught). Guns (Skoda) : 2—4·7 inch, 45 cal., 4—3 inch, 6—1 pdr. (Vickers), 4 M.G. Torpedo tubes : 2—18 inch *above water.* Armour : $\frac{2}{3}''$ nickel steel over boilers and engines. 4 Normand boilers. I.H.P. : 8,000 = 23 kts. Coal : 210 tons = 3,000 miles at 10 kts.

Note.—Is fitted for service as Training Ship for midshipmen.

1932 *Photo, Official.*

18 DE JULIO. Displacement : 764 tons. Complement : 85. Dimensions : 194 (pp.) $\times$ 26 $\times$ 15·5 feet. I.H.P. : 600 = 12 kts. No guns at present. Coal : 140 tons.

1939, *Official.*

ASPIRANTE (ex-*Exir-Dallen*). Purchased 1938, for use as a Training Ship.

Surveying Vessel.

1932 *Photo, Official,*

CAPITAN MIRANDA (S.E. de C.N., Matagorda, Cadiz, 1930). 516 tons. Dimensions : 148 (*p.p.*)×28×10 feet. 1 Diesel (M.A.N.). H.P. 500 = 10·5 kts. Oil fuel : 45 tons.

Tenders. (rated as Despatch Vessels)

1939, *Official.*

HURACÁN. Displacement : 197 tons. Dimensions : 114¾ × 25¾ × — feet. I.H.P. : 384 = 12 kts.

1918 *Photo, A. J. Carbone.*

CORSARIO. Displacement : 130 tons. Guns : 2—37 mm. Speed : 10 kts. (Employed on Survey Service, Rio de la Plata).

1939, *Official.*

ZAPICÁN. Displacement : 162 tons. Dimensions : 91 × 23⅔ × — feet. I.H.P. 422 = 10 kts.

1918 *Photo, A. J. Carbone.*

VANGUARDIA (Glasgow, 1908). Displacement : 95 tons. Guns : 2—37 mm. I.H.P. : 200 = 12 kts.

VENEZUELA.

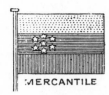

ENSIGN   MERCANTILE

Minister of War and Marine : Colonel don Isaias Medina.

Warship Port : Puerto Cabello. Steel floating dock here 282 × 90 × 22 feet. (2400 tons capacity) built in five sections on self-docking system, and worked by electricity. Also a wooden floating dock, 180 × 60 × 19 feet (1200 tons capacity). Both these docks are Government property.

Mercantile Marine: ("Lloyd's Register," 1939 figures). 54 vessels of 77,322 gross tonnage.

Gunboats

GEN. SOUBLETTE.   1938, *courtesy Lieut. L. F. Bouman.*

GEN. URDANETA.   1939, *courtesy W. H. Davis, Esq.*

GENERAL SOUBLETTE (ex-*Milazzo*), **GENERAL URDANETA** (ex-*Dardanelli*). (1925). Both built at Monfalcone for the Royal Italian Navy, and sold to Venezuela in 1938. Displacement : 615 tons (*full load*, 850 tons). Dimensions : 204 × 28½ × 8½ feet. Guns : 2—4 inch, 35 cal., 1—3 inch AA. H.P. : 1,500 = 15 kts. Oil-fired boilers (converted from coal in 1938). Fitted for minelaying.

Note.—It has been proposed to purchase two more vessels of this type.

Gunboats—*Continued.*

1933 *Photo, Official.*

MIRANDA (Clydebank, 1895 ; purchased from Spain, 1898). 200 tons. Dimensions : 140 × 17½ × 7½ feet. Guns : 2—6 pdr. 2 M.G. H.P. : 315 = 10 kts. Coal : 36 tons. Endurance : 850 miles at 8 kts. Complement : 55.

1933 *Photo, Official.*

MARISCAL SUCRE (ex-Spanish *Isla de Cuba*, 1886, captured by U.S., 1898, and sold to Venezuela, 1912). 1125 tons. Dimensions : 192 × 30 × 12¼ feet (*mean* draught) 13 feet (*max.* draught). Guns : 2—4 inch, 2—6 pdr., 4—3 pdr., 2—1* pdr. H.P. 2000 = 11 kts., *max.* continuous speed, 8 kts. Coal: 200 tons. Endurance : 885 miles at 9·5 kts. Complement, 100 Built by Armstrongs.

*1—1 pdr. transferable to boat mounting.

Note.—Likely to be scrapped soon.

Gunboats—*continued*.

(Classed as *Crucero*.)   1933 *Photo, Official*.

GENERAL SALOM (ex-*Restaurador*, purchased 1900; built as U.S. private yacht *Atlanta*, 1884). 750 tons. Dimensions: 240 × 26 × 13 feet *(max.* draught). Guns: **1**—3 inch, **4**—6 pdr., **1** machine. H.P. 1500 = 12 kts., *max.* continuous speed 8 kts. Coal: 200 tons. Endurance: 1080 miles at 8 kts. Complement: 86. (Refitted, 1938).

Armed Tugs.

A new tug is building, dimensions: 60 × 11½ × 4½ feet.

1933 *Photo, Official*.

ARAGUA (ex-tug *Caroni*), purchased 1929. 154 tons. 1 M.G. I.H.P. 525 = 7 kts. 14 tons oil. Complement: 30.

Photo by favour of Ellis Greu & Co., N.Y.

JOSÉ FELIX RIBAS (ex-*Zumbador*, built 1894). 300 tons. Dimensions: 127 × 23 × 12 feet. Guns: **2**—6 pdr. Speed, 8 kts. Coal: 60 tons. Endurance: 850 miles. Complement, **55**.

Note.—Tug 21 *de Julio* was wrecked in 1939.

River Gunboats.

2 vessels reported to have been acquired in 1939.

Motor Launches.

CARIBE (ex-*Guardacosta III*), **ARAUCA, TACHIRA.** 30 tons.

Presidential Yacht.

EL LEANDRO (ex-*Dr. Brinkley II*,) (U.S.A., 1925). Displacement: 320 tons. Dimensions: 149 (*o.a.*) × 24¼ × 7½ feet. 2 small guns. 2 Winton Diesel engines. 2 shafts.

YUGOSLAVIA.

FLAGS.

ROYAL STANDARD

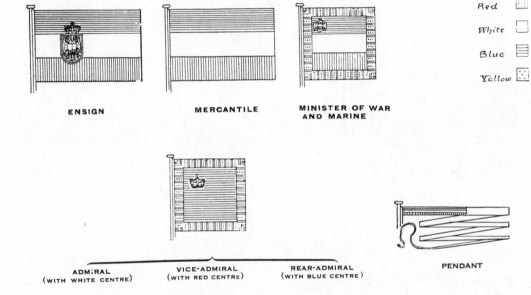

ENSIGN

MERCANTILE

MINISTER OF WAR
AND MARINE

Red
White
Blue
Yellow

ADMIRAL
(WITH WHITE CENTRE)

VICE-ADMIRAL
(WITH RED CENTRE)

REAR-ADMIRAL
(WITH BLUE CENTRE)

PENDANT

ADMINISTRATION.

Minister of War and Marine : General Milutin Dj. Nedić.

Commander in Chief of Fleet : Vice-Admiral Marjan L. Polić.

Naval Attaché in London :

Personnel : 625 officers. 5,700 petty officers and men.

(Reserve) : 400 officers. 720 petty officers and men.

Colour of Ships : Light grey.

Mercantile Marine : From " Lloyd's Register," 1939. 190 vessels of 411,384 gross tonnage.

Displacements are " standard."

UNIFORMS.

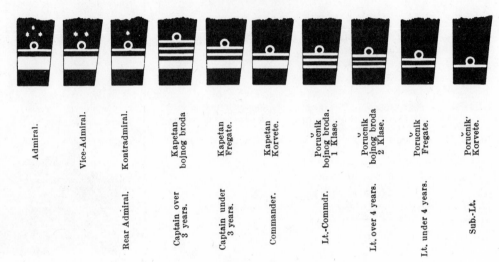

Admiral.

Vice-Admiral.

Kontradmiral.

Rear Admiral.

Kapetan
bojnog broda

Captain over
3 years.

Kapetan
Fregate.

Captain under
3 years.

Kapetan
Korvete.

Commander.

Poručnik
bojnog broda.
1 Klase.

Lt.-Commdr.

Poručnik
bojnog broda
2 Klase.

Lt. over 4 years.

Poručnik
Fregate.

Lt. under 4 years.

Poručnik
Korvete.

Sub.-Lt.

For relative ranks :

   Engineers have silver grey between the stripes.

   Paymasters have red between the stripes.

   Constructors have purple between the stripes.

   Warrant Officers have brown between the stripes.

   Surgeons have an Æsculapius snake on the curl.

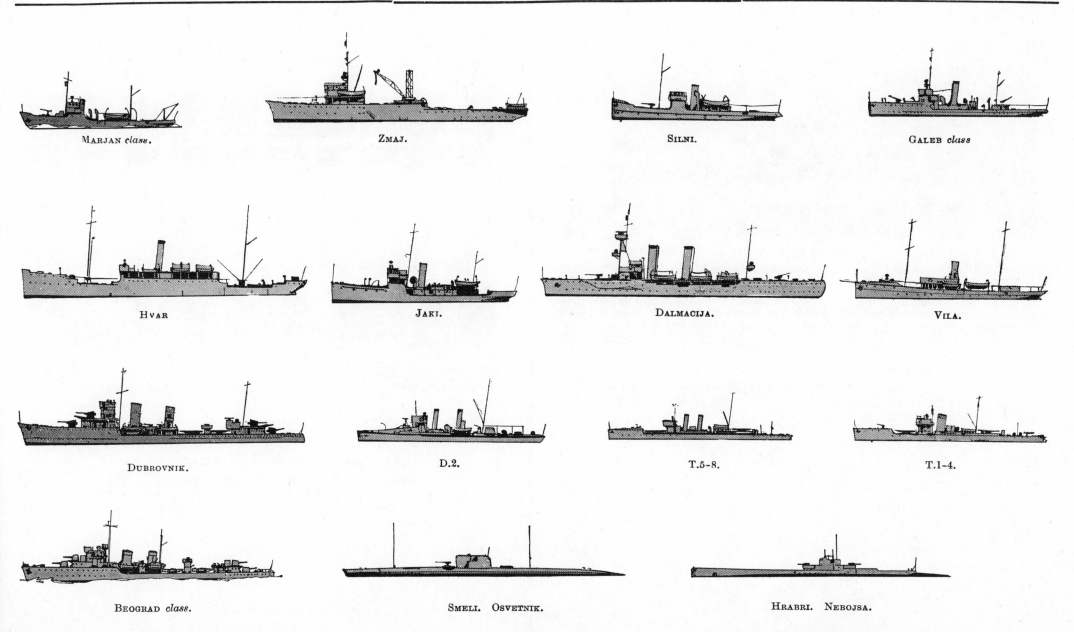

MARJAN *class*.

ZMAJ.

SILNI.

GALEB *class*

HVAR

JAKI.

DALMACIJA.

VILA.

DUBROVNIK.

D.2.

T.5-8.

T.1-4.

BEOGRAD *class*.

SMELI. OSVETNIK.

HRABRI. NEBOJSA.

YUGOSLAVIA—Destroyers (*Razarač*).

A new Flotilla Leader was laid down at Split in Oct., 1938. Engines and boilers to be supplied by Messrs. Yarrow.
Displacement: 1,875 tons (*standard*), 2,400 tons (*full load*). Guns: (Skoda) **5**—5·5 inch, **10**—40 mm. AA., **8** M.G. AA. Tubes: **6**—21 inch. Machinery: Parsons geared turbines. S.H.P.: 50,000 = 37 kts. Boilers: 4 Yarrow, working pressure 400 lb. Oil fuel: 590 tons.

BEOGRAD.

1939, *Wright & Logan.*

1932 *Photo, Messrs. Yarrow.*

DUBROVNIK (Oct. 11, 1931, Yarrow). Displacement: 1,880 tons (*standard*), 2,400 (*full load*). Complement: 200. Dimensions: 345 (*p.p.*). 371½ (*o.a.*) × 35 × 11¾ feet (*mean* draught). Guns: (Skoda) **4**—5·5 inch, **2**—3·4 inch AA., **6**—40 mm. AA. (2 single and 2 twin mounts). **2** M.G. AA. Tubes: **6**—21 inch. Fitted for minelaying. Machinery: Parsons geared Turbines. 3 Yarrow boilers. S.H.P: 42,000 = 37 kts. Radius: 7,000 miles at economical speed.

Note.—Designed to meet particular specifications and has proved a fast and economical steamer. Note the position of the AA. guns by after shelter deck, after control position and removal of searchlight from the bridge to athwart second funnel. S.L. platforms are stayed away from funnel to avoid all vibration. She is the first Yarrow destroyer to have a clipper bow.

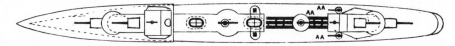

DUBROVNIK.

BEOGRAD.

1939, *courtesy Messrs. Yarrow & Co., Ltd.*

3 *French* type: **Beograd** (Dec. 23, 1937). Built by At. et Ch. de la Loire, St. Nazaire. **Ljubljana,** (June 28, 1938), **Zagreb** (March 30, 1938). Built at Split. Displacement: 1,210 tons. Dimensions: 313 × 31 × 9⅔ feet. Guns (Skoda): **4**—4·7 inch (paired), **4**—40 mm. AA. Tubes: **6**—21 inch (tripled), **30** mines carried. Machinery: Parsons geared turbines, S.H.P.: 44,000 = 38 kts. Boilers: 3 Yarrow, working pressure 400 lb.

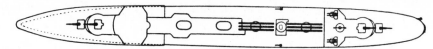

8 Torpedo Boats (*Torpiljarke*) (ex-Austrian).

1931 *Photo, Official.*

Ex-Austrian boats: **T1—T4** (ex-*76 T—79 T*, Stab. Tecnico, Trieste 1913-15). Displacement: 262 tons. Fuel: 18 tons coal, 24 tons oil. Dimensions : 188·3 ×18·7 × 4·9 feet.

1931 *Photo, Official.*

4 Ex-Austrian boats: **T5—T8** (ex-*87 F, 93 F, 96 F, 97 F*, Ganz-Danubius Co., Porte Ré, Fiume 1913-15). Displacement : 266 tons, Fuel: 20 tons coal, 34 tons oil.

Details of **T1—T8.** Dimensions: 188·3 × 18·7 × 4·9 feet. Guns: 2—66 m/m. and 1 M.G. Torpedo tubes: 4—18 inch (paired). Designed H.P. (turbines) : 5,000 = 28 kts. (24 reported best speed now). Yarrow boilers.

Motor Torpedo Boats (*Borbeni Čamci*).

VELEBIT.

1939, *Official.*

Orjen, Velebit, Dinara, Triglav, Suvobor, Rudnik, Kaimakcalan, Durmitor. (Lürssen, Vegesack, 1936-37). Displacement: 60 tons. Complement, 14. Dimensions : 92 × 14 × 5 feet. Armament: 1 M.G. A.A., 2 18-inch torpedo tubes. Machinery: Mercedes-Benz motors. H.P. 3,000 = 34 kts.

Note.—Distinguished by numbers 1 to 8, respectively, painted on bows.

Added 1938, *courtesy Messrs. Thornycroft.*

Uskok, Cetnik. Delivered by Messrs. John I. Thornycroft & Co., Ltd., in May, 1927. Dimensions: 55 × 11 feet. Machinery : 2 Thornycroft motors of 375 H.P. each=37 kts. *nominal* (40 kts. actually obtained). Auxiliary engine fitted for cruising, equal to 800 miles radius. 2 Lewis guns, 2—18 inch torpedoes. 4 D.C., and smoke floats.

4 Submarines (*Podmornice*).

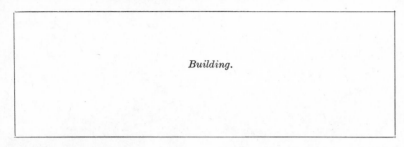

Building.

2 *Germania* type: Laid down at Kiel, 1939. Displacement: 280/335 tons. Complement: 17. Dimensions: 148⅝ × 15¾ × 12⅝ feet. Armament: 1—15 mm. AA., 4—21 inch tubes. Machinery: 4-stroke Krupp Diesels. H.P.: 830/— = 13/7 kts.

HRABRI. (Showing lowered gun positions).   1934, *Lieut. D. C. Beatty, R.N.*

Hrabri, Nebojša, (Armstrong. 1927). Displacement: $\frac{975}{1164}$ tons. Complement: 45. Dimensions: 236¼ × 24 × 13 feet. Armament: 2—4 inch AA., 6—21 inch torpedo tubes. H.P.: 2,400/1,600 = $\frac{15}{10}$ kts. Radius: 5,000 miles at 9 kts.

Names mean *Gallant* and *Dreadnought*. Are modified versions of British " L " type, materials having been assembled originally for *L* 67 and *L* 68, never built.

OSVETNIK.   1930 *Photo, M. Bar.*

Smeli (Dec. 1st, 1928). **Osvetnik** (Feb. 14th, 1929). Laid down at Nantes, 1927, by At. & Ch. de la Loire. Displacement: 600/809 tons. Dimensions: 227 × 18 × 14 feet. Armament: 1—3.9 inch Skoda, 1—1 pdr. AA., 1 M.G., 6—21.7 inch tubes (4 bow, 2 stern). H.P.: $\frac{1440}{1000}$ = $\frac{14}{9}$ kts. Complement: 43.

Names mean *Ardent* and *Vindictive*.

Training Ship (*Skolski brodovi.*)

DALMACIJA.   1931 *Photo, Official.*

1931 *Photo, Official.*

DALMACIJA (ex-German *Niobe*, Weser Yard, 18th July, 1899). Displacement: 2370 tons. Dimensions: 342¼ × 38½ × 17¼ feet (*max.* draught). Guns: 6—3.4 inch, 55 cal. (87 mm.) AA. (These are guns of a new and powerful Skoda model, with a maximum range of 18,000 yds.) Torpedo tubes: originally carried 2—19.7 inch, *above* water. Armour (Krupp): 2″ deck (amidships), ¾″ deck (ends), 3½″ glacis to engine room hatches, 3″ C.T. Machinery: 2 sets 4-cylinder triple expansion, 2 screws. Boilers: 5 Schulz-Thornycroft. Designed H.P. 8000 = 21 kts. Coal, *normal*, 380 tons; *maximum*, 580 tons.

Note.—Purchased from German Government in 1926 and underwent extensive refit and alterations at Kotor. Tripod mast fitted 1931.

Mine Layers (*Minonosci*).

SOKOL.

1924 *Photo, by courtesy of the Navy Department.*

6 boats : **GALEB** (ex-*M* 100), **LABUD** (ex-*M* 106), **JASTREB** (ex-*M* 112), **KOBAC** (ex-*M* 121), **ORAO** (ex-*M* 97), **SOKOL** (ex-*M* 144) (1917–18). Displacement : 330 tons. *standard*, 525 tons *full load*. Dimensions : 182 (*w.l.*), 192 (*o.a*) × 23½ × 7 feet. Guns : 2—3·9 inch AA., 4—3 pdrs. Complement : 71. I.H.P. : 1,800 = 15 kts. Oil : 160 tons. Names mean *Seagull, Swan, Hawk, Sparrowhawk, Eagle* and *Falcon* respectively.

Note.—Identification letters painted on bows : **AO**, *Orao* ; **JS**, *Jastreb* ; **LB**, *Labud* ; **KC**, *Kobac* ; **CK**, *Sokol* ; **ME**, *Meljine* ; **MN**, *Marjan* ; **MT**, *Mljet* ; **MO**, *Mosor*.

Mine Sweeper (*Drager*).

D 2.

1931 *Official Photo.*

D 2 (ex-Austrian T.B., *No.* 36., 1888). Displacement : 78 tons. Dimensions : 128 × 14¾ × 3¼ feet. Guns : 2—37 m/m. Triple expansion engines. H.P.: 700 = 17 kts. Complement : 16.

Aircraft Tender.

(*Matica za pomocni vazd*).

1931 *Official Photo.*

ZMAJ. Built in 1928 by Deutsche Werft, Hamburg : burnt out and re-built in 1929-30. Displacement : 1,870 tons. Dimensions : 249⅓ × 42⅔ × 11¼ feet. Guns : 1—4 inch AA. Machinery : 2 compressorless M.A.N. Diesels each 1,630 H.P. 3,260 H.P. = 15 kts. 2 screws. 10 aircraft carried. (*Zmaj* means *Kite*).

Patrol Vessel.

BJELI ORAO (C. R. dell' Adriatico, June 3, 1939).

Displacement : 640 tons.
Dimensions : 197 × 26 × 9 feet.

YUGOSLAVIA

Submarine Depot Ships (*Matica za Podmornice*).

HVAR.   1928 *Photo.*

HVAR (ex-*Solun*, ex-*Umtali*). Sir Jas. Laing & Sons, Ltd., Sunderland, 1896 (Rebuilt 1927). 3,600 tons. Dimensions: $318\frac{1}{4} \times 39 \times 13$ feet. Machinery: Triple expansion. H.P.: 1,100 = 12 kts.

SITNICA (ex-*Najade*, 1891). 370 tons. Dimensions: $157\frac{1}{2} \times 23 \times 6\frac{1}{2}$ feet. Machinery: Triple expansion. H.P.: 500 = 9 kts. Guns: 2—3 pdr. Name means *Dew*.

Mining Tenders (*Tenderi minopolagaci*)

MARJAN.   1939 *Official.*

5 boats: **MALINSKA, MARJAN, MELJINE, MLJET, MOSOR** (1931, Yarrow's Adriatic Yard, Kralyevica). Displacement: 130 tons. Dimensions: $174 \times 26\frac{1}{4} \times 13$ feet. Machinery: Triple expansion. H.P.: 280 = 9 kts. Guns: 1—11 pdr.

Oiler.

<table>
<tr><td>Photo wanted.</td></tr>
</table>

PERUN (March 8, 1939). Built by Cockerill, Antwerp. Displacement: 4,500 tons (3,006 tons *gross*). Complement: 100. Dimensions: 291 (*pp.*), $311\frac{1}{2}$ (*o.a.*) $\times 45\frac{1}{2} \times 20$ feet. Guns: 4—40 mm. AA., 2—15 mm. AA. Machinery: Burmeister & Wain 2-stroke Diesels. B.H.P.: 1,250 = 10 kts. *Deadweight capacity*: 3,000 tons.

Salvage Vessel (*Brod za Spasavanje*).

1936.

SPASILAC (1929). 740 tons. Dimensions: $174 \times 26\frac{1}{4} \times 13$ feet. Machinery: Triple expansion. H.P.: 2,000 = 15 kts. Name means *Salvor*.

Yacht (*Jahta*).

1931 *Photo, Official.*

VILA (ex-*Dalmata*) (1896). 230 tons. H.P. 325 = 12 kts. Name means *Nymph*.

Training Ship (*Skolski Brodovi*).

1933 *Photo, Official.*

JADRAN (1932). Displacement: 720 tons. Dimensions: $190\frac{1}{4} \times 29 \times 13\frac{3}{4}$ feet. One Linke-Hofmann Diesel. H.P.: 375 = 8 kts. Sail area, 8,600 sq. feet. Accommodation for 150 cadets. Name means *Adriatic*.

Tugs (*Remorkeri*).

MOCNI (Cockerill, Antwerp, 1939).

Note.—This tug replaces one of same name and characteristics launched at Antwerp in Nov., 1938, which was lost on passage. Name means *Mighty*.

1931 *Official Photo.*

SILNI (1914). Displacement : 200 tons. Guns : 2—47 mm. H.P. : 670 = 10 kts. Name means *Powerful*.

Jaki   1931 *Photo, Official.*

JAKI (1915). Displacement : 370 tons. H.P. 1,200=15 kts.

SNAZNI (1917). 100 tons. H.P. 300=10 kts.

USTRAJNI (1917). 160 tons. H.P. 250=9 kts.

MARLJIVI (1898). 130 tons. H.P. 300=12 kts.

Note.—Respective meanings of above names are *Forceful, Strong, Durable, Industrious.*

Water Carrier (*Vodonosac*).

Photo wanted.

LOVCEN (1932). Particulars required.

River Patrol Vessels.

1939 *Official.*

DRAGOR (1928). Displacement : 250 tons. Dimensions : 164 × 26¼ × 3¾ feet. H.P. : 480 = 10 kts. Serves as Royal Yacht on Danube.

CER (1909). 256 tons. Dimensions : 170½ × 23 × 3 feet. 2 M.G. H.P. : 400 = 15 kts.

SISAK (ex-*Triglav*), (1915). 90 tons. Dimensions : 118 × 19¼ × 6 feet. 2 M.G. H.P. : 350 = 11 kts.

SABAC (ex-*Avala*), (1914). 90 tons. Dimensions : 101¾ × 23 × 4½ feet. H.P. : 360 = 8 kts.

(Latter three vessels are converted tugs.)

Note.—Two 36-ton motor vedette boats, speed 9 kts., are maintained on Lake Ohrid. Names are *Graničar* and *Stražar*, meaning Frontier Guard and Sentinel, respectively. They were built in 1929.

River Flotilla.—(*Rečna Flotila*)

1933 *Photo, Official.*

VARDAR (ex-Austrian *Bosna*, 1915). 530 tons. Dimensions : 200 × 34½ × 4¼ feet. Guns : 2—4·7 inch, 45 cal., 2—4·7 inch, 10 cal. howitzers, 2—66 mm. AA., **7** M.G. Armour : 1½ inch belt and bulkheads, 1 inch deck, 2 inch C.T., 2 inch turrets and cupolas. H.P. 1,600 = 13 kts. Oil : 75 tons. Complement, 100. Sister to *Bucovina*, now in Roumanian Navy.

1933 *Photo, Official.*

SAVA (ex-Austrian *Bodrog*, Neupest, March, 1904). 380 tons. Dimensions : 183¾ × 31¼ × 4 feet. Designed H.P. 1,200 = 9 kts. Boilers : Yarrow. Armament : 2—4·7 inch, 35 cal., 1—4·7 inch howitzer, 1—66 mm. AA., 2 M.G., **1 or 3 machine.** Armour : 1½″ Belt and Bulkheads, 1″ Deck, 3″—1½″ Turrets and Conning Tower. Complement, 79. Coal : 62 tons.

DRAVA. 1933 *Photo, by courtesy of the Navy Dept.*

DRAVA (ex-Austrian *Enns*, 1913). 450 tons. Dimensions : 190¼ × 34½ × 4¼ feet. Guns : 2—4·7 inch **+ 3**—4·7 inch howitzers, 2—66 m/m., **7** M.G. Armour : 1½″ Belt and Bulkheads, 1″ Deck, 2″ C.T. and Turrets. Designed H.P. 1500 = 13 kts. Boilers : Yarrow. Fuel : Oil only, 70 tons. Complement, 86. Built under Austro-Hungarian 1912 Naval Programme ; ceded to Yugoslavia 1920. Sister ship *Basarabia* now in Roumanian Navy.

MORAVA. (Gun on superstructure since removed.) 1924 *Photo by courtesy of the Navy Dept.* Note overhanging rails at stern, for launching and hauling in boats.

MORAVA (ex-Austrian *Körös*, Budapest, 1892). 390 tons. Dimensions : 177⅛ × 29½ × 4 feet. Designed H.P. 1200 = 9 kts. Boilers : Yarrow. Guns : 2—4.7 inch (35 cal.), 1—66 m/m. 2 M.G. Armour : 2″ Belt, ¾″ Deck, 3″ Turret, 2″ C.T. Complement, 79-80. Coal : 54 tons.

ADDENDA.

BRITISH

Additional Names of British Warships (page 12).

ACACIA (2nd), 1915	HAZEL (2nd), 1914
ALMOND (1st), 1939	HICKORY (1st), 1939
ASH (1st), 1939	JUNIPER (2nd), 1813
BAY (1st), 1939	MANGROVE (1st), 1939
BIRCH (2nd), 1915	OLIVE (2nd), 1914
BLACKTHORN (2nd), 1915	PINE (1st), 1939
CHESTNUT (2nd), 1656	ROWAN (2nd), 1914
DEODAR (1st), 1939	WALNUT (1st), 1939
ELM (2nd), 1914	WHITETHORN (1st), 1939
FIR (1st), 1939	WISTARIA (2nd), 1915

Patrol vessel **KITTIWAKE** damaged through striking a mine, September 20, 1939 (page 82).

STRAITS SETTLEMENTS (page 111).

Motor Patrol Boats.

PAHLAWAN.   1939, *courtesy Messrs. Thornycroft.*

2 *Thornycroft type :* **PAHLAWAN, PANGLIMA.**
Dimensions : $76\frac{1}{2}$ (*o.a.*) × $13\frac{1}{2}$ × $4\frac{3}{4}$ feet.
Armament : 1 Small Gun, and D.C. Fitted for minesweeping.
Machinery : 1 RY/12 petrol engine and 2 RL/6 Diesels. Total B.H.P. : 780.

CRASSULA.   1939, *courtesy the Navy League.*

KOMMETJE.   1939, *Sport and General.*

KENYA, ETC.

NDOVU. Ex-tug, used for sea training of Kenya Division, R.N.V.R.
ATHALHARI. Ex-tug, used for a similar purpose at Zanzibar.

BELGIUM.

MERCATOR (page 127).   1939, *Official.*

BRAZIL.

CARIOCA. (Page 133).   1939, *Official.*

All 6 destroyers of *Javary* class have been acquired by the British Government (page 131).

FRANCE.

New Flags. (Page 169).

AMIRAL DE LA   VICE-AMIRAL
FLOTTE   D'ESCADRE

I A TOUR D'AUVERGNE destroyed by internal explosion at Casablanca, September 18, 1939 (page 192).

NETHERLANDS.

Minesweeper **JAN VAN GELDER** was badly damaged by a mine on September 30, 1939 (page 371).

HEEMSKERCK launched, Sept. 16, 1939 (page 361)

Destroyers **GERARD CALLENBURGH** and **TJERK HIDDES** both launched by Rotterdam Dry Dock Co., October 12, 1939. (page 365).

GERMANY.

According to American Press reports, the ship damaged by British air bombs on Sept. 4, 1939, was *Admiral Scheer* (page 223).

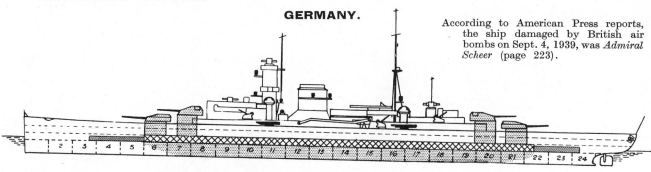

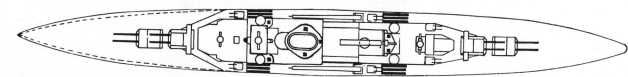

ADMIRAL HIPPER *class.* (Page 225).

Total of U-boats destroyed up to middle of October believed to be not less than 15, mostly ocean-going vessels (pages 231–2). A patrol vessel, possibly an armed merchant vessel or trawler, was sunk by mine in the Western Baltic, October 21, 1939. BISMARCK CLASS (Page 221) Length (*w.l.*) 729⅓ feet *should read* 792⅓ feet.

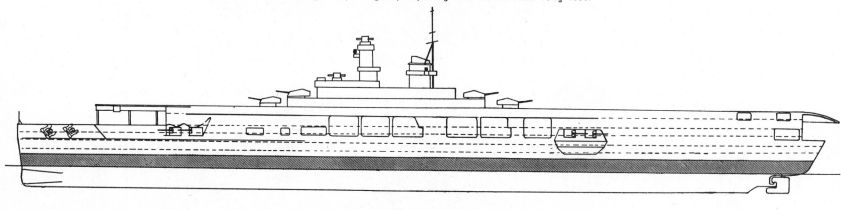

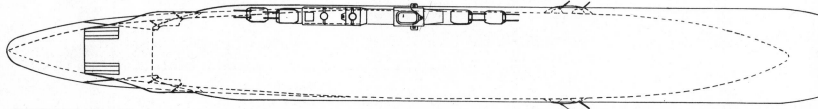

GRAF ZEPPELIN. (Page 225).

JAPAN.

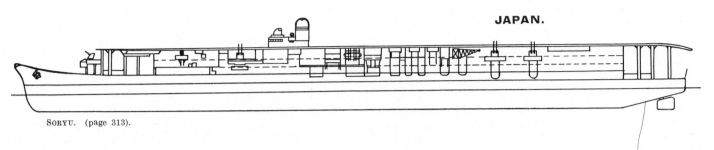

SORYU. (page 313).

Aircraft Carrier **AKAGI** has been recommissioned on completion of reconstruction. She has had flight deck extended and an island superstructure added on similar lines to *Kaga* (page 316).

KATORI is reported to be designed as a seagoing cruiser for midshipmen and cadets (page 322).

A third minelayer of *Sokuten* type launched at Mitubisi Yard, Yokohama, on Aug. 28, 1939, and named **NARIFU** (page 346).

Destroyer **AMATUKAZE** of *Kagero* class, launched at Maiduru, October 19, 1939 (page 331).

MIDUHO. (Page 328).   1939.

1939.

KAMIKAWA MARU.   Auxiliary seaplane carrier.   Guns   2—3 inch.   12 aircraft carried.

MIDUHO. (Page 328).   1939.

RUSSIA.

The warship mentioned on page 417 as completed at Vladivostok may be the destroyer *Volochevka* (described on page 418).

PROVODNIK (page 425).

1939, *Associated Press.*

SPAIN.

MOLA and **SANJURJO** are now believed to be of the Italian *Archimede* type (page 438).

1939.

Above photo is believed to represent one of the unidentified torpedo boats, either **C. PÉREZ, BADAJOZ, OVIEDO** or **TOLEDO,** referred to on p. 437.

SWEDEN.

1939 *Illustration, courtesy " Sveriges Flotta."*

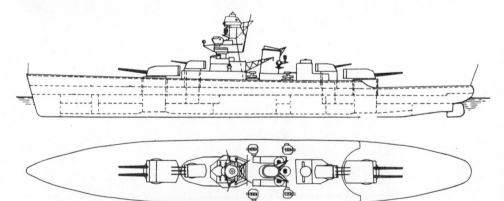

New Swedish Coast Defence Ships (described on p. 444).

SWEDEN—*continued.*

ÄRAN (as reconstructed)   1939, *Redak ör K.-E. Westerlund.*

U.S.A.

WICHITA (showing **8**—5 inch guns mounted). (Page 490).   1939, " *Ships and Aircraft.*"

U.S.A.

PENNSYLVANIA   1939, *Bear Photo Service.*

IOWA and **NEW JERSEY** are not expected to be laid down before July, 1940. Radius of action is reported to be 9,000 miles (page 476).

Latest reports credit the *Atlanta* class with an armament of **9**—6 inch and **6**—5 inch, 25 cal. guns (page 496).

FULTON design is reported unofficially to include Diesel engines of B.H.P. 12,000=20 kts. (page 513).

WICHITA. (Page 490).   1939.

CANADA.

H.M.S. KEMPENFELT has been transferred to the Royal Canadian Navy and re-named **H.M.C.S. ASSINIBOINE.**

ITALY.

IMPERO launched October 28, 1939 (page 263).

POLAND.

WICHER, GRYF, GEN. HALLER, KOM. PILSUDSKI, MAZUR and all ships on pages 392 and 393 except *Wilja* and *Iskra* are believed to have been lost.

TURKEY.

SALDIRAY (page 463)

1939, *Official*.

ROUMANIA.

MIRCEA. (Page 406).

1939.